THE CRIMINAL JURISDICTION
OF MAGISTRATES

THE CRIMINAL JURISDICTION OF MAGISTRATES

BY

BRIAN HARRIS, OBE, QC, LLB,

Clerk to the Poole Justices

NINTH EDITION

CHICHESTER

BARRY ROSE PUBLISHERS LTD.
JUSTICE OF THE PEACE LTD.
1984

BARRY ROSE PUBLISHERS LTD.
JUSTICE OF THE PEACE LTD.
LITTLE LONDON, CHICHESTER, WEST SUSSEX
ENGLAND

©

BARRY ROSE PUBLISHERS LTD.
1984

ISBN 0-85992-394-0 Hard Back Edition
ISBN 0-85992-399-1 Limp Edition

The Publishers are indebted for permission to reproduce in this book extracts from various Command Papers, Home Office Circulars, and other publications where the copyright vests in Her Majesty's Stationery Office, to the Controller.

Typeset by Margaret Spooner Typesetting, Dorset; Articulate Studios, Emsworth; City Technical Services, Chichester; EntaPrint Ltd., Cranleigh. Designed by Paul Sharp. Art work by City Technical Services and EntaPrint Ltd. Printed and bound by EntaPrint Ltd., Cranleigh, Surrey.

For My Father

INTRODUCTION

In the field of criminal procedure and sentencing the pace of legislative change continues unabated. There have been Criminal Justice or Criminal Law Acts in 1948, 1961, 1967, 1972, 1977 and 1982. No one can deny that profound changes have been made by the latest in the series but the most important of these have all been negative in content, in the sense that they are merely stripping from our laws the recently discarded myth of rehabilitation, the notion that it was somehow possible to make men better by order of the court. Worthy motive though that may be, it is no substitute for a re-moulding of our ancient structure of punishments and prevarications which passes for a criminal justice sytem.

As a society we are profoundly ignorant of the causes of crime and of the means of preventing it, although informed opinion nowadays suspects that the criminal justice system has a less than central part to play in the latter. Indeed, the nicest thing the critics would say of the courts is that a failure on their part to sentence convicted offenders would be marginally more inimical to the good health of society than the effects of many of the sentences that are imposed. It is tempting to think that our present chaos results from a pragmatic approach to unsolvable problems, and maybe it does, but it is difficult to believe that even Parliament would have hit upon the present arrangements if called upon to design a criminal justice system from scratch. In the meantime we must live with what we have.

As well as the Criminal Justice Act 1982 I have had to cope in this edition with two major statutes, the Legal Aid Act 1982 and the Mental Health Act 1983.

The new Legal Aid Act provides for the setting up of duty solicitor schemes on a statutory basis, changes radically the basis of legal aid contribution orders and provides for the possibility of a "through" legal aid order to cover both committal proceedings and the trial at the Crown Court. It is expected to be brought into force by the time this edition is in print and has therefore been incorporated as if it were fully in force. Unfortunately, the new regulations are not yet available for inclusion.

The Mental Health Act 1983 is a new code replacing that in the Act of 1959. Hospital and guardianship orders may still be made by the court on conviction of an offence punishable with imprisonment but the procedure and the medical grounds have been largely re-written. There is a new interim hospital order and the possibility of a remand to hospital for medical reports. Except for these last two provisions the Act will be brought into force on September 30, 1983.

However, it is the Criminal Justice Act 1982 which has given rise to the greatest changes. Hardly a chapter of this book escapes its effects. Borstal training has been abolished and imprisonment removed as a sentence for offenders under 21. Instead, there is a new sentence of youth custody. The law of detention centres has been completely re-drawn in such a way that these two sentences present a single custodial continuum into which the court is expected to fit the offender according to the length of his sentence. The Act introduces a strict set of criteria designed to avoid unnecessary and undesirable custodial sentences and requires the opportunity of legal representation before a custodial sentence is passed. Breach of supervision after release from these sentences will no longer be a matter for the Home Office, but for the courts.

The Act aims to strengthen the alternatives to custody by introducing locally run day centres and by a complex new set of requirements in probation orders designed to get round the decision of the House of Lords in *Cullen v Rogers*. Community service is extended to 16 year olds with a reduced minimum period. The Act gives greater emphasis to compensation, although the provision that compensation can be a sentence in its own right was untidy and unnecessary. For those who offend while in care there is a new "charge and control" order. The Act completes the last step towards a standard scale of fines for summary offences and makes a number of increases in the maximum fines, although the way in which this has been done could hardly be more tortuous. The attendance centre provisions have been repealed and re-enacted with minor improvements.

Against opposition from some parts of the legal profession a modest scheme for remand in the absence of the prisoner was introduced and appears to be working smoothly. The Crown Court has at last been given the power to grant bail in every case in which it may be refused by magistrates. The right of an accused to make an unsworn statement was finally killed off without a tear being shed, as was the need for a solicitor to be present at a paper committal. The much criticized decision in *R. v. Gilby* was reversed allowing magistrates to commit for sentence after a deferment which went wrong. Changes were also made in the law of suspended and partly suspended sentences.

The number of decided cases added to this edition are too many to be enumerated here, but they include:

R. v. Dunnington (aiding and abetting an attempt)
R. v. Canterbury & St. Augustine Justices, ex parte Turner (abuse of process)
R. v. Lambeth Metropolitan Stipendiary Magistrate, ex parte McComb (exhibits)
R. v. Leeds Justices, ex parte Sykes (restrictions on publicity of committal proceedings)
R. v. St. Helens Justices, ex parte McClorie (trial of criminal damage offences)
Chief Constable of Norfolk v. Clayton (joinder of offences and defendants)
R. v. Epsom Justices, ex parte Gibbons (ditto)
R. v. Seisdon Justices, ex parte Dougan (adjournment of trial)
R. v. Aramah (sentencing in drug offences)
R. v. Holloway (sentencing in obscene publications offences)
R. v. Amey (compensation)
Bond v. Chief Constable of Kent (compensation)
Haime v. Walklett (special reasons)
R. v. Kent (Peter) (penalty points)
Johnson v. Finbow (penalty points)
R. v. Clerkenwell Metropolitan Stipendiary Magistrate, ex parte Director of Public Prosecutions (refusal of jurisdiction)
R. v. Reigate Justices, ex parte Argus Newspapers Ltd. & Another (hearing mitigation in camera)

Finally, I have continued the process of amplifying and improving the introductions to each chapter. The aim is that the reader wishing to have a clear statement of the principles of any subject should go first to the appropriate introduction. This will refer him in turn to the annotated statute or other source which will supply more detail. Those who already know which statutory provision to refer to may go directly there where they will find cross references to the introduction should they need to consider the subject in context.

Except where otherwise noted I have attempted to state the law as at February 1 1984.

Poole   Brian Harris

CONTENTS

A

B

G

H

N

Q

R

S

U

V

CHAPTER 1.

COMMENCING THE PROSECUTION

INTRODUCTION

The Right to Prosecute

Subject to any statutory restrictions, any person may seek to prosecute another for an offence. (*See* the remarks of Lord Wilberforce in *Gouriet* v. *Union of Post Office Workers* (1977) 141 J.P. 205, 552). This power is preserved by the Prosecution of Offences Act 1979, s.4. In this respect the police officer is in no different position from any other citizen. So far as the police are concerned, the primary responsibility for the prosecution probably resides in the chief constable. (*See* the report of the Royal Commission on Criminal Procedure, Vol. II at paras 136 and 137 and the case of *Hawkins* v. *Bepey* (1980) 144 J.P. 203.) Exceptionally, a prosecution for common assault under the Offences Against the Persons Act 1861, s. 42, can be brought only "by or on behalf of the person aggrieved."

There is no statutory definition of the term, "prosecutor". In general, the prosecutor is the person named as informant. Where an officer of a local authority purports (wrongly) to act on its behalf he is to be regarded personally as the prosecutor: *Cole* v. *Coulton* (1860) 24 J.P. 596; *R.* v. *Bushell* (1888) 52 J.P. 136; *Giebler* v. *Manning* (1906) 70 J.P. 181; *Lake* v. *Smith* (1911) 76 J.P. 71; *Duchesne* v. *Finch* (1912) 76 J.P. 377; *Snodgrass* v. *Topping* (1952) 166 J.P. 332; *Lund* v. *Thompson* (1958) 122 J.P. 489.

Where a prosecution may only be brought with the consent or authority of another it is the duty of the person issuing the summons to see that that consent is available. There is a presumption that this has been done and at the trial there is no need for the prosecution to take any further step unless objection is taken. If objection is taken the prosecution must be in a position to prove the necessary consent or authority. If the defence want to challenge this they should take their objection before the prosecution case is closed because otherwise it will be presumed to be a good one and properly authorised: *Price* v. *Humphries* (1958) 122 J.P. 423; *Frost* v. *Frank Hoyles Transport Ltd.* (1983) May 11 (unreported).

The fiat (or consent) of the Attorney General is required before proceedings are instituted or continued for certain offences. The consent of the Director of Public Prosecutions is required for the prosecution of other offences. Some offences may not be prosecuted save by or on behalf of certain officials. Lists of these offences are contained in a booklet, *The Prosecution of Offences Regulations* 1978, published by the Director of Public Prosecutions. The Solicitor General may exercise any of the functions of the Attorney General if the latter is absent or incapacitated or if he is specifically authorized to do so. (Law Officers Act 1944, s. 1). The consent, etc., of a law officer or the Director may be in written form in accordance with the Prosecution of Offences Act 1979, s. 7.

The Director of Public Prosecutions is empowered by the Prosecution of Offences Act 1979, s. 2, to assume responsibility for the conduct of any prosecution.

Bringing the Accused to Court

A person may be compelled to appear before a magistrates' court in respect of a criminal prosecution in one of two ways: he may be arrested (with or without warrant) or he may appear in answer to a summons. The laying of an information is a pre-requisite to the issue of a summons or warrant. In the case of a person arrested otherwise than upon warrant the information is usually laid at the first appearance in court.

The process of charging an arrested person at the police station is an internal police procedure. Although it has been held to amount to the commencement of proceedings for a limited purpose *(see R.* v. *Brentwood Justices, ex parte Jones* [1979] R.T.R. 155), a charge at a police station does not constitute the laying of an information and does not, it is submitted, represent the commencement of time for jurisdictional purposes. *(See* the report of the Royal Commission on Criminal Procedure, Vol. II, para. 182 and the case of *Rees* v. *Barlow* [1974] Crim. L.R. 713.

The issue of process to compel appearance is not a necessary preliminary to the trial of an information. An information may be laid by a prosecutor against someone present in court, although in such a case he is probably entitled to an adjournment in order to prepare his defence. If such an adjournment is granted a summons should issue.

The Information

An information is simply "the statement by which the magistrate is informed of the offence", *per* Huddleston B. in *R.* v. *Hughes* (1897) 43 J.P. 556. The information need not be in writing or on oath (Magistrates' Courts Rules 1981, r 4(2)) except when a warrant is sought: Magistrates' Courts Act 1980, s.1(3).

The information is sufficient if it describes the specific offence in ordinary language avoiding as far as possible the use of technical terms and without necessarily stating all the elements of the offence and giving such particulars as may be necessary for giving reasonable information of the nature of the charge: Magistrates' Courts Rules 1981, r. 100(1). It must contain reference to the section and Act or other instrument: r. 100(2), *ibid*, but it is not necessary to negative any exception, proviso, excuse or qualification: r. 4(3), *ibid*. A court may not try an information charging more than one offence: Magistrates' Courts Rules 1981, r. 12(1) *(See* the introduction to ch. 5 under the Duplicity Rule.) But there is nothing to prevent a number of informations being laid on one piece of paper: *ibid,* r.12(2).

The practice of laying alternative informations when there is doubt was commended in *R.* v. *Newcastle Justices, ex parte Boyce* [1976] R.T.R. 325.

Defective informations may sometimes be cured by the Magistrates' Courts Act 1980, s. 123. See Defective Process, in the introduction to ch. 5.

Laying the Information

An information may be laid by the prosecutor in person or by his counsel or other person authorized in that behalf: Magistrates' Courts Rules 1981, r. 4(1).

An information may be laid before a justice of the peace (Magistrates' Court Act 1980, s. 1) or before a clerk to the justices (Justices' Clerks Rules 1970).

An information is laid for the purpose of s. 127 of the Magistrates' Courts Act 1980 when it is received at the office of the clerk to the justices for the relevant area. It is not necessary for the information to be personally received by a justice of the peace or by the clerk to the justices. It is enough that it is received by any member of the staff of the clerk to the justices, expressly or impliedly authorized to receive it, for onward transmission to a justice of the peace or the clerk to the justices: *Hill* v. *Anderton* (1982) 146 J.P. 348. The House found it unnecessary to decide whether similar reasoning applies to an information laid orally, but expressed the view that in the ordinary course such oral information will in practice and should as a matter of prudence be addressed by the informant or his authorized agent to a justice of the peace or the clerk to the justices in person.

The "precautionary" laying of an information before the prosecutor has decided to prosecute may be an abuse of the process of the court: *R*. v. *Brentford Justices, ex parte Wong* [1981] 1 All E.R. 884; *R*. v. *Fairford Justices, ex parte Brewster* (1975) 139 J.P. 574, except where there are administrative difficulties in getting the case together. See for example *R*. v. *South Western Magistrates' Court, ex parte Benton* [1980] R.T.R. 35, and *see* Oppression and Abuse of Process in the introduction to ch. 5.

Prosecuting a Juvenile

Anyone who decides to lay an information against someone he has reason to believe to be a juvenile is under a duty to notify the appropriate local authority: Children and Young Persons Act 1969, s. 5(8). In the case of a juvenile of 13 years or older a probation officer must also be notified: Children and Young Persons Act 1969, s. 34(2). Whenever a juvenile is charged with an offence his parents or guardians must be required to attend court unless this is unreasonable: Children and Young Persons Act 1933, s. 34. A summons or warrant may issue in the same manner as if it were laid against them or the summons to the juvenile may include a summons to the parent or guardian: Magistrates' Courts (Children and Young Persons) Rules 1970, r. 26.

The Issue of a Summons

Unlike the laying of an information, the issue of a summons thereupon "is the result of a judicial act", *per* Lord Goddard C.J. in *R*. v. *Wilson, ex parte Battersea B.C.* [1947] 2 All E.R. 569; *Hill* v. *Anderton* (1982) 146 J.P. 348.

The circumstances in which a summons may be issued are set out in the Magistrates' Courts Act 1980, s. 1(2). They should be distinguished from the jurisdiction to try offences which is contained in ss. 2, 3, *ibid*.

A summons may be issued by a justice of the peace: Magistrates' Courts Act 1980, s. 1; or by a justices' clerk: Justices' Clerks Rules 1970. This duty cannot be delegated by the clerk to any of his assistants: *R*. v. *Gateshead Justices, ex parte Tesco Stores* (1981) 145 J.P. 200; *Hill* v. *Anderton* (1982) 146 J.P. 348. When the clerk acts under these Rules he acts as a justice, *per* Donaldson LJ in *R*. v. *Worthing Justices, ex parte Norvell* [1981] 1 W.L.R. 413. He may thus refuse as well as grant.

If a justice authorizes the issue of a summons without having applied his mind to the information then he is guilty of dereliction of duty, *per* Lord Widgery CJ in *R*. v. *Brentford Justices, ex parte Catlin* (1975) 139 J.P. 516.

"In the exercise of his discretion whether or not to accede to an application for the issue of a summons a justice must at the very least ascertain:

(i) whether the allegation is of an offence known to the law and if so whether the essential ingredients of the offence are *prima facie* present;
(ii) that the offence alleged is not out of time;
(iii) that the court has jurisdiction;
(iv) whether the informant has the necessary authority to prosecute.

"In addition to these specific matters it is clear that he may and indeed should consider whether the allegation is vexatious. Since the matter is properly within the magistrate's discretion it would be inappropriate to attempt to lay down an exhaustive catalogue of matters to which consideration should be given. Plainly he should consider the whole of the relevant circumstances. The magistrate must be able to satisfy himself that it is a proper case in which to issue a summons. There can be no question, however, of conducting a preliminary hearing. Until a summons has been issued there is no allegation to meet: no charge has been made. A proposed defendant has no *locus standi* and no right at this stage to be heard. Whilst it is conceivable that a magistrate might seek information from him in exceptional circumstances it must be entirely within the discretion of the magistrate whether to do so," *per* Lord Widgery CJ in *R.* v. *West London Justices, ex parte Klahn* (1979) 143 J.P. 390; *R.* v. *Gateshead Justices, ex parte Tesco Stores* (1981) 145 J.P. 200.

Examples of magistrates *wrongly refusing* to issue process are: *R.* v. *Adamson* [1875] 1 Q.B.D. 201 (distaste for views expressed at public meeting); *R.* v. *Byrde and Pontypool Gas Co., ex parte Williams* (1980) 65 J.P. 310 (having previously dismissed a summons based on similar facts, justices declined process without exercising judicial discretion); *R.* v. *Bennett and Bond, ex parte Bennett* (1908) 72 J.P. 362 (first summons having been dismissed in the absence of the prosecutor who had knowledge of the hearing, the magistrates declined a second, commenting that the prosecutor had a civil remedy) and *R.* v. *Beacontree Justices, ex parte Mercer* [1970] Crim. L.R. 103 (practice always to refuse applications of a particular nature).

The refusal to grant process has been *upheld* in the following cases: *Ex parte Lewis* (1888) 52 J.P. 773 (where the High Court had earlier decided that the facts did not disclose an offence); *Utting* v. *Berney* (1888) 52 J.P. 806 (two informations laid against two different people for the same offence, informant refusing to select either). An order of *mandamus* will not be issued unless it can be shown that in declining to grant process a magistrate's decision was governed by extraneous or irregular matters: *R.* v. *Metropolitan Magistrate, ex parte Bennion* (1971) 135 J.P.N. 491.

In *R.* v. *Mead, ex parte National Insurance Commissioners* (1916) 80 J.P. 332, it was held that a magistrate could not decline to issue process against an employer simply because his servants were not being prosecuted. In the course of his judgment, Ridley J said: "It is quite true that in considering the matter brought before him the magistrate may decline to issue a summons because he thinks that there will not be evidence by which the offence could be proved if it were brought before a jury."

It may be doubted whether it is proper for justices to decide, as a matter of discretion, to entertain a second application for a summons on exactly the same material as has been considered by other justices of the same bench. *Per* Donaldson, LJ, in *R.* v. *Worthing Justices, ex parte Norvell* [1981] 1 W.L.R. 413. Although it may sometimes be useful to give reasons for the refusal of a summons there is no obligation to do so and it is not usually done, *per* Donaldon, LJ, *ibid*.

The charge to be preferred is in the discretion of the prosecution, not the justices: *R.* v. *Nuneaton Justices, ex parte Parker* (1954) 118 J.P. 524 (Magistrate refused summons for careless driving where he felt dangerous driving more appropriate), and *see* the remarks of Lord Roskill in *R.* v. *Seymour* [1983] 3 W.L.R. 349 at p. 359. But in *R.* v. *Old Street Magistrate, ex parte Simons* (1976) 140 J.P.N. 25, a magistrate's decision to refuse a summons for criminal damage after he had granted one for common assault arising out of the same incident was upheld where he considered that this could satisfactorily dispose of the case.

Summons Not Essential to Jurisdiction

A summons, as distinct from an information, is not essential to jurisdiction. In *R.* v. *Hughes* (1879) 43 J.P. 556, Hawkins, J in a considered judgment in the Court for Crown Cases Reserved approved also by Coleridge LCJ said "There is a marked distinction between the jurisdiction to take cognizance of an offence and the jurisdiction to issue a particular process to compel the accused to answer it. The former may exist, the latter may be wanting . . . Process is not essential to the jurisdiction of the justices to hear and adjudicate." This still seems concisely to state the rule of law. *See* also *R.* v. *Shaw* (1865) 29 J.P. 339; *R.* v. *Tabrum and Quayle, ex parte Dash* (1907) 71 J.P. 325;*Gray* v. *Customs Commissioners* (1884) 48 J.P. 343.

The effect of this is that an oral information may be laid against a person present in court and the trial begun immediately. This is of course subject to the principles of natural justice and if the accused seeks an adjournment it is submitted that he is entitled to it, whereupon a summons should issue.

The Contents of a Summons

A summons must state shortly the matter of the information and the time and place at which the defendant is required to appear: Magistrates' Courts Rules 1981, r. 4(2). The summons is sufficient if it describes the specific offence in ordinary language avoiding as far as possible the use of technical terms and without necessarily stating all the elements of the offence, and gives such particulars as may be necessary for giving reasonable information of the nature of the charge: *ibid.*, r. 100(1). If a statutory offence it must refer to the section of the Act etc: *ibid.*, r. 100(2). A single summons may contain a number of informations: *ibid.*, r. 4(3). It must be signed by the justice issuing it or be authenticated by the clerk: *ibid.*, r. 4(1). If issued by the clerk it must be signed by him.

Challenging the Sufficiency of a Summons

Certain defects in a summons may be cured by the Magistrates' Courts Act 1980 s. 123. (*See* under Defective Process in the introduction to ch. 5.).

If a summons does not give sufficient particulars the proper course for the defendant is to apply for an adjournment, and if the justices are satisfied that he has in any way been misled they would always be willing to grant such an application: *Neal* v. *Devenish* (1894) 58 J.P. 246. If the prosecution reject an adjournment to enable them to supply sufficient particulars the information may be dismissed: *Robertson* v. *Rosenburg* (1951) 115 J.P. 128.

Application for particulars may be made any time after the charge is preferred, but the accused is not in general entitled to see the information before committal for trial: *R.* v. *Aylesbury Justices, ex parte Wisbey* (1965) 129 J.P. 287. In *Hickmott* v. *Curd* (1971) 135 J.P. 519 a conviction was upheld on particulars different from those stated in the charge where the alternative particulars had been "sufficiently ventilated" in argument. It is suggested that this decision is one which should be regarded very much as being dependent on its particular facts.

The Service of a Summons

A distinction must be made between the methods by which a summons may be served and the means by which service of a summons may be proved.

A summons may be served

(a) by delivering it to the person to whom it is directed;

(b) by leaving it for him with some person at his last known or usual place of abode or at an address given by him for that purpose; or

(c) by sending it by post in a letter addressed to him at such place of abode or address:

Magistrates' Courts Rules 1981, r.99(1),(8).

However, in the case of an indictable offence service by method (b) or (c) must not be treated as proved unless it is proved that the summons came to the defendant's knowledge and for that purpose any letter or other communication purporting to be written by him or on his behalf in such terms as reasonably to justify the inference that the summons came to his knowledge is admissible as evidence of that fact: *ibid,* r.99(2). There is no need for proof that the summons came to the defendant's knowledge in the case of a summary offence, but where service is by post it must be by recorded delivery or registered letter: *ibid,* r.99(2), proviso.

A witness summons and certain other summonses may not be served by methods (b) or (c): *ibid,* r.99(6).

A summons to a corporation may be served by delivery to, or sending it by post to, the registered office: *ibid,* r. 99(3).

The fact that a summons has been properly served may be proved by evidence on oath or in any other admissible form, but the most usual way is a certificate under the Magistrates' Courts Rules, 1981, r. 67.

Voiding Proceedings Unknown to Accused

When a summons has been issued and a magistrates' court has begun to try the information the accused may make a statutory declaration that he did not know of the proceedings or summons until a date after the court had begun to try the information. If this declaration is served on the clerk to the justices within 21 days of the date mentioned in the declaration the summons and all subsequent proceedings are void: Magistrates' Courts Act 1980, s. 14(1). The date for service may be extended if the court (or the justices' clerk: Justices' Clerks Rules 1970) is satisfied that it was not reasonable to expect the accused to serve the statement within time: *ibid.,* s. 14(3).

When a statutory declaration is made a fresh summons may issue on the original information but the information cannot be tried by the same justices: *ibid.,* s. 14(1), (4).

The Issue of a Warrant

The vast majority of summary offenders are proceeded against by way of summons, but a warrant is usually issued in a serious case or when the accused is unlikely to attend as a result of a summons: *O'Brien* v. *Brabner* (1885) 49 J.P.N. 227; *Dumbell* v. *Roberts* (1944) 108 J.P. 139. In the case of an adult the power to issue a warrant in the first instance is confined to (i) indictable offences: (ii) offences punishable with imprisonment; and (iii) cases where the address of the defendant is not sufficiently established for a summons to be served on him: Magistrates' Courts Act 1980, s. 1(4).

The circumstances in which a warrant may issue are set out in The Magistrates' Courts Act 1980, s. 1(2), (5). They should be distinguished from the jurisdiction to try offences which is contained in ss. 2, 3 *ibid.* Where the offence is indictable a warrant may issue at any time notwithstanding that a summons has previously been issued: s. 1(6), *ibid.*

The Contents of a Warrant

A warrant of arrest must require the persons to whom it is directed to arrest the person against whom the warrant is issued: Magistrates' Courts Rules 1981, r. 96(1). It must name or otherwise describe the person to be arrested and must contain a statement of the offence charged: *ibid.,* r. 96(2). The warrant is sufficient if it describes the offence charged in ordinary language avoiding as far as possible the use of technical terms and without necessarily stating all the elements of the offence, and gives such particulars as may be necessary for giving reasonable information of the nature of the charge: *ibid.,* r. 100(1). It must refer to the section of the Act: *ibid.,* r. 100(2). The warrant must be signed by the justice or, in certain cases, his clerk: *ibid.,* r. 95. The warrant may be endorsed for bail: Magistrates' Courts Act 1980, s. 117; except in a case of treason: *ibid.,* s. 47. Certain defects in a warrant may be cured by the Magistrates' Courts Act 1980, s. 123. *See* Defective Process in the introduction to ch. 5.

The Execution of a Warrant

A warrant may be executed anywhere in England and Wales by any person to whom it is directed or by any constable acting within his police area: Magistrates' Courts Act 1980, s. 125(2). It remains in force until executed or withdrawn: subs. (1), *ibid*.; notwithstanding the death of the issuing justice: s. 124, *ibid*. When a warrant is lost or destroyed a duplicate may be issued after proper inquiry: *R.* v. *Leigh Justices, ex parte Kara [1981]* 72 Cr. App. R. 327.

Process Outside England and Wales

A *warrant* issued in England and Wales for the arrest of a person charged with an offence may be executed in Scotland or Northern Ireland and *vice versa* without endorsement: Criminal Law Act 1977, s. 38. No endorsement is required.

A warrant issued in England and Wales for the arrest of a person in any part of the United Kingdom including the Channel Islands and the Isle of Man may be executed after endorsement in those places (and *vice versa*) under the Indictable Offences Act 1848, ss 12-14. Effectively, because of the simpler machinery of the Criminal Law Act 1977, s. 38, the Act of 1848 is used now only in respect of the Channel Islands and the Isle of Man and for civil process. The Act of 1848 has been extended to a wider range of warrants of arrest and to warrants of commitment by the Magistrates' Courts Act 1980, s. 126.

A *summons* requiring a person charged with an offence to appear before a court in England or Wales may be served on him in Scotland or Northern Ireland: Criminal Law Act 1977, s. 39(1). Methods of service and proof of service are dealt with in the Magistrates' Courts Rules 1981, rr. 67 and 99. Such a summons issued for appearance in a court in Northern Ireland may similarly be served in England and Wales: Criminal Law Act 1977, s 39(2). Service is prescribed in the Magistrates' Courts (Amendment) Rules (Northern Ireland) 1980 (not contained herein).

Citation of a person charged with a crime or offence to appear before a Scottish court may be effected in England or Wales or Northern Ireland in like manner as it may be in Scotland: Criminal Law Act 1977, s. 39(3).

The endorsement and execution in England and Wales of warrants granted in the Republic of Ireland is dealt with in a separate code laid down in the Backing of Warrants (Republic of Ireland) Act 1965, and rules made thereunder. There are no reciprocal arrangements between the two countries for the execution of summonses.

The ordinary process of a magistrates' court in criminal cases (*i.e.* summonses and warrants) cannot be executed outside the United Kingdom and the Republic of Ireland except under the Extradition Acts 1870 and 1873, or the Fugitive Offenders Act 1967 (which are not dealt with in this work).

Arrest without Warrant

The general powers of a constable or anyone else to arrest without warrant are codified in the Criminal Law Act 1967, s. 2. They are expressed in relation to arrestable offences, that is to say offences for which the sentence is fixed by law or for which a person (not previously convicted) may under or by virtue of any enactment be sentenced to imprisonment for a term of five years and attempts to commit such offences. In addition, specific powers of arrest without warrant are conferred by a variety of statutes.

Jurisdiction

Jurisdiction is both territorial and temporal.

Territorial Jurisdiction

Indictable offences may, in general, be dealt with by magistrates either as examining justices or (where they have jurisdiction) on summary trial, wherever committed in England and Wales: Magistrates' Courts Act, 1980, ss 2(3) and (4) and 155(6). (Various statutes extending the powers of English courts over acts committed abroad are outside the scope of this work).

As to acts committed outside this country, the rules of international comity do not call for more than that each sovereign state should refrain from punishing persons for their conduct within the territory of another sovereign state where that conduct has had no harmful consequences within the territory of the state which imposes the punishment, *per* Lord Diplock in *Treacy* v. *Director of Public Prosecutions* (1971) 135 J.P. 112 (defendant could be tried for black-mail where he posted in England a letter received by someone in Germany). An attempt to obtain property by deception is committed within the jurisdiction where letters posted in Northern Ireland were received in England: *R.* v. *Baxter* (1971) 135 J.P. 345. And *see R.* v. *Wall* [1974] 2 All E.R. 245 (knowingly concerned in fraudulent evasion of import restriction) and *R.* v. *Markus* (1975) 139 J.P. 19 (fraudulent inducement to invest). In *D.P.P.* v. *Stonehouse* (1977) 141 J.P. 473 Lord Edmund Davies approved the proposition that "If a person, being outside England, initiates an offence, part of the essential elements of which take effect in England, he is amenable to English jurisdiction". That case concerned an attempted deception to obtain insurance monies where acts committed abroad had resulted in the intended payment of those monies in England.

"Where a crime is committed in England a secondary party (accessory or abettor) can be punished even though he was not within British territorial jurisdiction at the time when the crime was committed or when he gave his assistance, *at least if he is a citizen of the United Kingdom*": Professor Glanville Williams, quoted with approval by the court in *R.* v. *Robert Millar (Contractors) Ltd* (1970) 134 J.P. 240. (Scottish company convicted of counselling and procuring death by dangerous driving in England when tyre of vehicle driven by their employee was defective).

The jurisdiction of English courts in indictable cases extends over British ships on the high seas or waters where great ships go, as far as the tide ebbs and flows: *R.* v *Anderson* [1861-73] All E.R. 999. This jurisdiction is extended by the Merchant Shipping Act, 1894, s. 686 over aliens committing offences on board British ships and British subjects committing offences on board any foreign ship to which they do not belong. *See R.* v. *Kelly* [1981] 2 All E.R. 1098. Justices are given jurisdiction over ships lying off the coast by s. 685, *ibid*. And *see R.* v. *Liverpool Justices, ex parte Molyneux* (1972) 136 J.P. 477. For jurisdiction in territorial waters see the Territorial Waters Jurisdiction Act 1878, s. 2 (not reproduced herein) and *R.* v. *Kent Justices, ex parte Lye and Others* (1967) 131 J.P. 212.

For jurisdiction over criminal acts committed in aircraft see the Tokyo Convention Act 1967 (not reproduced herein).

Local Jurisdiction

Summary offences may be tried only by the justices of the county within which they were committed: Magistrates' Courts Act 1980, s. 2(1); except when process was issued under s. 2(1)(b), *ibid*., in order to allow a person accused of an offence committed elsewhere to be charged jointly with or in the same place as a person for whose alleged offence the justices already have jurisdiction: s. 2(2), *ibid*. Similarly, when a defendant is already being tried for an offence before magistrates they have jurisdiction to try him for any summary offence committed elsewhere: s. 2(6), *ibid*. Special rules apply to offences committed on boundaries, on journeys or begun in one jurisdiction and completed in another: s. 3, *ibid*. For the purpose of the Magistrates' Courts Act 1980 the Isles of Scilly form part of the County of Cornwall: *ibid*., s. 149.

Jurisdiction of the London Courts

Greater London is divided into five London commission areas by the Justices of the Peace Act 1979, s. 2. Each commission area is "deemed to be a county for all purposes of the law relating to commissions of the peace, justices of the peace, magistrates' courts, the *custos rotulorum*, justices' clerks and matters connected with any of these matters" by subs. (3), *ibid.* Thus, magistrates for any London commission area may try any summary offence arising within the area in accordance with the Magistrates' Courts Act, 1980, s. 2(1). (It should be noted that the jurisdiction of all magistrates' courts in respect of summary offences is extended by subs. (6), *ibid.*). A justice in any London commission area may act as a justice for his area in any other commission area or county adjoining his own area by virtue of s. 133, *ibid.*

The InnerLondon area is in turn divided into a number of petty sessional divisions by virtue of the Justices of the Peace Act 1979, s. 36 and Orders made thereunder.

Before the coming into operation of the Administration of Justice Act 1964 there were two separate and, geographically at least, coextensive systems of petty sessional courts in the metropolitan area—the courts of the metropolitan stipendiary magistrates and those of the lay justices for the county of London. The effect of that Act was, substantially, to merge these two jurisdictions. The present position is as follows:

The Metropolitan Stipendiary Magistrates

— exercise the jurisdiction conferred on them by statute except that the inner London area replaces the metropolitan police courts area: Justices of the Peace Act 1979, s. 33(2).
— have the jurisdiction conferred on any two justices of the peace sitting together by any enactment, their commission or by the common law (s. 33(1), *ibid.*).
— are by virtue of their office justices of the peace for each of the London commission areas and for the counties of Essex, Hertfordshire, Kent and Surrey (s. 31(4)); notwithstanding that they may be assigned by the Lord Chancellor to particular petty sessional division (s. 32(1), *ibid.*).

Lay Justices

— share the jurisdiction conferred on all justices of the peace, by any enactment, by their commission and by the common law (s. 33(1), *ibid*).
—when sitting with at least one other, are given the jurisdiction conferred on metropolitan stipendiary magistrates as such by any enactment except:

(a) the Extradition Acts, 1870-1935
(b) s. 40 of the Pawnbrokers Act, 1872
(c) the Fugitive Offenders Act 1967
(d) s. 28 of the Pilotage Act, 1913
(e) s. 25 of the Children and Young Persons Act, 1933.(s. 33(3). *ibid).*

Limitation of Time

Nullum tempus occurrit regi (time never runs against the Crown) is the rule with regard to any indictable offence when tried on indictment and this rule is applied by the Magistrates' Courts Act 1980, ss 127(2) and (3), to the summary trial of an offence triable either way. However, where any enactment imposes a limitation on the time for taking proceedings on indictment for that offence no summary proceedings may be taken after the latest time for taking proceedings on indictment: *ibid.*, s. 127(4).

Subject only to the exception concerning indictable offences, a magistrates' court may not try an information within six months from the time when the offence was committed: *ibid.*, s. 127(1). It is always necessary to consult the statute concerned to ensure that no special period of limitation applies.

The purpose of the six months' limitation is to ensure that summary offences are charged and tried as soon as reasonably possible after their alleged commission so that the recollection of witnesses may still be reasonably clear and so that there shall be no unnecessary delay in the disposal of summary offences, *per* May J in *R.* v. *Newcastle-upon-Tyne Justices, ex parte Bryce (Contractors) Ltd* (1976) 140 J.P. 440; and *per* Donaldson LJ in *R.* v. *Brentford Justices, ex parte Wong* [1981] 1 All E.R. 884. Thus, undue delay between the laying of an information and the issue of process may amount to Oppression and an Abuse of the Process of the Court: (*See* under that heading in the introduction to ch. 5.).

The laying of a subsequent information out of time was held not to bar the reissue of a warrant on an earlier information laid within time: *R.* v. *Leigh Justices, ex parte Kara* [1981] 72 Cr. App. R. 327. The Act lays down no period within which a summons must issue upon the information but it cannot be delayed indefinitely to the prejudice of the defendant: *R.* v. *Fairford Justices, ex parte Brewster* (1975) 139 J.P. 574.

For calculating the period of limitation the day on which the offence was committed is to be excluded and the day the information was laid included: *Radcliffe* v. *Bartholomew* (1892) 56 J.P. 262; *Stewart* v. *Chapman* (1951) 115 J.P. 473; *Marren* v. *Dawson, Bentley and Co., Ltd* [1961] 2 All E.R. 270.

The relevant date is that of the information and not that of the hearing: *Beardsley* v. *Giddings* (1904) 68 J.P. 222; *Abraham* v. *Jutson* (1962) 106 Sol. J. 880; *Morris* v. *Duncan* (1899) 62 J.P. 823. Where a doubt is raised as to whether an information was laid in time, the defendant is entitled to be acquitted: *Lloyd* v. *Young* [1963] Crim. L.R. 703. When the evidence fails to show that the offence was committed within the time, it is immaterial that the evidence available to the prosecution at the time of instituting the proceedings did: *R.* v. *Lewis* (1979) 143 J.P. 588.

Certain enactments have their own time limits. In some cases these are dependent upon the date upon which information had come to the prosecutor's knowledge. Where an information was laid within time but not accompanied by the necessary certificate as to knowledge it was held that the magistrate had been wrong to decline jurisdiction: *R.* v. *Clerkenwell Metropolitan Stipendiary Magistrate, ex parte Director of Public Prosecutions* (1983) The Times, August 4.

Aiders and abettors are subject to the same time limit as the principal offenders: *Gould and Co.* v. *Houghton* (1921) 85 J.P. 93; *Homolka* v. *Osmond* [1939] 1 All E.R. 154.

The same, but no other, justice may issue a second summons out of time ("or a series of summonses, if necessary"), when the information was laid in time and the first summons not served: *R.* v. *Pickford* (1861) 25 J.P. 549 (a bastardy case). And *see* also *Ex parte Fielding* (1861) 25 J.P. 759.

Continuing Offences

With continuing offences, time runs not from first discovery but from each day on which the offence was committed: *Barrett* v. *Barrow-in-Furness Corporation* (1887) 51 J.P. 803; *Rowley* v. *Everton (T.A.) and Sons, Ltd* (1940) 104 J.P. 461; *R.* v. *Chertsey Justices, ex parte Franks* (1961) 125 J.P. 305. A continuing offence is one which is committed afresh each day, not a single transaction, albeit taking place over a length of time: *Anderton* v. *Cooper* (1981) 145 J.P. 128 (distinguishing *Parry* v. *Forest of Dean District Council* (1976) 34 P&CR 209, which however is still binding on magistrates' courts in respect of its particular facts, i.e. covering s. 89(5) of the Town and Country Planning Act 1971). The illegal erection of a partition wall is not a continuing offence: *Marshall* v. *Smith* (1873) 29 J.P. 36; and neither is letting at an excessive rent: *R.* v. *Wimbledon Justices, ex parte Derwent* (1953) 117 J.P. 113; nor "depositing and leaving" litter contrary to the Litter Act, 1958: *Vaughan* v. *Biggs* (1960) 124 J.P. 341. There is a Scottish decision to the effect that acts required by statute to be performed "forthwith" are not continuing offences and time runs from the date the act falls to be performed: *A. and C McLennan (Blairgowrie) Ltd* v. *MacMillan* (1964) S.L.T. 2. It is not a continuing offence for a non-patrial to remain unlawfully in this country contrary to the Immigration Act 1971, s. 24(1)(b)(i): *Singh (Gurdev)* v. *The Queen* [1974] 1 All E.R. 26. The offence of knowingly remaining in the U.K. beyond time in s. 24(1)(b) of the Immigration Act 1971 can only be committed on the day following the expiry of the limited leave: *Grant* v. *Borg* [1982] 2 All E.R. 257. (*See* generally the article by J.N. Spencer at 146 J.P.N. 542.)

The Crown and Diplomatic Immunity

The court may be deprived of jurisdiction in cases involving a head of state. "The doctrine of regal immunity really rests upon the fact that no British tribunal has a jurisdiction under which the Sovereign can be tried. That this is so is shown by the rules . . . under which the servants of the Crown cannot plead superior orders as an excuse for any offence which they may have committed": *Russell on Crime*, 12th edn. at p. 96. The principle that statutes do not bind the Crown except by clear expression to the contrary is not derogated from by the many Acts of Parliament protecting the Crown or saving Crown rights: *Hornsey Urban District Council* v. *Hennell* [1900-3] All E.R. 392; *Cooper* v. *Hawkins* (1904) 68 J.P. 25. An example of a statute being applied to persons and property in the service of the Crown is the Road Traffic Act 1972, s. 188.

A diplomatic agent as defined in art. 1 of sch. I of the Diplomatic Privileges Act 1964 enjoys immunity from the criminal jurisdiction of this country (art. 31, *ibid.*), but such immunity may be waived by his State (art. 32, *ibid.*). For the corresponding provisions concerning consular officers and employees see the Consular Relations Act 1968, and for representatives of Commonwealth countries the Diplomatic and Other Privileges Act 1971. Proceedings brought against anyone entitled to diplomatic immunity are without jurisdiction and null and void until there is a valid waiver, but immunity is a procedural bar which can be lost by change of circumstances: *R.* v. *Madan* (1961) 125 J.P. 246; as explained in *Empson* v. *Smith* [1965] 2 All E.R. 881.

THE INDICTABLE OFFENCES ACT 1848

English warrants may be backed in Ireland and vice versa

12. That if any person against whom a warrant shall be issued in any county, riding, division, liberty, city, borough, or place in England or Wales, by any justice of the peace, or by any Judge of Her Majesty's court of Queen's Bench, or the Crown Court, for any indictable offence against the laws of that part of the United Kingdom, shall escape, go into, reside, or be, or be supposed or suspected to be, in any county or place in that part of the United Kingdom called Ireland, or if any person against whom a warrant shall be issued in any county or place in Ireland, by any justice of the peace, or by any Judge of Her Majesty's Court of Queen's Bench there, to any justice of oyer and terminer or goal delivery, for any crime or offence against the laws of that part of the United Kingdom, shall escape, go into, reside, or be, or be supposed or suspected to be, in any county, riding, division, liberty, city, borough, or place in that part of the United Kingdom called England or Wales, it shall and may be lawful for any justice of the peace in and for the county or place into which such person shall escape or go, or where he shall reside or be, or be supposed or suspected to be, to make an endorsement on the warrant, signed with his name, authorizing the execution of the warrant within the jurisdiction of the justice making the endorsement, or to the like effect, and which warrant so endorsed shall be a sufficient authority to the person or persons bringing such warrant, and to all persons to whom such warrant was originally directed, and also to all constables or other peace officers of the county or place where such warrant shall be so endorsed, to execute the said warrant in the county or place where the justice so endorsing it shall have jurisdiction, by apprehending the person against whom such warrant shall have been granted, and to convey him before the justice or justices who granted the same, or before some other justice or justices of the peace in and for the same county or place, and which the said justice or justices before whom he shall be so brought shall thereupon proceed in such manner as if the said person had been apprehended in the said last-mentioned county or place.

(*as amended by the Magistrates' Courts Act, 1952, sch. 5, the Courts Act 1971, sch. 8*).

COMMENTARY

Sections 12-14 of this Act have been applied to (a) warrants of arrest issued under s. 1 of the Magistrates' Courts Act 1980 for offences other than those referred to in this section; (b) warrants of arrest issued under s. 13, *ibid*., and (c) warrants of commitment issued under the Act of 1980: s. 126, *ibid*.

This Act is effectively superseded so far as concerns a warrant of arrest of a person charged with an offence by the Criminal Law Act 1977, s. 38, *infra*.

By s. 32 of the Act the town of Berwick upon Tweed is deemed to be within England.

Indictable offence. Defined in the Interpretation Act 1978, sch. 1.

Ireland. This is to be construed as referring to Northern Ireland only: Backing of Warrants (Republic of Ireland) Act 1965, s. 9.

Backing English warrants in the Isles of Man, Guernsey, Jersey, Alderney, or Sark, and vice versa

13. That if any person against whom a warrant shall be issued in any county, riding, division, liberty, city, borough, or place in England or Wales, by any justice of the peace, or by any Judge of Her Majesty's Court of Queen's Bench, or the Crown Court, for any indictable offence, shall escape, go into, reside, or be, or supposed to be, or suspected to be, in any of the Isles of Man, Guernsey, Jersey, Alderney, or Sark, it shall be lawful for any officer within the district into which such accused person shall escape or go, or where he shall reside or be, or be supposed or suspected to be, who shall have jurisdiction to issue any warrant or process in the nature of a warrant for the apprehension of offenders within such district, to endorse such warrant in the manner hereinbefore mentioned, or to the like effect; or if any person against whom any warrant, or process in the nature of a warrant, shall be issued in any of the Isles aforesaid, shall escape, go into, reside, or be, or be supposed or suspected to be, in any county, riding, division, liberty, city, borough, or place in England or Wales, it shall be lawful for any justice of the peace in and for the county or place into which such person shall escape or go, or where he shall reside or be, or be supposed or suspected to be, to endorse such warrant or process in the nature of a warrant in manner hereinbefore mentioned, and every such warrant or process, so endorsed, shall be a sufficient authority to the person or persons bringing the same, and to all persons to whom the same respectively was originally directed, and also to all constables and peace officers in the county, district, or jurisdiction within which such warrant or process shall be so endorsed, to execute the same within the county, district, or place where the justice or officer endorsing the same has jurisdiction, and to convey such offender, when apprehended, into the county or district wherein the justice or person who issued such warrant or process shall have jurisdiction and carry him before such justice or person, or before some other justice or person within the same county or district who shall have jurisdiction to commit such offender to prison for trial, and such justice or person may thereupon proceed in such and the same manner as if the said offender had been apprehended within his jurisdiction.

(*as amended by the Courts Act 1971, sch. 8*).

COMMENTARY

This section has been extended by the Magistrates' Courts Act 1980, s. 126. *See* the commentary to s. 12, *supra.*. It is still necessary to use this provision because the Criminal Law Act 1977, s. 38, does not apply to the territories named herein.

Channel Islands. For the endorsement of warrants in the Channel Islands *see* the Criminal Justice Administration Act, 1851, s. 18.

English or Irish warrants may be backed in Scotland

14. That if any person against whom a warrant shall be issued by any justice of the peace for any county or place within England or Wales or Ireland, or by any Judge of Her Majesty's Court of Queen's Bench or in England the Crown Court or in Ireland any justice of oyer and terminer or goal delivery for any crime or offence against the laws of those parts respectively of the United Kingdom of Great Britain and Ireland, shall escape, go into, reside, or be, or be supposed or suspected to be, in any place in Scotland it shall be lawful for the sheriff or steward depute or substitute, or any justice of the peace of the county or place where such person or persons shall go into, reside, or be, or be supposed or suspected to be, to endorse the said warrant in manner hereinbefore mentioned, or to the like effect, which warrant so endorsed shall be a sufficient authority to the person or persons bringing such warrant, and to all persons to whom such warrant was originally directed, and also to all sheriffs' officers, stewards' officers, constables, and other peace officers of the county or place where such warrant shall be so endorsed, to execute the same within the county or place where it shall have been so endorsed, by apprehending the person against whom such warrant shall have been granted, and to convey him into the county or place in England, Wales or Ireland where the justice or justices who first issued the said warrant shall have jurisdiction in that behalf, and to carry him before such justice or justices, or before any other justice or justices of the peace of and for the same county or place, to be there dealt with according to law, and which said justice or justices are hereby authorized and required thereupon to proceed in such and the same manner as if the said offender had been apprehended within his or their jurisdiction.

(*as amended by the Courts Act 1971, sch. 8*).

COMMENTARY

See the *Commentary* to s. 12, *supra*.

Ireland. This is to be construed as referring to Northern Ireland only: Backing of Warrants (Republic of Ireland) Act 1965, s. 9.

Scottish warrants may be backed in England or Ireland

15. That if any person against whom a warrant shall be issued by the Lord Justice General, Lord Chief Justice Clerk, or any of the Lords Commissioners of Justiciary, or by any sheriff or steward depute or sustitute, or justice of the peace, of Scotland, for any crime or offence against the laws of that part of the United Kingdom, shall escape, go into, reside, or be, or shall be supposed or suspected to be, in any county or place in England or in Ireland, it shall be lawful for any justice of the peace in and for the county or place into which such person shall escape or go, or where he shall reside or be, or shall be supposed or suspected to be, to endorse the said warrant in manner hereinbefore mentioned, and which said warrant so endorsed shall be a sufficient authority to the person or persons bringing the same, and to all persons to whom the same was originally directed, and also to all constables and other peace officers of the county or place where the justice so endorsing such warrant shall have jurisdiction, to execute the said warrant in the county or place where it is so endorsed, by apprehending the person against whom such warrant shall have been granted, and to convey him into the county or place in Scotland next adjoining England, and carry him before the sheriff or steward depute or substitute or one of the justices of the peace, of such county or place, and which said sheriff, steward depute or substitute, or justice of the peace, is hereby authorized and required thereupon to proceed in such and the same manner according to the rules and practice of the law of Scotland, as if the said offender had been apprehended within such county or place in Scotland last aforesaid.

COMMENTARY

See the Commentary to s. 12, *supra*. By s. 32 of this Act the town of Berwick upon Tweed is deemed to be within England.

Ireland. This is to be construed as referring to Northern Ireland only: Backing of Warrants (Republic of Ireland) Act 1965, s. 9.

THE CHILDREN AND YOUNG PERSONS ACT 1933

Attendance at court of parents of child or young person brought before court

34. (1) Where a child or young person is charged with any offence or is for any other reason brought before a court, any person who is a parent or guardian of his may be required to attend at the court before which the case is heard or determined during all stages of the proceedings, and any such person shall be so required at any stage where the court thinks it desirable, unless the court is satisfied that it would be unreasonable to require his attendance.

(2) Where a child or young person is arrested, such steps shall be taken by the person who arrested him as may be practicable to inform at least one person whose attendance may be required under this section.

(*as substituted by the Children and Young Persons Act 1963, s. 25, as amended by the Children and Young Persons Act 1969, schs 5 and 6*).

COMMENTARY

"Where a child or young person is charged with an offence, or is for any other reason brought before a court, a summons or warrant may be issued by a court to enforce the attendance of a parent or guardian under s. 34 of the Act of 1933, in the same manner as if an information were laid upon which a summons or warrant could be issued against a defendant under the (Magistrates' Courts Act, 1980) and a summons to the child or young person may include a summons to the parent or guardian to enforce his attendance for the said purpose.": Magistrates' Courts (Children & Young Persons) Rules 1970, r. 26.

Child. Means a person under the age of 14 years: s. 107(1) of the Act.

Young person. Means a person who has attained the age of 14 years and is under the age of 17 years: s. 107(1) of the Act.

Parent. This term is not defined. It is submitted that it is restricted to natural and adoptive parents, whether having legal custody or not and does not apply to step-parents or others having custody. As to adoptive parents *see* the Children Act 1975, sch. 1, para 3.

Guardian. In relation to a child or young person, "guardian" includes any person who, in the opinion of the court having cognizance of any case in relation to the child or young person or in which the child or young person is concerned, has for the time being the charge of or control over the child or young person: Children and Young Persons Act 1933, s. 107(1).

THE BACKING OF WARRANTS (REPUBLIC OF IRELAND) ACT 1965

Endorsement of warrants issued in Republic of Ireland

1. (1) Where—

(a)   a warrant has been issued by a judicial authority in the Republic of Ireland (in this Act referred to as the Republic) for the arrest of a person accused or convicted of an offence against the laws of the Republic, being an indictable offence or an offence punishable on summary conviction with imprisonment for six months; and

(b)   an application for the endorsement of the warrant is made to a justice of the peace in the United Kingdom by a constable who produces the warrant and states on oath that he has reason to believe the person named or described therein to be within the area for which the justice acts;

then, subject to the provisions of this section, the justice shall endorse the warrant in the prescribed form for execution within the part of the United Kingdom comprising the area for which he acts.

(2) A warrant for the arrest of a person accused of an offence which under the laws of the Republic is not an indictable offence but is punishable on summary conviction with imprisonment for six months shall not be endorsed under this section unless—

(a)   he has failed to appear in answer to a summons issued by or on behalf of a court in the Republic requiring his presence before the court for the trial of the offence and, not less than 14 days before the date named in the summons for his appearance, the summons was served on him personally in the Republic or a notice of the issue of the summons, together with a copy of the summons, was served on him personally in the United Kingdom; or

(b)   having entered into a recognizance for his appearance before a court in the Republic for the trial of the offence, he has failed to appear in pursuance of the recognizance; or

(c)   having appeared before a court in the Republic for the trial of the offence, he has subsequently failed to appear on any date to which the proceedings were adjourned.

(3) A warrant for the arrest of a person convicted of any offence against the laws of the Republic shall not be endorsed under this section unless the purpose of the arrest is to enable him—

(a)   to be brought before a court in the Republic for sentence in respect of the conviction;or

(b)   to be taken to a place where he is to undergo imprisonment under such a sentence, not being imprisonment in default of the payment of a fine or other sum.

(4) The endorsement of a warrant under this section by a justice of the peace in any part of the United Kingdom shall be treated for the purposes of any enactment or rule of law relating to warrants of arrest as if it were for the arrest of a person charged with an offence committed in that part.

COMMENTARY

This Act was introduced following the case of *R.* v. *Metropolitan Police Commissioner, ex parte*

Hammond (1964) 128 J.P. 299, which disclosed defects in the pre-existing law. It is complemented by Part III of the Extradition Act 1965, an Act of the Republic of Ireland (as to which *see* Home Office circ. 178/1965 dated August 13, 1965). *See* generally Home Office circ. No. 240/1965 dated November 9, 1965.

The task of the justices is to look first at the warrant and any certificate or affidavit in support of it and to decide whether it comes within s. 1(1). If the matter is raised that it is a case within s. 1(3) the justices ought to look at the matter and examine it in some detail and with such evidence as may be placed before them, *per* Michael Davies J in *Re Lawlor* [1978] 66 Cr. App. R. 75 at p. 79.

A judicial authority. This means a court, judge or justice of a court or peace commissioner: s. 10, *infra*.

Republic of Ireland. Defined in the Ireland Act, 1949, s. 1 and the Eire (Confirmation of Agreements) Act, 1938, s. 1.

Indictable offence. This term is defined in s. 10(1), *infra*.

United Kingdom. That is England and Wales, Scotland or Northern Ireland: s. 10(2). It also extends to Jersey and Guernsey: s. 12.

Shall endorse. Once the matters mentioned in subs. (1) are proved the magistrate is obliged to endorse the warrant: *Re Arkins* (1966) 130 J.P. 427.

The prescribed form. *See* form No. 1 of the Magistrates' Courts (Backing of Warrants) Rules 1965.

Subsection (2). For evidence by affidavit *see* s. 7 and r. 5, *infra*.

Not less than 14 days before the date. This means at least 14 clear days exclusive of the day of service and exclusive of the return date: *R.* v. *Turner* (1910) 74 J.P. 81; *Re Hector Whaling, Ltd* [1935] All E.R. Rep. 302; *Thompson* v. *Stimpson* [1960] 3 All E.R. 500.

Imprisonment. Includes any form of detention: s. 10, *infra*.

Proceedings before magistrates' court

2. (1) So soon as is practicable after a person is arrested under a warrant endorsed in accordance with s. 1 of this Act, he shall be brought before a magistrates' court and the court shall, subject to the following provisions of this section, order him to be delivered at some convenient point of departure from the United Kingdom into the custody of a member of the police force (Garda Síochána) of the Republic, and remand him until so delivered.

(2) An order shall not be made under subs. (1) of this section if it appears to the court that the offence specified in the warrant does not correspond with any offence under the law of the part of the United Kingdom in which the court acts' which is an indictable offence or is punishable on summary conviction with imprisonment for six months; nor shall such an order be made if it is shown to the satisfaction of the court—

    (*a*)   that the offence specified in the warrant is an offence of a political character, or an offence under military law which is not also an offence under the general criminal law, or an offence under an enactment relating to taxes, duties or exchange control; or

    (*b*)   that there are substantial grounds for believing that the person named or described in the warrant will, if taken to the Republic, be prosecuted or detained for another offence, being an offence of a political character or an offence under military law which is not also an offence under the general criminal law; or

    (*c*)   that the warrant is for the arrest of a person accused of an offence committed in Northern Ireland which constitutes an extra-territorial offence under the law of the Republic of Ireland as defined in s. 3 of the Criminal Jurisdiction Act, 1975; or

    (*d*)   that the person named or described in the warrant has been acquitted or convicted in a trial in Northern Ireland for an extra-territorial offence as defined in s. 1 of the said Act of 1975 in respect of which the warrant is issued.

(3)In any case where the court does not make an order under subs.(1) of this section, the court shall order the person named or. described in the warrant to be discharged.

(4) The provisions of the schedule to this Act shall apply in relation to proceedings under this section.

(*as amended by the Criminal Jurisdiction Act, 1975, sch. 3*).

COMMENTARY

Subsection (1): A magistrates' court. For the composition and powers of the court *see* the schedule, *infra*.

Remand. *See* s. 5 and r. 3 *infra*.

Correspond with any offence. These words refer to the ingredients of the offence, whether it be murder, grievous bodily harm, child neglect or whatever it may be, and in no sense dealing with the classification of the offence according to whether it is indictable or both summary and indictable or summary only, *per* Lord Parker CJ in *Re Arkins* (1966) 130 J.P. 427. As to proof of the laws of the Republic, *see* s. 7(*b*), *infra*.

United Kingdom. *See* the note to s. 1, *supra*.

Indictable offence. Defined in s. 10, *infra*.

Subsection (2). In relation to any warrant issued in the Republic ofIreland which specified an offence to which s. 1 of the Suppression of Terrorism Act 1978 applies, being a warrant to which para. (c) of subs. (3) of that section applies this section has effect as if at the end of s. 2(2) there were added the following words:

> "or
> (*e*) that there are substantial grounds for believing—

> (i)   that the warrant was in fact issued in order to secure the return of the person named or described in it to the Republic for the purpose of prosecuting or punishing him on account of his race, religion, nationality or political opinions; or

> (ii)   that he would, if returned there, be prejudiced at his trial or punished, detained or restricted in his personal liberty by reason of his race, religion, nationality or political opinions."

(Suppression of Terrorism Act 1978, s. 2(2)).

Offence of a political character. The fact that the defendant will be tried by a court set up under the (Irish) Offences Against the State Act 1939 is no acknowledgement that the offence is a political one: *R.* v. *Governor of Winson Green Prison, Birmingham, ex parte Littlejohn* [1975] 3 All E.R. 208. Unless this issue is raised before the justice it is not a matter upon which fresh or additional evidence is admissible in an application for *habeas corpus: Re Nobbs* (1978) 142 J.P. 624.

In relation to extradition it has been held that (i) burglaries by members of the Church of Scientology which had not taken place in order to challenge the political control or government of the United States of America but simply to further the interests of the Church and its members were not offences of a political character; (ii) when the offence had not been shown to be of a political character, our courts would not entertain allegations of bad faith on the part of the requesting country: *R.* v. *Budlong and Kember* (1980) N.L.J. 90.

Genocide is not an offence of a political character: Genocide Act 1969, s. 2(2).

For the purposes of this Act

(*a*)   no offence to which this section applies shall be regarded as an offence of a political character; and

(*b*)   no proceedings in respect of an offence to which this section applies shall be regarded as a criminal matter of a political character or as criminal proceedings of a political character. (Suppression of Terrorism Act 1978, s. 1(2)).

Subsection (2)(b): Another offence. This must be an offence already committed or alleged to have been already committed: *Keane* v. *Governor of Brixton Prison* (1971) 135 J.P. 340.

Review of orders of magistrates' courts

3. (1) Where an order is made by a magistrates' court under s. 2(1) of this Act in respect of any person—

    (a)   he shall not be delivered up under the order until the expiration of the period of 15 days beginning with the date on which the order is made, unless he gives notice in the prescribed manner that he consents to his earlier removal;

    (b)   if within that period an application is made by him or on his behalf for a writ of habeas corpus *ad subjiciendum* or, in the case of an order made in Scotland, an application for review is made by him under subs. (2) of this section, he shall not be so delivered up while proceedings on the application are pending;

and the magistrates' court shall inform him that he will not be delivered up under the order during the said period of 15 days unless he gives notice as aforesaid, and that he has the right to apply for a writ of habeas corpus *ad subjiciendum* or, as the case may be, to make an application for review under subs. (2) of this section.

(2). . . .

(3) For the purposes of this section proceedings on an application for a writ of habeas corpus *ad subjiciendum* shall be treated as pending until any appeal in those proceedings is disposed of; and an appeal shall be treated as disposed of at the expiration of the time within which the appeal may be brought or, where leave to appeal is required, within which the application for leave may be made, if not brought or made within that time.

COMMENTARY

Notice in the prescribed manner. To be signed in the presence of a justice or justices' clerk: r. 2(1) of the Magistrates Courts (Backing of Warrants) Rules 1965.

Provisional warrants

4. (1) A justice of the peace in the United Kingdom, on the application of a constable who states on oath—

    (a)   that he has reason to believe that a warrant has been issued by a judicial authority in the Republic for the arrest of a person accused or convicted of an indictable offence against the laws of the Republic, but that the warrant is not yet in his possession; and

    (b)   that he has received a request made on grounds of urgency by a member of the police force of the Republic holding the rank of inspector or above for the issue in the United Kingdom of a warrant for the arrest of that person; and

    (c)   that he has reason to believe that person to be within the area for which the justice acts;

may issue a warrant in the prescribed form (in this section referred to as a provisional warrant) for the arrest of that person:

Provided that where the warrant issued in the Republic was for the arrest of a convicted person, a provisional warrant shall not be issued unless the applicant states on oath that he has reason to believe the requirements of s. 1(3) of this Act to be satisfied.

(2) A provisional warrant issued in any part of the United Kingdom shall be treated for the purposes of any enactment or rule of law relating to warrants of arrest as if it were a warrant for the arrest of a person charged with an offence

committed in that part, but the warrant shall not be authority for the making of an arrest more than five days after the date of its issue.

(3) So soon as is practicable after a person is arrested under a provisional warrant he shall be brought before a magistrates' court, and—

(a) if there is produced to the court the warrant issued in respect of him in the Republic, endorsed in accordance with s. 1 of this Act, the court shall proceed as if he had been arrested under that warrant;

(b) in any other case the court may remand him for not more than three days.

(4) Where at any time there is produced to a constable having custody of a person remanded under this section the warrant issued in respect of that person in the Republic, endorsed in accordance with s. 1 of this Act, the period of the remand shall determine, and he shall thereafter be treated as if arrested at that time under that warrant.

(5) If the period of a remand under this section is not determined under subs. (4) thereof the person remanded shall be discharged at the end of the period.

COMMENTARY

Subsection (1): A judicial authority. Defined in s. 10, *infra*.

Indictable offence. Defined in s. 10 *infra*.

The prescribed form. *See* form 3 of the Magistrates' Courts (Backing of Warrants) Rules 1965.

Subsection (3): Remand. *See* s. 5 and r. 3, *infra*.

Remand

5. (1) Where under s. 2(1) or s. 4(3) of this Act a magistrates' court has power to remand a person, the court may—

(a) remand him in custody, that is to say, commit him for the period of the remand to prison or, in the case of a remand under s. 4(3) of this Act, to the custody of a constable; or

(b) remand him on bail in accordance with the Bail Act 1976, that is to say, direct him to surrender himself into the custody of the officer in charge of a specified police station at the time to be appointed by that officer and notified in writing to the person so remanded;

and where his release on bail is conditional on his providing one or more surety or sureties and, in accordance with s. 8(3) of that Act, the court fixes the amount in which the surety is to be bound with a view to his entering into his recognizance susequently in accordance with subs. (4) and (5) or (6) of that section the court shall in the meantime commit him to the custody of a constable.

(2) The time to be appointed for the purpose of subs. (1) above by the officer and notified to the person so remanded shall not be more than 24 hours before the time at which it appears to the officer in charge of the police station that the period of remand is likely to end.

(3) During the period between the surrender of a person as aforesaid and the end of the period of remand he shall be treated as if committed to the custody of a constable, but where it appears to the officer to whom he surrenders that the end of the period of remand will be unexpectedly delayed, the officer shall grant him bail in accordance with the Bail Act, 1976 subject to a duty to surrender himself into the custody of the officer in charge of the station specified under subs. (1) above at the time appointed by that officer and notified in writing to him; and subs. (2)

above shall apply to the appointment of a time for the purposes of this subsection as it applies to the appointment of a time for the purposes of subs. (1) above.

(4) If a person fails to surrender as aforesaid, the court by which he was remanded may issue a warrant in the prescribed form for his arrest; and on his arrest under the warrant subs. (3) of this section shall apply as if he had surrendered to the officer in charge of the police station specified under subs. (1) above, but that officer shall not grant him bail as provided by that subsection unless he is satisfied that it is proper to do so.

A warrant issued under this subsection in any part of the United Kingdom shall be treated for the purposes of any enactment or rule of law relating to warrants of arrest as if it were a warrant for the arrest of a person charged with an offence committed in that part.

(5). . . .

(as amended by the Bail Act, 1976, sch. 2 and 3).

COMMENTARY

Commit him . . . to prison. Persons under the age of 21 shall be committed to the institution to which they would be committed if charged with an offence: Criminal Justice Act 1967, s. 34, *infra.* As to which institution *see* the Criminal Justice Act, 1948, s. 27

Warrant in the prescribed form. *See* form 9 of the Rules.
As to where the warrant should be sent *see* r. 4, *infra.*

Discharge of persons not taken to Republic

6. (1) If the person in respect of whom an order has been made by a magistrates' court under s. 2(1) of this Act is not delivered up under the order within one month after it was made, a superior court exercising jurisdiction in the part of the United Kingdom within which it was made, upon application by or on behalf of that person, may, unless reasonable cause is shown for the delay, order him to be discharged.

In this subsection "superior court" means the High Court, the High Court of Justiciary in Scotland or the High Court of Northern Ireland.

(2) If, in the case of a person in respect of whom an order has been made under s. 2(1) of this Act, it appears to a justice of the peace acting for the same area as that of the court by which the order was made, or in Scotland to the sheriff, that for any reason the police force of the Republic no longer require the delivery of that person into their custody he shall order him to be discharged.

COMMENTARY

Within one month. That is, one calendar month: Interpretation Act 1978, sch. 1. The first day is to be excluded and the last included: *Goldsmiths' Co.* v. *West Metropolitan Rail Co.* [1900-03] All E.R. Rep. 667; *Stewart* v. *Chapman* (1951) 115 J.P. 473.

Evidence as to matters originating in Republic

7. For the purposes of this Act—

    (1)   a document purporting to be a warrant issued by a judicial authority in the Republic or a copy of a summons issued by or on behalf of a court in the Republic, if verified in the prescribed manner, may be taken to be such a warrant or, as the case may be, a copy of such a summons, and the warrant or summons shall be taken to have been duly issued;

    (*b*)   evidence with respect to the laws of the Republic may be given by affidavit or other written statement on oath, but a certificate purporting to be issued by or on behalf of the judicial authority in the Republic by whom a warrant was issued, or another judicial authority acting for the same area, and certifying that the offence specified in the warrant can be dealt with under the laws of the Republic in the manner described in the certificate shall be sufficient evidence of matters so certified;

(c) a deposition purporting to have been made in the Republic, or affidavit or written statement purporting to have been sworn therein, may be admitted if verified in the prescribed manner.

COMMENTARY

For the verification of warrants, summonses and depositions under this section, *see* r. 5, *infra*.

Interpretation

10. (1) In this Act—

"imprisonment" includes any form of detention;

"indictable offence" does not include an offence which is triable on indictment only at the instance or with the consent of the accused;

"judicial authority" means a court, judge or justice of a court, or peace commissioner;

"prescribed" means prescribed in accordance with s. 8 of this Act;

"the Republic" means the Republic of Ireland.

(2) Subject to s. 12(1) of this Act, references in this Act to a part of the United Kingdom are references to England and Wales, to Scotland, or to Northern Ireland.

(3). . . .

(4) Any reference in this Act to any other enactment is a reference thereto as amended, and includes a reference thereto as extended or applied, by or under any other enactment.

COMMENTARY

Subsection (1): Indictable offence. This definition would not include an offence triable either way. As such it is inconsistent with the definition of this term in the Interpretation Act 1978, sch. 1 which can thus have no application to this statute.

Application to Channel Islands and Isle of Man

12. (1) Subject to the provisions of this section, this Act shall extend to the Channel Islands and the Isle of Man (in this section collectively referred to as the Islands) and shall have effect as if each of them were a part of the United Kingdom.

(2), (3). (*Orders in Council*).

COMMENTARY

S.I. 1965, Nos. 1874 (Guernsey), 1875 (Isle of Man), 1876 (Jersey) apply this Act to those areas.

SCHEDULE

SUPPLEMENTARY PROVISIONS AS TO PROCEEDINGS UNDER S. 2

Proceedings in England or Wales

1. Paragraphs 2 to 4 of this schedule shall apply to proceedings in England or

Wales under s. 2 of this Act.

2. The court shall consist of at least two justices and shall sit in open court in a petty-sessional court-house or an occasional court-house: provided that s. 16(1) of the Justices of the Peace Act 1979 (which exempts stipendiary magistrates from certain restrictions imposed by the Magistrates' Courts Act 1980) shall apply as if the foregoing provisions of this paragraph were contained in the Magistrates' Courts Act 1980.

3. Subject to para. 2 of this schedule, the court shall have the like powers, including power to adjourn the case and meanwhile to remand the person arrested under the warrant either in custody or on bail, and the proceedings shall be conducted as nearly as may be in the like manner, as if the court were acting as examining justices inquiring into an indictable offence alleged to have been committed by that person.

4. Without prejudice to the generality of para. 3 of this schedule, s. 1 of the Costs in Criminal Cases Act 1973 (award of costs by examining justices out of central funds) and s. 2 of the Poor Prisoners Defence Act, 1930 (legal aid before examining justices) shall apply in relation to the proceedings as if the person arrested under the warrant were charged with an indictable offence on the prosecution of the constable on whose application the warrant was endorsed and, where the court discharges that person, as if it had determined not to commit for trial.

5.-10. . . .

(*as amended by the Costs in Criminal Cases Act 1973, sch. 1, Justices of the Peace Act 1979, s. 71, sch. 2, Magistrates' Courts Act 1980, sch. 7*).

COMMENTARY

Paragraph 3. The caution required by the Magistrates' Courts Rules 1981, is inapt to proceedings under this Act; nor is there any need for any inquiry into whether there is strong or probable presumption of guilt: *Re Arkins* (1966) 130 J.P. 427. The words "in like manner" refer to the manner in which proceedings are to be conducted and not to issues to be tried. The schedule does not provide for any inquiry by the magistrate into the merits of the charges: *Keane* v. *Governor of Brixton Prison* (1971) 135 J.P. 340. It is submitted that this phrase does not import the restrictions on publication contained in the Magistrates' Courts Act 1980, s. 8.

Paragraph 4: Section 2 of the Poor Prisoners Defence Act, 1930. Now the Legal Aid Act 1974, .s. 28.

THE CRIMINAL JUSTICE ACT 1967

Committal of persons under 21 accused of extradition crimes, etc.

34. Any person under the age of 21 who apart from this section would be committed to prison under s. 10 of the Extradition Act, 1870 (committal of a person alleged to have committed an extradition crime) or s. 5(1)(a) of the Backing of Warrants (Republic of Ireland) Act 1965 (remand in custody of a person for whose arrest a warrant has or is alleged to have been issued in the Republic of Ireland) shall be committed to an institution to which he could be committed if he were charged with an offence before the court which commits him, and any reference in those provisions to prison shall be construed accordingly.

COMMENTARY

Under the age of 21. For the determination of age *see* the Magistrates' Courts Act 1980, s. 150(4).

An institution. For the appropriate institutions *see* the Criminal Justice Act, 1948, s. 27 in ch. 3.

THE CRIMINAL LAW ACT 1967

Arrest without warrant

2. (1) The powers of summary arrest conferred by the following subsections shall apply to offences for which the sentence is fixed by law or for which a person (not previously convicted) may under or by virtue of any enactment be sentenced to imprisonment for a term of five years (or might be so sentenced but for the restrictions imposed by s. 33 of the Magistrates' Courts Act 1980, and to attempts to commit any such offence; and in this Act, including any amendment made by this Act in any other enactment, "arrestable offence" means any such offence or attempt. The said restrictions are those which apply where, in pursuance of subsection (2) of s. 22 of the said Act of 1980 (certain offences to be tried summarily if value involved is small) a magistrates' court summarily convicts a person of a scheduled offence within the meaning of the said s. 22.

(2) Any person may arrest without warrant anyone who is, or whom he, with reasonable cause, suspects to be, in the act of committing an arrestable offence.

(3) Where an arrestable offence has been committed, any person may arrest without warrant anyone who is, or whom he, with reasonable cause, suspects to be, guilty of the offence.

(4) Where a constable, with reasonable cause, suspects that an arrestable offence has been committed, he may arrest without warrant anyone whom he, with reasonable cause, suspects to be guilty of the offence.

(5) A constable may arrest without warrant any person who is, or whom he, with reasonable cause, suspects to be, about to commit an arrestable offence.

(6) For the purpose of arresting a person under any power conferred by this section a constable may enter (if need be, by force) and search any place where that person is or where the constable, with reasonable cause, suspects him to be.

(7) This section shall not prejudice any power of arrest conferred by law apart from this section.

(as amended by the Criminal Law Act 1977, s. 65, sch. 12, the Criminal Jurisdiction Act 1975, s. 14(5), sch. 6, the Magistrates' Courts Act 1980, sch. 7).

COMMENTARY

This provision derives from the proposals of the Criminal Law Revision Committee's seventh report, Cmnd. 2659.

Subsection (4): Constable. That is, any member of a police force of whatever rank.

Subsection (6). It is not necessary that the constable who first suspects an arrestable offence and seeks to arrest under subs. (4) should be the one who effects entry under subs. (6): *R.* v. *Francis* (1972) *The Times*, July 4.

Force. The word "force" means the application of energy to an obstacle: *Swales* v. *Cox* [1981] 1 All E.R. 1115.

THE CHILDREN AND YOUNG PERSONS ACT 1969

Restrictions on criminal proceedings for offences by young persons

5. (1)-(7) *(Not yet in force).*

(8) It shall be the duty of a person who decides to lay an information in respect of an offence in a case where he has reason to believe that the alleged offender is a young person to give notice of the decision to the appropriate local authority unless he is himself that authority.

(9) In this section—

"the appropriate local authority", in relation to a young person, means the local authority for the area in which it appears to the informant in question that the young person resides or, if the young person appears to the informant not to reside in the area of a local authority, the local authority in whose area it is alleged that the relevant offence or one of the relevant offences was committed; . . .

COMMENTARY

Young person. Includes a child who has attained the age of 10 years: S.I. 1970 No. 1882.

Resides. Means "habitually resides": s. 70.

Transitional modifications of Part I for persons of specified ages

34. (1) . . .

(2) In the case of a person who has not attained the age of 17 but has attained such lower age as the Secretary of State may by order specify, no proceedings under s. 1 of this Act or for an offence shall be begun in any court unless the person proposing to begin the proceedings has, in addition to any notice falling to be given by him to a local authority in pursuance of s. 2(3) or 5(8) of this Act, given notice of the proceedings to a probation officer for the area for which the court acts: and accordingly in the case of such a person the reference in s. 1(1) of this Act to the said s. 2(3) shall be construed as including a reference to this subsection.

(3), (4). . .

(5) (*Repealed*).

(6), (7). . .

(*as amended by the Criminal Law Act 1977, sch. 12, the Criminal Justice Act 1982, sch. 16.*)

COMMENTARY

Such lower age. The age of 13 has been specified in S.I. 1970 No. 1882, as amended by S.I. 1973 No. 485 and S.I. 1974 No. 1083.

THE CRIMINAL LAW ACT 1977

Execution throughout United Kingdom of warrants of arrest

38. (1) A warrant issued in Scotland or Northern Ireland for the arrest of a person charged with an offence may be executed in England or Wales by any constable acting within his police area; and subs. (3) of s. 125 of the Magistrates' Courts Act 1980 (execution without possession of the warrant) shall apply to the execution in England or Wales of any such warrant.

(2) A warrant issued in England, Wales or Northern Ireland for the arrest of a person charged with an offence may be executed in Scotland by any constable appointed for a police area in the like manner as any such warrant issued in Scotland.

(3) A warrant issued in England, Wales or Scotland for the arrest of a person charged with an offence may be executed in Northern Ireland by any member of

the Royal Ulster Constabulary or the Royal Ulster Constabulary Reserve; and paras (4) and (5) of Art. 158 of the Magistrates' Courts (Northern Ireland) Order 1981 (execution without possession of the warrant and execution on Sunday) shall apply to the execution in Northern Ireland of any such warrant.

(4) A warrant may be executed by virtue of this section whether or not it has been endorsed under ss 12, 14 or 15 of the Indictable Offences Act 1848 or under ss 27, 28 or 29 of the Petty Sessions (Ireland) Act 1851.

(5) Nothing in this section affects the execution in Scotland or Northern Ireland of a warrant to which s. 123 of the Bankruptcy Act 1914 applies.

(as amended by the Magistrates' Courts Act 1980, sch. 7, the Magistrates' Courts (Northern Ireland) Order 1981.)

COMMENTARY

The effects of this section are described in Home Office cir. 44/1980.

Subsection (2): Charged with an offence. These words distinguish between civil and criminal cases. A warrant for the arrest of a convicted person for the purpose of passing sentence is a warrant for the arrest of a person "charged with an offence": *cf. Evans* v. *Macklen* [1976] Crim. L.R. 120.

Service of summonses and citation throughout United Kingdom

39. (1) A summons requiring a person charged with an offence to appear before a court in England or Wales may, in such manner as may be prescribed by rules of court, be served on him in Scotland or Northern Ireland.

(2) A summons requiring a person charged with an offence to appear before a court in Northern Ireland may, in such manner as may be prescribed by rules of court, be served on him in England, Wales or Scotland.

(3) Citation of a person charged with a crime or offence to appear beore a court in Scotland may be effected in any other part of the United Kingdom in like manner as it may be done in Scotland, and for this purpose the persons authorized to effect such citation shall include (a) in England and Wales and Northern Ireland, constables and prison officers serving in those parts of the United Kingdom (b) persons authorized by a chief officer of police in England or Wales to serve summonses there.

(as amended by the Criminal Justice (Scotland) Act 1980, sch. 7.)

COMMENTARY

The effects of this section are described in Home Office cirs 44/1980 and 105/1980, which latter contains details of the procedure which has been agreed with the Northern Ireland court service for personal service of a non-police summons in Northern Ireland.

THE PROSECUTION OF OFFENCES ACT 1979

Delivery of recognizances, etc. to Director

5. (1) Where the Director gives notice to any justice that he has instituted or undertaken or is carrying on any criminal proceedings, the justice shall, at the prescribed time and in the prescribed manner or at the time and in the manner directed, in a special case, by the Attorney General, send the Director every recognizance, information, certificate, deposition, document and thing connected with those proceedings which the justice is required by law to deliver to the appropriate officer of the Crown Court.

(2) The Director shall—

(*a*)   subject to the regulations, cause anything that is sent to him under subs. (1) above to be delivered to the appropriate officer of the Crown Court; and

(*b*)   be under the same obligation (on the same payment) to deliver to an applicant copies of anything so sent as the said officer.

(3) It shall be the duty of every justices' clerk to send the Director, in accordance with the regulations, a copy of the information and of any depositions and other documents relating to any case in which a prosecution for an offence before the magistrates' court to which he is clerk is withdrawn or is not proceeded with within a reasonable time.

COMMENTARY

The Director. Means the Director of Public Prosecutions: ss. 1 and 100 of the Act.
Subsection (3).
    " 8. Every justice of the peace to whom a notice shall have been given under s. 5 of the Prosecution of Offences Act 1879 shall within three days of receipt of the notice deliver or transmit by post or other means to the Director of Public Prosecutions all documents and things which are required to be transmitted by that section.

    " 9. In any case in which the prosecution for any offence instituted before examining justices or a court of summary jurisdiction is wholly withdrawn or is not proceeded with within a reasonable time and there is some ground for suspecting that there is no satisfactory reason for the withdrawal or failure to proceed it shall be the duty of the clerk of the court to send to the Director of Public Prosecutions a report of the case and to supply him with such information or documents in relation to the case as he may specify." (Prosecution of Offences Regulations 1978).

Consents to prosecutions, etc.

6. (1) This section applies to any enactment which prohibits the institution or carrying on of proceedings for any offence except—

(*a*)   with the consent (however expressed) of a Law Officer of the Crown or of the Director; or

(*b*)   where the proceedings are instituted or carried on by or on behalf of a Law Officer of the Crown or the Director,

and so applies whether or not there are other exceptions to the prohibition (and in particular whether or not the consent is an alternative to the consent of any other authority or person).

(2) An enactment to which this section applies—

(*a*)   shall not prevent the arrest without warrant, or the issue or execution of a warrant for the arrest, of a person for any offence, or the remand in custody or on bail of a person charged with any ofence; and

(*b*)   shall be subject to any enactment concerning the apprehension or detention of children or young persons.

(3) In this section "enactment" includes any provision having effect under or by virtue of any Act; and this section applies to enactments passed or made before the passing of this Act, or later.

Consents to be admissible in evidence

7. Any document purporting to be the consent of a Law Officer of the Crown or the Director for, or to, the institution of any criminal proceedings or the institution of criminal proceedings in any particular form and to be signed by a Law Officer of the Crown, the Director or an Assistant Director, as the case may be, shall be admissible as prima facie evidence without further proof.

THE MAGISTRATES' COURTS ACT 1980

Issue of summons to accused or warrant for his arrest

1. (1) Upon an information being laid before a justice of the peace for an area to which this section applies that any person has, or is suspected of having, committed an offence, the justice may, in any of the events mentioned in subs. (2) below, but subject to subs. (3) to (5) below—

> (*a*) issue a summons directed to that person requiring him to appear before a magistrates' court for the area to answer to the information, or
>
> (*b*) issue a warrant to arrest that person and bring him before a magistrates' court for the area or such magistrates' court as is provided in subs. (5) below.

(2) A justice of the peace for an area to which this section applies may issue a summons or warrant under this section—

> (*a*) if the offence was committed or is suspected to have been committed within the area, or
>
> (*b*) if it appears to the justice necessary or expedient, with a view to the better administration of justice, that the person charged should be tried jointly with, or in the same place as, some other person who is charged with an offence, and who is in custody, or is being or is to be proceeded against, within the area, or
>
> (*c*) if the person charged resides or is, or is believed to reside or be, within the area, or
>
> (*d*) if under any enactment a magistrates' court for the area has jurisdiction to try the offence, or
>
> (*e*) if the offence was committed outside England and Wales and, where it is an offence exclusively punishable on summary conviction, if a magistrates' court for the area would have jurisdiction to try the offence if the offender were before it.

(3) No warrant shall be issued under this section unless the information is in writing and substantiated on oath.

(4) No warrant shall be issued under this section for the arrest of any person who has attained the age of 17 unless—

> (*a*) the offence to which the warrant relates is an indictable offence or is punishable with imprisonment, or
>
> (*b*) the person's address is not sufficiently established for a summons to be served on him.

(5) Where the offence charged is not an indictable offence—

> (*a*) no summons shall be issued by virtue only of para. (*c*) of subs. (2) above, and
>
> (*b*) any warrant issued by virtue only of that paragraph shall require the person charged to be brought before a magistrates' court having jurisdiction to try the offence.

(6) Where the offence charged is an indictable offence, a warrant under this section may be issued at any time notwithstanding that a summons has previously been issued.

(7) A justice of the peace may issue a summons or warrant under this section upon an information being laid before him notwithstanding any enactment requiring the information to be laid before two or more justices.

(8) The areas to which this section applies are any county, any London commission area and the City of London.

COMMENTARY

Subsection (1): Information. *See* under The Information in the introduction.

Laid before a justice. Informations, other than those substantiated on oath, may be laid before a clerk to justices who may issue any summons thereon: Justices' Clerks Rules 1970. In exercising this power the clerk is acting as a justice and may refuse as well as grant: *R.* v. *Worthing Justices, ex parte Norvell* [1981] 1 W.L.R. 413. As to what constitutes the Laying of an Information *see* under that title in the introduction.

A summons was held to be invalid where it was considered by two justices and signed by a third who had not considered the complaint: *Dixon* v. *Wells* (1980) L.R. 25 Q.B. 249. When a summons is granted by a justice it may be signed by him or authenticated by a. justices' clerk: r. 98(1) of the Magistrates' Courts Rules, 1981. It is the duty of the clerk to see that any necessary formalities are in order, *per* Dibben J in *Price* v. *Humphreys* (1958) 122 J.P. 423.

Any person. Includes a body corporate and incorporate: Interpretation Act, 1978, sch. 1.

Offence. An Act prohibited on pain of an excise penalty is not an offence: *Brown* v. *Allweather Mechanical Grouting Co., Ltd* (1953) 117 J.P. 136. But *see* now the Customs and Excise Management Act 1979, s. 156(2). Non-compliance with an abatement notice under the Public Health Act, 1936, constitutes an offence: *Northern Ireland Trailers Ltd* v. *County Borough of Preston* (1972) 136 J.P. 149.

Issue a summons. *See* under that title in the introduction.

Issue a warrant. *See* under that title in the introduction.

Subsection (2): If it appears to the justice necessary or expedient. That is, to the justice issuing the warrant, not the justice hearing the case: *Turf Publishers, Ltd* v. *Davies* [1927] W.N. 190.

Subsection (2)(b). A receiver may thus be charged along with the thief: *R.* v. *Blandford, R.* v. *Freestone* (1955) 119 J.P. 306.

Subsection (2)(c): Resides. "A person resides where he lives, where he has his bed and where he dwells." It includes the place where one works provided the work is not merely temporary: *Stoke-on-Trent Borough Council* v. *Cheshire County Council* (1915) 79 J.P. 452; *South Shields Corporation* v. *Liverpool Corporation* (1943) 107 J.P. 77.

"'To reside' is a somewhat elegant expression for what used to be called 'to live'", *per* Cockburn CJ in *R.* v. *St Leonards* (1865) 29 J.P. 728. It is essentially a question of fact, *per* Lord Buckmaster in *I.R.C.* v. *Lysaght* [1928] All E.R. Rep. 575 at p. 582. To constitute constructive residence there must be both an intention to return and a place to return to: *R.* v. *Guardians of Glossop Union* (1886) 30 J.P. 215 (a pauper case). It may include residence in an institution: *Worcestershire County Council* v. *Warwickshire County Council* (1934) 98 J.P. 347.

The House of Lords, in a taxation case, has expressed the view that a man may have two homes, one abroad and one in the United Kingdom (and *see* also *Langford Property Co., Ltd* v. *Athamassoglou* [1948] 2 All E.R. 722); but if he is a wanderer spending most of his time in hotels then it is a question of fact and of degree which must be determined on the circumstances of the case: *Levene* v. *I.R.C.* [1928] All E.R. Rep. 746.

Is, or is believed to. . . be. A person does not "happen to be" at a place to which he comes in response to a summons: *Johnson* v. *Colam* (1875) 40 J.P. 135. In *R.* v. *Hitchin Justices, ex parte Hilton* (1975) 139 J.P. 252, similar words in the Transport Act, 1968 were held to relate to the point at which the proceedings were commenced.

Subsection (2)(e). *See* Home Office cir. 162/1971 dated July 30, 1971.

Subsection (3): Substantiated on oath. Not necessarily by the original informant.

Subsection (4): Indictable offence. This means an offence, which, if committed by an adult, is triable on indictment, whether it is exclusively so triable or triable either way: Interpretation Act 1978, s. 5, sch. 1.

Subsection (7). It is submitted that the effect of this subsection, when read with s. 11, *ibid.*, is to allow a court to issue a warrant under s. 1 for an indictable offence prior to the return date of a summons already granted, and not, impliedly, to preclude the grant of a warrant for a non-indictable offence after the return date of a summons previously issued.

Jurisdiction to deal with charges

2. (1) A magistrates' court for a county, a London commission area or the City of London shall have jurisdiction to try all summary offences committed within the county, the London commission area or the City (as the case may be).

(2) Where a person charged with a summary offence appears or is brought before a magistrates' court in answer to a summons issued under paragraph (*b*) of s. 1(2) above, or under a warrant issued under that paragraph, the court shall have jurisdiction to try the offence.

(3) A magistrates' court for a county, a London commission area or the City of London shall have jurisdiction as examining justices over any offence committed by a person who appears or is brought before the court, whether or not the offence was committed within the county, the London commission area or the City (as the case may be).

(4) Subject to ss 18 to 22 below and any other enactment (wherever contained) relating to the mode of trial of offences triable either way, a magistrates' court shall have jurisdiction to try summarily an offence triable either way in any case in which under subs. (3) above it would have jurisdiction as examining justices.

(5) A magistrates' court shall, in the exercise of its powers under s. 24 below, have jurisdiction to try summarily an indictable offence in any case in which under subs. (3) above it would have jurisdiction as examining justices.

(6) A magistrates' court for any area by which a person is tried for an offence shall have jurisdiction to try him for any summary offence for which he could be tried by a magistrates' court for any other area.

(7) Nothing in this section shall effect any jurisdiction over offences conferred on a magistrates' court by any enactment not contained in this Act.

COMMENTARY

It is a principle engrained in our law that jurisdiction cannot be conferred by consent, *per* Davey LJ in *Farquharson* v. *Morgan* (1894) 58 J.P. 495 (a civil case).

Subsection (1): Summary offence. This means an offence which, if committed by an adult, is triable only summarily: Interpretation Act 1978, s. 5, Sch. 1.

Committed within the county. Jurisdiction is not, therefore, confined to the petty sessional division: *R.* v. *Beacontree JJ* [1914-15] All E.R. Rep. 1180. The Isles of Scilly form part of the county of Cornwall: s. 149, *infra*.

Subsection (3). For the extent of the court's indictable jurisdiction see *Territorial Jurisdiction* in the introduction.

Subsection (4): An offence triable either way. This means an offence which, if committed by an adult, is triable either on indictment or summarily: Interpretation Act 1978, s. 5, sch. 1.

Subsection (5): Indictable offence. This means an offence which, if committed by an adult, is triable on indictment, whether it is exclusively so triable or triable either way: Interpretation Act 1978, s. 5, sch. 1.

Offences committed on boundaries, etc

3. (1) Where an offence has been committed on the boundary between two or more areas to which this section applies, or within 500 yards of such a boundary, or in any harbour, river, arm of the sea or other water lying between two or more such areas, the offence may be treated for the purposes of the preceding provisions of this Act as having been committed in any of those areas.

(2) An offence begun in one area to which this section applies and completed in another may be treated for the purposes of the preceding provisions of this Act as having been wholly committed in either.

(3) Where an offence has been committed on any person, or on or in respect of any property, in or on a vehicle or vessel engaged on any journey or voyage through two or more areas to which this section applies, the offence may be treated for the purposes of the preceding provisions of this Act as having been committed in any of those areas; and where the side or any part of a road or any water along which the vehicle or vessel passed in the course of the journey or voyage forms the boundary between two or more areas to which this section applies, the offence may be treated for the purposes of the preceding provisions of this Act as having been committed in any of those areas.

(4) The areas to which this section applies are any county, any London commission area and the City of London.

COMMENTARY

Subsection (1): Five hundred yards. That is, measured in a straight line on a horizontal plane: *Interpretation Act,* 1978, s. 8; *Stokes* v. *Grissell* (1854) 18 J.P. 378.

Subsection (2): Begun in one county. Normally an offence takes place where it is completed: *Athersmith* v. *Dewry* (1858) 22 J.P. 735. But, by the operation of this section, a letter seeking to obtain money by false pretences, posted in one jurisdiction and delivered in another, may be the subject of a prosecution in either: *R.* v. *Leech* (1856) 20 J.P. 278. The offence of exacting an excessive cab fare, however, is committed where the fare is exacted, although the journey may have begun in another jurisdiction: *Ely* v. *Godfrey* (1922) 86 J.P. 82. The offence of forwarding cattle into a prohibited area is committed only in the latter area: *Midland Rail Co.* v. *Freeman* (1884) 48 J.P. 660. See also under *Territorial Jurisdiction* in the introduction.

Subsection (3): In or on a vehicle. Not the mere unlawful use of the vehicle: *Wardhaugh (A.F.), Ltd* v. *Mace* (1952) 116 J.P. 360.

Proceedings invalid where accused did not know of them

14. (1) Where a summons has been issued under s. 1 above and a magistrates' court has begun to try the information to which the summons relates, then if—

> (a) the accused, at any time during or after the trial, makes a statutory declaration that he did not know of the summons or the proceedings until a date specified in the declaration, being a date after the court has begun to try information; and
>
> (b) within 21 days of that date the declaration is served on the clerk to the justices,

without prejudice to the validity of the information, the summons and all subsequent proceedings shall be void.

(2) For the purposes of subs. (1) above a statutory declaration shall be deemed to be duly served on the clerk to the justices if it is delivered to him, or left at his office, or is sent in a registered letter or the recorded delivery service addressed to him at his office,

(3) If on the application of the accused it appears to a magistrates' court (which

for this purpose may be composed of a single justice) that it was not reasonable to expect the accused to serve such a statutory declaration as is mentioned in subs. (1) above within the period allowed by that subsection, the court may accept service of such a declaration by the accused after that period has expired; and a statutory declaration accepted under this subsection shall be deemed to have been served as required by that subsection.

(4) Where any proceedings have become void by virtue of subs. (1) above, the information shall not be tried again by any of the same justices.

COMMENTARY

Subsection (1): Statutory declaration. This means a declaration made by virtue of the Statutory Declarations Act, 1835: Interpretation Act, 1978, sch. 1. This procedure is to be used where applicable in preference to *certiorari*, which will not normally be granted in such a case: *R. v. Brighton Justices, ex parte Robinson* [1973] 1 W.L.R. 69.

Within 21 days. The date specified is to be excluded and the 21st day included: *Goldsmiths Co. v. Metropolitan Rail Co.,* (1904) 68 J.P. 41; *Stewart v. Chapman* (1951) 115 J.P. 473. Note that time runs from the date mentioned in the declaration, not the date of conviction. See also subs. (3).

Served on the clerk. Who must note it in the register and inform the prosecutor or in the case of a private prosecutor the chief officer of police: Magistrates' Courts Rules 1981, r. 20.

Without prejudice. This allows a second summons to be issued upon the original information without the necessity for a further information which might be out of time.

Subsection (3). A justices' clerk may perform the function of a single justice under this subsection (Justices' Clerks Rules 1970).

Service of summons out of time after failure to prove service by post

47. Where any enactment requires, expressly or by implication, that a summons in respect of an offence shall be issued or served within a specified period after the commission of the offence, and service of the summons may under the rules be effected by post, then, if under the rules service of the summons is not treated as proved, but it is shown that a letter containing the summons was posted at such time as to enable it to be delivered in the ordinary course of post within that period, a second summons may be issued on the same information; and the enactment shall have effect, in relation to that summons, as if the specified period were a period running from the return day of the original summons.

COMMENTARY

Any enactment. For example, the Road Traffic Act, 1972, s. 179.

Construction of references to complaint in enactments dealing with offences

50. In any enactment conferring power on a magistrates' court to deal with an offence, or to issue a summons or warrant against a person suspected of an offence, on the complaint of any person, for references to a complaint there shall be substituted references to an information.

COMMENTARY

This provision standardized nomenclature so as to confine the term "complaint" to civil and the term "information" to criminal proceedings. It does not affect the substantive law by converting a ground for civil complaint into an offence: *R. v. Nottingham Justices, ex parte Brown* [1960] 3 All E.R. 625 (dangerous dogs). *See* also *Northern Ireland Trailers Ltd v. County Borough of Preston* (1972) 136 J.P. 142.

False statements in declaration proving service, etc

107. If, in any solemn declaration, certificate or other writing made or given for the purpose of its being used in pursuance of the rules as evidence of the service of any document or the handwriting or seal of any person, a person makes a statement that he knows to be false in a material particular, or recklessly makes any statement that is false in a material particular, he shall be liable on summary conviction to imprisonment for a term not exceeding six months or a fine not exceeding level 3 on the standard scale or both.

(as amended by the Criminal Justice Act 1982, ss. 38, 46).

Warrant endorsed for bail

117. (1) A justice of the peace on issuing a warrant for the arrest of any person may grant him bail by endorsing the warrant for bail, that is to say, by endorsing the warrant with a direction in accordance with subs. (2) below.

(2) A direction for bail endorsed on a warrant under subs. (1) above shall—

    (*a*)   in the case of bail in criminal proceedings, state that the person arrested is to be released on bail subject to a duty to appear before such magistrates' court and at such time as may be specified in the endorsement;

    (*b*)   in the case of bail otherwise than in criminal proceedings, state that the person arrested is to be released on bail on his entering into such a recognizance (with or without sureties) conditioned for his appearance before a magistrates' court as may be specified in the endorsement;

and the endorsement shall fix the amounts in which sureties and, in the case falling within para. (*b*) above, that person is or are to be bound.

(3) Where a warrant has been endorsed for bail under subs. (1) above, then, on the person referred to in the warrant being taken to a police station on arrest under the warrant, the officer in charge of the police station shall (subject to his approving any surety tendered in compliance with the endorsement) release him from custody as directed in the endorsement.

COMMENTARY

The general right to bail (Bail Act, 1976, s. 4) does not apply to the endorsement of a warrant.
Subsection (1): A warrant for the arrest of any person. Thus if a warrant is merely for the arrest of person to which this section applies: *Coughtry* v. *Porter* (1950) 114 J.P. 129 (which dealt with a warrant under the Gaming Act, 1845, now replaced by s. 51 of the Betting, Gaming and Lotteries Act, 1963). See also the Magistrates' Courts Rules 1981, r. 96.
Betting, Gaming and Lotteries Act, 1963). See also the Magistrates' Courts Rules 1981, r. 96.

Endorsing. Pinning a separate document to the warrant is not endorsement: *R.* v. *Metropolitan Police Commissioner, ex parte Melia* (1958) 122 J.P. 23.

Subsection (2): Released on bail. For the conditions of bail, see the Bail Act, 1976, s. 3, *supra.*

Process valid notwithstanding death, etc., of justice

124. A warrant or summons issued by a justice of the peace shall not cease to have effect by reason of his death or his ceasing to be a justice.

Warrants

125. (1) A warrant of arrest issued by a justice of the peace shall remain in force until it is executed or withdrawn.

(2) A warrant of arrest, warrant of commitment, warrant of distress or search warrant issued by a justice of the peace may be executed anywhere in England

and Wales by any person to whom it is directed or by any constable acting within his police area.

This subsection does not apply to a warrant of commitment or a warrant of distress issued under Part VI of the General Rate Act 1967.

(3) A warrant to arrest a person charged with an offence may be executed by a constable notwithstanding that it is not in his possession at the time; but the warrant shall, on the demand of the person arrested, be shown to him as soon as practicable.

COMMENTARY

Subsection (2): Constable. That is a police officer of any rank.

Police area. Defined in the Police Act 1964, s. 62 and sch. 8.

Subsection (3). This subsection does not apply to the arrest of a fine defaulter: *De Costa Small* v. *Kirkpatrick* [1978] 68 Cr. App. R. 186; applying *R.* v. *Purdy* (1974) 138 J.P. 771. (And see *Horsfield* v. *Brown* (1932) 96 J.P. 123). The decision to the contrary in *Evans* v. *Macklin* [1976] Crim. L.R. 120 is implicitly over-ruled. (But *see* the criticism at 144 J.P.N. 534).

Execution of certain warrants outside England and Wales

126. Sections 12 to 14 of the Indictable Offences Act 1848 (which relate, among other things, to the execution in Scotland, Northern Ireland, the Isle of Man and the Channel Islands of warrants of arrest for the offences referred to in those sections) shall, so far as applicable, apply to—

(*a*)   warrants of arrest issued under s. 1 above for offences other than those referred to in the said ss 12 to 14;

(*b*)   warrants of arrest issued under s. 13 above;

(*c*)   warrants of arrest issued under s. 97 above other than warrants issued in bastardy proceedings to arrest a witness; and

(*d*)   warrants of commitment issued under this Act.

Limitation of time

127. (1) Except as otherwise expressly provided by any enactment and subject to subs. (2) below, a magistrates' court shall not try an information or hear a complaint unless the information was laid, or the complaint made, within six months from the time when the offence was committed, or the matter of complaint arose.

(2) Nothing in—

(*a*)   subs. (1) above; or

(*b*)   subject to subs. (4) below, any other enactment (however framed or worded) which, as regards any offence to which it applies, would but for this section impose a time-limit on the power of a magistrates' court to try an information summarily or impose a limitation on the time for taking summary proceedings,

shall apply in relation to any indictable offence.

(3) Without prejudice to the generality of para. (*b*) of subs. (2) above, that paragraph includes enactments which impose a time-limit that applies only in certain circumstances (for example, where the proceedings are not instituted by or with the consent of the Director of Public Prosecutions or some other specified authority).

(4) Where, as regards any indictable offence, there is imposed by any enactment (however framed or worded, and whether falling within subs. (2) (*b*) above or not) a limitation on the time for taking proceedings on indictment for that

offence no summary proceedings for that offence shall be taken after the latest time for taking proceedings on indictment.

COMMENTARY

See generally under Limitation of Time in the introduction.

While this section may bar an information laid against a third party outside the time limit under a statutory third party procedure it does not prevent the original defendant from invoking that procedure: *R.* v. *Bicester Justices, ex parte Unigate Ltd* (1975) 139 J.P. 216.

Subsection (1): Try an information. This does not apply to the preferment of a charge under para. 4 of Part IV of sch. 4 to the Road Traffic Act 1972: *R.* v. *Coventry Justices, ex parte Sayers* [1979] R.T.R. 22.

Six months. That is, calendar months: Interpretation Act 1978, sch. 1.

The information was laid. *See* under Laying the Information in the introduction.

Subsection (2): Indictable offence. *See* the note to s. 2(5), *supra*.

Isles of Scilly

149. For the purposes of this Act the Isles of Scilly form part of the county of Cornwall.

THE MAGISTRATES' COURTS (BACKING OF WARRANTS) RULES 1965

S.I. 1965, No. 1906

1.(1) (Forms).

(2) Where a requirement is imposed by the Act for the use of a prescribed form, and an appropriate form is contained in the schedule to these rules, that form or a form to the like effect shall be used.

2.(1) A notice given under s. 3(1)(a) of the Act (consent to surrender earlier than is otherwise permitted) shall be signed in the presence of a justice of the peace or a justices' clerk.

(2) Any such notice given by a person in custody shall be delivered to the governor of the prison in whose custody he is.

(3) If a person on bail gives such notice, he shall deliver it to, or send it by post in a registered letter or by recorded delivery service addressed to, the police officer in charge of the police station specified in his recognizance.

(4) Any such notice shall be attached to the warrant ordering the surrender of that person.

3. (1) The person taking the recognizance of a person remanded on bail under s. 2(1) or s. 4(3) of the Act shall furnish a copy of the recognizance to the police officer in charge of the police station specified in the recognizance.

(2) The clerk of a magistrates' court which ordered a person to be surrendered and remanded him on bail shall deliver to, or send by post in a registered letter or by recorded delivery service addressed to, the police officer in charge of the police station specified in the recognizance the warrant ordering the person to be surrendered.

4 (1) The clerk of the magistrates' court which ordered a person to be surrendered shall deliver to, or send by post in a registered letter or by recorded delivery service addressed to—

(a) if he is remanded in custody under s. 5(1)(a) of the Act, the prison governor to whose custody he is committed,

(b) if he is remanded on bail under s. 5(1)(b) of the Act, the police officer in charge of the police station specified in the recognizance,

(c) if he is committed to the custody of a constable pending the taking from him of a recognizance under s. 5(1) of the Act, the police officer in charge of the police station specified in the warrant of commitment,

the warrant of arrest issued by a judicial authority in the Republic and endorsed in accordance with s. 1 of the Act.

(2) The governor or police officer to whom the said warrant of arrest is delivered or sent shall arrange for it to be given to the member of the police force of the Republic into whose custody the person is delivered when the person is so delivered.

5 (1) A document purporting to be a warrant issued by a judicial authority in the Republic shall, for the purposes of s. 7(a) of the Act, be verified by a certificate purporting to be signed by a judicial authority, a clerk of a court or a member of the police force of the Republic and certifying that the document is a warrant and is issued by a Judge or justice of a court or a peace commissioner.

(2) A document purporting to be a copy of a summons issued by a judicial

authority in the Republic shall, for the purposes of the said s. 7(a), be verified by a certificate purporting to be signed by a judicial authority, a clerk of a court or a member of the police force of the Republic and certifying that the document is a true copy of such a summons.

(3) A deposition purporting to have been made in the Republic, or affidavit or written statement purporting to have been sworn therein, shall, for the purposes of s. 7 (c) of the Act, be verified by a certificate purporting to be signed by the person before whom it was sworn and certifying that it was so sworn.

6. *(1) In these Rules—*

"the Act" means the Backing of Warrants (Republic of Ireland) Act 1965;

a reference to a person ordered to be surrendered means a reference to a person ordered by a magistrates' court to be delivered into the custody of a member of the police force of the Republic under s. 2(1) of the Act; and cognate expressions shall be construed accordingly;

"the Republic" means the Republic of Ireland.

(2) The Interpretation Act, 1978, shall apply to the interpretation of these rules as it applies to the interpretation of an Act of Parliament.

THE MAGISTRATES' COURTS RULES 1981

S.I. 1981 No. 552 as amended by S.I. 1983 No. 523

Information and complaint

4. *(1) An information may be laid or complaint made by the prosecutor or complainant in person or by his counsel or solicitor or other person authorized in that behalf.*

(2) Subject to any provision of the Act of 1980 and any other enactment, an information or complaint need not be in writing or on oath.

(3) It shall not be necessary in an information or complaint to specify or negative an exception, exemption, proviso, excuse or qualification, whether or not it accompanies the description of the offence or matter of complaint contained in the enactment creating the offence or on which the complaint is founded.

COMMENTARY

For the laying of the information *see* the Magistrates' Courts Act, 1980, s. 1. For the contents of the information *see* r. 100 of the Magistrates' Courts Rules 1981 and form 1.

Paragraph (1): The prosecutor. *See* The Right to Prosecute in the introduction.

Other person authorized. For example, authorized officers of local authorities and Ministries. The informant is the person named in the information, not the one who actually lays the information: Glanville Williams at [1956] Crim. L.R. 169.

Paragraph (2): Any provision of the Act. *See* the Magistrates' Courts Act 1980, s. 1(3).

Paragraph (3). *See* s. 101 of the Act for the substantive law. The words "proviso", "exception" have no technical meaning, and the word "unless' is equally covered by this provision: *Roche* v. *Willis* (1934) 98 J.P. 227.

Duty of clerk receiving statutory declaration under s. 14(1) of Act of 1980

20. *Where the clerk of a magistrates' court receives a statutory declaration which complies with s. 14(1) of the Act of 1980, he shall—*

    (a)   *note the receipt of the declaration in the register against the entry in respect of the trial of the information to which the declaration relates; and*

    (b)   *inform the prosecutor and, if the prosecutor is not a constable, the chief officer of police of the receipt of the declaration.*

Proof of service, handwriting, etc.

67. *(1) The service on any person of a summons, process, notice or document required or authorized to be served in any proceedings before a magistrates' court, and the handwriting or seal of a justice of the peace or other person on any warrant, summons, notice, process or documents issued or made in any such proceedings, may be proved in any legal proceedings by a document purporting to be a solemn declaration in the prescribed form made before a justice of the peace, commissioner for oaths, clerk of a magistrates' court or registrar of a county court or a sheriff or sheriff clerk (in Scotland) or a clerk of petty sessions (in Northern Ireland).*

(2) The service of any process or other document required or authorized to be served, the proper addressing, pre-paying and posting or registration for the purposes of service of a letter containing such a document, and the place, date and time of posting or registration of any such letter, may be proved in any proceedings before a magistrates' court by a document purporting to be a certificate signed by the person by whom the service was effected or the letter posted or registered.

(3) References in para. (2) to the service of any process shall, in their application to a witness summons, be construed as including references to the payment or tender to the witness of his costs and expenses.

COMMENTARY

False statements in documents made under this rule are punishable in accordance with the Magistrates' Courts Act 1980, s. 37.

Paragraph (1): Seal of a justice. This means court stamps which are used as seals: *R.* v. *Wolverhampton Deputy Recorder, ex parte Director of Public Prosecutions* (1951) 115 J.P. 212.

Prescribed form. *See* forms 136 and 139.

Paragraph (2): Certificate. *See* forms 140 and 141.

Warrant to be signed

95 *Except where signature by the clerk of a magistrates' court is permitted by r. 109 or by the Magistrates' Courts (Forms) Rules 1981, every warrant under the Act of 1980 shall be signed by the justice issuing it.*

Warrant of arrest

96. *(1) A warrant issued by a justice of the peace for the arrest of any person shall require the persons to whom it is directed, that is to say, the constables of the police area in which the warrant is issued, or the authorized persons for the police area specified in the warrant, or any persons named in that behalf in the warrant, to arrest the person against whom the warrant is issued.*

(2) The warrant shall name or otherwise describe the person for whose arrest it is issued, and shall contain a statement of the offence charged in the information or, as the case may be, the ground on which the warrant is issued.

COMMENTARY

Paragraph (1): Police area. Defined in s. 62 and sch. 8 of the Police Act 1964 (not reproduced herein).

The authorized persons. This is a reference to the persons employed by a local authority in that area or by the chief officer of police or the police authority for that area who are authorized by the chief officer of police to execute warrants: r. 2(4).

Paragraph (2): Name or otherwise describe. A constable is liable to an action for false imprisonment if he arrests a person not properly named in the warrant even though that is the person against whom it was desired the warrant should issue: *Hoye* v. *Bush* [1835-42] All E.R. Rep. 286. A conviction for wounding in the course of resisting arrest upon a warrant which merely stated the defendant's surname and the name of his father was quashed where the father had four sons living at the same address: *R.* v. *Hood* (1830) 1 M.C.C. 281.

It is not improper to issue a warrant on description, but justices should be careful that the description is specific (and substantiated by the information) and not capable of application to a substantial proportion of the population, *e.g.* "dark-haired male, aged about 30".

Statement of the offence. *See* r. 100, *infra*.

Form of summons

98. *(1) A summons shall be signed by the justice issuing it or state his name and be authenticated by the signature of the clerk of a magistrates' court.*

(2) A summons requiring a person to appear before a magistrates' court to answer to an information or complaint shall state shortly the matter of the information or complaint and shall state the time and place at which the defendant is required by the summons to appear.

(3) A single summons may be issued against a person in respect of several informations or complaints; but the summons shall state the matter of each information or complaint separately and shall have effect as several summonses, each issued in respect of one information or complaint.

COMMENTARY

Paragraph (1). A summons may also be issued (and thus signed in his own right) by the clerk to justices: Justices' Clerks Rules 1970.

A summons. *See* form 2.

Signed. A signature may be affixed by a rubber stamp facsimile not only by the justice himself but also by another person expressly authorized to do so or, if he is subject to the directions and control of the justices, if he is acting in accordance with an established practice in the justices' office. In no case may a document to be signed in blank: *R.* v. *Brentford Justices, ex parte Catlin* (1975) 139 J.P. 516.

State shortly. *See* r. 100, *infra*.

Service of summons, etc.

99. *(1) Service of a summons issued by a justice of the peace on a person other than a corporation may be effected—*

(a)   *by delivering it to the person to whom it is directed; or*
(b)   *by leaving it for him with some person at his last known or usual*

place of abode; or

 (c) by sending it by post in a letter addressed to him at his last known or usual place of abode.

(2) If the person summoned fails to appear, service of a summons in manner authorized by sub-paras. (b) or (c) of para. (1) shall not be treated as proved unless it is proved that the summons came to his knowledge; and for that purpose any letter or other communication purporting to be written by him or on his behalf in such terms as reasonably to justify the inference that the summons came to his knowledge shall be admissible as evidence of that fact; Provided that this paragraph shall not apply to any summons in respect of a summary offence served in the manner authorised by—

 (a) the said sub-para (b); or

 (b) the said sub-para (c) in a registered letter or by recorded delivery service.

(3) Service for the purposes of the Act of 1980 of a summons issued by a justice of the peace on a corporation may be effected by delivering it at, or sending it by post to, the registered office of the corporation, if that office is in the United Kingdom, any place in the United Kingdom where the corporation trades or conducts its business.

(4) Paragraph (3) shall have effect in relation to a document (other than a summons) issued by a justice of the peace as it has effect in relation to a summons so issued, but with the substitution of references to England and Wales for the references to the United Kingdom.

(5) Any summons or other document served in a manner authorized by the preceding provisions of this rule shall, for the purposes of any enactment other than the Act of 1980 or these rules requiring a summons or other document to be served in any particular manner, be deemed to have been as effectively served as if it had been served in that manner; and nothing in this rule shall render invalid the service of a summons or other document in that manner.

(6) Sub-paragraph (c) of para. (1) shall not authorize the service by post of—

 (a) a summons requiring the attendance of any person to give evidence or produce a document or thing; or

 (b) a summons issued under any enactment relating to the liability of members of the naval, military or air forces of the Crown for the maintenance of their wives and children, whether legitimate or illegitimate.

(7) . . .

(8) Where this rule or any other of the rules provides that a summons or other document may be sent by post to a person's last known or usual place of abode that rule shall have effect as if it provided also for the summons or other document to be sent in the manner specified in the rule to an address given by that person for that purpose.

(9) This rule shall not apply to a judgment summons.

COMMENTARY

The effects of this rule are summarized under Service of the Summons in the introduction. So far as a summons for a summary offence is concerned, ordinary post may be used in the first instance, but if the accused fails to acknowledge in the manner referred to in para. (2) the hearing of a summary offence may be adjourned for service by registered letter or recorded delivery, in which case the lack of acknowledgment at the adjourned date will not be a bar to trial in the absence of the accused. The trial of an indictable offence cannot proceed in the absence of the accused without either proof of service, normally personal service (sub-para. (a) of para. (1)), or acknowledgment or other proof of service in acordance with para (2).

Paragraph (1). Service upon the defendant's solicitor would not appear to be good service in criminal proceedings: 136 J.P.N. 796.

Leaving it for him. This may include posting: *Stylo Shoes Ltd* v. *Price Tailors Ltd*, [1959] 3 All E.R. 901. If a summons is served by leaving it with another person such person should be told who it is for and made to understand the nature of the summons, *per* Quain J, in *R.* v. *Smith* (1875) 39 J.P. 313.

Last known or usual place of abode. Does not include a shop where the defendant does not reside: *R.* v. *Lilley, ex parte Taylor* (1910) 75 J.P. 95; nor a lock-up shop: *R.* v. *Rhodes, ex parte McVittie* (1915) 79 J.P. 527. "Place of abode" includes the last place of abode if the defendant no longer has one: *R.* v. *Evans and Yale* (1850) 1 L.M. & P. 357; 19 L.J.M.C. 151. But where the defendant has obtained a fixed place of abode abroad his last address in England is not his "last known place of abode": *R.* v. *Farmer* (1892) 56 J.P. 341.

In view of the change of wording in the modern statutes the old cases should be approached with caution. And *see* also the comments of the court in *R.* v. *Rose, ex parte London County Council* (1948) 122 J.P.N. 548.

Sending it by post. Where an Act passed on or after January 1, 1890, authorizes or requires any document to be served by post, whether the expression "serve" or the expression "give" or "send" or any other expression is used, then, unless the contrary intention appears, the service shall be deemed to be effected by properly addressing, prepaying and posting a letter containing the document, and, unless the contrary is proved, to have been effected at the time at which the letter would be delivered in the ordinary course of post: Interpretation Act 1978, s. 7.

For proof of such service *see* para. (2).

Proviso to paragraph (2). Note as a corollary the provisions of the Magistrates' Courts Act 1980, s. 14 (proceedings may be made invalid when accused did not know of them).

Summary offence. Defined in the Interpretation Act 1978, sch. 1.

Principal office. That is, the place where the company's business is managed and controlled as a whole: *Garton* v. *G.W.R. Co.* (1858) E.B. & E. 837; *Palmer* v. *Caledonian Rail Co.* [1892] 1 Q.B. 823. When a summons is improperly served on an assistant at a shop occupied by a limited company and the company answers the summons simply to point out the irregularity this is not an appearance sufficient to effect a waiver of the irregularity: *Pearks, Gunston, Tee and Co.* v. *Richardson* (1902) 66 J.P. 774.

Statement of offence

100. *(1) Every information, summons, warrant or other document laid, issued or made for the purposes of, or in connexion with, any proceedings before a magistrates' court for an offence shall be sufficient if it describes the specific offence with which the accused is charged, or of which he is convicted, in ordinary language avoiding as far as possible the use of technical terms and without necessarily stating all the elements of the offence, and gives such particulars as may be necessary for giving reasonable information of the nature of the charge.*

(2) If the offence charged is one created by or under any Act, the description of the offence shall contain a reference to the section of the Act, or, as the case may be, the rule, order, regulation, byelaw or other instrument creating the offence.

COMMENTARY

Defects in an information, summons or warrant may be cured by the Magistrates' Courts Act 1980, s. 123.

Technical terms. In *Lomas* v. *Peek* (1947) 112 J.P. 13, the Court held that the words "knowingly and wilfully" were technical terms, omission of which was permissible in an information. This rule was not considered in the later case of *Waring* v. *Wheatley* (1951) 115 J.P. 630, which came to the contrary conclusion on special facts.

1. COMMENCING THE PROSECUTION 41

Such particulars as may be necessary for giving reasonable information of the nature of the charge. In *Stephenson* v. *Johnson* (1954) 118 J.P. 199, a conviction for failing to pay a minimum wage was quashed when the information failed to quote the statutory order involved, the nature of the worker's employment, the amounts paid and alleged to be due, etc. Other examples of insufficient information are given in *Herniman* v. *Smith* [1938] 1 All E.R. 1 at p. 7; *Atterton* v. *Browne* (1945) 109 J.P. 25; *Cording* v. *Halse* (1954) 118 J.P. 558.

When the date of offence is not known it is sufficient to allege commission between specified dates: *R.* v. *Simpson* (1715) 10 Mod. Rep. 248; *Onley* v. *Gee* (1861) 25 J.P. 342. The place of offence may be omitted if unknown and immaterial, as in an indictable offence: *R.* v. *Wallwork* (1958) 122 J.P. 299. First hand knowledge of the offence is not essential: the informant need not see the party injured, *per* Blackburn J in *Ralph* v. *Hurrell* (1875) 40 J.P. 119.

Paragraph (2). "When the elements of an old common law offence are plainly covered by the words of a modern statute, it is preferable that the indictment should be framed, to use the old expression, *contra formam statuti*", *per* Veale J in *R.* v. *Pollock and Divers* (1966) 130 J.P. 287.

A failure to comply with this rule may be cured under s. 123 of the Magistrates' Courts Act 1980 where the accused has not been misled: *Thornley* v. *Clegg* [1982] Crim. L.R. 523; [1982] R.T.R. 405 (information recited the precise words of the statute and quoted the regulations but not the statute). The rule is directory only.

CHAPTER 2

PROVING THE CASE

CONTENTS

INTRODUCTION

Before discussing *how* facts in issue can be proved it is first necessary to consider who has to prove what (the burden of proof) and to what extent (the standard of proof).

The Burden of Proof

This term may be used in two different senses. On the one hand, there is the *evidential* burden or the onus of adducing evidence to prove specific issues or facts which may devolve upon either prosecutor or defendant and may shift from one to another during the trial. On the other, there is the *legal* or *persuasive* burden of proof, sometimes referred to, inaccurately, as the presumption of innocence, which in an English criminal trial is always borne by the prosecution: *R.* v. *Schama* (1914) 79 J.P. 184; *Woolmington* v. *Director of Public Prosecutions* [1935] A.C. 462. In the words of Sankey, LC in the latter case, "Throughout the web of the English criminal law one golden thread is always to be seen, that is the duty of the prosecution to prove the prisoner's guilt, subject to . . . the defence of insanity and subject also to any statutory exceptions . . . No attempt to whittle it down will be entertained."

In some statutes an evidential burden may be placed on the accused once the prosecution have established certain facts, as, for example, the establishment of lawful authority or reasonable excuse for the possession of an offensive weapon contrary to the Prevention of Crime Act, 1953, s. 1.

Negative Averments

When an accused relies for his defence on any exception, exemption, proviso, excuse or qualification the burden of proving it lies on him: Magistrates' Courts Act 1980, s. 101. This section sets out the common law rule in statutory form. It does not depend on either the fact or the presumption that the defendant has peculiar knowledge enabling him to prove the positive of any negative averment. The section shifts the persuasive, but not the evidential, burden of proof to the defendant: *R.* v. *Edwards* (1974) 138 J.P. 621. For a general review of the common law position *see R.* v. *Oliver*, (1943) 108 J.P. 30.

It has been held that the burden of proof that a defendant held a driving licence lies upon him: *John* v. *Humphreys* (1955) 119 J.P. 39; *Tynan* v. *Jones* [1975] R.T.R. 465. Similarly, with unauthorized possession of game: *R.* v. *Turner* (1816) 5 M. & S. 511, supplying drugs without a licence: *R.* v. *Scott* (1921) 86 J.P. 69, selling sugar without a licence: *R.* v. *Oliver, supra,* possessing drugs without a prescription: *R.* v. *Ewens* [1966] 2 All E.R. 470; using a motor vehicle without insurance: *Leathley* v. *Drummond* [1972] R.T.R. 293; or without a test certificate: *Davey* v. *Towle* [1973] R.T.R. 328, offering taxi service without authority: *Robertson* v. *Bannister* [1973] R.T.R. 109 and selling liquor without a licence: *R.* v. *Edwards, supra.*

It is not necessary in an information to specify or negative an exemption, etc.: Magistrates' Courts Rules 1981, r. 4(3).

The Standard of Proof

The rule is that the prosecution must prove their case "beyond reasonable doubt." It is often said that this term is designed to exclude the "fanciful" or "remote" or, as Sir James Stephen would have had it, "improbable" doubt. Doubts were cast on the value of the "reasonable doubt" test in *R.* v. *Summers* (1952) 116 J.P. 240; but in *R.* v. *Hepworth; R.* v. *Fearnley* (1955) 119 J.P. 516, its use was confirmed by Lord Goddard, CJ who, nevertheless, said to refer to "fanciful" doubts was no real guidance: "One would be on safe ground if one said in a criminal case to a jury: 'You must be satisfied beyond reasonable doubt' and one could also say 'You, the jury, must be completely satisfied' or, better still, 'You must feel sure of the prisoner's guilt'." It is best not to put any gloss on these terms: *R.* v. *Yap Chuan Ching* [1976] 63 Cr. App. R. 7. It is, however, quite clear that proof beyond reasonable doubt is not proof beyond a shadow of a doubt, *per* Denning, J in *Miller* v. *Minister of Pensions* [1947] 2 All E.R. 372. In directing a jury it is generally sufficient and safe to say that they must be satisfied beyond reasonable doubt so that they feel sure of the defendant's guilt: *Ferguson* v. *The Queen* [1979] 1 All E.R. 877.

When the evidential burden is upon the defendant in respect of any issue it is well established that the test is not the same as that upon the prosecutor, but is akin to that in civil cases, namely the balance of probabilities: *Sodeman* v. *R.* [1936] 2 All E.R. 1138; *Islington London Borough* v. *Panico* [1973] 3 All E.R. 485.

Challenging Admissibility of Evidence

Where matters are being conducted before magistrates there is no question of a trial within a trial because magistrates are the judges both of fact and law and determine questions of admissibility as well as guilt and innocence. Incidental matters should be decided as separate issues and not as trials within trials and consequently there is no need for evidence to be repeated after the issue of admissibility has been determined. It is quite impossible to lay down rules as to when magistrates should announce their decision on this type of point. Each case is different and the object of magistrates is to ensure that what is done is fair to the defendant and just to the prosecution: *S.J.F. (an infant)* v. *Chief Constable of Kent, ex parte Margate Juvenile Court* (1982) *The Times*, June 17; [1982] Crim. L.R. 682.

Witnesses

It is the task of the party calling a witness to ensure his attendance at court. However, if a justice of the peace is satisfied that a person in England or Wales is likely to be able to give material evidence or to produce any document or thing likely to be material evidence and that that person will not voluntarily attend as a witness or produce the document or thing the justice must issue a witness summons: Magistrates' Courts Act 1980, s. 97(1). The justices' clerk has a similar duty under the Justices' Clerks Rules 1980. A warrant may be issued for this purpose by a justice if he is satisfied by evidence on oath of these matters and that it is probable that a summons would not produce attendance of the witness: Magistrates' Courts Act 1980, s. 97(2). Witnesses, whether appearing on process under this section or not, may be compelled to give evidence, etc., under s. 97(4), *ibid.*

The Exclusion of Witnesses

It is time honoured practice, but not a rule of law, that persons who are to be called as witnesses (with the exception of professional men giving evidence in that capacity) should be ordered out of court before they are called: *Southey* v. *Nash*

(1837) 7 C. & P. 632; *R.* v. *Bexley Justices, ex parte King* [1980] R.T.R. 49. No
rule of law exists as to the presence of witnesses which is a matter purely within
the discretion of the court. But if they remain in court even in disobedience of the
court's order the court has no right to refuse to hear their evidence: *Moore*
v. *The Registrar of Lambeth County Court* [1969] 1 All E.R. 782 (a civil
case); *Cobbett* v. *Hudson* (1852) 17 J.P. 39.

Particulars of Witnesses

The normal rule is that a witness giving evidence must state publicly his name and
address. However, this rule may be departed from when there are overwhelming
reasons, as for example in the case of a victim of blackmail. See *per* Lord Widgery
CJ in *R.* v. *Socialist Worker and others, ex parte Attorney General* [1975] 1 All
E.R. 142 at p. 144. There is statutory provision concerning victims of rape in the
Sexual Offences (Amendment) Act 1976. Where the court may sit in camera it is
an acceptable alternative in a proper case to allow a witness to conceal his identity
by a pseudonym ("Col. X"): *Attorney General* v. *Leveller Magazine Limited
and Others* (1979) 143 J.P. 260. In any case when a court allows a name or
other matter to be withheld from the public it may give such directions
prohibiting its publication in connexion with the proceedings as appear
necessry for the purpose for which it was withheld: Contempt of Court Act
1981, s. 11. (*See* ch. 14.)

Evidence on Oath

The general rule is that evidence given before a magistrates' court must be
given on oath: Magistrates' Courts Act 1980, s. 98. The accused is not entitled to make a statement without being sworn: Criminal Justice Act 1982,
s. 72. *See* ch. 5. The general form of Christian oath (Oaths Act 1978, s.
1(1)) is administered to a witness without question unless he voluntarily
objects (subs. (2), *ibid.*) An oath may be administered to anyone not a
Christian or a Jew in any lawful manner (subs. (3), *ibid.*) Anyone who objects to being sworn must be permitted to make a solemn affirmation instead of taking oath (Oaths Act 1978, s. 5(1)). The affirmation may also be
used when it is not reasonably practical without inconvenience or delay to
administer the oath in the proper manner (subs. (2), *ibid.*). The form of affirmation is prescribed in s. 6, *ibid.*

Every person called as a witness in pursuance of the Criminal Evidence
Act 1898 must, unless otherwise ordered by the court, give his evidence from the
witness box or other place from which the other witnesses give their evidence: s. 1
(*g*),*ibid*.

The Evidence of Children

A child of tender years may give unsworn evidence when he does not understand
the nature of the oath if possessed of sufficient intelligence to justify the reception
of the evidence and if he understands the duty of speaking the truth: Children and
Young Persons Act, 1933, s. 38. For the problems which can arise with regard to
corroboration in respect of such unsworn evidence *see* the note to that section.
The evidence of a child witness in committal proceedings concerning sexual
offences must be in the form of a written statement produced as an exhibit unless
the defendant objects, the prosecutor requires the attendance of the child for the
purposes of establishing identity, where it has been impossible to obtain such a
statement, or where the proceedings began as a summary trial in the course of
which the child gave evidence: Children and Young Persons Act, 1963, s. 27. It
is submitted that this rule does not apply to committal proceedings without
consideration of the evidence.

Refreshing Memory out of Court

It is the practice of the courts not to allow a witness to refresh his memory in the witness box by reference to a written statement unless it was made contemporaneously with the event or as soon as possible after the event. But witnesses for the prosecution are normally (though not in all circumstances) entitled, if they so request, to copies of any statement taken from them by police officers. Witnesses for the defence are normally allowed to have copies of their statements and refresh their memories from them at any time up to the moment they go into the witness box. While it would be wrong for a number of witnesses to be handed statements in circumstances which allowed one to compare with another what each had said, there can be no general rule that witnesses may not before trial see the statement they made at some period reasonably close to the time of the event which is the object of the trial, *per* Sachs, LJ, in *R*. v. *Richardson* (1971) 135 J.P. 371; *Warley* v. *Bentley* [1976] Crim. L.R. 31. But there is no rule that witnesses must be allowed to see their statements, nor need the prosecution inform the defence that a witness has seen his statement: *R*. v. *Westwell* [1976] Crim. L.R. 441. (But *cf. R*. v. *Webb* [1975] Crim. L.R. 159).

Refreshing Memory in Court

A witness should not be shown his statement once he is in the witness box: *R*. v. *Graham* [1973] Crim. L.R. 628. However, a witness may refresh his memory by reference to any writing made or verified by himself concerning and contemporaneously with the facts to which he testifies: *Archbold*, 4th ed. at para 515; approved in *Attorney General's Reference No. 3 of 1979* [1979] 69 Cr. App. R. 411, (a police officer may refer to a full note of questions and answers where drawn up accurately from brief notes made at the time). And see *R*. v. *Cheng* [1976] 63 Cr. App. R. 2 (fuller transcription of notes made at the time). The document must have been written either at the time of the transaction or so shortly afterwards that the facts were fresh in (the witness') memory: *Phipson on Evidence*, 11th ed. at p. 1528, approved in *R*. v. *Richardson* [1971] 2 All E.R. 773 at p. 777, wherein it was said that that definition does provide a measure of elasticity and should not be taken to confine witnesses to an over-short period. In *R*. v. *Fotheringham* [1975] Crim. L.R. 710, a witness was allowed to look at a statement made 27 days after the event.

The rules which apply to refreshing memory in the witness box should be the same as those which apply if memory has been refreshed outside the door of the court. Thus, the defence is entitled to see such documents, including notebooks and statements, from which memory has been refreshed subject, of course, only to the well established rules that a witness can be cross-examined having refreshed his memory upon the material in his notebook from which he has refreshed his memory without the notebook being made evidence in the case, whereas if he is cross-examined beyond those limits into other matters, the cross examiner takes the risk of the material being evidence and the document being exhibited and therefore available for use by the fact finding tribunal: *Owen* v. *Edwards* (1983) 147 J.P. 245.

It suffices if the note was made by someone else so long as the witness adopted it contemporaneously as his own: *Groves* v. *Redbart* [1975] Crim. L.R. 158 (another officer's notebook which the witness had checked and signed at the time); *R*. v. *Kelsey* [1982] 74 Cr. App. R. 213 (witness allowed to refresh memory from note he had dictated to a policeman who then read it back to him without showing it). "What must be shown is that witness A has verified in the sense of satisfying himself whilst the matters are fresh in his mind, (1) that a record has been made, and (2) that it is accurate. If A makes a "contemporaneous" note himself, or if A reads and adopts at the time a "contemporaneous" note made by B, A may refresh his memory from it without need of another witness. In a case such as the present a second witness will be required.":*ibid.*

Interpreters

"When a foreigner is on trial on an indictment for a criminal offence, and he is ignorant of the English language and is undefended, the evidence given at the trial must be translated to him. If he states that he understands part of the evidence and does not wish that part translated it need not be translated unless the judge in his discretion thinks otherwise, because the object of the translation is already achieved. For example, if an agreement in writing signed by the accused is put in evidence by the Crown, it might well be that the accused knew the contents and did not wish a translation. He is not thereby admitting any part of the case against him, but merely that he understands that part of the evidence. If he does not understand the English language he cannot waive compliance with the rule that the evidence must be translated; he cannot dispense with it by express or implied consent, and it matters not that no application is made by him for the assistance of an interpreter. It is for the court to see that the necessary means are adopted to convey the evidence to his intelligence, notwithstanding that, either through ignorance or timidity or disregard of his own interests, he makes no application to the court," per Lord Reading, CJ in *R. v. Lee Kun* (1916) 80 J.P. 166. It is submitted that the same principles apply nowadays in summary trial and to the deaf and dumb.

A conviction was quashed when the interpreter was a waiter at the same restaurant as waiters who served witnesses for the prosecution: *R. v. Mitchell* [1970] Crim. L.R. 153. A police officer's evidence of what a witness said out of court as translated to him by an interpreter is hearsay and inadmissible: *R. v. Attard* [1958] 43 Cr. App. R. 90.

Although it will be open to the court to assign an interpreter, it is understood that chief officers of police are prepared to continue the existing arrangements for the obtaining of interpreters where this is desired: Home Office circ. 86/1973 dated May 1, 1973.

The customary form of oath for interpreters is:

"I swear by Almighty God that I will well and faithfully interpret and true explanation make of all such matters and things as shall be required of me according to the best of my skill and understanding." (*cf.* Welsh Courts' (Oaths and Interpreters) Rules 1943-72).

In any legal proceeding in Wales or Monmouthshire the Welsh language may be spoken by any party, witness or other person who desires to use it; and any necessary provision for interpretation shall be made accordingly: Welsh Language Act 1967, s. 1(1).

When an interpreter is needed in criminal proceedings because of the *defendant's* lack of English his expenses must be ordered by the court out of central funds and any costs the defendant may have incurred for this purpose where an information is not proceeded with must on application be the subject of such an order: Administration of Justice Act 1973, s. 17. Interpreters may be paid whatever allowance from central funds the court considers reasonable: Costs in Criminal Cases (Allowances) Regulations 1977.

The Home Office will meet expenditure on a sign language interpreter employed to assist a defendant who is deaf and dumb where the provisions of s. 17 of the Act of 1973 otherwise apply: Home Office cir. 3/1979 dated February 1, 1979.

Proof by Written Statement

A written statement by any person is, if certain conditions are satisfied, admissible as evidence to the like extent as oral evidence to the like effect in summary trial (Criminal Justice Act 1967, s. 9) and in committal proceedings (Magistrates' Courts Act 1980, s. 102). The form of the statement is the same in both types of proceedings, so any statement taken from a witness under these provisions may be used in either.

The conditions so far as form are:
(a)   the statement purports to be signed by the person who made it;
(b)   it contains a prescribed declaration as to its truth: Criminal Justice Act 1967, s. 9(2); Magistrates' Courts Act 1980, s. 102(2);
(c)   if made by a person under 21 it must give his age;
(d)   if made by a person who cannot read it it must be read to him before signature and must contain a declaration that this has been done: Criminal Justice Act 1967, s. 9(3); Magistrates' Courts Act 1980, s. 102(3).

The procedure for dealing with the statement differs according to the type of proceedings:

In committal proceedings (Magistrates' Courts Act 1980, s. 102(2))
(i)   before it is tendered in evidence a copy of the statement must be given to each of the other parties along with a copy of any exhibit or details of how to inspect it; and
(ii)   none of the other parties objects before the statement is tendered.

In summary trial (Criminal Justice Act 1967, s. 9(2).)
(i)   before the hearing a copy of the statement mst be given to each of the other parties along with a copy of any exhibit or details of how to inspect it. (This may be waived by agreement of the parties.)
(ii)   none of the other parties or their solicitor serves notice of objection within 7 days of service. (This condition may be waived by agreement of the parties.)

In addition, a copy of the statement and any exhibit must be given to the justices' clerk as soon as practicable after it is given to or served on the parties: Magistrates' Courts Rules 1981, r. 70(2)

The court may of its own motion or on the application of a party require the maker of any statement to attend and give evidence: Criminal Justice Act 1967, s. 9(4); Magistrates' Courts Act 1980, s. 102(4). Additionally, in the case of summary trial the party tendering the statement may call the person who made it: Criminal Justice Act 1967, s. 9(4).

Except in the case of a s. 6(2) committal the statement mustbe read aloud unless the court directs otherwise, when an oral account must be given of so much of the statement as is not read aloud: Criminal Justice Act 1967, s. 9(6); Magistrates' Courts Act 1980, s. 102(5). The name and address of the person who made the statement must be read aloud unless the court otherwise directs: Magistrates' Courts Rules 1981, r. 70(6).

The method of dealing with inadmissible material in written statements is laid down in the Magistrates' Courts Rules 1981, r. 70(5).

Written statements may be edited in accordance with the Practice Note [1969] 3 All E.R. 133:

> "Where a witness has made one or more written statements to the police (described in this direction as 'original statements') it is not proper but it is often necessary for the orderly presentation of the evidence to tender as written evidence under this section of the Criminal Justice Act 1967, s. 9, a prepared statement based on the original statement or statements but excluding prejudicial and inadmissible matter contained

therein and/or giving the combined effect of the original statements. Where there is a legal representative of the prosecutor, any such statement should be prepared by him and not by a police officer, and must have been signed by the witness and the requirements of this section or s. 9 of the Criminal Justice Act 1967, as the case may be, must have been complied with in respect thereof. The prosecutor or his legal representative, as the case may be, must exercise a discretion to notify the defence in a suitable manner of any matter arising from the preparation of a statement, *e.g.* where it is material, of the existence and contents of the original statements or the exclusion of some matter. The duty is the same as that which may arise where original statements materially differ from depositions of evidence given orally".

Formal Admissions

Any fact of which oral evidence may be given may be admitted by or on behalf of the prosecutor or defendant and the admission is, as against that party, conclusive evidence of the fact admitted: Criminal Justice Act 1967, s. 10(1)

An admission may be made before or at the proceedings: *ibid*, s. 10(2). If made otherwise than in court it must be written down and signed: Magistrates' Courts Rules 1981, r. 71. It must purport to be signed by the person making it or, if a body corporate, by a director or manager, the secretary or clerk or some other similar officer: Criminal Justice Act 1967, s. 10(2). Only counsel or a solicitor may make an admission on behalf of an individual. If made before the trial by an individual it must be approved by counsel or solicitor: *ibid*, s. 10(2).

An admission may with the leave of the court be withdrawn: Criminal Justice Act 1967, s. 10(4).

Proving Previous Convictions

Previous convictions may be proved under any of the following statutes:

— *the Evidence Act, 1851, s. 13 (proof of previous convictions by certified copy of record);
— the Criminal Procedure Act, 1865, s. 6 (proof of conviction of witness);
— *the Prevention of Crimes Act, 1871, s. 18 (evidence of previous convictions);
— the Criminal Justice Act, 1948, s. 39 (proof of previous convictions by finger print);
— the Magistrates' Courts Act 1980, s. 14, and the Magistrates' Courts Rules 1981, r. 72 (proof of previous convictions);
— the Magistrates' Courts Rules 1981, r. 68 (proof of proceedings).
— the Road Traffic Act 1972, s. 11(4A) (endorsement of licences).
— the Road Traffic Act 1972, s. 182(records of the Secretary of State).

Spent Convictions

The *Practice Note* [1975] 2 All E.R. 172, reads:
    1. The effect of s. 4(1) of the Rehabilitation of Offenders Act 1974 is that a person who has become a rehabilitated person for the purpose of the Act in respect of a conviction (known as a 'spent' conviction) shall be treated for all purposes in law as a person who has not committed or been charged with or prosecuted for or convicted of or sentenced for the offence or offences which were the subject of that conviction.
    2. Section 4(1) of the 1974 Act does not apply however to evidence given in criminal proceedings (s. 7(2)(a)). Convictions are often disclosed in such criminal proceedings. When the Bill was before the House of Commons on 28th June 1974 the

* Rarely used and therefore not printed herein.

hope was expressed that the Lord Chief Justice would issue a practice direction for the guidance of the Crown Court with a view to reducing disclosure of spent convictions to a minimum and securing uniformity of approach.

3. During the trial of a criminal charge reference to previous convictions (and therefore to spent convictions) can arise in a number of ways. The most common is when the character of the accused or a witness is sought to be attacked by reference to his criminal record, but there are, of course, cases where previous convictions are relevant and admissible as, for instance, to prove system.

4. It is not possible to give general directions which will govern all these different situations, but it is recommended that both court and counsel should give effect to the general intention of Parliament by never referring to a spent conviction when such reference can be reasonably avoided. If unnecessary references to spent convictions are eliminated much will have been achieved.

5. After a verdict of guilty the court must be provided with a statement of the defendant's record for the purposes of sentence. The record supplied should contain all previous convictions, but those which are spent should, so far as practicable, be marked as such.

6. No one should refer in open court to a spent conviction without the authority of the judge, which authority should not be given unless the interests of justice so require.

7. When passing sentence the judge should make no reference to a spent conviction unless it is necessary to do so for the purpose of explaining the sentence to be passed.

A breach of para. 6 of this Note cannot be a ground for upsetting a conviction which would otherwise be perfectly proper: *R.* v. *Smallman* [1982] Crim. L.R. 175 (prosecution cross-examined defence witness as to previous conviction.)

Proving plans and drawings

Undisputed plans and drawings may be proved by certificate in accordance with the Criminal Justice Act, 1948, s. 41.

Proving Banker's Books

A banker or bank officer is not compellable to produce any bank book in proceedings to which the bank is not a party except by order of a judge: Banker's Books Evidence Act, 1879, s. 6. Once criminal proceedings are begun against any person a magistrates' court may make an order under s. 7, *ibid.*, that either the prosecutor or the defendant shall be at liberty to inspect and take copies of any entries in a banker's book.

The purpose of the provision is that, to save bankers from the inconvenience of having their books and their staff in courts for the purposes of supplying evidence, it shall be possible for the police officers concerned to obtain an order from the court, and by virtue of that order to be at liberty to inspect the accounts and take notes from them in the bank. Then when the trial comes on the bank will be undisturbed in its business, *per* Lord Widgery CJ in *R.* v. *Marlborough Street Magistrates' Court Metropolitan Stipendiary Magistrate, ex parte Simpson and Others* [1980] 70 Cr. App. R. 291.

"In criminal proceedings, justices should warn themselves of the importance of the step which they are taking in making an order under s. 7: should always recognize the care with which the jurisdiction should be exercised; should take into account amongst other things whether there is other evidence in the possession of the prosecution to support the charge; or whether the application under s. 7 is a fishing expedition in the hope of finding some material on which the charge can be hung. If justices approach these applications with a due sense of responsibility and a recognition of the importance of that which they are being asked to do, if they are always alive to the requirement of not making the order extend beyond the true purposes of the charge before them, and if in consequence they limit the period of the disclosure of the bank account to a period which is strictly relevant to the charge before them; and if finally they recognize the importance of considering whether there is other evidence in the possession of the prosecution before they provide the bank account as perhaps the only evidence, I feel if they observe those precautions and pay heed to those warnings, they will in fact produce a situation in which the section is used properly, wisely, and in support of the interests of justice, and will not allow it to be used as an instrument of oppression which on its face it might very well be ... it would be perfectly proper when justices are faced with a difficult case in which they are genuinely disturbed whether they should use this jurisdiction or not, for them to decline to make the order and to say that they decline because they feel that it is an application more appropriate to the High Court," *per* Lord Widgery, CJ in *Williams and Others* v. *Summerfield* (1972) 136 J.P. 616; *R.* v. *Marlborough Street Magistrates' Court Metropolitan Stipendiary Magistrate, ex parte Simpson and Others, supra.*

It is the duty of magistrates to take great care, when deciding whether or not to issue an order under this section, to ensure that the person whose bank account is to be inspected is not oppressed and, with a view to seeing that that is not the case, they must limit the period of time in respect of which disclosure is made. They must also be very wary that the prosecution are not using the section for ulterior purposes; that is to say for purposes other than inquiring into the matters with which the person concerned is charged. Nevertheless, the fact that a defendant intends to plead guilty does not mean that the prosecution should cease their efforts to collect sufficient evidence or that magistrates should refuse an order, *per* Donaldson LJ in *Owen* v. *Sambrook* (1980) 145 J.P.N. 18; [1981] Crim. L.R. 329.

Accomplices

Since the Criminal Law Act 1967, s. 1, (which abolished all distinctions between felonies and misdemeanours and provided that on all matters in which a distinction had previously been made the law and practice should be that applicable to felony), the only categories of accomplice have been principals in the first degree and principals in the second degree (or aiders and abettors). A person may no longer be charged as an accessory after the fact, although s. 4 of the Act of 1967 makes it an offence to assist persons who have committed an arrestable offence.

By the Accessories and Abettors Act 1861, s. 8, every person who aids, abets, counsels or procures the commission of a misdemeanour (and thus, now, any offence) is liable to be tried, indicted and punished as a principal. By the Magistrates' Courts Act 1980, s. 44(1), a person who aids, abets, counsels or procures the commission by another of a summary offence is guilty of the like offence and may be tried (whether or not charged as a principal) either by a court having jurisdiction to try the other person or by a court having jurisdiction to try him.

"Two things must be proved before an accused can be held to be guilty of aiding and abetting the commission of the offence: first, he must have full knowledge of the facts which constitute the offence ... Secondly, there must be some form of voluntary assistance in the commission of the offence. Sometimes the word used is 'encouragement' ..." *per* Parker LCJ in *Tuck* v. *Robson* (1970) 134 J.P. 389, in which was approved the dictum of Devlin J in *National Coal Board* v. *Gamble* (1958) 122 J.P. 453, where he said: "It would be wrong to conclude . . . that proof of encouragement is necessary to every form of aiding and abetting . . . Presence on the scene of the crime without encouragement or assistance is no aid to the criminal; the supply of essential material is . . . If voluntary presence is *prima facie* evidence of encouragement and therefore aiding and abetting, it appears to me to be *a fortiori* that the intentional supply of an essential article must be *prima facie* evidence of aiding and abetting. And see *Cassady* v. *Reg. Morris (Transport) Ltd* [1975] Crim L.R. 398. Mere presence at the scene of a crime is not enough. In *R.* v. *Coney* (1882) 8 Q.B.D. at 557, Hawkins, J, said:

'In my opinion, to constitute an aider and abettor some active steps must be taken by word, or action, with the intent to instigate the principal, or principals. Encouragement does not of necessity amount to aiding and abetting, it may be intentional or unintentional, a man may unwittingly encourage another in fact by his presence, by misinterpreted words, or gestures, or by his silence, or non-interference, or he may encourage intentionally by expressions, gestures, or actions intended to signify approval. In the latter case he aids and abets, in the former he does not. It is no criminal offence to stand by, a mere passive spectator of a crime, even of a murder. Non-interference to prevent a crime is not itself a crime. But the fact that a person was voluntarily and purposely present witnessing the commission of a crime, and offered no opposition to it, though he might reasonably be expected to prevent and had the power to do so, or at least to express his dissent, might under some circumstances, afford cogent evidence upon which a jury would be justified in finding that he wilfully encouraged and so aided and abetted. But it would be purely a question for the jury whether he did so or not.'

And *see R.* v. *Clarkson* (1971) 135 J.P. 533.

In the case of *D. Stanton and Sons Ltd.* v. *Webber* (1972) 136 J.P.N. 68, it was said that to convict a person as an aider and abettor it must be proved that he knew the material and relevant facts which constituted a substantive offence either by actual knowledge or from knowledge deemed to be had from the fact that he deliberately shut his eyes to the obvious.

It is still necessary to distinguish between principals in the first and second degree (even if not charged as such) in the case of offences of strict liability, owing to the fact that *mens rea* will in general attach to the latter but not to the former. *See*, for example, *John Henshall (Quarries), Ltd.* v. *Harvey* (1965) 129 J.P. 224.

Aiders and abettors are liable to the same time limit as principal offenders: *Gould and Co., Ltd* v. *Houghton* (1921) 85 J.P. 93; *Homolka* v. *Osmond* [1939] 1 All E.R. 154.

Can an accomplice be convicted when the alleged principal has been acquitted?

In misdemeanors (and now, by virtue of the Criminal Law Act 1967, s. 1, all offences) the acquittal or conviction of the principal in the second degree is a matter of evidence so that, for example, notwithstanding that the principal offender has been acquitted for lack of admissible evidence, the offence can be proved to have taken place by evidence which, as against the aider and abettor, is admissible and cogent: *per* Judge Chapman in *R.* v. *Humphreys and Turner* (1965) 130 J.P. 45; affirmed by the Court of Appeal in *R.* v. *Cogan R.* v. *Leak* (1975) 139 J.P. 608. But an accomplice cannot be convicted when the principal offender has not committed the offence: *R.* v. *Davis* [1977] Crim. L.R. 542.

The Offence of Incitement

It is an offence at common law to incite the commission of any offence. It matters not whether the offence is committed or not but, if committed, the inciter will become guilty of the substantive offence.

Any offence consisting in the incitement to commit a summary offence is triable only summarily: Magistrates' Courts Act 1980, s. 45(1).

The Offence of Attempt

If, with intent to commit an indictable offence, a person does an act which is more than merely preparatory to the commission of the offence, he is guilty of attempting to commit the offence: Criminal Attempts Act 1981, s. 1(1). By virtue of s. 1(4), *ibid*., attempts to commit conspiracy, aiding and abetting, counselling, procuring or suborning the commission of an offence and offences under ss. 4(1) and 5(1) of the Criminal Law Act 1967 are excluded. A person may be guilty of attempting to commit an offence even though the facts are such that the commission of the offence is impossible: s. 1(2), *ibid*. He is also regarded as having had an intent to commit an offence where, apart from the act, his intention would not be regarded as having amounted to an intent to commit an offence, so long as, if the facts of the case had been as he believed them to be, his intention would have been so regarded: s. 1(3), *ibid*. These subsections are applied to offences of attempt under other enactments by s. 3, *ibid*.

Certain penal and procedural provisions governing the substantive offences are applied to attempts by virtue of s. 2, *ibid*.

If the offence attempted is triable only on indictment the attempt is also so triable: s. 4(1), *ibid*. If the offence attempted is triable either way the accused is liable on summary conviction to any penalty to which he would have been liable on summary conviction of that offence: s. 4(1), *ibid*. Where the court may proceed to summary trial of an information charging a person with an offence and an information charging him with an attempt to commit it the court may, without his consent, try the informations together: s. 4(2), *ibid*.

Husbands and Wives

A husband and wife cannot conspire together to commit a crime: Criminal Law Act 1977, s. 2(2)(a). Nor can there be any publication of a criminal libel between them: *R. v. Lord Mayor of London* [1886] 16 Q.B.D. 772. A husband may not be convicted of rape upon his wife: 1 Hale 629; except after a separation order: *R. v. Clarke* (1949) 114 J.P. 192; a decree *nisi*: *R. v. O'Brien (Edward)* (1974) 138 J.P. 798; or an undertaking not to molest: *R. v. Steele* [1977] 65 Cr. App. R. 22

Except in treason or murder it is a defence for a wife to prove that the offence was committed in the presence of and under the coercion of her husband: Criminal Justice Act 1925, s. 47.

The common law rule that husbands and wives could not steal from one another, at least when living together, modified by the Larceny Act, 1916, has been reversed altogether by the Theft Act 1968, s. 30. In the words of the Criminal Law Revision Committee (8th Report, Cmnd. 2977), the effect of s. 30 is to make "husbands and wives liable for offences under the [Act] as if they were not married . . . It enables spouses to prosecute each other for any offence and amends the law as to when a spouse is competent to give evidence in proceedings against the other spouse." The consent of the Director of Public Prosecutions is necessary to certain prosecutions made possible by this section.

A wife is in principle not a competent witness against her husband: *Hoskyn v. Commissioner of Police for the Metropolis* (1978) 142 J.P. 291. This applies even if they have been judicially separated: *Moss v. Moss* [1963] 2 Q.B. 799. At common law the only clear exception is that she is competent in cases of personal violence against her, but even here she is not compellable: *Hoskyn v. Commissioner of Police for the Metropolis, supra*. There are also possible exceptions in the case of treason and of abduction (even if the accused has married the woman abducted). By various enactments, including s. 4 of the Criminal Evidence Act 1898 the wife is competent for the prosecution in the case of a number of offences, but in these cases she is not compellable (*Leach v. R.* (1912) 76 J.P. 203). The most important offences are offences against the property of the wife, failure to maintain wife or children, many other offences relating to children (including cruelty), bigamy and most sexual offences against a third person (not including unnatural offences). If the wife herself brings the proceedings against her husband (which s. 30(2) of the Theft Act 1968 enables her to do for any offence except that the consent of the Director of Public Prosecutions is required for a prosecution for stealing or damaging her property), she is competent under that provision to give evidence against him.

The accused's wife is competent as a witness for him, under s. 1 of the 1898 Act, in all cases, but she is compellable for him only in cases where she is competent (and compellable) for the prosecution at common law. Comment by the prosecution on her failure to give evidence for her husband is prohibited by s. 1(b) of the 1898 Act.

The wife of the accused is competent to give evidence under s. 1 of the 1898 Act for a person accused (and tried) jointly with her husband in all cases with her husband's consent. Where the wife is made competent for the prosecution by s. 4 of the 1898 Act she is competent for the co-accused under that section, even without her husband's consent. In the cases where she is competent (and compellable) for the prosecution at common law she is probably also compellable for the co-accused.

Once the issue of competence is raised the onus of proof is on the prosecution: *R*. v. *Yacoob* [1981] 72 Cr. App. R. 313.

Up to the point where she goes into the witness box, the wife has a choice: she may refuse to give evidence or waive her right of refusal. The waiver is effective only if made with full knowledge of her right to refuse. If she waives her right of refusal, she becomes an ordinary witness. She is by analogy in the same position as a witness who waives privilege which would entitle him to refuse to answer questions on a certain topic. If the nature of her evidence justifies it, an application may be made to treat her as a hostile witness, *per* Peter Pain, J in *R*. v. *Pitt* [1982] 3 All E.R. 63.

Criminal Evidence Statutes

The subject of evidence in criminal cases is too big to include in a book of this compass, particularly since most of it is still to be found in the cases. However there are a small number of statutes dealing with evidence in criminal cases and these are included for convenience. They are:

— *The Criminal Procedure Act* 1865, which deals with adverse and hostile witnesses and the comparison of disputed writing.

— *The Criminal Evidence Act* 1898, which provides for the accused to be a competent witness and where he should give evidence, deals partially with the competence of his spouse and retains his right to make an unsworn statement. It also prohibits cross examination as to bad character of the accused save in certain excepted cases.

— *The Criminal Evidence Act* 1965, which allows documentary hearsay evidence in certain narrowly defined circumstances.

— *The Rehabilitation of Offenders Act 1974*, which precludes reference to spent convictions. It does not apply to any criminal proceedings before a court in Great Britain: s. 7(2)(a), *ibid*.

The Judges' Rules

The Judges' Rules are set out in Appendix A. These are not rules of law. Their non-observance may lead to the exclusion of an alleged confession, but the ultimate test is whether, breach or no breach, the confession is voluntary, *per* Edmund Davies L.J. in *R*. v. *Prager* (1972) 136 J.P. 287.

Evidence of Identification

The guidance given by the Court in *R*. v. *Turnbull* (1976) 140 J.P. 648 is set out in Appendix B.

THE CRIMINAL PROCEDURE ACT 1865

How far witness may be discredited by the party producing

3.   A party producing a witness shall not be allowed to impeach his credit by general evidence of bad character; but he may, in case the witness shall in the opinion of the judge prove adverse, contradict him by other evidence, or by leave of the judge, prove that he has made at other times a statement inconsistent with his present testimony; but before such last-mentioned proof can be given the circumstances of the supposed statement, sufficient to designate the particular occasion, must be mentioned to the witness, and he must be asked whether or not he has made such a statement.

COMMENTARY

This provision has not removed the common law right of the court to allow at its discretion cross-examination of a hostile witness: *R.* v. *Thompson* [1977] 64 Cr. App. R. 96.

As to proof of contradictory statements of adverse witness

4.   If a witness, upon cross-examination as to a former statement made by him relative to the subject matter of the indictment or proceeding, and inconsistent with his present testimony, does not distinctly admit that he has made such statement, proof may be given that he did in fact make it; but before such proof can be given the circumstances of the supposed statement, sufficient to designate the particular occasion, must be mentioned to the witness, and he must be asked whether or not he has made such statement.

Cross-examinations as to previous statements in writing

5.   A witness may be cross-examined as to previous statements made by him in writing, or reduced into writing, relative to the subject matter of the indictment or proceeding, without such writing being shown to him; but if it is intended to contradict such witness by the writing, his attention must, before such contradictory proof can be given, be called to those parts of the writing which are to be used for the purpose of so contradicting him: Provided always, that it shall be competent for the judge, at any time during the trial, to require the production of the writing for his inspection, and he may thereupon make such use of it for the purposes of the trial as he may think fit.

Proof of conviction of witness for felony or misdemeanor may be given

6.   A witness may be questioned as to whether he has been convicted of any felony or misdemeanor, and upon being so questioned, if he either denies or does not admit the fact, or refuses to answer, it shall be lawful for the cross-examining party to prove such conviction; and a certificate containing the substance and effect only (omitting the formal part) of the indictment and conviction for such offence, purporting to be signed by the clerk of the court or other officer having the custody of the records of the court where the offender was convicted, or by the deputy of such clerk or officer, (for which certificate a fee of five shillings and no more shall be demanded or taken) shall, upon proof of the identity of the person, be sufficient evidence of the said conviction, without proof of the signature or official character of the person appearing to have signed the same.

Proof of instrument to validity of which whereof attestation is not necessary.

7.   It shall not be necessary to prove by the attesting witness any instrument to the validity of which attestation is not requisite, and such instrument may be proved as if there had been no attesting witness thereto.

Comparison of disputed writing with writing proved to be genuine

8.   Comparison of a disputed writing with any writing proved to the satisfaction of the judge to be genuine shall be permitted to be made by witnesses; and such writings, and the evidence of witnesses respecting the same, may be permitted to the court and jury as evidence of the genuineness or otherwise of the writing in dispute.

COMMENTARY

Proof beyond reasonable doubt is required under this section in criminal proceedings: *R*. v. *Ewing* (1983) *The Times*, March 15.

THE BANKER'S BOOKS EVIDENCE ACT, 1879

Mode of proof of entries in bankers' books.

3. Subject to the provisions of this Act, a copy of any entry in a banker's book shall in all legal proceedings be received as prima facie evidence of such entry, and of the matters, transactions, and accounts therein recorded.

Proof that book is a banker's book.

4. A copy of an entry in a banker's book shall not be received in evidence under this Act unless it be first proved that the book was at the time of the making of the entry one of the ordinary books of the bank, and that the entry was made in the usual and ordinary course of business, and that the book is in the custody or control of the bank.

Such proof may be given by a partner or officer of the bank, and may be given orally or by an affidavit sworn before any commissioner or person authorized to take affidavits.

Verification of copy.

5. A copy of an entry in a banker's book shall not be received under this Act unless it be further proved that the copy has been examined with the original entry and is correct.

Such proof shall be given by some person who has examined the copy with the original entry, and may be given either orally or by an affidavit sworn before any commissioner or person authorized to take affidavits.

Case in which banker, etc., not compellable to produce book, etc.

6. A banker or officer of a bank shall not, in any legal proceeding to which the bank is not a party, be compellable to produce any banker's book the contents of which, can be proved under this Act, or to appear as a witness to prove the matters, transactions, and accounts therein recorded, unless by order of a judge made for special cause.

COMMENTARY

Banker, bank. Defined in s. 9, *infra*.

Proved under this Act. A copy of an entry in a banker's book cannot be received in evidence under this Act unless it be first proved that the book was at the time of the making of the entry one of the ordinary books of the bank, and that the entry was made in the usual and ordinary course on business, and that the book is in the custody or control of the bank. Such proof may be given by a partner or officer of the bank, and may be given orally or by an affidavit sworn before any commissioner or person authorized to take affidavits: s. 4 of the Act. A copy of an entry in a banker's book cannot be received in evidence under this Act unless it be further proved that the copy has been examined with the original entry and is correct. Such proof may be given by some person who has examined the copy with the original entry, either orally or by affidavit: s. 5, *ibid*.

Court or judge may order inspection, etc.

7. On the application of any party to a legal proceeding a court or judge may order that such party be at liberty to inspect and take copies of any entries in a banker's book for any of the purposes of such proceedings. An order under this section, may be made either with or without summoning the bank or any other party, and shall be served on the bank three clear days before the same is to be obeyed, unless the court or judge otherwise directs.

COMMENTARY

For the principles upon which the court should act *see* the introduction.

The power under this section extends to banks in Scotland and Northern Ireland: *Kissam* v. *Link* (1896) 1 Q.B. 574. For the Isle of Man *see R.* v. *Grossman* [1981] Crim. L.R. 396.

The court (including the justice), has power to order the costs of any application against the bank: s. 8, *infra*.

Legal proceeding. Defined in s. 10, *infra*.
A court or judge may. The terms "court" and "judge" are defined in s. 10, *infra*.

Order. Discharge need not be limited to the periods charged: *Owen* v. *Sambrook* (1980) 145 J.P.N. 18; [1981] Crim. L.R. 329. The order should be limited in time: *Williams and Others* v. *Summerfield* (1972) 136 J.P. 616; *R.* v. *Marlborough St. Magistrates' Court Metropolitan Stipendiary Magistrate, ex parte Simpson and Others* [1980] 70 Cr. App. R. 291.

A banker's book. Defined in s. 9, *infra.*. This is not confined to the books of the defendant, but extends to third parties: *Waterhouse* v. *Wilson Baker* [1924] All E.R. Rep. 777 (a civil case); *R.* v. *Andover Justices, ex parte Rhodes* [1980] Crim. LR. 644 (husband of accused).

Summoning the bank or any other person. It is in the court's discretion whether to issue a summons or to make the order *ex parte* although *ex parte* orders are more common. A summons would appear to be indicated when the books are those of someone other than the accused. *Cf. R.* v. *Grossman* [1981] Crim. L.R. 396.

Three clear days. That is, excluding the day of service and the day on which the order is to be obeyed.

Costs

8. The costs of any application to a court or judge under or for the purposes of this Act, and the costs of anything done or to be done under an order of a court or judge made under or for the purposes of this Act shall be in the discretion of the court or judge, who may order the same or any part thereof to be paid to any party by the bank where the same have been occasioned by any default or delay on the part of the bank. Any such order against a bank may be enforced as if the bank was a party to the proceeding.

Interpretation of "bank","banker" and "banker's books"

9. (1) In this Act the expressions "bank" and "banker" mean–
(*a*) a recognised bank, licensed institution or municipal bank, within the meaning of the Banking Act 1979;
(*b*) a trustee savings bank within the meaning of the Trustee Savings Banks Act 1981;
(*c*) the National Savings Bank; and
(*d*) the Post Office, in the exercise of its powers to provide banking services.

(2) Expressions in this Act relating to "bankers' books" include ledgers, day books, cash books, account books and other records used in the ordinary business of the bank, whether those records are in written form or are kept on microfilm, magnetic tape or any other form of mechanical or electronic data retrieval mechanism.

(as substituted by the Banking Act 1979, sch. 6, as amended by the Trustee Savings Bank Act 1981, sch. 6.)

COMMENTARY

Letters contained in a bank correspondence file are not banker's books: *R. v. Dadson* (1983) 147 J.P. 509.

Interpretation of "legal proceeding", "court", "judge"

10. In this Act—

The expression "legal proceeding" means any civil or criminal proceeding or inquiry in which evidence is or may be given, and includes an arbitration and an application to, or an inquiry or other proceeding before, the Solicitors Disciplinary Tribunal or any body exercising functions in relation to solicitors in Scotland or Northern Ireland corresponding to the functions of that Tribunal;

The expression "the court" means the court, judge, arbitrator, persons or person before whom a legal proceeding is held or taken;

The expression "a judge" means with respect to England a judge of the High Court . . .

(*as amended by the Solicitors Act, 1974, s. 86*).

COMMENTARY

Persons or person. Includes a magistrates' court: *R. v. Kinghorn* (1908) 72 J.P. 478.

THE CRIMINAL EVIDENCE ACT 1898

Competency of witnesses in criminal cases

1. Every person charged with an offence, and the wife or husband, as the case may be, of the person so charged, shall be a competent witness for the defence at every stage of the proceedings, whether the person so charged is charged solely or jointly with any other person. Provided as follows-

(*a*) A person so charged shall not be called as a witness in pursuance of this Act except upon his own application:

(*b*) The failure of any person charged with an offence, or of the wife or husband, as the case may be, of the person so charged, to give evidence shall not be made the subject of any comment by the prosecution:

(*c*) The wife or husband of the person charged shall not, save as in this Act mentioned, be called as a witness in pursuance of this Act except upon the application of the person so charged:

(*d*) Nothing in this Act shall make a husband compellable to disclose any communication made to him by his wife during the marriage, or a wife compellable to disclose any communication made to her by her husband during the marriage:

(*e*) A person charged and being a witness in pursuance of this Act may be asked any question in cross-examination notwithstanding that it would tend to criminate him as to the offence charged:

(*f*) A person charged and called as a witness in pursuance of this Act shall not be asked, and if asked shall not be required to answer, any question tending to show that he has committed or been convicted of or been charged with any offence other than that wherewith he is then charged, or is of bad character, unless—

    (i) the proof that he has committed or been convicted of such other offence is admissible evidence to show that he is guilty of the offence wherewith he is then charged; or

    (ii) he has personally or by his advocate asked questions of the witnesses for the prosecution with a view to establish his own good character, or has given evidence of his good character, or the nature or conduct of the defence is such as to involve imputations on the character of the prosecutor or the witnesses for the prosecution; or

(iii) he has given evidence against any other person charged in the same proceedings:

(g) Every person called as a witness in pursuance of this Act shall, unless otherwise ordered by the court, give his evidence from the witness box or other place from which the other witnesses give their evidence.

(as amended by the Criminal Evidence Act 1979, s. 1, the Criminal Justice Act 1982, sch. 16).

COMMENTARY

Wife or husband. See the introduction.

Witness for the defence. Including the defence of a co-defendant. But the person charged is not a compellable witness: see proviso (a).

Proviso (a). Once a co-defendant is acquitted she becomes a compellable witness: *R.* v. *Conti* [1974] 85 Cr. App. R. 387.

Proviso (e). The phrase "tend to criminate him as to the offence charged" means "tend to connect him with the commision of the offence charged" rather than "tend to convince or persuade the jury that he is guilty," *per* Lord Reid and Viscount Simonds in *Jones* v. *Director of Public Prosecutions* (1962) 126 J.P. 216.

Proviso (e): Any question. When the accused gives evidence on behalf of another accused he may be cross-examined to show that he is guilty of the offence charged: *R.* v. *Rowland* (1910) 74 J.P. 144.

Charged. Means "charged before a court": *Stirland* v. *Director of Public Prosecutions* (1945) 109 J.P. 1. This prohibits questions in regard to a charge of which the accused was acquitted: *R.* v. *Cokar* (1960) 124 J.P. 313. The mere fact that a man has been charged with an offence is no proof that he committed the offence and is irrelevant unless asked as a step in cross-examination leading to a question of whether the witness was convicted, or in order to elicit some evidence of statements made or evidence given by the prisoner on the trial of a charge which failed which tends to throw doubt on evidence which he is giving or in order to show anger on the part of the accused against the person attacked for having brought a charge against the accused which proved to b unfounded. *per* Viscount Sankey LC in *Maxwell* v. *Director of Public Prosecutions* (1934) 98 J.P. 387.

Proviso (f). "The substantive part of (proviso (f)) is negative in form and as such is universal and is absolute unless the exceptions come into play. Then come the three exceptions, but it does not follow that when the absolute prohibition is superseded by a permission, the permission is as absolute as the prohibition. When it is sought to justify a question it must not only be brought within the terms of the permission, but also must be capable of justification according to the general rules of evidence and in particular must satisfy the test of relevance. Exception (i) deals with evidence falling within the rule that where issues of intention or design are involved in the charge or defence, the prisoner may be asked questions relevant to these matters, even though he has himself raised no question of his good character. Exceptions (ii) and (iii) come into play when the prisoner by himself or his witnesses has put his character in issue, or has attacked the character of others. Dealing with exceptions (i) and (ii), it is clear that the test of relevance is wider in (ii) than in (i). In the latter, proof that the prisoner has committed or been convicted of some other offence can only be admitted if it goes to show that he was guilty of the offence charged. In the former (exception (ii)) the questions permissible must be relevant to the issue of his own good character and if not so relevant cannot be admissible", *per* Lord Sankey LC in *Maxwell* v. *Director of Public Prosecutions, supra.*

Ignoring exception (i), the rules governing cross-examination of the accused were summarized by Viscount Simonds in *Stirland* v. *Director of Public Prosecutions* (1945) 109 J.P. 1 as follows:

(1) The accused in the witness box may not be asked any question "tending to show that he had committed or been convicted of or been charged with any offence other than that wherewith he is then charged, or is a bad character, unless" one or other of the three conditions set out in s. 1 (*f*) of the Act of 1898 is fulfilled.

(2) He may however be cross-examined as to any of the evidence he has given in chief, including statements as to his good record, with a view to testing his veracity or accuracy, or to showing that he is not to be believed on his oath.

(3) An accused who "puts his character in issue" must be regarded as putting the whole of his past record in issue. He cannot assert his good character in certain respects without exposing himself to inquiry as to the rest of his record so far as this tends to disprove a claim for good character.

(4) An accused is not to be regarded as depriving himself of the protection of the section, because the proper conduct of his defence necessitates the making of injurious reflections on the prosecutor or his witnesses: *R.* v. *Turner* [1944] 1 All E.R. 599.

(5) It is no disproof of good character that a man has been suspected, or accused, of a previous crime. Such questions as "Were you suspected?" or "Were you accused?" are inadmissible because they are irrelevant to the issue of character, and can only be asked if the accused has sworn expressly to the contrary. (See r. 2 above).

(6) The fact that a question put to the accused is irrelevant is in itself no reason for quashing his conviction, though it should have been disallowed by the judge. If the question is not only irrelevant but is unfair to the accused as being likely to distract the jury from considering the real issues, and so lead to "a miscarriage of justice" (Criminal Appeal Act, 1907, s. 4(1)), it should be disallowed, and, if not disallowed, is a ground on which an appeal against conviction may be based.

And *see R.* v. *Nelson* [1979] 68 Cr. App. R. 12. (Cross-examination should not have been allowed when defence put it to police officer that conversation recorded in his notebook never took place).

It is necessary that an unrepresented defendant should be warned of the risk he runs if he persists in attacking prosecution witnesses. The proper practice should be for those representing the prosecution, who alone know whether the defendant has got previous convictions, to ask for an adjournment and, when the justices have retired, to enlist the help, which I am sure would only too readily be given, of the justices' clerk in order that they may both explain, as simply as possible, to the unrepresented defendant the risk which he runs if he continues in that course of conduct, *per* Lord Parker CJ in *R.* v. *Weston-Super-Mare Justices, ex parte Townsend* (1968) 132 J.P. 526. Where justices hear inadmissible evidence they should not dismiss the case but should adjourn it for a re-hearing before a different bench: *Elkington* v. *Kesley* (1948) 112 J.P. 228. Where the defendant has forfeited his shield he may be cross-examined about subsequent as well as previous convictions: *R.* v. *Coltress* [1979] 68 Cr. App. R. 193.

Proviso (f) (i). Sometimes known as the similar facts rule.

The present test was described as follows: is the evidence capable of tending to persuade a jury of the accused's guilt on some ground other than his bad character and disposition to commit the sort of crime with which he is charged? In the case of an alleged homosexual offence, just as in the case of an alleged burglary, evidence which proves merely that the accused has committed crimes in the past and is therefore disposed to commit the crime charged is clearly inadmissible. It has, however, never been doubted that if the crime charged is committed in an uniquely or strikingly similar manner to other crimes committed by the accused the manner in which the other crimes were committed may be evidence upon which a jury could reasonably conclude that the accused was guilty of the crime charged. The similarity would have to be so unique or striking that commonsense makes it inexplicable on the basis of coincidence.

per Lord Salmon in *Boardman* v. *Director of Public Prosecutions* (1975) 139 J.P. 52. In *R.* v. *Rance and Herron* [1976] 62 Cr. App. R. 118 at p. 121, Lord Widgery CJ was forced to say that "one must be careful not to attach too much importance to Lord Salmon's vivid phrase 'uniquely or strikingly similar'. The gist of what is being said both by Lord Cross (at p. 185) and by Lord Salmon, is that evidence is admissible as similar fact evidence if, but only if, it goes beyond showing a tendency to commit crimes of this kind and is positively probative in regard to the crime now charged." And *see R.* v. *Scarrott* (1978) 142 J.P. 198.

In *R.* v. *Seaman* [1978] 67 Cr. App. R. 234, the appellant had gone into a supermarket carrying a shopping bag, ordered a packet of bacon which the assistant had given him and placed it in a wire basket. He then bought some bottles of beer and slipped the bacon into the same bag. He left the supermarket without paying for the bacon and was stopped outside. At his trial for the theft of the bacon evidence was given of two previous occasions. On the first the store detective had seen the appellant buying bacon and put it in a wire basket which was later seen to be empty. However, as he had been lost sight of for a minute or so, no action had been taken against him. On the second occasion, the appellant, noticing that he was being watched, had returned the bacon on the shelf. Although it was said to be a borderline case, the evidence of the prior acts was held to have been properly admitted.

62   2.   PROVING THE CASE

Evidence may be admitted of facts subsequent to the offence: *R. v. Armstrong* (1922) 86 J.P. 209. *See also R. v. Barrington,* (1980) *The Times,* 3 December and *Thompson v. R.* (1917) 81 J.P. 266.

Proviso (f) (ii) The following guidelines have been set out for the exercise of discretion in favour of defendants:

First, it should be used if there is nothing more than a denial, however emphatic or offensively made, of an act or even a short series of acts amounting to one incident or in what was said to have been a short interview. Examples are provided by the kind of evidence given in pickpocket cases and where the defendant is alleged to have said: 'Who grassed on me this time?' The position would be different however if there were a denial of evidence of a long period of detailed observation extending over hours and just as in this case and in *R. v. Tanner,* where there were denials of long conversations. Second, cross-examination should only be allowed if the judge is sure that there is no possibility of mistake, misunderstanding or confusion and that the jury will inevitably have to decide whether the prosecution witnesses have fabricated evidence. Defendants sometimes make wild allegations when giving evidence. Allowance should be made for the strain of being in the witness box and the exaggerated use of language which sometimes results from such strain or lack of education or mental instability. Particular care should be used when a defendant is led into making allegations during cross-examination. The defendant who, during cross-examination, is driven to explaining away the evidence by saying it has been made up or planted on him usually convicts himself without having his previous convictions brought out. Finally, there is no need for the prosecution to rely on s. 1(f)(ii) if the evidence against a defendant is overwhelming.

per Lawton LJ. in *R. v. Britzman. R. v. Hall* [1983] 1 All E.R. 369.

Cross-examination of the accused is permissible under this exception notwithstanding that the imputations are a necessary part of the accused's defence, but the court has a discretion to refuse to permit cross-examination: *Selvey v. Director of Public Prosecutions* (1968) 132 J.P. 43. A statement that amounts to no more than a denial of the charge expressed in emphatic language should not be regarded as coming within this section: *Selvey v. Director of Public Prosecutions, supra.* It is wrong in principle to allow cross-examination as to character and previous convictions where the convictions are minor and took place long before: *R. v. Nye* [1982] 75 Cr. App. R. 247 (spent convictions).

Proviso (f)(iii): Evidence against. The following guidelines were laid down for deciding whether evidence by an accused was "evidence against" his co-accused: (1) If it is established that a person jointly charged has given evidence against the co-defendant that defendant has a right to cross-examine the other as to previous convictions and the trial judge has no discretion to refuse an application. (2) Such evidence may be given either in chief or during cross-examination. (3) It has to be objectively decided whether the evidence either supports the prosecution case in a material respect or undermines the defence of the co-accused. A hostile intent is irrelevant. (4) If consideration has to be given to the undermining of the other's defence care must be taken to see that the evidence clearly undermines the defence. Inconvenience to or inconsistency with the other's defence is not of itself sufficient. (5) Mere denial of participation in a joint venture is not of itself sufficient to rank as evidence against the co-defendant. For the proviso to apply, such denial must lead to the conclusion that if the witness did not participate then it must have been the other who did. (6) Where the one defendant asserts or in due course would assert one view of the joint venture which is directly contradicted by the other such contradiction may be evidence against the co-defendant: *R. v. Varley* [1982] 2 All E.R. 519.

Evidence of person charged

2.   Where the only witness to the facts of the case called by the defence is the person charged, he shall be called as a witness immediately after the close of the evidence for the prosecution.

Right of reply

3.   The fact that the person charged has been called as a witness shall not of itself confer on the prosecution the right of reply.

Calling of wife or husband in certain cases

4. (1) The wife or husband of a person charged with an offence under any enactment mentioned in the schedule to this Act may be called as a witness either for the prosecution or defence and without the consent of the person charged.

(2) Nothing in this Act shall affect a case where the wife or husband of a person charged with an offence may at common law be called as a witness without the consent of that person.

COMMENTARY

Subsection (2): At common law. *See* Husbands and Wives in the Introduction.

SCHEDULE

(Section 4)

ENACTMENTS REFERRED TO

Session and Chapter Short Title   *Enactments referred to*

19 & 2 Geo. 5 c. 34	The Infant Life (Preservation) Act, 1929	The whole Act.
11 & 12 Geo. 6 c. 29	National Assistance Act, 1948	Section 51.

(as amended by the Infant Life (Preservation) Act 1929, s. 2(5), the National Assistance (Adaptation of Enactments) Regulations 1952, the Sexual Offences Act 1956, s. 51, sch. 4, the Theft Act 1968, sch. 3, the Statute Law (Revision) Act 1981, sch. 1)

THE CRIMINAL JUSTICE ACT 1925

Abolition of presumption of coercion of married woman by husband

47. Any presumption of law that an offence committed by a wife in the presence of her husband is committed under the coercion of the husband is hereby abolished, but on a charge against a wife for any offence other than treason or murder it shall be a good defence to prove that the offence was committed in the presence of, and under the coercion of, the husband.

COMMENTARY

See Husbands and Wives in the Introduction.

THE CHILDREN AND YOUNG PERSONS ACT, 1933

Evidence of child of tender years

38. (1) Where, in any proceedings against any person for any offence, any child of tender years called as a witness does not in the opinion of the court understand the nature of the oath, his evidence may be received, though not given upon oath, if, in the opinion of the court, he is possessed of sufficient intelligence to justify the reception of his evidence, though not given on oath, but otherwise taken and reduced into writing in accordance with the provisions of s. 17 of the Indictable Offences Act, 1848, or of this Part of this Act, shall be deemed to be a deposition within the meaning of that section and that Part respectively:

Provided that where evidence admitted by virtue of this section is given on behalf of the prosecution the accused shall not liable to be convicted of the offence unless that evidence is corroborated by some other material evidence in support thereof implicating him.

(2) If any child whose evidence is received as aforesaid wilfully gives false evidence in such circumstances that he would, if the evidence had been given on oath, have been guilty of perjury, he shall be liable on summary conviction to be dealt with as if he had been summarily convicted of an indictable offence punishable in the case of an adult with imprisonment.

COMMENTARY

Subsection (1). This was always a rule of the common law: *R.* v. *Southern* [1930] All E.R. Rep. 16.
There may be cases in which witnesses should be called on the child's capacity to take the oath: *R.* v. *Reynolds* (1950) 114 J.P. 115. For an example of the examination of a child on this point *see R.* v. *Dent* (1907) 71 J.P. 511. And *see* also *R.* v. *Lyons* [1921] 15 Cr. App. R. 144. Recently the Court of Appeal has tended to play down the importance of an awareness of the divine sanction. The important consideration, it was said in *R.* v. *Hayes* [1977] 64 Cr. App. R. 194 at p. 186, is whether the child has a sufficient appreciation of the solemnity of the occasion and the added responsibility to tell the truth which is involved in taking an ·oath over and above the duty to tell the truth which is an ordinary duty of normal social conduct. There are two aspects when considering whether a child should properly be sworn: first that the child has sufficient appreciation of the particular nature of the case and, secondly, a realization that taking the oath involves more than the ordinary duty of telling the truth in ordinary day to day life: *R.* v. *Campbell* (1982) *The Times*, December 10. Where a court admits the unsworn evidence of a child without first satisfying itself of the factors set out in subs. (1) the conviction will not necessarily be quashed: *R.* v. *Surgenor* (1940) 104 J.P. 213. The assessment should be made in open court.
The evidence of a child before examining justices in sexual cases must in general be tendered in writing under the Children and Young Persons Act, 1963, s. 27, *infra*.
The public, but not the press, may be excluded during the evidence of a juvenile witness in proceedings in relation to an offence against or any conduct contrary to, decency or morality: Children and Young Persons Act, 1933, s. 37.

Of tender years. "Whether a child is of tender years is a matter for the good sense of the court": *R.* v. *Campbell* (1956) 120 J.P. 359. What "tender years" means differs according to the child. In general for a profferred witness under the age of 14 the precautions are necessary: *R.* v. *Khan* [1981] Crim. L.R. 33. In *R.* v. *Hayes* [1977] 64 Cr. App. R. 82 it was said that the borderline dividing children who are not normally considered old enough to take the oath properly falls between the ages of eight and 10. It is undesirable in any circumstances to call a child of five years old: *R.* v. *Wallwork* (1958) 122 J.P. 299.

On oath. Includes an affirmation: Interpretation Act 1978, sch. 1.

Section 17 of the Indictable Offences Act, 1848. Now the Magistrates' Courts Rules 1981, r. 7.

Corroborated. *(a)* The unsworn evidence of a child must be corroborated by sworn evidence: if then the only evidence implicating the accused is that of unsworn children the judge must stop the case.
(*b*) It makes no difference whether the child's evidence relates to an assault on himself or herself or to any other charge, for example, when an unsworn child says that he saw the accused person steal an article.
(*c*) The sworn evidence of a child need not as a matter of law be corroborated, but a jury should be warned, not that they must find corroboration, but that there is a risk in acting on the uncorroborated evidence of young boys or girls, though they may do so if convinced that the witness is telling the truth.
(*d*) Such warning should also be given when a young boy or girl is called to corroborate the evidence either of another child whether sworn or unsworn or of an adult.
(*e*) As the statute which permits a child of tender years to give unsworn evidence expressly provides for such evidence being given in any proceeding against any person for any offence, the unsworn evidence of a child can be given to corroborate the evidence of another person given on oath, but in such a case a particularly careful warning should be given, *per* Lord Goddard CJ in *R.* v. *Campbell ex parte Nomikos* (1956) 120 J.P. 359; approved by the House of Lords in *Director of Public Prosecutions* v. *Hester* (1973) 137 J.P. 45, in which it was further decided that the evidence of an unsworn child (admitted pursuant to s. 38(1)) could amount to corroboration

of evidence given on oath by another child (the complainant) provided that the unsworn evidence was corroborated as required by the proviso: "What was principally contemplated by the proviso was the situation where a child of tender years had been assaulted and the child's unsworn evidence was received. Corroboration of 'that' evidence was then essential before a conviction could result."

There is no rule of law that the sworn evidence of a child which requires corroboration cannot corroborate the sworn evidence of another child which requires corroboration: *Director of Public Prosecutions* v. *Kilbourne* (1973) 137 J.P. 193.

THE CRIMINAL JUSTICE ACT, 1948

Proof of previous convictions by fingerprints

39. (1) A previous conviction may be proved against any person in any criminal proceedings by the production of such evidence of the conviction as is mentioned in this section, and by showing that his fingerprints and those of the person convicted are the fingerprints of the same person.

(2) A certificate purporting to be signed by or on behalf of the Commissioner of Police of the Metropolis, containing particulars relating to a conviction extracted from the criminal records kept by him, and certifying that the copies of the fingerprints exhibited to the certificate are copies of the fingerprints appearing from the said records to have been taken under or by virtue of any enactment in that behalf in force in any part of the United Kingdom (including an enactment of the Parliament of Northern Ireland), from the person convicted on the occasion of the conviction, shall be evidence of the conviction and evidence that the copies of the fingerprints exhibited to the certificate are copies of the fingerprints of the person convicted.

(3) A certificate purporting to be signed by or on behalf of the governor of a prison or remand centre in which any person has been detained in connexion with any criminal proceedings, certifying that the fingerprints exhibited thereto were taken from him while he was so detained, shall be evidence in those proceedings that the fingerprints exhibited to the certificate are the fingerprints of that person.

(4) A certificate, purporting to be signed by or on behalf of the Commissioner of Police of the Metropolis, and certifying that the fingerprints, copies of which are certified as aforesaid by or on behalf of the Commissioner to be copies of the fingerprints of a person previously convicted and the fingerprints certified by or on behalf of the governor as aforesaid, or otherwise shown, to be the fingerprints of the person aginst whom the previous conviction is sought to be proved are the fingerprints of the same person shall be evidence of the matter so certified.

(5) The method of proving a previous conviction authorized by this section shall be in addition to any other method of proving the conviction.

(as amended by the Criminal Justice Act, 1961, sch. 4).

COMMENTARY

Previous conviction. To be construed as including a reference to a previous conviction by a court in any part of Great Britain: Criminal Justice Act, 1948, s. 8(2).

Fingerprints. To be construed as including a reference to palm prints: Criminal Justice Act 1967, s. 33.

Any other method. *See* Proving Previous Convictions in the introduction.

Evidence by certificate

41. (1) In any criminal proceedings, a certificate purporting to be signed by a constable, or by a person having the prescribed qualifications, and certifying that a plan or drawing exhibited thereto is a plan or drawing made by him of the place or object specified in the certificate, and that the plan or drawing is correctly drawn to a scale so specified, shall be evidence of the relative position of the things shown on the plan or drawing.

(2),(3) (*Repealed*).

(4) Nothing in this section shall be deemed to make a certificate admissible as evidence in proceedings for an offence except in a case where and to the extent to which oral evidence to the like effect would have been admissible in those proceedings.

(5) Nothing in this section shall be deemed to make a certificate admissible as evidence in proceedings for any offence—

> (*a*) unless a copy thereof has, not less than seven days before the hearing or trial, been served in the prescribed manner on the person charged with the offence; or
> (*b*) if that person, not later than three days before the hearing or trial or within such further time as the court may in special circumstances allow, serves notice in the prescribed form and manner on the prosecutor requiring the attendance at the trial of the person who signed the certificate.

(6) In this section the expression 'prescribed" means prescribed by rules made by the Secretary of State.
(*as amended by the Road Traffic Act, 1960, sch. 18 and the Theft Act 1968, sch. 3*).

COMMENTARY

Constable That is, a police officer of any rank.
The prescribed qualifications. The Evidence by Certificate Rules, 1961 (S.I. 1961 No. 248) prescribe:
> (*a*)   registration as an architect under the Architects (Registration) Acts, 1931 to 1938; or
> (*b*)   membership of any of the following bodies, that is to say, the Royal Institution of Chartered Surveyors, the Institution of Civil Engineers, the Institution of Municipal Engineers and the Land Agents Society.

Not less than seven days before. That is, seven clear or intervening days: *R.* v. *Turner* (1910) 74 J.P. 81; *Re Hector Whaling, Ltd* [1935] All E.R. Rep. 302; *Thompson* v. *Stimpson* [1960] 3 All E.R. 500.

The prescribed manner. The Evidence by Certificate Rules, 1961 (S.I. 1961, No. 248) prescribe:

> "(*a*)   where the person to be served is a corporation, by addressing it to the corporation and leaving it at, or sending it by registered post or by recorded delivery service to, the registered office of the corporation or, if there is no such office, its principal office or place at which it conducts its business;
> (*b*)   in any other case, by delivering it personally to the person to be served or by addressing it to him and leaving it at, or sending it by registered post or by the recorded delivery service to, his last or usual place of abode or place of business."

THE CHILDREN AND YOUNG PERSONS ACT 1963

Form of oath for use in juvenile courts and by children and young persons in other courts

28. (1) Subject to subs. (2) of this section, in relation to any oath administered to and taken by any person before a juvenile court or administered to and taken by any child or young person before any other court, s. 1 of the Oaths Act 1978, shall have effect as if the words "I promise before Almighty God" were set out in it instead of the words "I swear by Almighty God that."

(2) Where in any oath otherwise duly administered and taken either of the forms mentioned in this section is used instead of the other, the oath shall nevertheless be deemed to have been duly administered and taken.
(*as amended by the Oaths Act 1978, s. 2*).

COMMENTARY

This section shall be construed as one with the Children and Young Persons Act, 1933: s. 65(3) of the 1963 Act.

THE CRIMINAL EVIDENCE ACT 1965

Admissibility of certain trade or business records

1. (1) In any criminal proceedings where direct oral evidence of a fact would be admissible, any statement contained in a document and tending to establish that fact shall, on production of the document, be admissible as evidence of that fact if—

> (a) the document is, or forms part of, a record relating to any trade or business and compiled, in the course of that trade or business, from information supplied (whether direcly or indirectly) by persons who have, or may reasonably be supposed to have, personal knowledge of the matters dealt with in the information they supply; and
>
> (b) the person who supplied the information recorded in the statement in question is dead, or beyond the seas, or unfit by reason of his bodily or mental condition to attend as a witness, or cannot with reasonable diligence be identified or found, or cannot reasonably be expected (having regard to the time which has elapsed since he supplied the information and to all the circumstances) to have any recollection of the matters dealt with in the information he supplied.

For the purpose of deciding whether or not a statement is admissible as evidence by virtue of this section, the court may draw any reasonable inference from the form or content of the document in which the statement is contained, and may, in deciding or not a person is fit to attend as a witness, act on a certificate purporting to be a certificate of a fully registered medical practitioner.

(3) In estimating the weight, if any, to be attached to a statement admissible as evidence by virtue of this section regard shall be had to all the circumstances from which any inference can reasonably be drawn as to the accuracy or otherwise of the statement, and, in particular, to the question whether or not the person who supplied the information recorded in the statement did so contemporaneously with the occurrence or existence of the facts stated, and to the question whether or not that person, or any person concerned with making or keeping the record containing the statement, had any incentive to conceal or misrepresent the facts.

(4) In this section "statement" includes any representation of fact, whether made in words or otherwise, "document" includes any device by means of which information is recorded or stored and "business" includes any public transport, public utility or similar undertaking carried on by a local authority and the activities of the Post Office.

COMMENTARY

This enactment deals with the problem revealed in *Myers* v. *Director of Public Prosecutions* (1964) 128 J.P. 481.
"This particular Act was passed in order to simplify the course of a trial, in order to provide a means of establishing facts without the necessity of calling a large body of witnesses or making detailed

investigations and obtaining statements from a considerable number of persons who would then have to come to the trial to give evidence in respect of those facts which were within their personal knowledge and it is important that the Act is operated to the end that its purpose is achieved—the simplification of proceedings. In many cases where evidence is sought to be adduced as admissible pursuant to the terms of s. 1 of the Criminal Evidence Act 1965, it may have been possible for the facts to be agreed as between prosecution and defence provided the proper preparation of the case was followed. It occurs to us that one sensible step would be the service of a notice to admit facts in the early stages of the case. The accused is not bound to admit facts but if he does admit facts then those admitted facts can form part of the evidence. If he does not admit the facts stated in the notice then witness statements can be taken and served upon him on the basis that those witnesses need not attend the trial unless the Crown or the accused desire their attendance, in which case notice should be served, and at that stage the accused has an opportunity of deciding whether to challenge the evidence or not. If he does not challenge the evidence and seek the attendance of the witnesses, then their witness statements can be read in the course of the trial. If he does challenge the evidence then the Crown can take advantage, in the proper case, of the provisions of the Act and it is for the Crown then to lay the foundation by which the Court can be satisfied that the evidence that they seek to adduce can properly be adduced by reason of that enactment," per James LJ in R. v. Nicholls [1976] 63 Cr. App. R. 187 at p. 192. By virtue of s. 2(2) of the Act nothing therein prejudices the admissibility of any evidence which would be admissible apart from the provisions of the Act.

Subsection (1): Record. "Although it is not an exhaustive definition of the word, 'record' in this context means a history of events in some form which is not evanescent. How long the record is likely to be kept is immaterial: it may be something which will not survive the end of the transaction in question; it may be something which is indeed more lasting than bronze, but the degree of permanence does not seem to us to make or mar the fulfilment of the definition of the word 'record'. The record in each individual case will last as long as commercial necessity may demand," per Geoffrey Lane LJ in R. v. Jones (1978) 142 J.P. 453; (bills of lading and cargo manifests held to be records). Records made outside the jurisdiction are admissible under s. 1(1): ibid. In R. v. Tirado [1974] 59 Cr. App. R. 80 it was doubted whether a file of correspondence maintained simply as a file of correspondence and added to from time to time as letters came in is or could be a record. "The language of s. 1 seems on its face to contemplate the making or keeping of a record. That means the keeping of a book or file or card index into which information is deliberately put in order that it may be available to others another day. A cash book, a ledger, a stockbook: all these may be records because they contain information deliberately entered in order that the information may be preserved", per Lord Widgery CJ, ibid.

Subsection (4): Business. Includes the activities of the Director of Savings: Post Office Act, 1969, s. 93(4). It also includes the activities of the Secretary of State in relation to proceedings for any offence which is connected with (a) the obtaining of any benefit under the Family Income Supplement Act 1970, the Industrial Injuries and Diseases (Old Cases) Act 1975, the Child Benefit Act 1975, the Social Security Act 1975 or the Supplementary Benefit Act 1976; or (b) the failure to pay any Class 1 or Class 2 contribution (within the meaning of Part I of the Social Security Act 1975): Social Security Act 1979, s. 16. The services provided by a hospital do not have the commercial connotation of the service described in this subsection: R. v. Crayden (1978) 142 J.P. 441 (medical records excluded).

Post Office. To be construed as including reference to the British Telecommunications Authority: British Telecommunications Act 1981, sch. 3.

THE WELSH LANGUAGE ACT, 1967

Use of Welsh in legal proceedings

1. (1) In any legal proceeding in Wales or Monmouthshire the Welsh language may be spoken by any party, witness or other person who desires to use it, subject in the case of proceedings in a court other than a magistrates' court to such prior notice as may be required by rules of court; and any necessary provision for interpretation shall be made accordingly.

(2) . . .

COMMENTARY

The Lord Chancellor has powers under the Welsh Courts Act 1942, s. 2 to prescribe translations in the Welsh language of any form of oath or affirmation and has done so in the Welsh Courts (Oaths and Interpreters) Rules 1943, S.R. & O. 1943 No. 683, as amended by S.I. 1959 No. 157.

THE CRIMINAL JUSTICE ACT 1967

Proof by written statement

9. (1) In any criminal proceedings, other than committal proceedings, a written statement by any person shall, if such of the conditions mentioned in the next following subsection as are applicable are satisfied, be admissible as evidence to the like extent as oral evidence to the like effect by that person.

(2) The said conditions are—

(a) the statement purports to be signed by the person who made it;

(b) the statement contains a declaration by that person to the effect that it is true to the best of his knowledge and belief and that he made the statement knowing that, if it were tendered in evidence, he would be liable to prosecution if he wilfully stated in it anything which he knew to be false or did not believe to be true;

(c) before the hearing at which the statement is tendered in evidence, a copy of the statement is served, by or on behalf of the party proposing to tender it, on each of the other parties to the proceedings; and

(d) none of the other parties or their solicitors, within seven days from the service of the copy of the statement, serves a notice on the party so proposing objecting to the statement being tendered in evidence under this section:

Provided that the conditions mentioned in paras. (c) and (d) of this subsection shall not apply if the parties agree before or during the hearing that the statement shall be so tendered.

(3) The following provisions shall also have effect in relation to any written statement tendered in evidence under this section, that is to say—

(a) if the statement is made by a person under the age of 21, it shall give his age;

(b) if it is made by a person who cannot read it, it shall be read to him before he signs it and shall be accompanied by a declaration by the person who so read the statement to the effect that it was so read; and

(c) if it refers to any other document as an exhibit, the copy served on any other party to the proceedings under para. (c) of the last foregoing subsection shall be accompanied by a copy of that document or by such information as may be necessary in order to enable the party on whom it as served to inspect that document or a copy thereof.

(4) Notwithstanding that a written statement made by any person may be admissible as evidence by virtue of this section—

(a) the party by whom or on whose behalf a copy of the statement was served may call that person to give evidence; and

(b) the court may, of its own motion or on the application of any party to the proceedings, require that person to attend before the court and give evidence.

(5) . . .

(6) So much of any statement as is admitted in evidence by virtue of this section shall, unless the court otherwise directs, be read aloud at the hearing and where the court so directs an account shall be given orally of so much of any statement as is not read aloud.

(7) Any document or object referred to as an exhibit and identified in a written statement tendered in evidence under this section shall be treated as if it had been

produced as an exhibit and identified in court by the maker of the statement.

(8) A document required by this section to be served on any person may be served—

(*a*) by delivering it to him or to his solicitor; or

(*b*) by addressing it to him and leaving it at his usual or last known place of abode or place of business or by addressing it to his solicitor and leaving at his office; or

(*c*) by sending it in a registered letter or by the recorded delivery service addressed to him at his usual or last place of abode or place of business or addressed to his solicitor at his office; or

(*d*) in the case of a body corporate, by delivering it to the secretary or clerk of the body at its registered office or sending it in a registered letter or by the recorded delivery service addressed to the secretary or clerk of that body at that office.

COMMENTARY

See under Proof by Written Statement in the introduction.

So far as admissibility of the statements is concerned, a distinction is apparently to be drawn between the "conditions" referred to in subs. (2) and the "provisions" referred to in subs. (3). Any failure to comply with the former renders the statement wholly inadmissible under this section. (It may of course be admissible for other purposes). Breach of the "provisions" on the other hand would, it is submitted, give the court a discretion to exclude the statement. For the background to this section *see* the 9th Report of the Criminal Law Revision Committee, Cmnd. 3145.

Expressions used in this section have the same meaning as in the Magistrates' Courts Act, 1980: Criminal Justice Act 1967, s. 36(2).

This section, except subss. (2), (6) and (3A), applies to written statements made in the Isle of Man: Isle of Man Act 1979, s. 5(3)(9). This section applies to written statements made in Scotland and Northern Ireland as well as to written statements made in England and Wales: Criminal Justice Act 1972, s. 46.

Subsection (1): Committal proceedings. Means proceedings before a magistrates' court acting as examining justices: s. 36(1) of the Act.

A written statement. For the editing of statements *see* the *Practice Note* [1969] 3 All E.R. 133 noted under Proof by Written Statement in the introduction. For the use of a written statement for the purpose of Refreshing Memory out of Court and in Court *see* under those titles in the introduction. It is desirable for the prosecution to call witnesses in person who are central to their case and not use s. 9 statements, *per* Stephen Brown J, in *Lister* v. *Quaife* (1982) *The Times,* May 1.

Admissible as evidence to the like extent as oral evidence. Thus a written statement under this section which identifies the accused by name only has the same effect as if evidence had been given orally from the witness box to the like effect, and in the absence of any suggestion that the person named is not the accused, is sufficient to constitute a case to answer: *Ellis* v. *Jones* (1973) 137 J.P. 581. And *see* the note to the Magistrates' Courts Act 1980, s. 12, *infra.*

Subsection (2)(b): Contains a declaration. Unlike the statement itself, this declaration need not be signed and may be at the beginning or (preferably) the end of the statement: *Chapman* v. *Ingleton* [1973] 57 Cr. App. R. 476.

Liable to prosecution. *See* the note to the Magistrates' Courts Act 1980, s. 12, *post.*

A copy of the statement is served . . . on each of the other parties. Together with a notice of the accused's right to object. A copy of the statement must as soon as practicable be given to the clerk: Magistrates' Courts Rules 1981, r. 7(2). For the method of service *see* subs. (8). No minimum period is prescribed: it is left to the party seeking to tender the statement to serve it within seven days in accordance with subs. (2)(*d*). For proof of service *see* r. 67. Service may be waived by agreement: *see* the proviso to subs. (2).

Within seven days from. This term implies that the first day is to be excluded and the last included:

2. PROVING THE CASE 71

Goldsmiths' Co. v. *West Metropolitan Rail Co.* (1904) 68 J.P. 41;*Stewart* v. *Chapman* (1951) 115 J.P. 473.

Under the age of 21. For the determination of age *see* the Magistrates' Courts Act 1980, s. 150(4).

Exhibit. For the identification of exhibits *see* r. 70(4) of the Magistrates' Courts Rules 1981.

Subsection (4). The provisions of this subsection do not over-ride the general rule that once justices have retired to consider the evidence further evidence should be admitted only in the most exceptional cases: *French's Dairies (Sevenoaks) Ltd* v. *Davis* [1973] Crim. L.R. 630. And *see* the note to subs. (4) of the Magistrates' Courts Act 1980, s. 12, *post.*

Subsection (6). The statement must be read aloud or, with the consent of the court, summarized by the party tendering it: Magistrates' Courts Rules 1981, r. 70(7). The name and address of the witness must, unless the court directs otherwise, be read out: r. 70(6), *ibid.*

Proof by formal admission

10. (1) Subject to the provisions of this section, any fact of which oral evidence may be given in any criminal proceedings may be admitted for the purpose of those proceedings by or on behalf of the prosecutor or defendant, and the admission by any party of any such fact under this section shall as against that party be conclusive evidence in those proceedings of the fact admitted.

(2) An admission under this section—

(a) may be made before or at the proceedings;

(b) if made otherwise than in court, shall be in writing;

(c) if made in writing by an individual, shall purport to be signed by the person making it and, if so made by a body corporate, shall purport to be signed by a director or manager, or the secretary or clerk, or some other similar officer of the body corporate;

(d) if made on behalf of a defendant who is an individual, shall be made by his counsel or solicitor;

(e) if made at any stage before the trial by a defendant who is an individual must be approved by his counsel or solicitor (whether at the time it was made or subsequently) before or at the proceedings in question.

An admission under this section for the purpose of proceedings relating to any matter shall be treated as an admission for the purpose of any subsequent criminal proceedings relating to that matter (including any appeal or retrial).

(4) An admission under this section may with the leave of the court be withdrawn in the proceedings for the purpose of which it is made or any subsequent criminal proceedings relating to the same matter.

COMMENTARY

Expressions used in this section have the same meaning as in the Magistrates' Courts Act, 1980: Criminal Justice Act 1967, s. 36(2).

Admissions made orally in court must be written down and signed: Magistrates' Courts Rules 1981, r. 71.

Any fact of which oral evidence may be given. In a trial on indictment it was held that the practice of admitting the contents of the prosecutor's opening speech should be adopted rarely and with extreme caution because of the difficulties of jurors distinguishing facts, law and comment: *R.* v. *Lewis* [1971] 55 Cr. App. R. 386. It is not possible for a layman to admit what only an expert can know: *R.* v. *Lang and Evans* [1977] Crim. L.R. 286 (whether substance was cannabis).

In writing. Includes typing, printing, lithography, photography, and other modes of representing or reproducing words in a visible form: Interpretation Act, 1978, sch. 1. This document should be retained as it must be sent to the Crown Court in the event of an appeal: Magistrates' Courts Rules 1981, r. 74 (6).

Director. In relation to a body corporate which is established by or under any enactment for the purpose of carrying on under national ownership any industry or part of an industry or undertaking and whose affairs are managed by the members thereof means a member of that body: s. 36(1) of the Act.

Made/approved by his counsel or solicitor. This does not imply that an unrepresented defendant may not make an admission, merely that admissions by represented defendants must be made or approved by their legal representatives—*see* para. 28 of the 9th Report of the Criminal Law Revision Committee, Cmnd. 3145.

Subsection (4): Withdrawn. "If necessary the court, in allowing a withdrawal, might adjourn the hearing for a witness to prove the fact admitted": 9th Report of the Criminal Law Revision Committee, Cmnd. 3145, para. 29. For a discussion of the effects of a withdrawn admission *see* para. 3, *ibid.*

Taking and use of fingerprints and palmprints

33. In s. 39 of the Criminal Justice Act, 1948 (proof of previous convictions by fingerprints) any reference to fingerprints shall be construed as including a reference to palmprints.

(*as amended by the Magistrates' Courts Act 1980, sch. 1*).

THE THEFT ACT 1968

Prosecution of husband or wife.

30. (1) This Act shall apply in relation to the parties to a marriage, and to the property belonging to the wife or husband whether or not by reason of an interest derived from the marriage, as it would apply if they were not married and any such interest subsisted independently of the marriage.

(2) Subject to subsection (4) below, a person shall have the same right to bring proceedings against that person's wife or husband for any offence (whether under this Act or otherwise) as if they were married, and a person bringing any such proceedings shall be competent to give evidence for the prosecution at every stage of the proceedings.

(3) Where a person is charged in proceedings not brought by that person's wife or husband with having committed any offence with reference to that person's wife or husband or to property belonging to the wife or husband, the wife or husband shall be competent to give evidence at every stage of the proceedings whether for the defence or for the prosecution, and whether the accused is charged solely or jointly with any other person:
Provided that—
  (*a*)   the wife or husband (unless compellable at common law) shall not be compellable either to give evidence or, in giving evidence, to disclose any communication made to her or him during the marriage by the accused; and
  (*b*)   her or his failure to give evidence shall not be made the subject of any comment by the prosecution.

(4) Proceedings shall not be instituted against a person for any offence of stealing or doing unlawful damage to property which at the time of the offence belongs to that person's wife or husband, or for any attempt, incitement or conspiracy to commit such an offence, unless the proceedings are instituted by or with the consent of the Director of Public Prosecutions.
Provided that—
  (*a*)   this subsection shall not apply to proceedings against a person for an offence—
  (i)   if that person is charged with committing the offence jointly with the wife or husband; or

(ii)   if by virtue of any judicial decree or order (wherever made) that person and the wife or husband are at the time of the offence under no obligation to cohabit;
(b)   (*Repealed.*)
(5) Notwithstanding section 6 of the Prosecution of Offences Act 1979 subsection (4) of this section shall apply–
(a)   to an arrest (if without warrant) made by the wife or husband, and
(b)   to a warrant of arrest issued on an information laid by the wife or husband.
(*as amended by the Criminal Jurisdiction Act 1975, sch. 5 and the Prosecution of Offences Act 1979, sch. 1.*)

COMMENTARY

See under Husband and Wives in the introduction.

THE CRIMINAL JUSTICE ACT 1972

Admissibility of written statements made outside England and Wales

46. (1) Section 12 of the Magistrates' Courts Act 1980 and s. 9 of the Criminal Justice Act 1967 (which respectively allow written statements to be used as evidence in committal proceedings and in other criminal proceedings) and s. 16 of the said Act of 1980 and s. 89 of the said Act of 1967 (which punishes the making of false statements which are tendered in evidence under the said ss 12 or 9, as the case may be) shall apply to written statements made in Scotland or Northern Ireland as well as to written statements made in England and Wales.

(2) The said s. 12 shall apply also to written statements made outside the United Kingdom, but, in relation to such statements, that section shall have effect with the omission of subss (2)(b), (3A) and (7).
(*as amended by the Magistrates' Courts Act 1980, sch. 7*).

THE ADMINISTRATION OF JUSTICE ACT 1973

Payment of interpreters in criminal cases (England and Wales)

17. (1) Where in any criminal proceedings an interpreter is required because of a defendant's lack of English, the expenses properly incurred on his employment shall be ordered by the court to be paid out of central funds; and—

(a)   where there is laid before a justice of the peace for any area an information charging with an offence a person who because of his lack of English would require an interpreter on his trial, but the information is not proceeded with, then, if he has incurred expenses on the employment of an interpreter for the proceedings on the information, he may apply to a magistrates' court for that area and the court shall order payment out of central funds of the expenses properly so incurred by him; and
(b)   where such a person is committed for trial but is not ultimately tried, then if he has incurred expenses on the employment of an interpreter for the proceedings in the Crown Court, he may apply to the Crown Court and the court shall order the payment out of central funds of the expenses properly so incurred by him.

(2) In this section "criminal proceedings" means any proceedings in which a court has power under the Costs in Criminal Cases Act 1973 to make an order for

payment of costs out of central funds or would have power to do so if any reference in that Act to an indictable offence were a reference to any offence; and ss 13 to 17 of that Act (which relate to the procedure for implementing orders under the Act and other supplemental matters) shall apply in relations to this section as they apply in relation to that Act, except that—

> (a)   in s. 15 (costs ordered by magistrates' court to be paid out of central funds) subs. (1) shall apply as if the reference in para. (a) to an indictable offence included any offence,(and shall also apply where an order is made by a magistrates' court under subs. (1)(a) above; and
> (b)   s. 16(2) (payment of costs ordered to be paid out of central funds and by accused or prosecutor) shall not apply so as to require a defendant to reimburse any costs paid out of central funds by virtue of this section.

(3) In this section "court" includes the House of Lords, and "defendant" means the person (whether convicted or not) who is alleged to be guilty of an offence.

COMMENTARY

This provision gives effect to the European Convention of 1950 for the Protection of Human Rights and Fundamental Freedoms. For interpreters generally, *see* the introduction.

Interpretation of and into the Welsh language is dealt with in the Welsh Language Act 1967, *supra*. *See* generally the introduction.

Subsection (1): Because of a defendant's lack of English. Thus this section has no application where an interpreter is required because of a *witness's* lack of English, nor because anyone is deaf and dumb. For sign language interpreters *see* Interpreters in the introduction.

Paid out of central funds. And may be accounted for as if they were witnesses' expenditure in indictable cases: Home Office circ. 86/1973 dated May 1, 1973.

Criminal proceedings. Defined in subs. (2).

THE OATHS ACT 1978

Manner of administration of oaths

1. (1) Any oath may be administered and taken in England, Wales or Northern Ireland in the following form and manner:-

> The person taking the oath shall hold the New Testament, or, in the case of a Jew, the Old Testament, in his uplifted hand, and shall say or repeat after the officer administering oath the words "I swear by Almighty God that . . .", followed by the words of the oath prescribed by law.

(2) The officer shall (unless the person about to take the oath voluntarily objects thereto, or is physically incapable of so taking the oath) administer the oath in the form and manner aforesaid without question.

(3) In the case of a person who is neither a Christian nor a Jew, the oath shall be administered in any lawful manner.

(4) In this section "officer" means any person duly authorized to administer oaths.

COMMENTARY

Subsection (1): His uplifted hand. The requirement that the Bible shall be held in the uplifted hand is directive only so that a failure to comply does not invalidate the witness's testimony: *R. v. Chapman*

[1980] Crim. L.R. 42. There is no requirement that only the right hand should be used.

"I swear by Almight God." For the words to be substituted in the case of children and young persons *see* the Children and Young Persons Act 1963, s. 28, *supra*.

Subsection (2): **Voluntarily objects.** This places the onus upon the witness to object.

A person objecting may be entitled to affirm under s. 5, *infra*, or he may be sworn in any lawful manner (subs. (3)).

Subsection (3): Any lawful manner. That is to say, adapted to his religious beliefs. See also ss. 4(1) and 5(2), *infra*.

Swearing with uplifted hand

3. If any person to whom an oath is administered desires to swear with uplifted hand, in the form and manner in which an oath is usually administered in Scotland, he shall be permitted so to do, and the oath shall be administered to him in such form and manner without further question.

Validity of oaths

4. (1) In any case in which an oath may lawfully be and has been administered to any person, if it has been administered in a form and manner other than that prescribed by law, he is bound by it if it has been administered in such form and with such ceremonies as he may have declared to be binding.

(2) Where an oath has been administered and taken, the fact that the person to whom it was administered had, at the time of taking it, no religious belief, shall not for any purpose affect the validity of the oath.

COMMENTARY

For a list of oaths binding upon persons of different religions *see A Handbook of Cautions, Oaths and Recognizances Etc.* by Shannon. For doubts as to the validity of commonly used Hindu, Sikh and Muhammedan oaths *see* 136 J.P.N. 831.

Making of solemn affirmations

5. (1) Any person who objects to being sworn shall be permitted to make his solemn affirmation instead of taking an oath.

(2) Subsection (1) above shall apply in relation to a person to whom it is not reasonably practicable without inconvenience or delay to administer an oath in the manner appropriate to his religious belief as it applies in relation to a person objecting to be sworn.

(3) A person who may be permitted under subs. (2) above to make his solemn affirmation may also be required to do so.

(4) A solemn affirmation shall be of the same force and effect as an oath.

COMMENTARY

The form of the affirmation is prescribed in s. 6, *infra*.

Form of affirmation

6. (1) Subject to subs. (2) below, every affirmation shall be as follows:

"I, ... do solemnly, sincerely and truly declare and affirm," and then proceed with the words of the oath prescribed by law omitting any words of imprecation or calling to witness.

(2) Every affirmation in writing shall commence:
  "I, of , do solemnly and sincerely affirm,"
and the form in lieu of jurat shall be:
  "Affirmed at this day of 19 , Before me"

THE MAGISTRATES' COURTS ACT 1980

Aiders and abettors

44. (1) A person who aids, abets, counsels or procures the commission by another person of a summary offence shall be guilty of the like offence and may be tried (whether or not he is charged as a principal) either by a court having jurisdiction to try that other person or by a court having by virtue of his own offence jurisdiction to try him.

(2) Any offence consisting in aiding, abetting, counselling or procuring the commission of an offence triable either way (other than an offence listed in sch. 1 to this Act) shall by virtue of this subsection be triable either way.

COMMENTARY

See generally the introduction under Accomplices.

Aids, abets, counsels or procures. These words may properly be used conjunctively ("aids, abets, counsels *and* procures") "to charge a person who is alleged to have participated in an offence otherwise than as a principal in the first degree": *Ex parte Smith* (1858) 22 J.P. 45; *Ferguson* v. *Weaving* (1951) 115 J.P. 142.

The words "aid and abet" refer to principals in the second degree. The words "counsel and procure" refer to accessories before the fact as they were formerly called.

The word "procure" means to produce by endeavour, thus there may be a procuring of a crime by another even though there is no sort of conspiracy or even discussion between the two: *Attorney General's Reference* (*No. 1 of 1975*) (1975) 139 J.P. 569, (laced drink).

A summary offence. Defined in the Interpretation Act 1978, sch. 1 as meaning an offence which, if committed by an adult, is triable only summarily.

Guilty of the like offence. And subject to the same penalties. This section, like s. 8 of the Accessories and Abettors Act, 1861, is declaratory of the common law at which there was no distinction between the principal and accessory in misdemeanour. Thus the fact that a defendant was an accomplice other than a principal in the first degree does not prevent him from being convicted as such: *Stacey* v. *Whitehurst* (1865) 29 J.P. 136; *Du Cros* v. *Lambourne* (1970) 70 J.P. 525. The Criminal Law Act 1967, s. 1, assimilated the law of felony to that of misdemeanour, and the same rules now apply to all offences.

Subsection (2): Offence triable either way. Defined in the Interpretation Act 1978, sch. 1, as an offence which, if committed by an adult, is triable either on indictment or summarily.

Incitement

45. (1) Any offence consisting in the incitement to commit a summary offence shall be triable only summarily.

(2) Subsection (1) above is without prejudice to any other enactment by virtue of which any offence is triable only summarily.

(3) On conviction of an offence consisting in the incitement to commit a summary offence a person shall be liable to the same penalties as he would be liable to on conviction of the last-mentioned offence.

Summons to witness and warrant for his arrest

97. (1) Where a justice of the peace for any county, any London commission area or the City of London is satisfied that any person in England or Wales is likely to be able to give material evidence, or produce any document or thing likely to be material evidence, at an inquiry into an indictable offence by a magistrates' court for that county, that London commission area or the City (as the case may be) or at the summary trial of an information òr hearing of a complaint by such a court and that that person will not voluntarily attend as a witness or will not voluntarily produce the document or thing, the justice shall issue a summons directed to that person requiring him to attend before the court at the time and place appointed in the summons to give evidence or to produce the document or thing.

(2) If a justice of the peace is satisfied by evidence on oath of the matters mentioned in subs. (1) above, and also that it is probable that a summons under that subsection would not procure the attendance of the person in question, the justice may instead of issuing a summons issue a warrant to arrest that person and bring him before such a court as aforesaid at a time and place specified in the warrant; but a warrant shall not be issued under this subsection where the attendance is required for the hearing of a complaint.

(3) On the failure of any person to attend before a magistrates' court in answer to a summons under this section, if—

(a) the court is satisfied by evidence on oath that he is likely to be able to give material evidence or produce any document or thing likely to be material evidence in the proceedings; and

(b) it is proved on oath, or in such other manner as may be prescribed, that he has been duly served with the summons, and that a reasonable sum has been paid or tendered to him for costs and expenses; and

(c) it appears to the court that there is no just excuse for the failure,

the court may issue a warrant to arrest him and bring him before the court at a time and place specified in the warrant.

(4) If any person attending or brought before a magistrates' court refuses without just excuse to be sworn or give evidence, or to produce any document or thing, the court may commit him to custody until the expiration of such period not exceeding one month as may be specified in the warrant or until he sooner gives evidence or produces the document or thing or impose on him a fine not exceeding £1,000 or both.

(*as amended by the Contempt of Court Act 1981, sch. 2*).

COMMENTARY

Application for process may be made either personally or by the applicant's counsel or solicitor and may in the case of a summons be in writing to the clerk: Magistrates Courts Rules 1981, r. 17(1). The clerk himself may issue a witness summons: Justices' Clerks Rules 1970.

"No process for the production of any document kept by the Registrar of Companies shall issue from any court without the leave of that court and any such process, if issued, shall bear thereon a statement that it is issued with the leave of that court": Companies Act, 1948, s. 426(2).

The former prohibition of process against members of H.M. Forces was not reenacted in 1955.

Process may issue under this section against a juvenile notwithstanding that someone of that age may not be imprisoned for disobedience to the order: *R. v. Greenwich JJ, ex parte Carter* (1973) Crim. L.R. 444.

Subsection (1): A justice of the peace. Or a justices' clerk by virtue of the Justices' Clerks Rules 1970.

London commission area. Has the same meaning as in the Justices of the Peace Act 1979: Magistrates' Courts Act 1980, s. 15(1).

Give material evidence. It is within the inherent jurisdiction of the Divisional Court to set aside a witness summons where there has been an abuse of the process of the court or if it is clear in fact that the witness cannot give relevant evidence. An application could also be made to the magistrates' court for this purpose: *per* Lord Parker CJ in *R. v. Lewes Justices, ex parte The Gaming Board of Great*

Britain (1971) 135 J.P. 442. (Crown privilege invoked.) And *see* also *R.* v. *Howe JJ, ex parte Donne* (1967) 131 J.P. 460. There is no right to demand production of documents which are inadmissible as evidence: *R.* v. *Cheltenham JJ, ex parte Secretary of State for Trade* (1977) 141 J.P. 175 (copies of transcripts of evidence which could only be used in cross examination).

Document. A cinematograph film was held to be a document for the purposes of a county court summons *duces tecum: Senior and Others* v. *Holdsworth* [1975] 2 All E.R. 1009 (I.T.N. film). The machinery of this section is intended merely to get the document into court. It does not allow the party to inspect it before it is produced: *R.* v. *Greenwich Juvenile Court, ex parte Greenwich L.B.C.* (1977) *The Times*, May 11. Each document has to be considered individually by the magistrate granting the summons. There is no general power of discovery in magistrates' courts: *ibid*.

Indictable offence. Defined in the Interpretation Act 1978, sch. 1.

Issue a summons. *See* form 136. A witness summons may not be served by post: *see* the Magistrates' Courts Rules 1981, r. 99. Note that the summons cannot later be enforced by warrant unless conduct money is tendered under subs. (3)(*b*). No subpoena *ad testificandum* or *duces tecum* shall issue in respect of any proceedings for the purpose of which a witness summons may be issued under this section: Criminal Procedure (Attendance of Witness) Act 1965, s. 8. For an example of a case in which such a subpoena may still be appropriate *see* 123 J.C.L. 16.

Issue a warrant. *See* forms 137, 138. For the signature, contents and execution of a warrant see rr 95, 96 of the Magistrates' Courts Rules 1981. The warrant may be backed for bail: s. 117 of the Magistrates' Courts Act 1980. Since bail on a warrant issued under this section is not bail in criminal proceedings within the meaning of the Bail Act 1976, s. 1 the provisions of that Act do not apply. A warrant remains in force until it is executed or withdrawn: Magistrates' Courts Act 1980, s. 125; notwithstanding the death of the issuing justice: s. 124, *ibid*.

A person brought before the court on a "forthwith" warrant may not seemingly be remanded by the court: [1955] Crim. L.R. 561.

Subsection (3): Such other manner as may be prescribed. *See* the Magistrates' Courts Rules 1981, r. 67.

Subsection (4): Any person attending. The power to commit is not confined to persons attending in answer to a witness summons or warrant: *R.* v. *Flavell* (1884) 49 J.P. 406.

Without just excuse. For example, where he had reasonable grounds for believing that he would be criminated by his answers: *Ex parte Reynolds* (1882) 46 J.P. 533.

Produce any document or thing. The fact that a document is deposited by two persons on condition that it is not to be given up except with permission of both is no ground for refusing to produce it: *R.* v. *Daye* (1908) 72 J.P. 269.

Commit him to custody. Means commit to prison or, where any enactment authorizes or requires committal to some other place of detention instead of to prison, to that other place: s. 150(1) of the Act. In the case of young offenders this means detention under the Criminal Justice Act 1982, s. 9. (*See* ch. 6). Note the restraint in *ibid*, s. 1(5) which in turn attracts *ibid*, ss. 2(1), (5) and 7.

Evidence on oath

98. Subject to the provisions of any enactment or rule of law authorizing the reception of unsworn evidence, evidence given before a magistrates' court shall be given on oath.

COMMENTARY

Any enactment. For example, the Children and Young Persons Act 1933, s. 38 (evidence of children of tender years), the Criminal Justice Act 1967, s. 9 and the Magistrates' Courts Act 1980, s. 12.

A magistrates' court. This means any justice or justices of the peace acting under any enactment or by the virtue of his or their commission or under common law: s. 148 (1) of the Act.

On oath. This term includes affirmations and declarations: Interpretation Act, 1978, sch. 1.

Onus of proving exceptions, etc

101. Where the defendant to an information or complaint relies on his defence on any exception, exemption, proviso, excuse or qualification, whether or not it accompanies the description of the offence or matter of complaint in the enactment creating the offence or on which the complaint is founded, the burden of proving the exception, exemption, proviso, excuse or qualification shall be on him; and notwithstanding that the information or complaint contains an allegation negativing the exception, exemption, proviso, excuse or qualification.

COMMENTARY

See under Negative Averments in the introduction.

Written statements before examining justices

102. In committal proceedings a written statement by any person shall, if the conditions mentioned in subs. (2) below are satisfied, be admissible as evidence to the like extent as oral evidence to the like effect by that person.

(2) The said conditions are—

(a) the statement purports to be signed by the person who made it;

(b) the statement contains a declaration by that person to the effect that it is true to the best of his knowledge and belief and that he made the statement knowing that, if it were tendered in evidence, he would be liable to prosecution if he wilfully stated in it anything which he knew to be false or did not believe to be true;

(c) before the statement is tendered in evidence, a copy of the statement is given, by or on behalf of the party proposing to tender it, to each of the parties to the proceedings; and

(d) none of the other parties, before the statement is tendered in evidence at the committal proceedings, objects to the statement being so tendered under this section.

(3) The following provisions shall also have effect in relation to any written statement tendered in evidence under this section, that is to say—

(a) if the statement is made by a person under 21 years old, it shall give his age;

(b) if it is made by a person who cannot read it, it shall be read to him before he signs it and shall be accompanied by a declaration by the person who so read the statement to the effect that it was so read; and

(c) if it refers to any other document as an exhibit, the copy given to any other party to the proceedings under subs. (2)(c) above shall be accompanied by a copy of that document or by such information as may be necessary in order to enable the party to whom it is given to inspect that document or a copy thereof.

(4) Notwithstanding that a written statement made by any person may be admissible in committal proceedings by virtue of this section, the court before which the proceedings are held may, of its own motion or on the application of any party to the proceedings, require that person to attend before the court and give evidence.

(5) So much of any statement as is admitted in evidence by virtue of this section shall, unless the court commits the accused for trial by virtue of s. 6(2) above or the court otherwise directs, be read aloud at the hearing, and where the court so directs an account shall be given orally of so much of any statement as is not read aloud.

(6) Any document or object referred to as an exhibit and identified in a written statement tendered in evidence under this section shall be treated as if it had been produced as an exhibit and identified in court by the maker of the statement.

(7) Subsection (3) of s. 13 of the Criminal Justice Act 1925 (reading of deposition as evidence at the trial) shall apply to any written statement tendered in evidence in committal proceedings under this section as it applies to a deposition taken in such proceedings, but in its application to any such statement that subsection shall have effect as if para. (b) thereof were omitted.

(8) In s. 2(2) of the Administration of Justice (Miscellaneous Provisions) Act 1933 (procedure for preferring bills of indictment) the reference in proviso (i) to facts disclosed in any deposition taken before a justice in the presence of the accused shall be construed as including a reference to facts disclosed in any such written statement as aforesaid.

(9) Section 28 above shall not apply to any such statement as aforesaid.

(10) A person whose written statement is tendered in evidence in committal proceedings under this section shall be treated for the purposes of s. 1 of the Criminal Procedure (Attendance of Witnesses) Act 1965 (witness orders) as a witness who has been examined by the court.

COMMENTARY

See under Proof by Written Statement in the introduction.

Subsection (1): Committal proceedings. Means proceedings before a magistrates' court acting as examining justices: s. 150(1) of the Act.

A written statement. In the prescribed form: Magistrates' Courts Rules 1981, r. 70(1). See form 13. For the editing of written statements see the Practice Note [1969] 3 All E.R. 133 under Proof by Written Statements in the introduction.

Admissible as evidence to the like extent as oral evidence. For the method of excluding inadmissible evidence see the Magistrates Courts Rules 1981, r. 70.

Subsection (2): Liable to prosecution. This would be under s. 16 of the Act. The Home Office take the view (circular 29/1967) that since a child under the age of 1 is not liable to prosecution his evidence cannot be put in by way of a statement under this section.

Written statements made in Scotland or Northern Ireland are included in this provision: Criminal Justice Act 1972, s. 46(1). Written statements made outside the United Kingdom are also admissible with the omission of subss (2)(b), (3A) and (7): Criminal Justice Act 1972, s. 46(2).

A copy of the statement is given. Not "served" as in statements under the Criminal Justice Act 1967, s. 9. No minimum period of time is prescribed, but of course the other parties have a complete right to object to the statement being put in. A copy must also be given to the clerk: Magistrates' Courts Rules 1981, r. 70(2).

The other parties to the proceedings. It is sufficient if the statement is given to the party's solicitor, per Veale J in R. v. Bott (1968) 132 J.P. 199.

Objects. Where the accused objects without having given notice of objection the court must, if necessary, adjourn to enable the witness to be called: Magistrates' Courts Rules 1981, r. 70(3).

Subsection (3): Under 21 years old. For the determination of age see s. 150(4) of the Act.

Subsection (4). It is suggested that the statement may first be put in as evidence under this section (not as an exhibit) and the witness then sworn for cross examination.

Subsection (5). The effect of this subsection and the Magistrates' Courts Rules 1981, r. 70(6) is that the statement must be read aloud or, with the consent of the court, summarized by the party tendering it, except where it is put in in proceedings under s. 6(2) of the Act, where only the names and addresses of the witnesses should be read out, but even these particulars may be omitted by direction of the court.

Subsection (6). The statement must be read aloud or, with the consent of the court, summarized by the party tendering it: Magistrates' Courts Rules 1981, r. 70(7). The name and address of the witness must, unless the court directs otherwise, be read out: r. 70(6), ibid.

THE CRIMINAL ATTEMPTS ACT 1981

Attempting to commit an offence

1. (1) If, with intent to commit an offence to which this section applies, a person does an act which is more than merely preparatory to the commission of the offence, he is guilty of attempting to commit the offence.

(2) A person may be guilty of attempting to commit an offence to which this section applies even though the facts are such that the commission of the offence is impossible.

(3) In any case where—

(a) apart from this subsection a person's intention would not be regarded as having amounted to an intent to commit an offence; but

(b) if the facts of the case had been as he believed them to be, his intention would be so regarded,

then, for the purposes of subs. (1) above, he shall be regarded as having had an intent to commit that offence.

(4) This section applies to any offence which, if it were completed, would be triable in England and Wales as an indictable offence, other than—

(a) conspiracy (at common law or under s. 1 of the Criminal Law Act 1977 or any other enactment);

(b) aiding, abetting, counselling, procuring or suborning the commission of an offence;

(c) offences under s. 4(1) (assisting offenders) or 5(1) (accepting or agreeing to accept consideration for not disclosing information about an arrestable offence) of the Criminal Law Act 1967.

COMMENTARY

This provision is based on the Law Commission report, *Attempt and Impossibility in Relation to Attempt, Conspiracy and Incitement,* Law Com. No. 12.

Subsection (2). This overrules the decision in *Haughton* v. *Smith* [1975] A.C. 476.

Subsection (4): Indictable offence. Defined in the Interpretation Act 1978, schedule. Thus there is no offence of attempting to commit a summary offence.

Subsection (4)(b). This subsection avoids the creation of an offence of attempting to aid and abet an offence: it does not rule out the offence of aiding and abetting an attempt to commit an offence: *R.* v. *Dunnington* (1983) *The Times,* August 11; [1984] 2 W.L.R. 125.

Application of procedural and other provisions to offences under s. 1

2. (1) Any provision to which this section applies shall have effect with respect to the offence attempted.

(2) This section applies to provisions of any of the following descriptions made by or under any enactment (whenever passed)—

(a) provisions whereby proceedings may not be instituted or carried on otherwise than by, or on behalf or with the consent of, any person (including any provisions which also make other exceptions to the prohibition);

(b) provisions conferring power to institute proceedings;

(c) provisions as to the venue of proceedings;

(d) provisions whereby proceedings may not be instituted after the expiration of a time limit;
(e) provisions conferring a power of arrest or search;
(f) provisions conferring a power of seizure and detention of property;
(g) provisions whereby a person may not be convicted or committed for trial on the uncorroborated evidence of one witness (including any provision requiring the evidence of not less than two credible witnesses);
(h) provisions conferring a power of forfeiture, including any power to deal with anything liable to be forfeited;
(i) provisions whereby, if an offence committed by a body corporate is proved to have been committed with the consent or connivance of another person, that person also is guilty of the offence.

Offences of attempt under other enactments

3. (1) Subsections (2) to (5) below shall have effect, subject to subs. (6) below and to any inconsistent provision in any other enactment, for the purpose of determining whether a person is guilty of an attempt under a special statutory provision.

(2) For the purposes of this Act an attempt under a special statutory provision is an offence which—

(a) is created by an enactment other than s. 1 above, including an enactment passed after this Act; and
(b) is expressed as an offence of attempting to commit another offence (in this section referred to as "the relevant full offence").

(3) A person is guilty of an attempt under a special statutory provision if, with intent to commit the relevant full offence, he does an act which is more than merely preparatory to the commission of that offence.

(4) A person may be guilty of an attempt under a special statutory provision even though the facts are such that the commission of the relevant full offence is impossible.

(5) In any case where—

(a) apart from this subsection a person's intention would not be regarded as having amounted to an intent to commit the relevant full offence; but
(b) if the facts of the case had been as he believed them to be, his intention would be so regarded,

then, for the purposes of subs.(3) above, he shall be regarded as having had an intent to commit that offence.

(6) Subsections (2) to (5) above shall not have this effect in relation to an act done before the commencement of the Act.

COMMENTARY

This section applies the provisions of subss (2) and (3) of s. 1 to offences of attempt already specially created by statute. The procedural provision of s. 2, *supra*, have not been applied to these offences.

Trial and penalties

4. (1) A person guilty by virtue of s. 1 above of attempting to commit an offence shall—

(a) if the offence attempted is murder or any other offence the sentence for which is fixed by law, be liable on conviction on indictment to imprisonment for life; and

(b) if the offence attempted is indictable but does not fall within para. (a) above, be liable on conviction on indictment to any penalty to which he would have been liable on conviction on indictment of that offence; and .

(c) if the offence attempted is triable either way, be liable on summary conviction to any penalty to which he would have been liable on summary conviction of that offence.

(2) In any case in which a court may proceed to summary trial of an information charging a person with an offence and an information charging him with an offence under s. 1 above of attempting to commit it or an attempt under a special statutory provision, the court may, without his consent, try the informations together.

(3) Where, in proceedings against a person for an offence under s. 1 above, there is evidence sufficient in law to support a finding that he did an act falling within subs. (1) of that section, the question whether or not his act fell within that subsection is a question of fact.

(4) Where, in proceedings against a person for an attempt under a special statutory provision, there is evidence sufficient in law to support a finding that he did an act falling within subs. (3) of s. 3 above, the question whether or not his act fell within that subsection is a question of fact.

(5) Subsection (1) above shall have effect—

(a) subject to s. 37 of and sch. 2 to the Sexual Offences Act 1956 (mode of trial of and penalties for attempts to commit certain offences under that Act); and

(b) notwithstanding anything—

(i) in s. 32(1) (no limit to fine on conviction on indictment) of the Criminal Law Act 1977; or

(ii) in s. 31(1) and (2) (maximum of six months' imprisonment on summary conviction unless express provision made to the contrary) of the Magistrates' Courts Act 1980.

COMMENTARY

Subsection (1). An attempt to commit an offence triable either way is by virtue of this subsection triable and punishable in the same way as the substantive offence and is itself an offence triable either way.

THE MAGISTRATES' COURTS RULES 1981

S.I. 1981 No. 552 as amended by S.I. 1983 No. 523

Written statements in committal proceedings or summary trial

70. *(1) Written statements to be tendered in evidence under s. 12 of the Act of 1980 or s. 9 of the Criminal Justice Act 1967 shall be in the prescribed form.*

(2) When a copy of such a statement is given to or served on any party to the proceedings a copy of the statement and of any exhibit which accompanied it shall be given to the clerk of the magistrates' court as soon as practicable thereafter, and where a copy of any such statement is given or served by or on behalf of the prosecutor, the accused shall be given notice by or on behalf of the prosecutor of his right to object to the statement being tendered in evidence.

(3) Where before a magistrates' court enquiring into an offence as examining justices the accused objects to a written statement being tendered in evidence and he has been given a copy of the statement but has not given notice of his intention to object to the statement being tendered in evidence, the court shall if necessary, adjourn to enable the witness to be called.

(4) Where a written statement to be tendered in evidence under the said s. 12 or 9 refers to any document or object as an exhibit, that document or object shall wherever possible be identified by means of a label or other mark of identification signed by the maker of the statement, and before a magistrates' court treats any document or object referred to as an exhibit in such a written statement as an exhibit produced and identified in court by the maker of the statement, the court shall be satisfied that the document or object is sufficiently described in the statement for it to be identified.

(5) If it appears to a magistrates' court that any part of a written statement is inadmissible there shall be written against that part—
   (a)   in the case of a written statement tendered in evidence under the said s. 102 the words "Treated as inadmissible" together with the signature and name of the examining justice or, where there is more than one examining justice, the signature and name of one of the examining justices by whom the statement is so treated;
   (b)   in the case of a written statement tendered in evidence under the said s. 9 the words "Ruled inadmissible" together with the signature and name of the justice or, where there is more than one justice, the signature and name of one of the justices who ruled the statement to be inadmissible.

(6) Where a written statement is tendered in evidence under the said s. 12 or 9 before a magistrates' court the name and address of the maker of the statement shall be read aloud unless the court otherwise directs.

(7) Where under subs. (5) of the said s. 12 or subs. (6) of the said s. 9 in any proceedings before a magistrates' court any part of a written statement has to be read aloud, or on account has to be given orally of so much of any written statement as is not read aloud, the statement shall be read or the account given by or on behalf of the party which has tendered the statement in evidence.

(8) Written statements tendered in evidence under the said s. 12 before a magistrates' court acting as examining justices shall be authenticated by a certificate signed by one of the examining justices.

(9) A written statement tendered in evidence under the said s. 12 or 9 before a magistrates' court and not sent to the Crown Court under r. 11, 17 or 18 shall be preserved for a period of three years by the clerk of the magistrates' court.

2. PROVING THE CASE   85

COMMENTARY

Paragraph 1: The prescribed form . See form 13.

Paragraph (8): Written statements. Failure of one of the examining justices to sign the certificate does not invalidate a committal: *R*. v. *Carey* [1983] Crim. L.R. 111.

Proof by formal admission

71. *Where under s. 10 of the Criminal Justice Act 1967 a fact is admitted orally in court by or on behalf of the prosecutor or defendant for the purposes of the summary trial of an offence or proceedings before a magistrates' court acting as examining justices the court shall cause the admission to be written down and signed by or on behalf of the party making the admission.*

Proof of previous convictions

72. *Service on any person of a notice of intention to cite previous convictions under s. 14 of the Act of 1980 or s. 182(2A)(c) of the Road Traffic Act 1972 may be effected by delivering it it him or by sending it by post in a registered letter or by recorded delivery service addressed to him at his last known or usual place of abode.*

Application for summons to witness or warrant for his arrest

107. *(1) An application for the issue of a summons or warrant under s. 97 of the Act of 1980 may be made by the applicant in person or by his counsel or solicitor.*

(2) An application for an issue of such a summons may be made by delivering or sending the application in writing to the clerk of the magistrates' court.

CHAPTER 3

BAIL

CONTENTS

INTRODUCTION

When the hearing of criminal proceedings is adjourned the defendant may (and in some circumstances must) be remanded, that is, he must be granted bail or committed to custody. Bail may also be granted or refused by the court on a committal for trial or sentence, on appeal and in a number of other circumstances. Furthermore, the police may grant bail to an arrested person prior to his first appearance in court. The rules concerning remands are dealt with mainly in the Magistrates' Court Act 1980 and the principles upon which bail may be granted or refused in the Bail Act, 1976.

"Police Bail"

Anyone arrested without warrant for an offence must be brought before a magistrates' court as soon as practicable. If this is not practicable within 24 hours, he must be bailed by police to appear before a magistrates' court unless the offence appears to be serious: Magistrates' Courts Act 1980, s. 43(1). A juvenile must, as a general rule, be brought before a court within 72 hours of arrest unless he is bailed or the station officer or another officer not below the rank of inspector certifies that he cannot be brought before the court by reason of illness or accident: Children and Young Persons Act, 1969, s. 29.

"Police bail" is governed by the Bail Act, 1976 except that the general right to bail (s. 4) does not apply. Security may be demanded in the circumstances mentioned in s. 3(5), but requirements may not be imposed under s. 3(6).

Adjournments and Remands

While a magistrates' court had power at common law to adjourn the hearing of an information, that power is now regulated by statute and depends, as does the power to remand the defendant, upon the stage of the proceedings as follows:

Mode of trial proceedings (for an offence triable either way). The power of adjournment is contained in the Magistrates' Courts Act 1980, s. 18, which also permits an adult to be remanded whenever he is present and requires him to be remanded in certain circumstances. There is no obligation to remand where these proceedings are conducted by a legal representative in accordance with s. 25 *ibid*., or when the court changes over to act as examining justices.

Committal proceedings. The power of adjournment is contained in the Magistrates' Courts Act 1980, s. 5, which also requires the accused to be remanded.

Summary trial. The power of adjournment is contained in the Magistrates' Courts Act 1980, s. 10, which permits the accused to be remanded in any case and requires an adult to be remanded on an offence triable either way in certain circumstances.

A remand is an order of a court disposing of the person of someone appearing before it during the period of an adjournment. A remand may be either on bail or in custody: Magistrates' Courts Act 1980, s. 128.

Maximum periods apply to different types of remand, of which the following are the more important:

before conviction
—in custody   —eight clear days
—on bail   —eight clear days unless } Magistrates' Courts Act
                 both sides consent to   1980, s. 128(6)
                 longer period

In either case the eight-day period may be exceeded in the case of an offence triable either way where necessary to obtain a properly constituted court.

after conviction or for medical reports
—in custody   —three weeks   } Magistrates' Courts Act
                                             1980,
—on bail   —four weeks   ss 10 and 128(6).

When the accused is already serving a custodial sentence there is power in certain circumstances to remand in custody for up to 28 days: Magistrates' Courts Act 1980, s. 131.

There is power to remand further: s. 128(3), *ibid.* which may be exercised in the absence of the defendant: s. 129, *ibid.*

Remand in Absence of the Defendant

A magistrates' court may remand an accused in his absence where:
 (i)   he is aged 17 or over;
 (ii) he has already been remanded in custody;
 (iii) he has given his consent to this course (and was 17 when he did so);
 (iv) that consent has not been withdrawn;
 (v)   not more than two immediately preceding remands have been in his absence under this provision (Magistrates' Courts Act 1980, s. 128(3A)).

This provision must be explained on all relevant remands in custody where the accused is 17 or over and legally represented (*ibid*, s. 128(1A)). His consent must then be sought (*ibid*, s. 128(1C)).

Where on an adjourned hearing the court is not satisfied that these conditions are or were met it must adjourn the case for the shortest period possible to allow the accused to be produced (*ibid*, s. 128(3C), (3D), (3E)).

Young Persons and Juveniles

The places to which a person aged 17-20 years may be remanded in custody are dealt with in the Criminal Justice Act, 1948, s. 27. A juvenile not granted bail is committed to the care of the local authority in accordance with the Children and Young Persons Act, 1969, s. 23, except if he is a boy aged 15 years or older when in certain narrowly prescribed circumstances be may be committed to prison. See the Certificates of Unruly Character (Conditions) Order 1977, *post*.

The Custody of a Constable

As an alternative to a remand to a prison or other institution a court having power to remand anyone in custody, may, if the remand is for a period not exceeding three clear days commit him instead to the custody of a constable: Magistrates' Courts Act 1980, s. 128(7). The maximum period for such a remand in the case of a juvenile is 24 hours: Children and Young Persons Act, 1969, s. 23(5).

Bail

The remand of an adult defendant otherwise than in custody must be on bail.

The General Right to Bail

Anyone accused of an offence who appears or is brought before a magistrates' court in the course of or in connexion with proceedings for the offence or who applies to a court for bail in connexion with an offence must be granted bail unless his case falls within one of the exceptions in sch. 1 of the Bail Act, 1976 when the court has a discretion to grant or refuse bail: s. 4(1), *ibid.*

The general right to bail does not apply

(i)   (by virtue of s. 4(2), *ibid.*) after "conviction" (a term widely defined in s. 2(1), *ibid.*) unless the adjournment is for the purpose of enabling enquiries to be made to assist the court in dealing with him for the offence (s. 4(4), *ibid.*) or for proceedings under ss 6 or 16 of the Powers of Criminal Courts Act, 1973 (breach of requirement of probation and community service respectively). (s. 4(3), *ibid.*) Thus while the general right to bail applies on a committal to the Crown Court for trial is does not upon an appeal or a committal to the Crown Court for sentence or to be dealt with for breach of a suspended sentence;

(ii)   to warrants for the appearance of a defendant, nor, it is submitted, to warrants for fine defaulters; and

(iii)   to appeals to the Crown Court or the High Court.

Bail may not be granted by a magistrate in cases of treason: Magistrates' Courts Act 1980, s. 41: Bail Act, 1976, s. 4(7).

Exceptions to the General Right to Bail

Where the general right to bail applies a defendant may be refused bail only in the following circumstances:

in all cases:

(i)   if he has been arrested under s. 7 of the Bail Act, 1976 for absconding or breaching bail conditions in the present proceedings (para. 2 of Part I and para. 5 of Part II of sch. I);

(ii)   for his own protection or, if a juvenile, for his welfare (para. 3 of Part I and para. 3 of Part II of sch. I);

(iii)   if he is in custody in pursuance of a sentence of a court or under the Services Acts (para. 4 of Part I and para. 4 of Part II of sch. I);

in the case of non-imprisonable offences only:

(iv)   if he has previously failed to answer bail *and* the court believes that, if released, he would fail to surrender to custody (para. 2 of Part II of sch. I);

in the case of imprisonable offences only:

if there are "substantial grounds" for believing that he would—

(v)   fail to surrender to custody (para. 2 of Part I of sch. 1);

The court must however weigh the gravity of the charge and all the other facts of the case against the likelihood of the accused absconding: *R.* v. *Phillips* (1947) 111 J.P. 333.

(vi)   commit an offence while on bail (para. 2 of Part I of sch. 1);

In *R.* v. *Phillips* (1947) 111 J.P. 333, Atkinson J in the Court of Appeal said that housebreaking particularly is a crime which will very probably be repeated if a prisoner is released on bail, especially in the case of a man who has a record of housebreaking. It is an offence which can be committed with a considerable measure of safety. Referring to a defendant who had committed nine offences while on bail, he said: "To turn such a man loose on society until he has received his punishment for an offence which is not in dispute is, in the view of the court, a very inadvisable step to take. The court wish justices who release on bail young housebreakers such as this to know that in 19 cases out of 20 it is a very wrong step to take." This applies, *a fortiori* in the case of offenders with bad records: *R.* v. *Gentry; R.* v. *Wharton* [1955] Crim. L.R. 565; *R.* v. *Pegg* [1955] Crim. L.R. 308.

The Home Office working party on bail agreed with this view and commented that there were indications that there is a significantly greater risk of offences being committed on bail by persons charged with robbery or burglary than those charged with other offences (para. 67 of the report). At the other extreme, they added, if a person is charged with a comparatively minor offence a greater risk of similar offences being committed if bail is granted can reasonably be accepted (para. 68).

(vii)   interfere with witnesses or otherwise obstruct the course of justice (para. 2 of Part I of sch. I);

The Home Office working party on bail commented: The possibility of the defendant interfering with witnesses arises less frequently and will usually be relevant only when the alleged offence is comparatively serious and there is some other indication, such as a past record of violence or threatening behaviour by the defendant. When there is a substantial ground for fearing such interference, this seems to us to be a very strong reason for refusing bail (para. 69).

It is submitted that the requirement that there should be "substantial grounds" connotes something more than a mere possibility and something less than proof beyond reasonable doubt. Indeed, it would not appear to connote any particular degree of "proof" because much of the information put before a court in a remand application, for example is necessarily incapable of proof in an evidential sense. And compare *R.* v. *Guest, ex parte Metropolitan Police Commissioner* (1962) 126 J.P. 21 (evidence of arrest unnecessary).

if the court is "satisfied" that—

(viii)   it has not been practicable since the proceedings were instituted to obtain sufficient information to take the bail decision (para. 5 of Part I of sch. I);
(ix)   he has been convicted and it is impracticable to complete any necessary inquiries or report on bail (para. 7 of Part I of sch. I).

Factors to be Considered

In taking a bail decision in the case of an imprisonable offence the court may consider the following factors as well as any others which may be relevant (para. 9 of Part I of sch. 1):

the nature and seriousness of the offence or default

The following observations were made by Dunn L. J., in the Court of Appeal in respect of committal proceedings on a charge of murder:

"We understand that, pursuant to the provisions of the Bail Act 1976, it is not uncommon for persons charged with murder to be granted bail on their committal. If that is done, the kind of difficulties which arose in this case may arise in future cases. It is unnecessary to say that it is in the interests of the accused himself that he should be examined by a prison doctor whenever there is a charge of murder so that the various relevant matters affecting his state of mind at the time of the offence may be considered by the doctor, and in particular the possibility of a defence of diminished responsibility. This situation is not expressly provided for in the 1976 Act, which gives a right to bail, subject to the exceptions set out in Part I of sch. 1. Nothing that we say is intended to derogate from the terms of the 1976 Act so far as those exceptions are concerned. However, in para. 9 of Part I of sch. 1, it is provided that in taking the decision required by para. 2 of Part I of the schedule (that is to say the decision whether or not to grant bail) the court shall have regard to four specified considerations as well as to any others which appear to be relevant. It appears to this court that the consideration in a charge of murder that in his own interests an accused should be examined by a prison doctor is a proper consideration for the magistrates to take into account. They should consider, before granting bail, whether it would not be desirable to remand the accused in custody at any rate for a period long enough for the necessary reports to be prepared. Once that is done, the accused will then of course be in a position to apply for bail to the Crown Court:" *R.* v. *Vernege* [1982] 1 All E.R. 403. And *see* now the Bail Act 1976, s. 3(6A), (6B).

The Home Office working party on bail commented:

" . . ., the more serious the offence charged, the stronger the temptation to abscond is likely to be, since a defendant who is liable, if convicted, to receive a long sentence of imprisonment has more incentive to abscond than one facing a less serious charge. Moreover, the more serious the offence, the smaller is the risk than can justifiably be taken either of the defendant's absconding or of his committing offences similar to that with which he is charged. . . . At the other extreme, the comparative triviality of the offence may of itself indicate that a remand in custody is not justified, whatever the other considerations.

"57. While the seriousness of the class of offence is an important factor, it is not necessarily conclusive. The nature of the particular offence may also be relevant. The circumstances of a domestic murder, for example, may of themselves preclude any likelihood of repetition and there may be virtually no risk of the defendant's absconding. Similarly, in the case of certain types of fraud, the possibility of repetition may not be a factor, although a remand in custody may, of course, be justifiable on other grounds."

"Default" is defined in para. 4 of Part III of sch. I.

the probable method of dealing with the defendant
The Home Office working party on bail commented:

"60. The court should also have regard to the likely sentence if the defendant is convicted, since his perception of the likely consequences of a conviction may be expected to have a considerable influence on his reaction to bail. The defendant will have much less incentive to abscond if the likely penalty is a fine or probation than if a custodial sentence is in prospect. If a person is remanded in custody and subsequently receives a sentence of imprisonment, the time spent on remand counts towards the sentence by virtue of s. 67 of the Criminal Justice Act, 1967. If, however, he does not receive a sentence of imprisonment, he cannot of course gain "credit" for his period in custody. Although it is wrong to assume that where a custodial remand is followed by a non-custodial sentence bail should have been granted initially, it is clearly desirable that, where an eventual custodial sentence is unlikely, bail should be granted unless there are strong grounds for a remand in custody. We would suggest that in a borderline case the court might give the defendant the benefit of the doubt, if a non-custodial sentence seems the likeliest outcome.

"61. This is not to say that a person who is likely to receive a custodial sentence if convicted should necessarily be refused bail. It has been suggested that, where a defendant is likely to receive a custodial sentence, it is doing him no kindness to give him a preliminary period of liberty. We do not think that this is a conclusive argument; much depends on whether the likely sentence of imprisonment will be short or long, since there is a danger, if the sentence is likely to be short, that the period on remand may exceed it. It seems to us, therefore, that the likely sentence if the defendant is convicted should be considered more in relation to the danger of his absconding than as a factor in its own right."

defendant's character and antecedents
The Home Office working party on bail commented:

"59. The court should next consider the defendant's antecedents. These are a valuable guide, but need to be interpreted with some care. If the defendant has abused the grant of bail in the past or is already on bail in respect of another charge, these facts should count strongly against him. In other cases, however, the defendant's previous convictions may not provide a reliable guide to his likely reaction to the grant of bail, unless, for example, they disclose a large number of serious offences. A long string of petty offences does not automatically justify a remand in custody. Clearly a man who, although convicted on a number of occasions in the past, has always answered his bail, is likely to be a good bail risk."

Antecedents include previous convictions. They should be submitted to the court in writing and not *viva voce: R. v. Dyson* (1943) 107 J.P. 178. "Antecedents" is as wide a term as can be conceived, *per* Lord Goddard CJ in *R. v. Vallett* (1951) 115 J.P. 113 (where it was held in another context to extend to offences taken into consideration).

A justice who has been informed of a defendant's previous convictions must not take part in trying the issue of his guilt: Magistrates' Courts Act 1980, s.42(1).

defendant's associations and community ties
The Home Office working party on bail commented:
"The extent to which the defendant has a stable background and settled employment—what are generally called his "community ties"—is likely to be of considerable influence in determining whether he is a good bail risk.

"65. One aspect of the defendant's community ties is the type of accommodation in which he lives. The fact that a defendant has no fixed abode is often advanced as a good reason for opposing bail. We accept that this is a material consideration, but we think it important that courts should ascertain precisely what is meant when a person is said to have no fixed abode. Does it mean that he is sleeping rough or that he is staying with friends or in a hostel or merely that he is living in a furnished flat to which he has only moved very recently?"

defendant's record as respects previous grants of bail
Even before the coming into force of the Act: para. 2 of Part III of sch. I.

(before conviction only) the strength of the evidence
The Home Office working party on bail commented:

"58. Where the nature of the prosecution evidence of the alleged offence is known, this should be considered in conjunction with the seriousness and nature of the offence. If the case against the defendant appears to the court to be weak, this should be an additional ground for considering the grant of bail. In many cases the evidence will not be available at the time the court is considering the bail application, particularly if it is the defendant's first appearance in court. Where, however, the court is considering the question of bail on committal for trial, it may at that stage have a good idea of the strength of the evidence."

Procedure on a Bail Decision

Neither the Act nor the Rules lays down the procedure whereby the question of bail should be considered. The Home Office working party envisaged that after it had been decided whether to adjourn the case, the prosecution would be asked whether it was aware of any reasons why bail should not be granted. The defendant should also be given the opportunity to put forward considerations in favour of bail which he wished the court to take account of and to comment on any points made by the prosecution. Evidence is not essential on either side. In any event the strict rules of evidence do not apply: *In re Moles* [1981] Crim. L.R. 170.

A decision about bail is not, like a trial, a contest between two parties with the court neutrally holding the ring. The court is under a duty to consider the question of bail properly and it may grant bail against the objection of the prosecutor as much as it may refuse bail in the absence of such objection. As the working party said, "the decision whether to remand on bail or in custody must be the court's and the court's alone". In pursuance of this duty the court may seek the views, not only of the prosecutor and defendant, but also of anyone else who, it believes can offer useful assistance. Thus, the court may properly direct a probation officer to make inquiries, for example about the defendant's background and the possibility of bail accommodation.

In the case of a bail decision taken after conviction (which the working party did not contemplate as it had no proposal for a right to bail in those circumstances) the facts of the case and the circumstances of the defendant will usually be within the court's knowledge and the role of the parties will accordingly be much less.

Subsequent Bail Applications

Once a bench has been satisfied that one of the statutory exceptions to the general right to bail exists it is a finding of the court analogous to *res judicata*. Thereafter a subsequent bench can only investigate whether that situation has changed: *R.* v. *Nottingham Justices, ex parte Davies* (1980) 144 J.P. 233. The question is not "Has there been a change?" It is "Are there any new considerations which were not before the court when the accused was last remanded in custody?" The lapse of time may amount to fresh circumstances, particularly, but by no means only, because of delay on the part of the prosecution. It is submitted that for a decision to have this binding effect it must be one taken after the accused has had the opportunity to mount a fully prepared application for bail. The first appearance, which may take place soon after arrest and without legal representation, is seldom such an occasion. The later court is bound to investigate any alleged change of circumstances: *In re Moles, supra.*

In many cases there will be a material change in circumstances at the committal for trial stage justifying a review of the bail decision, e.g. the strength of the prosecution case may be better known or it may be possible to re-evaluate the seriousness of the offence or the time likely to elapse before the case comes to trial, but the fact that the committal stage has been reached is not *ipso facto* a material change: *R. v. Slough Justices, ex parte Duncan and Embling* (1983) 147 J.P. 2.

Conditions of Bail

The defendant's own recognizance may not be taken in criminal

proceedings (Bail Act 1976, s. 3(2)), but he may be required to:
  (*a*)   provide sureties;
  (*b*)   comply with requirements imposed by the court; and
  (*c*)   give security (*see* below).
When the offence is an imprisonable one sureties, requirements of bail and
security may only be required where necessary to prevent the defendant:
  – failing to surrender
  – committing an offence
  – interfering with witnesses or otherwise obstructing the course of
    justice (para. 8 of Part I of sch. 1.)

Sureties

A bailed person may be required to provide sureties: Bail Act 1976, s. 3(4).
In considering the suitability of a surety regard may be had among other things to:

  —   his financial resources
  —   his character and any previous convictions
  —   his proximity to the bailed person (Bail Act 1976, s. 8(2)).

As the section makes clear, these are not the only matters which may be
considered in assessing the suitability of a surety. It is essential that the person
giving bail should be interested in looking after and, if necessary, using powers he
has to prevent the accused from escaping: *Petersdorff on Bail* quoted with
approval by North J in *Consolidated Exploration and Finance Co.* v.*Musgrave*
(1900) 64 J.P. 89. It would therefore appear incumbent upon anyone accepting
the recognizance of a surety to satisfy himself, not only of his pecuniary
sufficiency, but also of his ability and willingness to perform all the duties of a
surety. (*See* the article at 136 J.P.N. 400). But a court may not refuse a surety for
his political opinions or otherwise inquire into his private interest or character: *R.*
v. *Badger* (1843) 7 J.P. 128. "Excessive" bail is forbidden by the Bill of
Rights, 1688. The Queen's Bench Division have disapproved of a solicitor
standing bail for his client: *R.* v. *Scott Jervis* (1876) *The Times*, November
20.
    As well as being an illegal contract (*R.* v. *Porter* (1910) 74 J.P. 159) it is
an offence to agree to indemnify a surety in criminal proceedings: Bail Act
1976, s. 9(1).

Forfeiture of Recognizance

Where a surety's recognizance appears to be forfeited the court may declare
it forfeited: Magistrates' Courts Act 1980, s. 120(1). No procedure is laid
down for the forfeiture of a recognizance other than one conditioned to
keep the peace or be of good behaviour, but, since the section confers a
discretion on the justices whether to forfeit in whole or in part or not at all
(subs. (3)), it would seem essential that the surety should have an opportunity to show cause why the recognizances should be estreated. A
notice of hearing would appear to be sufficient for this purpose provided
there is proof of service.
    In exercising their discretion justices must consider to what extent the
surety has been at fault with regard to the accused's failure to appear: *R.* v.
Southampton Justices, ex parte Green (1975) 135 J.P. 667. But the onus of
showing absence of culpability is on the surety: *R.* v. *Southampton Justices,
ex parte Corker* (1976) *The Times* February 11. The problem of forfeiture is
to be approached on the footing that the surety was entering into a serious
obligation and ought to pay the amount promised unless there are circumstances which made it fair or just to make the surety pay a smaller

sum (or, *semble*, no sum at all): *R.* v. *Horseferry Road Magistrates' Court, ex parte Pearson* (1976) 140 J.P. 382. The burden of satisfying the court that the full sum should be forfeited is a very heavy one. Only in a wholly extreme and exceptional case should it be remitted entirely, *per* Donaldson L. J. in *R.* v. *Waltham Forest Justices, ex parte Parfrey* [1980] 2 Cr. App. R. (S) 208. Provided these principles are followed by the magistrates the High Court will not exercise its prerogative jurisdiction to interfere with their discretion: *R.* v. *Tottenham Magistrates' Court, ex parte Riccardi* [1978] 66 Cr. App. R. 150.

Means other than the surety's own must be disregarded: *R.* v. *Southampton Justices, ex parte Green, supra.*; but the system of sureties would be defeated if the amount to be forfeited was limited to the defendant's means: *R.* v. *Southampton Justices, ex parte Corker, supra.* The justices are under no obligation to inquire as to the ability of the surety to pay: *R.* v. *Waltham Forest Justices, ex parte Parfrey* [1980] 2 Cr. App. R. (S) 208. However, an order of forfeiture was quashed where justices declined to hear evidence of means: *R.* v. *Uxbridge Justices, ex parte Heward-Mills* (1983) 147 J.P. 225.

It is the duty of the surety to stay in touch with the bailed person to see that he will appear in court. The court in considering the culpability of the surety will look to what he did to see that the accused surrendered and what he did to alert the police if there was any known risk of absconding. It is the duty of the surety to keep himself informed of the bail conditions and he can help himself by entering into the recognizance only from one remand to another rather than on continuous bail: *R.* v. *Wells St. Magistrates' Court, ex parte Albanese.* [1981] 3 All E.R. 769. While the fact that a surety has reported to the police under s. 7(3) of the Act does not relieve the surety of his obligations it is a factor which the court may take into account when considering forfeiture: *R.* v. *Ipswich Crown Court, ex parte Reddington* [1981] Crim. L.R. 618.

There is no right of appeal to the Crown Court against an order to forfeit a recognizance: *R.* v. *Durham JJ, ex parte Laurent* (1945) 109 J.P. 21. But *certiorari* will lie where an error in law is disclosed in the affidavits: *R.* v. *Southampton Justices, ex parte Green, supra.*

Requirements of Bail

A person bailed by the court may be required to comply with requirements necessary to secure that;

> —he surrenders to custody
> — he does not commit an offence while on bail
> — he does not interfere with witnesses or otherwise obstruct the course of justice
> — he makes himself available for the purpose of inquiries or a report: Bail Act 1976, s. 3(6).

A parent or guardian who stands as surety may additionally be required to secure that the child or young person complies with any such requirement except where the child or young person will become 17 before he is required to surrender and not in respect of a sum greater than £50: s. 3(7), *ibid.*

Home Office circ. 206/1977 dated November 18, 1977 asks courts "to ensure that the defendant is able to comply with any conditions they intend to impose under s. 3(6) and that any such conditions are enforceable. Difficulty has been encountered where, for example, a court has required residence at a particular address without first checking that accommodation was available there; a court has delegated the approval of a place of residence to the police or probation service; a court has required the defendant not to enter any licensed premises for the period of bail; a court has imposed a reporting condition without specifying the police station or has named a station without checking that it is continuously manned. Courts are requested to be especially selective in requiring regular reporting to a police station since this can be burdensome for the police and also raise identification problems. A condition of bail sometimes imposed by courts is that the defendant surrender his passport prior to release. Since this is simply a device to prevent the defendant from absconding abroad it should be accompanied by a post-release condition stipulating that the defendant shall not leave Great Britain during the period of bail. When a passport condition is imposed but the defendant is committed to custody pending its surrender or the finding of sureties, it would be of assistance to prison governors and help to avoid unnecessary delay in releasing the defendant if any information available to the court about the whereabouts of the passport (e.g. that it is already in the hands of airport police or Customs and Excise authorities) could be noted on the committal warrant."

A condition that the accused should not drive is lawful, but courts ought to consider whether it might have unexpected and possibly unjust results: *R.* v. *Kwame* [1975] 60 Cr. App. R. 65.

Security

A bailed person may be required to give security where he is unlikely to remain in Great Britain: Bail Act 1976, s. 3(5).

The term "security" is not defined in the Act. Home Office circ. 206/1977 dated November 18, 1977 comments that "it may take the form of cash, travellers' cheques or any other article of value. In exercising their discretion in a particular case, courts or the police should have regard to the ease with which the security could be held and converted into pounds sterling in the event of forfeiture. For example it would be unwise to accept as security any perishable articles or any article which would create problems of storage or valuation." The court may direct how the requirement to give security is to be complied with: Magistrates' Courts Rules 1981, r. 85. For advice on this matter see Home Office circ. 11/1978 dated February 17, 1978.

Security may be forfeited in whole or part upon a failure to surrender: s. 5(7) and (8), *infra*. The order does not take effect until 21 days after it is made (s. 5(8A)) and the court may in this period revoke or vary it if the defendant shows that he did, after all, have good reason for failing to surrender to custody. The court may also remit or reduce the amount of the forfeiture after the order has taken effect (s. 5(8B)). Home Office circ. 206/1977 comments that it is expected that an application for variation or remission would normally be made within the 21 day period, but there may be occasions when this is not possible and when it would, therefore, be unreasonable for a period which is fixed for administrative convenience to act as a fetter to the rights of the individual.

Information for the Defendant

Whenever bail is granted in criminal proceedings or withheld from anyone enjoying the general right to bail a record of the decision must be made in prescribed manner and a copy given on request to the defendant: Bail Act, 1976 s. 5(1).

When in criminal proceedings a court dealing with anyone enjoying the general right to bail (*see* above), withholds bail or imposes or varies conditions of bail it must give its reasons for the purpose of enabling him to consider making an application to another court: Bail Act, 1976, s. 5(3). A note of the reasons must be recorded in the court register and a copy given to the defendant: s. 5(4), *ibid*.

When a magistrates' court withholds bail to anyone who is not legally represented it must tell him of his right to apply to the High Court and, where appropriate, the Crown Court Bail Act, 1976, s. 5(6).
Bail Act, 1976, s. 5(6).

Variation of Bail Terms

A court may vary the conditions of any bail it has granted or impose conditions where there were none before on application by or on behalf of the bailed person or by the prosecutor or a constable: Bail Act, 1976, s. 3(8).

Application to the High Court for Bail

Where in criminal proceedings a magistrates' court withholds bail or imposes conditions in granting bail the High Court may grant bail or vary the conditions: Criminal Justice Act 1967, s. 22(1).

Application to the Crown Court for Bail

The Crown Court may grant bail, *inter alia*, to anyone:
  (i)   who has been committed in custody for appearance before that court;
  (ii) who is in custody pursuant to a sentence of a magistrates' court and who has appealed to the Crown Court; or
  (iii) who has been remanded in custody by a magistrates' court and who has a full argument certificate: Supreme Court Act 1981, s. 81(1), (1J). (Such a certificate must be granted by a magistrates'· court upon hearing full argument on a bail application for the first time and on hearing argument after a change in circumstances or on new considerations: Bail Act 1976, s. 5(6A).)

The Duty to Surrender

A person granted bail in criminal proceedings is under a duty to surrender to custody (Bail Act, 1976, s. 3(1)), failure to comply with which constitutes an offence under s. 6(1) or (2), *ibid*. A remand on bail is a direction to appear before the court:

— at the end of the period of remand, or
— at every time and place to which the hearing may be adjourned: Magistrates' Courts Act 1980, s. 128(1), (4).

Arrest of a Bailed Person Without Warrant

A constable may arrest without warrant a bailed person where he has reasonable grounds for believing that he will abscond or is likely to break or has broken any bail condition or where he is notified in writing by a surety that the bailed person is unlikely to surrender and the surety wishes to be relieved of his obligations: Bail Act 1976, s. 7(3). As soon as practicable (and in any event within 24 hours) a person so arrested must be brought before a justice for the petty sessions area in which he was arrested unless he was arrested within 24 hours of the time appointed for surrender: *ibid*, s. 7(4). The justice must give him bail on the same conditions unless satisfied that he is not likely to surrender or has broken a bail condition, when the defendant may be remanded on bail or in custody: *ibid*, s. 7(5).

At common law the surety of a bailed person had a power to detain. Thus, "if it comes to (the knowledge of sureties) that (the bailed person) is about to abscond they should at once inform the police of the fact," *per* Lord Alverstone CJ in *R.* v. *Porter, supra.* "Hence, they may seize his person at any time (as on a Sunday) or at any place to carry him to a justice to find new sureties, or be committed in their discharge, and in surrendering the principal they may command the co-operation of the sheriff and any of his officers": *Petersdorff on Bail* cited in *Consolidated Exploration and Finance Co.* v. *Musgrave* (1900) 64 J.P. 89. It is submitted that this power of the surety has not been superseded by the Act of 1976, although a constable would normally be wise to use the procedure provided in the Bail Act 1976, s. 7(3).

Arrest of a Bailed Person on Warrant

If a person released on bail in criminal proceedings fails to surrender, a warrant may be issued for his arrest: Bail Act 1976, s. 7(1). There is a similar power when a defendant who has surrendered absents himself without leave from the court: *ibid*, s. 7(2).

The Offence of Absconding from Bail

It is an offence for a bailed person to fail without reasonable cause to surrender to custody: Bail Act 1976, s. 6(1). Similarly, it is an offence, having had reasonable cause to fail to surrender, to fail to surrender as soon as reasonably practicable thereafter: *ibid*, s. 6(2). The burden of proof of reasonable cause lies on the bailed person: *ibid*, s. 6(3). Both offences are punishable either on summary conviction or as a criminal contempt of court: *ibid*, s. 6(5). On summary conviction the offender may be liable to imprisonment for up to three months or a fine not exceeding level 5 on the standard scale or both: *ibid*, s. 6(7).

It should be noted that breach of a bail condition (as opposed to a failure to surrender) is not an offence under s.6 or otherwise.

Absconder from the Crown Court

A person in custody in pursuance of a Crown Court warrant with a view to his appearance before that court must be brought before either the Crown Court or a magistrates' court: Supreme Court Act 1981, s. 81. Where such a person is brought before a magistrates' court he must be dealt with in accordance with the Magistrates' Courts Act 1980, s. 43A.

Legal Aid

An application for legal aid must be granted, subject to means, when a defendant is brought before the court in pursuance of a remand in custody on an occasion when he may be again remanded or committed in custody and is not (but wishes to be) legally represented, not having been legally represented on the first occasion: Legal Aid Act, 1974, s. 29(1)(c). This requirement does not apply after conviction s. 29(1A), *ibid*. Such a legal aid order may be confined to so much of the procedings as relates to the grant of bail: s. 29(1A), *ibid*. Legal aid confined to bail applications does not extend to the services of counsel: Legal Aid Act 1974,, s. 30(2).

Legal aid must similarly be granted, subject to means, when it is applied for by a person who is to be sentenced or dealt with for an offence by a magistrates' court or the Crown Court and is to be kept in custody for inquiries or report: Legal Aid Act 1974,s. 29(1)(d).

Fingerprint Orders

When a defendant other than a child is before the court, whether in answer to a summons for an offence punishable with imprisonment or to a charge, the magistrates have power on application of a police officer not below the rank of

Inspector to direct that his finger and palm prints shall be taken, by force if necessary: Magistrates' Courts Act 1980, s. 49. The prints are destroyed in the event of an acquittal or discharge.

"The purpose of this provision is to assist the police in their investigation of crime. The police may have in their possession finger-prints taken in the course of inquiries into the offence with which the accused is charged, or in the course of inquiries into other offences, e.g. finger-prints left at the scene of the crime, and the taking of the finger-prints of the accused will enable the police to determine whether these finger-prints are the finger-prints of the accused. The taking of finger-prints is not only a means by which the identity of the perpetrator of an offence may be established: it is also a means by which an innocent person suspected of committing an offence may be cleared of suspicion. It will be for the court to decide in its discretion whether to make an order upon application by the police in such a case, but it will not always be possible for the police to give reasons for their application, since this might prejudice the hearing of the charge before the court, e.g. when the person charged is believed to have previous convictions and the police wish to have the finger-prints for comparison with the records at Scotland Yard, or where he is suspected of having committed other offences and the police wish to ascertain whether his finger-prints are identical with those found at the scene of these offences." Home Office circ. 265/1948 dated December 13, 1948.

Justices have the right to make an order under this section whenever in their judicial discretion they think fit. Thus, it was held not to be an objection to the making of an order that the evidence obtained from a finger-print taken thereunder was evidence of identity and that an accused person could not be compelled to make a confession: *George* v. *Coombe* [1978] Crim. L.R. 47.

THE CRIMINAL JUSTICE ACT, 1948

Remand of persons aged 17 to 20

27. (1) Where a court remands a person charged with or convicted of an offence or commits him for trial or sentence and he is not less than 17 but under 21 years old and is not released on bail, then, if the court has been notified by the Secretary of State that a remand centre is available for the reception from the court of persons of his class or description, it shall commit him to a remand centre and, if it has not been so notified, it shall commit him to prison.

(2) Where a person is committed to a remand centre in pursuance of this section, the centre shall be specified in the warrant and he shall be detained there for the period for which he is remanded or until he is delivered thence in due course of law.

(3) In this section "court" includes a justice; and nothing in this section affects the provisions of s. 128(7) of the Magistrates' Courts Act, 1980 (which provides for remands to the custody of a constable).

(*as substituted by the Children and Young Persons Act 1969, sch. 5, as amended by the Magistrates' Courts Act 1980, sch. 7.*)

COMMENTARY

For the determination of age *see* the Criminal Justice Act, 1948, s. 80(3).

For the disposal of juveniles remanded or committed for trial or sentence *see* the Children and Young Persons Act 1969, s. 23, *infra.*

Subsection (1): Remand centre. Defined in the Prison Act 1952, s. 43, as substituted by the Criminal Justice Act 1982, s. 11. (*See* s. 80 of the Act of 1948).

3. BAIL   101

THE CHILDREN AND YOUNG PERSONS ACT 1969

Remand to care of local authorities etc.

23. (1) Where a court—

(a) remands or commits for trial a child charged with homicide or remands a child convicted of homicide; or

(b) remands a young person charged with or convicted of one or more offences or commits him for trial or sentence,

and he is not released on bail, then, subject to the following provisions of this section, the court shall commit him to the care of a local authority in whose area it appears to the court that he resides or that the offence or one of the offences was committed.

(2) If the court aforesaid certifies that a young person is of so unruly a character that he cannot safely be committed to the care of a local authority under the preceding subsection, then if the court has been notified by the Secretary of State that a remand centre is available for the reception from the court of persons of his class or description, it shall commit him to a remand centre and, if it has not been so notified, it shall commit him to a prison.

(3) If, on the application of the local authority to whose care a young person is committed by a warrant under subs. (1) of this section, the court by which he was so committed or any magistrates' court having jurisdiction in the place where he is for the time being certifies as mentioned in subs. (2) of this section, the provisions of the said subs. (2) relating to committal shall apply in relation to him and he shall cease to be committed in pursuance of the said subs. (1).

(4) The preceding provisions of this section shall have effect subject to the provisions of s. 37 of the Magistrates' Courts Act 1980 (which relates to committal to the Crown Court with a view to a youth custody sentence).

(5) In this section "court" and "magistrates' court" include a justice; and notwithstanding anything in the preceding provisions of this section, s. 128(7) of the said Act of 1980 (which provides for remands to the custody of a constable for periods not exceeding three clear days) shall have effect in relation to a child or young person as if for the reference to three clear days there were substituted a reference to 24 hours.

(as amended by the Courts Act 1971, sch. 8, the Magistrates' Courts Act 1980, sch. 7, the Criminal Justice Act 1982, sch. 14.)

COMMENTARY

Subsection (1): A court. *See* subs. (5).

A child. Means a person under the age of 14: s. 70(1) of the Act.

A young person. Includes in subs. (1) a child who has attained the age of 10 years: The Children and Young Persons Act 1969 (Transitional Modifications of Part 1) Order 1970. For the determination of age *see* the Children and Young Persons Act, 1933, s. 99.

The care of a local authority. Except when the contrary intentions appears a child in the care of a local authority under a warrant under subs. (1) of this section is treated in accordance with Part II of the Child Care Act 1980: s. 17, *ibid.* Note, particularly, s. 18(3), *ibid.*, which states that: "If it appears to the local authority that it is necessary, for the purpose of protecting members of the public, to exercise their powers in relation to a particular child in their care in a manner which may not be consistent with their duty . . . the authority may, notwithstanding that duty, act in that manner." For other powers and duties of the authority *see* s. 24 of the 1969 Act.

Resides. Means "habitually resides": s. 70(1) of the Act.

Subsection (2): So unruly a character. When a young person is committed to a remand centre or a prison under subs. (2), the court shall include in the order of committal a cerficate that the young person is of so unruly a character that he cannot safely be committed to the care of a local authority: Magistrates' Courts (Children and Young Persons) Rules 1970, r. 27.

Certifies. The court may not make a certificate under this subsection unless one or more of the conditions in the Certificates of Unruly Character (Conditions) Order 1977, *post,* is satisfied.

Young person. Means a person who has attained the age of 14 and is under the age of 17: s. 70(1) of the Act. The references in subss (2) and (3) to a young person do not include a female person under the age of 17: Children and Young Persons Act 1979 (Transitional Modifications of Part I) Order 1979, S.I. 1979 No. 125. They also exclude references to a male person who has not attained the age of 15 years: Children and Young Persons Act (Transitional Modifications of Part I) Order 1981, S.I. 1981, No. 81.

Subsection (3): Certifies. *See* the note to subs.(2). *supra.*

Young person. See the note to subs.(2) above.

Release or further detention of arrested child or young person

29. (1) Where a person is arrested with or without a warrant and cannot be brought immediately before a magistrates' court, then if either—

    (*a*)   he appears to be a child and his arrest is for homicide; or

    (*b*)   he appears to be a young person and his arrest is for any offence,

the police officer in charge of the police station to which he is brought or another police officer not below the rank of inspector shall forthwith inquire into the case and, subject to subs. (2) of this section, shall release him unless—

    (i)   the officer considers that he ought in his own interests to be further detained; or

    (ii)   the officer has reason to believe that he has committed homicide or another grave crime or that his release would defeat the ends of justice or that if he were released (in a case where he was arrested without a warrant) he would fail to appear to answer to any charge which might be made.

(2) Where a parent or guardian enters into a recognizance to secure that the child or young person appears at the hearing of the charge, the recognizance may, if the said officer thinks fit, be conditioned for the attendance of the parent or guardian at the hearing in addition to the person arrested.

(3) An officer who inquires into a case in pursuance of subs. (1) of this section and does not release the person to whom the inquiry relates shall, unless the officer certifies that it is impracticable to do so or that he is of so unruly a character as to make it inappropriate to do so, make arrangements for him to be taken into the care of a local authority and detained by the authority, and it shall be lawful to detain him in pursuance of the arrangements; and a certificate made under this subsection in respect of any person shall be produced to the court before which that person is first brought thereafter.

(4) (*Not yet implemented*).

(5) A person detained by virtue of subs. (3) of this section shall be brought before a magistrates' court within 72 hours from the time of his arrest unless within that period a police officer not below the rank of inspector certifies to a magistrates' court that by reason of illness or accident he cannot be brought before a magistrates' court within that period.

(6) *(Repealed)*.

(as amended by the Bail Act, 1976, sch. 2 & 3).

COMMENTARY

Subsection (1): A child. Means a person under the age of 14: s. 70(1) of the Act.
A young person. Includes a child who has attained the age of 10 years: The Children and Young Persons Act 1969 (Transitional Modifications of Part I) Order 1970. For the determination of age *see* the Children and Young Persons Act, 1933, s. 99.

Subsection (5): Accident. See the note to the Magistrates' Courts Act, 1980, s. 129, *infra*.

THE BAIL ACT 1976

Meaning of "bail in criminal proceedings"

1. (1) In this Act "bail in criminal proceedings" means—

(*a*) bail grantable in or in connexion with proceedings for an offence to a person who is accused or convicted of the offence, or

(*b*) bail grantable in connexion with an offence to a person who is under arrest for the offence or for whose arrest for the offence a warrant (endorsed for bail) is being issued.   '

(2) In this Act "bail" means bail grantable under the law (including common law) for the time being in force.

(3) Except as provided by s. 13(3) of this Act, this section does not apply to bail in or in connexion with proceedings outside England and Wales.

(4) This section does not apply to bail granted before the coming into force of this Act.

(5) This section applies—

(*a*) whether the offence was committed in England or Wales or elsewhere, and

(*b*) whether it is an offence under the law of England and Wales, or of any other country or territory.

(6) Bail in criminal proceedings shall be granted (and in particular shall be granted unconditionally or conditionally) in accordance with this Act.

COMMENTARY

Subsection (1): Bail. Defined in subs. (2).

An offence. Includes an alleged offence: s. 2(2), *infra*. It does not seemingly include a breach of the peace which does not itself constitute an offence.

Convicted. Partially defined in s. 2 (1), *infra*.

Other definitions

2. (1) In this Act, unless the context otherwise requires, "conviction" includes—

(*a*) a finding of guilt,

(*b*) a finding that a person is not guilty by reason of insanity,

(*c*) a finding under s. 30(1) of the Magistrates' Courts Act, 1980 (remand for medical examination) that the person in question did the act or made the omission charged, and

(*d*) a conviction of an offence for which an order is made placing the offender on probation or discharging him absolutely or conditionally,

and "convicted" shall be construed accordingly.

(2) In this Act, unless the context otherwise requires—

"child" means a person under the age of 14,

"court" includes a Judge of a court, or a justice of the peace and, in the case of a specified court, includes a Judge or (as the case may be) justice having powers to act in connexion with proceedings before that court,

"Courts-Martial Appeal rules" means rules made under s. 49 of the Courts-Martial (Appeals) Act, 1968,

"Crown Court rules" means rules made under s. 15 of the Courts Act, 1971,

"magistrates' courts rules" means rules made under s. 15 of the Justices of the Peace Act, 1949,

"offence" includes an alleged offence,

"proceedings against a fugitive offender" means proceedings under s. 9 of the Extradition Act, 1870, s. 7 of the Fugitive Offenders Act, 1967 or s. 2(1) or s. 4(3) of the Backing of Warrants (Republic of Ireland) Act, 1965,

"Supreme Court rules" means rules made under s. 99 of the Supreme Court of Judicature (Consolidation) Act, 1925,

"surrender to custody" means, in relation to a person released on bail, surrendering himself into the custody of the court or of the constable (according to the requirements of the grant of bail) at the time and place for the time being appointed for him to do so,

"vary", in relation to bail, means imposing further conditions after bail is granted, or varying or rescinding conditions,

"young person" means a person who has attained the age of 14 and is under the age of 17.

(3) Where an enactment (whenever passed) which relates to bail in criminal proceedings refers to the person bailed appearing before a court it is to be construed unless the context otherwise requires as referring to his surrendering himself into custody of the court.

(4) Any reference in this Act to any other enactment is a reference thereto as amended, and includes a reference thereto as extended or applied, by or under any other enactment, including this Act.

(*as amended by the Criminal Law Act 1977, sch. 12, the Magistrates' Courts Act 1980, sch. 7*).

COMMENTARY

Subsection (2): Surrendering to custody. Thus, a defendant answers to his bail when he reports his presence at the place and time appointed. If there is any gap between that moment and his appearance in court he is, for that period, not on bail but in the custody of the court. If he absents himself from the court without leave during that period a warrant for his arrest may be issued (s. 7(2)). Unless there is some special reason, Home Office cir. 206/1977 dated November 18, 1977 suggests that defendants surrendering to the custody of the court as required by their bail should not be held in the secure area pending the beginning of their case since it is undesirable that a person who has been at liberty prior to the hearing should be locked up upon his arrival at the court.

General provisions

3. (1) A person granted bail in criminal proceedings shall be under a duty to surrender to custody, and that duty is enforceable in accordance with s. 6 of this Act.

(2) No recognizance for his surrender to custody shall be taken from him.

(3) Except as provided by this section—

(*a*) no security for his surrender to custody shall be taken from him,
(*b*) he shall not be required to provide a surety or sureties for his surrender to custody, and
(*c*) no other requirement shall be imposed on him as a condition of bail.

(4) He may be required, before release on bail, to provide a surety or sureties to secure his surrender to custody.

(5) If it appears that he is unlikely to remain in Great Britain until the time appointed for him to surrender to custody, he may be required, before release on bail, to give security for his surrender to custody.

The security may be given by him or on his behalf.

(6) He may be required (but only by a court) to comply, before release on bail or later, with such requirements as appear to the court to be necessary to secure that—

(*a*) he surrenders to custody,
(*b*) he does not commit an offence while on bail,
(*c*) he does not interfere with witnesses or otherwise obstruct the course of justice whether in relation to himself or any other person,
(*d*) he makes himself available for the purpose of enabling inquiries or a report to be made to assist the court in dealing with him for the offence.

(6A) In the case of a person accused of murder the court granting bail shall, unless it considers that satisfactory reports on his mental condition have already been obtained, impose as conditions of bail—

(*a*) a requirement that the accused shall undergo examination by two medical practitioners for the purpose of enabling such reports to be prepared; and
(*b*) a requirement that he shall for that purpose attend such an institution or place as the court directs and comply with any other directions which may be given to him for that purpose by either of those practitioners.

(6B) Of the medical practitioners referred to in subs. (6A) above at least one shall be a practitioner approved for the purposes of s. 12 of the Mental Health Act 1983.

(7) If a parent or guardian of a child or young person consents to be surety for the child or young person for the purposes of this subsection, the parent or guardian may be required to secure that the child or young person complies with any requirement imposed on him by virtue of subs. (6) or (6A) above, but—

(*a*) no requirement shall be imposed on the parent or the guardian of a young person by virtue of this subsection where it appears that the young person will attain the age of seventeen before the time to be appointed for him to surrender to custody; and
(*b*) the parent or guardian shall not be required to secure compliance with any requirement to which his consent does not extend and shall not, in

(8) Where a court has granted bail in criminal proceedings that court, or, where that court has committed a person on bail to the Crown Court for trial or to be
respect of those requirements to which his consent does extend, be bound in a sum greater than £50.

(9) This section is subject to subs. (2) of s. 30 of the Magistrates' Courts

(9) This section is subject to subs. (2) of s. 30 of the Magistrates' Courts Act 1980 (conditions of bail on remand for medical examination).
(as amended by the Criminal Law Act 1977, sch. 12, the Magistrates' Courts Act 1980, sch. 7, the Mental Health (Amendment) Act 1982, s. 34, the Mental Health Act 1983, sch. 4).

COMMENTARY

Subsection (1): Surrender to custody. Defined in s. 2(2), *supra.*

Subsection (2). This rules out the defendant's own recognizances.

Subsection (3): Security. Except as provided for in subs. (5) this rules out cash bail.

Surety. The effect of para. (b) and subs. (4) is to rule out sureties for any purpose other than securing the surrender to custody of the bailed person, but note subs. (7).

Subsections (4)-(7). No condition may be imposed under these subsections in the case of an imprisonable offence save for the purpose of preventing any of the events in para. 2 of Part I of sch. I, *infra* or, in the case of a condition under subs. (6)(d), where it is necessary to enable inquiries or a report concerning the defendant's physical or mental condition: para. 8(1), *ibid.* This would not seemingly permit a remand to assess suitability for a bail hostel. (See 142 J.P.N. 287).

Subsection (4): Surety. See the introduction and s. 8, *infra.*
In the event of non-appearance the recognizance of a surety may be estreated in accordance with the Magistrates' Courts Act 1980, s. 120. For the persons who may take the recognizance of a surety see r. 86.

Subsection (5): Security. *See* under this title in the introduction.

Great Britain. That is, England, Scotland and Wales: Union with Scotland Act 1706, Wales and Berwick Act 1746, s. 3. Great Britain is specified rather than the United Kingdom because there is power to arrest and return an absconder who has gone to Scotland: Home Office cir. 706/1977 dated April 18, 1977.

Subsection (6). *See* under Requirements of Bail in the introduction.
A requirement under this subsection amounts to a "condition" of bail, breach of which would justify the bailed person's arrest under s. 7, *infra.*
When the requirement has to be complied with before release the court may give directions as to the manner in which and the person(s) before whom they are to be complied with: Magistrates' Courts Rules 1981, r. 85.

A court. Defined in s. 2(2), *supra.*

Subsection (6A). *See* also the comments of Dunn L.J. in *R.* v. *Vernege* [1982] 1 All E.R. 403 in the introduction under Factors to be Considered in Questions of Bail.

Subsection (7). This places a limit on the extent to which a parent or guardian may be required to stand surety for his child (in this case anyone who will be under 17 at the adjourned date) in respect of any requirements under subs. (6). It does not limit the amount of the parent or guardian's recognizance for the appearance of his child.

Parent/guardian. These terms are not defined in this Act. Compare the definition of "guardian" in the Children and Young Persons Act, 1933, s. 107.

Child/young person. Defined in s. 2(2), *supra.*

Conditions of bail. These include, not merely the special requirements under subs. (6), but the number and value of any sureties. Note also the restrictions in para. 8 of Part I of sch. I, *infra.*

Subsection (8): Vary. Defined in s. 2(2). There is no duty in the court to notify a surety of variation of bail conditions but the court might wish to warn the surety of this fact and, where it thinks that a variation might affect a surety's willingness to continue, might decline to continue bail unless the surety agrees knowingly to continue: *R.* v. *Wells St. Magistrates' Court, ex parte Albanese* [1981] 3 All E.R. 769.

General right to bail of accused persons and others

4. (1) A person to whom this section applies shall be granted bail except as provided in sch. 1 to this Act.

(2) This section applies to a person who is accused of an offence when—

    (*a*)   he appears or is brought before a magistrates' court or the Crown Court in the course of or in connexion with proceedings for the offence, or

    (*b*)   he applies to a court for bail in connexion with the proceedings.

This subsection does not apply as respects proceedings on or after a person's conviction of the offence or proceedings against a fugitive offender for the offence.

(3) This section also applies to a person who, having been convicted of an offence, appears or is brought before a magistrates' court to be dealt with under s. 6 or s. 16 of the Powers of Criminal Courts Act, 1973 (breach of requirement of probation or community service order).

(4) This section also applies to a person who has been convicted of an offence and whose case is adjourned by the court for the purpose of enabling inquiries or a report to be made to assist the court in dealing with him for the offence.

(5) Schedule 1 to this Act also has effect as respects conditions of bail for a person to whom this section applies.

(6) In sch. 1 to this Act "the defendant" means a person to whom this section applies and any reference to a defendant whose case is adjourned for inquiries or a report is a reference to a person to whom this section applies by virtue of subs. (4) above.

(7) This section is subject to s. 41 of the Magistrates' Courts Act, 1980 (restriction of bail by magistrates' court in cases of treason).
(as amended by the Magistrates' Courts Act 1980, sch. 7).

COMMENTARY

Subsection (2). One effect of the concluding sentence of subs. (2) is that sch. I does not apply after conviction except in the cases referred to in subss (3) and (4).

Offence. See the note to s. 1, *supra.*

Conviction. Partially defined in s. 2(1), *supra.*

Proceedings against a fugitive offender. Defined in s. 2(1), *supra.*

Subsection (4). This refers to an adjournment under the Magistrates' Courts Act, 1980, s. 10.

Supplementary provisions about decisions on bail

5. (1) Subject to subs. (2) below, where—

    (*a*)   a court or constable grants bail in criminal proceedings, or

    (*b*)   a court withholds bail in criminal proceedings from a person to whom s. 4 of this Act applies, or

    (*c*)   a court, officer of a court or constable appoints a time or place or a court or officer of a court appoints a different time or place for a person granted bail in criminal proceedings to surrender to custody, or

    (*d*)   a court varies any conditions of bail or imposes conditions in respect of bail in criminal proceedings,

that court, officer or constable shall make a record of the decision in the prescribed manner and containing the prescribed particulars and, if requested to do so by the person in relation to whom the decision was taken, shall cause him to be given a copy of the record of the decision as soon as practicable after the record is made.

(2) Where bail in criminal proceedings is granted by endorsing a warrant of arrest for bail the constable who releases on bail the person arrested shall make

the record required by subs. (1) above instead of the Judge or justice who issued the warrant.

(3) Where a magistrates' court or the Crown Court—

    (a)   withholds bail in criminal proceedings, or

    (b)   imposes conditions in granting bail in criminal proceedings, or

    (c)   varies any condition of bail or imposes conditions in respect of bail in criminal proceedings,

and does so in relation to a person to whom s. 4 of this Act applies, then the court shall, with a view to enabling him to consider making an application in the matter to another court, give reasons for withholding bail or for imposing or varying the conditions.

(4) A court which is by virtue of subs. (3) above required to give reasons for its decision shall include a note of those reasons in the record of its decision and shall (except in a case where, by virtue of subs. (5) below, this need not be done) give a copy of that note to the person in relation to whom the decision was taken.

(5) . . .

(6) Where a magistrates' court withholds bail in criminal proceedings from a person who is not represented by counsel or a solicitor, the court shall—

    (a)   if it is committing him for trial to the Crown Court, or if it issues a certificate under subs. (6A) below, inform him that he may apply to the High Court or to the Crown Court to be granted bail;

    (b)   in any other case, inform him that he may apply to the High Court for that purpose.

(6A) Where in criminal proceedings—

    (a)   a magistrates' court remands a person in custody under any of the following provisions of the Magistrates' Court Act 1980—

        (i)   s. 5 (adjournment of inquiry into offence);

        (ii)   s. 10 (adjournment of trial);

        (iii)   s. 18 (initial procedure on information against adult for offence triable either way); or

        (iv)   s. 30 (remand for medical examination),

    after hearing full argument on an application for bail from him; and

    (b)   either—

        (i)   it has not previously heard such argument on an application for bail from him in those proceedings; or

        (ii)   it has previously heard full argument from him on such an application but it is satisfied that there has been a change in his circumstances or that new considerations have been placed before it,

it shall be the duty of the court to issue a certificate in the prescribed form that they heard full argument on his application for bail before they refused the application.

(6B) Where the court issues a certificate under subs. (6A) above in a case to which para. (b)(ii) of that subsection applies, it shall state in the certificate the nature of the change of circumstances or the new considerations which caused it to hear a further fully argued bail application.

(6C) Where a court issues a certificate under subs. (6A) above it shall cause the person to whom it refuses bail to be given a copy of the certificate.

(7) Where a person has given security in pursuance of s. 3(5) above and a court is satisfied that he failed to surrender to custody then, unless it appears that he had reasonable cause for his failure, the court may order the forfeiture of the security.

(8) If a court orders the forfeiture of a security under subs. (7) above, the court may declare that the fortfeiture extends to such amount less than the full value of the security as it thinks fit to order.

(8A) An order under subs. (7) above shall, unless previously revoked, take effect at the end of 21 days beginning with the day on which it is made.

(8B) A court which has ordered the forfeiture of a security under subs. (7) above may, if satisfied on an application made by or on behalf of the person who gave it that he did after all have reasonable cause for his failure to surrender to custody, by order remit the forfeiture or declare that it extends to such amount less than the full value of the security as it thinks fit to order.

(8C) An application under subs. (8B) above may be made before or after the order for forfeiture has taken effect, but shall not be entertained unless the court is satisfied that the prosecution was given reasonable notice of the applicant's intention to make it.

(9) A security which has been ordered to be forfeited by a court under subs. (7) above shall, to the extent of the forfeiture—

>   (a)   if is consists of money, be accounted for and paid in the same manner as a fine imposed by that court would be;
>   (b)   if it does not consist of money, be enforced by such magistrates' court as may be specified in the order.

(9A) Where an order is made under subs. (8B) above after the order for forfeiture of the security in question has taken effect, any money which would have fallen to be repaid or paid over to the person who gave the security if the order under subs. (8B) had been made before the order for fortfeiture took effect shall be repaid or paid over to him.

(10) (*Rules*).

(as amended by the Criminal Law Act 1977, sch. 12, the Criminal Justice Act 1982, s. 60.)

COMMENTARY

Records required by this section must be made by way of an entry in the register: Magistrates' Courts Rules 1981, r. 90.

Subsection (1): A court. Defined in s. 2(2), *supra*.

Bail in criminal proceedings. Defined in s. 1(1), *supra*.

The prescribed manner/particulars. See forms 149-152.

Subsection (2): Give reasons. Advice as to the form the reasons should take is contained in Home Office cir. 11/1978 dated February 17, 1978.

Subsection (3): Varies. Defined in s. 2(2), *supra*.

Conditions of bail. Seemingly under subss (4)-(7) of s. 4, *supra*.

Subsection (4): The record of its decision. The record must be made by way of an entry in the court register: Magistrates' Courts Rules 1981, r. 90.

A note of those reasons. Incorporated in forms 149-153.

Subsection (6). The right to apply to the Crown Court is contained in the Courts Act 1971, s. 13(4) and the Supreme Court Act 1981, s. 81, and to the High Court in the Criminal Justice Act 1967, s. 22.

Subsection (6A). The purpose of the certificate is to facilitate an application to the Crown Court for bail under the Supreme Court Act 1981, s. 81. The reference to changed circumstances and new considerations seems to import the principles laid down by the

Divisional Court in the *Nottingham Justices* case. *See* under *Subsequent Bail Decisions* in the introduction.

Subsection (7): Forfeiture. Note subss (8)-(9A).

Offence of absconding by person released on bail

6. (1) If a person who has been released on bail in criminal proceedings fails without reasonable cause to surrender to custody he shall be guilty of an offence.

(2) If a person who—

(*a*)   has been released on bail in criminal proceedings, and

(*b*)   having reasonable cause therefor, has failed to surrender to custody,

fails to surrender to custody at the appointed place as soon after the appointed time as is reasonably practicable he shall be guilty of an offence.

(3) It shall be for the accused to prove that he had reasonable cause for his failure to surrender to custody.

(4) A failure to give to a person granted bail in criminal proceedings a copy of the record of the decision shall not constitute a reasonable cause for that person's failure to surrender to custody.

(5) An offence under subs. (1) or (2) above shall be punishable either on summary conviction or as if it were a criminal contempt of court.

(6) Where a magistrates' court convicts a person of an offence under subss (1) or (2) above the court may, if it thinks—

(*a*)   that the circumstances of the offence are such that greater punishment should be inflicted for that offence than the court has power to inflict, or

(*b*)   in a case where it commits that person for trial to the Crown Court for another offence, that it would be appropriate for him to be dealt with for the offence under subss (1) or (2) above by the court before which he is tried for the other offence,

commit him in custody or on bail to the Crown Court for sentence.

(7) A person who is convicted summarily of an offence under subss (1) or (2) above and is not committed to the Crown Court for sentence shall be liable to imprisonment for a term not exceeding three months or to a fine not exceeding level 5 on the standard scale or to both and a person who is so committed for sentence or is dealt with as for such a contempt shall be liable to imprisonment for a term not exceeding 12 months or to a fine or to both.

(8) In any proceedings for an offence under subss (1) or (2) above a document purporting to be a copy of the part of the prescribed record which relates to the time and place appointed for the person specified in the record to surrender to

(9) For the purposes of subs (8) above—

(*a*)   "the prescribed record" means the record of the decision of the court, officer or constable made in pursuance of s. 5(1) of this Act;

(*b*)   the copy of the prescribed record is duly certified if it is certified by the appropriate officer of the court or, as the case may be, by the constable who took the decision or a constable designated for the purpose by the officer in charge of the police station from which the person to whom the record relates was released;

(*c*)   "the appropriate oficer" of the court is—

(i) in the case of a magistrates' court, the justices' clerk or such other officer as may be authorized by him to act for the purpose;

(ii) in the case of the Crown Court, such officer as may be

designated for the purpose in accordance with arrangements
made by the Lord Chancellor;
(iii) in the case of the High Court, such officer as may be
designated for the purpose in accordance with arrangements
made by the Lord Chancellor;
(iv) in the case of the Court of Appeal, the registrar of criminal
appeals or such other officer as may be authorized by him to act
for the purpose;
(v) in the case of the Courts-Martial Appeal Court, the registrar
or such other officer as may be authorized by him to act for the
purpose.

(as amended by the Criminal Justice Act 1982, ss. 38, 46).

COMMENTARY

This section makes it an offence for a bailed person to fail without reasonable cause to surrender to
custody at the time appointed (subs. (1)) or (if he had a reasonable cause for such failure) as soon as
reasonably practicable thereafter (subs. (2)). It is submitted that sub. (3) applies to a prosecution
under both subss (1) and (2) otherwise a subs. (2) prosecution would fail unless the prosecution could
prove reasonable cause for the defendant's failure to appear on the original date.

It is wrong for the clerk to the justices' to prosecute for an offence under this section, *per* Donaldson
J. in: *R.* v. *Gateshead Justices, ex parte Usher and Another* [1981] Crim. L.R. 491.

Although this offence may be dealt with *ab initio* at the Crown Court, it would, by virtue of subs.
(5), not be triable on indictment. It is not therefore an offence triable either way within the meaning of
the Interpretation Act 1978, sch. 1.

A magistrates' court has power in certain circumstances to commit an offender to the Crown Court
to be dealt with: subs. (6).

Subsection (1). In *R.* v. *Gateshead Justices, ex parte Usher and Another, supra* it was held that no
offence had been committed where the accused had arrived at court seven minutes late. It is submitted
that this decision may perhaps be viewed as special to its context.

Bail in criminal proceedings. Defined in s. 1 (1), *supra.*

Without reasonable cause. See subss (3) and (4).

Surrender to custody. Defined in s. 2(2), *supra.*

Subsection (4): Copy of the record. Presumably that referred to in subs. (4) of s. 5, *supra.* The
legislature appear to have taken the view that it was unnecessary to provide that a failure on the part of
the court to perform its duty under s.5(3) constitutes reasonable cause within the meaning of the
subs. (1).

Subsection (5). The purpose of the provision is to create swift and simple alternative remedies, either
by way of proceedings for a summary offence or by way of committal for what is to be treated as a
criminal contempt of court, without the necessity for more elaborate proceedings of a kind which
sometimes are necessary when questions of criminal contempt of court arise. It is designed to give a
court other than a magistrates' court, that is the Crown Court, power to deal with an offender as if he
had committed a criminal contempt of court, leaving the Crown Court to deal with him in whatever
way as the Crown Court could do if he were guilty of criminal contempt of court. In some cases it may
not be appropriate to deal with the offender summarily in this way, e.g. where there is a dispute
whether or not particular facts amounted to absconding; the judge might then direct that summary
proceedings should be begun before a magistrates' court, or he might think he could deal with the
matter adequately himself: *R.* v. *Harbax Singh* (1979) 143 J.P. 214.

An offence. Sufficient to activate a suspended sentence: *R.* v. *Tyson* [1979] 68 Cr. App. R.
314.

Subsection (6). The power to commit to the Crown Court for sentence otherwise than on a committal
for trial is confined to "the circumstances of the offence." The past record of the defendant, including
any previous failures to surrender to bail, would not appear to justify such a committal. Home Office
cir. 206/1977 dated November 18, 1977 comments: "The mode of trial procedure is designed to give
maximum flexibility, to take account of both the seriousness of the offence and the stage in the
proceedings at which it occurs: on occasions it will be better to deal with a relatively minor

infringement immediately after the person is rearrested; on other occasions it will be appropriate for sentence to be passed for the absconding offence at the same time as the main offence is finally disposed of."

There is nothing to prevent a defendant convicted summarily of an offence under this section being committed to the Crown Court to be dealt with (Criminal Justice Act 1967, s. 56.)

Subsection (7): Convicted. Partially defined in s. 2(1).

Level 5. That is, £1,000.

Liability to arrest for absconding or breaking conditions of bail

7. (1) If a person who has been released on bail in criminal proceedings and is under a duty to surrender into the custody of a court fails to surrender to custody at the time appointed for him to do so the court may issue a warrant for his arrest.

(2) If a person who has been released on bail in criminal proceedings absents himself from the court at any time after he has surrendered into the custody of the court and before the court is ready to begin or to resume the hearing of the proceedings, the court may issue a warrant for his arrest; but no warrant shall be issued under this subsection where that person is absent in accordance with leave given to him by or on behalf of the court.

(3) A person who has been released on bail in criminal proceedings and is under a duty to surrender into the custody of a court may be arrested without warrant by a constable—

(*a*)   if the constable has reasonable grounds for believing that that person is not likely to surrender to custody;

(*b*)   if the constable has reasonable grounds for believing that that person is likely to break any of the conditions of his bail or has reasonable grounds for suspecting that that person has broken any of those conditions; or

(*c*)   in a case where that person was released on bail with one or more surety or sureties, if a surety notifies a constable in writing that that person is unlikely to surrender to custody and that for that reason the surety wishes to be relieved of his obligations as a surety.

(4) A person arrested in pursuance of subs. (3) above—

(*a*)   shall, except where he was arrested within 24 hours of the time appointed for him to surrender to custody, be brought as soon as practicable and in any event within 24 hours after his arrest before a justice of the peace for the petty sessions area in which he was arrested; and

(*b*)   in the said excepted case shall be brought before the court at which he was to have surrendered to custody.

In reckoning for the purposes of this subsection any period of 24 hours, no account shall be taken of Christmas Day, Good Friday or any Sunday.

(5) A justice of the peace before whom a person is brought under subs. (4) above may, subject to subs. (6) below, if of the opinion that that person—

(*a*)   is not likely to surrender to custody, or

(*b*)   has broken or is likely to break any condition of his bail,

remand him in custody or commit him to custody, as the case may require, or alternatively, grant him bail subject to the same or to different conditions, but if not of that opinion shall grant him bail subject to the same conditions (if any) as were originally imposed.

(6) Where the person so brought before the justice is a child or young person and the justice does not grant him bail, subs. (5) above shall have effect subject to the provisions of s. 23 of the Children and Young Persons Act, 1969 (remands to the care of local authorities).

(*as amended by the Criminal Law Act 1977, sch. 12*).

COMMENTARY

Subsection (1): Bail in criminal proceedings. Defined in s. 1(1), *supra*.

Surrender to custody. Defined in s. 2(2), *supra*.

Warrant. No information is necessary.

Subsection (2). By absenting himself in this manner the accused is not committing an offence under s. 6.

Subsection (3): Constable. All members of a police force are, in law, constables.

Reasonable grounds for believing. By analogy these words should be read as "has reasonable grounds for believing and believes" c.f. *R.* v. *Banks.* (1916) 80 J.P. 432; *R.* v. *Harrison* [1938] 3 All E.R. 134.

The conditions of his bail. In this context this phrase appears to relate solely to requirements imposed under s. 3(6), *supra*.

Subsection (3)(c): Relieved of his obligations. But not, it is submitted, of the liability to have his recognizances estreated. *See* 143 J.P.N. 585. *See R. v. Ipswich Crown Court, ex parte Reddington* [1981] Crim. L.R. 618, noted under the Magistrates' Courts Act 1980, s. 20, *infra*.

Subsection (4)(a). The justice must cause a copy of the bail record to be sent to the clerk of the court: Magistrates' Courts Rules 1981, r. 92.

Subsection (5). Note that the power to remand only arises if the justice forms either opinion (a) or (b) or both. It does not require these matters to be proved and, while it is open to the parties to call evidence on these matters it is submitted that the justice can in a proper case form an opinion on the basis solely of representations made to him.

Commit him to custody. Defined in the Magistrates' Courts Act 1980, s. 150(1). For the place to which persons aged 17-20 years of age should be committed see the Criminal Justice Act 1948, s. 27. For the treatment of juveniles see subs. (6). Committals to custody must be by warrant: Magistrates' Courts Rules 1981, r. 94.

Subsection (6). A suggested procedure and specimen letter for the use of courts are contained in Home Office cir. 11/1978 dated February 17, 1978.

Child or young person. Defined in s. 2(2), *supra*.

Bail with sureties

8. (1) This section applies where a person is granted bail in criminal proceedings on condition that he provides one or more surety or sureties for the purpose of securing that he surrenders to custody.

(2) In considering the suitability for that purpose of a proposed surety, regard may be had (amongst other things) to—

  (*a*)   the surety's financial resources;
  (*b*)   his character and any previous convictions of his; and
  (*c*)   his proximity (whether in point of kinship, place of residence or otherwise) to the person for whom he is to be surety.

(3) Where a court grants a person bail in criminal proceedings on such a condition but is unable to release him because no surety or no suitable surety is available, the court shall fix the amount in which the surety is to be bound and subss (4) and (5) below, or in a case where the proposed surety resides in Scotland subs. (6) below, shall apply for the purpose of enabling the recognizance of the

surety to be entered into subsequently.

(4) Where this subsection applies the recognizance of the surety may be entered into before such of the following persons or descriptions of persons as the court may by order specify or if it makes no such order, before any of the following persons, that is to say—

(a)   where the decision is taken by a magistrates' court, before a justice of the peace, a justices' clerk or a police officer who either is of the rank of inspector or above or is in charge of a police station or, if magistrates' courts rules so provide, by a person of such other description as is specified in the rules;

(b)   where the decision is taken by the Crown Court, before any of the persons specified in para. (a) above or, if Crown Court rules so provide, by a person of such other description as is specified in the rules;

(c)   where the decision is taken by the High Court or the Court of Appeal, before any of the persons specified in para. (a) above or, if Supreme Court rules so provide, by a person of such other description as is specified in the rules;

(d)   where the decision is taken by the Courts-Martial Appeal Court, before any of the persons specified in paragraph (a) above or, if Courts-Martial Appeal rules so provide, by a person of such other description as is specified in the rules;

and Supreme Court rules, Crown Court rules, Courts-Martial Appeal rules or magistrates' courts rules may also prescribe the manner in which a recognizance which is to be entered into before such a person is to be entered into and the persons by whom and the manner in which the recognizance may be enforced.

(5) Where a surety seeks to enter into his recognizance before any person in accordance with subs. (4) above but that person declines to take his recognizance because he is not satisfied of the surety's suitability, the surety may apply to—

(a)   the court which fixed the amount of the recognizance in which the surety was to be bound, or

(b)   a magistrates' court for the petty sessions area in which he resides,

for that court to take his recognizance and that court shall, if satisfied of his suitability, take his recognizance.

(6) Where this subsection applies, the court, if satisfied of the suitability of the proposed surety, may direct that arrangements be made for the recognizance of the surety to be entered into in Scotland before any constable, within the meaning of the Police (Scotland) Act, 1967, having charge at any police office or station in like manner as the recognizance would be entered into in England or Wales.

(7) Where, in pursuance of subss (4) or (6) above, a recognizance is entered into otherwise than before the court that fixed the amount of the recognizance, the same consequences shall follow as if it had been entered into before that court.

COMMENTARY

Subsection (2): Among other things. For other factors which may be considered see the note "Sureties" in the introduction.

Subsection (3): Fix the amount. The court will supply a certificate of the amount and conditions of the recognizance or a statement of the requirement: Magistrates' Courts Rules 1981, r. 86(2).

Subsection (4). The effect of this is that in the absence of any special direction a recognizance of a surety may be taken before anyone in categories (a)-(d), but the court may reserve this function to any one or more of those categories. Presumably a court can also reserve this function to itself.

Magistrates' Courts Rules. See rr. 86-88, *infra*.

Subsection (6). Home Office cir. 11/1978 suggests the arrangements referred to.

Offence of agreeing to indemnify sureties in criminal proceedings

9. (1) If a person agrees with another to indemnify that other against any liability which that other may incur as a surety to secure the surrender to custody of a person accused or convicted of or under arrest for an offence, he and that other person shall be guilty of an offence.

(2) An offence under subs. (1) above is committed whether the agreement is made before or after the person to be indemnified becomes a surety and whether or not he becomes a surety and whether the agreement contemplates compensation in money or in money's worth.

(3) Where a magistrates' court convicts a person of an offence under subs. (1) above the court may, if it thinks—

(a) that the circumstances of the offence are such that greater punishment should be inflicted for that offence than the court has power to inflict, or

(b) in a case where it commits that person for trial to the Crown Court for another offence, that it would be appropriate for him to be dealt with for the offence under subs. (1) above by the court before which he is tried for the other offence,

commit him to custody or on bail to the Crown Court for sentence.

(4) A person guilty of an offence under subs. (1) above shall be liable—

(a) on summary conviction, to imprisonment for a term not exceeding three months or to a fine not exceeding £1,000 or to both; or

(b) on conviction on indictment or if sentenced by the Crown Court on committal for sentence under subs. (3) above, to imprisonment for a term not exceeding 12 months or to a fine or to both.

(5) No proceedings for an offence under subs. (1) above shall be instituted except by or with the consent of the Director of Public Prosecutions.

(as amended by the Magistrates' Courts Act 1980, s. 32(2).)

SCHEDULE 1

PERSONS ENTITLED TO BAIL: SUPPLEMENTARY PROVISIONS

PART I

DEFENDANTS ACCUSED OR CONVICTED OF IMPRISONABLE OFFENCES

Defendants to whom Part I applies

1. Where the offence or one of the offences of which the defendant is accused or convicted in the proceedings is punishable with imprisonment the following provisions of this Part of this schedule apply.

Exceptions to right to bail

2. The defendant need not be granted bail if the court is satisfied that there are substantial grounds for believing that the defendant, if released on bail (whether subject to conditions or not) would—

(*a*)   fail to surrender to custody, or
(*b*)   commit an offence while on bail, or
(*c*)   interfere with witnesses or otherwise obstruct the course of justice,
         whether in relation to himself or any other person.

3. The defendant need not be granted bail if the court is satisfied that the defendant should be kept in custody for his own protection or, if he is a child or young person, for his own welfare.

4. The defendant need not be granted bail if he is in custody in pursuance of the sentence of a court or of any authority acting under any of the Services Acts.

5. The defendant need not be granted bail where the court is satisfied that it has not been practicable to obtain sufficient information for the purpose of taking the decisions required by this Part of this schedule for want of time since the institution of the proceedings against him.

6. The defendant need not be granted bail if, having been released on bail in or in connexion with the proceedings for the offence, he has been arrested in pursuance of s. 7 of this Act.

Exception applicable only to defendant whose case is adjourned for inquiries or a report

7. Where his case is adjourned for inquiries or a report, the defendant need not be granted bail if it appears to the court that it would be impracticable to complete the inquiries or make the report without keeping the defendant in custody.

Restrictions of conditions of bail

8. (1) Subject to sub-para. (3) below, where the defendant is granted bail, no conditions shall be imposed under subss (4) to (7) of s. 3 of this Act unless it appears to the court that it is necessary to do so for the purposes of preventing the occurrence of any of the events mentioned in para. 2 of this Part of this schedule or, in the case of a condition under subs. (6)(*d*) of that section, that it is necessary to impose it to enable inquiries or a report to be made into the defendant's physical or mental condition.

(2) Sub-paragraph (1) above also applies on any application to the court to vary the conditions of bail or to impose conditions in respect of bail which has been granted unconditionally.

(3) The restriction imposed by sub-para. (1) above shall not operate to override the direction in s. 30(2) of the Magistrates' Courts Act, 1980 to a magistrates' court to impose conditions of bail under s. 3(6)(*d*) of this Act of the description specified in the said s. 30(2) in the circumstances so specified.

Decisions under para. 2

9. In taking the decisions required by para. 2 of this Part of this schedule, the court shall have regard to such of the following considerations as appear to it to be relevant, that is to say—

(*a*)   the nature and seriousness of the offence or default (and the probable method of dealing with the defendant for it),
(*b*)   the character, antecedents, associations and community ties of the defendant,
(*c*)   the defendant's record as respects the fulfilment of his obligations under previous grants of bail in criminal proceedings,
(*d*)   except in the case of a defendant whose case is adjourned for inquiries

or a report, the strength of the evidence of his having committed the offence or having defaulted,

as well as to any others which appear to be relevant.
(*as amended by the Magistrates' Courts Act 1980, sch. 7*).

COMMENTARY

In this schedule the term "defendant" means a person to whom s. 4 applies (s. 4(6)), that is to say someone who enjoys the general right to bail.

Paragraph 1: Punishable with imprisonment. See para. 1 of Part III, *infra*.

Paragraph 2. In taking a decision under this paragraph the court may have regard to the considerations referred to in para. 9.

See generally under "Exceptions to the General Right to Bail" in the introduction.

Paragraph 3: Kept in custody. Includes in the case of a juvenile in the care of a local authority: para. 3 of part III, *infra*.

His welfare. The court must in a proper case take steps for removing a juvenile from undesirable surroundings: Children and Young Persons Act 1933, s. 44.

Paragraph 4: Court. See para. 4 of Part III, *infra*.

Services Acts. See para. 4 of Part III, *infra*.

Paragraph 5: Sufficient information. Home Office cir. 155/1975 recommended a standardized procedure for the collection of this information. The Home Office working party on bail commented that the length of remands of this nature should be kept to the minimum necessary to enable the inquiries to be completed. A week's remand should not be ordered as a matter of course (para. 72). They recommended for this purpose greater use of remands in police custody under s. 128(7) of the Magistrates' Courts Act 1980.

Paragraph 6. Failures to surrender to custody in proceedings for earlier offences are evidence to support a refusal to bail under para. 2(a).

Paragraph 7. Unlike para. 5 (which deals with inquiries concerning the bail application) this paragraph appears to relate to inquiries after conviction under the Magistrates' Courts Act 1980, s. 10.

Paragraph 9. See "Factors to be Considered" in the introduction.

PART II

DEFENDANTS ACCUSED OR CONVICTED OF NON-IMPRISONABLE OFFENCES

Defendants to whom Part II applies

1. Where the offence or every offence of which the defendant is accused or convicted in the proceedings is one which is not punishable with imprisonment the following provisions of this Part of this schedule apply.

Exceptions to right to bail

2. The defendant need not be granted bail if—

    (*a*)   it appears to the court that, having been previously granted bail in criminal proceedings, he has failed to surrender to custody in accordance with his obligations under the grant of bail; and

    (*b*)   the court believes, in view of that failure, that the defendant, if released on bail (whether subject to conditions or not) would fail to surrender to custody.

3. The defendant need not be granted bail if the court is satisfied that the defendant should be kept in custody for his own protection or, if he is a child or young person, for his own welfare.

4. The defendant need not be granted bail if he is in custody in pursuance of the sentence of a court or of any authority acting under any of the Services Act.

5. The defendant need not be granted bail if, having been released on bail or in connexion with the proceedings for the offence, he has been arrested in pursuance of s. 7 of this Act.

COMMENTARY

In this schedule the term "the defendant" means a person to whom s. 4 of the Act applies by virtue of subs. (4), *ibid.*: subs. (6), *ibid.*, that is to say, a person who enjoys the general right to bail.

Paragraph 1: Punishable with imprisonment. See the note to para. 1 of Part I, *supra.*

Paragraph 2. Note that both (a) and (b) must be satisfied before bail may be refused. Condition (a) however is not restricted to absconsions in proceedings for the present offence.

Bail in criminal proceedings. Defined in s. 1(1), *supra.*.

Paragraph 3: In custody. In the case of a juvenile see para. 3 of Part III, *infra.*

Paragraph 4: The sentence of a court. This does not seemingly extend to a remand in custody for another offence nor to a commitment to prison in default of payment of a fine etc. *Cf.* Magistrates' Courts Act 1980, s. 150(1).

The Services Acts. Defined in para. 4 of Part III, *infra.*

PART III

Interpretation

1. For the purposes of this schedule the question whether an offence is one which is punishable with imprisonment shall be determined without regard to any enactment prohibiting or restricting the imprisonment of young offenders or first offenders.

2. References in this schedule to previous grants of bail in criminal proceedings include references to bail granted before the coming into force of this Act.

3. References in this schedule to a defendant's being kept in custody or being in custody include (where the defendant is a child or young person) references to his being kept or being in the care of a local authority in pursuance of a warrant of commitment under s. 23(1) of the Children and Young Persons Act, 1969.

4. In this schedule—

"court", in the expression "sentence of a court", includes a service court as defined in s. 12(1) of the Visiting Forces Act, 1952 and "sentence" in that expression, shall be construed in accordance with that definition;

"default", in relation to the defendant, means the default for which he is to be dealt with under s. 6 or s. 16 of the Powers of Criminal Courts Act, 1973;

"the Services Acts" means the Army Act, 1955, the Air Force Act, 1955 and the Naval Discipline Act, 1957.

THE MAGISTRATES' COURTS ACT 1980

Restriction on grant of bail in treason

41. A person charged with treason shall not be granted bail except by order of a judge of the High Court or the Secretary of State.

COMMENTARY

By order of a judge of the High Court. Such an order cannot be altered by magistrates: s. 119(3) of the Act.

Restriction on justices sitting after dealing with bail

42. (1) A justice of the peace shall not take part in trying the issue of an accused's guilt on the summary trial of an information if in the course of the same proceedings the justice has been informed, for the purpose of determining whether the accused shall be granted bail, that he has one or more previous convictions.

(2) For the purposes of this section any committal proceedings from which the proceedings on the summary trial arose shall be treated as part of the trial.

COMMENTARY

This is a mandatory provision, breach of which would give rise to an order of prohibition, *per* Lord Widgery CJ in *R. v. McLean, ex parte Aikens and Others* (1975) 139 J.P. 261 at p. 264.

Trying the issue of an accused's guilt on the summary trial of an information. Thus, this section does not operate to prevent a justice from dealing with subsequent remands, from sentencing a convicted offender, nor from acting as an examining justice.

Subsection (2). This deals with the situation where the court had begun to inquire into the information as examining justices and had then reverted to summary trial under s. 25 of the Act.

Committal proceedings. Defined in s. 150(1) of the Act.

Bail on arrest without warrant

43. (1) On a person's being taken into custody for an offence without a warrant, a police officer not below the rank of inspector, or the police officer in charge of the police station to which the person is brought, may, and, if it will not be practicable to bring him before a magistrates' court within 24 hours after his being taken into custody, shall, inquire into the case and, unless the offence appears to the officer to be a serious one, grant him bail in accordance with the Bail Act 1976 subject to a duty to appear before a magistrates' court at such time and place as the officer appoints.

(2) Where a person has been granted bail under subs. (1) above, the magistrates' court before which he is to appear may appoint a later time at which he is to appear and may enlarge the recognizances of any sureties for him to that time.

(3) Where, on a person's being taken into custody for an offence without a warrant, it appears to any such officer as aforesaid that the inquiry into the case cannot be completed forthwith, he may grant him bail in accordance with the Bail Act 1976 subject to a duty to appear at such a police station and at such a time as the officer appoints unless he previously receives a notice in writing from the officer in charge of that police station that his attendance is not required; and the recognizance of any surety for that person may be enforced before a magistrates' court for the petty sessions area in which the police station named in the recognizance is situated.

(4) Where a person is taken into custody for an offence without a warrant and is retained in custody, he shall be brought before a magistrates' court as soon as practicable.

COMMENTARY

This section does not contain a complete code laying down what is to follow after arrest. It deals with two cases: (i) where the inquiry at the police station discloses a case to be answered and (ii) where the inquiry cannot be completed forthwith. In cases where on inquiry at the police station it appears there is not sufficient ground on which to proceed further against the man he should be released forthwith: *Wiltshire* v. *Barrett* (1965) 129 J.P. 348.

Special rules apply to the bail or detention of arrested juveniles—*see* the Children and Young Persons Act 1969, s. 29.

Subsection (1): Taken into custody for an offence. An arrest without warrant under (what is now) s. 8(4) of the Road Traffic Act 1972 following a positive breathalyser test does not fall within this provision: *R.* v. *McKenzie* (1971) 135 J.P. 26. "Offence" includes an alleged offence: s. 150(5) of the Act.

Grant him bail. By the terms of subs. (6) of s. 3 of the Bail Act 1976 no requirements other than those in subss (4), (5) or (7), *ibid.* may be attached to bail granted by police.

Appear before a magistrates' court. To be construed as surrendering himself into the custody of the court: Bail Act 1976, s. 2(3).

Subsection (2). The court must give notice to the accused and his sureties: Magistrates' Courts Rules 1981, r. 91.

Subsection (3). Since a special provision, *viz* s. 129, *infra*, is necessary for further remands on bail ordered by a court, it must be doubted whether there is power in a police officer to bail an offender twice under this subsection.

Subsection (4): A magistrates' court. Means any justice or justices of the peace acting under any enactment or by virtue of his or their commission or under common law: s. 148(1) of the Act.

As soon as practicable. This means "as speedily as is reasonably possible". Those who arrest cannot bolster up their assurance or the strength of the case by seeking further evidence and detaining the man arrested meanwhile, but the fact that they delay to seek the advice of a senior official or do not take the most direct route is not necessarily conclusive of delay: *John Lewis and Co., Ltd* v. *Tims* (1952) 116 J.P. 275, (a civil action for false imprisonment). Costs were awarded against police in a civil action when a person arrested on Sunday was not brought before magistrates until Tuesday: 135 J.P.N. 767. While this provision must be strictly complied with the court has a discretion to admit confessions obtained from the accused while he was illegally held: *R.* v. *Houghton* [1979] 68 Cr. App. R. 197 (detention for purpose of finding out what had happened to missing money).

The remark of Donaldson LJ in *Re Sherman and Apps* (1981) 145 J.P. 337, that "save in a wholly exceptional case the period between arrest and appearance before a magistrates' court should not exceed 48 hours" was disapproved in *R.* v. *Malcherek and Steel* (1981) 145 J.P. 329.

Functions of magistrates' court where a person in custody is brought before it with a view to his appearance before the Crown Court

43A. (1) Where a person in custody in pursuance of a warrant issued by the Crown Court with a view to his appearance before the Crown Court is brought before a magistrates' court in pursuance of s. 81(5) of the Supreme Court Act 1981—

> (*a*) the magistrates' court shall commit him in custody or release him on bail until he can be brought or appear before the Crown Court at the time and place appointed by the Crown Court;
>
> (*b*) if the warrant is endorsed for bail, but the person in custody is unable to satisfy the conditions endorsed, the magistrates' court may vary those conditions, if satisfied that it is proper to do so.

(2) A magistrates' court shall have jurisdiction under subs. (1) whether or not the offence was committed, or the arrest was made, within the court's area. (*as inserted by the Supreme Court Act 1981, sch. 5*).

COMMENTARY

For the duties of the clerk to the justices *see* the Magistrates' Courts Rules 1981, r. 89, *infra*.

Taking of finger-prints

49. (1) Where any person not less than 14 years old—

    (*a*)   who has been taken into custody is charged with an offence before a magistrates' court; or

    (*b*)   appears before a magistrates' court in answer to a summons for an offence punishable with imprisonment,

the court may, if it thinks fit, on the application of a police officer not below the rank of inspector, order the finger-prints of that person to be taken by a constable.

(2) Finger-prints taken in pursuance of an order under this section shall be taken either at the place where the court is sitting or, if the person to whom the order relates is remanded in custody, at any place to which he is committed; and a constable may use such reasonable force as may be necessary for that purpose.

(3) The provisions of this section shall be in addition to those of any other enactment under which finger-prints may be taken.

(4) Where the finger-prints of any person have been taken in pursuance of an order under this section, then, if he is acquitted, or the examining justices determine not to commit him for trial, or if the information against him is dismissed, the finger-prints and all copies and records of them shall be destroyed.

(5) In this section "finger-prints" includes palm-prints.

COMMENTARY

See under Finger-Print Orders in the introduction.

Subsection (1): Not less than 14 years old. For the determination of age *see* s. 150(4) of the Act.

A magistrates' court. Means any justice or justices of the peace acting under any enactment or by virtue of his or their commission or under the common law: s. 148(1) of the Act.

Order. *See* form 11.

Subsection (2). Fingerprints may be taken by an order under this section only at the places mentioned in this subsection. Thus where an accused is bailed her finger-prints may not be taken under this section at the police station: *R. v. Jones* (1978) *The Times*, February 6; [1978] R.T.R. 137.

Postponement of taking recognizance

119. (1) Where a magistrates' court has power to take any recognizance, the court may, instead of taking it, fix the amount in which the principal and his sureties, if any, are to be bound; and thereafter the recognizance may be taken by any such person as may be prescribed.

(2) Where, in pursuance of this section, a recognizance is entered into otherwise than before the court that fixed the amount of it, the same consequences shall follow as if it had been entered into before that court; and references in this or any other Act to the court before which a recognizance was entered into shall be construed accordingly.

(3) Nothing in this section shall enable a magistrates' court to alter the amount of a recognizance fixed by the High Court or the Crown Court.

(as amended by the Criminal Justice Act 1982, sch. 14.)

COMMENTARY

Subsection (1): Such person as may be prescribed. In the Magistrates' Courts Rules 1981, r. 86(1).

Forfeiture of recognizance

120. (1) Where a recognizance to keep the peace or to be of good behaviour has been entered into before a magistrates' court or any recognizance is conditioned for the appearance of a person before a magistrates' court or for his doing any other thing connected with a proceeding before a magistrates' court, and the recognizance appears to the court to be forfeited, the court may, subject to subs. (2) below, declare the recognizance to be forfeited and adjudge the persons bound thereby, whether as principal or sureties, or any of them, to pay the sum in which they are respectively bound.

(2) . . .

(3) The court which declares the recognizance to be forfeited may, instead of adjudging any person to pay the whole sum in which he is bound, adjudge him to pay part only of the sum or remit the sum.

(4) Payment of any sum adjudged to be paid under this section, including any costs awarded against the defendant, may be enforced, and any such sum be applied, as if it were a fine and as if the adjudication were a summary conviction of an offence not punishable with imprisonment and so much of s. 85(1) above as empowers a court to remit fines shall not apply to the sum but so much thereof as relates to remission after a term of imprisonment has been imposed shall so apply; but at any time before the issue of a warrant of commitment to enforce payment of the sum, or before the sale of goods under a warrant of distress to satisfy the sum, the court may remit the whole or any part of the sum either absolutely or on such conditions as the court thinks just.

(5) A recognizance such as is mentioned in this section shall not be enforced otherwise than in accordance with this section, and accordingly shall not be transmitted to the Crown Court nor shall its forfeiture be certified to that Court.

COMMENTARY

Subsection (1): Any recognizance . . . conditioned for the appearance of a person before a magistrates' court. That is under the Magistrates' Courts Act 1980, s. 43 and the Children and Young Persons Act 1969, s. 29 (bail by police) or the Magistrates' Courts Act 1980, ss 128, 129, the Criminal Justice Act 1967, s. 23 and the Courts Act 1971, s. 13 (bail by the court).

Forfeited. *See* under Forfeiture of the Recognizance in the introduction.

Subsection (4): Enforced as if it were a fine. Notice must be given to the defendant if he is absent or time to pay is allowed: r. 46, Magistrates' Courts Rules 1981.

An order of discharge in bankruptcy does not release the debt on the recognizance: Bankruptcy Act, 1914, s. 28(1)(a).

Remit. Recognizances estreated by the Crown Court may not be remitted by magistrates except with the permission of that court: Criminal Justice Act 1967, s. 47(8). Any order of remission must be entered in the register or separate record: Magistrates' Courts Rules 1981, r. 65.

Remand in custody or on bail

128. (1) Where a magistrates' court has power to remand any person, then, subject to s. 4 of the Bail Act 1976 and to any other enactment modifying that power, the court may—

    (a)   remand him in custody, that is to say, commit him to custody to be brought before the court subject to subs. (3A) below at the end of the period of remand or at such earlier time as the court may require; or

    (b)   where it is inquiring into or trying an offence alleged to have been committed by that person or has convicted him of an offence, remand him on bail in accordance with the Bail Act 1976, that is to say, by directing him to appear as provided in subs. (4) below; or

(*c*)   except in a case falling within para. (*b*) above, remand him on bail by taking from him a recognizance (with or without sureties) conditioned as provided in this subsection;

and may, in a case falling within para. (*c*) above, instead of taking recognizances in accordance with that paragraph, fix the amount of the recognizances with a view to their being taken subsequently in accordance with s. 119 above.

(1A) Where—

(*a*)   on adjourning a case under ss. 5, 10(1) or 18(4) above the court proposes to remand or further remand a person in custody; and

(*b*)   he is before the court; and

(*c*)   he has attained the age of 17; and

(*d*)   he is legally represented in that court,

it shall be the duty of the court—

(i)   to explain the effect of subss. (3A) and (3B) below to him in ordinary language; and

(ii)   to inform him in ordinary language that, notwithstanding the procedure for a remand without his being brought before a court, he would be brought before a court for the hearing and determination of at least every fourth application for his remand, and of every application for his remand heard at a time when it appeared to the court that he had no solicitor acting for him in the case.

(1B) For the purposes of subs. (1A) above a person is to be treated as legally represented in a court if, but only if, he has the assistance of counsel or a solicitor to represent him in the proceedings in that court.

(1C) After explaining to an accused as provided by subs. (1A) above the court shall ask him whether he consents to the hearing and determination of such applications in his absence.

(2) Where the court fixes the amount of a recognizance under subs. (1) above or s. 8(3) of the Bail Act 1976 with a view to its being taken subsequently the court shall in the meantime commit the person so remanded to custody in accordance with para. (*a*) of the said subs. (1).

(3) Where a person is brought before the court after remand, the court may further remand him.

(3A) Subject to subs. (3B) below, where a person has been remanded in custody, the court may further remand him on an adjournment under ss. 5, 10(1) or 18(4) above without his being brought before it if it is satisfied—

(*a*)   that he gave his consent, either in response to a question under subs. (1C) above or otherwise, to the hearing and determination in his absence of any application for his remand on an adjournment of the case under any of those provisions; and

(*b*)   that he has not by virtue of this subsection been remanded without being brought before the court on more than two such applications immediately preceding the application which the court is hearing; and

(*c*)   that he had attained the age of 17 years when he gave his consent to the hearing and determination of such applications in his absence; and

(*d*)   that he has not withdrawn his consent to their being so heard and determined.

(3B) The court may not exercise the power conferred by subs. (3A) above if it appears to the court on an application for a further remand being made to it, that the person to whom the application relates has no solicitor acting for him in the case (whether present in court or not).

(3C) Where—

    (a)   a person has been remanded in custody on an adjournment of a case under ss. 5, 10(1) or 18(4) above; and

    (b)   an application is subsequently made for his further remand on such an adjournment; and

    (c)   he is not brought before the court which hears and determines the application; and

    (d)   that court is not satisfied as mentioned in subs. (3A) above,

the court shall adjourn the case and remand him in custody for the period for which it stands adjourned.

(3D) An adjournment under subs. (3C) above shall be for the shortest period that appears to the court to make it possible for the accused to be brought before it.

(3E) Where—

    (a)   on an adjournment of a case under ss. 5, 10(1) or 18(4) above a person has been remanded in custody without being brought before the court; and

    (b)   it subsequently appears—

        (i)   to the court which remanded him in custody; or

        (ii)   to an alternate magistrates' court to which he is remanded under s. 130 below,

that he ought not to have been remanded in custody in his absence, the court shall require him to be brought before it at the earliest time that appears to the court to be possible.

(4) Where a person is remanded on bail under subs. (1) above the court may, where it remands him on bail in accordance with the Bail Act 1976 direct him to appear or, in any other case, direct that his recognizance be conditioned for his appearance—

    (a)   before that court at the end of the period of remand; or

    (b)   at every time and place to which during the course of the proceedings the hearing may be from time to time adjourned;

and, where it remands him on bail conditionally on his providing a surety during an inquiry into an offence alleged to have been committed by him, may direct that the recognizance of the surety be conditioned to secure that the person so bailed appears—

    (c)   at every time and place to which during the course of the proceedings the hearing may be from time to time adjourned and also before the Crown Court in the event of the person so bailed being committed for trial there.

(5) Where a person is directed to appear or a recognizance is conditioned for a person's appearance in accordance with para. (b) or (c) of subs. (4) above, the fixing at any time of the time for him next to appear shall be deemed to be a remand; but nothing in this subsection or subs. (4) above shall deprive the court of power at any subsequent hearing to remand him afresh.

(6) Subject to the provisions of s. 129 below, a magistrates' court shall not remand a person for a period exceeding eight clear days, except that—

    (a)   if the court remands him on bail, it may remand him for a longer period if he and the other party consent;

(*b*) where the court adjourns a trial under ss 10(3) or 30 above, the court may remand him for the period of the adjournment;

(*c*) where a person is charged with an offence triable either way, then, if it falls to the court to try the case summarily but the court is not at the time so constituted, and sitting in such a place, as will enable it to proceed with the trial, the court may remand him until the next occasion on which it will be practicable for the court to be so constituted, and to sit in such a place, as aforesaid, notwithstanding that the remand is for a period exceeding eight clear days.

(7) A magistrates' court having power to remand a person in custody may, if the remand is for a period not exceeding three clear days, commit him to the custody of a constable.

(as amended by the Criminal Justice Act 1982, sch. 9.)

COMMENTARY

Subsection (1): Power to remand any person. For example, during committal proceedings (s. 5(1) of the Act), summary trial (s. 10(3) of the Act) and for medical reports (s. 30(1) of the Act).

In custody. It is not necessary for sworn "evidence of arrest" to be given before remanding in custody: *R.* v. *Guest, ex parte Metropolitan Police Commissioner* (1962) 126 J.P. 21.

The committal must be by warrant: Magistrates' Courts Rules, 1981, r. 94. For the contents of the warrant *see* r. 97, *ibid.* For the place to which persons aged 17-20 years of age should be remanded in custody *see* the Criminal Justice Act 1948, s. 27. For the remand of juveniles otherwise than on bail *see* the Children and Young Persons Act 1969, s. 23, *supra.*

Such earlier time. This allows a defendant to be brought back earlier than the remand date if the court so orders. Home Office circ. 107/1971 dated May 14, 1971 recommends that this power should be used where reports after conviction are available earlier than the remand date. *See* also circ. 116/1972 dated June 16, 1972.

A recognizance. A recognizance may not be required of the defendant himself in criminal proceedings: Bail Act 1976, s. 3(3).

Subsection (3): Further remand. There is power to remand further in the absence of the defendant under s. 129, *infra.* The justices' clerk may order such remands on bail: Justices' Clerks Rules 1970. When a transfer direction has been made by the Secretary of State the managers of the hospital must be notified in writing of any further remand: Magistrates' Courts Rules 1981, r. 26.

Subsection (3A). Where the court is satisfied under this subsection the power to further remand is adapted in accordance with s. 130(4A), *infra.*

Subsection (4): Appear . . . before that court. To be construed as referring to surrendering himself into the custody of the court: Bail Act 1976, s. 2(3).

Every time and place. Such a remand is sometimes described as continuous bail and avoids the need for sureties attending at each remand.

Subsection (5): Remand afresh. Thus a court is empowered to fix different terms of remand at an adjourned hearing despite the fact that the defendant is on "continuous bail."

Subsection (6). This subsection does not apply to further remands arising from illness or accident: s. 129, *infra.* When the accused is committed to custody in default of sureties the warrant must direct production at the end of eight clear days or sooner unless the sureties enter into their recognizances: Magistrates' Courts Rules 1981, r. 23. For the power to remand in custody up to 28 days where the accused is serving a custodial sentence, see s. 131, *infra.*

Eight clear days. That is, disregarding the day of remand and the day of the adjourned hearing.

Exception (b). Both these sections are subject to their own time limits.

Exception (c). This proviso is appropriate where a single magistrate sits to deal with the mode of trial procedure.

Offence triable either way. Defined in the Interpretation Act 1978, sch. 1.

Subsection (7). A warrant is required by r. 94 of the Magistrates' Courts Rules 1981, *see* form 5.

Three clear days. That is, disregarding the day of remand and the day of the adjourned hearing. This subsection has effect in relation to a juvenile as if for the reference to three clear days there were substituted a reference to twenty four hours: Children and Young Persons Act 1969, s. 23(5).

Further remand

129. (1) If a magistrates' court is satisfied that any person who has been remanded is unable by reason of illness or accident to appear or be brought before the court at the expiration of the period for which he was remanded, the court may, in his absence, remand him for a further time; and s. 128(6) above shall not apply.

(2) Notwithstanding anything in s. 128(1) above, the power of a court under subs. (1) above to remand a person on bail for a further time—

> (a) where he was granted bail in criminal proceedings, includes power to enlarge the recognizance of any surety for him to a later time;
>
> (b) where he was granted bail otherwise than in criminal proceedings, may be exercised by enlarging his recognizance and those of any sureties for him to a later time.

(3) Where a person remanded on bail is bound to appear before a magistrates' court at any time and the court has no power to remand him under subs. (1) above, the court may in his absence—

> (a) where he was granted bail in criminal proceedings, appoint a later time as the time at which he is to appear and enlarge the recognizances of any sureties for him to that time;
>
> (b) where he was granted bail otherwise than in criminal proceedings, enlarge his recognizance and those of any sureties for him to a later time;

and the appointment of the time or the enlargement of his recognizance shall be deemed to be a further remand.

(4) Where a magistrates' court commits a person for trial on bail and the recognizance of any surety for him has been conditioned in accordance with para. (a) of subs. (4) of s. 128 above the court may, in the absence of the surety enlarge his recognizance so that he is bound to secure that the person so committed for trial appears also before the Crown Court.

COMMENTARY

This is an unnecessarily confusing section. Subsection (1) gives power to remand for a further time persons unable to appear through illness or accident. Subsection (2) gives the court the option in such circumstances to enlarge the recognizance of any surety, while subs. (3) gives a general power to appoint a later date for the appearance of the accused and to enlarge the recognizances of his sureties where the non-appearance is due to circumstances other than illness or accident. Subsection (1) is not subject to the general prohibition (and exceptions) against remands for more than eight clear days contained in s. 128(6). Subsection (1) applies to remands on bail and in custody, subss (2) and (3) to remands on bail only.

Subsection (1): A magistrates' court. The clerk to justices may order the further adjournment of criminal proceedings with the consent of the prosecutor and the accused if, but only if, . . . (b) the accused, having been remanded on bail on the previous adjournment, is remanded on bail on the like terms and conditions. When the clerk adjourns proceedings under this rule he may also remand the accused on bail in pursuance of (b) above: The Justices' Clerks Rules 1970. Remands under this rule may be ordered by the clerk in the absence of the defendant under subss (2) or (3) above. The clerk may not fix bail in the first instance, strangely enough, even when the defendant has been bailed by police under s. 43(1) of the Act.

Accident. The first definitions in the *Concise Oxford Dictionary* are: "Event without apparent cause, unexpected, unforeseen course of events." It has been held in Northern Ireland that an industrial dispute cannot constitute an "accident" for the purpose of similarly phrased legislations: 143 J.P.N. 23.

Remand . . . for a further time. *See* form 10. Notice must be given to the accused and his sureties under the Magistrates' Courts Rules 1981, r. 91.

Subsection (4): Enlarging his recognizance. Notice must be given to the surety: Magistrates' Courts Rudes 1981, r. 84.

Transfer of remand hearings

130. (1) A magistrates' court adjourning a case under ss. 5, 10(1) or 18(4) above, and remanding the accused in custody may, if he has attained the age of 17, order that he be brought up for any subsequent remands before an alternate magistrates' court nearer to the prison where he is to be confined while on remand.

(2) The order shall require the accused to be brought before the alternate court at the end of the period of remand or at such earlier time as the alternate court may require.

(3) While the order is in force, the alternate court shall, to the exclusion of the court which made the order, have all the powers in relation to further remand (whether in custody or on bail) and the grant of legal aid which that court would have had but for the order.

(4) The alternate court may, on remanding the accused in custody, require him to be brought before the court which made the order at the end of the period of remand or at such earlier time as that court may require; and, if the alternate court does so, or the accused is released on bail, the order under subs (1) above shall cease to be inforce.

(4A) Where a magistrates' court is satisfied as mentioned in s. 128(3A) above–
- (*a*)   subs. (1) above shall have effect as if for the words "he be brought up for any subsequent remands before" there were substituted the words "applications for any subsequent remands be made to";
- (*b*)   subs. (2) above shall have effect as if for the words "the accused to be brought before" there were substituted the words "an application for a further remand to be made to"; and
- (*c*)   subs. (4) above shall have effect as if for the words "him to be brought before" there were substituted the words "an application for a further remand to be made to".

(5) Schedule 5 to this Act shall have effect to supplement this section.

(as amended by the Criminal Justice Act 1982, sch. 9.)

COMMENTARY

This section must be read in conjunction with sch. 5 *infra*.

   The Home Office advise that the cases in which transfer under this provision seem likely to provide positive advantages are those where bail is not likely to be granted, when several remands in custody are likely to be necessary before trial or committal, and transport to and from the prison:

   (1)   is likely to involve a significant security risk; in the main, these are likely to involve prisoners who are provisionally in category A (a category A prisoner is one whose escape would be highly dangerous to the public, the police or the security of the state): or

128   3. BAIL

(2)   when the journey between the original magistrates' court and the prison or remand centre is particularly lengthy or in some other way inconvenient. (When, however, the original magistrates' court is on or close to the route of a daily prison van to a Crown Court centre, this consideration is less likely to apply). (Home Office cir. dated July 10, 1978).

The consent of the accused is not necessary.
For the documents to be sent to the alternate court *see* the Magistrates' Courts Rules 1981, r. 25.

Remand of accused already in custody

131. (1) When a magistrates' court remands an accused person in custody and he is already detained under a custodial sentence, the period for which he is remanded may be up to 28 clear days.

(2) But the court shall inquire as to the expected date of his release from that detention; and if it appears that it will be before 28 clear days have expired, he shall not be remanded in custody for more than eight clear days or (if longer) a period ending with that date.

(3) (Repealed)
(as amended by the Criminal Justice Act 1982, sch. 9, 16.)

COMMENTARY

The practice of remanding a sentenced prisoner on "notional bail" in order to avoid the need to have him produced to court every eight days for a further remand in custody was criticized by the Chief Inspector of the Prison Service in his report of March, 1977, on the escape of William Thomas Hughes on the grounds that not only does it involve a legal fiction but it may also mislead people into thinking that the court has a real intention of granting bail at the end of the custodial sentence. This provision avoids the need to use notional bail in these circumstances.

Subsection (1): A custodial sentence. And not a mere remand.

28 clear days. That is, disregarding the day of the remand and the day of the adjourned hearing.

SCHEDULE 5

Section 130

TRANSFER OF REMAND HEARINGS

1. A court which, on adjourning a case, makes an order under s. 130(1) of this Act is not required at that time to fix the time and place at which the case is to be resumed but shall do so as soon as practicable after the order ceases to be in force.
2. Where an order under subs. (1) of s. 130 of this Act is made in the course of proceedings which, for the purpose of s. 8 of this Act, are committal proceedings, proceedings relating to the accused before the alternate court are also committal proceedings for these purposes.
3. A court making an order under subs. (1) of s. 130 of this Act or remanding the accused under subs. (4) shall at once notify the terms of the order or remand to the court before which the accused is to be brought for the hearing on any application for a subsequent remand or, as the case may be, before which any such application is to be made without his being brought before it.
4. A person to whom an order under s. 130(1) of this Act applies shall, if released on bail, be bailed to appear before the court which made the order.
5. Section 130 of this Act and this schedule have effect notwithstanding anything in ss. 5, 10 or 18(4) of this Act.

(as amended by the Criminal Justice Act 1982, sch. 9).

3.　BAIL　　　　　　　　　　　　　　　129

COMMENTARY

The memorandum accompanying Home Office cir. 39/1978 dated March 31 1978 comments on the paragraphs of this schedule as follows:

"1. When a magistrates' court adjourns a case and makes an order under s. 130 it will have to specify a date on which the accused is to be brought up before the alternate court (subject to the alternate court specifying an earlier date). The first court is not, however, required, when making the order, to fix the date and time on which the case will be resumed before it—indeed it would seldom know at that stage when the case would be ready to proceed. Instead, it is required to fix a date for resumption as soon as possible after the order ceases to be in force (which occurs either when the accused is remanded back to the alternate court or when the accused is released on bail).

"2. The effect of para. 2 of (sch. 5) is that when an order under (s. 130) is made in the course of proceedings for such an offence, the provisions of (s. 8 of the Act) will apply equally to proceedings before the alternate court. Thus if an order lifting those restrictions has been made by the original court that order will continue to have effect during the proceedings before the alternate court; similarly if no such order has been made when the case is transferred, the reporting restrictions will continue in force at the alternate court unless the accused applies to the alternate court to have them lifted.

"3.When remand hearings are transferred to or from the alternate court, under (ss 130 (1) and (4)) respectively, the court making the transfer must notify the court before which the defendant will next appear.

"4. When a person is *released* on bail the transfer order ceases to have effect by virtue of (s. 130(4)). The order granting bail must therefore require him to surrender to the custody of the court which made the transfer order and not the alternate court. Where the alternate court *grants* bail for surrender to the original court but commits the defendant to custody until he complies with pre-release conditions, he is to be produced to the alternate court after eight days if he has been unable to comply with those conditions and is consequently still in custody. He returns to the jurisdiction of the original court only after his release on bail (or on transfer back by the alternate court).

"5. This paragraph contains a saving for (s. 130) from specified enactments which require that a person who is remanded on an adjournment must be brought back before the same court at the end of the period of remand."

THE SUPREME COURT ACT 1981

Bail

81. (1) The Crown Court may grant bail to any person–
- (*a*) who has been committed for appearance before the Crown Court; or
- (*b*) who is in custody, pursuant to a sentence imposed by a magistrates' court, and who has appealed to the Crown Court against his conviction or sentence; or
- (*c*) who is in the custody of the Crown Court pending the disposal of his case by that court; or
- (*d*) who, after the decision of his case by the Crown Court, has applied to that court for the statement of a case for the High Court on that decision; or
- (*e*) who has applied to the High Court for an order of certiorari to remove proceedings in the Crown Court in his case into the High Court, or has applied to the High Court for leave to make such an application;
- (*f*) to whom the Crown Court has granted a certificate under ss. 1(2) or 11(1A) of the Criminal Appeal Act 1968 or under subs. (1B) below; or
- (*g*) who has been remanded in custody by a magistrates' court on adjourning a case under–
  - (i)   s. 5 (adjournment of inquiry into offence);
  - (ii) s. 10 (adjournment of trial);
  - (iii) s. 18 (initial procedure on information against adult for offence triable either way);
  - (iv) s. 30 (remand for medical examination) of the Magistrates'

Courts Act 1980; and the time during which a person is released on bail under any provision of this subsection shall not count as part of any term of imprisonment or detention under his sentence.

(1A) – (1G) . . .

(1H) Where the Crown Court grants a person bail under subs. 1(g) it may direct him to appear at a time and place which the magistrates' court could have directed and the recognizance of any surety shall be conditioned accordingly.
(1J) The Crown Court may only grant bail to a person under subs. (1)(g) if the magistrates' court which remanded him in custody has certified under s. 5(6A) of the Bail Act 1976 that it heard full argument on his application for bail before it refused the application.

(2) (Rules)

(3) Any reference in any enactment to a recognizance shall include, unless the context otherwise requires, a reference to any other description of security given instead of a recognizance, whether in pursuance of subs. (2)(a) or otherwise.
(4) The Crown Court, on issuing a warrant for the arrest of any person, may endorse the warrant for bail, and in any such case–
- (*a*) the person arrested under the warrant shall, unless the Crown Court otherwise directs, be taken to a police station; and
- (*b*) the officer in charge of the station shall release him for custody if

he, and any sureties required by the endorsement and approved by
the officer, enter into recognizance of such amount as may be fixed
by the endorsement:

Provided that in the case of bail in criminal proceedings (within the
meaning of the Bail Act 1976) the person arrested shall not be required to
enter into a recognizance.

(5) A person in custody in pursuance of a warrant issued by the Crown
Court with a view to his appearance before that court shall be brought forthwith before either the Crown Court or a magistrates' court.

(6) A magistrates' court shall have jurisdiction, and a justice of the peace
may act, under or in pursuance of rules under subs. (2) whether or not the
offence was committed, or the arrest was made, within the court's area, or
the area for which he was appointed.

(as amended by the Criminal Justice Act 1982, ss. 29, 60.)

COMMENTARY

The procedure for an application under this section is dealt with in the *Practice Direction*
[1983] 77 Cr. App. R. 69.

Subsection (4). A person arrested in pursuance of this subsection and brought before a
magistrates' court must be dealt with in accordance with the Magistrates' Courts Act 1980,
s. 43A, *supra.*

THE CERTIFICATES OF UNRULY CHARACTER (CONDITIONS) ORDER 1977

S.I. 1977 No. 1037

2. *(1) In this Order—*

"appropriate local authority" means the local authority in whose area the court is sitting or the young person resides.
"court" includes a justice; and
"local authority" means the council of a county (other than a metropolitan county), a metropolitan district or a London borough, or the Common Council of the City of London.
"young person" means a person who has attained the age of 14 and is under the age of 17.

(2) The Interpretation Act [1978] shall apply to the interpretation of this Order as it applies to the interpretation of an Act of Parliament.

3. *The court shall not certify under s. 22(5) or s. 23(2) or (3) of the Children and Young Persons Act 1969 (committals to remand centres or prisons) that a young person is of so unruly a character that he cannot safely be committed to the care of a local authority unless one or more of the following conditions is satisfied in relation to him—*

    (a)   *the young person is charged with an offence punishable in the case of an adult with imprisonment for 14 years or more, and—*

        (i) the court is remanding him for the first time in the proceedings and is satisfied that there has not been time to obtain a written report from the appropriate local authority on the availability of suitable accommodation for him in a community home, or
        (ii) the court is satisfied on the basis of such a report that no suitable accommodation is available for him in a community home where he could be accommodated without substantial risk to himself or others;

    (b)   *the young person is charged with an offence of violence or has been found guilty on a previous occasion of an offence of violence, and—*

        (i) the court is remanding him for the first tme in the proceedings and is satisfied that there has not been time to obtain a written report from the appropriate local authority on the availability of suitable accommodation for him in a community home, or
        (ii) the court is satisfied on the basis of such a report that no suitable accommodation is available for him in a community home where he could be accommodated without substantial risk to himself or others;

    (c)   *the young person has persistently absconded from a community home or, while accommodated in a community home, has seriously disrupted the running of the home, and the court is satisfied on the basis of a written report from the appropriate local authority that accommodation cannot be found for him in a suitable community home where he could be accommodated without risk of his absconding or seriously disrupting the running of the home.*

COMMENTARY

"The Secretaries of State suggest that where the court is satisfied that a young person before it cannot properly be released on bail, and where it has reason to think that it might not be appropriate to commit him to the care of the local authority under s. 23(1) of the Children and Young Persons Act 1969, the court will wish to make such inquiries as it thinks relevant concerning the previous history of the young person in respect of the matters mentioned in the prescribed conditions; that is, whether he has any previous findings of guilt for offences of violence, or a history of absconding from local authority care or of particularly disruptive behaviour while in such care. The court may also consider it a matter of good practice to state the grounds on which it is proposed to issue the certificate and give the young person and his parents (if present) or legal adviser an opportunity to address the court.": Home Office circ. 91/1977 dated June 29, 1977.

THE MAGISTRATES' COURTS RULES 1981

S.I. 1981 No. 552

Remand on bail for more than eight days where sureties have not entered into recognizances

23. *Where the court, with a view to a person's being remanded on bail under para. (a) of s. 128(6) of the Act of 1980 for a period exceeding eight days, has fixed the amount of the recognizances to be taken for that purpose but commits that person to custody because the recognizances of the sureties have not yet been taken, the warrant of commitment shall direct the governor or keeper of the prison or place to which he is committed to bring him before the court at the end of eight clear days or at such earlier time as may be specified in the warrant, unless in the meantime the sureties have entered into their recognizances.*

Transfer of remand hearings

25. *(1) Where a magistrates' court, under s. 130(1) of the Act of 1980, orders that an accused who has been remanded in custody be brought up for any subsequent remands before an alternate magistrates' court, the clerk of the first-mentioned court shall, as soon as practicable after the making of the order and in any case within two days thereafter (not counting Sundays, Good Friday, Christmas Day or bank holidays), send to the clerk of the alternate court—*

> *(a) a statement indicating the offence or offences charged;*
> *(b) a copy of the record made by the first-mentioned court in pursuance of s. 5 of the Bail Act 1976 relating to the withholding of bail in respect of the accused when he was last remanded in custody;*
> *(c) a copy of any legal aid order previously made in the same case;*
> *(d) a copy of any legal aid application;*
> *(ee) a copy of any contribution order previously made in the case under s. 7 of the Legal Aid Act 1982.*
> *(f) if the first-mentioned court has made an order under s. 8(2) of the Act of 1980 (removal of restrictions on reports of committal proceedings), a statement to that effect;*
> *(g) a statement whether or not the accused has a solicitor acting for him in the case and has consented to the hearing and determination in his absence of any application for his remand on an adjournment of the case under ss. 5, 10(1) and 18(4) of the Act of 1980 together with a statement indicating whether or not that consent has been withdrawn;*
> *(h) a statement indicating the occasions, if any, on which the accused has been remanded under s. 128(3A) of the Act of 1980 without being brought before the first-mentioned court.*

(1A) Where the first-mentioned court is satisfied as mentioned in s. 128(3A) of the Act of 1980, para. (1) shall have effect as if for the words "an accused who has been remanded in custody be brought up for any subsequent remands before" there were substituted the words "applications for any subsequent remands of the accused be made to".

(2) The clerk of an alternate magistrates' court before which an accused who has been remanded in custody is brought up for any subsequent remands in pursuance of an order made as aforesaid shall, as soon as practicable after the order ceases to be in force and in any case within two days thereafter (not counting Sundays, Good Friday, Christmas Day or bank holidays), send to the clerk of the magistrates' court which made the order—

(a) the documents referred to in sub-paras (c), (d) and (e) of para. (1);

(b) a copy of the record made by the alternate court in pursuance of s. 5 of the Bail Act 1976 relating to the grant or withholding of bail in respect of the accused when he was last remanded in custody or on bail;

(c) a copy of any legal aid order made by the alternate court;

(d) a copy of any legal aid application made to the alternate court;

(e) any statement of means submitted to the alternate court; and

(ee) a copy of any contribution order made in the case by the alternate court under s. 7 of the Legal Aid Act 1982;

(f) if the first-mentioned court has made an order under s. 8(2) of the Act of 1980 (removal of restrictions on reports of committal proceedings), a statement to that effect.

(g) a statement indicating whether or not the accused has a solicitor acting for him in the case and has consented to the hearing and determination in his absence of any application for his remand on an adjournment of the case under ss. 5, 10(1) and 18(4) of the Act of 1980 together with a statement indicating whether or not that consent has been withdrawn;

(h) a statement indicating the occasions, if any, on which the accused has been remanded by the alternate court under s. 128(3A) of the Act of 1980 without being brought before that court.

(2A) Where the alternate court is satisfied as mentioned in s. 128(3A) of the Act of 1980 para. (2) shall have effect as if for the words "an accused who has been remanded in custody is brought up for any subsequent remands" there shall be substituted the words "applications for the further remand of the accused are to be made".

Notice of further remand in certain cases

26. Where a transfer direction has been given by the Secretary of State under s. 73 of the Mental Health Act 1959 in respect of a person remanded in custody by a magistrates' court and the direction has not ceased to have effect, the clerk of the court shall give notice in writing to the managers of the hospital where he is detained of any further remand under s. 128 of the Act of 1980.

Notice of enlargement of recognizances

84. (1) If a magistrates' court before which any person is bound by a recognizance to appear enlarges the recognizance to a later time under s. 129 of the Act in his absence, it shall give him and his sureties, if any, notice thereof.

(2) If a magistrates' court, under s. 129(4) of the Act of 1980, enlarges the recognizance of a surety for a person committed for trial on bail, it shall give the surety notice thereof.

Directions as to security, etc.

85. Where a magistrates' court, under s. 3(5) or (6) of the Bail Act 1976, imposes any requirement to be complied with before a person's release on bail, the court may give directions as to the manner in which and the person or persons before whom the requirement may be complied with.

Requirements to be complied with before release

86. (1) Where a magistrates' court has fixed the amount in which a person (including any surety) is to be bound by a recognizance, the recognizance may be entered into—

(a)   in the case of a surety in connexion with bail in criminal proceedings where the accused is in a prison or other place of detention, before the governor or keeper of the prison or place as well as before the persons mentioned in s. 8(4)(a) of the Bail Act 1976;

(b)   in any other case, before a justice of the peace, a justices' clerk, a police officer who either is of the rank of inspector or above or is in charge of a police station or, if the person to be bound is in prison or other place of detention, before the governor or keeper of the prison or place.

(2) The clerk of a magistrates' court which has fixed the amount in which a person (including any surety) is to be bound by a recognizance or, under s. 3(5) or (6) of the Bail Act 1976, has imposed any requirement to be complied with before a person's release on bail shall issue a certificate in the prescribed form showing the amount and conditions, if any, of the recognizance or, as the case may be, containing a statement of the requirement; and a person authorized to take the recognizance or do anything in relation to the compliance with such requirement shall not be required to take or do it without production of such a certificate as aforesaid.

(3) If any person proposed as a surety for a person committed to custody by a magistrates' court produces to the governor or keeper of the prison or other place of detention in which the person so committed is detained a certificate in the prescribed form to the effect that he is acceptable as a surety, signed by any of the justices composing the court or the clerk of the court and signed in the margin by the person proposed as surety, the governor or keeper shall take the recognizance of the person so proposed.

(4) Where the recognizance of any person committed to custody by a magistrates' court or of any surety of such a person is taken by any person other than the court which committed the first-mentioned person to custody, the person taking the recognizance shall send it to the clerk of that court:

Provided that, in the case of a surety, if the person committed has been committed to the Crown Court for trial or under any of the enactments mentioned in r. 17(1), the person taking the recognizance shall send it to the appropriate officer of the Crown Court.

Notice to governor of prison, etc. where release from custody is ordered
87. Where a magistrates' court has, with a view to the release on bail of a person in custody, fixed the amount in which he or any surety of such a person shall be bound or, under s. 3(5) or (6) of the Bail Act 1976, imposed any requirement to be complied with before his release—

(a)   the clerk of the court shall give notice thereof to the governor or keeper of the prison or place where that person is detained by sending him such a certificate as is mentioned in r. 86(2);

(b)   any person authorized to take the recognizance of a surety or do anything in relation to the compliance with such requirement shall, on taking or doing it, send notice thereof by post to the said governor or keeper in the prescribed form and, in the case of a recognizance of a surety, shall give a copy of the notice to the surety.

COMMENTARY

(b) Notice . . . in the prescribed form. *See* forms 129 and 130. The Home Office request that the prison governor should also be notified by telephone in cases where it is impracticable for the surety's copy to be presented at the prison the same day: Home Office cir. 104/1972 dated June 13, 1972.

Release when recognizances have been taken or requirements complied with

88. *Where a magistrates' court has, with a view to the release on bail of a person in custody, fixed the amount in which he or any surety of such a person shall be bound or, under s. 3(5) or (6) of the Bail Act 1976, imposed any requirement to be complied with before his release and given notice thereof in accordance with these rules to the governor or keeper of the prison or place where that person is detained, the governor or keeper shall, when satisfied that the recognizances of all sureties required have been taken and that all such requirements have been complied with—*

  (a)   *in the case of bail in criminal proceedings, unless he is in custody for some other cause, release him;*

  (b)   *in the case of bail otherwise than in criminal proceedings, take the recognizances of that person if this has not already been done and, unless he is in custody for some other cause, release him.*

Procedure under [s. 43A of the Magistrates' Courts Act 1980]

89. *Where under [s. 43A of the Magistrates' Courts Act 1980] a magistrates' court commits to custody or releases on bail a person who has been arrested in pursuance of a warrant issued by the Crown Court, or the officer in charge of a police station releases such a person on bail under s. 13(6) of that Act, the clerk of the magistrates' court or the officer, as the case may be, shall forthwith notify the appropriate officer of the Crown Court of the action which has been taken and, if that person has been released, shall transmit to the appropriate officer of the Crown Court as soon as practicable—*

  (a)   *in the case of bail in criminal proceedings, a copy of the record made in pursuance of s. 5 of the Bail Act 1976 relating to such bail;*

  (b)   *in the case of bail otherwise than in criminal proceedings, the recognizance of that person.*

Bail records to be entered in register

90. *Any record required by s. 5 of the Bail Act 1976 to be made by a magistrates' court (together with any note of reasons required by subs. (4) of that section to be included) and the particulars set out in any certificate granted under subs. (6A) of that section shall be made by way of an entry in the register and shall contain the particulars set out in the appropriate form prescribed for the purpose.*

Notice of change of time for appearance

91. *Where—*

  (a)   *a person has been granted bail under s. 43(1) of the Act of 1980 and the magistrates' court before which he is to appear appoints, under s. 43(2), a later time as the time at which he is to appear; or*

  (b)   *a magistrates' court further remands a person on bail under s. 129 of that Act in his absence,*

it shall give him and his sureties, if any, notice thereof.

Notification of bail decision after arrest while on bail

92. *Where a person who has been released on bail and is under a duty to surrender into the custody of a court is brought under s. 7(4)(a) of the Bail Act 1976 before a justice of the peace, the justice shall cause a copy of the record made in pursuance of s. 5 of that Act relating to his decision under s. 7(5) of that Act in respect of that person to be sent—*

  (a)   *in the case of a magistrates' court, to the clerk thereof; or*

  (b)   *in the case of any other court, to the appropriate officer thereof:*

CHAPTER 4

COMMITTAL PROCEEDINGS

CONTENTS

INTRODUCTION

There are two methods of trial at English law, trial on indictment and summary trial: the first takes place at the Crown Court, the second at a magistrates' court. For the purpose of ascertaining how they are to be tried, therefore, offences are divided into three types:

offences triable only on indictment;
offences triable only summarily; and
offences triable either way

So far as adults are concerned, the function of a magistrates' court, as respects offences triable only on indictment, is solely the holding of a preliminary inquiry or committal proceedings: the actual trial takes place at the Crown Court. Offences triable only summarily proceed to trial in a magistrates' court: they cannot be tried in the Crown Court. Offences triable either way may be tried either in the Crown Court or in a magistrates' court.

The Classification of Offences

For the purposes of statutory drafting there are three categories of offence as follows:

— *an indictable offence*, which means an offence which, if committed by an adult, is triable on indictment, whether it is exclusively so triable or triable either way;
— *a summary offence*, which means an offence which, if committed by an adult, is triable only summarily; and
— *an offence triable either way*, which means an offence which if committed by an adult, is triable either on indictment or summarily. (Interpretation Act 1978, s. 5, sch. 1)

Offences Triable Either Way

Offences triable either way consist of:

(i)   those offences which are triable either summarily or on indictment by virtue of any statutory provision (the Magistrates' Courts Act 1980, s. 17(2));and
(ii)   the offences listed in the Magistrates' Courts Act 1980, (s. 17(1), *ibid*, refers).

The maximum penalty on summary conviction of an offence listed in sch. 1 is imprisonment for a term not exceeding six months and a fine of £1000 unless the penalty on indictment is less: Magistrates' Courts Act 1980, s. 32(1). For all other offences triable either way the maximum fine is £2000 or any larger sum prescribed by statute: *ibid*, s. 32(2), (7). The maximum term of imprisonment is six months unless the statute prescribes a shorter term: *ibid*, s. 31(1), (2). The six-months' period of limitation does not apply to an offence triable either way: Magistrates' Courts Act 1980, s. 127(2).

Selecting the Mode of Trial

When a person who has attained the age of 17 years appears or is brought before a magistrates' court on an information charging him with an offence triable either way, the court (which may consist of a single justice: Magistrates' Courts Act 1980, s. 18(5)) must cause the charge to be written down and read to the accused: s. 19(2), *ibid*. First, the prosecution and then the accused must be given opportunity to make representations as to the mode of trial (*ibid*). The court must then make an initial decision as to which mode of trial is more suitable having regard to the criteria listed in s. 19(3), *ibid*. For guidance as to the application of those criteria see the commentary to that subsection. If the court decides that trial on indictment is more appropriate, it will proceed with the inquiry without more ado: s. 21, *ibid*. If, on the other hand, it decides that summary trial is more appropriate, the accused must be so informed and cautioned as to his rights in accordance with s. 20(2), *ibid*. If he then consents to summary trial the matter proceeds accordingly; if he does not, the court will begin to inquire into the information as examining justices: s. 20(3), *ibid*.

If the prosecution is carried on by a law officer or the Director of Public Prosecutions and he applies for trial on indictment, neither the court nor the accused has any discretion in the matter: s. 19(4), *ibid*.

The restrictions on the reporting of committal proceedings (see below) apply to the mode of trial proceedings: Magistrates' Courts Act 1980, s. 8(8).

Offences of Criminal Damage

Special rules apply to the selection of the mode of trial of certain offences of criminal damage except arson. The offences concerned are set out in the Magistrates' Courts Act 1980, sch. 2 (s. 22(1), *ibid*).

Before any evidence is called (s. 18(2)) the court must first consider, having regard to any representations made by the prosecutor or accused, whether the value (as defined in s. 22(10) and sch. 2) involved exceeds £200: Magistrates' Courts Act 1980, s. 22(1). When the accused is jointly charged with a juvenile, the latter may also make representations: s. 22(9), *ibid*. If the value involved is £200 or less the offence (which would otherwise be triable either way in accordance with the mode of trial procedure set out above) is tried summarily. The maximum penalty in such cases is £1,000 and six months' imprisonment and there is no power to commit to the Crown Court for greater sentence: s. 33, *ibid*. If the value involved *exceeds* £200 the ordinary mode of trial procedure described above applies.

But if it is *not clear* whether the value does or does not exceed £200, a special procedure takes place before any representations are heard: s. 22(4), *ibid*. The purpose of this procedure appears to be to induce the offender to accept summary trial by offering him a reduced maximum penalty should he be convicted. Under this procedure the charge is written down and read to the accused who is then cautioned as to his right to trial by jury and informed that if he consents to summary trial his liability to punishment will be limited. The limitation consists of a lower maximum penalty (three months and £500) and removal of the possibility of being committed to the Crown Court for greater sentence: s. 33, *ibid*. If the accused consents to summary trial the proceedings continue accordingly. If he does not, the mode of trial procedure described above is followed: s. 22(6), *ibid*. There is no right of appeal to the Crown Court against the magistrates' decision as to value: s. 22(8), *ibid*.

This procedure does not apply when the offence charged is one of two or more criminal damage offences charged on the same occasion appearing to constitute or form part of a series of offences of like character or where the offence consists in the incitement to commit two or more offences listed in sch. 2, *ibid*: s. 22(7), *ibid*.

All offences of criminal damage are indictable offences, no matter that they may be triable only summarily. Costs may therefore be ordered from central funds in accordance with the Costs in Criminal Cases Act 1973, s. 1.

The Presence of the Accused

Selection of the mode of trial must take place before any evidence is called and in the presence of the accused (Magistrates' Courts Act 1980, s. 18(2)), except

(i)   when this is impracticable by reason of his orderly conduct before the court (s. 18(3) *ibid.*); or

(ii) when the accused is represented by counsel or a solicitor who in his absence signifies the accused's consent for the proceedings for determining the mode of trial to take place in his absence and the court is satisfied there is good reason for so proceeding (s. 23(1), *ibid.*).

In both these cases the proceedings may take place in the absence of the accused, the caution need not be put and the legal representative, if any, may signify his consent to summary trial. If there is no legal representative (in a disorderly conduct case) or if the legal representative does not consent to summary trial or if, in accordance with s. 21, *ibid.*, the court considers trial on indictment more appropriate, the magistrates will proceed to inquire into the information as examining justices and may adjourn the hearing without remanding the accused: s. 23(5). *ibid.*

If the court is not satisfied that there is good reason for proceeding in the absence of the accused or if for any reason the court decides to proceed as examining justices, process may issue to compel the personal attendance of the accused: s. 26, *ibid*.

Corporations

A representative may on behalf of a corporation consent to the corporation being tried summarily: Magistrates' Courts Act 1980, sch. 3, para. 1(2). Any requirement that anything shall be done in the presence of the accused or said to him applies to a representative if he appears: *ibid*, para. 3.

Changing the Procedure

The fact that a court has embarked upon summary trial or has commenced to act as examining justices does not necessarily fix the procedure irrevocably. Except in the case of the special criminal damage procedure where the accused has opted for summary trial under s. 22(6), the court may change from summary trial to inquiry at any time before the conclusion of the evidence for the prosecution: s. 25(2), *ibid*. To change from an inquiry to summary trial the court must first explain its decision to the accused and obtain his consent, informing him, if this has not already been done, of its power to commit him to the Crown Court for sentence: s. 25(3), *ibid*. If the prosecution is being carried on by a law officer or the Director of Public Prosecutions his consent is essential to a conversion to summary trial: s. 25(3), *ibid*. Evidence given during the inquiry is deemed to have been given in and for the purposes of the summary trial: Magistrates' Courts Act 1980, s. 28. However, witnesses must be recalled for cross-examination unless not required by the accused or the prosecutor: Magistrates' Courts Rules 1981, r. 21.

Adjournments and Remands

Procedurally, the trial of an offence triable either way is divided into three possible stages. The first, which is common to all, is the mode of trial procedure. This commences as soon as the accused appears or is brought before a magistrates' court (Magistrates' Courts Act 1980, s. 18(1)). From that time until the decision as to mode of trial is taken the power to adjourn is contained in s. 18(4), *ibid*. On such an adjournment the accused *may* be remanded whenever he is present and *must* be remanded if (a) on the occasion on which he first appeared or was brought before the court he was in custody or, having been released on bail, surrendered to the custody of the court; or (b) if he has been remanded at any time in the course of the proceedings (*ibid.*).

Juveniles

A juvenile charged with an indictable offence other than homicide must be tried summarily unless (i) he is aged 14-16 and charged with certain grave offences and the court feels that if found guilty it ought to be possible for him to be detained for the longer periods available in such cases *or* (ii) he is charged jointly with an adult and the court considers it necessary to commit both: Magistrates' Courts Act 1980, s. 24(1).

In the latter case the juvenile may also be committed for trial for any other indictable offence with which he is charged (whether jointly or not) arising out of the same or connected circumstances: s.24(2), *ibid*.

If the juvenile is tried summarily for such an offence the maximum fine may not exceed £400 if a young person: s. 24(3), *ibid*; or £100 if a child: s. 24(3), *ibid*.

Ouster of Jurisdiction

There are certain circumstances in which justices have no jurisdiction in matters involving a *bona fide* claim of title: *R.* v. *Speed* (1700) 1 Ld. Raym. 583. In cases such as this the magistrates must commit for trial to a higher court: *R.* v. *Holsworthy and Another, ex parte Edwards* (1952) 116 J.P. 130. At common law the main effect of the rule was in respect of prosecutions for malicious damage. However, the Criminal Damage Act 1971, s. 7(2), specially excludes the rule from prosecutions under that Act or any other offences of destroying or damaging property. A rule of ouster in relation to charges of assault or battery still obtains by virtue of the Offences Against the Person Act, 1861, s. 46. The elements of the rule at common law are that:

(i) it is confined to claims of title to *real* property: *Eagling* v. *Wheatley* (1977) 141 J.P. 514

(ii) It is confined to claims to *private* title. Thus magistrates can properly hear informations in which are raised disputes over public highways: *R.* v. *Critchlow* (1878) 26 W.R. 681; *White* v. *Fox* (1880) 44 J.P. 618 (but compare *Edwards* v. *Cock* (1894) 58 J.P. 398). Nor are they excluded by mere contractual claims to enter land: *Lucan* v. *Barrett* (1915) 79 J.P. 463.

(iii) There must be a *bona fide* claim to title and not a mere pretence or assertion. Assertions may be disregarded where upon either the defendant's own showing or other manifest grounds, it is apparent the claim is baseless: *R.* v. *Sandford* (1874) 39 J.P. 118. The justices must decide whether the claim is *bona fide*: *Legg* v. *Pardoe* (1860) 25 J.P. 39; *Birnie* v. *Marshall* (1876) 41 J.P. 22 (a borderline case where ouster was upheld); *Hudson* v. *Macrea* (1863) 33 L.J.M.C. 65; *Croyden R.D.C.* v. *Cowley and Another* (1909) 73 J.P. 205; *Burton* v. *Hudson* (1909) 73 J.P. 401. But if, in order to decide whether a legal claim exists, it is necessary to determine some disputed question of fact, the jurisdiction of magistrates is ousted, *per* Ridley J in *Arnold* v. *Morgan* (1911) 75 J.P. 105.

(iv) The claim must be part of the defendant's case: *Cornwell* v. *Sanders* (1862) 27 J.P. 148.

It is important to distinguish the principles by which the jurisdiction of magistrates is ousted from a claim of right which may be pleaded as a defence to certain offences. Such claims are matters of substantive law and are thus not dealt with in this work.

There are other cases where a statute may give jurisdiction to decide questions of title: *Duplex Settled Investment Trust, Ltd* v. *Worthing Borough Council* (1952) 116 J.P. 176; *London, Brighton and South Coast Railway* v. *Fairbrother* (1900) 16 T.L.R. 167.

COMMITTAL PROCEEDINGS

A person may be tried on indictment by a bill of indictment preferred:

- (i)   by the direction or with the consent of the Court of Appeal or a judge of the High Court;
- (ii) pursuant to an order made under s. 9 of the Perjury Act, 1911; or
- (iii) upon committal for trial following a preliminary inquiry.

(Administration of Justice (Miscellaneous Provisions) Act, 1933, s. 2(2).) Of these, by far the most usual procedure is committal by an examining justice.

There are two types of committal proceedings, namely committal without consideration of the evidence under the Magistrates' Courts Act 1980, s. 6(2) and "conventional" committal proceedings under *ibid*, s. 6(1).

A single justice may discharge the functions of an examining justice: Magistrates' Courts Act 1980, s. 4(1).

Committal without Consideration of the Evidence

A person can be committed to the Crown Court for trial by an examining justice without consideration of the evidence where,

- (i)   all the evidence consists of written statements under the Magistrates' Courts Act 1980, s. 102;
- (ii) the accused has a solicitor acting for him; and
- (iii) no submission is made that the evidence is insufficient: Magistrates' Courts Act 1980, s. 6(2).

The procedure for such a committal is set out in the Magistrates' Courts Rules, 1981, r. 6. If the conditions set out above do not obtain the proceedings take the conventional form: *ibid*, r. 6(3).

"Conventional" Committal Proceedings

In committal proceedings of the conventional form the examining justice has to consider the evidence and if there is sufficient evidence to put the accused on trial for any indictable offence the accused must be committed for trial. If not, he must be discharged: Magistrates' Courts Act 1980, s. 6(1).

The procedure for such a committal is set out in the Magistrates' Courts Rules, 1981, r. 7.

The function of committal proceedings is to ensure that no one shall stand his trial unless a *prima facie* case has been made out, not a rehearsal for the defence to try out their cross-examination on the prosecution witnesses with a view to using the results to their advantage in the Crown Court. It is thus not incumbent upon the prosecutor to call even a very important witness if they deem this unnecessary or undesirable: *R.* v. *Epping and Harlow Justices, ex parte Massaro* (1973) 137 J.P. 373 (girl victim of sex assault). In the course of his judgment in *R.* v. *Colchester Justices, ex parte Beck and Others, infra,* Kilner Brown, J said, "There is regrettably a tendency in committals under both (subs. (1) and (2) of s. 6 of this Act) for quantities of irrelevant or inadmissible, or it may be highly prejudicial, material to be collected by prosecuting authorities and served without any attempt to remove such material before consideration by the court. It may place an intolerable burden on committing magistrates, and it certainly does on trial judges in cases of committals under (subs. (2)). Speaking for myself, I would hope that more careful selection would be made in appropriate cases. It would be preferable if there is a concentration on the essential evidence to be tendered at committal stages. Any lacunae can always be corrected by a notice of additional evidence."

"To ask a court to call witnesses for any other purpose than to ask them to consider whether the evidence is sufficient to commit for trial would be an improper use of that section. The section is not intended to allow the accused to explore the evidence as a rehearsal for trial. It is to consider the situation when the magistrates may have properly argued before them the sufficiency of the evidence and for no other purpose," *per* Eveleigh LJ in *R.* v. *Grays Justices, ex parte Tetley* [1980] 70 Cr. App. R. 11 (prosecutor went back on undertaking to call witness).

"The duty of the magistrate [in committal proceedings] is simply upon hearing the evidence for the prosecution, and evidence, if it is to be adduced, on the part of the defence, to consider and decide whether there is a presumption of guilt . . . It is no part of his duty or his province to try the case", *per* Cockburn CJ in *R.* v. *Carden* (1879) 44 J.P. 122 at p. 137.

What constitutes a *prima facie* case is usually described in the following terms: "There must be such evidence that, if uncontradicted at the trial, a reasonably minded jury could convict upon it," *per* Swift J in *R.* v. *Brixton Prison Governor, ex parte Bidwell* (1936) 100 J.P. 458; approved by the House of Lords in *Schtraks* v. *Government of Israel* (1962) 126 J.P. 277. (and *see* also *Armah* v. *Government of Ghana* (1967) 131 J.P. 43), all cases turning upon extradition or the like proceedings in which the court held that the test is the same as in committal proceedings. When a defendant gives evidence in committal proceedings in support of a defence it is open to the justices to refuse to commit if, on the whole of the evidence, they are satisfied no reasonable jury would convict: *Re Roberts* [1967] Crim. L.R. 304.

Oppression and Abuse of Process

Committal for trial cannot be refused on the ground that it would be unjust, oppressive or contrary to natural justice, *per* Lords Reid & Upjohn in *Atkinson* v. *United States Government* [1969] 3 All E.R. 1317 at pp. 1322, 1334 (an extradition case). However in *R.* v. *Canterbury & St. Augustine Justices, ex parte Turner* (1983) 147 J.P. 193 McNeill J., while accepting that examining justices must have some power to prevent abuse of their process, held that delay alone is not sufficient, on the balance of the authorities reviewed under this title in the introduction to Ch. 5. (*See* also *R.* v. *Horsham Justices, ex parte Reeves* [1982] 75 Cr. App. R. 236 where the question was reserved.)

The Evidence

Evidence at conventional committal proceedings may be in the form either of depositions or of written statements taken under the Magistrates' Courts Act 1980, s. 102, or both. Admissions may also be made under the Criminal Justice Act 1967, s. 10.

Despite the fact that it is improper to take a deposition by means of leading questions, this will not invalidate a committal: *R.* v. *Walker* (1950) 114 J.P. 578. And, in general, a committal for trial is not invalidated simply because inadmissible evidence was admitted by the examining justices: *R.* v. *Norfolk Quarter Sessions, ex parte Brunson* (1953) 117 J.P. 100; *R.* v. *Ipswich Justices, ex parte Edwards* (1979) 143 J.P. 699. A prerogative order will issue only when a magistrate has refused to exercise discretion and not when the matter complained of is the exercise of that discretion: *R.* v. *Wells Street Stipendiary Magistrate, ex parte Seillon and Others* [1980] 69 Cr. App. R. 78 (refusal to allow questions of witness). In committal proceedings magistrates have no discretion to admit or reject evidence on the ground that its prejudicial effect outweighs its probative value: *R*. v. *Horsham Justices, ex parte Bukhari* [1981] 74 Cr. App. R. 291 (dock identification). In all other respects, it is submitted, the normal rules of evidence apply in committal proceedings.

The evidence of a child in committal proceedings for a sexual offence must be dealt with in accordance with the Magistrates' Courts Act 1980, s. 103, except, it is submitted, in the case of proceedings under s. 6(1), *ibid*.

The Presence of the Offender

Evidence in committal proceedings must be given in the presence of the accused unless (a) the court considers this impracticable by reason of his diorderly conduct or (b) he cannot be present for health reasons, but is represented by counsel or solicitor and has consented to that course: Magistrates' Courts Act 1980, s. 4(4). s. 4(3). This does not prevent the magistrate from reading the papers in advance of the hearing: *R*. v. *Colchester Magistrate, ex parte Beck and Others* (1979) 143 J.P. 202.

Open Court

Examining justices must sit in open court except when statute allows otherwise or when it appears to them as respects the whole or part of the proceedings that the ends of justice would not be served by sitting in open court: Magistrates' Courts Act 1980, s. 4(2).

Multiple Charges and Defendants

Two charges (even against different defendants) can be properly committed jointly for trial wherever two offences can be properly tried jointly on indictment: *R*. v. *Camberwell Green Justices, ex parte Christie* (1978) 142 J.P. 345.

Adjournment of Inquiry

Examining justices may adjourn their inquiry at any time and on doing so must remand the accused to a fixed date: Magistrates' Courts Act 1980, s. 5

Examining justices have a discretion to allow the prosecutor an adjournment: *R*. v. *West London Metropolitan Stipendiary Magistrate, ex parte Karminski* [1983] Crim. L.R. 40.

Place of Trial

The examining justice must specify the location of the Crown Court at which the accused will be tried in accordance with the criteria in the Magistrates' Courts Act 1980, s. 7. His discretion is also governed by Directions given by the Lord Chief Justice. *See* Appx. B.

Bail or Custody

A committal for trial must be either in custody or on bail (Magistrates' Courts Act 1980, s. 6(3)), although magistrates may review their decision to commit in custody at a later date: *ibid,* s. 6(4). The defendant enjoys the general right to bail: Bail Act, 1976, s. 4. Magistrates may not grant bail to a person charged with treason: Magistrates' Courts Act 1980, s. 41; Bail Act 1976, s. 4(7). Once a person has been committed in custody by a magistrates' court the Crown Court may admit him to bail: Supreme Court Act 1981, s. 81.

Corporations

A corporation may be committed for trial by an order in writing empowering the prosecutor to prefer a bill of indictment: Magistrates' Courts Act 1980, sch. 3, para. 1 The requirement that evidence must be given in the presence of the defendant applies if the corporation appears by a representative but not otherwise: *ibid*, para. 3.

Reporting Restrictions

The press are allowed to report no more than certain prescribed formalities unless the court makes an order removing the restrictions. Such an order may be made only on the application of a defendant: and if an application is made the court must so order; it has no discretion in the matter Magistrates' Courts Act 1980, s. 8. As a corollary, even in cases where the press restrictions are lifted, the clerk must, subject to the Sexual Offences (Amendment) Act 1976 (see below), display particulars of the proceedings in or near the court house: Magistrates' Courts Act 1980, s. 6(5). That notice may not identify any juvenile concerned unless by direction of the justices for the purpose of avoiding injustice to him: s. 6(6), *ibid*.

For the purposes of this provision committal proceedings are deemed to include any proceedings in the magistrates' court before the court proceeds to inquire into the information as examining justices: Magistrates' Courts Act 1980, s. 8(8).

In any legal proceedings held in public the court may, where it appears to be necessary for avoiding a substantial risk of prejudice to the administration of justice in those proceedings, or in any other proceedings pending or imminent, order that the publication of any report of the proceedings, or any part of the proceedings be postponed for such period as the court thinks necessary for that purpose: Contempt of Court Act 1981, s. 4(2). *See* Ch. 14.

Rape Offences

Restrictions on the identification of the complainant and defendant in committal proceedings for a rape offence are contained in the Sexual Offences (Amendment) Act, 1976, which defines the term "rape offence" in s. 7, *ibid*.

Upon the application of the defendant a magistrates' court may at any time before the commencement of the trial remove the restrictions upon his identification: s. 6(2), *ibid*. Otherwise, the only person who can remove the restrictions is a judge of the Crown Court.

The Alibi Warning

On a trial on indictment the defendant may not without the leave of the court adduce evidence in support of an alibi unless within seven days from the end of the proceedings before the examining justices he gives notice of particulars of the alibi: Criminal Justice Act 1967, s. 11(1), (8). During committal proceedings the court is obliged to warn the defendant of this fact unless, having regard to the nature of the offence, it appears to the court unnecessary to do so: Magistrates' Courts Rules 1981, rr. 6(4), 7(9).

Witness Orders

Witnesses at committal proceedings, even those whose evidence is in the form of written statements, must be made the subject of an order to attend the trial, which may or may not be conditional upon their being given notice: Criminal Procedure (Attendance of Witnesses) Act 1965, s. 1.

Exhibits

Once an article has become an exhibit, the court has a responsibility in relation to it. That responsibility is to preserve and retain it, or to arrange for its preservation and retention, for the purposes of justice. The usual course is for the court to entrust the exhibits to the police or to the Director of‚Public Prosecutions subject to the same responsibility. That responsibility is (1) to take all proper care to preserve the exhibits safe from loss or damage, (2) to co-operate with the defence in order to allow them reasonable access to the exhibits for the purpose of inspection and examination, and (3) to produce the exhibits at the trial. Where a court entrusts exhibits to the police or the prosecutor, it can impose such restrictions as it considers proper in all circumstances. In the case of a private prosecutor it would be more likely to impose such restrictions than in the case of a public prosecutor and indeed might well decide to retain the exhibits itself or to deliver them into the custody of the police. But if the court imposes no restrictions, it is for the recipient of the exhibits to deal with them in whatever way appears best for the purposes of justice. If the recipient has doubts as to where his duty lies, he can apply to the court for directions, but he is under no obligation so to do. Equally, the accused can apply to the court for directions if he thinks it appropriate, *per* Sir John Donaldson M.R. in *R.* v. *Lambeth Metropolitan Stipendiary Magistrate, ex parte McComb* [1983] 2 W.L.R. 259. And *see* the Magistrates' Courts Rules 1981, r. 11(1), (2), *infra.*

Autrefois Acquit *and* Convict

The discharge of a defendant in committal proceedings is not an acquittal and does not bar the bringing of futher proceedings in respect of the same offence, but the High Court has a discretion to see that the use of repeated committal proceedings is not allowed to become vexatious or an abuse of the court: *R.* v. *Manchester City Magistrates' Court, ex parte Snelson* (1978) 142 J.P. 274.

A defendant committed for trial in respect of offences triable only summarily cannot claim *autrefois acquit*. The committal is a nullity and the justices may proceed to convict the defendant summarily: *Bannister* v. *Clarke* (1920) 85 J.P. 12. Conversely, an acquittal by justices of an offence triable only on indictment is not a bar to the justices committing the defendant for trial: *R.* v. *West* (1962) 126 J.P. 352.

Despite *dicta* in *R.* v. *West* (1962) 126 J.P. 352, it would appear that the doctrines of *autrefois acquit* and *convict* can debar examining justices from committing for trial: *cf. Re Roberts* [1967] Crim. L.R. 304.

THE CRIMINAL PROCEDURE (ATTENDANCE OF WITNESSES) ACT 1965

Order by examining justices for attendance of witness at court of trial

1. (1) A magistrates' court acting as examining justices shall in respect of each witness examined by the court, other than the accused and any witness of his merely to his character, make an order (in this Act referred to as a witness order) requiring him to attend and give evidence before the Crown Court.

(2) Where it appears to the court, after taking into account any representation made by the accused or the prosecutor, that the attendance at the trial of any witness is unnecessary on the ground that his evidence is unlikely to be required or is unlikely to be disputed, then—

    (a)   any witness order to be made by the court in his case shall be a conditional order requiring him to attend the trial if notice in that behalf is given to him and not otherwise; and

    (b)   if a witness order other than a conditional order has previously been made by the court in his case, the court shall direct that that order be treated as a conditional order.

(3) A magistrates' court on committing any person for trial shall inform him of his right to require the attendance at the trial of any witness in respect of whom a conditional witness order, or an order treated as a conditional witness order, has been made, and of the steps he must take for the purpose of enforcing the attendance.

(4) (*Repealed).*

(as amended by the Courts Act, 1971, sch. 8, the Statute Law (Repeals) Act 1974).

COMMENTARY

If a witness fails to appear at the Crown Court in response to a witness order that Court has power to issue a warrant under s. 14 of the Act. The Home Office have expressed the view (in circ. 118/1970 dated June 10, 1970) that no attempt should be made to effect service upon a witness outside the UK, but that the prosecutor or defendant should be asked to make suitable arrangements for his attendance.

Subsection (1): A witness order. *See* generally the Magistrates' Courts Rules 1981, r. 8 and form 17. Disobedience to a witness order is punishable as a contempt: s. 3 of the Act. **Subsection (2): Evidence ... unlikely to be disputed.** For example, a medical man whose evidence is unchallenged and really only formal, as is often the case in cases of carnal knowledge, or of wounding, where there is no dispute as to the nature and extent of the injuries: *Practice Note* [1952] W.N. 245.

A conditional order. A conditional order must be served on a witness who has been examined as soon as practicable after committal for trial except where made at the conclusion of his examination when it must be served on him immediately after the deposition is signed: Magistrates' Courts Rules 1981, r. 8(1). For the admissibility of the deposition of such a witness at the trial *see* the Criminal Justice Act, 1925, s. 13(3) and the Criminal Justice Act 1967, s. 7 (not reproduced herein). Inability to warn a conditional witness does not necessarily prevent his deposition being read at the trial: *R.* v. *Dadlani* (1970) 54 Cr. App. R. 305. And *see* also *R.* v. *Schaffer* [1960] Crim. L.R. 124 and *R.* v. *Meyrow* [1974] Crim. L.R. 627. Unless there are reasons for not doing so exhibits produced by a witness subject to a conditional witness order must be retained by the court: Magistrates' Courts Rules 1981, r. 11(1).

Subsection (3). Presumably, the steps consist of informing the appropriate officer of the Crown Court.

THE CRIMINAL JUSTICE ACT 1967

Signature of depositions

7. An examining justice who signs a certificate authenticating one or more depositions or statements tendered under s. 102 of the Magistrates' Courts Act 1980 shall be treated for the purposes of s. 13(3)(*c*) of the Criminal Justice Act, 1925 (requirement that depositions read at the trial must have been signed by an examining justice) as signing that deposition or statement or each of those depositions and statements.

(as amended by the Magistrates' Courts Act 1980, sch. 7).

COMMENTARY

Expressions used in this section have the same meaning as in the Magistrates' Courts Act, 1980: Criminal Justice Act 1967, s. 36(2).

A certificate. *See* form 11.

Section 13(3)(c) of the Criminal Justice Act, 1925. (Not reproduced herein.) Provides that the depositions and statements shall be admissible in a trial on indictment provided, *inter alia*, that they are signed by the justices.

Notice of alibi

11. (1) On a trial on indictment the defendant shall not without the leave of the court adduce evidence in support of an alibi unless, before the end of the prescribed period, he gives notice of particulars of the alibi.

(2) Without prejudice to the foregoing subsection, on any such trial the defendant shall not without the leave of the court call any other person to give such evidence—

> (a) the notice under that subsection includes the name and address of the witness or, if the name or address is not known to the defendant at the time he gives the notice, any information in his possession which might be of material assistance in finding the witness;
>
> (b) if the name or the address is not included in that notice, the court is satisfied that the defendant, before giving the notice, took and thereafter continued to take all reasonable steps to secure that the name or address would be ascertained;
>
> (c) if the name or the address is not included in that notice, but the defendant subsequently discovers the name or address or receives other information which might be of material assistance in finding the witness, he forthwith gives notice of the name, address or other information, as the case may be; and
>
> (d) if the defendant is notified by or on behalf of the prosecutor that the witness has not been traced by the name or at the address given, he forthwith gives notice of any such information which is then in his possession or, on subsequently receiving any such information, forthwith gives notice of it.

(3) The court shall not refuse leave under this section if it appears to the court that the defendant was not informed in accordance with rules under s. 144 of the Magistrates' Courts Act 1980 (rules of procedure for magistrates' courts) of the requirements of this section.

(4) Any evidence tendered to disprove an alibi may, subject to any directions by the court as to the time it is to be given, be given before or after evidence is given in support of the alibi.

(5) Any notice purporting to be given under this section on behalf of the defendant by his solicitor shall, unless the contrary is proved, be deemed to be given with the authority of the defendant.

(6) A notice under subs. (1) of this section shall either be given in court during, or at the end of, the proceedings before the examining justices or be given in writing to the solicitor for the prosecutor, and a notice under para. (c) or (d) of subs. (2) of this section shall be given in writing to that solicitor.

(7) A notice required by this section to be given to the solicitor for the prosecutor may be given by delivering it to him, or by leaving it at his office, or by sending it in a registered letter or by the recorded delivery service addressed to him at his office.

(8) In this section—

> "evidence in support of an alibi" means evidence tending to show that by reason of the presence of the defendant at a particular place or in a particular area at a particular time he was not, or was unlikely to have been, at the place where the offence is alleged to have been committed at the time of its alleged commission.

> "the prescribed period" means the period of seven days from the end of the proceedings before the examining justices.

(9) In computing the said period a Sunday, Christmas Day, Good Friday, a

4. COMMITTAL PROCEEDINGS

day which is a bank holiday under the Bank Holidays Act, 1871, in England and Wales or a day appointed for public thanksgiving or mourning shall be disregarded.

(as amended by the Magistrates' Courts Act 1980, sch. 7).

COMMENTARY

For the proposals on which this provision was based, *see* the Ninth Report of the Criminal Law Revision Committee, Cmnd. 3145. The provisions of this section do not apply to summary trials wherein sprung alibis may be readily met by an adjournment.

Expressions used in this section have the same meaning as in the Magistrates' Courts Act, 1980: Criminal Justice Act 1967, s. 36(2).

Subsection (1) includes evidence which the defendant himself may give; subs. (2) deals with evidence given by persons other than the accused: *R. v. Jackson and Robertson* [1973] Crim. L.R. 356.

"In order to enable clerks of assize to make more reliable estimates of the length of criminal trials, the prosecution are requested, so soon as any notice of alibi is given to them under s. 11 of the Criminal Justice Act 1967 to send a copy thereof to the court of trial": *Practice Note* [1969] 1 All E.R. 1042.

Subsection (1): Evidence in support of an alibi. *See* subs. (8). This applied only to evidence relative to the whereabouts of the accused at the time when the crime is alleged to have been committed: evidence relative to another occasion is not subject to the restrictions however significant to the issues of the case: *R. v. Lewis* [1969] 1 All E.R. 79. Any question as to the place or date at or on which the offence was committed must be resolved on the material then available to the accused, namely, the committal charges and the depositions: *ibid.*

"This phrase envisages an offence which necessarily involves the accused being at a particular place at a particular time. Thus s. 11 is inapplicable to an offence of a continuing nature such as living on the earnings of prostitution alleged to have been committed 'in the city of Cardiff'": *R. v. Hassan* (1970) 134 J.P. 266. The defence of alibi is inapplicable to a person charged with driving while disqualified who admits that he was in the car but denies that he was the driver: *R. v. Westlake* [1970] Crim. L.R. 652.

Before the end of the prescribed period. *See* subss. (8) and (9).

Subsection (3): Informed in accordance with rules. *See* the Magistrates' Courts Rules, 1981, rr. 6(4), (5) and 7(9), (13) and form 23.

Subsection (7): A notice may be given. This term implies that these are not the only methods whereby the notice may be given.

Subsection (8): Evidence in support of an alibi. Includes evidence by the accused himself: *R. v. Jackson and Robertson* [1973] Crim. L.R. 356.

THE SEXUAL OFFENCES (AMENDMENT) ACT, 1976

Restrictions on evidence at trials for rape etc.

2. (1) If at a trial any person is for the time being charged with a rape offence to which he pleads not guilty, then, except with the leave of the judge, no evidence and no question in cross-examination shall be adduced or asked at the trial, by or on behalf of any defendant at the trial, about any sexual experience of a complainant with a person other than that defendant.

(2) The judge shall not give leave in pursuance of the preceding subsection for any evidence or question except on an application made to him in the absence of the jury by or on behalf of a defendant; and on such an application the judge shall give leave if and only if he is satisfied that it would be unfair to that defendant to refuse to allow the evidence to be adduced or the question to be asked.

(3) In subs. (1) of this section "complainant" means a woman upon whom, in a charge of a rape offence to which the trial in question relates, it is alleged that rape was committed, attempted or proposed.

(4) Nothing in this section authorizes evidence to be adduced or a question to be asked which cannot be adduced or asked apart from this section.

4. COMMITTAL PROCEEDINGS

COMMENTARY

Subsection (1): A rape offence. Defined in s. 7, *infra*.

The leave of the judge. The ultimate question for the judge is whether he is "satisfied" that to refuse to allow a particular question of a series of questions in cross-examination would be unfair to the defendant on the view that it was more likely than not that that cross-examination, if allowed, might reasonably lead the jury, properly directed, in the summing up to take a different view of the complainant's evidence from that which they might take if that cross-examination were not allowed. The judge's decision is a judgment, not an exercise of discretion; if he concluded that it would be unfair to exclude a question, it had to be admitted and allowed. Generally speaking, if the proposed questions merely sought to establish that the complainant has had sexual experiences with other men so as to suggest that, therefore, she ought not be be believed on oath the judge would refuse to allow them: *R.* v. *Viola* [1982] 3 All E.R. 73.

Complainant. Defined in subs. (3).

Other than that defendant. Thus a defendant is restricted in respect of evidence of sexual experience with a co-defendant. The defendant may be of good character and able to put his character in issue by attacking the character of a prosecution witness even though the co-defendant is of bad character and therefore does not wish to do so. This may be a ground for an application to lift the restriction.

Subsection (2): Unfair to that defendant. Unfairness to another defendant or even prejudice to another defendant are not material.

Application of s. 2 to committal proceedings, courts-martial and summary trials

3. (1) Where a magistrates' court inquires into a rape offence as examining justices, then, except with the consent of the court, evidence shall not be adduced and a question shall not be asked at the inquiry which, if the inquiry were a trial at which a person is charged as mentioned in subs. (1) of the preceding section and each of the accused at the inquiry were charged at the trial with the offences of which he is accused at the inquiry, could not be adduced or asked without leave in pursuance of that section.

(2) On an application for consent in pursuance of the preceding subsection for any evidence or question the court shall—

> (a)   refuse the consent unless the court is satisfied that leave in respect of the evidence or question would be likely to be given at a relevant time; and
>
> (b)   give the consent if the court is so satisfied.

(3) *(Courts-martial and juvenile court).*

COMMENTARY

Subsection (1): A magistrates' court. Includes a single justice: Magistrates' Courts Act 1980, s. 4(1).

A rape offence. Defined in s. 7, *infra*.

Subsection (2). The criteria are the same as in s. 2, *supra*.

An application for consent. That is, by the defendant. The prosecutor does not need consent.

Anonymity of complainants in rape etc. cases

4. (1) Subject to subs. (7)(a) of this section, after a person is accused of a rape offence no matter likely to lead members of the public to identify a woman as the complainant in relation to that accusation shall either be published in England and Wales in a written publication available to the public or be broadcast in England and Wales except as authorized by a direction given in pursuance of this section.

(2)-(5) . . .

(6) For the purposes of this section a person is accused of a rape offence if—

(a) an information is laid alleging that he has committed a rape offence; or
(b) he appears before a court charged with a rape offence; or
(c) a court before which he is appearing commits him for trial on a new charge alleging a rape offence; or
(d) a bill of indictment charging him with a rape offence is preferred before a court in which he may lawfully be indicted for the offence;

and references in this section and s. 7(5) on this Act to an accusation alleging a rape offence shall be construed accordingly; and in this section—

"a broadcast" means a broadcast by wireless telegraphy of sound or visual images intended for general reception, and cognate expressions shall be construed accordingly;
"complainant", in relation to a person accused of a rape or an accusation alleging a rape offence, means the woman against whom the offence is alleged to have been committed; and
"written publication" includes a film, a sound track and any other record in permanent form but does not include an indictment or other document prepared for use in particular legal proceedings.

(7) Nothing in this section—

(a) prohibits the publication or broadcasting, in consequence of an accusation alleging a rape offence, of matter consisting only of a report of legal proceedings other than proceedings at, or intended to lead to, or on an appeal arising out of, a trial at which the accused is charged with that offence; or
(b) affects any prohibition or restriction imposed by virtue of any other enactment upon a publication or broadcast;

and a direction in pursuance of this section does not effect the operation of subs. (1) of this section at any time before the direction is given.

COMMENTARY

The following guidance was given to clerks to justices in an annex to Home Office cir. 194/1976 dated December 16, 1976.
"It may be considered appropriate if, at the commencement of committal proceedings in respect of a rape offence, the Chairman or the Clerk reminds all persons present that, notwithstanding that the court may make an order under [s. 6(5) of the Magistrates' Courts Act 1980] removing the restrictions on reports of committal proceedings,

(i) it is a criminal offence to publish or broadcast at any time in the future any report of the proceedings or indeed any matter which is likely to identify the complainant except as authorized by a direction of the Crown Court; and

(ii) no such report or matter may be published, except as authorized by the court, which is likely to lead members of the public to identify the defendant in those proceedings unless and until the defendant is convicted of the offence by the Crown Court.

"The duty imposed upon the clerk to the justices by [s. 6(5) of the Magistrates' Courts Act 1980] in respect of giving notice of the result of committal proceedings no longer applies in respect of rape offences, so far as the inclusion in such notice of the defendant's name, address and age. The notice should not contain any particulars which identify or are likely to identify the complainant. Although there will be no breach of anonymity under the Act if names are used in court, nevertheless clerks to the justices may consider it expedient to advise justices and advocates to refrain from addressing the complainant and the defendant by name whenever possible. Clerks are also advised that in notices posted in the courthouse giving details of the cases to be heard in the various courtrooms, the name of the defendant should not—as is the usual practice—be included where a rape offence is charged. Therefore the notice should indicate in which courtroom such a case is being heard by some other names, for example:

4. COMMITTAL PROCEEDINGS

COURT 1

10 a.m.

Case 1—Committal Proceedings
        (Officer in charge of case on behalf of Police—Det:/Sgt: Smith)

"With regard to the citing of such cases, it is recommended that the current practice used in respect of cases involving juveniles should be followed with the addition of the symbol "[R]" indicating that it is a rape case."

Subsection (1): A rape offence. Defined in s. 7, *infra*.

Complainant/written publication/broadcast. Defined in subs. (6).

A direction given in pursuance of this section. That is by a judge of the Crown Court under subss. (2) or (3) or by the Court of Appeal under subs. (4).

Anonymity of defendants in rape etc. cases

6. (1) After a person is accused of a rape offence no matter likely to lead members of the public to identify him as the person against whom the accusation is made shall either be published in England and Wales in a written publication available to the public or be broadcast in England and Wales except—

- (a) as authorized by a direction given in pursuance of this section or by s. 4(7)(a) of this Act as applied by subs. (6) of this section; or
- (b) after he has been convicted of the offence at a trial before the Crown Court.

(2) If person accused of a rape offence applies to a magistrates' court, before the commencement of his trial for that offence, for a direction in pursuance of this subsection, the court shall direct that the preceding subsection shall not apply to him in consequence of the accusation; and if at a trial before the Crown Court at which a person is charged with a rape offence in respect of which he has not obtained such a direction—

- (a) the judge is satisfied that the effect of the preceding subsection is to impose a substantial and unreasonable restriction on the reporting of proceedings at the trial and that it is in the public interest to remove the restrictionof that person; or
- (b) that person applies to the judge for a direction in pursuance of this subsection,

the judge shall direct that the preceding subsection shall not apply to that person in consequence of the accusation alleging that offence.

(3) (*Crown Court*).

(4) (*Services Acts*).

(5) (*Juvenile Court*).

(6) Subsections (5) to (7) of s. 4 of this Act shall have effect for the purposes of this section as if for references to that section there were substituted references to this section; and—

- (a) in relation to a person charged as mentioned in subs. (4) of this section, s. 4(6) of this Act, as applied by this subsection, shall have effect as if for paras. (a) to (d) there were substituted the words "he is charged with a rape offence in pursuance of any provision of the Naval Discipline Act, 1957, the Army Act, 1955 or the Air Force Act, 1955";
- (b) in s. 5(2) of this Act the reference to the purposes of s. 4(2) of this Act shall be construed as including a reference to the purposes of subs. (2)

and (3) of this section; and

(c)   in relation to a person charged by virtue of this subsection with such an offence as is mentioned in subs. (5) of s. 5 of this Act, that subsection shall have effect as if for the reference to s. 4(1) of this Act there were substituted a reference to subs. (1) of this section.

COMMENTARY

Subsection (2): A rape offence. Defined in s. 7, *infra*.

A magistrates' court. Includes a single justice: Magistrates' Courts Act 1980, s. 4(1).

Citation, interpretation, commencement and extent

7. (1) (*Short title*).

(2) In this Act—

"a rape offence" means any of the following, namely rape, attempted rape, aiding, abetting, counselling and procuring rape or attempted rape, and incitement to rape; and

references to sexual intercourse shall be construed in accordance with s. 44 of the Sexual Offences Act, 1956 so far as it relates to natural intercourse (under which such intercourse is deemed complete on proof of penetration only);

and s. 46 of that Act (which relates to the meaning of "man" and "woman" in that Act) shall have effect as if the reference to that Act included a reference to this Act.

(3)-(6) . . .

COMMENTARY

Section 44 of the Sexual Offences Act 1956. Reads: "Where on the trial of an offence under this Act it is necessary to prove sexual intercourse (whether natural or unnatural) it shall not be necessary to prove the completion of the intercourse by the emission of seed, but the intercourse shall be deemed complete upon proof of penetration only."

Section 46 of that Act. Reads: "The use in any provision of this Act of the word "man" without the addition of the word "boy", or *vice versa*, shall not prevent the provision applying to any person to whom it would have applied if both words had been used, and similarly with the words "woman" and "girl.""

THE MAGISTRATES' COURTS ACT 1980

General nature of committal proceedings

4. (1) The functions of examining justices may be discharged by a single justice.

(2) Examining justices shall sit in open court except where any enactment contains an express provision to the contrary and except where it appears to them as respects the whole or any part of committal proceedings that the ends of justice would not be served by their sitting in open court.

(3) Subject to subs. (4) below and s. 102 below, evidence given before examining justices shall be given in the presence of the accused, and the defence shall be at liberty to put questions to any witness at the inquiry.

(4) Examining justices may allow evidence to be given before them in the absence of the accused if—

(a)   they consider that by reason of his disorderly conduct before them it is not practicable for the evidence to be given in his presence, or

(b)   he cannot be present for reasons of health but is represented by counsel or a solicitor and has consented to the evidence being given in his absence.

COMMENTARY

Subsection (2): Express provision to the contrary. *See* the Children and Young Persons Act 1933, s. 37, the Magistrates' Courts Act 1980, s. 105 and the Official Secrets Act 1920, s. 8(4).

Subsection (3). See in the introduction under Evidence and The Presence of the Accused.

Evidence given before examining justices. Since written statements put in under s. 102 of the Act are evidence, this section applies equally to committals under both subs. (1) and (2) of s. 6, *infra*.

The defence shall be at liberty. There is no corresponding provision in the Act or Rules in respect of the prosecution, but they are in practice always accorded the privilege of cross-examination of any witnesses called by the defendant.

Adjournment of inquiry

5. (1) A magistrates' court may, before beginning to inquire into an offence as examining justices, or at any time during the inquiry, adjourn the hearing, and if it does so shall remand the accused.

(2) The court shall when adjourning fix the time and place at which the hearing is to be resumed; and the time fixed shall be that at which the accused is required to appear or be brought before the court in pursuance of the remand or would be required to be brought before the court but for s. 128 (3A) below.

(as amended by the Criminal Justice Act 1982, sch. 9)

COMMENTARY

Subsection (1): May . . . adjourn. The justices' clerk has power further to adjourn criminal proceedings in certain circumstances with the consent of the prosecutor and the accused: Justices' Clerks Rules 1970.

Shall remand the accused. *See* form 5. The remand must be on bail or in custody: s. 128 of the Act. The general right to bail applies: Bail Act, 1976, s. 4.

Subsection (2): Fix the time. It is not therefore possible to adjourn a preliminary inquiry without fixing a date.

Discharge or committal for trial

6. (1) Subject to the provisions of this and any other Act relating to the summary trial of indictable offences, if a magistrates' court inquiring into an offence as examining justices is of opinion, on consideration of the evidence [and of any statement of the accused], that there is sufficient evidence to put the accused on trial by jury for any indictable offence, the court shall commit him for trial; and, if it is not of that opinion, it shall, if he is in custody for no other cause than the offence under inquiry, discharge him.

(2) A magistrates' court inquiring into an offence as examining justices may, if satisfied that all the evidence before the court (whether for the prosecution or the defence) consists of written statements tendered to the court under s. 102 below, with or without exhibits, commit the accused for trial for the offence without consideration of the contents of those statements, unless—

    (*a*)   the accused or one of the accused has no solicitor acting for him in the case (whether present in court or not);

    (*b*)   counsel or a solicitor for the accused or one of the accused , as the case may be, has requested the court to consider a submission that the statements disclose insufficient evidence to put that accused on trial by jury for the offence;

4. COMMITTAL PROCEEDINGS   157

and subs. (1) above shall not apply to a committal for trial under this subsection.

(3) Subject to s. 4 of the Bail Act 1976 and s. 41 below, the court may commit a person for trial—

> (a)   in custody, that is to say, by committing him to custody there to be safely kept until delivered in due course of law, or
> (b)   on bail in accordance with the Bail Act 1976, that is to say, by directing him to appear before the Crown Court for trial;

and where his release on bail is conditional on his providing one or more surety or surities and, in accordance with s. 8(3) of the Bail Act 1976, the court fixes the amount in which the surety is to be bound with a view to his entering into his recognizance subsequently in accordance with subss. (4) and (5) or (6) of that section the court shall in the meantime commit the accused to custody in accordance with para. (a) of this subsection.

(4) Where the court has committed a person to custody in accordance with para. (a) of subs. (3) above, then, if that person is in custody for no other cause, the court may, at any time before his first appearance before the Crown Court, grant him bail in accordance with the Bail Act 1976 subject to a duty to appear before the Crown Court for trial.

(5) Where a magistrates' court acting as examining justices commits any person for trial or determines to discharge him, the clerk of the court shall, on the day on which the committal proceedings are concluded or the next day, cause to be displayed in a part of the court house to which the public have access a notice—

> (a)   in either case giving that person's name, address, and age (if known);
> (b)   in a case where the court so commits him, stating the charge or charges on which he is committed and the court to which he is committed;
> (c)   in a case where the court determines to discharge him, describing the offence charged and stating that it has so determined;

but this subsection shall have effect subject to ss. 4 and 6 of the Sexual Offences (Amendment) Act 1976 (anonymity of complainant and accused in rape etc. cases).

(6) A notice displayed in pursuance of subs. (5) above shall not contain the name or address of any person under the age of 17 unless the justices in question have stated that in their opinion he would be mentioned in the notice apart from the preceding provisions of this subsection and should be mentioned in it for the purpose of avoiding injustice to him.

(as amended by the Criminal Justice Act 1982, s. 61.)

COMMENTARY

This section provides for two types of committal proceedings, (a) on consideration of the evidence (or conventional committal proceedings) under subs. (1); and (b) without consideration of the evidence under subs. (2).

The court's permission is not needed for the prosecutor to offer no evidence on a charge in committal proceedings: *R. v. Canterbury and St. Augustine's Justices, ex parte Klisiak (1981) 145 J.P. 344.*

Legal aid may be granted in the proceedings: Legal Aid Act 1974, s. 28.

Prosecution costs may be awarded out of central funds and the defendant's costs in the event of his not being committed: Costs in Criminal Cases Act 1973, s. 1 The prosecutor may also be ordered to pay the defendant's costs if the latter is discharged, but only when the examining justice is of opinion the charge was not made in good faith: s. 2(4), *ibid.* For costs where the prosecution is not proceeded with, see s. 12, *ibid.*

The provisions of s. 42 of this Act (restriction of justices sitting after dealing with bail) do not apply to committals for trial, nor is there apparently any objection in principle to magistrates who are aware of previous convictions acting as examining justices. If the committal proceedings are discontinued and the matter dealt with summarily then by s. 42 such a magistrate is debarred from trying the issue of guilt: *R.* v. *Brixton Prison Governor, ex parte Thompson* (1970) 134 J.P.N. 371 (an extradition case).

Subsection (1). For the procedure to be followed in a committal under this subsection *see* the Magistrates' Courts Rules 1981, r. 7, *infra*.

Indictable offence. Defined in the Interpretation Act 1978, sch. 1, as an offence which, if committed by an adult, is triable on indictment, whether it is exclusively so triable or not.

Examining justices. This term is defined in the Criminal Justice Act, 1925, s. 49(2) as "the justices before whom a charge is made against any person for an indictable offence, and references to examining justices include a reference to a single examining justice."

Of opinion. Justices evenly divided may adjourn for re-hearing before a differently constituted bench: *R.* v. *Hertfordshire Justices, ex parte Larsen* (1926) 89 J.P. 205; in which it was also said to be desirable that the bench should preferably consist of an odd number of justices.

The evidence. *See* under this title in the introduction.

Statement of the accused. It is submitted that the words in square brackets have been repealed by the Criminal Justice Act 1982, s. 72. *See* Ch. 5.

Sufficient evidence. *See* the introduction under "Conventional Committal Proceedings".

For any indictable offence. And not merely the offences charged by the prosecutor, but any disclosed in the evidence. If the defendant is committed in respect of a different offence from that charged it must be read to him: r. 7(12) of the Magistrates' Courts Rules 1981.

Other and additional counts may be subsequently be added to the indictment under the proviso to s. 2(2) of the Administration of Justice (Miscellaneous Provisions) Act, 1933.

Commit him for trial. The committing magistrate must specify the place of trial in accordance with the Supreme Court Act 1981, s. 75.

Legal aid may be granted by magistrates in respect of the trial in the Crown Court: Legal Aid Act 1974, s. 28.

"It shall be the duty of the clerk to the examining justices before whom a person is charged with murder, manslaughter or infanticide to inform the coroner who is responsible for holding an inquest upon the body of the making of the charge, and of the committal for trial or discharge, as the case may be, of the person charged": Coroners (Amendment) Act, 1926, s. 20(5). This section has been applied to the offence of causing death by reckless driving by the Road Traffic Act 1972, s. 1(2) and to aiding, abetting, counselling or procuring suicide by the Suicide Act, 1961, sch. 1.

The court shall ... discharge him. There is power to order costs against the prosecutor on a discharge only when the court is of opinion that the charge was not made in good faith: Costs in Criminal Cases Act 1973, s. 2(4). Costs may be awarded from central funds without that restriction: s. 1, *ibid*.

Subsection(2). For the procedure in a committal under this subsection *see* the Magistrates' Courts Rules 1981, r. 6, *infra*.

A magistrates' court . . . may. This terminology would appear to give the court an overriding discretion to refuse to deal with the proceedings under the procedure laid down in this section.

All the evidence before the court. This is merely a reference to the statements and not to the nature or admissibility of their contents: *R.* v. *Brooker* [1977] 65 Cr. App. R. 181. It is submitted that the wording of this subsection precludes the use of a written statement by a child taken in accordance with the Children and Young Persons Act 1963, s. 27.

Commit ... for trial. *See* the corresponding note to subs. (1), *supra*.

For the offence. That is, unlike committal proceedings under subs. (1), *supra,* a committal under this subsection may only be in respect of the charge or charges preferred by the prosecutor. Other and additional counts may be added to the indictment later under the proviso to s. 2(2) of the Administration of Justice (Miscellaneous Provisions) Act, 1933: *R.* v. *James William* [1972] Crim. L.R. 436. But the indictment will be quashed where the defendant is committed for trial in the respect of an offence which has been repealed: *R.* v. *Lamb (Thomas)* (1969) 133 J.P. 89.

A solicitor. The fact that the solicitor has no practising certificate is irrelevant to the validity of the committal: *R.* v. *Scott (John)* [1978] L.S. Gaz., July 12.

Subsection (3): In custody. *See* form 18. Juveniles not granted bail are committed to the care of the local authority: Children and Young Persons Act, 1969, s. 23. Unless certified as unruly: Children and Young Persons Act, 1969, s. 23(2). For the committal to custody of persons aged 17-20 *see* the Criminal Justice Act, 1948, s. 27. The reasons for refusing bail are set out in the Bail Act 1976. Bail may be granted by the High Court (Criminal Justice Act 1967, s. 22) and the Crown Court (Supreme Court Act 1981, s. 81) and the defendant if unrepresented must be informed that he may apply thereto: Bail Act 1976, s. 5(6).

On bail. Except in treason: Magistrates' Courts Act 1980, s. 41. The conditions and other incidents of bail are governed by the Bail Act 1976. The general right to bail applies: s. 4, *ibid.* If bail is offered on unacceptable terms the High Court have power to admit to bail: Criminal Justice Act 1967, s. 22. Notice must be sent to the prison governor, etc.: Magistrates' Courts Rules 1981, r. 9.

Subsection (5): Cause to be displayed. No minimum period of display is prescribed. Home Office circ. 209/1967 recommends "at least (*sic*) two to three days" and adds: "If it is not practicable to post up the notice in the building in which the court sits, it should be posted as near as possible to the entrance of the building."

Place of trial on indictment

7. A magistrates' court committing a person for trial shall specify the place at which he is to be tried, and in selecting that place shall have regard to—

    (*a*)   the convenience of the defence, the prosecution and the witnesses,

    (*b*)   the expediting of the trial, and

    (*c*)   any direction given by or on behalf of the Lord Chief Justice with the concurrence of the Lord Chancellor under s. 4(5) of the Courts Act 1971.

COMMENTARY

The Directions of the Lord Chief Justice are printed in Appx. C.

Restrictions on reports of committal proceedings

8. (1) Except as provided by subs. (2), (3) and (8) below, it shall not be lawful to publish in Great Britain a written report, or to broadcast in Great Britain a report, of any committal proceedings in England and Wales containing any matter other than that permitted by subs. (4) below.

(2) Subject to subs. (2A) below a magistrates' court shall, on application for the purpose made with reference to any committal proceedings by the accused or one of the accused, as the case may be, order that subs. (1) above shall not apply to reports of those proceedings.

(2A) Where in the case of two or more accused one of them objects to the making of an order under subs. (2) above, the court shall make the order if, and only if, it is satisfied, after hearing the representations of the accused, that it is in the interests of justice to do so.

(2B) An order under subs. (2) above shall not apply to reports of proceedings under subs. (2A) above, but any decision of the court to make or not to make such an order may be contained in reports published or broadcast before the time authorized by subs. (3) below.

(3) It shall not be unlawful under this section to publish or broadcast a report of committal proceedings containing any matter other than that permitted by subs. (4) below.—

    (*a*)   where the magistrates' court determines not to commit the accused, or determines to commit none of the accused, for trial after it so determines;

    (*b*)   where the court commits the accused or any of the accused for trial, after the conclusion of his trial or, as the case may be, the trial of the last to be tried;

and where at any time during the inquiry the court proceeds to try summarily the case of one or more of the accused under s. 25(3) or (7) below, while committing the other accused or one or more of the other accused for trial, it shall not be unlawful under this section to publish or broadcast as part of a report of the summary trial, after the court determines to proceed as aforesaid, a report of so much of the committal proceedings containing any such matter as takes place before the determination.

(4) The following matters may be contained in a report of committal proceedings published or broadcast without an order under subs. (2) before the time authorized by subs. (3) above, that is to say—

(a) the identity of the court and the names of the examining justices;
(b) the names, addresses and occupations of the parties and witnesses and the ages of the accused and witnesses;
(c) the offence or offences, or a summary of them, with which the accused is or are charged;
(d) the names of counsel and solicitors engaged in the proceedings;
(e) any decision of the court to commit the accused or any of the accused for trial, and any decision of the court on the disposal of the case of any accused not committed;
(f) where the court commits the accused or any of the accused for trial, the charge or charges, or a summary of them, on which he is committed and the court to which he is committed;
(g) where the committal proceedings are adjourned, the date and place to which they are adjourned;
(h) any arrangements as to bail on committal or adjournment;
(i) whether legal aid was granted to the accused or any of the accused.

(5) If a report is published or broadcast in contravention of this section, the following persons, that is to say—

(a) in the case of a publication of a written report as part of a newspaper or periodical, any proprietor, editor or publisher of the newspaper or periodical;
(b) in the case of a publication of a written report otherwise than as part of a newspaper or periodical, the person who publishes it;
(c) in the case of a broadcast of a report, any body corporate which transmits or provides the programme in which the report is broadcast and any person having functions in relation to the programme corresponding to those of the editor of a newspaper or periodical,

shall be liable on summary conviction to a fine not exceeding £500.

(6) Proceedings for an offence under this section shall not, in England and Wales, be instituted otherwise than by or with the consent of the Attorney-General.

(7) Subsection (1) above shall be in addition to, and not in derogation from, the provisions of any other enactment with respect to the publication of reports and proceedings of magistrates' and other courts.

(8) For the purposes of this section committal proceedings shall, in relation to an information charging an indictable offence, be deemed to include any proceedings in the magistrates' court before the court proceeds to inquire into the information as examining justices; but where a magistrates' court which has begun to try an information summarily discontinues the summary trial in

pursuance of s. 25(2) or (6) below and proceeds to inquire into the information as examining justices, that circumstance shall not make it unlawful under this section for a report of any proceedings on the information which was published or broadcast before the court determined to proceed as aforesaid to have been so published or broadcast.

(9) (*Repealed*)

(10) In this section—

"broadcast" means broadcast by wireless telegraphy sounds or visual images intended for general reception;

"publish", in relation to a report, means publish the report, either by itself or as part of a newspaper or periodical, for distribution to the public.

(*as amended by the Criminal Justice (Amendment) Act 1981, s. 1, the Contempt of Court Act 1981, s. 4(4)*).

COMMENTARY

The court is required to give the defendant, whether legally represented or not, an explanation of the effects of this section: Magistrates' Courts Rules 1981, r. 5(1). The existence of this section does not prevent the court from making an order under the Contempt of Court Act 1981, s. 4(2): *R. v. Horsham Justices, ex parte Farquharson and Another* (1981) *The Times*, December 22.

Subsection (1): Great Britain. That is, England, Scotland and Wales: Union with Scotland Act, 1706; Wales and Berwick Act, 1746, s. 3.

A written report. Writing includes typing, printing, lithography, photography and other modes of representing or reproducing words in a visible form: Interpretation Act, 1978.

Committal proceedings. Defined in s. 150(1) of the Act as meaning proceedings before a magistrates' court acting as examining justices.

Subsection (2). Once a court has made an order under this subsection this fact must be stated at any adjourned hearing on a later date: Magistrates' Courts Rules 1981, r. 5(3).
The order must be recorded in the register: *ibid*, r. 5(2).
Jurisdiction to make the order is not confined to magistrates sitting as examining justices, but may be made at an earlier stage of the proceedings. When an order is made the particular committal proceedings to which it relates must be ascertained in the light of the circumstances prevailing at the time when the order was made: *R. v. Bow Street Magistrate, ex parte Kray* (1969) 133 J.P. 54; *R. v. Blackpool Justices, ex parte Beaverbrook Newspapers, Ltd.* (1972) 136 J.P. 225. An order under this subsection applied to a variety of charges being heard together is not extinguished by reason of the fact that the charges are later dealt with separately: *R. v. Bow Street Magistrate, ex parte Kray, supra.*
There is, seemingly, no power to reimpose the restrictions once they have been removed. *See R. v. Blackpool JJ, supra.*

Subsection 2A: The interests of justice. It is the interests of justice as affecting the defendant that the court must consider, *per* Shaw L.J. in *R. v. Horsham Justices, ex parte Farquharson* [1982] 2 All E.R. 269 (application by newspaper reporter and union). *Dictum* approved in *R. v. Leeds Justices, ex parte Sykes* [1983] 1 All E.R. 460. The phrase "the interests of justice" incorporates as a paramount consideration that the defendant should have a fair trial. Only if a powerful case is made out should justices lift reporting restrictions if one of the defendants objects: *R. v. Leeds Justices, supra.* (Magistrates wrong to lift restrictions in order to give publicity to a defendant's grievance against the police where a co-defendant feared publicity would prejudice a fair trial.)

Subsection (4)(h): Arrangements as to bail. That is to say, the terms and conditions and not the evidence or submissions.

Subsection (6): The consent of the Attorney-General. "Any document purporting to be the consent of a law officer of the Crown or the director for, or to, the institution of any criminal proceedings or the institution of criminal proceedings in any particular form and to be signed by a law officer of the Crown, the director or an assistant director, as the case may be, shall be admissible as *prima facie* evidence without further proof.": Prosecution of Offences Act 1979, s. 7. For the Solicitor General's powers to discharge his functions *see* the Law Officers Act 1944, s. 1 (not reproduced herein).

Subsection (7): Any other enactment. *See*, for example, the Judicial Proceedings (Regulation of Reports) Act 1926 (in relation to indecent details), the Children and Young Persons Act, 1933 s. 39 (identification of juveniles) and the Sexual Offences (Amendment) Act 1976, s. 6, *supra*.

Subsection (8). This means that the restrictions of this section apply from the first moment the defendant is brought before the court. Compare the remarks of Widgery LCJ, in *R.* v. *Bow Street Magistrate, ex parte Kray* (1969) 133 J.P. 54.

Indictable offence. Defined in the Interpretation Act 1978, sch. 1.

Certain offences triable either way

17 (1) The offences listed in sch. 1 to this Act shall be triable either way.

(2) Subsection (1) above is without prejudice to any other enactment by virtue of which any offence is triable either way.

COMMENTARY

Subsection (1): Triable either way. Defined in the Interpretation Act 1978, sch. 1 (see the Commentary to s. 18, *infra*).

Subsection (2). There are many statutes which create offences triable either on indictment or summarily. Such offences are also "triable either way."

Initial procedure on information against adult for offence triable either way

18. (1) Sections 19 to 23 below shall have effect where a person who has attained the age of 17 appears or is brought before a magistrates' court on an information charging him with an offence triable either way.

(2) Without prejudice to s. 11(1) above, everything that the court is required to do under ss. 19 to 22 below must be done before any evidence is called and, subject to subs. (3) below and s. 23 below, with the accused present in court.

(3) The court may proceed in the absence of the accused in accordance with such of the provisions of ss. 19 to 22 below as are applicable in the circumstances if the court considers that by reason of his disorderly conduct before the court it is not practicable for the proceedings to be conducted in his presence; and subss. (3) to (5) of s. 23 below, so far as applicable, shall have effect in relation to proceedings conducted in the absence of the accused by virtue of this subsection (references in those subsections to the person representing the accused being for this purpose read as references to the person, if any, representing him).

(4) A magistrates' court proceeding under ss 19 to 23 below may adjourn the proceedings at any time, and on doing so on any occasion when the accused is present may remand the accused, and shall remand him if—

> (*a*)   on the occasion on which he first appeared, or was brought, before the court to answer to the information he was in custody or, having been released on bail, surrendered to the custody of the court; or
> (*b*)   he has been remanded at any time in the course of proceedings on the information;

and where the court remands the accused, the time fixed for the resumption of the proceedings shall be that at which he is required to appear or be brought before the court in pursuance of the remand or would be required to be brought before the court but for s. 128 (3A) below

(5) The functions of a magistrates' court under ss 19 to 23 below may be discharged by a single justice, but the foregoing provision shall not be taken to authorize the summary trial of an information by a magistrates' court composed of less than two justices.

(as amended by the Criminal Justice Act 1982, sch. 9).

COMMENTARY

This section and ss 19 to 23 *infra*, do not apply where the defendant is charged with an offence under the Firearms Act 1968, s. 17(1) or (2) (using firearm to resist arrest and possessing firearms while committing certain offences) and is also charged with a sch. 1 offence. For the procedure in such cases see the Firearms Act 1968, sch. 6, Part II.

Failure to follow the procedure in ss. 19-24 will result in any ensuing conviction being quashed: *R. v. Tottenham Justices, ex parte Arthur's Transport Services* [1981] Crim. L.R. 180.

Subsection (1): Attained the age of 17. For the determination of age see the Magistrates' Courts Act 1980, s. 150(4). For the mode of trial of juveniles see the Children and Young Persons Act 1969, s. 6.

Subsection (1): Offence triable either way. This phrase is defined in the Interpretation Act 1978, sch. 1, as meaning an offence which, if committed by an adult, is triable either on indictment or summarily.

Subsection (2): Before any evidence is called. This would appear to relate to evidence in the trial and not to statements made on oath during a bail application.

The accused present in court. The effect of this is that the decision as to mode of trial may not be taken without the defendant being personally present in court unless he is legally represented and the conditions of s. 23 are satisfied. (This subsection is drafted so as to exclude the general right of an accused contained in s. 122 of the Act to appear by a legal representative). This subsection does not affect s. 11 of the Act which prescribes what may take place if the defendant does not appear, but in that case appearance by a legal representative under s. 122, is sufficient unless for any other purpose the accused's appearance in person is required, e.g. to surrender to bail.

Subsection (3). This allows the court to exclude the defendant personally in the circumstances referred to and as such is an exception to the common law right of a defendant to be present at his trial. This subsection ceases to operate after evidence has been called: subs. (2). The comparable provisions in s. 4(4) apply only when committal proceedings begin. Note the powers of a legal representative under s. 23, *infra*, as applied by this subsection.

Subsection (4). The remand will be in accordance with s. 128 of the Act. The general right to bail applies: Bail Act 1970, s. 4. The period of the remand must be co-terminous with the adjournment. The powers of adjournment contained in ss. 5 and 10 of the Act are not available at this stage of the proceedings.

There is no overriding necessity for evidence of arrest before a remand in custody: *R. v. Guest, ex parte Metropolitan Police Commissioner* (1962) 126 J.P. 21.

Court to begin by considering which mode of trial appears more suitable

19. (1) The court shall consider having regard to the matters mentioned in subs. (3) below and any representations made by the prosecutor or the accused, the offence appears to the court more suitable for summary trial or for trial on indictment.

(2) Before so considering, the court—

    (*a*)   shall cause the charge to be written down, if this has not already been done, and read to the accused; and

    (*b*)   shall afford first the prosecutor and then the accused an opportunity to make representations as to which mode of trial would be more suitable.

(3) The matters to which the court is to have regard under subs. (1) above are the nature of the case; whether the circumstances make the offence one of serious character; whether the punishment which a magistrates' court would have power to inflict for it would be adequate; and any other circumstances which appear to the court to make it more suitable for the offence to be tried in one way rather than the other.

(4) If the prosecution is being carried on by the Attorney General, the Solicitor General or the Director of Public Prosecutions and he applies for the offence to be

tried on indictment, the preceding provisions of this section and ss 20 and 21 below shall not apply, and the court shall proceed to inquire into the information as examining justices.

COMMENTARY

This section applies in the circumstances set out in s. 18(1), *supra*. Its requirements must be completed before any evidence is called and, subject to s. 23 *infra*, with the accused present in court: s. 18(2).

Subsection (1): Representations. The court is not bound by these (unless subs. (4) applies) but must consider them, if made. The court may not at this stage investigate whether the accused has any previous convictions: *R.* v. *Colchester Justices, ex parte North Essex Building Co. Ltd.* (1977) 141 J.P. 713 (limited company which could not be committed for sentence). It is a matter of fundamental importance that this provision should be complied with and the clerk should make a record of the fact the accused was asked for representations and of his response: *R.* v. *Horseferry Road Magistrates' Court, ex parte Constable* [1981] Crim. L.R. 504, (form of words used by the clerk statisfactory but preferable to follow the statutory wording). It is submitted that the fact that the accused wishes other offences to be taken into consideration is not a matter which should be relied upon by the court in taking its decision under this section because this is a matter which can justify a committal to the Crown Court for sentence. *See* the articles at 145 J.P.N. 647 and 735 in which latter the case of *R.* v. *Derby and South Derbyshire Magistrates, ex parte McCarthy and McGovern* (1981) April 28, is considered.

Subsection (2): Cause the charge to be written down. The charge sheet or summons will usually suffice.

Subsection (3): The nature of the case. For example, the trial of a councillor in a small borough: *Afford* v. *Pettit* (1949) 133 J.P. 433.

Offence . . . of serious character. Justices must exercise their discretion judicially. Grave offences, such as stabbing which barely falls short of murder, were not intended to be tried summarily; although the Divisional Court will not in such a case interfere by means of *certiorari*. In *R.* v. *Middlesex Quarter Sessions, ex parte Director of Public Prosecutions* (1950) 114 J.P. 276 Lord Goddard CJ said "Serious cases ought to be dealt with by the superior courts", and in *R.* v. *South Greenhoe Justices, ex parte Director of Public Prosecutions* (1950) 114 J.P. 312: "When a case is of a serious character – and surely a case of a man committing 13 bankruptcy offences is one of a serious character – that case ought to go for trial. It is not merely a matter of what the sentence may be . . . serious cases ought to be dealt with by a superior court." In *R.* v. *Everest* (1968) 118 Sol. Jo. 820, Lord Parker CJ said: "Serious offences must be dealt with on indictment, which would enable appropriate sentences to be given." And see also *R.* v. *Coe* (1969) 133 J.P. 103 and *R.* v. *Pitson* [1972] 56 Cr. App. R. 391: "Large scale thieving and receiving" should be dealt with by the Crown Court. While trivial burglaries may be tried by magistrates, cases of breaking and entering, particularly at night, should not, *per* Lord Lane CJ in *R.* v. *Hardman* (1982) *The Times*, November 10.

Punishment. Appears to include the award of compensation: *R.* v. *McLean, ex parte Metropolitan Commissioner of Police* [1975] Crim. L.R. 289.

Subsection (4). *See* the commentary to s. 18(6), *supra*.

Procedure where summary trial appears more suitable

20. (1) If, where the court has considered as required by s. 19(1) above, it appears to the court that the offence is more suitable for summary trial, the following provisions of this section shall apply (unless excluded by s. 23 below).

(2) The court shall explain to the accused in ordinary language—

    (a)   that it appears to the court more suitable for him to be tried summarily for the offence, and that he can either consent to be so tried or, if he wishes, be tried by a jury; and

    (b)   that if he is tried summarily and is convicted by the court, he may be committed for sentence to the Crown Court under s. 38 below if the convicting court, on obtaining information about his character and antecedents, is of opinion that they are such that greater punishment should be inflicted than the convicting court has power to inflict for the offence.

(3) After explaining to the accused as provided by subs. (2) above the court shall ask him whether he consents to be tried summarily or wishes to be tried by a jury, and—

(a) if he consents to be tried summarily, shall proceed to the summary trial of the information;

(b) if he does not so consent, shall proceed to inquire into the information as examining justices.

COMMENTARY

This section applies in the circumstances set out in s. 18(1), *supra.*. It does not apply where the presence of the accused has been dispensed with under s. 18(3) or when the accused's legal representative has signalled his consent under s. 23, *infra*. The requirements of this section must be complied with before any evidence is called and, subject to s. 23, *infra*, with the accused present in court: s. 18(2).

Subsection (2): Explain to the accused. Failure to give the caution would seemingly render a committal for sentence invalid: *cf. R. v. Kent Justices, ex parte Machin* (1952) 116 J.P. 242; *R. v. Newcastle under Lyme Justices, ex parte Whitehouse* [1952] 2 All E.R. 531. Where the omission of the caution is discovered and the proceedings withdrawn a fresh information may seemingly be laid: *Davis v. Morton* (1913) 77 J.P. 223.

Character and antecedents. This term has been considered judicially in relation to its use in s. 38 of the Act.

Subsection (3): If he consents. Although the caution must be put to the defendant in person it was held under the pre-existing provisions that a consent to summary trial by counsel or solicitor in the presence and the hearing of the defendant is sufficient if not contradicted at the time: *R. v. Latham, ex parte Roberts* (1943) 41 L.G.R. 99. And see also *R. v. Salisbury and Amesbury Justices, ex parte Greatbatch* (1954) 118 J.P. 392. A legal representative may act in the absence of the accused in the circumstances set out in s. 23, *infra*. A representative may consent to summary trial on behalf of a corporation: para. 2 of sch. 3 of the Act. Where a representative does not appear the corporation's consent to summary trial is not required: para. 3, *ibid*.

Consent may be withdrawn at any time before evidence is given: *R. v. Craske, ex parte Metropolitan Police Commissioner* (1957) 121 J.P. 502; confirmed by the Court of Criminal Appeal in *R. v. Ibrahim* (1958) 122 J.P. 119, and re-affirmed in *R. v. Southampton City Justices, ex parte Robins* (1981) 144 J.P. 288. Following *R. v. Craske, supra*, the Divisional Court made it clear that the justices have a discretion whether or not to permit withdrawal of consent which will depend on how they see the broad justice of the whole situation: *R. v. Southampton Justices, ex parte Briggs* (1972) 136 J.P. 237. Consent may not be withdrawn after evidence has been given: *R. v. Bennett, ex parte R.* [1960] 1 All E.R. 335. However, the court now has the power to abandon summary trial at this stage and convert to committal proceedings under s. 25(2), *infra*. [N.B. The effects of this provision, which first appeared in the Criminal Justice Administration Act 1962, have not been considered expressly in any of the subsequent cases dealing with the discretion to change the mode of trial.] The court's refusal to allow consent to be withdrawn cannot be attacked by an application for prerogative orders unless it was wrongly exercised, that is to say, exercised on a wrong principle or exercised having regard to factors which ought to have been ignored or exercised without reference to factors which ought to have been included, or indeed not exercised at all: *R. v. Lambeth Metropolitan Stipendiary Magistrate, ex parte Wright* (1974) *The Times*, April 29; [1974] Crim. L.R. 444; 138 J.P.N. 313. When a person is tried summarily under this section "the court shall cause his consent to be entered in a register and if the consent was signified by a person representing him in his absence" that fact too: Magistrates' Courts Rules 1981, r. 66(5).

The summary trial. Any subsequent adjournment must be in accordance with s. 10 of the Act and not s. 18(4). The court may subsequently discontinue the summary trial and proceed as examining justices in accordance with s. 25(2), *infra*.

Examining justices. Any subsequent adjournment must be in accordance with s. 5 of the Act and not s. 18(4). The court may with the defendant's consent subsequently change over to summary trial in accordance with s. 25(3), *infra*. *See* the note to s. 2, *supra*.

Procedure where trial on indictment appears more suitable

21. If, where the court has considered as required by s. 19(1) above, it appears to the court that the offence is more suitable for trial on indictment, the court shall tell the accused that the court has decided that it is more suitable for him to be tried for the offence by a jury, and shall proceed to inquire into the information as examining justices.

COMMENTARY

The requirements of this section must be complied with before any evidence is called, and subject to s. 23, *infra*, with the accused present in court: s. 18(2). This section does not apply when the accused has been excluded under s. 18(3), *supra*, or when the accused's legal representative has signified his consent under s. 23, *infra*.

Examining justices. See the note to s. 20.

Certain offences triable either way to be tried summarily if value involved is small

22. (1) If the offence charged by the information is one of those mentioned in the first column of sch. 2 to the Act (in this section referred to as "scheduled offences") then, subject to subs. 17 below, the court shall, before proceeding in accordance with s. 19 above consider whether, having regard to any representations made by the prosecutor or the accused, the value involved (as defined in subs. (10) below) appears to the court to exceed the relevant sum.

For the purpose of this section the relevant sum is £200.

(2) If, where subs. (1) above applies, it appears to the court clear that, for the offence charged, the value involved does not exceed the relevant sum, the court shall proceed as if the offence were triable only summarily, and ss. 19 to 21 above shall not apply.

(3) If, where subs. (1) above applies, it appears to the court clear that, for the offence charged, the value involved exceeds the relevant sum, the court shall thereupon proceed in accordance with s. 19 above in the ordinary way without further regard to the provisions of this section.

(4) If, where subs. (1) above applies, it appears to the court for any reason not clear whether, for the offence charged, the value involved does or does not exceed the relevant sum, the provisions of subs. (5) and (6) below shall apply.

(5) The court shall cause the charge to be written down, if this has not already been done, and read to the accused, and shall explain to him in ordinary language—

　　(*a*)　that he can, if he wishes to be tried summarily for the offence and that if he consents to be so tried, he will definitely be tried in that way; and

　　(*b*)　that if he is tried summarily and is convicted by the court, his liability to imprisonment or a fine will be limited as provided in s. 33 below.

(6) After explaining to the accused as provided by subs. (5) above the court shall ask him whether he consents to be tried summarily and—

　　(*a*)　if he so consents, shall proceed in accordance with subs. (2) above as if that subsection applied;

　　(*b*)　if he does not so consent, shall proceed in accordance with subs. (3)

above as if that subsection applied.

(7) Subsection (1) above shall not apply where the offence charged—

(a)   is one of two or more offences with which the accused is charged on the same occasion and which appear to the court to constitute or form part of a series of two or more offences of the same or a similar character; or

(b)   consists in the incitement to commit two or more scheduled offences.

(8) Where a person is convicted by a magistrates' court of a scheduled offence, it shall not be open to him to appeal to the Crown Court against the conviction on the ground that the convicting court's decision as to the value involved was mistaken.

(9) If, where subs. (1) above applies, the offence charged is one with which the accused is charged jointly with a person who has not attained the age of 17, the reference in that subsection to any representations made by the accused shall be read as including any representations made by the person under 17.

(10) In this section "the value involved", in relation to any scheduled offence, means the value indicated in the second column of sch. 2 to this Act, measured as indicated in the third column of that schedule; and in that schedule "the material time" means the time of the alleged offence.

COMMENTARY

This section applies to most offences of criminal damage except arson (see sch. 2), except in the circumstances referred to in subs. (7). It contemplates three contingencies:

(i)   when it appears clear to the court that the value involved (as defined in subs. (10) and sch. 2) is £200 or less, in which case the court proceeds according to summary trial in accordance with subs. (2);

(ii)   when it appears clear to the court that the value involved exceeds £200, in which case the court proceeds according to the provisions of ss 19-21, which govern the selection of method of trial offences triable either way; and

(iii)   when it is not clear whether the value involved does or does not exceed £200, in which case the special procedure of subss. (5) and (6) is applied by subs. (4). If the accused does not consent to summary trial thereunder the procedure under s. 19 is followed in accordance with s. 22(3). Under this he has a second opportunity to consent to summary trial but will suffer disadvantages if he does consent; in particular, he will be subject on conviction to a greater maximum penalty, he can be committed to the Crown Court for sentence and the magistrates can revert to trial on indictment in accordance with s. 24.

There is no appeal to the Crown Court against the court's decision as to value: subs. (8).

By virtue of subs. (1) the procedure of this section takes place before representations are heard from prosecutor and defendant under s. 19, *supra*. Its requirements must be complied with before any evidence is called and, subject to s. 23, *infra*, with the accused present in court: s. 18(2). The court's decision as to value must be recorded in the register: Magistrates' Courts Rules 1981, r. 66(7).

Subsection (1): Representations. Representations under this section are confined to value only. The court is not bound by these but must consider them, if made. Unlike the "single procedure" neither side has the right to speak first. A juvenile jointly charged with an adult is entitled to make representations: subs. (9).

While the court may in its discretion hear evidence on the value involved it need not do so. Representations imply something less than evidence. The nearest analogy is a speech in mitigation: *R. v. Canterbury and St. Augustine's Justices, ex parte Klisiak* (1981) 145 J.P. 344.

Subsection (2). The maximum penalty for an offence tried summarily is three months' imprisonment and £500: s. 33.

Subsection (4). This is a procedural device which seeks to avoid argument about the value of the property involved by giving the accused the right to select the mode of trial wherever there is doubt in the matter. In such cases s. 33 encourages the accused to opt for summary trial by limiting the maximum penalties thereon, by removing the power of the court to commit an offender to the Crown Court for greater sentence and by taking away the power of the court to change to committal proceedings.

Subsection (5). See the notes to ss 18 and 20, *supra*. Subsections (5) and (6) do not apply where the accused has been excluded from the court under s. 18(3), *supra*, or where his legal representative signals consent in accordance with s. 23. The maximum penalty on summary trial is limited to three months' imprisonment and a fine of not more than £500. There is no power to commit for sentence under s. 38 of the Act.

Fine. Includes any pecuniary penalty: s. 150(1) of the Act.

Definitely. The power in s. 25 *infra*, to change from summary trial to committal proceedings does not apply to summary trial under subs. (2) of this section.

Subsection (6). See the note to subs. (5).

Subsection (7). The object of this subsection is to allow the defendant to be tried on indictment when, although the criminal damage charge is a very minor one, there are other charges which may make a minor matter more serious: *per* Lord Lane CJ, in *R.* v. *Tottenham Justices, ex parte Tibble* (1981) 145 J.P. 269.

A series of offences. To form part of a series the offences must be separated in time: *R.* v. *Hatfield Justices, ex parte Castle* (1981) 145 J.P. 265; *R.* v. *Canterbury and St. Augustine's Justices, ex parte Klisiak, supra.* In *R.* v. *St. Helens Justices, ex parte McClorie* [1983] 1 W.L.R. 1332 two criminal damage offences were held to be a series. In such a case the value of the damage was immaterial.

The same or similar character. An offence of common assault is not of similar character to an offence of criminal damage. Generally speaking, similar offences will be other offences under s. 1 of the Criminal Damage Act 1971: *R.* v. *Tottenham Justices, ex parte Tibble, supra*, disapproving *R.* v. *Leicester Justices, ex parte Lord* (1980) *The Times*, June 20. In *re Prescott* [1980] 70 Cr. App. R. 244, it was held that an offence of obstructing a police officer was not of the same or similar character as an offence of criminal damage to the officer's trousers. In, *R.* v. *Hatfield Justices, ex parte Castle, supra*, it was held that threatening behaviour and obstruction were not similar to criminal damage. To be of similar character the other offence must be triable either way: *R.* v. *Hatfield Justices, ex parte Castle, supra; R.* v. *Considine* [1980] Crim. L.R. 179.

Incitement to commit a scheduled offence. Is itself a scheduled offence: sch. 1, para. 35.

Subsection (8). This would not rule out an appeal to the High Court by way of case stated, for example, if the court came to a decision as to value for which there were no possible grounds. Nor would it prevent an appeal to the Crown Court against the making of a compensation order in a particular amount.

Power of court, with consent of legally represented accused, to proceed in his absence

23 (1) Where—

   (a) the accused is represented by counsel or a solicitor who in his absence signifies to the court the accused's consent to the proceedings for determining how he is to be tried for the offence being conducted in his absence; and

   (b) the court is satisfied that there is good reason for proceeding in the absence of the accused

the following provisions of this section shall apply.

(2) Subject to the following provisions of this section, the court may proceed in the absence of the accused in accordance with such of the provisions of ss 19 to 22 above as are applicable in the circumstances.

(3) If, in a case where subs. (1) of s. 22 above applies, it appears to the court as

mentioned in subs. (4) of that section, subss. (5) and (6) of that section shall not apply and the court—

(*a*)   if the accused's consent to be tried summarily has been or is signified by the person representing him, shall proceed in accordance with subs. (2) of that section as if that subsection applied; or

(*b*)   if that consent has not been and is not so signified, shall proceed in accordance with subs. (3) of that section as if that subsection applied.

(4) If, where the court has considered as required by s. 19(1) above, it appears to the court that the offence is more suitable for summary trial then—

(*a*)   if the accused's consent to be tried summarily has been or is signified by the person representing him, s. 20 above shall not apply, and the court shall proceed to the summary trial of the information; or

(*b*)   if that consent has not been and is not so signified, s. 20 above shall not apply and the court shall proceed to inquire into the information as examining justices and may adjourn the hearing without remanding the accused.

(5) If, where the court has considered as required by s. 19(1) above, it appears to the court that the offence is more suitable for trial on indictment, s. 21 above shall not apply, and the court shall proceed to inquire into the information as examining justices and may adjourn the hearing without remanding the accused.

COMMENTARY

This section allows the accused's legal representative to signify his consent to the mode of trial proceedings being conducted in his absence. However, the court must also be satisfied that there is good reason for so proceeding. It is an exception to the general rule in s. 18(2) that the accused must be personally present during the selection of the mode of trial. The court register must show whether the accused was present: Magistrates' Courts Rules 1981, r. 66(6).

This section does not relieve the accused, if he has been bailed to attend court, from his duty to surrender.

This section has effect for the purposes set out in s. 18(1), *supra*.

Subsection (1)(a). When the court is not satisfied there is good reason for proceeding in the absence of the accused it may issue a summons or warrant under s. 25, *infra*.

Subsection (4)(a): Section 20. That is, the caution must not be put.

Subsections (4)(b)(5). When the hearing is adjourned without the accused being remanded a summons or warrant may issue under s. 25, *infra*.

Summary trial of information against child or young person for indictable offence

24. (1) Where a person under the age of 17 appears or is brought before a magistrates' court on an information charging him with an indictable offence other than homicide, he shall be tried summarily unless—

(*a*)   he has attained the age of 14 and the offence is such as is mentioned in subs. (2) of s. 53 of the Children and Young Persons Act 1933 (under which young persons convicted on indictment of certain grave crimes may be sentenced to be detained for long periods) and the court considers that if he is found guilty of the offence it ought to be possible to sentence him in pursuance of that subsection; or

(*b*)   he is charged jointly with a person who has attained the age of 17 and the court considers it necessary in the interests of justace to commit them both for trial;

and accordingly in a case falling within para. (*a*) or (*b*) of this subsection the court shall commit the accused for trial if either it is of the opinion that there is sufficient evidence to put him on trial or it has power under s. 6(2) above so to commit him without consideration of the evidence.

(2) Where, in a case falling within subs. (1)(*b*) above, a magistrates' court commits a person under the age of 17 for trial for an offence with which he is charged jointly with a person who has attained that age, the court may also commit him for trial for any other indictable offence with which he is charged at the same time (whether jointly with the person who has attained that age or not) if that other offence arises out of circumstances which are the same as or connected with those giving rise to the first-mentioned offence.

(3) If on trying a person summarily in pursuance of subs. (1) above the court finds him guilty, it may impose a fine of an amount not exceeding £400 or may exercise the same powers as it could have exercised if he had been found guilty of an offence for which, but for s. 1(1) of the Criminal Justice Act 1982, it could have sentenced him to imprisonment for a term not exceeding–
   (*a*)   the maximum term of imprisonment for the offence on con-
           viction on indictment; or
   (*b*)   six months,
whichever is the less.

(4) In relation to a person under the age of 14 subs. (3) above shall have effect as if for the words "£400" there were substituted the words "£100"; but this subsection shall cease to have effect on the coming into force of s. 4 of the Children and Young Persons Act 1969 (which prohibits criminal proceedings against children).

(as amended by the Criminal Justice Act 1982, sch. 14).

COMMENTARY

There are now no circumstances in which juveniles have a right to claim trial by jury but they must be so tried in the circumstances specified in subs. (1) of this section.

Subsection (1). In *Re Daley* (1982) 146 J.P. 363; it was held that the date at which to determine whether an accused person has attained an age which entitles him to elect to be tried by a jury for an offence triable either way is the date of his appearance before the magistrates' court on the occasion when the court makes its decision as to the mode of trial. *Daley's* case concerned a 16 year old charged with an either way offence who, after pleading not guilty before a juvenile court, had subsequently attained the age of 17 at an adjourned hearing when he claimed trial by jury. *See* generally the article at 146 J.P.N. 540.
   For the restrictions upon evidence concerned with the sexual experience of a complainant in a rape offence see the Sexual Offences (Amendment) Act 1976, s. 2 and for their application to the trial of a juvenile under this section, s. 3(3), *ibid.*

The age of 17. For the determination of age *see* the Magistrates' Courts Act 1980, s. 150(4).

A magistrates' court. Not necessarily a juvenile court: *see* the Children and Young Persons Act, 1933, s. 46 and the 1963 Act, s. 18.

Indictable offence. Defined in the Interpretation Act 1978, sch. 1.

Homicide. Homicide would appear to include the offence of causing death by reckless driving.

Subsection (2) of s. 53 of the Act of 1933. This reads:

   "Where a child or young person is convicted on indictment of (any offence punishable in the case of an adult with imprisonment for 14 years or more, not being an offence the sentence for which is fixed by law) and the court is of opinion that none of the other methods in which the case may legally be dealt with is suitable, the court may sentence the offender to be detained for such period (not exceeding the maximum term of imprisonment with which the offence is punishable in the case of an adult) as may be specified in the sentence; and where such sentence has been passed the child or young person shall, during that period . . . be liable to be detained in such place and on such conditions as the Secretary of State may direct."

Charged jointly. It has been said in another connexion that "the use of the word 'jointly' or 'together' is not necessary to make the offence charged in the count a joint offence," *per* Stephenson LJ, in *R.* v.

LJ, in *R*. v. *Rowlands* (1972) 136 J.P. 106. In *R*. v. *Newham Justices, ex parte Knight* [1976] Crim. L.R. 323, the court accepted that a mother and child involved in the same incident but separately charged with theft could be regarded as having been jointly charged.

Sufficient evidence. This relates to a committal under s. 6(1), *supra*.

Subsection (3). The powers of the adult court in dealing with a juvenile are restricted in accordance with the Children and Young Persons Act 1969, s. 7(8).

Power to change from summary trial to committal proceedings and vice versa

25. (1) Subsections (2) to (4) below shall have effect where a person who has attained the age of 17 appears or is brought before a magistrates' court on an information charging him with an offence triable either way.

(2) Where the court has (otherwise than in pursuance of s. 22(2) above) begun to try the information summarily, the court may, at any time before the conclusion of the evidence for the prosecution, discontinue the summary trial and proceed to inquire into the information as examining justices and, on doing so, may adjourn the hearing without remanding the accused.

(3) Where the court has begun to inquire into the information as examining justices, then, if at any time during the inquiry it appears to the court, having regard to any representations made in the presence of the accused by the prosecutor, or made by the accused, and to the nature of the case, that the offence is after all more suitable for summary trial, the court may, after doing as provided in subs. (4) below, ask the accused whether he consents to be tried summarily and, if he so consents, may proceed to try the information summarily; but if the prosecution is being carried on by the Attorney General, the Solicitor General or the Director of Public Prosecutions, the court shall not act under this subsection without his consent.

(4) Before asking the accused under subs. (3) above whether he consents to be tried summarily, the court shall in ordinary language—

> (*a*)   explain to him that it appears to the court more suitable for him to be tried summarily for the offence, but that this can only be done if he consents to be so tried; and
>
> (*b*)   unless it has already done so, explain to him, as provided in s. 20(2)(*b*) above, about the court's power to commit to the Crown Court for sentence.

(5) Where a person under the age of 17 appears or is brought before a magistrates' court on an information charging him with an indictable offence other than homicide, and the court—

> (*a*)   has begun to try the information summarily on the footing that the case does not fall within para. (*a*) or (*b*) of s. 24(1) above and must therefore be tried summarily, as required by the said s. 24(1); or
>
> (*b*)   has begun to inquire into the case as examining justices on the footing that the case does so fall,

subss (6) or (7) below, as the case may be, shall have effect.

(6) If, in a case falling within subs. (5)(*a*) above, it appears to the court at any time before the conclusion of the evidence for the prosecution that the case is after all one which under the said s. 24(1) ought not to be tried summarily, the court may discontinue the summary trial and proceed to inquire into the information as examining justices and, on doing so, may adjourn the hearing without remanding the accused.

(7) If, in a case falling within subs. (5)(*b*) above, it appears to the court at any

time during the inquiry that the case is after all one which under the said s. 24(1) ought to be tried summarily, the court may proceed to try the information summarily.

COMMENTARY

Subsection (1): Attained the age of 17. For the determination of age, see s. 150(4) of the Act.

Subsection (2): The conclusion of the evidence for the prosecution. This contemplates a plea of not guilty. Presumably there is no power to change over following a plea of guilty. The restrictions on press publicity do not apply to reports of a summary trial published or broadcast before a decision to change over to inquiry: s. 8(8), *supra.* Where a bench of two justices failed to agree and the case had been put back for re-hearing it could not be said that the prosecution case had been concluded: *R.* v *Coventry City Justices, ex parte Wilson* [1981] Crim. L.R. 787.

Examining justice. See the note to s. 6, *supra.*

Subsection (3). Witnesses who have already given evidence must be recalled for cross-examination: Magistrates' Courts Rules 1981, r. 21.

Representations. Except in the cases mentioned later in this subsection the court is not bound by the representations but must consider them, if made. There would seem to be nothing to preclude the court from taking the initiative to effect a change-over to an inquiry so long as it gives the parties opportunity to make representations.

Justices are entitled to refuse an application to change to summary trial where the election for trial on indictment was made in order to obtain the prosecution statements: *R.* v. *Warrington Justices, ex parte McDonagh* [1981] Crim. L.R. 629.

The nature of the case. Compare the note to s. 19.

If he consents. See the note to s. 20.

Try the information summarily. As to the receipt of evidence given in the inquiry see s. 28 of the Act, *post.*

Subsection (7). *See* the note to subs.(3), *supra.*

Power to issue summons to accused in certain circumstances

26. (1) Where—

(a)   in the circumstances mentioned in s. 23(1)(a) above the court is not satisfied that there is good reason for proceeding in the absence of the accused; or

(b)   subsections (4)(b) or (5) of s. 23 or subss (2) or (6) of s. 25 above applies, and the court adjourns the hearing in pursuance of that subsection without remanding the accused,

the justice or any of the justices of which the court is composed may issue a summons directed to the accused requiring his presence before the court.

(2) If the accused is not present at the time and place appointed—

(a)   in a case within subs. (1)(a) above, for the proceedings under ss 19(1) above, as the case may be; or

(b)   in a case within subs. (1)(b) above, for the resumption of the hearing,

the court may issue a warrant for his arrest.

COMMENTARY

Subsection (1): Issue a summons. There is no power to issue a warrant at this stage.

Subsection (2): Issue a warrant. No further information is called for nor need the information be substantiated on oath.

Effect of dismissal of information for offence triable either way

27. Where on the summary trial of an information for an offence triable either way the court dismisses the information, the dismissal shall have the same effect as an acquittal on indictment.

COMMENTARY

Thus the defendant can plead *autrefois acquit* if subsequently indicted on the same offence: *Wemyss* v. *Hopkins* (1875) 39 J.P. 549.

An offence triable either way. Defined in the Interpretation Act 1978, sch. 1.

Using in summary trial evidence given in committal proceedings

28. Where under ss 25(3) or (7) above a magistrates' court, having begun to inquire into an information as examining justices, proceeds to try the information summarily, then, subject to ss 102(9) and 103(3) below, any evidence already given before the court shall be deemed to have been given in and for the purposes of the summary trial.

COMMENTARY

Witnesses must be recalled for cross-examination unless not required by the accused or the prosecutor: Magistrates' Courts Rules 1981, r. 21. This section does not apply to written statements before examining justices under s. 102 of the Act: subs. (9), *ibid*.

Any evidence. This section does not not apply to written statements of child witnesses in sexual cases tendered under s. 103 of the Act: subs. (3), *ibid*.

Penalties on summary conviction for offences triable either way

32. On summary conviction of any of the offences triable either way listed in sch. 1 to this Act a person shall be liable to imprisonment for a term not exceeding six months or to a fine not exceeding the prescribed sum or both, except that—

> (*a*)   a magistrates' court shall not have power to impose imprisonment for an offence so listed if the Crown Court would not have that power in the case of an adult convicted of it on indictment;
>
> (*b*)   on summary conviction of an offence consisting in the incitement to commit an offence triable either way a person shall not be liable to any greater penalty than he would be liable to on summary conviction of the last-mentioned offence.

(2) For any offence triable either way which is not listed in sch. 1 to this Act, being an offence under a relevant enactment, the maximum fine which may be imposed on summary conviction shall by virtue of this subsection be the prescribed sum unless the offence is one for which by virtue of an enactment other than this subsection a larger fine may be imposed on summary conviction.

(3) Where, by virtue of any relevant enactment, a person summarily convicted of an offence triable either way would, apart from this section, be liable to a maximum fine of one amount in the case of a first conviction and of a different amount in the case of a second or subsequent conviction, subs. (2) above shall apply irrespective of whether the conviction is a first, second or subsequent one.

(4) Subsection (2) above shall not affect so much of any enactment as (in whatever words) makes a person liable on summary conviction to a fine not exceeding a specified amount for each day on which a continuing offence is continued after conviction or the occurrence of any other specified event.

(5) Subsection (2) above shall not apply on summary conviction of any of the following offences:-

> (*a*)   offences under s. 5(2) of the Misuse of Drugs Act 1971 (having possession of a controlled drug) where the controlled drug in relation to which the offence was committed was a Class B or Class C drug;

(b)   offences under the following provisions of that Act, where the controlled drug in relation to which the offence was committed was a Class C drug, namely—

   (i) section 4(2) (production, or being concerned in the production, of a controlled drug);
   (ii) section 4(3) (supplying or offering a controlled drug or being concerned in the doing or either activity by another;
   (iii) section 5(3) (having possession of a controlled drug with intent to supply it to another);
   (iv) section 8 (being the occupier, or concerned in the management, of premises and permitting or suffering certain activities to take place there);
   (v) section 12(6) (contravention of direction prohibiting practitioner etc. from possessing, supplying etc. controlled drugs).

(6) Where, as regards any offence triable either way, there is under any enactment (however framed or worded) a power by subordinate instrument to restrict the amount of the fine which on summary conviction can be imposed in respect of that offence—

(a)   subsection (2) above shall not affect that power or override any restriction imposed in the exercise of that power; and
(b)   the amount to which that fine may be restricted in the exercise of that power shall be any amount less than the maximum fine which could be imposed on summary conviction in respect of the offence apart from any restriction so imposed.

(7) Where there is under any relevant enactment (however framed or worded) a power by subordinate instrument to impose penal provisions, being a power which allows the creation of offences triable either way—

(a)   the maximum fine which may in the exercise of that power be authorized on summary conviction in respect of an offence triable either way shall by virtue of this subsection be the prescribed sum unless some larger maximum fine can be authorized on summary conviction in respect of such an offence by virtue of an enactment other than this subsection; and
(b)   subsection (2) above shall not override any restriction imposed in the exercise of that power on the amount of the fine which on summary conviction can be imposed in respect of an offence triable either way created in the exercise of the power.

(8) In subs. (5) above "controlled drug", "Class B drug" and "Class C drug" have the same meaning as in the Misuse of Drugs Act 1971.

(9) In this section—

"fine" includes a pecuniary penalty but does not include a pecuniary forfeiture or pecuniary compensation;
"the prescribed sum" means £2,000 or such sum as is for the time being substituted in this definition by an order in force under s. 143(1) below;
"relevant enactment" means an enactment contained in the Criminal Law Act 1977 or in any Act passed before, or in the same Session as, that Act.
(as amended by the Criminal Attempts Act 1981, sch.).

COMMENTARY

Subsection(1): A fine. See subs. (9).

The prescribed sum. £1000: subs. (9).

Subsection (2). This does not affect (a) continuing penalties (see subs. (4)); (b) limitations by subordinate instrument (see subs (6) and (7); or (c) the maximum term of imprisonment available which continues to be that prescribed in the relevant enactment, but not exceeding six months (s. 31).

A relevant enactment. See subs. (9).

Subsection (3). Thus where the statute prescribes higher fines for second or subsequent convictions the effect of subs. (2) is to apply the figure of £1000 unless exceeded by any figure in the statute. *See* now the Criminal Justice Act 1982, s. 35 in Ch. 8.

Subsection (6). "Provides that where there is a power to stipulate in subordinate instruments a maximum summary fine for an offence triable either way than the maximum provided in the primary statute, that power shall remain unaltered despite the increase of the maximum summary fine in the primary statute to £1000": Home Office cir. 1978 dated March 31, 1978.

Subsection (7). "Provides that where a statute limits the sum which may be stipulated as the maximum summary fine for offences triable either way in subordinate legislation, that maximum shall be the prescribed sum, £1000, but shall apply only to offences in subordinate legislation made after this section comes into force and shall not affect the maximum summary fines for offences in subordinate legislation already in force on that date": Home Office cir. 39/1978 dated March 31, 1978.

Maximum penalties on summary conviction in pursuance of section 22

33. (1) Where in pursuance of subs. (2) of s. 22 above a magistrates' court proceeds to the summary trial of an information, then, if the accused is summarily convicted of the offence—

(a) the court shall not have power to impose on him in respect of that offence imprisonment for more than three months or a fine greater than £1,000; and

(b) section 38 below shall not apply as regards that offence.

(2) In subs. (1) above "fine" includes a pecuniary penalty but does not include a pecuniary forfeiture or pecuniary compensation.

COMMENTARY

Subsection (1). Note that the terms of para. (a) do not prescribe the maximum penalty available in a trial under s. 22(2): they are merely limitations on the penalty allowed in s. 32. The effect of the two sections read together therefore is that the maximum penalty in a s. 22(2) case is imprisonment for a term not exceeding three months or a fine of £500 or both.

This section does not appear to preclude a committal to the Crown Court to be dealt with (Criminal Justice Act 1967, s. 56).

Evidence of children in committal proceedings for sexual offences

103. (1) In any proceedings before a magistrates' court inquiring into a sexual offence as examining justices—

(a) a child shall not be called as a witness for the prosecution; but

(b) any statement made in writing by or taken in writing from the child shall be admissible in evidence of any matter of which his oral testimony would be admissible,

except in a case where the application of this subsection is excluded under subs. (2) below.

(2) Subsection (1) above shall not apply—

(a) where at or before the time when such a statement is tendered in evidence the defence objects to the application of that subsection; or

(b) where the prosecution requires the attendance of the child for the purpose of establishing the identity of any person; or

(c)   where the court is satisfied that it has not been possible to obtain from the child a statement that may be given in evidence under this section; or

(d)   where the inquiry into the offence takes place after the court has discontinued to try it summarily and the child has given evidence in the summary trial.

(3) Section 28 above shall not apply to any statement admitted in pursuance of subs. (1) above.

(4) In this section "child" has the same meaning as in the Children and Young Persons Act 1933 and "sexual offence" means any offence under the Sexual Offences Act 1956 or the Indecency with Children Act 1960 or s. 1(1)(a) of the Protection of Children Act 1978, or any attempt to commit such an offence.

COMMENTARY

Subsection (1). Before a statement is received in evidence under this subsection its effect must be explained to an unrepresented defendant in ordinary language and, if he does not object to its operation, he must be informed that he may ask questions about the circumstances in which the statement was made or taken: Magistrates' Courts Rules 1981, r. 7(4).

Child. See subs. (4) and note thereto.

Sexual offence. *See* subs. (4).

Shall not be called as a witness. This does not seemingly preclude the use of written statements under s. 102, *supra,* but note the comments thereto under the heading "Liable to Prosecution."

In writing. Includes typing, printing, lithography, photography and other modes of representing or reproducing words in a visible form: Interpretation Act 1978, sch. 1 The statement must be made an exhibit: Magistrates' Courts Rules 1981, r. 7(5).

Subsection (4): Child. Defined in the Children and Young Persons Act, 1933, s. 107, as "a person under the age of 14 years".

Deposition of person dangerously ill

105. (1) Where a person appears to a justice of the peace to be able and willing to give material information relating to an indictable offence, and—

(a)   the justice is satisfied, on a representation made by a duly qualified medical practitioner, that the person able and willing to make the statement is dangerously ill and unlikely to recover; and

(b)   it is not practicable for examining justices to take the evidence of the sick person in accordance with the provisions of this Act and the rules,

the justice may take in writing the deposition of the sick person on oath.

(2) A deposition taken under this section may be given in evidence before examining justices inquiring into an information against the offender or in respect of the offence to which the deposition relates, but subject to the same conditions as apply, under s. 6 of the Criminal Law Amendment Act 1867, to its being given in evidence upon the trial of the offender or offence.

COMMENTARY

Subsection (1): A justice of the peace. Not necessarily one of the examining justices.

Indictable offence. Defined in the Interpretation Act 1978, sch. 1.

Representation made. Presumably either orally or in writing.

Duly qualified medical practitioner. That is, a person fully registered under the Medical Act, 1956: the Medical Act, 1956, s. 52.

The justice may take. It was held under the previously existing provisions that a magistrate was bound to attend a witness who is dangerously ill: *R. v. Bros, ex parte Hardy* (1910) 74 J.P. 483. Reasonable notice must be given to the other side of the intention to take the deposition, and full opportunity of cross-examining allowed. The procedure for taking the deposition is set out in the Magistrates' Courts Rules, 1981, r. 33(1), (2). The depositions must be sent to the examining justice or the court of trial: r. 33(3), *ibid.*

In writing. Includes typing, printing, lithography, photography and other modes of representing or reproducing words in a visible form: Interpretation Act, 1978, sch. 1.

Subsection (2): Section 6 of the Criminal Law Amendment Act 1867. This permits the deposition to be read at the trial if the person who made it is dead or there is no reasonable probability that such person will ever be able to travel or give evidence, provided certain conditions are satisfied.

False written statements tendered in evidence

106. (1) If any person in a written statement tendered in evidence in criminal proceedings by virtue of s. 102 above wilfully makes a statement material in those proceedings which he knows to be false or does not believe to be true, he shall be liable on conviction on indictment to imprisonment for a term not exceeding two years or a fine or both.

(2) The Perjury Act 1911 shall have effect as if this section were contained in that Act.

COMMENTARY

Subsection (2). An effect of this subsection is that an offence under subs. (1) is triable either way: sch. 1, para. 14, *infra.*

SCHEDULE 1

OFFENCES TRIABLE EITHER WAY BY VIRTUE OF S. 17

1. Offences at common law of public nuisance.

2. Offences under s. 8 of the Disorderly Houses Act 1751 (appearing to be keeper of bawdy house etc.).

3. Offences consisting in contravention of s. 13 of the Statutory Declarations Act 1835 (administration by a person of an oath etc. touching matters in which he has no jursidiction).

4. Offences under s. 36 of the Malicious Damage Act 1861 (obstructing engines or carriages on railways).

5. Offences under the following provisions of the Offences against the Person Act 1861—

    (*a*)   section 16 (threats to kill);
    (*b*)   section 20 (inflicting bodily injury, with or without a weapon);
    (*c*)   section 26 (not providing apprentices or servants with food etc.);
    (*d*)   section 27 (abandoning or exposing child);
    (*e*)   section 34 (doing or omitting to do anything so as to endanger railway passengers);
    (*f*)   section 36 (assaulting a clergyman at a place of worship etc.);
    (*g*)   section 38 (assault with intent to resist apprehension);
    (*h*)   section 47 (assault occasioning bodily harm—common assault);
    (*i*)   section 57 (bigamy);
    (*j*)   section 60 (concealing birth of a child).

6. Offences under s. 20 of the Telegraph Act 1868 (disclosing or intercepting messages).

7. Offences under section 13 of the Debtors Act 1868 (transactions intended to defraud creditors).

8. Offences under s. 5 of the Public Stores Act 1875 (obliteration of marks with intent to conceal).

9. Offences under s. 12 of the Corn Returns Act 1882 (false returns).

10. Offences under s. 22 of the Electric Lighting Act 1882 (injuring works with intent to cut off electricity supply).

11. Offences under s. 3 of the Submarine Telegraph Act 1885 (damaging submarine cables).

12. Offences under s. 13 of the Stamp Duties Management Act 1891 (offences in relation to dies and stamps).

13. Offences under s. 8(2) of the Cremation Act 1902 (making false representations etc. with a view to procuring the burning of any human remains).

14. All offences under the Perjury Act 1911 except offences under—

(a)   section 1 (perjury in judicial proceedings);
(b)   section 3 (false statements etc. with reference to marriage);
(c)   section 4 (false statements etc. as to births or deaths).

15. (Repealed).

16. Offences under s. 17 of the Deeds of Arrangement Act 1914 (trustee making preferential payments).

17. Offences under s. 3(4) of the Checkweighing in Various Industries Act 1919 (false statements).

18. Offences under s. 8(2) of the Census Act 1920 (disclosing census information).

19. Offences under s. 36 of the Criminal Justice Act 1925 (forgery of passports etc.).

20. Offences under s. 11 of the Agricultural credits Act 1928 (frauds by farmers).

21. (Repealed).

22. Offences under the following provisions of the Post Office Act 1953—

(a)   section 53 (unlawfully taking away or opening mail bag)
(b)   section 55 (fraudulent retention of mail bag or postal packet);
(c)   section 57 (stealing, embezzlement, destruction etc. by officer of Post Office of postal packet);
(d)   section 58 (opening or delaying of postal packets by officers of the Post Office).

23. Offences under the following provisions of the Sexual Offences Act 1956—

(a)   section 6 (unlawful sexual intercourse with a girl under 16);
(b)   section 13 (indecency between men);
(c)   section 26 (permitting a girl under 16 to use premises for sexual intercourse).

24. Offences under s. 3(1) of the Shipping Contracts and Commercial Documents Act 1964 (offences), so far as it relates to the contravention of any directions given under that Act before March 20, 1980.

25. Offences under s. 24B(7) of the Housing Subsidies Act 1967 (failure to notify lender that residence condition not fulfilled or ceased to be fulfilled).

26. The following offences under the Criminal Law Act 1967—

(a) offences under s. 4(1) (assisting offenders); and
(b) offences under s. 5(1) (concealing arrestable offences and giving false information),

where the offence to which they relate is triable either way.

27. Offences under s. 4(1) of the Sexual Offences Act 1967 (procuring others to commit homosexual acts).

28. All indictable offences under the Theft Act 1968 except—

(a) robbery, aggravated burglary, blackmail and assault with intent to rob;
(b) burglary comprising the commission of, or an intention to commit, an offence which is triable only on indictment;
(c) burglary in a dwelling if any person in the dwelling was subjected to violence or the threat of violence.

29. Offences under the following provisions of the Criminal Damage Act 1971—

section 1(1) (destroying or damaging property);
section 1(1) and (3) (arson);
section 2 (threats to destroy or damage property);
section 3 (possessing anything with intent to destroy or damage property).

30. Offences in relation to stamps issued for the purpose of national insurance under the provisions of any enactments as applied to those stamps.

31. (Repealed).

32. Committing an indecent assault upon a person whether male or female.

33. Aiding, abetting, counselling or procuring the commission of any offence listed in the preceding paragraphs of this schedule except para. 26.

34. (Repealed).

35. Any offence consisting in the incitement to commit an offence triable either way except an offence mentioned in para. 33.

(as amended by the Criminal Attempts Act 1981, sch., the Forgery and Counterfeiting Act 1981, sch.)

COMMENTARY

This schedule is not a complete list of all offences triable either way. See the commentary to s. 17, *supra*.

Paragraph 5(h): s. 47 of the Offences Against the Person Act 1861. Section 47 provides penalties for conviction on indictment of (i) any assault occasioning actual bodily harm and (ii) common assault. Both offences are, by virtue of this schedule, triable either way. It was held under the former legislation that s. 42 also provides for the summary trial of common assault with the accused's consent, but this does not create a summary offence since common assault, even so tried, remains an indictable offence: *R. v. Tower Bridge Justices, ex parte Fray* (1975) 140 J.P.N. 204.

Paragraph 33: Aiding, abetting. Any offence consisting in aiding, abetting, counselling or procuring the commission of an offence triable either way *not* listed in this schedule is triable either way: s. 44(2) of the Act.

Paragraph 35: Incitement. The offender is not liable to any greater penalty than if convicted summarily of the completed act: s. 32(1)(b) of the Act.

SCHEDULE 2

OFFENCES FOR WHICH THE VALUE INVOLVED IS RELEVANT TO THE MODE OF TRIAL

Offence	Value involved	How measured
1.Offences under s. 1 of the Criminal Damage Act 1971 (destroying or damaging property) excluding any offence committed by destroying or damaging property by fire.	As regards property alleged to have been destroyed, its value. As regards property alleged to have been damaged, the value of the alleged damage.	What the property would probably have cost to buy in the open market at the material time, (a) If immediately after the material time the damage was capable of repair— (i)what would probably then have been the market price for the repair of the damage, or (ii) what the property alleged to have been damaged would probably have cost to buy in the open market at the material time, whichever is the less; or (b) if immediately after the material time the damage was beyond repair, what the said property would probably have cost to buy in the open market at the material time.
2.The following offences, namely— (a) aiding, abetting, counselling or procuring the commission of any offence mentioned in para. 1 above; (b) attempting to commit any offence so mentioned; and (c) inciting another to commit any offence so mentioned.	The value indicated in para. 1 above for the offence alleged to have been aided, abetted, counselled or procured, or attempted or incited.	As for the corresponding entry in para. 1 above.

THE MAGISTRATES' COURTS RULES 1981

S.I. 1981 No. 552 as amended by S.I. 1983 No. 523

Restrictions on reports of committal proceedings

5. *(1) Except in a case where evidence is, with the consent of the accused, to be given in his absence under s. 4(4)(b) of the Act of 1980 (absence caused by ill health), a magistrates' court acting as examining justices shall before admitting in evidence any written statement or taking depositions of witnesses in accordance with r. 7 explain to the accused the restrictions on reports of committal proceedings imposed by s. 8 of the Act of 1980 and inform him of his right to apply to the court for an order removing those restrictions.*

(2) Where a magistrates' court has made an order under s. 8(2) of the Act of 1980 removing restrictions on the reports of committal proceedings, such order shall be entered in the register.

(3) Where the court adjourns any such proceedings to another day, the court shall, at the beginning of any adjourned hearing, state that the order has been made.

COMMENTARY

Paragraph (1): Explain to the accused. The Home Office memorandum on this rule comments:

It is not intended that this should be done at hearings which are only remand proceedings and at which the prosecution does not present the evidence against the accused; at these hearings the accused may not be represented; it might be unfair to expect him to make this decision without proper advice at so early a stage; and the case may, in the event, be tried summarily. It is therefore suggested that the information should be given to the accused at the beginning of the committal proceedings proper, *i.e.* before depositions are taken or written statements tendered in evidence. It should be borne in mind that the accused may apply to the court for an order at any time during the proceedings (in which event the order will be applied retrospectively), but the court may think it advisable, in appropriate cases, to remind the accused that if his application is deferred until a later stage in the proceedings there is likely to be less opportunity for the evidence to be reported.

Where no reporter is present in court when the restrictions are lifted the Home Office suggest that the court should consider adjourning the case for a short period to enable the press to attend: Home Office circ. 109/1968 dated May 2, 1968.

Committal for trial without consideration of evidence

6. *(1) This rule applies to committal proceedings where the accused has a solicitor acting for him in the case (whether present in court or not) and where the court has been informed that all the evidence for the prosecution is in the form of written statements copies of which have been given to the accused.*

(2) A magistrates' court inquiring into an offence in committal proceedings to which this rule applies shall cause the charge to be written down, if this has not already been done, and read to the accused and shall then ascertain whether he wishes to—

(a) object to any of the prosecution statements being tendered in evidence;

(b) give evidence himself or call witnesses; or

(c) submit that the prosecution statements disclose insufficient evidence to put him on trial by jury for the offence with which he is charged.

(3) If the court is satisfied that the accused or, as the case may be, each of the accused does not wish to take any of the steps mentioned in sub-paras

(a), (b) and (c) of para. (2) and determines, after receiving any written statements tendered by the prosecution and the defence under s. 102 of the Act of 1980, to commit the accused for trial without consideration of the evidence, the court shall proceed in accordance with para. (4) and in any other case shall proceed in accordance with r. 7.

(4) The court shall then say to the accused—

> *"You will be committed for trial but I must warn you that at that trial you may not be permitted to give evidence of an alibi or to call witnesses in support of an alibi unless you have earlier given particulars of the alibi and of the witnesses. You or your solicitor may give those particulars now to this court or at any time in the next seven days to the solicitor for the prosecution.",*

or words to that effect:

Provided that the court shall not be required to give this warning in any case where it appears to the court that, having regard to the nature of the offence with which the accused is charged, it is unnecessary to do so.

(5) Where the court has given to the accused the warning required by para. (4) the clerk of the court shall give to him written notice of the provisions of s. 11 of the Criminal Justice Act 1967 about giving notice of particulars of alibi to the solicitor for the prosecution and the solicitor's name and address shall be stated in the notice.

COMMENTARY

This rule applies to committal proceedings under the Magistrates' Courts Act 1980, s. 6(2).

The effect of this and the preceding rule is that a committal by consent proceeds as follows:

(i)	The court explains the restrictions on reports of committal proceedings and informs the defendant of his right to apply for an order removing them.
(ii)	The prosecution informs the court that all their evidence is in the form of written statements, copies of which have been given to all defendants.
(iii)	The court verifies that the defendant has a solicitor acting for him (whether present or not).
(iv)	The clerk reads the charge.
(v)	The court asks the defendant if he:

> (a) objects to any of the written statements being put in;
> (b) wishes to give evidence or call witnesses; or
> (c) is making a submission of no case.

Provided that none of these questions is answered in the affirmative, the defendant is given the alibi warning: otherwise the proceedings revert to the conventional form under r. 7, *infra: R. v. Pontypool JJ, ex parte McCann* (1968) 113 Sol. Jo. 52.

The magistrate may delegate to his clerk his duty to inform the defendant of his rights at a committal: *R. v. Horseferry Road Justices, ex parte Farooki* (1982) *The Times*, October 29. **Proviso to para. (4).** The discretion resides in the court, not the parties.

Paragraph (5): Written notice of the provisions of s. 11. *See* form 24.

Taking depositions of witnesses and statement of accused

7. *(1) This rule does not apply to committal proceedings where under s. 6(2) of the Act of 1980 a magistrates' court commits a person for trial without consideration of the evidence.*

(2) A magistrates' court inquiring into an offence as examining justices shall cause the evidence of each witness, including the evidence of the accused, but not including any witness of his merely to his character, to be put into writing; and as soon as may be after the examination of such a witness shall cause his deposition to be read to him in the presence and hearing of the accused, and shall require the witness to sign the deposition:

Provided that where the evidence has been given in the absence of the accused under s. 4(4) of the Act of 1980 this shall be recorded on the deposition of the witness and the deposition need not be read in the presence and hearing of the accused.

(3) The depositions shall be authenticated by a certificate signed by one of the examining justices.

(4) Where the accused is not represented by counsel or a solicitor, before a statement made in writing by or taken in writing from a child is received in evidence under subs. (1) of s. 103 of the Act of 1980 the court shall cause the effect of that subsection to be explained to the accused in ordinary language and, if the defence does not object to the application of that subsection, shall inform him that he may ask questions about the circumstances in which the statement was made or taken.

(5) Any such statement as aforesaid which is received in evidence shall be made an exhibit.

(6) After the evidence for the prosecution (including any statements tendered under s. 102 of the Act of 1980, has been given and after hearing any submission, if any is made, the court shall, unless it then decides not to commit for trial, cause the charge to be written down, if this has not already been done, and, if the accused is not represented by counsel or a solicitor, shall read the charge to him and explain it in ordinary language.

*[(7) The courts shall then ask the accused whether he wishes to say anything in answer to the charge and, if he is not represented by counsel or a solicitor, shall before asking the question say to him—

> *"You will have an opportunity to give evidence on oath before us and to call witnesses. But first I am going to ask you whether you wish to say anything in answer to the charge. You need not say anything unless you wish to do so. Anything you say will be taken down and may be used in evidence at your trial. You should take no notice of any promise or threat which any person may have made to persuade you to say anything",*

or words to that effect.]

*[(8) Whatever the accused says in answer to the charge shall be put into writing, read over to him and signed by one of the examining justices and also, if the accused wishes, by him.]

(9) The court shall then say to the accused—

> *"I must warn you that if this court should commit you for trial you may not be permitted at that trial to give evidence of an alibi or to call witnesses in support of an alibi unless you have earlier given particulars of the alibi and of the witnesses. You may give those particulars now to this court or to the solicitor for the prosecution not later than seven days from the end of these committal proceedings.",*

or words to that effect and, if it appears to the court that the accused may not understand the meaning of the term "alibi", the court shall explain it to him:

Provided that the court shall not be required to give this warning in any case where it appears to the court that, having regard to the nature of the offence with which the accused is charged, it is unnecessary to do so.

(10) After complying with the requirements of this rule relating to the statement of the accused, and whether or not he has made a statement in answer to the charge, the court shall give him an opportunity to give

---

*It is submitted that both these paragraphs have been repealed by the Criminal Justice Act 1982, s. 72.

evidence himself and to call witnesses.

(11) Where the accused is represented by counsel or a solicitor, his counsel or solicitor shall be heard on his behalf, either before or after the evidence for the defence is taken, at his discretion, and may, if the accused gives evidence himself and calls witnesses, be heard on his behalf with the leave of the court both before and after the evidence is taken:

Provided that, where the court gives leave to counsel or the solicitor for the accused to be heard after, as well as before, the evidence is taken, counsel or the solicitor for the prosecution shall be entitled to be heard immediately before counsel or the solicitor for the accused is heard for the second time.

(12) Where the court determines to commit the accused for trial in respect of a charge which differs from that which was read to him in accordance with the provisions of para. (6), the court shall cause the new charge to be read to him.

(13) Where the court has given to the accused the warning required by para. (9) the clerk of the court shall give to him written notice of the provisions of s. 11 of the Criminal Justice Act 1967 about giving notice of particulars of alibi to the solicitor for the prosecution and the solicitor's name and address shall be stated in the notice.

COMMENTARY

Paragraph (2): Cause the evidence ... to be put in writing. Statements voluntarily interposed by the defendant should, if material, be taken down: *R. v. Weller* (1846) 2 Car. & Kir. 223; *R. v. Watson* (1851) 3 Car & Kir. 111.

It is improper for depositions taken in respect of one defendant to be read over and confirmed in the inquiry respecting another co-defendant subsequently joined: *R. v. Phillips, R. v. Quayle* (1938) 102 J.P. 467. In *Ex parte Bottomley* (1909) 73 J.P. 246, it was held that where in a preliminary inquiry a magistrate was unable to conclude a case the witnesses who had already given evidence might affirm their earlier depositions before a different justice if the depositions were read over to them and they were given the opportunity to correct inaccuracies and make additions. The defendant must be allowed to cross-examine even if he did so on the earlier occasion. *Bottomley's* case was partially distinguished in *R. v. Phillips, supra,* and the force of this decision must now be doubted.

Prejudicial evidence should go "unvarnished" into the depositions; any editing may be done at the trial: *R. v. Weaver, R. v. Weaver* (1967) 131 J.P. 173.

Read to him in the presence and hearing of the accused. Where the depositions were not taken in the presence of the justice or defendant the fact that they were subsequently read over in their presence does not cure the defect: *R. v. Christopher, Smith and Thornton* (1850) 14 J.P. 83; and this applies equally to the practice of giving the heads of evidence before the magistrate and detailed depositions before the clerk: *R. v. Watts* (1863) 27 J.P. 821. In *R. v. Bates* (1860) 2 F. & F. 317, the practice of taking abbreviated notes before the justice which were copied out in full, read before the justice and defendant and signed was not condemned. But in *R. v. Gee, R. v. Bibby, R. v. Dunscombe* (1936) 100 J.P. 227, (in which *R. v. Bates, supra,* was not referred to) the practice of checking in court a proof of evidence which had been taken otherwise than in the presence of the defendant was disapproved, and this is certainly the safer view. (*See* also *R. v. Wharmby, Lindley and Lindley* [1946] 31 Cr. App. R. 174.)

Require the witness to sign the deposition. This is merely directory and not a condition of admissibility at the trial on indictment, *per* Wills, J, in *R. v. Holloway* (1901) 65 J.P. 712.

Paragraph (3): A certificate. *See* form 16.

The Court of Criminal Appeal refused to set aside convictions on the ground that depositions taken on three separate days were not signed as to one of those days: *R. v. Edgar, etc.* (1958) 122 J.P. 342.

Paragraphs (7), (8). *See* the footnote in the text.

Paragraph (9): The meaning of the term "alibi". *See* s. 11(8) of the Criminal Justice Act 1967.

Paragraph (10): Opportunity to give evidence himself and to call witnesses. Justices should not discourage witnesses for the defence from giving evidence at this stage, *per* Channell J, in *R.* v. *Nicholson* (1909) 73 J.P. 347. The defendant is not precluded from giving evidence simply because his submission of no case has been overruled: *R.* v. *Horseferry Rd. Magistrates' Court, ex parte Adams* (1978) 142 J.P. 127

Paragraph (13): Written notice. *See* form 24.

Order for attendance of witness at court of trial

8. *(1) A witness order under s. 1 of the Criminal Procedure (Attendance of Witnesses) Act 1965 shall be in the prescribed form and shall be served on the witnesses as soon as practicable after the accused has been committed for trial:*

Provided that where, at the conclusion of the examination of a witness, the court determines that the witness order shall be a conditional order, the order shall be served on him immediately after the deposition has been signed.

(2) Where a court has directed under subs. (2)(b) of the said s. 1 that a witness order shall be treated as a conditional order, it shall give notice to the witness in the prescribed form.

(3) If a witness order has been made as aforesaid and the court determines not to commit the accused for trial, it shall give notice to the witness that he is no longer required to attend.

(4) A notice given under this rule shall be in writing and signed by one of the justices composing the court or the clerk of the court.

(5) A witness order under the said s. 1 and a notice given under this rule shall be served by delivering it to the witness or by leaving it for him with some person at his last known or usual place of abode or by sending it by post in a letter addressed to him at his last known or usual place of abode.

COMMENTARY

Paragraph (1): Witness order. *See* form 22.

Paragraph (2). *See* form 23.

Notice to governor of prison of committal on bail

9. *(1) Where the accused is committed for trial on bail, the clerk of the court shall give notice thereof in writing to the governor of the prison to which persons of the sex of the person committed are committed by that court if committed in custody for trial and also, if the person committed is under 21, to the governor of the remand centre to which he would have been committed if the court had refused him bail.*

(2) Where a corporation is committed for trial, the clerk of the court shall gave notice thereof to the governor of the prison to which would be committed a man committed by that court in custody for trial.

Paragraph (1): Notice. *See* form 19.

Paragraph (2): Notice. *See* form 20.

Notices on committal of person subject to transfer direction

10. *Where a transfer direction has been given by the Secretary of State under s. 73 of the Mental Health Act 1959 in respect of a person remanded in custody by a magistrates' court, and before the direction ceases to have effect, that person is committed for trial, the clerk of the court shall give notice in the prescribed form—*

> (a)   *to the governor of the prison to which persons of the sex of that person are committed by that court if committed in custody for trial; and*
>
> (b)   *to the managers of the hospital where he is detained.*

Notice. *See* form 21.

Documents and exhibits to be retained and sent to court of trial

11. *(1) A magistrates' court that commits a person for trial shall, unless there are reasons for not doing so, retain any documents and articles produced by a witness who is subject to a conditional witness order or in whose case the court has directed that a witness order be treated as a conditional order.*

(2) As soon as practicable after the committal of any person for trial, and in any case within four days from the date of his committal (not counting Sundays, Good Friday, Christmas Day or Bank Holidays), the clerk of the magistrates' court that committed him shall, subject to the provisions of s. 5 of the Prosecution of Offences Act 1979 (which relates to the sending of documents and things to the Director of Public Prosecutions), send to the appropriate officer of the Crown Court—

> (a)   *the information, if it is in writing;*
>
> (b)   *the depositions and written statements tendered in evidence, together with a certificate authenticating the depositions and statements, and any admission of facts made for the purposes of the committal proceedings under s. 10 of the Criminal Justice Act 1967 and not withdrawn;*
>
> (c)   *all statements made by the accused before the magistrates' court;*
>
> (d)   *a list of the names, addresses and occupations of the witnesses in respect of whom witness orders have been made;*
>
> (e)   *a copy of the record made in pursuance of s. 5 of the Bail Act 1976 relating to the grant or withholding of bail in respect of the accused on the occasion of the committal;*
>
> (f)   *any recognizance entered into by any person as surety for the accused together with a statement of any enlargement thereof under s. 129(4) of the Act of 1980;*
>
> (g)   *a list of the documents and articles produced in evidence before the justices or treated as so produced;*
>
> (h)   *such of the documents and articles referred to in the last preceding sub-paragraph as have been retained by the justices;*
>
> (i)   *a certificate showing whether the accused was informed at the committal proceedings of the requirements of s. 11 of the*

Criminal Justice Act 1967 (notice of alibi) and a record of any particulars given by him to the magistrates' court under that section; -

(j)   *if the committal was under s. 6(2) of the Act of 1980 (committal for trial without consideration of the evidence), a statement to that effect;*

(k)   *if the magistrates' court has made an order under s. 8(2) of the Act of 1980 (removal of restrictions on reports of committal proceedings), a statement to that effect;*

(l)   *the certificate of the examining justices as to costs of prosecution (Form B in the Schedule to the Costs in Criminal Cases Regulations 1908);*

(m) *if any person under the age of 17 is concerned in the committal proceedings, a statement whether the magistrates' court has given a direction under s. 39 of the Children and Young Persons Act 1933 (prohibition of publication of certain matter in newspapers).*

(n)   *a copy of any legal aid order previously made in the case;*

(o)   *a copy of any contribution order previously made in the case under section 7 of the Legal Aid Act 1982;*

(p)   *a copy of any legal aid application previously made in the case which has been refused;*

(q)   *any statement of means already submitted.*

(3) The clerk shall retain a copy of any list sent in pursuance of para. (2)(d).

(4) The period of four days specified in para. (2) may be extended in relation to any committal for so long as the appropriate officer of the Crown Court directs, having regard to the length of any document mentioned in that paragraph or any other relevant circumstances.

COMMENTARY

The Home Office also asks justices' clerks to notify the liaison probation officer at the Crown Court of the matters specified in Home Office cir. 28/71, para. 36.

Paragraph (1): Reasons for not doing so. For example, that the exhibit is perishable.

Paragraph (2)

>   **(b) A certificate authenticating the depositions and statements.** *See* form 16.

>   **(c) Statements made by the accused.** *See* form 17.

>   **(d) A list of the names, addresses and occupations of witnesses.** This must be drawn up with care: *Practice Note* [1961] 1 All E.R. 875 (relating to the former document).

>   **(g) A list of documents and articles.** *See* form 25.

>   **(h)** No means of identification is prescribed, but a signed label is commonly used: *cf.* r. 70(4). As to what should be done with the exhibits *see* under Exhibits in the introduction.

>   (i)   **Certificate of committal.** An erroneous certificate under r. 11 (2) (j) does not invalidate a lawful committal: *R.* v. *Hall* [1981] 1 W.L.R. 1510.

Duty to recall witnesses who have given evidence before examining justices

21. *Where under s. 25(3) or (7) of the Act of 1980 a magistrates' court, having begun to inquire into an information as examining justices, proceeds to try the information summarily, then, unless the accused pleads guilty, the court shall recall for cross-examination any witnesses who have already given evidence, except any not required by the accused or the prosecutor to be recalled for that purpose.*

Preservation of depositions where offence triable either way is dealt with summarily

22. *The clerk of the magistrates' court by which any person charged with an offence triable either way has been tried summarily shall preserve for a period of three years such depositions as have been taken.*

Deposition of person dangerously ill

33.(*1*) *Where a justice of the peace takes the deposition of a person under s. 105 of the Act of 1980 and the deposition relates to an offence with which a person has been charged, the justice shall give the person, whether prosecutor or accused, against whom it is proposed to use it reasonable notice of the intention to take the deposition, and shall give that person or his counsel or solicitor full opportunity of cross-examining the deponent.*

(*2*) *The justice shall sign the deposition and add to it a statement of his reason for taking it, the day when, and the place where it was taken and the names of any persons present when it was taken.*

(*3*) *The justice shall send the deposition, with the statement, to the clerk to the justices for the petty sessions area for which the justice acts and the clerk shall—*

(*a*)   *if the deposition relates to an offence for which a person has been committed for trial, send the deposition and statement to the appropriate officer of the Crown Court;*

(*b*)   *if the deposition relates to proceedings which are pending before a magistrates' court acting for another area, send the deposition and statement to the clerk of that court.*

COMMENTARY

Paragraph (1): Give . . . reasonable notice. The notice should be in writing: *R.* v. *Harris* (1918) 82 J.P. 196 (in which it was held that one hour's notice was not reasonable).

Full opportunity of cross-examining. Includes cross-examination following questions put by the magistrate: *R.* v. *Prestridge* (1881) 72 L.T.N. 93. In *R.* v. *Harris* (1918) 82 J.P. 196, it was held that by being without counsel or solicitor, the defendant did not have "a full opportunity to cross-examine." But in this case the lack of legal representation was due to inadequate notice on the part of the prosecutor and it is certainly not a general principle.

Paragraph (2): Persons present. It was ruled in *R.* v. *May* (1891) *The Times*, December 7, that omission of the name of the prisoner's husband did not render the deposition inadmissible.

CHAPTER 5

TRIAL AND SENTENCE

CONTENTS

Remission of Juveniles
Deferment of Sentence
The Presence of the Offender
The Power to Alter Sentence

INTRODUCTION

Subject to the statutory provisions, "magistrates have always had an inherent power to regulate the procedure in their courts in the interests of justice and a fair and expeditious trial:" *per* Lord Parker CJ, in *Simms* v. *Moore* (1970) 134 J.P. 573.

THE TRIAL

Legal Representation

Either party may be represented by counsel or solicitor: Magistrates' Courts Act 1980, s.122(1). A party so represented is deemed not to be absent except for any enactment or any condition of a recognisance expressly requiring his presence: *ibid*, s.122(2),(3). Thus, for example, the accused must be personally present:
- at committal proceedings: *ibid*, s.4(4)
- at the mode of trial proceedings: *ibid*, s.18(2).

Representation Otherwise than by a Lawyer

The Privy Council have decided (in relation to an appeal from New South Wales) that the enactment which was replaced by the Magistrates' Courts Act 1952 "did not deprive magistrates of their pre-existing discretionary power to allow a person, not being the informant or his counsel or attorney, to conduct the case for the informant," *per* Lord Pearson in *O'Toole* v. *Scott* [1965] 2 All E.R. at p. 246. Furthermore, there is no limitation on the magistrates' discretion: "it can be exercised on general grounds common to many cases or on special grounds arising in a particular case ... It should be regarded as proper for a magistrate to exercise the discretion in order to secure or promote convenience or expedition and efficiency in the administration of justice." These comments apply to prosecutors before magistrates' courts in this country: *R.* v. *Uxbridge Justices, ex parte Smith* [1977] R.T.R. 93. That case dealt with a particular instance where in an emergency it was sought to allow someone other than the named prosecutor to read out in his absence the statement of facts. The court stressed the need for each case to be considered on its merits. It did not, however, appear to consider the widespread practice whereby a court inspector is, by a general dispensation of the magistrates in a particular court, allowed to act on behalf of each named prosecuting officer. (See the article by Glanville Williams at [1956] Crim. L.R. 169.) This practice has seemingly superseded the disapproval of one police officer acting for another which was expressed in such cases as *Webb* v. *Catchlove* (1886) 50 J.P.N. 705; *Duncan* v. *Toms* (1887) 51 J.P. 631 and *May* v. *Beeley* (1910) 74 J.P. 111).

Silent Assistance (The McKenzie Friend)

Legal representation is to be distinguished from assistance in presenting the case by a person who does not act as an advocate. "Any person, whether he be a professional man or not, may attend as a friend of either party, may take notes, may quietly make suggestions, and give advice; but no-one can demand to take part in the proceedings as an advocate contrary to the regulations of the court as settled by the discretion of the justices," *per* Lord Tenterden CJ in *Collier* v. *Hicks* (1831) 2 B. & Ad. 663, L.J.O.S.M.C. 138; approved by the Court Appeal in *McKenzie* v. *McKenzie* [1970] 3 All E.R. 1034. (*See* the article at 138 J.P.N. 428).

The Duties of the Prosecutor
In the words of the *Code of Conduct for the Bar of England and Wales:*

> It is not the duty of the prosecuting counsel to obtain a conviction by all means at his command but rather to lay before the jury fairly and impartially the whole of the facts which comprise the case for the prosecution and to see that the jury are properly instructed in the law applicable to those facts.

It follows that there are certain duties laid upon the prosecutor which are not imposed on the defence.

According to the Law Society *Guide to the Professional Conduct of Solicitors:*

3.(2) The prosecutor must state the relevant facts dispassionately and should not attempt by advocacy to induce the court to impose a more severe sentence. He should, particularly where the accused is unrepresented, mention to the court any mitigating circumstances. He must not in his opening address state as a fact anything which he does not believe himself able to prove.

3.(3) The advocate who is prosecuting must not conceal from his opponent facts which are within his knowledge which are inconsistent with the facts which he, as a prosecutor, has presented to the court. . . . Before any commencement of the trial where the prosecutor obtains evidence which may assist the defence, or learns of witnesses who may do so, he must supply the defence with particulars of the witnesses. During the trial, if he obtains evidence which he does not intend to use which may assist the defence he must supply it to them.

3.(4) In opening the prosecution case, the advocate must not deliberately withhold anything which tells in favour of the accused. In a criminal case the duty of the advocate in respect of matters of law is the same as in a civil case, namely to reveal all decided law known to him whether it be for or against his case. This is so whether he has been called upon to argue or not, and, in the opinion of the Council, even where the judge or magistrate is proposing to act of his own volition without hearing the advocate.

When the police have taken a statement from a witness but decide not to call him they are under a duty to make that person available as a witness for the defence: *R.* v. *Bryant and Dickson* [1946] 31 Cr. App. R. 146; *R.* v. *Leyland Justices, ex parte Hawthorn* [1979] 1 All E.R. 209. However they are not obliged to supply the defence with a copy of the statement they took: *R.* v. *Bryant and Dickson, supra.*

When a witness whom the prosecution call or tender gives evidence in the box on a material issue and the prosecution have in their possession an earlier statement from that witness which is materially inconsistent with such evidence the prosecution should at any rate inform the defence of that fact: *Archbold*, 40th edn. at para. 443a, citing *R.* v. *Howes*, March 27, 1950, unreported.

When a prosecution witness is of known bad character the prosecution must inform the defence of this fact: *R.* v. *Colliston and Warhurst* [1955] 39 Cr. App. R. 100; *R.* v. *Matthews* [1975] 60 Cr. App. R. 292.

The prosecution is under a duty to supply the defence with the previous convictions of the accused in accordance with the *Practice Direction* [1966] 2 All E.R. 929, which deals with trial on indictment.

For the duties of the prosecutor following conviction see under "Ascertaining the Facts on a Plea of Guilty", *infra*.

Trial in the Absence of the Accused

An accused has, in general, a right to be present at his trial. This right is subject to the discretion of the court to proceed in his absence if it is voluntarily waived, for example, (i) where the accused abuses his right to be present for the purpose of obstructing the proceedings of the court by unseemly, indecent or outrageous behaviour; or (ii) where he ceases to claim his right to be present by deliberately jumping bail. This is a discretion which (in serious cases at least) should be exercised with great reluctance and with a view rather to the due administration of justice than to the comfort or convenience of anyone: *R.* v. *Jones (REW), (No. 2)* (1972) 136 J.P. In an appropriate case the court has a discretion to continue a trial in the absence of the accused through illness, but it is a discretion which should be sparingly exercised and never if the accused's defence could be prejudiced by his absence: *R.* v. *Howson* [1982] 74 Cr. App. R. 172.

Subject to these considerations the court may proceed with the trial of an information in the absence of the accused (Magistrates' Courts Act 1980, s.11(1)) but where a summons was issued the information may not be tried unless (a) it is proved that the summons was served a reasonable time before the trial or (b) the accused has appeared on a previous occasion: *ibid,* s.11(2).

Where neither prosecutor nor the accused appears the court may dismiss the information or, if evidence was received on a previous occasion, proceed in their absence: s. 16, *ibid*.

A warrant may issue for the arrest of the accused if the information has been substantiated on oath (*ibid*, s. 13(1)), subject to the restrictions in subs. (2), (5), *ibid*.

Adjournment

Magistrates have always had power at common law to adjourn their proceedings and it is now enacted in the Magistrates' Courts Act 1980, s. 10, that a trial may be adjourned both before and after the court has began to try the information. The clerk to the justices may order the further adjournment of criminal proceedings with the consent of the prosecutor and the accused if, but only if (a) the accused, not having been remanded on the previous adjournment, is not remanded on this further adjournment; or (b) the accused having been remanded on bail on the previous adjournment, is remanded on bail on the like terms and conditions: Justices' Clerks' Rules 1970.

On any adjournment of a trial the accused may be remanded. In certain circumstances on the trial of an offence triable either way he *must* be remanded: Magistrates' Courts Act 1980, s.10(4).

All the justices composing the court must be present during the whole proceedings, but if any justice absents himself he must cease to act further therein and if the remaining justices are enough to satisfy the Magistrates' Courts Act 1980, s. 121 the proceedings may continue before them: *ibid*, s. 121 (6). If at an adjourned hearing the court comprises different magistrates the trial must be recommenced: *Re Guerin* (1888) 53 J.P. 468; *R.* v. *Walton, ex parte Dutton* (1911) 75 J.P. 558. Evidence already given must be repeated and not read over: *Fulker* v. *Fulker* (1937) 101 J.P. 8.

The accused has no claim to an adjournment as a matter of right for the purpose of obtaining legal assistance: *R.* v. *Lipscombe, ex parte Biggins* (1882) 26 J.P. 244; nor will the High Court interfere where justices have refused adjournment after being satisfied that the defendant had sufficient time to instruct a solicitor: *R.* v. *Cambridgeshire JJ* (1880) 44 J.P. 168. It is a breach of natural justice if a party, especially a defendant in a criminal case, is not given a reasonable opportunity to present his case. This is not confined to addressing the court, but entails a reasonable opportunity to prepare the case before presentation: *R.* v. *Thames Magistrates' Court, ex parte Polemis* (1974) 138 J.P. 672. The question magistrates should ask themselves is: if we proceed now, can the inquiry be conducted with due regard to natural justice?

Magistrates' refusal to allow a further adjournment to an accused who had already received one and who had been notified that the case would go ahead was upheld in *R*. v. *Macclesfield Justices, ex parte Jones* [1983] R.T.R. 143. It was otherwise in *R*. v. *Afan Justices, ex parte Chaplin* [1983] R.T.R. 168 where the justices had overlooked a sentencing formality. Magistrates' refusal to allow an adjournment to the prosecutor was upheld in *Taylor* v. *Baird and Watters* (1983) *The Times*, May 3 (owing to a confusion the prosecutor's case had been in disarray).

As to the impropriety of making an adjournment conditional upon payment of costs *see* the Irish case of *R*. (*Roche*) v. *County Clare JJ* (1912) 46 I.L.T. 80. When a case is dismissed because an adjournment is refused to the prosecutor he may challenge it by application for judicial review; not by preferring further process before the magistrates, *per* Donaldson LJ in *R*. v. *Swansea Justices, ex parte Purvis* (1981) 145 J.P. 252.

Where a prosecutor declines to accept a medical certificate tendered in support of the defendant's absence he should notify the defendant's solicitors so as to give them an opportunity of calling the doctor to give evidence: *R*. v. *King's Lynne Justices, ex parte Whitelam* (1982) *The Times*, June 23.

A hearing should not be adjourned for long periods for the purposes of civil litigation: *R*. v. *Evans* (1980) 54 J.P. 47. The High Court would interfere in the case of an unduly long adjournment which was in effect a refusal of jurisdiction, *per* Alverstone J, in *R*. v. *Southampton JJ, ex parte Lebern* (1907) 71 J.P. 332.

Preliminary Points

It is permissible for the accused to address the court before the prosecutor when he wishes to raise a preliminary point. Preliminary points may concern three types of defect:

(1) those which go to jurisdiction and which cannot be waived, such as where the information is not laid in time or at all or where any necessary consent to jurisdiction has not been obtained. If these matters are not raised by the defence they should be by the court;

(2) those which may be cured by amendment under the Magistrates' Courts Act 1980, s. 123, but if not amended or waived should result in an acquittal, such as lack of a summons, insufficient (or insufficiently correct) particularity of the information or duplicity; and

(3) those which are so trivial as not even to require amendment, such as minor misdescriptions of property, persons or venue. The test is whether the defendant has been misled or injustice might otherwise occur.

Preliminary points should be taken as early as possible, preferably before any evidence is given: *R*. v. *Brown* (1857) 21 J.P. 357; *R*. v. *Salop JJ*. (1859) 2 El. & El. 386; but may be raised at any time before the decision is pronounced. A solicitor should as a matter of courtesy inform the other party that he intends to take a preliminary point: *Re Mundy, ex parte Shead* (1885) 15 Q.B.D. 338.

If there is objection "the magistrates may or may not at that stage be in a position to decide whether the act complained of was or was not done (*in circumstances which render it outside their jurisdiction*). It is however always within the jurisdiction of magistrates to inquire whether they have jurisdiction to try the case before them, and in circumstances such as these the magistrates ought to continue the hearing despite the objection until they have reached the stage in which the facts are sufficiently clear for them to reach a conclusion on this point. If at that point they decide that (*they have jurisdiction*), they will complete the hearing and the matter can be tested if necessary by way of appeal. If, on the other hand, the magistrates conclude that (*they have not*), and that the proceedings before them cannot continue, they will discontinue the proceedings accordingly and leave the disappointed prosecutor to move for *mandamus* if so advised": *R*. v. *Bracknell Justices, ex parte Griffiths* (1975) 139 J.P. 368. Justices should be extremely careful before agreeing to treat submissions as preliminary points: *Williams* v. *Mohamed* [1977] R.T.R. 12.

Where justices decline jurisdiction on a preliminary point the proper remedy in *mandamus*: *Davies* v. *May* (1937) 101 J.P. 250.

A case dismissed on a preliminary objection is not decided on its merits: *R.* v. *Middlesex JJ* (1877) 41 J.P. 261, 629.

Waiver of Objections

Informalities may be waived if prior to the close of the prosecution case an accused with knowledge of the defect makes no objection: *Grimble & Co.* v. *Preston* (1914) 78 J.P. 72; *R.* v. *Banks* (1972) 136 J.P. 306.

An appearance to answer the charge without objection cures the want of information or summons: *Eggington* v. *Pearl* (1875) 40 J.P. 56; *Gray* v. *Customs Commissioners* (1886) 48 J.P. 343; *R.* v. *Garrett Pegge, ex parte Brown* (1911) 75 J.P. 169. In the words of Blackburn J in *R.* v. *Shaw* (1865) 29 J.P. 339 (quoted with approval in *R.* v. *Hughes* (1879) 43 J.P. 556): "When a man appears before justices and a charge is then made against him, if he has not been summoned, he has a good ground for asking for an adjournment; if he waives that and answers the charge, a conviction would be perfectly good against him . . .". An appearance simply in order to point out an irregularity of service is not a waiver: *Pearks, Gunston & Tee Ltd.* v. *Richardson* (1902) 56 J.P. 119.

There is no waiver where the accused was ignorant of the objection or his right to raise it: *R.* v. *Essex JJ, ex parte Perkins* (1927) 91 J.P. 94. Objection to certain formalities, once waived, may not be renewed: *Turner* v. *Postmaster General* (1864) 34 L.J.M.C. 10; but only where jurisdiction is otherwise satisfied.

Defective Process

No objection may be allowed to any information, summons or warrant for any defect in it in substance or form or for any variance between it and the evidence at the hearing: Magistrates' Courts Act 1980, s.123(1). If it appears that any variance between a summons or warrant and the evidence adduced by the prosecutor at the hearing has misled the defendant the court must on his application adjourn the hearing: *ibid*, s.123(2).

"It of course as always been held that (subs (1)) cannot be read literally as meaning: there can be no attack on an information however fundamental the defect. It depends in every case whether, for instance, the variance between it and the evidence is such as to require an amendment: a misdescription of premises might not even require an amendment. (If), unless the information is amended there might be grave injustice to the accused, an amendment is called for. Once an amendment is called for and granted, then (s. 123(2)) operates, which requires the court on the application of the defendant to adjourn", *per* Lord Parker CJ in *Wright* v. *Nicholson* (1970) 134 J.P. 85, (conviction quashed where failure to amend date of offence).

"It seems to me that one might find an information which was so defective, so fundamentally bad, that it could not be cured at all and the only proper course would be for the justices to dismiss the information. At the other end of the scale there may be informations which are deficient in some minor particular, a misdescription of premises or data, where there could be no prejudice and where no amendment or further particulars are required at all. In between there are informations, which are perfectly good as informations, albeit deficient, and can be cured, not merely by a formal amendment, but by the delivery of particulars to supplement their contents", *per* Lord Parker CJ in *Hutchinson (Cinemas) Ltd and Others* v. *Tyson* (1969) 134 J.P. 202. (Informations cured by delivery of particulars of statutory conditions said to be contravened by unlawful gaming). And *see*

Lee v. *Coles* (1972) 136 J.P.N. 226. If the court is minded to rely on this section the defendant must be made aware of this, *per* Lord Widgery CJ in *Morriss* v. *Lawrence* [1977] R.T.R. 205.

Justices are entitled to amend under this section after conviction and at any time they are *functi officio: Allen* v. *Wiseman* [1975] R.T.R. 217. But not afterwards: *Cole* v. *Wolkind* [1981] Crim. L.R. 252.

For examples of defects and variations which can and cannot be cured by this provision *see* the commentary to the Magistrates' Courts Act 1980, s.123, *infra*.

Joinder of Offences and Defendants

"The practice in magistrates' courts should be analogous to the practice prescribed in *Assim's* case in relation to trials on indictment. Where a defendant is charged on several informations and the facts are connected, for example motoring offences or several charges of shoplifting, I can see no reason why those informations should not, if the justices think fit, be heard together. Similarly, if two or more defendants are charged on separate informations but the facts are connected, I can see no reason why they should not, if the justices think fit, be heard together. In the present cases there were separate informations against the husband and the wife and a joint information against them both. I can see no rational objection to all those informations being heard and determined together. Of course, when this question arises, as from time to time it will arise, justices will be well advised to inquire both of the prosecution and of the defence whether either side has any objection to all the informations being heard together. If consent is forthcoming on both sides there is no problem. If such consent is not forthcoming, the justices should then consider the rival submissions and, under any necessary advice from their clerk, rule as they think right in the overall interests of justice. If the defendant is absent or not represented, the justices, of course, should seek the views of the prosecution and again if necessary the advice of their clerk and then rule as they think fit in the overall interests of justice. Absence of consent, either express where the defendant is present or represented and objects or necessarily brought about by his absence or the absence of representation, should no longer in practice be regarded as a complete and automatic bar to hearing more than one information at the same time or informations against more than one defendant charged on separate informations at the same time when in the justices' view the facts are sufficiently closely connected to justify this course and there is no risk of injustice to the defendants by its adoption. Accordingly, the justices should always ask themselves whether it would be fair and just to the defendant or defendants to allow a joint trial. Only if the answer is clearly in the affirmative should they order joint trial in the absence of consent by or on behalf of the defendant. To give magistrates' courts this discretion and to change the practice and procedure which has seemingly prevailed in recent years is not to invite magistrates' courts to embark on long and complicated summary trials with many charges being heard and many offenders being tried all at the same time. As Sachs J said in *Assim's* case, it is impossible to lay down general rules applicable to every case which may arise, but if justices ask themselves, before finally ruling, the single question, what is the fairest thing to do in all the circumstances in the interests of everyone concerned, they are unlikely to err in their conclusion, for the aim of the judicial process is to secure a fair trial and rules of practice and procedure are designed to that end and not otherwise": *per* Lord Roskill in *Chief Constable of Norfolk* v. *Clayton* [1983] 1 All E.R. 984 (No reason why separate informations against a husband and wife and a joint information against them both should not be heard together).

In *R*. v. *Assim* [1966] 2 All E.R. 881 Sachs J. said: "As a general rule it is, of course, no more proper to have tried by the same jury several offenders on charges of committing individual offences that have nothing to do with each other, than it is to try before the same jury offences committed by the same person that have nothing to do with each other. Where, however, the matters which constitute the individual offences of the several offenders are on the available evidence so related, whether in time or by other factors, that the interests of justice are best served by their being tried together, then they can properly be the subject of counts in one indictment and can, subject always to the discretion of the court, be tried together. Such a rule, of course, includes cases where there is evidence that several offenders acted in concert but is not limited to such cases. Again, while the court has in mind the classes of case that have been particularly the subject of discussion before it, such as incidents which, irrespective of there appearing in a joint charge in the indictment, are contemporaneous (as where there has been something in the nature of an affray), or successive (as in protection racket cases), or linked in a similar manner as where two persons individually in the course of the same trial commit perjury as regards the same or a closely connected fact, the court does not intend the operation of the rule to be restricted so as to apply only to such cases as have been discussed before it."

The rule on indictment is that accused who are jointly charged may apply to be tried separately, but in the majority of cases, however, it is in the public interest for persons jointly charged to be tried together: *R*. v. *Hoggins and Others* (1967) 131 J.P. 515. There is no rule of law that separate trials should be ordered where the defence of one accused consists of an attack on the other: *R*. v. *Marion Grondkowski and Henryck Malinowski* (1946) 110 J.P. 19.

When two accused are charged with a joint offence it is open to the prosecution to secure a conviction of both on the ground that they acted *jointly* or, no matter how either pleaded, of *either* or *both* on the ground of an *independent* commission of the offence: *Director of Public Prosecutions* v. *Merriman* (1972) 136 J.P. 659.

When two accused charged with a joint offence are tried together and one gives evidence against the other he is liable to be cross-examined by the other's counsel: *R*. v. *Hadwen* (1902) 66 J.P. 456; and this applies equally to the summary trial of co-accused: *Rigby* v. *Woodward* (1957) 121 J.P. 120. The rule is not dependent upon the one accused implicating his co-accused: *R*. v. *Hilton* (1971) 135 J.P. 590.

Use of the word "jointly" or "together" is not necessary to make the offence charged a joint offence, *per* Stephenson LJ, in *R*. v. *Rowlands* (1972) 136 J.P. 106.

An information should not be tried at the same time as a civil complaint: *R*. v. *Dunmow JJ, ex parte Anderson* (1964) (dangerous dog). In that case it was suggested that the criminal proceedings should be heard first, and the parties invited to accept the evidence given therein in the subsequent civil proceedings.

Justices do not have power even with consent to permit the simultaneous trial of cross-summonses: *R*. v. *Epsom Justices, ex parte Gibbons* (1983) *The Times*, July 28.

The Rule against Duplicity

The court may not proceed to the trial of an information that charges more than one offence: Magistrates' Courts Rules 1981, r. 12(1).

This rule arises in practice in three main circumstances: (i) where it is difficult to know from the wording of the statute whether Parliament intended to create one or more offences; (ii) in relation to continuing offences; and (iii) where a number of similar offences are charged as one.

So far as (i) is concerned, it has been held that it is legitimate to charge in a single charge one activity even though that activity may involve more than one act: *Jemmison* v. *Priddle* (1972) 136 J.P. 230, (taking or killing deer without a licence). Where a section creates two offences they may in a proper case be charged conjunctively where they arise out of a single act or incident: *R.* v. *Clow* (1963) 127 J.P. 371 (driving at a speed and in a manner dangerous to the public); *Vernon* v. *Paddon* (1978) 137 J.P. 758. For a narrow approach to the rule *see Shah* v. *Swallow* (1983) *The Times,* November 9.

Concerning (ii), earlier cases have used the term "continuing offence" in two senses. A statute which creates a series of separate offences is caught by this rule but one which charges one transaction, albeit taking place over a length of time, is not: *Anderton* v. *Cooper* [1980] 72 Cr. App. R. 232 (managing a brothel).

Concerning (iii) it has been held in *R.* v. *Ballysingh* [1953] 37 Cr. App. R. 28, that where, in a case of shoplifting, the evidence shows that a number of articles had been taken from different parts of a large store the proper course was to make each taking the subject of a separate count for larceny. In *Jemmison* v. *Priddle* (1972) 136 J.P. 230, Lord Widgery CJ, after referring to this case, said that "Thus, if the accused is alleged to have gone to one department and picked up a handful of tomatoes, or whatever it might be, it is perfectly legitimate to charge that as a single offence, whereas if the accused spends a substantial time going round the floors picking up a separate article here and another article there those individual articles ought to be charged separately." The test traditionally used to distinguish these two types of conduct is whether the acts were all one transaction, although on the facts of *Jemmison* v. *Priddle* His Lordship did not find that particularly helpful. In *R.* v. *Jones & Others* [1974] 59 Cr. App. R. 120, at p. 122, the Court of Appeal applied the approach of Lord Parker in *Ware* v. *Fox* (1967) 131 J.P. 113, by asking the question "Does the single count charge more than one activity even though that activity may involve more than one act?" (acts of unlawful assembly). In *Horrix* v. *Malam* [1984] R.T.R. 112 the rule was held to apply to an information for careless driving which alleged driving on different roads over a period of some 35 minutes.

Curing a Duplicitous Information

The prosecutor should be invited before the trial begins to decide on which offence he elects to proceed and the remaining offence should be struck out. If the prosecutor refuses to elect, the information should be dismissed: *Edwards* v. *Jones* (1947) 111 J.P. 324.

There is no power to amend the information to cure duplicity once the trial has begun; *Hargreaves* v. *Alderson* [1962] 3 All E.R. 1019. If the summons is not amended, either forthwith or after an adjournment, and the justices proceed to conviction on a bad information it will be quashed: *Hunter* v. *Coombs* (1962) 126 J.P. 300.

Where a question of duplicity was not taken before the magistrates and their conviction was a good one if certain dates were to be regarded as surplusage, the Divisional Court would not interfere: *Blakey Transport Ltd.* v. *Baggott* [1973] Crim. L.R. 776.

Putting the Charge

If the accused appears the court must state to him the substance of the information and ask him whether he pleads guilty or not guilty: Magistrates' Courts Act 1980, s. 9.

The court is under a duty not to accept a plea of guilty which is not unambiguous. By contrast the court has a discretion to permit an unambiguous plea of guilty to be changed to one of not guilty.

Ambiguous Pleas

A plea of guilty accompanied by words denying an essential element of the offence is really a plea of not guilty: *R.* v. *Golathon* (1915) 79 J.P. 270; *R.* v. *Durham Quarter Sessions, ex parte Virgo* (1952) 116 J.P. 157. This applies equally to statements made in mitigation: *R.* v. *Ingleson* (1915) 1 K.B. 512; to statements made to the police and read to the court by the prosecutor: *R.* v. *Tottenham Justices, ex parte Rubens* (1970) 134 J.P. 285 and to reported statements of the accused in a social inquiry report: *Maurice Leahy* v. *Rawlinson* [1978] Crim. L.R. 106.

A plea is not unequivocal if, after a represented accused pleads guilty, his counsel interrupts and states that his client does not precisely understand the proceedings: *R.* v. *Halliwell* [1980] Crim. L.R. 49.

Change of Plea

The accused can apply at any time before final adjudication to change his plea of guilty and it is for the court then to decide whether justice requires that that should be permitted. There is no difference in this respect in the practice of the superior and inferior courts and the doctrine of *functus officio* has no application to the acceptance of a plea: *S (an infant)* v. *Manchester City Recorder and Others* (1970) 134 J.P. 3. The court refused to upset an advocate's application to change a plea of guilty to one of not guilty in *R.* v. *Ali Tasamulug* [1971] Crim. L.R. 441. Magistrates should only allow a change of plea where justified by the interests of justice and not by expediency: *R.* v. *Uxbridge Justices, ex parte Smith* [1977] R.T.R. 93. The court's power to allow an unequivocal plea of guilty to be changed at a later stage of the proceedings to one of not guilty should only be exercised in clear cases and very sparingly, *per* O'Connor J in *P. Foster (Haulage) Ltd.* v. *Roberts* (1978) 142 J.P. 447 (solicitor mistakenly thought offence was absolute).

Magistrates cannot entertain an application to change a plea after sentence: *R.* v. *Campbell, ex parte Hoy* (1953) 117 J.P. 189; *R.* v. *McNally* [1954] 2 All E.R. 372; nor should they do so after a committal to the Crown Court for sentence: *R.* v. *Mutford & Lothingland Justices, ex parte Harber* (1971) 135 J.P. 107, (except where the committal was invalid: *R.* v. *Norfolk Justices, ex parte Director of Public Prosecutions* [1950] 2 K.B. 558).

Although the circumstances in which it would be proper to admit it are rare, the fact that a plea of guilty was entered (though subsequently withdrawn) may have some degree of probative value according to the circumstances of the case: *R.* v. *Rimmer* (1972) 136 J.P. 242.

Standing Mute and Fitness to Plead

In a trial on indictment a jury is empanelled to determine the issue of fitness to plead (Criminal Procedure (Insanity) Act 1964, s. 4) but there is no analogous procedure which can be applied to magistrates' courts. (*See* the Butler Committee report on Mentally Abnormal Offenders, paras. 10-33.) Sometimes the prosecution, on hearing of the defendant's state of mind, will discontinue the proceedings and call in the mental welfare officer. If they do not it is suggested that the preferred course is for magistrates to commit the defendant for trial in the case of an indictable offence and to enter a plea of not guilty in the case of a summary offence. Legal aid is indicated in either event. Alternatively, the magistrates could proceed to hear the case and rely upon the provisions of the Mental Health Act 1983, s. 37 (power to make hospital order when satisfied accused did the act or made the omission charged).

Proceedings Following a Plea of "Not Guilty"

The order of proceedings following a plea of Not Guilty is mainly (but not entirely) set out in the Magistrates' Courts Rules 1981, r. 13. Following any *preliminary points* which may be raised (*see* under that heading above) the prosecutor may first "open his case" in what is technically described as the opening speech, and then proceed to call his witnesses as well as producing any written statements or admissions in accordance with the Criminal Justice Act 1967, ss. 9, 10. At the close of his case the court should consider whether a *prima facie* case has been made out and for this purpose hear any submission of no case to answer.

No Case to Answer

"(1) If there is no evidence that the crime alleged has been committed by the defendant, there is no difficulty. The judge will of course stop the case. (2) The difficulty arises where there is some evidence but it is of a tenuous character, for example because of inherent weakness or vagueness or because it is inconsistent with other evidence. (*a*) Where the judge comes to the conclusion that the prosecution evidence, taken at its highest, is such that a jury properly directed could not properly convict upon it, it is his duty, upon a submission being made, to stop the case. (*b*) Where however the prosecution evidence is such that its strength or weakness depends on the view to be taken of a witness's reliability, or other matters which are generally speaking within the province of the jury and where on one possible view of the facts there *is* evidence upon which a jury could properly come to the conclusion that the defendant is guilty, then the judge should allow the matter to be tried by the jury."

per Lord Lane CJ in *R.* v. *Galbraith* (1981) 145 J.P. 406.

This direction is supplemented in magistrates' courts by the *Practice Note* [1962] 1 All E.R. 448 (which, it was said in *Stonely* v. *Coleman* (1974) *The Times*, February 1; [1974] Crim. L.R. 25, should always be brought to the attention of the presiding justice). That *Note* reads:

"A submission that there is no answer may properly be made and upheld:

(*a*) when there has been no evidence to prove an essential element in the alleged offence;

(*b*) when the evidence adduced by the prosecution has been so discredited as a result of cross-examination or is so manifestly unreliable that no reasonable tribunal could safely convict on it.

Apart from these two situations a tribunal should not in general be called on to reach a decision as to conviction or acquittal until the whole of the evidence which either side wishes to tender has been placed before it. If, however, a submission is made that there is no case to answer the decision should depend not so much on whether the adjudicating tribunal (if compelled to do so) would at that stage convict or acquit, but on whether the evidence is such that a reasonable tribunal might convict. If a reasonable tribunal might convict on the evidence so far laid before it, there is a case to answer".

Despite the fact that the defence made no submission at the close of the prosecution case, it will, in appropriate cases, be the duty of the court to take the initiative itself: *R.* v. *Burdett* [1820] 4 B. & Ald. 95. It has been held in relation to civil proceedings that justices have a power at common law rather than under these rules to stop a case at the conclusion of the complainant's case, either on their own motion or on the complainant's submission: *Mayes* v. *Mayes* (1971) 135 J.P. 487. A submission of "no case" is a submission of law. The prosecutor is thus seemingly entitled to reply to it and the clerk to advise upon it.

There is a case to answer when the only evidence of identification is the fact that the defendant who appears in answer to the summons bears the same name as appeared on a driving licence produced by the offender to a traffic warden: *Cooke* v. *McCann* [1973] Crim. L.R. 522. Or even when counsel appears in answer to a summons and there is evidence that the driver gave the same name as the defendant: *Creed* v. *Scott* [1976] Crim. L.R. 381. And *see Stickings* v. *George* [1980] R.T.R. 237 (identity of driver).

In civil proceedings upon a submission of no case the court may have a discretion to insist that the defendant elects either to rely upon his submission or call evidence, but not both. But so far as criminal prosecutions are concerned, "there is no question of putting a man to his election in a magistrates' court", *per* Lord Parker CJ, in *Jones* v. *Metcalfe* (1967) 131 J.P. 494.

It is, however, important that justices should ascertain whether what is submitted is part of the final speech of the defence advocate or whether he makes the submission while reserving his right to call evidence thereafter. The proper practice should be to ask a defendant: "Are you making a final speech or are you making a submission and reserving the right to call evidence hereafter?", *per* Lord Parker CJ, in *R.* v. *Gravesend JJ, ex parte Sheldon* (1968) 132 J.P. 553. (And *see* also *R.* v. *Birkenhead JJ, ex parte Fisher* (1963) 127 J.P. 15, and *R.* v. *Essex JJ, ex parte Final; Same* v. *Same* (1963) 127 J.P. 39.)

Where, through a misunderstanding, justices, having retired to consider a submission of no case, return and announce a conviction, and the error is subsequently pointed out to them, they may on the authority of *S (an infant)* v. *Manchester City Recorder* (1970) 134 J.P. 3, direct a re-hearing of the case by a differently constituted bench: *R.* v. *Midhurst JJ, ex parte Thompson* (1974) 138 J.P. 359.

The court may dismiss a case after rejecting a submission, even where no evidence is given for the defence: *Lyons Maid, Ltd* v. *John Hardy Burrows* (1974) November 7; 138 J.P.N. 701 and *De Filipo* v. *De Filipo* (1963) 108 Sol. Jo. 56 (a civil case).

The Case for the Accused

Following the close of the prosecution case the accused may give evidence and call witnesses in accordance with the Magistrates' Courts Rules 1981, r. 13.

The accused is not entitled to make a statement without being sworn, but an unrepresented accused may address the court otherwise than on oath on any matter on which, if he were represented, his advocate could address the court: Criminal Justice Act 1982, s. 72(1), (2).

Evidence to Rebut

At the conclusion of the evidence for the defence the prosecutor may call evidence to rebut that evidence: Magistrates' Courts Rules 1981, r. 13(3). Such evidence must be confined to matters arising unexpectedly: *R.* v. *Whelan* (1881) 14 Cox C.C. 595; 8 L.R. Ir. 314. That is to say, "matters arising *ex improviso* which no human ingenuity can foresee": *R.* v. *Harris* (1927) 91 J.P. 152. Although the court has a discretion, evidence which is clearly relevant to the issues and in the possession of the prosecution should be adduced as part of their case and cannot properly be admitted in rebuttal: *R.* v. *Levy & Tait* [1966] Crim. L.R. 454.

Re-opening Otherwise than in Rebuttal

There are circumstances where the prosecution may make application to re-open their case otherwise than in rebuttal of the defence evidence.

Justices should always allow a case to be re-opened where the matter is one "of technicality such as the proof of a statutory rule or order", *per* Devlin J, in *Price* v. *Humphrys* (1958) 122 J.P. 423. And *see* also *Palastanga* v. *Solman* [1962] Crim. L.R. 334. "In all ordinary circumstances and in the absence of any conduct on the part of the prosecution which might properly be described as misconduct or election not to call other evidence and in the absence of any grave potential prejudice to the accused, there is only one way in which the discretion (*i.e.* to grant an adjournment) can properly be exercised", *per* Winn LJ, in *Royal* v. *Prescott Clarke & Another* (1966) 130 J.P. 274 (proof of notices and regulations allowed after submission of no case to answer).

But this applies only to highly technical or formal evidence. Where the prosecution omit to give any evidence on a matter of substance, such as the identity of the driver in a charge of careless driving, the justices have a discretion in the matter which they need not automatically exercise in favour of the prosecutor: *Middleton* v. *Rowlett* (1954) 118 J.P. 362; *Jones* v. *Carter* [1956] Crim. L.R. 275. In *Saunders* v. *Johns* [1965] Crim. L.R. 49, the Divisional Court held that while evidence of identity could be called by the prosecutor or the court following the close of the prosecution case and even after a submission of no case, it could not be called after the defence had closed their case. In *Piggott* v. *Simms* [1972] Crim. L.R. 595, the failure of the prosecution to put in the analyst's certificate in a drunken driving case was treated as a matter of substance rather than a procedural error. *See Matthews* v. *Morris* (1981) 145 J.P. 262.

The power to re-open is not confined to evidence of a formal nature. Justices have power to allow a case to be re-opened and to adjourn to enable any necessary proof to be obtained. This extends to any evidence omitted owing to accident or mistake or lack of foresight: *Duffin* v. *Markham* (1981) 82 J.P. 281 (magistrates' dismissal on a submission of no case reversed where prosecutor failed to prove order). Similarly, when after two defence witnesses had been called, two of six other witnesses in court discovered their own capacity to contribute something to the trial the judge's decision to allow the prosecutor to re-open his case was upheld: *R.* v. *Doran* [1972] 56 Cr. Ap. R. 429.

As a general rule and in the absence of some special circumstances, it would certainly be wholly wrong for justices to purport to exercise a discretion to allow evidence to be called *once they had retired: Webb* v. *Leadbitter* (1966) 130 J.P. 277; followed in *Phelan* v. *Back* (1972) 136 J.P. 298; *French's Dairies (Sevenoaks) Ltd.* v. *Davis* [1973] Crim. L.R. 630. This applies even where the irregularity takes place at the request of the defence: *R.* v. *Nixon* (1968) 132 J.P. 309 (motor car viewed after retirement of jury. Although the appeal was dismissed on the ground that there had been no miscarriage of justice, the court stressed that there had been an irregularity); *R.* v. *Corless* [1972] 56 Cr. App. R. 341 (evidence by formal admission wrongly admitted after jury had retired).

No question about re-opening arises where what is in issue is whether the proceedings were properly authorized and the prosecution have been allowed to close their case without objection: such an objection should have been made by the defence before the prosecution close their case: *Price* v. *Humphries* (1958) 122 J.P. 423.

Majority Decision

The decision of justices is that of the majority and the chairman has no casting vote. It has been said that if, on a division of opinion, one justice withdraws there is no objection to the ensuing majority verdict: *Ex parte Evans* (1894) 58 J.P. 260 (a licensing case). But this was disapproved in *Barnsley* v. *Marsh, infra*, and the better course for justices equally divided is to adjourn the case for hearing before another bench: *Bagg* v. *Colquhoun* (1904) 68 J.P. 159. It is desirable that the reconstituted bench should consist of an uneven number of justices: *R.* v. *Hertfordshire JJ, ex parte Larsen* (1925) 89 J.P. 205; *Barnsley* v. *Marsh* (1947) 111 J.P. 463. If they do not adjourn, the information should be dismissed: *R.* v. *Ashplant* (1888) 52 J.P. 474. A further summons cannot be preferred after a dismissal in these circumstances: *Kinnis* v. *Graves* (1898) 67 L.J.Q.B. 583. Where there was an uneven number of justices *mandamus* has issued to compel them to hear a case and come to a decision and *prohibition* to prevent them remitting to another bench: *R.* v. *Bridgend Justices, ex parte Randall* [1975] Crim. L.R. 287.

The High Court will not look behind the recorded decision of magistrates: *Ex parte Attorney General* (1877) 41 J.P. 118. Thus where a stipendiary disagreed with a lay justice the High Court presumed that the latter had withdrawn from the adjudication: *R.* v. *Thomas, ex parte O'Hare* (1914) 78 J.P. 55.

Ordering a Re-trial

When the accused is convicted following a plea of not guilty or after the hearing has proceeded in his absence the same court or, if the court consisted of three or more justices, a court consisting of or including a majority of that court, may within 28 days beginning with the day of conviction order a re-trial before a different bench: Magistrates' Courts Act 1980, s. 142(2).

In no other case can a finding of guilt once pronounced in open court be changed because the magistrates are *functi officio*: cf. *R.* v. *Manchester JJ, ex parte Lever* (1937) 101 J.P. 407; *R.* v. *Essex JJ, ex parte Final* (1963) 127 J.P. 39.

Written Pleas of "Guilty"

A plea of guilty may be received in writing in the absence of the accused under the procedure laid down in the Magistrates' Courts Act, 1980, s. 12. Briefly, this procedure, which is confined to summary offences, requires:

(*a*) service on the accused along with the summons of a statement of facts and an explanatory note;

(*b*) notification of this fact to the clerk of the court;

(*c*) receipt by the clerk of a written plea of guilty purporting to come from the accused or his solicitor;

(*d*) proof to the court of (*a*);

(*e*) the reading out in court of the plea, the statement of facts and any written submission in mitigation from the accused.

The court may of its own volition discontinue the procedure under s. 12, but while it is in operation no information may be given to the court by or on behalf of the prosecutor other than that contained in the documents already referred to except following an adjournment after conviction and notice. The plea of guilty may be withdrawn by the accused at any time before sentence.

Autrefois Acquit and Convict

When a magistrates' court dismisses an information for an offence triable either way the effect is the same as acquittal on indictment: Magistrates' Courts Act 1980, s. 27. This corresponds to the special pleas in bar of *autrefois acquit* and *autrefois convict*, by pleading which on indictment the accused asserts that the charge has already been the subject of a prior acquittal or conviction, as the case may be, of a court of competent jurisdiction. Most of the cases concern trial on indictment and for this reason these terms are commonly used in relation to summary trial to which, strictly speaking, they are not applicable.

Thus, in *Wemyss* v. *Hopkins* (1875) 39 J.P. 549, Blackburn J, said of a previous conviction by justices: "The defence does not arise on a plea of *autrefois convict* but on the well established rule at common law, that where a person has been convicted and punished for an offence by a court of competent jurisdiction *transit in rem judicatem*, that is, the conviction shall be a bar to all further proceedings for the same offence, and he shall not be punished again for the same matter; otherwise there might be two different punishments for the same offence." And *see* also the remarks of counsel in *Welton* v. *Taneborne* (1908) 72 J.P. 419, and of Lord Goddard CJ, in *Flatman* v. *Light* (1946) 110 J.P. 273.

The whole subject of *autrefois acquit* and *convict* was reviewed by the House of Lords in *Connelly* v. *Director of Public Prosecutions* (1964) 128 J.P. 418 in which Lord Morris quoted with approval the following dictum of Lawrence J: "For a plea of *autrefois acquit* to be maintainable, the offence of which the accused has been acquitted and that with which he is charged must be the same in the sense that each must have the same essential ingredients. The factors which constitute the one must be sufficient to justify a conviction for the other": *R.* v. *Kupferberg* [1918] 3 Cr. App. R. 166. In *Connelly's* case the House held that an acquittal of murder in the course of armed robbery did not preclude a subsequent indictment for robbery where the accused had relied on a defence of alibi at the earlier trial. Commenting on the case of *Connelly* v. *Director of Public Prosecutions, supra,* Lord Parker CJ, said in *United States Government* v. *Atkinson* [1969] 2 All E.R. 1151: "The question is not a question of whether the actual facts examined on the trial of each of the offences are the same, but whether the facts necessary to support a conviction for each offence are the same." (N.B. certain other aspects of this judgment were disapproved on appeal by the House of Lords in *Atkinson* v. *United States Government* [1969] 3 All E.R. 1317).

It is an essential ingredient of the plea that the defendant should have been in peril at the earlier proceedings. An acquittal on the merits simply means that the accused must have been in jeopardy of conviction. It does not necessarily imply that there was a hearing and balancing of evidence but merely that the acquittal was not on some technical or jurisdictional point: *British Railways Board* v. *Warwick and Others* (1980) June 17 (unreported); 145 J.P.N. 214; *R.* v. *The Swansea Justices, ex parte Purvis* (1981) 145 J.P. 252 (case dismissed where prosecution witness not available). Thus the doctrine does not apply to a summons which was dismissed for irregularities in the prosecution: *Foster* v. *Hull* (1869) 33 J.P. 629; or in respect of a conviction based on unsworn evidence: *R.* v. *Marsham, ex parte Pethick Lawrence* (1912) 76 J.P. 284; or following a committal for trial of an offence triable only summarily: *Bannister* v. *Clarke* (1920) 85 J.P. 12; or which could have been quashed for reciting the wrong date: *R.* v. *West* (1962) 126 J.P. 352. The doctrine does not apply to a summons which has been withdrawn: *Brooks* v. *Bagshaw* (1904) J.P. 514; *Davies* v. *Morton* (1913) 77 J.P. 223; unless the withdrawal was on the merits of the case: *Pickavance* v. *Pickavance* (1901) P. 60 (cited in *Davies* v. *Morton, supra*). In *R.* v. *Bedford and Sharnbrook JJ, ex parte Ward* [1974] Crim. L.R. 109, prohibition was refused to prevent the prosecution of a person against whom no evidence had been offered when he had previously answered a charge against someone of the same name. The doctrine does not apply to convictions reversed through errors of law: *R.* v. *Drury* (1849) 18 L.J.M.C. 189; but a conviction quashed on appeal becomes an acquittal.

The court must be a court of competent jurisdiction: *R.* v. *Bitton* (1833) 6 C. & P. 92; *R.* v. *Flower* [1956] 40 Cr. App. Rep. 189. But a conviction for a summary offence will act equally as a bar to subsequent proceedings for what is, effectively, the same offence, even though under a different statute: *Wemyss* v. *Hopkins, supra.* And *see* the Magistrates' Courts Act 1980, s. 27. The fact that the earlier conviction was not recorded in the court register does not prevent application of the doctrine of *autrefois convict: R.* v. *Manchester Justices, ex parte Lever* (1937) 101 J.P. 407. It is necessary for the accused to call evidence of the previous conviction (or acquittal): a statement by counsel is not sufficient: *Iremonger* v. *Vissenga and Another* [1976] Crim. L.R. 524. The burden of proof lies upon the accused and must be discharged on balance of probabilities: *R.* v. *Coughlin (Martin)* [1976] 63 Cr. App. R. 33.

The doctrine of issue estoppel is no part of the criminal law: *Director of Public Prosecutions* v. *Humphrys* (1976) 140 J.P. 386.

Nemo Debet and Road Traffic Offences

The rule against double punishment (*nemo debet bis puniri*) frequently arises in relation to traffic offences where the defendant is charged both with a substantive offence of bad driving, such as reckless or careless driving, and with an offence of strict liability arising out of the same facts, such as excess speed or failure to conform to traffic lights.

The prohibition against double punishment is now contained in statutory form in the Interpretation Act, 1978, s. 18, as follows: "Where an act or omission constitutes an offence under two or more Acts or both under an Act and at common law, whether any such Act was passed before or after the commencement of this Act, the offender shall unless the contrary intention appears, be liable to be prosecuted and punished under either or any of those Acts or at common law but shall not be liable to be punished twice for the same offence."

The proper course to follow in cases where there has been a plea of guilty to the more serious offence has been laid down by Lord Parker CJ, in *R.* v. *Burnham JJ., ex parte Ansorge* (1959) 123 J.P. 539, as follows: "Before the magistrates can decide whether to convict or not on the second information they must inquire into the matter to see what are the facts. If, having inquired into the matter, they find that the facts are the very facts which have given rise to the conviction on the first information their proper course would be to *proceed no further*" (author's italics).

This course was first laid down in respect of summary proceedings in *Welton* v. *Taneborne* (1908) 72 J.P. 419, where the Divisional Court held that a conviction for dangerous driving was a bar to a conviction for exceeding the speed limit. The magistrate in his case said that "in deciding the first information I took into consideration, besides other circumstances, the question of speed which I considered to be an element of danger". The Court by a majority held that the magistrate after convicting on the first information was right in refusing to hear the second. Lawrence J, in the course of his judgment pointed out that this was not an inflexible rule: "You might have a case [of dangerous driving] in which you might have a man convicted of driving to the danger of the public without there being any evidence of excessive speed. Then a policemen might come and say he was driving at over 20 miles an hour (the speed limit in 1908), and then the magistrate could convict [of speeding]."

In *R.* v. *Burnham JJ, supra*, the Divisional Court quashed a conviction for causing a motor car to wait in a restricted area when the defendant had already been convicted on the same facts and on the same occasion of having caused a motor car to wait on a road so as to cause unnecessary obstruction. The proper course in these circumstances, it is submitted , is to adjourn the less serious information *sine die* and to convict only on the more serious offence: *see* the article at 130 J.P.N. 298. The practice of marking the register "no separate penalty" has no statutory or judicial authority in summary proceedings.

Where charges of both careless and reckless driving are preferred in respect of the same incident and the prosecutor indicates his willingness to accept a plea to the lesser charge this is subject to the agreement of the bench. If after inquiring into the facts as they would be presented by the prosecutor, they appear to warrant the more serious charge, the magistrates can properly refuse to accept the plea to the lesser offence: *R.* v. *Bedwellty Justices, ex parte Munday* (1970) 134 J.P.N. 483; [1970] Crim. L.R. 601. If the prosecutor then declined to proceed the court should seemingly adjourn and report the matter to the Director of Public Prosecutions in accordance with the Prosecution of Offences Act 1979.

It was held in *Pilgram* v. *Dean* (1974) 138 J.P. 502 that magistrates could convict a motorist of both using a vehicle without a current excise licence and of failing to display such a licence. (But *see* 138 J.P.N. 74.)

A request by the defendant that two charges should be tried together may preclude him from objecting to a dual conviction on the same evidence: *Williams* v. *Hallam* (1943) 112 L.J.K.B. 353.

Military and Civil Convictions

A special application of the rule against double punishment is contained in the Army Act 1955, s. 133, as substituted by the Armed Forces Act 1966, s. 25, "Where a person subject to military law (*a*) has been tried for an offence by a court-martial or has had an offence committed by him taken into consideration by a court martial in sentencing him, or (*b*) has been charged with an offence under this Act and has had the charge dealt with summarily by his commanding officer or the appropriate superior authority, a civil court shall be debarred from trying him subsequently for an offence substantially the same as that offence; but except as aforesaid nothing in this Act shall be construed as restricting the jurisdiction of any civil court to try a person subject to this Act for an offence."

There is a provision in the Air Force Act, 1955, s. 133, in identical terms but with the substitution of "air force law" for "military law", and in similar but not identical terms in the Naval Discipline Act, 1957, s. 129, as amended by the Armed Forces Act 1966, s. 35.

And *see* also the Visiting Forces Act, 1952, ss. 3 and 4 (not printed herein).

Oppression and Abuse of Process

The court may of its own motion stay proceedings which are oppressive or an abuse of the process of the court: *Connelly* v. *Director of Public Prosecutions* (1964) 128 J.P. 418; *Mills* v. *Cooper* (1967) 131 J.P. 349; *Director of Public Prosecutions* v. *Humphrys* (1976) 140 J.P. 386. Although Viscount Dilhorne took the view in the case of *Humphrys, supra,* that the power to stay for abuse of process was not shared by a magistrates' court, a Divisional Court of the Queen's Bench thought otherwise in *R.* v. *Brentford Justices, ex parte Wong* [1981] 1 All E.R. 884. (Late issue of summons following "precautionary" laying of an information).

Magistrates were wrong in agreeing to hear a prosecution for driving with excess alcohol where there had been unjustified delay due to police inefficiency of such a length that it could be said to be unconscionable: *R.* v. *Oxford City Justices, ex parte Smith* [1982] RTR 201. This was followed in *R.* v. *Watford Justices, ex parte Outrim* [1983] R.T.R. 26 where it was said that in the case of unconscionable delay even in the absence of abuse justices were entitled and in appropriate cases bound to refuse to proceed. In *Doyle* v. *Leroux* [1981] R.T.R. 438, it was held that abuse of process must mean something had been done, deliberately or by accident, by the prosecution which had seriously prejudiced the possibility of the accused defending himself successfully. In that case the writing of a letter by the prosecution indicating that no further action was to be taken by them on a careless driving charge led to the defendant destroying a blood sample. It was held that this was not such an abuse of process as to justify refusing to hear the case. In *R.* v. *Grays Justices, ex parte Graham* [1982] 3 W.L.R. 596, it was held that delay of itself if sufficiently long can be an abuse of process but the delay in that case (four months between committal proceedings and two years since date of offence) was not sufficient.

For the application of this doctrine to committal proceedings *see* under the same title in Ch. 4.

There is no power in a magistrates' court to dismiss an information without hearing evidence: *R.* v. *Birmingham Justices, ex parte Lamb* (1983) 147 J.P. 75.

Withdrawal

Process may with the leave of the court be withdrawn: *R.* v. *Broad* [1970] 68 Cr. App. R. 281. The power to permit withdrawal is shared by a magistrates' court: *R.* v. *Phipps, ex parte Alton* (1964) 128 J.P. 283; *R.* v. *Redbridge Justices, ex parte Sainty* [1981] R.T.R. 13. (And *see Pickavance* v. *Pickavance* (1901) P. 60). However, the justices' consent is not necessary to withdrawal of charges in committal proceedings: *R.* v. *Canterbury and St. Augustine's Justices, ex parte Klisiak* (1981) 145 J.P. 344. Costs may be ordered against the prosecutor or (in the case of an indictable offence) out of central funds in proceedings which are not proceeded with: Costs in Criminal Cases Act 1973, s. 12.

An information, as distinct from a summons, once laid, may not be withdrawn: *R.* v. *Leigh Justices, ex parte Kara* [1981] Crim. L.R. 628.

The justices' clerk must send to the Director of Public Prosecutions details in accordance with regulations of any case which is withdrawn or not proceeded with within a reasonable time: Prosecution of Offences Act 1979, s. 5(3).

The power of the Director of Public Prosecutions under the Prosecution of Offences Act 1979, s.4, to intervene to "conduct" proceedings includes power to abort the proceedings: *Raymond* v. *Attorney General* [1982] 2 All E.R. 849.

Trial of Juveniles

Charges against juveniles must be heard in the juvenile court, except that magistrates in the adult court *may* deal with juveniles charged with aiding and abetting an adult or *vice versa*, and where the offence arose out of circumstances which are the same as or connected with those giving rise to an offence with which an adult is at the same time charged; and *must* hear an information against a juvenile jointly charged with an adult: Children and Young Persons Act, 1933, s. 46(1) and 1963, s. 18. There is, additionally, a saving in the former provision whereby a defendant who is discovered to be a juvenile only in the course of proceedings in the adult court may nevertheless be dealt with thereby. The restrictions on the jurisdiction of the adult court do not prevent it from hearing remand applications: subs. (2) of s. 46 of the 1933 Act. Notwithstanding these provisions, when a juvenile is jointly charged with an adult or a corporation and the latter pleads guilty and is committed for trial or is discharged and the juvenile pleads not guilty the juvenile may be remitted to the juvenile court for trial before evidence is called: Magistrates' Courts Act 1980, s. 29.

Juveniles unwittingly dealt with in the adult court on a written plea of guilty under the Magistrates' Courts Act 1980, s. 12, are deemed to have attained the age of 17: Children and Young Persons Act, 1933, s. 46(1A).

A juvenile appearing in court must be prevented from associating with adults who have been charged and, if a girl, must be under the care of a woman: Children and Young Persons Act, 1933, s. 31. The terms "conviction" and "sentence" are replaced for juveniles by the clumsy euphemisms "finding of guilt" and "order made upon a finding of guilt": Children and Young Persons Act, 1933, s. 59. A special form of oath is prescribed for juveniles by the Children and Young Persons Act 1963, s. 28. At every stage of the proceedings the court must have regard (among other things) to the welfare of a juvenile and must take steps in a proper case to remove him from undesirable surroundings: Children and Young Persons Act 1933, s. 44.

The rule that the names of juveniles inovolved in proceedings in the juvenile court may not be reported in the press (Children and Young Persons Act, 1933, s. 49) does not apply to the adult court except in cases involving the variation of supervision orders (Children and Young Persons Act 1969, s. 10). But in any proceedings the court may make an order preventing the press from identifying any juvenile concerned in any way therein: s. 39 of the 1933 Act. Furthermore, the public, but not the press, may be excluded by direction of the court when a juvenile gives evidence in proceedings in relation to an offence against or conduct contrary to, decency or morality: s. 37, *ibid.*

The Presumption of Incapacity

At common law all children under 14 were presumed not to know right from wrong and thus to be *doli incapax*, a presumption which, in the case of those of (now) 10 years and over may be rebuttable by strong proof of mischievous disposition: *malitia supplet aetatem: R.* v. *Gorrie* (1918) 83 J.P. 136. The younger the child the stronger the evidence required: *B.* v. *R.* (1958) 123 J.P. 61. But it is dangerous to deduce capacity from the demeanour of the accused in court: while this may be evidence it is evidence to which very little weight should be given: *Ex parte N* [1959] Crim. L.R. 523. Evidence of the boy's background should be heard to decide whether a child has been brought up with a knowledge of right or wrong: *R.* v. *Padwick* [1959] Crim. L.R. 439; *The Times*, April 24.

The prosecution can call any relevant evidence, including previous convictions, to rebut the presumption: *R.* v. *B.* [1979] 3 All E.R. 360. If the prosecution fail to call evidence to rebut the presumption of incapacity the information must be dismissed upon the close of the prosecution case: *J.B.H. and J.H. (minors)* v. *O'Connell* [1981] Crim. L.R. 632.

There is a conclusive presumption against sexual capacity in the case of children under 14 years in respect of certain sexual and unnatural offences such as rape: *R.* v. *Phillips* (1839) 8 C. & P. 736; *R.* v. *Waite* [1892] 2 Q.B. 600. But children are capable of aiding and abetting such offences.

It is conclusively presumed that no child under the age of 10 can be guilty of any offence: Children and Young Persons Act 1933, s. 50.

Reference to the European Court

Under the EEC Treaty (the Treaty of Rome), art. 177:

> The Court of Justice shall have jurisdiction to give preliminary rulings concerning: (*a*) the interpretation of this Treaty; (*b*) the validity and interpretation of acts of the institutions of the Community; (*c*) the interpretation of the statutes of bodies established by an act of the Council, where those statutes so provide.
>
> Where such a question is raised before any court or tribunal of a member state, that court or tribunal may, if it considers that a decision on the question is necessary to enable it to give judgment, request the Court of Justice to give ruling thereon.
>
> Where any such question is raised in a case pending before a court or tribunal of a member state, against whose decisions there is no judicial remedy under national law, that court or tribunal shall bring the matter before the Court of Justice.

This treaty is incorporated into English law by the European Communities Act 1972, s.2.

A magistrates' court is a "court or tribunal" falling within the second paragraph of the article which has a discretion to refer a question if it considers it "necessary to enable it to give judgment." The position of the magistrates' court is to be contrasted with that of a court against whose decision there is no judicial remedy who must refer such a matter to the European Court: *R.* v. *Plymouth Justices, ex parte Rogers* [1982] 3 W.L.R. 1. The word "necessary" is stronger than "convenient" or "desirable". The point must be such that, whichever way it is decided, it is conclusive of the case. In general therefore it is best to decide the facts first, *per* Denning, L.J., in *H.P. Bulmer Ltd.* v. *J. Bollinger SA* [1974] Ch. 401. Necessary means "reasonably necessary" and not "unavoidable", *per* Ormrod, L.J. in *Polydor Ltd. and RSO Records* v. *Harlequin Record Shops Ltd.* (1980) 2 C.M.L.R. 413. The test is not more stringent in a magistrates' court but in the ordinary case it would be highly undesirable for the justices to decide to refer until all the evidence had been called and until they could be satisfied that there was no question of the respondent being acquitted on the facts (but in this case the justices were correct in not so waiting). In the ordinary way justices should exercise considerable caution before referring even after they heard all the evidence. If they come to a wrong decision on Community law, a higher court can make the reference and frequently the higher court would be the more suitable forum to do so. The higher court is as a rule in a better position to assess whether any reference is desirable. On references the form of the question referred is of importance and the higher court will normally be in a better position to assess the appropriateness of the question and to assist in formulating it clearly. Leaving it to the higher court will often also avoid delay, *per* Donaldson, L.J. in *R.* v. *Plymouth Justices, ex parte Rogers, supra.*

SENTENCING

Once an accused person has been convicted then, unless the court adjourns his case (see below) or defers the passing of sentence in accordance with its statutory power (see below), it must proceed to impose a sentence upon him or make an order in lieu of sentence (see below).

Procedure on a Plea of Guilty

Following a plea of guilty it is the duty of the prosecutor: (a) to outline dispassionately but fully the facts of the case laying before the court any statements made by the accused; (b) to inform the court of the defendant's previous convictions; and (c) to inform the court of the defendant's antecedent history including his work record and family circumstances. The prosecution are entitled to correct erroneous statements of law concerning sentence. They should also be prepared to address the court on the maximum sentence permitted by law in the particular case. Finally, the prosecutor may indicate any claims for compensation, restitution or the like. As the *Code of Conduct for the Bar of England and Wales* comments, "prosecuting counsel should not attempt by advocacy to influence the court in regard to sentence. If, however, an accused person is unrepresented, it is proper for prosecuting counsel to inform the court of any mitigating circumstances as to which he is instructed." And *see* the comments of Lord Scarman in *R.* v. *Atkinson (Leslie)* (1978) 142 J.P. 378.

Ascertaining the Facts on a Plea of Guilty

"Often it may be desirable to hear some evidence on oath, but this is not necessary in the many cases which are very trivial and the facts can be stated informally. Of course, if the accused person says that the facts have not been stated correctly, the justices would be well advised to have the informant sworn so that he can be cross-examined", *per* Lord Goddard CJ in *R.* v. *Recorder of Grimsby, ex parte Purser* (1951) 115 J.P. 637, and *see R.* v. *Milligan* [1982] 4 Cr. App. R. (S) 2.

When there is conflict between the prosecution and the defence version of the facts the only thing the court can do unless it is minded, as some courts are, to hear the conflicting evidence on each side and make up its mind where the truth lies, is to form the best picture it can of the circumstances of the offence. It is in no way bound to accept as gospel truth everything that is said in mitigation on behalf of the defendant who is pleading guilty, *per* Bridge LJ in *R.* v. *Depledge* [1979] 1 Cr. App. R. (S) 183. And *see R.* v. *Newton* [1983] 77 Cr. App. R. 13.

Previous Convictions and Antecedents

Previous convictions are convictions which antedate the offence in question. Convictions after that date and prior to the court hearing should be referred to in the antecedents. (*See* the *Practice Direction* at [1966] 2 All E.R. 929 which concerns trial on indictment and *R.* v. *Van Pelz* (1943) 107 J.P. 24. Findings of guilt while under the age of 14 must be disregarded for the purposes of previous convictions of persons over 21: Children and Young Persons Act, 1963, s. 16, but they may be referred to as antecedent history: *Practice Direction* (1966) 130 J.P. 387.

Where an alleged previous conviction which is in dispute is trivial or irrelevant the court should state that it will ignore it, *per* Lord Goddard CJ, in *R.* v. *Butterwasser* (1947) 111 J.P. 527. (Also *R.* v. *Campbell* (1911) 75 J.P. 216.)

A previous conviction should never be mentioned to magistrates in circumstances which prevent its being challenged by the defendant: *Hastings* v. *Ostle* (1930) 94 J.P. 209. Details of antecedents need not be based strictly on the laws of evidence: *R.* v. *Elley* (1921) 85 J.P. 144; but the officer should not be allowed or invited to make allegations which are incapable of proof and which he has reason to think will be denied by the defendant: *R.* v. *Van Pelz* (1943) 107 J.P. 24; *R.* v. *Robinson* (1969) 113 Sol. Jo. 143; [1969] Crim. L.R. 207; *R.* v. *Bibby* [1972] Crim. L.R. 513; *R.* v. *Sargeant* [1974] 60 Cr. App. R. 74; *R.* v. *Wilkins* [1978] 66 Cr. App. R. 49.

The defence advocate is under no duty to disclose facts known to him regarding his client's character or antecedents, or to correct any information which may be given to the court by the prosecution if the correction would be to his client's detriment, unless, in either case, the failure to disclose amounts, in the context of the language used by the advocate, to a positive deception of the court. Generally, it is not part of his duty to advise his client to disclose a previous conviction; but this is not so if the language used by the advocate involves a deception of the court, e.g. in mitigating against disqualification by using words implying an unblemished motoring record when the advocate knows of the existence of one or more convictions. Where facts relate to the jurisdiction of the court, the advocate may need to exercise special care, for example, where disqualification is mandatory and the advocate knows, but the court does not, of the existence of convictions which would thus render it mandatory upon the court to disqualify in the absence of special reasons or circumstancnces. Whilst the advocate cannot breach the client's privilege by disclosing the true position to the court, he should refuse to mitigate on a question of disqualification or to act further unless the client agrees to allow him to disclose the true position.

Law Society's *Guide to the Professional Conduct of Solicitors.* *See* also under Proving Previous Convictions in the introduction to Ch. 2.

Spent convictions

The Secretary of State considers that magistrates' courts will wish to follow, so far as possible, a practice which reflects the tenor of the Lord Chief Justice's Practice Direction [1975] 2 All E.R. 172 printed under Spent Convictions in the introduction to Ch. 2. What this implies, broadly speaking, is that when evidence of antecedents is given following conviction, no oral reference should be made to any spent conviction unless it has influenced the court in determining sentence: Home Office circ. 98/1975 dated June 24, 1975.

Offences Taken into Consideration

As a matter of practice the court may, when passing sentence, take into consideration certain other offences committed by the accused of which he has not been convicted: *R. v. Syres* (1908) 73 J.P. 13; *Director of Public Prosecutions* v. *Anderson* (1978) 142 J.P. 391; and this is a power which is shared by magistrates: *R. v. Marquis* (1951) 115 J.P. 329. An offence should not be taken into consideration:

(*i*)   if the offence is triable only by a higher court: *R. v. Warn* (1938) 102 J.P. 46; *R. v. Simons* (1953) 117 J.P. 422;

(*ii*) unless the offence was committed within the territorial jurisdiction, *i.e.* not in a foreign country: *R. v. Warn, supra*; *R. v. Davies* (1912) 28 T.L.R. 431;

(*iii*) if the offence is not of the same class as that of which the defendant stands convicted: *R. v. Davies, supra*;

(*iv*) if disqualification or endorsement may be ordered thereupon under the Road Traffic Act 1972: *R. v. Collins* (1947) 111 J.P. 154; *R. v. Simons, supra.* This objection does not apply where the principal offence is also disqualifiable: *R. v. Jones* [1970] 3 All E.R. 815;

(*v*)   in respect of breaches of probation or of conditions of discharge: *R. v. Webb* (1953) 117 J.P. 147.

The court has a discretion whether to take other offences into consideration, but where they are similar to those on which the defendant has just been convicted it is "practically the duty" of the court to take this course: *R. v. Smith* (1921) 85 J.P. 224.

As to the procedure which should be followed, Lord Goddard CJ, in *R. v. Marquis* (1951) 115 J.P. 329 said:

> It is not enough for the court to be told that the prisoner has signed a form on which the other offences are mentioned. The prisoner should be told what those other offences are, and himself asked whether he admits them and desires them to be taken into consideration. It is not necessary in every case to put the details of each offence, but he may be asked: "Have you received and signed this list of cases showing the other offences which are outstanding against you?" If he says "Yes", he should then be asked: "Do you admit those offences and wish them to be taken into consideration"? Then he can say "Yes" or "No" as the case may be, or he can say: "Yes, I admit some, and I do not admit others."

When "sample" charges are preferred the ordinary procedure for taking other offences into consideration should be followed: *Director of Public Prosecutions* v. *Anderson* (1978) 142 J.P. 391.

It is essential that there shall be no suggestion of pressure being put on the offender to ask for other offences to be taken into consideration: *R. v. Nelson*

[1947] 1 All E.R. 358. (Recorder criticized for explaining that if prisoner did not wish offences taken into consideration prosecution would be entitled to have them tried.)

It is for the accused himself and not his counsel or solicitor to admit the other offences and ask for them to be considered: *R.* v. *Davis* (1943) 107 J.P. 75. (But the court refused to upset sentence where the accused had heard his counsel speak and had himself signed the form).

Offences taken into consideration do not rank as convictions and are probably not sufficient upon which to found a plea of *autrefois convict*; although "normally no proceedings follow on them": *R.* v. *Nicholson* [1947] 1 All E.R. 535; *R.* v. *Neal* (1949) 113 J.P. 468.

Note that the maximum sentence allowed by law is unaffected, however many offences may be taken into consideration. Compensation may, however, be ordered in respect of offences taken into consideration: Powers of Criminal Courts Act 1973, s. 35.

Adjournment for Inquiries

There is power in the Magistrates' Courts Act 1980, s. 10(3), to adjourn for limited periods after conviction for the purpose of enabling inquiries to be made or of determining the most suitable method of dealing with the case. Such adjournments can be repeated and there is no overall period prescribed within which sentence must follow upon conviction. The general right to bail applies: Bail Act 1976, s. 4(4). In such circumstances and subject to means legal aid must be granted on application by anyone remanded in custody: Legal Aid Act 1974, s. 29(1).

An adjournment for the purpose of reports does not imply a lenient sentence: *R.* v. *Hatherall* [1977] Crim. L.R. 755. However, when a court adjourns a case after conviction for the purpose of obtaining a probation report in order to ascertain the offender's suitability for community service and the report shows the offender to be suitable for such an order, the court ought to make it because otherwise a feeling of injustice would be aroused: *R.* v. *Gillam* [1981] Crim. L.R. 55. *See* also *R.* v. *Ward* [1982] 4 Cr. App. R. (S) 103, (report on suitability for bail hostel followed by borstal sentence) and *R.* v. *Moss and others* [1983] Crim. L.R. 751.

Part Sentencing Improper

It is improper to fine a convicted offender and adjourn the case for consideration of the rest of the sentence: *R.* v. *Talgarth JJ, ex parte Bithell* (1973) 139 J.P. 666.

Social Inquiry Reports

In order to determine whether there is any appropriate method other than a sentence of imprisonment of dealing with an offender aged 21 or over who has not previously received such a sentence, the court must, unless it considers it unnecessary, obtain a social inquiry report: Powers of Criminal Courts Act 1973, s. 20A(1), (2). A social inquiry report means in this context a report about a person and his circumstances made by a probation officer: *ibid*, s. 20A(7). In order to determine whether there is any appropriate method other than youth custody or a detention centre order of dealing with an offender under 21 the court must, unless it considers it unnecessary, obtain a social inquiry report: Criminal Justice Act 1982, s. 2(2), (3). A social inquiry report in this context means a report about a person and his circumstances made by a probation officer or by a social worker of a local authority social services department: *ibid*, s. 2(10). A community service order cannot be made unless the court has considered a report by a probation officer or by a social worker of a local authority social services department about the offender and his circumstances: Powers of Criminal Courts Act 1973, s. 14(2).

A probation officer is under a duty to inquire in accordance with any directions of the court into the circumstances or home surroundings of any person with a view to assisting the court in determining the most suitable method of dealing with his case: Powers of Criminal Courts Act 1973, sch. 3, para 8(1).

A copy of any probation officer's report must be given by the court to the offender or his legal representative or, if under 17 and unrepresented, to his parent or guardian: Powers of Criminal Courts Act 1973, s. 46.

Solicitors representing an accused person should not make a request for a report direct to the probation service. Any such request must be made through the court: *R. v. Adams* [1970] Crim. L.R. 693.

In the case of a juvenile a local authority notified that criminal proceedings are being brought is, unless it considers it unnecessary, under a duty to make investigations and produce certain reports to the court: Children and Young Persons Act 1969, s. 9(1). The court may request such investigations and reports when the local authority is obliged to respond: *ibid*, s. 9(2).

The Home Office have given the following advice on the *manner of presentation* of probation reports:

"27. The Secretary of State shares the view of the Morison Committee that the probation officer's report should be provided to the defendant or his adviser by the court itself, and that it is not the probation officer's responsibility to do so. The court will wish to bear in mind the desirability of allowing the defence to see a copy of the report in sufficient time to digest its contents and to clarify or challenge any points of doubt. A copy of a prison report is, under s. 37 of the Criminal Justice Act, 1961, similarly required to be provided by the court. It will not normally be necessary to supply a copy of a social inquiry report to the prosecution, though there may be cases where the court thinks it right to do so—*e.g.* if it considers that the prosecution can assist in clearing up any conflict between the report and the police antecedents. If a copy of the report is given to the prosecution arrangements should be made for it to be returned to the court .. . when the prosecution has given such assistance as may be required.

"28. The Secretary of State's view, with which the Lord Chief Justice agrees, is that, as a general rule, it is undesirable that reports by probation officers should be read aloud in open court: it is likely to be only in exceptional circumstances that the court will wish to depart from normal practice in this respect. (This view is supported by judicial remarks made in the Court of Appeal in the unreported case of *R. v. Albert Edwin Smith* (1967), on the ground that a report usually contains many things which, for the prisoner's sake, are better not emphasized). If it is known that a report may be read aloud, the frankness of the defendant in talking to the probation officer, and of the latter in preparing his report, may be impaired.

"29. The Streatfeild Committee expressed the view that ordinarily the prison reporting officer need not be in court to present his report; and both the Streatfeild and Morison Committees recognized that it was impracticable for the reporting probation officer to attend court in every case. The reporting officer will, however, attend if the accused is already under supervision, or if requested to do so by either the court or the defence; . . .

"30. The Streatfeild and Morison Committees further expressed the view, with which the Secretary of State agrees, that, when a probation officer gives evidence, he should not appear as a witness for the defence or prosecution, but should be called by the court (para. 367 of the Streatfeild report and para. 44 of the Morison report)." (Extracts from H.O. circ. 28/1971 dated February 8, 1971).

As to *recommendations* in probation reports the Home Office advise:

The Secretary of State and Lord Widgery CJ, shared the view that a probation officer can go further in commenting on an offender's "treatment needs". They suggested that if an experienced probation officer feels able to make a specific recommendation in favour of (or against) any particular form of decision being reached he should state it clearly in his report. Further, when offering advice in a report on the suitability of an offender for probation, probation officers should be encouraged to suggest the terms of an order, taking into account their assessment of the offender's needs, his likely response to supervision and any other relevant factors: Home Office circ. 195/1974 dated October 25, 1974. (*See* generally the article at [1979] Crim. L.R. 373).

The following further guidance on recommendations in probation reports was given in Home Office circular 18/1983:

2. The purpose of such a recommendation, offered by a probation officer as an officer of the court, is to assist the Judge or magistrates in deciding what is the best way of dealing with the offender. It will be one of a number of factors which they must take into account, and final responsibility for weighing the recommendation along with all other relevant considerations rests with the court.

3. The particular value of such a recommendation is that it takes account of knowledge and experience gained from social work. Furthermore, the probation officer may be the only person connected with the case who has met the defendant in a comparatively informal setting. As a result of professional training and dealing with a wide range of offenders, an experienced probation officer is equipped to understand and interpret a defendant's attitude and disposition. In particular this may apply to the defendant's attitude to the current offence and to any previous sentences or orders. The officer may thus – subject perhaps to qualifications which should always be made explicit – be able to offer an informed assessment of the likely consequences of a particular decision in the present case.

4. A recommendation is likely to be more helpful, and carry more weight, if it is supported with reasons related to the consequences which the probation officer's experience indicates are likely to follow if the recommended course is – or is not – taken. For example, if a probation order is recommended, it is useful for the court to be told, in terms that are as specific as possible, how probation may be expected to affect the offender's conduct or environment. (It is not sufficient to say that the offender "could benefit from supervision"). Similarly, in relation to every sentence or order which the court is likely to (or might with advantage) consider, an assessment of the likely consequences of that decision for the offender – whether beneficial or adverse – could be of great assistance. If a report recommends a course of action to the court which may in the circumstances appear unusual, it is important that the reason for that proposal should be carefully explained.

5. It will be particularly helpful when making recommendations if the court is aware of the various non-custodial facilities which are available in the area. In recent years the probation service has made increasing use of the local groups and activities in supervising offenders, and it is important that sentencers should be informed of these resources. Where this is done the court will be better prepared to understand and consider specific recommendations. The most suitable method of keeping such information up to date is a matter for local arrangements.

Guidance on the *contents* of probation reports was given in Home Ofice circular 17/1983.

Medical and Mental Reports

Reports on the physical and mental condition of an accused person may be called for:

(a) where the court is satisfied that the accused did the act or made the omission charged in the case of an offence punishable with imprisonment: Magistrates' Courts Act, 1980, s. 30; and

(b) after a finding of guilt in the case of any offence: Magistrates' Courts Act 1980, s. 10(3). *See Boaks* v. *Reece* (1956) 121 J.P. 51.

There is power to remand an accused to a hospital for a report on his mental condition if he has:

(i) been convicted of an offence punishable on summary conviction with imprisonment;

(ii) been charged with such an offence and the court is satisfied he did that act or made the omission charged; or

(iii) been charged with such an offence and has consented to the remand: *see* the Mental Health Act 1983, s. 35(1), (2) in Ch. 7.

For provisions concerning medical evidence *see ibid*, s. 54, in Ch. 7.

The costs of a doctor giving oral evidence under the Magistrates' Courts Act 1980, s. 10(3), may be ordered from central funds in the case of an indictable offence: Costs in Criminal Cases Act 1973; and in the case of a summary offence: Magistrates' Courts Act 1980, s. 30(3). Similar provision is made for written reports in the Criminal Justice Act 1967, s. 32(2).

Sentencing Co-accused

Special problems arise when two or more accused with different backgrounds and criminal records and, perhaps, ages, are convicted of the same offence. Normally a court will strive to apply uniform sentences on co-defendants unless there are grounds for discriminating between them: *R.* v. *Richards* [1955] 39 Cr. App. R. 1915; *R.* v. *Gardiner. R.* v. *Ryall* [1962] Crim. L.R. 853. "But when two persons are convicted together of a crime or series of crimes in which they have been acting in concert, it may be right, and very often is right, to discriminate between the two and to be lenient to the one and not to the other . . . The argument that a severe sentence on one prisoner must be unjust because his fellow prisoner, who was convicted of the same crime, received a light sentence or none at all, has neither validity nor force. The differentiation in treatment is justified if the court, in considering the public interest, has regard to the difference in characters and antecedents of the two convicted men and discriminates between them because of those differences", *per* Hilbery J. in *R.* v. *Ball* [1951] 35 Cr. App. R. 164. And *see R.* v. *Coe* [1969] 1 All E.R. 65.

The fact that a co-accused has had to be dealt with more leniently because of the Criminal Justice Act, 1961, s. 3, even though the ring-leader, is no reason for reducing sentence: *R.* v. *Jones* [1973] 57 Cr. App. R. 140.

The fact that one of the defendants is a woman is not of itself sufficient to warrant discriminating in her favour unless she was a young woman operating under the influence of a man: *R.* v. *Williams* [1953] 37 Cr. App. R. 71.

Complete legal consistency is impossible and it may not be wrong for a young man to go to a detention centre when older men were treated more leniently: *R.* v. *Midgley* [1975] Crim. L.R. 469. What must be avoided is such disparity between sentences as would leave a reasonable man with a burning sense of grievance: *R.* v. *Dickinson* [1977] Crim. L.R. 303.

When deterrent sentences are passed individual circumstances may be irrelevant: *R.* v. *Goldsmith & Oakey* [1964] Crim. L.R. 729; *R.* v. *Colley, Mills & Greenland* (1967) *The Times*, March 20.

It is undesirable if it can be avoided that members of a gang should be dealt with at different times and by different judges: *R.* v. *Pitson* [1972] Cr. App. R. 391; *R.* v. *Stroud* [1977] 65 Cr. App. R. 150; *R.* v. *Weekes and Others* [1982] 74 Cr. App. R. 161.

When one of a number of co-accused is convicted before the others sentence should be postponed until the trial is concluded except in the rare case where it is necessary to sentence one accused in order to allow him to be called against his co-accused without any suspicion that his evidence will be coloured by considerations of sentence: *R.* v. *Payne* (1950) 114 J.P. 68.

The object of sentencing in advance a co-accused who is going to give evidence for the prosecution is that there should be no suggestion that he is under any inducement which will result in his getting a lesser sentence than otherwise: *R.* v. *Stone* (1970) 134 J.P. 567. This practice is not obligatory: *R.* v. *Potter* (1977) September 15. There may be exceptions: *R.* v. *Woods* (1977) October 25. There is no corresponding rule where it is proposed to call one accused as a witness for another: *R.* v. *Coffey* [1977] Crim. L.R. 45. Where one accused is sentenced before his co-accused the later court should be fully informed of the sentence passed at the first trial: *R.* v. *Pleasance* [1974] Crim. L.R. 20.

Mitigation

After any reports have been read the accused must be given an opportunity to address the court in mitigation. Failure to afford the accused an opportunity to address the court in mitigation is a breach of the rules of natural justice: *R.* v. *Billericay Justices, ex parte Rumsey* [1978] Crim. L.R. 305. The right of the offender to address the court in mitigation otherwise than on oath is preserved by the Criminal Justice Act 1982, s. 72(2). In appropriate circumstances there is no reason why the accused should not give evidence in mitigation: *R.* v. *Cross* [1975] Crim. L.R. 591. Certain aspects of mitigation, as for example special reasons for not disqualifying in a traffic case, require that the defendant discharge a burden of proof. On a plea of guilty therefore such reasons should be advanced on oath: *Jones* v. *English* (1951) 115 J.P. 609.

The form of oath (the *voire dire*) for statements made after conviction is as follows:

> "You shall true answer make to all such questions as the court shall demand of you."

The court can then demand any information it thinks fit, *per* Lord Goddard CJ, in *R.* v. *Butterwasser* (1947) 111 J.P. 527.

When the accused gives evidence on oath after conviction he can be subject to cross-examination by the prosecutor, who may, if necessary, call rebutting evidence. Where statements are made in mitigation not on oath which the prosecutor wishes to challenge it is suggested that he has the same duty as he bears throughout the trial to intervene and point out any inaccuracy of facts so as to give the accused an opportunity to substantiate what he says by sworn testimony.

Before the court is addressed in mitigation it should receive and read any social inquiry reports which are available: *R.* v. *Kirkham* (1968) 112 Sol. Jo. 151.

Powers Available to the Court

Upon conviction of a criminal offence it is the duty of the court, after taking such steps as it desires or is required to inform itself of the circumstances of the case and of the offender and subject to its powers to defer sentence, to remit to another magistrates' court or to a juvenile court for sentence or to commit to the Crown Court for sentence, to proceed to impose a *sentence* or *order in lieu of sentence* in respect of each offence, with or without any order or *orders ancillary to sentence* as it may be required or see fit to make. There is in other words a duty to proceed to sentence a convicted offender and a magistrates' court which makes an order ancillary to sentence without passing a sentence or making an order in lieu of sentence has not discharged its function in relation to that conviction.

What sentences and orders are available will depend on the offence and on any statutory rules concerning elgibility for particular sentences and orders. However, the following is a comprehensive list of powers available to magistrates sitting in the adult court:

Sentences (properly so called)

A sentence of imprisonment, including a suspended and partly suspended sentence.

A youth custody sentence.

A detention centre order.

A hospital or guardianship order.

An attendance centre order.

An order of detention in cells of police station or court.

A community service order.

A fine.

A compensation order.

A bind-over of a parent.

A statutory bind-over (*i.e.* a bind-over specially provided for by the statute creating the offence).

A charge and control order (in respect of someone already in care).

Orders in lieu of sentence

A probation order.

An order of absolute or conditional discharge.

Orders ancillary to sentence

Costs.

Disqualification.

Disqualification until test passed.

Endorsement of driving licence.

Compensation.

Restitution.

Forfeiture.

Deprivation of property.

Bind-over.

Recommendation for deportation.

Combination of Sentences

Except where permitted by statute, only one sentence or order in lieu of sentence may be passed or made in respect of any one offence. Any number of orders ancillary to sentence may however be added to a sentence.

A court which passes a suspended sentence for an offence may not make a probation order in respect of another offence: Powers of Criminal Courts Act 1973, s. 22(1). There is a similar rule with regard to partly suspended sentences: *ibid*, sch. 9, para. 1.

It is wrong to impose over a period of time a number of sentences or orders upon an offender each of which could give rise to punishment in default because the commission thereafter of a relatively minor offence could result in the imposition of sentences which in aggregate would be disproportionate to the offence: *R.* v. *Docker* [1979] 1 Cr. App. R. (S) 151.

Remission to Another Court for Sentence

When an adult convicted by a magistrates' court of an offence punishable by imprisonment or a motoring offence for which he may be disqualified is also convicted of such an offence at another magistrates' court he may be remitted to the latter court for sentence either on bail or in custody: Magistrates' Courts Act 1980, s. 39. The remitting court may at the same time make an order of restitution: subs. (4). *ibid.* The other court may deal with the offender in any way he could have been dealt with by the convicting court including the remission of the offender to the convicting or any other magistrates' court.

Remission of Juveniles

After a finding of guilt the adult court must remit a juvenile offender to a juvenile court to be dealt with *unless* satisfied this would be undesirable: Children and Young Persons Act 1933, s. 56; *and* that the case can properly be dealt with by means of a fine, absolute or conditional discharge or the binding over of a parent with or without any ancillary orders: Children and Young Persons Act 1969, s. 7(8).

Deferment of Sentence

A court may defer passing sentence on a convicted offender for a single period up to six months for the purpose of enabling the court to have regard in determining his sentence to his conduct after conviction (including, where appropriate, the making by him of reparation for his offence) or to any change of circumstances: Powers of Criminal Courts Act 1973, s. 1(1). This can only be done with the offender's consent and if the court is satisfied, having regard to the nature of the offence and the character and circumstances of the offender that it would be in the interests of justice to do so: *ibid*, s. 1(3). This provision does not give a general discretion to defer sentence: *R.* v. *McQuaide* [1975] 60 Cr. App. R. 239. Examples of circumstances suitable for deferment are given in *R.* v. *Crosby and Hayes* [1975] 60 Cr. App. R. 234. Deferment cannot be used to require an offender to keep in touch with a probation officer or pay fines: *R.* v. *Dwyer* [1975] 60 Cr. App. R. 39; nor may it be subject to any condition or undertaking: *R.* v. *Skelton* (1983) L.S. Gaz 1659; *The Times*, May 18. "However, it will be desirable for a court that defers sentence to make it clear to the offender, and to record for its own future reference, what specific object it has in mind (e.g. to see if the offender obtains and keeps the job he says he has been offered). It will also be desirable for a court to make it clear when it defers sentence how it expects to be informed at the end of the period of deferment, about the offender's progress. Often the best course will be to ask for a report from a probation officer at the end of the period; other possible sources of information are the offender's legal representative if he has one, and the police." (Home Office circular on the Criminal Justice Act 1972).

All aspects of sentencing must be deferred: *R. v. Dwyer, supra*; including disqualification: *R. v. Fairhead* (1975) 139 J.P. 537. An exception is the power to order restitution under the Theft Act 1968, s. 28.

Following deferment the offender may be dealt with in any way in which the court which deferred sentence could have dealt with him, including the power to commit him to the Crown Court for sentence: Powers of Criminal Courts Act 1973, s. 1(8).

A decision to defer contains the implication—that is, if the report called for by the court is favourable to the accused (even though the accused has not achieved all that was hoped for)—that the court will not pass so severe a sentence as it might otherwise have imposed. As a matter of principle a substantial custodial sentence is not appropriate after deferment under s. 1 in a case in which the report to the court on the conduct and on any change of circumstances of the offender after conviction is not unfavourable to the offender, *per* James LJ, in *R. v. Gilby* (1975) 139 J.P. 537. But these remarks do not amount to an absolute rule of law: *R. v. Head* [1976] 63 Cr. App. R. 157. Thus, it would not necessarily be wrong for the court subsequently to impose a suspended sentence for a prior offence which was inadvertently not disclosed at the time of deferment: *R. v. Harling* [1977] 65 Cr. App. R. 320.

It is normally desirable for the offender to be sentenced by the bench which deferred passing sentence, but this is not essential: cf. Magistrates' Court Act 1980, s. 121. To guard against this possibility it is advisable for the clerk to make a note of the court's reasons for deferment: cf. *R. v. Jacobs* [1976] 62 Cr. App. R. 116.

If a person the subject of a deferred sentence is convicted in Great Britain of any offence prior to the adjourned date the court which deferred sentence (Powers of Criminal Courts Act 1973, s. 1(4)) or the convicting court, if different (*ibid*, s. 1(4A)), may proceed to sentence for the original offence except that a magistrates' court may not pass sentence where the Crown Court deferred: *ibid*, s. 1(4A).

When a person is convicted of a further offence during the operational period of a suspended sentence and the passing of sentence for the further offence is deferred no action should be taken on the suspended sentence during the period of deferment. Furthermore, where the suspended sentence was imposed by the Crown Court and the subsequent conviction is before a magistrates' court the better course is to commit the offender to the Crown Court: *R. v. Salmon* [1973] 57 Cr. App. R. 953.

Despite the terms of the statute a failure to sentence the offender on the due date is not fatal, whether it arises from administrative difficulties (*R. v. Ingle* (1975) 139 J.P. 81) or error (*R. v. Anderson* (1983) 147 J.P. 499.

The Presence of the Offender

A sentence of imprisonment, an order that a suspended sentence shall take effect, and a sentence of detention in a detention centre, may not be passed or made in the absence of the accused, and anyone convicted of an endorsable traffic offence may not be disqualified in his absence without notice and an opportunity of attending: Magistrates' Courts Act 1980, s. 11(3), (4).

The Power to Alter Sentence

Within 28 days beginning with the day on which a sentence or order was imposed or made a magistrates' court may vary or rescind that sentence or order and this power extends to the alteration of invalid sentences or orders: Magistrates' Courts Act 1980, s. 142(1). The power is exercisable only by the court which passed sentence or, if three or more justices sat originally, by a court consisting of or including a majority of that court (subs. (4), *ibid.*). Unless there is a direction to the contrary, the revised sentence, etc., takes effect from the beginning of the day it was originally imposed.

THE CHILDREN & YOUNG PERSONS ACT, 1933

Separation of children and young persons from adults in police stations, courts, &c.

31. Arrangements shall be made for preventing a child or young person while detained in a police station, or while being conveyed to or from any criminal court, or while waiting before or after attendance in any criminal court, from associating with an adult (not being a relative) who is charged with any offence other than an offence with which the child or young person is jointly charged, and for ensuring that a girl (being a child or young person) shall while so detained, being conveyed, or waiting, be under the care of a woman.

COMMENTARY

Waiting. "It is desirable that a child witness should be able to wait in privacy and comfort—if possible in a separate room— and should have a trusted adult close at hand at all times, especially when giving evidence"; Home Office circ. No. 208/1964, dated September 9, 1965.

Prohibition against children being present in court during the trial of other persons

36. No child (other than an infant in arms) shall be permitted to be present in court during the trial of any other person charged with an offence, or during any proceedings preliminary thereto, except during such time as his presence is required as a witness or otherwise for the purposes of justice; and any child present in court when under this section he is not to be permitted to be so shall be ordered to be removed:

Provided that this section shall not apply to messengers, clerks, and other persons required to attend at any court for purposes connected with their employment.

Power to clear court while child or young person is giving evidence in certain cases

37. (1) Where, in any proceedings in relation to an offence against, or any conduct contrary to, decency or morality, a person who, in the opinion of the court, is a child or young person is called as a witness, the court may direct that all or any persons, not being members or officers of the court or parties to the case, their counsel or solicitors, or persons otherwise directly concerned in the case, be excluded from the court during the taking of the evidence of that witness:

Provided that nothing in this section shall authorize the exclusion of *bonâ fide* representatives of a newspaper or news agency.

(2) The powers conferred on a court by this section shall be in addition and without prejudice to any other powers of the court to hear proceedings in camera.

COMMENTARY

The object of this section is more likely to be attained if the court is closed before the witness enters: Home Office circ. No. 208/1964, dated September 9, 1964. The Home Office also recommend that the attention of justices should be drawn to their powers under this section in certain cases: *see* the Commentary on s. 39, *infra*.

Subsection (1): Provided that. Without a direction under s. 39, *infra*, the press are not prevented from publishing what is said simply by virtue of the fact that an order is made under this section.

Subsection (2): Any other powers. For example the Magistrates' Courts Act 1980, s. 4(2) (committal proceedings) and the Official Secrets Act, 1920, s. 8(4) (proceedings under the Official Secrets Acts).

Power to prohibit publication of certain matter in newspaper

39. (1) In relation to any proceedings in any court, the court may direct that—

(a) no newspaper report of the proceedings shall reveal the name, address, or school, or include any particulars calculated to lead to the identification, of any child or young person concerned in the proceedings, either as being the person by or against or in respect of whom the proceedings are taken, or as being a witness therein;

(b) no picture shall be published in any newspaper as being or including a picture of any child or young person so concerned in the proceedings as aforesaid;

except in so far (if at all) as may be permitted by the direction of the court.

(2) Any person who publishes any matter in contravention of any such direction shall on summary conviction be liable in respect of each offence to a fine not exceeding level 5 on the standard scale

(as amended by the Children and Young Persons Act, 1963, s. 57(1), the Criminal Law Act 1977, sch. 6, the Criminal Justice Act 1982, ss. 39, 46, sch. 3).

COMMENTARY

This section, with the necessary modifications, applies in relation to sound and television broadcasts as it applies in relation to newspapers: Children and Young Persons Act 1963, s. 57(4).

"In Home Office Circular No. 18/1956 the Secretary of State suggested that, in all cases to which s. 39 applied, the clerk to the justices should remind the court of its powers under that section and, in a case committed for trial, include with the depositions a statement that the examining justices, having had their attention drawn to those powers, did or did not exercise them. Section 39, as extended by s. 57(1) of the 1963 Act, will apply in any proceedings against or in respect of a person under 17, or in which such a person is a witness. The Secretary of State thinks that it would be sufficient to draw the court's attention especially to its powers under that section only in cases where:—

(a) one of the defendants before an ordinary magistrates' court is under the age of 17, or

(b) the proceedings arise (in the current phrase) "out of an offence against or conduct contrary to decency or morality."

"In the second class of case the justices' attention might also be drawn to their power under s.37 of the Act of 1933 to exclude the public while a witness under 17 gives evidence. If in a case of the kinds mentioned at (a) and (b) above (or in any other case in which the justices have given a direction under s. 37 or s. 39) the defendant is committed to a superior court for trial or for sentence, it would be helpful if the statement suggested in Home Office Circular No. 18/1956 could be included with the depositions or other documents sent to the clerk of that court." Home Office circ. 17/1964 dated January 22, 1964.

In order that the clerk may be aware in advance of those criminal cases to which the section is likely to apply, chief officers of police have been asked to inform him before the proceedings if it is intended to call juvenile witnesses to give evidence for the prosecution: Home Office circ. No. 18/1956 dated February 14, 1956.

The Magistrates' Courts Rules 1981, r. 11(2)(m) requires the justices' clerk to send to the court of trial a statement whether the court has given a direction under s. 39 in every case where a person under 17 is concerned in the committal proceedings (whether as defendant or witness).

General considerations

44. (1) Every court in dealing with a child or young person who is brought before it, either as an offender or otherwise, shall have regard to the welfare of the child or young person and shall in a proper case take steps for removing him from undesirable surroundings, and for securing that proper provision is made for his education and training.

(2) (*Repealed*)

(as amended by the Children & Young Persons Act 1969, sch. 6).

Assignment of certain matters to juvenile courts

46. (1) Subject as hereinafter provided, no charge against a child or young person, and no application whereof the hearing is by rules made under this section assigned to juvenile courts, shall be heard by a court of summary jurisdiction which is not a juvenile court:

Provided that—

(a) a charge made jointly against a child or young person and a person who has attained the age of 17 years shall be heard by a court of summary jurisdiction other than a juvenile court; and

(b) where a child or young person is charged with an offence, the charge may be heard by a court of summary jurisdiction which is not a juvenile court if a person who has attained the age of 17 years is charged at the same time with aiding, abetting, causing, procuring, allowing or permitting that offence; and

(c) where, in the course of any proceedings before any court of summary jurisdiction other than a juvenile court, it appears that the person to whom the proceedings relate is a child or young person, nothing in this subsection shall be construed as preventing the court, if it thinks fit so to do, from proceeding with the hearing and determination of those proceedings.

(1A) If a notification that the accused desires to plead guilty without appearing before the court is received by the clerk of a court in pursuance of s. 12 of the Magistrates' Courst Act 1980 and the court has no reason to believe that the accused is a child or young person, then, if he is a child or young person he shall be deemed to have attained the age of 17 for the purposes of subs. (1) of this section in its application to the proceedings in question.

(2) No direction, whether contained in this or any other Act, that a charge shall be brought before a juvenile court shall be construed as restricting the powers of any justice or justices to entertain an application for bail or for a remand, and to hear such evidence as may be necessary for that purpose.

(3) (*Repealed*)

(*as amended by the Education Act, 1944, sch. 9, the Justices of the Peace Act, 1949, sch. 7, the Children and Young Persons Act 1969, sch. 5, the Magistrates' Courts Act 1980, sch. 7*).

COMMENTARY

The powers of an adult court to hear cases involving juveniles have been extended largely by the Children & Young Persons Act 1963, s. 18, *infra*. For the *power* to remit a juvenile for trial to a juvenile court in certain circumstances see the Magistrates' Courts Act 1980, s. 29, *infra*. For the *duty* to remit to the juvenile court after a finding of guilt *see* s. 56 of the 1933 Act and s. 7(8) of the 1969 Act.

Subsection (1): Charge. It is submitted that this does not extend to a complaint for a bind-over under the Magistrates' Courts Act 1980, s. 115, or even to a juvenile arrested for the breach of the peace without such a complaint or any charge being preferred.

Rules made under this section. None has been made.

Proviso (a). But *see* the Magistrates' Courts Act 1980, s. 29, *infra*. (Power to remit to juvenile court).

Charge made jointly. See the note to the Children and Young Persons Act 1969, s. 6, *infra*.

Attained the age of 17 years. For the determination of age *see* s. 99. *See* also subs. (1A).

Shall be heard/may be heard. The difference in wording clearly implies that the court has a discretion in para. (*b*) but not in para. (*a*).

Aiding, abetting. *See* the Magistrates' Courts Act 1980, s. 44.

Age of criminal responsibility

50. It shall be conclusively presumed that no child under the age of 10 years can be guilty of any offence.
(*as amended by the Children and Young Persons Act 1963, s. 16(1)*).

COMMENTARY

The provisions of s. 4 of the Children & Young Persons Act 1969 (which would prevent prosecutions for offences committed by children) have not been brought into effect.

For the Presumption of Incapacity in the case of children *see* under that title in the introduction.

Power of other courts to remit juvenile offenders to juvenile courts

56. (1) Any court by or before which a child or young person is found guilty of an offence other than homicide, may, and, if it is not a juvenile court, shall, unless satisfied that it would be undesirable to do so, remit the case to a juvenile court acting for the place where the offender was committed for trial, or, if he was not committed for trial, to a juvenile court acting either for the same place as the remitting court or for the place where the offender habitually resides; and, where any such case is so remitted, the offender shall be brought before a juvenile court accordingly, and that court may deal with him in any way in which it might have dealt with him if he had been tried and found guilty by that court.

(2) Where any case is so remitted the offender shall have the same right of appeal against any order of the court to which the case is remitted as if he had been found guilty by that court, but shall have no right of appeal against the order of remission.

(3) A court by which an order remitting a case to a juvenile court is made under this section may give such directions as appear necessary with respect to the custody of the offender or for his release on bail until he can be brought before the juvenile court, and shall cause to be transmitted to the clerk of the juvenile court a certificate setting out the nature of the offence and stating that the offender has been found guilty thereof, and that the case has been remitted for the purpose of being dealt with under this section.

(*as amended by the Children & Young Persons Act 1963, sch. 3, the Children & Young Persons Act 1969, sch. 5, the Courts Act 1971, sch. 11*).

COMMENTARY

The power to remit under this section only arises after and not before a finding of guilt.

Undesirable to do so. The court has no discretion but to remit unless it proposes to make one or more of the orders contained in the Children & Young Persons Act 1969, s. 7(8), *infra*.

Remit. For the form of order *see* form 51 of the Magistrates' Courts (Children & Young Persons) Rules 1970.
There is no right of appeal against an order of remission.

The custody of the offender. The Home Office booklet on Part 1 of the Children & Young Persons Act 1969 states:

> "Courts may wish to use the remand procedure for this purpose. If there is no release on bail, remand would be in accordance with s. 23 of the 1969 Act, if the person was under 17, or with s.23 of the 1969 Act, if the person was under 17, or with s.27 of the Criminal Justice Act 1948, if he had reached the age of 17 since the proceedings were begun."

Miscellaneous provisions as to summary proceedings against juvenile offenders

59. (1) The words "conviction" and "sentence" shall cease to be used in relation to children and young persons dealt with summarily and any reference to any enactment whether passed before or after the commencement of this Act to a person convicted, a conviction or a sentence shall, in the case of a child or young person, be construed as including a reference to a person found guilty of an offence, a finding of guilt or an order made upon such a finding, as the case may be.

(2) *(Repealed)*

(*as amended by the Criminal Justice Act 1948, sch. 9, the Costs in Criminal Cases Act 1952, s. 8(1)*).

COMMENTARY

The effect of this section is purely terminological; thus a finding of guilt remains a previous conviction for the purpose of attracting higher penalties, for the "totting" procedure under the Transport Act 1981, and for all other purposes. But *see* the Children & Young Persons Act 1963, s. 16, *infra*, as to the citation of findings of guilt which occurred when the offender was under the age of 14.

Presumption and determination of age.

99. (1) Where a person, whether charged with an offence or not, is brought before any court otherwise than for the purpose of giving evidence, and it appears to the court that he is a child or young person, the court shall make due enquiry as to the age of that person, and for that purpose shall take such evidence as may be forthcoming at the hearing of the case, but an order or judgment of the court shall not be invalidated by any subsequent proof that the age presumed or declared by the court to be the age of the person so brought before it shall, for the purposes of the Act, be deemed to be the true age of that person, and, where it appears to the court that the person so brought before it has attained the age of 17 years, that person shall for the purposes of this Act be deemed not to be a child or young person.

(2) Where in any charge or indictment for any offence under this Act or any of the offences mentioned in the First Schedule to this Act, except as provided in that Schedule, it is alleged that the person by or in respect of whom the offence was committed was a child or young person or was under or had attained any specified age, and he appears to the court to have been at the date of the commission of the alleged offence a child or young person, or to have been under or to have attained the specific age, as the case may be, he shall for the purpose of this Act be presumed at that date to have been a child or young person or to have been under or to have attained that age, as the case may be, unless the contrary is proved.

(3) Where, in any charge or indictment for any offence under this Act or any of the offences mentioned in the First Schedule to this Act, it is alleged that the person in respect of whom the offence was committed was a child or was a young person, it shall not be a defence to prove that the person alleged to have been a child was a young person or the person alleged to have been a young person was a child in any case where the acts constituting the alleged offence would equally have been an offence if committed in respect of a young person or child respectively.

(4) Where a person is charged with an offence under this Act in respect of a person apparently under a specified age it shall be a defence to prove that the person was actually of or over that age.

(*as amended by the Sexual Offences Act, 1956, sch. 3*).

5. TRIAL AND SENTENCE 225

COMMENTARY

Subsection (1): This Act. Includes the 1969 Act: Children & Young Persons Act 1969, s. 70(3).

First Schedule

Offences Against Children and Young Persons, With Respect to Which Special Provisions of This Act Apply

Offences Against Children and Young Persons, With Respect to Which Special Provisions of This Act Apply
The murder or manslaughter of a child or young person.
Infanticide.
Any offence under ss. 27, 56, of the Offences against the Persons Act 1861, and any offences against a child or young person under ss. 5, 42, 43, of that Act.
Any offence under ss. 1, 3, 4, 11 or 23, of this Act.
Any offence against a child or young person under any of the following sections of the Sexual Offences Act 1956, that is to say, ss. 2 to 7, 10 to 16, 19, 20, 22 to 26, and 28 and any attempt to commit against a child or young person an offence under ss. 2, 5, 6, 7, 10, 11, 12, 22 or 23 of that Act. Provided that for the purposes of s. 99(2) of this Act this entry shall apply so far only as it relates to offences under ss. 10, 11, 12, 14, 15, 16, 20 and 28 of the Sexual Offences Act 1956, and attempts to commit offences under ss. 10, 11 and 12 of that Act.
Any other offence involving bodily injury to a child or young person.

(as amended by the Sexual Offences Act 1956, sch. 3)

THE CHILDREN AND YOUNG PERSONS ACT, 1963

Offences committed by children
16. (1)...

(2) In any proceedings for an offence committed or alleged to have been committed by a person of or over the age of 21, any offence of which he was found guilty while under the age of 14 shall be disregarded for the purposes of any evidence relating to his previous convictions; and he shall not be asked, and if asked shall not be required to answer, any question relating to such an offence, notwithstanding that the question would otherwise be admissible under s. 1 of the Criminal Evidence Act, 1898.

COMMENTARY

This Act is to be construed as one with the Children & Young Persons Act 1933: s. 65(3) of the 1963 Act.

The age of 21. For the determination of age *see* the Magistrates' Courts Act 1980, s. 150(4), and the Children and Young Persons Act 1933, s. 99, *supra*.

Disregarded for the purposes of any evidence relating to his previous convictions. But not for the purposes of informing the court as to antecedents: *Practice Direction* [1966] 2 All E.R. 929. (*See* article at 135 J.P.N. 656).

Section 1 of the Criminal Evidence Act, 1898. Proviso (*f*) thereof lists the cases in which a witness may be questioned as to previous offences.

THE CHILDREN AND YOUNG PERSONS ACT 1969

Alterations in treatment of young offenders etc.

7. (1)-(4) *(Repealed)*

(5), (6) . . .

(7) Subject to subs. (7A) of this section and to the enactments requiring cases to be remitted to juvenile courts and to s. 53(1) of the Act of 1933 (which provides for detention for certain grave crimes), where a child is found guilty of homicide or a young person is found guilty of any offence by or before any court, that court or the court to which his case is remitted shall have power–

> (*a*), (*b*) *(Refer to juvenile court*), or

> (*c*) with the consent of his parent or guardian, to order the parent or guardian to enter into a recognizance to take proper care of him and exercise proper control over him,

and, if it makes such an order as is mentioned in this subsection while another such order made by any court is in force in respect of the child or young person, shall also have power to discharge the earlier order; and subs. (13) of s. 2 of this Act shall apply to an order under para. (*c*) of this subsection as it applies to such an order as is mentioned in that subsection.

(7A) . . .

(8) Without prejudice to the power to remit any case to a juvenile court which is conferred on a magistrates' court other than a juvenile court by s. 56(1) of the Act of 1933, in a case where such a magistrates' court finds a person guilty of an offence and either he is a young person or was a young person when the proceedings in question were begun, it shall be the duty of the court to exercise that power unless the court is of the opinion that the case is one which can properly be dealt with by means of—

> (*a*) an order discharging him absolutely or conditionally, or
> (*b*) an order for the payment of a fine; or
> (*c*) an order requiring his parent or guardian to enter into a recognizance to take proper care of him and exercise proper control over him,

with or without any other order that the court has power to make when absolutely or conditionally discharging an offender.

(*as amended by the Criminal Justice Act 1972, sch. 5, the Powers of Criminal Courts Act 1973, sch. 6, the Criminal Justice Act 1982, s. 23, sch. 16).*

COMMENTARY

The enactments requiring cases to be remitted. *See* the Children & Young Persons Act 1933, s. 56 and subs. (8).

Young person. The definition in s. 70 of the Act has been extended to include in this subsection and in subs. (8) a child who has attained the age of 10 years: The Children and Young Persons Act 1969 (Transitional Modifications of Part 1) Order 1970, S.I. 1970, no. 1882.

Enter into a recognizance. This power is in addition to the common law powers of magistrates. Note that it may only be made by consent of the parent or guardian and is subject to the limitations of s. 2(13) of the Act.

Section 2(13) of this Act. This reads as follows:

> "Such an order is as mentioned in subs. (3)(a) of the preceding section shall not require the parent or guardian in question to enter into a recognizance for an amount exceeding £50 or for a period exceeding three years or, where the relevant infant will attain the age of 18 in a period shorter than three years, for a period exceeding that shorter period; and s. 120 of the Magistrates' Courts Act 1980 (which relates to the forfeiture of recognizances) shall apply to a recognizance to keep the peace."

Subsection (8). Thus an adult court may not make a supervision or detention centre order in respect of a juvenile offender or even commit him to the Crown Court for sentence.

Was a young person when the proceedings were begun. Thus an adult court must remit even an adult to a juvenile court if he was a juvenile when the proceedings began, unless it proposes to make one or more of the specified orders. *See* also the note "Young Person" above. It has been held that proceedings were begun on the date the accused was served with the summons: *R.* v. *Billericay Justices, ex parte Johnson* (1979) 143 J.P. 697.

A recognizance to take proper care. *See* subs. (7).

Investigations by local authorities

9. (1) Where a local authority or a local education authority bring proceedings under s. 1 of this Act or proceedings for an offence alleged to have been committed by a young person or are notified that any such proceedings are being brought, it shall be the duty of the authority, unless they are of the opinion that it is unnecessary to do so, to make such investigations and provide the court before which the proceedings are heard with such information relating to the home surroundings, school record, health and character of the person in respect of whom the proceedings are brought as appear to the authority likely to assist the court.

(2) If the court mentioned in subs. (1) of this section requests the authority aforesaid to make investigations and provide information or to make further investigations and provide further information relating to the matters aforesaid, it shall be the duty of the authority to comply with the request.

COMMENTARY

Subsection (1): Proceedings under s. 1 of this Act. That is, care proceedings.

Young person. The definition in s. 70 of the Act has been extended to include a child who has attained the age of 10 years: Children & Young Persons Act 1969 (Transitional Modifications of Part 1) Order 1970. S.I. 1970 No 1882. Where local arrangements allow of reports by the probation service of young persons to the age of 13 the duty of the local authority under this section is removed by s. 34(3) of the Act. (S.I. 1970 No 1882 refers).

Notified. The prosecutor is under a duty to notify the local authority when he decides to lay an information against a juvenile: s. 5(8) of the Act.

THE POWERS OF CRIMINAL COURTS ACT 1973

Deferment of Sentence

1. (1) Subject to the provisions of this section, the Crown Court or a magistrates' court may defer passing sentence on an offender for the purpose of enabling the court or any other court to which it falls to deal with him to have regard, in dealing with him, to his conduct after conviction (including, where appropriate, the making by him of reparation for his offence) or to any change in his circumstances.

(2) Any deferment under this section shall be until such date as may be specified by the court, not being more than six months after the date on which the deferment is announced by the court; and subject to subs. (8A) below where the passing of sentence has been deferred under this section it shall not be further deferred thereunder.

(3) The power conferred by this section shall be exercisable only if the offender consents and the court is satisfied, having regard to the nature of the offence and the character and circumstances of the offender, that it would be in the interests of justice to exercise the power.

(4) A court which under this section has deferred passing sentence on an offender may deal with him before the expiration of the period of deferment if during that period he is convicted in Great Britain of any offence.

(4A) If an offender on whom a court has under this section deferred passing sentence in respect of one or more offences is during the period of deferment convicted in England or Wales of any offence ("the subsequent offence"), then. without prejudice to subs. (4) above, the court which (whether during that period or not) passes sentence on him for the subsequent offence may also, if this has not already been done, deal with him for the first-mentioned offence or offences:
Provided that—

    (a) the power conferred by this subsection shall not be exercised by a magistrates'court if the court which deferred passing sentence was the Crown Court; and

    (b) the Crown Court, in exercising that power in a case in which the court which deferred passing sentence was a magistrates' court, shall not pass any sentence which could not have been passed by a magistrates' court in exercising it.

(5) Where a court which under this section has deferred passing sentence on an offender proposes to deal with him, whether on the date originally specified by the court or by virtue of subs. (4) above before that date, or where the offender does not appear on the date so specified, the court may issue a summons requiring him to appear before the court, or may issue a warrant for his arrest.

(6) It is hereby declared that in deferring the passing of sentence under this section a magistrates' court is to be regarded as exercising the power of adjourning the trial which is conferred by s. 10(1) of the Magistrates' Courts Act 1980, and that accordingly ss. 11(1) and 13(1), (2) and (5) of that Act (non-appearance of the accused) apply (without prejudice to subs. (5) above) if the offender does not appear on the date specified in pursuance of subs. (2) above.

(6A) Notwithstanding any enactment, a court which under this section defers passing sentence on an offender shall not on the same occasion remand him.

(7) . . .

(8) The power of a court under this section to deal with an offender in a case where the passing of sentence has been deferred thereunder–
    (a)   includes power to deal with him in any way in which the court which deferred passing sentence could have dealt with him; and
    (b)   without prejudice to the generality of the foregoing, in the case of a magistrates' court, includes the power conferred by ss. 37 or 38 of the Magistrates' Courts Act 1980 to commit him to the Crown Court for sentence.

(8A) Where, in a case where the passing of sentence on an offender in respect of one or more offences has been deferred under this section, a magistrates' court deals with him by committing him to the Crown Court under ss. 37 or 38 of the Act of 1980, the power of the Crown Court to deal with him includes the same power to defer passing sentence on him as if he had just been convicted of the offence or offences on indictment before the court.

(*as amended by the Criminal Law Act 1977, sch. 12; the Magistrates' Courts Act 1980, sch. 7, the Criminal Justice Act 1982, s. 63*).

COMMENTARY

See generally the introduction, under Deferment of Sentence.

Subsection (2). The prohibition of further deferment beyond the six months period is confined to deferments "under this section". It would not seem to exclude, for example, a remand under the Magistrates' Courts Act 1980, ss. 10 or 30 if, even at this late date, it became clear that such a remand was desirable. Cf. *R.* v. *Ingle* (1975) 139 J.P. 81.

Subsection (3). Consents. Consent should be obtained from the accused personally: *R.* v. *Gilby* (1975) 139 J.P. 552; but where counsel appeared and requested deferment lack of a personal consent was not held to be fatal: *R.* v. *Fairhead* (1975) 139 J.P. 537.

Subsection (4). Any offence. Whether committed before or after the date of conviction of the present offence. The clerk of the convicting court must notify the clerk of the court which has deferred sentence: Magistrates' Courts Rules 1981, r. 27.

Great Britain. That is England, Scotland and Wales: Union with Scotland Act, 1706; Wales & Berwick Act, 1746, s. 3. Excluding the Channel Isles and the Isle of Man.

Subsection (4A). *See* the note to subs. (4).

Subsection (6A). Thus, a deferment is an adjournment (subs. (6)) upon which the defendant cannot be bailed or remanded in custody.

Subsection (8). This reverses the decision in *R.* v. *Gilby* (1975) 139 J.P. 552.

Reports of Probation Officers

46. (1) Subject to subs. (2) below, where a report by a probation officer is made to any court (other than a juvenile court) with a view to assisting the court in determining the most suitable method of dealing with any person in respect of an offence, a copy of the report shall be given by the court to the offender or his counsel or solicitor.

(2) If the offender is under 17 years of age and is not represented by counsel or a solicitor, a copy of the report need not be given to him but shall be given to his parent or guardian if present in court.

COMMENTARY

A probation officer's report should be read by the court before it is addressed by counsel or solicitor: *R.* v. *Kirkham* (1968) *The Times*, February 10; [1968] Crim. L.R. 210. Failure to comply with the provisions of this section is probably not in itself a ground for upsetting the order of the court: *Re Philpot* (1960) 124 J.P. 124.
    See generally the heading Social Inquiry Reports in the introduction.

Subsection (2). A juvenile offender must be remitted to a juvenile court for sentence *unless* the court is satisfied this would be undesirable: Children & Young Persons Act, 1933, s. 56 *and* the court is of the opinion the case can properly be dealt with in one or more of a number of specified ways: Children and Young Persons Act 1969, s. 7(8).

Shall be given. Whether this implies a transfer of ownership or not, it must, it is submitted, involve at least the right to take a copy of the whole or any part of the report and to retain it until the conclusion of the trial and, probably, beyond, for the purpose of any appeal against sentence.

Parent or guardian. For their attendance at court *see* the Children & Young Persons Act 1933, s. 34.

THE MAGISTRATES' COURTS ACT 1980

Procedure on trial

9. (1) On the summary trial of an information, the court shall, if the accused appears, state to him the substance of the information and ask him whether he pleads guilty or not guilty.

(2) The court, after hearing the evidence and the parties, shall convict the accused or dismiss the information.

(3) If the accused pleads guilty, the court may convict him without hearing evidence.

COMMENTARY

Subsection (1): An information. *See* under this title in the introduction.

For the trial of two or more informations at the same time *see* under *Joinder of Defendants and Offences* in the introduction.

State . . . the substance of the information. Loquacity rather than justice is served by reading out the formal wording of the information in full and this applies *a fortiori* to the young and inarticulate.

Ask him. The question must be asked personally of the accused whether he pleads guilty or not and a plea of guilty by a solicitor without the question being so put will be quashed: *R.* v. *Wakefield JJ., ex parte Butterworth* (1970) 134 J.P. 347. So long as the charges are put to the accused personally there is nothing wrong in his solicitor pleading guilty even if such a plea was not justified by his instructions, provided the accused did not show dissatisfaction with the plea: *ibid.* and *R.* v. *Gowerton JJ., ex parte Davies* [1974] Crim. L.R. 253.

Despite the wording of this provision it has long been universal practice in magistrates' courts to accept a plea of guilty from a solicitor or counsel representing under s. 122 of the Act an accused who is not personally present.

Pleads guilty. The plea must be entered in the register: Magistrates' Courts Rules 1981, r. 66(4).

For the conduct of a trial following a plea of guilty, *see* the note "Ascertaining the Facts on a Plea of Guilty" in the introduction. For Ambiguous Pleas and Change of Plea *see* under those headings in the introduction.

Or not guilty. The plea must be entered in the register: Magistrates' Courts Rules 1981, r. 66(4).

Subsection (2): Hearing the evidence and the parties. As to the order of speeches on a plea of not guilty *see* the Magistrates' Courts Rules 1981, r. 13. The court must hear the evidence of the accused before that of his witnesses: *R.* v. *Morrison* (1911) 75 J.P. 272; *R.* v. *Smith* (1968) 132 J.P. 312 (both cases on indictment).

Convict the accused or dismiss the information. The term "conviction" may not be used in relation to juveniles, for whom the term "finding of guilt" has been prescribed by s. 59(1) of the Children and Young Persons Act 1933.

There is no power in a magistrates' court to substitute a conviction for a lesser offence: *Martin* v. *Brickhill* (1864) 28 J.P. 359. In *Lawrence* v. *Same* (1968) 132 J.P. 277, Lord Parker CJ said that if the justices consider that the accused was guilty of some lesser offence, they can always acquit him of the offence charged and direct that a summons be served forthwith on the accused for the offence of which they consider him to be guilty. That charge can then be heard.

It has always been accepted (in relation to a charge of stealing a number of articles) that it is unnecessary that the prosecution should prove that all the articles mentioned in the information have been stolen. The register should note a conviction in respect only of the property found to be stolen and not the other items: *Machent* v. *Quinn* (1970) 134 J.P. 501.

For the powers of the court to re-open a case after a finding of guilt *see* the note "Ordering a Retrial" in the introduction.

For the form of conviction *see* the Magistrates' Courts Rules 1981, r. 16. For an order of dismissal *see* form 37.

Adjournment of trial

10. (1) A magistrates' court may at any time, whether before or after beginning to try an information, adjourn the trial, and may do so, notwithstanding anything in this Act, when composed of a single justice.

(2) The court may when adjourning either fix the time and place at which the trial is to be resumed, or, unless it remands the accused, leave the time and place to be determined later by the court; but the trial shall not be resumed at that time and place unless the court is satisfied that the parties have had adequate notice thereof.

(3) A magistrates' court may, for the purpose of enabling inquiries to be made or of determining the most suitable method of dealing with the case, exercise its power to adjourn after convicting the accused and before sentencing him or otherwise dealing with him; but, if it does so, the adjournment shall not be for more than four weeks at a time unless the court remands the accused in custody and, where it so remands him, the adjournment shall not be for more than three weeks at a time.

(4) On adjourning the trial of an information the court may remand the accused and, where the accused has attained the age of 17, shall do so if the offence is triable either way and—

(a) on the occasion on which the accused first appeared, or was brought, before the court to answer the information he was in custody or, having been released on bail, surrendered to the custody of the court; or

(b) the accused has been remanded at any time in the course of proceedings on the information;

and, where the court remands the accused, the time fixed for the resumption of the trial shall be that at which he is required to appear or be brought before the court in pursuance of the remand or would be required to be brought before the court but for s. 128(3A) below.

(as amended by the Criminal Justice Act 1982, sch. 9).

COMMENTARY

For guidance on the exercise of discretion in granting and refusing *Adjournments see* under that title in the introduction.

Note that the powers of adjournment and remand contained in this section apply only to the trial of an information. They do not apply to committal proceedings or to proceedings for determining the mode of trial (as to which see the Magistrates' Courts Act 1980, ss. 5, 18).

Subsection (1): May . . . adjourn the trial. This subsection is restricted to an adjournment before a verdict is returned, *per* Lord Widgery CJ in *R. v. Talgarth JJ., ex parte Bithell* (1973) 137 J.P. 666.

Subsection (2): Unless it remands the accused. An adjournment where the defendant is remanded may not, therefore, be without a date. Certain cases *must be* remanded in accordance with subs. (4). A remand in custody of an adult may be to an alternate magistrates' court nearer to the prison: s. 130 of Act, *infra.* An accused already detained under a custodial sentence may be remanded for up to 28 clear days: s. 131 of the Act.

Adequate notice. The clerk must give written notice of the time and place at which the trial is to be resumed and this may be served in accordance with paras. (1) and (3) of r. 99, of the Magistrates' Courts Rules 1981 proof of which may be given under para. (2) of r. 99, *ibid.* A trial which is resumed without service of such a notice is a nullity: *R. v. Seisdon Justices, ex parte Dougan* [1983] 1 All E.R. 6.

When the adjournment follows a decision not to proceed under s. 12 of the Act the notice must give the reason for the adjournment: s. 12(6), *post.*

When a court proposes to disqualify an absent offender and adjourns the trial in accordance with this section and s. 11(4) the notice of resumption must include notice of the reason for the adjournment: *ibid*.

Notice is required to advance the date of hearing even when the accused has indicated his intention not to attend on the original date: *R.* v. *Haverfordwest JJ., ex parte George* (1964) 108 Sol. J. 199.

Subsection (3). This sub-section is directory not mandatory and an excessively long adjournment does not necessarily deprive the court of jurisdiction: *R.* v. *Manchester City Justices, ex parte Miley and Another* (1977) 16 February. As to the composition of the bench after conviction *see* s. 121(7) of the Act.

Justices adjourning under this subsection should adjourn "the whole question of sentencing" and should not, for example, impose a fine and adjourn to consider disqualification: *R.* v. *Talgarth JJ., ex parte Bithell* (1973) 137 J.P. 666. (This decision was apparently overlooked in the case of *Dyson* v. *Ellison* [1974] 1 All E.R. 276).

The periods of limitation in this subsection have no application to a deferment of sentence under the Powers of Criminal Courts Act 1973, s. 1.

Any remand must be on bail or in custody: s. 128(1) of the Act. The general right to bail applies: Bail Act 1976, s. 4.

For the effects of an adjournment under this subsection see Adjournment for Inquiries in the introduction.

Subsection (4). A remand for the purposes of s. 10(4) may be for the period of the adjournment: s. 128(6).

Offence triable either way. Defined in the Interpretation Act 1978, sch. 1.

Non-appearance of accused: general provisions

11.   (1) Subject to the provisions of this Act, where at the time and place appointed for the trial or adjourned trial of an information the prosecutor appears but the accused does not, the court may proceed in his absence.

(2) Where a summons has been issued, the court shall not begin to try the information in the absence of the accused unless either it is proved to the satisfaction of the court, on oath or in such other manner as may be prescribed, that the summons was served on the accused within what appears to the court to be a reasonable time before the trial or adjourned trial or the accused has appeared on a previous occasion to answer to the information.

(3) A magistrates' court shall not in a person's absence sentence him to imprisonment or detention in a detention centre or make an order under s. 23 of the Powers of Criminal Courts Act 1973 that a suspended sentence passed on him shall take effect.

(4) A magistrates' court shall not in a person's absence impose any disqualification on him, except on resumption of the hearing after an adjournment under s. 10(3) above; and where a trial is adjourned in pursuance of this subsection the notice required by s. 10(2) above shall include notice of the reason for the adjournment.

COMMENTARY

Subsection (1): Appears. Appearance may be counsel or solicitor: s. 122 of the Act.

Proceed in his absence. This course should only be taken where the court has strong grounds for believing that the defendant is wilfully disobeying the summons, *per* Cockburn, J, in *R.* v. *Smith* (1875) 39 J.P. 613. And, obviously, at the accused's request in trivial cases. For the right of the accused to be present at his trial and the qualifications thereto *see Trial in the Absence of the Accused* in the introduction. The Divisional Court refused *certiorari* when the defending solicitor could not establish that he had been misled into thinking that the case would be adjourned to a later date: *R.* v. *Pembroke JJ, ex parte Perrins* October 26, (1961).

Magistrates have power to deal with summary offences on a summons served by registered post or recorded delivery without proof that the summons came to the knowledge of the defendant: Magistrates' Courts Rules 1981, r. 99(1), (2).

When an accused is found guilty after the court has proceeded in his absence under subs. (1) the same bench of justices or (if there were three or more) a court consisting of or comprising a majority thereof may direct a retrial before a differently constituted bench where this appears to be in the interest of justice: s. 142 of the Act.

Subsection (2). Section 1(6) of the Act provides that a warrant may be issued under that section in respect of an indictable offence even where a summons has already issued. There is no express provision prohibiting a warrant being issued in respect of a summary offence under that section where a summons has been issued earlier.

Such other manner as may be prescribed. That is, under the Magistrates' Courts Rules 1981, r. 67.

A reasonable time before the trial. "In considering the reasonableness of the time the justices are the proper judges", *per* Erle, J, in *Ex parte Williams* (1851) 15 J.P. 757 (a 19th century case which upheld the reasonableness of a summons to appear the following day). But the justices' decision may be upset if they were not in full possession of the facts: *Ex parte Smith* (1875) 39 J.P. 613; *R.* v. *Anwyl & Others, Merionethshire JJ, ex parte Cookson* (1909) 73 J.P. 485.

Subsection (3): A person's absence. By virtue of s. 122 of the Act an accused represented by counsel or solicitor is deemed not to be absent.

Subsection (4): Notice of the reason for the adjournment. If notice was given in respect of one course of action the court may not take any other course without first adjourning and giving further notice: *R.* v. *Mason* [1965] 2 All E.R. 308.

Non-appearance of accused: plea of guilty

12. (1) Subject to subs. (7) below, this section shall apply where a summons has been issued requiring a person to appear before a magistrates' court, other than a juvenile court, to answer to an information for a summary offence, not being an offence for which the accused is liable to be sentenced to be imprisoned for a term exceeding three months, and the clerk of the court is notified by or on behalf of the prosecutor that the following documents have been served upon the accused with the summons, that is to say—

    (*a*) a notice containing such statement of the effect of this section as may be prescribed; and

    (*b*) a concise statement in the prescribed form of such facts relating to the charge as will be placed before the court by or on behalf of the prosecutor if the accused pleads guilty without appearing before the court.

(2) Subject to subs. (3) to (5) below, when the clerk of the court receives a notification in writing purporting to be given by the accused or by a solicitor acting on his behalf that the accused desires to plead guilty without appearing before the court, the clerk of the court shall inform the prosecutor of the receipt of the notification and if at the time and place appointed for the trial or adjourned trial of the information the accused does not appear and it is proved to the satisfaction of the court, on oath or in such other manner as may be prescribed, that the notice and statement of facts referred to in subs. (1) above have been served upon the accused with the summons, then—

    (*a*) subject to s. 11(3) and (4) above, the court may proceed to hear and dispose of the case in the absence of the accused, whether or not the prosecutor is also absent, in like manner as if both parties had appeared and the accused had pleaded guilty; or

    (*b*) if the court decides not to proceed as aforesaid, the court shall adjourn or further adjourn the trial for the purpose of dealing with the information as if the notification aforesaid had not been given.

(3) If at any time before the hearing the clerk of the court receives an intimation in writing purporting to be given by or on behalf of the accused that he wishes to withdraw the notification aforesaid, the clerk of the court shall inform the prosecutor thereof and the court shall deal with the information as if this section had not been passed.

(4) Before accepting the plea of guilty and convicting the accused in his absence under subs. (2) above, the court shall cause the notification and statement of facts aforesaid, including any submission received with the notification which the accused wishes to be brought to the attention of the court with a view to mitigation of sentence, to be read out before the court.

(5) If the court proceeds under subs. (2) above to hear and dispose of the case in the absence of the accused, the court shall not permit any statement to be made by or on behalf of the prosecutor with respect to any facts relating to the offence charged other than the statement of facts aforesaid except on a resumption of the trial after an adjournment under s. 10(3) above.

(6) In relation to an adjournment by reason of the requirements of para. (b) of subs. (2) above or to an adjournment on the occasion of the accused's conviction in his absence under that subsection, the notice required by s. 10(2) above shall include notice of the reason for the adjournment.

(7), (8) . . .

COMMENTARY

Juveniles. Since, following conviction, a juvenile must often be remitted to the juvenile court (s. 56 of the 1933 Act and s. 7(8) of the 1969 Act) it will seldom be appropriate to use the procedure of this Act with regard to juveniles even in the rare cases when they may or must appear in the adult court (s. 46(1) of the 1933 Act and s. 18 of the 1963 Act). But note s. 46(1A) of the 1933 Act: "If a notification that the accused desires to plead guilty without appearing before the court is received by the clerk of a court in pursuance of s. 12 of the Magistrates' Courts Act 1980, and the court has no reason to believe that the accused is a child or young person, then, if he is a child or young person he shall be deemed to have attained the age of 17, for the purposes of subs. (1) of this section in its application to the proceedings in question."

Subsection (1): Summary offence. Defined in the Interpretation Act 1978, sch. 1 as meaning an offence which, if committed by an adult, is triable only summarily.

Statement in the prescribed form. *See* form 30. A copy of the statement must be sent to the clerk of the magistrates' court: Magistrates' Courts Rules 1981, r. 73.

Subsection (2): The clerk of the court receives. Once the procedure of this Act is invoked "an accused has the right up to the very last moment to enter a plea of guilty on the conditions laid down", and not merely at the return date of the summons, *per* Lord Parker CJ, in *R.* v. *Norham & Islandshire JJ, ex parte Sunter Bros., Ltd.* (1961) 125 J.P. 181.

Notification in writing. No form of notice is prescribed, but a form of notice is suggested in Home Office circ. 151/1957 dated August 14, 1957. If the accused ignores this and writes his own letter pleading guilty it is equally effective.
    In the case of a corporation, notification of a plea or intimation of withdrawal may be given by a director or the secretary: sch. 3, para. 4(1) of the Act.

Desires to plead guilty. One set of forms may properly be used for two or more offences, but a conviction will be quashed unless it is clear that the accused intended to plead guilty to all the offences: *R.* v. *Burnham JJ, ex parte Ansorge* (1959) 123 J.P. 539.

Proved . . . in the prescribed manner. *See* the Magistrates' Courts Rules 1981, r. 67.

Served upon the accused. Certain methods of service are prescribed in r. 99(5) of the Magistrates' Courts Rules 1981.

Decides not to proceed as aforesaid. *Certiorari* issued where magistrates so adjourned but subsequently reverted to the procedure under this section because of a misapprehension: *R.* v. *Liverpool City JJ, ex parte Wallace* (1973) December 12 (unreported). Where the court declines to use the procedure of this section the statement of facts is inadmissible in evidence or cross examination of a witness of fact who had taken no part in its preparation and cannot be put to him as an inconsistent statement: *Roger* v. *Sullivan* [1978] R.T.R. 181.

Subsection (4): Accepting the plea of guilty. *See* the note "Pleads Guilty" to s.9, *supra*.

Read out before the court. Failure to observe this provision deprives the court of jurisdiction: *R.* v.

Oldham JJ, ex parte Morrissey (1959) 123 J.P. 38. The onus of proving failure to read aloud rests on the defendant: *R*. v. *Davies* [1958] 3 All E.R. 559.

Subsection (5). Thus the court may not even inquire of the prosecutor whether the facts of a no driving licence offence make it an endorsable matter or not: *R*. v. *Liskerett JJ, ex parte Child* [1972] R.T.R. 141.

A court may not sentence an accused to imprisonment or detention in his absence. Nor can it order disqualification without first giving the accused opportunity to attend: s. 11(4), *supra*.

Subsection (6): Notice of the reason for the adjournment. If there has been any adjournment for a particular reason of which the defendant was notified, the court may not deal with him in any other way without adjourning again and giving further notice: *R*. v. *Mason* (1965) 129 J.P. 363.

Non-appearance of the accused: issue of warrant

13.   (1) Subject to the provisions of this section, where the court, instead of proceeding in the absence of the accused, adjourns or further adjourns the trial, the court may, if the information has been substantiated on oath, issue a warrant for his arrest.

(2) Where a summons has been issued, the court shall not issue a warrant under this section unless it is proved to the satisfaction of the court, on oath or in such other manner as may be prescribed, that the summons was served on the accused within what appears to the court to be a reasonable time before the trial or adjourned trial or the accused has appeared on a previous occasion to answer the information.

(3) A warrant for the arrest of any person who has attained the age of 17 shall not be issued under this section unless—

(a) the offence to which the warrant relates is punishable with imprisonment; or

(b) the court, having convicted the accused, proposes to impose a disqualification on him.

(4) This section shall not apply to an adjournment by reason of the requirements of para. (b) of s. 12 above or to an adjournment on the occasion of the accused's conviction in his absence under that subsection.

(5) Where the court adjourns the trial—

(a) after having, either on that or on a previous occasion, received any evidence or convicted the accused without hearing evidence on his pleading guilty under s. 9(3) above; or

(b) after having on a previous occasion convicted the accused without hearing evidence on his pleading guilty under s. 12(2) above,

the court shall not issue a warrant under this section unless it thinks it undesirable, by reason of the gravity of the offence, to continue the trial in the absence of the accused.

COMMENTARY

Subsection (1): Adjourns the trial. Subsection (4) makes it clear that a trial for the purposes of this section begins even before evidence is heard. As to the composition of the bench at an adjourned trial *see* s. 121(6) of the Act. Written notice of the time and place of the adjourned hearing must be given to the accused, if absent: Magistrates' Courts Rules 1981, r. 15. *See* form 32.

Issue a warrant. For the signature, contents and execution of the warrant *see* the Magistrates' Courts Rules 1981, r. 95, 96. For execution in Scotland *see* the Criminal Procedure (Scotland) Act, 1975, s. 17. For execution in other parts of the United Kingdom *see* the Magistrates' Courts Act 1980, s. 126. Warrants remain in force until executed or withdrawn: s. 125, *ibid*.; notwithstanding the death of the issuing justice: s. 124, *ibid*. The warrant may be backed for bail: s. 117, *ibid*.

Subsection (2). Section 1(6) of the Act provides that a warrant may be issued under that section in respect of an indictable offence even where a summons has already issued. There is no express provision prohibiting a warrant being issued in respect of a summary offence under that section where a summons has been issued earlier.

Such other manner as may be prescribed. That is, under the Magistrates' Courts Rules 1981, r. 67.

A reasonable time before the trial. "In considering the reasonableness of the time the justices are the proper judges", *per* Erle J, in *Ex parte Williams* (1851) 15 J.P. 757 (a 19th century case which upheld the reasonableness of a summons to appear the following day). But the justices' decision may be upset if they were not in full possession of the facts: *Ex parte Smith* (1875) 39 J.P. 613; *R. v. Anwyl & Others, Merionethshire JJ., ex parte Cookson* (1909) 73 J.P. 485.

Subsection (3): Punishable with imprisonment. Partially defined in s. 150(6) of the Act.

Non-appearance of prosecutor

15. (1) Where at the time and place appointed for the trial or adjourned trial of an information the accused appears or is brought before the court and the prosecutor does not appear, the court may dismiss the information or, if evidence has been received on a previous occasion, proceed in the absence of the prosecutor.

(2) Where, instead of dismissing the information or proceeding in the absence of the prosecutor, the court adjourns the trial, it shall not remand the accused in custody unless he has been brought from custody or cannot be remanded on bail by reason of his failure to find sureties.

COMMENTARY

Subsection (1): The prosecutor does not appear. Appearance may be by counsel or solicitor: Magistrates' Courts Act 1980, s. 122.

Dismiss the information. For a discussion of the effects of such a dismissal on future proceedings *see* under the title *Autrefois Acquit and Convict* in the introduction.

Non-appearance of both parties

16. Subject to s. 11(3) and (4) and to s. 12 above, where at the time and place appointed for the trial or adjourned trial of an information neither the prosecutor nor the accused appears, the court may dismiss the information or, if evidence has been received on a previous occasion, proceed in their absence.

COMMENTARY

Appears. Appearance may be by counsel or solicitor: Magistrates' Courts Act 1980, s. 122.

Dismiss the information. *See* the note to s. 15, *supra*.

Proceed in their absence. Witnesses cannot be called by absent parties, but they can be called by the court. The only other proceedings which can be undertaken in the absence of both parties are adjournments and for the court to announce its adjudication following an adjourned hearing.

Power of magistrates' court to remit a person under 17 for trial to a juvenile court in certain circumstances

29. (1) Where—

    (*a*) a person under the age of 17 ("the juvenile") appears or is brought before a magistrates' court on an information jointly charging him and one or more other persons with an offence; and (*b*) that other person, or any of those other persons, has attained that age,

subs. (2) below shall have effect notwithstanding proviso (*a*) in s. 46(1) of the Children and Young Persons Act 1933 (which would otherwise require the charge against the juvenile to be heard by a magistrates' court other than a juvenile court).

In the following provisions of this section "the older accused" means such one or more of the accused as have attained the age of 17.

(2) If—

    (*a*) the court proceeds to the summary trial of the information in the case of both or all of the accused, and the older accused or each of the older accused pleads guilty; or

    (*b*) the court—

        (i) in the case of the older accused or each of the older accused, proceeds to inquire into the information as examining justices and either commits him for trial or discharges him; and
        (ii) in the case of the juvenile, proceeds to the summary trial of the information,

then, if in either situation the juvenile pleads not guilty, the court may before any evidence is called in his case remit him for trial to a juvenile court acting for the same place as the remitting court or for the place where he habitually resides.

(3) A person remitted to a juvenile court under subs. (2) above shall be brought before and tried by a juvenile court accordingly.

(4) Where a person is so remitted to a juvenile court—

    (*a*) he shall have no right of appeal against the order of remission; and

    (*b*) the remitting court may give such directions as appear to be necessary with respect to his custody or for his release on bail until he can be brought before the juvenile court.

(5) The preceding provisions of this section shall apply in relation to a corporation as if it were an individual who has attained the age of 17.

COMMENTARY

This section gives an adult court power to remit a juvenile where (a) he had been jointly charged with an adult or a corporation, (b) the adult or corporation pleads guilty or is committed for trial or is discharged, and (c) the juvenile pleads not guilty. Without these provisions, the charge against the juvenile would have to be heard in the adult court in accordance with the Children & Young Persons Act 1933, s. 46(1)(*a*). There is no right of appeal against an order under this section: subs (4).

For the power to remit to a juvenile court a juvenile who has been found guilty or who has pleaded guilty, see the Children & Young Persons Act 1933, s. 56 and the Children & Young Persons Act 1969, s. 7(8), *supra*.

Subsection (1): Age. For the determination of age see the Children & Young Persons Act 1933, s. 99.

Remand for medical examination

30. (1) If, on the trial by a magistrates' court of an offence punishable on summary conviction with imprisonment, the court is satisfied that the accused did the act or made the omission charged but is of opinion that an inquiry ought to be made into his physical or mental condition before the method of dealing with him is determined, the court shall adjourn the case to enable a medical examination and report to be made and shall remand him; but the adjournment shall not be for more than three weeks at a time where the court remands him in custody nor for more than four weeks at a time where it remands him on bail.

(2) Where on an adjournment under subs. (1) above the accused is remanded on bail, the court shall impose conditions under para. (d) of s. 3(6) of the Bail Act 1976 and the requirements imposed as conditions under that paragraph shall be or shall include requirements that the accused—

(a) undergo medical examination by a duly qualified medical practitioner or, where the inquiry is into his mental condition and the court so directs, two such practitioners; and

(b) for that purpose attend such an institution or place, or on such practitioner, as the court directs and, where the inquiry is into his mental condition, comply with any other directions which may be given to him for that purpose by any person specified by the court or by a person of any class so specified.

(3) The Costs in Criminal Cases Act 1973 shall apply to a duly qualified medical practitioner who makes a report otherwise than in writing for the purposes of this section as it applies to a person called to give evidence, and shall so apply notwithstanding that the proceedings for the purposes of which the report is made are not proceedings to which s. 1 of the Act applies.

COMMENTARY

When the examination is completed some time before the remand date the prison will inform the clerk of the court to enable the hearing to be advanced where practicable in accordance with the Magistrates' Courts Act 1980, s. 128(1)(a) or the accused released on bail if the court considers this appropriate: Home Office circ. 28/1971, dated February 2, 1971. Most reports by prison governors and medical officers can be prepared within 14 days: H.O. circ. 116/1972 dated June 16, 1972.

Subsection (1): Offence punishable on summary conviction with imprisonment. There is power to remand for medical reports under s. 10(3) of the Act in the case of offences not so punishable: *Boaks* v. *Reece* (1957) 121 J.P. 51.

Shall remand him. Either in custody or on bail: Magistrates' Courts Act 1980, s. 128. If on bail note subs. (2) of this section. The general right to bail applies: Bail Act 1976, s. 4, but para. 7 of sch. 1, *ibid.*, allows bail to be refused in the case of an imprisonable offence if it appears impracticable to make the report otherwise. Home Office circular 206/1977 dated November 18, 1977 suggests the use of outpatient facilities (circular 155/1975 refers), and, in the case of reports on suitability for detention centre training, the police surgeon (circular 179/1972 refers).

The institution or place of remand must be given a statement of the reasons for the remand and any information before the court about his physical or mental condition: Magistrates' Courts Rules 1981, r. 24.

Subsection (2): Para. (d) of s. 3(6). That is, a condition that the offender makes himself available for the purpose of enabling inquiries to be made to assist the court in dealing with him for the offence.

Duly qualified medical practitioner. That is, a fully registered person, namely a person registered under ss. 7 or 8 of the Medical Act, 1956.

Subsection (3). The effect of this subsection is to enable the costs of a doctor giving oral evidence under this section to be paid from central funds even where the offence charged is not indictable. The Criminal Justice Act 1967, s. 32(3), extends this provision to the written reports of doctors. See the Costs in Criminal Cases (Allowances) Regulations 1977.

Mitigation of penalties, etc.

34. (1) Where under any enactment whether passed before or after the commencement of this Act a magistrates' court has power to sentence an offender to imprisonment for a period specified by the enactment, or to a fine of an amount specified by the enactment, then, except where an Act passed after December, 31, 1879 expressly provides to the contrary, the court may sentence him to imprisonment for less than that period or, as the case may be, to a fine of less than that amount.

5. TRIAL AND SENTENCE

(2) Where under any such enactment an offender sentenced on summary conviction to imprisonment or a fine is required to enter into a recognizance with or without sureties to keep the peace or observe any other condition, the court convicting him may dispense with or modify the requirement.

(3) Where under any such enactment a magistrates' court has power to sentence an offender to imprisonment or other detention but not to a fine, then, except where an Act passed after December, 31, 1879 expressly provides to the contrary, the court may, instead of sentencing him to imprisonment or other detention, impose a fine which—

(a) for an offence triable either way, shall not exceed the prescribed sum within the meaning of s. 32 above; and
(b) for a summary offence, shall—

(i) not exceed £200;and
(ii) not be of such an amount as would subject the offender, in default of payment of the fine, to a longer term of imprisonment or detention than the term to which he is liable on conviction of the offence.

COMMENTARY

Subsection (1). This power does not extend to the reduction of any minimum penalty prescribed by statute: *Osborn* v. *Wood Bros.* (1897) 61 J.P. 118. *See,* for example, s. 78(3), Reserve Forces Act 1980.

December 31, 1879. The date upon which the Summary Jurisdiction Act 1879 came into force.

A fine. Arrears of national insurance, although "recoverable as a penalty", are neither a "penalty" nor "pecuniary compensation" so as to make them a fine under s. 126(1) of the Act: *Leach* v. *Litchfield* (1961) 126 J.P. 115.

Subsection (3): An offence triable either way / a summary offence. Defined in the Interpretation Act 1978, sch. 1.

Cases where magistrates' court may remit offender to another such court for sentence

39. (1) Where a person who has attained the age of 17 ("the offender") has been convicted by a magistrates' court ("the convicting court") of an offence to which this section applies ("the instant offence") and—

(a) it appears to the convicting court that some other magistrates' court ("the other court") has convicted him of another such offence in respect of which the other court has neither passed sentence on him nor committed him to the Crown Court for sentence nor dealt with him in any other way; and
(b) the other court consents to his being remitted under this section to the other court,

the convicting court may remit him to the other court to be dealt with in respect of the instant offence by the other court instead of by the convicting court.

(2) The offender, if remitted under this section, shall have no right of appeal against the order of remission.

(3) Where the convicting court remits the offender to the other court under this section, it shall adjourn the trial of the information charging him with the instant offence, and—

(a) section 128 below and all other enactments (whenever passed) relating to remand or the granting of bail in criminal proceedings shall have effect in relation to the convicting court's power or duty to remand the offender on that adjournment as if any reference to the court to or before which the person remanded is to be brought or appear after remand were a reference to the court to which he is being remitted; and

240   5. TRIAL AND SENTENCE

(b) subject to subs. (4) below, the other court may deal with the case in any way in which it would have power to deal with it (including, where applicable, the remission of the offender under this section to another magistrates' court in respect of the instant offence) if all proceedings relating to that offence which took place before the convicting court had taken place before the other court.

(4) Nothing in this section shall preclude the convicting court from making any order which it has power to make under s. 28 of the Theft Act 1968 (orders for restitution) by virtue of the offender's conviction of the instant offence.

(5) Where the convicting court has remitted the offender under this section to the other court, the other court may remit him back to the convicting court; and the provisions of subs. (3) above (so far as applicable) shall apply with the necessary modifications in relation to any remission under this subsection.

(6) This section applies to—

(a) any offence punishable with imprisonment; and
(b) any offence in respect of which the convicting court has a power or duty to order the offender to be disqualified under s. 93 of the Road Traffic Act 1972 (disqualification for certain motoring offences);

and in this section "conviction" includes a finding under s. 30(1) above that the person in question did the act or made the omission charged, and "convicted" shall be construed accordingly.

COMMENTARY

Note that both the instant offence and the offence at the other court must fall within the categories of subs. (6). For the documents to be transmitted to the other court see the Magistrates' Courts Rules 1981, r. 19(1).

Subsection (1): Attained the age of 17.   For the determination of age see the Children and Young Persons Act 1933, s. 99.

Convicted.   Includes a finding under s. 30(1) of the Act: subs. (6).

Dealt with him in any other way.   It is submitted that this does not prevent remission where the other court has deferred sentence upon the offender.

Subsection (3): Remand.   The general right to bail (Bail Act 1976, s. 4) only applies if the case is also adjourned for inquiries or a report.

Subsection (5).   For the documents to be sent to the other court see the Magistrates' Courts Rules 1981, r. 30(2).

Corporations

46.   The provision of sch. 3 to this Act shall have effect where a corporation is charged with an offence before a magistrates' court.

Proof of previous convictions

104.   Where a person is convicted of a summary offence by a magistrates' court, other than a juvenile court, and—

(a) it is proved to the satisfaction of the court, on oath or in such other manner as may be prescribed, that not less than seven days previously a notice was served on the accused in the prescribed form and manner specifying any alleged previous conviction of the accused of a summary offence proposed to be brought to the notice of the court in the event of his conviction of the offence charged; and
(b) the accused is not present in person before the court,

the court may take account of any such previous conviction so specified as if the accused had appeared and admitted it.

COMMENTARY

This section is confined to the proof of previous convictions of summary offences after conviction of a summary offence.

Summary offence. Defined in the Interpretation Act 1978, sch. 1, as meaning an offence which, if committed by an adult, is triable only summarily.

Proved . . . in the prescribed manner. See the Magistrates' Courts Rules 1981, r. 67.

Not less than seven days previously. That is, seven clear or intervening days: R. v. Turner (1910) 74 J.P. 81; Re Hector Whaling Ltd. [1935] All E.R. Rep. 302; Thompson v. Stimpson [1960] 3 All E.R. 500.

Notice . . . in the prescribed form. See form 29.

Previous conviction. Although in the ordinary procedure a court is permitted to hear subsequent convictions as antecedents, there is no means of adducing them under this section. For the contrary opinion, see 125 J.P.N. 404.

Appearance by counsel or solicitor

122. (1) A party to any proceedings before a magistrates' court may be represented by counsel or solicitor.

(2) Subject to subs. (3) below, an absent party so represented shall be deemed not to be absent.

(3) Appearance of a party by counsel or solicitor shall not satisfy any provision of any enactment or any condition of a recognizance expressly requiring his presence.

COMMENTARY

The effects of this section are summarized in the introduction under Legal Representation.

When can magistrates issue a warrant under s. 13 of this Act to compel personal appearance of an accused who appears by his legal representative only? The issue of such a warrant was held successfully to found an action for trespass in Bessell v. Wilson (1853) 17 J.P. 567, but this case appears to have concerned fine enforcement proceedings now dealt with by statute. Certiorari issued to quash a similar warrant against an accused who appeared by solicitor in answer to a speeding charge, the court having considered the pre-existing legislation which was framed in similar but not identical terms to s. 13: R. v. Montgomery & Others, ex parte Long (1910) 74 J.P. 110. Nevertheless, the judgment of Alverstone LCJ, was hedged about by the following qualifications: "Where there is a proper appearance and where the justices must hear and determine, and where there is an admission by the defendant of what the prosecution desire to prove, and the defendant has not been shown to be contumacious, no warrant ought to be issued by the justices". The position may be different after conviction. See generally the article at 135 J.P.N. 861.

Subsection (1): Represented by counsel or solicitor. "Acting properly upon his client's instructions" must, it is submitted, be added by inference.

Subsection (3): Any provision of any enactment. When a representative of a corporation appears "any requirement of this Act that anything shall be done in the presence of the accused, or shall be read or said to the accused, shall be construed as a requirement that that thing shall be done in the presence of the representative or read or said to the representative": para. 3(1) of sch. 3 to the Act.

Defect in process

123. (1) No objection shall be allowed to any information or complaint, or to any summons or warrant to procure the presence of the defendant, for any defect in it in substance or in form, or for any variance between it and the evidence adduced on behalf of the prosecutor or complainant at the hearing of the information or complaint.

(2) If it appears to a magistrates' court that any variance between a summons or warrant and the evidence adduced on behalf of the prosecutor or complainant is such that the defendant has been misled by the variance, the court shall, on the application of the defendant, adjourn the hearing.

COMMENTARY

The effects of this section are described under Defective Process in the introduction.

A dismissal after a refusal to allow amendment of a summons *on the grounds of inadequacy of evidence* is sufficient to found a plea of *autrefois acquit: Halstead* v. *Clark* (1944) 108 J.P. 70.

Subsection (1): Any defect . . . in substance or in form. The section has been held to apply where the defendant's proper name was wrongly spelt, the court adding that such a defect does not even require amendment: *Dring* v. *Mann* (1948) 112 J.P. 270. The section does not contemplate a different defendant: *City of Oxford Tramway Co.* v. *Sankey* (1890) 54 J.P. 564; but when summonses intended for a man were mistakenly addressed to his wife and he wrote to the court for an adjournment of "the summonses against me", the convictions were upheld: *R.* v. *Norkett, ex parte Geach* (1915) 139 L.T.Jo. 316. And *see* also *R.* v. – (1825) R. & R. 489 (defendant refused name). Amendment of the defendant's surname was allowed under this section where it was not disputed that he was the accused: *Allen* v. *Wiseman, supra*.

Superfluous words may be deleted: *Rogerson* v. *Stephens* (1950) 114 J.P. 372; *Roberts* v. *Griffiths* [1978] R.T.R. 362. However, no amendment is required to delete purely superfluous words when the defendant has not been misled: *Roberts* v. *Griffiths* [1978] R.T.R. 362. An information which referred to the Act but not the section was held to be curable under this section: *R.* v. *Doncaster Justices, ex parte Doncaster Corpn.* (1962) 106 Sol. Jo. 879.

A justice's failure to sign the copy of a summons served on the defendant is not fatal when an original was in fact signed: *R.* v. *Hay Halkett, ex parte Rush* (1929) 93 J.P. 209. (The Court expressly refrained from deciding whether an unsigned original could be saved by this provision). Omission from the summons of the date on which the information was laid is a defect curable by this section where there is no reason for thinking that it had any relevance to the case: *R.* v. *Godstone Justices, ex parte Secretary of State for the Environment* [1974] Crim. L.R. 110.

The fact that two offences are charged in one information has been held to be a defect in substance which can be remedied under this section: *Rodgers* v. *Richards* [1891-4] All E.R. Rep. 394. But not when the summons is void *ab initio: Garman* v. *Plaice* (1969) 133 J.P. 114, (language of the information disclosed no offence). By virtue of the Magistrates' Courts Rules 1981 r. 12, an information bad for duplicity may not be amended under this section after the trial has begun: *Hargreaves* v. *Alderson* (1963) 127 J.P. 99.

A failure to refer in the information to the Act and section can be cured under this provision where the accused is not misled: *Thornley* v. *Clegg* [1982] R.T.R. 405. (*See* the Magistrates' Courts Rules 1981, r. 100(2)).

Subsection (2): Variance. That is, some difference between the allegation and the evidence, not where there is a different offence: *Martin* v. *Pridgeon* (1859) 23 J.P. 630; *R.* v. *Brickill* (1864) 28 J.P. 359 (but see the doubts cast on the reasoning of these cases in *Lawrence* v. *Same* [1968] (1968) 132 J.P. 277; *Loadman* v. *Cragg* (1862) 26 J.P. 743. "The section does not operate to prevent an objection being effective where the error alleged is fundamental, such as, for instance, where one offence is charged in the information and a different offence is found in the conviction recorded by the justices", *per* Humphreys J in *Atterton* v. *Browne* (1945) 109 J.P. 25. But in *R.* v. *Newcastle-upon-Tyne Justices, ex parte Bryce (Contractors) Ltd.* (1976) 140 J.P. 440 amendment of an information was allowed so as to allege a different offence even after the expiry of six months from its commission. Prohibition was refused to prevent justices from hearing informations which had been amended after the six months' period of limitation so as to alter the description of the tyres concerned in offences of using tyres with insufficient tread: *R.* v. *Sandwell Justices, ex parte West Midlands Passenger Transport Executive* [1979] R.T.R. 17.

"It seems to me to be quite plain that if a person is charged before justices under a repealed statute, they have a choice which they can exercise. They can say, in effect, to the defendant: "If you do not object to an amendment, this summons can be amended forthwith" and if there is no objection that can be done. They can say: "We will adjourn this case so that this summons may be amended" and put the prosecution on whatever terms they please as the result of the adjournment. Or they can dismiss the summons leaving it to the prosecution to charge the offence under the correct statute in a fresh summons", *per* Byrne J in *Meek* v. *Powell* (1952) 116 J.P. 116; quoted with approval in *Hunter* v. *Coombs* (1962) 126 J.P. 300; *R.* v. *Crook* [1977] 65 Cr. App. R. 66.

This provision has been applied to variance between the date charged and the evidence: *Exeter Corporation* v. *Heaman* (1877) 42 J.P. 503; *Wright* v. *Nicholson, supra; Wright* v. *Eldred* (1971) 135 J.P.N. 491; the place of the offence: *Fowler* v. *St Mary Abbott's Vestry* (1872) 36 J.P. 69; *Lee* v. *Coles* (1972) 136 J.P.N. 226; *Moulder* v. *Judd* [1974] Crim. L.R. 111; *Darnell* v. *Holliday* [1973] R.T.R. 276; *Taylor* v. *Grey* [1973] R.T.R. 281; and as to ownership of property maliciously damaged: *Ralph* v. *Hurrell* (1875) 40 J.P. 119; *Pike* v. *Morrison* [1981] Crim. L.R. 492. Magistrates erred in refusing to allow an information to be amended so as to correct the name of the street in which the offence was committed: *Cotterill* v. *Johal* [1982] Crim. L.R. 523.

Power of magistrates' court to re-open cases to rectify mistakes etc

142. (1) Subject to subs. (4) below, a magistrates' court may vary or rescind a sentence or other order imposed or made by it when dealing with an offender; and it is hereby declared that this power extends to replacing a sentence or order which for any reason appears to be invalid by another which the court has power to impose or make.

(2) Where a person is found guilty by a magistrates' court in a case in which he has pleaded not guilty or the court has proceeded in his absence under s. 11(1) above, and it subsequently appears to the court that it would be in the interests of justice that the case should be heard again by different justices, the court may, subject to subs. (4) below, so direct.

(3) Where a court gives a direction under subs. (2) above—

(a) the finding of guilty and any sentence or other order imposed or made in consequence thereof shall be of no effect; and

(b) section 10(4) above shall apply as if the trial of the person in question had been adjourned.

(4) The powers conferred by subs. (1) and (2) above shall be exercisable only within the period of 28 days beginning with the day on which the sentence or order was imposed or made or the person was found guilty, as the case may be, and only—

(a) by a court constituted in the same manner as the court by which the sentence or order was imposed or made or, as the case may be, by which the person in question was found guilty, or

(b) where that court comprised three or more justices of the peace, by a court which consists of or comprises a majority of those justices.

(5) Where a sentence or order is varied under subs. (1) above, the sentence or other order, as so varied, shall take effect from the beginning of the day on which it was originally imposed or made, unless the court otherwise directs.

COMMENTARY

Whatever the powers of justices to re-open conviction at common law their only powers in this regard now are contained in this section the terms of which must be strictly complied with: *R.* v. *Maidstone Justices, ex parte Booth* (1980) 144 J.P. 354.

Subsection (1). It is submitted that the power to vary sentence is not confined to reducing sentence but includes in a proper case the imposition of a more severe sentence or of an additional order ancillary to sentence: Cf. *R.* v. *Reilly* [1982] 3 W.L.R. 149; *R.* v. *May* [1981] 3 Cr. App. R. (S) 165.

The power to vary sentence must be exercised in the presence of the offender, unless it is waived either expressly or impliedly, e.g. by absconding: *R.* v. *May, supra.*

Subsection (2). The powers under this subsection arise in two circumstances: a finding of guilt following a plea of not guilty or a finding of guilt in the absence of the accused (whether a plea of not guilty was entered at an earlier stage or not). It has no application to a plea of guilty, as to which *see* the note "Pleads Guilty" to s. 9, *supra*.

The Home Office circular on the Act quotes "examples of situations where the use of this power might be appropriate . . . where a conviction is announced prematurely, perhaps because a submission of no case to answer is misunderstood as constituting the whole defence case, or where a defendant is convicted in his absence but then arrives and presents new facts justifying a rehearing. The subsection does not apply where a defendant has pleaded guilty in person and seeks to change his plea after sentence." Home Office Circular No. 230/1972 dated December 8, 1972.

Found guilty. Not acquitted: *R.* v. *Gravesend Justices, ex parte Dexter* [1977] Crim. L.R. 298.

The court may . . . so direct. As to the composition of the court, *see* subs. (4).

Subsection (3): Section 10(4) . . . shall apply. Thus the accused may be remanded in all cases and must be remanded where the offence is triable either way and the accused was first brought to court in custody or surrendered to custody or the accused had earlier been remanded.

Subsection (4). The effect of this subsection is that the bench of justices which convicted the accused may direct that he should be tried before a bench of justices containing none of themselves, but where the convicting court comprised three or more justices it is sufficient if the directing court either consists of or includes a majority of them. A bench of justices cannot direct a retrial before themselves.

Within the period of 28 days beginning. That is at any time during the 28 days starting with and including the day of conviction or sentence: cf. *Trow* v. *Ind Coope* [1967] 2 All E.R. 900. The period cannot be extended by the clerk giving written notice of the court's intention to act under this section: *Bradburn* v. *Richards* [1976] Crim. L.R. 62.

SCHEDULE 3

(Section 46.)

CORPORATIONS

1. (1) A magistrates' court may commit a corporation for trial by an order in writing empowering the prosecutor to prefer a bill of indictment in respect of the offence named in the order.

(2) An order under this paragraph shall not prohibit the inclusion in the bill of indictment of counts that under s. 2 of the Administration of Justice (Miscellaneous Provisions) Act 1933 may be included in the bill in substitution for, or in addition to, counts charging the offence named in the order.

2. A representative may on behalf of a corporation—

(*a*) make a statement before examining justices in answer to the charge;
(*b*) consent to the corporation being tried summarily;
(*c*) enter a plea of guilty or not guilty on the trial by a magistrate's court of an information.

3. (1) Where a representative appears, any requirement of this Act that anything shall be done in the presence of the accused, or shall be read or said to the accused, shall be construed as a requirement that that thing shall be done in the presence of the representative or read or said to the representative.

(2) Where a representative does not appear, any such requirement, and any requirement that the consent of the accused shall be obtained for summary trial, shall not apply.

4. (1) Notification or intimation for the purposes of subs. (2) and (3) of s. 12 above may be given on behalf of a corporation by a director or the secretary of the corporation; and those subsections shall apply in relation to a notification or intimation purporting to be so given as they apply to a notification or intimation purporting to be given by an individual accused.

8. Subsection (6) of s. 33 of the Criminal Justice Act 1925 shall apply to a representative for the purposes of this Schedule as it applies to a representative for the purposes of that section.

(2) In this paragraph "director", in relation to a corporation which is established by or under any enactment for the purpose of carrying on under national ownership any industry or part of an industry or undertaking and whose affairs are managed by the members thereof, means a member of that corporation.

5. The provisions of this Act relating to committal to the Crown Court for sentence shall not apply to a corporation.

6. Subject to the preceding provisions of this schedule, the provisions of this Act relating to the inquiry into, and trial of, indictable offences shall apply to a corporation as they apply to an adult.

7. Where a corporation and an individual who has attained the age of 17 are jointly charged before a magistrates' court with an offence triable either way, the court shall not try either of the accused summarily unless each of them consents to be so tried.

COMMENTARY

Paragraph 1(1): An order in writing. *See* form 14. Notice must be given to the prison governor: r. 9(2), Magistrates' Courts Rules 1981.

Paragraph (2): A representative. *See* para. 8.

Anything shall be done in the presence of the accused. For a list of such things *see* the notes to s. 122 of the Act.

Paragraph 6: Indictable offences. Defined in the Interpretation Act 1978, sch. 1.

An adult. That is a person aged 17 years and over.

An offence triable either way. Defined in the Interpretation Act 1978, sch. 1.

Paragraph 8: Section 33(6) of the Criminal Justice Act, 1925. This section, as amended, defines a "representative" as "a person duly appointed by the corporation to represent it for the purpose of doing any act or thing which the representative of a corporation is by this section authorized to do, but a person so appointed shall not, by virtue only of being so appointed, be qualified to act on behalf of the corporation before any court for any other purpose. A representative for the purposes of this section need not be appointed under the seal of the corporation, and a statement in writing purporting to be signed by a managing director of the corporation, or by any person (by whatever name called) having, or being one of the persons having, the management of the affairs of the corporation, to the effect that the person named in the statement has been appointed as the representative of the corporation for the purposes of this section shall be admissible without further proof as *prima facie* evidence that that person has been so appointed."

THE CRIMINAL JUSTICE ACT 1982

Abolition of right of accused to make unsworn statement.

72. (1) Subject to subss. (2) and (3) below, in any criminal proceedings the accused shall not be entitled to make a statement without being sworn, and accordingly, if he gives evidence, he shall do so on oath and be liable to cross-examination; but this section shall not affect the right of the accused, if not represented by counsel or a solicitor, to address the court or jury otherwise than on oath on any matter on which, if he were so represented, counsel or a solicitor could address the court or jury on his behalf.

(2) Nothing in subs. (1) above shall prevent the accused making a statement without being sworn—
    (a) if it is one which he is required by law to make personally; or

(b)   if he makes it by way of mitigation before the court passes sentence upon him.
(3) Nothing in this section applies–
   (a)   to a trial; or
   (b)   to proceedings before a magistrates' court acting as examining justices
which began before the commencement of this section.

THE MAGISTRATES COURTS' RULES 1981

S.I. 1981 No. 552 as amended by S.I. 1983 No. 523

Information to be for one offence only

12.   (1) *Subject to any Act passed after October 2, 1848, a magistrates' court shall not proceed to the trial of an information that charges more than one offence.*

(2) *Nothing in this rule shall prohibit two or more informations being set out in one document.*

COMMENTARY

Paragraph (1). *See* The Rule Against Duplicity in the introduction.

Paragraph (2). Thus, two or more informations may be laid in writing on the same sheet provided they are set out separately.

Order of evidence and speeches: information

13.   (1) *On the summary trial of an information, where the accused does not plead guilty, the prosecutor shall call the evidence for the prosecution, and before doing so may address the court.*

(2) *At the conclusion of the evidence for the prosecution, the accused may address the court, whether or not he afterwards calls evidence.*

(3) *At the conclusion of the evidence, if any, for the defence, the prosecutor may call evidence to rebut that evidence.*

(4) *At the conclusion of the evidence for the defence and the evidence, if any, in rebuttal, the accused may address the court if he has not already done so.*

(5) *Either party may, with the leave of the court, address the court a second time, but where the court grants leave to one party it shall not refuse leave to the other.*

(6) *Where both parties address the court twice the prosecutor shall address the court for the second time before the accused does so.*

COMMENTARY

Paras (2) and (4) have been amended in accordance with the Criminal Justices Act 1982, s. 72, *supra*.

The provisions of this rule deal only with the order of proceedings, and are merely directory rather than mandatory: *per* Lord Parker CJ, in *Simms* v. *Moore* (1970) 134 J.P. 573. Thus where the prosecutor was also a witness it was open to the justices to take the view that the examination of prosecution witnesses should be taken out of his hands.
   This rule does not provide a comprehensive code of procedure on summary trial. For *No Case to Answer* see under that title in the introduction.

Paragraph (3): Evidence ... for the defence.   "It was important for the prisoner to be called before any of his witnesses. He ought to give his evidence before he heard the evidence and cross-examination of any witnesses he was going to call *per* Lord Alverstone CJ, in *R.* v. *Morrison*

(1911) 75 J.P. 272, confirmed in *R.* v. *Smith* (1968) 132 J.P. 312.

By s. 1(*g*) of the Criminal Evidence Act, 1898, "Every person called as a witness in pursuance of this Act (that is, the defendant and his spouse) shall, unless otherwise ordered by the court, give his evidence from the witness box or other place from which the other witnesses give their evidence." The accused is not to be deprived of this right without good reason: *R.* v. *Symonds* [1924] Cr. App. R. 100.

Evidence to rebut. *See* under this title in the introduction.

Paragraph (4): The accused may address the court. This includes an unrepresented person who has a right to make a speech as well as give evidence: *R.* v. *Great Marlborough St. Magistrates' Court, ex parte Fraser* [1974] Crim. L.R. 47; *R.* v. *Middlesex Crown Court, ex parte Riddle* [1976] Crim. L.R. 731 (a case on indictment). But in *R.* v. *Knightsbridge Crown Court, ex parte Martin* [1976] Crim. L.R. 463, the High Court refused to intervene where the Crown Court failed to give an opportunity to an unrepresented appellant to address them, distinguishing *Fraser's* case on the basis that the accused was positively denied the right to make a further speech. [N.B. The appellant in this case was a solicitor and a justices' clerk who might have been expected to make the point at the time.] Where the justices omit to give the accused opportunity to address them and announce a conviction they cannot thereafter rectify the fault but should order a re-trial: *R.* v. *Marylebone Justices, ex parte Yasmin Farras* [1981] Crim. L.R. 182.

Paragraph (5). The peremptory nature of this rule is different from the procedure on indictment: cf. *R.* v. *Bryant* (1978) 142 J.P. 460.

Adjournment of trial of information

15. (1) *Where in the absence of the accused a magistrates' court adjourns the trial of an information, the clerk of the court shall give to the accused notice in writing of the time and place at which the trial is to be resumed.*

(2) *Service of the notice required to be given by paragraph (1) may be effected in any manner in which service of a summons may be effected under para. (1) or (3) of r. 99 and para. (2) of that rule shall apply to the proof of service of the notice as it applies to the proof of service of a summons in respect of the offence charged in the information.*

COMMENTARY

Paragraph (1): The absence of the accused. An accused who is legally represented in court is deemed not to be absent: Magistrates' Courts Act 1980, s. 122(2).

Remittals to another magistrates' court for sentence, etc

19. (1) *Where a magistrates' court remits an offender to some other magistrates' court under s. 39 of the Act of 1980 after convicting him of an offence, the clerk of the convicting court shall send to the clerk of the other court—*

(a) *a copy signed by the clerk of the convicting court of the minute or memorandum of the conviction and remittal entered in the register;*

(b) *a copy of any note of the evidence given at the trial of the offender, any written statement tendered in evidence and any deposition;*

(c) *such documents and articles produced in evidence before the convicting court as have been retained by that court;*

(d) *any report relating to the offender considered by the convicting court;*

(e) *if the offender is remitted on bail, a copy of the record made by the convicting court in pursuance of s. 5 of the Bail Act 1976 relating to such bail and also any recognizance entered into by any person as his surety;*

(f) *if the convicting court makes an order under s. 28 of the Theft Act 1968 (orders for restitution), a copy signed by the clerk of the convicting court of the minute or memorandum of the order entered in the register;*

(g)　a copy of any legal aid order previously made in the same case;

(h)　a copy of any legal aid application; and

(i)　any statement of means already submitted.

(2)　Where a magistrates' court remits an offender to some other magistrates' court as aforesaid and the other court remits him back to the convicting court under subs. (5) of the said s. 39, the clerk of the other court shall send to the clerk of the convicting court—

(a)　a copy signed by the clerk of the other court of the minute or memorandum of the remittal back entered in the register;

(b)　if the offender is remitted back on bail, a copy of the record made by the other court in pursuance of s. 5 of the Bail Act 1976 relating to such bail and also any recognizance entered into by any person as his surety;

(c)　all documents and articles sent in pursuance of para. (1).

(3)　In this rule "the offender", "the convicting court" and "the other court" have the same meanings as in the said s. 39.

Documents to be sent on remand for medical inquiry

24.　On exercising the powers conferred by s. 30 of the Act of 1980 a court shall—

(a)　where the accused is remanded in custody, send to the institution or place to which he is committed;

(b)　where the accused is remanded on bail, send to the institution or place at which, or the person by whom, he is to be examined,

a statement of the reasons why the court is of opinion that an inquiry ought to be made into his physical or mental condition and of any information before the court about his physical or mental condition.

COMMENTARY

A form of statement is recommended in Home Office circulars 113/73 and 1/75.

Notification of conviction before expiration of period of deferment

27.　Where under s. 1 of the Powers of Criminal Courts Act 1973 a court has deferred passing sentence on an offender and before the expiration of the period of deferment he is convicted of any offence by a magistrates' court, the clerk of the court shall, if the court which deferred passing sentence on the earlier occasion was another magistrates' court or the Crown Court, give notice of the conviction to the clerk of that magistrates' court or the appropriate officer of the Crown Court, as the case may be.

Clerk to have copies of documents sent to defendant under s. 12(1) of the Act of 1980

73.　Where the prosecutor notifies the clerk of the court that the documents mentioned in paras. (a) and (b) of s. 12(1) of the Act of 1980 have been served upon the accused, the prosecutor shall send to the clerk a copy of the document mentioned in para. (b).

CUSTODIAL SENTENCES

CONTENTS

INTRODUCTION

According to the Home Office:

> The aims of the courts in imposing custodial sentences may include the expression of public condemnation of a particular act or course of conduct; the protection of the public by the removal of a dangerous or persistent offender from among them; the prevention of future offences on the part of the convicted offender himself or other potential offenders, through the deterrent effect of being held in custody; and the reformation or improvement of the offender through programmes of training or treatment ("*The Sentence of the Court*").

Lawton LJ said that the four classic principles of sentencing are summed up in four words, retribution, deterrence, prevention and rehabilitation:

> I will start with retribution. The Old Testament concept of an eye for an eye and tooth for tooth no longer plays any part in our criminal law. There is, however, another aspect of retribution which is frequently overlooked: it is that society, through the courts, must show its abhorrence of particular types of crime, and the only way in which the courts can show this is by the sentences they pass. The courts do not have to reflect public opinion. On the other hand courts must not disregard it. Perhaps the main duty of the court is to lead public opinion. Anyone who surveys the criminal scene at the present time must be alive to the appalling problem of violence. Society, we are satisfied, expects the courts to deal with violence. The weapons which the courts have at their disposal for doing so are few. We are satisfied that in most cases fines are not sufficient punishment for senseless violence. . . .
>
> I turn now to the element of deterrence, because it seems to us the trial judge probably passed this sentence as a deterrent one. There are two aspects of deterrence: deterrence of the offender and deterrence of likely offenders. Experience has shown over the years that deterrence of the offender is not a very useful approach, because those who have their wits about them usually find the closing of prison gates an experience which they do not want again. If they learn that lesson, there is likely to be a high degree of recidivism anyway. So far as deterrence of others is concerned, it is the experience of the courts that deterrent sentences are of little value in respect of offences which are committed on the spur of the moment, either in hot blood or in drink or both. Deterrent sentences may very well be of considerable value where crime is premeditated. Burglars, robbers and users of firearms and weapons may very well be put off by deterrent sentences. . . .
>
> We come now to the element of prevention. Unfortunately it is one of the facts of life that there are some offenders for whom neither deterrence nor rehabilitation works. They will go on committing crimes as long as they are able to do so. In those cases the only protection which the public has is that such persons should be locked up for a long period . . .
>
> Finally, there is the principle of rehabilitation. Some 20 to 25 years ago there was a view abroad, held by many people in executive authority, that short sentences were of little value, because there was not enough time to give in prison the benefit of training. That view is no longer held as firmly as it was.

R. v.*Sargeant* [1975] 60 Cr. App. R. 74 at p.77 (two years for affray "much too long").

Factors Affecting Sentence

The Relevance of Previous Convictions

So far as a prison sentence is concerned previous convictions are relevant to the likelihood of redemption and the effectiveness of training, but where the object of a sentence is punitive or deterrent (as in imprisonment) "a man must not be sentenced on his record, he must be sentenced on the facts which have come out in evidence, or, alternatively, have been put before the court after a plea of guilty": *R.* v. *Griffiths* (1966) November 29 (unreported). And *see R.* v. *Queen*[1981] 3 Cr. App. R (S) 245. Or, in other words, "a man has to be sentenced for the offences which he has committed": *R.* v. *Disbrey* [1967] Crim. L.R. 431.

Dealing with a man who, the court said, it was manifest had been sentenced on his record, Lawton, L.J., said in the case of *R.* v. *Lister* October 5, 1972 (unreported): "That is not a correct way of sentencing and the court wishes to emphasize that the proper way of sentencing is to look first at the offence itself and the circumstances in which it was committed, then to assess the proper sentence for the offence on the basis that there are no mitigating circumstances; and finally to look to see what the mitigating circumstances are, if any, to reduce the assessed sentence to give effect to the mitigating circumstances." (But note that the power to commit for sentence under the Magistrates' Courts Act, 1980, s. 38, depends entirely on the character and antecedents of the offender, not the gravity of the offence).

The Effect of the Plea on Sentence

In *R.* v. *Harper* [1967] 3 All E.R. 619, reducing a sentence of imprisonment, Lord Parker CJ said of the inferior court: "It is quite improper to use language which may convey that an accused is being sentenced because he has pleaded not guilty or because he has run his defence in a particular way. It is, however, proper to give an accused a lesser sentence if he has shown genuine remorse, amongst other things, by pleading guilty." And *see* also *R.* v. *Behman* (1967) 117 N.L.Jo. 834. However, "It is undoubtedly right that a confession of guilt [in the context a plea changed from not guilty to guilty] should tell in favour of an accused person, for that is clearly in the public interest", *per* Edmund Davies LJ in *R.* v. *de Haan* [1967] 3 All E.R. 618. (Sentence varied from four-and-a-half to three years when there was a change of plea after four prosecution witnesses had given evidence). The reduction cannot be expressed in percentage terms because of the individual nature of sentencing: *R.* v. *Williams* (1983) *The Times,* July 14. The principle applies to youth custody sentences also: *R.* v. *Stewart* [1983] Crim. L.R. 830.

There are conflicting decisions whether it is proper to suspend a sentence of imprisonment on an offender who pleaded guilty, while not suspending it on a co-defendant who did not. See *R.* v. *Hollymen* [1979] 1 Cr. App. R. (S) 289 and *R.* v. *Tonks* [1979] 1 Cr. App. R. (S) 293.

Remorse (*see,* for example, *R.* v. *Alcock* [1966] Crim. L.R. 66) or the lack of it (for example, *R.* v. *O'Leary* [1965] Crim. L.R. 56) has long been held to be relevant to the sentence.

Failure to name an accomplice may be material to sentence if it is in defiance of the law, but not if through fear: *R.* v. *Hogwood* [1969] Crim. L.R. 209.

The Conduct of the Defence

It is well established that the fact that the defence consisted of an attack on the integrity of a police officer or the character of the prosecution witnesses should not to be taken into account when passing sentence: *R.* v. *Harper* [1967] 3 All E.R. 619; *R.* v. *Scott* [1983] Crim. L.R. 568.

Similarly, it is wrong to increase the sentence simply because the court believes the defendant to have committed perjury during his trial: *R. v. Quinn* [1932] 23 Cr. App. R. 196; *R. v. Dunbar* [1966] 51 Cr. App. R. 57.

The Prevalence of the Offence

The prevalence of a particular type of offence in a locality may be a ground for increasing the sentence: *R. v. Green* (1912) 76 J.P. 351; *R. v. Withers* [1935] 25 Cr. App. R. 53. But for a single court deliberately to adopt a change of policy (for example, by determining to sentence first offenders to imprisonment for driving under the influence of alcohol) in matters which affect every part of the country alike is improper: *R. v. Lavin* [1967] 51 Cr. App. R. 378.

The Wealth of the Offender

It is wrong to impose a prison sentence simply because the offender is too rich to be hurt by a fine: *R. v. Hanbury* [1979] 1 Cr. App. R. (S) 243. Or because he is too poor to pay an adequate fine: *R. v. Reeves* [1972] 56 Cr. App. R. 366; *R. v. McGowan* [1975] Crim. L.R. 113. The case of *R. v. Gormley* [1973] Crim. L.R. 644 suggests that this course is not wrong where imprisonment is being imposed on another offence.

The Different Standards of Immigrants

Once in this country this country's laws must apply, and, while the first transgression may be treated sympathetically, thereafter the defendant would be expected to conform strictly with English standards: *R. v. Derriviere* [1969] 53 Cr. App. R. 637. The same standards of conduct are expected of all colours: *R. v. Mack* [1974] Crim. L.R. 557.

The Curative Element

In relation to offences of dishonesty, sentences of imprisonment—except when there is an element of protection of the public involved—are normally intended to be the correct sentence for the particular crime and not to include a curative element. This has nothing to do with special cases such as possessing drugs or cases where the protection of the public is involved: *R. v. Ford* (1969) 133 J.P. 701 (sentence of imprisonment on chronic alcoholic wrongly invoked to allow for treatment). But when there is a background of alcoholism the court must determine what are the limits of a proper sentence in respect of the offence charged. Within those limits it may be proper to increase sentence in order to enable a cure to be undertaken whilst the accused is in prison, *per* Lord Widgery CJ, in *R. v. Moylan* (1969) 133 J.P. 709.

It is not the function of the courts to use their sentencing powers to dispose of those who are socially inconvenient: *R. v. Clarke* [1975] 61 Cr. App. R. 320.

"Political" Offences

Strongly held opinions and high motives do not justify deliberate dis-obedience of the law: *R. v. Gruffydd and Others* [1972] 56 Cr. App. R. 585 (a Welsh road signs case). But the fact that the accused may be a danger to society by reason of his political views is not a reason for increasing sentence: *R. v. King and Simpkins* [1973] 57 Cr. App. R. 696.

Young men in universities or in any walk of life have no licence to assault policeman and deliberate use of violence, when in support of political issues, should, save for wholly exceptional mitigation, result in immediate custodial sentences: *R. v. Coleman* [1975] Crim. L.R. 349.

Sentencing for Particular Offences

From time to time the High Court have offered guidance on how the courts should approach sentencing in particular classes of offence. The following is a selection of comments concerning offences dealt with in magistrates' courts.

(i) *Dishonesty by Public Servants and Persons in Positions of Trust.* The amount stolen is not necessarily a conducive yardstick to the appropriate sentence: thefts by postmen erode confidence in a public service and cause at the least disappointment and sometimes distress or worse to those directly affected: *R.* v. *Rendall* [1973] Crim. L.R. 585; 57 Cr. App. R. 714. A suspended sentence is generally inappropriate: *R.* v. *Howard* [1979] 1 Cr. App. R. (S) 364 (postman), save where the sums involved are small: *R.* v. *Bowler* [1972] 57 Cr. App. R. 275 (bus conductor). In *R.* v. *Orsler* [1981] 3 Cr. App. R(S) 204 a sentence of 12 months' imprisonment was upheld on a postman for offences of stealing postal packets involving small sums of money.

(ii) *Thefts involving Danger to the Public.* Although the value of the goods stolen may be small the offence may be serious: *R.* v. *Holmes* [1966] Crim. L.R. 457 (larceny of battery from railway warning device); *R.* v. *Yardley* [1968] Crim. L.R. 48 (railway signal wire). The court will "uphold any substantial sentences that are given for these offences connected with telephone kiosks. It is something which must be stamped out, and deterrent sentences given": *R.* v. *French* 31.1.66 (unreported).

(iii) *Handling Stolen Property.* There would not be so many thieves if there were no receivers. Professional thieves do not steal goods merely for their own consumption; they steal them for disposal and it is essential to the success of the criminality that there should be receivers, big receivers and small receivers, like this appellant, who will dispose of their goods unobtrusively in various markets: *R.* v. *Battams* [1979] 1 Cr. App. R. (S) 15 (18 months not excessive on small scale but extensive receiver).

(iv) *Social Security Frauds.* This type of offence is prevalent and deterrent sentences have become essential: *R.* v. *Williams* [1970] Crim. L.R. 357. Where the public is swindled out of a large sum of money by a large and sustained deceit an immediate custodial sentence is inevitable: *R.* v. *Grafton* [1979] 1 Cr. App. R. (S) 305 (pretending to be unemployed when in work the defendant fraudulently obtained £3,000 over two years). But the sentence may be short: *R.* v. *McDonald* (1981) 144 J.P.N. 337. It must be observed that the great majority of social security frauds dealt with in magistrates' courts are not of this level of gravity.

(v) *Burglary* is too often lightly referred to as "just another crime" and not sufficient account is given of the misery and subsequent fear that result from it: *R.* v. *Luckhurst* [1971] 56 Cr. App. R. 209. Burglary in the form of housebreaking is a very serious crime indeed. The public are entitled to be protected against burglars. They are not likely to be protected if lenient sentences are passed. Unfortunately it is a matter of experience that nowadays a large number of housebreakers are adolescents and that when they break into houses, the house is frequently turned upside-down. Adolescents have got to be discouraged from housebreaking and they are not likely to be discouraged by sentences which do not involve loss of liberty: *R. v. Smith; R. v. Woollard* [1978] 67 Cr. App. R. 211 (sentence of borstal training upheld). In *R. v. Plant* (1982) 146 JPN 207 six months' imprisonment was held to be adequate for a man with no previous convictions convicted of a single burglary of a dwelling house.

(vi) *Going Equipped for Stealing.* This offence is a very important piece of protective justice and will lose its value and effect unless it is clearly recognised that it attracts a significant sentence which will deter others: *R. v. Person* [1969] Crim. L.R. 553.

(vii) *Crimes of Violence.* Deterrent sentences are called for for:
  (a) attacks on licensees: *R. v. Thompson* [1974] Crim. L.R. 720 (glasses and fittings smashed in public house; a glass thrown at landlord's face); *R. v. Williams* [1980] 2 Cr. App. R. (S) 150 (four months for kicking and punching which knocked out a tooth);
  (b) attacks on bus conductors: *R. v. Campbell* [1979] 1 Cr. App. R (S) 12; *R. v. Foster* [1982] 4 Cr. App. R. (S) 101 (six months' detention upheld for knocking head against window);
  (c) violence at football matches: *R. v. Motley* [1978] 66 Cr. App. R. 274; *R. v. Wood* (1984) *The Times,* Jan. 17;
  (d) violence at other public places, such as discotheques: *R. v. Evans* [1980] Crim. L.R. 64 and in the streets: *R. v. Wilkinson* (1981) 144 J.P.N. 566 (12 months upheld for actual bodily harm).

(viii) *Weapons.* Carrying a knife is a serious matter, and if it is used severe punishment must be imposed: *R. v. Nuttall* [1968] Crim. L.R. 282. Violence involving the use of weapons such as bottles in public or semi-public places will inevitably be visited with condign punishment: *R. v. Lachtay* [1983] Crim. L.R. 766 (six months upheld for hitting victim on head at dance with bottle).

(ix) *Assaults on Police.* A sentence of imprisonment for an attack deliberately made on a police officer inflicting upon him harm, no matter how slight, is never wrong in principle: *R. v. McKenlay* [1979] 1 Cr. App. R. (S) 161. (Sentence of six months suspended on a picketing journalist who punched and butted an officer). An immediate sentence is usually appropriate: *R. v. Bird* [1979] 1 Cr. App. R. (S) 348 (six months upheld for actual bodily harm at incident outside a dance hall). It is inappropriate to suspend a prison sentence when there is deliberate violence, even in the course of evading arrest: *R. v. Bell* [1973] Crim. L.R. 318 (knee in the groin).

(x) *Unlawful Sexual Intercourse.* A sentence of a punitive nature is inappropriate when there is a virtuous friendship which ends in unlawful sexual intercourse between young people, but a man who abuses a position of trust for sexual gratification ought to receive something near the maximum sentence of two years. In between there are various degrees of guilt. Thus, a casual pick-up by a youth of a girl at a dance is dealt with by a fine. A man in his twenties or older can expect a much stiffer fine, and if the girl is under 15, he can expect to go to prison for a short term. A young man who deliberately sets out to seduce a girl under 16 can expect to go to detention, the older man to prison: *R. v. Taylor* [1977] 64 Cr. App. R. 183. And see *R. v. O'Grady* [1978] 66 Cr. App. R. 279 (young man of good character had sex with passionate 14-year-old once. Given absolute discharge after he had spent Christmas in detention).

(xi) *Drugs Offences.* The following guidance was given by Lord Lane C.J. in *R. v. Aramah* (1983) 147 J.P. 217.

Class 'A' Drugs and particularly heroin and morphine:
It is common knowledge that these are the most dangerous of all the addictive drugs for a number of reasons: first of all, they are easy to handle. Small parcels can be made up into huge numbers of doses. Secondly, the profits are so enormous that they attract the worst type of criminal. Many of such criminals may think, and indeed do think, that it is less dangerous and more profitable to traffic in heroin or morphine than it is to rob a bank. It does not require much imagination to realize the consequential evils of corruption and bribery which the huge profits are likely to produce. This factor is also important when considering the advisability of granting bail. Sums which to the ordinary person, and indeed the ordinary defendant, might seem enormous are often trivial for the trafficker in drugs. Anything which the courts of this country can do by way of deterrent sentences on those found guilty of crimes involving these class 'A' drugs should be done. After dealing with the prison sentences for importers His Lordship turned to supplying heroin, morphine, etc.: It goes without saying that the sentence will largely depend on the degree of involvement, the amount of trafficking and the value of the drug being handled. It is seldom that a sentence of less than three years will be justified and the nearer the source of supply the defendant is shown to be, the heavier will be the sentence. There may well be cases where the sentences similar to those appropriate to large scale importers may be necessary. It is, however, unhappily all too seldom that those big fish amongst the suppliers get caught. Possession of heroin, morphine etc.: (Simple possession): It is at this level that the circumstances of the individual offender become of much greater importance. Indeed the possible variety of considerations is so wide, including often those of a medical nature, that we feel it impossible to lay down any practical guidelines. On the other hand the maximum penalty for simple possession of class 'A' drugs is seven years' imprisonment and/or a fine, and there will be very many cases where deprivation of liberty is both proper and expedient.
Class 'B' Drugs, particularly cannabis:
We select this from amongst the class 'B' drugs as being the drug most likely to be exercising the minds of the courts. Importation of cannabis: Importation of very small amounts for personal use can be dealt with as if it were simple possession, with which we will deal later. After dealing with the prison sentences appropriate to a number of sellers to importation and wholesale supply His Lordship said: Supplying a number of small sellers — wholesaling if you like — comes at the top of the bracket. At the lower end will be the retailer of a small amount to a consumer. Where there is no commercial motive (for example, where cannabis is supplied at a party), the offence may well be serious enough to justify a short custodial sentence. Possession of cannabis: When only small amounts are involved being for personal use, the offence can often be met by a fine. If the history shows, however, a persisting flouting of the law, imprisonment may become necessary.

It is not appropriate as a general rule to impose a sentence of imprisonment where the offence is possession of cannabis in very small quantities for personal consumption. The proper penalty in the ordinary course is a financial one. If however there was a continuous and persistent defiance of the law there might come a time where there would be no alternative to a custodial sentence: *R. v. Robinson-Coupar and Baxendale* [1982] Crim. L.R. 536.

(xii) *Obscene Publications*"In the judgment of this Court, the only way of stamping out this filthy trade is by imposing sentences of imprisonment on first offenders and all connected with the commercial exploitation of pornography: otherwise front men will be put up and the real villains will hide behind them. It follows, in our judgment, that the salesmen, projectionists, owners and suppliers behind the owners should on conviction lose their liberty. For first offenders sentences need only be comparatively short, but persistent offenders should get the full rigour of the law. In addition courts should take the profit out of this illegal filthy trade by imposing very substantial fines. Before leaving this matter we wish to make one or two further observations. We wish to make it clear that the guidelines we have indicated apply to those who commercially exploit pornography. We do not suggest that sentences of imprisonment would be appropriate for a newsagent who is carrying on a legitimate trade in selling newspapers and magazines and who has the odd pornographic magazine in his possession, probably because he has been careless in not looking to see what he is selling. If he is discovered to have the odd pornographic magazine in the midst of the articles of trade which he is properly and lawfully selling, he can be discouraged, and usually should be, by a substantial fine from repeating his carelessness. Nor do we suggest that a young man who comes into possession of a pornographic video tape and who takes it along to his rugby or cricket club to amuse his friends by showing it should be sentenced to imprisonment. On conviction he too can be dealt with by the imposition of a fine. The matter might be very different if owners or managers of clubs were to make a weekly practice of showing "blue" films to attract custom. Like the pornographers of Soho they would be engaging in the commercial exploitation of pornography," *per* Lawton J in *R. v. Holloway* [1982] 4 Cr. App. R. 128 (six months upheld on a man convicted of six offences of having obscene books and videos for sale). In *R. v. Cowan* [1982] Crim. L.R. 766, three months was considered appropriate for an owner of a sex shop with no similar previous convictions.

(xiii) *Drink and Driving.* There is no principle that a custodial sentence should not be imposed on a first conviction for driving with excess alcohol in the body, but the circumstances of these offences vary infinitely. The surrounding circumstances must also be looked at: *R. v. Nokes* [1978] R.T.R. 101 (183 mg alcohol/100 ml blood: six months' imprisonment upheld when defendant drove erratically at high speed in built-up-area. No previous convictions for drink). Circumstances which may indicate a custodial sentence (particularly when they occur together) are: high blood/alcohol reading: *R. v. Tupa* [1974] R.T.R. 153 (289 mg/100 ml): dangerous driving: *R. v. Jenkins* [1978] R.T.R. 104; *R. v. Pashley* [1974] R.T.R. 149 and repeated offending: *R. v. Sylvester* [1979] 1 Cr. App. R. (S) 250; *R. v. Peverill* (1975) December 4, unreported. Without such aggravating features a custodial sentence is inappropriate: *R. v. Thomas* [1973] R.T.R. 325.

(xiv) *Reckless Driving.* A short forthwith prison sentence is right in principle for deliberately ramming a car from behind in the fast lane of a motorway: *R. v. Till* [1982] 4 Cr. App. R. (S) 158 (but three months too long for a man of good character). And *see R. v. O'Sullivan. R. v. Burtoft* [1983] Crim. L.R. 827.

NOTE: The fact that the Lord Chief Justice or the higher courts have indicated that a particular offence should be visited by a particular sentence in no way fetters the discretion of magistrates: *R. v. Acting Deputy Chairman, South East London Quarter Sessions, ex parte Abraham* [1970] Crim. L.R. 116. (Sentence quashed where deputy chairman expressed himself as if so bound). In *R. v. DeHavilland* (1983) *The Times*, April 8, Dunn L.J. said that the sentencer retains his discretion within the guidelines laid down by the Court of Appeal or even to depart from them if the particular circumstances of the case justify it.

Imprisonment

For adults only

A sentence of imprisonment, which includes a suspended sentence and a partly suspended sentence, may not be passed on a person under 21, nor may such a person be committed to prison for any reason: Criminal Justice Act 1982, s.1(1). (This does not prevent the committal to prison of a person under 21 who is remanded in custody or committed to custody for trial or sentence: *ibid*, s. 1(2).)

Maximum and Minimum Sentences

The maximum term of imprisonment which may be imposed by a magistrates' court is usually set out in the statute creating the offence. However, a magistrates' court does not have power to impose imprisonment for more than six months in respect of any one offence: Magistrates' Courts Act 1980, s. 31. Section 34, *ibid,* makes it clear that the court is not bound to impose the maximum sentence. A magistrates' court may not impose imprisonment for less than five days: s. 132, *ibid.*

For Consecutive Sentences *see* under that title, *infra.*

The Need for Shorter Sentences

In recent years realization of the limited rehabilitative effects of imprisonment and the pressure on prison accommodation have led the judges to examine more carefully the types of offender who should receive a custodial sentence and the length of such sentences. In *R.* v. *Bibi* [1980] 71 Cr. App. R. 363 Lord Lane CJ said,

> "Many offenders can be dealt with equally justly and effectively by a sentence of six or nine months' imprisonment as by one of 18 months or three years. We have in mind not only the obvious case of the first offender for whom any prison sentence however short may be an adequate punishment and deterrent, but other types of case as well. The less serious types of factory or shopbreaking; the minor cases of sexual indecency; the more petty frauds where small amounts of money are involved; the fringe participant in more serious crime: all these are examples of cases where the shorter sentence would be appropriate. There are, on the other hand, some offences for which, generally speaking, only the medium or longer sentences will be appropriate. For example, most robberies; most offences involving serious violence; use of a weapon to wound; burglary of private dwelling-houses; planned crime for wholesale profit; active large scale trafficking in dangerous drugs. These are only examples. It would be impossible to set out a catalogue of those offences which do and those which do not merit more severe treatment. So much will, obviously, depend upon the circumstances of each individual offender and each individual offence. What the Court can and should do is to ask itself whether there is any compelling reason why a short sentence should not be passed. We are not aiming at uniformity of sentence; that would be impossible. We are aiming at uniformity of approach."

(18 months upheld for burglary of a department store).

In *R.* v. *Upton* [1980] 71 Cr. App. R. 102, Lord Lane CJ said,

> ". . . the time has come to appreciate that non-violent petty offenders should not be allowed to take up what has become valuable space in prison. If there really is no alternative, as we believe to be the case here, to an immediate prison sentence, then it should be as short as possible. Sentencing judges should appreciate that overcrowding in many of the penal establishments in this country is such that a prison sentence, however short, is a very unpleasant experience indeed for the inmates."

(six months' imprisonment too long for small theft by deputy manager of supermarket).

The Suspended Sentence

When passing a prison sentence of any length a magistrates' court may order that its operation shall be suspended for a period of one to two years: Powers of Criminal Courts Act 1973, s. 22; but only where a sentence of imprionment would have been appropriate in the absence of this power: subs. (2), *ibid.*

In *The Sentence of the Court* (HMSO), the Home Office advise that:
Suspended sentences are intended to give an offender an incentive to avoid trouble by making a set period of imprisonment contingent on his committing a further imprisonment offence. They also give the courts the opportunity to distinguish between the gravity of the offence, which they may mark by the length of the sentence, and the needs of the offender, which may be better served by release into the community with the knowledge that, should he re-offend, he will be liable to the original sentence.

A court which passes a supended sentence for one offence may not make a probation order in respect of another: Powers of Criminal Courts Act 1973, s. 22(3).

It has been held in relation to a trial on indictment that a fine may be imposed in addition to a suspended sentence on the same offence: *R.* v. *Leigh* [1970] 54 Cr. App. R. 169; *R.* v. *Ffoulkes* [1976] Crim. L.R. 458. It is submitted that the same principle applies to magistrates' courts wherever there is power to impose a fine in addition to a sentence of immediate imprisonment.

There is nothing wrong in principle in passing a forthwith sentence of imprisonment on an offender already subject to a suspended sentence, even when he is not in breach of the latter: *R.* v. *Gibbons* [1969] Crim. L.R. 210; *R.* v. *Sorrell* [1971] 55 Cr. App. R. 573. The former rule that it was wrong to pass two prison sentences, one suspended, the other forthwith (*see R.* v. *Butters, R.* v. *FitzGerald* [1971] 55 Cr. App. R. 515) must be regarded as superseded by the thinking in the Criminal Law Act 1977 which allows for partly suspended sentences: *R.* v. *Ipswich Crown Court, ex parte Williamson* [1982] 4 Cr. App. R. (S) 348.

Consecutive Suspended Sentences

Suspended sentences, like other prison sentences may be ordered to be either concurrent or consecutive: Magistrates' Courts Act, 1980, s. 133. It is imperative when passing two or more suspended sentences to indicate, *e.g.* for the purposes of s. 57(2) of the Act, whether as between themselves they are to be served consecutively or concurrently: *R.* v. *Wilkinson* (1970) 134 J.P. 676. But it is against the spirit and intention of the Act to impose a suspended sentence, whether consecutive to or concurrent with a prison sentence then being served: *R.* v. *Sapiano* [1968] 32 Cr. App. R. 674; *R.* v. *Morris* [1970] Crim. L.R. 172. Similarly, when passing a suspended sentence (as opposed to ordering that it shall be put into effect) it is wrong to order that it shall take effect consecutively to any other suspended sentence already imposed: *R.* v. *Blakeway* [1969] 2 All E.R. 1133; *R.* v. *Towner* [1970] Crim. L.R. 358.

As to ordering that suspended sentences *take effect* consecutively *see* the Powers of Criminal Courts Act 1973, s. 23(2), *infra* and notes thereto.

Breach of a Suspended Sentence

If within the operational period of a suspended sentence the offender commits in Great Britain an offence punishable with imprisonment the suspended sentence must be ordered to take effect unaltered, either consecutively to or concurrently with any other sentence, unless the court is of opinion that this would be unjust in view of all the circumstances, including the facts of the subsequent offence, when it may mitigate the sentence in prescribed manner or make no order: Powers of Criminal Courts Act 1973, s. 23.

The comparative triviality of an offence committed during the operational period of a suspended sentence may be a good ground for failing to put a suspended sentence into operation, particularly when the later offence is in a different category to the first offence: *R.* v. *Moylan* (1969) 133 J.P. 709. But the mere fact that it is of a different character to the original offence is no ground for refraining from bringing the suspended sentence into operation: *R.* v. *Saunders* [1970] 54 Cr. App. R. 247. (And see also *R.* v. *Williams* [1969] Crim. L.R. 669; *R.* v. *Griffiths* (1969) 133 J.P. 507; *R.* v. *Stevens* [1970] 55 Cr. App. R. 154; *R.* v. *Peck* [1970] Crim. L.R. 172; *R.* v. *Cobbold* [1971] Crim. L.R. 436; *R.* v. *Barton* [1974] Crim. L.R. 555; *R..* v. *Craine* [1981] 3 Cr. App. R. (S) 198.

Save only when it is unjust to do so, a suspended sentence must be put into effect on conviction of an imprisonable offence, whether a sentence of imprisonment is imposed therefor or not: *R.* v. *Cobbold* [1971] Crim. L.R. 436; *R.* v. *Isaacs* [1980] Crim. L.R. 666. (fine for subsequent offence). And compare *R.* v. *McElhorne* [1983] 5 Cr. App. R. (S) 53 and *R.* v. *Seymour* [1983] Crim. L.R. 410 (community service orders).

When the suspended sentence was passed by a superior court, a magistrates' court dealing with the offender may commit him to the Crown Court or take no action except to notify that court: Powers of Criminal Courts Act 1973, s. 24. There is power in s. 25, *ibid.*, to compel the appearance of an offender who falls to be dealt with in respect of a suspended sentence.

Suspended Sentence Supervision Order

Although a magistrates' court cannot make a suspended sentence supervision order it does have certain functions with respect to such orders.

When a suspended sentence of imprisonment is passed for a term in excess of six months *on a single offence* the Crown Court may at the same time make a suspended sentence supervision order in accordance with the Powers of Criminal Courts Act 1973, s. 26. Such an order may stipulate a period of supervision not longer than the operational period of the suspended sentence during which the offender will be under the supervision of a probation officer. The suspended sentence supervision order must specify the petty sessions area in which the offender resides. A copy of the order together with relevant documents and information must be sent to the clerk of the magistrates' court: *ibid.*, s. 26(4), (5).

The magistrates' court may, and on the application of the supervising officer, must amend the order when the offender moves to another area: *ibid.*, s. 26(6), (7). The order may be discharged by the magistrates' court unless the Crown Court included in the order a direction to the contrary: *ibid.*, s. 27(9). Failure without reasonable cause to comply with any requirement of a suspended sentence supervision order may be punished by a fine of up to £50: *ibid.*, s. 27.

Note that a suspended sentence supervision order is not a type of suspended sentence but an order ancillary to a suspended sentence.

The Partly Suspended Sentence

When passing a sentence of imprisonment on an offender who has attained the age of 21 for a term of not less than three months and not more than two years a court may order that, after he has served part of his sentence in prison, the remainder of it should be held in suspense: Criminal Law Act 1977, s. 47(1). The part to be served must be not less than 28 days and the part held in suspense not less than one quarter of the whole term: *ibid.*, s. 47(2). A partly suspended sentence may not be passed unless a wholly suspended sentence would be inappropriate: *ibid.*, s. 47(1A).

Partly suspended sentences are subject to the restrictions on passing any prison sentence (*see* above) and to the requirement concerning legal representation: *ibid.*, s. 47(1B).

Where a court passes a partly suspended sentence it may not make a probation order in respect of any other offence: *ibid.*, sch. 9, para. 1.

It is undesirable to sentence an offender to a substantive term of imprisonment and a partly suspended sentence at the same time: *R.* v. *McCarthy* [1982] 4 Cr. App. R. (S) 364.

Breach of Partly Suspended Sentence

If at any time after the making of the order an offender is convicted of an offence punishable with imprisonment committed during the whole period of the original sentence a competent court may restore the part of the sentence held in suspense and order him to serve it: Criminal Law Act 1977, s. 47(3). The "whole period" of a sentence is defined in s. 47(6), *ibid*, and the 'competent court' in sch. 9, para. 2, *ibid*. If the court is of the opinion that in view of all the circumstances, including the facts of the subsequent offence it would be unjust fully to restore the part of the sentence held in suspense it must either restore the lesser part or declare, with reasons given, its decision to make no order: *ibid.*, s. 47(4). The court restoring part of a partly suspended sentence may direct that it take effect immediately or consecutively to another sentence: s. 47(5) *ibid*. Once an order has been made restoring part of a sentence no further such order may be made: *ibid.*, s. 47(4A)

Guidelines

The following guidelines were laid down by Lord Lane CJ in *R.* v. *Clarke* [1983] 3 All E.R. 232:

> Before imposing a partly suspended sentence the Court should ask itself the following question: First of all, is this a case where a custodial sentence is really necessary? If it is not it should pass a non-custodial sentence. But if it is necessary then the Court should ask itself secondly this: can we make a community service order as an equivalent to imprisonment, or can we suspend the whole sentence? That problem requires very careful consideration. It is easy to slip into a partly suspended sentence because the Court does not have the courage of its own convictions. That temptation must be resisted. If it is possible to make a community service order or to suspend the whole of the sentence, then of course that should be done. If not, then the third point arises: what is the shortest sentence the Court can properly impose? In many cases, of which an obvious example is the case of the first offender for whom a short term of imprisonment is a sufficient shock, without any suspension, that would be enough. Sometimes 14 or 28 days may suffice, which is shorter than the shortest term which is at present available under s. 47, .

. .

> In that case that should be the order of the Court, without any partial suspension at all. The imposition of a very short term will also make possible the ordering of a fine or a compensation order in addition, when such a course is appropriate.

> If imprisonment is necessary, and if a very short sentence is not enough, and if it is not appropriate to suspend the sentence altogether, then partial suspension should be considered. Great care must be taken to ensure that the power is not used in a way which may serve to increase the length of sentence. It is not possible satisfactorily to forecast the precise way in which the provisions of s. 47 might be used. In general the type of case that we have in mind is where the gravity of the offence is such that at least three months' imprisonment is merited, but when there are mitigating circumstances which point towards a measure of leniency not sufficient to warrant total suspension. Examples are always dangerous, but we venture very tentatively to suggest a few: first of all, some

serious 'one off' acts of violence which are usually met with the immediate terms of imprisonment: some cases of burglary which at present warrant 18 months' or two years' imprisonment, where the offender is suitably qualified in terms of his record: some cases of fraud on public departments or some credit card frauds, where a short immediate sentence would be insufficient; some cases of handling involving medium-range sums of money; some thefts involving breach of trust; some cases of stealing from employers. All these are examples of cases where it may be possible to suspend part of the sentence without harm to the public and with benefit to the prisoner.

We would like to echo the words of the Advisory Council on the Penal System in para. 282 of their report on the review of maximum penalties: 'We view the partially suspended sentence as a legitimate means of exploiting one of the few reliable pieces of criminological knowledge – that many offenders sent to prison for the first time do not subsequently re-offend. We see it not as a means of administering a 'short, sharp shock', nor as a substitute for a wholly suspended sentence, but as especially applicable to serious first offenders or first-time prisoners who are bound to have to serve some time in prison, but who may well be effectively deterred by eventually serving only a small part of even the minimum sentence appropriate to the offence. This, in our view, must be its principal role.' We would like to add another type of offender: prisoners whose last term of imprisonment was some considerable time ago. We think that the power can be used on occasions where something more than a short sentence of immediate imprisonment is required to mark public disapproval and as a deterrent to others, but where the circumstances of the particular offender are such that some short term of immediate imprisonment, coupled with the threat involved in the suspension of the remainder, is enough to punish him for what he has done and to deter him in the future.

Restrictions on First Prison Sentence

A sentence of imprisonment may not be passed on a person on whom such a sentence has not previously been passed by any court in the United Kingdom unless the court is of the opinion that no other method of dealing with him is appropriate: Powers of Criminal Courts Act 1973, s. 20(1). For this purpose the court must obtain and consider information about the offender's circumstances and must take into account any information before the court which is relevant to his character and his physical and mental condition: *ibid*, s. 20(1). Where a sentence of imprisonment is passed in such a case the court must state the reason for its opinion that no other method is appropriate and the reason must be specified in the warrant and the register: *ibid*, s. 20(2).

For this purpose the court must obtain a social inquiry report unless of the opinion that this is unnecessary: Powers of Criminal Courts Act 1973, s. 20A(1), (2). The report must be from a probation officer: *ibid*, s. 20A(7). If the court does not obtain a social inquiry report it must state in open court the reason for its opinion why it was unnecessary: *ibid*, s. 20A(3). The reason must be specified in the warrant and entered in the register: *ibid*, s. 20A(4). Failure to obtain a social inquiry report does not invalidate sentence, but the appeal court must obtain one unless this is considered unnecessary: *ibid*, s. 20A(5).

Legal Representation

A court may not pass a sentence of imprisonment, including a suspended sentence and a partly suspended sentence on an unrepresented offender unless, having been informed of his right to apply for legal aid and having had the opportunity to do so, he refused or failed to apply or was refused legal aid on grounds of means: Powers of Criminal Courts Act 1973, s. 21.

Custodial Sentences for Young Offenders

The only custodial sentences for young offenders are detention centre orders and youth custody sentences. Broadly speaking, detention centre orders are for short sentences and youth custody for long. While training is provided as part of the regime of both types of sentence it is clear from government statements and official reports that training is not intended to be the purpose for which young offenders should receive these sentences. It is submitted that it would be wrong in principle therefore for a court to decide that a youth custody or a detention centre regime was the more suitable for the offender and then to fix a length of sentence which would allow of such a sentence. Instead, the court should first determine the length of sentence in accordance with the same principles as a sentence of imprisonment: the institution in which the young offender should serve a sentence of that length will then fall to be determined according to law.

Youth Custody

A sentence of youth custody may be passed on an offender under 21 years of age but not less than 15 years convicted of an offence which is punishable with imprisonment in the case of a person aged 21 or over where the court considers a sentence of more than four months (or sentences of more than 4 months in aggregate) to be appropriate: Criminal Justice Act 1982, s. 61(1). The court must consider, for reasons which must be stated in open court, that the only appropriate method of dealing with the offender is to pass a custodial sentence: *ibid*, s. 6(1). In addition, the Restrictions on Passing Custodial Sentences on Young Offenders (see *infra*) must be satisfied.

The usual term of youth custody is a term exceeding four months: Criminal Justice Act 1982, s. 7(5). By *ibid*, s. 7(6) the term may be for less than this period but not less than 21 days if one of the following circumstances applies:

(i) a sentence of four months or less would be appropriate, but a detention centre order is precluded because of the offender's physical or mental condition or because he is serving or has served a sentence of youth custody or certain other sentences: *ibid*, s. 6(2); or

(ii) the offender is female and has attained the age of 17: *ibid*, s. 6(4).

The maximum term of youth custody may not exceed the maximum period of imprisonment which may be imposed in the case of someone over 21: Criminal Justice Act 1982, s. 7(1). Magistrates' courts are limited to a maximum of six months youth custody for any one offence: Magistrates' Courts Act 1980, s. 31. If a longer sentence is called for they may in certain circumstances commit the offender to the Crown Court for sentence in accordance with *ibid*, s. 38. (*See* Committal for Sentence, *infra*.)

The court has the same power to pass consecutive sentences of youth custody as if they were sentences of imprisonment: Criminal Justice Act 1982, s. 7(2). *See* Consecutive Sentences of Imprisonment and Youth Custody, *infra*. A sentence of imprisonment on someone over 21 may be made consecutive to a sentence of youth custody already being served: *ibid*, s. 7(3).

The place in which a youth custody sentence is to be served is determined in accordance with the Criminal Justice Act 1982, s. 12. This gives effect to the Secretary of State's undertaking that anyone receiving a term of between four and 18 months youth custody will be guaranteed a place in a youth custody centre. Others may have to serve their sentence in a remand centre or prison.

There is no power to suspend a sentence of youth custody, but the issue of a warrant of commitment on a fine etc. defaulter may be postponed on terms: *see* Ch. 8:

According to Home office circular 42/1983:

Youth custody centres will be training establishments, based on the present borstals, those male young prisoner centres which operate a training regime and units in several female establishments. They will aim to lay emphasis on individual assessment and personal development in work, training, education and positive preparation for release to life in the community, and to offer a range of activities including employment, employment training courses, a group personal officer scheme (in which trainees come under the oversight of and are advised by particular officers) and a physical education programme. So far as possible the aim will be to prepare a programme suitable for the individual offender which takes account of the length of his sentence, bearing in mind that youth custody sentences, unlike sentences of borstal training, will be determinate. A youth custody sentence should not be regarded primarily as a means of securing that the offender receives training. The regime for young women and girls will generally operate on similar lines to those in the male youth custody centres. The legislation takes account of the likelihood that through pressure of numbers it will not be possible to accommodate all those sentenced to youth custody in youth custody centres (the provisions relating to allocation are in section 12). Offenders sentenced to more than four and up to and including 18 months will generally be held there, and others will be to the extent that vacancies are available, but some will have to serve their sentences in prison or remand centre accommodation providing only limited opportunities to operate training activities. These establishments will nevertheless endeavour so far as possible to cater for the particular requirements of young offenders, for example in relation to exercise, educational opportunities, access to employment facilities and preparation for release under supervision.

Consecutive Sentences of Imprisonment and Youth Custody

Sentences of imprisonment and youth custody may be ordered to take effect either concurrently or, subject to certain limits, consecutively: Magistrates' Courts Act 1980, s. 133. The effects of this section are that:

(i) sentences of imprisonment and youth custody, including suspended sentences and partly suspended sentences, imprisonment or detention in default of payment of a fine, may be consecutive to others imposed at the same time or earlier:

(ii) where two or more consecutive periods are imposed by the same magistrates' court they may not in total exceed six months, or 12 months if two or more of the sentences are for offences triable either way except offences tried summarily under s. 22(2); but

(iii) these limitations (of six or 12 months) do not apply when the sentence is consecutive to an earlier sentence.

The High Court have given the following guidance as to the form in which consecutive sentences should be pronounced:

Attention has been drawn to a difficulty which sometimes arises when a sentence is expressed to begin "at the expiration of the term of imprisonment you are now serving," or words to the same effect. If, as sometimes happens, the prisoner is already subject to two or more consecutive terms of imprisonment the effect of such a formula is that the new sentence will begin at the expiration of the term that he is *then* serving which may be the first of two consecutive terms. This will often not be the intention of the court giving the new sentence. It is suggested that the simplest course would be to use some such formula as "*consecutive to the total period of imprisonment to which you are already subject.*" The only exception to the use of such a formula

would be if the intention was that the new sentence should be concurrent with one of the previous sentences:
Practice Note [1959] 2 All E.R. 144.

As to the need to indicate clearly the total effective period of detention, the Court of Criminal Appeal has issued the following guidance in relation to trials on indictment:

> The attention of this court has been drawn to the fact that in many cases when a prisoner has been sentenced on more than one count only one sentence, say three years' imprisonment, is recorded on the indictment without indicating whether it is "concurrent on each count" or otherwise. No doubt this is because the court in question has been concentrating on the total period of imprisonment appropriate and has omitted specifically to say that it is intended to be concurrent on each count. While in the absence of any reference to a sentence being consecutive it is no doubt intended to be concurrent, we think that this should, to avoid confusion, be expressly stated in the presence of the prisoner and entered on the indictment. Clerks of the peace and clerks of assize should, therefore, in such a case consult the court before the prisoner leaves the dock and ask the court to state expressly that the sentence is concurrent on all counts, or as the case may be, and then make the appropriate entry on the indictment:

Practice Direction [1962] 1 All E.R. 417. And *see* also *Re Hastings* (1958) 122 J.P. 283.

In the ordinary way consecutive sentences should not be passed for what is in effect one act and one offence: *R. v. Cowburn* [1959] Crim. L.R. 590; *R. v. Hussain* [1962] Crim. L.R. 712. Thus, if two charges "arise out of precisely the same facts and involve, so to speak, the same criminality on the part of the (defendant)" there is no possible reason for passing consecutive sentences: *R. v. Torr* (1966) 130 J.P. 139 (obtaining goods by false pretences and obtaining credit by false pretences in respect of the same transaction). On the other hand consecutive sentences may properly be passed for the theft of a car and the subsequent obtaining of money by deception through its sale: *R. v. Bishoppe* [1973] Crim. L.R. 583; and for burglary and going equipped therefor: *R. v. Ferris* [1973] Crim. L.R. 642. If an assault on a police officer is part and parcel of a substantive offence (in the case robbery) and is to be treated as an aggravation of it this can be reflected in the sentence for the original offence and the sentence for the assault may be ordered concurrently. On the other hand when the offender assaults the police in an effort to escape, the sentence for the substantive offence can be fixed independently of that for the assault and the sentence for the assault can be dealt with by a separate and consecutive sentence: *R. v. Kastercum* [1972] 56 Cr. App. R. 298; *R. v. Hill* (1983) *The Times*, June 30. Similarly, where the offender (i) takes a vehicle without consent and (ii) drives it while disqualified and whilst unfit: *R. v. Dillon* (1984) *The Times*, Dec. 15.

A multiplicity of short consecutive sentences should not be passed in respect of a number of similar offences forming a series of transactions. It is the overall picture that matters and the court should decide what the overall sentence should be: *R. v. Brown* [1970] 50 Cr. App. R. 176; *R. v. Simpson* [1969] Crim. L.R. 383.

It is wrong (even if there were power in a magistrates' court) to impose a sentence of imprisonment consecutive to one of detention in a detention centre. The correct course is to order the imprisonment to commence forthwith: *R. v. Raisis* (1969) 133 J.P. 731.

It is wrong to make one sentence *partly* consecutive to another: *R. v. Gregory and Mills* (1969) 133 J.P. 337.

Detention Centres

A detention centre order may be made on a male offender aged 14 to 20 years convicted of an offence punishable in a person of 21 years with imprisonment: Criminal Justice Act 1982, s. 4(1). The court must consider that a custodial sentence of no more than four months is the only appropriate method of dealing with him: *ibid*, s. 4(1). The Restrictions on Passing Custodial Sentences on Young Offenders must also be satisfied: *see infra*.

There is no requirement for the offender to receive a medical examination before a detention centre order is made, but an order may not be made where detention would be unsuitable because of the offender's mental or physical condition: Criminal Justice Act 1982, s. 4(5)(a). Arrangements for securing a medical report from the police surgeon on the day of conviction are contained in Home Office circular 122/1983.

A detention centre order may not be made if the offender is serving or has ever served a sentence of youth custody or certain other sentences: *ibid*, s. 4(5)(b). This latter prohibition may be overriden where there are special circumstances, whether relating to the offence or to the offender, which warrant the making of a detention centre order in his case: *ibid*, s. 4(6). There is no prohibition on the making of a second or subsequent detention order.

The minimum period of a detention centre order is 21 days: Criminal Justice Act 1982, s. 4(3). The maximum term is four months: *ibid*, s. 4(1); so long as this does not exceed the maximum term of imprisonment available in the case of a person of 21 years: *ibid*, s. 4(2).

Consecutive detention centre orders are allowed by the Criminal Justice Act 1982, s. 5(1), so long as they do not exceed in aggregate a period in excess of four months: *ibid*, s. 5(2). Any excess is automatically remitted if the offender is younger than 15: *ibid*, s. 5(3). In the case of an offender aged 15 or older a sentence of excess length is deemed to be one of youth custody: *ibid*, s. 5(4).

There is no power to suspend a detention centre order, although the issue of a warrant of commitment to a detention centre of a defaulter may be postponed on terms: *see* Ch. 8.

A magistrates' court may not in a person's absence make a detention centre order: Magistrates' Courts Act 1980, s. 11(3).

Administratively, detention centres are divided into senior detention centres (for offenders aged 17 - 20) and junior detention centres (for offenders aged 14 - 16). There are no detention centres for females. The detention centres available to each court are listed in Home Office circular 3/1983, which also requests courts, *after* making a detention centre order, to ascertain whether a place is available and suggests the procedure to be followed if it is not.

According to Home Office circular 42/1983: The detention centre order is seen as providing a distinctive form of custodial sentence and although detention centres will now provide for shorter sentences than hitherto, it is not intended that there should be any major changes in the contents of regimes in detention centres. All the establishments will continue to be places for detention for short periods under discipline suitable to the age-range concerned. The regime will be based on the concept of a basic two-week programme founded on unskilled work, basic education, physical education, parade and inspections of a kind to which newly-sentenced young offenders can be introduced quickly so that they spend the greater part of the fortnight on a full regime. For those due to spend more than two weeks in custody each individual will undergo a programme building on the initial two weeks and involving a range of occupations appropriate to the length of sentence, including work with a greater element of skill, a broader education programme, and short basic training courses when these can be provided.

Restrictions on Custodial Sentences for Young Offenders

The court may not pass a youth custody sentence or make a detention centre order unless it is of the opinion that no other method of dealing with the offender is appropriate because:

(a) it appears to the court that he is unable or unwilling to respond to non-custodial penalties; or

(b) because a custodial sentence is necessary for the protection of the public,; or

(c) because the offence was so serious that a non-custodial sentence cannot be justified: Criminal Justice Act 1982, s. 14.

For this purpose the court must obtain a social inquiry report: Criminal Justice Act 1982, s. 2(2), save where in the circumstances of the case, it is of opinion that this is unnecessary: *ibid*, s. 2(3). The report can be either from a probation officer or a social worker of a local authority social services department: *ibid*, s. 2(10). The court must also obtain and consider information about the circumstances and take into account any information before the court relevant to the offender's character and his physical and mental condition: *ibid*, s. 2(1). The reason why no other method is appropriate must be stated in open court: Criminal Justice Act 1982, s. 2(4), and recorded in the warrant of commitment and the court register: *ibid*, s. 2(7). It would seem that these reasons must explain why the exceptions apply, not merely which exception applies.

Legal Representation

A youth custody sentence may not be passed or a detention centre order made on an unrepresented defendant unless he has knowingly refused or failed to apply for legal aid or has had an application for legal aid refused on the ground of means: Criminal Justice Act 1982, s. 3.

Supervision on Release

Anyone under 22 years of age released from youth custody or detention centre otherwise than on licence will be under the supervision of a probation officer or social worker for various periods of time between three to 12 months: Criminal Justice Act 1982, s. 15. Failure without reasonable excuse to comply with requirements laid down by the Secretary of State is a summary offence punishable by a fine of £200 or an appropriate custodial sentence not exceeding 30 days: *ibid*, s. 15(11). The appropriate custodial sentence is stipulated in *ibid*, s. 15(12) and the 21 day minimum period is waived for this offence, *ibid*, s. 7(7). If breach proceedings result in a custodial sentence such a sentence entails no extra supervision: *ibid*, s. 15(13).

Committal for Sentence

A magistrates' court has power to commit a convicted offender to the Crown Court for sentence:

(i) in the case of most offences triable either way, where it is of opinion that greater punishment should be inflicted than it has power to inflict (*see* below);

(ii) in the case of a wide range of offences when the offender is at the same time being committed to the Crown Court for sentence (*see* below); and

(iii)   in the case of an offender aged 15 or 16 convicted of an offence
         punishable on indictment in the case of a person with more than
         six months' imprisonment a magistrates' court which believes he
         should receive a greater term of youth custody than it has power to
         impose may commit him to the Crown Court for sentence:
         Magistrates' Courts Act 1980, s. 37(1). (Since this power is not
         available in the adult court by virtue of the Children and Young
         Persons Act 1969, s. 7(8), it is not dealt with in this book).

The offender must be committed to the most convenient location of the
Crown Court: *see* the Directions of the Lord Chief Justice, para. 8, in
Appx. C.

Committal for Greater Punishment

If upon summary conviction of anyone not less than 17 years old of an offence
triable either way other than one excluded by the Magistrates' Courts Act 1980,
s. 33 (offences of criminal damage tried summarily) a magistrates' court is of
opinion that the character and antecedents of the offender are such that greater
punishment should be inflicted than is within the court's powers, it may commit
him in custody or on bail to the Crown Court for sentence: s. 38, *ibid.* The power
to commit for sentence rests entirely upon the character and antecedents of the
offender and not the gravity of the offence. Grave offences, the High Court have
said repeatedly, should not be tried summarily.

Lord Parker CJ expressed the view that magistrates, when committing for
sentence, should state in open court any local reasons, such as that the crime had
become particularly prevalent in the area, which had led them to take this course,
and these should be sent by the clerk with the committal papers to the Crown
Court (XXV *The Magistrate* at p. 163). The communication of other
reasons was implied by approved in *R.* v. *Leith* (1983) March 1. 147 J.P.N.
193.

The Home Secretary recommends that courts should, as normal practice,
consider a social inquiry report before committing an offender to the Crown Court
for sentence: Home Office cir. 28/1971.

There is no power to commit a corporation to the Crown Court for sentence:
Magistrates' Courts Act 1980, s. 3.

The Crown Court upon such a committal may deal with the offender in any
manner in which it could deal with him if he had just been convicted of
the offence on indictment: Powers of Criminal Courts Act 1973, s. 42(1).

Committal to be Dealt With

A magistrates' court which commits an offender to the Crown Court for
sentence may at the same time commit him to be dealt with in respect of
any offence if the relevant offence is an offence triable either way, or in
respect of:

—any offence punishable with imprisonment;
—any disqualfiable traffic offence; and
—the commission of a further offence during the operational period of a
suspended sentence

if the relevant offence is a summary offence: Criminal Justice Act 1967, s.
56(1).

The Crown Court may then deal with the offender in respect of the other
offences in any way in which he could have been dealt with in the magistrates'
court: *ibid*, s. 56(5).

Other Offences

When an offender is committed for sentence under these or any other provisions other related offences which cannot be so committed should be dealt with by the magistrates or by adjournment until the decision of the Crown Court is known.

Ancillary Orders

There is power to order the interim disqualification of a road traffic offender upon committal to the Crown Court for sentence: Road Traffic Act 1972, s. 103. Any other powers which the magistrates might otherwise have exercised must on a committal for sentence or a committal to be dealt with be left to the Crown Court: Criminal Justice Act 1967, s. 56(5).

Attendance Centre Orders

Where a magistrates' court would in the case of someone over 21 have power to pass a sentence of imprisonment it may make an attendance centre order in respect of a person under 21: Criminal Justice Act 1982, s. 17(1). Such an order can only be made in respect of an offender if the court has been notified that an attendance centre (as defined in *ibid*, s. 16(2)) is available for the reception of persons of his description: *ibid*, s. 17(1). An attendance centre order may not be made on anyone who has been previously sentenced to youth custody, detention in a detention centre or to certain other custodial sentences unless there are special circumstances: *ibid*, s. 17(3). There is no bar on a second attendance centre order.

The number of hours must be specified in the order: *ibid*, s. 17(1). They may not be less than 12 in aggregate except where the offender is a child: *ibid*, s. 17(4). (An attendance centre order may not be made in the adult court on someone under 17: Children and Young Persons Act 1969, s. 7(8).) Nor may the aggregate number of hours exceed 12 except where the court is of opinion having regard to all the circumstances that 12 would be inadequate. Where 12 would be inadequate the aggregate number must not exceed 36 where the offender is aged 17-20: *ibid*, s. 17(5).

The attendance centre must be specified in the order (*ibid*, s. 17(1)), must be reasonably accessible to the person concerned having regard to his age, the means of access available to him and any circumstances: *ibid*, s. 17(7). The time of first attendance must be specified in the order: *ibid*, s. 17(9). Subsequent times are fixed by the officer in charge having regard to the offender's circumstances: *ibid*, s. 17(10). A copy of the order must be delivered or sent by the clerk of the court to the officer in charge of the attendance centre and a copy to the offender: *ibid*, s. 17(12).

Discharge and Variation

An attendance centre order may be discharged by the court on application by the offender or the officer in charge: *ibid*, s. 18(1). A magistrates' court acting for the petty sessions area in which the attendance centre is situated has jurisdiction, as well as the court which made the order (*ibid*, s. 18(3)) except where the order was made by the Crown Court and a direction is included in the order reserving this power to that court: *ibid*, s. 18(4). An attendance centre order may in like manner be varied as respects the time of first attendance or the centre specified: *ibid*, s. 18(5), (6). Where either type of application is made the court may deal with it without summoning the offender: *ibid*, s. 18(7). The order of discharge or variation must be delivered or served by the clerk of the court: *ibid*, s. 18(8).

Breach

Failure without reasonable excuse to attend an attendance centre or breach of its rules, if proved to the satisfaction of a magistrates' court, may result in the court:

(a) revoking the order (if made by a magistrates' court) and dealing with the offender for the original offence in any manner in which he could have been dealt with for that offence by the court which made the order if the order had not been made; or

(b) committal in custody or on bail to the Crown Court (if the order was made by that court) to be dealt with under *ibid*, s. 19(5): *ibid*, s. 19(3).

A summons or warrant may be issued to secure the attendance of the offender: *ibid*, s. 19(1). The magistrates' court in question is the one in the area of which the attendance centre is situated or the magistrates' court which made the order, *ibid*, s. 19(2). There is an appeal to the Crown Court against sentence under (a) above: *ibid*, s. 19(6).

The Home Office advise:

Attendance centres are designed to deal with young offenders whose future conduct may be expected to be influenced by the deprivation of leisure time involved, and by the endeavours of the staff to encourage them to make constructive use of leisure time and to guide them towards worthwhile recreational activities which they can continue on leaving the centre. An attendance centre order is not an appopriate sentence for offenders who require the sustained influence of a supervisor or removal from their home surroundings, or for those with a long record of offences.

(The Sentence of the Court)

Detention for Shorter Periods

A magistrates' court has various powers to detain for short periods under three separate provisions of the Magistrates' Court Act 1980 as follows:

	Detention in police cells s. 134	Detention in court or police station s. 135	Committal to custody overnight s. 136
Available in lieu of sentence of imprisonment and youth custody	Yes	Yes'	No
Available for non-payment of a fine	Yes 2	Yes· 2	Yes 1
Place of detention	Certified police cells, bridewell or similar place	Precincts of the courthouse or any police station	In a police station
Maximum period of detention	Four days	Until 8 *p.m.* or such earlier time as is necessary to give offender reasonable opportunity of returning to his abode the same day	Until 8 *p.m.* if arrested between midnight and 8 *a.m.* Otherwise until 8 *a.m.* next morning

1 For persons aged 21 and over only.
2 For persons aged 17 and over

Charge and Control Orders

Where a person, the subject of a care order made in criminal proceedings or in care proceedings based on the offence conditions, is convicted of an offence punishable with imprisonment the court may make an order restricting the classes of person who may have charge and control of the

offender for a period not exceeding six months: Children and Young Persons Act 1969, s. 20A(1). This is achieved by adding to the care order a condition that the power of the local authority to allow a parent, guardian, relative or friend to have charge or control
(a)   shall not be exercisable; or
(b)   shall not be exercisable except to allow charge and control to a specified parent, guardian, relative or friend.
Where such a direction has been given and the defendant commits another such offence the court may replace the condition with another: *ibid*, s. 20A(2).

These powers may not be exercised unless the court is of opinion that it is appropriate to do so because of the seriousness of the offence *and* that no other method of dealing with the person is appropriate. To determine this the court must obtain and consider information about the circumstances:*ibid*, s.20A(3). Nor may these powers be exercised with respect to an unrepresented defendant unless he has knowingly failed or refused to apply for legal aid or has been refused legal aid on grounds of means: *ibid*, s. 20A(4), (8). The order must be explained to the defendant before it is made: *ibid*, s. 20A(5).

The subject of the order, his parent or guardian and the local authority may apply to the juvenile court for its revocation: *ibid*, s. 20A(6). The local authority may appeal to the Crown Court against the making of the order: *ibid*, s. 20A(7). The subject of the order may appeal under the Magistrates' Courts Act 1980, s. 108.

Juveniles

Magistrates sitting in the adult court may not pass any custodial sentence, commit for sentence, make an attendance centre order or a charge and control order in respect of a juvenile; instead, they should remit the offender to the juvenile court to be dealt with: Children and Young Persons Act 1969, s. 7(8). *See* Ch. 5.

THE CRIMINAL JUSTICE ACT 1967

Committal for sentence for offences tried summarily

56.   (1) Where a magistrates' court ("the committing court") commits a person in custody or on bail to the Crown Court under any enactment to which this section applies to be sentenced or otherwise dealt with in respect of an offence ("the relevant offence"), the committing court—

(a)   if the relevant offence is an offence triable either way, may also commit him, in custody or on bail as the case may require, to the Crown Court to be dealt with in respect of any other offence whatsoever in respect of which the committing court has power to deal with him (being an offence of which he has been convicted by that or any other court); or

(b)   if the relevant offence is a summary offence, may commit him, as aforesaid, to the Crown Court to be dealt with in respect of—

(i)   any other offence of which the committing court has convicted him, being either an offence punishable with imprisonment or an offence in respect of which the committing court has a power or duty to order him to be disqualified under s. 93 of the Road Traffic Act 1972 or s. 19 of the Transport Act 1981 (disqualification for certain motoring offences); or

(ii) any suspended sentence in respect of which the committing court has under s. 24(1) of the Powers of Criminal Courts Act 1973 power to deal with him.

(2) The enactments to which this section applies are the Vagrancy Act, 1824 (incorrigible rogues), ss 37 and 38 of the Magistrates' Courts Act 1980 (committal for sentence), s. 62(6) of this Act and s. 8(6) (probationer convicted of subsequent offence) and s. 24(2) (committal to be dealt with in respect of a suspended sentence) of the Powers of Criminal Courts Act 1973.

(3) . . .

(4) (Repealed).

(5) Where under subs. (1) of this section a magistrates' court commits a person to be dealt with by the Crown Court in respect of an offence, the latter court may after inquiring into the circumstances of the case deal with him in any way in which the magistrates' court might have dealt with him, and without prejudice to the foregoing provision, where under that subsection or any enactment to which this section applies a magistrates' court so commits a person, any duty or power which, apart from this subsection, would fall to be discharged or exercised by the magistrates' court shall not be discharged or exercised by that court but shall instead be discharged or may instead be exercised by the Crown Court.

(6) Any duty imposed or power conferred by virtue of the last foregoing subsection on the Crown Court, in a case where an offender has been committed to the court under s. 37 of the Magistrates' Courts Act, 1980, shall be discharged or may be exercised by the court notwithstanding that it sentences him to borstal training and in that or any other case shall be discharged or may be exercised notwithstanding anything in any other enactment and, in particular, in ss 93 and 101 of the Road Traffic Act 1972 or s. 19 of the Transport Act 1981.

(7)–(12) (Repealed).

(13) In this section—

"disqualified" means disqualified for holding or obtaining a licence under Part II of the Road Traffic Act 1972 or s. 19 of the Transport Act 1981, . . .

(as amended by the Vehicles and Driving Licences Act 1969, sch. 1, the Courts Act 1971, schs 8 and 11, the Road Traffic Act 1972, schs 7 and 9, the Powers of Criminal Courts Act 1973, sch. 5, the Criminal Law Act 1977, s. 46, the Magistrates' Courts Act 1980, sch. 7, the Transport Act 1981, sch. 9).

COMMENTARY

This section applies only where the defendant has been committed for sentence or to be dealt with under one of the enactments mentioned in subs. (2) and not to a committal for trial: R. v. Thorne [1969] Crim. L.R. 188.

Subsection (1): Any enactment to which this section applies. See subs. (2).

An offence triable either way/a summary offence. Defined in the Interpretation Act 1978, sch. 1.

Commit him in custody or on bail. See notes to the Magistrates' Court Act 1980, s. 38, infra. and form 96. For the location of the Crown Court to which the offender should be committed see paras 5–9 of the directions of the Lord Chief Justice in Appx. C.
For the documents to be sent to the higher court see the Magistrates' Courts Rules 1981, r. 17.

To be dealt with. On a committal under this section the Crown Court is restricted to the powers which the magistrates could have exercised: R. v. Ward [1969] 53 Cr. App. R. 23.

An offence punishable with imprisonment. To be construed in relation to any offender without regard to any prohibition or restriction imposed by or under any enactment on the imprisonment of offenders of his age: s. 104(4) of the Act.

Subsection (2): Section 62(6) of this Act. Deals with prisoners on licence: "If a person subject to a licence under ss 60 or 61 of this Act is convicted by a magistrates' court of an offence punishable on indictment with imprisonment, the court may commit him in custody or on bail to the Crown Court for sentence in accordance with s. 42 of the Powers of Criminal Courts Act 1973. (*Power of the Crown Court to sentence persons convicted by magistrates' courts of indictable offences*)".

Section 8(6). It is submitted that the words in brackets following this reference do not limit its scope and that it applies to persons committed to the Crown Court following commission of an offence during the operational period of an order of conditional discharge as well as a probation order.

Subsection (5). Thus the magistrates may not, for example, commit to the Crown Court for sentence while at the same time making a restitution order: *R.* v. *Blackpool Justices, ex parte Charlson and Gregory* (1973) 137 J.P. 25. Magistrates must be scrupulously careful to leave all questions of sentence to the Crown Court: *R.* v. *Brogan* (1975) 139 J.P. 296. But the magistrates have power to make an interim order of disqualification and endorsement – *see* the Road Traffic Act 1972, s. 103.

THE CHILDREN AND YOUNG PERSONS ACT 1969

Power of court to add condition as to charge and control of offender in care.

20A. (1) Where a person to whom a care order relates which was made–
  (a) by virtue of subs. (3) of s. 1 of this Act in a case where the court which made the order was of the opinion that the condition mentioned in subs. (2)(f) of that section was satisfied; or
  (b) by virtue of s. 7(7) of this Act, is convicted or found guilty of an offence punishable with imprisonment in the case of a person over 21,
the court which convicts or finds him guilty of that offence may add to the care order a condition under this section that the power conferred by s. 21(2) of the Child Care Act 1980 (power of local authority to allow a parent, guardian, relative or friend charge and control) shall for such period not exceeding six months as the court may specify in the condition–
  (c) not be exercisable; or
  (d) not be exercisable to allow the person to whom the order relates to be under the charge and control of a specified parent, guardian, relative or friend.
  (2) Where–
  (a) the power conferred by subs. (1) above has been exercised; and
  (b) before the period specified in the condition has expired the person to whom the care order relates is convicted or found guilty of another offence punishable with imprisonment in the case of a person over 21,
the court may replace the condition with another condition under this section.
  (3) A court shall not exercise the powers conferred by this section unless the court is of opinion that it is appropriate to exercise those powers because of the seriousness of the offence and that no other method of dealing with the person to whom the care order relates is appropriate; and for the purpose of determining whether any other method of dealing with him is appropriate the court shall obtain and consider information about the circumstances.
  (4) A court shall not exercise the said powers in respect of a person who is not legally represented in that court unless either–
  (a) he applied for legal aid and the application was refused on the ground that it did not appear his means were such that he

required assistance; or

(b)   having been informed of his right to apply for legal aid and had the opportunity to do so, he refused or failed to apply.

(5) Before adding a condition under this section to a care order a court shall explain to the person to whom the care order relates the purpose and effect of the condition.

(6) At any time when a care order includes a condition under this section—

(a)   the person to whom the order relates;

(b)   his parent or guardian, acting on his behalf; or

(c)   the local authority in whose care he is, may apply to a juvenile court for the revocation or variation of the condition.

(7) The local authority may appeal to the Crown Court against the imposition of a condition under this section by a magistrates' court or against the terms of such a condition.

(8) For the purposes of this section a person is to be treated as legally represented in a court if, but only if, he has the assistance of counsel or a solicitor to represent him in the proceedings in that court at some time after he is convicted or found guilty and before any power conferred by this section is exercised, and in this section "legal aid" means legal aid for the purposes of proceedings in that court, whether the whole proceedings or the proceedings on or in relation to the exercise of the power; but in the case of a person committed to the Crown Court for sentence or trial, it is immaterial whether he applied for legal aid in the Crown Court to, or was informed of his right to apply by, that court or the court which committed him.

(as inserted by the Criminal Justice Act 1982, s. 22)

COMMENTARY

The effect of this section is described under Charge and Control Orders in the introduction.

Subsection (1): Care order. Defined in s. 70(1) of the Act as "an order committing (a person) to the care of a local authority".

Section 1(3). This relates to care orders made in care proceedings based on the offence condition (s. 1(2)(f)).

Section 7(7). This relates to care orders made in criminal proceedings.

Section 21(2) of the Child Care Act 1980. Reads:

Without prejudice to the generality of subs. (1) above, a local authority may allow a child in their care, either for a fixed period or until the local authority otherwise determine, to be under the charge and control of a parent, guardian, relative or friend.

Subs. (1) of s. 21, *ibid*, reads:

A local authority shall discharge their duty to provide accommodation and maintenance for a child in their care in such one of the following ways as they think fit, namely,

(a)   by boarding him out on such terms as to payment by the authority and otherwise as the authority may, subject to the provisions of this Act and regulations thereunder, determine; or

(b)   by maintaining him in a community home or in any such home as is referred to in s. 80 of this Act; or

(c)   by maintaining him in a voluntary home (other than a community home) the managers of which are willing to receive him;

or by making such other arrangements as seem appropriate to the local authority.

Charge and control. DHSS circular LAC (83) 6 dated April 5, 1983 comments:
"Local authorities may make any arrangements for the juvenile's accommodation during the currency of the order except placement with parents, guardians, relatives or friends not specified in the order, and this will include boarding out or placement outside the community home system. The currency of an order does not prohibit home leave, provided that responsibility for the juvenile's charge and control is not transferred, and local authorities may make reasonable provision for home visits, though in doing so they are asked not to be insensitive to the wishes of the courts."

Subsection (3): The seriousness of the offence. Thus it could not be appropriate to make an order under this section in respect of a relatively trivial offence.

No other method . . . appropriate. This seems to indicate that an order under this section is a sentence in its own right and cannot, for example, be combined with an attendance centre order on the same offence. It is submitted that it does not rule out the making of orders for costs, compensation and other ancillary matters.

Subsection (7). The offender himself may appeal to the Crown Court under the Magistrates' Court Act 1980, s. 108.

THE POWERS OF CRIMINAL COURTS ACT 1973

Restriction on imposing sentences of imprisonment on persons who have not previously served prison sentences

20. (1) No court shall pass a sentence of imprisonment on a person of or over 21 years of age on whom such a sentence has not previously been passed by a court in any part of the United Kingdom unless the court is of opinion that no other method of dealing with him is appropriate; and for the purpose of determining whether any other method of dealing with any such person is appropriate the court shall obtain and consider information about the circumstances, and shall take into account any information before the court which is relevant to his character and his physical and mental condition.

(2) Where a magistrates' court passes a sentence of imprisonment on any such person as is mentioned in subs. (1) above, the court shall state the reason for its opinion that no other method of dealing with him is appropriate, and cause that reason to be specified in the warrant of commitment and to be entered in the register.

(3) For the purposes of this section—

(*a*) a previous sentence of imprisonment which has been suspended and which has not taken effect under s. 23 of this Act or under s. 19 of the Treatment of Offenders Act (Northern Ireland) 1968 shall be disregarded; and

(*b*) "sentence of imprisonment" does not include a committal or attachment for contempt of court.

(4) . . .

(5) For the purposes of this section the age of a person shall be deemed to be that which it appears to the court to be after considering any available evidence.

(as amended by the Criminal Justice Act 1982, sch. 14.)

COMMENTARY

Subsection (1): A sentence of imprisonment. Does not include a committal in default of payment of any sum of money, or for want of sufficient distress to satisfy any sum of money, or for failure to do or abstain from doing any thing required to be done or left undone: s. 57(1) of the Act. And note subs. (3) of this section.

21 years of age. *See* subs. (5).

United Kingdom. That is, Great Britain and Northern Ireland: Royal and Parliamentary Titles Act, 1927.

No other method of dealing with him is appropriate. The obligation is merely a duty to think twice before passing a prison sentence: *Vassall* v. *Harris* [1964] Crim. L.R. 322; *Morris* v. *The Crown Office* [1970] 1 All E.R. 1079.

Shall obtain and consider information. It is submitted that this provision goes primarily to the matters which the prosecutor normally lays before the court on a plea of guilty. (*See* the introduction to ch. 5.)

Subsection (2). The provisions of this subsection are not mandatory but directory only: Cf. *Morris* v. *The Crown Office* [1970] 1 All E.R. 1079. Failure to state reasons would not be sufficient grounds for quashing the sentence: *R.* v. *Jackson (alias Rintoul)* (1966) 130 J.P. 284; *R.* v. *Chesterfield Justices, ex parte Hewitt* (1972) *The Times*, December 12; [1973] Crim. L.R. 181.

The register. Means the register of proceedings before a magistrates' court required by rules made under s. 15 of the Justices of the Peace Act 1979 to be kept by the clerk of the court: Powers of Criminal Courts Act 1973, s. 57(1).

Social inquiry report for purposes of s. 20.

20A. (1) Subject to subs. (2) below, the court shall in every case obtain a social inquiry report for the purpose of determining under s. 20(1) above whether there is any appropriate method of dealing with an offender other than imprisonment.

(2) Subs. (1) above does not apply if, in the circumstances of the case, the court is of the opinion that it is unnecessary to obtain a social inquiry report.

(3) Where a magistrates' court passes a sentence of imprisonment on a person of or over 21 years of age on whom such a sentence has not previously been passed by a court in any part of the United Kingdom without obtaining a social inquiry report, it shall state in open court the reason for its opinion that it was unnecessary to obtain such a report.

(4) A magistrates' court shall cause a reason stated under subs. (3) above to be specified in the warrant of commitment and to be entered in the register.

(5) No sentence shall be invalidated by the failure of a court to comply with subs. (1) above, but any other court on appeal from that court shall obtain a social inquiry report if none was obtained by the court below, unless it is of the opinion that in the circumstances of the case it is unnecessary to do so.

(6) In determining whether it should deal with the appellant otherwise than by passing a sentence of imprisonment on him the court hearing the appeal shall consider any social inquiry report obtained by it or by the court below.

(7) In this section "social inquiry report" means a report about a person and his circumstances made by a probation officer.

(as inserted by the Criminal Justice Act 1982, s. 62.)

COMMENTARY

Subsection (1): Social inquiry report. Defined in subs. (7).

In every case. This phrase seems otiose.

Subsection (2): Unnecessary. Compare the comment to the Criminal Justice Act 1982, s. 2(3), *infra*.

Restriction on imposing sentences of imprisonment, [Borstal training] or detention on persons not legally represented

21.   (1) A magistrates' court on summary conviction or the Crown Court on committal for sentence or on conviction on indictment shall not pass a sentence of imprisonment, on a person who is not legally represented in that court and has not been previously sentenced to that punishment by a court in any part of the United Kingdom, unless either—

(a) he applied for legal aid and the application was refused on the ground that it did not appear his means were such that he required assistance;

or

(b) having been informed of his right to apply for legal aid and had the opportunity to do so, he refused or failed to apply.

(2) For the purposes of this section a person is to be treated as legally represented in court if, but only if, he has the assistance of counsel or a solicitor to represent him in the proceedings in that court at some time after he is found guilty and before he is sentenced, and in subs. (1)(a) and (b) above "legal aid" means legal aid for the purposes of proceedings in that court, whether the whole proceedings or the proceedings on or in relation to sentence; but in the case of a person committed to the Crown Court for sentence or trial, it is immaterial whether he applied for legal aid in the Crown Court to, or was informed of his right to apply by, that court or the court which committed him.

(3) For the purposes of this section—

(a) a previous sentence of imprisonment which has been suspended and which has not taken effect under s. 23 of this Act or under s. 19 of the Treatment of Offenders Act (Northern Ireland) 1968 shall be disregarded;

(b) "sentence of imprisonment" does not include a committal or attachment for contempt of court.

(as amended by the Criminal Justice Act 1982, sch. 16.)

COMMENTARY

Corresponding provisions for offenders under 21 are contained in the Criminal Justice Act 1982, s. 3, *infra*.

Failure to comply with the terms of this section renders a sentence invalid: *R.* v. *Birmingham Justices, ex parte Wyatt* (1975) 140 J.P. 46.

Subsection (1): Pass a sentence of imprisonment. Includes a suspended sentence. And *see* subs. (3)(a).

Not legally represented. Representation after conviction and before sentence is sufficient: subs. (2).

Has not been previously sentenced to that punishment. Suspended sentences which have not been served do not take the offender outside the protection of this section: subs. (3)(a).

United Kingdom. That is, Great Britain and Northern Ireland: Royal and Parliamentary Titles Act, 1927.

Subsection (2). In view of the terms of this subsection the magistrates' court should inform the Crown Court whether the accused had the opportunity to apply at the magistrates' court for legal aid in the Court whether the accused had the opportunity to apply at the magistrates' court for legal aid in the Crown Court proceedings and what the outcome was: Home Office circ. 237/1972 dated Dec. 19, 1972.

Suspended sentences of imprisonment

22. (1) Subject to subs. (2) below, a court which passes a sentence of imprisonment for a term of not more than two years for an offence may order that the sentence shall not take effect unless, during a period specified in the order, being not less than one year or more than two years from the date of the order, the offender commits in Great Britain another offence punishable with imprisonment and thereafter a court having power to do so orders under s. 23 of this Act that the original sentence shall take effect; and in this part of this Act "operational period", in relation to a suspended sentence, means the period so specified.

(2) A court shall not deal with an offender by means of a suspended sentence unless the case appears to the court to be one in which a sentence of imprisonment would have been appropriate in the absence of any power to suspend such a sentence by an order under subs. (1) above.

(3) A court which passes a suspended sentence on any person for an offence shall not make a probation order in his case in respect of another offence of which he is convicted by or before the court or for which he is dealt with by the court.

(4) On passing a suspended sentence the court shall explain to the offender in ordinary language his liability under s. 23 of this Act if during the operational period he commits an offence punishable with imprisonment.

(5) Where a court has passed a suspended sentence on any person, and that person is subsequently sentenced to borstal training, he shall cease to be liable to be dealt with in respect of the suspended sentence unless the subsequent sentence or any conviction or finding on which it was passed is quashed on appeal.

(6) Subject to any provision to the contrary contained in the Criminal Justice Act 1967, this Act or any enactment passed or instrument made under any enactment after December 31, 1967—

(a) a suspended sentence which has not taken effect under s. 23 of this Act shall be treated as a sentence of imprisonment for the purposes of all enactments and instruments made under enactments except any enactment or instrument which provides for disqualification for or loss of office, or forfeiture of pensions, of persons sentenced to imprisonment; and

(b) where a suspended sentence has taken effect under that section, the offender shall be treated for the purposes of the enactments and instruments excepted by para. (a) above as having been convicted on the ordinary date on which the period allowed for making an appeal against an order under that section expires or, if such an appeal is made, the date on which it is finally disposed of or abandoned or fails for non-prosecution.

COMMENTARY

See generally Suspended Sentences in the introduction.

Subsection (1): A sentence of imprisonment. Defined in s. 57(1) of the Act: *see* the note to s. 20, *supra*. It does not include a committal to prison for non-payment of a fine: *R.* v. *Nixon* [1976] Crim. L.R. 117; nor the imprisonment of an incorrigible rogue: *R.* v. *Graves* [1976] Crim. L.R. 697.

Great Britain. That is England, Scotland and Wales: Union with Scotland Act, 1706; Wales and Berwick Act, 1746, s. 3. Excluding the Channel Islands and the Isle of Man.

Offence punishable with imprisonment. To be construed in relation to any offender, without regard to any prohibition or restriction imposed by or under any enactment on the imprisonment of offenders of his age: s. 57(4) of the Act.

An offence triable either way which carries imprisonment in the Crown Court but not in the magistrates' court, such as an offence under the Trade Descriptions Act 1968, s. 14(1)(b), is only an offence punishable by imprisonment when the offender is convicted in the Crown Court: *R.* v. *Melbourne* [1980] Crim. L.R. 510; 144 J.P.N. 357. For the offence of failing to provide a laboratory speciment see *R.* v. *Hugsans* [1977] Crim. L.R. 684.

A certificate purporting to be signed by or on behalf of the Lord Advocate that an offence is punishable in Scotland with imprisonment or is so punishable on indictment for a specified term is evidence of the matter so specified: s. 52 of the Act.

This Part of this Act. That is ss. 1-46 inclusive.

Subsection (2): This subsection gives effect to the decision in *R.* v. *O'Keefe* (1969) 133 J.P. 160; in which it was said that before deciding to impose a suspended sentence all other possibilities must first be rejected. Only when the court has decided it is a case for imprisonment can it go on to the final question: is immediate imprisonment required or can it be suspended?

Subsection (4): For a model form of explanation *see R.* v. *Crosby and Hayes* [1975] 60 Cr. App. R. 234.

Power of court on conviction of further offence to deal with suspended sentence

23.   (1) Where an offender is convicted of an offence punishable with imprisonment committed during the operational period of a suspended sentence and either he is so convicted by or before a court having power under s. 24 of this Act to deal with him in respect of the suspended sentence or he subsequently appears or is brought before such a court, then, unless the sentence has already taken effect, the court shall consider his case and deal with him by one of the following methods—

(*a*)   the court may order that the suspended sentence shall take effect with the original term unaltered;

(*b*)   it may order that the sentence shall take effect with the substitution of a lesser term for the original term;

(*c*)   it may by order vary the orginal order under s. 22(1) of this Act by substituting for the period specified therein a period expiring not later than two years from the date of the variation; or

(*d*)   it may make no order with respect to the suspended sentence;

and a court shall make an order under para. (*a*) of this subsection unless the court is of opinion that it would be unjust to do so in view of all the circumstances, including the facts of the subsequent offence, and where it is of that opinion the court shall state its reasons.

(2) Where a court orders that a suspended sentence shall take effect, with or without any variation of the original term, the court may order that that sentence shall take effect immediately or that the term thereof shall commence on the expiration of another term of imprisonment passed on the offender by that or another court.

(3)-(5) (*Repealed.*)

(6) ...

(7) Where a court deals with an offender under this section in respect of a suspended sentence the appropriate officer of the court shall notify the appropriate officer of the court which passed the sentence of the method adopted.

(8) Where on consideration of the case of an offender a court makes no order with respect to a suspended sentence, the appropriate officer of the court shall record that fact.

(9) For the purposes of any enactment conferring rights of appeal in criminal cases any order made by a court with respect to a suspended sentence shall be treated as a sentence passed on the offender by that court for the offence for which the suspended sentence was passed.

(*as amended by the Criminal Justice Act 1982, s. 31, sch. 16*).

COMMENTARY

Legal aid may be granted in these proceedings: Legal Aid Act 1974, ss 28(2) and 30(12). Costs are regulated by the Costs in Criminal Cases Act 1973 as if the offender had been tried in those proceedings for the offence for which the sentence was passed: s. 18(4), *ibid.*

Subsection (1): Convicted.   A suspended sentence cannot be brought into operation as a result of a conviction during the period of suspension which resulted in a probation order or an order of absolute or conditional discharge, having regard to the fact that this is deemed not to be a "conviction" by s. 13(1) of the Powers of Criminal Courts Act 1973. It ought to be a rule of practice for magistrates' courts that whenever they are minded to make an order which will not enable a suspended sentence (passed by a higher court) to be brought into operation, namely absolute or conditional discharge or probation, their proper course is to refrain from making one or other of those orders and to commit under s. 56 of the 1967 Act so that the court that imposed the sentence can deal with the whole matter

Save only when it is unjust to do so, a suspended sentence must be put into effect on conviction of an imprisonable offence, whether a sentence of imprisonment is imposed therefor or not: *R.* v. *Cobbold* [1971] Crim. L.R. 436 (fine for subsequent offence); *R.* v. *Isaacs* [1980] Crim. L.R. 666. together: *R.* v. *Tarry* (1970) 134 J.P. 469; *R.* v. *Salmon* [1973] 57 Cr. App. R. 953.

The operational period.   Defined in s. 22(1), *supra.*

A suspended sentence.   Means a sentence to which s. 22(1) of the Act applies: s. 57(1), *ibid.*

An offence punishable with imprisonment.   *See* the note to s. 22.

Brought before such a court.   That is, under s. 25, *infra.*

Unless the sentence has already taken effect.   The extension of the operational period under subs. (1)(c) in respect of one offence committed in breach of a suspended sentence does not constitute a taking effect of that sentence for the purpose of a quite different offence in breach: *R.* v. *McDonald* [1971] 55 Cr. App. R. 575.

The court shall consider his case.   "Whilst, of course, it is never part of the function of a court which may have to consider activating a suspended sentence in any way to review its propriety, nonetheless, there are cases where justice cannot be done without fitting into the pattern of events leading to the further conviction the facts which led to the suspended sentence. To that extent, therefore, it may then be necessary on the second occasion for the court to inform itself of the circumstances in which the suspended sentence was passed in order that such proper assessment may be made of the overall position so as to determine the sentence to be passed and make plain the grounds on which it is acting." *per* Sachs, LJ in *R.* v. *Munday* [1971] 56 Cr. App. R. 220 (the revised judgment). And *see R.* v. *Metcalfe* [1971] Crim. L.R. 112.

Deal with him.   Whenever a person is dealt with under this subsection otherwise than by method (*a*) the court's reason must be entered in the register. When the sentence was passed by another court, the clerk of that court must be notified: Magistrates' Courts Rules 1981, r. 29(1). And *see* generally the note "Dealt With" to s. 25, *infra.*

Order that the suspended sentence shall take effect.   *See* forms 89, 90. Note that the court is not "imposing imprisonment". It follows that the power to impose consecutive sentences under the Magistrates' Courts Act, 1980, s. 133 does not apply—but *see* subs. (2). If the offender is subject to a suspended sentence supervision order the clerk must notify the court which made the order: Magistrates' Courts Rules 1981, r. 30(1).

A lesser term.   But not less than five days: Magistrates' Courts Act, 1980, s. 132. If the offender is subject to a suspended sentence supervision order the clerk must notify the court which made the order: Magistrates' Courts Rules 1981, r. 30(1). When two or more suspended sentences passed on the same occasion were ordered by the earlier court to be served consecutively, they are, by the operation of s. 57(2) of the Act, to be treated as a single term, for example, for the purposes of a reduction of length of sentence when a later court comes to put them into effect: *R.* v. *Gall* [1970] 54 Cr. App. R. 292. Periods spent in custody prior to the passing of the suspended sentence do not justify a later court from putting into effect a lesser term: *R.* v. *Deering* [1976] Crim. L.R. 638. The fact that the subsequent offence was committed near the end of the operational period of the suspended sentence may be a reason for reducing the length of the activated sentence: *R.* v. *Beacock* [1979] 1 Cr. App. R. (S) 198. Although not unlawful it is wrong in principle to pass an immediate sentence of imprisonment on the later offence and extend the operational period of a suspended sentence: *R.* v. *Treays* [1981] Crim. L.R. 511.

Vary the original order. *See* form 91. It is not good practice when passing a forthwith sentence of imprisonment to vary the operational period of an earlier suspended sentence: *R.* v. *Goodlad* (1973) 137 J.P. 704; following *R.* v. *Sapiano* [1968] 52 Cr. App. R. 674.

Make no order. For the effect of such a course *see* the note "Dealt With" to s. 25, *infra.*

When an offender in breach of suspended sentences is made the subject of a community service order on the occasion of the later offence, the court deciding under s. 23(1)(*d*) to make no order regarding the breach of the suspended sentences, a later court may not purport to activate the suspended sentences: *R.* v. *Peterborough Justices, ex parte Casey* [1979] 1 Cr. App. R. (S) 268; *R.* v. *Folan* [1980] 1 All E.R. 217.

The facts of the subsequent offence *see* under Breach of Suspended Sentences in the introduction.

Subsection (2). The sentence for the original offence may thus be consecutive to any passed by the court, whether on the same occasion or previously or passed by any other court. The proper course is to sentence the offender for the second offence first and then to order that the suspended sentence take effect either concurrently or consecutively: *R.* v. *Ithell* (1969) 133 J.P. 371. "It (is) wrong in principle when an order bringing into force a suspended sentence (is) made for that sentence to be made concurrent unless there (are) some very special circumstances", *per* Lord Parker CJ in *R.* v. *Brown* [1969] Crim. L.R. 20; *R.* v. *Smith* [1977] 64 Cr. App. R. 217. It is submitted that this power cannot extend to two or more suspended sentences passed on the same occasion and expressed by the earlier court to be concurrent. The maximum periods of imprisonment referred to in s. 133 of the Magistrates' Courts Act 1980, do not apply to an order under this subsection.

When an offender subject to a suspended sentence is convicted of a number of offences, some committed before and some after the date of the suspended sentence, the suspended sentence can be put into effect consecutively to the sentences for all the other offences: *R.* v. *Drablow* [1969] Crim. L.R. 501.

To avoid confusion, the *Practice Direction* [1962] 1 All E.R. 417 (noted under the Magistrates' Courts Act 1980, s. 133, *infra.*) should be followed: *R.* v. *Corry* [1973] Crim. L.R. 381. There is no power to antedate the commencement of a suspended sentence when ordering it to be put into effect: *R.* v. *Bell* [1969] Crim. L.R. 670.

When consecutive sentences are imposed the sentencer's duty is to make sure that the totality is not excessive, which he may do either by reducing the period of the instant or the suspended sentence: *R.* v. *Bocskei* [1970] 54 Cr. App. R. 519.

Subsection (7). For a recommended form of notice *see* Annex A to Home Office cir. 209/1967 dated November 13, 1967.

The appropriate officer of the court. Means in relation to a magistrates' court the clerk of the court: s. 57(1) of the Act.

Subsection (9). This subsection creates a right of appeal against orders made under this section.

Court by which suspended sentence may be dealt with

24. (1) An offender may be dealt with in respect of a suspended sentence by the Crown Court or, where the sentence was passed by a magistrates' court, by any magistrates' court before which he appears or is brought.

(2) Where an offender is convicted by a magistrates' court of an offence punishable with imprisonment and the court is satisfied that the offence was committed during the operational period of a suspended sentence passed by the Crown Court—

(*a*)   the court may, if it thinks fit, commit him in custody or on bail to the Crown Court; and

(*b*)   if it does not, shall give written notice of the conviction to the appropriate officer of the Crown Court.

(3) For the purposes of this section and of s. 25 of this Act a suspended sentence passed on an offender on appeal shall be treated as having been passed by the court by which he was originally sentenced.

COMMENTARY

Subsection (1): When the sentence was passed by a magistrates' court. As to suspended sentences passed on appeal *see* subs. (3).

Is brought. That is, under s. 25, *infra*.

Subsection (2): The operational period. Defined in s. 22(1), *supra*.

Commit. There is power to grant legal aid in respect of the proceedings in the Crown Court: Legal Aid Act 1974, ss 28(7) and 30(12).

When committing to the Crown Court under subs. (2), the court may also commit the offender to be dealt with in respect of (*a*) if the offence concerned was an offence triable either way any other offence whatsoever, and (*b*) if the offence concerned was a summary offence, (i) any offence punishable with imprisonment; (ii) any disqualifiable traffic offence and (iii) any breach of a suspended sentence imposed by magistrates: Criminal Justice Act 1967, s. 56(1).

For the power to impose interim disqualification of road traffic offenders *see* the Road Traffic Act 1972, s. 103.

For the location of the Crown Court *see* the Directions of the Lord Chief Justice, paras. 5-9, in Appendix C.

In custody or on bail. *See* the notes to the Magistrates' Courts Act 1980, s. 38, *infra*.

Procedure where court convicting of further offence does not deal with suspended sentence

25. (1) If it appears to the Crown Court, where that court has jurisdiction in accordance with subs. (2) below, or to a justice of the peace having jurisdiction in accordance with that subsection, that an offender has been convicted in Great Britain if an offence punishable with imprisonment committed during the operational period of a suspended sentence, that court or justice may, subject to the following provisions of this section, issue a summons requiring the offender to appear at the place and time specified therein, or a warrant for his arrest.

(2) Jurisdiction for the purposes of subs. (1) above may be exercised—

(*a*)   if the suspended sentence was passed by the Crown Court, by that court;
(*b*)   if it was passed by a magistrates' court, by a justice acting for the area for which that court acted.

(3) Where an offender is convicted by a court in Scotland of an offence punishable with imprisonment and the court is informed that the offence was committed during the operational period of a suspended sentence passed in England or Wales, the court shall give written notice of the conviction to the appropriate officer of the court by which the suspended sentence was passed.

(4) Unless he is acting in consequence of a notice under subs. (3) above, a justice of the peace shall not issue a summons under this section except on information and shall not issue a warrant under this section except on information in writing and on oath.

(5) A summons or warrant issued under this section shall direct the offender to appear or to be brought before the court by which the suspended sentence was passed.

COMMENTARY

Subsection (1).   For the location of the court to which the offender should be summoned or brought *see* subs. (5), and paras. 5-9 of the Directions given by the Lord Chief Justice in Appendix C.

Great Britain. *See* the note to s. 22, *supra*.

An offence punishable with imprisonment. *See* the note to s. 22, *supra*.

The operational period. Defined in s. 22(1), *supra*.

Dealt with. Under s. 23(1), *supra*. If an offender has been convicted of an imprisonable offence during the operational period of a suspended sentence and the convicting court decides to make no order under s. 23(1), *supra*, the effect of these words is to prevent any other court having concurrent jurisdiction from issuing process. It does not, it is submitted, prevent the suspended sentence being brought into force later if the offender should commit any further offence during the operational period.

Issue a summons. For the signature and contents of the summons *see* the Magistrates' Courts Rules 1981, rr. 98 and 100 and form 85. The Summary Jurisdiction (Process) Act, 1881, s. 4 is applied to process under this section by s. 53, *ibid*. And see subs. (4).

Warrant. For the signature execution and contents of a warrant *see* the Magistrates Courts Rules 1981, rr. 95, 96 and 100 and form 86. Warrants remain in force until executed or withdrawn: Magistrates' Courts Act, 1980, s. 125; notwithstanding the death of the issuing justice: s. 124, *ibid*. The warrant may be backed for bail: s. 167, *ibid*. And *see* subs. (4).

For execution in Scotland *see* the Criminal Procedure (Scotland) Act, 1975, s. 17 and in other parts of the United Kingdom, s. 126 of the Magistrates' Courts Act, 1980.

Subsection (3): The court by which the suspended sentence was passed. As to suspended sentences made on appeal *see* s. 24(3), *supra*.

The appropriate officer of the court. *See* the note to s. 23, *supra*.

Subsection (4): On information. *See* form 84.

G.S. Wilkinson in an article at 132 J.P.N. 529 suggested that the period of limitation prescribed by the Magistrates' Courts Act, 1980, s. 127(1) does not apply to an information laid under this section.

Suspended sentence supervision orders

26. (1) Where a court passes on an offender a suspended sentence for a term of more than six months for a single offence, the court may make a suspended sentence supervision order (in this Act referred to as "a supervision order") placing the offender under the supervision of a supervising officer for a period specified in the order, being a period not exceeding the operational period of the suspended sentence.

(2) (*Order making power*).

(3) A supervision order shall specify the petty sessions area in which the offender resides or will reside; and the supervising officer shall be a probation officer appointed for or assigned to the area for the time being specified in the order (whether under this subsection or by virtue of subs. (6) below).

(4) An offender in respect of whom a supervision order is in force shall keep in touch with the supervizing officer in accordance with such instructions as he may from time to time be given by that officer and shall notify him of any change of address.

(5) The court by which a supervision order is made shall forthwith give copies of the order to a probation officer assigned to the court, and he shall give a copy to the offender and the superising officer; and the court shall, except where it is itself a magistrates' court acting for the petty sessions area specified in the order, send to the clerk to the justices for the petty sessions area specified in the order a copy of the order, together with such documents and information relating to the case as it considers likely to be of assistance to a court acting for that area in exercising its functions in relation to the order.

(6) If a magistrates' court acting for the petty sessions area for the time being specified in a supervision order is satisfied that the offender proposes to change, or has changed, his residence from that petty sessions area to another petty sessions area, the court may, and on the application of the supervising officer shall, amend the order by substituting the other petty sessions area for the area specified in the order.

(7) Where a supervision order is amended by a court under subs. (6) above the court shall send to the clerk to the justices for the new area specified in the order a copy of the order, together with such documents and information relating to the case as it considers likely to be of assistance to a court acting for that area in exercising its functions in relation to the order.

(8) A supervision order shall cease to have effect if before the end of the period specified in it—

(a)   a court orders under s. 23 of this Act that a suspended sentence passed in the proceedings in which the order was made shall have effect; or

(b)   the order is discharged or replaced under the subsequent provisions of this section.

(9) A supervision order may be discharged, on the application of the supervising officer or the offender—

(a)   if it was made by the Crown Court and includes a direction reserving the power of discharging it to that court, by the Crown Court;

(b)   in any other case by a magistrates' court acting for the petty sessions area for the time being specified in the order.

(10) Where under s. 23 of this Act a court deals with an offender in respect of a suspended sentence by varying the operational period of the sentence or by making no order with respect to the sentence, the court may make a supervision order in respect of the offender—

(a)   in place of any such order made when the suspended sentence was passed; or

(b)   if the court which passed the sentence could have made such an order but did not do so; or

(c)   if that court could not then have made such an order but would have had power to do so if subs. (1) above had then had effect as it has effect at the time when the offender is dealt with under s. 23.

(11) On making a supervision order the court shall in ordinary language explain its effect to the offender.

COMMENTARY

Since a magistrates' court cannot impose a single sentence longer than six months (Magistrates' Courts Act 1980, s. 31) it cannot make a suspended sentence supervision order. The functions of magistrates with regard to such orders are confined to discharge, variation and breach proceedings.

Subsection (1). A suspended sentence. Means a sentence to which an order under s. 22(1) of this Act applies: s. 57(1), *ibid.*

Subsection (4). A summons or warrant may issue for breach of requirement and a fine imposed under s. 27, *infra.*

Subsection (9). The clerk of the discharging court must notify the court which made the original order: Magistrates' Courts Rules 1981, r. 30(2).

Breach of requirement of suspended sentence supervision order

27. (1) If at any time while a supervision order is in force in respect of an offender it appears on information to a justice of the peace acting for the petty sessions area for the time being specified in the order that the offender has failed to comply with any of the requirements of s. 26(4) of this Act, the justice may issue a summons requiring the offender to appear at the place and time specified therein, or may, if the information is in writing and on oath, issue a warrant for his arrest.

(2) Any summons or warrant issued under this section shall direct the offender

to appear or be brought before a magistrates' court acting for the petty sessions area for the time being specified in the supervision order.

(3) If it is proved to the satisfaction of the court before which an offender appears or is brought under this section that he has failed without reasonable cause to comply with any of the requirements of s. 26(4) the court may, without prejudice to the continuance of the order, impose on him a fine not exceeding £200.

(4) A fine imposed under this section shall be deemed for the purposes of any enactment to be a sum adjudged to be paid by a conviction.

(as amended by the Criminal Justice Act 1982, s. 39, sch. 4).

COMMENTARY

Process under this section may be served or executed in Scotland under s. 4 of the Summary Jurisdiction (Process) Act, 1881: s. 53 of the Act.

Subsection (1): At any time while a supervision order is in force. Thus no action may be taken for breach of requirements after the expiry of the supervision order. Supervision order is defined in s. 26(1), *supra.*

Issue a summons. For the contents and service of the summons see the Magistrates' Courts Rules 1981, rr. 98, 100.

Issue a warrant. For the contents of the warrant see the Magistrates Courts Rules 1981, rr. 95, 96, 100.

Subsection (3). Legal aid may be granted in these proceedings: Legal Aid Act 1974, ss 28(7) and 30(12).

The Costs in Criminal Cases Act 1973, applies: s. 18(4), *ibid.*

A fine. The clerk of the fining court must notify the court which made the original order: Magistrates' Courts Rules 1981, r. 30(3).

Power of Crown Court on committal for sentence

42. (1) Where an offender is committed by a magistrates' court for sentence under s. 38 of the Magistrates' Courts Act, 1980, or s. 62 of the Criminal Justice Act 1967, the Crown Court shall inquire into the circumstances of the case and shall have power to deal with the offender in any manner in which it could deal with him if he had just been convicted of the offence on indictment before the court.

(2) . . .

(as amended by the Magistrates' Courts Act, 1980, sch. 7, the Criminal Justice Act 1982, sch. 14).

COMMENTARY

The Crown Court may issue a warrant for the arrest of a person bailed who fails to appear: Courts Act 1971, s. 13(3).

Evidence with respect of offences punishable in Scotland

52. For the purposes of this Act a certificate purporting to be signed by or on behalf of the Lord Advocate that an offence is punishable in Scotland with imprisonment or is punishable in Scotland on indictment with imprisonment for a term specified in the certificate shall be evidence of the matter so certified.

THE CRIMINAL LAW ACT 1977

Prison sentence partly served and partly suspended

47. (1) Subject to subs. (1A) below, where a court passed on an adult a sentence of imprisonment for a term of not less than three months and not more than two years, it may order that, after he has served part of the sentence in prison, the remainder of it shall be held in suspense.

(1A) A court shall not make an order under this section unless the case appears to the court to be one in which an order under s. 22 of the Powers of Criminal Courts Act 1973 (sentences wholly suspended) would be inappropriate.

(1B) Subs. (1A) above is without prejudice to s. 20 of the Powers of Criminal Courts Act 1973 (restriction on imposing sentences of imprisonment on persons who have not previously served prison sentences).

(2) The part of the sentence to be served in prison shall be not less than twentyeight days and the part to be held in suspense shall be not less than one-quarter of the whole term, and the offender shall not be required to serve the latter part unless it is restored under subs. (3) below; and this shall be explained to him by the court, using ordinary language and stating the substantial effect of that subsection.

(3) If at any time after the making of the order he is convicted of an offence punishable with imprisonment and committed during the whole period of the original sentence, then (subject to subs. (4) and (4A) below) a court which is competent under this subsection may restore the part of the sentence held in suspense and order him to serve it.

(4) If a court considering the offender's case with a view to exercising the powers of subs. (3) above, is of opinion that (in view of all the circumstances, including the facts of the subsequent offence) it would be unjust fully to restore the part of the sentence held in suspense, it shall either restore a lesser part or declare, with reasons given, its decision to make no order under the subsection.

(4A) If an order restoring part of a sentence has been made under subs. (3) above, no order restoring any further part of it may be made.

(5) Where a court exercises those powers, it may direct that the restored part of the original sentence is to take effect as a term to be served either immediately or on the expiration of another term of imprisonment passed on the offender by that or another court.

(6) "Adult" in this section means a person who has attained the age of 21; and "the whole period" of a sentence is the time which the offender would have had to serve in prison if the sentence had been passed without an order under subs. (1) above and he had no remission under s. 25(1) of the Prison Act 1952 (industry and good conduct in prison).

(7) Schedule 9 to this Act has effect with respect to procedural, sentencing and miscellaneous matters ancillary to those dealt with above in this section, including in particular the courts which are competent under subs. (3) above.

(8) This section and paras. 1 to 6 of sch. 9 to this Act and the Powers of Criminal Courts Act 1973 shall be construed and have effect as if this section and those paragraphs of the Schedule were contained in that Act.

(9)-(11) (*Orders*)

(*as amended by the Criminal Justice Act 1982, s. 30.*)

COMMENTARY

See generally the introduction under Partly Suspended Sentences.

Subsection (1): A sentence of imprisonment. By virtue of the Powers of Criminal Courts Act 1973, as applied by subs. (8) of this section, this term does not include a committal in default of payment of any sum of money or for want of sufficient distress to satisfy any sum of money, or for failure to do or abstain from doing anything required to be left undone.

For consecutive terms *see* sch. 9, para. 3A, *infra*.

Subsection (2). There is no rule of law requiring that if part of a sentence is to be suspended it is to be the greater part: *R.* v. *Lunn* [1982] 4 Cr. App. R. (S) 343.

Subsection (4): Make no order. The reasons for the court's decision must be entered in the register: Magistrates' Courts Rules 1981, r. 29(1A).

Subsection (6): Attained the age. A person attains a given age at the commencement of the relevant anniversary of the date of his birth: Family Law Reform Act 1969, s. 9.

SCHEDULE 9

(Section 47)

MATTERS ANCILLARY TO Section 47

Probation orders

1. Where a court makes an order under s. 47(1) above with respect to a sentence of imprisonment, it shall not make a probation order in the offender's case in respect of another offence of which he is convicted by or before that court, or for which he is dealt with by that court.

Courts competent to restore sentence held in suspense

2. (1) In relation to a sentence of imprisonment part of which is held in suspense, the courts competent under s. 47(3) above are—

(*a*)   the Crown Court; and
(*b*)   where the sentence was passed by a magistrates' court, any magistrates' court before which the offender appears or is brought.

(2) Where an offender is convicted by a magistrates' court of an offence punishable with imprisonment and the court is satisfied that the offence was committed during the whole period of a sentence passed by the Crown Court with an order under s. 47(1) above—

(*a*)   it may, if it thinks fit, commit him to custody or on bail to the Crown Court; and
(*b*)   if it does not, it shall give written notice of the conviction to the appropriate officer of that court.

(3) For the purposes of this and the next following paragraph, a sentence of imprisonment passed on an offender with an order under s. 47(1) above shall be treated as having been passed (with such an order) by the court which originally sentenced him.

Recall of offender on re-conviction

3. (1) If it appears to the Crown Court, where that court has jurisdiction in accordance with sub-para. (2) below, or to a justice of the peace having jurisdiction in accordance with that sub-paragraph that an offender has been convicted in Great Britain of an offence punishable with imprisonment committed during the whole period of a sentence passed with an order under s. 47(1) above and that he has not been dealt with in respect of the part cf the sentence held in suspense, that court or justice may, subject to the following provisions of this

paragraph, issue a summons requiring the offender to appear at the place and time specified therein, or a warrant for his arrest.

(2) Jurisdiction for the purposes of sub-para. (1) above may be exercised—

(a)   if the sentence was passed by the Crown Court, by that court;
(b)   if it was passed by a magistrates' court, by a justice acting for the area for which that court acted.

(3)   Where an offender is convicted by a court in Scotland of an offence punishable with imprisonment and the court is informed that the offence was committed during the whole period of a sentence passed in England and Wales with an order under s. 47(1) above, the court shall give written notice of the conviction to the appropriate officer of the court by which the original sentence was passed.

(4)   Unless he is acting in consequence of a notice under sub-para. (3) above, a justice of the peace shall not issue a summons under this paragraph except on information and shall not issue a warrant under this paragraph except on information in writing and on oath.

(5)   A summons or warrant issued under this paragraph shall direct the offender to appear or to be brought before the court by which the original sentence of imprisonment was passed.

Consecutive sentences of imprisonment

3A (1) This paragraph applies where—
(a)   an offender is serving consecutive sentences of imprisonment; and
(b)   at least one of the sentences was passed with an order under s. 47(1) of this Act.

(2) Where this paragraph applies the offender shall, so far as the consecutive sentences are concerned, be treated for the purposes—
(a)   of computing the date when he should be released from prison; and
(b)   of calculating the term of imprisonment liable to be restored under s. 47(3) of this Act,

as if he had been sentenced to a single term of imprisonment with an order under s. 47(1) of this Act of which the part which he is immediately required to serve in prison were the aggregate—
(i)   of the part which he is required to serve in prison of any consecutive sentence passed with an order under s. 47(1) of this Act; and
(ii)   of the whole term of any other consecutive sentence,

and of which the part which is held in suspense were the aggregate of all parts of the sentences which were ordered to be held in suspense under that section.

(3) S. 47(6) of this Act shall have effect, in relation to any consecutive sentence passed with an order under s. 47(1) of this Act, as if for the words following the word "prison" there were substituted the following words "if—
(a)   none of the sentences to which he is subject had been passed with an order under subs. (1) above; and
(b)   he had not had, in respect of any sentence passed with such an order, any remission under s. 25(1) of the Prison Act 1952 (industry and good conduct in prison)".

(4) In this paragraph "a consecutive sentence" means a sentence which is one of two or more sentences of imprisonment the terms of which have

been ordered to run consecutively.

Miscellaneous (procedural)

4. Where the offender is before the Crown Court with a view to the exercise by that court of its powers under s. 47(3) above, any question whether and, if so, when he has been convicted of an offence shall be determined by the court and not by the verdict of a jury.

5. Where the offender has been before a court with a view to its exercising those powers, the appropriate officer shall—

(a) if the court decided not to exercise the powers, record that fact; and
(b) whether or not it exercised them, notify the appropriate officer of the court which passed the original sentence as to the manner in which the offender was dealt with.

6. For the purposes of any enactment conferring rights of appeal in criminal cases, the restoration by a court under s. 47(3) above of a part of a sentence held in suspense shall be treated as a sentence passed on the offender by that court for the original offence, that is to say the offence for which the original sentence was passed with an order under s. 47(1) above.

Miscellaneous (consequential)

7. Subject to s. 60(1C) of the Criminal Justice Act 1967 (release on licence) where a sentence of imprisonment is passed with an order under s. 47(1) above, it is still to be regarded for all purposes as a sentence of imprisonment for the term stated by the court, notwithstanding that part of it is held in suspense by virtue of the order; and, for the avoidance of doubt, a sentence of which part is held in suspense by virtue of such an order is not to be regarded as falling within the expression "suspended sentence" for the purposes of any legislation, instrument or document.

8. Where an offender is sentenced to imprisonment with an order under s. 47 above and, having served part of the sentence in prison, is discharged under s. 25(1) of the Prison Act 1952 (remission for industry and good conduct), the remainder of the sentence being held in suspense, the sentence is not to be regarded as expiring under that section.

9.–11. . . .

(as amended by the Criminal Justice Act 1982, sch. 14.)

THE MAGISTRATES' COURTS ACT 1980

General limit on power of magistrates' court to impose imprisonment

31. (1) Without prejudice to s. 133 below, a magistrates' court shall not have power to impose imprisonment or youth custody for more than six months in respect of any one offence.

(2) Unless expressly excluded, subs. (1) above shall apply even if the offence in question is one for which a person would otherwise be liable on summary conviction to imprisonment or youth custody for more than six months.

(3) Any power of a magistrates' court to impose a term of imprisonment for non-payment of a fine, or for want of sufficient distress to satisfy a fine, shall not be limited by virtue of subs. (1) above.

(4) In subs. (3) above "fine" includes a pecuniary penalty but does not include a pecuniary forfeiture for pecuniary compensation.

(as amended by the Criminal Justice Act 1982, sch. 14.)

COMMENTARY

Subsection (1).   This does not affect the power in the Magistrates' Courts Act 1980 s. 133, to pass consecutive sentences in excess of six months in aggregate.

Impose imprisonment.   Means pass a sentence of imprisonment or fix a term of imprisonment for failure to pay any sum of money, or for want of sufficient distress to satisfy any sum of money, or for failure to do or abstain from doing anything required to be done or left undone: s. 150(1) of the Act.

Subsection (3): Fine.   See subs. (4).

Committal for sentence on summary trial of offence triable either way

38.   Where on the summary trial of an offence triable either way (not being an offence as regards which this section is excluded by s. 33 above) a person who is not less than 17 years old is convicted of the offence, then, if on obtaining information about his character and antecedents the court is of opinion that they are such that greater punishment should be inflicted for the offence than the court has power to inflict, the court may, in accordance with s. 56 of the Criminal Justice Act 1967, commit him in custody or on bail to the Crown Court for sentence in accordance with the provisions of s. 42 of the Powers of Criminal Courts Act 1973.

COMMENTARY

Failure to warn the accused of the court's powers to commit for sentence before taking his consent to summary trial invalidates any subsequent committal under this section.

Where justices purport to commit for sentence in a case where they have no such power the proceedings are a nullity: *R. v. South Greenhoe JJ, ex parte Director of Public Prosecutions* (1950) 114 J.P. 312; *R. v. Jones (Gwyn)* (1969) 133 J.P. 144.

An order may be made under this section in addition to a committal to the Crown Court with a view to a restriction order: Mental Health Act 1983, s. 37.

When magistrates commit an offender to the Crown Court under this section they may also commit him in respect of any other offence whatsoever: Criminal Justice Act 1967, s. 56(1).

When committing under this power the magistrates relinquish all other powers and duties with respect to the offender to the Crown Court: Criminal Justice Act, 1967, s. 56(5), *infra*. But they do have power to order interim disqualification under the Road Traffic Act, 1972, s. 103.

Appeal. A committal under this section is not an "order made on conviction" and there is, therefore, no right to appeal against such a committal: *R. v. London Sessions Appeal Committee, ex parte Rogers* (1951) 115 J.P. 108; the remedy of a man wrongly committed is by way of prerogative order: *R. v. Warren* (1954) 118 J.P. 238; *R. v. Jones (Gwyn), supra.* But there is a right of appeal against conviction on a plea of not guilty and if dealt with before the normal time for appeal has expired the Crown Court should, before passing sentence, ascertain whether the defendant intends to appeal against conviction: *R. v. Faithful* (1950) 115 J.P. 20. A plea of guilty which is not unambiguous may be changed even after a committal for sentence, but the proper court to order this at that late stage is the Crown Court and not the magistrates' court: *R. v. Mutford and Lothingland Justices, ex parte Harber* (1971) 135 J.P. 107; *R. v. Inner London Crown Court, ex parte Sloper* [1979] 69 Cr. App. R. 1.

Legal Aid. The magistrates have power to grant legal aid in respect of the proceedings in the Crown Court: Legal Aid Act 1974, s. 28(7). "If a lower court has it in mind, having regard to the gravity of the offence charged or the number of offences which are charged or for other reasons, that a heavy sentence is called for, it is most desirable that the accused should be offered legal aid . . . and we take the view that, in the circumstances already indicated, the court should take it on itself to offer legal aid to the accused so that, albeit there may be guilty pleas before the court, any matters which even remotely tell in favour of the accused may be properly advanced through a skilled advocate to the court and so may be properly brought adequately to their attention and then considered by them", *per* Edmund Davies LJ in *R. v. Serghiou* [1966] 3 All E.R. 637. And *see* also *R. v. Green* [1968] 2 All E.R. 77, at p. 80.

The Justices' duty. It is the duty of justices to make proper inquiry of the facts before agreeing to summary trial, particularly in the case of assaults: *R. v. Hartlepool Justices, ex parte King* [1973] Crim. L.R. 637 (*certiorari* issued to quash a committal for sentence when the justices regretted their decision for summary trial after hearing the facts of the case).

However, in *R. v. Lymm JJ, ex parte Brown* (1973) 137 J.P. 269 it was held that failure to make inquiry about the sufficiency of punishment did not inhibit the power to commit for sentence where the court later learnt that the offender was a police officer. When, following a plea of guilty, the magistrates learned that the circumstances of the offence were graver than they had believed (head injuries) and that the accused had failed to show remorse, these factors did not justify a committal for sentence because they did not relate to the character and antecedents of the offender: *R. v. Warrington Justices, ex parte Mooney* [1980] 2 Cr. App. R. (S) 40. There must be some change of circumstances from the situation as it was known to the magistrates when they decided to try the case summarily: *R. v. Derby Magistrates, ex parte McCarthy* [1980] 2 Cr. App. R. (S) 140; *R. v. Derby and South Derbyshire Magistrates, ex parte McCarthy and McGovern* (1981) April 28; 145 JP.N. 735.

An offence triable either way. Defined in the Interpretation Act 1978, sch. 1, as meaning an offence which, if committed by an adult, is triable either on indictment or summarily.

Excluded by s. 33. This relates to certain offences of criminal damage tried summarily.

A person. The powers under this section do not apply to a corporation: para. 5 of sch. 3 of the Act.

Not less than 17 years old. For the determination of age *see* the Magistrates' Courts Act, 1980, s. 150(4).

Character and antecedents. "'character'. . .relates to something more than the fact that a person has been previously convicted, and the word 'antecedents' is as wide as can be conceived", *per* Lord Goddard CJ in *R. v. Vallett* (1951) 115 J.P. 103 (a "shameless thief" who asked for 96 other offences to be taken into consideration). Thus, an offender who asked for 19 other offences to be taken into consideration involving a systematic fraud of £5,000 can be committed under this section: *R. v. Harlow Justices, ex parte Galway* [1975] Crim. L.R. 288. Equally, a defendant with no previous convictions not asking for offences to be taken into consideration may be committed under this section in respect of a series of thefts over a long period: *R. v. King's Lynn Justices, ex parte Carter* (1969) 133 J.P. 103. That decision is not a charter for magistrates to deal with cases summarily rather than commit them for trial: *per* Lord Parker CJ in *R. v. Tower Bridge Magistrate, ex parte Osman* (1971) 135 J.P. 427. *See* also under The Justices' Duty above.

Greater punishment. A suspended sentence coupled with a supervision order (which can only be for a period in excess of six months) is greater punishment than a forthwith sentence for a lesser period: *R. v. Rugby Justices, ex parte Prince* [1974] 2 All E.R. 116.

In accordance with s. 56 of the Criminal Justice Act 1967. For the documents to be sent to the Crown Court, *see* the Magistrates' Courts Rules 1981, r. 17(1).

On bail. "In the opinion of this court the cases must be rare when justices can properly commit (under this section) on bail because the whole purpose of the committal is to have the man sent to prison for a longer period than the justices can send him to prison", *per* Lord Parker CJ in *R. v. Coe* (1969) 133 J.P. 103. The general right to bail does not apply: Bail Act, 1976, s. 4(2).

The High Court has power to admit to bail where it is offered on unacceptable terms: Criminal Justice Act 1967, s. 22. The Crown Court has similar powers under the Courts Act 1971, s. 13(4). If the defendant is committed on bail, the governor of the appropriate prison, etc., must be notified: Magistrates' Courts Rules 1981, r. 17(3). Forfeiture of recognizances is a matter for the Crown Court.

In custody. The general right to bail does not apply: Bail Act, 1976, s. 4(2).

Committals must be by warrant: Magistrates' Courts Rules 1981, r. 94. For the form of warrant *see* form 39. For the place of commitment of persons under 21 years *see* the Criminal Justice Act, 1948, s. 27.

To the Crown Court. For the location of the Crown Court to which the offender should be committed see paras. 5-9 of the Directions of the Lord Chief Justice in Appendix C.

Minimum term

132. A magistrates' court shall not impose imprisonment for less than five days.

COMMENTARY

Impose imprisonment.   *See* the note to s. 31, *supra.*

Committals in default following part payment of a fine are not subject to this restriction: Magistrates' Courts Rules 1981, r. 55(5). Nor are orders of detention under ss 134, 135, 136 of the Act.

Consecutive terms of imprisonment

133.   (1) A magistrates' court imposing imprisonment or youth custody on any person may order that the term of imprisonment or youth custody shall commence on the expiration of any other term of imprisonment or youth custody imposed by that or any other court; but where a magistrates' court imposes two or more terms of imprisonment or youth custody to run consecutively the aggregate of such terms shall not, subject to the provisions of this section, exceed six months.

(2) If two or more of the terms imposed by the court are imposed in respect of an offence triable either way which was tried summarily otherwise than in pursuance of s. 22(2) above, the aggregate of the terms so imposed and any other terms imposed by the court may exceed six months but shall not, subject to the following provisions of this section, exceed 12 months.

(3) The limitations imposed by the preceding subsections shall not operate to reduce the aggregate of the terms that the court may impose in respect of any offences below the term which the court has power to impose in respect of any one of those offences.

(4) Where a person has been sentenced by a magistrates' court to imprisonment and a fine for the same offence a period of imprisonment imposed for non-payment of the fine, or for want of sufficient distress to satisfy the fine, shall not be subject to the limitations imposed by the preceding subsections.

(5) For the purposes of this section a term of imprisonment shall be deemed to be imposed in respect of an offence if it is imposed as a sentence or in default of payment of a sum adjudged to be paid by the conviction or for want of sufficient distress to satisfy such a sum.

(as amended by the Criminal Justice Act 1982, sch. 14.)

COMMENTARY

For the use of Consecutive Sentences *see* the introduction.

Subsection (1). This subsection limits only the total imprisonment etc. imposed on the same occasion: *Forrest* v. *Brighton Justices* [1981] 2 All E.R. 711 (alternatives of imprisonment in default of payment of fine).

Imposing imprisonment. See the note to s. 31, *supra* and *see R.* v. *Metropolitan Stipendiary Magistrate for South Westminster, ex parte Green* (1977) 141 J.P. 151.

Subsection (2): An offence triable either way.   See the note to s. 38, *supra.*

In pursuance of s. 22(2).   This refers to certain offences of criminal damage.

Detention in police cells, etc

134.   (1) A magistrates' court having power to impose imprisonment on any person may instead of doing so order him to be detained for any period not exceeding four days in a place certified by the Secretary of State to be suitable for the purpose.

(2) The Secretary of State may certify under this section any police cells, bridewell or similar place provided by him and on the application of any other

police authority, any such place provided by that authority.

(3) A woman or girl shall not be detained in any such place except under the supervision of women.

Section 6(*b*) of the Interpretation Act 1978 (feminine includes masculine) does not apply for the purposes of this subsection.

(4) (*Regulations*).

(5), (6)...

(7) Subsection (2) above shall, in its application to the City of London, have effect as if for the references therein to the police authority there were substituted references to the Commissioner of Police for the City of London.

(8) This section shall have effect in relation to a person aged 17 or over but less than 21 as if references in it to imprisonment were references to youth custody.

(*as amended by the Criminal Justice Act 1982, sch. 14.*)

COMMENTARY

Subsection (1): Power to impose imprisonment.   *See* the note to s. 31, *supra*.

Imprisonment here includes youth custody: subs. (8).

Detained . . . in a place certified.   An order under this section is not a sentence of imprisonment and may not be suspended under the Powers of Criminal Courts Act 1973, s. 22. Committal must be by warrant: Magistrates' Courts Rules 1981, r. 94. *See* form 57. The order of detention should be so described in the register: Home Office cir. 35/52/C dated February 15, 1952.

The making of such an order does not deprive the court of its powers to order costs or compensation: Magistrates' Courts Act 1980, s. 150(7).

Subsection (2): Police authority.   Defined in s. 62 and sch. 8 of the Police Act 1964. And *see* subs. (7).

Detention of offender for one day in court-house or police station

135.   (1) A magistrates' court that has power to commit to prison a person convicted of an offence, or would have that power but for ss 82 or 88 above, may order him to be detained within the precincts of the court-house or at any police station until such hour, not later than 8 o'clock in the evening of the day on which the order is made, as the court may direct, and, if it does so, shall not, where it has power to commit him to prison, exercise that power.

(2) A court shall not make such an order under this section as will deprive the offender of a reasonable opportunity of returning to his abode on the day of the order.

(3) This section shall have effect in relation to a person aged 17 or over but less than 21 as if references in it to prison were references to detention under s. 9 of the Criminal Justice Act 1982 (detention of persons aged 17 to 20 for default).

(*as amended by the Criminal Justice Act 1982, sch. 14.*)

COMMENTARY

Subsection (1): Power to commit to prison.   For example, by way of sentence of imprisonment or in default of payment of fines or under the Magistrates' Courts Act 1980, ss. 75(3) or 84. This term includes detention under s. 9 of the Criminal Justice Act (detention of persons aged 17-20 for default) but not, seemingly, as a sentence for persons of that age.

Or would have that power but for.   Thus, an order under this section is not subject to the restrictions on imposing alternatives to a fine on conviction, the need to hold a means inquiry, nor the need to receive a report from a fines supervision officer.

Order him to be detained.   No warrant is necessary. The order of detention should be so described in the register: Home Office cir. 35/53/C, dated February 15, 1952.

The making of such an order does not deprive the court of the power to order payment of costs or compensation: s. 150(7) of the Act.

Committal to custody overnight at police station for non-payment of sum adjudged by conviction

136. (1) A magistrates' court that has power to commit to prison a person in default of payment of a sum adjudged to be paid by a summary conviction, or would have that power but for ss 82 or 88 above, may issue a warrant for his detention in a police station, and, if it does so, shall not, where it has power to commit him to prison, exercise that power.

(2) A warrant under this section, unless the sum adjudged to be paid by the conviction is sooner paid—

(*a*)   shall authorize any police constable to arrest the defaulter and take him to a police station, and

(*b*)   shall require the officer in charge of the station to detain him there until 8 o'clock in the morning of the day following that on which he is arrested, or, if he is arrested between midnight and 8 o'clock in the morning, until 8 o'clock in the morning of the day on which he is arrested.

(4) The Secretary of State may make regulations for the inspection of places certified by him under this section, for the treatment of persons detained in them and generally for the purpose of carrying this section into effect.

(5) Any expenses incurred in the maintenance of persons detained under this section shall be defrayed out of moneys provided by Parliament.

(6) . . .

(7) Subsection (2) above shall, in its application to the City of London, have effect as if for the references therein to the police authority there were substituted references to the Commissioner of Police for the City of London.

COMMENTARY

The power under this section may be used for enforcing payment of fines compensation and costs but not as an alternative to a sentence of imprisonment.

Or would have that power but for. *See* the note to s. 135, *supra*.

Subsection (1): Power to commit to prison. This excludes offenders under 21: Criminal Justice Act 1982, s. 1(1).

Issue a warrant. *See* form 58.

THE CRIMINAL JUSTICE ACT 1982

General restriction on custodial sentences.

1. (1) Subject to subs. (2) below, no court shall pass a sentence of imprisonment on a person under 21 years of age or commit such a person to prison for any reason.

(2) Nothing in subs. (1) above shall prevent the committal to prison of a person under 21 years of age who is remanded in custody or committal in custody for trial or sentence.

(3) No court shall pass a sentence of Borstal training.

(4) Where a person under 21 years of age is convicted or found guilty of an offence, the court may not—

(a) make a detention centre order in respect of him under s. 4 below;
(b) pass a youth custody sentence on him under s. 6 below; or
(c) pass a sentence of custody for life on him under s. 8(2) below,
unless it is of the opinion that no other method of dealing with him is appropriate because it appears to the court that he is unable or unwilling to respond to non-custodial penalties or because a custodial sentence is necessary for the protection of the public or because the offence was so serious that a non-custodial sentence cannot be justified.

(5) No court shall commit a person under 21 years of age to be detained under s. 9 below unless it is of the opinion that no other method of dealing with him is appropriate.

(6) For the purpose of any provision of this Act which requires the determination of the age of a person by the court or the Secretary of State his age shall be deemed to be that which it appears to the court or the Secretary of State (as the case may be) to be after considering any available evidence.

COMMENTARY

For the effects of this section *see* Restrictions on Custodial Sentences on Young Offenders in the introduction.

Subsection (4). For the purpose of this subsection the court must obtain and consider certain information (s. 2(1), *infra*) and, unless it is unnecessary, obtain a social inquiry report (s. 2(2), (3), *infra*.)

Further restrictions on imposing the sentences mentioned in this subsection on an unrepresented defendant are contained in s. 3, *infra*.

Before making a detention centre order or passing a youth custody sentence the court must consider that a custodial sentence is the only appropriate method of dealing with the offender: ss. 4(1), 6(1), *infra*, respectively.

Subsection (5). For the purpose of this subsection the court must obtain and consider certain information: subs. 2(1), *infra*.

Social inquiry reports etc.

2. (1) For the purpose of determining whether there is any appropriate method of dealing with a person under 21 years of age other than a method whose use in the case of such a person is restricted by s. 1(4) or (5) above the court shall obtain and consider information about the circumstances and shall take into account any information before the court which is relevant to his character and his physical and mental condition.

(2) Subject to subs. (3) below, the court shall in every case obtain a social inquiry report for the purpose of determining whether there is any appropriate method of dealing with a person other than a method whose use is restricted by s. 1(4) above.

(3) Subsection (2) above does not apply if, in the circumstances of the case, the court is of the opinion that it is unnecessary to obtain a social inquiry report.

(4) Where a magistrates' court deals with a person under 21 years of age by a method whose use in the case of such a person is restricted by section 1(4) above, it shall state in open court the reason for its opinion that no other method of dealing with him is appropriate because it appears to the court that he is unable or unwilling to respond to non-custodial penalties or because a custodial sentence is necessary for the protection of the public or

because the offence was so serious that a non-custodial sentence cannot be justified.

(5) Where a magistrates' court deals with a person under 21 years of age by a method whose use in the case of such a person is restricted by s. 1(5) above, it shall state in open court the reason for its opinion that no other method of dealing with him is appropriate.

(6) Where a magistrates' court deals with a person under 21 years of age by a method whose use in the case of such a person is restricted by s. 1(4) above without obtaining a social inquiry report, it shall state in open court the reason for its opinion that it was unnecessary to obtain such a report.

(7) A magistrates' court shall cause a reason stated under subss. (4), (5) or (6) above to be specified in the warrant of commitment and to be entered in the register.

(8) No sentence or order shall be invalidated by the failure of a court to comply with subs. (2) above, but any other court on appeal from that court shall obtain a social inquiry report if none was obtained by the court below, unless it is of the opinion that in the circumstances of the case it is unnecessary to do so.

(9) In determining whether it should deal with the appellant by a method different from that by which the court below dealt with him the court hearing the appeal shall consider any social inquiry report obtained by it or by the court below.

(10) In this section "social inquiry report" means a report about a person and his circumstances made by a probation officer or by a social worker of a local authority social services department.

COMMENTARY

Subsection (1). It is submitted that this merely re-enacts the practice at common law concerning the usual matters presented to the court by the prosecution and the defence.

Subsection (2). The words "in every case" seem otiose. *See* also subs. (8).

Social inquiry report. Defined in subs. (1) in terms which are not confined to a written report. However, unless the defendant and his circumstances are already well known to the reporting officer the calling for a "stand-down" report is regarded as bad practice where a full report is needed.

Subsection (3): Unnecessary. Not merely inconvenient. Where a defendant in the course of a long trial put his character in and the judge went into his background a report was held to be unnecessary: *R.* v. *Peter* [1975] Crim. L.R. 593. And *see* subss. (6) and (7).

Subsection (4). This appears to require the court to stipulate, not only which of the s. 1(4) criteria it relies on, but the reason why it does so. *See* also subs. (7).

Subsection (5). *See* also subs. (7).

Subsection (6). *See* also subs. (7).

Subsection (10). *See* the note "Social inquiry report" above.

Restriction on imposing custodial sentences on persons under 21 not legally represented.

3. (1) A magistrates' court on summary conviction or the Crown Court on committal for sentence or on conviction on indictment shall not—
    (*a*) make a detention centre order under s. 4 below;
    (*b*) pass a youth custody sentence under s. 6 below;

(c)   pass a sentence of custody for life under s. 8(2) below; or
(d)   make an order for detention under s. 53(2) of the Children and
      Young Persons Act 1933,
in respect of or on a person who is not legally represented in that court,
unless either—
   (i)   he applied for legal aid and the application was refused on the
         ground that it did not appear his means were such that he
         required assistance; or
   (ii) having been informed of his right to apply for legal aid and had
         the opportunity to do so, he refused or failed to apply.
(2) For the purposes of this section a person is to be treated as legally
represented in a court if, but only if, he has the assistance of counsel or a
solicitor to represent him in the proceedings in that court at some time after
he is found guilty and before he is sentenced, and in subs. (1)(i) and (ii)
above "legal aid" means legal aid for the purposes of proceedings in that
court, whether the whole proceedings or the proceedings on or in relation
to sentence; but in the case of a person committed to the Crown Court for
sentence or trial, it is immaterial whether he applied for legal aid in the
Crown Court to, or was informed of his right to apply by, that court or the
court which committed him.

COMMENTARY

Compare the notes to the Powers of Criminal Courts Act 1973, s. 21, *supra*.

Orders for detention of male offenders aged 14 to 20.

4. (1) Where—
   (a)   a male offender under 21 but not less than 14 years of age is con-
         victed of an offence which is punishable with imprisonment in
         the case of a person aged 21 or over; and
   (b)   the court considers—
      (i)   that the only appropriate method of dealing with him is to pass
            a custodial sentence on him; but
      (ii) that the term of such a sentence should be no more than four
            months,
the order that the court is to make, subject to the provisions of this section
and to s. 5(2) below, is an order for his detention centre for such period,
not exceeding four months, as it considers appropriate.
   (2) If the maximum term of imprisonment that a court could impose for
an offence is less than four months, the maximum term of detention it may
specify for that offence in a detention centre order is the same as the
maximum term of imprisonment.
   (3) Subject to subs. (4) below, no order may be made under this section
for the detention of an offender in a detention centre for less than 21 days.
   (4) A court may order the detention of an offender in a detention centre
for less than 21 days for an offence under s. 15(11) below.
   (5) Subject to subs. (6) below, a court shall not make an order under this
section for the detention of an offender in a detention centre—
   (a)   if it considers that his detention in such a centre would be un-
         suitable because of his mental or physical condition; or
   (b)   if he is serving or has ever served a sentence—
      (i)   of imprisonment;
      (ii) of detention under s. 53 of the Children and Young Persons
            Act 1933 (detention on conviction of certain grave crimes);

    (iii) of Borstal training;
    (iv) of youth custody under s. 6 below; or
    (v) of custody for life under s. 8 below.

(6) A court may make an order under this section for the detention in a detention centre of an offender who has served a sentence of a description specified in subs. 5(*b*) above if it appears to the court that there are special circumstances (whether relating to the offence or to the offender) which warrant the making of such an order in his case.

(7) An order under this section is referred to in this Act as a "detention centre order".

COMMENTARY

The effects of this section are summarized in the introduction under Detention Centres.

For the limitations of passing a detention centre sentence *see* ss. 1(4), 2(1)-(4), (6), (7). For restrictions on sentencing an unrepresented defendant *see* s. 3.

For the determination of age *see* s. 1(6), *supra*.

Section (1): Four months. That is, calendar months: Interpretation Act 1978, sch.

Subsection (5). Where a detention centre order is precluded by this subsection a youth custody sentence may be passed for less than the usual period of youth custody: ss. 6(2) and 7(6).

Consecutive terms and aggregate periods of detention.

5. (1) Subject to the provisions of this section, any court which makes a detention centre order may direct that the term of detention under the order shall commence on the expiration of a term of detention under another detention centre order.

(2) No court shall—
    (*a*) make a detention centre order in respect of an offender who is subject to another such order; or
    (*b*) give a direction under subs. (1) above,
if the effect would be that the offender would be ordered to be detained in a detention centre for more than four months at a time.

(3) If a court makes such an order or gives such a direction in respect of an offender aged less than 15 years, so much of the aggregate of all the terms of detention in a detention centre to which he is subject as exceeds four months shall be treated as remitted.

(4) If a court makes such an order or gives such a direction in respect of an offender aged 15 years or over, he shall be treated for all purposes as if he had been sentenced to a term of youth custody equal to the aggregate of all the terms of detention in a detention centre to which he is subject.

(5) Where—
    (*a*) an offender not less than 15 years of age is serving a term of detention in a detention centre; and
    (*b*) on his conviction of an offence the court by which he is convicted considers that the only appropriate method of dealing with him is to pass a custodial sentence on him; and
    (*c*) the length of sentence which the court considers appropriate is such that the period for which he would be ordered to be detained by virtue of the sentence, together with the period for which any detention centre order to which he is subject directed

that he should be detained, would exceed four months,
the sentence that the court is to pass is a youth custody sentence for the
term which it considers appropriate.

(6) Where a court passes a youth custody sentence on an offender under
subs. (5) above, it shall direct that any detention centre order to which he is
subject at the time of the conviction for which the youth custody sentence
is imposed shall be treated for all purposes as if it had been a sentence of
youth custody.

(7) Where a detention centre order is treated as a sentence of youth
custody by virtue of this section, the portion of the term of detention imposed by the order which the offender has already served shall be deemed
to have been a portion of a term of youth custody.

COMMENTARY

The effect of this section is to permit consecutive detention centre orders to be made subject
to an overriding aggregate of four months. Excess terms are automatically converted to
youth custody if the offender is 15 or older (subs. (4)). The excess is remitted if he is under
that age (subs. (3)).

Youth custody: offenders aged 15 to 20.

6. (1) Subject to s. 8 below and to s. 53 of the Children and Young Persons Act 1933, where—
- (a)   a person under 21 but not less than 15 years of age is convicted
  of an offence which is punishable with imprisonment in the case
  of a person aged 21 or over; and
- (b)   the court considers for reasons which shall be stated in open
  court that the only appropriate method of dealing with the offender is to pass a custodial sentence; and
- (c)   either—
  - (i)   the court considers that it would be appropriate to sentence the
    offender to a term of more than four months, or where the of-
    fender has been convicted of more than one offence, to terms
    of more than four months in the aggregate; or
  - (ii)   the case falls within subss. (2) or (4) below, the sentence that
    the court is to pass is a sentence of youth custody.

(2) A case falls within this subsection where the offender is male and the
court determines—
- (a)   that a sentence of four months or less would be appropriate; but
- (b)   that a detention centre order is precluded by s. 4(5) above.

(3) If a court passes a sentence of youth custody on an offender because
it considers that his detention in a detention centre would be unsuitable
because of his mental condition, it shall certify in the warrant of commitment that it passed the sentence of youth custody for that reason.

(4) A case falls within this subsection if the offender is female and has attained the age of 17 years.

(5) A sentence under this section is referred to in this Act as a "youth
custody sentence".

COMMENTARY

For the effects of this section *see* Youth Custody in the introduction.

For the determination of age *see* s. 1(6), *supra*. For the place of detention *see* s. 12, *infra*.

300   6.   CUSTODIAL SENTENCES

Subsection (1): Reasons. *See* s. 1(4), *supra*.

Subsection (2). If the offender is sentenced to youth custody because a detention centre order would be unsuitable by reason of his mental condition the place of detention is to be determined in accordance with s. 12(3), *infra*.

Youth custody: length of term.

7. (1) Subject to subs. (8) below, the maximum term of youth custody that a court may impose for an offence is the same as the maximum term of imprisonment that it may impose for that offence.

(2) Subject to subs. (8) below, where—
   (a)   an offender is convicted of more than one offence for which he is liable to a sentence of youth custody; or
   (b)   an offender who is serving a youth custody sentence is convicted of one or more further offences for which he is liable to such a sentence,

the court shall have the same power to pass consecutive youth custody sentences as if they were sentences of imprisonment.

(3) Where an offender who—
   (a)   is serving a youth custody sentence; and
   (b)   is aged over 21 years.

is convicted of one or more further offences for which he is liable to imprisonment, the court shall have the power to pass one or more sentences of imprisonment to run consecutively upon the youth custody sentence.

(4) Subject to subss. (6) and (7) below, a court shall not pass a youth custody sentence on an offender whose effect would be that he would be sentenced to a total term which is less than the usual term of youth custody.

(5) The usual term of youth custody is a term exceeding four months.

(6) If a case falls within s. 6(2) or (4) above, the term of youth custody to which the offender is sentenced may be less than the usual term but not less than 21 days.

(7) A court may pass a sentence of youth custody for less than 21 days for an offence under s. 15(11) below.

(8) (*Juvenile court.*)

(9) In subs. (4) above "total term" means—
   (a)   in the case of an offender sentenced to two or more terms of youth custody which are consecutive or wholly or partly concurrent, the aggregate of those terms;
   (b)   in the case of any other offender, the term of the youth custody sentence in question.

COMMENTARY

For the determination of age *see* s. 1(6), *supra*.

Subsection (2): The same power. That is, consecutive terms may be passed up to six months in aggregate or twelve months if two or more of the offences are triable either way: Magistrates' Courts Act 1980, s. 133, *supra*.

Subsection (4): Total term. *See* subs. (9).

The usual term of youth custody. *See* subs. (5).

Detention of persons aged 17 to 20 for default or contempt.

9. (1) In any case where, but for s. 1(1) above, a court would have power—

(a)   to commit a person under 21 but not less than 17 years of age to prison for default in payment of a fine or any other sum of money; or

(b)   to make an order fixing a term of imprisonment in the event of such a default by such a person; or

(c)   to commit such a person to prison for contempt of court or any kindred offence,

the court shall have power, subject to s. 1(5) above, to commit him to be detained under this section or, as the case may be, to make an order fixing a term of detention under this section in the event of default, for a term not exceeding the term of imprisonment.

(2) (*County Court*).

COMMENTARY

For the determination of age *see* s. 1(6), *supra.*

Subsection (1). Note that the making of an order under this section is subject to s. 1(5), *supra* (no other method appropriate). That in turn attracts ss. 2(1), (5) and (7).

Contempt of court. That is, under the Contempt of Court Act 1981, s. 12 or under the Magistrates' Courts Act 1980, s. 97(4).

Kindred offence. This clearly applies to offences under the Magistrates' Courts Act 1980, s. 63(3) (disobedience of an order of the court). *See* Ch. 14.

Detained under this section. *See* s. 12(10), *infra.*

Accommodation of young offenders and defaulters etc.

12. (1) Subject to subs. (11) below, a male offender sentenced to youth custody shall be detained in a youth custody centre—

(a)   if the term of his youth custody sentence is more than four but not more than 18 months; and

(b)   if the term is not treated by virtue of s. 67 of the Criminal Justice Act 1967 as reduced to less than 21 days,

unless the Secretary of State gives a direction for his detention in a prison under subs. (4) below.

(2) (*Juveniles*)

(3) Subject to subs. (11) below, an offender who has been sentenced to youth custody because the court considered that his detention in a detention centre would be unsuitable because of his mental condition is to be detained in a youth custody centre or in a remand centre as the Secretary of State may from time to time direct unless—

(a)   the term of his youth custody sentence is treated by virtue of s. 67 of the Criminal Justice Act 1967 as reduced to less than 21 days; or

(b)   he has been sentenced under s. 15(11) below to youth custody for less than 21 days; or

(c)   the Secretary of State gives a direction for his detention in a prison under subs. (4) below.

(4) The Secretary of State may from time to time direct that—

(a)   an offender who falls to be detained in a youth custody centre by

virtue of subs. (1) above; or
  (b)   an offender who falls to be detained in a youth custody centre or
        a remand centre by virtue of subss. (2) or (3) above,
is instead to be detained for any temporary purpose in a prison.
  (5) Any offender sentenced to youth custody, other than an offender
who falls to be detained in a youth custody centre by virtue of subs. (1)
above or an offender who falls to be detained in a youth custody centre or
a remand centre by virtue of subss. (2) or (3) above, is to be detained—
  (a)   in a youth custody centre;
  (b)   in a remand centre; or
  (c)   in a prison,
as the Secretary of State may from time to time direct.
  (6), (7) . . .
  (8) Where a detention centre order has been made in respect of an offender aged 15 years or over, the Secretary of State may from time to time
direct that he shall be detained for any temporary purpose in a youth
custody centre of a prison instead of a detention centre.
  (9)   Where   in   the   case   of   an   offender   aged   15   years   or
over—   (a)   either—
        (i)   a detention centre order has been made; and
        (ii) the term for which he is ordered to be detained is treated by
              virtue of s. 67 of the Criminal Justice Act 1967 as reduced to
              less than 21 days; or
  (b)   he is ordered under s. 15(11) below to be detained in a detention
        centre for less than 21 days,
the Secretary of State may from time to time direct that he is to be detained
(otherwise than for a temporary purpose) in a remand centre, a youth
custody centre or (where the offender is aged 17 or over) a prison instead
of a detention centre.
  (10) A person in respect of whom an order has been made under s. 9
above is to be detained—
  (a)   in a remand centre;
  (b)   in a detention centre;
  (c)   in a youth custody centre; or
  (d)   in any place in which a person aged 21 years or over could be
        imprisoned or detained for default in payment of a fine or any
        other sum of money,
as the Secretary of State may from time to time direct.
  (11) This section is without prejudice—
  (a)   to s. 22(2)(b) of the Prison Act 1952 (removal to hospital etc.);
        and
  (b)   to s. 43(3) of that Act (detention in remand centre for a tem-
        porary purpose or for the purpose of providing maintenance and
        domestic services).

Release of young offenders.

  15. (1) Subject to subs. (13) below, if subss. (2), (3) or (4) below applies to
a person under 22 years of age who is released from a term of detention
under a detention centre order of a term of youth custody, he shall be under the supervision of a probation officer or a social worker of a local
authority social services department.
  (2) This subsection applies to a person who was neither granted
remission nor released on licence.
  (3) This subsection applies to a person who was granted remission.

6. Custodial Sentences

(4) This subsection applies to a person—
  (a) who was under 21 years of age when sentence was passed on him; and
  (b) who is released on licence; and
  (c) whose licence expires less than 12 months after his release.

(5) The supervision period ends on the offender's 22nd birthday if it has not ended before.

(6) Subject to subs. (5) above, where subs. (2) above applies, the supervision period begins on the offender's release and ends three months from his release.

(7) Subject to subs. (5) above and to subs. (9) below, where subs. (3) above applies, the supervision period begins on the offender's release and ends—
  (a) three months from his release; or
  (b) on the date on which his sentence would have expired if he had not been granted remission,
whichever is the later.

(8) Subject to subs. (5) above and to subs. (9) below, where subs. (4) above applies, the supervision period begins when the offender's licence expires and ends on the date on which he would have been released if he had never been granted remission or released on licence.

(9) If the date mentioned in subss. (7)(b) or (8) above is more than 12 months from the date of the offender's release, the supervision period ends 12 months from the date of his release.

(10) While a person is under supervision by virtue of this section, he shall comply with such requirements, if any, as may for the time being be specified in a notice from the Secretary of State.

(11) A person who without reasonable excuse fails to comply with a requirement imposed under subs. (10) above shall be guilty of an offence and liable on summary conviction—
  (a) to a fine not exceeding £200; or
  (b) to an appropriate custodial sentence for a period not exceeding 30 days.

(12) In subsection (11) above "appropriate custodial sentence" means—
  (a) a sentence of imprisonment, if the offender has attained the age of 21 years when he is sentenced; and
  (b) a detention centre order or a youth custody sentence, if he has not then attained that age.

(13) A person released from a custodial sentence passed under subs. (11) above shall not be liable to a period of supervision in consequence of his conviction under that subsection, but his conviction shall not prejudice any liability to supervision to which he was previously subject, and that liability shall accordingly continue until the end of the supervision period.

(14) In this section—
  "licence" means a licence under s. 60 of the Criminal Justice Act 1967; and
  "remission" means remission under rules made by virtue of s. 47 of the Prison Act 1952.

COMMENTARY

For the determination of age *see* s. 1(6).

Subsection (11): An appropriate custodial sentence. *See* subs. (12).

Provision, regulation and management of attendance centres.

16. (1) The Secretary of State may continue to provide attendance centres.

(2) In this Act "attendance centre" means a place at which offenders under 21 years of age may be required to attend and be given under supervision appropriate occupation or instruction, in pursuance of orders made—

(*a*)   by the Crown Court or magistrates' courts under section 17 below;

(*b*)   by juvenile courts or other magistrates' courts under ss. 15(2A) or (4) of the Children and Young Persons Act 1969 (attendance centre orders made on breach of requirements in ssuervision orders); or

(*c*)   by magistrates' courts under s. 6(3)(*c*) of the Powers of Criminal Courts Act 1973 (attendance centre orders made on breach of requirements in probation orders).

(3)-(5) . . .

Attendance centre orders.

17. (1) Subject to subss. (3) and (4) below, where a court—

(*a*)   would have power, but for s. 1 above, to pass a sentence of imprisonment on a person who is under 21 years of age or to commit such a person to prison in default of payment of any sum of money or for failing to do or abstain from doing anything required to be done or left undone; or

(*b*)   has power to deal with any such person under s. 6 of the Powers of Criminal Courts Act 1973 for failure to comply with any of the requirements of a probation order,

the court may, if it has been notified by the Secretary of State that an attendance centre is available for the reception of persons of his description, order him to attend at such a centre, to be specified in the order, for such number of hours as may be so specified.

(2) An order under this section is referred to in this Act as an "attendance centre order".

(3) No attendance centre order shall be made in the case of an offender who has been previously sentenced—

(*a*)   to imprisonment;

(*b*)   to detention under s. 53 of the Children and Young Persons Act 1933;

(*c*)   to Borstal training;

(*d*)   to youth custody or custody for life under this Act; or

(*e*)   to detention in a detention centre,

unless it appears to the court that there are special circumstaancs (whether relating to the offence or to the offender) which warrant the making of such an order in his case.

(4) The aggregate number of hours for which an attendance centre order may require an offender to attend at an attendance centre shall not be less than 12 except where he is under 14 years of age and the court is of opinion that 12 hours would be excessive, having regard to his age or any other circumstances.

(5) The aggregate number of hours shall not exceed 12 except where the court is of opinion, having regard to all the circumstances, that 12 hours would be inadequate, and in that case shall not exceed 24 where the offender is under 17 years of age, or 36 hours where the offender is under 21 but not less than 17 years of age.

(6) A court may make an attendance centre order in respect of an offender before a previous attendance centre order made in respect of him has ceased to have effect, and may determine the number of hours to be specified in the order without regard—

. (a) to the number specified in the previous order; or

(b) to the fact that that order is still in effect.

(7) An attendance centre order shall not be made unless the court is satisfied that the attendance centre to be specified in it is reasonably accessible to the person concerned, having regard to his age, the means of access available to him and any other circumstances.

(8) The times at which an offender is required to attend at an attendance centre shall be such as to avoid interference, so far as practicable, with his school hours or working hours.

(9) The first such time shall be a time at which the centre is available for the attendance of the offender in accordance with the notification of the Secretary of State and shall be specified in the order.

(10) The subsequent times shall be fixed by the officer in charge of the centre, having regard to the offender's circumstances.

(11) An offender shall not be required under this section to attend at an attendance centre on more than one occasion on any day, or for more than three hours on any occasion.

(12) Where a court makes an attendance centre order, the clerk of the court shall deliver or send a copy of the order to the officer in charge of the attendance centre specified in it, and shall also deliver a copy to the officer or send a copy by registered post or the recorded delivery service addressed to the offender's last or usual place of abode.

(13) Where an offender has been ordered to attend at an attendance centre in default of the payment of any sum of money—

(a) on payment of the whole sum to any person authorised to receive it, the attendance centre order shall cease to have effect;

(b) on payment of a part of the sum to any such person, the total number of hours for which the offender is required to attend at the centre shall be reduced proportionately, that is to say by such number of complete hours as bears to the total number the proportion most nearly approximating to, without exceeding, the proportion which the part bears to the said sum.

COMMENTARY

For the effects of this section *see* Attendance Centres in the introduction.

Subsection (1): Attendance Centre. Defined in s. 16(2), *supra*.

21 years of age. For the determination of age *see* s. 1(6), *supra*.

Notified by the Secretary of State. In Home Office circ. 64/1983.

Subsection (3): Sentenced to Imprisonment. Including a suspended and partly suspended sentence.

Subsection (7): Reasonably accessible. The Home Office consider 10 miles or a journey of 45 minutes to be the most that a boy could reasonably be expected to travel (15 miles or 90 minutes in the case of a 14 year old): Home Office circular 136/1977.

Discharge and variation of attendance centre orders.

18. (1) An attendance centre order may be discharged on an application made by the offender or the officer in charge of the relevant attendance centre.

(2) An application under subs. (1) above shall be made to one of the courts specified in subs. (3) below or to the Crown Court under subs. (4) below, and the discharge of such an order shall be by order of the court.

(3) Subject to subs. (4) below, the power to discharge an attendance centre order shall be exercised—

(a)   by a magistrates' court acting for the petty sessions area in which the relevant attendance centre is situated; or

(b)   by the court which made the order.

(4) Where the court which made the order is the Crown Court and there is included in the order a direction that the power to discharge the order is reserved to that court, the power shall be exercised by that court.

(5) An attendance centre order may, on the application of the offender or of the officer in charge of the relevant attendance centre, be varied by a magistrates' court acting for the petty sessions area in which the relevant attendance centre is situated; and an attendance centre order made by a magistrates' court may also be varied, on such an application, by that court.

(6) The power to vary an attendance centre order is a power by order—

(a)   to vary the day or hour specified in the order for the offender's first attendance at the relevant attendance centre; or

(b)   if the court is satisfied that the offender proposes to change or has changed his residence, to substitute for the relevant attendance centre an attendance centre which the court is satisfied is reasonably accessible to the offender, having regard to his age, the means of access available to him and any other circumstances.

(7) Where an application is made under this section by the officer in charge of an attendance centre, the court may deal with it without summoning the offender.

(8) It shall be the duty of the clerk to a court which makes an order under this section—

(a)   to deliver a copy to the offender or send a copy by registered post or the recorded delivery service addressed to the offender's last or usual place of abode; and

(b)   to deliver or send a copy—

(i)   if the order is made by virtue of subss. (1) or (6)(a) above, to the officer in charge of the relevant attendance centre; and

(ii)   if it is made by virtue of subs. (6)(b) above, to the officer in charge of the attendance centre which the order as varied will require the offender to attend.

(9) In this section "the relevant attendance centre", in relation to an attendance centre order, means the attendance centre specified in the order or substituted for the attendance centre so specified by an order made by virtue of subs. (6)(b) above.

Breaches of attendance centre orders or attendance centre rules.

19. (1) Where an attendance centre order has been made and it appears on information to a justice acting for a relevant petty sessions area that the offender—

(a)   has failed to attend in accordance with the order; or

(b)   while attending has committed a breach of rules made under s. 16(3) above which cannot be adequately dealt with under those rules,

the justice may issue a summons requiring the offender to appear at the place and time specified in the summons before a magistrates' court acting

6. CUSTODIAL SENTENCES

for the area or, if the information is in writing and on oath, may issue a warrant for the offender's arrest requiring him to be brought before such a court.

(2) For the purposes of this section a petty sessions area is a relevant petty sessions area in relation to an attendance centre order—

    (*a*)   if the attendance centre which the offender is required to attend by an order made by virtue of ss. 17(1) or 18(6)(*b*) above is situated in it; or

    (*b*)   if the order was made by a magistrates' court acting for it.

(3) If it is proved to the satisfaction of the magistrates' court before which an offender appears or is brought under this section that he has failed without reasonable excuse to attend as mentioned in paragraph (*a*) of subs. (1) above or has committed such a breach of rules as is mentioned in para. (*b*) of that subsection, that court—

    (*a*)   if the attendance centre order was made by a magistrates' court, may revoke it and deal with him, for the offence in respect of which the order was made, in any manner in which he could have been dealt with for that offence by the court which made the order if the order had not been made;

    (*b*)   if the order was made by the Crown Court, may commit him in custody or release him on bail until he can be brought or appear before the Crown Court.

(4) A magistrates' court which deals with an offender's case under subs. (3)(*b*) above shall send to the Crown Court a certificate signed by a justice of the peace giving particulars of the offender's failure to attend or, as the case may be, the breach of the rules which he has committed, together with such other particulars of the case as may be desirable; and a certificate purporting to be so signed shall be admissible as evidence of the failure or the breach before the Crown Court.

(5) Where by virtue of subs. (3)(*b*) above the offender is brought or appears before the Crown Court and it is proved to the satisfaction of the court that he has failed to attend as mentioned in para. (*a*) of subs. (1) above or has committed such a breach of rules as is mentioned in para. (*b*) of that subsection, that court may revoke the attendance centre order and deal with him, for the offence in respect of which the order was made, in any manner in which it could have dealt with him for that offence if it had not made the order.

(6) A person sentenced under subs. (3)(*a*) above for an offence may appeal to the Crown Court against the sentence.

(7) . . .

THE MAGISTRATES' COURTS RULES 1981

S.I. 1981 No 552, as amended by S.I. 1982 No. 245, S.I. 1983 No. 523

Committals for sentence, etc

17. *(1) Where a magistrates' court commits an offender to the Crown Court under the Vagrancy Act 1824, ss 37 or 38 of the Act of 1980, ss 56(1) or 61(6) of the Criminal Justice Act 1967, s. 24(2)(a) of the Powers of Criminal Courts Act 1973 or s. 6 of the Bail Act 1976 after convicting him of an offence, the clerk of the magistrates' court shall send to the appropriate officer of the Crown Court—*

    (a)   *a copy signed by the clerk of the magistrates' court of the minute or memorandum of the conviction entered in the register;*

    (b)   *a copy of any note of the evidence given at the trial of the offender, any*

written statement tendered in evidence and any deposition;

(c)   *such documents and articles produced in evidence before the court as have been retained by the court;*

(d)   *any report relating to the offender considered by the court;*

(e)   *if the offender is committed on bail, a copy of the record made in pursuance of s. 5 of the said Act of 1976 relating to such bail and also any recognizance entered into by any person as his surety;*

(f)   *if the court imposes under s. 56(8) of the Criminal Justice Act 1967 an interim disqualification for holding or obtaining a licence under Part III of the Road Traffic Act 1972, a statement of the date of birth and sex of the offender;*

(g)   *if the court makes an order under s. 28 of the Theft Act 1968 (orders for restitution), a copy signed by the clerk of the convicting court of the minute or memorandum of the order entered in the register;*

(h)   *a copy of any contribution order previously made in the case under s. 7 of the Legal Aid Act 1982.*

(2) Where a magistrates' court commits an offender to the Crown Court under the Vagrancy Act 1824, ss 8(6) or 24(2) of the Powers of Criminal Courts Act 1973, ss 37 or 38 of the Act of 1980 or ss 56(1) or 62(6) of the Criminal Justice Act 1967 and the magistrates court on that occasion imposes, under s. 56(8) of the Criminal Justice Act 1967, an interim disqualification for holding or obtaining a licence under Part III of the Road Traffic Act 1972, the clerk of the magistrates' court shall give notice of the interim disqualification to the appropriate officer of the Crown Court.

(3) Where a magistrates' court commits a person on bail to the Crown Court under any of the enactments mentioned in para. (2) or under s. 6(4) of the Powers of Criminal Courts Act 1973 or under s. 6 of the Bail Act 1976 the clerk of the magistrates' court shall give notice thereof in writing to the governor of the prison to which persons of the sex of the person committed are committed by that court if committed in custody for trial and also, if the person committed is under the age of 21, to the governor of the remand centre to which he would have been committed if the court had refused him bail.

COMMENTARY

The Home Office also request justices' clerks to notify the liaison probation officer at the Crown Court of the particulars contained in Home Office cir. No. 28/71, para. 36.

Any note of the evidence. "In the case of committal for sentence or borstal training it is really essential that all the information that was before the committing justices should be before the (Crown Court), and accordingly, any notes of evidence taken by the clerk and any documents put in at the hearing should be sent, as no doubt they generally are. Our opinion on this matter was, we think, made clear in the case of *R. v. Dorset Quarter Sessions, ex parte O'Brien.": Practice Note* [1956] 1 All E.R. 448.

Entries in register in respect of suspended sentences

29.   *(1) Where under s. 23 of the Powers of Criminal Courts Act 1973 a magistrates' court deals with a person in respect of a suspended sentence otherwise than by making an order under subs. (1)(a) of that section, the court shall cause to be entered in the register its reasons for its opinion that it would be unjust to make such an order.*

(1A)   Where a magistrates' court, in dealing with a person under s. 47(3) to (5) of the Criminal Law Act 1977 in respect of a partly suspended sentence, decides under subs. (4) to make no order under subs. (3), the court shall cause to be entered in the register its reasons for its decision.

(2) Where an offender is dealt with under the said s. 23 or the said s. 47(3) to

6. CUSTODIAL SENTENCES

(5) in respect of a suspended or partly suspended sentence passed by a magistrates' court, the clerk of the court shall note this in the register against the original entry in respect of the suspended or partly suspended sentence, or where the suspended or partly suspended sentence was not passed by that court, shall notify the clerk of the court by which it was passed who shall note it in the register against the original entry in respect of the suspended or partly suspended sentence.

(3)   In this Rule "partly suspended sentence" means a sentence of which part has been ordered under s. 47(1) of the Criminal Law Act 1977 to be held in suspense.

Suspended sentence supervision orders

30.   *(1)   Where a magistrates' court makes an order under s. 23(1)(a) or (b) of the Powers of Criminal Courts Act 1973 in respect of a person who is subject to a suspended sentence supervision order, the clerk of the court shall note this in the register against the original entry in respect of the suspended sentence supervision order, or where that order was not made by that court, shall—*

(a)   *if the order was made by another magistrates' court, notify the clerk of that court who shall note the court register accordingly; or*

(b)   *if the order was made by the Crown Court, notify the appropriate officer of the Crown Court.*

(2)   Where a magistrates' court discharges a suspended sentence supervision order under s. 26(9) of the said Act of 1973, the clerk of the court shall note this in the register against the original entry in respect of that order, or where that order was not made by that court, shall—

(a)   *if the order was made by another magistrates' court, notify the clerk of that court who shall note the court register accordingly; or*

(b)   *if the order was made by the Crown Court, notify the appropriate officer of the Crown Court.*

(3)   Where a magistrates' court fines a person under s. 27 of the said Act of 1973 for breach of the requirements of a suspended sentence supervision order which was not made by that court, the clerk of the court shall—

(a)   *if the order was made by another magistrates' court, notify the clerk of that court; or*

(b)   *if the order was made by the Crown Court, notify the appropriate officer of the Crown Court.*

Committal to custody to be by warrant

94.   *A justice of the peace shall not commit any person to a prison, detention centre, remand centre or place certified under s. 134 of the Act of 1980 or to the custody of a constable under s. 128(7) of the Act except by a warrant of commitment.*

Warrant of commitment

97.   *(1)   A warrant of commitment issued by a justice of the peace—*

(a)   *shall name or otherwise describe the person committed;*

(b)   *shall contain a statement of the offence with which the person committed is charged, or of which he has been convicted, or of any other ground on which he is committed;*

(c)   *shall be directed to a person named in the warrant or to the constables of the police area in which the warrant is issued or to the authorized persons for the police area specified in the warrant and to the governor or keeper of the prison or place of detention specified in the warrant, and shall require—*

    (i)   the named person or the constables or authorized persons to arrest the person committed, if he is at large, and convey him to that prison or place and deliver him with the warrant to the governor or keeper;

    (ii)   the governor or keeper to keep in custody the person committed until that person be delivered in due course of law, or until the happening of an event specified in the warrant, or for the period specified in the warrant, as the case may be.

(2) A warrant of commitment may be executed by conveying the person committed to any prison or place of detention in which he may lawfully be detained and delivering him there together with the warrant; and so long as any person is detained in any such prison or place other than that specified in the warrant, the warrant shall have effect as if that other prison or place were the prison or place specified in it.

(3) Notwithstanding the preceding provisions of this rule, a warrant of commitment issued in pursuance of a valid conviction, or of a valid order requiring the person committed to do or abstain from doing anything, shall not, if alleges that the person committed has been convicted, or ordered to do or abstain from doing that thing, be held void by reason of any defect in the warrant.

(4) The governor or keeper of the prison or place of detention at which any person is delivered in pursuance of a warrant of commitment shall give to the constable or other person making the delivery a receipt for that person.

(5) Notwithstanding the preceding provisions of this rule, a warrant of a justice of the peace to commit to custody any person who to the justice's knowledge is already detained in a prison or other place of detention shall be delivered to the governor or keeper of the prison or place of detention in which that person is detained.

COMMENTARY

Paragraph (1): A statement of the offence.   As to what constitutes a sufficient statement of offence *see* r. 100.

Paragraph (3): Any defect.   It is "good sense and good law" to lodge a fresh warrant after the defendant has been committed to correct a defect or informality: *Ex parte Cross* (1857) 21 J.P. 407; *Ex parte Smith* (1858) 27 L.J.M.C. 186.

    "When magistrates commit . . . on several charges, the committals are several and distinct and, if one is bad, the others are not necessarily invalidated", *per* Lord Hewart, CJ in *R.* v. *Phillips. R.* v. *Quayle* (1938) 102 J.P. 467.

Paragraph (5).   The provisions of this paragraph are administrative in content and do not prevent a warrant being executed later which was not lodged with a prison while the subject was there on remand: *R.* v. *Leeds Prison Governor and Another, ex parte Huntley* (1972) 136 J.P. 551.

NON-CUSTODIAL ORDERS

CONTENTS

PROBATION

As an alternative to sentencing an offender aged 17 or over a court can place him on probation, that is to say, direct that for a specified period of from six months to three years he shall be under the supervision of a probation officer and subject to the conditions of the order: Powers of Criminal Courts Act 1973, s. 2.

Explanation and Willingness to Comply

Before making a probation order the court must first explain in ordinary language the effect of the order and of any breach. An order may not be made unless the offender expresses his willingness to comply with its requirements: *ibid*, s. 2(6).

Probation Requirements

A probation order may require the probationer to comply during all or any part of the probation period with such requirements as the court, having regard to the circumstances of the case, considers necessary for securing the offender's good conduct or for preventing a repetition by him of the same or of other offences: Powers of Criminal Courts Act 1973, s. 2(3). These requirements must be read in light of the observations of the House of Lords in *Cullen* v. *Rogers* (1982) 146 J.P. 257, noted under that section. The power to add requirements in *ibid*, s. 2(3), includes power to impose requirements that the probationer:

(a) presents himself to a specified person or persons at a specified place or places;

(b) participates, or

(c) refrains from participating in specified activities: *ibid*, s. 4A.

This power is subject to stringent statutory conditions, including the willingness of the defendant to comply and, in the case of a "presenting" requirement, the consent of anyone else whose co-operation is involved: *ibid*, s. 4A(3). A probation officer must be consulted about the offender's circumstances and the feasibility of securing compliance with the requirement and the court must be satisfied, having regard to his report, as to feasibility: *ibid*, s. 4A(2).

A "participating" and a "refraining" order will take effect on a day or days specified in the probation order or, if the order so specifies, throughout the probation period: *ibid*, s. 4A(1).

A "presenting" and a "participating" requirement operates to require the probationer in accordance with the probation officer's instructions to present himself at a place or to participate in the activities, for not more than 60 days and, while there or while participating, to comply with the instructions of those in charge: *ibid*, s. 4A(4) and (6).

Requirements as to residence may be imposed under *ibid*, s. 2(5) and requirements as to treatment for a mental condition under *ibid*, s. 3 (*see* below). Finally, there is power to add a day centre requirement under *ibid*, s. 4B. (*See* below). The payment of compensation and damages must not form part of the order (*ibid*, s. 2(4)), although these may be ordered separately under *ibid*, s. 35.

Treatment for Mental Condition

On making a probation order the court may include a requirement that the offender shall submit during the whole or a specified part of the probation period to treatment by or under the direction of a duly qualified medical practitioner with a view to the improvement of his mental condition: Powers of Criminal Courts Act 1973, s. 3(1).

For this purpose the court must be satisfied:

(i) on the evidence of an approved medical practitioner that the offender's mental condition is such as requires and may be susceptible to treatment but is not such as to warrant his detention under a hospital order; and

(ii) that arrangements have been made for the treatment (including where appropriate reception): *ibid*, s. 3(1).

The treatment must be:

(a) as a resident patient in a hospital other than a special hospital or a mental nursing home;

(b) as a non-resident patient at a specified institution or place; or

(c) by or under the direction of a duly qualified medical practitioner: *ibid*, s. 3(2).

While the probationer is a resident patient supervision is only nominal: *ibid*, s. 3(4).

The medical practitioner may change the institution or place of treatment (*ibid*, s. 3(5)) subject to notifying the probation officer: *ibid*, s. 3(6).

An offender's mental condition may be proved in accordance with the Mental Health Act 1983, s. 54(2), (3): *ibid*, s. 3(7).

A requirement to submit to mental treatment may be added to a probation order once made, but only within three months of the original order: *ibid*, sch. 1, para. 3(2).

A reasonable refusal to comply with a requirement to submit to treatment for a mental condition may not constitute a breach of the order in the circumstance mentioned in *ibid*, s. 6(7).

The supervising officer is under a duty to apply for the variation or cancellation of the requirement on receipt of certain reports in writing from the medical practitioner: *ibid*, sch. 1, para. 4.

Day Centre

A probation order may require the probationer during the probation period to attend at a specified day centre: Powers of Criminal Courts Act 1973, s. 4B(1). A day centre means premises at which non-residential facilities are provided for use in connexion with the rehabilitation of offenders and which are provided or approved by the probation committee: *ibid*, s. 4B(6).

Before imposing such a requirement a probation officer must be consulted and the court must be satisfied that (a) arrangements can be made for attendance; and (b) the person in charge consents: *ibid*, s. 4B(2).

Such a requirement operates to require the probationer in accordance with instructions from the probation officer to attend on not more than 60 days at the day centre and, while there, to comply with the instructions of the person in charge: *ibid*, s. 4B(3). It includes a duty to attend elsewhere for activities in accordance with the instructions of those in charge: *ibid*, s. 4B(5). The probation officer's instructions must so far as practicable avoid interference with work and education: *ibid*, s. 4B(4).

Social Inquiry Report

There is no requirement for a social inquiry report before a probation order is made except to the extent that this is necessary in regard to "presenting", "participating" and "refraining" requirements (Powers of Criminal Courts Act 1973, s. 4A(2)) and day centre requirements (*ibid*, s. 4B(2)). However, the Home Secretary has reminded magistrates of the view expressed by the Departmental Committee on the Probation Service that a social inquiry report should normally be obtained before a probation order is made: Home Office circ. 28/1971.

The Aims of Probation

The Home Office advise that:—
  The fundamental aim of probation, as of all methods of penal treatment, is to uphold the law and protect society. The particular object of placing an offender on probation is to leave him at liberty in the community but subject to certain conditions regarding his way of life, with skilled help available to him from the probation service to cope with the problems and difficulties that may have led to his offending, and with an obligation to co-operate with his supervising probation officer as regards reporting, receiving visits and heeding the advice given to him. Through the discipline of submission to supervision by a probation officer, this method of treatments seeks both to protect society and to strengthen the probationer's resources so that he becomes a more responsible person. As regards the situations in which the making of a probation order is appropriate, the views of the Departmental Committee on the Probation Service are still valid: they concluded (para. 15 of their report) that there was an *a priori* case for using probation where:—
  (*a*) the circumstances of the offence and the offender's record are not such as to demand, in the interests of society, that some more severe method be adopted in dealing with him;
  (*b*) the risk, if any, to society through setting the offender at liberty is outweighed by the moral, social and economic arguments for not depriving him of it;
  (*c*) the offender needs continuing attention, (since otherwise, if condition (*b*) is satisfied, a fine or discharge will suffice);
  (*d*) the offender is capable of responding to this attention while at liberty.
                                        (The Sentence of the Court)

Combining Probation with Other Orders

Since a probation order is made "instead of sentence" it cannot be combined with any other sentence or order in lieu of sentence *on the same offence: R.* v. *McClelland* (1951) 115 J.P. 179 (wrong to combine fine and probation). Ancillary orders such as disqualification (Road Traffic Act 1972, s. 102) and compensation (Powers of Criminal Courts Act 1973, s. 12(4)) may however be made on the same offence as a probation order.
  A probation order may not be made on one offence and a suspended sentence on another: Powers of Criminal Courts Act, 1973, s. 22(3).
  In the ordinary way a probation order must operate forthwith. It is, therefore, wrong to make such an order at the same time as passing a sentence of detention centre training which will postpone the effective commencement of probation: *R.* v. *Evans* (1959) 123 J.P. 128; or at the same time as a sentence of imprisonment: *R.* v. *Emmett* (1968) *The Times*, December 21. Otherwise, there seems to be no reason why a probation order on one offence should not be combined with a different disposition on another offence, such as a fine: *R.* v. *Bainbridge* [1979] L.S. Gaz. 28.

Breach of Probation

Breach of any of the requirements of a probation order renders the probationer liable to:

  (a)   a fine of up to £200; or
  (b)   an attendance centre order (if available).

  Alternatively, unless the order was made by the Crown Court, he may be dealt with in any manner in which the court could deal with him if it had just convicted him of the original offence: Powers of Criminal Courts Act 1973, s. 6(3). In the first two cases the probation order continues unaffected; in the third it is replaced by the subsequent order. If the probation order was made by the Crown Court the magistrates' court may commit the offender to that court on bail or in custody to be dealt with: *ibid*, s. 6(4) and (5). A summons or warrant may issue to compel the attendance of a probationer at court for the purpose of dealing with an alleged breach provided the information is laid during the probation period: *ibid*, s. 6(1). Breach proceedings are to be distinguished from the powers of the court upon the commission of an offence during the probation period.

For breach resulting from refusal to undergo treatment for a mental condition, *see ibid*, s. 6(7).

Commission of a Further Offence

Since a probation order is an alternative to sentence the commission of a further offence during the probationary period followed by conviction therefor renders the offender liable to be dealt with as for the original offence (but in this case the court has no option of punishing the offender and allowing the probation order to continue): Powers of Criminal Courts Act 1973, s. 8. In the case of a probationer who commits further offences during the currency of a probation order made by the Crown Court magistrates' powers are confined to committing him to the Crown Court or taking no action. Where one magistrates' court sentences an offender who was placed on probation by another magistrates' court the consent of the latter or of the supervising court is necessary: s. 8(9), *ibid*.

Amendment

A probation order may be amended in accordance with sch. 1 to the Powers of Criminal Courts Act 1973: s. 5, *ibid*. Where the amendment is to substitute a different division the court is required to act upon the application of the probation officer: para. 2(1) of sch. 1, *ibid*. No summons is necessary. A justices' clerk may amend a petty sessions area: Justices' Clerks Rules 1970. Other amendments, except where cancelling or reducing the period of any requirement or on the application of the probationer, must be by summons and with the consent of the probationer: para. 5(1) and (2) of sch. 1, *ibid*. Any requirement of a probation order may be cancelled or inserted: *ibid*, sch. 1, para. 3(1). The probation period may not be reduced: *ibid*, sch. 1, para. 3(2). A requirement to submit to treatment for a mental condition may only be inserted within three months of the original order: *ibid*, sch. 1, para. 3(2).

Discharge

A probation order may be discharged on the application of the probation officer or probationer: para. 1 of sch. 1. No summons is necessary.

It is the supervising court which has jurisdiction to amend a probation order: *ibid*, sch. 1, para. 2. It is the supervising court which can discharge the order where it was made by the court by or before which the probationer was convicted (para. 1(2) of sch. 1) except when the order was made by the Crown Court and it includes a direction reserving that power to the Crown Court. Orders made by the Crown Court following a committal for sentence may also be discharged by the supervising court. In all other cases the power to discharge resides in the court which made the order: para. 1(4) of sch. 1.

Conversion to Conditional Discharge

When a probation order ceases to be appropriate the unexpired portion may be converted to a conditional discharge on the application either of the probationer or the probation officer: Powers of Criminal Courts Act 1973, s. 11(1). The hearing may be conducted in the absence of the probationer if the probation officer producing a written statement from him to the effect that he understands and consents to the proceedings: *ibid*, s. 11(3). Application may not be made while an appeal against the making of the probation order is pending: *ibid*, s. 11 (1A).

Scotland

For a Scottish order relating to a person residing in England *see* the Criminal Procedure (Scotland) Act 1975, s. 389 and for English orders relating to persons residing in Scotland, the Powers of Criminal Courts Act 1973, s. 10.

Absolute and Conditional Discharge

When punishment is inexpedient and probation inappropriate an offender may be discharged either absolutely or conditionally, under s. 7 of the Powers of Criminal Courts Act 1973. Upon conviction of a further offence, a conditional discharge (which may be for up to three years but, unlike a probation order, has no minimum period) has the same consequences as a probation order—*see* s. 8, *ibid*.

The Effects of Probation and Discharge

Neither probation nor discharge, absolute or conditional, counts as a conviction, except for the purposes of the proceedings in which the order was made and certain specifically exempted purposes: Powers of Criminal Courts Act 1973, s. 13. But this immunity is removed if the offender is subsequently sentenced for the original offence.

Appeal

There is a right of appeal to the Crown Court against the making of a probation order and an order for conditional or absolute discharge: Magistrates' Courts Act 1980, s. 108 (1), (1A).

SUPERVISION ORDER

A juvenile may not be made the subject of a probation order, and if supervision is considered desirable should be remitted to the juvenile court under the provisions of the Children and Young Persons Act 1969, s 7(8).

Supervision orders may be made in both care and criminal proceedings. An order made in criminal proceedings may fall to be considered in the adult court when the supervised person has attained the age of 18 and either (1) there is an application for the terms of the order to be varied; or (2) the supervised person has failed to comply with any requirement of the order: s. 15, *ibid*. (Proceedings of this nature in respect of 17-year-olds and younger are dealt with in the juvenile court). The supervised person may be brought before the court by summons or warrant under s. 16(2) of the Act, but his attendance is unnecessary in the cases listed in subs. (5), *ibid*.

The restrictions in the Children & Young Persons Act 1933 on the reporting of juvenile court proceedings are applied to the adult court in relation to proceedings resulting from supervision orders by virtue of s. 10(1)(b) of the Children and Young Persons Act 1969. This fact must be announced by the court in the course of the proceedings: *ibid*, s. 10(2).

Community Service

A magistrates' court convicting anyone aged 16 or over of an offence punishable with imprisonment may, instead of dealing with him in any other way, make a community service order, that is an order that he should perform unpaid work under the direction of "the relevant officer": Powers of Criminal Courts Act 1973, s. 14(1). The power to make such an order is subject to the following pre-requisites:

(a)   the offender consents;
(b)   the court being satisfied, after consideration of a report by a probation officer or by a social worker of a local authority social services department and after hearing from them, if necessary, that the offender is a suitable person to perform work under such an order; and
(c)   (in the case of an offender aged 17 or over) being satisfied that provision can be made for the work in the area in which the offender resides:*ibid*, s. 14(2), (2A).

Juveniles

The adult court has no power to make a community service order in respect of a juvenile: Children and Young Persons Act 1969, s. 7(8).

Social Inquiry Report

The report the court is required to obtain must be about the offender and his circumstances: Powers of Criminal Courts Act 1973, s. 14(2). In practice it will usually be a full social inquiry report. When a court adjourns a case after conviction for the purpose of obtaining a report in order to ascertain the offender's suitability for community service and the report shows the offender to be suitable for such an order, the court ought to make it because otherwise a feeling of injustice would be aroused: *R. v. Gillam* [1981] Crim. L.R. 55; *R. v. Millwood* [1982] Crim. L.R. 832.

Explanation

Before making a community service order the court must explain in ordinary language its purpose and effect, what is required of the offender, the consequences of breach and the possibility of review: Powers of Criminal Courts Act 1973, s. 14(5).

The Length of a Community Service Order

The number of hours must be specified in a community service order and, in the case of an offender aged 17 or over, must be not less than 40 nor more than 240: Powers of Criminal Courts Act 1973, s. 14(1A). Generally speaking, it is wrong to order a small number of community service hours where the alternative to the order would have been a sentence of imprisonment. A short period of community service would usually be reserved in cases where the court was not minded otherwise to impose a custodial sentence: *R. v. Lawrence* [1982] 4 Cr. App. R. (S) 69, (190 hours would have been sufficient where 18 month sentence contemplated).

When two or more community service orders are made at the same time the court may order that the hours shall be served concurrently or additionally, so a later order may be made consecutive to an earlier order: *R. v. Evans* (1977) 141 J.P. 141, so that the total period does not exceed 240 hours. Because of the administrative difficulties to which additional hours orders can give rise, concurrent hours are normally to be preferred.

The Relevant Officer

The community service order must specify the relevant officer, that is a probation officer or a person appointed by the probation committee: Powers of Criminal Courts Act 1973, s. 14(4).

The Work

The work under a community service order must be performed within 12 months of the making of the order: Powers of Criminal Courts Act 1973, s. 15(2). The offender must perform such work at such times as he may be instructed by the relevant officer: *ibid*, s. 15(1). The instructions must, so far as practicable, avoid any conflict with the offender's religious beliefs and any interference with his normal working or school hours: *ibid*, s. 15(3).

The Aims of Community Service

The Home Office describe the aims of community service as follows:

> The community service order was introduced with the primary purpose of providing a constructive alternative for those offenders who would otherwise have received a short custodial sentence. An order can be made in respect of any offender convicted of an offence "punishable with imprisonment"—it is not a requirement of the law that the court would have imposed a prison sentence on that particular offender had it not given him a community service order. Nevertheless it was the emphasis both of the Advisory Council on the Penal System in its report on Non-Custodial and Semi-Custodial Penalties (often referred to as "the Wootton Report") in proposing the introduction of community service, and of Parliament in giving effect to the recommendations of the Council, that community service should be seen as a penal sanction that made serious demands on the offender and could thus be regarded as a viable alternative to a custodial sentence. The offender is penalized by being deprived of his leisure time, but for a constructive and outward-looking purpose; he has an opportunity to make reparation to the community against which he has offended by working for its benefit; and in some cases he will be brought into direct contact with members of the community who most need help and support. Whilst the main aim is to ensure that an offender completes satisfactorily the number of hours' service ordered by the court, it is hoped that working for the benefit of the community will also have a positive effect on the future attitudes and conduct of the offender.
>
> *(The Sentence of the Court)*

Combining Community Service and Other Orders

Community service is a sentence and as such may not be combined with any other sentence or order in lieu of sentence on the same offence. Thus it cannot be combined *on the same offence* with a fine: *R.* v. *Carnwell* [1979] Crim. L.R. 59; 68 Cr. App. R. 58. It would not seemingly be wrong to make a community service order on one offence and a fine on another. However, it is bad sentencing practice to make a community service order on one offence and a suspended prison sentence on another: *R.* v. *Starie* [1979] Crim. L.R. 731: L.S. Gaz., June 13. And *a fortiori* on implementing a suspended sentence: *R.* v. *Seymour* [1983] Crim. L.R. 410.

Breach of Community Service

Breach without reasonable excuse of any requirement of a community service order may be dealt with by a magistrates' court:

(a)   imposing a fine of up to £200 (which does not prejudice the continuance of the order) or, if the order was made by a magistrates' court,

(b)   dealing with the offender in any way in which he could have been dealt with on conviction if the order had not been made;

or, if the order was made by the Crown Court, by
(c)   committing the offender to the Crown Court to be dealt with: Powers of Criminal Courts Act 1973, s. 16(3).

A custodial sentence may be expected on breach of a community service order where the making of the order had saved the offender from an immediate custodial sentence: *R. v. Howard and Wade* [1977] Crim. L.R. 683. However, a custodial sentence is usually inappropriate where an offender has completed a substantial proportion of the work required: *R. v. Paisley* [1979] 1 Cr. App. R. (S) 196; *R. v. Baines* [1983] Crim. L.R. 756.

Where the breach of community service is not sufficiently grave to warrant a prison sentence the court will rarely be justified in activating a suspended sentence: *R. v. McElhorne* [1983] Crim. L.R. 487.

Revocation Consequent upon a Custodial Sentence

Where a person the subject of a community service order receives a custodial sentence from a magistrates' court other than the court named in the order and it appears on the application of the offender or the relevant officer that it would be in the interests of justice to do so having regard to circumstances which have arisen since the order was made the court may:
(a)   (if the order was made by a magistrates' court) revoke it; or
(b)   (if the order was made by the Crown Court) commit the offender to that court: Powers of Criminal Courts Act 1973, s. 17(4A).

Other Revocations

Upon application by the offender or the relevant officer at any time while the order is in force the magistrates' court specified in the order may if it appears to be in the interests of justice to do so,
(a)   (if the order was made by a magistrates' court) revoke the order or revoke the order and deal with the offender in any manner in which he could have been dealt with by the court of conviction if the order had not been made; or
(b)   (if the order was made by the Crown Court) commit the offender to that court: Powers of Criminal Courts Act 1973, s. 17(2)

Extension

Either the offender or the relevant officer may at any time while the order is in force apply for the 12 month period to be extended and the court may so order if this appears in the interests of justice having regard to circumstances which have arisen since it was made: Powers of Criminal Courts Act 1973, s. 17(1).

Petty Sessions Area

The petty sessions area in which the offender resides or will reside must be specified in the order: Powers of Criminal Courts Act 1973, s. 14(4); and on his removal to another area may be amended in accordance with s. 17(5), (5A), *ibid*.

Scotland

A Scottish court may make a community service order in respect of an offender residing in England and Wales by virtue of the Community Service by Offenders (Scotland) Act 1978, s. 6 (not reproduced herein). Breach of such an order may be punished by a court in this country: Powers of Criminal Courts Act 1973, s. 16(3). A court in England or Wales may make a community service service order in respect of an offender residing in Scotland: *ibid*, ss. 14, 17A.

Northern Ireland

A Northern Ireland court may make a community service order in respect of an offender residing in England or Wales: Treatment of Offenders (Northern Ireland) Order 1976, as amended by the Criminal Justice Act 1982, sch. 13 (not reproduced herein). A magistrates' court in England or Wales may make a community service order in respect of an offender residing in Northern Ireland: Powers of Criminal Courts Act 1973, s. 17B.

MEDICAL TREATMENT

The mental condition of a defendant may affect both the issue of his guilt or innocence and the disposition of his case upon conviction.

Insanity under the M'Naghten rules is probably a defence to all crimes; though for obvious reasons it is in practice pleaded only in cases of homicide. A special defence statutorily confined to murder is that of "diminished responsibility" under s. 2 of the Homicide Act, 1957. Neither of these defences has any significant part to play in summary jurisdiction and they are thus not dealt with in this work.

Magistrates may be concerned with two categories of abnormal mental condition:

> (1) mental disorder (of certain specified forms) of a nature and degree which warrants detention in a hospital for medical treatment; and
>
> (2) a mental condition such as requires and may be susceptible to treatment, but which is not sufficient to warrant such detention.

In the second category of case, however trivial the offence, the magistrates may, if they make a probation order, include in it a requirement that the offender shall submit, for the probation period or any lesser period fixed by the court, to treatment, whether residential or otherwise, by or under the direction of a doctor: Powers of Criminal Courts Act, 1973, s. 3. (See above).

Hospital and Guardianship Orders

A hospital order is an order for the admission of an offender to a hospital: Mental Health Act 1983, s. 37(4). A guardianship order is an order placing an offender under the guardianship of a local social services authority or of any other person: *ibid*, s. 37(6). The effects of these orders are prescribed in *ibid*, s. 40.

A hospital order or a guardianship order may be made by a magistrates' court where a person is convicted of an offence punishable on summary conviction with imprisonment and where certain conditions are satisfied: Mental Health Act 1983, s. 37(1). The court must be satisfied on the evidence of two registered medical practitioners that the offender is suffering from mental illness, psychopathic disorder, severe mental impairment or mental impairment and that either:

> (a) the mental disorder is of a nature or degree which makes it appropriate for him to be detained in hospital for medical treatment and, in the case of psychopathic disorder or mental impairment, that the treatment is likely to alleviate or prevent a deterioration of his condition; or
>
> (b) in the case of an offender aged 16 or over, that the mental disorder is of a nature or degree which warrants his reception into guardianship; and
>
> (c) in either case the court must also be of the opinion that the most suitable method of disposing of the case is a hospital or guardianship order, *ibid*, s. 37(2).

Where the accused is suffering from mental illness or severe mental im-

pairment and the court is satisfied that he did the act or made the omission
charged it may if it thinks fit make the order without convicting the accused: *ibid*, s. 37(3).

In addition to the evidence required at (*a*) or (*b*) above the court must be
satisfied on the evidence of the registered medical practitioner who would
be in charge of the treatment, or of some other person representing the
managers of the hospital, that arrangements have been made for admission
within 28 days: *ibid*, s. 37(4). For the requirements concerning medical
evidence see *ibid*, s. 54.

Pending admission the court may give directions for the offender's conveyance to and detention in a place of safety: *ibid*, s. 37(4)

Before making a guardianship order the court must be satisfied that the
authority or other person is willing to receive the offender into guardianship: *ibid*, s. 57(6).

When making a hospital or guardianship order the court may not pass a
sentence of imprisonment or other detention or impose a fine or make a
supervision order concerning a juvenile or bind over his parent or guardian: *ibid*, s. 37(8). This does not rule out any other order which the court
has power to make.

*Interim Hospital Order**

Where a person is convicted by a magistrates' court of an offence
punishable on summary conviction with imprisonment it may make an interim hospital order if satisfied on the evidence of two registered medical
practitioners that
   (*a*)   he is suffering from mental illness, psychopathic disorder, severe
          mental impairment or mental impairment; and
   (*b*)   there is no reason to suppose that the mental disorder is such that it
          may be appropriate for a hospital order to be made: Mental Health
          Act 1983, s. 38(1). An interim hospital order is an order authorising
          admission to a specified hospital and detention there in accordance
          with the Mental Health Act 1983, s. 38(1): *ibid*, s. 38(1). For the
          requirements concerning medical evidence *see* the Mental Health
          Act 1983, s. 38(3) and (4), and s. 54.

A further interim order may be made without the offender being
brought before the court if he is represented by counsel or solicitor who is
given an opportunity of being heard: *ibid*, s. 38(2)

An interim hospital order remains in force for such period as the court
specifies not exceeding 12 weeks: *ibid*, s. 38(5). It may be renewed for further periods of not more than 28 days at a time if it appears on the
evidence of the responsible medical officer that continuation is warranted:
ibid. An interim hospital order may not continue in force for more than six
months in all and the court must terminate it on making a hospital order or
deciding to deal with the offender in some other way: *ibid*, s. 38(5).

Information about Hospitals

The court may obtain, on request from the Regional Health Authority, information about hospitals which could receive persons under a hospital order or an interim hospital order: Mental Health Act 1983, s. 39.

Commitment for a Restriction Order

Where the conditions for the making of a hospital order are satisfied but it

---

*At the time of preparation of this book no date had been fixed for
bringing this provision into force.

appears having regard to the nature of the offence, the antecedents of the offender and the risk of his committing further offences if set at large that a restriction order should accompany the hospital order a magistrates' court may, instead of making a hospital order, commit the offender in custody to the Crown Court to be dealt with: Mental Health Act 1983, s. 43(1). The powers of the Crown Court on such a committal are set out in *ibid*, s. 43(2).

The magistrates' court may at the same time commit the offender for sentence under the Magistrates' Courts Act 1980, s. 38, where of the opinion that greater punishment should be inflicted on the offender unless a hospital order is made: *ibid*, s. 43(4).

Instead of committing the offender in custody he may be committed to a specified hospital if the court is satisfied on medical evidence that arrangements have been made for his reception: *ibid*, s. 44.

Appeal

Where a hospital order or a guardianship order is made without convicting the accused he has a right of appeal against the order under the Mental Health Act 1983, s. 45. In other cases there is a right of appeal under the Magistrates' Courts Act 1980, s. 108.

*Remand to Hospital for Mental Report**

There is power to remand an accused to a hospital for a report on his mental condition if he has:
  (a)   been convicted of an offence punishable on summary conviction with imprisonment;
  (b)   been charged with such an offence and the court is satisfied he did the act or made the omission charged; or
  (c)   been charged with such an offence and has consented to the remand: Mental Health Act 1983, s. 35(1), (2): *see* Ch. 5.

Before making the order the court must (a) be satisfied on medical evidence of certain matters; (b) be of opinion that it would be impracticable to make the report if the accused were on bail; and (c) be satisfied on medical evidence that arrangements have been made for admission within seven days; *ibid*, s. 35(4).

An accused so remanded may be further remanded if this appears necessary on medical evidence: *ibid*, s. 35(5). This may take place in the absence of the accused if he is legally represented: *ibid*, s. 35(6).

Remands may not be for more than 28 days at a time or more than 12 weeks in all: *ibid*, s. 35(7). The accused is entitled to obtain at his own expense an independent medical report and to apply on the basis of it for his remand to be terminated: *ibid*, s. 35(8).

For other powers to obtain Medical and Mental Reports *see* under that title in the introduction to Ch. 5.

DEPORTATION

A person aged 17 or over who is not a British citizen is liable to deportation if he is convicted of an offence for which he is punishable by imprisonment and a competent court recommends deportation: Immigration Act 1971, s. 3(6). Such a person may be recommended for deportation by any court having power to sentence him for the offence unless the court commits him to be sentenced or further dealt with by another court: *ibid*, s.

*At the time of preparation of this book no date had been fixed for the bringing into force of this provision.

6(1). There are exceptions for certain existing residents in *ibid*, s. 7, and for seamen, aircrew and other special cases in *ibid*, s. 8. When any question arises whether or not a person is a British citizen or is entitled to any exemption it lies in the person asserting it to prove that he is: *ibid*, s. 3(8). A court may not recommend deportation unless the offender has been given not less than seven days written notice of the legal provisions and the hearing may be adjourned for this purpose: *ibid*, s. 6(2).

The following guidelines for courts were laid down by Lawton, LJ, in *R. v. Nazari and Others* (1981) 145 J.P. 102:

> First, the court must consider, as was said by Sachs, LJ, in *R. v. Caird* [1970] 54 Cr. App. R. 499, whether the accused's continued presence in the United Kingdom is to its detriment. This country has no use for criminals of other nationalities, particularly if they have committed serious crimes or have long criminal records. That is self-evident. The more serious the crime and the longer the record the more obvious it is that there should be an order recommending deportation. On the other hand, a minor offence would not merit an order recommending deportation. In the Greater London area, for example, shoplifting is an offence which is frequently committed by visitors to this country. Normally an arrest for shoplifting followed by conviction, even if there were more than one offence being dealt with, would not merit a recommendation for deportation. But a series of shoplifting offences on different occasions may justify a recommendation for deportation. Even a first offence of shoplifting might merit a recommendation if the offender were a member of a gang carrying out a planned raid on a department store. Second, the courts are not concerned with the political systems which operate in other countries. They may be harsh; they may be soft; they may be oppressive; they may be the quintessence of democracy. The court has no knowledge of those matters over and above that which is common knowledge, and that may be wrong. In our judgment it would be undesirable for this court or any other court to express views about regimes which exist outside the United Kingdom of Great Britain and Northern Ireland. It is for the Home Secretary to decide in each case whether an offender's return to his country of origin would have consequences which would make his compulsory return unduly harsh. The Home Secretary has opportunities of informing himself about what is happening in other countries which the courts do not have. The sort of argument which was put in Nazari's case is one which we did not find attractive. It may well be that the regime in Iran at the present time is likely to be unfavourable from his point of view. Whether and how long it will continue to be so we do not know. Whether it will be so by the end of this man's sentence of imprisonment must be a matter of speculation. When the time comes for him to be released from prison the Home Secretary, we are sure, will bear in mind the very matters which we have been urged to consider, namely whether it would be unduly harsh to send him back to his country of origin. The next matter to which we invite attention by way of guidelines is the effect that an order recommending deportation will have on others who are not before the court and who are innocent persons. This court and all other courts would have no wish to break up families or impose hardship on innocent people.

The sentencer may consider the consequences of deportation on the offender: *R. v. Thoseby and Krawczyk* [1979] 1 Cr. App. R. (S) 280, (defendants had married residents of UK.). However, fears of the treatment the offender will receive if deported are matters for the Secretary of State and not the court: *R.* v. *Caird and Others* [1970] 54 Cr. App. R. 499; *R.* v. *Antypas* [1972] 57 Cr. App. R. 207; *R.* v. *Sabharwal* [1973] Crim. L.R. 132; *R.* v. *Nazari, supra.*

It was not the intention of the (pre-existing legislation) that a recommendation for deportation should be part of the punishment for the offence in the sense that the court should give a reduced sentence when a recommendation was made. Courts should sentence the prisoner to the penalty he deserves and then deal with the recommendation quite separately: *R.* v. *Edgehill* [1963] 1 All E.R. 181.

There is no power to make a recommendation when the executive act cannot follow thereupon. Thus a recommendation may not be made where a deportation order is still in force: *R.* v. *Kelly* (1966) 130 J.P. 424.

A recommendation under this section may be made in respect of a national of an E.E.C. member state. However the Secretary of State's powers are limited by the E.E.C. restrictions upon interference with the free movement of workers in accordance with art. 48 of the treaty. By virtue of art. 3(2) of Directive 62/221 previous criminal convictions do not by themselves justify a recommendation although they may be evidence that the continued presence of the accused represents a present threat to public policy: *R.* v. *Bouchereau* [1978] 2 W.L.R. 251 (European Ct.). And *see R.* v *Secretary of State for the Home Department, ex parte Santillo* [1981] 2 All E.R. 897.

It is inappropriate to make a recommendation for deportation on a national of a member state of the E.E.C. solely for failure to obtain a special residence permit: *R.* **v.** *Pieck* [1981] 3 All E.R. 46 (European Ct.).

The Attitude of the Secretary of State

The Secretary of State has made the following statement of principle:

STATEMENT OF IMMIGRATION RULES
FOR CONTROL
AFTER ENTRY
Laid before Parliament under s. 3(2) of the Act.

Consideration of the merits
48. In considering whether deportation is the right course on the merits, the public interest will be balanced against any compassionate circumstances of the case. While each case will be considered in the light of the particular circumstances, the aim is an exercise of the power of deportation that is consistent and fair as between one person and another, although one case will rarely be identical with another in all material respects.

49. Most of the cases in which deportation may be the appropriate course fall into two main categories. There are, first, those cases which come to notice following a conviction for a criminal offence and in which it is fitting that, because of his conduct, a person should no longer be allowed to remain here, in defiance of the immigration control.

Deportation following a conviction
50. In considering whether to give effect to a recommendation for deportation made by a court on conviction the Secretary of State will take into account every relevant factor, including—

> age
> length of residence in the United Kingdom
> personal history, including character, conduct and employment record
> domestic circumstances
> the nature of the offence of which the person was convicted
> previous criminal record
> compassionate circumstances
> any representations received on the person's behalf.

In certain circumstances, particularly in the case of young or first offenders, supervised departure, with a prohibition on re-entry, may be arranged as an alternative to the deportation recommended by the court provided that the person is willing to leave the country.

51. Where the court has not recommended deportation there may nevertheless be grounds, in the light of all the relevant information and subject to the right of appeal, for curtailment of stay or a refusal to extend stay followed, after departure, by a prohibition on re-entry.

"While any recommendation of a court will of course be most carefully considered in relation to the circumstances of the case, he would not normally think it right to deport an offender sentenced to borstal training or to be sent to a detention centre; it would, in his view, be inappropriate to require an offender to serve either of these sentences, which would be designed to fit him for future life in this country, and then to deport him at the end of it.": Home Office cir. 215/1972 dated December 15, 1972.

Detention Pending Deportation

When a recommendation for deportation is in force in respect of anyone not detained pursuant to a sentence or released on bail and the court fails to direct otherwise he must be detained pending the making of the order unless the Secretary of State directs his release: Immigration Act 1971, sch. 3, para. (1).

The court may direct the release of a person recommended for deportation but only on prescribed conditions: *ibid*, sch. 3, para. 4.

Appeal

A recommendation for deportation is treated as a sentence for the purpose of appeal: s. 6(5)(*a*) of the Immigration Act 1971; and an appeal against a recommendation lies therefore to the Crown Court under the Magistrates' Courts Act 1980, s. 108. No deportation order may be made until the expiration of the period for appeal (21 days) or pending the determination of the appeal: s. 6(6) of the Immigration Act 1971.

A person ordered to be deported following a recommendation has a right of appeal under s. 17 of the Act of 1971 (not included herein) to the appellate authorities set up under the Immigration Appeals Act 1969 on the ground only that he ought to be removed to a country or territory other than that specified in the removal directions.

THE CHILDREN AND YOUNG PERSONS ACT 1969

Variation and discharge of supervision orders

15. (1), (2), (2A) (*Concern the juvenile court*).

(3) If while a supervision order is in force in respect of a supervised person who has attained the age of 18 it appears to a magistrates' court other than a juvenile court, on the application of the supervisor or the supervised person, that it is appropriate to make an order under this subsection, the court may make an order discharging the supervision order or varying it by—

(*a*)   inserting in it a provision specifying the duration of the order or altering or cancelling such a provision already included in it; or

(*b*)   substituting for the provisions of the order by which the supervisor is designated or by virtue of which he is selected such other provisions in that behalf as could have been included in the order if the court had then had power to make it and were exercising the power; or

(*c*)   substituting for the name of an area included in the order in pursuance of s. 18(2)(*a*) of this Act the name of any other area of a local authority or petty sessions area, as the case may be, in which it appears to the court that the supervised person resides or will reside; or

(*d*)   cancelling any provision included in the order by virtue of s. 18(2)(*b*) of this Act or inserting in it any provision prescribed for the purposes of that paragraph; or

(*e*)   cancelling any requirement included in pursuance of s. 12(1) or (2) of this Act.

(4) If while a supervision order is in force in respect of a supervised person who has attained the age of eighteen it is proved to the satisfaction of a magistrates' court other than juvenile court, on the application of the supervisor, that the supervised person has failed to comply with any requirement included in the supervision order in pursuance of s. 12 or s. 18(2)(*b*) of this Act, the court may—

(*a*)   whether or not it also makes an order under subs. (3) of this section, order him to pay a fine of an amount not exceeding £100 or, subject to subs. (10) of the following section, make an attendance centre order in respect of him;

(*b*)   if it also discharges the supervision order, make an order imposing on him any punishment which it could have imposed on him if it had then had power to try him for the offence in consequence of which the supervision order was made and had convicted him in the exercise of that power;

and in a case where the offence in question is of a kind which the court has no power to try without appropriate consents, the punishment imposed by virtue of para. (*b*) of this subsection shall not exceed that which any court having power to try such an offence could have imposed in respect of it and shall not in any event exceed imprisonment for a term of six months and a fine of £2,000.

(5) (*Concerns the juvenile court*).

(6) The preceding provisions of this section shall have effect subject to the provisions of the following section.
(*as amended by the Criminal Law Act 1977, ss. 37, 58(5)*).

COMMENTARY

Proceedings under this section in the adult court are governed by the restrictions on reporting applicable to juvenile courts: Children and Young Persons Act 1933, s. 49 as applied by 1969, s. 10; and this fact must be announced in the course of the proceedings: 1969, s. 10(2).

For the right to appeal against an order under this section *see* s. 16(8), *infra*.

Subsection (3): Supervision order. Has the meaning assigned to it by s. 11 of the Act: s. 70(1), *ibid*. Supervision orders to which this subsection apply will have been made by the juvenile court under s. 7(7) of the Act.

Attained the age of 18. For the determination of age *see* s. 99 of the 1933 Act. Variations under the age of 18 are made in the juvenile court under subs. (1), even though the supervised person is no longer a juvenile.

A magistrates' court. As to which court *see* s. 16(11), *infra*.

The application of . . . a supervised person. Or his parent or guardian: s. 70(2).

Subsection (3)(b): Such other provisions. *See* ss 12 and 18 of the Act.

Make an attendance centre order. Under the Criminal Justice Act 1982, s. 17. *See* Ch. 6. *See* also subs. (10) of s. 16.

Provisions supplementary to s. 15

16. (1) Where the supervisor makes an application or reference under the preceding section to a court he may bring the supervised person before the court and subject to subs. (5) of this section a court shall not make an order under that section unless the supervised person is present before the court.

(2) Without prejudice to any power to issue a summons or warrant apart from this subsection, a justice may issue a summons or warrant for the purpose of securing the attendance of a supervised person before the court to which any application or reference in respect of him is made under the preceding section; but subss (3) and (4) of s. 55 of the Magistrates' Courts Act, 1980 (which among other things restrict the circumstances in which a warrant may be issued) shall apply with the necessary modifications to a warrant under this subsection as they apply to a warrant under that section and as if in subs. (3) after the work "summons" there were inserted the words "cannot be served or".

(3) Where the supervised person is arrested in pursuance of a warrant issued by virtue of the preceding subsection and cannot be brought immediately before the court referred to in that subsection, the person in whose custody he is—

(a)   may make arrangements for his detention in a place of safety for a period of not more than 72 hours from the time of the arrest (and it shall be lawful for him to be detained in pursuance of the arrangements); and

(b)   shall within that period, unless within it the relevant infant is brought before the court aforesaid, bring him before a justice;

and the justice shall either direct that he be released forthwith or—

(i)   if he has not attained the age of 18, make an interim order in respect of him;

(ii)   if he has attained that age. remand him.

(4) (*Concerns the juvenile court*).

(5) A court may make an order under the preceding section in the absence of the supervised person if the effect of the order is confined to one or more of the following, that is to say—

(a)   discharging the supervision order;

(b)   cancelling a provision included in the supervision order in pursuance of s. 12 or s. 18(2)(b) of this Act;

(c)   reducing the duration of the supervision order or any provision included in it in pursuance of the said s. 12;

(d)   altering in the supervision order the name of any area;

(e)   changing the supervisor.

(6) (*Concerns the juvenile court*).

(7) Where the supervised person has attained the age of 14, then except with his consent a court shall not make an order under the preceding section containing provisions which insert in the supervision order a requirement authorized by s. 12(4) of this Act or which alter such a requirement already included in the supervision order otherwise than by removing it or reducing its duration.

(8) The supervised person may appeal to the Crown Court against—

(a)   any order made under the preceding section, except an order made or which could have been made in the absence of the supervised person and an order containing only provisions to which he consented in pursuance of the preceding subsection;

(b)   the dismissal of an application under that section to discharge a supervision order.

(9) Where an application under the preceding section for the discharge of a supervision order is dismissed, no further application for its discharge shall be made under that section by any person during the period of three months beginning with the date of the dismissal except with the consent of a court having jurisdiction to entertain such an application.

(10) In para. (b) of subs. (2A) and para. (a) of subs. (4) of the preceding section "attendance centre order" means such an order to attend an attendance centre as is mentioned in subs. (1) of s. 17 of the Criminal Justice Act 1982; and the provisions of that section shall accordingly apply for the purpose of each of those paragraphs as if for the words from "has power" to "probation order" in subs. (1) there were substituted the words "considers it appropriate to make an attendance centre order in respect of any person in pursuance of s. 15(2A) or (4) of the Children and Young Persons Act 1969" and for references to an offender there were substituted references to the supervised person and as if subs. (13) were omitted.

(11) In this and the preceding section references to a juvenile court or any other magistrates' court, in relation to a supervision order, are references to such a court acting for the petty sessions area for the time being named in the order in pursuance of s. 18(2)(a) of this Act; and if while an application to a juvenile court in pursuance of the preceding section is pending the supervised person to whom it related attains the age of 17 or 18, the court shall deal with the application as if he had not attained the age in question.

(as amended by the Courts Act 1971, sch. 9, the Criminal Law Act 1977, sch. 12, the Magistrates' Courts Act 1980, sch. 7, the Criminal Justice Act 1982, sch. 14).

COMMENTARY

Proceedings under this section in the adult court are governed by the restrictions on reporting applicable to juvenile courts: Children and Young Persons Act, 1933, s. 40, as applied by 1969, s. 10. This fact must be announced in the course of the proceedings: 1969, s. 10(2).

Subsection (2): Subsections (3) and (4) of s. 55 of the Magistrates' Courts Act, 1980. It is submitted that, despite the reference in subs. (3) to the summons being served and the wording of the prescribed form of warrant (form 6), a warrant may be issued without a summons first being issued if the supervisor states that it would be impracticable to serve a summons.

Subsection (3): Place of safety. This means a community home provided by a local authority or a controlled community home, any police station or any hospital, surgery or any other suitable place, the occupier of which is willing temporarily to receive a child or young person: s. 107(1) of the Act of 1933.

Remand him. That is, under the Magistrates' Courts Act 1980, s. 128.

Is present. Appearance by counsel or solicitor under the Magistrates' Courts Act 1980, s. 122 is not enough.

Requirements authorized by s. 12(4). This relates to medical treatment.

Order which could have been made in the absence. *See* subs. (5).

Supplementary provisions relating to supervision orders
18. (1), (2) . . .

(3) A court which makes a supervision order or an order varying or discharging a supervision order shall forthwith send a copy of its order—

> (a)   to the supervised person and, if the supervised person is a child, to his parent or guardian; and

> (b)   to the supervisor and any person who has ceased to be the supervisor by virtue of the order; and

(*c*) to any local authority who is not entitled by virtue of the preceding paragraph to such a copy and whose area is named in the supervision order in pursuance of the preceding subsection or has ceased to be so named by virtue of the court's order; and

(*d*) where the supervised person is required by the order, or was required by the supervision order before it was varied or discharged, to reside with an individual or to undergo treatment by or under the direction of an individual or at any place, to the individual or the person in charge of that place; and

(*e*) where a petty sessions area named in the order or discharged order in pursuance of subs. (2) of this section is not that for which the court acts, to the clerk to the justices for the petty sessions area so named;

and, in a case falling within para. (*e*) of this subsection, shall also send to the clerk to the justices in question such documents and information relating to the case as the court considers likely to be of assistance to them.

(4) . . .

THE IMMIGRATION ACT 1971

General provisions for regulation and control

3   (1) - (5) . . .

(6) Without prejudice to the operation of subs. (5) above, a person who is not a British citizen shall also be liable to deportation from the United Kingdom if, after he has attained the age of 17, he is convicted of an offence for which he is punishable with imprisonment and on his conviction is recommended for deportation by a court empowered by this Act to do so.

(7) (*Power to make orders in Council*).

(8) When any question arises under this Act whether or not a person is a British citizen, or is entitled to any exemption under this Act, it shall lie on the person asserting it to prove that he is.

(9), (9A) . . .

(as amended by the British Nationality Act 1981, s. 39 (3), sch. 4.)

COMMENTARY

Subsection (6): Liable to deportation. By order of the Secretary of State in accordance with s. 5.

Attained the age of 17. That is, on the relevant anniversary of his birth: Family Law Reform Act 1969, s. 9. And *see* s. 6(3)(a), *infra*.

Convicted. A conviction followed by an order of probation, absolute or conditional discharge is a conviction for the purposes of deportation recommendations notwithstanding the Powers of Criminal Courts Act 1973, s. 13: *R.* v. *Akan* (1972) 136 J.P. 766. And see also s. 6(3), *infra*.

An offence for which he is punishable by imprisonment. To be determined without regard to the statutory restrictions on the imprisonment of young offenders or of persons not previously sentenced to imprisonment: s. 6(3)(b).

An offence triable either way punishable by imprisonment only on conviction on indictment would not appear to fall within the terms of the statute if tried summarily.

An offender dealt with otherwise than by imprisonment in respect of an offence punishable by imprisonment would however be liable to be recommended for deportation. Although the occasions must be rare when it would be right for justices not to make a recommendation in the case of an offender convicted of an offence under s. 24 of the Act (remaining in the United Kingdom without leave) justices have a complete discretion in the matter: *Khan* v. *Shea* (1968) *The Times*, November 1; 112 Sol. Jo. 908.

Recommended for deportation. That is under s. 6(1), *infra*.

Recommendations by court for deportation

6. (1) Where under s. 3(6) above a person convicted of an offence is liable to deportation on the recommendation of a court, he may be recommended for deportation by any court having power to sentence him for the offence unless the court commits him to be sentenced or further dealt with for that offence by another court:

(Proviso applies to Scotland).

(2) A court shall not recommend a person for deportation unless he has been given not less than seven days notice in writing stating that a person is not liable to deportation if he is a British citizen, describing the persons who are patrial and stating (so far as material) the effect of s. 3(8) above and s. 7 below; but the powers of adjournment conferred by s. 10(3) of the Magistrates' Courts Act 1980, ss. 179 or 380 of the Criminal Procedure (Scotland) Act 1975 or any corresponding enactment for the time being in force in Northern Ireland shall include power to adjourn, after convicting an offender, for the purpose of enabling a notice to be given to him under this subsection or, if a notice was given to him less than seven days previously, for the purpose of enabling the necessary seven days to elapse.

(3) For purposes of s. 3(6) above—

(*a*)   a person shall be deemed to have attained the age of 17 at the time of his conviction if, on consideration of any available evidence, he appears to have done so to the court making or considering a recommendation for deportation; and

(*b*)   the question whether an offence is one for which a person is punishable with imprisonment shall be determined without regard to any enactment restricting the imprisonment of young offenders or persons who have not previously been sentenced to imprisonment;

and for purposes of deportation a person who on being charged with an offence is found to have committed it shall, notwithstanding any enactment to the contrary and notwithstanding that the court does not proceed to conviction, be regarded as a person convicted of the offence, and references to conviction shall be construed accordingly.

(4) . . .

(5) Where a court recommends or purports to recommend a person for deportation, the validity of the recommendation shall not be called in question except on an appeal against the recommendation or against the conviction on which it is made; but the recommendation shall be treated as a sentence for the purpose of any enactment providing an appeal against sentence.

(6) A deportation order shall not be made on the recommendation of a court so long as an appeal or further appeal is pending against the recommendation or against the conviction on which it was made; and for this purpose an appeal or

further appeal shall be treated as pending (where one is competent but has not been brought) until the expiration of the time for bringing that appeal or, in Scotland, until the expiration of 28 days from the date of the recommendation.

(7) (*Applies to Scotland*).

(*as amended by the Criminal Justice Act 1972, sch. 5, the Criminal Procedure (Scotland) Act 1975, sch. 9, the Magistrates' Courts Act 1980, sch. 7, the British Nationality Act 1981, sch. 4, the Criminal Justice Act 1982, sch. 16.*)

COMMENTARY

Subsection (1). For the principles upon which the court should exercize its discretion *see* the introduction.

It is advisable in general that legal aid should be granted when a recommendation is being considered: *R.* v. *Edgehill,* [1963] 1 All E.R. 181. Normally if a court is minded to make a recommendation it would be desirable for his advocate to be given the opportunity of making any submissions they may wish in that respect, *per* Megaw, LJ in *R.* v. *Antypas* [1972] 57 Cr. App. R. 207; but this is not a rule of law: *R.* v. *Newham Justices, ex parte Akhtar* (1982) 25 June.

A suggested certificate of recommendation is attached to Home Office circ. 215/1972 dated December 15, 1972.

Once a recommendation has been made the provisions of sch. 3 apply with respect to detention or control.

Commits him to be sentenced or further dealt with. Thus where magistrates commit an offender to the Crown Court they may not at the same time make a recommendation for deportation.

Subsection (2): Notice.

"12. The service of a notice will, as at present, be the duty of the police, and the Secretary of State has suggested to chief officers of police the use of the form of notice which is enclosed with this circular. He has suggested, further, that where a person is charged with an offence of illegal entry under *s.* 24(1)(a) of the Act, or of overstaying or breach of conditions under *s.* 24(1)(b) or where, in a particular case, they consider it desirable to do so, the police should normally serve the notice forthwith, as a matter of course; but that, in all other cases, where notice has not been served on a person who appears to the police to be liable for deportation, and who is charged with an offence punishable with imprisonment, they should be prepared to provide the court with whatever information they have about his liability, and should seek the court's direction on whether the notice should be served. The direction will be sought at the end of the accused person's first court appearance on the charge, i.e. when he is convicted or, as the case may be, when he is remanded or committed for sentence or trial.

"13. Where a notice has been served on a person, the prosecution will so inform the court when giving, after conviction, particulars of the character and antecedents of the offender. The court will also be given any information that the prosecution may have bearing on the offender's liability to deportation.

"14. It is also desirable that the governor of a prison or remand centre should be informed whenever a person in his custody has been, or is about to be, served with a notice under *s.* 6(2) of the Act. Accordingly, it is requested that, when proceedings are adjourned to enable a notice to be given to the prisoner or to enable the necessary seven days after the service of a notice to elapse, the purpose of the adjournment should be indicated on the warrant of commitment on remand.":

Home Office circ. 215/1972 dated December 15, 1972 (which also contains a recommended form of notice).

Acknowledgment of the notice should be attached to the papers sent to the appeal court: *R.* v. *Edgehill, supra.*

Subsection (4): Any rule of practice. *See R.* v. *Assa Singh* [1965] 1 All E.R. 938.

Exemption from deportation for certain existing residents

7. (1) Notwithstanding anything in s. 3(5) or (6) above but subject to the provisions of this section, a Commonwealth citizen or citizen of the Republic of Ireland who was such a citizen at the coming into force of this Act and was then ordinarily resident in the United Kingdom—

(*a*), (*b*) . . .; and
(*c*)   shall not on conviction of an offence be recommended for deportation
         under s. 3(6) if at the time of the conviction he had for the last five
         years been ordinarily resident in the United Kingdom and Islands.

(2) A person who has at any time become ordinarily resident in the United
Kingdom or in any of the Islands shall not be treated for the purposes of this
section as having ceased to be so by reason only of his having remained there in
breach of the immigration laws.

(3) The "last five years" before the material time under subs. (1)(*b*) or(*c*) above
is to be taken as a period amounting in total to five years exclusive of any time
during which the person claiming exemption under this section was undergoing
imprisonment or detention by virtue of a sentence passed for an offence on a
conviction in the United Kingdom and Islands, and the period for which he was
imprisoned or detained by virtue of the sentence amounted to six months or more.

(4) For purposes of subs. (3) above—

(*a*)   "sentence" includes any order made on conviction of an offence; and
(*b*)   two or more sentences for consecutive (or partly consecutive) terms
         shall be treated as a single sentence; and
(*c*)   a person shall be deemed to be detained by virtue of a sentence—

         (i) at any time when he is liable to imprisonment or detention by
         virtue of the sentence, but is unlawfully at large; and
         (ii) (unless the sentence is passed after the material time) during
         any period of custody by which under any relevant enactment
         the term to be served under the sentence is reduced.

In paragraph (*c*) (ii) above "relevant enactment" means s. 67 of the Criminal
Justice Act 1967 (or, before that section operated, s. 17(2) of the Criminal
Justice Administration Act, 1962) and any similar enactment which is for the
time being or has (before or after the passing of this Act) been in force in any part
of the United Kingdom and Islands.

(5) Nothing in this section shall be taken to exclude the operation of s. 3(8)
above in relation to an exemption under this section.

COMMENTARY

Exemptions transitional upon withdrawal of Pakistan from the Commonwealth are contained in the
Pakistan Act 1973, sch. 3.

Subsection 1(c): Islands. Defined in s. 33, *infra*.

Ordinarily resident. Illegal residence cannot amount to ordinary residence: *R*. v. *Bangoo*
[1976] Crim. L.R. 746.

Exceptions for seamen, aircrews and other special cases

8(1) . . .

(2) (*Rule making power*).

(3) The provisions of this Act relating to those who are not British
citizens shall not apply to any person so long as he is a member of a
mission (within the meaning of the Diplomatic Privileges Act 1964), a person who is a member of the family and forms part of the household of
such a member, or a person otherwise entitled to the like immunity from
jurisdiction as is conferred by that Act on a diplomatic agent.

(4) ...

(5) Where a person having a limited leave to enter or remain in the United Kingdom becomes entitled to an exemption under this section, that leave shall continue to apply after he ceases to be entitled to the exemption, unless it has by then expired; and a person is not to be regarded for purposes of this Act as having been settled in the United Kingdom at any time when he was entitled under the former immigration laws to any exemption corresponding to any of those afforded by subss. (3) or (4)(b) or (c) above or by any order under subs. (2) above.

(5A) (*Rules.*)

(6) In this section "the home forces" means any of Her Majesty's forces other than a Commonwealth force or a force raised under the law of any associated state, colony, protectorate or protected state; "Commonwealth force" means a force of any country to which provisions of the Visiting Forces Act, 1952, apply without an Order in Council under s. 1 of the Act; and "visiting force" means a body, contingent or detachment for the time being present in the United Kingdom on the invitation of Her Majesty's Government in the United Kingdom.

(*as amended by the British Nationality Act 1981, s. 39(4), sch. 4.*)

COMMENTARY

Subsection (3). Consular officers, etc., are exempted by the Immigration (Exemption from Control) Order 1972, S.I. 1972 No. 1613.

Interpretation

33. (1) For purposes of this Act, except in so far as the context otherwise requires—

"aircraft" includes hovercraft, "airport" includes hoverport and "port" includes airport;

"captain" means master (of a ship) or commander (of an aircraft);

"certificate of patriality" means such a certificate as is referred to in s. 3(9) above;

"crew", in relation to a ship or aircraft, means all persons actually employed in the working or service of the ship or aircraft, including the captain, and "member of the crew" shall be construed accordingly;

"entrant" means a person entering or seeking to enter the United Kingdom, and "illegal entrant" means a person unlawfully entering or seeking to enter in breach of a deportation order or of the immigration laws, and includes also a person who has so entered;

"entry clearance" means a visa, entry certificate or other document which, in accordance with the immigration rules, is to be taken as evidence of a person's eligibility, though not a British citizen, for entry into the United Kingdom (but does not include a work permit);

"immigration laws" means this Act and any law for purposes similar to this Act which is for the time being or has (before or after the passing of this Act) been in force in any part of the United Kingdom and Islands;

"immigration rules" means the rules for the time being laid down as mentioned in s. 3(2) above;

"the Islands" means the Channel Islands and the Isle of Man, and "the United Kingdom and Islands" means the United Kingdom and the Islands taken together;

"legally adopted" means adopted in pursuance of an order made by any court in the United Kingdom and Islands or by any adoption specified as an overseas adoption by order of the Secretary of State under s. 4 of the Adoption Act, 1958;

"limited leave" and "indefinite leave" mean respectively leave under this Act to enter or remain in the United Kingdom which is, and one which is not, limited as to duration;

"settled" shall be construed in accordance with subs. (2A) below;

"ship" includes every description of vessel used in navigation;

"United Kingdom passport" means a current passport issued by the Government of the United Kingdom, or by the Lieutenant Governor of any of the Islands or by the Government of any territory which is for the time being a dependent territory within the meaning of the British Nationality Act 1981;

"work permit" means a permit indicating in accordance with the immigration rules, that a person named in it is eligible, though not a British citizen, for entry into the United Kingdom for the purpose of taking employment.

(2) It is hereby declared that, except as otherwise provided in this Act, a person is not to be treated for the purposes of any provision of this Act as ordinarily resident in the United Kingdom or in any of the Islands at a time when he is there in breach of the immigration laws.

(2A) Subject to s. 8(5) above, references to a person being settled in the United Kingdom are references to his being ordinarily resident there without being subject under the immigration laws to any restriction on the period for which he may remain.

(3), (4) . . .

(5) This Act shall not be taken to supersede or impair any power exercisable by Her Majesty in relation to aliens by virtue of Her prerogative.

(as amended by the British Nationality Act 1981, sch. 4.)

COMMENTARY

Settled. By virtue of s. 33(2) an illegal entrant is not settled in this country: *Azam* v *Secretary of State* (1973) 137 J.P. 626.

SCHEDULE 3
(Section 5(5))

1. . . .

Detention or control pending deportation

2. (1) Where a recommendation for deportation made by a court is in force in respect of any person, and that person is neither detained in pursuance of the sentence or order of any court nor for the time being released on bail by any court having power so to release him, he shall, unless the court by which the recommendation is made otherwise directs or a direction is given under sub-para. (1A) below, be detained pending the making of a deportation order in pursuance of the recommendation, unless the Secretary of State directs him to be released pending further consideration of his case.

(2)-(4) . . .

3. . . . .

Powers of Courts Pending Deportation

4. Where the release of a person recommended for deportation is directed by a court, he shall be subject to such restrictions as to residence and as to reporting to the police as the court may direct.

5.−(1) On an application made−
   (a) by or on behalf of a person recommended for deportation whose release was so directed; or
   (b) by a constable; or
   (c) by an immigration officer,
the appropriate court shall have the powers specified in sub-para. (2) below.

   (2) The powers mentioned in sub-para. (1) above are−
   (a) if the person to whom the application relates is not subject to any such restrictions imposed by a court as are mentioned in para. 4 above, to order that he shall be subject at any such restrictions as the court may direct; and
   (b) if he is subject to such restrictions imposed by a court by virtue of that paragraph or this paragraph−
       (i)   to direct that any of them shall be varied or shall cease to have effect; or
       (ii) to give further directions as to his residence and reporting.

6.−(1) In this Schedule "the appropriate court" means, except in a case to which sub-para. (2) below applies, the court which directed release.

   (2) This sub-paragraph applies where the court which directed release was−
   (a) the Crown Court;
   (b) the Court of Appeal;
   (c) the High Court of Justiciary;
   (d) the Crown Court in Northern Ireland; or
   (e) the Court of Appeal in Northern Ireland.

   (3) Where the Crown Court or the Crown Court in Northern Ireland directed release, the appropriate court is−
   (a) the court that directed release; or
   (b) a magistrates' court acting for the commission area or county court division where the person to whom the application relates resides.

   (4), (5) . . .

7.−(1) A constable or immigration officer may arrest with warrant any person who is subject to restrictions imposed by a court under this Schedule and who at the time of the arrest is in the relevant part of the United Kingdom−
   (a) if he has reasonable grounds to suspect that that person is contravening or has contravened any of those restrictions; or
   (b) if he has reasonable grounds for believing that that person is likely to contravene any of them.

   (2) In sub-para. (1) above "the relevant part of the United Kingdom" means−
   (a) England and Wales, in a case where a court with jurisdiction in England or Wales imposed the restrictions;
   (b) Scotland, in a case where a court with jurisdiction in Scotland imposed them; and
   (c) Northern Ireland, in a case where a court in Northern Ireland imposed them.

8.−(1) A person arrested in England or Wales or Northern Ireland in pursuance of para. 7 above shall be brought as soon as practicable and in any event within 24 hours after his arrest before a justice of the peace for the petty sessions area or district in which he was arrested.

(2) In reckoning for the purposes of this paragraph any period of 24 hours, no account shall be taken of Christmas Day, Good Friday or any Sunday.

9. (*Scotland.*)

10. Any justice of the peace or court before whom a person is brought by virtue of paras. 8 or 9 above—

    (*a*)   if of the opinion that that person is contravening, has contravened or is likely to contravene any restriction imposed on him by a court under this Schedule, may direct—

        (i)   that he be detained; or

        (ii) that he be released subject to such restrictions as to his residence and reporting to the police as the court may direct; and

    (*b*)   if not of that opinion, shall release him without altering the restrictions as to his residence and his reporting to the police.

(*as amended by the Criminal Justice Act 1982, sch. 10*).

COMMENTARY

Para. 2. The exclusion in para. 2(1) of sch. 3 from the need to detain persons "released on bail by any court" does not apply to bail on an irrelevant charge: *R*. v. *Secretary of State for the Home Office, ex parte Giambe* [1981] 3 Cr. App. R. (S) 260. It is nowhere stated where persons shall be detained in pursuance of para. 2 or who shall convey them there. The paragraph has effect without any order or warrant of the court.

Para. 4. The power to direct release is not a power to grant bail. Thus, the court cannot demand the defendant's recognizances, take a surety or impose conditions other than those allowed in para. 4.

THE POWERS OF CRIMINAL COURTS ACT 1973

Probation

2. (1) Where a court by or before which a person of or over 17 years of age is convicted of an offence (not being an offence the sentence for which is fixed by law) is of opinion that having regard to the circumstances, including the nature of the offence and the character of the offender, it is expedient to do so, the court may, instead of sentencing him, make a probation order, that is to say, an order requiring him to be under the supervision of a probation officer for a period to be specified in the order of not less than six months nor more than three years.

For the purposes of this subsection the age of a person shall be deemed to be that which it appears to the court to be after considering any available evidence.

(2) A probation order shall name the petty sessions area in which the offender resides or will reside; and the offender shall (subject to the provisions of sch. 1 to this Act relating to probationers who change their residence) be required to be under the supervision of a probation officer appointed for or assigned to that area.

In this Act "supervising court" means, in relation to a probation order, a magistrates' court acting for the petty sessions area for the time being named in the order.

(3) Subject to the provisions of subs. (4) below and ss. 3, 4A and 4B of this Act a probation order may in addition require the offender to comply during the whole or any part of the probation period with such requirements as the court, having regard to the circumstances of the case, considers necessary for securing the good conduct of the offender or for preventing a repetition by him of the same offence or the commission of other offences.

(4) Without prejudice to the power of the court under s. 35 of this Act to make a compensation order, the payment of sums by way of damages for injury or compensation for loss shall not be included among the requirements of a probation order.

(5) Without prejudice to the generality of subs. (3) above, a probation order may include requirements relating to the residence of the offender, but—

(a) before making an order containing any such requirements, the court shall consider the home surroundings of the offender; and

(b) where the order requires the offender to reside in an approved probation hostel or any other institution, the period for which he is so required to reside shall be specified in the order.

(6) Before making a probation order, the court shall explain to the offender in ordinary language the effect of the order (including any additional requirements proposed to be inserted therein and that if he fails to comply with it or commits another offence he will be liable to be sentenced for the original offence; and the court shall not make the order unless he expresses his willingness to comply with its requirements.

(7) The court by which a probation order is made shall forthwith give copies of the order to a probation officer assigned to the court, and he shall give a copy to the offender, to the probation officer responsible for the supervision of the offender and to the person in charge of any institution in which the probationer is required by the order to reside; and the court shall, except where it is itself the supervising court, send to the clerk to the justices for the petty sessions area named in the order a copy of the order, together with such documents and information relating to the case as it considers likely to be of assistance to the supervising court.

(8). (Repealed)

(9), (10) . . .

(as amended by the Criminal Law Act 1977, s. 57, schs. 12, 13, the Probation Orders (Variation of Statutory Limits) Order 1978, S.I. 1978, No. 474, the Criminal Justice Act 1982, schs. 11, 16.)

COMMENTARY

For the use of probation see the introduction.

Subsection (1): Convicted. For the effects of a probation order upon the conviction see s. 13, infra.

Instead of sentencing him. These words to not take away the court's power to order the offender to pay costs or compensation: s. 12(4), infra.

Probation order. See form 64.

A probation officer. Selected in accordance with sch. 3, Part I, para. 9. His duties are set out in para. 8, ibid.

A period. The period may not be reduced by amendment or extended more than three years from the original date, but the order may be discharged altogether (sch. 1 to the Act, infra) or its unexpired portion converted to a conditional discharge under s. 11, infra.

The minimum period (now six months) was reduced from one year by the Probation Orders (Variation of Statutory Limits) Order 1978, S.I. 1978 No. 474. (Home Office circ. 67/1978 refers.)

Subsection (3): Such requirements as the court . . . considers necessary. Common requirements are: to be of good behaviour and lead an industrious life; to keep in touch with the probation officer, notifying him of any change of address; to report to the probation officer from time to time in accordance with his instructions; and for the offender to receive visits in his home from the probation officer. (The Sentence of the Court)

Requirements cannot be added to a probation order which are not otherwise authorized by the terms of the statute. The language of s. 2(3) is very wide, but the power to impose requirements is subject to limitations, viz: (1) "Since the making of a probation order is a course taken by the court to avoid the passing of a custodial sentence a requirement must not introduce such a custodial or other element as will amount in substance to the imposition of a sentence". (2) "Since it is the court alone which can define the requirements of the order, any discretion conferred on the probation officer must itself be confined within well defined limits". Thus "a court cannot under the guise of a requirement imposed pursuant to s. 2(3) require a probationer to perform such unpaid work as would appropriately be the subject of a community service order". No requirement to reside in any sort of institution could properly be imposed under s. 2(3). A requirement to attend for a given number of hours at an institutional establishment and there to comply with instructions of a wholly unspecified character given by the probation officer would go far beyond the range of proper requirements on the ground both that it would involve a substantial element of custodial punishment and that it would subject the probationer to the unfettered discretionary control of the probation officer: *Cullen* v. *Rogers* (1982) 146 J.P. 25. These limitations on the power to impose requirements under s. 2(3) must now be read in light of the power to impose certain carefully limited requirements under s. 4A, *infra*, ("presenting", "participating", and "refraining" requirements) and under s. 4B, *infra*, (day training centre requirement). Requirements as to residence may be imposed under s. 2(5). Requirements as to treatment for a mental condition are dealt with in s. 3(8).

There is no power to include a condition that the defendant leaves the country and does not return: *R.* v. *McCartan* (1958) 122 J.P. 465 (an Irish youth). Although it was stated in that case that such an order should be made under the Justices of the Peace Act, 1361, there is in fact no such power: *R.* v. *Ayu* (1959) 123 J.P. 76. The condition that the probationer should lead an "honest and industrious life" was criticized by the Court of Criminal Appeal at (1952) 116 J.P.N. 145.

There is no power to include a condition that the defendant leaves the country and does not return: *R.* v. *McCartan* (1958) 122 J.P. 465; [1958] 3 All E.R. 140; (an Irish youth). Although it was stated in that case that such an order should be made under the Justices of the Peace Act, 1361, there is in fact no such power: *R.* v. *Ayu* (1159) 123 J.P. 76; [1958] 3 All E.R. 636. The condition that the probationer should lead an "honest and industrious life" was criticized by the Court of Criminal Appeal at (1952) 116 J.P.N. 145.

Requirements may be cancelled or inserted by amendment under sch. 1 to the Act, *infra*.

Subsection (5): Approved probation hostel. The Home Office advise:

> Approved probation hostels (run by the probation service or by voluntary organizations and approved by the Secretary of State) provide a stable and supportive environment in which groups of between 15 and 25 offenders may learn how to get on with their contemporaries and other people, including those in authority, and may be helped to develop regular work habits and to achieve satisfaction in work and at leisure. The emphasis is upon helping the resident through group and individual contact both inside and outside the hostel to move towards a more adequate way of life and away from a pattern of offending. Probationers in hostels are expected to go to daily employment (or to full-time education or training) outside the hostel. They contribute from their earnings towards their board and lodging and are helped to take responsibility for their own affairs.
>
> A number of hostels however provide for more inadequate offenders who are unlikely to be able to obtain and keep ordinary employment in the community. Residents in these hostels initially receive full-time training on the premises aimed at the acquisition of basic work habits, but commonly go to outside employment during the later stages of their stay.
>
> Residence in a probation hostel is likely to be of benefit to offenders who are socially or emotionally immature or who, by reason of their background, are likely to be socially isolated and to lack family or community support. It is expected that offenders will have had a number of previous convictions and may also have had experience of custodial treatment. However, residents are not in legal custody, and hostels are unlikely to be suitable for the more serious offenders or those who require special care by reason of a high degree of personal disturbance or addiction to drugs or alcohol.
>
> *(The Sentence of the Court)*

Subsection (6): Willingness to comply. This is not exactly the same as the offender's consent. Note also that the court should explain, not only the normal conditions of a probation order, but also any special requirements imposed in the particular case. There is no consent where the offender is not given a free choice: *R.* v. *Marquis* [1974] 2 All E.R. 1216 (given the impression that the only alternative was a custodial one).

Subsection (7). This subsection does not apply to orders made in respect of offenders who reside or will reside in Scotland: as to which *see* s. 10(7), *infra.*   The normal rule that orders made on appeal are made by the court from which the appeal is brought does not apply to this subsection: s. 12(2), *infra.*

Probation orders requiring treatment for mental condition

3. (1) Where the court is satisfied, on the evidence of a duly qualified medical practitioner approved for the purpose of s. 12 of the Mental Health Act, 1983, that the mental condition of an offender is such as requires and may be susceptible to treatment but is not such as to warrant his detention in pursuance of a hospital order under Part III of that Act, the court may, if it makes a probation order, include in it a requirement that the offender shall submit, during the whole of the probation period or during such part of that period as may be specified in the order, to treatment by or under the direction of a duly qualified medical practitioner with a view to the improvement of the offender's mental condition.

(2) The treatment required by any such order shall be such one of the following kinds of treatment as may be specified in the order, that is to say—

(*a*)   treatment as a resident patient in a hospital within the meaning of the Mental Health Act, 1983, or mental nursing home within the meaning of the Nursing Homes Act 1975, not being a special hospital within the meaning of the National Health Service Act 1977;

(*b*)   treatment as a non-resident patient at such institution or place as may be specified in the order; or

(*c*)   treatment by or under the direction of such duly qualified medical practitioner as may be specified in the order;

but the nature of the treatment shall not be specified in the order except as mentioned in paras (*a*), (*b*) or (*c*) above.

(3) A court shall not by virtue of this section include in a probation order a requirement that an offender shall submit to treatment for his mental condition unless it is satisfied that arrangements have been made for the treatment intended to be specified in the order (including arrangements for the reception of the offender where he is to be required to submit to treatment as a resident patient).

(4) While the probationer is under treatment as a resident patient in pursuance of a requirement of the probation order, the probation officer responsible for his supervision shall carry out the supervision to such extent only as may be necessary for the purpose of the discharge or amendment of the order.

(5) Where the medical practitioner by whom or under whose direction a probationer is being treated for his mental condition in pursuance of a probation order is of opinion that part of the treatment can be better or more conveniently given in or at an institution or place not specified in the order, being an institution or place in or at which the treatment of the probationer will be given by or under the direction of a duly qualified medical practitioner, he may, with the consent of the probationer, make arrangements for him to be treated accordingly; and the arrangements may provide for the probationer to receive part of his treatment as a resident patient in an institution or place notwithstanding that the institution or place is not one which could have been specified for that purpose in the probation order.

(6) Where any such arrangements as are mentioned in subs. (5) above are made for the treatment of a probationer—

(*a*)   the medical practitioner by whom the arrangements are made shall give notice in writing to the probation officer responsible for the supervision of the probationer, specifying the institution or place in or at which the treatment is to be carried out; and

(b)   the treatment provided for by the arrangements shall be deemed to be treatment to which he is required to submit in pursuance of the probation order.

(7) Subsections (2) and (3) of s. 54 of the Mental Health Act, 1983, shall have effect with respect to proof for the purposes of subs. (1) above of an offender's mental condition as they have effect with respect to proof of an offender's mental condition for the purposes of s. 37(2)(a) of that Act.

(8) The provisions of this section shall apply in relation to a probation order made or amended by virtue of s. 10 of this Act only so far as indicated in subs. (3) of that section, and except as provided by this section or s. 10 a court shall not include in a probation order a requirement that the probationer shall submit to treatment for his mental condition.

(as amended by the Mental Health Act 1983, sch. 4.)

COMMENTARY

For the effects of this section see Treatment for Mental Condition in the introduction.

Subsection (1): A duly qualified medical practitioner. *See* the Medical Act 1983, s. 55.

Subsection (5). It is not necessary to amend the order. Notice must however be given under subs. (6).

Requirements in probation orders.

4A (1) Without prejudice to the generality of s. 2(3) above, the power conferred by that subsection includes power, subject to the provisions of this section, to require the probationer—

(a)   to present himself to a person or persons specified in the order at a place or places so specified;

(b)   to participate or refrain from participating in activities specified in the order—
    (i)   on a day or days so specified; or
    (ii) during the probation period or such portion of it as may be so specified.

(2) A court shall not include in a probation order a requirement such as is mentioned in subs. (1) above unless it has first consulted a probation officer as to—

(a)   the offender's circumstances; and

(b)   the feasibility of securing compliance with the requirements, and is satisfied, having regard to the probation officer's report, that it is feasible to secure compliance with them.

(3) A court shall not include a requirement such as is mentioned in subs. (1)(a) above or a requirement to participate in activities if it would involve the co-operation of a person other than the probationer and the probation officer responsible for his supervision, unless that other person consents to its inclusion.

(4) A requirement such as is mentioned in subs. (1)(a) above shall operate to require the probationer—

(a)   in accordance with instructions given by the probation officer responsible for his supervision, to present himself at a place for not more than 60 days; and

(b)   while there, to comply with instructions given by, or under the authority of, the person in charge of the place.

(5) A place specified in the order shall have been approved by the probation committee for the area in which the premises are situated as providing facilities suitable for persons subject to probation orders.

(6) A requirement to participate in activities shall operate to require the probationer–

(a)   in accordance with instructions given by the probation officer responsible for his supervision, to participate in the activities for not more than 60 days; and

(b)   while participating, to comply with instructions given by, or under the authority of, the person in charge of the activities.

(7) Instructions given by a probation officer under subss. (4) or (6) above shall, as far as practicable, be such as to avoid any interference with the times, if any, at which the probationer normally works or attends a school or other educational establishment.

(as inserted by the Criminal Justice Act 1982, sch. 11.)

COMMENTARY

See under Probation Requirements in the introduction.

Subsection (1). All three types of requirement authorized by this subsection may be included in the same probation order. These requirements must however be carefully formulated and may not exceed the clear words of the statute.

Subsection (2): Consulted a probation officer. Presumably concerning the requirement. Normally the "consultation" will take the form of a social inquiry report, but a written report is not essential, for example where the offender and the offender's present circumstances are already sufficiently known to the probation officer. Where this is not the case the use of "stand down" report procedures is, it is submitted, bad practice.

The feasibility of compliance. Note that the court's conclusion must "have regard" to the probation officer's report. This does not mean that the probation officer has a veto, but the circumstances in which a court could be satisfied as to the feasibility of compliance in face of clear advice from a probation officer that compliance would not be feasible must be rare.

Subsection (3): Consents. There is no prescribed procedure for obtaining or proving consent but the court will clearly be satisfied if the probation officer reports that he has explained what is contemplated to the person concerned and that the latter has given his consent. The court would also accept such a statement from an advocate where he speaks of his own knowledge.

Subsection (4): 60 days. It is submitted that the effect of this subsection is that directions may be given by the probation officer in respect of not more than 60 days. It is not seemingly intended that the court should stipulate a period. The probation officer is under no obligation to use all the days.

Subsection (6). See the note to subs. (4). In this case however overall length of time must be specified by the court. *See* subs. (1).

Probation orders requiring attendance at day centre.

4B (1) Without prejudice to the generality of ss. 2(3) and 4A above, the power conferred by s. 2(3) above includes power, subject to the provisions of this section, to require the probationer during the probation period to attend at a day centre specified in the order.

(2) A court shall not include such a requirement in a probation order unless–

(*a*)   it has consulted a probation officer; and

(*b*)   it is satisfied—
    (i)   that arrangements can be made for the probationer's attendance at a centre; and
    (ii)   that the person in charge of the centre consents to the inclusion of the requirements.

(3) A requirement under subsection (1) above shall operate to require the probationer—

(*a*)   in accordance with instructions given by the probation officer responsible for his supervision, to attend on not more than 60 days at the centre specified in the order; and

(*b*)   while attending there to comply with instructions given by, or under the authority of, the person in charge of the centre.

(4) Instructions given by a probation officer under subsection (3) above shall, so far as is practicable, be such as to avoid any interference with the times, if any, at which the probationer normally works or attends a school or other educational establishment.

(5) References in this section to attendance at a day centre include references to attendance elsewhere than at the centre for the purpose of participating in activities in accordance with instructions given by, or under the authority of, the person in charge of the centre.

(6) In this section "day centre" means premises at which non-residential facilities are provided for use in connection with the rehabilitation of offenders and which—

(*a*)   are provided by a probation committee; or

(*b*)   have been approved by the probation committee for the area in which the premises are situated as providing facilities suitable for persons subject to probation orders.

(as inserted by the Criminal Justice Act 1982, sch. 11)

COMMENTARY

See under Day Centre in the introduction.

Subsection (2): Consulted a probation officer. *See* the note to s. 4A, *supra.*

Consents. *See* the note to s. 4A(3), *supra.*

Subsection (3): 60 days. *See* the note to s. 4A(4), *supra.*

Discharge and amendment of probation orders

5. (1) The provisions of sch. 1 to this Act shall have effect in relation to the discharge and amendment of probation orders.

(2) Where, under the following provisions of this Part of this Act, a probationer is sentenced for the offence for which he was placed on probation, the probation order shall cease to have effect.

COMMENTARY

The making of a deportation order does not discharge a probation order: *R.* v. *Bissett* [1973] Crim. L.R. 132.

Subsection (2): Sentenced. A further probation order is not a sentence: s. 2(1), *supra.*

Cease to have effect. But not any order for costs or compensation: *R.* v. *Evans* (1961) 125 J.P. 134.

Breach of requirement of probation order

6. (1) If at any time during the probation period it appears on information to a justice of the peace on whom jurisdiction is conferred by subs. (2) below that the probationer has failed to comply with any of the requirements of the order, the justice may issue a summons requiring the probationer to appear at the place and time specified therein, or may, if the information is in writing and on oath, issue a warrant for his arrest.

(2) The following justices shall have jurisdiction for the purposes of subs. (1) above, that is to say—

    (a)   if the probation order was made by a magistrates' court any justice acting for the petty sessions area for which that court or the supervising court acts;

    (b)   in any other case, any justice acting for the petty sessions area for which the supervising court acts;

and any summons or warrant issued under this section shall direct the probationer to appear or be brought before a magistrates' court acting for the petty sessions area for which the justice issuing the summons or warrants acts.

(3) If it is proved to the satisfaction of the magistrates' court before which a probationer appears or is brought under this section that the probationer has failed to comply with any of the requirements of the probation order, then, subject to the following provisions of this subsection, that court may deal with him in respect of the failure in any one of the following ways, that is to say:

    (a)   it may impose on him a fine not exceeding £400;

    (b)   [subject to subs. (10) below, it may make a community service order in respect of him;]

    (c)   in a case to which s. 17 of the Criminal Justice Act 1982 applies, it may make an order under that section requiring him to attend at an attendance centre; or

    (d)   where the probation order was made by a magistrates' court, it may deal with him for the offence in respect of which the probation order was made, in any manner in which it could deal with him if it had just convicted him of that offence.

(4) Where the probation order was made by the Crown Court and a magistrates' court has power to deal with the probationer under subs. (3)(a), (b) or (c) above in respect of a failure to comply with any of the requirements of the order, the magistrates' court may instead commit him to custody or release him on bail until he can be brought or appear before the Crown Court.

(5) A magistrates' court which deals with a probationer's case under subs. (4) above shall send to the Crown Court a certificate signed by a justice of the peace, certifying that the probationer has failed to comply with such of the requirements of the probation order as may be specified in the certificate, together with such other particulars of the case as may be desirable; and a certificate purporting to be so signed shall be admissible as evidence of the failure before the Crown Court.

(6) Where by virtue of subs. (4) above the probationer is brought or appears before the Crown Court, and it is proved to the satisfaction of the court that he has failed to comply with any of the requirements of the probation order, the court may deal with him in respect of the failure in any one of the following ways, that is to say:

    (a)   it may impose on him a fine not exceeding £400;

    (b)   [subject to subs. (10) below, it may make a community service order in respect of him;] or

    (c)   it may deal with him for the offence in respect of which the probation order was made in any manner in which it could deal with him if he had just been convicted before the Crown Court of that offence.

(7) A probationer who is required by the probation order to submit to treatment for his mental condition shall not be treated for the purposes of this section as having failed to comply with that requirement on the ground only that he has refused to undergo any surgical, electrical or other treatment if, in the opinion of the court, his refusal was reasonable having regard to all the circumstances; and without prejudice to the provisions of s. 8 of this Act, a probationer who is convicted of an offence committed during the probation period shall not on that account be liable to be dealt with under this section in respect of a failure to comply with any requirement of the probation order.

(8) Any exercise by a court of its powers under subss. (3)(a), (b) or (c) or (6)(a) or (b) above shall be without prejudice to the continuance of the probation order.

(9) A fine imposed under subs. (3)(a) above in respect of a failure to comply with the requirements of a probation order shall be deemed for the purposes of any enactment to be a sum adjudged to be paid by a conviction.

(10) Section 14(2) of this Act and, so far as applicable, the other provisions of this Act relating to community service orders shall have effect in relation to a community service order under this section as they have effect in relation to a community service order in respect of an offender, but as if the power conferred by ss. 16 and 17 of this Act to deal with the offender for the offence in respect of which the community service order was made were a power to deal with the probationer for the failure to comply with the requirements of the probation order in respect of which the community service order was made.

(as amended by the Criminal Justice Act 1982, sch. 14.)

COMMENTARY

The Costs in Criminal Cases Act 1973, applies to proceedings under this section as if the offender had been tried in those proceedings for the offence for which the order was made: s. 18(4), *ibid.*

Legal aid may be granted in proceedings under this section: Legal Aid Act 1974, ss 28 and 30(12).

Where a magistrates' court deals with a person under this section in respect of an order made by another court the clerk must notify the other court: Magistrates' Courts Rules 1981, r. 28(2).

Subsection (1): Any time during the probation period. Thus an information laid after the probation period is out of time.

Issue a summons. For the contents and service of the summons *see* the Magistrates' Courts Rules 1981, rr. 98, 99, and form 71. The Summary Jurisdiction (Process) Act 1881, s. 4 applies to this section as it applies to process issued under the Magistrates' Courts Act: s. 53 of the Act of 1973.

Issue a warrant. for the contents of the warrant, *see* the Magistrates' Courts Rules 1981 rr. 95, 96, and form 72. The warrant may be endorsed for bail: Magistrates' Courts Act 1980, s. 118..

The supervising court. Defined in s. 2(2), *supra.* Whenever a probationer is dealt with under this section by a magistrates' court other than the court which made the order, the clerk of that court shall notify the original court: Magistrates' Courts Rules 1981, r. 28(2).

Subsection (3): Proved to the satisfaction of the court. The Court of Criminal Appeal have laid down the following procedure:

"Where a prisoner is brought before a court for breach of a probation order (the breach alleged) should be put to him . . . in the clearest possible terms and he should be asked to say whether he admits it or not. The terms in which the matter should be put to him are: first, to say where he was convicted and what happened to him, then to tell him how the breach is alleged to have taken place, and, if it be by a further conviction, then to tell him the time of the conviction and the adjudication of the court. He should next be asked to say whether he admits those acts. If that is done, there is no further difficulty. If that is not done, then, of course, it being a trial, albeit without a jury, the prisoner will have to be asked whether he desires to give evidence or call witnesses, and the court will have to pronounce on whether they find the breach of the order has been proved. But it is desirable that the proceedings should begin by the matter being put clearly to the prisoner and for him to be asked whether he admits the allegation with regard to it":

per Byrne J in *R*. v. *Devine* (1956) 120 J.P. 238; *R*. v. *Long* (1960) 124 J.P. 4; *R*. v. *Chapman and Pidgley* (1960) 124 J.P. 219; *R*. v. *Holmes* (1966) 130 J.P. 102; and *R*. v. *Bruce* [1967] Crim. L.R. 356.

For the court's powers under this subsection when dealing with an adult offender convicted under s. 17 of an offence which, if he had been an adult, could not have been tried summarily, *see* s. 9, *infra*.

Subsection (3)(b). Has not yet been brought into force.

Subsection (3)(d). This includes power to make a further probation order, the original order becoming ineffective by virtue of s. 5(2), *supra: R*. v. *Havant Justices, ex parte Jacobs* (1957) 121 J.P. 197.   But, if a man who has broken the terms of a probation order is again put on probation without proper reflection: "it greatly weakens the force of probation orders, it brings the machinery of the probation service into contempt and public harm would result therefrom": *R*. v. *Thompson* [1969] 1 All E.R. 60.

In the event of the offender being sentenced in respect of the original offence any order for compensation made at the same time will continue in force: *R*. v. *Evans* (1961) 125 J.P. 134.

The defendant has a right to appeal to the Crown Court against sentence: Magistrates' Courts Act 1980, s. 108.

Subsection (4). Legal aid may be granted by magistrates' in respect of the proceedings in the Crown Court: Legal Aid Act 1974, ss 28 and 30(12).

Commit him to custody. The general right to bail applies: Bail Act 1976, s. 4(3) and sch. 1.

For the place to which defendants under 21 years of age should be committed *see* s. 27 of the Criminal Justice Act 1948. Committals to prison must be by warrant: Magistrates' Courts Rules 1981, r. 94. For the contents of the warrant *see* rr. 95, 96, *ibid*.

The Crown Court. The location of the Crown Court is specified in the Directions of the Lord Chief Justice, paras. 5-9. *See* Appx. C.

Subsection (5): A certificate. *See* form 74.

Admissible as evidence. But not conclusive evidence: *R*. v. *Devine* (1956) 120 J.P. 238; *R*. v. *Chapman and Pidgley* (1960) 124 J.P. 219; *R*. v. *Tucker* [1967] Crim. L.R. 473.

Subsection (7): A probationer who is convicted of an offence. For the method of dealing with such offenders *see* s. 8, *infra*.

Absolute and conditional discharge

7. (1) Where a court by or before which a person is convicted of an offence (not being an offence the sentence for which is fixed by law) is of opinion, having regard to the circumstances including the nature of the offence and the character of the offender, that it is inexpedient to inflict punishment and that a probation order is not appropriate, the court may make an order discharging him absolutely, or, if the court thinks fit, discharging him subject to the condition that he commits no offence during such period, not exceeding three years from the date of the order, as may be specified therein.

(2) An order discharging a person subject to such a condition is in this Act referred to as "an order for condtional discharge", and the period specified in any such order (subject to s. 8(1) of this Act) as "the period of conditional discharge".

(3) Before making an order for conditional discharge the court shall explain to the offender in ordinary language that if he commits another offence during the period of conditional discharge he will be liable to be sentenced for the original offence.

(4) Where, under the following provisions of this Part of this Act, a person conditionally discharged under this section is sentenced for the offence in respect of which the order for conditional discharge was made, that order shall cease to have effect.

(5) ...

(*as amended by the Criminal Law Act 1977, s. 57(2)*).

COMMENTARY

An order under this section may be combined with a disqualification for holding or obtaining a driving licence: Road Traffic Act 1972, s. 102. Costs and compensation may also be ordered: s. 12(4), *infra*.

On making an order of conditional discharge the court may allow persons who consent to do so to give security for the good behaviour of the offender: s. 12(1), *infra*. No other conditions may be imposed by virtue of this section. An order for conditional discharge cannot be made except in the presence of the defendant in view of the terms of subs. (3). An order for conditional discharge is not a "sentence" from which appeal may be made to the Crown Court: Magistrates' Courts Act 1980, s. 108, although the conviction itself may be challenged where the plea was one of not guilty: subs. (1), *ibid*.

Subsection (1): Convicted. To be construed in the case of a child or young person as including a reference to a person found guilty of an offence: Children and Young Persons Act 1933, s. 59(1).

For the effects of an order under this section upon conviction *see* s. 13, *infra*.

Inexpedient to inflict punishment. Thus, by analogy with a probation order, an order for conditional discharge may not be accompanied by a fine except in respect of a separate offence. An order under this section cannot be coupled with an order of deprivation of property: *R.* v. *Hunt* [1978] Crim. L.R. 697; *R.* v. *Savage* [1983] 147 J.P.N. 667.

Subsection (3). The requirement for the court to give the explanation is merely a statement of good practice and in *R.* v. *Wehner* (1977) 141 J.P. 24, an order was upheld where the task of explanation had been delegated to counsel.

Liable to be sentenced for the original offence. For the power to deal with an offender who has committed a further offence during the period of conditional discharge, *see* s. 8, *infra*.

Commission of further offence by probationer or person conditionally discharged

8. (1) If it appears to the Crown Court, where that court has jurisdiction in accordance with subs. (2) below, or to a justice of the peace having jurisdiction in accordance with that subsection, that a person in whose case a probation order or an order for conditional discharge has been made has been convicted by a court in any part of Great Britain of an offence committed during the relevant period, and has been dealt with in respect of that offence, that court or justice may, subject to subs. (3) below, issue a summons requiring that person to appear at the place and time specified therein or a warrant for his arrest.

In this section "the relevant period" means, in relation to a probation order, the probation period, and in relation to an order for conditional discharge, the period of conditional discharge.

(2) Jurisdiction for the purposes of sub. (1) above may be exercised—

    (*a*)   if the probation order or order for conditional discharge was made by the Crown Court, by that court;

    (*b*)   if the order was made by a magistrates' court, by a justice acting for the petty sessions area for which that court acts;

    (*c*)   in the case of a probation order, by whatever court it was made, by a justice acting for the petty sessions area for which the supervising court acts.

(3) A justice of the peace shall not issue a summons under this section except on information and shall not issue a warrant under this section except on information in writing and on oath.

(4) Subject to subs. (5) below, a summons or warrant issued under this section shall direct the person to whom it relates to appear or to be brought before the court by which the probation order or the order for conditional discharge was made.

(5) In the case of a probation order made by a magistrates' court, a summons or warrant issued by a justice acting for the petty sessions area for which the supervising court acts may specify the supervising court instead of the court which made the order.

(6) If a person in whose case a probation order or an order for conditional discharge has been made by the Crown Court is convicted by a magistrates' court

of an offence committed during the relevant period, the magistrates' court may commit him to custody or release him on bail until he can be brought or appear before the Crown Court; and if it does so the magistrates' court shall send to the Crown Court a copy of the minute or memorandum of the conviction entered in the register, signed by the clerk of the court by whom the register is kept.

(7) Where it is proved to the satisfaction of the court by which a probation order or an order for conditional discharge was made, or to the satisfaction of that court or the supervising court in the case of a probation order made by a magistrates' court, that the person in whose case the order was made has been convicted of an offence committed during the relevant period, the court may deal with him, for the offence for which the order was made, in any manner in which it could deal with him if he had just been convicted by or before that court of that offence.

(8) If a person in whose case a probation order or an order for conditional discharge has been made by a magistrates' court is convicted before the Crown Court of an offence committed during the relevant period, or is dealt with by the Crown Court for any such offence in respect of which he was committed for sentence to the Crown Court, the Crown Court may deal with him, for the offence for which the order was made, in any manner in which the magistrates' court could deal with him if it had just convicted him of that offence.

(9) If a person in whose case a probation order or an order for conditional discharge has been made by a magistrates' court is convicted by another magistrates' court of any offence committed during the relevant period, that court may, with the consent of the court which made the order or, in the case of a probation order, with the consent of that court or of the supervising court, deal with him, for the offence for which the order was made, in any manner in which the court could deal with him if it had just convicted him of that offence.

COMMENTARY

Although the commission of a further offence is, technically, a breach of a requirement of a probation order it may not be so dealt with under s. 6, but under this section: s. 6(7), *supra*.

"When an accused commits an offence while on probation it is usually desirable that a court should consider whether he is to be dealt with for the original offence, for if he is not, two consequences ensue. First, the original offence cannot thereafter be treated as a conviction. Second, the probation officer's responsibilities under the probation order continue, even though the accused may have been sent to prison for the offence in respect of which he is before the court, unless and until the probation order is discharged." *R. v. Calvert* (1961) 127 J.P. 61.

Legal aid may be granted in these proceedings: Legal Aid Act 1974, ss 28 and 30(12). Costs are regulated by the Costs in Criminal Cases Act 1973, as if the offender had been tried for the offence for which the order was made: s. 18(4), *ibid.*

Subsection (1): Great Britain. That is, England, Scotland and Wales: Union with Scotland Act, 1706; Wales and Berwick Act, 1746, s. 3.

Has been dealt with. And not "sentenced". Therefore if an offender is placed on probation or discharged absolutely or conditionally in respect of the second offence he may still be dealt with under this section. The terms of s. 13(1), *infra,* exempt "any subsequent proceedings which may be taken against the offender under the preceding provisions of this Act." *See R. v. Wilcox* (1964) November 21, unreported.

Issue a summons/warrant. *See* the notes to s. 6, *supra,* and forms 78, 79.

Subsection (2): Petty sessions area. *See* the note to s. 6, *supra.*

Subsection (3): On information. *See* form 77. Unlike proceedings under s. 6, *supra* this may be laid after the relevant period has expired.

Subsection (6): Commit him to custody. The general right to bail (Bail Act 1976, s. 4) does not apply.

For the place to which defendants under 21 years should be committed *see* the Criminal Justice Act, 1948, s. 27. Committals to custody must be by warrant: Magistrates' Courts Rules 1981, r. 94. For the contents of the warrant *see* rr. 95, 96, and form 82.

Release him on bail. *See* the note to s. 6, *supra.*

The Crown Court. For the location of the Crown Court *see* paras 5-9 of the directions of the Lord Chief Justice in Appendix C.

When committing under subs. (6) there is power to commit for sentence also in respect of certain other offences at the same time under the Criminal Justice Act 1967, s. 56.

Legal aid may be granted in respect of the proceedings in the Crown Court: Legal Aid Act 1974, ss. 28 and 30(12).

Subsection (7): Proved to the satisfaction of the court. *See* the Commentary on s. 6, *supra.*

The supervising court. Defined in s. 2(2). If that court deals with the probationer under this section, it must notify the court which made the order: Magistrates' Courts Rules 1981, r. 28(2).

An offence committed during the relevant period. Even though the conviction may be outside that period: *R. v. Lee* [1976] Crim. L.R. 521.

Any manner in which the court could deal with him. The court should first make proper inquiry of the facts of the earlier offence: *R. v. Laval* [1977] Crim. L.R. 627. By analogy with s. 6, *supra*, this includes the power to make a further probation order, as a result of which the original order becomes ineffective: *R. v. Havant Justices, ex parte Jacobs* (1957) 121 J.P. 197. But such an order should not be made lightly: *R. v. Thompson* [1969] 1 All E.R. 60. Where an offender is put on probation on two separate occasions, a sentence for the original offence not being imposed at the second occasion, the offender falls to be dealt with under this section for both if he should later commit a third offence: *R. v. Keeley* (1960) 124 J.P. 325; (the second probation order being "ineffective" only in so far as supervision is concerned in respect of orders which are concurrent).

"The sentence (upon commission of a further offence) should in general be made consecutive and should be more than a nominal one": *R. v. Stuart* (1965) 129 J.P. 197. And *see* also *R. v. Fry* (1955) 119 J.P. 75.

The sentence does not affect any order for compensation made on the original occasion: *R. v. Evans* (1961) 125 J.P. 134. (Although this was a case under s. 6, *supra*, the court expressed the view that it seemed immaterial in this respect whether the offender was dealt with under s. 6 or s. 8).

For the court's powers when dealing with an adult offender convicted when under 17 of an offence which, if he had been an adult, could not have been dealt with summarily, *see* s. 9, *infra.*

The defendant has a right to appeal to the Crown Court against sentence when dealt with by magistrates for the original offence: Magistrates' Courts Act 1980 s, 108.

Subsection (9): The consent of the court. The justices' clerk may give consent when the order was made after the offender attained the age of 17: Justices' Clerks Rules 1970.

Any manner in which the court could deal with him. *See* the note to subs. (7), *supra.*

Breach of conditional discharge by young offenders

9. (1) Where an order for conditional discharge has been made by a magistrates' court in the case of an offender under 17 years of age in respect of an offence triable only on indictment in the case of an adult any powers exercisable by that or any other court in respect of the offender after he has attained the age of 17 years under subss. (7), (8) or (9) of s. 8 of this Act shall be those which would be exercisable if that offence were an offence triable either way and had been tried summarily.

For the purposes of this section the age of an offender at a particular time shall be deemed to be or to have been that which appears to the court after considering any available evidence to be or to have been his age at that time.
(*as amended by the Criminal Law Act 1977, sch. 12*).

COMMENTARY

The effect of this section is that when a juvenile offender is given a conditional discharge for an offence triable, in the case of an adult, on indictment only, and later commits a further offence as an adult, the court will have the same powers as in the case of an offender convicted summarily of an indictable offence, namely imprisonment for a term not exceeding six months or a fine not exceeding £1,000, or both, or any alternative to those sentences.

An offence triable either way. Defined in the Interpretation Act 1978, sch. 1

Probation orders relating to persons residing in Scotland

10. (1) Where the court by which a probation order is made under s. 2 of this Act is satisfied that the offender resides or will reside in Scotland, subs. (2) of that section shall not apply to the order, but the order shall specify as the appropriate court for the purposes of this section a court summary jurisdiction (which, in the case of an offender convicted on indictment, shall be the sheriff court) having jurisdiction in the place in Scotland in which the offender resides or will reside.

(2) Where a probation order has been made under s. 2 of this Act and the supervising court is satisfied that the probationer proposes to reside or is residing in Scotland, the power of that court to amend the order under sch. 1 to this Act shall include power to amend it by substituting for the provisions required by s. 2(2) of this Act the provisions required by subs. (1) above; and the court may so amend the order without summoning the probationer and without his consent.

(3) A probationer order made or amended by virtue of this section may include a requirement that the probationer shall submit to treatment for his mental condition, and—

(a)   subsections (1), (3) and (7) of s. 3 of this Act and ss 184(2) or 385(2) of the Criminal Procedure (Scotland) Act 1975 (which makes equivalent provision to that made by s. 3(2) of this Act) shall apply to the making of an order which includes any such requirement by virtue of this subsection as they apply to the making of an order which includes any such requirement by virtue of s. 3 of this Act and ss 184 or 385 of that Act respectively; and

(b)   subsections (4) to (6) of ss 184 or 385 of that Act (functions of supervising officer and medical practitioner where such a requirement has been imposed) shall apply in relation to a probationer who is undergoing treatment in Scotland in pursuance of a requirement imposed by virtue of this subsection as they apply in relation to a probationer undergoing such treatment in pursuance of a requirement imposed by virtue of ss 184 or 385 of that Act.

(4) Sections 5(1) and 6(1) and (2) of this Act shall not apply to any order made or amended by virtue of this section; but the provisions of the Criminal Procedure (Scotland) Act, 1975 except ss 186(2)(b), 187, 387(2)(b) and 388 (sentencing the probationer for the offence for which the order was made), shall apply to the order as if it were a probation order made under ss 183 or 384 of that Act and as if the court specified in the order as the appropriate court had been named as such under subs. (2) of that section.

(5) If in the case of a probation order made or amended by virtue of this section the appropriate court (as defined by the Criminal Justice (Scotland) Act, 1975) is satisfied that the probationer has failed to comply with any requirement of the probation order, the court may, instead of dealing with him in any manner authorized by that Act, commit him to custody or release him on bail until he can be brought or appear before the court in England and Wales by which the probation order was made, and, if it so commits him or releases him on bail,—

(a)   the court shall send to the court in England and Wales a certificate certifying that the probationer has failed to comply with such of the requirements of the probation order as may be specified in the certificate, together with such other particulars of the case as may be desirable;

(b)   that court shall have the same powers as if the probationer had been brought or appeared before it in pursuance of a warrant or summons issued under s. 6(1) of this Act;

and a certificate purporting to be signed by the clerk of the appropriate court shall be admissible as evidence of the failure before the court which made the probation order.

(6) In relation to a probation order made or amended by virtue of this section, the appropriate court (as defined by the Criminal Justice (Scotland) Act, 1975) shall have jurisdiction for the purposes of s. 8(1) of this Act.

(7) The court by which a probation order is made or amended by virtue of this section shall send three copies of the order as made or amended to the clerk of the court specified in the order as the appropriate court, together with such documents and information relating to the case as it considers likely to be of assistance to that court; and s. 2(7) of this Act, or para. 6 of sch. 1 to this Act, as the case may be, shall not apply to any such order.

(8) Where a probation order which is amended by virtue of subs. (2) above is an order to which the provisions of this Act apply by virtue of ss 188 or 389 of the Criminal Procedure (Scotland) Act, 1975 (probation orders under that Act relating to persons residing in England and Wales) then, notwithstanding anything in that section or this section, the order shall, as from the date of the amendment, have effect in all respects as if it were an order made under ss 183 or 384 of that Act in the case of a person residing in Scotland, and as if the court specified as the appropriate court in the order as so amended had been named as such under subs. (2) of that section.

(as amended by the Criminal Procedure (Scotland) Act, 1975, sch. 9).

COMMENTARY

Costs in proceedings under this section are regulated by the Costs in Criminal Cases Act, 1973, as if the offender had been tried in those proceedings for the offence for which the order was made: s. 18(4), *ibid.*

The appropriate court. Defined in the Criminal Procedure (Scotland) Act, 1975, s. 462(1).

Subsection (5). *See* the notes to s. 8, *supra.*

Substitution of conditional discharge for probation

11. (1) Where on an application made by the probationer or the probation officer it appears to the court having power to discharge a probation order that the order is no longer appropriate in the case of the probationer, the court may make, in substitution for the probation order, an order discharging him in respect of the original offence, subject to the condition that he commits no offence between the making of the order under this section and the expiration of the probation period.

(1A) No application may be made under subs. (1) above while an appeal against the probation order is pending.

(2) A person in respect of whom an order is made under this section shall so long as the condition mentioned in subs. (1) above continues in force be treated in all respects and in particular for the purposes of s. 8 of this Act as if the original order made in his case had been an order for conditional discharge made by the court which made the original order and as if the period of conditional discharge were the same as the probation period.

(3) Where an application under this section is made by the probation officer, it may be heard in the absence of the probationer if the officer produces to the court a statement by him that he understands the effect of an order under this section and consents to the application being made.

(4) On the making of an order under this section the appropriate officer of the court shall forthwith give copies of the order to the probation officer, who shall give a copy to the person in respect of whom the order is made and to the person in charge of any institution in which that person was required by the probation order to reside.

(as amended by the Criminal Justice Act 1982, s. 66.)

COMMENTARY

When a magistrates' court makes an order under this section the clerk must notify the court which made the original order: Magistrates' Courts Rules 1981, r. 28(1).

Subsection (1). The application must be by complaint: Magistrates' Courts Rules 1981, r. 103. For the order *see* form 69.

The court having power to discharge. That is, the supervising court except where the convicting court was the Crown Court which included in the order a direction to the contrary: sch. 1, *infra*.

Supplementary provision as to probation and discharge

12. (1) Any court may, on making a probation order or an order for conditional discharge under this Part of this Act, if it thinks it expedient for the purpose of the reformation of the offender, allow any person who consents to do so to give security for the good behaviour of the offender.

(2) For the purposes of this Act, except s. 2(7) and para. 1 of sch. 1, where a probation order or an order for conditional discharge has been made on appeal, the order shall be deemed to have been made by the court from which the appeal was brought.

(3) . . .

(4) Nothing in ss 2 or 7 of this Act shall be construed as taking away any power of the court, on making a probation order in respect of an offender or discharging an offender absolutely or conditionally, to order him to pay costs or compensation.

COMMENTARY

Security for . . . good behaviour. A statutory provision in addition to the court's common law powers.

13. (1) Subject to subs. (2) below and to s. 50(1A) of the Criminal Appeal Act 1968 and s. 108(1A) of the Magistrates' Courts Act 1980, a conviction of an offence for which an order is made under the Part of this Act placing the offender on probation or discharging him absolutely or conditionally shall be deemed not to be a conviction for any purpose other than the purposes of the proceedings in which the order is made and of any subsequent proceedings which may be taken against the offender under the preceding provisions of this Act.

(2) Where the offender was of or over 17 years of age at the time of his conviction of the offence in question and is subsequently sentenced under this Part of this Act for that offence, subs. (1) above shall cease to apply to the conviction.

(3) Without prejudice to the preceding provisions of this section, the conviction of an offender who is placed on probation or discharged absolutely or conditionally under this Part of this Act shall in any event be disregarded for the purposes of any enactment or instrument which imposes any disqualification or disability upon convicted persons, or authorizes or requires the imposition of any such disqualification or disability.

(4) The preceding provisions of this section shall not effect—

    (a)   any right of any offender placed on probation or discharged absolutely or conditionally under this Part of this Act to rely on his conviction, in bar of any subsequent proceedings for the same offence;

(b)   the restoration of any property in consequence of the conviction of any such offender; or

(c)   the operation, in relation to any such offender, of any enactment or instrument in force at the commencement of this Act which is expressed to extend to persons dealt with under s. 1(1) of the Probation of Offenders Act, 1907, as well as to convicted persons.

(5) In this section "enactment" includes an enactment contained in a local Act and "instrument" means an instrument having effect by virtue of an Act.

(as amended by the Criminal Justice Act 1982, sch. 14.)

COMMENTARY

"The section absolves the offender from legal consequences which otherwise would flow from the conviction": Morrison and Hughes on *The Criminal Justice Act, 1948,* cited with approval in *R.* v. *Harris* (1950) 114 J.P. 535.

An applicant for a firearms certificate may thus truthfully deny a conviction for which he was given a conditional discharge: *R.* v. *Kitt* [1977] Crim. L.R. 220. And see *R.* v. *Maizone* [1974] Crim. L.R. 112.

This section is excluded by the Rehabilitation of Offenders Act 1974, s. 1(4) so as to permit offenders whose convictions are spent to rely upon the additional protection of that Act.

This section is excluded by the Civil Evidence Act 1968, s. 11(5), so as to allow a conviction which would otherwise be caught by it to be admissible to prove in civil proceedings the commission of the offence. The other effects of this section are not excluded.

For the purpose of proving "known character" under s. 15 of the Prevention of Crimes Act, 1871, a certificate of conviction which resulted in an order of conditional discharge is not admissible by virtue of this section, but it would not be objectionable if a witness gave "evidence to the following effect: 'I was present at the court on the day named when the accused was there. I heard him confess to a charge of having been found in possession of certain implements of housebreaking and he was discharged subject to the condition that he commit no further offence during the period of 12 months thereafter'": *R.* v. *Harris, supra.*

Subsection (1). Notwithstanding this subsection, convictions resulting in a probation order or order of absolute or conditional discharge must be taken into account in determining liability to punishment or disqualification under the Road Traffic Acts: Road Traffic Act 1972. s. 102(2). This section does not prevent an appeal against the making of an order for conditional discharge or a probation order: Magistrates' Courts Act 1980, s. 108(1A).

Because of the effects of this subsection it is "undesirable and, indeed, wrong, to take breaches of probation or of conditional discharge into consideration. They should be separately dealt with and separate sentences passed so that the original offences may rank as convictions". *R.* v. *Webb* (1953) 117 J.P. 319.

The preceding provisions of this Act. Notably, s. 8, *supra,* which deals with the commission of a further offence during the probation period.

Subsection (2): 17 years of age. For the determination of age *see* the Magistrates' Courts Act 1980, s. 150(4).

The time of his conviction. That is, when his plea of guilty is accepted or when the charge is found proved: *R.* v. *Sheridan* (1936) 100 J.P. 319. The reasoning in *R.* v. *Sheridan* was disapproved of by the House of Lords in the case of S. *(an infant)* v. *Manchester City Recorder and Others* (1970) 134 J.P. 3. This does not affect the fact that the term "conviction" in subs. (1) is used in what Lord Upjohn described as its secondary sense, *i.e.* the time at which a plea of guilty is made or when the case is proved.

Subsection (3). Notwithstanding this subsection, disqualification and endorsement under the Road Traffic Act may be ordered at the same time as a probation order or order of absolute or conditional discharge: Road Traffic Act 1972, s. 102(1).

A recommendation for deportation by a court is not a disqualification or disability within the meaning of this subsection: *R.* v. *Akan* [1972] 3 All E.R. 285.

This provision does not prevent a disciplinary tribunal from looking at the facts which led to the conviction: *R.* v. *Statutory Committee of Pharmaceutical Society of Great Britain, ex parte Pharmaceutical Society of Great Britain* [1981] 2 All E.R. 805.

Community service orders in respect of convicted persons

14. (1) Where a person of or over 16 years of age is convicted of an offence punishable with imprisonment, the court by or before which he is convicted may, instead of dealing with him in any other way (but subject to subs. (2) below) make an order (in this Act referred to as "a community service order") requiring him to perform unpaid work in accordance with the subsequent provisions of this Act.

The reference in this subsection to an offence punishable with imprisonment shall be construed without regard to any prohibition or restriction imposed or under any enactment on the imprisonment of young offenders.

(1A) The number of hours which a person may be required to work under a community service order shall be specified in the order and shall be in the aggregate—

  (a)   not less than 40; and
  (b)   not more—
      (i)   in the case of an offender aged sixteen, than 120; and
      (ii) in other cases, than 240.

(2) A court shall not make a community service order in respect of any offender unless the offender consents and after considering a report by a probation officer or by a social worker of a local authority social services department about the offender and his circumstances and, if the court thinks it necessary, hearing a probation officer or a social worker of a local authority social services department, the court is satisfied that the offender is a suitable person to perform work under such an order.

(2A) Subject to ss. 17A and 17B below,—

  (a)   a court shall not make a community service order in respect of an offender who is of or over seventeen years of age unless the court is satisfied that provision for him to perform work under such an order can be made under the arrangements for persons to perform work under such orders which exist in the petty sessions area in which he resides or will reside: and
  (b)   a court shall not make a community service order in respect of an offender who is under seventeen years of age unless—
      (i)   it has been notified by the Secretary of State that arrangements exist for persons of the offender's age who reside in the petty sessions area in which the offender resides or will reside to perform work under such orders; and
      (ii) it is satisfied that provision can be made under the arrangements for him to do so.

(3) Where a court makes community service orders in respect of two or more offences of which the offender has been convicted by or before the court, the court may direct that the hours of work specified in any of those orders shall be concurrent with or additional to those specified in any other of those orders, but so that the total number of hours which are not concurrent shall not exceed the maximum specified in para. (b)(i) or (ii) of subs. (1A) above.

(4) A community service order shall specify the petty sessions area in which the offender resides or will reside; and the functions conferred by the subsequent provisions of this Act on the relevant officer shall be discharged by a probation officer appointed for or assigned to the area for the time being specified in the order (whether under this subsection or by virtue of s. 17(5) of this Act), or by a person appointed for the purposes of those provisions by the probation and after-care committee for that area.

(5) Before making a community service order the court shall explain to the offender in ordinary language—

    (a)   the purpose and effect of the order (and in particular the requirements of the order as specified in s. 15 of this Act);

    (b)   the consequences which may follow under s. 16 if he fails to comply with any of those requirements; and

    (c)   that the court has under s. 17 the power to review the order on the application either of the offender or of a probation officer.

(6) The court by which a community service order is made shall forthwith give copies of the order to a probation officer assigned to the court and he shall give a copy to the offender and to the relevant officer; and the court shall, except where it is itself a magistrates' court acting for the petty sessions area specified in the order, send a copy to the clerk to the justices for the petty sessions area specified in the order a copy of the order, together with such documents and information relating to the case as it considers likely to be of assistance to the court acting for that area in exercising its functions in relation to the order.

(7) . . .

(8) Nothing in subs. (1) above shall be construed as preventing a court which makes a community service order in respect of any offence from making an order for costs against, or imposing any disqualification on, the offender or from making in respect of the offence an order under ss 35, 39, 43 or 44 of this Act, or under s. 28 of the Theft Act 1968.

(as amended by the Criminal Justice Act 1982, sch. 11, 16.)

COMMENTARY

For the use of community service *see* the introduction.

    Community service orders may be amended or revoked in accordance with s. 17 of the Act, *infra*. Breach is punishable under s. 16, *ibid*.

Scotland. For the adaptation of this section to an offender residing in Scotland *see* s. 17A, *infra*.

Northern Ireland. For the adaptation of this section to an offender residing in Northern Ireland *see* s. 17B, *infra*

Subsection (1): 16 years of age. For the determination of age *see* the Magistrates' Courts Act 1980, s. 150(4).

A community service order. *See* form 92.

In the aggregate. This apparently refers to the possibility of consecutive orders being made under subs. (3). Thus, it would appear possible to have two consecutive orders of 20 hours each, although this course is not recommended because of its administrative inconvenience. There is no objection in principle to one order being made consecutive to another made on an earlier occasion: *R. v. Evans* (1977) 141 J.P. 441.

Subsection (3): Where a court makes. This appears to be confined to orders made on the same occasion. But there is no objection to a later order being made consecutive to an earlier order: *R. v. Evans, supra,* so, however, that the total period does not exceed 240 hours.

Subsection (6). Judge Kershaw has held in the Crown Court that the effect of this subsection is to prevent the enforcement of a community service order when the defendant léft court before a copy of the order could be given to him: *R. v. Dugdale* [1981] Crim. L.R. 105. It is suggested that this is a decision which should be confined to its special facts.

Subsection (8): The sections quoted refer to orders of compensation, restitution, criminal bankruptcy and deprivation of property.

Obligations of persons subject to community service order

15. (1) An offender in respect of whom a community service order is in force shall—

    (*a*)   report to the relevant officer and subsequently from time to time notify him of any change of address; and

    (*b*)   perform for the number of hours specified in the order such work at such times as he may be instructed by the relevant officer.

(2) Subject to s. 17(1) of this Act, the work required to be performed under a community service order shall be performed during the period of 12 months beginning with the date of the order but, unless revoked, the order shall remain in force until the offender has worked under it for the number of hours specified in it.

(3) The instructions given by the relevant officer under this section shall, so far as practicable, be such as to avoid any conflict with the offender's religious beliefs and any interference with the times, if any, at which he normally works or attends a school or other educational establishment.

(*as amended by the Criminal Law Act 1977, sch. 12*).

COMMENTARY

For breach of the requirements of a community service order *see* s. 16, *infra*.

Subsection (1): The relevant officer. *See* s. 14(4), *supra*.

Subsection (2): Remain in force. By virtue of subs. (2) of this section an order remains in force until the hours are worked.

Breach of requirements of community service order

16. (1) If at any time while a community service order is in force in respect of an offender it appears on information to a justice of the peace acting for the petty sessions area for the time being specified in the order that the offender has failed to comply with any of the requirements of s. 15 of this Act (including any failure satisfactorily to perform the work which he has been instructed to do), the justice may issue a summons requiring the offender to appear at the place and time specified therein, or may, if the information is in writing and on oath, issue a warrant for his arrest.

(2) Any summons or warrant issued under this section shall direct the offender to appear or be brought before a magistrates' court acting for the petty sessions area for the time being specified in the community service order.

(3) If it is proved to the satisfaction of the magistrates' court before which an offender appears or is brought under this section that he has failed without reasonable excuse to comply with any of the requirements of s. 15 the court may, without prejudice to the continuance of the order, impose on him a fine not exceeding £400 or may—

    (*a*)   if the community service order was made by a magistrates' court, revoke the order and deal with the offender, for the offence in respect of which the order was made, in any manner in which he could have been dealt with for that offence by the court which made the order if the order had not been made;

    (*b*)   if the order was made by the Crown Court, commit him to custody or release him on bail until he can be brought or appear before the Crown Court.

(4) A magistrates' court which deals with an offender's case under subs. (3)(*b*) above shall send to the Crown Court a certificate signed by a justice of the peace

certifying that the offender has failed to comply with the requirements of s. 15 in the respect specified in the certificate, together with such other particulars of the case as may be desirable; and a certificate purporting to be so signed shall be admissible as evidence of the failure before the Crown Court.

(5) . . .

(6) A person sentenced under subs. (3)(*a*) above for an offence may appeal to the Crown Court against the sentence.

(7) . . .

(8) A fine imposed under this section shall be deemed for the purposes of any enactment to be a sum adjudged to be paid by a conviction.

COMMENTARY

Legal aid may be granted in proceedings under this section: Legal Aid Act 1974. ss 28 and 30(12).
    The Costs in Criminal Cases Act 1973 applies to proceedings under this section: s. 18, *ibid.*

Scottish Orders
    In the case of a community service order made by a Scottish court under the Community Service by Offenders (Scotland) Act 1978, s. 6, in respect of an offender residing in England or Wales this section has effect as if for subss (3)-(7) there were substituted:

"(3) If it is proved to the satisfaction of the magistrates' court before which an offender appears or is brought under this section that he has failed without reasonable excuse to comply with any of the requirements of s. 15 of this Act, the court may, without prejudice to the continuance of the order, impose on him a fine not exceeding £50 or issue a summons requiring him to appear before the court in Scotland by which the order was made".

Subsection (1): At any time while a community service order is in force. *See* the note to s. 15(2), *supra.*

Issue a summons. For the content and service of the summons *see* the Magistrates' Courts Rules 1981, rr. 98,99.

    Process may be served in Scotland in accordance with s. 4 of the Summary Jurisdiction (Process) Act 1881: s. 53 of the Act.

Issue a warrant. For the contents of the warrant, *see* the Magistrates' Courts Rules 1981, rr. 95, 96. The warrant may be backed for bail: Magistrates' Courts Act 1980, s. 118.

Subsection (3). For the purposes of this Act a community service order made on appeal from a magistrates' court shall be treated as if made by a magistrates' court: s. 57(5) of the Act.

Proved to the satisfaction of the court. Formal proof of breach is required, so that, once the prosecution have closed their case, they may not, save for purely technical matters, be allowed to re-open it: *R.* v. *Gainsborough Justices, ex parte Green* (1983) *The Times*, June 20. Cf. the note to s. 6(3), *supra.* Note that s. 15 contains a multiplicity of requirements, viz. (a) to report to the relevant officer; (b) subsequently from time to time to notify him of any change of address; (c) to perform for the number of hours specified in the order such work at such times as he may be instructed; and (d) to perform the work during the period of twelve months beginning with the date of the order. The first three requirements arise under subs. (1), the fourth under subs. (2).

Subsection (3)(a). The terms of this subsection appear to preclude a further community service order. Otherwise the powers of the court are limited to those available to the original court at the time the order was made.
    In the event of the offender being sentenced in respect of the original offence any compensation order made at the same time will continue in force: *cf. R.* v. *Evans* (1961) 126 J.P. 134.
    There is a right of appeal to the Crown Court against a sentence under this sub-para: subs. (6).

Commit him to custody. The general right to bail applies: Bail Act 1976, s. 4(4) and bail may only be withheld in the circumstances mentioned in sch. 1, *ibid.*
    For the place to which defendants under 21 years of age should be committed see s. 27 of

the Criminal Justice Act 1948. Committals to prison must be by warrant: Magistrates' Courts Rules 1981, r. 94. For the contents of the warrant see form 95.

Release him on bail. If the defendant is released on bail the clerk must notify the governor of the appropriate prison, etc.: Magistrates' Courts Rules 1981, r. 87. Forfeiture of recognizances is a matter for the Crown Court.

Subsection (4): A certificate. *See* form 93. May be signed by the justices' clerk: Justices' Clerks' Rules 1970.

Amendment and revocation of community service orders, and substitution of other sentences

17. (1) Where a community service order is in force in respect of any offender and, on the application of the offender or the relevant officer, it appears to a magistrates' court acting for the petty sessions area for the time being specified in the order that it would be in the interests of justice to do so having regard to circumstances which have arisen since the order was made, the court may extend, in relation to the order, the period of 12 months specified in s. 15(2) of this Act.

(2) Where such an order is in force and on any such application it appears to a magistrates' court acting for the petty sessions area so specified that, having regard to such circumstances, it would be in the interests of justice that the order should be revoked or that the offender should be dealt with in some other manner for the offence in respect of which the order was made, the court may—

(a) if the order was made by a magistrates' court, revoke the order or revoke it and deal with the offender for that offence in any manner in which he could have been dealt with for that offence by the court which made the order if the order had not been made;

(b) if the order was made by the Crown Court, commit him to custody or release him on bail until he can be brought or appear before the Crown Court;

and where the court deals with his case under para. (b) above it shall send to the Crown Court such particulars of the case as may be desirable.

(3) Where an offender in respect of whom such an order is in force—

(a) is convicted of an offence before the Crown Court; or

(b) is committed by a magistrates' court to the Crown Court for sentence and is brought or appears before the Crown Court; or

(c) by virtue of subs. (2)(b) above, is brought or appears before the Crown Court;

and it appears to the Crown Court to be in the interests of justice to do so, having regard to circumstances which have arisen since the order was made, the Crown Court may revoke the order or revoke the order and deal with the offender, for the offence in respect of which the order was made, in any manner in which he could have been dealt with for that offence by the court which made the order if the order had not been made.

(4) A person sentenced under subs. (2)(a) above for an offence may appeal to the Crown Court against the sentence.

(4A) Where—

(a) an offender in respect of whom a community service order is in force is convicted of an offence before a magistrates' court other than a magistrates' court acting for the petty sessions area for the time being specified in the order; and

(b) it appears to the court, on the application of the offender or the

relevant officer, that it would be in the interests of justice to do so having regard to circumstances which have arisen since the order was made,
the court may–
      (i)   if the order was made by a magistrates' court, revoke it; and
     (ii)   if the order was made by the Crown Court, commit him in custody or release him on bail until he can be brought or appear before the Crown Court;
and where the court deals with his case under sub-paragraph (ii) above, it shall send to the Crown Court such particulars of the case as may be, desirable.

(4B) Where by virtue of subs. (4A)(c)(ii) above the offender is brought or appears before the Crown Court and it appears to the Crown Court to be in the interests of justice to do so, having regard to circumstances which have arisen since the order was made, the Crown Court may revoke the order.

(5) If–
    (a)   a magistrates' court acting for the petty sessions area for the time being specified in a community service order is satisfied that the offender proposes to change, or has changed, his residence from that petty sessions area to another petty sessions area; and
    (b)   the conditions specified in subs. (5A) below are satisfied,
the court may, and on the application of the relevant officer shall, amend the order by substituting the other petty sessions area for the area specified in the order.

(5A) The conditions referred to in subs. (5) above are–
    (a)   if the offender is of or over 17 years of age, that it appears to the court that provision can be made for him to perform work under the community service order under the arrangements which exist for persons who reside in the other petty sessions area to perform work under such orders; and
    (b)   if the offender is under 17 years of age–
      (i)   that the court has been notified by the Secretary of State that arrangements exist for persons of his age who reside in the other petty sessions area to perform work under such orders; and
     (ii)   it appears to the court that provision can be made under the arrangements for him to do so.

(6) Where a community service order is amended by a court under subs. (5) above the court shall send to the clerk to the justices for the new area specified in the order a copy of the order, together with such documents and information relating to the case as it considers likely to be of assistance to a court acting for that area in exercising its functions in relation to the order.

(7) Where a magistrates' court proposes to exercise its powers under subs. (1) or (2) above otherwise than on the application of the offender it shall summon him to appear before the court and, if he does not appear in answer to the summons, may issue a warrant for his arrest.

(as amended by the Criminal Law Act 1977, sch. 12, the Criminal Justice Act 1982, sch. 12.)

COMMENTARY

Legal aid may be granted in respect of proceedings under subs. (1) and (2): Legal Aid Act 1974, ss 28 and 30(12).

The Costs in Criminal Cases Act 1973 applies: s. 18(4), *ibid.*

Note that the exercise of the court's powers under subss (1) or (2) is dependent upon circumstances having arisen "since the order was made."

7.　NON-CUSTODIAL ORDERS　　　　359

For the purposes of this Act a community service order made on appeal from a magistrates' court shall be treated as if made by a magistrates' court: s. 57(5) of the Act.

Northern Ireland. For the adaptation of this section for persons residing in Northern Ireland *see* s. 17B, *infra*.

Scottish orders. In the case of a community service order made by a Scottish court under the Community Service by Offenders (Scotland) Act 1978, s. 6, in respect of an offender residing in England or Wales this section has effect as if for subss. (2)-(4) there were substituted the following:

"(2) Where, on the application of the offender of the relevant officer, it appears to a magistrates' court acting for the petty sessions area for the time being specified in the order that it would be in the interests of justice (having regard to circumstances which have arisen since the order was made or amended, as the case may be, by virtue of s. 6 of the Community Service by Offenders (Scotland) Act 1978) that the order should be revoked or that the offender should be dealt with in some other manner for the offence in respect of which the order was made, the magistrates' court shall refer the case to the court in Scotland by which the order was made.";

and as if in subs. (7) the words "or (2)" were omitted.

For the adaptation of this section to orders made in respect of persons residing in Scotland *see* s. 17A, *infra*.

Subsection (1): In force. See s. 15(2).

On the application of . . . the relevant officer. A summons must issue under subs. (7). The issue of a warrant, however, is contingent upon non-appearance in answer to a summons. Relevant officer is defined in s. 14(4), *supra*. Note that the court has no power to act on its own motion.

Subsection (2): In force. See s. 15(2).

Subsection (2)(a): Deal with the offender . . . in any manner in which he could have been dealt with. *See* the note to s. 16(3)(a) *supra*. Subsection (4) of this section gives a right of appeal to the Crown Court against sentence.

Commit him to custody or release him on bail. The general right to bail (Bail Act 1976, s. 4) does not seemingly apply. Otherwise *see* the notes to s. 16, *supra*.

Subsection (3): Convicted. Does not include probation orders and orders of absolute and conditional discharge: s. 13 of the Act.

Subsection (4A). Note that the conviction need not be in respect of a subsequent offence but the interests of justice test relates to circumstances which have arisen since the order was made. These circumstances may relate to the offence but need not.

Subsection (7). Process may be served in Scotland in accordance with the Summary Jurisdiction (Process) Act, 1881, s. 4: s. 53 of the Act.

Making and amendment of community service orders relating to persons residing in Scotland.

17A.–(1) Where a court considering the making of a community service order is satisfied that the offender resides, or will be residing when the order comes into force, in Scotland, section 14 above shall have effect as if the following subsection were substituted for subs. (2A)–

"(2A) A court shall not make a community service order in respect of any offender unless–

(a) the court has been notified by the Secretary of State that arrangements exist for persons who reside in the locality in Scotland in which the offender resides, or will be residing when the order comes into force, to perform work under community service orders made under section 1 of the Community Service by Offenders (Scotland) Act 1978; and

(b) it appears to the court that provision can be made for him to perform work under those arrangements.".

(2) Where a community service order has been made and–

(a) a magistrates' court acting for a petty sessions area for the time being specified in it is satisfied that the offender proposes to reside or is residing in Scotland;

(b)   that court has been notified by the Secretary of State that arrangements exist for persons who reside in the locality in Scotland in which the offender proposes to reside or is residing to perform work under community service orders made under s. 1 of the Community Service by Offenders (Scotland) Act 1978;

(c)   it appears to that court that provision can be made for him to perform work under the community service order under those arrangements,

it may amend the order by specifying that the unpaid work required to be performed by the order be so performed.

(3) A community service order made or amended in accordance with this section shall—

(a)   specify the locality in Scotland in which the offender resides or will be residing when the order or the amendment comes into force; and

(b)   require the regional or islands council in whose area the locality specified under paragraph (a) above is situated to appoint or assign an officer who will discharge in respect of the order the functions in respect of community service orders conferred on the local authority officer by the Community Service by Offenders (Scotland) Act 1978.

(as inserted by the Criminal Justice Act 1982, sch. 13).

Making and amendment of community service orders relating to persons residing in Northern Ireland.

17B.—(1) Where a court considering the making of a community service order is satisfied that the offender resides or will be residing when the order comes into force, in Northern Ireland, it shall not make the order unless it is also satisfied that he is of or over 17 years of age.

(2) Where the court is satisfied that he is of or over that age, section 14 above shall have effect as if the following subsection were substituted for subsection (2A)—

"(2A) A court shall not make a community service order in respect of any offender unless it appears to the court that provision can be made by the Probation Board for Northern Ireland (in this section referred to as "the Probation Board") for him to perform work under the order.".

(3) Where a community service order has been made and—

(a)   a magistrates' court acting for a petty sessions area for the time being specified in it is satisfied that the offender has attained the age of 17 years and proposes to reside or is residing in Northern Ireland;

(b)   it appears to that court that provision can be made by the Probation Board for him to perform work under the order,

it may amend the order by specifying that the unpaid work required to be performed by the order be so performed.

(4) A community service order made or amended in accordance with this section shall—

(a)   specify the petty sessions district in Northern Ireland in which the offender resides or will be residing when the order or the amendment comes into force; and

(b)   require the Probation Board to select an officer who will discharge in respect of the order the functions in respect of community service orders conferred on the relevant officer by the

Treatment of Offenders (Northern Ireland) Order 1976.

(as inserted by the Criminal Justice Act 1982, sch. 13.)

Community service orders relating to persons residing in Scotland or Northern Ireland–general

17C.–(1) Where a community service order is made or amended in the circumstances specified in ss. 17A or 17B of this Act, the court which makes or amends the order shall send three copies of it as made or amended to the home court, together with such documents and information relating to the case as it considers likely to be of assistance to that court.

(2) In this section–

"home court" means–

(a)   if the offender resides in Scotland, or will be residing in Scotland at the relevant time, the sheriff court having jurisdiction in the locality in which he resides or proposes to reside; and

(b)   if he resides in Northern Ireland, or will be residing in Northern Ireland at the relevant time, the court of summary jurisdiction acting for the petty sessions district in which he resides or proposes to reside; and

"the relevant time" means the time when the order or the amendment to it comes into force.

(3) A community service order made or amended in the circumstances specified in ss. 17A or 17B of this Act shall be treated, subject to the following provisions of this section, as if it were a community service order made in the part of the United Kindom in which the offender resides, or will be residing at the relevant time; and the legislation relating to community service orders which has effect in part of the United Kingdom shall apply accordingly.

(4) Before making or amending a community service order in those circumstances the court shall explain to the offender in ordinary language–

(a)   the requirements of the legislation relating to community service orders which has effect in the part of the United Kingdom in which he resides or will be residing at the relevant time;

(b)   the powers of the home court under that legislation, as modified by this section; and

(c)   its own powers under this section,

and an explanation given in accordance with this section shall be sufficient without the addition of an explanation under s. 14(5) above.

(5) The home court may exercise in relation to the community service order any power which it could exercise in relation to a community service order made by a court in the part of the United Kingdom in which the home court exercises jurisdiction, by virtue of the legislation relating to such orders which has effect in the part of the United Kingdom in which it has jurisdiction except–

(a)   a power to vary the order by substituting for the number of hours' work specified in it any greater number than the court which made the order could have specified;

(b)   a power to revoke the order; and

(c)   a power to revoke the order and deal with the offender for the offence in respect of which it was made in any manner in which he could have been dealt with for that offence by the court which made the order if the order had not been made.

(6) If at any time while legislation relating to community service orders which has effect in one part of the United Kingdom applies by virtue of subs. (3) above to a community service order made in another part–

(a) it appears to the home court—
- (i) if that court is in Scotland, on evidence on oath from the local authority officer under the Community Service by Offenders (Scotland) Act 1978; and
- (ii) if it is in Northern Ireland, upon a complaint being made to a justice of the peace acting for the petty sessions district for the time being specified in the order, that the offender has failed to comply with any of the requirements of the legislation applicable to the order; or

(b) it appears to the home court on the application of the offender or—
- (i) if that court is in Scotland, of the local authority officer; and
- (ii) if it is in Northern Ireland, of the relevant officer, as defined in the Treatment of Offenders (Northern Ireland) Order 1976, that it would be in the interests of justice to exercise a power mentioned in subss. (5)(b) or (c) above,

the home court may require the offender to appear before the court by which the order was made.

(7) Where an offender is required by virtue of subs. (6) above to appear before the court which made a community service order, that court—
- (a) may issue a warrant for his arrest; and
- (b) may exercise any power which it could exercise in respect of the community service order if the offender resides in the part of the United Kingdom where the court has jurisdiction.

and any enactment relating to the exercise of such powers shall have effect accordingly.

(as inserted by the Criminal Justice Act 1982, sch. 13.)

SCHEDULE 1

(Section 5)

DISCHARGE AND AMENDMENT OF PROBATION ORDERS

Discharge

1. (1) A probation order may be discharged, in accordance with the following provisions of this paragraph, on an application made by the probation officer or by the probationer.

(1A) No application may be made under sub-para. (1) above while an appeal against the probation order is pending.

(2) Where the probation order was made by the court by or before which the probationer was convicted, or on appeal or by the Crown Court, where a magistrates' court has committed an offender to it for sentence, or by a magistrates' court to which the offender has been remitted for sentence under s. 39 of the Magistrates' Courts Act 1980, the power to discharge the order shall, subject to sub-para. (3) below, be exercised by the supervising court.

(3) Where the court before which the probationer was convicted or the court from which the appeal is brought is the Crown Court or where the Crown Court made the order following the offender's committal to it for sentence by a magistrates' court and there is included in the order a direction that the power be reserved to that court, the power to discharge the order shall be exercised by the Crown Court.

(4) In any other case the power to discharge the order shall be exercised by the court by which the order was made.

Amendment

2. (1) Subject to sub-para. (2) below, if the supervising court is satisfied that a probationer proposes to change, or has changed his residence from the petty sessions area named in the probation order to another petty sessions area, the court may, and on the application of the probation order officer shall, by order amend the probation order by substituting for the petty sessions area named in the order the petty sessions area where the probationer proposes to reside or is residing.

(1A) No order may be made under sub-para. (1) above while an appeal against the probation order is pending.

(2) If the probation order contains requirements which, in the opinion of the court, cannot be complied with unless the probationer continues to reside in the area named in the order, the court shall not amend the order under this paragraph unless, in accordance with the following provisions of this schedule, it cancels those requirements or substitutes for those requirements other requirements which can be complied with if the probationer ceases to reside in that area.

(3) Where a probation order is amended under this paragraph, the old supervising court shall send to the clerk to the justices for the new area named in the order a copy of the order, together with such documents and information relating to the case as it considers likely to be of assistance to the new supervising court.

3. (1) Without prejudice to the provisions of para. 2 above, but subject to sub-para. (2) below, the supervising court may, on an application made by the probation officer or by the probationer, by order amend a probation order by cancelling any of the requirements of the order or by inserting in the order (either in addition to or in substitution for any such requirement) any requirement which the court could include under ss. 2, 3, 4A or 4B of this Act if it were then making the order.

(1A) No application may be made under sub-para. (1) above while an appeal against the probation order is pending.

(2) The power of the supervising court under this paragraph to amend a probation order shall be subject to the following restrictions—

(*a*)   the court shall not amend a probation order by reducing the probation period, or by extending that period beyond the end of three years from the date of the original order;

(*b*)   (*Repealed*).

(*c*)   the court shall not amend a probation order by inserting therein a requirement that the probationer shall submit to treatment for his mental condition unless the amending order is made within three months after the date of the original order.

4. Subject to para. 4A below, where the medical practitioner by whom or under whose direction a probationer is being treated for his mental condition in pursuance of any requirement of the probation order is of opinion–

(*a*)   that the treatment of the probationer should be continued beyond the period specified in that behalf in the order, or

(*b*)   that the probationer needs different treatment, being treatment of a kind to which he could be required to submit in pursuance of a probation order, or

(*c*)   that the probationer is not susceptible to treatment, or

(*d*)   that the probationer does not require further treatment, or where the practitioner is for any reason unwilling to continue to treat or direct the treatment of the probationer, he shall make a report in writing to that effect to the probation officer and the probation officer shall apply to the supervising court for the variation or cancellation of the requirement.

4A. No application may be made under para. 4 above while an appeal against the probation order is pending.

General

5. (1) Subject to sub-para. (2) below, where the supervising court proposes to amend a probation order under this schedule, otherwise than on the application of the probationer, it shall summon him to appear before the court; and the court shall not amend a probation order unless the probationer expresses his willingness to comply with the requirements of the order as amended.

(2) This paragraph shall not apply to an order cancelling a requirement of the probation order or reducing the period of any requirement, or substituting a new petty sessions area for the area named in the probation order.

6. (1) On the making of an order discharging or amending a probation order, the clerk to the court shall forthwith—

(*a*)   if the order discharges the probation order or amends it otherwise than by substituting a new petty session area for the area named in the probation order, give copies of the discharging or amending order to the probation officer;

(*b*)   if the order amends the probation order in the manner excepted by head (*a*) above, send copies of the amending order to the clerk to the justices for the new petty sessions area;

and in the case falling within head (*b*) above the clerk to the justices for the new petty sessions area shall give copies of the amending order to the probation officer.

(2) A probation officer to whom in accordance with sub-para. (1) above copies of an order are given shall give a copy to the probationer and to the person in charge of any institution in which the probationer is or was required by the order to reside.

7. Section 2(8) of this Act shall apply to any order made under this schedule by virtue of which a probationer is required to reside in an institution as it applies to a probation order made under that section.

(as amended by the Criminal Law Act 1977, schs. 12, 13, the Criminal Justice Act 1982, s. 66, sch. 11).

COMMENTARY

This schedule has effect by virtue of s. 5, *supra.*

Paragraph 1. No procedure is prescribed for discharge, in particular it is not stated to be on complaint. Copies of the order must be given to the probation officer and by him to the former probationer: paras 6(1) and (2) of this schedule. The normal rule that orders made on appeal are deemed to be made by the court appealed against does not apply to this paragraph: s. 12(2), *supra.*

Paragraph 2(1). "(1) If a probation officer becomes aware that a person under his supervision has changed his residence from the petty sessions area named in the order placing him under his supervision to another petty session area, he shall apply . . . to the supervising court to amend the order in accordance with para. 2(1) of sch. 1 to the Criminal Justice Act, 1948 . . . unless—

(*a*)   the probation officer has reason to believe that the person under supervision is unlikely to reside there for a reasonable time; or

(b)   the probation officer has ascertained from, in the case of a probationer, the supervising court, . . . that that court and the court having jurisdiction in the petty sessions area where the person under supervision is residing are satisfied that, having regard to the special circumstances of the case, it is desirable that the person should remain under his supervision.

"(2) Where it appears to a probation officer that an application can properly be made for the discharge or amendment (otherwise than as provided by the foregoing paragraph of this rule) of a probation or supervision order relating to a person under his supervision, the probation officer shall make such application unless the person under supervision or any other person makes the application": Probation Rules 1965, para. 39.

The justices' clerk may amend a probation order by substituting a different petty sessions area under para. 2(1): Justices' Clerks Rules 1970.

Paragraph 3. Certain applications by the probation officer must be by way of summons: para. 5. There would, however, seem to be no power to issue a warrant on non-appearance.

Paragraph 5. Failure to secure an expression of "willingness to comply" renders the variation void: *R.* v. *Emmett* (1968) *The Times,* December 21.

SCHEDULE 3

PART I

Probation officers

8. (1) It shall be the duty of probation officers to supervise the probationers and other persons placed under their supervision and to advise, assist and befriend them, to inquire, in accordance with any directions of the court, into the circumstances or home surroundings of any person with a view to assisting the court in determining the most suitable method of dealing with his case, to advise, assist and befriend, in such cases and in such manner as may be prescribed, persons who have been released from custody and to perform such other duties as may be prescribed or may be imposed by any enactment or instrument.

(2) In sub-para. (1) above "enactment" includes an enactment contained in a local Act and "instrument" means an instrument having effect by virtue of an Act.

9. The probation officer who is to be responsible for the supervision of any probationer shall be selected under arrangements made by the probation and after-care committee for the probation and after-care area which includes the petty sessions area for the time being named in the order from among the probation officers appointed for or assigned to that petty sessions area; and, if the probation officer so selected dies or is unable for any reason to carry out his duties, another probation officer shall be selected in like manner from among the probation officers appointed for or assigned to that petty sessions area.

(*as amended by the Criminal Law Act 1977, sch. 12*).

THE CRIMINAL PROCEDURE (SCOTLAND) ACT 1975

Probation orders relating to persons residing in England

389. (1) Where the court by which a probation order is made under s. 384 of this Act is satisfied that the offender has attained the age of 17 years and resides or will reside in England, subs. (2) of the said section shall not apply to the order, but the order shall contain a requirement that he be under the supervision of a probation officer appointed for or assigned to the petty sessions area in which the offender resides or will reside; and that area shall be named in the order.

(2) Where a probation order has been made under s. 384 of this Act and the court in Scotland by which the order was made or the appropriate court is satisfied that the probationer has attained the age of 17 years and proposes to reside or is residing in England, the power of that court to amend the order under sch. 5 to this

Act shall include power to insert the provisions required by subs. (1) of this section; and the court may so amend the order without summoning the probationer and without his consent.

(3) A probation order made or amended by virtue of this section may, notwithstanding s. 385(8) of this Act, include a requirement that the probationer shall submit to treatment for his mental condition, and—

(a)   subsection (1), (3) and (7) of the said s. 385 and s. 3(2) of the Powers of Criminal Courts Act 1973 (all of which regulate the making of probation orders which include any such requirement) shall apply to the making of an order which includes any such requirement by virtue of this subsection as they apply to the making of an order which includes any such requirement by virtue of s. 385 of this Act and s. 3 of the said Act of 1973 respectively; and

(b)   subsections (4) to (6) of s. 3 of the said Act of 1973 (functions of supervising officer and medical practitioner where such a requirement has been imposed) shall apply in relation to a probationer who is undergoing treatment in England in pursuance of a requirement imposed by virtue of this subsection as they apply in relation to a probationer undergoing such treatment in pursuance of a requirement imposed by virtue of that section.

(4) Sections 386(1) and 387(1) of this Act shall not apply to any order made or amended under this section; but subject as hereinafter provided the provisions of the Powers of Criminal Courts Act 1973 (except s. 8 of that Act) shall apply to the order as if it were a probation order made under s. 2 of that Act:

Provided that s. 6(2)(a), (3)(d) and (6) of that Act shall not apply to any such order and s. 6(4) and (5) of that Act shall have effect respectively in relation to any such order as if for the first reference in s. 6(4) to the Crown Court there were substituted a reference to a court in Scotland and as if for the second such reference therein and for both such references in s. 6(5) there were substituted references to the court in Scotland by which the probation order was made or amended under this section.

(5) If it appears on information to a justice acting for the petty sessions area for which the supervising court within the meaning of the Powers of Criminal Court Act 1973 acts that a person in whose case a probation order has been made or amended under this section has been convicted by a court in any part of Great Britain of an offence committed during the period specified in the order, he may issue a summons requiring that person to appear, at the place and time specified therein, before the court in Scotland by which the probation order was made or, if the information is in writing and on oath, may issue a warrant for his arrest, directing that person to be brought before the last-mentioned court.

(6) If a warrant for the arrest of a probationer issued under s. 388 of this Act by a court is executed in England, and the probationer cannot forthwith be brought before that court, the warrant shall have effect as if it directed him to be brought before a magistrates' court for the place where he is arrested; and the magistrates' court shall commit him to custody or release him on bail (with or without sureties) until he can be brought or appear before the court in Scotland.

(7) The court by which a probation order is made or amended in accordance with the provisions of this section shall send three copies of the order to the clerk to the justices for the petty sessions area named therein, together with such documents and information relating to the case as it considers likely to be of assistance to the court acting for that petty sessions area.

(8) Where a probation order which is amended under subs. (2) of this section is an order to which the provisions of this Act apply by virtue of s. 10 of the Powers

of Criminal Courts Act 1973 (which relates to probation orders under that Act relating to persons residing in Scotland) then notwithstanding anything in that section or this section, the order shall, as from the date of the amendment, have effect in all respects as if it were an order made under s. 2 of that Act in the case of a person residing in England.

COMMENTARY

Subsection (1): Petty sessions area. This has the same meaning as in the Children and Young Persons Act 1969: s. 390(8).

Subsection (6): Warrant issued under s. 388. That is, in respect of the commission of a further offence by a probationer.

THE MENTAL HEALTH ACT 1983

Application of Act: "mental disorder".

1.—(1) The provisions of this Act shall have effect with respect to the reception, care and treatment of mentally disordered patients, the management of their property and other related matters.

(2) In this Act— "mental disorder" means mental illness, arrested or incomplete development of mind, psychopathic disorder and any other disorder or disability of mind and "mentally disordered" shall be construed accordingly; "severe mental impairment" means a state of arrested or incomplete development of mind which includes severe impairment of intelligence and social functioning and is associated with abnormally aggressive or seriously irresponsible conduct on the part of the person concerned and "severely mentally impaired" shall be construed accordingly; "mental impairment" means a state of arrested or incomplete development of mind (not amounting to severe mental impairment) which includes significant impairment of intelligence and social functioning and is associated with abnormally aggressive or seriously irresponsible conduct on the part of the person concerned and "mentally impaired" shall be construed accordingly; "psychopathic disorder" means a persistent disorder or disability of mind (whether or not including significant impairment of intelligence) which results in abnormally aggressive or seriously irresponsible conduct on the part of the person concerned; and other expressions shall have the meanings assigned to them in s. 145 below.

(3) Nothing in subs. (2) above shall be construed as implying that a person may be dealt with under this Act as suffering from mental disorder, or from any form of mental disorder described in this section, by reason only of promiscuity or other immoral conduct, sexual deviancy or dependence on alcohol or drugs.

COMMENTARY

Mental illness. Is not further defined.

Remand to hospital for report on accused's mental condition.

35.—(1) Subject to the provisions of this section, the Crown Court or a magistrates' court may remand an accused person to a hospital specified by the court for a report on his mental condition.

(2) For the purposes of this section an accused person is—

(a) (Crown Court)

(b)   in relation to a magistrates' court, any person who has been convicted by the court of an offence punishable on summary conviction with imprisonment and any person charged with such an
offence if the court is satisfied that he did the act or made the
omission charged or he has consented to the exercise by the court
of the powers conferred by this section.

(3) Subject to subs. (4) below, the powers conferred by this section may
be exercised if—

(a)   the court is satisfied, on the written or oral evidence of a
registered medical practitioner, that there is reason to suspect that
the accused person is suffering from mental illness, psychopathic
disorder, severe mental impairment or mental impairment; and

(b)   the court is of the opinion that it would be impracticable for a
report on his mental condition to be made if he were remanded
on bail;

but those powers shall not be exercised by the Crown Court in respect of a
person who has been convicted before the court if the sentence for the offence of which he has been convicted is fixed by law.

(4) The court shall not remand an accused person to a hospital under this
section unless satisfied, on the written or oral evidence of the registered
medical practitioner who would be responsible for making the report or of
some other person representing the managers of the hospital, that
arrangements have been made for his admission to that hospital and for his
admission to it within the period of seven days beginning with the date of
the remand; and if the court is so satisfied it may, pending his admission,
give directions for his conveyance to and detention in a place of safety.

(5) Where a court has remanded an accused person under this section it
may further remand him if it appears to the court, on the written or oral
evidence of the registered medical practitioner responsible for making the
report, that a further remand is necessary for completing the assessment of
the accused person's mental condition.

(6) The power of further remanding an accused person under this section
may be exercised by the court without his being brought before the court if
he is represented by counsel or a solicitor and his counsel or solicitor is
given an opportunity of being heard.

(7) An accused person shall not be remanded or further remanded under
this section for more than 28 days at a time or for more than 12 weeks in
all; and the court may at any time terminate the remand if it appears to the
court that it is appropriate to do so.

(8) An accused person remanded to hospital under this section shall be
entitled to obtain at his own expense an independent report on his mental
condition from a registered medical practitioner chosen by him and to apply to the court on the basis of it for his remand to be terminated under
subs. (7) above.

(9) Where an accused person is remanded under this section—

(a)   a constable or any other person directed to do so by the court
shall convey the accused person to the hospital specified by the
court within the period mentioned in subs. (4) above; and

(b)   the managers of the hospital shall admit him within that period
and thereafter detain him in accordance with the provisions of
this section.

(10) If an accused person absconds from a hospital to which he has been
remanded under this section, or while being conveyed to or from that
hospital, he may be arrested without warrant by any constable and shall,
after being arrested, be brought as soon as practicable before the court that
remanded him; and the court may thereupon terminate the remand and

deal with him in any way in which it could have dealt with him if he had
not been remanded under this section.

COMMENTARY

Subsection (2): An offence punishable . . with imprisonment. *See* s. 55(2), *infra.*

Subsection (3): Evidence. *See* s. 54, *infra.*

Psychopathic disorder / severe mental impairment / mental impairment. Defined in s. 1 of
the Act (s. 145(1)).

Subsection (4): Hospital. Defined in s. 145(1) of the Act. For information about hospitals *see*
s. 39, *infra.*

Evidence. *See* s. 54, *infra.*

Place of safety. Defined in s. 55(1), *infra.*

Subsection (9): Constable. That is, a police officer of any rank.

The manager. Defined in s. 145(1) of the Act.

Powers of courts to order hospital admission or guardianship.

37.–(1) Where a person is convicted before the Crown Court of an offence punishable with imprisonment other than an offence the sentence for
which is fixed by law, or is convicted by a magistrates' court of an offence
punishable on summary conviction with imprisonment, and the conditions
mentioned in subs. (2) below are satisfied, the court may by order authorise
his admission to and detention in such hospital as may be specified in the
order or, as the case may be, place him under the guardianship of a local
social services authority or of such other person approved by a local social
services authority as may be so specified.

(2) The conditions referred to in subs. (1) above are that–
  (a) the court is satisfied, on the written or oral evidence of two
       registered medical practitioners, that the offender is suffering
       from mental illness, psychopathic disorder, severe mental im-
       pairment or mental impairment and that either–
       (i)   the mental disorder from which the offender is suffering is
             of a nature or degree which makes it appropriate for him to
             be detained in a hospital for medical treatment and, in the
             case of psychopathic disorder or mental impairment, that
             such treatment is likely to alleviate or prevent a
             deterioration of his condition; or
       (ii) in the case of an offender who has attained the age of 16
             years, the mental disorder is of a nature or degree which
             warrants his reception into guardianship under this Act; and
  (b) the court is of the opinion, having regard to all the circumstances
       including the nature of the offence and the character and an-
       tecedents of the offender, and to the other available methods of
       dealing with him, that the most suitable method of disposing of
       the case is by means of an order under this section.

(3) Where a person is charged before a magistrates' court with any act or
omission as an offence and the court would have power, on convicting him
of that offence, to make an order under subs. (1) above in his case as being

a person suffering from mental illness or severe mental impairment, then, if the court is satisfied that the accused did the act or made the omission charged, the court may, if it thinks fit, make such an order without convicting him.

(4) An order for the admission of an offender to a hospital (in this Act referred to as "a hospital order") shall not be made under this section unless the court is satisfied on the written or oral evidence of the registered medical practitioner who would be in charge of his treatment or of some other person representing the managers of the hospital that arrangements have been made for his admission to that hospital in the event of such an order being made by the court, and for his admission to it within the period of 28 days beginning with the date of the making of such an order; and the court may, pending his admission within that period, give such directions as it thinks fit for his conveyance to and detention in a place of safety.

(5) If within the said period of 28 days it appears to the Secretary of State that by reason of an emergency or other special circumstances it is not practicable for the patient to be received into the hospital specified in the order, he may give directions for the admission of the patient to such other hospital as appears to be appropriate instead of the hospital so specified; and where such directions are given—

(a)   the Secretary of State shall cause the person having the custody of the patient to be informed, and

(b)   the hospital order shall have effect as if the hospital specified in the directions were substituted for the hospital specified in the order.

(6) An order placing an offender under the guardianship of a local social services authority or of any other person (in this Act referred to as "a guardianship order") shall not be made under this section unless the court is satisfied that that authority or person is willing to receive the offender into guardianship.

(7) A hospital order or guardianship order shall specify the form or forms of mental disorder referred to in subs. (2)(a) above from which, upon the evidence taken into account under that subsection, the offender is found by the court to be suffering; and no such order shall be made unless the offender is described by each of the practitioners whose evidence is taken into account under that subsection as suffering from the same one of those forms of mental disorder, whether or not he is also described by either of them as suffering from another of them.

(8) Where an order is made under this section, the court shall not pass sentence of imprisonment or impose a fine or make a probation order in respect of the offence or make any such order as is mentioned in paras. (b) or (c) of s. 7(7) of the Children and Young Persons Act 1969 in respect of the offender, but may make any other order which the court has power to make apart from this section; and for the purposes of this subsection "sentence of imprisonment" includes any sentence or order for detention.

COMMENTARY

This section allows the court to make a hospital order or a guardianship order on anyone convicted of an offence punishable with imprisonment. Alternatively, a magistrates' court may make either order without proceeding to conviction if satisfied under subs. (3) that the accused is suffering from mental illness or severe mental impairment and that he did the act or made the omission charged.

For the effects of a hospital order and a guardianship order *see* s. 40, *infra*.

7. NON-CUSTODIAL ORDERS   371

Legal aid should be offered when magistrates are considering making a hospital order: *R.* v. *King's Lynn Justices, ex parte Fysh* [1964] Crim. L.R. 143.

The disorder need not be the cause of the offencer in question: *R.* v. *Hatt* [1962] Crim. L.R. 647.

For the information to be sent to the hospital (or the local authority in the case of a guardianship order) *see* the Magistrates' Courts Rules 1981, r. 31(1), (2). The adult court may not make an order under this section in respect of a juvenile but should remit him to a juvenile court: Children and Young Persons Act 1969, s. 7(8).

For the direction which should be added to an order under this section *see* s. 64(1), *infra*, and notes.

Subsection (1): Offence punishable on summary conviction with imprisonment. To be construed without regard to any prohibition or restriction imposed by or under any enactment relating to the imprisonment of young offenders: s. 55(2) of the Act.

Hospital. Defined in s. 145, *infra*. For information about hospitals *see* s. 39, *infra*.

Local social services authority. Defined in s. 145(1) of the Act.

Subsection (2): Written or oral evidence. *See* s. 54, *infra*. Note subs. (7) of this section also.

Justices act outside their jurisdiction if they make a hospital order without disclosing to an unrepresented defendant the substance of the reports or fail to inform her of her rights of cross-examination: *R.* v. *King's Lynn Justices, ex parte Fysh* [1964] Crim. L.R. 143. There is power to order costs from central funds in respect of the doctor's reports: Magistrates' Courts Act 1980, s. 30(3) (oral reports) and Criminal Justice Act 1967, s. 32 (written reports).

Psychopathic disorder / severe mental impairment / mental impairment. Defined in s. 1(2), *supra*. And note s. 1(3) also.

Subsection (3). Where a trial takes place it would seem that this provision is designed to allow the court to make a hospital order where the *actus reus* of the offence is proved but, because of the defendant's mental state, it is not possible to establish the necessary *mens rea*. However, in *R.* v. *Lincolnshire (Kesteven) Justices, ex parte O'Connor* [1983] 1 All E.R. 901 it was held that this provision allows a magistrates' court to make a hospital order without embarking on a trial and without (in the case of an offence triable either way) the defendant's consent to summary trial. Lord Lane C.J. stressed that the circumstances in which such a course would be appropriate will be rare and will usually require the assent of the defendant's legal representative.

Subsection (4): Written or oral evidence. *See* s. 54, *infra*.

Managers. Defined in s. 145(1), *infra*.

Subsection (8): Order . . . mentioned in paras. (b) or (c) of s. 7(7). That is, a supervision order or an order that a parent or guardian be bound over to keep proper control.

Interim hospital orders.

38.–(1) Where a person is convicted before the Crown Court of an offence punishable with imprisonment (other than an offence the sentence for which is fixed by law) or is convicted by a magistrates' court of an offence punishable on summary conviction with imprisonment and the court before or by which he is convicted is satisfied, on the written or oral evidence of two registered medical practitioners–

    (*a*) that the offender is suffering from mental illness, psychopathic disorder, severe mental impairment or mental impairment; and

    (*b*) that there is reason to suppose that the mental disorder from

which the offender is suffering is such that it may be appropriate
for a hospital order to be made in his case,
the court may, before making a hospital order or dealing with him in some
other way, make an order (in this Act referred to as "an interim hospital
order") authorising his admission to such hospital as may be specified in
the order and his detention there in accordance with this section.

(2) In the case of an offender who is subject to an interim hospital order
the court may make a hospital order without his being brought before the
court if he is represented by counsel or a solicitor and his counsel or
solicitor is given an opportunity of being heard.

(3) At least one of the registered medical practitioners whose evidence is
taken into account under subs. (1) above shall be employed at the hospital
which is to be specified in the order.

(4) An interim hospital order shall not be made for the admission of an
offender to a hospital unless the court is satisfied, on the written or oral
evidence of the registered medical practitioner who would be in charge of
his treatment or of some other person representing the managers of the
hospital, that arrangements have been made for his admission to that
hospital and for his admission to it within the period of 28 days beginning
with the date of the order; and if the court is so satisfied the court may,
pending his admission, give directions for his conveyance to and detention
in a place of safety.

(5) An interim hospital order–
   (a)   shall be in force for such period, not exceeding 12 weeks, as the
         court may specify when making the order; but
   (b)   may be renewed for further periods of not more than 28 days at
         a time if it appears to the court, on the written or oral evidence of
         the responsible medical officer, that the continuation of the order
         is warranted;
but no such order shall continue in force for more than six months in all
and the court shall terminate the order if it makes a hospital order in
respect of the offender or decides after considering the written or oral
evidence of the responsible medical officer to deal with the offender in
some other way.

(6) The power of renewing an interim hospital order may be exercised
without the offender being brought before the court if he is represented by
counsel or a solicitor and his counsel or solicitor is given an opportunity of
being heard.

(7) If an offender absconds from a hospital in which he is detained in
pursuance of an interim hospital order, or while being conveyed to or from
such a hospital, he may be arrested without warrant by a constable and
shall, after being arrested, be brought as soon as practicable before the
court that made the order; and the court may thereupon terminate the order and deal with him in any way in which it could have dealt with him if
no such order had been made.

COMMENTARY

Subsection (1): An offence punishable . . . with imprisonment. *See* the note to s. 37, *supra*.

Written or oral evidence. *See* s. 54, *infra*. And *see* subs. (3) of this section.

Psychopathic disorder / severe mental impairment / mental impairment. Defined in s. 1(1),
supra. And note s. 1(3).

Hospital. Defined in s. 145(1), *infra*.

Subsection (2): A hospital order. Defined in s. 37(4): s. 145(1).

Subsection (4): Written or oral evidence. *See* s. 54, *infra.*

Information as to hospitals.

39.–(1) Where a court is minded to make a hospital order or interim hospital order in respect of any person it may request–

(a) the Regional Health Authority for the region in which that person resides or last resided; or

(b) any other Regional Health Authority that appears to the court to be appropriate,

to furnish the court with such information as that Authority has or can reasonably obtain with respect to the hospital or hospitals (if any) in its region or elsewhere at which arrangements could be made for the admission of that person in pursuance of the order, and that Authority shall comply with any such request.

(2) In its application to Wales subs. (1) above shall have effect as if for any reference to any such Authority as is mentioned in paras. (a) or (b) of that subsection there were substituted a reference to the Secretary of State, and as if for the words "in its region or elsewhere" there were substituted the words "in Wales".

COMMENTARY

The clerk of the court should contact the Regional Medical Officer for the Regional Health Authority covering the area from which the offender seems to come: Home Office circular 69/1983.

Subsection (1): Hospital order / interim hospital order. Defined in s. 37,*supra*: s. 145(1).

Effect of hospital orders, guardianship orders and interim hospital orders.

40.–(1) A hospital order shall be sufficient authority–

(a) for a constable, an approved social worker or any other person directed to do so by the court to convey the patient to the hospital specified in the order within a period of 28 days; and

(b) for the managers of the hospital to admit him at any time within that period and thereafter detain him in accordance with the provisions of this Act.

(2) A guardianship order shall confer on the authority or person named in the order as guardian the same powers as a guardianship application made and accepted under Part II of this Act.

(3) Where an interim hospital order is made in respect of an offender–

(a) a constable or any other person directed to do so by the court shall convey the offender to the hospital specified in the order within the period mentioned in s. 38(4) above; and

(b) the managers of the hospital shall admit him within that period and thereafter detain him in accordance with the provisions of s. 38 above.

(4) A patient who is admitted to a hospital in pursuance of a hospital order, or placed under guardianship by a guardianship order, shall, subject to the provisions of this subsection, be treated for the purposes of the provisions of this Act mentioned in Part I of Sch. 1 to this Act as if he had

been so admitted or placed on the date of the order in pursuance of an application for admission for treatment or a guardianship application, as the case may be, duly made under Part II of this Act, but subject to any modifications of those provisions specified in that Part of that Schedule.

(5) Where a patient is admitted to a hospital in pursuance of a hospital order, or placed under guardianship by a guardianship order, any previous application, hospital order or guardianship order by virtue of which he was liable to be detained in a hospital or subject to guardianship shall cease to have effect; but if the first-mentioned order, or the conviction on which it was made, is quashed on appeal, this subsection shall not apply and s. 22 above shall have effect as if during any period for which the patient was liable to be detained or subject to guardianship under the order, he had been detained in custody as mentioned in that section.

COMMENTARY

After consultation with the Home Office, the Department of Health and Social Security and the Lord Chancellor's Department, the Lord Chief Justice directed that an additional direction be given by the court under this section addressed to the governor of the prison which is to hold the person pending admission to hospital, which reads as follows:

"but if at any time it appears to the person in whose custody the defendant is detained in a place of safety that the defendant might not be admitted to hospital in pursuance of this order within 28 days of this date, that person shall within 21 days of this date (or at once if it becomes apparent only after 21 days that the defendant might not be admitted to hospital) report the circumstances to the Chief Clerk of the Court and unless otherwise directed by the Chief Clerk shall bring the defendant before the Court forthwith so as to enable it within 28 days of this date to make such order as may be necessary."

The Home Office have advised that:

"Magistrates' courts have re-sentencing powers, analogous to those of the Crown Court, under [s. 142 of the Magistrates' Courts Act 1980.] The Secretary of State has no authority to interpret the law, but he takes the view that this provision can properly be applied in these circumstances. It is open to magistrates' courts to make a request in similar terms by means of an addendum to [Form 35 of the Magistrates' Courts (Forms) Rules 1981]. Prison authorities have been asked to inform the clerk to the justices of the impending possible frustration of a hospital order, but the suggested addendum for Form 35 would be a useful additional safeguard.": Home Office circ. 66/1980 dated June 25, 1980.

Subsection (1): A constable. That is, a police officer of any rank.

Approved social worker. Defined in s. 145(1), *infra*.

Powers of magistrates' courts to commit for restriction order.

43.—(1) If in the case of a person of or over the age of 14 years who is convicted by a magistrates' court of an offence punishable on summary conviction with imprisonment—

    (a)   the conditions which under s. 37(1) above are required to be satisfied for the making of a hospital order are satisfied in respect of the offender; but

    (b)   it appears to the court, having regard to the nature of the offence, the antecedents of the offender and the risk of his committing further offences if set at large, that if a hospital order is made a restriction order should also be made,

the court may, instead of making a hospital order or dealing with him in any other manner, commit him in custody to the Crown Court to be dealt with in respect of the offence.

(2) Where an offender is committed to the Crown Court under this section, the Crown Court shall inquire into the circumstances of the case and
may—

(a)   if that court would have power so to do under the foregoing
      provisions of this Part of this Act upon the conviction of the of-
      fender before that court of such an offence as is described in s.
      37(1) above, make a hospital order in his case, with or without a
      restriction order;

(b)   if the court does not make such an order, deal with the offender
      in any other manner in which the magistrates' court might have
      dealt with him.

(3) The Crown Court shall have the same power to make orders under
ss. 35, 36 and 38 above in the case of a person committed to the court under this section as the Crown Court has under those sections in the case of
an accused person within the meaning of ss. 35 or 36 above or of a person
convicted before that court as mentioned in s. 38 above.

(4) The power of a magistrates' court under s. 38 of the Magistrates'
Courts Act 1980 (which enables such a court to commit an offender to the
Crown Court where the court is of the opinion that greater punishment
should be inflicted for the offence than the court has power to inflict) shall
also be exercisable by a magistrates' court where it is of the opinion that
greater punishment should be inflicted as aforesaid on the offender unless a
hospital order is made in his case with a restriction order.

(5) The power of the Crown Court to make a hospital order, with or
without a restriction order, in the case of a person convicted before that
court of an offence may, in the same circumstances and subject to the same
conditions, be exercised by such a court in the case of a person committed
to the court under s. 5 of the Vagrancy Act 1824 (which provides for the
committal to the Crown Court of persons who are incorrigible rogues
within the meaning of that section.)

COMMENTARY

The magistrates have power to grant legal aid in respect of the proceedings in the Crown
Court: Legal Aid Act 1974, s. 28(7). As to the desirability of legal aid *see* the note to s. 60,
supra.

For the documents to be sent to the Crown Court *see* the Magistrates' Courts Rules 1981,
r.18,

A restriction order was upheld against a subnormal psychopath with a persistent history
of absconding in *R. v. Toland* [1974] Crim. L.R. 196.

Subsection (1): An offence punishable on summary conviction with imprisonment. To be construed without regard to any prohibition or restriction imposed by or under any enactment
relating to the imprisonment of young offenders: s. 55(2).

Commit him to custody. Alternatively, if satisfied that arrangements have been made for his
admission, the court may direct that the offender be admitted to hospital and give instructions for his production at the Crown Court: s. 44, *infra.*

Committal to hospital under s. 43.

44.—(1) Where an offender is committed under s. 43(1) above and the
magistrates' court by which he is committed is satisfied on written or oral
evidence that arrangements have been made for the admission of the offender to a hospital in the event of an order being made under this section,
the court may, instead of committing him in custody, by order direct him
to be admitted to that hospital, specifying it, and to be detained there until

the case is disposed of by the Crown Court, and may give such directions as it thinks fit for his production from the hospital to attend the Crown Court by which his case is to be dealt with.

(2) The evidence required by subs. (1) above shall be given by the registered medical practitioner who would be in charge of the offender's treatment or by some other person representing the managers of the hospital in question.

(3) The power to give directions under s. 37(4) above, s. 37(5) above and s. 40(1) above shall apply in relation to an order under this section as they apply in relation to a hospital order, but as if references to the period of 28 days mentioned in s. 40(1) above were omitted; and subject as aforesaid an order under this section shall, until the offender's case is disposed of by the Crown Court, have the same effect as a hospital order together with a restriction order, made without limitation of time.

COMMENTARY

Subsection (2): Evidence. *See* s. 54, *infra*.

Appeals from magistrates' courts.

45.—(1) Where on the trial of an information charging a person with an offence a magistrates' court makes a hospital order or guardianship order in respect of him without convicting him, he shall have the same right of appeal against the order as if it had been made on his conviction; and on any such appeal the Crown Court shall have the same powers as if the appeal had been against both conviction and sentence.

(2) An appeal by a child or young person with respect to whom any such order has been made, whether the appeal is against the order or against the finding upon which the order was made, may be brought by him or by his parent or guardian on his behalf.

COMMENTARY

Where there is a conviction, appeal is under the Magistrates' Courts Act 1980, s. 108.

Further provisions as to persons remanded by magistrates' courts.

52.—(1) This section has effect where a transfer direction has been given in respect of any such person as is described in para. (*b*) of s. 48(2) above; and that person is in this section referred to as "the accused".

(2) Subject to subs. (5) below, the transfer direction shall cease to have effect on the expiration of the period of remand unless the accused is committed in custody to the Crown Court for trial or to be otherwise dealt with.

(3) Subject to subs. (4) below, the power of further remanding the accused under s. 128 of the Magistrates' Courts Act 1980 may be exercised by the court without his being brought before the court; and if the court further remands the accused in custody (whether or not he is brought before the court) the period of remand shall, for the purposes of this section, be deemed not to have expired.

(4) The court shall not under subs. (3) above further remand the accused in his absence unless he has appeared before the court within the previous six months.

(5) If the magistrates' court is satisfied, on the written or oral evidence of the responsible medical officer—

(a)   that the accused no longer requires treatment in hospital for mental disorder; or

(b)   that no effective treatment for his disorder can be given in the hospital to which he has been removed,

the court may direct that the transfer direction shall cease to have effect notwithstanding that the period of remand has not expired or that the accused is committed to the Crown Court as mentioned in subs. (2) above.

(6) If the accused is committed to the Crown Court as mentioned in subs. (2) above and the transfer direction has not ceased to have effect under subs. (5) above, s. 51 above shall apply as if the transfer direction given in his case were a direction given in respect of a person falling within that section.

(7) The magistrates' court may, in the absence of the accused, inquire as examining justices into an offence alleged to have been committed by him and commit him for trial in accordance with s. 6 of the Magistrates' Courts Act 1980 if—

(a)   the court is satisfied, on the written or oral evidence of the responsible medical officer, that the accused is unfit to take part in the proceedings; and

(b)   where the court proceeds under subs. (1) of that section, the accused is represented by counsel or a solicitor.

COMMENTARY

Subsection (1): A transfer direction. That is, a direction by the Secretary of State under s. 48 of the Act removing a prisoner to a hospital.

Para. (b) of s. 48(2). This deals with persons remanded in custody by a magistrates' court.

Subsection (4): Written or oral evidence. *See* s. 54, *infra*.

Requirements as to medical evidence.

54.—(1) The registered medical practitioner whose evidence is taken into account under s. 35(3)(a) above and at least one of the registered medical practitioners whose evidence is taken into account under ss. 36(1), 37(2)(a), 38(1) and 51(6)(a) above and whose reports are taken into account under ss. 47(1) and 48(1) above shall be a practitioner approved for the purposes of s. 12 above by the Secretary of State as having special experience in the diagnosis or treatment of mental disorder.

(2) For the purposes of any provision of this Part of this Act under which a court may act on the written evidence of—

(a)   a registered medical practitioner or a registered medical practitioner of any description; or

(b)   a person representing the managers of a hospital,

a report in writing purporting to be signed by a registered medical practitioner or a registered medical practitioner of such a description or by a person representing the managers of a hospital may, subject to the provisions of this section, be received in evidence without proof of the signature of the practitioner or that person and without proof that he has the requisite qualifications or authority or is of the requisite description; but the court may require the signatory of any such report to be called to give oral evidence.

(3) Where, in pursuance of a direction of the court, any such report is tendered in evidence otherwise than by or on behalf of the person who is the subject of the report, then—

(a)   if that person is represented by counsel or a solicitor, a copy of the report shall be given to his counsel or solicitor;

(b)   if that person is not so represented, the substance of the report shall be disclosed to him or, where he is a child or young person, to his parent or guardian if present in court; and

(c)   except where the report relates only to arrangements for his admission to a hospital, that person may require the signatory of the report to be called to give oral evidence, and evidence to rebut the evidence contained in the report may be called by or on behalf of that person.

COMMENTARY

Justices act outside their jurisdiction if they make a hospital order without disclosing to an unrepresented defendant the substance of the reports or fail to inform her of her rights of cross-examination: R. v. King's Lynn Justices, ex parte Fysh [1964] Crim. L.R. 143.

Interpretation of Part III.

55.–(1) In this Part of this Act—

"child" and "young person" have the same meaning as in the Children and Young Persons Act 1933;

"civil prisoner" has the meaning given to it by s. 48(2)(c) above;

"guardian", in relation to a child or young person, has the same meaning as in the Children and Young Persons Act 1933;

"place of safety", in relation to a person who is not a child or young person, means any police station, prison or remand centre, or any hospital the managers of which are willing temporarily to receive him, and in relation to a child or young person has the same meaning as in the Children and Young Persons Act 1933;

"responsible medical officer", in relation to a person liable to be detained in a hospital within the meaning of Part II of this Act, means the registered medical practitioner in charge of the treatment of the patient.

(2) Any reference in this Part of this Act to an offence punishable on summary conviction with imprisonment shall be construed without regard to any prohibition or restriction imposed by or under any enactment relating to the imprisonment of young offenders.

(3) Where a patient who is liable to be detained in a hospital in pursuance of an order or direction under this Part of this Act is treated by virtue of any provision of this Part of this Act as if he had been admitted to the hospital in pursuance of a subsequent order or direction nder this Part of this Act or a subsequent application for admission for treatment under Part II of this Act, he shall be treated as if the subsequent order, direction or application had described him as suffering from the form or forms of mental disorder specified in the earlier order or direction or, where he is treated as if he had been so admitted by virtue of a direction under s. 42(1) above, such form of mental disorder as may be specified in the direction under that section.

(4) Any reference to a hospital order, a guardianship order or a restriction order in s. 40(2), (4) or (5), s. 41(3) to (5), or s. 42 above or s. 69(1)

below shall be construed as including a reference to any order or direction under this Part of this Act having the same effect as the first-mentioned order; and the exceptions and modifications set out in Sch. 1 to this Act in respect of the provisions of this Act described in that Schedule accordingly include those which are consequential on the provisions of this subsection.

(5) Section 34(2) above shall apply for the purposes of this Part of this Act as it applies for the purposes of Part II of this Act.

(6) References in this Part of this Act to persons serving a sentence of imprisonment shall be construed in accordance with s. 47(5) above.

(7) Section 99 of the Children and Young Persons Act 1933 (which relates to the presumption and determination of age) shall apply for the purposes of this Part of this Act as it applies for the purposes of that Act.

Interpretation

145.–(1) In this Act, unless the context otherwise requires–

"absent without leave" has the meaning given to it by s. 18 above and related expressions shall be construed accordingly;

"aplication for admission for assessment" has the meaning given in s. 2 above;

"application for admission for treatment" has the meaning given in s. 3 above;

"approved social worker" means an officer of a local social services authority appointed to act as an approved social worker for the purposes of this Act;

"hospital" means–

(a)   any health service hospital within the meaning of the National Health Service Act 1977; and

(b)   any accommodation provided by a local authority and used as a hospital by or on behalf of the Secretary of State under that Act;

and "hospital within the meaning of Part II of this Act" has the meaning given in s. 34 above;

"hospital order" and "guardianship order" have the meanings respectively given in s. 37 above;

"interim hospital order" has the meaning given in s. 38 above;

"local social services authority" means a council which is a local authority for the purpose of the Local Authority Social Services Act 1970;

"the managers" means–

(a)   in relation to a hospital vested in the Secretary of State for the purposes of his functions under the National Health Service Act 1977, and in relation to any accommodation provided by a local authority and used as a hospital by or on behalf of the Secretary of State under that Act, the District Health Authority or special health authority responsible for the administration of the hospital;

(b)   in relation to a special hospital, the Secretary of State;

(c)   in relation to a mental nursing home registered in pursuance of the Nursing Homes Act 1975, the person or persons registered in respect of the home;

and in this definition "hospital" means a hospital within the meaning of Part II of this Act;

"medical treatment" includes nursing, and also includes care, habilitation and rehabilitation under medical supervision;

"mental disorder", "severe mental impairment", "mental impairment" and "psychopathic disorder" have the meanings given in s. 1 above;

"mental nursing home" has the same meaning as in the Nursing Homes Act 1975;

"nearest relative", in relation to a patient, has the meaning given in Part II of this Act;

"patient" (except in Part VII of this Act) means a person suffering or appearing to be suffering from mental disorder;

"restriction direction" has the meaning given to it by s. 49 above;

"restriction order" has the meaning given to it by s. 41 above;

"special hospital" has the same meaning as in the National Health Service Act 1977;

"standard scale" has the meaning given in s. 75 of the Criminal Justice Act 1982;

"transfer direction" has the meaning given to it by s. 47 above.   ·

(2) "Statutory maximum" has the meaning given in s. 74 of the Criminal Justice Act 1982 and for the purpose of s. 128(4)(a) above—

    (a)   subs. (1) of s. 74 shall have effect as if after the words "England and Wales" there were inserted the words "or Northern Ireland"; and

    (b)   s. 32 of the Magistrates' Courts Act 1980 shall extend to Northern Ireland.

(3) In relation to a person who is liable to be detained or subject to guardianship by virtue of an order or direction under Part III of this Act (other than under ss. 35, 36 or 38), any reference in this Act to any enactment contained in Part II of this Act or in ss. 66 or 67 above shall be construed as a reference to that enactment as it applies to that person by virtue of Part III of this Act.

THE MAGISTRATES' COURTS RULES 1981

S.I. 1981 No. 552

Committal to Crown Court for order restricting discharge, etc.

18. *Where a magistrates' court commits an offender to the Crown Court either—*

    (a)   *under s. 43(1) of the Mental Health Act 1983 with a view to the making of a hospital order with an order restricting his discharge; or*

    (b)   *under s. 38 of the Act of 1980, as modified by subs. (4) of the said s. 67, with a view to the passing of a more severe sentence than the magistrates' court has power to inflict if such an order is not made*

the clerk of the court shall send to the appropriate officer of the Crown Court—

    ii(i)   *the copies, documents and articles specified in r. 17;*

    i(ii)   *any written evidence about the offender given by a medical practitioner under s. 37(2)(a) of the Mental Health Act 1983 or a copy of a note of any oral evidence so given;*

    (iii)   *the name and address of the hospital the managers of which have agreed to admit the offender if a hospital order is made; and*

    (iv)   *if the offender has been admitted to a hospital under s. 68 of that Act, the name and address of that hospital.*

Notification of discharge, etc., of probation order or order for conditional discharge

28. *(1) Where a magistrates' court discharges a probation order or makes an order under s. 11 of the Powers of Criminal Courts Act 1973 substituting an order for conditional discharge for a probation order and, in either case, the* *probation order was not made by that court, the clerk of the court shall—*

(a) *if the probation order was made by another magistrates' court, notify the clerk of that court; or*

(b) *if the probation order was made by the Crown Court, notify the appropriate officer of the Crown Court.*

(2) Where a magistrates' court deals with a person under ss 6 or 8 of the said Act of 1973 in relation to a probation order or order for conditional discharge which was not made by that court the clerk of the court shall give notice of the result of the proceedings to the clerk of the court by which the order was made.

(3) The clerk of a magistrates' court receiving a notice under this rule shall note the decision of the other court in the register against the entry in respect of the original order.

Documents to be sent under Mental Health Act 1983

31. *(1) The court by which a hospital order is made under s. 37 of the Mental Health Act 1983 shall send to the hospital named in the order such information in the possession of the court as it considers likely to be of assistance in dealing with the patient to whom the order relates, and in particular such information about the mental condition, character and antecedents of the patient and the nature of the offence.*

(2) The court by which a guardianship order is made under the said s. 60 shall send to the local health authority named therein as guardian or, as the case may be, the local health authority for the area in which the person so named resides, such information in the possession of the court as it considers likely to be of assistance in dealing with the patient to whom the order relates and in particular such information about the mental condition, character and antecedents of the patient and the nature of the offence.

(3) The court by which an offender is ordered to be admitted to hospital under s. 43 of the said Act of 1983 shall send to the hospital such information in the possession of the court as it considers likely to assist in the treatment of the offender until his case is dealt with by the Crown Court.

Application for substitution of conditional discharge for probation

103. *An application to a magistrates' court under s. 11 of the Powers of Criminal Courts Act 1973 for the substitution of an order of conditional discharge for a probation order shall be by complaint.*

CHAPTER 8.

FINES, COMPENSATION AND PROPERTY ORDERS

CONTENTS

INTRODUCTION

THE FINE

The fine is far and away the most commonly used penalty in magistrates' courts, even for indictable offences. As a sentence, the fine has no remedial effect, its function being one of punishment or deterrence or both. In a report submitted to the Home Secretary in 1957 the Advisory Council on the Treatment of Offenders made the following observations which are still very pertinent:

> A number of witnesses have pointed out to us that fines of an amount higher than that now imposed might be used in some cases where the courts at present feel that they must impose imprisonment. The representatives of the police were firmly of the opinion that the deterrent value of the fine is underrated by the courts and that fines are more appropriate for many acquisitive and personal offences than the courts apparently think, although they warned that in unsuitable cases a heavy fine would serve only as an inducement to commit further offences . . .
>
> . . .We feel that within the maxima the courts might well consider in suitable cases whether a heavy fine would not be an adequate alternative to imprisonment, and we recommend that this possibility should be brought to their attention. We think it right to say at the same time that such a fine should be carefully related to the means of the offender— as indeed should all fines— because if the offender cannot pay he will no doubt be committed to prison in default and there will be no advantage.

The Standard Scale

There is a standard scale of fines for summary offences as follows:

Level on the scale	*Amount of fine*
1	£50
2	£100
3	£400
4	£1,000
5	£2,000

per Criminal Justice Act, 1982, s. 37(2). References in any enactment to a fine on the standard scale are to be construed accordingly: *ibid*, s. 37(3).

Maximum Fine

The maximum fine for an offence triable either way included in the Magistrates' Courts Act 1980, sch. 1 is £2000, except that a magistrates' court's powers may not in this respect exceed those of the Crown Court: Magistrates' Courts Act 1980, s. 32(1), (9). The maximum fine for an offence triable either way not listed in sch. 1, *ibid*., is £1000 or such larger sum as may be prescribed by the statute creating the offence. (*Ibid*., s. 32(2). Certain offences under the Misuse of Drugs Act 1971 are excluded: s. 32(5), *ibid*. The maximum fine for incitement or attempt of an offence triable either way may not exceed the maximum available on conviction of the completed offence: *ibid*., s. 32(1).

There is an overriding maximum fine for young persons of £400 (*ibid*., ss. 24(3), 36(1) and for children of £100 (*ibid*., ss. 24(4) and 36(2)).

The Means of the Offender

A magistrates' court is required in fixing the amount of a fine to take into consideration the means of the offender so far as they appear or are known to the court: Magistrates' Court Act 1980, s. 35.

The means of the offender must be investigated before the amount of the fine is fixed: *R. v. Rizvi* [1979] 1 Cr. App. R. (S) 307: it is not enough simply to adjust the rate of payment. Although there is no clear pronouncement on this, the balance of judicial authority is probably best summarised by Devlin (*Sentencing Offenders in Magistrates' Courts* at p. 69): "Although the fine may be mitigated by the offender's lack of means, it cannot be inflated by his wealth." (And *see* also Thomas at [1967] Crim. L.R. 523 and his commentary on the case of *R. v. Tester* [1969] Crim. L.R. 274 at p. 275 and the case of *R. v. Fairbairn* (1981) 145 J.P. 198.) In considering the offender's means the court is not necessarily confined to his present capacity: *R. v. Lewis* [1965] Crim. L.R. 121. However, it is wrong when sentencing an undischarged bankrupt to take his wife's means into account when fixing the amount of a fine: *R. v. Baxter* [1974] Crim. L.R. 611.

Compensation

Upon conviction of any offence a court may, instead of or in addition to dealing with the offender in any other way, make a compensation order requiring him to pay compensation for any personal injury, loss, or damage resulting from that offence or any other offence taken into consideration: Powers of Criminal Courts Act 1973, s. 35(1). It will be noted that compensation may thus be imposed as an order ancillary to a sentence or as a sentence in its own right. Where the court considers that it would be appropriate both to impose a fine and make a compensation order but the offender has insufficient means to pay both the court must give preference to compensation, though it may impose a fine as well: *ibid*, s. 35(4A).

A compensation order may be made on application or on the court's own motion: *ibid*, s. 35(1). It must be of such amount as the court considers appropriate having regard to any evidence and representations made by the parties: *ibid*, s. 35(1A).

In a magistrates' court the amount of a compensation order may not exceed £2,000 in respect of any offence of which the court has convicted the offender: Magistrates' Courts Act 1980, s. 40. A compensation order may include any damage accruing to the property while out of the owner's possession by whomsoever caused in the case of offences under the Theft Act 1968 (Powers of Criminal Courts Act 1973, s. 35(2)), but except in these cases a motor vehicle accident may not be the subject of a compensation order (*ibid*, s. 35(3)). Loss suffered by dependants of the dead is excluded (*ibid*,s. 35(3)).

Consideration of the offender's means in so far as they appear or are known to the court is required by the Powers of Criminal Courts Act 1973, s. 35(4).

It has been said that,

> (1) A compensation order is not an alternative to a sentence; (2) an order should only be made when the legal position is quite clear; (3) regard must be had to the defendant's means; (4) the order must be precise— relate to an offence, specify the amount, and the instalments if there is to be payment by instalment; (5) the order must not be oppressive. The court has to bear in mind that a discharged prisoner is often short of money, and he must not be tempted to commit further offences to provide the cash to satisfy an order; (6) there might, however, be good moral grounds for making an order, including payment by instalments, to remind the defendant of the evil he had done. This might apply particularly when a non-custodial sentence was imposed and the order was for not too great a sum; (7) an order must be

realistic. An order for payment by instalments over a long period was to be avoided: *R.* v. *Miller [1976] 68 Cr. App. R. 58.*

The machinery of the compensation order is a quick and simple way of dealing with the claim in simple cases, *per* Lord Widgery CJ in *R.* v. *Daly* (1974) 138 J.P. 245; and *see R.* v. *Grundy* (1974) 138 J.P. 242. It must be remembered that the civil rights of the victim remain. In a great majority of cases the appropriate court to deal with the extent of the loss is in the appropriate civil proceedings, *per* Lord Widgery CJ in *R.* v. *Kneeshaw* (1974) 138 J.P. 291.

Compensation for loss of a hired car was quashed in *R.* v. *Donovan* [1982] RTR 126 because the amount of damages in such a case is notoriously open to argument.

It is inappropriate to make a substantial compensation order together with a significant sentence of immediate imprisonment because if a man is saddled with such an order which he will have to meet when he comes out of prison he will be tempted to return to crime to meet it. If there is reason to suppose that he has proceeds of his crime (or presumably other capital), that is a different matter, *per* Dunn L.J. in *R.* v. *Morgan* [1982] 4 Cr. App. R. (S) 358.

The court may at any later time discharge a compensation order or reduce the amount payable in the light of civil proceedings or any recovery of property Powers of Criminal Courts Act 1973, s. 37. The effect of the order upon civil proceedings is described in s. 38, *ibid.*

A compensation order is treated for purposes of collection and enforcement as if adjudged to be paid on a conviction by a magistrates' court: Administration of Justice Act 1970, s. 41 and sch. 9.

PARENT'S RESPONSIBILITY FOR A JUVENILE

The parent or guardian of a juvenile must be ordered to pay any fine, compensation or costs ordered: Children and Young Persons Act 1983, s. 55(1). This duty does not arise if the court is satisfied that,

   (a)   the parent or guardian cannot be found; or
   (b)   that in the circumstances of the case it would be unreasonable to do so: *ibid*, s. 35(1). The parent or guardian must first be given an opportunity of being heard unless, having been required to attend, he has failed to do so: s. 55(3), *ibid.*

RESTITUTION

A magistrates' court has a power under the Theft Act 1968, s. 28, to order the restitution of (*a*) stolen property (as widely defined in s. 24 of the Act); or (*b*) of goods directly or indirectly representing stolen goods; or (*c*) of the offender's money taken from him on arrest representing the value of the goods; or may make any combination of those orders. When an order is made under (*a*) above, the court may also order the payment out of the offender's money of a sum not greater than the amount by which the offender sold the goods to a purchaser in good faith or raised money on them from a lender in good faith: *ibid*, s. 28(3).

This power extends to offences taken into consideration: Criminal Justice Act 1972, s. 6(3) and (4).

DEPRIVATION OF PROPERTY ORDER

A magistrates' court convicting anyone of an offence punishable on indictment with not less than two years' imprisonment may, in addition to any other sentence or order, make an order under the Powers of Criminal Courts Act 1973, s. 43 depriving the offender of his rights in any property which:

(a) was in his possession or under his control, at the time of his apprehension and which has been

(b) used for the purpose of committing or facilitating the commission of any offence; or

(c) was intended by him for that purpose.

The taking of steps after an offence has been committed for the purpose of disposing of any property to which it relates or of avoiding apprehension or detection is to be regarded as facilitating the commission of the offence: *ibid*, s. 42(2).

Orders under this section have been upheld by the Court of Appeal when the use of the property was an integral part of the offence: *R. v. Lidster* [1976] R.T.R. 240 (car necessary to transport goods away from place of theft); but not when the offence was committed on the spur of the moment: *R. v. Miele* [1976] R.T.R. 238. Like a compensation order, a deprivation of property order should not be made if there are complicating factors: *R. v. Troth* [1980] R.T.R. 389 (partnership property). The court should consider the value of any property to be forfeited so that, together with any fine imposed, it does not represent an undue penalty on the accused: *R. v. Miele, supra*. The intention of s. 43 is to provide an additional penalty: *R. v. Kingston upon Hull Stipendiary Magistrate, ex parte Hartung* [1981] R.T.R. 262 (order that proceeds of sale of van be applied to fine and compensation with balance to defendant quashed). The power does not extend to real property: *R. v. Khan* [1982] 3 All E.R. 969. It refers to the accoutrements of crime, i.e. the tools, instruments or other physical means used to commit the crime.

Not later than six months from the date of the order anyone may apply to a magistrates' court for an order under the Police (Property) Act 1897 (*see* below) if he can satisfy the court that he did not consent to the offender having possession of the property or did not know and had no reason to suspect that it was to be used for the prohibited purpose: Powers of Criminal Courts Act 1973, s. 43(4).

RIGHT OF APPEAL

There is a right of appeal to the Crown Court against the making of a fine and a compensation, restitution and deprivation order: Magistrates' Courts Act 1980, s. 108.

It would be "exceedingly improper" to issue process to enforce a fine where notice of appeal has been lodged: *Kendall v. Wilkinson* (1855) 19 J.P. 467.

In the case of both compensation and, with certain exceptions, restitution orders enforcement is stayed automatically until the expiry of the normal time for appeal of the determination of any appeal entered: Powers of Criminal Courts Act 1973, s. 36(2) and the Criminal Justice Act 1972, s. 6(5) respectively.

PROPERTY IN POSSESSION OF POLICE

When any property has come into the possession of police in connexion with their investigation of a suspected offence or under certain statutes a magistrates' court other order with respect to the property as may seem meet: Police (Property) Act 1897, s. 1

Justices are discouraged from attempting to use the procedure of this Act in cases which involve a real issue of law or any real difficulty in determining whether a particular person was or was not the owner: *Raymond Lyons and Co. Ltd. v. Metropolitan Police Commissioner* (1975) 139 J.P. 213.

There is, except by way of case stated, no right of appeal against an order under this Act: *Stupple J.W. & F.T. v. Royal Insurance Co. Ltd.* [1970] 1 All E.R. 390. Civil proceedings may however be instituted, but not later than six months after the order: s. 1(2), *ibid*.

PRISONER'S PROPERTY

A magistrates' court has power under the Magistrates' Courts Act 1980, s.48 to direct the return of property taken from an accused person on arrest without warrant or after the issue of process where this is consistent with the interests of justice and the safe custody of the accused.

TIME TO PAY

A fine or other sum ordered by the court is payable immediately. However, the court may allow time for payment or order payment by instalment of any sum adjudged to be paid by conviction: Magistrates' Courts Act 1980, s. 75(1). When payment by instalment is ordered enforcement proceedings may be brought if there is default in any one payment: *ibid*, s. 75(3). Further time to pay may be allowed under *ibid*, s. 75(2) and instalments may be varied under *ibid*, s. 85A. In practice, applications under these provisions are usually made to the justices' clerk who may make similar orders under the Justices Clerks' Rules 1970. When time is allowed for payment or payment is allowed in instalments the court may at the same time fix a day on which, if the court's order is not complied with, the defaulter must attend court for a means inquiry or hearing: *ibid*, s. 86.

Search

When a magistrates' court has adjudged a sum to be paid by a conviction, it may order that the offender be searched. Any money found on him may, unless the court otherwise directs, be applied towards payment: Magistrates' Courts Act 1980, s. 80.

Transfer of Fine

When a person has been adjudged by a summary conviction to pay a sum and it appears that he is resident in a different petty sessions area, the court may make a transfer of fine order making payment enforceable in the other area: Magistrates' Courts Act 1980, s. 89. The other court may make a further transfer of fine order: s. 89(3), *ibid*. A transfer of fine order may be made to and from courts in Scotland and Northern Ireland, ss 90, 91, *ibid*.

Money Payment Supervision Order

A person adjudged to pay a sum by a summary conviction may be placed under the supervision of such person as the court may from time to time appoint: Magistrates' Courts Act 1980, s. 88(1).

Such an order may be made on conviction or subsequently. A defaulter under 21 years of age may not be committed to detention unless placed under such supervision unless the court is satisfied that it is undesirable or impracticable: s. 88(4), *ibid*.

ENFORCEMENT

There is a common system for the enforcement of all sums adjudged to be paid by a conviction of a magistrates' court, a term which includes, not only the fine, but also costs and compensation: Magistrates' Courts Act 1980, s. 150(3).

The following sanctions are available to the court to secure payment of a sum adjudged to be paid on conviction:

Attachment of earnings (*see* below)
Attendance at an attendance centre (*see* Ch. 6)
Detention in police cells etc. (*see* Ch. 6)

A garnishee order (*see* below)
Distraint of goods (*see* below)
Imprisonment and other detention (*see* below)

It may be doubted whether it is open to a justices' clerk to bring proceedings to wind up a limited company as a means of enforcing a fine: cf. *In re a Company* (1915) 1 Ch. 520.

Notice of Fine

Neither a warrant of distress nor a warrant of commitment may be issued until a notice of fine has been served on the offender where:
- (*a*) the court is enforcing a Crown Court or coroner's court order;
- (*b*) time was allowed for payment or payment by instalment is ordered; or
- (*c*) where the offender was absent when the sum was adjudged to be paid: Magistrates' Courts Rules 1981, r. 46(1).

Distraint of Goods

Where default is made in paying a sum adjudged to be paid by a conviction or order of a magistrates' court the court may issue a distress warrant: Magistrates' Courts Act 1980, s. 76(1). The issue of such a warrant may be postponed until such time and on such conditions as the court thinks just: *ibid*, s. 78.

For the rules governing warrants of distress *see* the Magistrates' Courts Rules 1981, r. 54. The warrant cannot usually issue unless a notice of fine has been served on the offender: r. 46, *ibid*. For defects in a warrant of distress and irregularity in execution *see* The Magistrates' Courts Act 1980, s. 78. A distress warrant may be executed anywhere in England and Wales: *ibid*, s. 125. Justices may refuse to issue a warrant of distress where it is known that there are no goods: *R. v. German* (1892) 56 J.P. 258.

There is no authority for the use of force in entering under a distress warrant, but entry may be gained by an unsecured door or window: *Long v. Clarke* (1894) 58 J.P. 150, or by opening an outer door in the usual manner: *Ryan v. Shilcock* (1851) 16 J.P. 213. A closed but unsecured window may not be opened: *Nash v. Lucas* (1867) L.R. 2 Q.B. 590, but a partly opened window may be further opened: *Crabtree v. Robinson* (1885) 50 J.P. 70. Once inside, an internal door may be forced: *Browning v. Dann* (1735) 95 E.R. 107 (all cases of landlord's right of distress).

It has been said *obiter* that in order to exercise their discretion whether to enforce payment by prison or distraint of goods justices must inquire into the means of the defaulter. They do not, however, have to be satisfied that there is no doubt about the defaulter's ability to pay. If the evidence reveals that there is a reasonable likelihood that the defaulter has assets available to satisfy the sum he owes, justices should proceed by way of distress rather than by way of committing the defaulter to prison. In the case of a defaulter already serving a prison sentence, a concurrent prison sentence is no penalty at all: *R. v. Birmingham Justices, ex parte Bennett* (1983) *The Times*, November 13.

Imprisonment

Where a default is made in payment of a sum adjudged to be paid by a conviction or order of a magistrates' court the court may issue a warrant committing the defaulter to prison: Magistrates' Courts Act 1980, s. 76(1). A warrant may issue either where the return on a distress warrant has been insufficient or instead of a distress warrant: *ibid*, s. 76(2). The period for which a person may be committed to prison may not exceed the period

applicable to the case in *ibid*, sch. 4: *ibid*, s. 76(2). Consecutive terms may
be imposed by virtue of *ibid*, s. 133, but *see* the commentary to *ibid*, s.
76(3). The court may not impose imprisonment for less than five days: *ibid*,
s. 132; but committals following part payment are not subject to this rule:
Magistrates' Courts Rules 1981, r. 55(5).

Where a court has power to issue a warrant of commitment it may, if it
thinks it expedient to do so, fix a term of imprisonment or detention and
postpone the issue of the warrant until such time and on such conditions as
it thinks just: Magistrates' Courts Act 1980, s.77(2).

Restrictions on Commitment

A warrant of commitment may issue in respect of a defaulter:

at the time of conviction only:

(a)   in the case of an offence punishable with imprisonment if the
defaulter appears to have sufficient means to pay forthwith;

(b)   it appears that he is unlikely to remain long enough at a place of
abode in the United Kingdom to enable payment to be enforced
by other methods; or

(c)   he is sentenced to or is already serving a custodial sentence:

Magistrates' Courts Act 1980, s. 82(1).

after conviction only:

(a)   When the defaulter is serving a custodial sentence; or

(b)   after a means inquiry (*see* below):

Magistrates' Courts Act 1980, s. 82(3).

Means Enquiry

After conviction a warrant of commitment may not be issued or a term of
imprisonment fixed in default except at a hearing at which the defaulter is present
unless,

(a)   he is in breach of postponed terms; or

(b)   he is serving a custodial sentence:

Magistrates' Courts Act 1980, s. 82(5). This provision does not mean that the
defaulter is not entitled to a hearing in case (b), merely that he is not entitled to be
present at the hearing: *Forrest* v. *Brighton Justices. Hamilton* v. *Marylebone
Magistrates' Court* (1981) 145 J.P. 356. There is no requirement for a hearing in
case (a): *R.* v. *Chichester Justices, ex parte Collins* (1981) 146 J.P. 109.

Attendance of a defaulter at a means inquiry may be secured by the issue of a
summons or warrant: Magistrates' Courts Act 1980, s. 83(1), (2). Either before
or at the inquiry the magistrates' court or a justice of the peace may order the
defaulter to furnish to the court, within a specified period, such statement of his
means as the court may require: *ibid.*, s. 84(1). Any written statement of wages
by an employer is evidence in the inquiry: *ibid.*, s. 100.

When a means inquiry is held the warrant may not issue except,

(a)   in the case of an offence punishable with imprisonment the defaulter
appears to have sufficient means to pay forthwith; or

(b)   the court
(i)   is satisfied that the default is due to the offender's wilful
refusal or culpable neglect; and (ii) has considered or tried all
other methods of enforcing payment and they appear inappropriate or unsuccessful:

Magistrates' Courts Act 1980, ss. 77(2), 82(2).

Part Payment

When a defaulter has been imprisoned for his default payment of the sum due will secure his release: Magistrates' Courts Act 1980, s. 79(1). Part payment secures a proportionate reduction of the term calculated in accordance with s. 79(2), (3), *ibid.*

Defaulter under 21 Years

In the case of a defaulter under 21, references to detention under s. 9 of the Criminal Justice Act 1982 are to be substituted for references to prison: Magistrates' Courts Act 1980, s. 96A. Anyone committed to such detention is to be detained in a remand centre, detention centre, youth custody centre or certain other places as the Secretary of State may from time to time direct: Criminal Justice Act 1982, s. 12(10). A defaulter may not be so detained unless the court is of the opinion that no other method of dealing with him is appropriate: *ibid*, s. 1(5). The alternative of detention under s. 9 of the Act of 1982 may not be imposed or a warrant of distress issued in the case of a defaulter under 21 unless he has been placed under supervision in respect of the sum or the court is satisfied that supervision is undesirable or impracticable: Magistrates' Courts Act 1980, s. 88(4). Where a supervision order is made the defaulter may not be committed to custody without taking all reasonable steps to obtain a report: *ibid*, s. 88(6).

Garnishee Order

Payment of a sum adjudged to be paid by a conviction or order of a magistrates' court may be enforced by the High Court and County Court as if the sum were due to the clerk of the magistrates' court in pursuance of a judgment or order of the High Court of County Court: Magistrates' Courts Act 1980, s. 87(1). This authority does not extend to the issue of a writ of *fieri facias* or other process against goods or by imprisonment or attachment of earnings because these proceedings are available in the magistrates' court.

The clerk must first be authorised by the court to bring these proceedings after a means inquiry: *ibid*, s. 87(3).

Northern Ireland

Warrants of commitment to prison etc. for fine default issued in England and Wales may be executed in Northern Ireland and *vice versa*: Criminal Law Act 1977, s. 38B.

Scotland

Warrants of commitment to prison etc. for fine default issued in England and Wales may be executed in Scotland and *vice versa*: Criminal Law Act, 1977, s. 38A.

Remission

A fine may be remitted in whole or in part at a means inquiry if the court thinks it just to do so having regard to any change in the offender's circumstances since the conviction: Magistrates' Courts Act 1980, s. 85(1). "Fine" is defined narrowly in this context: s. 85(2), *ibid*. Crown Court fines and recognizances may not be remitted except with the consent of that court: Powers of Criminal Courts Act 1973, s. 32(4).

ATTACHMENT OF EARNINGS

The procedure for making and administering attachment of earnings orders in all types of courts and proceedings is contained in the Attachment of Earnings Act 1971. The Act is supplemented so far as magistrates' courts are concerned by the Magistrates' Courts (Attachment of Earnings) Rules 1971. Only the provisions relevant to the criminal jurisdiction of magistrates are printed herein.

Attachment of earnings is a procedure whereby the court orders that an employer shall deduct money from the earnings of the debtor. The sums which can be recovered in this way include:

— fines and other sums adjudged to be paid on conviction
— sums treated as so adjudged, a term which includes costs, compensation, and recognizances, and
— legal aid contribution orders (s. 1).

An attachment of earnings order may be made:

— on the application of the debtor or, if there has been default, creditor (s. 3); or, it is submitted,
— after a means inquiry (s. 1).

In any proceedings where the court has power to make or vary an attachment of earnings order it can order the debtor or anyone appearing to be his employer to supply details of his earnings (s. 14).

An attachment of earnings order may be made against the employer of an employed person only as defined in s. 6(2). It cannot be used in respect of:

— the self employed; or
— servicemen's pay, seamen's wages and certain other sums excepted by s. 24.

The fact that a person is employed by the Crown does not exclude him from this procedure: s. 22. The court has power to determine under s. 16 whether payments to the debtor constitute earnings as defined in s. 24.

An attachment of earnings order must name the employer to whom it is directed, stipulate a normal deduction rate and a protected earnings rate, as well as the particulars specified in r. 7. The detailed rules by which these deductions are made are set out in sch. 3 of the Act and the employer is allowed to deduct 50p a week from the employee's earnings (not from the debt) for his pains: s. 7(4).

An attachment of earnings order "ceases to have effect" when a warrant of commitment is issued: s. 8 and it "lapses" when the debtor leaves his employer (s. 9). The employer is required to notify the court when this happens: s. 7(2). The debtor is required to notify the court when he is re-employed (s. 15) and the court may then re-direct the order to that employer under r. 12. This power may be exercised by the justices' clerk: r. 22(2)(d).

The court may discharge or vary an attachment of earnings order by order on complaint (ss. 9 and 19(1)).

Frequently, a debtor may be under more than one attachment of earnings order. All orders in respect of fines and other sums adjudged to be paid on conviction may be consolidated under s. 17 of the Act, when the procedure set out in rr. 15 and 17 applies. Orders made to obtain maintenance payments cannot be consolidated.

THE JUSTICES' CLERK

The enforcement of fines is the responsibility of the clerk to the justices— not only the fines imposed by his own magistrates and those of other magistrates' courts transferred to him by transfer of fines orders (Magistrates' Courts Act 1980, ss. 89, 90, 91), but also the fines of the Crown Court, the Court of Appeal and the House of Lords (Powers of Criminal Courts Act 1973, s. 32) and of coroners (Criminal Justice Act 1967, s. 49).

SERVICEMEN

Advice on the collection of fines from servicemen is given in Home Office circ. 149/70.

If a financial penalty has been awarded against any person under the Army Act 1955, the Air Force Act 1955 or the Naval Discipline 1957 on his being convicted of a qualifying offence or as the parent or guardian of a person so convicted and no term of imprisonment was imposed in default, the military authorities can make a financial penalty enforcement order which is enforceable in a magistrates' court as if it had been a fine. See the Army Act 1955, s. 133A, and the Magistrates' Courts Rules 1981, r. 47. This provision is only available when the person concerned is neither subject to service law nor is among certain categories of civilian. In practice it is of use mainly with regard to discharged servicemen.

BANKRUPTCY

A fine is a debt of record due to the Crown: *Re Pascoe, Trustee in Bankruptcy* v. *The Lords Commissioners of H.M. Treasury* (1944) 108 J.P. 126. What then is the effect of a receiving order upon a fine? Under the Bankruptcy Act 1914, s. 30(3): "All debts and liabilities, present or future, certain or contingent, to which the debtor is subject at the date of the receiving order, or to which he may become subject before his discharge by reason of any obligation incurred before the date of the receiving order, shall be deemed to be debts provable in bankruptcy." By s. 7(1), *ibid*, "On the making of a receiving order an official receiver shall be thereby constituted receiver of the property of the debtor, and thereafter, except as directed by (the) Act, no creditor to whom the debtor is indebted in respect of any debt in bankruptcy shall have any remedy against the property or person of the debtor in respect of the debt, or shall commence any action or other legal proceedings, unless with the leave of the court and on such terms as the court may impose." By s. 151, *ibid*, it is enacted that the provisions of the Act relating to the remedies against the property of a debtor, the priorities of debts, the effect of a composition or scheme of arrangement, and the effect of a discharge shall bind the Crown.
made should be rendered to the trustee in bankruptcy (*see The Justices' Clerk*, Winter, 1963, at p. 14), but the better view is that this duty is overridden by s. 61 of the Justices of the Peace Act 1979 (see *The Justices' Clerk*, May, 1964, at p. 51).

The omission from the list of remedies against the *person* of the debtor, therefore, probably implies that a criminal court is not, by reason of bankruptcy, deprived of its power to enforce fines (*see* the articles at 114 J.P.N. 644 and 127 J.P.N. 235) although the trustee in bankruptcy may have a claim on after acquired property.

Thus, the fact that bankruptcy proceedings are in progress does not prevent the court conducting a means inquiry, although the making of a receiving order, may be evidence of lack of means which prevents enforcement of the fine: *R.* v. *Woking JJ, ex parte Johnstone* (1942) 106 J.P. 232. However, it is not necessarily conclusive: *James* v. *James* (1963) 127 J.P. 352 (a case of maintenance arrears). Where an alternative of imprisonment has been imposed in default of payment of a fine the fact of bankruptcy proceedings is no bar to the issue of the warrant of commitment.

The Crown is not obliged to prove a fine in bankruptcy and when it does not do so and an alternative of imprisonment is imposed in default *habeas corpus* will not issue to secure the release of the defaulter: *Re Savundra* [1973] 58 Cr. App. R. 54.

Fines imposed on a company have no priority in a winding up: *Food Controller* v. *Cork* [1923] A.C. 647; 39 T.L.R. 699.

An order of discharge does not release the debtor from any debt on a recognizance nor from any debt with which the bankrupt may be chargeable at the suit of the Crown or of any person for an offence against a statute relating to any branch of the public revenue or at the suit of the sheriff or other public officer on a bail bond entered into for the appearance of any person prosecuted for any such offence; and he is not discharged from such excepted debts unless the Treasury certify in writing their consent: Bankruptcy Act 1914, s. 28(1)(a). By s. 28(2), *ibid.*, "an order of discharge shall release the bankrupt from all other debts provable in bankruptcy."

THE POLICE (PROPERTY) ACT, 1897

Power to make orders with respect to property in possession of Police

1. (1) Where any property has come into the possession of the police in connexion with their investigation of a suspected offence or under s. 66 of the Metropolitan Police Act 1839, s. 48 of the Act of the session of the second and third years of Her present Majesty, ch. 94 (local), for regulating the police in the city of London or s. 34 of the Pawnbrokers Act 1872, a court of summary jurisdiction may, on application, either by an officer of police or by a claimant of the property, make an order for the delivery of the property to the person appearing to the magistrate or court to be the owner thereof, or, if the owner cannot be ascertained, make such order with respect to the property as to the magistrate or court may seem meet.

(2) An order under this section shall not affect the right of any person to take within six months from the date of the order legal proceedings against any person in possession of property delivered by virtue of the order for the recovery of the property, but on the expiration of those six months the right shall cease.

(3) In any part of the metropolitan police district for which a police court is established under the Metropolitan Police Courts Acts 1839 and 1840, the powers of a court of summary jurisdiction under this section shall be exercised by a metropolitan police magistrate.

(*as amended by the Theft Act 1968, sch. 3, the Criminal Justice Act 1972, s. 58*).

COMMENTARY

This Act is excluded in relation to things retained by the police under the Customs and Excise Management Act 1979, s. 139(3): s. 139(4), *ibid.*

The Police (Disposal of Property) Regulations 1975, S.I. 1975 No 1474 provide for the disposal of property which has come into possession of police under s. 43 of the Powers of Criminal Courts Act 1973 and for which no successful application has been made within six months of the making of the order, as well as of property in any other case in respect of which the owner has not been ascertained and no order of a competent court has been made.

Subsection (1): Any property. A wide definition of this term was adopted by a stipendiary magistrate: *see* the article at 123 J.P.N. 640.

In connexion with their investigation of a suspected offence. These words are wide enough to cover property seized on arrest or under a search warrant or in proceedings under the Children & Young Persons Act 1969, s. 3 where the offence condition is alleged.

A court of summary jurisdiction. This provision is not confined to the court by or before which an offender was convicted.

On application. The procedure under this Act should commence by complaint. Costs may accordingly be ordered against the unsuccessful party under the Magistrates' Courts Act 1980, s. 64, at least where there is a dispute between parties and not simply where police seek directions as to disposal of property without involving others: *R.* v. *Uxbridge Justices, ex parte Commissioner of Police for the Metropolis* [1981] 3 All E.R. 129. An order of costs is however inappropriate when police do not object to the making of an order sought by the claimant, *per* Rees J, *ibid.*

An officer of police. This is designed to protect the police from actions of trover such as *Winter* v. *Bancks* (1901) 65 J.P. 468.

8. FINES, COMPENSATION AND PROPERTY ORDERS

A claimant. Presumably not an offender who has been deprived of the property by an order of a court under the Powers of Criminal Courts Act 1973, s. 43, having regard to the terms of subs. (3), *ibid*.

An owner. To be given its popular meaning. It does not include jewellers to whom a diamond ring was handed for valuation by a youth who was never seen again: *Raymond Lyons and Co. Ltd* v. *Metropolitan Police Commissioner, supra.* The magistrates are not bound by any determination of ownership made in excess of jurisdiction by the court of trial: *R.* v. *Chester Justices, ex parte Smith* (1978) 142 J.P. 282.

Subsection (2). The effect of this subsection is "to make it clear that, after the period of six months, the right to possession, even against the true owner, enures irrevocably for the benefit of the claimant . . . For six months the defendant has a title defeasible at the suit of the true owner", *per* Holroyd Pearce, J in *Irving* v. *National Provincial Bank Ltd.* (1962) 126 J.P. 76. Professor Smith (*The Law of Theft*, 2nd ed., para. 528) submits that this subsection "should defeat the title only of one who might have asserted a better right to possess before the magistrates' court".

THE CHILDREN AND YOUNG PERSONS ACT 1933

Power to order parent or guardian to pay fine etc.

55. (1) Where—
- (a) a child or young person is convicted or found guilty of any offence for the commission of which a fine or costs may be imposed or a compensation order may be made under s. 35 of the Powers of Criminal Courts Act 1973; and
- (b) the court is of opinion that the case would best be met by the imposition of a fine or costs or the making of such an order, whether with or without any other punishment,

it shall be the duty of the court to order that the fine, compensation or costs awarded be paid by the parent or guardian of the child or young person instead of by the child or young person himself, unless the court is satisfied—
- (i) that the parent or guardian cannot be found; or
- (ii) that it would be unreasonable to make an order for payment, having regard to the circumstances of the case.

(2) An order under this section may be made against a parent or guardian who, having been required to attend, has failed to do so, but, save as aforesaid, no such order shall be made without giving the parent or guardian an opportunity of being heard.

(3) A parent or guardian may appeal to the Crown Court against an order under this section made by a magistrates' court.

(4) . . .

(as substituted by the Criminal Justice Act 1982, s. 26.)

COMMENTARY

The effects of this section are summarised under Parent's Responsibility in the introduction.

It is wrong to use information contained in a probation report to decide a parent's responsibility under this section: *Lenihan* v. *West Yorkshire Metropolitan Police* [1981] 3 Cr. App. R. (S) 42. However, it is submitted that it would be proper for the court, if alerted to a fact by a comment in the report, to verify it by inquiry of the parent or otherwise and act upon whatever is disclosed thereby.

Orders under this section are enforceable as if adjudged to be paid on a conviction by a magistrates' court by virtue of s. 41 of the Administration of Justice Act 1970 and sch. 9, *ibid*.

Subsection (1): Child. Means a person under the age of 14 years: s. 107(1) of the Act.

Young person. Means a person who has attained the age of 14 years and is under the age of 17 years: s. 107(1) of the Act.

396   8.   FINES, COMPENSATION AND PROPERTY ORDERS

Fine. Subject to a maximum of £400 in the case of a young person (Magistrates' Courts Act 1980, s. 24(3) and 36(1)); £100 in the case of a child (s. 24(4) and 36(2), *ibid.*).

Costs. When the fine is *not* imposed on the parent or guardian the costs may not exceed the fine: Costs in Criminal Cases Act 1973, s. 2(2).

Guardian. Includes any person who in the opinion of the court having recognizance of any case in relation to a child or young person as in which the child or young person is concerned, has for the time being the charge of and control over the child or young person: s. 107(1) of the Act. This term has no application to a local authority which has a child in its care or to anyone except an individual human person: *Leeds City Council* v. *West Yorkshire Metropolitan Police and Others* [1982] 1 All E.R. 274, in which Lord Diplock said: "(1) a local authority which allows a child, accommodated and maintained in a community home which it manages, to visit a parent (or other person) on holiday or for a weekend does not, merely by giving the leave, transfer charge and control to the parent (or other person); (2) but a local authority may, without terminating its statutory care, arrange with a parent (or guardian or relative or friend) to transfer charge and control to that person, in which event that person, willingly, accepts the de facto guardianship of the child and so assumes (or, if a parent, reassumes) the role of a 'parent or guardian' within the meaning of s. 55; (3) it is, as the Divisional Court recognized in the present case, a question of fact whether the arrangements made between the parties constitute such a transfer of control".

Unreasonable. While the court will usually be concerned with the degree of control exercised by or the responsibility shown by the parent or guardian towards his child it would, it is submitted, be unreasonable to order a parent or guardian to pay a sum of money which was beyond his means. (And *see* also the Magistrates' Courts Act 1980, s. 35 – the court must consider in fixing amount of fine the means of the person on whom it is imposed – and the Powers of Criminal Courts Act 1973, s. 35(4) – compensation orders).

Subsection (2): Opportunity of being heard. Presumably on the question of whether he should be ordered to pay.

THE ARMY ACT 1955

Financial penalty enforcement orders

133A. (1) If—

(a)   a financial penalty has been awarded against any person under this Act, and

(b)   it was awarded against him on his being convicted of a qualifying offence or as the parent or guardian of a person convicted of such an offence, and

(c)   no term of imprisonment was imposed in default of payment, and

(d)   no appeal is outstanding and the time provided for the giving of notice of appeal against the award has expired, and

(e)   the whole or any part of the penalty remains unpaid or unrecovered, and

(f)   the person against whom the award was made is a person to whom this section applies,

the Defence Council or an officer authorized by them may make an order (in this section referred to as a "financial penalty enforcement order") for the registration of the penalty by the relevant court.

(2)   This section applies to a person who is, or would be but for s. 131 above, neither subject to service law nor a civilian to whom Part III of this Act is applied

by s. 209 below, Part II of the Air Force Act 1955 is applied by s. 209 of that Act or Parts I and II of the Naval Discipline Act 1957, are applied by s. 118 of that Act.

(3)   In this section "qualifying offence" means—

    (a)   an offence under s. 36 above committed outside the United Kingdom and consisting of or including act or omissions that would constitute a comparable foreign offence or a local road traffic offence;

    (b)   an offence under s. 70 above;

    (c)   an offence under any provision of this Act other than s. 70 above consisting of or including acts or omissions which would also constitute an offence under s. 70 above;

and for the purposes of this definition—

    "comparable foreign offence" means an offence under the civil law of any place outside the United Kingdom which is comparable to an offence under the law of England and Wales; and

    "local road traffic offence" means an offence under the civil law of any place outside the United Kingdom relating to road traffic.

(4)   A financial penalty enforcement order shall contain a certificate issued on behalf of the Defence Council or by an officer authorized by them and stating—

    (a)   that a financial penalty has been awarded against the person named in the order;

    (b)   that the conditions specified in paras. (b) to (f) of subs. (1) above are satisfied;

    (c)   the nature and amount of the penalty;

    (d)   the date on which and the charge or charges in respect of which it was awarded;

    (e)   if it was awarded against the person named in the order as the parent or guardian of some other person, the fact that it was so awarded and the name of that other person;

    (f)   sufficient particulars of the case (including particulars of any offences taken into consideration at the trial);

    (g)   the date of any payment or recovery of a sum on account of the penalty;

    (h)   the sum outstanding; and

    (j)   the authority to whom and address to which any stoppages or compensation included in the penalty will fall, on recovery, to be remitted under subs. (7) below.

(5)   A document purporting to be a financial penalty enforcement order and to be signed on behalf of the Defence Council or by an officer authorized by them shall be deemed to be such an order unless the contrary is proved, and a certificate under subs. (4) above shall be evidence of the matters stated.

(6)   Subject to subs. (7) below, upon registration of a financial penalty enforcement order—

    (a)   service enforcement procedures shall cease to be available for the recovery of the sum certified as outstanding, and

    (b)   that sum shall be treated for all purposes as if it had been a fine imposed upon a conviction by the relevant court.

(7)   Stoppages or compensation recovered under this section shall be remitted to the authority at the address specified in the certificate under subs. (4) above.

(8)   Where it appears from a financial penalty enforcement order that the penalty was imposed in respect of more than one offence, it shall be deemed for

the purposes of enforcement to be a single penalty only.

(9)   Where—

(a)   a financial penalty enforcement order has been made against any person, and

(b)   he ceases to be a person to whom this section applies at a time when the whole or any part of the certified sum is still outstanding,

service enforcement procedures shall apply to the amount outstanding as if it were a sum payable by way of a fine imposed by a civil court.

(10)   In this section—

"financial penalty" means—

(a)   a fine, including a fine imposed by virtue of para. 13 of sch. 5A below;

(b)   stoppages;

(c)   a compensation order imposed by virtue of para. 11 or 13 of sch. 5A below; or

(d)   a fine together with stoppages or a compensation order;

"the relevant court" means—

(a)   the magistrates' court in England or Wales,

(b)   (Scotland), or

(c)   (Northern Ireland).

Within whose jurisdiction the person against whom a financial penalty enforcement order is made appears to the Defence Council or an officer authorized by them to reside or to be likely to reside;

"service enforcement procedures" means any procedure available by virtue of any of the following enactments, namely—

(a)   ss. 144, 146 and 209(4) and (4A) below and ss. 144, 146 and 209(4) and (4A) of the Air Force Act 1955, and

(b)   ss. 128A and 128B of the Naval Discipline Act 1957; and

"stoppages" does not include sums awarded by virtue of s. 147 or 148 below. (as inserted by the Armed Forces Act 1976, sch. 8).

COMMENTARY

Similar provisions are contained in the Air Force Act 1955, s. 133A and the Naval Discipline Act, 1957, s. 128F, with suitable modifications.

For the duties of the clerk of a magistrates' court receiving a financial penalty enforcement order see the Magistrates' Courts Rules 1981, r. 47.

THE CRIMINAL JUSTICE ACT 1967

Fines imposed by coroners

49.   A fine imposed by a coroner after the commencement of the Act under s. 19 of the Coroners Act 1887, shall be treated for purposes of its collection, enforcement and remission as having been imposed by the magistrates' court for the area in which the coroner's court was held, and the coroner shall as soon as practicable after imposing the fine give particulars of the fine to the clerk of that court.

COMMENTARY

The magistrates' clerk must serve written notice on the person fined: Magistrates' Courts Rules 1981, r. 46(1).

Section 19 of the Coroners Act 1887. Subsection (5) reads: "Where a recognizance is forfeited at an inquest before a coroner, the coroner shall proceed in like manner under this section as if he had imposed a fine under this section upon the person forfeiting that recognizance, and the provisions of this section shall apply accordingly."

8. FINES, COMPENSATION AND PROPERTY ORDERS   399

THE THEFT ACT 1968

Orders for restitution

28. (1) Where goods have been stolen and either a person is convicted of any offence with reference to the theft (whether or not the stealing is the gist of his offence) or a person is convicted of any other offence but such offence as aforesaid is taken into consideration in determining his sentence, the court by or before which the offender is convicted may on the conviction whether or not the passing of sentence is in other respects deferred exercise any of the following powers—

(a) the court may order anyone having possession or control of the goods to restore them to any person entitled to recover them from him; or

(b) on the application of a person entitled to recover from the person convicted any other goods directly or indirectly representing the first-mentioned goods (as being the proceeds of any disposal or realization of the whole or part of them or of goods so representing them), the court may order those other goods to be delivered or transferred to the applicant; or

(c) the court may order that a sum not exceeding the value of the first-mentioned goods shall be paid, out of any money of the person convicted which was taken out of his possession on his apprehension, to any person, who, if those goods were in possession of the person convicted, would be entitled to recover them from him.

(2) Where under subs. (1) above the court has power on a person's conviction to make an order against him both under para. (b) and under para (c) with reference to the stealing of the same goods, the court may make orders under both paragraphs provided that the person in whose favour the orders are made does not thereby recover more than the value of those goods.

(3) Where under subs. (1) above the court on a person's conviction makes an order under para. (a) for the restoration of any goods, and it appears to the court that the person convicted has sold the goods to a person acting in good faith, or has borrowed money on the security of them from a person so acting, the court may order that there shall be paid to the purchaser or lender, out of any money of the person convicted which was taken out of his possession on his apprehension, a sum not exceeding the amount paid for the purchase by the purchaser or, as the case may be, the amount owed to the lender in respect of the loan.

(4) The court shall not exercise the powers conferred by this section unless in the opinion of the court the relevant facts sufficiently appear from evidence given at the trial or the available documents, together with admissions made by or on behalf of any person in connexion with any proposed exercise of the powers; and for this purpose "the available documents" means any written statements or admissions which were made for use, and would have been admissible, as evidence at the trial, the depositions taken at any committal proceedings and any written statements or admissions used as evidence in those proceedings.

(5) ...

(6) References in this section to stealing are to be construed in accordance with s. 24(1) and (4) of this Act.
(as amended by the Criminal Justice Act 1972, sch. 5; the Criminal Law Act 1977, sch. 12).

COMMENTARY

For the extension of the powers conferred by this section to offences taken into consideration *see* the Criminal Justice Act 1972, s. 6(3) and (4), *infra.*.

With certain exceptions orders made under this section are suspended until the expiration of the appeal period or the determination of any appeal: see the Criminal Justice Act 1972, s. 6(5), *infra*.

The police have no power to retain property seized from an accused person in anticipation of an order under this section: *Malone* v. *Commissioner of Police of the Metropolis* (1979) 143 J.P. 161.

Subsection (1).   When the whole of the goods the subject of the charge are recovered, it is an incorrect exercise of discretion to make the offender pay compensation in respect of other goods: *R.* v. *Parker* (1970) 134 J.P. 497.

Goods.   Defined in s. 40 of the Act as including (except in so far as the context otherwise requires) money and every other description of property except land and including things severed from land by stealing.

Stolen.   *See* subs. (6), and note thereto.

On the conviction.   This means immediately after the conviction: *R.* v. *Church* [1970] 54 Cr. App. R. 35.

Whether or not. . .deferred.   Thus an order may be made under this section as an exception to the general rule in *R.* v. *Dwyer* [1975] 60 Cr. App. R. 39, that on a deferment all aspects of sentencing must be deferred.

Subsection (1)(a).   "In other words, if the convicted man is found in possession of some specific goods, and goods includes money, there is power to order its restitution", *per* Parker LCJ in *R.* v. *Thebith* [1970] 54 Cr. App. R. 35.

Order.   Disobedience to the order is punishable under the Magistrates' Courts Act 1980, s. 63.

Entitled to recover.   Professor Smith (*The Law of Theft*, 2nd ed., para. 508) argues that this should be given "a broad interpretation to extend to cases in which the claimant would be able to sue in an action based upon his proprietary rights in the things in question".

Subsection (1)(b).   This envisages a case where the original specific goods have been realized or exchanged or have been, as it were, converted into other specific goods, *per* Parker LCJ in *R.* v. *Thebith, supra.*

Subsection (1)(c).   The powers conferred by this paragraph are exercisable without application: Criminal Justice Act 1972, s.6(2).

Taken out of his possession on his apprehension.   This phrase envisages a case where on apprehension the offender is found in possession of money which cannot be shown to be money representing the realization of the goods that were stolen, *per* Parker LCJ in *R.* v. *Thebith, supra*. It includes money in a safe deposit, even though not opened between deposit and apprehension: *R.* v. *Ferguson* (1970) 134 J.P. 608.

Subsection (3).   The powers conferred by this subsection are exercisable without application: Criminal Justice Act 1972, s. 6(2).

Subsection (4).   Referring to the pre-existing powers in the Larceny Act 1916, Widgery J said, in *Stamp* v. *United Dominions Trust* (1967) 131 J.P. 177:

> "Justices should hesitate before exercising this jurisdiction if the value of the goods in question is substantial, or if the application for an order is likely to raise difficult questions of law. There are many cases. . . where the civil courts are really better equipped to try an issue of this kind, and I would deprecate any suggestions in the future that magistrates should be too anxious to exercise their discretion to deal with such issues."

Lord Parker CJ went further in saying: "It seems to me that whenever difficult questions of law affecting title are likely to arise, as, for instance– and this is only an illustration– by a reason of the Hire Purchase Act 1964, no criminal court, whether Assizes, quarter sessions or magistrates, should embark on the consideration of making a restitution order."

Similarly, Salmon J said in another case:

> "It is only in the plainest cases, when there can be no doubt that the money belonged to the convicted man, that the court would be justified in exercising its discretion in making an order for restitution. To do so in any case of doubt might cause the gravest injustice to a third party because the third party to whom the money may belong has no *locus standi* to appear before a criminal court. Nor is there any appropriate machinery available in the criminal courts for deciding the issue of who is the true owner. Discovery is sometimes a very important part of the necessary machinery for resolving issues of that sort, and discovery for this purpose can be

obtained only in the civil courts. The civil courts are the correct forum for deciding matters of this kind": *R. v. Ferguson, supra.* (Order should not have been made where defendant raised the issue that the money belonged not to him but to his mistress and where there was no evidence by which the contrary could have been proved beyond all reasonable doubt).

At the trial. The trial comes to a conclusion when sentence is passed: *R. v. Church, supra.*

Subsection (6). These provisions read as follows:

"24(1) The provisions of this Act relating to goods which have been stolen shall apply whether the stealing occurred in England or Wales or elsewhere, and whether it occurred before or after the commencement of this Act, provided that the stealing (if not an offence under this Act) amounted to an offence where and at the time when the goods were stolen; and references to stolen goods shall be construed accordingly." "24(4) For purposes of the provisions of this Act relating to goods which have been stolen (including subss. (1) to (3) above) goods obtained in England or Wales or elsewhere either by blackmail or in the circumstances described in s. 15(1) of this Act shall be regarded as stolen; and 'steal', 'theft' and 'thief' shall be construed accordingly."

Section 15(1) of the Act refers to goods obtained by criminal deception.

Effect on civil proceedings and rights

31. (1) . . .

(2) Notwithstanding any enactment to the contrary, when property has been stolen or obtained by fraud or other wrongful means, the title to that or any other property shall not be affected by reason only of the conviction of the offender.

THE ADMINISTRATION OF JUSTICE ACT 1970

Schedule 9

Enforcement of orders for costs, compensation etc

PART I
CASES WHERE PAYMENT ENFORCEABLE AS ON SUMMARY CONVICTION

Miscellaneous orders for costs, compensation, damages etc.
9.   Where a court makes an order by virtue of s. 18 of the Costs in Criminal Cases Act 1973 for the payment of costs by an offender.

10.   Where under s. 35 of the Powers of Criminal Courts Act 1973 a court orders the payment of compensation.

12.   Where under s. 55 of the Children & Young Persons Act 1933, a court orders any fine, compensation or costs, or any sum awarded by way of satisfaction or compensation to be paid by the parent or guardian of a child or young person.

13-21. . . .

(as amended by the Criminal Damage Act 1971, s. 8(4), the Criminal Justice Act 1972, sch. 5, 6, the Costs in Criminal Cases Act 1973, sch. 1, the Powers of Criminal Courts Act 1973, sch. 5).

COMMENTARY

The above orders are treated for the purposes of collection and enforcement as if adjudged to be paid on a conviction by a magistrates' court being:

(a)   when the order is made by a magistrates' court, that court and
(b)   in any other case such magistrates' court as may be specified in the order: Administration of Justice Act 1970, s. 41(1).

THE ATTACHMENT OF EARNINGS ACT 1971

Courts with power to attach earnings.

1. (1), (2) . . .

(3) A magistrates' court may make an attachment of earnings order to secure—

    (a)   . . .;

    (b)   the payment of any sum adjudged to be paid by a conviction or treated (by any enactment relating to the collection and enforcement of fines, costs, compensation or forfeited recognisances) as so adjudged to be paid; or

    (c)   the payment of any sum required to be paid by a legal aid contribution order.

(4) The following provisions of this Act apply, except where otherwise stated, to attachment of earnings orders made, or to be made, by any court.

(5) Any power conferred by this Act to make an attachment of earnings order includes a power to make such an order to secure the discharge of liabilities arising before the coming into force of this Act.

COMMENTARY

Subsection (3). It is submitted that, having regard to the legislative history of this measure, this provision is authority for a magistrates' court to make an attachment of earnings order on its own motion to secure the payment of a fine etc. without need for application under s. 3. *See* the article at 135 J.P.N. 671. A contrary opinion, however, is expressed in the September, 1971 issue of the *Justices' Clerk* at p. 114.

Sums adjudged to be paid by a conviction. Defined in s. 150(3) of the Magistrates' Courts Act 1980 as applied by s. 25(6) of this Act as including a reference to any costs, damages or compensation adjudged to be paid by the conviction of order of which the amount is ascertained by the conviction or order.

Treated. . . .as so adjudged. *See*, for example, the Administration of Justice Act 1970, s. 41(1).

Legal aid contribution order. *See* the Legal Aid Act 1982, ss. 7 and 8(2). *See* s. 25, *infra*.

Principal definitions

2. In this Act—

    (a), (b) . . .

    (c)   "judgment debt" means a sum payable under—

        (i)   a judgment or order enforceable by a court in England and Wales (not being a magistrates' court);

        (ii) an order of a magistrates' court for the payment of money recoverable summarily as a civil debt; or

        (iii) an order of any court which is enforceable as if it were for the payment of money so recoverable,

but does not include any sum payable under a maintenance order or an administration order;

    (d)   "the relevant adjudication", in relation to any payment secured or to be secured by an attachment of earnings order, means the conviction, judgment, order or other adjudication from which there arises the liability to make the payment; and

    (e)   "the debtor", in relation to an attachment of earnings order, or to

8.   FINES, COMPENSATION AND PROPERTY ORDERS   403

proceedings in which a court has power to make an attachment of earnings order, or to proceedings arising out of such an order, means the person by whom payment is required by the relevant adjudication to be made.

COMMENTARY

Judgment debt. May be enforced by attachment in the county court, but not in the magistrates' court: s. 1, *supra*.

Application for order and conditions of court's power to make it.

3. (1) The following persons may apply for an attachment of earnings order—

(*a*)   the person to whom payment under the relevant adjudication is required to be made (whether directly or through an officer of any court);

(*b*), (*c*) . . .

(*d*   in the following cases the debtor—

  (i)   where the application is to a magistrates' court; or
  (ii)   where the application is to the High Court or a county court for an order to secure maintenance payments.

(2) . . .

(3)   For an attachment of earnings order to be made on the application of any person other than the debtor it must appear to the court that the debtor has failed to make one or more payments required by the relevant adjudication.

(4)-(7) . . .

COMMENTARY

Relevant adjudication.   *See* s. 2, *supra*.

Apply.   Application is by way of complaint: s. 19. For the court having jurisdiction, *see* r. 4, *infra*.

Effect and contents of order

6. (1) An attachment of earnings order shall be an order directed to a person who appears to the court to have the debtor in his employment and shall operate as an instruction to that person—

(*a*)   to make periodical deductions from the debtor's earnings in accordance with Part I of sch. 3 to this Act;   and

(*b*)   at such times as the order may require, or as the court may allow, to pay the amounts deducted to the collecting officer of the court, as specified in the order.

(2)   For the purposes of this Act, the relationship of employer and employee shall be treated as subsisting between two persons if one of them, as a principal and not as a servant or agent, pays to the other any sums defined as earnings by s. 24 of this Act.

(3)   An attachment of earnings order shall contain prescribed particulars enabling the debtor to be identified by the employer.

(4)   Except where it is made to secure maintenance payments, the order shall specify the whole amount payable under the relevant adjudication (or so much of that amount as remains unpaid), including any relevant costs.

(5)   The order shall specify—

(*a*)   the normal deduction rate, that is to say, the rate (expressed as a sum of money per week, month or other period) at which the court thinks it reasonable for the debtor's earnings to be applied to meeting his liability under the relevant adjudication; and

(b)   the protected earnings rate, that is to say the rate (so expressed) below which, having regard to the debtor's resources and needs, the court thinks it reasonable that the earnings actually paid to him should not be reduced.

(6) . . .

(7)   For the purposes of an attachment of earnings order, the collecting officer of the court shall be (subject to later variation of the order under s. 9 of this Act)—

(a)   in the case of an order made by the High Court, either—
(i)   the proper officer of the High Court, or
(ii)   the appropriate officer of such county court as the order may specify;

(b)   in the case of an order made by a county court, the appropriate officer of that court; and

(c)   in the case of an order made by a magistrates' court, the clerk either of that court or of another magistrates' court specified in the order.

(8)   In subs. (7) above "appropriate officer" means an officer designated by the Lord Chancellor.

(as amended by the Administration of Justice Act 1977, s. 19(5).

COMMENTARY

Effect of bankruptcy
Directly the money deducted by the employer is paid into court it is held to the order of the judgment creditor: *Re Green (a bankrupt), ex parte Official Receiver v. Cutting and Others* [1979] 1 All E.R. 832. Where the creditor has no notice of any act of bankruptcy he is protected by s.45 of the Bankruptcy Act 1914.

Subsection (1): Employment. See the commentary to s. 24, *infra.*

Collecting officer. *See* subs. (7).

Subsection (3): Prescribed particulars. *See* r. 7.

Subsection (4): Relevant costs. *See* s. 25(2).

Subsection (5): Debtor's resources. It was held in a civil case that in fixing the normal deduction rate the court should not consider the potential earnings of the debtor in some other occupation than that in which it is sought to attach his earnings: *Pepper* v. *Pepper* [1960] 1 All E.R. 529.

Debtor's needs. *See* s. 25(3). It was said in a civil case that there is no principle which prevents a protected earnings rate being fixed below the rate prescribed by the Supplementary Benefits Commission, but that in most cases it would be unreasonable to do so: *Billington* v. *Billington* (1974) 138 J.P. 228.

Compliance with order by employer

7. (1) Where an attachment of earnings order has been made, the employer shall, if he has been served with the order, comply with it; but he shall be under no liability for non-compliance before seven days have elapsed since the service.

(2)   Where a person is served with an attachment of earnings order directed to him and he has not the debtor in his employment, or the debtor subsequently ceases to be in his employment, he shall (in either case), within ten days from the date of service or, as the case may be, the cesser, give notice of that fact to the court.

(3)   Part II of sch. 3 to this Act shall have effect with respect to the priority to be accorded as between two or more attachment of earnings orders directed to a person in respect of the same debtor.

(4)   On any occasion when the employer makes, in compliance with the order a deduction from the debtor's earnings—

(*a*)   he shall be entitled to deduct, in addition, [50p], or such other sum as may be prescribed by order made by the Lord Chancellor, towards his clerical and administration costs; and

(*b*)   he shall give to the debtor a statement in writing of the total amount of the deduction.

(5) . . .

COMMENTARY

Employer. Defined in s. 25, *infra*.

Comply. Failure to comply with an order is an offence under s. 23(2)(*a*).

Give notice. Failure to give notice is an offence under s. 23(2)(*b*)

In his employment.   *See* s. 6(2).

Subsection (4): Such other sum.   S.I. 1980 No. 558 substitutes 50p for the 5p originally mentioned in this subsection.

Interrelation with alternative remedies open to creditor

8.   (1)-(3) . . .

(4)   An attachment or earnings order made to secure the payment of a judgment debt shall cease to have effect on the making of an order of commitment or the issue of a warrant of commitment for the enforcement of the debt.

(5)   An attachment of earnings order made to secure any payment specified in s. 1(3)(*b*) or (*c*) of this Act shall cease to have effect on the issue of a warrant committing the debtor to prison for default in making that payment.

COMMENTARY

When an order ceases to have effect notice must be given to the employer: r. 6(2).

Judgment debt. defined in s. 2, *supra*.

Variation, lapse and discharge of orders

9.   (1) The court may make an order discharging or varying an attachment of earnings order.

(2)   Where an order is varied, the employer shall, if he has been served with notice of the variation, comply with the order as varied; but he shall be under no liability for non-compliance before seven days have elapsed since the service.

(3)   (*Rules*).

(4)   Where an attachment of earnings order has been made and the person to whom it is directed ceases to have the debtor in his employment, the order shall lapse (except as respects deduction from earnings paid after the cesser and payment to the collecting officer of amounts deducted at any time) and be of no effect unless and until the court again directs it to a person (whether the same as before or another) who appears to the court to have the debtor in his employment.

(5)   The lapse of an order under subs. (4) above shall not prevent its being treated as remaining in force for other purposes.

COMMENTARY

The court. *See* s. 25, *infra*.

Discharge or vary. By complaint: s. 19(1). For temporary variations *see* r. 14, *infra*.

Comply. Failure to comply is an offence under s. 23(2)(*a*).

In his employment. *See* s. 6(2).

The court again directs it to a person. The employer is required to notify the court when the debtor leaves his employment: s. 7(2), and there is a corresponding duty on the debtor, who is also required to notify when he becomes re-employed: s. 15. The court may of its own volition redirect an order to a new employer: r. 12; and this power may be exercised by the justices' clerk: r. 22(2)(*d*).

Termination of employer's liability to make deductions

12. (1) Where an attachment of earnings order ceases to have effect under s. 8 or s. 11 of the Act, the proper officer of the prescribed court shall give notice of the cesser to the person to whom the order was directed.

(2) Where, in the case of an attachment of earnings order made otherwise than to secure maintenance payments, the whole amount payable under the relevant adjudication has been paid, and also any relevant costs, the court shall give notice to the employer that no further compliance with the order is required.

(3) Where an attachment of earnings order—

  (*a*) ceases to have effect under s. 8 or s. 11 of this Act; or
  (*b*) is discharged under s. 9

the person to whom the order has been directed shall be under no liability in consequence of his treating the order as still in force at any time before the expiration of seven days from the date on which the notice required by subs. (1) above or, as the case may be, a copy of the discharging order is served on him.

COMMENTARY

The prescribed court. *See* r. 6(3),*infra*.

Relevant costs. *See* s. 25(2).

The court. *See* s. 25, *infra*.

Application of sums received by collecting officer

13. (1) Subject to subs. (3) below, the collecting officer to whom a person makes payments in compliance with an attachment of earnings order shall, after deducting such court fees, if any, in respect of proceedings for or arising out of the order, as are deductible from those payments, deal with the sums paid in the same was as he would if they had been paid by the debtor to satisfy the relevant adjudication.

(2), (3) . . .

COMMENTARY

Collecting officer. *See* s. 6(7), *supra*.

Power of court to obtain statements of earnings etc.

14. (1) Where in any proceedings a court has power to make an attachment of earnings order, it may—

  (*a*) order the debtor to give to the court, within a specified period, a statement signed by him of—

> > (i) the name and address of any person by whom earnings are paid to him;
> > (ii) specified particulars as to his earnings and anticipated earnings and as to his resources and needs; and
> > (iii) specified particulars for the purpose of enabling the debtor to be identified by any employer of his;
>
> (b) order any person appearing to the court to have the debtor in his employment to give to the court, within a specified period, a statement signed by him or on his behalf of specified particulars of the debtor's earnings and anticipated earnings.

(2) Where an attachment of earnings order has been made, the court may at any time thereafter while the order is in force (a) make such an order as described in subs. (1)(a) or (b) above; and (b) order the debtor to attend before it on a day and at a time specified in the order to give the information described in subs. (1)(a) above.

(3) In the case of an application to a magistrates' court for an attachment of earnings order, or for the variation or discharge of such an order, the power to make an order under subs. (1) or subs. (2) above shall be exercisable also, before the hearing of the application, by a single justice.

(4) (*Rules*).

(5) In any proceedings in which a court has power to make an attachment of earnings order, and in any proceedings for the making, variation or discharge of such an order, a document purporting to be a statement given to the court in compliance with an order under subs. (1)(*a*) or (*b*) above, or with any such requirement of a notice of application for an attachment of earnings order as is mentioned in subs. (4) above, shall, in the absence of proof to the contrary, be deemed to be a statement so given and shall be evidence of the facts stated therein.
(*as amended by the Administrations of Justice Act 1982, s. 53(1)*)

COMMENTARY

Order. For service of the order, *see* r. 20. Failure to comply is an offence under s. 23(2)(*c*).

Earnings. Defined in s. 24, *infra*.

Debtor's needs. *See* s. 25 (3), *infra*.

In his employment. *See* s. 6(2), *supra*.

Single justice. That is, for the same petty sessions area as the court: s. 25(1). For the justices' clerk's powers to make orders under subss (1) and (2) *see* r. 22(2)(*a*), *infra*.

Obligation of debtor and his employers to notify changes of employment and earnings

15. While an attachment of earnings order is in force—

> (*a*) the debtor shall from time to time notify the court in writing of every occasion on which he leaves any employment, or becomes employed or re-employed, not later (in each case) than seven days from the date on which he did so;
>
> (*b*) the debtor shall, on any occasion when he becomes employed or re-employed, include in his notification under para. (*a*) above particulars of his earnings and anticipated earnings from the relevant employment; and
>
> (*c*) any person who becomes the debtor's employer and knows that the order is in force and by what court it was made shall, within seven days of his becoming the debtor's employer or of acquiring that knowledge (whichever is the later) notify that court in writing that he is the debtor's employer, and include in his notification a statement of the debtor's earnings and anticipated earnings.

COMMENTARY

The court.   *See* s. 25(1), *infra*.

Notify. Failure to comply may be an offence under s. 23(2)(*d*)-(*f*).

Earnings. Defined in s. 24, *infra*.

Power of court to determine whether particular payments are earnings

16.   (1) Where an attachment of earnings order is in force, the court shall, on the application of a person specified in subs. (2) below, determine whether payments to the debtor of a particular class or description specified by the application are earnings for the purpose of the order; and the employer shall be entitled to give effect to any determination for the time being in force under this section.

(2)   The persons referred to in subs. (1) above are —

    (*a*)   the employer;
    (*b*)   the debtor;
    (*c*)   the person to whom payment under the relevant adjudication is required to be made (whether directly or through an officer of any court); and
    (*d*)   . . .

(3)   Where an application under this section is made by the employer he shall not incur any liability for non-compliance with the order as respects any payments of the class or description specified by the application which are made by him to the debtor while the application, or any appeal in consequence thereof, is pending; but this subsection shall not, unless the court otherwise orders, apply as respects such payments if the employer subsequently withdraws the application or, as the case may be, abandons the appeal.

COMMENTARY

The court. *See* s. 25(1), *infra*.

Application. By complaint: s. 19(3). For the power to award costs *see* s. 21.

Employer. *See* s. 25(1), *infra*.

Consolidated attachment orders

17.   (1) The powers of a county court under ss 1 and 3 of this Act shall include power to make an attachment of earnings order to secure the payment of any number of judgment debts; and the powers of a magistrates' court under those sections shall include power to make an attachment of earnings order to secure the discharge of any number of such liabilities as are specified in s. 1(3).

(2)   An attachment of earnings order made by virtue of this section shall be known as a consolidated attachment order.

(3)   (*Rules*).

COMMENTARY

A magistrates' court may only consolidate orders for the payment of sums adjudged to be paid by a conviction and sums treated as so adjudged as well as legal aid contribution orders. Rule 15(1) excludes payments under a magistrates' courts maintenance order from the consolidation procedure.

For the jurisdiction and procedure concerning consolidated orders *see* rr. 15 and 17. For the transfer of fines for this purpose *see* r. 16. Before the court consolidates two or more orders of its own motion written notice must first be given to the debtor: r. 15(8), *infra*.

8.   FINES, COMPENSATION AND PROPERTY ORDERS   409

Procedure on applications

19.   (1)   Subject to rules of court made by virtue of the following subsection, an application to a magistrates' court for an attachment of earnings order, or an order discharging or varying an attachment of earnings order, shall be made by complaint.

(2)   (*Rules*).

(3)   An application to a magistrates' court for a determination under s. 16 of this Act shall be made by complaint.

(4)   For the purposes of s. 51 of the Magistrates' Courts Act 1980 (which provides for the issue of a summons directed to the person against whom an order may be made in pursuance of a complaint)—

(*a*)   the power to make an order in pursuance of a complaint by the debtor for an attachment of earnings order, or the discharge or variation of such an order, shall be deemed to be a power to make an order against the person to whom payment under the relevant adjudication is required to be made (whether directly or through an officer of any court); and

(*b*)   the power to make an attachment of earnings order, or an order discharging or varying an attachment of earnings order, in pursuance of a complaint by any other person (including a complaint in proceedings to which s. 3(4)(*b*) of this Act applies) shall be deemed to be a power to make an order against the debtor.

(5)   A complaint for an attachment of earnings order may be heard notwithstanding that it was not made within the six months allowed by s. 127(1) of the Magistrates' Courts Act 1980.

(*as amended by the Magistrates' Courts Act 1980, sch. 7.*)

COMMENTARY

Rules of court.   *See* r. 14(1), *infra*, concerning temporary variations of protected earnings rate.

Complaint.   *See* the Magistrates' Courts Act 1980, s. 51

Costs on application under s. 16

21.   (1)   On making a determination under s. 16 of the Act, a magistrates' court may in its discretion make such an order as it thinks just and reasonable for payment by any of the persons mentioned in subs. (2) of that section of the whole or any part of the costs of the determination (but subject to s. 18(2)(*b*) of this Act).

(2)   Costs ordered to be paid under this section shall—

(*a*)   in the case of costs to be paid by the debtor to the person in whose favour the attachment of earnings order in question was made, be deemed—

(i)   if the attachment of earnings order was made to secure maintenance payments, to be a sum due under the related maintenance order, and

(ii)   otherwise, to be a sum due to the clerk of the court; and

(*b*)   in any other case, be enforceable as a civil debt.

COMMENTARY

Section 18(2)(b).   Relates to payments under a maintenance order.

Sum due to the clerk of the court.   The clerk may deduct court fees by virtue of s. 13(1).

Enforceable as a civil debt. That is, by order on complaint under the Magistrates' Courts Act 1980, s. 96.

Persons employed under the Crown

22.   (1) The fact that an attachment of earnings order is made at the suit of the Crown shall not prevent its operation at any time when the debtor is in the employment of the Crown.

(2)   Where a debtor is in the employment of the Crown and an attachment of earnings order is made in respect of him, then for the purposes of this Act—

> (a)   the chief officer for the time being of the department, office or other body in which the debtor is employed shall be treated as having the debtor in his employment (any transfer of the debtor from one department, office or body to another being treated as a change of employment); and
>
> (b)   any earnings paid by the Crown or a Minister of the Crown or out of the public revenue of the United Kingdom, shall be treated as paid by the said chief officer.

(3)   If any question arises, in proceedings for or arising out of an attachment of earnings order, as to what department, office or other body is concerned for the purposes of this section, or as to who for those purposes is the chief officer thereof, the question shall be referred to and determined by the Minister for the Civil Service; but that Minister shall not be under any obligation to consider a reference under this subsection unless it is made by the court.

(4)   A document purporting to set out a determination of the said Minister under subs. (3) above and to be signed by an official of the Management and Personnel Office shall, in any such proceedings as are mentioned in that subsection, be admissible in evidence and be deemed to contain an accurate statement of such a determination unless the contrary is shown.

(5)   This Act shall have effect notwithstanding any enactment passed before May 29, 1970 and preventing or avoiding the attachment or diversion of sums due to a person in respect of service under the Crown, whether by way of remuneration, pension or otherwise.

(as amended by the Transfer of Functions (Minister for the Civil Service and Treasury) Order 1981.)

COMMENTARY

In the employment. *See* s. 6(2), *supra.*

Meanings of "earnings"

24.   (1) For the purposes of this Act, but subject to the following subsection, "earnings" are any sums payable to a person—

> (a)   by way of wages or salary (including any fees, bonus, commission, overtime pay or other emoluments payable in addition to wages or salary or payable under a contract of service);
>
> (b)   by way of pension (including an annuity in respect of past services, whether or not rendered to the person paying the annuity, and including periodical payments by way of compensation for the loss, abolition or relinquishment, or diminution in the emoluments, of any office or employment).

(2)   The following shall not be treated as earnings—

> (a)   sums payable by any public department of the Government of Northern Ireland or of a territory outside the United Kingdom;

8. FINES, COMPENSATION AND PROPERTY ORDERS   411

(b)   pay or allowances payable to the debtor as a member of Her Majesty's forces;

(c)   pension, allowances, or benefit payable under any of the enactments specified in sch. 4 to this Act (being enactments relating to social security);

(d)   pension or allowances payable in respect of disablement or disability;

(e)   except in relation to a maintenance order wages payable to a person as a seaman, other than wages payable to him as a seaman of a fishing boat;

(f)   guaranteed minimum pension within the meaning of the Social Security Pensions Act 1975.

(3) In subs. (2)(e) above, expressions used in the Merchant Shipping Act, 1894, have the same meanings as in that Act.

(as amended by the Social Security Pensions Act 1975, sch. 4, the Merchant Shipping Act 1979, s. 39(1)).

COMMENTARY

The fact that the parties regard themselves as not in the relationship of employer/employee is not conclusive: cf. *Maurice Graham* v. *Brunswick* (1974) 16 K.I.R. 158 D.C.; (1974) 7 C.L. 116 and *Ferguson* v. *John Dawson and Partners (Contractors) Ltd* (1976) *The Times*, July 22.

Subsection (1): Pension. An ill-health pension calculated by reference to length of service was held not to be excluded by reason of s. 24(2)(*d*) of the Act from the definition of a pension in s. 24(1)(*b*): *Miles* v. *Miles* [1979] 1 All E.R. 865.

Subsection 2(e): A seaman. This apparently includes the crews of cross Channel ferries.

General interpretation

25. (1) In this Act, except where the context otherwise requires—

"administration order" means an order made under, and so referred to in, Part VII of the County Courts Act 1959;

"the court", in relation to an attachment of earnings order, means the court which made the order, subject to rules of court as to the venue for, and the transfer of, proceedings in county courts and magistrates' courts;

"debtor" and "relevant adjudication" have the meanings given by s. 2 of this Act;

"the employer", in relation to an attachment of earnings order, means the person who is required by the order to make deductions from earnings paid by him to the debtor;

"judgment debt" has the meaning given by s. 2 of this Act;

"legal aid contribution order" means an order under ss. 7 or 8(2) of the Legal Aid Act 1982;

"maintenance order" has the meaning given by s. 2 of this Act;

"maintenance payments" means payments required under a maintenance order;

"prescribed" means prescribed by rules of court; and

"rules of court", in relation to a magistrates' court, means rules under s. 144 of the Magistrates' Courts Act 1980;

and, in relation to a magistrates' court, references to a single justice are to a justice of the peace acting for the same petty sessions area as the court.

(2)   Any reference in this Act to sums payable under a judgment or order, or to the payment of such sums, includes a reference to costs and the payment of them; and the references in ss 6(4) and 12(2) to relevant costs are to any costs of the proceedings in which the attachment of earnings order in question was made, being costs which the debtor is liable to pay.

(3)   References in ss 6(5)(*b*) and 14(1)(*a*) of this Act to the debtor's needs include references to the needs of any person for whom he must, or reasonably may, provide.

(4)   Earnings which, in pursuance of a scheme under the Dock Workers (Regulation of Employment) Act 1946, are paid to a debtor by a body responsible for the local administration of the scheme acting as agent for the debtor's employer or as delegate of the body responsible for the general administration of the scheme shall be treated for the purposes of this Act as paid to the debtor by the last-mentioned body acting as principal.

(5)   Any power to make rules which is conferred by this Act is without prejudice to any other power to make rules of court.

(6)   This Act, so far as it relates to magistrates' courts, and Part III of the Magistrates' Courts Act 1980 shall be construed as if this Act were contained in that Part.

(7)   References in this Act to any enactment include references to that enactment as amended by or under any other enactment, including this Act.

(as amended by the Legal Aid Act 1974, sch. 4, the Magistrates' Courts Act 1980, sch. 7, the Legal Aid Act 1982, s. 14).

SCHEDULE 3

DEDUCTIONS BY EMPLOYER UNDER ATTACHMENT OF EARNINGS ORDER

PART I

SCHEME OF DEDUCTIONS

Preliminary definitions

1. The following three paragraphs have effect for defining and explaining, for purposes of this schedule, expressions used therein.

2. "Pay-day", in relation to earnings paid to a debtor, means an occasion on which they are paid.

3. "Attachable earnings", in relation to a pay-day, are the earnings which remain payable to the debtor on that day after deduction by the employer of—

(*a*)   income tax;
(*bb*) primary Class I contributions under Part I of the Social Security Act 1975;
(*c*)   amounts deductible under any enactment, or in pursuance of a request in writing by the debtor, for the purposes of a superannuation scheme within the meaning of the Wages Councils Act 1979.

4. (1) On any pay-day—
(a)   "the normal deduction" is arrived at by applying the normal deduction rate (as specified in the relevant attachment of earnings order) with respect to the relevant period; and

(b) "the protected earnings" are arrived at by applying the protected
earnings rate (as so specified) with respect to the relevant period.

(2) For the purposes of this paragraph the relevant period in relation to
any pay-day is the period beginning—

(a) if it is the first pay-day of the debtor's employment with the employer, with the first day of the employment; or

(b) if on the last pay-day earnings were paid in respect of a period
falling wholly or partly after that pay-day, with the first day after
the end of that period; or

(c) in any other case, with the first day after the last pay-day, and
ending—

(i)   where earnings are paid in respect of a period falling wholly
or partly after the pay-day, with the last day of that period;
or

(ii) in any other case, with the pay-day.

5. . .

Employer's deduction (other cases)

6. (1) The following provision shall have effect in the case of an attachment of
earnings order to which para. 5 above does not apply.

(2) If on a pay-day the attachable earnings exceed the sum of—

(a) the protected earnings; and

(b) so much of any amount by which the attachable earnings on any
previous pay-day fell short of the protected earnings as has not been
made good by virtue of this subparagraph on another previous pay-
day,

then, in so far as the excess allows, the employer shall deduct from the attachable
earnings the amount specified in the following subparagraph.

(3) The said amount is the sum of—

(a) the normal deduction; and

(b) so much of the normal deduction on any previous pay-day as was not
deducted on that day and has not been paid by virtue of this
subparagraph on any other previous pay-day.

(4) No deduction shall be made on any pay-day when the attachable earnings
are equal to, or less than, the protected earnings.

PART II

PRIORITY AS BETWEEN ORDERS

7. Where the employer is required to comply with two or more attachment of
earnings orders in respect of the same debtor, all or none of which orders are made
to secure either the payment of judgment debts or payments under an administration
order, then on any pay-day the employer shall, for the purpose of complying with
Part I of this schedule,—

(a) deal with the orders according to the respective dates on which they
were made, disregarding any later order until an earlier one has been
dealt with;

(b) deal with any later order as if the earnings to which it relates were the
residue of the debtor's earnings after the making of any deduction to
comply with any earlier order.

8. Where the employer is required to comply with two or more attachment of
earnings orders, and one or more (but not all) of those orders are made to secure
either the payment of judgment debts or payments under an administration order,

then on any pay-day the employer shall, for the purpose of complying with Part I of this schedule—

(a)   deal first with any order which is not made to secure the payment of a judgment debt or payments under an administration order (complying with para. 7 above if there are two or more such orders); and

(b)   deal thereafter with any order which is made to secure the payment of a judgment debt or payments under an administration order as if the earnings to which it relates were the residue of the debtor's earnings after the making of any deduction to comply with an order having priority by virtue of subpara. (a) above; and

(c)   if there are two or more orders to which subpara. (b) above applies, comply with para. 7 above in respect of those orders.

(as amended by the Social Security (Consequential Provisions) Act 1975, the Social Security Pensions Act 1975, sch. 5, the Wages Councils Act 1979, sch. 6, the Administration of Justice Act 1982, s. 54.)

SCHEDULE 4

ENACTMENTS PROVIDING BENEFITS WHICH ARE NOT TO BE TREATED AS DEBTOR'S EARNINGS

The Supplementary Benefits Act 1976.
The Family Income Supplements Act 1970.
The Social Security Act 1975.
The Industrial Injuries and Diseases (Old Cases) Act 1975.
The Child Benefit Act 1975.

(as substituted by the Social Security (Consequential Provisions) Act 1975, the Child Benefit Act 1975, sch. 4, the Supplementary Benefits Act 1976, sch. 7).

THE CRIMINAL JUSTICE ACT 1972

Restitution orders

6. (1) The following provisions of this section shall have effect with respect to s. 28 of the Theft Act 1968 (which enables orders for the restitution and certain other orders to be made in relation to stolen property).

(2) The powers conferred by—

(a)   subsection (1)(c) of the said s. 28 (payment to owner of stolen goods out of money taken from the offender on his apprehension); and

(b)   subsection (3) of that section (payment to purchaser of, and lender on the security of, stolen goods out of money so taken),

shall be exercisable without any application being made in that behalf or on the application of any person appearing to the court to be interested in the property concerned.

(3) The powers conferred by the said s. 28 shall be exercisable not only where a person is convicted of an offence with reference to the theft of the goods in question but also where, on the conviction of a person of any other offence, the court takes an offence with reference to the theft of those goods into consideration in determining sentence.

(4) Where an order is made under the said s. 28 against any person in respect to an offence taken into consideration in determining his sentence—

(*a*) the order shall cease to have effect if he successfully appeals against his conviction of the offence or, if more than one, all the offences, of which he was convicted in the proceedings in which the order was made;

(*b*) he may appeal against the order as if it were part of the sentence imposed in respect of the offence or, if more than one, any of the offences, of which he was so convicted.

(5) Any order under the said s. 28 made by a magistrates' court shall be suspended—

(*a*) in any case until the expiration of the period for the time being prescribed by law for the giving of notice of appeal against a decision of a magistrates' court;

(*b*) where notice of appeal is given within the period so prescribed, until the determination of the appeal;

but this subsection shall not apply where the order is made under s. 28(1)(*a*) or (*b*) and the court so directs, being of the opinion that the title to the goods to be restored or, as the case may be, delivered or transferred under the order is not in dispute.

THE POWERS OF CRIMINAL COURTS ACT 1973

Powers, etc., of Crown Court in relation to fines and forfeited recognizances.
3. (1) Subject to the provisions of this section, if the Crown Court imposes a fine on any person or forfeits his recognizance, the court may make an order—

(*a*) allowing time for the payment of the amount of the fine or the amount due under the recognizance;

(*b*) directing payment of that amount by instalments of such amounts and on such dates respectively as may be specified in the order;

(*c*) in the case of a recognizance, discharging the recognizance or reducing the amount due thereunder.

(2) Subject to the provisions of this section, if the Crown Court imposes a fine on any person or forfeits his recognizance, the court shall make an order fixing a term of imprisonment or of detention under s. 9 of the Criminal Justice Act 1982 (detention of persons aged 17 to 20 for default) which he is to undergo if any sum which he is liable to pay is not duly paid or recovered.

(3) No person shall on the occasion when a fine is imposed on him or his recognizance is forfeited by the Crown Court be committed to prison or detained in pursuance of an order under subs. (2) above unless—

(*a*) in the case of an offence punishable with imprisonment, he appears to the court to have sufficient means to pay the sum forthwith;

(*b*) it appears to the court that he is unlikely to remain long enough at a place of abode in the United Kingdom to enable payment of the sum to be enforced by other methods; or

(*c*) on the occasion when the order is made the court sentences him to immediate imprisonment, custody for life, youth custody or detention in a detention centre for that or another offence, or sentences him as aforesaid for an offence in addition to forfeiting his recognizance, or he is already serving a sentence of custody for life or a term—

(i) of imprisonment;

(ii) of youth custody;

(iii) of detention in a detention centre; or

(iv)   of detention under s. 9 of the Criminal Justice Act 1982.

(3A) Subject to subss. (3B) and (3C) below, the periods set out in the second column of the following Table shall be the maximum periods of imprisonment or detention under subs. (2) above applicable respectively to the amounts set out opposite thereto.

TABLE

An amount not exceeding £50	7 days
An amount exceeding £50 but not exceeding £100	14 days
An amount exceeding £100 but not exceeding £400	30 days
An amount exceeding £400 but not exceeding £1,000	60 days
An amount exceeding £1,000 but not exceeding £2,000	90 days
An amount exceeding £2,000 but not exceeding £5,000	6 months
An amount exceeding £5,000 but not exceeding £10,000	9 months
An amount exceeding £10,000	12 months

(3B) Where the amount due at the time imprisonment or detention is imposed is so much of a fine or forfeited recognizance as remains due after part payment, then, subject to subs. (3C) below, the maximum period applicable to the amount shall be the period applicable to the whole sum reduced by such number of days as bears to the total number of days therein the same proportion as the part paid bears to the total sum.

(3C) In calculating the reduction required under subs. (3B) above any fraction of a day shall be left out of account and the maximum period shall not be reduced to less than five days.

(4) Where any person liable for the payment of a fine or a sum due under a recognizance to which this section applies is sentenced by the court to, or is serving or otherwise liable to serve, a term of imprisonment or youth custody or a term of detention under ss. 4 or 9 of the Criminal Justice Act 1982, the court may order that any term of imprisonment or detention fixed under subs. (2) above shall not begin to run until after the end of the first-mentioned term.

(5) The power conferred by this section to discharge a recognizance or reduce the amount due thereunder shall be in addition to the powers conferred by any other Act relating to the discharge, cancellation, mitigation or reduction of recognizances or sums forfeited thereunder.

(6) Subject to subs. (7) below, the powers conferred by this section shall not be taken as restricted by any enactment about committal by a magistrates' court to the Crown Court which authorises the Crown Court to deal with an offender in any way in which the magistrates' court might have dealt with him.

(7) Any term fixed under subs. (2) above as respects a fine imposed in pursuance of such an enactment, that is to say a fine which the magistrates' court could have imposed, shall not exceed the period applicable to that fine (if imposed by the magistrates' court) under s. 149(1) of the Customs and Excise Management Act 1979.

(8) This section shall not apply to a fine imposed by the Crown Court on appeal against a decision of a magistrates' court, but subss. (2) to (3C) above shall apply in relation to a fine imposed or recognizance forfeited by the criminal division of the Court of Appeal, or by the House of Lords on appeal from that division, as they apply in relation to a fine imposed or recognizance forfeited by the Crown Court, and the references to the Crown Court in subss. (2) and (3) above shall be construed accordingly.

(as amended by the Customs and Excise Management Act 1979. sch. 4. the Criminal Justice Act 1982, s. 69 S.I. 1984 No. 447.)

Enforcement, etc., of fines imposed and recognizances forfeited by Crown Court

32.   (1) Subject to the provisions of subs. (4) below, a fine imposed or a recognizance forfeited by the Crown Court after December 31, 1967, shall be treated for the purposes of collection, enforcement and remission of the fine or other sum as having been imposed or forfeited—

> (*a*)   by a magistrates' court specified in an order made by the Crown Court; or
>
> (*b*)   if no such order is made, by the magistrates' court by which the offender was committed to the Crown Court to be tried or dealt with;

and in the case of a fine as having been so imposed on conviction by the magistrates' court in question.

(2) The term of imprisonment or detention under s. 9 of the Criminal Justice Act 1982 specified in any warrant of commitment issued by a magistrates' court on a default in the payment of a fine imposed, or sum due under a recognizance forfeited, by the Crown Court as the term which the offender is liable to serve shall be the term fixed by the latter court under s. 31(2) of this Act or, if that term has been reduced under s. 79(2) of the Magistrates' Courts Act 1980 (part payment) or s. 85(1) of that Act (remission) that term as so reduced, notwithstanding that that term exceeds the period applicable to the case under s. 149(1) of the Customs and Excise Management Act 1979 (maximum periods of imprisonment in default of payment of fines, etc.).

(3)   The preceding provisions of this section shall apply in relation to a fine imposed or recognizance forfeited by the criminal division of the Court of Appeal, or by the House of Lords on appeal from that division, as they apply in relation to a fine imposed or recognizance forfeited by the Crown Court, and references in those provisions to the Crown Court shall be construed accordingly.

(4)   A magistrates' court shall not under s. 85(1) or 120 of the Magistrates' Courts Act 1980, as applied by subs.(1) above, remit the whole or any part of a fine imposed or a sum due under a recognizance forfeited by the Crown Court without the consent of that court, and s. 85(1) shall have effect accordingly.

(5) A fine imposed or a recognizance forfeited by the criminal division of the Court of Appeal on appeal from the Crown Court or by the House of Lords on appeal from that division shall be treated for the purposes of collection, enforcement and remission of the fine or other sum as having been imposed or forfeited by the Crown Court.

(6) . . .

(*as amended by the Customs and Excise Management Act 1979, sch. 4, the Magistrates' Courts Act 1980, sch. 7, the Criminal Justice Act 1982, schs. 14 and 16.*)

COMMENTARY

Despite the side note, these provisions apply equally to fines and recognizances imposed by the Criminal Division of the Court of Appeal and the House of Lords: subs. (5).

Fines and recognizances may be transferred to Scotland notwithstanding that an alternative of imprisonment has been imposed by the higher court: s. 33, *infra*.

Subsection (1). Written notice must be served by the clerk of the court: Magistrates' Courts Rules 1981, r. 46(1).

A fine. The wide definition of this term in the Magistrates' Courts Act 1980, s. 150(1), does not apply to this provision, wherein this term bears its narrow meaning.

Treated . . . as having been so imposed on conviction by the magistrates' court. The effect of these words, it is suggested, is to import all the enforcement powers that magistrates possess *vis-a-vis* their own fines. The Crown Court is required by s. 31 of this Act to impose an alternative of imprisonment in default of payment of any fine or recognizance. Occasionally it fails to do so through an oversight. In such cases, it is submitted, magistrates may in exercise of their powers under s. 76 of the Act of 1980 impose an alternative of imprisonment not exceeding the periods set out in sch. 4, *ibid.* It would appear that in all cases a means inquiry is necessary before the issue of a warrant of commitment in view of the fact that s. 82(5) of the Magistrates' Courts Act 1980 speaks of "the court" fixing an alternative of imprisonment. Written notice must usually be served on the person fined: Magistrates' Courts Rules 1981, r. 46(1).

Collection. Thus, the justices' clerk has power to extend the time in which payment is to be made: Justices' Clerks Rules 1970.

Enforcement. See the note "Treated . . . as having been so imposed on conviction by a magistrates' court", *supra*.

Remission. This applies s. 85 of the Magistrates' Courts Act 1980, subject to subs. (4) of this section.

Compensation orders against convicted persons

35. (1) Subject to the provisions of this Part of this Act and to s. 40 of the Magistrates' Courts Act 1980 (which imposes a monetary limit on the powers of a magistrates court under this section), a court by or before which a person is a convicted of an offence, instead of or in addition to dealing with him in any other way, may, on application or otherwise, make an order (in this Act referred to as "a compensation order") requiring him to pay compensation for any personal injury, loss or damage resulting from that offence or any other offence which is taken into consideration by the court in determining sentence.

(1A) Compensation under subs. (1) above shall be of such amount as the court considers appropriate, having regard to any evidence and to any representations that are made by or on behalf of the accused or the prosecutor.

(2) In the case of an offence under the Theft Act 1968, where the property in question is recovered, any damage to the property occurring while it was out of the owner's possession shall be treated for the purposes of subs. (1) above as having resulted from the offence, however and by whomsoever the damage was caused.

(3) No compensation order shall be made in respect of loss suffered by the dependants of a person in consequence of his death, and no such order shall be made in respect of injury, loss or damage due to an accident arising out of the presence of a motor vehicle on a road, except such damage as is treated by subs. (2) above as resulting from an offence under the Theft Act 1968.

(4) In determining whether to make a compensation order against any person, and in determining the amount to be paid by any person under such an order, the court shall have regard to his means so far as they appear or are known to the court.

(4A) Where the court considers–
  (a) that it would be appropriate both to impose a fine and to make a compensation order; but
  (b) that the offender has insufficient means to pay both an appropriate fine and appropriate compensation,
the court shall give preference to compensation (though it may impose a fine as well).

(5) (*Repealed*).

8.   FINES, COMPENSATION AND PROPERTY ORDERS   419

(as amended by the Criminal Law Act 1977, s. 60, the Magistrates' Courts Act 1980, sch. 8, the Criminal Justice Act 1982, s. 67.)

COMMENTARY

For the principles upon which compensation orders should be made *see* the introduction.

For the making of a compensation order against a juvenile see the Children and Young Persons Act, 1933, s. 55.

An order of compensation may not be made by magistrates at the same time as committing an offender to the Crown Court for sentence: CriminalJustice Act 1967, s. 56(5): *cf. R.* v. *Blackpool Justices, ex parte Charlson and Gregory* (1973) 137 J.P. 25.

An order of compensation made under this section continues in force even though the offender be dealt with later under s. 6 of the Powers of Criminal Courts Act 1973 (breach of requirements of probation order), in respect of the original offence: *R.* v. *Evans* (1961) 125 J.P. 134. The court expressed the view that similar considerations would apply in the case of a probationer dealt with under s. 8, *ibid,* (subsequent offence). However, where a probationer subsequently receives a substantial sentence of imprisonment it is contrary to justice that a compensation order should remain hanging over his head if he has no means of paying it: *R.* v. *Wallis* [1979] Crim. L.R. 732.

For the effect of a compensation order on subsequent civil proceedings, see s. 38, *infra.*.

There is a maximum of £2000 on any compensation order made by a magistrates' court: Magistrates' Courts Act 1980, s. 40.

Orders under this section may be enforced as sums adjudged to be paid on a conviction by a magistrates' court: Administration of Justice Act 1970, s. 41(1) and sch. 9. But only after the period of suspension referred to in s. 36(2) of this Act.

For the priority of payment of compensation orders see the Magistrates' Courts Act 1980, s. 139.

The Ancient Monuments and Archeological Areas Act 1979, s. 29 provides that: "Where the owner or any other person is convicted of an offence involving damage to a monument situated in England and Wales which was at the time of the offence under the guardianship of the Secretary of State or any local authority by virtue of this Act, any compensation order made under s. 35 of the Powers of Criminal Courts Act 1973 (compensation orders against convicted persons) in respect of that damage shall be made in favour of the Secretary of State or (as the case may require) in favour of the local authority in question."

Subsection (1): Instead of. This makes it clear that a compensation order may be a sentence in its own right. However, in view of the power to make a compensation order in addition to discharging an offender absolutely or conditionally it would seem that most compensation orders will continue to be made as ancillary to some other sentence.

A person. An order against two persons involving joint and several liability is not inconsistent with the Act, but in view of the payment difficulties to which it could give rise, should be made only with reserve and not if substantial justice can be achieved by orders made, severally: *R.* v. *Grundy* (1974) 138 J.P. 242.

Where there are a number of claimants for compensation and the offender has insufficient means to satisfy them all, as a general rule the compensation should be apportioned pro rata but this principle may be departed from where there are strong grounds, for example where it would lead to one or more small claimants being compensated to a wholly inadequate degree. Similarly all co-defendants ought to be ordered to pay pro rata unless one of them is more responsible than the others or where the ability to pay is markedly different: *R.* v. *Amey* (1983) 147 J.P. 124.

Convicted. Includes a conviction resulting in a probation order or order of absolute or conditional discharge. (Such orders are not excluded by the effects of s. 13(1) of the Act, because the making of a compensation order is a "purpose of the proceedings in which the order is made").

Personal injury. Compensation for distress and anxiety was upheld in *Bond* v. *Chief Constable of Kent* (1973) 147 J.P. 107, although it was left undecided whether this was personal injury or damage.

Loss. The word "loss" is to be given its ordinary meaning and includes any loss resulting from the offence provided it is not too remote. It is wide enough to allow the award of interest, at least where the amount involved is large, the time elapsed is long and the defendant's means warrant the additional sum: *R.* v. *Schofield* (1978) 142 J.P. 426. Compensation should not be asked for in respect of costs in related civil proceedings: *Hammerton Cars Ltd.* v. *Redbridge L.B.C. and Another* [1974] 2 All E.R. 216. In *R.* v. *Lester* [1976] 63 Cr. App. R. 144, doubts were expressed about the propriety of ordering compensation in respect of offences under the Trade Descriptions Act, 1968; but *see R. v. Thomson Holidays Ltd, infra.* Compensation is inappropriate in a handling charge where there is no evidence that the goods have suffered any damage or are of less value: *R. v. Sharkey* [1976] Crim. L.R. 388 (car disassembled into component parts.) Seemingly this does not prevent an order for the cost of re-assembly or an order for loss where the parts cannot be re-assembled.

Resulting from that offence. Thus, any order must be related to a specific offence, whether convicted or taken into consideration: *R. v. Oddy* (1974) 138 J.P. 515; *R. v. Inwood* [1974] 50 Cr. App. R. 70; *R. v. Parker* [1982] 3 Cr. App. R. (S) 279; *R. v. Making* [1982] Crim. L.R. 613.

This term is to be given a wide meaning. In particular, Parliament did not intend to introduce into the criminal law the concepts of causation which apply to the assessment of civil damages: *R. v. Thomson Holidays Ltd* (1974) 138 J.P. 284 (compensation for lost holiday). The court must ask itself whether loss or damage can fairly be said to have resulted to anyone from the offence for which the accused has been convicted or taken into consideration (*ibid*). Thus, a handler of stolen goods may be ordered to pay compensation to someone who purchased those goods from him innocently who has had to return them to the owner: *R. v. Howell* [1978] 66 Cr. App. R. 179. Similarly, the court could make a compensation order in respect of sums fraudulently obtained over a number of weeks from the Department of Health and Social Security where the defendant was charged only with the first fraud: *Rowlston* v. *Kenny* [1982] 4 Cr. App. R. (S) 85. However, suffering if caused by taking a controlled drug does not result from the offence of its possession: *Berkeley* v. *Orchard* [1975] Crim. L.R. 225 (but see Professor Smith's comments on that case.)

Any other offence which is taken into consideration. This is confined to offences taken into consideration under formalized practice and does not extend to other offences not the subject of sample charges: *Director of Public Prosecutions* v. *Anderson* (1978) 142 J.P. 391.

Subsection (1A). This reverses the decision in *R. v. Vivian* (1979) 143 J.P. 102. It does not rule out the calling of evidence, but if the court is unable readily to settle any dispute about the extent of the loss or damage it should refrain from making an order, at least beyond the level which is admitted.

Subsection (2). Note that compensation for damage under this subsection is not subject to the exclusion concerning road accident damage contained in subs. (3).

Since the subsection refers to damage to "the property", damage to other property, for example other cars involved in an accident with a stolen car (where this falls within subs. (3)), may not be awarded: *Quigley* v. *Stokes* [1977] 2 All E.R. 317.

Subsection (3): Accident. Where two young men were convicted of criminal damage following their having driven a stolen car into a wall it was held that there is no power to order compensation under this section because that was properly described as an "accident" even though recklessness was proved: *M (a minor) and Another* v. *Oxford* [1981] R.T.R. 246.

Subsection (4). As long as a man has his normal health and is capable of earning something it is perfectly proper to make an order against him even though he is temporarily unemployed, although the court may have to be restricted by reason of the probability that his earnings will be small, *per* Lord Widgery CJ in *R. v. Bradburn* [1973] 57 Cr. App. R. 948. In saying this Lord Widgery was merely inviting courts to keep in mind all the common sense features, and rehabilitation is one of these. This subsection does not assimilate the principles on which compensation is assessed to those used for the assessment of fines, but orders should not be counterproductive in the sense that they result in the accused committing further offences in order to pay: *R v. Oddy* (1974) 138 J.P. 515. (Order which would take four years to pay disapproved). And *see R. v. Daly* (1974) 138 J.P. 245. In *R. v. Makin* [1982] 4 Cr. App. R. (S) 180 the Court ordered compensation to be repaid over two years. Compensation payable by 90 weekly instalments was upheld in *R. v. Pellant* [1984] *The Times,* March 16. Subject to this rule, it is not improper to make a compensation order, even when a person has been sentenced to a substantial term of imprisonment: *R. v. Wylie* [1975] R.T.R. 94. In *R. v. Dallas-Cope* (1975) 139 J.P.N. 171, the Court of Appeal upheld a trial Judge's decision to treat as the appellant's means money which his father said he was prepared to pay. Potential earning capacity may be considered: *R. v. Ford* [1976] Crim. L.R. 114. The court must take a broad picture of the defendant's assets; it need not make a precise calculation: *R. v. Howell* [1978] 66 Cr. App. R. 179. In *R. v. Workman* [1979] 1 Cr. App. R. (S) 335 a Crown. Court compensation order was upheld where the offender had bought a house with the

8. FINES, COMPENSATION AND PROPERTY ORDERS 421

proceeds of crime even though there was no evidence that she could pay within a reasonable time.

This subsection places no duty on the prosecutor to establish the defendant's means or to conduct a means inquiry: *R.* v. *Johnstone* [1982] 4 Cr. App. R. (S) 141.

Appeals in the case of compensation orders

36. (1) ...

(2) A compensation order made by a magistrates' court shall be suspended—

(*a*) in any case until the expiration of the period for the time being prescribed by law for the giving of notice of appeal against a decision of a magistrates' court;

(*b*) where notice of appeal is given within the period so prescribed, until the determination of the appeal.

(3) Where a compensation order has been made against any person in respect of an offence taken into consideration in determining his sentence—

(*a*) the order shall cease to have effect if he successfully appeals against his conviction of the offence or, if more than one, all the offences, of which he was convicted in the proceedings in which the order was made;

(*b*) he may appeal against the order as if it were part of the sentence imposed in respect of the offence or, if more than one, any of the offences, of which he was so convicted.

COMMENTARY

Subsection (2). It is submitted that this does not prevent a justices' clerk accepting payment of compensation within this period, but it should not be paid out to the person entitled until the period has expired or any appeal determined.

Made by a magistrates' court. A compensation order made on appeal from a magistrates' court shall be treated for the purposes of this Act as if it had been made by a magistrates' court: s. 57(5).

The period for the time being prescribed. That is, 21 days: Crown Court Rules 1971, r. 7.

The determination of the appeal. There may, of course, be no determination of an appeal by way of case stated which is not proceeded with. In such a case it is suggested that enforcement may properly be commenced from the expiration of the period when the case should have been lodged in the Crown Office, provided only that no application is being made for an extension of that time.

Review of compensation orders

37. At any time before a compensation order has been complied with or fully complied with, the magistrates' court for the time being having functions in reaction to the enforcement of the order (by virtue of s. 41(1) of the Administration of Justice Act 1970, may, on the application of the person against whom it was made, discharge the order, or reduce the amount which remains to be paid, if it appears to the court—

(*a*) that the injury, loss or damage in respect of which the order was made has been held in civil proceedings to be less than it was taken to be for the purposes of the order; or

(*b*) in the case of an order in respect of the loss of any property, that the property has been recovered by the person in whose favour the order was made.

COMMENTARY

There is power to grant legal aid in respect of proceedings under this section: Legal Aid Act 1974, s. 28(4).

The magistrates' court for the time being having functions in relation to the enforcement of the order. *See* the Administration of Justice Act 1970, s. 41(1).

Application.   To be by way of complaint: the Magistrates' Courts Rules 1981, r. 104. That incorporates the provisions of the Magistrates' Courts Act 1980, ss 51-57. The terms of the rule would appear to leave the justice no discretion but to issue a summons whenever a complaint is made.

The property has been recovered. The amount of the compensation order may seemingly be reduced for partial recovery.

Effect of compensation order on subsequent award of damages in civil proceedings

38.   (1) This section shall have effect where a compensation order has been made in favour of any person in respect of any injury, loss or damage and a claim by him in civil proceedings for damages in respect thereof subsequently falls to be determined.

(2)   The damages in the civil proceedings shall be assessed without regard to the order; but where the whole or part of the amount awarded by the order has been paid; the damages awarded in the civil proceedings shall not exceed the amount (if any) by which, as so assessed, they exceed the amount paid under the order.

(3)   Where the whole or part of the amount awarded by the order remains unpaid and the court awards damages in the civil proceedings, then, unless the person against whom the order was made has ceased to be liable to pay the amount unpaid (whether in consequence of an appeal, of his imprisonment for default or otherwise), the court shall direct that the judgment—

(a)   if it is for an amount not exceeding the amount unpaid under the order, shall not be enforced; or

(b)   if it is for an amount exceeding the amount unpaid under the order, shall not be enforced as to a corresponding amount;

without the leave of the court.

Power to deprive offender of property used, or intended for use, for purposes of crime

43.   (1) Where a person is convicted of an offence punishable on indictment with imprisonment for a term of two years or more and the court by or before which he is convicted is satisfied that any property which was in his possession or under his control at the time of his apprehension—

(a)   has been used for the purpose of committing, or facilitating the commission of, any offence; or

(b)   was intended by him to be used for that purpose;

the court may make an order under this section in respect of that property.

(2)   Facilitating the commission of an offence shall be taken for the purposes of this section and s. 44 of this Act to include the taking of any steps after it has been committed for the purpose of disposing of any property to which it relates or of avoiding apprehension or detection, and references in this or that section to an offence punishable with imprisonment shall be construed without regard to any prohibition or restriction imposed by or under any enactment on the imprisonment of young offenders.

(3)   An order under this section shall operate to deprive the offender of his rights, if any, in the property to which it relates, and the property shall (if not already in their possession) be taken into the possession of the police.

(4)   The Police (Property) Act, 1897, shall apply, with the following modifications, to property which is in the possession of the police by virtue of this section—

(a)   no application shall be made under s. 1(1) of that Act by any claimant of the property after the expiration of six months from the date on which the order in respect of the property was made under this section; and

(b)   no such application shall succeed unless the claimant satisfies the court either that he had not consented to the offender having possession of the property or that he did not know, and had no reason to suspect, that the property was likely to be used for the purpose mentioned in subs. (1) above.

(5)   (*Regulations*).

COMMENTARY

See under Deprivation of Property in the introduction.

An order under this section cannot be complied with a conditional discharge: *R.* v. *Savage* (1983) 147 J.P.N. 667.

Subsection (1): An offence punishable on indictment. Even if tried summarily. And *see* subs. (2).

At the time of his apprehension. Thus, if the property was seized before the defendant was arrested no order may be made under this section: *R.* v. *Hinde* [1977] 64 Cr. App. R. 213; *R.* v. *McFarlane* [1982] 4 Cr. App. R. (S) 264.

Facilitating the commission of any offence. *See* subs. (2). An order was quashed because a car used to transport a woman to a place where she was indecently assaulted was not used for the purpose of committing or facilitating the commission of an offence: *R.* v. *Lucas* [1976] R.T.R. 235.

Subsection (3). The property will, subject to subs. (4), be disposed of in accordance with the Magistrates' Courts Act 1980, s. 140. However, an order under this section may not be made as a means of securing payment of a fine: *R.* v. *Kingston Upon Hull Stipendiary Magistrate, ex parte Hartnung* [1981] R.T.R. 262.

Subsection (4): The Police (Property) Act 1897. *See* above. The effect of this subsection is to apply the s. 1 procedure for application to a magistrates' court subject to the six months' limitation imposed by para. (*a*) of this subsection.

THE CRIMINAL LAW ACT 1977

Execution in different part of United Kingdom of warrants for imprisonment for non-payment of fine

38A.   (1) Subject to subs. (6) below, a person against whom an extract conviction is issued in Scotland for imprisonment in default of payment of a fine may be arrested—

(a)   in England and Wales, by any constable acting within his police area;

(b)   in Northern Ireland, by any member of the Royal Ulster Constabulary or the Royal Ulster Constabulary Reserve;

and subs. (4) and (5) of s. 159 of the Magistrates' Courts Act (Northern Ireland) 1964 (execution without possession of the warrant and execution on Sunday) shall apply to the execution in Northern Ireland of any such extract conviction as those subsections apply in relation to the execution of a warrant for arrest.

(2)   Subject to subs. (6) below, a person against whom there has been issued in England, Wales or Northern Ireland a warrant committing him to prison in default of payment of a sum adjudged to be paid by a conviction may be arrested in Scotland, by any constable appointed for a police area, in like manner as if the warrant were an extract conviction for imprisonment issued in Scotland in default of payment of a fine.

(3)   A person arrested by virtue of subs. (1) above under an extract conviction or by virtue of subs. (2) above under a warrant of commitment may be detained under it in any prison in the part of the United Kingdom in which he was arrested; and while so detained he shall be treated for all purposes as if he were detained under a warrant of commitment or extract conviction issued in that part of the United Kingdom.

(4)   An extract conviction or a warrant of commitment may be executed by virtue of this section whether or not it has been endorsed under s. 4 of the Summary Jurisdiction (Process) Act 1881 or under s. 27 of the Petty Sessions (Ireland) Act 1851.

(5)   In this section—
'fine' includes any sum treated by any enactment as a fine for the purposes of its enforcement and any sum to be found as caution;

'imprisonment' includes, in the case of a person who is under the age of 21 years, detention;

'part of the United Kingdom' means England and Wales, Scotland or Northern Ireland;

'prison' means—
- (i)   in the case of a person who is under the age of 21 years arrested in Scotland, a young offenders institution; and
- (i)   in the case of a person under that age arrested in England and Wales, any place in which he could be detained under s. 12(10) of the Criminal Justice Act 1982;
- (ii) in the case of a person under that age arrested in Northern Ireland, a young offenders centre; and

'sum adjudged to be paid by a conviction' has the meaning given by s. 150(3) of the Magistrates' Courts Act 1980 or, in Northern Ireland, s. 169(2) of the Magistrates' Courts (Northern Ireland) Act 1964.

(6)   This section shall not apply to the arrest of persons under the age of 17 years.

(as inserted by the Criminal Justice (Scotland) Act 1980, s. 51 and as amended by the Criminal Justice Act 1982, sch. 14.)

COMMENTARY

The effects of this section are described in Home Office Circular 58/1981.

Subsection (1): Extract conviction. This is the Scottish equivalent of a warrant of commitment.

Further provision for execution of warrants of commitment for non-payment of sum adjudged to be paid by conviction in England and Wales or Northern Ireland.

38B. (1) Subject to subs. (6) below, a person against whom there has been issued in England and Wales a warrant committing him to prison in default of payment of a sum adjudged to be paid by a conviction may be arrested in Northern Ireland by any member of the Royal Ulster Constabulary Reserve in like manner as if the warrant committing him to prison in default of payment of a sum adjudged to be paid by a conviction in Northern Ireland; and Art. 158(4) and (5) of the Magistrates' Courts (Northern Ireland) Order 1981 (execution without possession of the warrant and execution on Sunday) shall apply to the execution in Northern Ireland of any such warrant which has been issued in England and Wales as they apply in relation to the execution of a warrant for arrest.

8. FINES, COMPENSATION AND PROPERTY ORDERS   425

(2) Subject to subs. (6) below, a person against whom there has been issued in Northern Ireland a warrant committing him to prison in default of payment of a sum adjudged to be paid by a conviction may be arrested in England and Wales by any constable acting within his police area in like manner as if the warrant were a warrant committing him to prison in default of payment of a sum adjudged to be paid by a conviction in England and Wales.

(3) A person arrested by virtue of subss. (1) or (2) above under a warrant of commitment may be detained under it in any prison in the part of the United Kingdom in which he was arrested; and while so detained he shall be treated for all purposes as if he were detained under a warrant of commitment issued in that part of the United Kingdom.

(4) A warrant of commitment issued by a court in Northern Ireland may be executed in England and Wales by virtue of this section whether or not it has been endorsed under s. 27 of the Petty Sessions (Ireland) Act 1851.

(5) In this section—

"part of the United Kingdom" means England and Wales or Northern Ireland;

"prison" means—

   (a) in the case of a person who is under the age of 21 years arrested in England and Wales, any place in which he could be detained under s. 12(10) of the Criminal Justice Act 1982; and

   (b) in the case of a person under that age arrested in Northern Ireland, a young offenders centre; and

"sum adjudged to be paid by a conviction" has the meaning given by s. 150(3) of the Magistrates' Courts Act 1980 or, in Northern Ireland, Art. 2(5) of the Magistrates' Courts (Northern Ireland) Order 1981.

(6) This section shall not apply to the arrest of persons under the age of 17 years.

(as inserted by the Criminal Justice Act 1982, s. 52.)

COMMENTARY

"Both subsections (1) and (2) (like subsections (1) and (2) of section 38A) are intended to meet the situation where, after a court in one jurisdiction has issued a warrant committing a defaulter to prison, it becomes known that he is living in the other. (Prior to the issue of a warrant a transfer of fine order may be made under sections 90 and 91 of the Magistrates' Courts Act 1980.)" (Home Office circular 13/1983).

THE MAGISTRATES' COURTS ACT 1980

Fixing amount of fine

35. In fixing the amount of a fine, a magistrates' court shall take into consideration among other things the means of the person on whom the fine is imposed so far as they appear or are known to the court.

COMMENTARY

See The Means of the Offender in the introduction.

A fine. This includes any pecuniary penalty or pecuniary forfeiture or pecuniary compensation payable under a conviction: s. 150(1) of the Act.

Restriction on fines in respect of young persons

36. (1) Where a person under 17 years of age is found guilty by a magistrates' court of an offence for which, apart from this section, the court would have power to impose a fine of an amount exceeding £400, the amount of any fine imposed by the court shall not exceed £400.

(2) In relation to a person under the age of 14 subs. (1) above shall have effect as if for the words "£200", in both the places where they occur, there were substituted the words "£100"; but this subsection shall cease to have effect on the coming into force of s. 4 of the Children and Young Persons Act 1969 (which prohibits criminal proceedings against children).
(as amended by S.I. 1984 No. 447)

COMMENTARY

A fine. The wide definition of this term in s. 150(1) of the Act is inapplicable. It therefore bears its ordinary or narrow meaning.

Restriction on amount payable under compensation order of magistrates' court

40. (1) The compensation to be paid under a compensation order made by a magistrates' court in respect of any offence of which the court has convicted the offender shall not exceed £2,000; and the compensation or total compensation to be paid under a compensation order or compensation orders made by a magistrates' court in respect of any offence or offences taken into consideration in determining sentence shall not exceed the difference (if any) between the amount or total amount which under the preceding provisions of this subsection is the maximum for the offence or offences of which the offender has been convicted and the amount or total amounts (if any) which are in fact ordered to be paid in respect of that offence or those offences.

(2) In subs. (1) above "compensation order" has the meaning assigned to it by s. 35(1) of the Powers of Criminal Courts Act 1973.
(as amended by S.I. 1984 No. 447)

COMMENTARY

Subsection (1). The second part of this subsection merely extends the existing rule that the maximum financial burden which can be imposed on a defendant when offences are taken into consideration cannot exceed the maximum permitted without such other offences, except that where there are two or more substantive offences the amount available for compensation is the aggregate of the amounts allowable for each offence. Thus where, for example, there are two offences one of which involves damage of say, £100, the court may order a total of up to £3900 compensation in respect of offences taken into consideration being £2000 on each offence.

Return of property taken from accused

48. Where a summons or warrant has been issued requiring any person to appear or be brought before a magistrates' court to answer to an information, or where any person has been arrested without a warrant for an offence and property has been taken from him after the issue of the summons or warrant or, as the case may be, on or after his arrest without a warrant, the police shall report the taking of the property, with particulars of the property, to the magistrates' court which deals with the case; and, if the court, being of opinion that the whole or any part of the property can be returned to the accused consistently with the interests of justice and the safe custody of the accused, so directs, the property, or such part of it as the court directs, shall be returned to the accused or to such other person as he may require.

COMMENTARY

This section may be used, for example, when a person committed for trial needs access to his money to pay for his defence. *Cf. R.* v. *D'Eyncourt* [1888] 21 Q.B.D. 109.

After the issue of the summons etc. Not before: *Arnell* v. *Harris* (1945) 109 J.P. 14.

Power to dispense with immediate payment

75. (1) A magistrates' court by whose conviction or order a sum is adjudged to be paid may, instead of requiring immediate payment, allow time for payment, or order payment by instalments.

8. FINES, COMPENSATION AND PROPERTY ORDERS 427

(2) Where a magistrates' court has allowed time for payment, the court may, on application by or on behalf of the person liable to make the payment, allow further time or order payment by instalments.

(3) Where a court has ordered payment by instalments and default is made in the payment of any one instalment, proceedings may be taken as if the default has been made in the payment of all the instalments then unpaid.

COMMENTARY

Subsection (1). The clerk must give notice to the offender unless the offender is present and the fine is ordered to be paid forthwith: Magistrates' Courts Rules 1981, r. 46(1). Payment is to the clerk unless the court directs otherwise: r. 48, *ibid*.

Save in exceptional circumstances it is desirable that fines should be capable of being paid within about 12 months: *R.* v. *Knight* [1980] 2 Cr. App. R. (S) 82.

A sum is adjudged to be paid (on conviction). This term is defined in s. 150(3) of the Act, *infra*.

Subsection (2): On application. Unless the court requires the applicant to attend the application may be in writing: Magistrates' Courts Rules 1981, r. 51. And to any magistrates' court acting for the same petty sessions area: Magistrates' Courts Act 1980, s. 148(2).

Allow further time or order payment by instalments. Either order must be recorded in the court register or any separate record kept for the purpose: Magistrates' Courts Rules 1981, r. 65. The defaulter must be notified in writing: r. 46(1), *ibid*. The clerk to the justices may allow further time for payment of a sum enforceable by a magistrates' court: Justices' Clerks Rules 1970.

Enforcement of sums adjudged to be paid

76. (1) Subject to the following provisions of this Part of this Act, and to s. 132 below, where default is made in paying a sum adjudged to be paid by a conviction or order of a magistrates' court, the court may issue a warrant of distress for the purpose of levying the sum or issue a warrant committing the defaulter to prison.

(2) A warrant of commitment may be issued as aforesaid either—

    (*a*)   where it appears on the return to a warrant of distress that the money and goods of the defaulter are insufficient to satisfy the sum with the costs and charges of levying the sum; or

    (*b*)   instead of a warrant of distress.

(3) The period for which a person may be committed to prison under such a warrant as aforesaid shall not, subject to the provisions of any enactment passed after December 31, 1879, exceed the period applicable to the case under sch. 4 to this Act.

(as amended by the Criminal Justice Act 1982, sch. 16.)

COMMENTARY

For defaulters under 21 years *see* under that title in the introduction.

Subsection (1): Default in paying. A certificate signed by the clerk is admissible to prove non-payment: s. 99 of the Act.

Sum adjudged to be paid by a conviction. Defined in s. 150(3) of the Act, *infra*.

The court. Not necessarily the justices or even the court which imposed the fine, but any court acting for the same petty sessions area: s. 148(2) of the Act.

Warrant of distress. *See* Distraint of Goods in the introduction.

Warrant committing the defaulter to prison. *See* under Imprisonment in the introduction.

The warrant may be executed anywhere in England and Wales: Magistrates' Courts Act 1980, s. 125(2). The warrant remains in force until executed or withdrawn: Magistrates' Courts Act 1980, s. 125(1). For the contents of the warrant *see* the Magistrates' Courts Rules 1981, rr. 95, 96 and forms 51, 52.

When a warrant of commitment is issued or an alternative of imprisonment is fixed on the occasion of conviction, the reasons for the court's action must be recorded in the register or separate record: Magistrates' Courts Rules 1981, r. 65.

A warrant of commitment in default cannot be suspended under the Powers of Criminal Courts Act 1973, s. 22: *R.* v. *Nixon* [1969] 54 Cr. App R. 179; but it can be postponed under s. 77, *infra*.

Imprisonment runs from the date the prisoner is received by the prison: *Henderson* v. *Preston* (1888) 52 J.P. 820. Where a prisoner cannot be taken to prison the same day an express order should be inserted in the warrant that the sentence is to be reckoned from the date on which it was passed: Home Office circ., April 22, 1889 (56 J.P.N. 586). It is not an abuse of power for an officer to fail to execute a warrant of commitment until after the defaulter has been released from a period of remand: *R.* v. *Leeds Prison Governor and Another, ex parte Huntley* (1972) 136 J.P. 551.

Dealing with the arrest of an absconding debtor, Vaughan Williams LJ was of opinion that a warrant would authorize the officer to break the door and go in and arrest the debtor inside: *Re Von Weissenfeld, ex parte Hendry* (1892) 36 Sol. J. 276.

Subsection (3). Terms may be consecutive up to a maximum of six months, or 12 months if two or more of the sentences are indictable: s. 133 of the Act. The period fixed by the court must not exceed the maximum for the aggregated sum found on the warrant. If separate periods for separate fines are fixed the separate warrants have to be issued: *R.* v. *Southampton Justices, ex parte Davies* (1981) 145 J.P. 247. Although doubted by the House of Lords in *Forrest* v. *Brighton Justices, infra,* this decision was nevertheless followed in *R.* v. *Midhurst Justices, ex parte Seymour* (1983) *The Times,* March 24, wherein it was said that the proper course for justices is to look at the whole of the circumstances, including the offence and the amount sought to be enforced. If they are satisfied that justice can be done by a term not exceeding the statutory maximum, it would be appropriate for it to be done on a single sheet. If after full consideration it was felt right that the aggregate of sentences imposed should be such that it would exceed the maximum, it was inevitable that separate warrants in respect of each committal would have to be issued.

Provided that sentences are imposed on different days there is in theory no limit to the aggregate of the terms of imprisonment that may be imposed: *Forrest* v. *Brighton Justices. Hamilton* v. *Marylebone Magistrates Court* (1981) 145 J.P. 356. Thus, when a fine was imposed at the same time as a sentence of imprisonment and an alternative in default of payment fixed at a later hearing the total period of imprisonment was not limited in accordance with s. 133(1) of the Act: *R.* v. *Metropolitan Stipendiary Magistrate for South Westminster, ex parte Green* (1977) 141 J.P. 151.

Postponement of issue of warrant

77. (1) Where a magistrates' court has power to issue a warrant of distress under this Part of this Act, it may, if it thinks it expedient to do so, postpone the issue of the warrant until such time and on such conditions, if any, as the court thinks just.

(2)   Where a magistrates' court has power to issue a warrant of commitment under this Part of this Act, it may, if it thinks it expedient to do so, fix a term of imprisonment or detention under s. 9 of the Criminal Justice Act 1982 (detention of persons aged 17 to 20 for default) and postpone the issue of the warrant until such time and on such conditions, if any, as the court thinks just.

(as amended by the Criminal Justice Act 1982, sch. 14.)

COMMENTARY

Subsection (1): Power ... under this Part of this Act. *See* s. 76, *supra* and s. 82, *infra*.

Subsection (2). There is no power to vary the conditions of postponement under this subsection: *R.* v. *Clerkenwell Stipendiary Magistrate, ex parte Mays* (1975) 139 J.P. 151.

Defect in distress warrant and irregularity in its execution

78. (1) A warrant of distress issued for the purpose of levying a sum adjudged to be paid by the conviction or order of a magistrates' court shall not, if it states that the sum has been so adjudged to be paid, be held void by reason of any defect in the warrant.

(2) A person acting under a warrant of distress shall not be deemed to be a trespasser from the beginning by reason only of any irregularity in the execution of the warrant.

(3) Nothing in this section shall prejudice the claim of any person for special damages in respect of any loss caused by a defect in the warrant or irregularity in its execution.

(4) If any person removes any goods marked in accordance with the rules as articles impounded in the execution of a warrant of distress, or defaces or removes any such mark, he shall be liable on summary conviction to a fine not exceeding level 1 on the standard scale.

(5) If any person charged with the execution of a warrant of distress wilfully retains from the proceeds of a sale of the goods on which distress is levied, or otherwise exacts, any greater costs and charges than those properly payable, or makes any improper charge, he shall be liable on summary conviction to a fine not exceeding level 1 on the standard scale.

(as amended by the Criminal Justice Act 1982, s. 46).

COMMENTARY

Warrants of distress may be issued under s. 76,*supra.*

Subsection (1): Any defect. Presumably this is not to be taken literally: compare the cases on s. 123 of the Act.

Subsection (2): Trespasser from the beginning. That is a trespasser *ab initio.* But *cf. Chic Fashions (West Wales) Ltd* v. *Jones* (1968) 132 J.P. 175.

Subsection (4): Goods marked in accordance with the rules. That is, in accordance with r. 54(8) of the Magistrates' Courts Rules 1981.

Release from custody and reduction of detention on payment

79. (1) Where imprisonment or other detention has been imposed on any person by the order of a magistrates' court in default of payment of any sum adjudged to be paid by the conviction or order of a magistrates' court or for want of sufficient distress to satisfy such a sum, then ,on the payment of the sum, together with the costs and charges, if any, of the commitment and distress, the order shall cease to have effect; and if the person has been committed to custody he shall be released unless he is in custody for some other cause.

(2) Where, after a period of imprisonment or other detention has been imposed on any person in default of payment of any sum adjudged to be paid by the conviction or order of a magistrates' court or for want of sufficient distress to satisfy such a sum, payment is made in accordance with the rules of part of the sum, the period of detention shall be reduced by such number of days as bears to the total number of days in that period less one day the same proportion as the amount so paid bears to so much of the said sum, and the costs and charges of any distress levied to satisfy that sum, as was due at the time the period of detention was imposed.

(3) In calculating the reduction required under subs. (2) above any fraction of a day shall be left out of account.

COMMENTARY

Subsection (1): Other detention. In the case of a defaulter aged 17 - 20 *see* s. 96A, *infra*. For detention in police cells etc., *see* the Magistrates' Courts Act 1980, ss. 134, 135, 136 in Ch. 6.

Subsections (2) and (3). The calculation is as follows:

$$\frac{\text{Sum paid}}{\text{Sum adjudged to be paid}} \times \quad \text{Days of imprisonment less one}$$

From the product deduct any fraction, then take the remaining whole number from the total days' imprisonment. The answer is the period of imprisonment still to be served. Note the difference between this calculation and that for reducing the maximum period of imprisonment set out in para. 2 of sch. 4, *infra*.

When the period of imprisonment is reduced by part payment to less than five days, the offender may alternatively be detained in a place certified by the Secretary of State under s. 134 of the Act: Magistrates' Courts Rules 1981, r. 55(5).

Payment is made in accordance with the rules. For the persons entitled to receive part payment *see* the Magistrates' Courts Rules 1981, r. 55.

Application of money found on defaulter to satisfy sum adjudged

80. (1) Where a magistrates' court has adjudged a person to pay a sum by a conviction or has ordered the enforcement of a sum due from a person under an affiliation order or an order enforceable as an affiliation order, the court may order him to be searched.

(2) Any money found on the arrest of a person adjudged to pay such a sum as aforesaid, or on a search as aforesaid, or on his being taken to a prison or other place of detention in default of payment of such a sum or for want of sufficient distress to satisfy such a sum, may, unless the court otherwise directs, be applied towards payment of the said sum; and the balance, if any, shall be returned to him.

(3) A magistrates' court shall not allow the application as aforesaid of any money found on a person if it is satisfied that the money does not belong to him or that the loss of the money would be more injurious to his family than would be his detention.

COMMENTARY

Subsection (1): Adjudged .. to pay a sum by conviction. This term is defined in s. 150(3) of the Act, *infra*.

Subsection (2): Other place of detention. *See* the note to s. 79.

For want of sufficient distress. *See* s. 76, *supra*.

Unless the court otherwise directs. Such a direction must be endorsed on the warrant of commitment: Magistrates' Courts Rules 1981, r. 64.

Restriction on power to impose imprisonment for default

82. (1) A magistrates' court shall not on the occasion of convicting an offender of an offence issue a warrant of commitment for a default in paying any sum adjudged to be paid by the conviction unless—

(a)   in the case of an offence punishable with imprisonment, he appears to the court to have sufficient means to pay the sum forthwith;

(b)   it appears to the court that he is unlikely to remain long enough at a place of abode in the United Kingdom to enable payment of the sum to be enforced by other methods; or

(c)   on the occasion of that conviction the court sentences him to im-

8. FINES, COMPENSATION AND PROPERTY ORDERS 431

mediate imprisonment, youth custody or detention in a detention centre for that or another offence or he is already serving a sentence of custody for life, or a term of imprisonment, youth custody, detention under s. 9 of the Criminal Justice Act 1982 or detention in a detention centre.

(2) A magistrates' court shall not in advance of the issue of a warrant of commitment fix a term of imprisonment which is to be served by an offender in the event of a default in paying a sum adjudged to be paid by a conviction, except where it has power to issue a warrant of commitment forthwith, but postpones issuing the warrant under s. 77(2) above.

(3) Where on the occasion of the offender's conviction a magistrates' court does not issue a warrant of commitment for a default in paying any such sum as aforesaid or fix a term of imprisonment under the said s. 77(2) which is to be served by him in the event of any such default it shall not thereafter issue a warrant of commitment for any such default or for want of sufficient distress to satisfy such a sum unless—
  (a) he is already serving a sentence of custody for life, a term of imprisonment, youth custody, detention under s. 9 of the Criminal Justice Act 1982 or detention in a detention centre; or
  (b) the court has since the conviction inquired into his means in his presence on at least one occasion.

(4) Where a magistrates' court is required by subs. (3) above to inquire into a person's means, the court may not on the occasion of the inquiry or at any time thereafter issue a warrant of commitment for a default in paying any such sum unless—

  (a) in the case of an offence punishable with imprisonment, the offender appears to the court to have sufficient means to pay the sum forthwith; or
  (b) the court—

      (i) is satisfied that the default is due to the offender's wilful refusal or culpable neglect; and
      (ii) has considered or tried all other methods of enforcing payment of the sum and it appears to the court that they are inappropriate or unsuccessful.

(5) After the occasion of an offender's conviction by a magistrates' court, the court shall not, unless—

  (a) the court has previously fixed a term of imprisonment under s. 77(2) above which is to be served by the offender in the event of a default in paying a sum adjudged to be paid by the conviction; or
  (b) the offender is serving a sentence of custody for life, a term of imprisonment, youth custody, detention under s. 9 of the Criminal Justice Act 1982 or detention in a detention centre,

issue a warrant of commitment for a default in paying the sum or fix such a term except at a hearing at which the offender is present.

(6) Where a magistrates' court issues a warrant of commitment on the ground that one of the conditions mentioned in subs. (1) or (4) above is satisfied, it shall state that fact, specifying the ground, in the warrant.

(as amended by the Criminal Justice Act 1982, sch. 14.)

COMMENTARY

Subsection (1). An alternative of imprisonment fixed at the time of conviction should be a true and not an illusory alternative in the sense that it should not be imposed on a defendant who cannot *possibly pay: R.* v. *Hall* [1968] Crim. L.R. 688.

Sum adjudged to be paid by the conviction. Defined in s. 150(3) of the Act as including costs, damages or compensation adjudged to be paid by the conviction or order of which the amount is ascertained by the conviction or order.

A warrant of commitment. That is, under s. 76, *supra.*

An offence punishable with imprisonment. To be construed without regard to any prohibition or restriction imposed by or under this or any other Act on imprisonment of young offenders: s. 150(6) of the Act.

Forthwith. It is submitted that the use of this term in this subsection indicates that Parliament intended exception (*a*) to apply not only to cases where the defendant has the money on him or in his possessions which are in police custody, but also where he can, by making a telephone call or the like, cause such a sum to be paid into court the same day.

United Kingdom. That is, Great Britain and Northern Ireland. It does not include the Channel Islands and the Isle of Man: Royal & Parliamentary Titles Act 1927, s. 2(2).
Immediate imprisonment. That is, a sentence of imprisonment which is not suspended under s. 22 of the Powers of Criminal Courts Act 1973. For application to defaulters aged 17 - 20 *see* s. 96A, *infra.*
Subsection (2). The effect of this subsection is that a court may fix a postponed alternative of custody only where it has power to issue a warrant of commitment forthwith.

Subsection (3). This includes a custodial sentence and a committal in default of payment of fine, but not periods on remand or on committal for trial.
Inquired into his means. By at least two justices in open court: Magistrates' Courts Act, s. 121. For process to compel appearance before such an inquiry see s. 83, *ibid.* Particulars of the inquiry must be entered in the court register or separate record: Magistrates' Courts Rules 1981, r. 65.

Subsection (4): All other methods. *See* the introduction.

Subsection (5). This does not relieve the court of the obligation of conducting a hearing, merely of the need for the accused to be present. The defaulter must be given opportunity either in person or through a representative or in writing to make representations to the court, particularly where it is proposed to lodge a warrant consecutively to another term: *Forrest* v. *Brighton Justices,* (1981) 145 J.P. 356 (a case under para. (*b*) of the subsection). There is no need for notice or hearing where the court has previously fixed a term of imprisonment under para. (*a*) of the subsection and postponed it on terms which have been broken: *R.* v. *Chichester Justices, ex parte Collins* [1982] 1 All E.R. 1000. Particulars of the hearing must be recorded in the court register or separate record: Magistrates' Courts Rules 1981, r. 65.

Process for securing attendance of offender for purposes of section 82

83.   (1) A magistrates' court may, for the purpose of enabling inquiry to be made under s. 82 above or for securing the attendance of an offender at a hearing required to be held by subs. (5) of that section—

(*a*)   issue a summons requiring the offender to appear before the court at the time and place appointed in the summons; or

(*b*)   issue a warrant to arrest him and bring him before the court.

(2)   On the failure of the offender to appear before the court in answer to a summons under this section the court may issue a warrant to arrest him and bring him before the court.

(3)   A warrant issued under this section may be executed in like manner, and the like proceedings may be taken with a view to its execution, in any part of the United Kingdom, as if it had been issued under s. 13 above.

(4)   Notwithstanding anything in s. 125 below, a warrant under this section shall cease to have effect when the sum in respect of which the warrant is issued is paid to the police officer holding the warrant.

COMMENTARY

Subsection (1): Issue a summons. For the form and service of the summons *see* the Magistrates' Courts Rules 1981, rr. 98, 99, 100.

Issue a warrant. For the signature and contents of the warrant *see* the Magistrates' Courts Rules 1981, rr. 95, 96, 100. The warrant may be backed for bail: Magistrates' Courts Act 1980 s. 117. It is submitted that the general right to bail (Bail Act 1976, s. 4) does not apply to the endorsement of a warrant.

Vaughan Williams LJ in the case of *re Von Weissenfeld, ex parte Hendry* (1892) 36 Sol. Jo. 276 expressed the opinion that a warrant for the arrest of an absconding debtor was authority to break open doors in pursuit thereof. For the need for the officer to be in possession of the warrant see the notes to the Magistrates Courts Act 1980, s. 125(3).

United Kingdom. That is, Great Britain and Northern Ireland: Royal and Parliamentary Titles Act 1927, s. 2(2). Isle of Man and Channel Islands not included.

Power to require statement of means

84. (1) A magistrates' court may, either before or on inquiring into a person's means under s. 82 above, and a justice of the peace acting for the same petty sessions area as that court may before any such inquiry, order him to furnish to the court within a period specified in the order such a statement of his means as the court may require.

(2)   A person who fails to comply with an order under subs. (1) above shall be liable on summary conviction to a fine not exceeding £50.

(3)   If a person in furnishing any statement in pursuance of an order under subs. (1) above makes a statement which he knows to be false in a material particular or recklessly furnishes a statement which is false in a material particular, or knowingly fails to disclose any material fact, he shall be liable on summary conviction to imprisonment for a term not exceeding four months or a fine not exceeding £100 or both.

(4)   Proceedings in respect of an offence under subs. (3) above may, notwithstanding anything in s. 127(1) below, be commenced at any time within two years from the date of the commission of the offence or within six months from its first discovery by the prosecutor, whichever period expires the earlier.

COMMENTARY

Subsection(1). An order under this subsection may be made before the means inquiry by the clerk to the justices: Justices' Clerks Rules 1970.

Power to remit fine

85. (1) Where a fine has been imposed on conviction of an offender by a magistrates' court, the court may, on inquiring into his means or at a hearing under s. 82(5) above, remit the whole or any part of the fine if the court thinks it just to do so having regard to any change in his circumstances since the conviction, and where the court remits the whole or part of the fine after a term of imprisonment has been fixed, it shall also reduce the term by an amount which bears the same proportion to the whole term as the amount remitted bears to the whole fine or, as the case may be, shall remit the whole term.

In calculating the reduction in a term of imprisonment required by this subsection any fraction of a day shall be left out of account.

(2) Notwithstanding the definition of "fine" in s. 150(1) below, references in this section to a fine do not include any other sum adjudged to be paid on conviction, whether as a pecuniary penalty, forfeiture, compensation or otherwise.

COMMENTARY

Note that in order for the court to exercise its powers under this subsection there must have been a change in the defendant's circumstances since the conviction. Orders of remission must be recorded in the court register or separate record: Magistrates' Courts Rules 1981, r. 65. Although this subsection does not refer to a means inquiry "at which the offender is present" it must first "inquire into his means". Possibly this could be done in the defendant's absence, *e.g.* on the basis of a probation officer's report. This subsection does not apply to the remission of forfeited recognizances: Magistrates' Courts Act 1980, s. 120(4).

Fines imposed by the Crown Court may only be remitted with the consent of that court: Powers of Criminal Courts Act 1973, s. 32(4).

Variation of instalments of sum adjudged to be paid by conviction.

85A. Where under s. 75 above a magistrates' court orders that a sum adjudged to be paid by a conviction shall be paid by instalments, the court, on an application made by the person liable to pay that sum, shall have power to vary that order by varying the number of instalments payable, the amount of any instalment payable, and the date on which any instalment becomes payable.

(as inserted by the Criminal Justice Act 1982, s. 51).

COMMENTARY

This power may be exercised by the justices' clerk: Justices' Clerks Rules 1970. Any direction under this section must be entered in the register: Magistrates' Courts Rules 1981, r. 65.

Power of magistrates' court to fix day for appearance of offender at means inquiry etc.

86. (1) A magistrates' court which has exercised in relation to a sum adjudged to be paid by a conviction either of the powers conferred by s. 75(1) above shall have power, either then or later, to fix a day on which, if the relevant condition is satisfied, the offender must appear in person before the court for either or both of the following purposes, namely—

    (*a*)   to enable an inquiry into his means to be made under s. 82 above;

    (*b*)   to enable a hearing required by subs. (5) of the said s. 82 to be held.

(1A) Where the power which the court has exercised is the power to allow time for payment of a sum ("the adjudged sum"), the relevant condition is satisfied if any part of that sum remains unpaid on the day fixed by the court.

(1B) Where the power which the court has exercised is the power to order payment by instalments, the relevant condition is satisfied if an instalment which has fallen due remains unpaid on the day fixed by the court.

    (*a*)   to enable an inquiry into his means to be made under s. 82 above;

    (*b*)   to enable a hearing required by subs. (5) of the said s. 82 to be held.

(2) Except as provided in subs. (3) below, the power to fix a day under this section shall be exercisable only in the presence of the offender.

(3) Where a day has been fixed under this section, the court may fix a later

day in substitution for the day previously fixed, and may do so—

    (*a*)   when composed of a single justice; and
    (*b*)   whether the offender is present or not.

  (4) Subject to subs. (5) below, if on the day fixed under this section—

    (*a*)   the relevant condition is satisfied; and
    (*b*)   the offender fails to appear in person before the court,

the court may issue a warrant to arrest him and bring him before the court; and subs. (3) and (4) of s. 83 above shall apply in relation to a warrant issued under this section.

  (5) Where under subs. (3) above a later day has in the absence of the offender been fixed in substitution for a day previously fixed under this section, the court shall not issue a warrant under this section unless it is proved to the satisfaction of the court, on oath or in such other manner as may be prescribed, that notice in writing of the substituted day was served on the offender not less than what appears to the court to be a reasonable time before that day.

(as amended by the Criminal Justice Act 1982, s. 51.)

COMMENTARY

This section applies not only to fines, but to all other sums adjudged to be paid on conviction, such as costs and compensation.

Subsection (1): Sum adjudged to be paid by a conviction. Defined in s. 150(3) of the Act, *infra*.

Subsection (2): The presence of the offender. Not merely of his counsel or solicitor: Magistrates' Courts Act 1980, s. 122.

Subsection (3). Service of the notice of the substituted day may be effected in any manner as service

Subsection (5). The notice may be served in any manner in which a summons may be served under the Magistrates' Courts Rules 1981 r. 52, *ibid*.

Enforcement of payment of fines by High Court and county court

87. (1) Subject to the provisions of subs. (2) below, payment of a sum adjudged to be paid by a conviction of a magistrates' court may be enforced by the High Court or county court (otherwise than by issue of a writ of fieri facias or other process against goods or by imprisonment or attachment of earnings) as if the sum were due to the clerk of the magistrates' court in pursuance of a judgment or order of the High Court or county court, as the case may be.

  (2) Subsection (1) above shall not be construed as authorizing the enforcement by a county court of payment of a fine exceeding the limit for the time being in force under s. 40 of the County Courts Act 1959 on the amount of any sum recoverable by statute in a county court.

  (3) The clerk of the magistrates' court shall not take proceedings by virtue of subs. (1) above to recover any sum adjudged to be paid by a conviction of the

  (4) Any expenses incurred by the clerk of a magistrates' court in recovering any such sum shall be treated for the purposes of Part VI of the Justices of the Peace Act 1979 as expenses of the magistrates' courts committee.

(as amended by the Supreme Court Act 1981, sch. 5.)

COMMENTARY

Subsection (1): A sum adjudged to be paid by a conviction. Defined in s. 150(3) of the Act, *infra*.

Authorized to do so. Such an order shall be entered in the court register or separate record: Magistrates' Courts Rules 1981, r. 65. *See* form 63.

Subsection (3). Presumably no means inquiry is necessary in the case of a corporation.

Supervision pending payment

88. (1) Where any person is adjudged to pay a sum by a summary conviction and the convicting court does not commit him to prison forthwith in default of payment, the court may either on the occasion of the conviction or on a subsequent occasion, order him to be placed under the supervision of such person as the court may from time to time appoint.

(2)   An order placing a person under supervision in respect of any sum shall remain in force so long as he remains liable to pay the sum or any part of it unless the order ceases to have effect or is discharged under subs. (3) below.

(3)   An order under this section shall cease to have effect on the making of a transfer of fine order under s. 89 below with respect to the sum adjudged to be paid and may be discharged by the court that made it, without prejudice in either case to the making of a new order.

(4)   Where a person under 21 years old has been adjudged to pay a sum by a summary conviction and the convicting court does not commit him to detention under s. 9 of the Criminal Justice Act 1982 forthwith in default of payment, the court shall not commit him to such detention in default of payment of the sum, or for want of sufficient distress to satisfy the sum, unless he has been placed under supervision in respect of the sum or the court is satisfied that it is undesirable or impracticable to place him under supervision.

(5) Where a court, being satisfied as aforesaid, commits a person under 21 years old to such detention without an order under this section having been made, the court shall state the grounds on which it is so satisfied in the warrant of commitment.

(6)   Where an order placing a person under supervision with respect to a sum is in force, a magistrates' court shall not commit him to prison in default of payment of the sum, or for want of sufficient distress to satisfy the sum, unless the court has before committing him taken such steps as may be reasonably practicable to obtain from the person appointed for his supervision an oral or written report on the offender's conduct and means and has considered any report so obtained, in addition, in a case where an inquiry is required by s. 82 above, to that inquiry.

(as amended by the Criminal Justice Act 1982, sch. 14.)

COMMENTARY

The Departmental Committee on the Probation Service pointed out (in paras. 94 and 95 of their report) that a money payment supervision order was designed to minimize committals to prison for default in paying fines, and that it was in no sense a substitute for a probation order. They recommended that a probation officer should be used for money payment supervision only where the limited supervision he could exercise might avoid a default otherwise likely to occur; for example, where the offender was too incompetent or feckless to put aside the necessary savings.

Subsection (1): Adjudged to pay a sum by a summary conviction. Defined in s. 150(3) of the Act, *infra.*

Order. Unless made in the offender's presence, notice of the order must be delivered to the offender or served by post: Magistrates' Courts Rules 1981, r. 56(1). It must be recorded in the register or any separate record kept for the purpose of recording fine enforcement: r. 65, *ibid.*

Such person as the court may from time to time appoint. First, therefore, the order must be to a named person; though this may, it is suggested, be by description, as for example, "the senior probation officer . . . petty sessional division". Secondly, the court is empowered from time to time to change the named person and this should, it is suggested, be effected by written order. The duties of the supervising officer are set out in the Magistrates' Courts Rules 1981, r. 56(2).

A supervising officer has authority to receive part payment of the fine unless a warrant of distress or commitment has issued: Magistrates' Courts Rules 1981, r. 55(1), but he must hand the money over

8. FINES, COMPENSATION AND PROPERTY ORDERS   437

to the clerk of the court, r. 55(4), *ibid*.

Subsection (4): Under 21 years old. For the determination of age *see* the Magistrates' Courts Act 1980, s. 150(4).

Subsection (6): Commit him to prison. That is the act of fixing the term of imprisonment, even where this is postponed on terms: *R. v. Clerkenwell Stipendiary Magistrate, ex parte Mays* (1975) 139 J.P. 151. For application to defaulters aged 17 - 20 *see* s. 96A, *infra*.

Transfer of fine order

89. (1) Where a magistrates' court has, or is treated by any enactment as having, adjudged a person by a conviction to pay a sum and it appears to the court that the person is residing in any petty sessions area other than that for which the court acted, the court may make a transfer of fine order, that is to say, an order making payment enforceable in the petty sessions area in which it appears to the court that he is residing; and that area shall be specified in the order.

(2) As from the date on which a transfer of fine order is made with respect to any sum, all functions under this Part of this Act relating to that sum which, if no such order had been made, would have been exercisable by the court which made the order, or the clerk of that court, shall be exercisable by a court acting for the petty sessions area specified in the order, or the clerk of that court, as the case may be, and not otherwise.

(3) Where it appears to a court by which functions in relation to any sum are for the time being exercisable by virtue of a transfer of fine order that the person liable to pay the sum is residing in a petty sessions area other than that for which the court is acting, the court may make a further transfer of fine order with respect to that sum.

(4) In this section and ss. 90 and 91 below, references to this Part of this Act do not include references to s. 81(1) above.

COMMENTARY

For the procedure for making a transfer of fine order *see* the Magistrates' Courts Rules 1981, r. 57. The defendant's presence or consent is not necessary.

An order under this section puts an end to any money payment supervision order: s. 88(3), *supra*.

For transfers to and from Scotland *see* ss. 90 and 91, *infra*, respectively as well as the Powers of Criminal Courts Act 1973, s. 33, *supra*.

Subsection (1): Treated by any enactment as having. *See*, for example the Administration of Justice Act 1970, s. 41(1).

Adjudged ... by a conviction to pay a sum. This term is defined in s. 150(3) of the Act, *infra*.

Residing. Corporations can have a residence. *See Halsbury's Laws*, 4th ed., vol. 9, at p. 731.

A transfer of fine order. The order must be entered in the register or any separate record kept for the purpose of recording particulars of fine enforcement: Magistrates' Courts Rules 1981, r. 65. For the form of order *see* form 59.

Subsection (2): This Part of this Act. This comprises ss. 75-96 inclusive except s. 81(1): *see* subs. (4).

Transfer of fines to Scotland or Northern Ireland

90. (1) Where a magistrates' court has, or is treated by any enactment as having, adjudged a person by a conviction to pay a sum, and it appears to the court that he is residing—

  (a) within the jurisdiction of a court of summary jurisdiction in Scotland, or

  (b) in any petty sessions district in Northern Ireland,

the court may order that payment of the sum shall be enforceable by that court of summary jurisdiction or, as the case may be, in that petty sessions district.

(2) An order under this section shall specify the court of summary jurisdiction by which or petty sessions district in which payment of the sum in question is to be enforceable; and if—

(a)   that sum is more than £100 or is a fine originally imposed by the Crown Court or the sheriff court, and

(b)   payment is to be enforceable in Scotland,

the court to be so specified shall be the sheriff court.

(3) Where an order is made under this section with respect to any sum, any functions under this Part of this Act relating to that sum which, if no such order has been made, would have been exercisable by the court which made the order or by the clerk of that court shall cease to be so exercisable.

COMMENTARY

For the duties on the clerk of the court see the Magistrates' Courts Rules 1981, r. 57.

Subsection (1): Adjudged . . . by a conviction to pay a sum. This term is defined in s. 150(3) of the Act, *infra*.

Treated by any enactment. See the note to s. 89.

Subsection (3): This Part of this Act. Does not include s. 81(1): s. 89(4).

Transfer of fines from Scotland or Northern Ireland

91.   (1) Where a transfer of fine order under s. 403 of the Criminal Procedure (Scotland) Act 1975 or Art. 95 of the Magistrates' Courts (Northern Ireland) Order 1981 provides that payment of a sum shall be enforceable in a specified petty sessions area in England and Wales, a magistrates' court acting for that area, and the clerk of that court, shall, subject to the provisions of this section, have all the like functions under this Part of this Act in respect of the sum (including power to make an order under s. 89 or 90 above) as if the sum were a sum adjudged to be paid by a conviction of that court and as if any order made under the said Act of 1975 or, as the case may be, the said Order of 1981 in respect of the sum before the making of the transfer of fine order had been made by that court.

(2)   For the purpose of determining the period of imprisonment which may be imposed under this Act in default of payment of a fine originally imposed by a court in Scotland, sch. 4 to this Act shall have effect as if for the Table set out in para. 1 there were substituted the Table set out in s. 407 of the Criminal Procedure (Scotland) Act 1975.

(3) Where a transfer of fine order under s. 403 of the Criminal Procedure (Scotland) Act 1975 or Art. 950 of the Magistrates' Courts (Northern Ireland) Order 1981 provides for the enforcement in a petty sessions area in England and Wales of a fine originally imposed by the Crown Court, a magistrates' court acting for that area shall have all the like functions under this Part of this Act, exercisable subject to the like restrictions, as if it were the magistrates' court by which payment of the fine fell to be enforced by virtue of s. 32(1) of the Powers of Criminal Courts Act 1973, and as if any order made under the said Act of 1975 or, as the case may be, the said Order of 1981 in respect of the fine before the making of the transfer of fine order had been made by that court.

(as amended by the Magistrates' Courts (Northern Ireland) Order 1981, sch. 6).

8. FINES, COMPENSATION AND PROPERTY ORDERS 439

COMMENTARY

For the duties of the clerk of the magistrates' court *see* the Magistrates' Courts Rules 1981, r. 57, (3), (4).

Subsection (1): This Part of this Act. Does not include s. 81(1): s. 89(4).

Subsection (2): The table. This corresponds with the Table in sch. 4, *infra*.

Application of Part III to persons aged 17 to 20.

96A. This Part of this Act shall have effect in relation to a person aged 17 or over but less than 21 as if any reference to committing a person to prison, or fixing a term of imprisonment for a default, were a reference to committing the person to, or, as the case may be, to fixing a term of, detention under s. 9 of the Criminal Justice Act 1982; and any reference to warrants of commitment, or to periods of imprisonment imposed for default, shall be construed accordingly.

(as inserted by the Criminal Justice Act 1982, sch. 14.)

COMMENTARY

This Part of this Act. That is, ss. 75-96.

Statement of wages to be evidence

100. A statement in writing to the effect that wages of any amount have been paid to a person during any period, purporting to be signed by or on behalf of his employer, shall be evidence of the facts therein stated in any proceedings taken before a magistrates' court—

(*a*) for enforcing payment by the person to whom the wages are stated to have been paid of a sum adjudged to be paid by a summary conviction or order; or

(*b*) on any application made by or against that person for the making of an order in any matter of bastardy or an order enforceable as an affiliation order, or for the variation, revocation, discharge or revival of such an order.

COMMENTARY

Sum adjudged to be paid by a summary conviction. This term is defined in s. 150(3), *infra*.

Disposal of non-pecuniary forfeitures

140. Subject to any enactment relating to customs or excise, anything other than money forfeited on a conviction by a magistrates' court or the forfeiture of which may be enforced by a magistrates' court shall be sold or otherwise disposed of in such manner as the court may direct; and the proceeds shall be applied as if they were a fine imposed under the enactment on which the proceedings for the forfeiture are founded.

Interpretation of other terms

150. (1), (2)...

(3) Any reference in this Act to a sum adjudged to be paid by a conviction or order of a magistrates' court shall be construed as including a reference to any costs, damages or compensation adjudged to be paid by the conviction or order of which the amount is ascertained by the conviction or order; but this subsection does not prejudice the definition of "sum adjudged to be paid by a conviction" contained in subs. (8) of s. 81 above for the purposes of that section.

(4)-(7)...

SCHEDULE 4

(Section 76)

MAXIMUM PERIODS OF IMPRISONMENT IN DEFAULT OF PAYMENT

1. Subject to the following provisions of this schedule, the periods set out in the second column of the following table shall be the maximum periods applicable respectively to the amounts set out opposite thereto, being amounts due at the time the imprisonment or detention is imposed.

TABLE

An amount not exceeding £50	7 days
An amount exceeding £50 but not exceeding £100	14 days
An amount exceeding £100 but not exceeding £400	30 days
An amount exceeding £400 but not exceeding £1,000	60 days
An amount exceeding £1,000 but not exceeding £2,000	90 days
An amount exceeding £2,000 but not exceeding £5,000	6 months
An amount exceeding £5,000 but not exceeding £10,000	9 months
An amount exceeding £10,000	12 months

2. (1) Where the amount due at the time imprisonment or detention is imposed is so much of a sum adjudged to be paid by a summary conviction as remains due after payment, then, subject to sub-para. (2) below, the maximum period applicable to the amount shall be the period applicable to the whole sum reduced by such number of days as bears to the total number of days therein the same proportion as the part paid bears to the whole sum.

(2)   In calculating the reduction required under sub-para. (1) above any fraction of a day shall be left out of account and the maximum period shall not be reduced to less than five days.

(3)   The maximum period applicable to a sum of any amount enforceable as a civil debt shall be six weeks.

(as amended by the Criminal Justice Act 1982, sch. 14, S.I. 1984 No. 447.)

COMMENTARY

For the calculation of the alternative see the commentary to s. 76(3) of the Act, *supra*.

THE CRIMINAL JUSTICE ACT 1982

Abolition of enhanced penalties on subsequent conviction of summary offences under Acts of Parliament.

35. (1) Subject to subs. (3) below, this section applies where under an Act a person convicted of a summary offence–

    (a)   is liable to a fine or maximum fine of one amount in the case of a first conviction and of a different amount in the case of a second or subsequent conviction; or

    (b)   is liable to imprisonment for a longer term in the case of a second or subsequent conviction; or

    (c)   is liable to imprisonment in the case of a second or subsequent conviction.

8. Fines, Compensation and Property Orders   441

(2) Where this section applies, a person guilty of such an offence shall be liable on summary conviction—

(a) to a fine or, as the case may be, a maximum fine of an amount not exceeding the greatest amount;

(b) to imprisonment for a term not exceeding the longest or only term,

to which he would have been liable before this section came into force if his conviction has satisfied the conditions required for the imposition of a fine or maximum fine of that amount or imprisonment for that term.

(3) This section does not apply to offences under—

(a) ss. 33 to 36 of the Sexual Offences Act 1956 (brothel-keeping and prostitution); or

(b) s. 1(2) of the Street Offences Act 1959 (loitering and soliciting for the purpose of prostitution).

COMMENTARY

Fine. Is defined in s. 47(1), *infra*.

The standard scale of fines for summary offences.

37. (1) There shall be a standard scale of fines for summary offences, which shall be known as "the standard scale".

(2) The scale at the commencement of this section is shown below.

Level on the scale	Amount of fine
1	£50
2	£100
3	£400
4	£1,000
5	£2,000

(3) Where any enactment (whether contained in an Act passed before or after this Act) provides—

(a) that a person convicted of a summary offence shall be liable on conviction to a fine or a maximum fine by reference to a specified level on the standard scale; or

(b) confers power by subordinate instrument to make a person liable on conviction of a summary offence (whether or not created by the instrument) to a fine or maximum fine by reference to a specified level on the standard scale,

it is to be construed as referring to the standard scale for which this section provides as that standard scale has effect from time to time by virtue either of this section or of an order under s. 143 of the Magistrates' Courts Act 1980.

(as amended by S.I. 1984 No. 447)

COMMENTARY

Fine. Is defined in s. 47(1), *infra*.

Conversion of references to amounts to references to levels on scale.

46. (1) Where—

(a) either—

(i) a relevant enactment makes a person liable to a fine or maximum fine on conviction of a summary offence; or

(ii)   a relevant enactment confers power by subordinate instrument to make a person liable to a fine or maximum fine
on conviction of a summary offence (whether or not created
by the instrument); and

(b)   the amount of the fine or maximum fine for the offence is,
whether by virtue of this Part of this Act or not, an amount
shown in the second column of the standard scale,

a reference to the level in the first column of the standard scale corresponding to that amount shall be substituted for the reference in the enactment
to the amount of the fine or maximum fine.

(2) Where a relevant enactment confers a power such as is mentioned in
subs. (1)(a)(ii) above, the power shall be construed as a power to make a
person liable to a fine or, as the case may be, a maximum fine not exceeding the amount corresponding to the level on the standard scale to
which the enactment refers by virtue of subs. (1) above or not exceeding a
lesser amount.

(3) If an order under s. 143 of the Magistrates' Courts Act 1980 alters the
sums specified in s. 37(2) above, the second reference to the standard scale
in subsection (1) above is to be construed as a reference to that scale as it
has effect by virtue of the order.

(4) In this section "relevant enactment" means–

(a)   any enactment contained in an Act passed before this Act except–
  (i)   an enactment mentioned in Sch. 2 to the Companies Act
1980;
  (ii)   an enactment contained in the Companies Act 1981;

(b)   any enactment contained in this Act;

(c)   any enactment contained in an Act passed on the same day as
this Act; and

(d)   any enactment contained in an Act passed after this Act but in
the same Session as this Act.

(5) This section shall not affect so much of any enactment as (in
whatever words) makes a person liable on summary conviction to a
maximum fine not exceeding a specified amount for each period of a
specified length during which a continuing offence is continued.

COMMENTARY

Fine. Is defined in s. 47(1), *infra.*

Provisions supplementary to sections 35 to 46.

47. (1) In ss. 35 to 40 and 46 above "fine" includes a pecuniary penalty
but does not include a pecuniary forfeiture or pecuniary compensation.

(2) Nothing in any provision contained in ss. 35 to 46 above shall affect
the punishment for an offence committed before that provision comes into
force.

Construction of references to "statutory maximum".

74. (1) In any enactment (whether contained in an Act passed before or
after this Act) "statutory maximum", in relation to a fine on summary conviction for an offence in England and Wales, means the prescribed sum
within the meaning of s. 32 of the Magistrates' Courts Act 1980 (£1,000 or
another sum fixed by order under s. 143 of that Act to take account of
changes in the value of money).

(2) (*Scotland*).

8.   FINES, COMPENSATION AND PROPERTY ORDERS   443

Construction of references to "the standard scale".

75. In any enactment (whether contained in an Act passed before or after this Act) "the standard scale"—

    (a)   in relation to England and Wales, has the meaning given by s. 37 of this Act;

    (b)   (*Scotland*).

THE MAGISTRATES' COURTS (ATTACHMENT OF EARNINGS)

RULES 1971

S.I. 1971, No. 809

Interpretation

2. *(1) Sections 2 and 25(1) of the Act shall apply to the interpretation of these rules as they apply to the interpretation of the Act.*

(2) The Interpretation Act 1978, shall apply to the interpretation of these Rules as it applies to the interpretation of an Act of Parliament.

(3) Any reference in these rules to "the Act" is a reference to the Attachment of Earnings Act 1971.

(4) Any reference in these rules to any enactment or rule is a reference to that enactment or rule as amended by any enactment or rule.

(5) Any reference in these rules to a form in the schedule to these rules shall include a reference to a form to the like effect with such variations as the circumstances may require.

(6) Any reference in these rules to an attachment of earnings order shall be construed subject to the provisions of r. 23.

Service or orders and notices

6. *(1) Where a magistrates' court makes an attachment of earnings order or an order varying or discharging such an order, the clerk of the court shall cause a copy of the order to be served on the employer and shall send a copy of the order to the debtor.*

(2) Where an attachment of earnings order made by a magistrates' court ceases to have effect as provided in s. 8 or s. 11 of the Act, notice of cessation shall be given to the employer.

(3) The notice required by the preceding paragraph shall be given by the clerk of the magistrates' court—

    (a)   *which made or confirmed the maintenance order (in a case to which s. 11(1)(c) of the Act applies;*

    (b)   *in which the maintenance order is registered under any enactment in a case to which s. 11(1)(a), (b) or (d) of the Act applies;*

    (c)   *which issued the warrant of commitment or exercised the power conferred by [s. 77(2) of the Magistrates' Courts Act 1980] (in a case to which s. 8 of the Act applies).*

Particulars of debtor

7. *The particulars of the debtor for the purpose of enabling him to be identified which, so far as they are known, are to be included in an attachment of earnings order under s. 6(3) of the Act shall be—*

    (a)   *full names and address;*

    (b)   *place of work;*

Variation of attachment of earnings order on change of employment

12. *Where an attachment of earnings order has lapsed under s. 9(4) of the Act on the debtor's ceasing to be in the employment of the person to whom the order was directed and it appears to a magistrates' court [1], acting for the same petty sessions area as the court which made the order, that the debtor has subsequently entered the employment of a person (whether the same as before or another), the court may, of its own motion, vary the order by directing it to that person and may make any consequential amendment to the order made necessary by this variation.*

Discharge of attachment of earnings order by court of its own motion

13. *(1) Where it appears to a magistrates' court [2] acting for the same petty sessions area as the magistrates' court which made the attachment of earnings order that the debtor is not in the employment of the person to whom the order is directed and that the likelihood of the debtor's entering the employment of any person is not such as to justify preserving the order, the court may, of its own motion, discharge the order.*

(2) . . .

Temporary variation of protected earnings rate

14. *(1) A justice of the peace[3] acting for the same petty sessions area as the magistrates' court which made the attachment of earnings order may, on a written application made by the debtor on the ground of a material change in the debtor's resources and needs since the order was made or last varied, by order (hereinafter referred to as a temporary variation order) vary the attachment of earnings order for a period of not more than four weeks by an increase of the protected earnings rate.*

(2) (Form)

(3) The clerk of the magistrates' court which made the attachment of earnings order shall cause a copy of any temporary variation order to be served on the employer and shall give him notice if the temporary variation order is discharged.

(4) Where an application for the variation or discharge of an attachment of earnings order is made to a magistrates' court and there is in existence a temporary variation order in respect of the attachment of earnings order, the court may, of its own motion, discharge the temporary variation order.

Consolidated attachment orders

15. *(1) In this rule references to an attachment of earnings order are references to such an order made by a magistrates' court and do not include such an order made to secure payments under a magistrates' court maintenance order.*

(2) Where a magistrates' court has power to make more than one attachment of earnings order in respect of the liabilities of a debtor, it may make a consolidated attachment order to discharge those liabilities.

(3) Where a magistrates' court has power to make an attachment of earnings order in respect of a debtor who is already subject to such an order (whether or not it is itself a consolidated attachment order) made by any magistrates' court, the court may, subject to the provisions of this rule, discharge the existing order and make a consolidated attachment order in respect of that debtor.

(4) Where two or more attachment of earnings orders (whether or not they are themselves consolidated attachment orders) made by magistrates' courts are in existence in respect of one debtor, a magistrates' court acting for the same

---

[1] See r. 22, *infra*.

[2] As applied by r. 23, *infra*.

[3] Or a justices' clerk. *See* r. 22.

[4] As adapted by r. 23(4)).

8. FINES, COMPENSATION AND PROPERTY ORDERS   445

petty sessions area as one of these courts may, subject to the provisions of this rule, discharge the existing orders and make a consolidated attachment order in respect of that debtor.

(5) A magistrates' court may exercise the powers conferred under paras (2) to (4) of this rule either of its own motion or on the application of the debtor.

(6) A debtor may apply to a magistrates' court for a consolidated attachment order—

(i) in a case to which paras (2) or (3) of this rule applies, during the hearing of the proceedings for the enforcement of the fine or other liability;

(ii) in a case to which para (4) of this rule applies, by complaint.

(7) Where an employer applies in writing to the clerk of a magistrates' court which has power to make a consolidated attachment order requesting the court to make such an order, the clerk shall bring the application before the court, and, if it appears to the court that the application is justified, the court shall proceed as if it had determined of its own motion to make such an order.

(8) Before a magistrates' court exercises of its own motion the powers conferred under para. (4) of this rule, it shall cause written notice to be given to the debtor of his right to make representations to the court.

(9) Where a magistrates' court has power to make a consolidated attachment order under paras (3) or (4) of this rule and a relevant attachment of earnings order has been made by a magistrates' court acting for another petty sessions area, the first mentioned court shall cause notice to be given to the clerk of the second mentioned court and shall not discharge that attachment of earnings order unless the enforcement of the sum to which the order relates is transferred to the first mentioned court under [s. 89 of the Magistrates' Courts Act 1980 (transfer of fines), para. 7 of sch. 3 to the Legal Aid Act 1974] (transfer of enforcement of legal aid contribution orders) or r. 16 of these rules as the case may be.

(10) Where a magistrates' court makes a consolidated attachment order, it shall specify in the order such normal deduction rate as the court thinks reasonable and this rate may be less than the sum of the normal deduction rates specified in any attachment of earnings orders discharged by the court.

Transfer of fines etc. with view to making consolidated attachment order

16. (1) Where a magistrates' court has made or has power to make an attachment of earnings order to secure—

(a) the payment of any sum adjudged to be paid by a conviction or treated (by any enactment relating to the collection and enforcement of fines, costs, compensation or forfeited recognizances) as so adjudged to be paid, or

(b) the payment of any sum required to be paid by a legal aid contribution order,

and a magistrates' court acting for some other petty sessions area has made an attachment of earnings order in respect of the debtor, then, if the debtor does not reside in either petty sessions area, the first mentioned court[1] may make an order making payment of that sum enforceable in the petty sessions area for which the second mentioned court acted.

(2) As from the date on which an order is made under para. (1) of this rule with respect to any sum, all functions under any enactment relating to that sum

which, if no such order has been made, would have been exercisable by a court acting for the petty sessions area specified in the order, or the clerk of that court, as the case may be, and not otherwise.

(3) The making of an order under para. (1) of this rule with respect to any sum shall not prejudice the power to make a subsequent order with respect to that sum under that paragraph or under [s. 89 or 90 of the Magistrates' Courts Act 1980 or para. 7 of sch. 3 to the Legal Aid Act 1974].

Disposal of sums paid under consolidated attachment orders

17. *(1) A clerk of a magistrates' court receiving a payment under a consolidated attachment order shall, subject to para. (2) below, apply the money in payment of the sums secured by the order, paying first any sums previously secured by an attachment of earnings order which was discharged in consequence of the making of the consolidated attachment order.*

(2) Where two or more attachment of earnings orders were discharged in consequence of the making of the consolidated attachment order the sums due under the orders shall be paid in the chronological order of the orders.

Method of making payment under attachment of earnings order

18. *(1) A clerk of a magistrates' court to whom any payment under an attachment of earnings order is to be made shall notify the employer[2] of the hours during which, and the place at which, payments are, subject to the provisions of this rule, to be made and received.*

(2) If an employer sends by post any payments under an attachment of earnings order to a clerk of a magistrates' court, he shall do so at his own risk and expense.

Service of orders and notices

20. *Where under s. 14 of the Act (which relates to statements of earnings, etc.) an order is directed to the debtor or to a person appearing to be an employer of the debtor or where under these rules a copy of an order is to be served or a notice is to be given to any person—*

   (a)   *service may be effected on, or notice may be given to a person, other than a corporation, be delivering it to the person to whom it is directed or by sending it by post in a letter addressed to him at his last known or usual place of abode or, in the case of an employer or a person appearing to be an employer of the debtor, at his place of business;*

   (b)   *service may be effected on, or notice given to, a corporation by delivering the document at, or sending it to—*

   (i)   *such office or place as the corporation may, for the purpose of this rule have specified in writing to the court in relation to the debtor or to a class or description of person to which he belongs, or*

   (ii)   *the registered office of the corporation if that office is in England and Wales or, if there is no registered office in England and Wales, any place therein where the corporation trades or conducts its business.*

County court records

21. *(1) Where a clerk of a magistrates' court causes a copy of an order or notice to be given to any person under r. 6 of these rules, he shall cause a copy of the order or notice to be given also to the County Court Registrar for the district in which the debtor resides.*

2. As adopted by r. 23(5).

8. FINES, COMPENSATION AND PROPERTY ORDERS   447

(2) Where the clerk of a magistrates' court which has made an attachment of earnings order is informed of a debtor's change of address, he shall notify the new address to the County Court Registrar for the district in which the debtor resided before the change of address.

Justices' clerks.

22. *(1) The things specified in para. (2) of this rule, being things authorized to be done by, to or before a single justice of the peace for a petty sessions area, may be done by, to or before the justices' clerk for that area.*

(2) The things referred to in para. (1) above are—

(a) *the power to make an order under s. 14(1) or (2) of the Act (power of court to obtain statements of earnings etc.) before the hearing of an application to a magistrates' court for an attachment of earnings order, or for the variation or discharge of such an order;*

(b) *the determination that a complaint for the discharge or variation of an attachment of earnings order be dealt with by a magistrates' court acting for another petty sessions area in accordance with r. 9 of these rules;*

(c) *the giving of directions under r. 10 or r. 11 of these rules;*

(d) *the discharge or variation by the court of its own motion of an attachment or earnings order in accordance with r. 12 or r. 13 of these rules;*

(e) *the temporary variation of an attachment of earnings order by an increase of the protected earnings rate in accordance with r. 14 of these rules;*

(f) *the making of an order under r. 16 of these rules (transfer of fines etc. with view to making consolidated attachment order).*

Application of these Rules to attachment of earnings orders in respect of fines etc.

23. *(1) In the application of these Rules to attachment of earnings orders to secure—*

(a) *the payment of any sum adjudged to be paid by a conviction or treated by any enactment relating to the collection and enforcement of fines, costs, compensation or forfeited recognizances) as to adjudged to be paid, or*

(b) *the payment of any sum required to be paid by a legal aid contribution order,*

the exceptions and modifications specified in the following provisions of this Rule shall apply.

(2) Rules 4, 5, 8, 9, 10, 11 and 19 shall not apply.

(3) An attachment of earnings order shall be in the form numbered 2 in the schedule to these Rules.

(4) Rule 14 (temporary variation of protected earnings rate) shall have effect as if in para. (3) the words "and the clerk shall also send a copy to the person entitled to receive payments under the related maintenance order whether directly or through an officer of any court" were omitted.

(5) Rule 18 (method of making payment under attachment of earnings order) shall have effect as if in paragraph (1) the words "and the person entitled to receive payments under the related maintenance order" and para. (3) were omitted.

THE MAGISTRATES' COURTS RULES 1981

S.I. 1981 No. 552, as amended by S.I. 1983 No. 523

Notice to defendant of fine or forfeited recognizance

46. *(1) Where under s. 3(1) of the Powers of Criminal Courts Act 1973, s. 49 of the Criminal Justice Act 1967 or s. 19(5) of the Coroners Act 1887 a magistrates' court is required to enforce payment of a fine imposed or recognizance forfeited by the Crown Court or by a coroner or where a magistrates' court allows time for payment of a sum adjudged to be paid by a summary conviction, or directs that the sum be paid by instalments, or where the offender is absent when a sum is adjudged to be paid by a summary conviction, the clerk of the court shall serve on the offender notice in writing stating the amount on the sum and, if it is to be paid by instalments, the amount of the instalments, the date on which the sum, or each of the instalments, is to be paid and the places and times at which payment may be made; and a warrant of distress or commitment shall not be issued until the preceding provisions of this rule have been complied with.*

(2) A notice under this rule shall be served by delivering it to the offender or by sending it to him by post in a letter addressed to him at his last known or usual place of abode.

COMMENTARY

Compliance with this rule is mandatory even on an adjourned means inquiry where the defendant is present in court: *R.* v. *Farnham Justices, ex parte Hunt* (1976) May 24; 140 J.P.N. 453.

Absent. A defendant who is legally represented is deemed not to be absent: Magistrates' Courts Act 1980, s. 122.

Notice in writing *See* forms 46 and 133.

Registration and notification of financial penalty enforcement order

47. *(1) The clerk of a magistrates' court receiving a financial penalty enforcement order made by the Defence Council or an officer authorized by them shall cause the said order to be registered in his courts by means of a memorandum entered in the register kept pursuant to r. 66 and signed by him and shall send notice in writing to the Defence Council or the authorized officer, as appropriate, stating that the order has been so registered.*

(2) Where a financial penalty enforcement order has been registered in accordance with the provisions of para. (1), the clerk shall forthwith serve on the person against whom the order was made a notice of registration in the prescribed form.

(3) A notice required by para. (2) shall be served on the person by delivering it to him or by sending it by post addressed to him at the address shown on the financial penalty enforcement order.

(4) In this rule "financial penalty enforcement order" means an order made under s. 133A(1) of the Army Act 1955, s. 133A(1) of the Air Force Act 1955 or s. 128F(1) of the Naval Discipline Act 1957.

COMMENTARY

Only the Army Act 1955, s. 133A is printed in this book. See generally Home Office circ. 129/1977 dated August 3, 1977 and form 47.

To whom payments are to be made

48. *(1) A person adjudged by the conviction or order of a magistrates' court to pay any sum shall, unless the court otherwise directs, pay that sum, or any instalment of that sum, to the clerk of the court.*

(2) Where payment of any sum or instalment of any sum adjudged to be paid by the conviction or order, of a magistrates' court is made to any person other than the clerk of the court, that person, unless he is the person to whom the court has directed payment to be made or, in the case of a child, is the person with whom the child has his home, shall, as soon as may be, account for and, if the clerk so requires, pay over the sum or instalment to the clerk of the court.

(3) Where payment of any sum adjudged to be paid by the conviction or order of a magistrates' court, or any instalment of such a sum, is directed to be made to the clerk of some other magistrates' court, the clerk of the court that adjudged the sum paid shall pay over any sums received by him on account of the said sum or instalment to the clerk of that other court.

Duty of clerk to give receipt

49. *The clerk of a magistrates' court shall give or send a receipt to any person who makes a payment to him in pursuance of a conviction or order of a magistrates' court and who asks for a receipt.*

Application for further time

51. *An application under s. 75(2) of the Act of 1980, s. 22 of the Act of 1978 s. 12B(5) of the Guardianship of Minors Act 1871 or s. 6A(5) of the Affiliation Proceedings Act 1957 may, unless the court requires the applicant to attend, be made in writing.*

Notice of date of hearing of means inquiry etc.

52. *Where a magistrates' court, under subs. (1) of s. 86 of the Act of 1980 (power of magistrates' court to fix day for appearance of offender at means inquiry etc.), has fixed a day on which an offender must appear in person before the court and, under subs. (3) of that section, fixes a later day in substitution for the day previously fixed, service of the notice of the substituted day may be effected in any manner in which service of a summons may be effected under r. 99(1).*

Execution of distress warrant

54. *(1) A warrant of distress issued for the purpose of levying a sum adjudged to be paid by a summary conviction or order—*

> (a)   shall name or otherwise describe the person against whom the distress is to be levied;
>
> (b)   shall be directed to the constables of the police area in which the warrant is issued or to the authorized persons for the police area specified in the warrant, or to a person named in the warrant and shall, subject to, and in accordance with, the provisions of this rule, require them to levy the said sum by distress and sale of the goods belonging to the said person;
>
> (c)   may where it is directed to the constables of a police area, instead of being executed by any of those persons be executed by any person under the direction of a constable.

(2) The warrant shall authorize the person charged with the execution of it to take any money as well as any goods of the person against whom the distress is levied; and any money so taken shall be treated as if it were the proceeds of the sale of goods taken under the warrant.

(3) The warrant shall require the person charged with the execution to pay the sum to be levied to the clerk of the court that issued the warrant.

(4) There shall not be taken under the warrant the wearing apparel or bedding of any person or his family or the tools and implements of his trade: so however that if the tools and implements of his trade exceed in value £150 it shall be lawful to take such of the tools and implements as will leave in that

person's possession tools and implements of his trade to the value of £150.

(5) The distress levied under any such warrant aforesaid shall be sold within such period beginning not earlier than the sixth day after the making of the distress as may be specified in the warrant, or if no period is specified in the warrant, within a period beginning on the sixth day and ending on the 14th day after the making of the distress:

Provided that with the consent in writing of the person against whom the distress is levied the distress may be sold before the beginning of the said period.

(6) The said distress shall be sold by public auction or in such other manner as the person against whom the distress is levied may in writing allow.

(7) Notwithstanding anything in the preceding provisions of this rule, the said distress shall not be sold if the sum for which the warrant was issued and the charges of taking and keeping the distress have been paid.

(8) Subject to any direction to the contrary in the warrant, where the distress is levied on household goods, the goods shall not, without the consent in writing of the person against whom the distress is levied, be removed from the house until the day of sale; and so much of the goods shall be impounded as is in the opinion of the person executing the warrant sufficient to satisfy the distress, by affixing to the articles impounded a conspicuous mark.

(9) The constable or other person charged with the execution of any such warrant as aforesaid shall cause the distress to be sold, and may deduct out of the amount realized by the sale all costs and charges incurred in effecting the sale; and he shall return to the owner the balance, if any, after retaining the amount of the sum for which the warrant was issued and the proper costs and charges of the execution of the warrant.

(10) The constable or other person charged with the execution of any such warrant as aforesaid shall as soon as practicable send to the clerk of the court that issued it a written account of the costs and charges incurred in executing it; and the clerk shall allow the person against whom the distress was levied to inspect the account within one month after the levy of the distress at any reasonable time to be appointed by the court.

(11) If any person pays or tenders to the constable or other person charged with the execution of any such warrant as aforesaid the sum mentioned in the warrant, or produces a receipt for that sum given by the clerk of the court that issued the warrant, and also pays the amount of the costs and charges of the distress up to the time of the payment or tender or the production of the receipt the constable or other person as aforesaid shall not execute the warrant, or shall cease to execute it, as the case may be.

COMMENTARY

The landlord does not have a first claim on the proceeds of sale: *Potts* v. *Hickman* (1940) 105 J.P. 26 (a distress warrant for rates).

Certain property of public utilities is exempted from distraint by various statutes, *viz.* the Water Act 1945, s. 35(2); the Gas Act 1972, sch. 4; the Electric Lighting Act 1882, s. 25; the Electric Lighting Act 1909, s. 16 and the Electricity Act 1947, s. 57 and sch. 4.

Paragraph(1): A warrant of distress. Issued under the Magistrates' Courts Act 1980, s. 76. See form 48.

The authorized persons. This is a reference to the persons employed by a local authority in that area or by the chief officer of police or the police authority for that area who are authorized by the chief officer of police to execute warrants: r. 2(4).

Paragraph (4): Bedding. Includes a bedstead: *Davis* v. *Harris* (1900) 64 J.P. 136.

Implements of his trade. Implements exceeding the prescribed value may not be taken if they are the only chattel on the premises: *Lavell* v. *Ritchings* [1906] 1 K.B. 480; 75 L.J.K.B. 287 (a cab used by a cab driver). A typewriter used as a "sample" is not so protected: *Addison* v. *Shepherd* (1908) 72 J.P. 239.

A written account of the costs and charges. *See* form 50.

Payment after imprisonment imposed

55. *(1) The persons authorized for the purposes of s. 79(2) of the Act of 1980 to receive a part payment are—*

(a)   *unless there has been issued a warrant of distress or commitment, the clerk of the court enforcing payment of the sum, or any person appointed under s. 88 of that Act to supervise the offender;*

(b)   *where the issue of a warrant of commitment has been suspended on conditions which provide for payment to be made to the clerk of some other magistrate' court, that clerk;*

(c)   *any constable holding a warrant of distress or commitment or, where the warrant is directed to some other person, that person;*

(d)   *the governor or keeper of the prison or place in which the defaulter is detained, or other person having lawful custody of the defaulter:*

Provided that—

(i)   *the said governor or keeper shall not be required to accept any sum tendered in part payment under the said subs. (2) except on a week-day between 9 o'clock in the morning and 5 o'clock in the afternoon; and*

(ii)   *no person shall be required to receive in part payment under the said subs. (2) an amount which, or so much of an amount as, will not procure a reduction of the period for which the defaulter is committed or ordered to be detained.*

(2) Where a person having custody of a defaulter receives payment of any sum he shall note receipt of the sum on the warrant of commitment.

(3) Where the clerk of a court other than the court enforcing payment of the sums receives payment of any sum he shall inform the clerk of the other court.

(4) Where a person appointed under s. 88 of the Act of 1980 to supervize an offender receives payment of any sum, he shall send it forthwith to the clerk of the court which appointed him.

(5) If the period of imprisonment imposed on any person in default of payment of a sum adjudged to be paid by a conviction or order of a magistrates' court, or for want of sufficient distress to satisfy such a sum, is reduced through part payments to less than five days, he may be committed either to a prison or to a place certified by the Secretary of State under s. 134 of the Act of 1980. or, if he is already in prison, the Secretary of State may transfer him to a place so certified.

Order for supervision

56. *(1) Unless an order under s. 88(1) of the Act of 1980 is made in the offender's presence, the clerk of the court making the order shall deliver to the offender, or serve on him by post, notice in writing of the order.*

(2) It shall be the duty of any person for the time being appointed under the said section to advise and befriend the offender with a view to inducing him to pay the sum adjudged to be paid and thereby avoid committal to custody and to give any information required by a magistrates' court about the offender's conduct and means.

COMMENTARY

Paragraph (1): An order under s. 88(1). That is, a money payment supervision order.

Serve on him by post. For proof of service *see* r. 67.
Notice in writing. *See* form 62.

Transfer of fine order

57. *(1) The clerk of a magistrates' court which has made a transfer of fine order under s. 89 or s. 90 or s. 90 as applied by s. 91 of the Act of 1980 shall send to the clerk of the court having jurisdiction under the order a copy of the order with a statement of the offence and the steps, if any, taken to recover the sum adjudged to be paid, and with such further information as is available and is in the opinion of the first-mentioned clerk likely to assist the last-mentioned court.*

(2) Where a magistrates' court has made a transfer of fine order in respect of a sum adjudged to be paid by a court in Scotland or in Northern Ireland the clerk of the magistrates' court shall send a copy of the order to the clerk of the Scottish court or to the clerk of the Northern Irish court, as the case may be.

(3) Where the clerk of a magistrates' court receives a copy of a transfer of fine order (whether made in England and Wales, or in Scotland or in Northern Ireland) specifying that court as the court by which payment of the sum in question is to be enforceable, he shall thereupon, if possible, deliver or send by post to the offender notice in writing in the prescribed form.

(4) Where under a transfer of fine order a sum adjudged to be paid by a Scottish court or by a Northern Irish court is enforceable by a magistrates' court—

(a) *if the sum is paid, the clerk of the magistrates' court shall send it to the clerk of the Scottish court or to the clerk of the Northern Irish court, as the case may be;*

(b) *if the sum is not paid, the clerk of the magistrates' court shall inform the clerk of the Scottish court or the clerk of the Northern Irish court, as the case may be, of the manner in which the adjudication has been satisfied or that the sum, or any balance thereof, appears to be irrecoverable.*

COMMENTARY

The order. *See* forms 59 and 60.

Notice in ... the prescribed form. *See* form 61.

Particulars of fine enforcement to be entered in register

65. *(1) Where the court on the occasion of convicting an offender of an offence issues a warrant of commitment for a default in paying a sum adjudged to be paid by the conviction or, having power to issue such a warrant, fixes a term of imprisonment under s. 77(2) of the Act of 1980, the reasons for the court's action shall be entered in the register, or any separate record kept for the purpose of recording particulars of fine enforcement.*

(2) There shall be entered in the register, or any such record, particulars of any—

(a) *means inquiry under s. 82 of the Act of 1980;*
(b) *hearing under subs. (5) of the said s. 82;*
(c) *allowance of further time for the payment of a sum adjudged to be paid by a conviction;*
(d) *direction that such a sum shall be paid by instalments including any direction varying the number of instalments payable, the amounts of any instalments payable and the date on which any instalment becomes payable;*

8. Fines, Compensation and Property Orders   453

(e)   distress for the enforcement of such a sum;
(f)   attachment of earnings order for the enforcement of such a sum;
(g)   order under that Act placing a person under supervision pending payment of such a sum;
(h)   order under s. 85(1) of that Act remitting the whole or any part of a fine;
(i)   order under s. 120(4) of that Act remitting the whole or any part of any sum enforceable under that section (forfeiture of recognizance);
(j)   authority granted under s. 87(3) of that Act authorizing the taking of proceedings in the High Court or county court for the recovery of any sum adjudged to be paid by a conviction;
(k)   transfer of fine order made by the court;
(l)   order transferring a fine to the court;
(m)   order under s. 32(1) of the Powers of Criminal Courts Act 1973 specifying the court for the purpose of enforcing a fine imposed or a recognizance forfeited by the Crown Court; and
(n)   any fine imposed or recognizance forfeited by a coroner which has to be treated as imposed or forfeited by the court.

Application for review of compensation order

104. *(1) An application under s. 37 of the Powers of Criminal Courts Act 1973 for the review of a compensation order shall be by complaint.*

(2) The justice to whom the complaint is made shall issue a summons directed to the person for whose benefit the compensation order was made, requiring him to show cause why the order should not be amended or revoked.

CHAPTER 9

ROAD TRAFFIC

CONTENTS

INTRODUCTION

Conviction of a wide range of road traffic offences renders an offender liable to disqualification for holding or obtaining a driving licence. These offences are commonly described as endorsable offences because the court is under a duty save for special reason to order that particulars of the conviction and any disqualification or penalty points shall be endorsed on the offender's driving licence.

Endorsement

Where a person is convicted of any offence mentioned in the Road Traffic Act 1972, s. 101(1) the court must order that there shall be endorsed on any licence held by him particulars of the conviction and of any disqualification or penalty points; *ibid*, s. 101(1). If the court does not order disqualification it need not order endorsement if for special reasons it thinks fit not to do so: *ibid*, s. 101(2). Such an endorsement may be produced as prima facie evidence of the matters endorsed: *ibid*, s. 101(1). Where a person is convicted of an offence involving obligatory endorsement and his licence is produced to the court the court may take into consideration endorsed particulars of any previous conviction or disqualification and of any penalty points which are to be taken into consideration: *ibid*, s. 101(4A).

A licence free of endorsements may be obtained after the end of the "effective period" of the endorsement: *ibid*, s. 101(7). The "effective periods" are set out in *ibid*, s. 101(7A).

Previous convictions may also be proved by an authenticated computer print-out under *ibid*, s. 182.

The mechanics of endorsement require that a person prosecuted for an endorsable offence shall cause his driving licence to be delivered to the court not later than the day before the hearing or post it by registered or recorded delivery at such a time that in the ordinary course of post it would arrive not later than that day, or in the alternative, have it with him at the hearing. Upon conviction the court must order the licence to be produced. Unless the accused satisfies the court that he has applied for a new licence and has not received it failure to produce a driving licence consitutes an offence and causes the operation of the licence to be suspended until such time as it is produced: Road Traffic Act 1972, s. 101(4). At the same time as ordering production of the licence the court must also order the defendant to disclose in writing his date of birth if not already known and, in the case of a written plea of guilty under the Magistrates' Courts Act 1980, s. 12, his sex also: Road Traffic Act 1972, s. 104.

Conviction of an endorsable offence carries a power and in the case of some offences a duty on the part of the court to order the offender to be disqualified for holding or obtaining a driving licence.

Disqualification

Official policy concerning the use of disqualification is described by the Home Office in the pamphlet *"The Sentence of the Court"* as follows:

> Disqualification is designed to be a road safety measure which will take off the road drivers who are a potential danger to other road users. The risk of disqualification either for a single offence or as a consequence of the "totting up" provisions . . . is widely regarded as a powerful influence towards compliance with road safety provisions.

The powers of the court were summarized thus by Lord Lane C.J. in *R. v. Kent (Peter)* [1983] 1 W.L.R. 794:

A person appearing before a court may be disqualified:

(a) because the offence of which he is convicted attracts obligatory or discretionary disqualification. Such offences are set out in Sch. 4 to the Road Traffic Act 1972. The power to disqualify is in s. 93(1) and (2) of that Act. Disqualifications run from the time of sentence and cannot be consecutive to one another; or

(b) (*in the Crown Court only*) because the court is satisfied that a motor vehicle was used by the person convicted or anyone else for the purpose of committing or facilitating the commission of the offence in question: s. 44 of the Powers of Criminal Courts Act 1973; or

(c) because he has committed repeated offences attracting obligatory or discretionary disqualification ("totting up"). The power to disqualify is set out in s. 19(2) of the Transport Act 1981. If the offender is liable to be disqualified under s. 19(2) for several offences, the disqualification is allocated to one offence only (s. 19(5)(a)) although for the purposes of an appeal the disqualification is treated as an order made on the conviction of each offence: s. 19(5)(c);

(d) for both (a) and (c) or (b) and (c) above; all disqualifications now run concurrently since the repeal of s. 93(5) of the Road Traffic Act 1972, which used to make disqualification for repeated offences consecutive to any other disqualification.

In addition there is power under the Road Traffic Act 1972, s. 93(7) to disqualify until a driving test has been passed. (*See* below).

Discretionary Disqualification

Where a person is convicted of an endorsable offence the court may order him to be disqualified for such period as the court thinks fit: Road Traffic Act 1972, s. 93(2).

There is no power to disqualify for an indefinite period: *R. v. Fowler* (1937) 101 J.P. 244. Disqualification for life is permissible as being for a fixed period: *R. v. Tunde-Olarinde* (1967) 131 J.P. 323. But long periods of disqualification do more harm than good in the case of a man whose occupation is that of a driver and whose offences do not include reckless or careless driving: *R. v. Bond* [1968] 1 All E.R. 1040 (12 month's disqualification substituted for life) and in *R. v. North* [1971] R.T.R. 366, it was said that disqualification for life is wrong in principle unless there are very unusual circumstances. Long periods of disqualification may prove a very severe handicap to a man when he comes out of prison and desires to pursue a different type of life to that which has led him into that prison. Such periods of disqualification may shut out a large sector of employments especially in certain areas. Moreover, if the length of disqualification is overlong and amounts to a period such as a decade the position may well seem hopeless to the man and that of itself sows the seeds of an incentive to disregard the law on this point. However wrong such an attitude may be it springs from a human factor which it is wise to take into account, *per* Sachs, LJ, in *R. v. Shirley* (1969) 133 J.P. 691.

Mandatory Disqualification

Where a person is convicted of certain offences specified in the Road Traffic Act 1972, sch. 4, the court must order him to be disqualified for such period not less than 12 months as it thinks fit unless for special reasons the court thinks fit to order a shorter period or not to disqualify at all: Road

Traffic Act 1972, s. 93(1). A second or subsequent conviction of certain offences within 10 years increases the minimum period of disqualification
from 12 months to three years: *ibid*, s. 93(4). Anyone convicted of aiding,
abetting, counselling or procuring or inciting to the commission of an offence involving mandatory disqualification is treated as if the offence were
one involving discretionary disqualification: *ibid*, s. 93(6).

Special Reasons

"A special reason within the exception is one which is special to the facts
of the particular case, that is special to the facts which constitute the offence. It is, in other words, a mitigating or extenuating circumstance, not
amounting in law to a defence to the charge, yet directly connected with
the commission of the offence, and one which the court ought properly to
take into consideration when imposing punishment. A circumstance
peculiar to the offence as distinguished from the offence is not a special
reason within the exception" *per* Lord Goddard CJ in *Whittall* v. *Kirby*
(1947) 111 J.P. 1; approved by the Court of Criminal Appeal in *R.* v.
Wickens [1958] 92 Cr. App. R. 236, and *R.* v. *Jackson* (1969) 133 J.P. 358.
   Whether special reasons exist is a question of law: *Rennison* v. *Knowler*
[1947] 1 All E.R. 302. Even when they do exist the court retains a
discretion to disqualify, for example in the interests of public safety owing
to age or infirmity: *R.* v. *Agnew* (1969) 13 Sol. J. 58; *R.* v. *Newton* [1974]
R.T.R. 451. In drink and driving cases it should rarely if ever fail to
disqualify if the alcohol content exceeded 100 mg./100 ml. of blood: *Taylor*
v. *Rajan* (1974) 138 J.P. 328.
Evidence. "Where on a plea of guilty or after evidence has been heard, a
defendant has been convicted of an offence for which the penalty of
disqualification is laid down by Act of Parliament and he seeks to rely on
special reasons for the non-imposition of disqualification he ought to give
evidence and the justices ought to hear evidence on the point and not
merely accept statements. This is highly desirable because the onus is on
the defendant to show special reasons why he should not be disqualified."
per Lord Goddard C.J. in *Jones* v. *English* (1951) 115 J.P. 609. A formal
admission by the prosecutor would be sufficient: *Brown* v. *Dyerson* (1968)
132 J.P. 495.
   Where the defence intend to call evidence to prove facts or medical
opinion in support of a plea of special reasons, notice of the nature of the
evidence to be called ought to be given to the prosecution at a sufficient in-
terval before the hearing to enable the prosecution to be prepared to deal
with it: *Pugsley* v. *Hunter* [1973] R.T.R. 284.
   For examples of special reasons *see* the commentary to the Road Traffic
Act 1972, s. 93.

Sentencing Practice

   All orders of disqualification (save for some imposed under former
legislation) take effect from the moment of conviction: *Taylor* v. *Kenyon*
(1952) 116 J.P. 599; *R.* v. *Phillips* (1955) 111 J.P. 455; *R.* v. *Graham* [1955]
Crim. L.R. 319; *R.* v. *Bradley* (1961) 125 J.P. 303; *R.* v. *Meese* (1973) 137
J.P. 674. Disqualification runs during periods of imprisonment: *R.* v.
Phillips (1955) 119 J.P. 499. There is no rule that persons who are sent to
prison have a right to have the period of disqualification coincide more or
less automatically with the period of the sentence: *R.* v. *Hansel* [1982] 4 Cr.
App. R. (S) 368.
   There is no power to limit disqualification to a particular class of motor
vehicle.
   In *R.* v. *Bignell* [1968] 52 Cr. App. R. 18, the Court of Appeal decided

that "an order for disqualification is good even though it is not attached to
a separate sentence of the court". However, this was apparently decided *per
incuriam* the argued decision of the Divisional Court in *R.* v. *Surrey Quarter
Sessions, ex parte Commissioner of Police of the Metropolis* (1962) 126 J.P.
269: *see* the article at 138 J.P.N. 632 and the decision in *R.* v. *Arundel
Justices, ex parte Jackson* (1957) 123 J.P. 346 (disqualification severable
from sentence).

Offences involving disqualification or endorsement ought not to be taken
into consideration when passing sentence but should be prosecuted
separately: *R.* v. *Collins* (1947) 111 J.P. 154; *R.* v. *Simons* (1953) 117 J.P.
422. This objection does not apply where the principal offence is also
disqualifiable: *R.* v. *Jones* (1970) 135 J.P. 36. The fact that a court makes a
probation order or order of absolute or conditional discharge does not
enable the offender to escape disqualification or endorsement. The court is
under the same obligation to endorse or disqualify as if it had dealt with
the offender by any other method: Road Traffic Act 1972, s. 102.
Magistrates have power on committing an offender to the Crown Court for
sentence to order interim disqualification until dealt with: Road Traffic Act
1972, s. 103.

Disqualification may not be imposed in the absence of the defendant
himself unless notice of adjournment has been sent to him specifying the
reason for the adjournment: Criminal Justice Act 1967, s. 26(2) and (3). It
is wrong to impose a fine and adjourn for the purpose of disqualification:
R. v. *Talgarth JJ, ex parte Bithell* (1973) 137 J.P. 666.

The licence of a disqualified person is suspended and of no effect: Road
Traffic Act 1972, s. 98. Driving in breach of a disqualification is an offence
under *ibid*, s. 99.

Penalty Points

For some years now the courts have been under an obligation, save for
mitigating circumstances, to disqualify an offender with a multiplicity of
convictions for endorsable offences (the "totting up" rule). The latest version of this rule is contained in the Transport Act 1981, s. 19 and is based
on a system of penalty points. It should be remembered that the purpose of
the penalty points system is to require the disqualification of the repeated
offender. For the serious road traffic offender the court has adequate
discretionary powers.

Where someone is convicted of an endorsable offence and the penalty
points to be taken into account number 12 or more the court must order
him to be disqualified for not less than the minimum period: Transport Act
1981, s. 19(2). The penalty points to be taken into account are any that on
that occasion will be ordered to be endorsed on his licence (or would be so
ordered if he were not disqualified) and any endorsed on a previous occasion unless the offender has since been disqualified: *ibid*, s. 19(3).
However, if any of the offences was committed more than three years
before another the points must be ignored: *ibid*, s. 19(3).

The penalty points in respect of each offence are listed in schedule 7:
ibid, s. 19(1). If a person is convicted of two or more endorsable offences
the number of penalty points in respect of those committed on the same occasion is the number or highest number that would be endorsed on a conviction of one of those offences: *ibid*, s. 19(1).

The minimum period of disualification is six months unless the offender
has a previous disqualification imposed within three years of commission
of the latest offence when the period is twelve months. If the offender has
two such disqualifications the period is two years: *ibid*, s. 19(4).

Where, having regard to all the circumstances, the court is satisfied that there are grounds for mitigating the normal consequences of the conviction it may if it thinks fit order the offender to be disqualified for a shorter period or not order him to be disqualified: *ibid*, s. 19(2). No account may be taken of any circumstances alleged to make the offence or any of the offences not a serious one, of hardship other than exceptional hardship and of any circumstances which within the three years immediately preceeding the conviction have already been taken into account: *ibid*, s. 19(6). This includes circumstances taken into account under the previous rule in the Road Traffic Act 1972, s. 93(3): *ibid*, s. 19(7), (b). The grounds for failing to disqualify for the minimum period must be stated in open court and entered in the register: Road Traffic Act 1972, s. 105(1).

Where the offender is convicted on the same occasion of more than one endorsable offence not more than one disqualification may be imposed on him under the penalty points rule, but in imposing the disqualification the court must take into account all the offences: Transport Act 1981, s. 19(5).

The penalty points system has been grafted directly onto the previous system of totting up under the Road Traffic Act 1972, s. 93(3), so that each endorsement imposed thereunder counts as three points no matter what the offence unless a disqualification was imposed on the offender on that or any subsequent occasion: *ibid*, s. 19(7) (a).

Disqualification until Test Passed

Under the Road Traffic Act 1972, s. 93(7) any court convicting an offender of any endorsable offence may order (whether with or without what might be called "ordinary" disqualification) that the offender shall be disqualified for holding or obtaining a driving licence until he has passed the ordinary driving test. This power is not intended as a punitive sanction but for the protection of the public against incompetent drivers: *Ashworth* v. *Johnson* [1959] Crim. LR 735. In *R.* v. *Donnelly* [1975] 139 JP 293 it was said that the object was to test drivers who have become disqualified and who may for some reason show some lack of competence or that some efficiency relating to their driving should be further tested.

The power is only appropriate in cases of age or infimity or where the circumstances of the offence are such that there is reason to suspect that the offending driver is not a competent driver, *per* Smith J in *R.* v. *Banks· (John)* [1978] RTR 535 at p. 536.

It is a misconception to regard this power as a means of keeping unsafe as opposed to incompetent drivers off the road: *Hughes* v. *Challes* (1983) *The Times*, November 8. In *R.* v. *Guilfoyle* (1975) 137 JP 568 an interruption of twelve months for reason of disqualification in the driving of a 19 year old convicted of causing death by dangerous driving was held to warrant an order under this section.

Notification of Disability

In the case of proceedings for (and not merely upon conviction of) *any* offence committed in respect of a motor vehicle (and not merely endorsable offences) the court is under a duty to notify the Secretary of State if it appears that the accused, whether or not he is convicted, may be suffering from any relevant disability or prospective disability, Road Traffic Act 1972, s. 92.

Appeal and Suspension

Appeal made against endorsement and against *mandatory* orders of disqualification may be made under the Road Traffic Act 1972, s. 94. Appeals against *discretionary* orders of disqualification may be made under the Magistrates' Courts Act 1980, s. 108. Pending hearing of the appeal the disqualification may be suspended by the magistrates' court (Road Traffic Act 1972, s. 94(2)) or by the appellate court (ss. 94 and 94A).

Removal of Disqualification

Application may be made for the removal of a disqualification to the court which made the order: Road Traffic Act 1972, s. 95(1). No application may be made within the following periods:
  (a) Two years if the disqualification is for less than four years.
  (b) Half the period of disqualification if it is for less than 10 years but not less than four.
  (c) Five years in any other case: *ibid*, s. 95(2).
Time when the disqualification was suspended does not count. There can be no application to remove a disqualification under *ibid*, s. 93(7) (disqualification until a test is passed): *ibid*, s. 95(3). Application is by way of complaint: Magistrates' Courts Rules 1981, r. 101(2). The court may remove the disqualification as from a specified date or may refuse the application: Road Traffic Act 1972, s. 95(1). If an application is refused a further application may not be made within three months: *ibid*, s. 95(3).

Foreign Driving Licences

Northern Irish driving licences must be produced to court and on disqualification sent to the Secretary of State: Road Traffic Act 1972, s. 111.

Particulars of endorsements may not be entered on any foreign driving permits, but must be sent to the Secretary of State: S.I. 1975 No. 1208.

Notice of Intended Prosecution

Where a person is prosecuted for an offence mentioned in the Road Traffic Act 1972, s. 179(1) he must not be convicted unless: (a) he was warned at the time the offence was committed that the question of prosecuting him for one or other of these offences would be taken into consideration; or (b) within 14 days a summons was served on him; or (c) within 14 days a notice of the intended prosecution was served on him or on the keeper of the vehicle: *ibid*, s. 179(2). (In the case of offences under *ibid*, ss. 17 and 18, (reckless and careless cycling) the notice must be served on the accused).

This requirement is deemed to have been complied with until the contrary is proved: *ibid*, s. 179(3).

The requirement does not apply to an offence if at the time of the offence or immediately thereafter an accident occurs owing to the presence on a road of the vehicle: *ibid*, s. 179(3A).

Failure to comply with this requirement is no bar to conviction where (a) neither the particulars of the accused nor those of the registered keeper could with reasonable diligence have been ascertained in time; or (b) the accused by his own conduct contributed to the failure: *ibid*, s. 179(4).

THE ROAD TRAFFIC ACT 1972

Requirements as to physical fitness of drivers

87.–(1) An application for the grant of a licence shall include a declaration by the applicant, in such form as the Secretary of State may require, stating whether he is suffering or has at any time (or, if a period is prescribed for the purposes of this subsection, had during that period) suffered–
  (*a*) from any prescribed disability or from any other disability likely to cause the driving of a vehicle by him in pursuance of the licence to be a source of danger to the public (such prescribed or other disability being hereafter in

this section referred to as a "relevant disability"); or

(b) from any other disability which at the time of the application is not of such a kind that it is a relevant disability but which, by virtue of the intermittent or progressive nature of the disability or otherwise, may become a relevant disability in course of time (such disability being hereafter in this section referred to as a "prospective disability").

(2) If it appears from the declaration aforesaid, or if on inquiry the Secretary of State is satisfied from other information, that the applicant is suffering from a relevant disability, then, subject to the following provisions of this section, the Secretary of State shall refuse to grant the licence.

(3) The Secretary of State shall not by virtue of subs. (2) above refuse to grant a licence—

(a) on account of any relevant disability which is prescribed for the purposes of this paragraph, if the applicant has at any time passed a relevant test and it does not appear to the Secretary of State that the disability has arisen or become more acute since that time or was, for whatever reason, not disclosed to the Secretary of State at that time;

(b) on account of any relevant disability which is prescribed for the purposes of this paragraph, if the applicant satisfies such conditions as may be prescribed with a view to authorizing the grant of a licence to a person in whose case the disability is appropriately controlled;

(c) on account of any relevant disability which is prescribed for the purposes of this paragraph, if the application is for a provisional licence.

(4) If as the result of a test of competence to drive the Secretary of State is satisfied that the person who took the test is suffering from a disability such that there is likely to be a danger to the public—

(a) if he drives any vehicle, or

(b) if he drives a vehicle other than a vehicle of a particular construction or design,

the Secretary of State shall serve notice in writing to that effect on that person and shall include in the notice a description of the disability; and where a notice is served in pursuance of this subsection, then—

(i) if the notice is in pursuance of para. (a) of this subsection and the disability is not prescribed under subs. (1) above, it shall be deemed to be so prescribed in relation to the person aforesaid and if the disability is prescribed for the purposes of subs. (3)(c) above it shall be deemed not to be so prescribed in relation to him; and

(ii) if the notice is in pursuance of para. (b) of this subsection, any licence granted to that person shall be limited to vehicles of the particular construction or design specified in the notice.

(5) If the Secretary of State is at any time satisfied on inquiry—

(a) that the licence holder is suffering from a relevant disability, and

(b) that the Secretary of State would be required by virtue of subs. (2) or (4)(ii) above to refuse an application for the licence made by him at that time,

the Secretary of State may serve notice in writing on the licence holder revoking the licence with effect from such date as may be specified in the notice, not being earlier than the date of service of the notice; and it shall be the duty of a person whose licence is revoked under this subsection to deliver up the licence to the Secretary of State forthwith after the revocation.

(5A) If the Secretary of State is at any time satisfied on inquiry that the licence holder is suffering from a prospective disability, the Secretary of State may—

(*a*) serve notice in writing on the licence holder revoking the licence with effect from such date as may be specified in the notice, not being earlier than the date of service of the notice; and

(*b*) on receipt of the licence so revoked and of an application made for the purposes of this subsection, grant to the licence holder, free of charge, a new licence for a period determined by the Secretary of State under s. 89(1)(*aa*) of this Act;

and it shall be the duty of a person whose licence is revoked under this subsection to deliver up the licence to the Secretary of State forthwith after the revocation.

(6) In this section—

"disability" includes disease; and

"relevant test", in relation to an application for a licence, means any such test of competence as is mentioned in s. 85 of this Act or a test as to fitness or agility in pursuance of s. 100 of the Road Traffic Act 1960 as originally enacted, being a test authorizing the grant of a licence in respect of vehicles of the classes to which the application relates;

and for the purposes of subs. (3)(*a*) above a person to whom a licence was granted after the making of a declaration under para. (*c*) of the proviso to s. 5(2) of the Road Traffic Act 1930 (which contained transitional provisions with respect to certain disabilities) shall be treated as having passed, at the time of the declaration, a relevant test in respect of vehicles of the classes to which the licence related.

(7) Without prejudice to subs. (6) above, for the purposes of subs. (3)(*a*) above—

(*a*) an applicant shall be treated as having passed a relevant test if, and on the day on which, he has passed a test of competence to drive which, under a provision of a relevant external law corresponding to subs. (2) or subs. (4) of s. 85 of this Act, either is prescribed in relation to vehicles of the classes to which the application relates or is sufficient under that law for the granting of a licence authorizing the driving of vehicles of those classes, and

(*b*) in the case of an applicant who is treated as having passed a relevant test by virtue of para. (*a*) above, disclosure of a disability to the authority having power under the relevant external law to grant a licence to drive a motor vehicle shall be treated as disclosure to the Secretary of State,

and in this subsection "relevant external law" has the meaning assigned to it in s. 85(1) of this Act.

(as amended by the Road Traffic Act 1974, sch. 3).

COMMENTARY

Subsection (1): Prescribed disability. Certain disabilities are prescribed in reg.22 of the Driving Licences Regulations, SI 1976 No. 1076.

Notification of [disease or] disability

92. (1) If, in any proceedings for an offence committed in respect of a motor vehicle it appears to the court that the accused may be suffering from any relevant disability or prospective disability within the meaning of s. 87 of the Act, the court shall notify the Secretary of State.

A notice sent by a court to the Secretary of State in pursuance of this section shall be sent in such manner and to such address and contain such particulars as the Secretary of State may determine.

(2) If an authorized insurer refuses to issue to any person such a policy of insurance as complies with the requirements of Part VI of this Act on the ground that the state of health of that person is not satisfactory, or on grounds which

include that ground, the insurer shall as soon as practicable notify the Secretary of State of that refusal and of the full name, address, sex and date of birth of that person as disclosed by him to the insurer.

(3) In subs. (2) above "authorized insurer" has the same meaning as in s. 145(2) of this Act.

(as amended by the Road Traffic Act 1974, sch. 3).

COMMENTARY

The Secretary of State has power under s. 87(2) to refuse a licence to applicants who he is satisfied are suffering from a relevant disability.

Note also the court's power under s. 93(7), *infra*.

Subsection (1): Relevant disability or prospective disability. *See* subs. (1) of s. 87, *supra*. Note that relevant disabilities are not limited to the prescribed disabilities. The existence of a drink problem in the past was held not to justify a notification under this section: *R.* v. *Chichester Justices, ex parte Crouch* (1981) 146 J.P. 26.

Disqualification on conviction of certain offences

93. (1) Where a person is convicted of an offence—

(a) under a provision of this Act specified in col. 1 of Part I of sch. 4 to this Act in relation to which there appears in col. 5 of that part the word "obligatory" or the word "obligatory" qualified by conditions or circumstances relating to the offence; and

(b) where the said word "obligatory" is so qualified, the conditions or circumstances are satisfied or obtain in the case of the offence of which he is convicted;

or where a person is convicted of the offence specified in Part II of that Schedule (any such offence being in this Part of this Act referred to as an "offence involving obligatory disqualification") the court shall order him to be disqualified for such period not less than 12 months as the court thinks fit unless the court for special reasons thinks fit to order him to be disqualified for a shorter period or not to order him to be disqualified.

(2) Where a person is convicted of an offence—

(a) under a provision of this Act specified in column 1 of Part I of sch. 4 to this Act in relation to which there appears in col. 5 of that part the word "discretionary" or the word "discretionary" qualified by conditions or circumstances relating to the offence; and

(b) where the said word "discretionary" is so qualified the conditions or circumstances are satisfied or obtain in the case of the offence of which he is convicted;

or where a person is convicted of an offence specified in Part III of that schedule (any such offence being in this part of this Act referred to as an "offence involving discretionary disqualification"), the court may order him to be disqualified for such period as the court thinks fit.

(3) *(Repealed)*

(4) Where a person convicted of an offence under any of the following provisions of this Act, namely s. 5(1), 6(1) or 8(7) (where the latter is an offence involving obligatory disqualification), has within the 10 years immediately preceding the commission of the offence been convicted of any such offence, subs. (1) above shall apply in relation to him with the substitution of three years for 12 months.

(5) *(Repealed)*

(6) The foregoing provisions of this section shall apply in relation to a conviction of an offence committed by aiding, abetting, counselling or procuring, or inciting to the commission of an offence involving obligatory disqualification as

if the offence were an offence involving discretionary disqualification.

(7) Where a person is convicted of an offence involving obligatory or discretionary disqualification the court may, whether or not he has previously passed the test of competence to drive prescribed under this Act, and whether or not the court makes an order under the foregoing provisions of this section, or under s. 19 of the Transport Act 1981, order him to be disqualified until he has, since the date of the order, passed that test; and a disqualification by virtue of an order under this subsection shall be deemed to have expired on production of the Secretary of State of evidence, in such form as may be prescribed by regulations under s. 107 of this Act, that the person disqualified has, since the order was made, passed that test.
(as amended by the Transport Act 1981, s. 12 sch. 9.)

COMMENTARY

Subsection (1): An offence. As to aiders and abettors *see* subs. (6).

Special reasons. For what constitutes special reasons and how they may be proved *see* under this title in the introduction.

Special reasons must be stated in open court and recorded in the register: s. 105, *infra*. Although what constitutes a special reason may vary from one offence to another it would appear that the following features can never justify a failure to invoke a mandatory disqualification:

financial hardship: *Lines* v. *Hersom* [1951] 2 All E.R. 650; *Whittall* v. *Kirby* (1946) 111 J.P. 1; good character: *Whittall* v. *Kirby, supra; Lines* v. *Hersom, supra*; hardship to the offender's family: *Reynolds* v. *Roche* [1972] R.T.R. 282; the fact that disqualification appears to severe a penalty for that class of offence: *Williamson* v. *Wilson* (1947) 111 J.P. 175; applying *Rennison* v. *Knowler* (1947) 111 J.P. 171; the public interest: *Holroyd* v. *Berry* [1973] R.T.R. 145 (doctor would have to resign and would be difficult to replace in unattractive area); the fact that the offender was earlier under a special condition of bail which forbade him to drive: *R.* v. *Kwame* [1975] 60 Cr. App. R. 65.

The following cases concern offences of driving (or being in charge) of a motor vehicle while *unfit* through drink or having consumed *excess* alcohol:

Ignorance of effects of drink

Ignorance of effect of small amount of alcohol combined with inhalation of fumes was held to be a special reason in *Brewer* v. *Metropolitan Police Commissioner* (1969) 133 J.P. 185 (unfit). Ignorance of the effect of diabetic lager was held to be a special reason where it had been offered to the defendant by the barman: *Alexander* v. *Latter* [1972] Crim. L.R. 646 (excess); but not where the defendant chose the drink himself: *Adams* v. *Bradley* [1975] R.T.R. 233. And *see R.* v. *Krebbs* [1977] R.T.R. 406. The fact that the offender was an inexperienced drinker who had miscalculated the quantity was held not to be a special reason in *Glendinning* v. *Batty* [1973] R.T.R. 405.

Short distance

The fact that the defendant drove only a short distance is not a special reason: *Coombs* v. *Kenhoe* (1972) 136 J.P. 387 (lorry drove 200 yards through busy streets);*Haime* v. *Walklett* (1983) *The Times*, May 19 (attempted to reverse across street); distinguishing *James* v. *Hall* [1972] R.T.R. 228 (drove 10-15 yards to park safely where no danger to public).

Degree of intoxication

The following have been held not to amount to special reasons: small degree by which blood/alcohol concentration exceeds legal limit: *Delaroy Hall* v. *Tadman* (1969) 133 J.P. 127 (excess); driving ability unimpaired: *Taylor* v. *Austin* (1969) 133 J.P. 182 (excess); *R.* v. *Jackson, supra*; the fact that the blood/alcohol concentration may have been below the limit at an earlier time: *Ferriby* v. *Sharman* [1971] Crim. L.R. 288 (excess).

Mitigation of effects

The following have been held not to amount to special reasons: the fact that the defendant stopped the car and went to sleep when he felt the effect of alcohol: *Duck* v. *Peacock* (1949) 113 J.P. 135 (in charge under the influence); calling the police to the accident: *Kerr* v. *Armstrong* (1973) Crim. L.R. 532 (excess).

"Laced" drink

The fact that the defendant's drink was unknowingly fortified by another can be a special reason: *Williams* v. *Neale* [1971] R.T.R. 149 (unfit). As to the difficulties of proving such a reason see *Flewitt* v. *Harvath* [1972] R.T.R. 121; *Pugsley* v. *Hunter* [1973] R.T.R. 284 and *Weatherson* v. *Connop* [1975] Crim. L.R. 239.

Medical conditions

Ignorance of a medical condition (diabetes) which exaggerates the effect of drink was held to be a special reason where the charge was one of driving while unfit through drink in *R.* v. *Wickens* [1958] Crim. L.R. 619. The un-known existence of a medical condition which aggravated the effects of drink was held not to amount to a special reason where the charge was one of excess alcohol in *R.* v. *Jackson. R.* v. *Hart* (1969) 133 J.P. 358; (liver complaint); *Goldsmith* v. *Laver* [1970] Crim. L.R. 286 (diabetes).

Similarly, while ignorance of the effects of combining drink and drugs may exceptionally be a special reason in charges of driving while unfit through drink: *Chapman* v. *O'Hagan* (1949) 113 J.P. 518; in charges of excess alcohol this can never be: *R.* v. *Scott* (1969) 133 J.P. 369. (In that case Widgery LCJ suggested that such ignorance might have amounted to special reasons in a charge of driving while unfit).

Sudden emergency

A sudden emergency which cannot reasonably be foreseen, namely the need to prevent a large dough-making machine from breaking down, was held to be a special reason in *Aichroth* v. *Cottee* (1954) 118 J.P. 499 (driving while disqualified); ambulance driver taking an emergency case: *R.* v. *Lundt Smith* (1964) 128 J.P. 534 (but note *Brown* v. *Dyerson* (1968) 132 J.P. 495—no evidence of medical emergency). In *R.* v. *Baines* [1970] 54 Cr. App. R. 481 (excess alcohol) a mission to help friend stranded with aged mother (where defendant could have tried to find a garage or contacted a motoring organization) was held not to constitute a special reason. A husband who drove home to his wife after hearing of the unexplained absence of their daughter was held not to have a special reason in *Jacobs* v. *Reed* [1973] Crim. L.R. 531 (excess alcohol), the court adding that it was an objective test considering the degree and character of the emergency and the extent to which alternative methods of transport were available. And *see Taylor* v. *Rajan* (1974) 138 J.P. 328. The word "emergency" is a convenient one to describe those cases where a motorist did not intend to drive any more, took drink in the belief that he would not so drive and then for some unexpected reason beyond his control was faced with a situation which appeared to require him to drive: *Fraser* v. *Barton* (1974) 138 J.P. 328. In *Evans* v. *Bray* [1977] R.T.R. 24 it was held not to be a special reason for a man to drive with tablets needed unexpectedly for his wife. The direr the emergency, it was said, the more obvious is the alternative course of dialling 999 or otherwise communicating with the local hospital or police. In assessing whether a crisis justified being regarded as a special reason the court should consider whether the defendant acted reasonably and responsibly in regard to the problem of driving when drink taken. It is important that an invented crisis should not be accepted: *Powell* v. *Gliha* [1979] R.T.R. 126. (Wife drove paraplegic husband away from party to home where he had specially fitted lavatory. Not special reason because she had failed to contemplate the possibility that he would need the facilities). A medical emergency must be established by the defendant with more than nebulous evidence: *Park* v. *Hicks* [1979] R.T.R. 259, (fear of recurrence of brain haemorrhage).

Driving on instructions

The following have been held to constitute special reasons: driving on the instructions of an employer: *Blows* v. *Chapman* (1948) 112 J.P. 8, (no insurance); driving at the direction of a constable: *Ambrose* v. *Jamison* [1967] Crim. L.R. 114 (driving while disqualified); This extends to a genuine but mistaken belief that a constable had ordered the defendant to move his car: *R.* v. *McIntyre* [1976] R.T.R. 330 (excess alcohol). However, the court must consider, not only the driving upon police request, but also any antecedent driving under the influence of alcohol on the defendant's own volition: *De Munthe* v. *Stewart* [1982] R.T.R. 27.

Subsection (6). The effect of this section is that participation in an offence involving obligatory disqualification otherwise than as a principal in the first degree attracts discretionary disqualification only. This subsection does not otherwise affect the rule in the Magistrates' Courts Act 1980, s. 44 that an aider and abettor is treated as a principal: *Ullah* v. *Luckhurst* [1977] Crim. L.R. 295. Thus someone convicted of aiding and abetting an excess alcohol offence is liable to the mandatory disqualification upon repeated conviction under s. 93(4): *Makeham* v. *Donaldson* [1981] R.T.R. 511.

Subsection (7). For the use of this power *see* Fitness to Drive in the introduction. A provisional driving licence may be obtained by a person so disqualified: s. 98(3). For the effects of driving in breach of such a licence *see* the commentary to that section.

Evidence in such form as may be prescribed. *See* the Motor Vehicles (Driving Licences) Regulations, 1971. S.I. 1971, No. 451.

Appeal against disqualification and rule for determining end of period thereof

94. (1) A person disqualified by an order of a magistrates' court under s. 93, of this Act or s. 19 of the Transport Act 1981 may appeal against the order in the same manner as against a conviction.

(2) Any court in England or Wales (whether a magistrates' court or another) which makes an order disqualifying a person may, if it thinks fit, suspend the disqualification pending an appeal against the order.

(3) (*Scotland.*)

(3A) Where a court exercises its power under subs. (2) or subs. (3) above it shall send notice of the suspension to the Secretary of State; and for the purposes of this section any such notice shall be sent in such manner and to such address and shall contain such particulars as the Secretary of State may determine.

(4) In determining the expiration of the period for which a person is disqualified by an order of a court made in consequence of a conviction, any time after the conviction during which the disqualification was suspended or he was not disqualified shall be disregarded.

(*as amended by the Road Traffic Act 1974, sch. 6, the Transport Act 1981, sch. 9*)

COMMENTARY

This section is necessary because the general right of appeal contained in the Magistrates' Courts Act 1980, s. 108 specifically excludes orders in the making of which magistrates have no discretion. Discretionary orders of disqualification carry a right of appeal under the Act of 1980; mandatory orders under this section.

The Crown Court and the High Court have power to suspend disqualification pending appeal or on application for certiorari under s. 94A of the Act (not contained herein).

Removal of disqualification

95. (1) Subject to the provisions of this section, a person who by an order of a court is disqualified may apply to the court by which the order was made to remove the disqualification, and on any such application the court may, as it thinks proper, having regard to the character of the person disqualified and his conduct subsequent to the order, the nature of the offence, and any other circumstances of the case, either by order remove the disqualification as from such date as may be specified in the order or refuse the application.

(2) No application shall be made under subs. (1) above for the removal of a disqualification before the expiration of whichever is relevant of the following periods from the date of the order by which the disqualification was imposed, that is to say—

(a) two years, if the disqualification is for less than four years,
(b) one half of the period of the disqualification if it is for less than 10 years but not less than four years,
(c) five years in any other case;

and in determining the expiration of the period after which under this subsection a person may apply for the removal of a disqualification, any time after the conviction during which the disqualification was suspended or he was not disqualified shall be disregarded.

(3) Where an application under subs. (1) above is refused, a further application thereunder shall not be entertained if made within three months after the date of the refusal.

(4) If under this section a court orders a disqualification to be removed, the court shall cause particulars of the order to be endorsed on the licence, if any, previously held by the applicant and the court shall in any case have power to order the applicant to pay the whole or any part of the costs of the application.

(5) The foregoing provisions of this section shall not apply where the disqualification was imposed by order under s. 93(7) of this Act, s. 5(7) of the Road Traffic Act, 1962, or s. 104(3) of the Road Traffic Act, 1960.

COMMENTARY

The procedure for making application under this section contained in the Magistrates' Courts Rules 1981, r. 101(2) is in mandatory terms and does not appear to permit the refusal of a summons upon application. Mandamus has issued where justices have refused a summons under this provision on the ground that a recent application was successful in reducing the period of disqualification: *R.* v. *Manchester JJ, ex parte Gaynor* [1956] 1 All E.R. 610. But note subs. (3). The procedure is by way of complaint which imports the provisions of the Magistrates' Courts Act 1980, ss. 51-57 and the Magistrates' Courts Rules 1981, r. 14, but note subs. (4) as to costs.

This provision should not be referred to by a court when passing sentence: *R.* v. *Lobley* [1974] 59 Cr. App. R. 63.

This section applies to all disqualifications, whether imposed under mandatory or discretionary powers: *Damer* v. *Davison* [1976] R.T.R. 44. However, justices may if they think fit regard a mandatory disqualification as one which they are somewhat less ready to remove than a discretionary disqualification, *per* Lord Widgery C.J. *ibid.*

Subsection (1): The court by which the order was made. Orders made by the Crown Court on appeal from a magistrates' court may seemingly be removed by the magistrates: Magistrates Courts Act 1980, s. 110.

Subsection (2). In determining the expiration of the period the words "by virtue of that order" should be read at the end of this subsection. Thus a period during which an earlier disqualification was operative should be regarded as a period during which the later disqualification was not effective: *R.* v. *Metropolitan Magistrates, ex parte Everett* (1968) 132 J.P. 6.

Where consecutive disqualifications were ordered under the Road Traffic Act 1972, s. 93(5) the periods must be treated as one continuous period for the purpose of this section: Transport Act 1981, s. 70.

Any other case. This includes a disqualification for life.

Disqualification to prevent duplication of licences

97. A person is disqualified for obtaining a licence authorizing him to drive a motor vehicle of any class so long as he is the holder of another licence authorizing him to drive a motor vehicle of that class, whether the licence is suspended or not.

Effect of disqualification

98. (1) Where the holder of a licence is disqualified by an order of court, the licence shall be treated as being revoked with effect from the beginning of the period of disqualification; and for this purpose, if the holder of the licence appeals against the order and the disqualification is suspended under s. 94 of this Act, the period of disqualification shall be treated as beginning on the day on which the disqualification ceases to be suspended.

(2) A licence obtained by any person who is disqualified shall be of no effect.

(3) Notwithstanding anything in this Part of this Act, a person disqualified by order of a court under s. 93(7) of this Act, s. 5(7) of the Road Traffic Act 1962 or s. 104(3) of the Road Traffic Act 1960 shall (unless he is disqualified otherwise than by virtue of such an order) be entitled to obtain and to hold a provisional licence and to drive a motor vehicle in accordance with the conditions subject to which the provisional licence is granted.

(*as amended by the Road Traffic Act 1974, sch. 3*).

COMMENTARY

Subsection (3): Disqualified . . . under s. 93(7). Driving in breach of a condition of a provisional licence while an order for disqualification under s. 93(7) is in force constitutes the offence of driving whilst disqualified: *Scott* v. *Jelf* [1974] Crim. L.R. 191. And *see Hunter* v. *Coombs* (1962) 126 J.P. 300.

Endorsement of Licences

101. (1) Subject to subs. (2) below, where a person is convicted of an offence—

(*a*) under a provision of this Act specified in col. 1 of Part I of sch. 4 to this Act in relation to which there appears in col. 6 of that Part the word "obligatory" or the word "obligatory" qualified by conditions relating to the offence; and

(*b*) where the said word "obligatory" is so qualified, the conditions are satisfied in the case of the offence of which he is convicted;

or where a person is convicted of such an offence specified in Part II or Part III of that schedule (any such offence being in this section referred to as an "offence involving obligatory endorsement"), the court shall order that there shall be endorsed on any licence held by him particulars of the conviction and, if the court orders him to be disqualified, particulars of the disqualification, and, if the court does not order him to be disqualified, the particulars and penalty points required by section 19(1) of the Transport Act 1981; and the endorsement may be produced as prima facie evidence of the matters endorsed.

(2) If the court does not order the said person to be disqualified, the court need not make an order under subs. (1) above as aforesaid if for special reasons it thinks fit not to do so.

(3) An order that any particulars or penalty points are to be endorsed on any licence held by the convicted person shall, whether he is at the time the holder of a licence or not, operate as an order that any licence he may then hold or may subsequently obtain shall be so endorsed until he becomes entitled under subs. (7) below to have a licence issued to him free from the particulars or penalty points.

(4) A person who is prosecuted for an offence involving obligatory endorsement and who is the holder of a licence, shall either—

(*a*) cause it to be delivered to the clerk of the court not later than the day before the date appointed for the hearing, or

(*b*) post it, at such a time that in the ordinary course of post it would be delivered not later than that day, in a letter duly addressed to the clerk and either registered or sent by the recorded delivery service, or

(c) have it with him at the hearing;

and if he is convicted of the offence the court shall, before making any order under subs. (1) above, require the licence to be produced to it; and if the offender has not posted the licence or caused it to be delivered as aforesaid and does not produce it as required then, unless he satisfies the court that he has applied for a new licence and has not received it, he shall be guilty of an offence and the licence shall be suspended from the time when its production was required until it is produced to the court and shall, while suspended, be of no effect.

(4A) Where a person is convicted of an offence involving obligatory endorsement and his licence is produced to the court, then in determining what order to make in pursuance of the conviction the court may take into consideration particulars of any previous conviction or disqualification endorsed on the licence and any penalty points endorsed on it which are to be taken into account under s. 19(3) of the Transport Act 1981.

(5) On the issue of a new licence to a person any particulars or penalty points ordered to be endorsed on any licence held by him shall be entered on the licence unless he has become entitled under subs. (7) below to have a licence issued to him free from these particulars or penalty points.

(6) If a person whose licence has been ordered to be endorsed with any particulars or penalty points and who has not previously become entitled under subs. (7) below to have a licence issued to him free from those particulars or penalty points applied for or obtains a licence without giving particulars of the order, he shall be guilty of an offence and any licence so obtained shall be of no effect.

(7) A person whose licence has been ordered to be endorsed (whether under this section or a previous enactment) shall be entitled to have a new licence issued to him free from the endorsement if, after the end of the period for which the endorsement remains effective, he applies for a new licence in pursuance of subsection (1) of section 88 of this Act, surrenders any subsisting licence, pays the prescribed fee and satisfies the other requirements of that subsection.

(7A) An endorsement ordered on a person's conviction of an offence remains effective—
(a) if an order is made for the disqualification of the offender, until four years have elapsed since the conviction; and
(b) if no such order is made, until either four years have elapsed since the commission of the offence or such an order is made;
but if the offence was one under section 1 or 2 of this Act the endorsement remains in any case effective until four years have elapsed since the conviction, and if it was one under section 5(1) or 6(1)(a) of this Act or was one under section 8(7) of this Act involving obligatory disqualfication, the endorsement remains effective until eleven years have elapsed since the conviction.

(8), (9) (Scotland.)

(as amended by the Road Traffic Act 1974, sch. 3, the Transport Act 1981, sch. 9.)

COMMENTARY

Subsection (1). The particulars to be endorsed on the licence are prescribed in the Magistrates' Courts Rules 1981, r. 32, infra. The requirements of this subsection as to statement and recording of reasons are directory and not mandatory: Brown v. Dyerson (1968) 132 J.P. 495.

In proceedings on a written plea of guilty under the Magistrates' Courts Act 1980, s. 12, the court may not look behind the prosecutor's statement of facts to determine whether an offence (of driving without a licence) is endorsable or not: *R. v. Liskerrett JJ, ex parte Child* [1972] R.T.R. 141.

Subsection (2): Special reasons. The grounds must be stated in open court and recorded in the register: s. 105(1), *infra*.

For a solicitor's articled clerk to exceed the speed limit in order to get to court to instruct counsel has been held to be a special reason for not endorsing on the ground that it is in the public interest that courts should not be kept waiting: *Police Prosecutor* v. *Humphreys* [1970] Crim. L.R. 234. The fact that an act of careless driving constitutes only a slight degree of blameworthiness cannot be a special reason for not ordering endorsement: *Nicholson* v. *Brown* [1974] R.T.R. 177; *Hawkins* v. *Roots*; *Hawkins* v. *Smith* [1976] R.T.R. 49. Ignorance of traffic regulations (significance of lamp post spacing) cannot be a special reason: *Walker* v. *Rawlinson* [1976] R.T.R. 94. Nor can the fact that the limit is often mistaken: *Jones* v. *Nicks* [1977] R.T.R. 72. The mere fact that the breach of the law is a little one cannot be a special reason any more than the lack of intention to commit an offence of strict liability (speeding). However the court must weigh the gravity of the offence against the gravity of the problem with which the driver had to deal (in this case anxiety about the passenger's state of health) and to this extent the minor nature of the offence cannot be ignored: *Marks* v. *West Midlands Police* [1981] R.T.R. 471.

While the prosecutor may not be heard on the quantum of sentence it is within his jurisdiction to bring to the justices' attention the jurisdictional limits on their powers to decide whether to endorse or disqualify, *per* Donaldson LJ in *Barnes* v. *Gevaux* [1981] R.T.R. 236 at p.241.

And *see* generally the note to s. 93, *supra*.

Subsection (4). This provision should work in this way: "The charge being one which involves an obligatory endorsement on conviction, the justices first of all proceed to the question of conviction or no. If they decide to convict, then it being an obligatory endorsement case, they order an endorsement under subs. (1), and the moment they have taken those two steps they can call for the licence and look at it. Having called for the licence and looked at it, they can then take whatever action is appropriate in regard to any endorsements which an inspection of the licence reveals," *per* Lord Widgery CJ in *Dyson* v. *Ellison* (1975) 139 J.P. 191.

The suspension arises automatically and not by direction of the court. The only case on which it does not arise is where the accused satisfies the court that he has applied for a new licence and not received it. Driving a motor vehicle while a licence is suspended under this provision is an offence contrary to s. 84(1) of the Act.

Where a person has been required under this subsection to produce a licence to the court and fails to do so a constable may require him to produce it and, upon it being produced, may seize it and deliver it to the court: Road Traffic Act 1972, s. 161(3A.)

Combination of disqualification and endorsement with probation orders and order for discharge in England and Wales

102. (1) Notwithstanding anything in s. 13(3) of the Powers of Criminal Courts Act 1973 (conviction of an offender placed on probation or discharged to be disregarded for the purposes of enactments relating to disqualification), a court in England or Wales which on convicting a person of an offence involving obligatory or discretionary disqualification makes a probation order or an order discharging him absolutely or conditionally may on that occasion also exercise any power conferred, and shall also discharge any duty imposed, on the court by ss. 93 or 101 of this Act or s. 19 of the Transport Act 1981.

(2) A conviction is respect of which a court in England or Wales has ordered a person to be disqualified or of which particulars have been endorsed on any licence held by him shall, notwithstanding anything in s. 13(1) of the said Act of 1973 (conviction of offender placed on probation or discharged to be disregarded for the purpose of subsequent proceedings), be taken into account in determining his liability to punishment or disqualification for any offence involving obligatory or discretionary disqualification committed subsequently.

(*as amended by the Powers of Criminal Courts Act 1973, sch. 5, the Transport Act 1981, sch. 9.*)

COMMENTARY

Subsection (1) For an application of this principle *see Owen* v. *Imes* [1972] R.T.R. 489.

Interim disqualification on committal in England or Wales under s. 56 of Criminal Justice Act 1967, etc.

103. (1) Where under s. 56(1) of the Criminal Justice Act 1967 or any enactment to which that section applies a magistrates' court commits an offender to the Crown Court and by reason of the provisions of the said s. 56 the magistrates' court does not exercise its power or discharge its duty under s. 93 of this Act or s. 19 of the Transport Act 1981 of ordering the offender to be disqualified, it may nevertheless order him to be disqualified until the court to which he is committed has dealt with him in respect of the offence.

(2) Where a court in England or Wales makes an order under subs. (1) above in respect of any person, it shall require him to produce to the court any licence, and any Northern Ireland licence, held by him and shall cause such licence to be sent to the clerk of the court to which he is committed; and if he does not produce any such licence as required he shall be guilty of an offence.

(3) Where a court in England or Wales makes any such order in respect of any person, ss. 101(1), 105(2) to (4) and 111(2) of this Act shall not apply in relation to the order, but the court shall send notice of the order to the Secretary of State; and the court to which he is committed shall, if it determines not to order him to be disqualified under s. 93 of this Act or s. 19 of the Transport Act 1981, send notice of the determination to the Secretary of State.

(4) Where a person is committed to the Crown Court under the said s. 56 or any enactment to which that section applies to be dealt with in respect of an offence involving obligatory or discretionary disqualification and no order is made in his case under subs. (1) above, s. 101(4) of this Act shall apply to him as it applies to a person who is prosecuted for such an offence and convicted before that court.

(5) A period of disqualification imposed on any person by virtue of s.56(5) of the said Act of 1967 (exercise by the court to which a person is committed for sentence, etc., of certain powers of magistrates' courts) shall be treated as reduced by any period during which he was disqualified by reason only of an order made under subs. (1) above; but a period during which he was so disqualified shall not be taken into account under this subsection for the purpose of reducing more than one other period of disqualification.

(6) A notice sent by a court to the Secretary of State in pursuance of subs. (3) above shall be sent in such manner and to such address and contain such particulars as the Secretary of State may determine.

(7) In this section "Northern Ireland licence" means a licence under any such provision as is mentioned in s. 111(1) of this Act.

(as amended by the Transport Act 1981, sch. 9)

COMMENTARY

Notice of an interim disqualification must be given to the Crown Court: Magistrates' Courts Rules 1981, r. 32(2).

Information as to date of birth and sex

104. (1) If on convicting a person of an offence involving obligatory or discretionary disqualification or of such other offence as may be prescribed, the court does not know his date of birth, the court shall order him to state that date in writing.

(2) It shall be the duty of a person giving a notification to the clerk of a court in pursuance of s. 12(2) of the Magistrates' Courts Act 1980 (which relates to pleas of guilty in the absence of the accused) in respect of an offence mentioned in subs. (1) above to include in the notification a statement of the date of birth and the sex of the accused; and in a case where the foregoing provisions of this subsection are not complied with the court shall, if on convicting the accused it does not know his date of birth or sex, order him to furnish that information in writing to the court.

(3) Nothing in s. 56(5) of the Criminal Justice Act 1967 (which provides that where a magistrates' court commits a person to another court under subs. (1) of that section, certain of its powers and duties are transferred to that other court) shall apply to any duty imposed upon a magistrates' court by the foregoing provisions of this section.

(4) A person who knowingly fails to comply with an order under subs. (1) or (2) above shall be guilty of an offence.

(5) Where in accordance with this section a person has stated his date of birth to a court or in such a notification as aforesaid, the Secretary of State may serve on that person a notice in writing requiring him to furnish the Secretary of State—

(a) with such evidence in that person's possession or obtainable by him as the Secretary of State may specify for the purpose of verifying that date; and

(b) if his name differs from his name at the time of his birth, with a statement in writing specifying his name at that time;

and a person who knowingly fails to comply with a notice under this subsection shall be guilty of an offence.

(6) (Scotland).

(as amended by the Road Traffic Act 1974, sch. 3; the Magistrates' Courts Act 1980, sch. 7).

COMMENTARY

Where the offender is not present in court a notice must be sent to him: Magistrates' Courts Rules 1981, r. 108.

Subsections (4) and (5): An offence. Punishable in accordance with sch. 4 of the Act.

Supplementary provisions as to disqualifications and endorsements

105. (1) In any case where a court exercises its powers under s.93 or 101 of this Act or s.19 of the Transport Act 1981 not to order any disqualification or endorsement or to order disqualification for a shorter period than would otherwise be required, it shall state the grounds for doing so in open court and, if it is a magistrates' court or, in Scotland, a court of summary jurisdiction, shall cause them to be entered in the register (or, in Scotland, record) of its proceedings.

(2) Where a court orders the endorsement of any licence held by a person it may, and if the court orders him to be disqualified it shall, send the licence, on its being produced to the court, to the Secretary of State; and if the court orders the endorsement but does not send the licence to the Secretary of State it shall send him notice of the endorsement.

(3) Where on an appeal against any such order the appeal is allowed, the court by which the appeal is allowed shall send notice thereof to the Secretary of State.

(4) Where a person is disqualified by order of a court under s. 93(7) of this Act, s. 5(7) of the Road Traffic Act 1962 or s. 104(3) of the Road Traffic Act 1960, then on the issue to him of a licence, there shall be added to the endorsed particulars of the disqualification a statement that the person disqualified has,

since the order was made, passed the prescribed test.

(5) A notice sent by a court to the Secretary of State in pursuance of this section shall be sent in such manner and to such address and contain such particulars as the Secretary of State may determine, and a licence so sent in pursuance of this section shall be sent to such address as the Secretary of State may determine.

(as amended by the Criminal Justice Act 1972, sch. 5, the Powers of Criminal Courts Act 1973, sch. 5, the Transport Act 1981, sch. 9.)

COMMENTARY

Subsection (1). The provisions of this subsection are directory only and not mandatory and non-compliance therewith is not therefore a ground of appeal: *Brown* v. *Dyerson* [1968[3 All E.R. 39; *Barnes* v. *Gevaux* [1981] R.T.R. 236.

Subsection (2). The codes for offences and sentences are set out at the end of this chapter.

Interpretation of Part III

110. In this Part of this Act, except where the context otherwise requires the following expressions have the meanings hereby assigned to them respectively, that is to say—

'Community licence' means a document issued in respect of a member State other than the United Kingdom by an authority of that or another member State (including the United Kingdom) authorising the holder to drive a motor vehicle, not being–

(a) a document containing a statement to the effect that that or a previous document was issued in exchange for a document issued in respect of a State other than a member State, or

(b) a document in any of the forms for an international driving permit annexed to the Paris Convention on Motor Traffic of 1926, the Geneva Convention on Road Traffic of 1949 or the Vienna Convention on Road Traffic of 1968;

. . .

"disqualified" means disqualified for holding or obtaining a licence, and "disqualification" shall be construed accordingly;
"licence" means a licence to drive a motor vehicle granted under this Part of this Act;

. . .

"offence involving obligatory disqualification" has the meaning given to it by s. 93(1) of this Act;
"offence involving discretionary disqualification" has the meaning given to it by s. 93(2) of this Act;

. . .

"prescribed" means prescribed by regulations;
"provisional licence" means a licence granted by virtue of s. 88(2) of this Act;
"regulations" means regulations made under s. 107 of this Act;

. . .

"test of competence to drive" means such a test conducted under s. 85 of this Act;

(as amended by the Road Traffic Act 1976, schs. 1 and 3, the Driving Licences (Community Driving Licence) Regulations 1982).

Provisions as to Northern Ireland drivers' licences

111. (1) If the Secretary of State certifies that satisfactory provision is made by the law of Northern Ireland for the granting of licences to drive and for a person to cause or permit the holder of such a licence to drive motor vehicles, it shall be lawful for the holder of such a licence to drive and for a person to cause or permit the holder of such a licence to drive in Great Britain a motor vehicle of any class which he is authorized by that licence to drive, and which he is not disqualified from driving under this Part of this Act, notwithstanding that he is not the holder of a licence under this Part of this Act:

Provided that any such driver shall be under the like obligation to produce such a licence as if it had been a licence granted under this Part of this Act, and the provisions of this Act as to the production of licences granted thereunder shall apply accordingly.

(2) The holder of any such licence who by an order of the court is disqualified for holding or obtaining a licence under this Part of this Act shall produce the licence so held by him to the court within such time as the court may determine, and the court shall, on production of the licence, forward it to the Secretary of State; and if the holder fails to produce the licence within such time as aforesaid, he shall be guilty of an offence.

(3) If the holder of any such licence is convicted of an offence and the court orders particulars of the conviction to be endorsed in accordance with s. 101 of this Act, the court shall send those particulars to the Secretary of State.

(*as amended by the Road Traffic Act 1976, sch. 1, the Road Traffic (Drivers' Ages and Hours of Work) Act 1976, sch. 1.*).

COMMENTARY

Subsection (1): Certifies. By the Northern Ireland Drivers Licence Certificate 1930 as applied by s. 205(2) and sch. 10.

Prosecution and punishment of offences

177. (1) Part I of sch.4 to this Act shall have effect with respect to the prosecution and punishment of the offences against the provisions of this Act specified in column 1 of that Part of that schedule or regulations made thereunder (of which the general nature is indicated in col. 2 thereof).

(2) In relation to any such offence—

(*a*) column 3 of that Part of that schedule shows whether the offence is punishable on summary conviction or on indictment or either in one way or the other;

(*b*) column 4 of that Part of that schedule shows the maximum punishment by way of fine or imprisonment which may be imposed on a person convicted of the offence in the way specified in relation thereto in col. 3 (that is to say, summarily or on indictment), any reference in col. 4 to a period of years or months being construed as a reference to a term of imprisonment of that duration;

(*c*) column 5 of that Part of that schedule shows in relation to which offences the court is required by s. 93(1) or empowered by s. 93(2) of this Act to order the person convicted to be disqualified for holding or obtaining a licence to drive a motor vehicle under Part 111 of this Act, any reference in col. 5 to obligatory disqualification importing such a requirement and any reference therein to discretionary disqualification importing such a power;

(*d*) column 6 of that Part of that schedule shows in relation to which offences the court is required by s. 101(1) of this Act to order that particulars of the conviction, and, if the court orders him to be disqualified, particulars of the disqualification, are to be endorsed on any licence held by him; and

(*e*) column 7 of that Part of that schedule applies to such of the offences against provisions of this Act specified in col. 1 as are indicated by entries against those offences in col. 7 the additional provisions of this Act (relating to the prosecution and trial of such offences) specified in those entries.

(3) Parts II and III of that schedule show offences which are not offences under this Act and are not punishable thereunder but on conviction of which the court is required by s. 93(1) or, as the case may be, empowered by s. 93(2) of this Act to order the person convicted to be disqualified for holding or obtaining a licence to drive a motor vehicle under Part III of the Act and, in either case, required by s. 101(1) of this Act to order that particulars of the conviction, and, if the court orders him to be disqualified, particulars of the disqualification, are to be endorsed on any licence held by him.

(4) The provisions contained in Part IV of that schedule (being provisions as the alternative verdicts, as to charges which may be preferred when a person is not convicted of an offence charged and as to the conviction of persons of certain offences despite the absence of a warning of prosecution of those offences) shall have effect in relation to such of the offences against provisions of this Act specified in col. 1 of Part I of that schedule as are indicated by entries against those offences in col. 7 of that Part; and in Scotland the provisions of para. 3 of Part IV shall have effect also in relation to the offence shown in Part II of that schedule.

(5) Part V of that schedule shall have effect for the interpretation of that schedule.

(6) Any reference in that schedule to a section by its number only is a reference to a section of this Act.

(*as amended by the Transport Act 1981, sch. 12.*)

Penalty for breach of regulations

178. If a person acts in contravention of or fails to comply with any regulations made by the Secretary of State under this Act (other than regulations made under s. 20, 43, 54, including that section as applied by s. 55, or 133 thereof) and contravention thereof, or failure to comply therewith, is not made an offence under any other provision of this Act, he shall for each offence be liable on summary conviction to a fine not exceeding level 3 on the standard scale.

(*as amended by the Road Traffic Act 1974, s. 21(2), the Criminal Justice Act 1982, ss. 40, 46*).

Restrictions on prosecutions for certain offences

179. (1) This section applies to—

(*a*) any offence under this Act to which it is applied by col. 7 of Part I of sch. 4 to this Act;

(*aa*) any offence under subs. (4) of s. 13 of the Road Traffic Regulation Act 1967 (traffic regulation on special roads) consisting of failure to observe a speed limit imposed by regulations under that section; and

(*b*) any offence under s. 77(7) of the Road Traffic Regulation Act 1967 or punishable by virtue of s. 78A of that Act.

(2) Subject to the following provisions of this section and to the provisions of para. 5, 6 and 7 of Part IV of the said sch. 4, where a person is prosecuted for an offence to which this section applies he shall not be convicted unless either—

(a) he was warned at the time the offence was committed that the question of prosecuting him for some one or other of the offences to which this section applies would be taken into consideration; or

(b) within 14 days of the commission of the offence a summons (or, in Scotland, a complaint) for the offence was served on him; or

(c) within the said 14 days a notice of the intended prosecution specifying the nature of the alleged offence and the time and place where it is alleged to have been committed, was—

(i) in the case of an offence against s. 17 or 18 of this Act, served on him,

(ii) in the case of any other offence, served on him or on the person, if any, registered as the keeper of the vehicle at the time of the commission of the offence;

and the notice shall be deemed for the purposes of para. (c) above to have been served on any person if it was sent by registered post or recorded delivery service addressed to him at his last known address, notwithstanding that the notice was returned as undelivered or was for any other reason not received by him.

(3) The requirement of subs. (2) above shall in every case be deemed to have been complied with unless and until the contrary is proved.

(3A) The requirement of subs. (2) above shall not apply in relation to an offence if, at the time of the offence or immediately thereafter, an accident occurs owing to the presence on a road of the vehicle in respect of which the offence was committed.

(4) Failure to comply with the requirement of subs. (2) above shall not be a bar to the conviction of the accused in a case where the court is satisfied—

(a) that neither the name and address of the accused nor the name and address of the registered keeper, if any, could with reasonable diligence have been ascertained in time for a summons or, as the case may be, a complaint to be served or for a notice to be served or sent in compliance with the said requirement; or

(b) that the accused by his own conduct contributed to the failure.

(as amended by the Road Traffic Act 1974, sch. 6, and the Criminal Law Act 1977, sch. 12.)

COMMENTARY

Subsection (2)(a): Warned at the time. This is a matter of fact: *Jeffs* v. *Wells* (1936) 100 J.P.N. 406; *Jollye* v. *Dale* (1960) 124 J.P. 333; *R.* v. *O'Kike* [1978] R.T.R. 489 (warning given 2 ½ hours later not unreasonable in circumstances). The question as to whether or not the chain of cir-cumstances was unbroken and all that took place was connected with the accident is a useful test: *R.* v. *Stacey* [1982] R.T.R. 20.
Subsection (2)(c): Specifying the nature of the offence. The notice need not quote the section, nor need the prosecutor at that time have made up his mind as to which offence to charge: *Milner* v. *Allen* (1933) 97 J.P. 111. (Summons for careless driving unobjectionable where notice referred to dangerous driving).
The time and place. It is a matter of degree whether the information is sufficient: *Young* v. *Day* (1959) 123 J.P. 317.
Subsection (2): Sent. The notice must be dispatched in time to reach the accused in the ordinary course of post within the 14-day period: *Nicholson* v. *Tapp* (1972) 136 J.P.N. 718.

Subsection (3). Although it may be convenient for the defendant to raise the objection under this section as a preliminary point he may do so at any time in the trial: *R.* v. *Edmonton Justices, ex parte Brooks* (1960) 124 J.P. 409. *Prima facie* a motorist is warned under this section if on an objective view, words addressed to him would be expected to have been heard and understood by him, but it is open to the motorist to prove that he did not hear, understand or appreciate the words and that he was not therefore warned: *Gibson* v. *Dalton* [1980] R.T.R. 410. The defence must show that neither alternative has been complied with: *Saunders* v. *Scott* (1961) 125 J.P. 419. It is not enough for the accused to raise a doubt: *Offen* v. *Ranson* [1980] R.T.R. 484.

Subsection (3A): Accident. *Cf.* the meaning of this term in *The Chief Constable of Staffordshire* v. *Lees* [1981] R.T.R. 506.

Subsection (4): Reasonable diligence. Provided that the prosecuting authority use reasonable diligence and cannot discover the name and address of the driver at the relevant time, or the name and address of the registered keeper within the 14 days thereafter, their failure, by reason of such inability, to serve the notice unders subs. (2) within that period of 14 days is no longer a bar to conviction. Under the section no such second period of 14 days is provided for at all. If the first period of 14 days passes, and if the prosecuting authority can bring themselves within the provisions of subs. (4), then the absence of any notice of intended prosecution within the first period of 14 days is neither here nor there, and the prosecution can proceed and be heard in the appropriate way: *Haughton* v. *Harrison* [1976] R.T.R. 208.

Time within which summary proceedings for certain offences must be commenced

180.   Summary proceedings for an offence under this Act to which this section is applied by col. 7 of Part I of sch. 4 to this Act may be brought within a period of six months from the date on which evidence sufficient in the opinion of the prosecutor to warrant the proceedings came to his knowledge; but no such proceedings shall be brought by virtue of this section more than three years after the commission of the offence.

For the purposes of this section a certificate signed by or on behalf of the prosecutor and stating the date on which such evidence as aforesaid came to his knowledge shall be conclusive evidence of that fact; and a certificate stating that matter and purporting to be signed shall be deemed to be so signed unless the contrary is proved.

Evidence by certificate

181   (1) In any proceedings in England or Wales for an offence under this Act to which this section is applied by col. 7 or Part I of sch. 4 to this Act or which is punishable by virtue of s. 178 thereof or for an offence against any other enactment relating to the use of vehicles on roads a certificate in the prescribed form, purporting to be signed by a constable and certifying that a person specified in the certificate stated to the constable—

(*a*)   that a particular motor vehcile was being driven or used by, or belonged to, that person on a particular occasion, or

(*b*)   that a particular motor vehicle on a particular occasion was used by, or belonged to, a firm in which that person also stated that he was at the time of the statement a partner, or

(*c*)   that a particular motor vehicle on a particular occasion was used by, or belonged to, a corporation of which that person also stated that he was at the time of the statement a director, officer or employee,

shall be admissible as evidence for the purpose of determining by whom the vehicle was being driven or used, or to whom it belonged, as the case may be, on that occasion.

(2) Nothing in subs. (1) above shall be deemed to make a certificate admissible as evidence in proceedings for an offence except in a case where and to the like extent to which oral evidence to the like effect would have been admissible in those proceedings.

(3) Nothing in subs. (1) above shall be deemed to make a certificate admissible as evidence in proceedings for an offence—

(a) unless a copy thereof has, not less than seven days before the hearing or trial, been served in the prescribed manner on the person charged with the offence, or

(b) if that person, not later than three days before the hearing or trial or within such further time as the court may in special circumstances allow, serves a notice in the prescribed form and manner on the prosecutor requiring attendance at the trial of the person who signed the certificate.

(4) In this section "prescribed" means prescribed by rules made by the Secretary of State by statutory instrument.

Admissibility of records as evidence

182. (1) A statement contained in a document purporting to be—

(a) a part of the records maintained by the Secretary of State in connexion with any functions exercisable by him by virtue of Part III of this Act or a part of any other records maintained by the Secretary of State with respect to vehicles; or

(b) a copy of a document forming part of those records; or

(c) a note of any information contained in those records,

and to be authenticated by a person authorized in that behalf by the Secretary of State shall be admissible in any proceedings as evidence of any fact stated therein to the same extent as oral evidence of that fact is admissible in those proceedings.

(2) In subs. (1) above "document" and "statement" have the same meanings as in s. 10(1) of the Civil Evidence Act 1968, and the reference to a copy of a document shall be construed in accordance with s. 10(2) of that Act; but nothing in this subsection shall be construed as limiting to civil proceedings the references to proceedings in subs. (1) above.

(2A) In any case where—

(a) any such statement as is referred to in subs. (1) above is produced to a magistrates' court in any proceedings for an offence involving obligatory or discretionary disqualification, within the meaning of Part III of this Act, and

(b) the statement specifies an alleged previous conviction of an accused person of any such offence or any order made on the conviction, and

(c) it is proved to the satisfaction of the court, on oath or in such manner as may be prescribed by rules under s. 15 of the Justices of the Peace Act 1949, that not less than seven days before the statement is so produced a notice was served on the accused, in such form and manner as may be so prescribed specifying the previous conviction or order and stating that it is proposed to bring it to the notice of the court in the event of, or, as the case may be, in view of his conviction, and

(d) the accused is not present in person before the court when the statement is so produced,

the court may take account of the previous conviction or order as if the accused had appeared and admitted it.

(3) Nothing in the foregoing provisions of this section shall enable evidence to be given with respect to any matter other than a matter of the prescribed description.

(4) (*Scotland*)

(*as amended by the Road Traffic Act 1974, s. 13(3), the Transport Act 1981, sch. 9.*)

COMMENTARY

Subsection (2A): Prescribed by Rules. In the Magistrates' Courts Rules 1981, r. 72.
Notice.... prescribed. In the Vehicle and Driving Licence Records (Evidence) Regulations 1970.

Proof, in summary proceedings, of identity of driver of vehicle.

183.   Where on the summary trial in England or Wales of an information an offence under this Act to which this section is applied by col. 7 of Part I of sch. 4 to this Act or which is punishable by virtue of s. 178 thereof or for an offence against any other enactment relating to the use of vehicles on roads—

(a) it is proved to the satisfaction of the court, on oath or in manner prescribed by rules made under s. 15 of the Justices of the Peace Act 1949, that a requirement under s. 168(2) of this Act to give information as to the identity of the driver of a particular vehicle on the particular occasion to which the information relates has been served on the accused by post; and

(b) a statement in writing is produced to the court purporting to be signed by the accused that the accused was the driver of that vehicle on that occasion

the court may accept that statement as evidence that the accused was the driver of that vehicle on that occasion.

THE ROAD TRAFFIC ACT 1972

SCHEDULE 4

(as amended by the Heavy Commercial Vehicles (Controls and Regulations) Act 1973, the Road Traffic Act 1974, the Road Traffic (Drivers' Ages and Hours of Work) Act 1976, sch. 1, and 3, the Secretary of State for Transport Order 1976, the Criminal Law Act 1977, s. 28, schs. 1, 5, 6, 12 and 13, the Transport Act 1978, sch. 3, the Magistrates' Courts Act 1980, sch. 7, the Transport Act 1981, ss. 26, 27(4), 28(2), sch. 9, the Criminal Justice Act 1982, ss. 38-40, 46, sch. 3, the Transport Act 1982, ss. 57(2), 63.)

(Sections 93, 101, 177, 179, 180, 181, 183.)

PROSECUTION AND PUNISHMENT OF OFFENCES
PART I OFFENCES UNDER THIS ACT

1 Provision creating offence	2 General nature of offence	3 Mode of prosecution	4 Punishment	5 Disqualification	6 Endorsement	7 Additional provisions
1	Causing death by reckless driving.	On indictment	5 years or, in the case of a conviction by a court in Scotland other than the High Court of Judiciary, 2 years.	Obligatory.	Obligatory.	s. 181 and para. 3 of Part IV of this schedule apply.
2	Reckless driving.	(a) Summarily	6 months or the prescribed sum (within the meaning of s. 32 of the Magistrates' Courts Act 1980) [£2,000] or both.	(a) Obligatory if committed within 3 years after a previous conviction of an offence under s. 1 or 2.	Obligatory.	ss. 179, 181 and 183 and paras. 1 2, 3, 5, and 6 of Part IV of this schedule apply.
		(b) On indictment	2 years or a fine or both.	(b) Discretionary if committed otherwise than as mentioned in para. (a) above.		

1 Provision creating offence	2 General nature of offence	3 Mode of prosecution	4 Punishment	5 Disqualification	6 Endorsement	7 Additional provisions
3	Careless and inconsiderate, driving.	Summarily.	Level 4 on the standard scale	Discretionary.	Obligatory.	ss. 179, 181 and paras. 3A, 4, 5 and 7 of Part IV of this schedule apply.
5(1)	Driving or attempting to drive when unfit to drive through drink or drugs.	Summarily.	6 months or level 5 on the standard scale or both.	Obligatory.	Obligatory.	ss. 181 and 183 and para. 3 of Part IV of this schedule apply.
5(2)	Being in charge of a motor vehicle when unfit to drive through drink or drugs.	Summarily.	3 months or level 4 on the standard scale or both.	Discretionary.	Obligatory.	ss. 181 and 183 and para. 3 of Part IV of this schedule apply.
6(1)	Driving or attempting to drive with blood-alcohol concentration above the prescribed limit.	Summarily.	6 months or level 5 on the standard scale or both.	Obligatory.	Obligatory.	ss. 181 and 183 and para. 3 of Part IV of this schedule apply.

6(2)	Being in charge of a motor vehicle with blood-alcohol concentration above the prescribed limit.	Summarily.	3 months or level 4 on the standard scale or both.	Discretionary.	Obligatory.	ss. 181 and 183 and para. 3 of Part IV of this schedule apply.
8(3)	Failing to provide a specimen of breath for a breath test.	Summarily.	Level 3 on the standard scale.	—	—	ss. 181 and 183 apply.
9(3)	Failing to provide a specimen of blood or urine for a laboratory test.*	Summarily.	(i) Where it is shown that at the relevant time (as defined in Part V of this schedule) the offender was driving or attempting to drive a motor vehicle on a road or other public place, 6 months or level 5 on the standard scale or both. (ii) Where in any other case it is shown that at that time the offender was in charge of a motor vehicle on a road or other public place, 3 months or level 4 on the standard scale or both.	(a) Obligatory if it is shown as mentioned in para. (i) of col. 4; (b) Discretionary if it is not so shown.	Obligatory.	ss. 181 and 183 and para. 3 of Part IV of this schedule apply.

1 Provision creating offence	2 General nature of offence	3 Mode of prosecution	4 Punishment	5 Disqualification	6 Endorsement	7 Additional provisions
14	Motor racing and speed trials on highways.	Summarily.	Level 4 on the standard scale	Obligatory.	Obligatory.	ss. 181 and 183 apply.
15	Other unauthorized or irregular competitions or trials on highways.	Summarily.	Level 3 on the standard scale	—	—	
16	Carrying passenger on motor cycle contrary to s. 16.	Summarily.	Level 3 on the standard scale	Discretionary.	Obligatory.	ss. 181 and 183 apply.
17	Reckless cycling.	Summarily.	Level 3 on the standard scale	—	—	ss. 179, 181 and 183 apply.
18	Careless and inconsiderate cycling.	Summarily.	Level 1 on the standard scale	—	—	ss. 179, 181 and 183 and paras. 3A, 4 and 7 of Part IV of this schedule apply.
19	Cycling when unfit through drink or drugs.	Summarily.	Level 1 on the standard scale	—	—	ss. 181 and 183 apply.

20	Unauthorized or irregular cycle racing or trials of speed on highways.	Summarily.	Level 1 on the standard scale	—	—	ss. 181 and 183 apply.
21	Carrying passenger on bicycle contrary to s. 21.	Summarily.	Level 1 on the standard scale	—	—	ss. 181 and 183 apply.
22	Failing to comply with traffic directions.	Summarily.	Level 3 on the standard scale	Discretionary, if committed in respect of motor vehicle described in the entry in col. 5 relating to offence.	Obligatory, if committed as described in failure to comply with a direction of a constable or traffic warden, or an indication given by a sign specified for the purposes of this paragraph in regulations made by the Secretary of State for Wales and the Secretary of State for Scotland acting jointly.	ss. 179, 181 and 183 apply.

The standard scale of fines is as follows:-

Level on the scale	Amount of fine
1	£50
2	£100
3	£400
4	£1,000
5	£2,000

Criminal Justice Act, 1982, s.37

1 Provision creating offence	2 General nature of offence	3 Mode of prosecution	4 Punishment	5 Disqualification	6 Endorsement	7 Additional provisions
23	Pedestrian failing to stop when directed by constable regulating traffic.	Summarily.	Level 3 on the standard scale	—	—	—
24	Leaving vehicles in dangerous positions.	Summarily.	Level 3 on the standard scale	Discretionary, if committed in respect of a motor vehicle.	Obligatory if committed in respect of a motor vehicle.	ss. 179, 181 and 183 apply.
25(4)	Failing to stop after accident and give particulars or report accident.	Summarily.	Level 5 on the standard scale	Discretionary.	Obligatory.	ss. 181 and 183 apply.
26(2)	Obstructing inspection of vehicles after accident.	Summarily.	Level 3 on the standard scale	—	—	—
29	Tampering with motor vehicles.	Summarily.	Level 3 on the standard scale	—	—	s. 181 applies.
30(1)	Holding or getting on to vehicle in order to be carried.	Summarily.	Level 1 on the standard scale	—	—	s. 181 applies.

30(2)	Holding on to vehicle in order to be towed.	Summarily.	Level 1 on the standard scale	—	ss. 181 and 183 apply.
31(1)	Dogs on designated roads without being held on lead.	Summarily.	Level 1 on the standard scale	—
32(3)	Driving or riding motor cycles in contravention of regulations requiring wearing of protective headgear.	Summarily.	Level 2 on the standard scale	—
33	Selling, etc., helmet not of prescribed type as helmet for affording protection for motor cyclists.	Summarily.	Level 3 on the standard scale	—
33AA(3)	Contravention of regulations with respect to use of head-worn appliances on motor cycles	Summarily.	Level 2 on the standard scale	—

The standard scale of fines is as follows:-

Level on the scale	Amount of fine
1	£50
2	£100
3	£400
4	£1,000
5	£2,000

Criminal Justice Act, 1982, s.37

1 Provision creating offence	2 General nature of offence	3 Mode of prosecution	4 Punishment	5 Disqualification	6 Endorsement	7 Additional provisions
33AA(4)	Selling, etc., appliance not of prescribed type as approved for use on motor cycles.	Summarily.	Level 3 on the standard scale			
33A	Driving or riding in a motor vehicle in contravention of regulations requiring wearing of seat belts.	Summarily.	Level 3 on the standard scale			Sections 181 and 183 apply.
33B	Driving motor vehicle with child in the front not wearing seat belt.	Summarily.	Level 3 on the standard scale			Sections 181 and 183 apply.
34(4)	Causing, etc., heavy motor vehicles to be driven or to haul without proper crew.	Summarily.	Level 3 on the —	—		s. 181 applies.
35(3)	Unauthorized motor vehicle trial on footpaths or bridleways.	Summarily.	Level 3 on the —	—		ss. 181 and 183 apply.
36	Driving motor vehicles elsewhere than on roads.	Summarily.	Level 3 on the —			ss. 181 and 183 apply.

36A	Prohibition of parking of vehicles on verges and footways.	Summarily.	Level 3 on the standard scale	—	ss. 181 and 183 apply.
36B	Prohibition of parking of vehicles on verges, central reservations and footways.	Summarily.	Level 3 on the standard scale	—	ss. 181 and 183 apply.
40(5)	Contravention of construction and use regulations.	Summarily.	Level 5 on the standard scale in the case of an offence of using, or causing or permitting the use of, a goods vehicle or a vehicle adapted to carry more than eight passengers— (a) so as to cause, or to be likely to cause danger by the condition of the vehicle or its parts or accessories, number of passengers carried by it, or the weight, distribution, packing or adjustment of its load; or	Discretionary if committed by using, or causing or permitting the use of, any motor vehicle or trailer— (a) as described in para. (a) or para. (c) in the entry in col. 4 relating to this offence; or (b) in breach of a construction and use requirement as to brakes, steering-gear or tyres; except where the offender proves that he did not know and had no reasonable cause to suspect that the facts of the case were such that the offence would be committed.	Obligatory if committed as described in the entry in col. 5 relating to this offence, but subject to the exception there mentioned.

The standard scale of fines is as follows:-

Level on the scale	Amount of fine
1	£50
2	£100
3	£400
4	£1,000
5	£2,000

Criminal Justice Act, 1982. s.37

1 Provision creating offence	2 General nature of offence	3 Mode of prosecution	4 Punishment	5 Disqualification	6 Endorsement	7 Additional provisions
	(b) in breach of a construction and use requirement as to brakes, steering gear, tyres or any description of weight; or (c) for any purpose for which it is so unsuitable as to cause or to be likely to cause danger;		Level 5 on the standard scale in the case of an offence of carrying on a goods vehicle a load which, by reason of its insecurity or its position, is likely to cause danger; level 4 on the standard scale in any other case.	Discretionary if committed by carrying on a motor vehicle or trailer a load which, by reason of its insecurity or position, is likely to cause danger, but subject to the exception above.		

44(1)	Using, etc., vehicle without required test certificate being in force.	Summarily.	(a) level 4 on the standard scale in the case of a vehicle adapted to carry more than 8 passengers; and (b) level 3 on the standard scale in any other case.	ss. 181 and 183 apply.
Regulations under 45(7)	Contravention of requirement of regulations that driver of goods vehicle being tested be present throughout test or drive vehicle, etc., which is declared by regulations to be an offence.	Summarily.	Level 3 on the standard scale.	ss. 181 and 183 apply.
46(1)	Using, etc., goods vehicle without required plating certificate being in force.	Summarily.	Level 3 on the standard scale	ss. 181 and 183 apply.
46(2)	Using, etc., goods vehicle without required goods vehicle test certificate being in force.	Summarily.	Level 4 on the standard scale.	ss. 181 and 183 apply.

The standard scale of fines is as follows:-

Level on the scale	Amount of fine
1	£50
2	£100
3	£400
4	£1,000
5	£2,000

Criminal Justice Act, 1982, s.37

1 Provision creating offence	2 General nature of offence	3 Mode of prosecution	4 Punishment	5 Disqualification	6 Endorsement	7 Additional provisions
46(3)	Using, etc., goods vehicle with alteration thereto required to be but not notified to Secretary of State under regulations under s. 45.	Summarily.	Level 3 on the standard scale	—	—	ss. 181 and 183 apply.
50(5)	Contravention of regulations requirement of regulations that driver of goods vehicle being tested after notifiable alteration be present throughout test and drive vehicle, etc., which is declared by regulations to be an offence.	Summarily.	Level 3 on the standard scale	—	—	—
51(1)	Using, etc., ...vehicle without required certificate being in force showing that it complies with type approval requirements applicable to it.	Summarily.	Level 4 on the standard scale	—	—	ss. 181 and 183 apply.

51(2)	Using, etc., certain ... vehicles for drawing trailer when plating certificate does not specify maximum laden weight for vehicle and trailer.	Summarily.	Level 3 on the standard scale	—	ss. 181 and 183 apply.
51(3)	Using, etc., ... vehicle with alterations thereto required to be put not notified to Secretary of State under regulations under s. 48.	Summarily.	Level 3 on the standard scale	—	ss. 181 and 183 apply.
53(4)	Obstructing testing of vehicle by examiner on road or failing to comply with requirements of s. 53 or sch. 3.	Summarily.	Level 3 on the standard scale	—	
54(5) (including application by 55 (3))	Failure of owner of vehicle discovered to be defective on roadside test or further test to give required certificate or declaration.	Summarily.	Level 3 on the standard scale	—	

The standard scale of fines is as follows:-

Level on the scale	Amount of fine
1	£50
2	£100
3	£400
4	£1,000
5	£2,000

Criminal Justice Act, 1982, s.37

1 Provision creating offence	2 General nature of offence	3 Mode of prosecution	4 Punishment	5 Disqualification	6 Endorsement	7 Additional provisions
54(6) (including application by 53 (3)	Failure of person in charge of vehicle on roadside test or further test to give particulars of owners.	Summarily.	Level 3 on the standard scale	—	—	—
55(5)	Obstructing further testing of vehicle by Secretary of State's officer or failing to comply with requirements of s. 55 of para. 3 or of sch. 3.	Summarily.	Level 3 on the standard scale	—	—	
56(3)	Obstructing goods vehicle examiner inspecting goods vehicle or entering premises where such vehicle believed to be.	Summarily.	Level 3 on the standard scale	—	—	
56(5)	Person in charge of stationary goods vehicle refusing etc., vehicle to proceed to nearby place of inspection.	Summarily.	Level 3 on the standard scale	—	—	

57(9)	Driving, etc., goods vehicle in contravention of prohibition on driving it as being unfit for service or refusal, neglecting or otherwise failing to comply with a direction to remove a goods vehicle found overloaded.	Summarily.	Level 5 on the standard scale	—	ss. 181 and 183 apply.
59(3)	Contravention of regulations requiring goods vehicle operator to inspect, and keep records of inspections of, goods vehicle.	Summarily.	Level 3 on the standard scale	—	—
60(3)	Selling, etc., unroadworthy vehicle or trailer or altering vehicle or trailer so as to make it unroadworthy.	Summarily.	Level 5 on the standard scale	—	—

The standard scale of fines is as follows:-

Level on the scale	Amount of fine
1	£50
2	£100
3	£400
4	£1,000
5	£2,000

Criminal Justice Act, 1982, s.37

1 Provision creating offence	2 General nature of offence	3 Mode of prosecution	4 Punishment	5 Disqualification	6 Endorsement	7 Additional provisions
60A(1)	Fitting of defective or unsuitable vehicle parts.	Summarily.	Level 5 on the standard scale	—	—	—
60A(3)	Selling defective or unsuitable vehicle parts.	Summarily.	Level 4 on the standard scale	—	—	—
60A(6)	Obstructing examiner testing vehicles to ascertain whether defective or unsuitable part has been fitted, etc.	Summarily.	Level 3 on the standard scale	—	—	—
61(2)	Obstructing examiner testing condition of used vehicles at sale rooms, etc.	Summarily.	Level 3 on the standard scale	—	—	—
62	Selling, etc., goods vehicle without required certificate being in force showing that it complies with type approval requirements applicable to it.	Summarily.	Level 5 on the standard scale	—	—	—

	Offence	Mode of prosecution	Punishment	Disqualification	Endorsement	
66(5)	Selling, etc., pedal cycle in contravention of regulations as to brakes, bells, etc.	Summarily.	Level 3 on the standard scale	—	—	
81(1)	Causing, etc., vehicle to be on road in contravention of provisions as to lighting etc., of vehicles.	Summarily.	Level 3 on the standard scale	—	—	ss. 181 and 183 apply.
81(2)	Selling, etc., wrongly made tail lamps or reflectors.	Summarily.	Level 5 on the standard scale	—	—	
84(1)	Driving without a licence.	Summarily.	Level 3 on the standard scale	Discretionary, if the offence is committed by driving a motor vehicle in a case where either no licence authorizing the driving of that vehicle could have been granted to the offender* or, if a provisional (but no other) licence to drive it could have been granted to him, the driving would not have complied with the conditions thereof.	Obligatory, if committed as described in the entry in col. 5 relating to this offence.*	ss. 181 and 183 apply.

The standard scale of fines is as follows:-

Level on the scale	Amount of fine
1	£50
2	£100
3	£400
4	£1,000
5	£2,000

Criminal Justice Act, 1982. s.37

*See R. v. Reading Justices, ex parte Bendall [1982] R.T.R. 30

1 Provision creating offence	2 General nature of offence	3 Mode of prosecution	4 Punishment	5 Disqualification	6 Endorsement	7 Additional provisions
84(2)	Causing or permitting a person to drive without a licence.	Summarily.	Level 3 on the standard scale	—	—	—
88(6)	Failing to comply with any conditions prescribed for driving under provisional licence or full licence treated as a provisional licence.	Summarily.	Level 3 on the standard scale	Discretionary.	Obligatory.	ss. 181 and 183 apply
89(3)	Driving licence holder failing, when his particulars become incorrect, to surrender licence and give particulars.	Summarily.	Level 3 on the standard scale	—	—	—
91(1)	Driving with uncorrected eyesight.	Summarily.	Level 3 on the standard scale	Discretionary.	Obligatory.	—

Provision	Offence	Mode of prosecution	Punishment	Disqualification	Endorsement
91(2)	Refusing to submit to test of eyesight.	Summarily.	Level 3 on the standard scale	Discretionary.	—
99(a)	Obtaining driving licence while disqualified.	Summarily.	Level 3 on the standard scale.	—	—
99(b)	Driving while disqualified.	(a) Summarily. 6 months or the prescribed sum (within the meaning of s.32 of the Magistrates' Courts Act 1980) £2,000 or both. (b) On indictment 12 months or a fine or both.	Discretionary.	Obligatory.	ss. 181 and 183 apply.
101(4) (including application by 103(4))	Failing to produce licence to court for endorsement on conviction of offence involving obligatory endorsement or on committal for sentence, etc., for offence involving obligatory or discretionary disqualification when no interim disqualification ordered.	Summarily.	Level 3 on the standard scale.	—	—

The standard scale of fines is as follows:-

Level on the scale	Amount of fine
1	£50
2	£100
3	£400
4	£1,000
5	£2,000

Criminal Justice Act, 1982, s.37

1 *Provision creating offence*	2 *General nature of offence*	3 *Mode of prosecution*	4 *Punishment*	5 *Disqualification*	6 *Endorsement*	7 *Additional provisions*
101(6)	Applying for or obtaining licence without giving particulars of current endorsement.	Summarily.	Level 3 on the standard scale	—	—	—
104(4)	Failing to state to court or give information as to date of birth or sex.	Summarily.	Level 3 on the standard scale	—	—	—
104(5)	Failing to furnish Secretary of State with evidence of date of birth, etc.	Summarily.	Level 3 on the standard scale	—	—	—
111(2)	Failing to produce to court Northern Ireland driving licence.	Summarily.	Level 4 on the standard scale	—	—	—
112(1)	Driving heavy goods vehicle without heavy goods vehicle licence.	Summarily.	Level 4 on the standard scale	—	—	—

112(2)	Causing or permitting a person to drive heavy goods vehicle without heavy goods vehicle licence.	Summarily.	Level 4 on the standard scale	s. 181 applies.
114(3)	Failing to comply with conditions of heavy goods vehicle driver's licence.	Summarily.	Level 3 on the standard scale	—
Regulations under 119(2)	Contravention of regulations about heavy goods vehicle driver's licences which is declared by regulation to be an offence.	Summarily.	Level 3 on the standard scale	ss. 181 and 183 apply.
126(3)	Giving of paid driving instruction by unregistered and unlicensed persons or their employees.	Summarily.	Level 4 on the standard scale	—

The standard scale of fines is as follows:-

Level on the scale	Amount of fine
1	£50
2	£100
3	£400
4	£1,000
5	£2,000

Criminal Justice Act, 1982, s.37

1 Provision creating offence	2 General nature of offence	3 Mode of prosecution	4 Punishment	5 Disqualification	6 Endorsement	7 Additional provisions
135 (2)	Unregistered instructors using title or displaying badge, etc., prescribed for registered instructor, and employers using such title, etc., in relation to his un-registered instructor or issuing misleading advertisement, etc.	Summarily.	Level 4 on the standard scale	—	—	—
136	Failure of instructor to surrender to Registrar certificate or licence.	Summarily.	Level 3 on the standard scale	—	—	—
143	Using motor vehicle while uninsured or unsecured against third party risks.	Summarily.	Level 4 on the standard scale	Discretionary.	Obligatory.	ss. 180, 181 and 183 apply.
147 (4)	Failing to surrender certificate of insurance or security to insurer on cancellation or make statutory declaration of loss or destruction.	Summarily.	Level 3 on the standard scale	—	—	—

151 (2)	Failing to give information, or wilfully making false statement, as to insurance or security when claim made.	Summarily.	Level 4 on the standard scale	—	—
159.	Failing to stop vehicle when required by constable.	Summarily.	Level 3 on the standard scale	—	ss. 181 and 183 apply.
160 (1)	Refusing or neglecting to allow motor vehicle or trailer to be weighed, etc.	Summarily.	Level 5 on the standard scale	—	ss. 181 and 183 apply.
161 (4)	Failing to produce driving licence to constable or to state date of birth.	Summarily.	Level 3 on the standard scale	—	ss. 181 and 183 apply.
161 (5)	Failing to furnish Secretary of State with evidence of date of birth, etc.	Summarily.	Level 3 on the standard scale	—	—

The standard scale of fines is as follows:-

Level on the scale	Amount of fine
1	£50
2	£100
3	£400
4	£1,000
5	£2,000

Criminal Justice Act, 1982. s.37

1 Provision creating offence	2 General nature of offence	3 Mode of prosecution	4 Punishment	5 Disqualification	6 Endorsement	7 Additional provisions
162.(1)	Failing to give constable certain names and addresses or to produce certificate of insurance or certain test and other like certificates.	Summarily.	Level 3 on the standard scale	—	—	ss. 181 and 183 apply.
162 (3)	Supervisor of learner-driver failing to give constable certain names and addresses.	Summarily.	Level 3 on the standard scale	—	—	s. 181 applies.
164 (1)	Refusing to give, or giving false, name and address in case of reckless, dangerous, careless or inconsiderate driving or cycling.	Summarily.	Level 3 on the standard scale	—	—	ss. 181 and 183 apply.
165	Pedestrian failing to give constable his name and address after failing to stop when directed by constable controlling traffic.	Summarily.	Level 1 on the standard scale	—	—	—

166 (1)	Failure by driver, in case of accident involving injury to another, to produce evidence of his insurance or security or to report accident.	Summarily.	Level 3 on the standard scale	—	ss. 181 and 183 apply.
167	Failure by owner of motor vehicle to give police information for verifying compliance with requirement of compulsory insurance or security.	Summarily.	Level 4 on the standard scale	—	ss. 181 and 183 apply.
168 (3)	Failure of person keeping vehicle and others to give police information as to identity of driver, etc., in the case of certain offences.	Summarily.	Level 3 on the standard scale	—	
169 (1)	Forgery, etc., of licences, certificates, test certificates, certificates of insurance and other documents and things.	(a) Summarily.	£2,000	—	s. 180 applies.
		(b) On indictment.	2 years.	—	

The standard scale of fines is as follows:-

Level on the scale	Amount of fine
1	£50
2	£100
3	£400
4	£1,000
5	£2,000

Criminal Justice Act, 1982, s.37

1 Provision creating offence	2 General nature of offence	3 Mode of prosecution	4 Punishment	5 Disqualification	6 Endorsement	7 Additional provisions
170 (1)	Making false statements in connection with licences under this Act and with registration as an approved driving instructor.	Summarily.	Level 4 on the standard scale	—	—	s. 170.(2)
170 (2)	Making or making use of false statements relating to goods vehicles.	Summarily.	Level 4 on the standard scale	—	—	
170 (3)	Producing false evidence or making false declaration in connection with applications for vehicle excise licences for vehicles required to have test certificates.	Summarily.	Level 4 on the standard scale	—	—	
170 (5)	Making false statements as to the remedying of defects discovered in vehicles on roadside tests.	Summarily.	Level 4 on the standard scale	—	—	

170(5)	Making, or making use of, false entry in records required to be kept in condition of goods vehicles.	Summarily.	Level 4 on the standard scale	—	—
170(5A)	Failure to notify Secretary of State of onset of, or deterioration in, relevant or prospective disability.	Summarily.	Level 3 on the standard scale	—	s. 180 applies.
170(6)	Making false statement or withholding material information in order to obtain the issue of insurance certificates, etc.	Summarily.	Level 4 on the standard scale	—	s. 180 applies.
171(1)	Issuing false insurance certificates, etc., or false test certificates.	Summarily.	Level 4 on the standard scale	—	s. 180 applies.

The standard scale of fines is as follows:—

Level on the scale	Amount of fine
1	£50
2	£100
3	£400
4	£1,000
5	£2,000

Criminal Justice Act, 1982, s.37

1 Provision creating offence	2 General nature of offence	3 Mode of prosecution	4 Punishment	5 Disqualification	6 Endorsement	7 Additional provisions
172	Using goods vehicle with unauthorised weights as well as authorised weights marked thereon.	Summarily.	Level 3 on the standard scale	—	—	s. 180 applies.
174	Personation of, or of person employed by, authorised examiner.	Summarily.	Level 3 on the standard scale	—	—	—
175	Taking, etc., in Scotland a motor vehicle without authority or, knowing that it has been so taken, driving it or allowing oneself to be carried in it without authority.	(a) Summarily. (b) On indictment	3 months or £2000. 12 months or a fine or both.	Discretionary.	Obligatory.	ss. 181 and 183 and para. 8 of Part IV of this schedule apply.
187(2)	Failing to attend, give evidence or produce documents to, inquiry held by Secretary of State, etc.	Summarily.	Level 3 on the standard scale	—	—	—

para. 5(1) Applying warranty to protective helmet in defending proceedings under section 33 where no warranty given.	Summarily.	Level 3 on the standard scale —
para. 5(2) Giving to purchaser of protective helmet a false warranty in case where warranty might be defence in proceedings under section 33.	Summarily.	Level 3 on the standard scale —

The standard scale of fines is as follows:-

1	£50
2	£100
3	£400
4	£1,000
5	£2,000

Criminal Justice Act, 1982, s.37

PART II

Other Offence Involving Obligatory Disqualification and Endorsement

Manslaughter or, in Scotland culpable homicide by driver of a motor vehicle.

PART III

Other Offences Involving Discretionary Disqualification and Obligatory Endorsement

1. Stealing or attempting to steal a motor vehicle.

2. An offence, or attempt to commit an offence, in respect of a motor vehicle under s, 12 of the Theft Act 1968 (taking conveyance without consent of owner etc. or, knowing it has been so taken, driving it or allowing oneself to be carried in it).

3. An offence under s, 25 of the Theft Act 1968 (going equipped for stealing, etc.) committed with reference to the theft or taking of motor vehicles.

4. An offence under s. 13(4) of the Road Traffic Regulation Act 1967 (contravention of traffic regulations on special roads) committed in respect of a motor vehicle otherwise than by unlawfully stopping or allowing the vehicle to remain at rest on a part of a special road on which vehicles are in certain circumstances permitted to remain at rest.

5. An offence under s. 23(5) of the Road Traffic Regulation Act 1967 (contravention of pedestrian crossing regulations) committed in respect of a motor vehicle.

6. An offence under s. 25(2) of the Road Traffic Regulation Act 1967 (failure to obey sign exhibited by school crossing patrol) committed in respect of a motor vehicle.

7. An offence under s. 26(6) or 26A(5) of the Road Traffic Regulation Act 1967 (contravention of order prohibiting or restricting use of street playground by vehicles) committed in respect of a motor vehicle.

8. An offence punishable by virtue of s. 78A of the Road Traffic Regulation Act 1967 (speeding offences under that and other Acts).

PART IV

Supplementary Provisions as to Prosecution, Trial and Punishment of Offences

1–3. (*Scotland*).

3A. (*Crown Court*)

4. Where a person is charged in England or Wales before a magistrates' court with an offence under s. 2 or with an offence under s. 17, and the court is of opinion that the offence is not proved, then, at any time during the hearing or immediately thereafter the court may, without prejudice to any other powers possessed by the court, direct or allow a charge for an offence under s. 3 or, as the case may be, s. 18 to be preferred forthwith against the defendant and may thereupon proceed with that charge, so however that he or his solicitor or counsel shall be informed of the new charge and be given an opportunity, whether by way of cross-examining any witness whose evidence has already been given against the defendant or otherwise, of answering the new charge, and the court shall, if it considers that the defendant is prejudiced in his defence by reason of the new charge's being so preferred, adjourn the hearing.

5. (*Crown Court*)

6. (*Scotland*)

7. A person may be convicted of an offence against ss. 3 or 18 notwithstanding that the requirement of s. 179(2) has not been satisfied as respects that offence where—

    (*a*) the charge for the offence has been preferred against him by virtue of para. 4 above, and

    (*b*) the said requirement has been satisfied, or does not apply, as respects the alleged offence against s. 2 or, as the case may be, s. 17.

8. (*Scotland*)

PART V

Interpretation

1. For the purposes of the entries in Part I of this Schedule relating to an offence under s. 5(1), 6(1) or 9(3) "the relevant time" means—

    (*a*) in relation to a person required under s. 8(1) to provide a specimen of breath for a breath test, the time when he was so required;

    (*b*) in relation to a person required under s. 8(2) to provide such a specimen, the time of the accident;

    (*c*) in relation to a person arrested under s. 5(5), the time of his arrest.

2. "Construction and use requirement" has the same meaning for the purposes of this schedule as it has for the purposes of Part II of this Act.

(*as amended by the Road Traffic Act 1974, sch. 5, the Road Traffic Act 1976, schs. 1 and 3, the Criminal Law Act 1977, sch. 1, 5, 6, 12.*)

COMMENTARY

Attempts at offences contained in this schedule (except where specifically listed) are not covered by its provisions: *Bell* v. *Ingham* [1968] 2 All E.R. 333. It is submitted that this decision must now be read in light of the Criminal Attempts Act 1981, s. 4 (1) (c), which provides that a person guilty of attempting to commit an offence triable either way shall be liable on summary conviction to any penalty to which he would have been liable on summary conviction of that offence. An aider and abettor of a scheduled offence, however, is punishable as a principal in the first degree: Magistrates' Courts Act 1980, s. 44, except as regards mandatory disqualifications: Road Traffic Act 1972, s. 3(6).

Part III. Stealing or attempting to steal a motor vehicle. It is submitted that this extends to other offences under the Theft Act when stealing comprises an essential part thereof, viz. burglary and stealing and robbery.

Part IV. The prohibition against prosecution of summary offences out of time contained in the Magistrates' Courts Act 1980, s. 127, does not apply to restrict the preferment of a charge under para. 4 of this Part of the schedule: *R.* v. *Coventry Justices, ex parte Sayers* [1979] R.T.R. 22.

THE TRANSPORT ACT 1981

By virtue of s. 30(2) of this Act these sections shall be construed as if they were contained in Part III of the Road Traffic Act 1972.

Disqualification for repeated offences.

19. (1) Where a person is convicted of an offence involving obligatory or discretionary disqualification and the court does not order him to be disqualified (whether on that or any other conviction) but orders particulars of the conviction to the endorsed under s. 101 of the 1972 Act, the endorsement ordered shall include—

(a) particulars of the offence, including the date when it was committed; and
(b) the number of penalty points shown in respect of the offence in sch. 7 to this Act (or, where a range of numbers is so shown, a number falling within the range);

but if a person is convicted of two or more such offences the number of penalty points to be endorsed in respect of those of them that were committed on the same occasion shall be the number or highest number that would be endorsed on a conviction of one of those offences.

(2) Where a person is convicted of an offence involving obligatory or discretionary disqualification and the penalty points to be taken into account under subs. (3) number 12 or more, the court shall order him to be disqualified for not less than the minimum period defined in subs. (4) unless the court is satisfied, having regard to all the circumstances not excluded by subs. (6), that there are grounds for mitigating the normal consequences of the conviction and thinks fit to order him to be disqualified for a shorter period or not to order him to be disqualified.

(3) The penalty points to be taken into account on the occasion of a person's conviction are—

(a) any that on that occasion will be ordered to be endorsed on any licence held by him or would be so ordered if he were not then ordered to be disqualified; and
(b) any that were on a previous occasion ordered to be so endorsed, unless the offender has since that occasion and before the conviction been disqualified, whether under subs. (2) or under s. 93 of the 1972 Act;

but if any of the offences was committed more than three years before another the penalty points in respect of that offence shall not be added to those in respect of the other.

(4) The minimum period referred to in subs. (2) is—

(a) six months if no previous disqualification imposed on the offender is to be taken into account; and
(b) one year if one, and two years if more than one, such disqualification is to be taken into account;

and a previous disqualification imposed on an offender is to be taken into account if it was imposed within the three years immediately preceding the commission of the latest offence in respect of which penalty points are taken into account under subs. (3).

(5) Where an offender is convicted on the same occasion of more than one offence involving obligatory or discretionary disqualification—

(a) not more than one disqualification shall be imposed on him under subs. (2); and
(b) in determining the period of the disqualification the court shall take into account all the offences; and
(c) for the purposes of any appeal any disqualification imposed under subs. (2) shall be treated as an order made on the conviction of each of the offences.

(6) No account is to be taken under subs. (2) of—

(a) any circumstances that are alleged to make the offence or any of the offences not a serious one;
(b) hardship, other than exceptional hardship; or
(c) any circumstances which, within the three years immediately preceding the conviction, have been taken into account under that subsection in ordering

the offender to be disqualified for a shorter period or not ordering him to be disqualified.

(7) For the purposes of this section—

(a) an order for endorsement which was made before the commencement of this section counts as an order made in pursuance of subs. (1) for the endorsement of three penalty points, unless a disqualification was imposed on the offender on that or any subsequent occasion; and

(b) circumstances which have been taken into account under s. 93(3) of the 1972 Act in ordering an offender to be disqualified for a shorter period or not ordering him to be disqualified shall be treated as having been so taken into account under subs. (2) of this section.

(8) (*Power to make orders*)

(9) References in this section to disqualification do not include a disqualification imposed under s. 103 of the 1972 Act (interim disqualification on committal to Crown Court) or s. 44 of the Powers of Criminal Courts Act 1973 (disqualification by Crown Court where vehicles was used for commission of offence).

COMMENTARY

A list of common mistakes made by the Crown Court in applying this section is contained in *R*. v. *Kent (Peter)* [1983] 1 W.L.R. 794. For the construction of this section *see* s. 30(2), *infra*.

Transitional proceedings. See *Porter* v. *Manning* (1984) *The Times*, March 23 and *King* v. *Lumgo* noted *infra*.

Subsection (1). This subsection contains the obligation to order endorsement of penalty points. The procedure for notifying D.V.L.C. is contained in Home Office circular 85/1982.

Does not order him to be disqualified. See subs. (9) and note thereto.

Committed on the same occasion. The construction of this term must be approached as a matter of common sense: *Johnson* v. *Finbow* [1983] 1 W.L.R. 879 (failing to stop and failing to report an accident held to be committed on the same occasion). It is submitted that strict simultaneity is not essential to the concept of one occasion: the ignoring of a stop sign may be followed almost immediately by an offence of failing to stop after an accident. On the other hand the fact that offences were committed on the same journey does not necessarily mean they were committed on the same occasion if, for example, one was committed in Wigan and one in London.

The highest number. Where one of the offences carries a range of penalty points it will be necessary for the court to determine the point on the range which would be ordered in case this is higher than the penalty points for any other offence committed on the same occasion.

Subsection (2): Convicted. Includes a conviction followed by probation, absolute or conditional discharge: s. 102, Road Traffic Act 1972, s. 102.

An offence. By virtue of the Magistrates' Courts Act 1980, s. 44, an aider and abettor is treated as a principal offender for the purpose of the totting up provisions: *Ullah* v. *Luckhurst* [1977] R.T.R. 401. But note Part I of sch. 7.

The minimum period. See subs. (4). Where the court fails to disqualify under this subsection through ignorance of the qualifying convictions where there is no inherent jurisdiction to re-open the matter on a subsequent conviction: cf. *R*. v. *Northants JJ, ex parte Nicholson* [1973] Crim. L.R. 702. But the Magistrates' Courts Act 1980, s. 142(1) may give such a power in certain circumstances. Where the failure was due to the defendant's deceit note the powers of the court under s. 21 of the Act, *infra*.

The terms of this subsection do not absolve the court from giving the defendant an opportunity to attend following a written plea of guilty under the Magistrates' Courts Act, 1980, s. 12: cf. *R*. v. *Llandrindod Wells JJ, ex parte Gibson* (1968) 132 J.P. 282.

Grounds for mitigating. It was held under the former legislation that, while in the ordinary way mitigating circumstances are largely circumstances pertaining to the offender, circumstances connected with the offence as opposed to the offender may equally be mitigating grounds: *Baker* v. *Cole* (1971) 135 J.P. 592. While little if any weight attaches to the relative triviality of the qualifying convictions evidence of such facts may not be excluded: *Lambie* v. *Woodage* (1972) 136 J.P. 554. The fact that a speed limit was a new one was held to be insufficient grounds under the previous legislation: *Hill* v. *Howell* [1976]

R.T.R. 270. The sentencing principle that a young offender particularly should not be made subject to a long period of disqualifiation may be grounds for mitigating the normal consequences of conviction: *R.* v. *Thomas (Kevin)* (1983) *The Times*, Oct. 17.

And thinks fit. Note that the mere existence of mitigating circumstances is not in itself sufficient to justify anything other than a disqualification for the minimum period: the court must also think fit to do otherwise.

Subs. (3): Would be so ordered. This refers to the fact that the requirement in subs. (1) that penalty points shall be endorsed does not apply where the court orders a disqualification.

Disqualified. This does not appear to be confined to disqualifications under this section. And see subs. (9).

Subs. (4): Disqualification. This does not appear to be confined to disqualifications under this section. And see subs (9).

Subs. (5): Convicted on the same occasion. It was said in another connection that summary convictions are convictions on separate occasions if they take place at sittings of a court of summary jurisdiction on different days: *R.* v. *Rogers* (1952) 117 J.P. 83.

Subs. (6)(a): Not a serious one. Thus the triviality of an offence cannot be a ground for mitigation.

(b): Exceptional hardship. It is submitted that this means hardship other than is inherent in the fact of being unable to drive.

(c): Under that subsection. And under the Road Traffic Act 1972, s. 93(3): Transport Act 1981, s. 19(7)(a).

Subsection (7)(a). An order for endorsement made prior to the commencement of this Act is counted as three penalty points even if it arises from offences committed on different occasions: *King* v. *Luongo* (1984) *The Times*, March 10.

Subsection (9). It is submitted that this section applies to a disqualification until test passed under the Road Traffic Act 1972, s. 93(7).

Removal of disqualification

20. Where, in pursuance of s. 93(5) of the 1972 Act, a period of disqualification was imposed on an offender in addition to any other period or periods then, for the purpose of determining whether an application may be made under s. 95 of that Act for the removal of either or any of the disqualifications the periods shall be treated as one continuous period of disqualification.

Offender escaping consequences of endorseable offence by deception.

21. (1) Where—

(*a*) in dealing with a person convicted of an endorseable offence a court was deceived regarding any circumstances that were or might have been taken into account in deciding whether or for how long to disqualify him; and

(*b*) the deception constituted or was due to an offence committed by that person;

then, if he is convicted of that offence, the court by or before which he is convicted shall have the same powers and duties regarding an order for disqualification as had the court which dealt with him for the endorseable offence but shall in dealing with him take into account any order made on his conviction of the endorseable offence.

(2) In this section "endorseable offence" means an offence involving obligatory or discretionary disqualification.

Interpretation of Part IV and consequential and minor amendments

30. (1) In this Part "the 1972 Act" means the Road Traffic Act 1972.

(2) Sections 19 to 21 shall be construed as if they were contained in Part III of the 1972 Act, and (without prejudice to the effect of the preceding provision) those sections shall apply to vehicles and persons in the public service of the Crown.

(3) . . .

(*as amended by the Transport Act 1982*)

SCHEDULE 7

PENALTY POINTS

(Section 19)

PART I

OFFENCES WHERE DISQUALIFICATION OBLIGATORY FOR
PRINCIPAL OFFENDERS EXCEPT FOR SPECIAL REASONS

Description of offence   *Number of*
                                             penalty points

Any offence involving obligatory disqualification (within the
meaning of Part III of the Road Traffic Act 1972) –

(a) in the case of an offence which is treated as an offence
     involving discretionary disqualification for the purposes
     of section 93 of that Act by virtue of subsection (6) of
     that section (offences committed by aiding, etc., the com-
     mission of an offence involving obligatory
     disqualification)   10

(b) in any other case   4

Part II

OFFENCES WHERE DISQUALIFICATION DISCRETIONARY

A—Offences under Road Traffic Act 1972

Section of 1972 Act creating offence	Description	Number of penalty points
2.	Reckless driving	10
3.	Careless or inconsiderate driving	2—5
5.(2)	Being in charge of motor vehicle when unfit through drink or drugs.	10
6.(1)(b)	Being in charge of motor vehicle with alcohol above prescribed limit.	10
7.(4)	Failing to provide specimen for breath test.	4
8.(7)	Failing to provide specimen for analysis.	10
16.	Carrying passenger on motor cycle contrary to section 16.	1
22.	Failing to comply with traffic directions.	3
24.	Leaving vehicle in dangerous position.	3
25.(4)	Failing to stop after accident.	5—9
25.(4)	Failing to give particulars or report accident.	4—9
40.(5)	Contravention of construction and use regulations.	3
84.(1)	Driving without licence.	2
88.(6)	Failing to comply with conditions of licence.	2
91.(1)	Driving with uncorrected defective eyesight.	2
91.(2)	Refusing to submit to test of eyesight.	2
99.(b)	Driving while disqualified or under age.	2
99.(b)	Driving while disqualified by order of court.	6
143.	Using, or causing or permitting use of, motor vehicle uninsured and unsecured against third-party risks.	4—8
175.	Taking in Scotland a motor vehicle without consent or lawful authority or driving, or allowing oneself to be carried in, a motor vehicle so taken.	8

9. ROAD TRAFFIC

B—Offences under other Acts
(or, where stated, attempts)

Act and section creating offence or providing for its punishment	Description	Number of penalty points
Road Traffic Regulation Act 1967 s. 13(4).	Contravention of traffic regulations on special roads.	3
Road Traffic Regulation Act 1967 s. 23(5).	Contravention of pedestrian crossing regulations.	3
Road Traffic Regulation Act 1967 s. 25(2).	Failure to obey sign exhibited by school crossing patrol.	3
Road Traffic Regulation Act 1967 s. 26(6), s. 26A(5).	Contravention of order prohibiting or restricting use of street playground by vehicles.	2
Road Traffic Regulation Act 1967, s. 78A.	Exceeding a speed limit.	3
Theft Act 1968, s. 12.	Taking or attempting to take conveyance without consent or lawful authority or driving or attempting to drive a motor vehicle so taken or allowing oneself to be carried in a motor vehicle so taken.	8
Theft Act 1968, s. 25.	Going equipped for stealing with reference to theft or taking of motor vehicle.	8

C—Thefts and attempted thefts

Description of offence	Number of penalty points
	8

Note: The descriptions of offences under A and B above indicate only their general nature.

(as amended and adapted by the Transport Act 1982, s. 58)

COMMENTARY

Offence involving obligatory disqualification. This term is defined in the Road Traffic Act 1972. s.110 and 93(2).

THE MAGISTRATES' COURTS RULES 1981
S.I. 1981 No 552

Endorsement of driving licence

32. (1) *Where a magistrates' court convicts a person of an offence and, under s. 101 of the Road Traffic Act 1972 orders that particulars of the conviction, and, if the court orders him to be disqualified, particulars of the disqualification, shall be endorsed on any licence held by him, the particulars to be endorsed shall include—*

(a) *the name of the petty sessions area for which the court is acting;*
(b) *the date of the conviction and the date on which sentence was passed (if different);*
(c) *particulars of the offence including the date on which it was committed;*
(d) *particulars of the sentence of the court (including the period of disqualification, if any).*

(2) *Where a magistrates' court orders that the licence of an offender be endorsed as mentioned in para. (1) or imposes an interim disqualification as mentioned in r. 17(1)(f) and the clerk of the court knows or is informed of the date of birth and sex of the offender, the clerk shall send the information to the licensing authority which granted the licence.*

COMMENTARY

Paragraph (1). In practice the Secretary of State asks courts to use codes for the petty sessions area, and the offence. *See* Home Office circular 85/1982 dated September 27, 1982. Appendix I of that circular "Endorsable Offence Codes and Penalty Points" is printed *infra*. The Home Office regard this rule as being "effectively amended" by s. 19(1) of the Transport Act 1981: circ. 85/1982.

Application for, and notice to be given of, order under s. 95 of, or para. 7 of Sch. 10 to, Road Traffic Act 1972

101. (1) *An application under s. 95 of, or para. 7 of sch. 10 to, the Road Traffic Act 1972 for an order removing a disqualification or disqualifications for holding or obtaining a licence shall be by complaint.*

(2) *The justice to whom the complaint is made shall issue a summons directed to the chief officer of police requiring him to appear before a magistrates' court acting for the petty sessions area for which the justice is acting to show cause why an order should not be made on the complaint.*

(3) *Where a magistrates' court makes an order under either of the provisions mentioned in para. (1) of the court shall cause notice of the making of the order and a copy of the particulars of the order endorsed on the licence, if any, previously held by the applicant for the order to be sent to the licensing authority to which notice of the applicant's disqualification was sent.*

COMMENTARY

Paragraph (1): By complaint. Thus a summons may issue under s. 51 of the Magistrates' Courts Act 1980 and the hearing will be conducted in accordance with s. 53.
Paragraph (2): Chief officer of police. This means the chief constable or, in the city of London, the commissioner of police of the metropolis: Police Act 1964, sch. 8

Notice of order under s. 104 of Road Traffic Act 1972

108. (1) *Where a magistrates' court makes an order under s. 104 of the Road Traffic Act 1972 that an offender shall inform the court of his date of birth or sex or both and the offender is not present in court, the clerk of the court shall serve notice in writing of the order on the offender.*

(2) *A notice under this rule shall be served by delivering it to the offender by sending it to him by post in a letter addressed to him at his last known or usual place of abode.*

9. ROAD TRAFFIC

ENDORSABLE OFFENCE CODES
AND PENALTY POINTS*

+ indicates obligatory disqualification
except for special reasons when 4 points imposed

Code	Offences	Penalty Points
	Offences in relation to accidents	
AC10	Failing to stop after an accident	5–9
AC20	Failing to give particulars or to report an accident within 24 hours	4–9
AC30	Undefined Accident Offence	4–9
	Offences of driving while disqualified	
BA10	Driving while disqualified	6
BA20	Driving while disqualified as under age	2
	Careless driving offences	
CD10	Driving without due care and attention	2–5
CD20	Driving without reasonable consideration for other road users	2–5
CD30	Driving without due care and attention or without reasonable consideration for other road users (primarily for use by Scottish Courts)	2–5
	Construction and use offences (vehicles or parts dangerous)	
CU10	Using a vehicle with defective brakes	3
CU20	Causing or likely to cause danger by reason of use of unsuitable vehicle or using a vehicle with parts or accessories (excluding brakes, steering or tyres) in dangerous condition	3
CU30	Using a vehicle with defective tyres	3
CU40	Using a vehicle with defective steering	3
CU50	Causing or likely to cause danger by reason of load or passengers	3
CU60	Undefined failure to comply with construction and use regulations	3
	Reckless driving offences	
DD30	Reckless driving	10
DD60	Manslaughter or, in Scotland, culpable homicide while driving a motor vehicle	+
DD70	Causing death by reckless driving	+
	Drink or drugs offences	
DR10	Driving or attempting to drive with alcohol concentration above limit	+

*Appendix 1 to the instructions endorsed with Home Office circular 85/1982.

DR20	Driving or attempting to drive when unfit through drink or drugs	+
DR30	Driving or attempting to drive then refusing to provide a specimen for analysis	+
DR40	In charge of a vehicle with alcohol concentration above limit	10
DR50	In charge of a vehicle when unfit through drink or drugs	10
DR60	Failure to provide a specimen for analysis in circumstances other than driving or attempting to drive	10
DR70	Failing to provide specimen for breath test	4

Insurance offences

| IN10 | Using a vehicle uninsured against third-party risks | 4–8 |

Licence offences

| LC10 | Driving without a licence | 2 |

Miscellaneous offences

MS10	Leaving vehicle in a dangerous position	3
MS20	Unlawful pillion riding	1
MS30	Playstreet offence	2
MS40*	Driving with uncorrected defective eyesight or refusing to submit to a test of eyesight	
MS50	Motor racing on the highway	+
MS60	Offences not covered by other codes	as approp.
MS70	Driving with uncorrected defective eyesight	2
MS80	Refusing to submit to an eye test	2

following the introduction of MS70 and MS80 the offence code MS40 can no longer be used but will continue to appear on existing licences for some time.

Motorway offences

| MW10 | Contravention of special roads regulations (excluding speed limits) | 3 |

Non-endorsable offence

| NE99 | A disqualification under section 24 of the Criminal Justice Act 1972 | |

Pedestrian crossing offences

| PC10 | Undefined contravention of pedestrian crossing regulations (primarily for use by Scottish courts) | 3 |

| PC20 | Contravention of pedestrian crossing regulations with moving vehicle | 3 |
| PC30 | Contravention of pedestrian crossing regulations with stationary vehicle | 3 |

Provisional Licence offences

PL10	Driving without L-plates	2
PL20	Not accompanied by a qualified person	2
PL30	Carrying a person not qualified	2
PL40	Drawing an unauthorised trailer	2
PL50	Undefined failure to comply with the conditions of provisional licence	2

Speed limits offences

SP10	Exceeding goods vehicle speed limit	3
SP20	Exceeding speed limit for type of vehicle (excluding goods/passenger vehicles)	3
SP30	Exceeding statutory speed limit on a public road	3
SP40	Exceeding passenger vehicle speed limit	3
SP50	Exceeding speed limit on a motorway	3
SP60	Undefined speed limit offence	3

TT99   **Special Code**
Only to be used to indicate a disqualification under the penalty points procedure i.e. where the number of penalty points totals 12 or more − including any penalty points "taken into account", but not endorsed because a driver has been disqualified. *NB* When using this code, a date of conviction must always be shown on the licence.

Aiding and/or Abetting and/or Counselling and/or Procuring
Offences as coded above but with zero changed to 2 e.g. UT10 becomes UT12.

Causing or Permitting
Offences as coded above but with zero changed to 4 e.g. PL10 becomes PL14.

Inciting
Offences as coded above but with zero changed to 6 e.g. DD30 becomes DD36.

XX99   **Obsolete Special Code**
To signify a disqualification under the old "totting up" procedure.
Following the introduction of the penalty points scheme this code can no longer be used but will continue to appear on existing licences for some time.

Aiding and/or Abetting and/or Counselling and/or Procuring
Offences as coded above but with zero changed to '2', e.g. UT10 becomes UT12.

Causing or Permitting
Offences as coded above but with zero changed to '4', e.g. PL10 becomes PL14.

Inciting
Offences as coded above but with zero changed to '6', e.g. DD30 becomes DD36.

CHAPTER 10

BINDING OVER

CONTENTS

INTRODUCTION

Since the earliest times it has been recognized that a magistrate has power to bind over persons appearing before him to keep the peace and be of good behaviour. This power is variously described as deriving from the common law or from his commission. In addition, there are a number of statutory powers to bind over, the oldest as well as the most widely used of which is contained in the Justices of the Peace Act, 1361. Whether magistrates' powers may be traced to this Act or to any pre-existing law or to their commission, the statute of Edward III is, in the words of Avory, J, in *Lansbury* v. *Riley* (1914) 77 J.P. 440, at p. 442, "not exhaustive of the jurisdiction of magistrates in such circumstances".

"A binding of a party is a precautionary measure to prevent a future crime, and is not by way of punishment for something past . . . ",*per* Blackburn J. in *Ex parte Davis* (1871) 35 J.P. 551. It is, as has frequently been said, an act of preventive justice. (*See*, for example, the comments of Lord Goddard CJ, in *Wilson* v. *Skeock* (1949) 113 J.P. at p. 295.) Thus a person brought before the court "charged" with conduct likely to cause a breach of the peace may not be fined: *Davies* v. *Griffiths* (1937) 101 J.P. 247.

A person may be bound over, as appropriate, to keep the peace or to be of good behaviour, or, more commonly, to keep the peace *and* be of good behaviour.

Surety of the Peace

"Surety for the peace is the acknowledging of a recognizance (or bond) to the King (taken by a competent judge of record) for the keeping of the peace; and it is called surety, of the word *securitas*, because the party that was in fear, is thereby the more secure and safe": Dalton's *Country Justice* at p. 263, quoted by Lord Lane C.J. in *Veater* v. *Glennon* (1981) 145 J.P. 158.

It has been said that ". . . the surety of the peace shall not be granted, but where there is a fear of some present or future danger, and not merely for a battery or trespass that is past or for any breach of the peace that is past, for this surety of the peace is only for the security of such as are in fear" (Dalt. c. 116). Thus, a threat alone is insufficient; the complainant must actually be in fear of bodily injury: *R.* v. *Dunn* (1840) 4 J.P. 728; even though this is believed to be merely contingent, for example, upon some act of the complainant: *R.* v. *Mallinson* (1851) 15 J.P. 66. However, the court may bind over where there is evidence that an accused had behaved in such a way as to bring about a likelihood of a breach of the peace and provided that the justices came to the conclusion that there was a danger of its repetition: *Mercer* v. *Cox* (1981) NLJ, April 2.

Surety to keep the peace may be required following the persistent holding of meetings likely to provoke disorder: *Davies* v. *Griffiths* (1937) 101 J.P. 247, even where the speaker commits no breach of the peace nor, directly, incites his followers to do so, so long as disorder is the natural consequence of the speaker's acts: *Wise* v. *Dunning* (1902) 66 J.P. 212.

Surety for Good Behaviour

This is wider than the surety of the peace and does not, for example, require proof of actual fear of bodily harm: *Lansbury* v. *Riley, supra*; *R.* v. *Sandbach, ex parte Williams* (1935) 99 J.P. 251 (apprehension only of act contrary to law).

Surety for good behaviour may be required for such acts as inciting persons not to pay their rent: *Dillon's Case* (1886) 31 Sol. Jo. 136; eavesdropping: *R.* v. *County of London Quarter Sessions, ex parte Metropolitan Police Commissioner* (1948) 112 J.P. 118, in circumstances where there is apprehension that the defendant may do anything contrary to law: *R.* v. *Sandbach Justices, ex parte Williams*, (1935) 99 J.P. 251 (persistently obstructing police); and for publishing a libel calculated to cause a breach of the peace: *Haylock* v. *Sparke* (1853) 17 J.P. 262.

No one ought to be bound to be of good behaviour for any rash, quarrelsome or unmannerly words unless they either lead directly to a breach of the peace or to scandalize the government: *Hawkin's Pleas of the Crown.*

Institution of Proceedings

A police officer has, like any citizen, power at common law to arrest anyone committing a breach of the peace in his presence or anyone reasonably suspected of being about to commit or renew a breach of the peace in his presence. Anyone so arrested may be brought before a magistrate to be dealt with in accordance with the Justices of the Peace Act 1361.

The power of a magistrates' court (as opposed to the power of a magistrate) on the complaint of any person to adjudge any other person to enter into a recognizance with or without sureties to keep the peace or be of good behaviour *towards the complainant* must be exercised by order on complaint: Magistrates' Courts Act 1980, s. 115(1). Although it is sometimes assumed that this statute creates a power to bind over it is submitted that it is merely regulatory of the procedure to bind over under pre-existing powers. Where a magistrate acts of his own motion as a measure of preventive justice there is no need for either a complaint or a complainant and the procedure is in the discretion of the magistrate, subject only to the rules of natural justice.

Under the procedure by way of complaint a summons may issue under the Magistrates' Courts Act 1980, s. 51, and if the defendant fails to appear in answer to the summons a warrant may be issued under s. 55, *ibid.* There is no statutory authority for the issue of a warrant at first instance, that is, without the prior issue of a summons, but, as *Stone's Justices' Manual*, 70th edn. (1938), observed at p. 249: "when a complainant satisfies a justice that he is in bodily fear, it is generally considered that the authority given by the Commission of the Peace is sufficient to justify the issue of a warrant."

Conduct of the Proceedings

It is important to distinguish between the court's power to act on the complaint of any person, which is governed by the Magistrates' Courts Act, 1980, s. 115, and its power to act on its own motion under the Act of 1361. "In the former case there must be proof; in the latter case there need not be proof of the matters complained of, but nevertheless the order cannot be made capriciously", *per* Edmund Davies LJ, in *R.* v. *Aubrey-Fletcher, ex parte Thompson* (1969) 133 J.P. 450.

The procedure on a complaint under the Magistrates' Courts Act 1980, s. 115 is laid down in ss. 51-57 of the Act, and the Magistrates' Court Rules 1981, r. 14.

At the hearing, the complainant may give evidence of earlier conduct of the defendant and previous orders: *R.* v. *Dunn* (1840) 4 J.P. 728.

The Taking of the Recognizance

The security offered by the process of binding over consists in the recognizance or bond, entered into either by the principal or by his sureties or both, *per* Lord Lane C.J. in *Veater* v. *Glennon* (1981) 145 J.P. 158. The recognizance need not be taken at the time but may be fixed by the court and taken later by another court or prescribed official: Magistrates' Courts Act 1980, s. 119. If anyone ordered by a magistrates' court under s. 115 of the Magistrates' Courts Act 1980 to enter into such a recognizance fails to comply with the order the court may commit him to custody for up to six months or until he sooner complies with the order: subs. (3), *ibid.* The sanction in the case of a failure to enter into a recognizance under the Act of 1361 is the same as under the Act of 1980, namely imprisonment, *per* Lord Lane C.J. in *Veater* v. *Glennon, supra.*

Where a person is committed in default of finding sureties under any power the court may on fresh evidence vary or dispense with the requirement for sureties: Magistrates' Courts Act 1980, s. 118.

Binding Over Without Complaint

Magistrates have power under the Act of 1361 to bind over any person appearing before them even though no formal complaint has been made against them: *Ex parte Davis* (1871) 35 J.P. 551; *R.* v. *Hughes* [1879] 4 Q.B.D. 614 at p. 625; *Wilson* v. *Skeock* (1949) 113 J.P. 294. Thus, they may bind over the complainant for a summons to show cause why another should not be bound over: *R.* v. *Wilkins, ex parte John* (1907) 71 J.P. 327. Unlike a bind-over on complaint under the Magistrates' Court Act 1980, s. 115 this power may be exercised by a single justice, *per* Lord Lane C.J. in *Veater* v. *Glennon* (1981) 145 J.P. 158.

It is elementary justice that particularly a mere witness should at any rate be told what is passing through the justices' minds and should have an opportunity of dealing with it, *per* Lord Parker CJ, in *Sheldon* v. *Bromfield JJ* [1964] 2 All E.R. 131 at p. 134; *R.* v. *Keighley Justices, ex parte Stoyles* [1976] Crim. L.R. 573. The same principles apply *a fortiori* to a private prosecutor. When magistrates bound over both prosecutor and defendant after the latter had been convicted of an assault arising from a motoring incident without giving either party prior opportunity to comment on this course of action the Divisional Court quashed by *certiorari* the order with regard to the prosecutor, Lord Widgery CJ, commenting that "it is high time that this particular error (*i.e.* of failing to warn the applicant of what was in the court's mind) should be eradicated because it is the easiest thing in the world for justices contemplating binding over to say what they have in mind and to ask the intended recipient what he has to say": *R.* v. *Hendon JJ, ex parte Gorchein* (1974) 138 J.P. 139.

There are many instances where, although the offence is not adequately proved, the conduct of the accused has, in the opinion of the bench, justified the use of preventive justice, *per* Lord Widgery CJ, in *R.* v. *Woking JJ, ex parte Gossage* (1973) 137 J.P. 565: where he commented that:

"... a very clear distinction is drawn between, on the one part, persons who come before the justices as witnesses, and on the other, persons who come before the justices as defendants. Not only do the witnesses come with no expected prospect of being subjected to any kind of penalty, but also witnesses as such, although they may speak in evidence, cannot represent themselves through counsel and cannot call evidence on their own behalf. By contrast, the defendant comes before the court knowing that allegations are to be made against him, knowing that he can be represented if appropriate, and knowing that he can call evidence if he wishes. It seems to me that a rule which requires a witness to be warned of the possibility of a binding-over should not necessarily apply to a defendant in that different position.... That is not to say that it would not be wise, and indeed courteous in these cases for justices to give such a warning; there certainly would be absolutely no harm in a case like the present if the justices, returning to court, had announced they were going to acquit, but had immediately said 'We are however contemplating a binding-over; what have you got to say?'."

Justices should make a binding-over order against a prosecutor only in an exceptional case when facts have emerged on a plea of guilty: *R.* v. *Preston Crown Court, ex parte Pamplin* [1981] Crim. L.R. 338.

But the justices' powers to bind over do not arise only at the conclusion of the case. In *R.* v. *Aubrey Fletcher, ex parte Thompson* (1969) 133 J.P. 450

a defendant was charged with using insulting words at Speakers' Corner, Hyde Park. The case had to be adjourned part heard before conviction and the magistrate granted bail. Being persuaded that it would be an invalid condition of bail that the defendant should not take part in meetings at Speakers' Corner, he bound him over to keep the peace for three months in the sum of £500. Granting *certiorari* to quash this order, the Divisional Court clearly accepted that such an order could be made at that stage in the proceedings provided it had by then emerged that there was likely to be a breach of the peace in the future.

While consent does not by itself confer jurisdiction to bind over, where there is reasonable apprehension of a breach of the peace the effect of consent is to relieve the magistrates of the duty to give the person bound opportunity to show cause why this should not be done: *R.* v. *South West London Magistrates' Court, ex parte Brown and Others* [1974] Crim. L.R. 313; (1974) 4 Fam. L. 158.

Disorder in Court

Prior to the Contempt of Court Act 1981 (*see* Ch. 14) the only order magistrates could make with respect to disorderly behaviour in court was a bind-over. This may still have a place where the Act of 1981 is inappropriate or to prevent future misbehaviour.

It was said in Hawk, PC, c. 61, s. 237 that surety for good behaviour could be required for disrespectful or unmannerly expressions in the face of the court or words out of court disparaging the magistrate in his office, and of obstructing officers of the court in the execution of their duty. Where the behaviour consists of defaming a particular justice he should not comprise the court which orders the bind-over: *R.* v. *Lee* (1701) 12 Mod. 514. In the case of other behaviour in court there is no objection to a magistrate who has witnessed it ordering the bind-over (*R.* v. *Butt*, 41 Cr. App. R. 82) unless the behaviour is disputed, when it should be tried by a different bench.

The need for a warning does not apply where the magistrate binds over applicants seeking cross summonses who engage in verbal argument in the face of the court which there is fear will lead to a breach of the peace: *R.* v. *North London Metropolitan Magistrate, ex parte Haywood* [1973] 3 All E.R. 50.

Statutory Powers

A bind-over is not a sentence, but there are various statutory provisions giving power to bind over on conviction, for example the Criminal Justice Act, 1925, s. 39(3), and the Powers of Criminal Courts Act 1973, s. 12 (this last with consent only).

The parent or guardian of a juvenile found guilty of any offence may, with his consent, be ordered to enter into a recognizance to take proper care of him and exercise proper control over him under the Children & Young Persons Act 1969, s. 7(7). Such an order can be made in the adult court: Children and Young Persons Act 1969, s. 7(8).

The Terms of the Order

A bind-over may be in respect of the world in general or with respect to a named individual or individuals (1 *Hawkins Pleas of the Crown* 129). A "particularized" bind-over was impliedly approved by the High Court in *Wilson* v. *Skeock* (1949) 113 J.P. 294, where the order commanded that the peace be kept "towards His Majesty and all his liege people and especially towards (the respondent)." It is not possible to insert other conditions into an order of bind-over: *R.* v. *Ayu* (1959) 123 J.P. 76; *Edward Lister* v. *David Healey Morgan* [1978] Crim. L.R. 292; *Goodlad* v. *Chief Constable of South Yorkshire* [1979] Crim. L.R. 51. Thus, it is not possible under the Act of 1361 or otherwise to bind over a convicted

offender to return to his country of origin: *R.* v. *Ayu, supra; R.* v. *East Grin-
stead JJ., ex parte Doeve* (1969) 133 J.P. 35; *R.* v. *Brixton Prison (Governor),
ex parte Havlide (otherwise Gruschwitz)* [1969] 1 All E.R. 109.

"There does not seem to be any authority or case in which a limitation (*i.e.* of
time) has not been inserted," *per* Pickford J, in *R.* v. *Edgar* (1913) 77 J.P. 356. In
that case the Court of Criminal Appeal inserted a limitation of five years in an
order made by the recorder of London. Six or 12 months are more usual periods in
the case of magistrates' orders.

There is no rule that the amount of the recognizance shall be no greater than the
maximum fine for the appropriate offence: *R.* v. *Sandbach Justices, ex parte
Williams* (1935) 99 J.P. 251.

Legal Aid

Legal aid may be granted in proceedings under the Magistrates' Courts Act 1980,
s. 115: Legal Aid Act 1974, s. 28(2) and 30(11), and in forfeiture proceedings
under s. 120 of the Act of 1980: Legal Aid Act 1974, ss. 28, 30(12).

Discharge

A surety to a bind-over may apply by complaint for his discharge on the
ground that the principal has been or is about to be in breach of the order:
Magistrates' Courts Act 1980, s. 116.

Forfeiture

Conduct in breach of a bind-over may be punished by estreatment of
recognizance: Magistrates' Courts Act 1980, s. 120.

Appeal

There is a right of appeal to the Crown Court against an order to enter into
recognizances to keep the peace or be of good behaviour under the Magistrates'
Courts (Appeals from Binding Over Orders) Act, 1956. There is no appeal from
an estreatment of recognizance: *R.* v. *Durham JJ, ex parte Laurent* (1945) 109
J.P. 21. There is seemingly no right of appeal against the bind-over of a
parent etc. under the Children & Young Persons Act 1969, s. 7(7).

THE JUSTICES OF THE PEACE ACT, 1361

First, that in every county of England shall be assigned for the keeping of the
peace, one lord, and with him three or four of the most worthy in the county, with
some learned in the law, and they shall have power to restrain the offenders,
rioters, and all other barators and to pursue, arrest, take, and chastise them
according to their trespass or offence; and to cause them to be imprisoned and
duly punished according to the law and customs of the realm, and according to
that which to them shall seem best to do by their discretions and good advisement;
. . . and to take and arrest all those that they may find by indictment, or by
suspicion, and to put them in prison; and to take of all them that be [not] of good
fame, where they shall be found, sufficient surety and mainprise of their good
behaviour towards the King and his people, and the other duly to punish; to the
intent that the people be not by such rioters or rebels troubled nor endamaged, nor
the peace blemished, nor merchants nor other passing by the highways of the
realm disturbed, nor [put in the peril which may happen] of such offenders.

(as amended by the Criminal Law Act 1967, sch. 3).

COMMENTARY

For procedure, enforcement and appeal *see* the introduction.

This Act does not create any offence, *per* Lord Goddard CJ, in *R.* v. *County of London Quarter Sessions, ex parte Commissioner of Metropolitan Police* [1948] 1 All E.R. 72; *R.* v. *London Sessions Appeal Committee, ex parte Beaumont* (1951) 115 J.P. 104.

Rioters . . . barators. These words "appear to me to mean people who create a disturbance or brawlers." And, whether or not the world "not" is properly inserted before the words "of good fame", "there is clear authority . . . that . . . justices can bind over, whether the person is or is not of good fame," *per* Lord Goddard CJ, in *R.* v. *County of London Quarter Sessions, ex parte Commissioner of Metropolitan Police, supra.*

[Not] of good fame. The negative is usually added to correct what some regard as a lacuna. For the opposite view *see* the article at 145 J.P.N. 500 and the previous note.

THE MAGISTRATES' COURTS (APPEALS FROM BINDING-OVER ORDERS) ACT, 1956

Right of appeal to the Crown Court

1. (1) Where, under the Justices of the Peace Act 1361, or otherwise, a person is ordered by a magistrates' court (as defined in the Magistrates' Courts Act, 1980) to enter into a recognizance with or without sureties to keep the peace or to be of good behaviour, he may appeal to the Crown Court.

(2) In the case of an appeal under this section—

(*a*) the other party to the proceedings which were the occasion of the making of the order shall be the respondent to the appeal;

(*b*) in relation to an appellant in custody for failure to comply with the order, so much of s. 37 of the Criminal Justice Act, 1948, as relates to the release of convicted persons from custody pending an appeal to the Crown Court shall, with the necessary adaptations, apply as if the appeal were an appeal against a conviction.

(3) Nothing in this section shall apply in relation to any order an appeal from which lies to the Crown Court apart from the provisions of this section.

(4) . . .

(*as amended by the Criminal Justice Act 1967, sch. 7, the Courts Act 1971, sch. 9, the Magistrates' Courts Act 1980, sch. 7*).

COMMENTARY

For the procedure on appeal, *see* the Crown Court Rules 1971, r. 7. An appeal against a bind-over is by way of re-hearing at which fresh evidence may be called as to whether the bind-over is necessary to prevent a future breach of the peace: *Shaw* v. *Hamilton* [1982] 2 All E.R. 718. For abandonment of appeal *see* the Magistrates' Courts Act 1980, s. 109.

Subsection (1): Magistrates' court. Defined in the Magistrates Courts Act 1980, s. 148.

Subsection (2): The other party to the proceedings. The justices themselves should appear and resist an appeal if they know that there is no one else who can do so: *R.* v. *Kent Justices, ex parte Metropolitan Police Commissioner* (1936) 100 J.P. 17. Where justices bound over a prosecutor they were entitled to appear at the appeal in the role of *amicus curiae* and should in an appropriate case state the surrounding circumstances so far as they are not in dispute: *R.* v. *Preston Crown Court, ex parte Pamplin* [1981] Crim. L.R. 338.

THE MAGISTRATES' COURT ACT 1980

Binding-over to keep the peace or be of good behaviour

115. (1) The power of a magistrates' court on the complaint of any person to adjudge any other person to enter into a recognizance, with or without sureties, to keep the peace or to be of good behaviour towards the complainant shall be exercised by order on complaint.

(2) Where a complaint is made under this section, the power of the court to remand the defendant under subs. (5) of s. 55 above shall not be subject to the restrictions imposed by subs. (6) of that section.

(3) If any person ordered by a magistrates' court under subs. (1) above to enter into a recognizance, with or without sureties, to keep the peace or to be of good behaviour fails to comply with the order, the court may commit him to custody for a period not exceeding six months or until he sooner complies with the order.

COMMENTARY

This provision would not appear to create a new power to bind-over, but merely to regulate the procedure under which bind-overs are made on the application of a party as opposed to bind-overs ordered on the court's initiative. *See* generally the introduction.

Legal aid may be granted by magistrates in these proceeding: Legal Aid Act 1974, ss. 28 (2) and 30(11).

Subsection (1): Magistrates' court. Defined in s. 148(1) of the Act.

A recognizance, with or without sureties. Instead of taking the recognizance at the time, the court may fix the amount in which principal and sureties are to be bound and thereafter the recognizances may be taken by another court or by prescribed officials: Magistrates' Courts Act 1980, s. 119. Where the offender is committed to custody in default of finding sureties, the court may later reduce or dispense with the sureties on fresh evidence: s. 118, *ibid*. For the forfeiture of the recognizances *see* s. 120, *ibid*.

Towards the complainant. This section appears to refer to a particularized bind-over and not a general one.

By order on complaint. The procedure on complaint is set out in ss. 51-57 of the Act (not printed here) and in the Magistrates' Courts Rules 1981, r. 14. Costs are accordingly available under s. 64, *ibid*.

Subsection (2). The effect of this is that the court may issue a warrant or remand the defendant notwithstanding that he has given evidence in the proceedings. Such a remand does not constitute bail in criminal proceedings and is not covered by the Bail Act 1976. The defendant's own recognizance may be taken.

Subsection (3): Fails to comply. That is, with the order to enter into recognizances, not breach of the recognizance. Breach of recognizances is dealt with under s. 120 of the Act and not otherwise: *R.* v. *Ossett Justices, ex parte Tebb* [1972] Crim. L.R. 39.

Commit him to custody. This means commit to prison or, where any enactment authorizes or requires committal to some other place of detention instead of committal to prison, to that other place: s. 150(1) of the Act. Committals to prison must be by warrant: Magistrates' Courts Rules 1981, r. 94. The requirement as to sureties may be varied or dispensed with by virtue of s. 118, *infra*.

Discharge of recognizance to keep the peace or be of good behaviour on complaint of surety

116. (1) On complaint being made to a justice of the peace for any area to which this section applies by a surety to a recognizance to keep the peace or to be of good behaviour entered into before a magistrates' court that the person bound by the recognizance as principal has been, or is about to be, guilty of conduct constituting a breach of the conditions of the recognizance, the justice may, if the complaint alleges that the principal is, or is believed to be, in that area, or if the recognizance was entered into before a magistrates' court for that area, issue a warrant to arrest the principal and bring him before a magistrates' court for that area or a summons requiring the principal to appear before such a court; but the justice shall not issue a warrant unless the complaint is in writing and substantiated on oath.

(2) The magistrates' court before which the principal appears or is brought in pursuance of such a summons or warrant as aforesaid may, unless it adjudges the recognizance to be forfeited, order the recognizance to be discharged and order the principal to enter into a new recognizance, with or without sureties, to keep the peace or to be of good behaviour.

(3) The areas to which this section applies are any county, any London commission area and the City of London.

COMMENTARY

Subsection (1): Complaint.   The procedure on complaint is set out in ss. 51-57 of the Act and in the Magistrates' Courts Rules 1981, r. 14.

Subsection (2): Forfeited.   That is, under s. 120 of the Act.

Discharged.   The clerk must send a copy of the order to the clerk of the court which made the order: Magistrates' Courts Rules 1981, r. 82.

Varying or dispensing with requirement as to sureties

118.   (1) Subject to subs. (2) below, where a magistrates' court has committed a person to custody in default of finding sureties, the court may, on application by or on behalf of the person committed, and after hearing fresh evidence, reduce the amount in which it is proposed that any surety should be bound or dispense with any of the sureties or otherwise deal with the case as it thinks just.

(2) Subsection (1) above does not apply in relation to a person granted bail in criminal proceedings.

COMMENTARY

For the order *see* form 117.

Subsection (1): The court.   A court of the same petty sessions area even though composed of a different justice or justices: s. 148(2) of the Act.

On application.   By complaint: Magistrates' Court Rules 1981, r. 83. For the summons *see* form 117.

Fresh evidence.   A restrictive view of this term has been adopted in the civil law as meaning something which has occurred subsequent to the original hearing and which was unknown to the party at that time. *See*, for example, *Johnson* v. *Johnson* (1900) 64 J.P. 72; *Weightman* v. *Weightman* (1906) 70 J.P. 120; and *Cross* v. *Cross* (1935) 95 J.P. 86. It is difficult to believe that the legislature would have used this technical term in a 1952 statute – re-enacted in 1980 – (changing it from the former "new evidence") otherwise than deliberately.

Subsection (2): Bail in criminal proceedings.   Defined in s. 150(1) of the Act as having the same meaning as in the Bail Act 1976.

Forfeiture of recognizance

120.   (1) Where a recognizance to keep the peace or to be of good behaviour has been entered into before a magistrates' court or any recognizance is conditioned for the appearance of a person before a magistrates' court or for his doing any other thing connected with a proceeding before a magistrates' court, and the recognizance appears to the court to be forfeited, the court may, subject to subs. (2) below, declare the recognizance to be forfeited and adjudge the persons bound thereby, whether as principal or sureties, or any of them, to pay the sum in which they are respectively bound.

(2) Where a recognizance is conditioned to keep the peace or to be of good behaviour, the court shall not declare it forfeited except by order made on

(4) Payment of any sum adjudged to be paid under this section, including any costs awarded against the defendant, may be enforced, and any such sum shall be applied, as if it were a fine and as if the adjudication were a summary conviction of an offence not punishable with imprisonment and so much of s. 85(1) above as empowers a court to remit fines shall not apply to the sum but so much thereof as relates to remission after a term of imprisonment has been imposed shall so apply; but at any time before the issue of a warrant of commitment to enforce payment of the sum, or before the sale of goods under a warrant of distress to satisfy the sum, the court may remit the whole or any part of the sum either absolutely or on such conditions as the court thinks just.

(5) A recognizance such as is mentioned in this section shall not be enforced otherwise than in accordance with this section, and accordingly shall not be transmitted to the Crown Court nor shall its forfeiture be certified to that Court.

COMMENTARY

Declare the recognizance forfeited. There is no right of appeal to the Crown Court against an order to forfeit a recognizance: *R*. v. *Durham JJ, ex parte Laurent* (1945) 109 J.P. 21. But *certiorari* will lie where an error in law is disclosed in the affidavits: *R*. v. *Southampton Justices, ex parte Green* (1975) 139 J.P. 667.

Subsection (2): By order made on complaint. For order, *see* form 133. The effect of these words is that to forfeit a recognizance to keep the peace or be of good behaviour a summons may be issued under s. 51 of the Act and the hearing must follow the procedure laid down in ss. 53-57 of the Act and in the Magistrates' Courts Rules 1981, r. 14. *Certiorari* will issue to quash an order of forfeiture made without complaint: *R*. v. *Ossett JJ, ex parte Tebb* [1972] Crim. L.R. 39.

The person summoned must be told precisely what it was he had been bound over to do; in what way it is alleged that he has failed to comply with his promise. Clear evidence must be given of the nature of the breach alleged. Most important, the defendant must be asked whether he desires to give evidence and explain his conduct, whether he has any witnesses to call; whether he has any explanation to make: *R*. v. *McGregor* (1945) 109 J.P. 136. The mere fact that a man the subject of a bind-over consents to a bind over on a subsequent charge (which was not proceeded with) does not amount to an admission of a breach of the peace justifying forfeiture of the earlier recognizance: *Jackson* v. *Lilley* (1982) 146 J.P. 132.

Legal aid may be granted in proceedings for failing to comply with a recognizance to keep the peace or be of good behaviour: Legal Aid Act 1974, ss. 28 and 30(12).

Subsection (4): Costs. Costs may, by virtue of subs. (2) be awarded to the successful party under s. 64 of the Act; but costs in alleged breaches of bind-over ordered upon conviction of an indictable offence may also be awarded out of central funds under the Costs in Criminal Cases Act 1973, as if the breach were an indictable offence committed in the same place as the offence: Costs in Criminal Cases Act 1973, s. 18(5).

Enforced as if it were a fine. Notice must be given to a defendant if he is absent or time to pay is allowed: Magistrates' Courts Rules 1981, r. 46.

An order of discharge in bankruptcy does not release the debt on the recognizance: Bankruptcy Act 1914, s. 28(1)(c).

Remit. Recognizances estreated by higher courts may not be remitted by magistrates except with the permission of that court: Criminal Justice Act 1967, s. 47(8). Any order of remission must be entered in the register or separate record: Magistrates' Courts Rules 1981, r. 65.

THE MAGISTRATES' COURTS RULES 1981

S.I. 1981 No. 552

Recognizance to keep the peace etc., taken by one court and discharged by another

82. *Where a magistrates' court acting for any petty sessions area makes an order under s. 116 of the Act of 1980 discharging a recognizance entered into before a magistrates' court acting for any other petty sessions area, the clerk of the court that orders the recognizance to be discharged shall send a copy of the order of discharge to the clerk of the court acting for that other petty sessions area.*

Application to vary order for sureties or dispense with them

83. *Where a person has been committed to custody in default of finding sureties and the order to find sureties was made at the instance of another person, an application under s. 118 of the Act of 1980 shall be made by complaint against that other person.*

COMMENTARY

By complaint. That is, in accordance with ss. 51-57 of the Magistrates' Courts Act 1980.

CHAPTER 11

COSTS

INTRODUCTION

In criminal cases magistrates have power to make orders of two different types concerning costs:

- (a)   an order that the costs of one of the parties be borne by the other (costs *inter partes*); and in some cases
- (b)   an order that the costs of one or more of the parties be borne by the public purse (costs from central funds).

Where available, both types of order may be made in the same case. (*See* Combined Orders below).

The circumstances in which magistrates may exercise their powers depend upon the nature of the proceedings (*i.e.* whether they constitute a summary trial or committal proceedings) and according to the character of the offence charged (indictable or summary). References, except where otherwise indicated, are to the Costs in Criminal Cases Act 1973.

On Summary Trial

If the information is dismissed the court may:

- make such order as to costs to be paid by the prosecutor to the accused as it thinks just and reasonable: s. 2(1); and
- if the offence charged is indictable, order payment out of central funds of the costs of the prosecution: s. 1(1); and
- if the offence charged is indictable, order payment out of central funds of the costs of the defence: s. 1(2).
  Even if no order is made for payment out of central funds of the costs of the defence the court may order payment out of those funds of the costs of defence witnesses: s. 1(4).

On conviction the court may:

- make such order as to costs to be paid by the accused to the prosecutor as it thinks just and reasonable, except that:
  - (a)   costs may not be ordered against a juvenile if the fine, penalty, forfeiture or compensation does not exceed 25p unless in any particular case the court thinks fit to do so; and
  - (b)   the amount of any costs ordered to be paid by a juvenile himself must not exceed the amount of the fine: s. 2(2); and
- if the offence charged is indictable, order payment out of central funds of the costs of the prosecution: s. 1(1).

In Committal Proceedings

If the accused is discharged the court may order:

- payment out of central funds of the costs of the prosecution: s. 1(1); and
- payment out of central funds of the costs of the defence: s. 1(2).
  Even if no order is made for payment out of central funds of the costs of the defence the court may order payment out of those funds of defence witnesses: s. 1(4); and
- the prosecutor to pay the whole or any part of the costs incurred in or about the defence if the justices are of opinion that the charge was not made in good faith: s. 2(4).

If the accused is committed for trial the court may order:

- payment out of central funds of the costs of the prosecution: s. 1(1).

Where the information is not proceeded with the court may:

- make such order as to costs to be paid by the prosecutor to the accused as it

thinks just and reasonable: s. 12(3); and
- in the case of an indictable offence, order payment out of central funds of the costs properly incurred in preparing a defence to the offence charged and such sums as appear reasonably sufficient to compensate any person attending to give evidence as a defence witness for the expense, trouble or loss of time properly incurred in or incidental to his attendance: s. 12(1).

Costs Inter Partes

In criminal proceedings the award of costs to the successful party is not automatic. Costs may only be awarded *inter partes* where it is just and reasonable. The court must always apply its mind to the fact of the particular case. A practice of always granting or refusing costs would thus be unlawful.

So far as costs against the prosecutor are concerned, every case depends on its own circumstances. The justices have first to decide whether the prosecution ought ever to have been brought and then to consider the question of costs: *R.* v. *Lytham Justices, ex parte Carter* [1975] Crim. L.R. 225 (*certiorari* issued where justices followed a practice of not awarding costs against police in certain cases). Magistrates should hear evidence if necessary before refusing the defendant costs where a material issue is in dispute: *Becker* v. *Purchase* (1950) 114 J.P. 550. Costs should not be used as a guise for the imposition of a penalty: *R.* v. *Highgate JJ, ex parte Petrou* (1954) 118 J.P. 151. It is undesirable to make an order for costs where the offender is committed to prison and may be unable to comply with it: *R.* v. *Murazzaman* [1979] 1 Cr. App. R. (S) 320.

The Amount of Costs Inter Partes

Costs are no more than an indemnity. They are not confined to disbursements and expenses properly so called, but extend to the cost of labour of a private detective or police officer: *R.* v. *Burt, ex parte Presburg* (1960) 124 J.P. 201. (Two guineas held to be reasonable costs for the attendance of one police constable for one afternoon). A lay litigant appearing in person is not entitled to remuneration for the time and labour expended in the preparation of his case, but a lawyer conducting his own case is in a different position: *Buckland* v. *Watts* [1969] 2 All E.R. 985. And *see Malloch* v. *Aberdeen Corpn. (No. 2)* [1973] 1 All E.R. 304 (both civil cases). The Litigants in Person Act 1976 does not apply to criminal proceedings in magistrates' courts.

The defendant's means would appear to be a material consideration in assessing costs: *R.* v. *Judd & Others* [1971] 1 All E.R. 127; *R.* v. *Gaston* [1971] 1 All E.R. 128; *R.* v. *Whalley* [1972] 56 Cr. App. R. 304; *R.* v. *Wright* [1977] Crim. L.R. 236; notwithstanding earlier dicta to the contrary (*see*, for example, *R.* v. *Churchill and Others (No. 2)* [1966] 2 All E.R. 215 at p. 221.) Costs may be justified where the offender has made a profit from the crime and it is impossible to say where the money has gone: *R.* v. *Cooper* [1974] Crim. L.R. 673.

Ascertaining Costs Inter Partes

The amount of costs *inter partes* must be specified in the order: (*ibid*, s. 2(3)). The court may order all or part of the costs but it must express its order as a sum of money which may take into account the expenses of witnesses: *Amalgamated Anthracite Collieries Ltd.* v. *Davies* (1946) 115 LJKB 185. Costs *inter partes* must therefore be ascertained by the justices: *R.* v. *Pwllheli JJ, ex parte Soane* (1948) 112 J.P. 441. They may not delegate this duty to their clerk although, where the necessary information is not available from the parties, the clerk may be called upon to obtain it: *Bunston* v. *Rawlings* (1982) 146 J.P. 386.

Enforcement of Costs Inter Partes

Costs payable by the parties are enforced:

(*a*) in the same way as a fine in the case of costs against the defendant;
(*b*) as a civil debt in the case of costs against the prosecutor: Administration of Justice Act 1970, s. 55.

Liability of Parents

The court is bound to order that any costs should be paid by the parent or guardian of a juvenile defendant unless this would be unreasonable or he cannot be found: Children and Young Persons Act 1933, s. 55. *See* Ch. 8.

Costs From Central Funds

The grant of costs from central funds to defendants in magistrates' courts is regulated by the following *Practice Note (Justices: Defendant's Costs)* [1982] 3 All E.R. 1152, *per* Lord Lane C.J.:

AWARD OF COSTS TO DEFENDANTS IN CRIMINAL CASES IN THE MAGISTRATES' COURTS

1. I understand that there is a need for guidance to magistrates in exercising their powers to order costs in indictable offences.
2. Under section 1 of the Costs in Criminal Cases Act 1973 a magistrates' court dealing summarily with an indictable offence and dismissing the information, or inquiring into any offence as examining justices and determining not to commit the accused for trial, may order the payment out of central funds of the costs of the defence. A similar power exists under section 12(1) of the Act where an information is not proceeded with.
3. Whether to make such an award is a matter in the unfettered discretion of the court in the light of the circumstances of each particular case.
4. It should be accepted as normal practice that such an award be made unless there are positive reasons for making a different order. Examples of such reasons are:—
    (*a*) Where the prosecution has acted spitefully or has instituted or continued proceedings without reasonable cause the defendant's costs should be paid by the prosecutor under section 2 of the Act. If there is any doubt whether payment will be forthcoming from the prosecutor the position of the defendant should be protected by making an order for costs from central funds in his favour as well.
    (*b*) Where the defendant's own conduct has brought suspicion on himself and has misled the prosecution into thinking that the case against him is stronger than it is the defendant can be left to pay his own costs.
    (*c*) Where there is ample evidence to support a conviction but the defendant is acquitted on a technicality which has no merit. Here again the defendant can be left to pay his own costs.
    (*d*) Where the defendant is acquitted on one charge but convicted on another. Here the court should make whatever order seems just

having regard to the relative importance of the two charges and the conduct of the parties generally.

Ascertaining the Amount of Costs from Central Funds

Once a court has exercised its discretion in favour of an award of costs from central funds, there is no further discretion to limit the amount awarded: *Practice Direction* [1968] 1 All E.R. 778 (dealing with trials on indictment); *R*. v. *Chertsey Justices, ex parte Edwards & Co. (The Provision Market) Ltd.* (1974) 138 J.P. 81.

The costs to be paid from central funds must be ascertained as soon as practicable by the justices' clerk: Costs in Criminal Cases Act 1973, s. 1(6). Save in the case mentioned by Lord Widgery, CJ in *R*. v. *Chertsey Justices, supra*. (See the commentary to s. 1(6), *infra*) the court plays no part in the ascertainment of costs from central funds.

Costs payable from central funds consist of such sums as appear reasonably sufficient to compensate the recipient for the expenses incurred by him in carrying on the prosecution or the defence and to compensate witnesses: s. 1(3). The allowances which may be paid to witnesses out of central funds are dealt with in the Costs in Criminal Cases (Allowances) Regulations 1977.

Medical Evidence

There are wide powers for the payment out of central funds of the costs of medical evidence: Magistrates' Courts Act 1980, s. 30(3) and the Criminal Justice Act 1967, s. 32(3).

Payment of Costs from Central Funds

Costs ordered out of central funds are paid by the Crown Court except in the following cases: (*a*) indictable offences tried summarily; (*b*) or not proceeded with; (*c*) committal proceedings where the defendant is discharged; and (*d*) travelling and personal expenses in all cases; when payment is made by the magistrates' clerk: Costs in Criminal Cases Act 1973, s. 15.

Combined Orders

The court may in an appropriate case make both an order of costs from central funds and an order of costs *inter partes*. Where it does so the costs are primarily payable out of central funds: s. 16(1).

Value Added Tax

For the effects of value added tax *see* Home Office Circular 55/1973 dated March 26, 1973.

Appeal

There is no appeal to the Crown Court against an order for costs except costs in excess of £25 against the prosecutor in committal proceedings: Costs in Criminal Cases Act 1973, s. 2(5). But *certiorari* may lie where no reasonable court could have made the order: *R*. v. *Tottenham Justices, ex parte Joshi* (1982) 75 Cr. App. R. 82.

THE CRIMINAL JUSTICE ACT 1967

Amendments of Costs in Criminal Cases Act, 1952

32. (1) (*Repealed*).

(2) Section 33 of the Courts Martial Appeals Act 1968 (payment out of moneys provided by Parliament of expenses of witnesses in connexion with appeals to the Courts Martial Appeals Court) and ss. 1, 3 and 8(1) of the Costs in

Criminal Cases Act 1973 (payment of costs out of central funds) shall apply in relation to a registered medical practitioner making a written report to a court in pursuance of a request to which this subsection applies as they apply in relation to a person called to give evidence at the instance of the court, and in the case of a report made in pursuance of such a request made by a magistrates' court shall so apply notwithstanding that the proceedings for the purposes of which the report is made are not proceedings to which the said s. 1 applies.

(3) The last foregoing subsection applies to a request to a registered medical practitioner to make a written or oral report on the medical condition of an offender or defendant, being a request made by a court—

    (a)   for the purposes of determining whether or not to make an order under s. 3 of the Powers of Criminal Courts Act 1973 (probation orders requiring treatment for mental condition) or s. 60 of the Mental Health Act 1959 (hospital orders and guardianship orders) or otherwise for the purpose of determining the most suitable method of dealing with an offender; or

    (b)   in exercise of the powers conferred by s. 30 of the Magistrates' Courts Act 1980 (remand of a defendant for medical examination and requirement of such an examination on committing a defendant for trial on bail).

(4) (*Repealed*).

(5) ...

(*as amended by the Courts Act 1971, schs. 6 and 11, the Costs in Criminal Cases Act 1973, schs. 1 and 2, the Powers of Criminal Courts Act 1973, sch. 5, the Magistrates' Courts Act 1980, sch. 7*).

COMMENTARY

The effects of this section are largely noted under the statutes affected.

    Expressions used in this section have the same meaning as in the Magistrates' Courts Act, 1980: Criminal Justice Act 1967, s. 36(2).

THE ADMINISTRATION OF JUSTICE ACT 1970

Recovery of costs and compensation awarded by magistrates, Crown Court, etc.

41. (1) In the cases specified in Part I of sch. 9 to this Act (being cases where, in criminal proceedings, a court makes an order against the accused for the payment of costs, compensation, etc.) any sum required to be paid by such an order as is there mentioned shall be treated, for the purposes of collection and enforcement, as if it had been adjudged to be paid on a conviction by a magistrates' court, being—

    (a)   where the order is made by a magistrates' court, that court; and

    (b)   in any other case, such magistrates' court as may be specified in the order.

(2) In the cases specified in Part II of the said schedule (being cases where a court makes an order against the prosecutor in criminal proceedings, and certain cases where an order for costs arises out of an appeal to the Crown Court in proceedings which are not criminal) any sum required to be paid by such an order as is there mentioned shall be enforceable as if the order were for the payment of money recoverable summarily as a civil debt.

(3) Without prejudice to the foregoing subsections, but subject to subs. (4) below, in the cases specified in sch. 9 to this Act any sum required to be paid by such an order as is there mentioned shall be enforceable by the High Court or a county court (otherwise than by issue of a writ of *fieri facias* or other process

against goods or by imprisonment or attachment of earnings) as if the sum were due in pursuance of a judgment or order of the High Court or county court, as the case may be.

(4) Subsection (3) above shall not authorize the enforcement by a county court of payment of any sum exceeding the limit for the time being in force under s. 40 of the County Courts Act 1959, on the amount of any penalty recoverable by statute in a county court.

(5) ...

(6), (7) (*Repealed*).

(8) In any of the cases specified in Part I of sch. 9 to this Act, a court (other than a magistrates' court) which makes such an order as is there mentioned may, if it thinks that the period for which the person subject to the order is liable apart from this subsection to be committed to prison for default under the order is insufficient, specify a longer period for that purpose, but not exceeding 12 months; and then, in the case of default—

(*a*) the specified period shall be substituted as the maximum for which the person may be imprisoned under s. 76 of the Magistrates' Courts Act 1980 (distress or committal); and

(*b*) paragraph 2 of sch. 4 to that Act shall apply, with the necessary modifications, for the reduction of the specified period where, at the time of imprisonment, he has made part payment under the order.

(9) Where a magistrates' court has power to commit a person to prison for default in paying a sum due under an order enforceable as mentioned in this section, the court shall not exercise the power unless it is satisfied that all other methods of enforcing payment have been tried or considered and either have proved unsuccessful or are likely to do so.

(*as amended by the Criminal Law Act 1977, sch. 13, the Magistrates' Courts Act 1980, schs. 7, 8*).

COMMENTARY

Subsection (2). Orders for the payment of money recoverable summarily as a civil debt may be enforced:

– *by distress* under the Magistrates' Courts Act 1980, s. 76.
– *in the High Court or County Court* under subss. (3) and (4).

The sum may be enforced by attachment of earnings in the County Court, but not in the magistrates' court.

The sanction of imprisonment for civil debt has been removed by the Administration of Justice Act 1970, s. 12.

Subsection (4). That is, £1000.

SCHEDULE 9

ENFORCEMENT OF ORDERS FOR COSTS, COMPENSATION, ETC.

PART I

CASES WHERE PAYMENT ENFORCEABLE AS ON SUMMARY CONVICTION

Costs awarded by magistrates

1. Where a magistrates' court, on the summary trial of an information, makes an order as to costs to be paid by the accused to the prosecutor.

2. Where an appellant to the Crown Court against conviction or sentence by a magistrates' court abandons his appeal and the magistrates' court orders him to pay costs to the other party to the appeal.

Costs awarded by the Crown Court

3. Where a person appeals to the Crown Court against conviction or sentence by a magistrates' court, and the Crown Court makes an order as to costs to be paid by him.

4. Where a person is prosecuted or tried on indictment before the Crown Court and is convicted, and the court orders him to pay the whole or part of the costs incurred in or about the prosecution and conviction.

5. (*Repealed*).

Costs awarded by Court of Appeal (Criminal Division) or House of Lords

6. Where the Criminal Division of the Court of Appeal dismisses an appeal or application for leave to appeal and orders the appellant or applicant to pay the whole or part of the costs of the appeal or application.

7. Where the Criminal Division of the Court of Appeal or the House of Lords dismisses an application for leave to appeal to that House being an application made by the person who was the appellant before the Criminal Division) and orders him to pay the whole or part of the costs of the application.

8. (*Repealed*).

9-12. ...

PART II

CASES WHERE COSTS ENFORCEABLE SUMMARILY AS CIVIL DEBT

Costs awarded by magistrates

13. Where a magistrate' court, on the summary trial of an information, makes an order as to costs to be paid by the prosecutor to the accused.

14. Where an appellant to the Crown Court from a magistrates' court (otherwise than against conviction or sentence) abandons his appeal and the magistrates' court orders him to pay costs to the other party to the appeal.

15. Where examining justices determine not to commit a person for trial and order the prosecutor to pay the whole or part of the costs incurred in or about the defence.

Costs awarded by the Crown Court

16. Any order for the payment of costs made by the Crown Court, other than an order falling within Part I above, or an order for costs to be paid out of money provided by Parliament.

17-21. (*Repealed*).

(*as amended by the Courts Act 1971, schs. 8 and 11, Costs in Criminal Cases Act 1973, schs. 1, 2 and 5, the Criminal Law Act 1977, sch. 13*).

THE COSTS IN CRIMINAL CASES ACT 1973

Awards by magistrates' courts out of central funds

1. (1) A magistrates' court dealing summarily with an indictable offence, or inquiring into any offence as examining justices, may, subject to the provisions of this section, order the payment out of central funds of the costs of the prosecution.

(2) A magistrates' court dealing summarily with an indictable offence and dismissing the information, or inquiring into any offence as examining justices and determining not to commit the accused for trial, may, subject to the provisions of this section, order the payment out of central funds of the costs of the defence.

(3) The costs payable out of central funds under the preceding provisions of this section shall be such sums as appear to the court reasonably sufficient to compensate the prosecutor, or as the case may be the accused, for the expenses properly incurred by him in carrying on the prosecution or the defence, and to compensate any witness for the prosecution, or as the case may be for the defence, for the expense, trouble or loss of time properly incurred in or incidental to his attendance.

(4) Notwithstanding that the court makes no order under subs. (2) above for the payment out of central funds of the costs of the defence, it may order the payment out of those funds of such sums as appear to the court reasonably sufficient to compensate any witness for the defence for the expense, trouble or loss of time properly incurred in or incidental to his attendance.

(5) References in subs. (3) and (4) above to a witness include any person who is a witness to character only and in respect of whom the court certifies that the interests of justice required his attendance, but no sums shall be payable in pursuance of an order made under this section to or in respect of any witness who is a witness to character only and in respect of whom no such certificate is given.

(6) The amount of costs ordered to be paid under this section shall be ascertained as soon as practicable by the proper officer of the court.

(7) In this section the expression "witness" means a person properly attending to give evidence, whether or not he gives evidence; and a person who, at the instance of the court, is called or properly attends to give evidence may be made the subject of an order under subs. (4) above whether or not he is a witness for the defence.

COMMENTARY

For guidance on the exercise of discretion under this section *see* the *Practice Note (Justices: Defendant's Costs)* [1982] 3 All E.R. 1152 in the introduction.

This section has been applied to certain doctors' reports by the Magistrates' Courts Act 1980, s. 30(3), (oral reports) and the Criminal Justice Act 1967, s. 32(2) (written reports).
    An order for costs is not a "sentence" from which appeal lies to the Crown Court: Magistrates Courts Act 1980, s. 108.
    Costs may be ordered from central funds even where the information is not proceeded with: s. 12(1), *infra*.
    The court may in addition to ordering costs from central funds under this section make an order for costs *inter partes*, in which case the provisions of s. 16, *infra*, apply.
    The term "costs ordered to be paid out of central funds" is partially defined in s. 20(2), *infra*.

Subsection (1): Magistrates' court.   Defined in s. 20(1), *infra*.

Indictable offence.   Defined in the Interpretation Act 1978, sch. 1, as meaning an offence which, if committed by an adult, is triable on indictment, whether it is exclusively so triable or triable either way.

Central funds.   Defined in s. 13, *infra*. Includes payment to witnesses and advocates: s. 20(2). For payment of such costs *see* s. 15.

Subsection (2): Dealing summarily.   While it is arguable that this phrase does not apply to committals for sentence having regard to the Criminal Justice Act 1967, s. 56(5), the Home Office Working Party on Magistrates' Courts recommend that justices' clerks should pay the costs on such committals: Home Office Circular MAG 71 dated November 26, 1974.

Indictable offence. *See* the note to subs. (1).

Subsection (3): The expenses properly incurred. The proper approach is to assume the defendant to be of adequate but not abundant means and to ask oneself whether the expenses were such as a sensible solicitor in the light of his then knowledge would consider reasonable to incur in the interests of his client: *Practice Direction* [1968] 1 All E.R 77. For the assessment of the costs of a salaried solicitor cf. *Re Eastwood, Lloyds Bank* v. *Eastwood and Others* [1973] 3 All E.R. 1079. Costs are incurred by a party if he was responsible or liable for them even though they were in fact paid by a third party who was also liable for them: *R.* v. *Miller and Glennie* (1983) *The Times*, 1 June (a case on s. 3 which concerned the relationship between solicitor and client.)

Witness. *See* subs. (7) and the Costs in Criminal Cases (Allowances) Regulations, 1977, *infra*.

Subsection (4). It is submitted that the power to order witness expenses is confined to the cases referred to in subs (2).

Subsection (6). The apparent inconsistency between this subsection and subs. (3) is to be resolved by giving subs. (6) its plain meaning, namely that the practice to be followed when an order for costs out of central funds is made is for the ascertainment of the amount to be made by the proper officer. The only instance when it is really feasible for a summary ascertainment of costs to be made in court is where the solicitor applying for costs mentions a figure and the justices, having their clerk in court, ask him if he thinks it appropriate and if he, as proper officer, agrees the court may there and then award the sum asked for: *R.* v. *Chertsey JJ, ex parte Edwards & Co. (The Provision Market) Ltd.* (1974) 138 J.P. 81.

The proper officer of the court. That is, the justices' clerk: Costs in Criminal Cases Regulations, 1908, and *R.* v. *Chertsey JJ, supra.* Guidance on the assessment of costs from central funds is to be found in the *Notes for Guidance of Justices' Clerks* issued by the Lord Chancellor's department under cover of LCD circular Central Funds (83) 1.

Awards by magistrates' courts as between parties

2. (1) On the summary trial of an information a magistrates' court shall, on dismissal of the informaiton, have power to make such order as to costs to be paid by the prosecutor to the accused as it thinks just and reasonable.

(2) On the summary trial of an information a magistrates' court shall, on conviction, have power to make such order as to costs to be paid by the accused to the prosecutor as it thinks just and reasonable, but—

(*a*)   where under the conviction the court orders payment of any sum as a fine, penalty, forfeiture or compensation, and the sum so ordered to be paid does not exceed 25p, the court shall not order the accused to pay any costs under this subsection unless in any particular case it thinks fit to do so;

(*b*)   where the accused is under 17 years old, the amount of the costs ordered to be paid by the accused himself under this subsection shall not exceed the amount of any fine ordered to be so paid.

(3) A court shall specify in the order of dismissal, or as the case may be the conviction, the amount of any costs that it orders to be paid under subs. (1) or (2) above.

(4) Where examining justices determine not to commit the accused for trial on the gound that the evidence is not sufficient to put him upon his trial, and are of opinion that the charge was not made in good faith, they may order the prosecutor to pay the whole or any part of the costs incurred in or about the defence.

(5) If the amount ordered to be paid under subs. (4) above exceeds £25, the prosecutor may appeal to the Crown Court; and no proceedings shall be taken upon the order until the time allowed for giving notice of appeal has elapsed, or, if within that time notice of appeal is given, until the appeal is determined or ceases to be prosecuted.

COMMENTARY

For the enforcement of costs, *see* the Administration of Justice Act 1970, s. 41, *supra*.

An order for costs is not a "sentence" from which appeal lies to the Crown Court: Magistrates' Courts Act 1980, s. 108; but *see* subs. (5), *supra*.

The judicial review procedure was used to quash a justices' order for costs against a defendant where no reasonable authority could have made the order: *R.* v. *Tottenham Justices, ex parte Joshi* [1982] 75 Cr. App. R. 72. (Legal aid rates wrongly used where neither party legally aided and prosecutor not legally represented). The question should have been what sum of money would reimburse the prosecuting authority for those items of time and trouble the offence committed had made necessary?

Subsection (1). *See* under Costs *Inter Partes* in the introduction.

Subsection (2): Conviction. Includes a finding of guilt in the case of a juvenile (Children and Young Persons Act 1933, s. 59) and orders of probation or of absolute or conditional discharge: Powers of Criminal Courts Act 1973, s. 13.

Under 17 years old. For the determination of age *see* the Children & Young Persons Act 1933, s. 99.

Paid by the accused himself. These words appear to distinguish deliberately the position where a parent or guardian is ordered to pay costs under the Children and Young Persons Act 1933, s. 55. In this respect the restriction under subs. (2)(*b*) seem to be different from that in subs. (2)(*a*) which does not employ these words.

Subsection (4): Determine not to commit for trial. This subsection is confined to cases where the accused is discharged under "conventional" committal proceedings and does not extend to information permitted to be withdrawn where justices have an unfettered discretion to order costs against the prosecutor: s. 12(1), *infra*.

Justices who order costs under this subsection may be compelled to state a case: *R.* v. *Allen* (1912) 76 J.P. 95.

Subsection (5). The prosecutor has no right to appeal under this subsection against an award of costs under s. 12, *infra*, where an information is not proceeded with: *R.* v. *Crown Court at Lewes, ex parte Rogers* (1974) 138 J.P. 249.

The time allowed for giving notice of appeal. That is, within 21 days of the decision: Crown Court Rules 1971, r. 7.

Awards where prosecution not proceeded with

12. (1) Where an information charging an indictable offence is laid before a justice of the peace for any area but the information is not proceeded with (either by summary trial or by an inquiry by examining justices) a magistrates' court for that area may order the payment out of central funds of—

(*a*)   the costs properly incurred in preparing a defence to the offence charged, and

(*b*)   such sums as appear to the court reasonably sufficient to compensate any person attending to give evidence as a witness for the defence for the expense, trouble or loss of time properly incurred in or incidental to his attendance.

(2) The amount of costs ordered to be paid under subs. (1) above shall be ascertained as soon as practicable by the proper officer of the court.

(3) Where an information is laid before a justice of the peace for any area but the information is not proceeded with (either by summary trial or by an inquiry by examining magistrates), a magistrates' court for that area may make such order as to costs to be paid by the prosecutor to the accused as it thinks just and reasonable.

(4) An order under subs. (3) above shall specify the amount of the costs ordered to be paid.

(5) Where a person committed for trial is not ultimately tried, the Crown Court shall have the same power to order payment of costs under this Act as if the accused had been tried and acquitted.

COMMENTARY

The prosecutor has no right of appeal against an order of costs made under this section: *R. v. The Crown Court at Lewes, ex parte Rogers, supra.*

Subsection (1): Indictable offence. Defined in the Interpretation Act 1978, sch. 1. *See* the Commentary to s. 1.

Laid before a justice of the peace. Or a justices' clerk: The Justices' Clerks Rules 1970.

Not proceeded with. This includes informations which are permitted to be withdrawn (thus overcoming the deficiency revealed in *R. v. Phipps, ex parte Alton* (1964) 128 J.P. 323), but not informations adjourned *sine die.*

Subsection (2): The proper officer of the court. *See* the note to s. 1.

Central funds

13. In this Act "central funds" means money provided by Parliament. (*as amended by the Interpretation Act 1978, sch. 3*).

Payment of costs ordered by magistrates' courts to be paid out of central funds

15. (1) As soon as there has been ascertained the amount due to any person as costs ordered to be paid out of central funds by a magistrates' court—

(a)   dealing summarily with an indictable offence, or
(b)   inquiring into an offence as examining justices and determining not to commit the accused for trial, or
(c)   where an information is not proceeded with, as mentioned in s. 12(1) above,

the justices' clerk shall pay to that person the amount so ascertained.

(2) As soon as there has been ascertained the amount due to any person as costs ordered to be paid out of central funds by a magistrates' court otherwise than as mentioned in subs. (1) above, the justices' clerk shall—

(a)   so far as the amount is due for travelling or personal expenses in respect of that person's attendance, pay to him the amount due forthwith, and
(b)   so far as the amount is not due for such expenses, send a certificate of the amount to the Crown Court, in accordance with arrangements made by the Lord Chancellor.

(3) Where a certificate is sent to the Crown Court under subs. (2) above the appropriate officer of the Crown Court shall pay to the person to whom the certificate relates, or to any person appearing to him to be acting on behalf of that person, the amount certified or any less amount which the Crown Court considers should have been allowed under this Act.

(4) The appropriate officer of the Crown Court shall, when practicable, include the amount payable as costs certified under this section in any order for payment of costs made by that court.

(*as amended by S.I. 1980 No. 705*).

Payment of costs ordered to be paid out of central funds and by accused or prosecutor

16. (1) Where a court orders the payment of costs by the accused or the prosecutor and also orders the payment of costs out of central funds, the costs, so far as they are payable under both orders, shall be primarily payable out of central funds; and the court shall give notice to the Lord Chancellor of the order for the payment of costs by the accused or the prosecutor.

(2) To the extent that any costs are primarily payable out of central funds by an order (under this or any other Act) and have been paid out of those funds, the Secretary of State shall be entitled to be reimbursed out of any money due under any other court order for the payment of those costs, and to take any proceedings for the enforcement of any such other order providing for payment of costs by the prosecutor.

(3) Subsection (4) of s. 61 of the Justices of the Peace Act 1979(regulations as to accounts of justices' clerks) shall apply in relation to sums payable to the Lord Chancellor by virtue of subs. (2) above as it applies in relation to sums payable to the Secretary of State under that section.

(as amended by S.I. 1980, No. 705).

Miscellaneous applications of Act

18. (1) This Act shall apply where a person is committed by a magistrates' court to the Crown Court—

(a) with a view to his being sentenced to borstal training under s. 20 of the Criminal Justice Act 1948, or

(b) with a view to his being sentenced for an indictable offence under s. 42 of the Powers of Criminal Courts Act 1973, or

(c) with a view to the making of a hospital order with a restriction order under Part III of the Mental Health Act 1983,

as it applies where a person is convicted before the Crown Court.

(2) This Act shall apply to a person committed by a magistrates' court as an incorrigible rogue under the Vagrancy Act 1824, as if he were committed for trial before the Crown Court and as if the committing court were examining justices.

(3) This Act shall apply to an appeal to the Crown Court under the Vagrancy Act 1824, as if the hearing of the appeal were a trial on indictment and as if the magistrates' court from which the appeal was brought were examining justices.

(4) This Act shall apply to—

(a) proceedings for dealing with an offender under ss. 6, 8 or 10 of the Powers of Criminal Courts Act 1973 (probation orders and orders for conditional discharge);

(b) proceedings under ss. 16 or 17 of that Act (community service orders) and

(c) proceedings under ss. 23(1) or 27 of that Act for dealing with an offender in respect of a suspended sentence or for breach of a suspended sentence supervision order

as if the offender had been tried in those proceedings for the offence for which the order was made or the sentence passed.

(5) The provisions of this Act, except those relating to costs as between parties, shall apply with all necessary modofications to proceedings in which it is alleged that an offender required on conviction of an indictable offence to enter into a recognizance to keep the peace or be of good behaviour has failed to comply with a condition of that recognizance, as if that failure were an indictable offence.

(as amended by the Powers of Criminal Courts Act 1973, sch. 5, the Mental Health (Amendment) Act 1982, sch. 3, the Mental Health Act 1983, sch. 4.)

COMMENTARY

Subsection (5): Indictable offence. Defined in the Interpretation Act 1978, sch. 1. *See* the commentary to s. 1.

Interpretation

20. (1) In this Act, except so far as the context otherwise requires, "magistrates' court" means a court of summary jurisdiction or examining justices and includes a single examining justice.

(2) References in this Act to costs paid or ordered to be paid out of central funds under this Act shall be construed as including references to any sums so paid or ordered to be paid as compensation to or expenses of a witness or other person or as counsel's or solicitor's fees.

(3) *(Repealed)*

(4) . . .

(as amended by the Criminal Law Act 1977, *sch.* 13).

COMMENTARY

Subsection (2): Central funds. Defined in s. 13, *supra.*

THE COSTS IN CRIMINAL CASES (ALLOWANCES) REGULATIONS 1977

S.I. 1977 No. 2069

2. *(1) In these regulations—*

"the Act" means the Costs in Criminal Cases Act 1973;

"relevant amount" in relation to an allowance referred to in these regulations means an amount calculated in accordance with rates or scales for the time being determined for that allowance under para. (2) of this regulation;

"witness" means a person properly attending to give evidence, whether or not he gives evidence.

(2) Rates of scales of allowances payable out of central funds under the Act shall be determined by the Lord Chancellor with the consent of the Minister for the Civil Service.

(3) In these regulations, a reference to any enactment shall be construed as a reference to that enactment as amended, extended or applied by any subsequent enactment.

(4) The Interpretation Act [1978] shall apply to the interpretation of these regulations as it applies to the interpretation of an Act of Parliament, and s. 38(2) of that Act shall apply as if these regulations were an Act of Parliament and the regulations revoked by these regulations were enactments repealed thereby.

3. . . .

4. *These regulations shall apply to costs payable out of central funds under the Act.*

5.   There may be allowed in respect of a witness practising as a member of the legal or medical profession or as a dentist or veterinary surgeon for attending to give professional evidence, whether in one or more cases, a professional witness allowance not exceeding the relevant amount.

6.   There may be allowed in respect of an expert witness for attending to give expert evidence and for work in connexion with its preparation an expert witness allowance of such amount as the court may consider reasonable having regard to the nature and difficulty of the case and the work necessarily involved.

7.   There may be allowed in respect of a witness, who attends to give evidence (other than professional or expert evidence), whether in one or more cases, and thereby—

  (a) incurs any expenditure (other than on travelling, lodging or subsistence) to which he would not otherwise be subject; or
  (b) suffers any loss of earnings, or of benefit under the enactments relating to National Insurance, which he would otherwise have received,

a loss allowance not exceeding the relevant amount in respect of that expense or loss.

8.   There may be allowed in respect of a witness (other than a witness who receives an allowance under regs. 5 or 6 of these regulations) who attends to give evidence, whether in one or more cases, a subsistence allowance not exceeding the relevant amount.

9.   There may be allowed in respect of a witness, who receives an allowance under regs. 5 or 6 above and is necessarily absent from his place of residence overnight for the purpose of attending as a witness, a night allowance not exceeding the relevant amount.

10.   (1) There may be allowed in respect of a seaman who is detained on shore for the purpose of attending to give evidence and thereby misses his ship, for the time during which he is, and is likely to be, necessarily detained on shore—

  (a) an allowance not exceeding, unless for special reason the court allows a greater sum, the relevant amount in respect of loss of wages, together with
  (b) an allowance not exceeding the sum actually and reasonably incurred for his maintenance.

    (2) Nothing in the last five preceding regulations shall apply to a person in respect of whom an allowance is made under this regulation.

11.   (1) Where a witness travels to or from court by railway or other public conveyance there may be allowed in respect thereof the fare actually paid:
    provided that, unless for a special reason the court otherwise directs, only second class fare shall be allowed for travel by railway.

    (2) Where a witness travels to or from court by a hired vehicle there may be allowed in respect thereof—

  (a) in a case of urgency or where no public service is reasonably available, the amount of the fare and any reasonable gratuity paid; and
  (b) in any other case, the amount of the fare for travel by the appropriate public service.

    (3) Subject to para. (4) below, where a witness travels to or from court by a private conveyance there may be allowed in respect thereof an allowance not exceeding the relevant amount.

    (4) There may be allowed—

(a) in respect of travelling expenses of a witness who, in the opinion of the court, is suffering from a serious illness; or

(b) in respect of the carriage of heavy exhibits

such sums, in excess of the sums allowable under the preceding paragraphs of this regulation, as appear to the court to have been reasonably incurred.

12. There may be allowed in respect of a person employed as an interpreter such allowances as the court may consider reasonable.

13. (1) There may be allowed in respect of any prosecutor, accused or appellant, or party to proceedings before the Divisional Court, whose costs are ordered to be paid out of central funds under the Act the same travelling and subsistence allowances as if he attended to give evidence other than professional or expert evidence.

(2) There may be allowed in respect of any other person who in the opinion of the court necessarily attends for the purpose of the case otherwise than to give evidence the same allowances as if he attended to give evidence other than professional or expert evidence.

14. Notwithstanding anything contained in the preceding regulations no sum shall be allowed under these regulations in the case of—

(a) a member of a police force attending court in his capacity as such;

(b) a whole-time officer of an institution to which the Prison Act 1952 applies attending court in his capacity as such;

(c) a prisoner in respect of any occasion on which he is conveyed to court in custody.

17. (1) There may be allowed in respect of a written report made by a registered medical practitioner to a court in pursuance of a request to which s. 32(2) of the Criminal Justice Act 1967 applies—

(a) if made for the purpose of determining whether or not to make an order under s. 3 of the Powers of Criminal Courts Act 1973 (probation orders requiring treatment for mental condition), s. 60 of the Mental Health Act 1959 (hospital orders and guardianship orders) or s. 12(4) of the Children and Young Persons Act 1969 (supervision order requiring treatment for mental condition) by a registered medical practitioner who holds an appointment to a post in the consultant grade in the National Health Service or is for the time being approved by a local health authority for the purposes of s. 28 of the Mental Health Act 1959, an allowance not exceeding the relevant amount;

(b) if made for any purpose referred to in sub-para. (a) above by a registered medical practitioner other than one referred to in that sub-paragraph, an allowance not exceeding the relevant amount;

(c) if made for any purpose other than one referred to in sub-para. (a) above by a registered medical practitioner who holds an appointment to a post in the consultant grade in the National Health Service, an allowance not exceeding the relevant amount;

(d) in any other case, an allowance not exceeding the relevant amount.

(2) Where a registered medical practitioner who makes a written report to a court, in pursuance of a request to which the said s. 32(2) applies, incurs travelling expenses in connexion with the preparation of that report, there may be allowed in respect thereof an allowance not exceeding the relevant amount.

(3) Nothing in this regulation shall apply to a report by the medical officer of an institution to which the Prison Act 1952 applies.

COMMENTARY

The "relevant amounts" (para. 2) are promulgated by government circular (presently HOC 147/1979 and L.C.D. circulars J.C.(81)2, J.C.(81)5, J.C.(81)7, J.C.(82)1, J.C.(82)5, J.C.(82)7, J.C.(83)4).

The absence of any reference to loss of earnings on the part of the defendant is deliberate. His are confined to travel and subsistence. (Taxing Master's decision in *R.* v. *Thompson* (1979) February 5, unreported).

CHAPTER 12

LEGAL AID

CONTENTS

INTRODUCTION

So far as criminal proceedings are concerned, a person unable to afford to instruct a solicitor privately may be assisted in the following ways:

(1)   by legal representation and advice under a legal aid order;
(2)   by legal advice and assistance under the "green form" scheme; and
(3)   by legal representation on the part of a solicitor acting under the "green form" scheme and authorized by the court.

Legal aid in civil proceedings and proceedings in the High Court arising from criminal proceedings, such as appeal by way of case stated and application for judicial review, is dealt with in Part I of the Legal Aid Act 1974

Legal Aid Orders

Not all proceedings which are criminal in nature are covered by criminal legal aid although it does extend to some quasi-criminal proceedings, for example bind-over to keep the peace, as well as to some purely civil matters, notably care proceedings in the juvenile court. It is therefore important in any case of doubt to check that the proceedings for which legal aid is sought fall within the ambit of s. 28 of the Legal Aid Act 1974. Magistrates can grant legal aid under *ibid*, Part II, not only for proceedings before their own courts, but also for certain proceedings in the Crown Court, including trial on indictment, appeals and committals for sentence.

Applying for legal aid

The power to determine an application for legal aid for proceedings in a magistrates' court may be exercised by:
(i)   the court (Legal Aid Act 1974, s.28); or
(ii)   the justices' clerk (Legal Aid in Criminal Proceedings (General) Regulations 1968, r.1(4)).

Application to the court may be made orally (r.1(2) of the Regs.) in which case it may be referred to the justices' clerk (r.1(5)). Application to the clerk must be in prescribed form (r.1(1)). The justices clerk may either:
(i)   make the order:
(ii)   refer the application to the court or to a justice of the peace; or
(iii) (where review by the criminal legal aid committee is available) refuse to make the order (r.1(6) of the Regs.).

Corresponding arrangements for legal aid for proceedings in the Crown Court are set out in r.2 of the Regulations except that, because of the absence of review by the criminal legal aid committee, the clerk may not refuse such an application.

Decisions on the grant of legal aid should be taken on the basis of an adequate knowledge of the facts and the arrangements must be such that the courts are properly acquainted with the precise nature of the charges and the grounds of the application, if necessary by calling upon the prosecution for information: *R*. v. *Highgate Justices, ex parte Lewis* (1978) 142 J.P. 78.

A parent or guardian may apply on behalf of a juvenile: Legal Aid Act 1974, s. 40(2).

There is power in the court to make a legal aid order without application: General Regulations, r. 5. This is useful, for example, in the case of the mentally ill. A statement of means (see below) is however still necessary under the Legal Aid Act 1974, s. 29(4).

General Regulations, r. 5. This is useful, for example, in the case of the mentally ill. A statement of means (see below) is however still necessary under the Legal Aid Act 1974, s. 29(4).

The Tests

If the applicant's means are such that he requires assistance in meeting the likely costs:

(*a*)   a legal aid order *must* be made
     (i)   when he is committed for trial on a charge of murder;
     (ii)   before conviction upon a remand or committal in custody if he has already been remanded in custody unrepresented; and
     (iii)   before a remand or committal in custody for inquiries before sentence;
     and
(*b*)   a legal aid order *may* be made if it appears desirable in the interests of justice (see below): Legal Aid Act 1974, s. 29(1), (1A) & (2).

Any doubt as to whether legal aid should be granted or not must be resolved in favour of the applicant: *ibid*, s. 29(6). In the case referred to in para. (a)(ii) above legal aid may be confined to the purposes of the bail proceedings: *ibid*, s. 29(1A). In such a case the order may not include the services of counsel: *ibid*, s. 30(2).

Any doubt as to whether legal aid should be granted or not must be resolved in favour of the applicant: s. 29(6). In the case referred to in para. (a)(ii) above legal aid may be confined to the purposes of the bail proceedings: s. 29(1A), *ibid*. In such a case the order may not include the services of counsel: s. 30(2).

The Interests of Justice (The Widgery Criteria)

The Departmental Committee on Legal Aid in Criminal Proceedings (the Widgery Committee) stated that in their view the following factors indicate that legal aid is desirable in the interests of justice:

(*a*)   the charge is a grave one in the sense that the accused is in real jeopardy of losing his liberty or livelihood or suffering serious damage to his reputation;
(*b*)   the charge raises a substantial question of law;
(*c*)   the accused is unable to follow the proceedings and state his own case because of his inadequate knowledge of English, mental illness or other mental or physical disability;
(*d*)   the nature of the defence involves the tracing and interviewing of witnesses or expert cross-examination of a witness for the prosecution; and
(*e*)   legal representation is desirable in the interest of someone other than the accused as, for example, in the case of sexual offences against young children when it is undesirable that the accused should cross-examine the witness in person.

Persons committed for trial or sentence. The Committee recommended that the general practice of the courts should be to grant legal aid to persons committed for trial or sentence who are financially eligible, and that while the courts should retain discretion to refuse legal aid on grounds other than means this should be exercised only in rare cases. They considered that the existing practice of assigning only counsel to unrepresented persons is unsatisfactory and that it is advisable that full legal aid should be provided in such cases. The Committee further recommended that the grant of legal aid in such cases should be considered by the justices at the time of committal.

Committal proceedings. The Committee recommended that (*a*) the application for legal aid should be considered before the plea is taken and before any election for summary trial or trial on indictment is made; (*b*) subject to the test of means, legal aid should normally be granted for the preliminary hearing in the case of offences triable only on indictment; and (c) where an offence can be tried either summarily or on indictment, the same criteria should be applied as for a summary trial.

Juvenile courts. The Committee took the view that the grant of legal aid in juvenile courts should be governed by the same general principles as in adult courts.

Appeals to the Crown Court. The Committee concluded that the only criteria, other than means, which it is practicable to apply are those suggested for the grant of legal aid in magistrates' courts.

Trials on indictment. The Committee also recommended that where a person who is charged with an offence triable only on indictment does not apply for legal aid before his appearance in court and is unrepresented, the examining justices should inquire on his first appearance whether he has been informed of the facilities for legal aid and whether he wishes to apply for it. On committing a person for trial or sentence the court should likewise inquire whether he wishes to apply for legal aid in the court of trial. In any other cases which appear to fulfil the criteria for the grant of legal aid, the court should satisfy itself that a failure to apply for legal aid is not the consequence of ignorance of the facilities available.

In addition, the High Court have stated that legal aid should be offered where:

(a) the magistrates are considering making a recommendation for deportation: *R. v. Edgehill* [1963] 1 All E.R. 181;
(b) where the defendant is resident abroad with no experience of English courts: *R. v. Phillips* [1965] Crim. L.R. 109;
(c) a hospital order is being considered: *R. v. King's Lynn JJ, ex parte Fysh* [1964] Crim. L.R. 143;
(d) on committal for sentence: *R. v. Serghiou* [1966] 3 All E.R. 637.

There is, apart from murder, no charge which of itself carries an automatic right to legal aid: *ibid.* (But see above as to the other circumstances in which, subject to means, a legal aid order must be made).

The High Court will not interefere to upset the exercise by magistrates of their discretion in the matter of legal aid: *R. v. Macclesfield Justices, ex parte Greenhalgh* (1980) 144 J.P. 142; *R. v. Cambridge Crown Court, ex parte Hagi* (1980) 144 J.P. 145. (And see the article at 144 J.P.N. 185).

Review of Refusal

An applicant refused legal aid on the interests of justice test for proceedings in a magistrates' court in respect of an indictable offence may apply for review to the appropriate legal aid committee. Such application must be made not later than 21 days before the date fixed for the trial or the enquiry, where such a date had been fixed when the application was made. (Legal Aid in Criminal Proceedings (General) Regulations 1968, r. 6E(2)). This time limit may be waived or altered by the committee for good reason (*ibid,* r. 6F(3)). The justices' clerk and the applicant must supply whatever further particulars the committee requires (*ibid.,* r. 6G).

The Statement of Means

Before making a legal aid order the court must require the applicant to furnish a statement of means in prescribed form unless it appears that he is by reason of his physical or mental condition incapable of doing so: Legal Aid Act 1974, s. 29(4). Where the applicant is under 16 the court has a discretion to call for a statement of means from him or any "appropriate contributor" or from both, or may waive the requirement altogether: *ibid,* s. 29(5). An appropriate contributor is defined in s. 40 in relation to a person under 16 as meaning his father, any person who has been adjudged to be his putative father and (whether or not he is legitimate) his mother.

Where an applicant fails to furnish a statement of means he may be treated as if his disposable income and disposable capital exceeded the prescribed limits and as if the amount of the contribution were such as the court might determine: Legal Aid Act 1982, s. 7(5). A legal aid application form should be seen by the trial court only after conviction and only for the purpose of dealing with a legal aid application: *R*. v. *Winter* [1980] Crim. L.R. 659. The form ought not to be used for the purpose of cross-examining the applicant as to his credit: *R*. v. *Stubbs* [1981] 1 All E.R. 424. Where a witness is properly cross-examined on his application form (e.g. in a prosecution arising from a statement therein) he is entitled to be given the normal warning against self-incrimination: *ibid*. It was also suggested *obiter* that applications for criminal legal aid may be privileged: *ibid*.

What Does Legal Aid Consist of?

Once a legal aid order is made the court must assign any solicitor selected by the assisted person who is willing to act, except that a single solicitor or counsel may be assigned to two or more persons whose cases are heard together, unless the interests of justice require separate representation: General Regulations, rr. 8, 14.

Legal aid consists of legal representation including advice on the preparation of the case. It also gives "authority" (*i.e.* a discretion on the part of the solicitor) to give advice on whether there appear to be reasonable grounds of appeal, as well as assistance in the preparation of a notice of appeal or in making application for a case to be stated, if given or made within the ordinary time: Legal Aid Act 1974, s. 30(1), (5).

Legal aid before a *magistrates' court* is normally confined to the services of a solicitor, but where in any indictable offence there are circumstances which make the case unusually grave or difficult the court may order representation by solicitor and counsel if this appears desirable: Legal Aid Act 1974, s. 30(2). Not more than one counsel may be assigned in magistrates' courts. Legal aid for proceedings in the *Crown Court* is limited to one counsel, but two may be ordered by a magistrates' court on a charge of murder: General Regulations, r. 13. (The Crown Court has power to order two counsel in other cases.) The selection of counsel is a matter for the solicitor: r. 9. On the other hand legal aid may be confined to the service of a solicitor (without counsel) in proceedings at which solicitors have a right to audience: Legal Aid Act 1974, s. 30(3). No payment may be made for work undertaken by a solicitor for a legally assisted person before the solicitor was assigned: *R*. v. *Rogers (Master Matthews)* [1979] 1 All E.R. 693.

Examining justices may make a legal aid order covering the committal proceedings and the proceedings in the Crown Court: Legal Aid Act 1982, s. 2.

Amending and Revoking Legal Aid Orders

A legal aid order may be *amended* by the court substituting a different solicitor or counsel, either on the application of the assisted person or otherwise: *ibid*, s. 31(1). An order may be *revoked* on the application of the legally assisted person or if the solicitor or counsel withdraws and the court thinks it undesirable by reason of the assisted person's conduct to substitute another: *ibid*, s. 31(2). A contribution order may be made in respect of an amended or revoked order: *ibid*, s. 31(3).

An application to amend or revoke may be referred to the appropriate criminal legal aid committee: Legal Aid in Criminal Proceedings (General) Regulations 1968, r.14A(2).

Legal Aid Contribution Orders

A legal aid contribution order means an order under the Legal Aid Act

1982, ss. 7 or 8(2): Legal Aid Act 1974, s. 40(1), as applied by the Legal Aid Act 1982, s. 16(4).

Where a court makes a legal aid order giving legal aid to a person whose disposable income or disposable capital exceeds prescribed limits it must make a legal aid contribution order: Legal Aid Act 1982, s. 7(1). The amount is determined by regulations: *ibid*, s. 7(2) namely rr. 18-20 of the Legal Aid in Criminal Proceedings (General) Regulations 1968 and the second Schedule. Payments out of disposable income are payable by instalments within a period not exceeding the contribution period: *ibid*, r. 22 (1). The contribution period is six months: *ibid*, r. 31. In the case of a legally assisted person who has not attained the age of 16 the court may instead of or in addition to making a legal aid contribution order against him make such an order against any appropriate contributor *ibid*, s. 7(3).

Where the cost of legal aid exceeds the contribution made under a legal aid contribution order the difference must be repaid: Legal Aid Act 1982, s. 7(6).

A legal aid contribution order may be varied in light of further information about the assisted person's disposable income or disposable capital or of any change in them: *ibid*, s. 8(1). Similarly, where no contribution order was made at first one may be made later if it subsequently appears that his means warrant it: *ibid*, s. 8(2).

A contribution order may be revoked: *ibid*, s. 8(3).

The court which may exercise these powers is specified in *ibid*, s. 8(4). At the conclusion of the proceedings the court may remit outstanding sums and in the event of acquittal order repayment: *ibid*, s. 8(5).

Enforcement of a Contribution Order

A legal aid contribution order is enforceable as if it were a sum ordered to be paid by the order of the collecting court: Legal Aid Act 1974, s. 35(1), sch. 3. The term "collecting court" is defined in *ibid*, s. 32(5).

Advice and Assistance (The "Green Form" Scheme)

A solicitor may give advice and assistance to a client who fulfils prescribed means qualifications. This scheme, which is known by the name of the green form used for ascertaining means, is provided for in the Legal Aid Act 1974, ss. 1, 2 and 2A. Advice and assistance under the green form scheme does not extend to legal representation unless given in compliance with a request made to the solicitor by the court or given in accordance with a proposal made by the solicitor and approved by the court, in either case at a time when the solicitor is present within the precincts of the court: Legal Advice and Assistance Regulations (No. 2) 1980, r. 19 (*See* the commentary to s. 2A of the Act, *infra*).

THE LEGAL AID ACT 1974

Persons eligible for advice and assistance

1. (1) Advice and assistance to which this section applies shall, subject to and in accordance with the provisions of this Part of this Act, be available in England and Wales for any person if—

(*a*)   his disposable income does not exceed £85 a week, or

(*b*)   he is (directly or indirectly) in receipt of supplementary benefit under the Supplementary Benefits Act 1976 or of family income supplement under the Family Income Supplements Act 1970.

and (in either case) his disposable income does not exceed £600.

(2) (*Regulations*).

(*as amended by the Supplementary Benefits Act* 1976, *sch.* 7, *the Legal Aid Act* 1979, *sch.* 1).

COMMENTARY

Disposable income/capital. Defined in s. 11 of the Act (not included here).
Any person. Corporate and unincorporated bodies are excluded by s. 25.

Scope and general conditions of advice and assistance

2. (1) Subject to subs. (2) and s. 2A below and to any prescribed exceptions or conditions, s. 1 above applies to any oral or written advice given by a solicitor, or, if and so far as may be necesary, by counsel—

(*a*)   on the application of English law to any particular circumstances which have arisen in relation to the person seeking advice, and

(*b*)   as to any steps which that person might appropriately take (whether by way of settling any claim, bringing or defending any proceedings, making an agreement, will or other instrument or transaction, obtaining further legal or other advice or assistance, or otherwise) having regard to the application of English law to those circumstances,

and applies to any assistance given by a solicitor, or, if and so far as may be necessary, by counsel to any person in taking any such steps as are mentioned in para. (*b*) above, whether the assistance is given by taking any such steps on his behalf or by assisting him in taking them on his own behalf.

(2) Notwithstanding anything in subs. (1) above, s. 1 above does not apply to any advice or assistance given to a person in connexion with any proceedings before a court or tribunal—

(*a*)   . . .

(*b*)   in the case of criminal proceedings, or any proceedings mentioned in subs. (3), (6), or (6A) of s. 28 below, at a time when a legal aid order made in respect of him for the purposes of those proceedings is in force.

(3), (4) (*Repealed*).

(5) Except as previously provided by this Part of this Act or by regulations made under it,—

(*a*)   the fact that the services of counsel or a solicitor are given by way of advice or assistance shall not affect the relationship between or the rights of counsel, solicitor and client or any privilege arising out of such relationship; and (*b*)   the rights conferred by this Part of this Act on a person receiving advice or assistance shall not affect the rights or liabilities of other parties to any proceedings or the principles on which the discretion of any court or tribunal is normally exercised.

(6)   In this section "legal aid certificate" means a certificate required, in accordance with regulations made under s. 20 below, to be obtained as a condition of entitlement to legal aid; "legal aid order" means an order made under s. 28 below.

(*as amended by the Legal Aid Act* 1979, *s.* 1(1), *sch.* 1).

COMMENTARY

It is for the solicitor to determine (by use of what is known as the Law Society's green form) whether the party to the proceedings falls within the financial limits meriting assistance as set out in s. 1 above. He is then entitled to give assistance up to £40. Before exceeding this limit he must first obtain approval of the area committee of the Law Society.

Advice and assistance may not be given under this section to a child, that is anyone under the upper limit of compulsory school age, unless authorized by the general committee: reg. 8(1) of the Legal Advice and Assistance Regulations (No. 2) 1980.

Subsection (1). Advice under this subsection can with the approval of the court be extended to legal representation in accordance witn the Legal Advice and Assistance Regulations (No. 2) 1980, *See* under s. 2A, *infra.* Where this is done payment for the advice and assistance is made as part of the costs of legal aid and any sum paid by the client is credited towards any legal aid contribution order: Legal Aid Act 1982, s. 12.

Representation in proceedings

2A.   (1) In this Part of this Act "assistance by way of representation" means any assistance given to a person by taking on his behalf any step in the institution or conduct of any proceedings before a court or tribunal, or of any proceedings in connexion with a statutory inquiry, whether by representing him in those proceedings or by otherwise taking any step on his behalf (as distinct from assisting him in taking such a step on his own behalf).

(2) Without prejudice to s. 2(2) above and subject to any prescribed exceptions, s. 1 above does not apply to any assistance by way of representation unless it is approved by an appropriate authority in accordance with regulations made for the purposes of this section; and regulations so made may make different provision for different cases or classes of cases.

(3), (4) (*Regulations*).

(5) Where a person receives any assistance by way of representation in any civil proceedings before a court or any proceedings before a tribunal, then, except in so far as regulations otherwise provide, his liability by virtue of an order for costs made against him with respect to the proceedings shall not exceed the amount (if any) which is a reasonable one for him to pay having regard to all the circumstances, including the means of all the parties and their conduct in connection with the dispute; and regulations shall make provision as to the court, tribunal or person by whom that amount is to be determined and the extent to which any determination of that amount is to be final.

(6) For the purposes of any inquiry under subs. (5) above as to the means of a person against whom an order for costs has been made, his dwelling house and household furniture and the tools and implements of his trade shall be left out of account except in such cases and to such extent as may be prescribed, and except as so prescribed they shall, in all parts of the United Kingdom, be protected from

seizure in execution to enforce the order.

(7) . . .

(*as inserted by the Legal Aid Act* 1979, *s.* 1).

COMMENTARY

Subsection (2): The appropriate authority. The Legal Advice and Assistance Regulations (No. 2) 1980, r. 16. This is normally the general committee, however, reg. 19 states that:

> "The approval of a general committee shall not be required for assistance by way of representation given by a solicitor to any party to proceedings (whether criminal or civil) before a magistrates' court or to proceedings before a county court, provided that the cost of such assistance does not exceed the limit imposed by virtue of s. 3(2) of the Act, where the assistance is given in compliance with a request which is made to the solicitor by the court or given in accordance with a proposal which is made by the solicitor and approved by the court and which (in either case)—

> (*a*)   is so made or approved at a time (whether at or after the beginning of the proceedings) when the solicitor is present within the precincts of the court, but
> (*b*)   is not made or approved at any such time as is mentioned in s. 2(2)(*a*) or (*b*) of the Act".

Regulation 27 and sch. 6 (costs) would not seem to apply to criminal proceedings.

Power to order legal aid to be given

28. (1) The following provisions of this section shall have effect with respect to the giving of legal aid in connexion with criminal proceedings and the proceedings mentioned in subss. (3), (6) and (6A) below, but any power conferred by those provisions to give such aid shall be exercisable only in the circumstances mentioned in subs. (1) of s. 19 below and subject to the provisions of subs. (1A) to (4) of that section.

(2) Where a person is charged with an offence before a magistrates' court or appears or is brought before a magistrates' court to be dealt with, the court may order that he shall be given legal aid for the purpose of the proceedings before the court and any juvenile court to which the case is remitted in pursuance of s. 56(1) of the Children and Young Persons Act 1933 or, in the circumstances mentioned in para. (*c*) of s. 28(1) below, for the purpose of so much of those proceedings as relates to the grant of bail.

(3) (*Juvenile Court*)

(4) Where a person makes an application to a magistrates' court under s. 37 of the Powers of Criminal Courts Act 1973 (review of compensation orders), the court may order that he shall be given legal aid for the purpose of the proceedings before the court.

(5) Where a person convicted or sentenced by a magistrates' court desires to appeal to the Crown Court, either of those courts may order that he shall be given legal aid for the purpose of the appeal, and, where any such person gives notice of appeal, either of those courts may order that the other party to the appeal shall be given legal aid for the purpose of resisting the appeal.

(6) Where a person desires to appeal to the Crown Court in pursuance of ss. 2(12), 3(8), 21(4) or 31(6) of the Children and Young Persons Act of 1969 or under s. 21A of the Child Care Act 1980, the Crown Court or the court from whose decision the appeal lies may order that he be given legal aid for the purposes of the appeal.

(6A) (*Juvenile Court*).

(7) Where a person is committed to or appears before the Crown Court for trial or sentence, or appears or is brought before the Crown Court to be dealt with, the

court which commits him or the Crown Court may order that he shall be given legal aid for the purpose of the trial or other proceedings before the Crown Court.

(8)–(11) . . .

(11A) In any case where a person is liable to be committed or fined–

   (a)   by a magistrates' court under s. 12 of the Contempt of Court Act 1981;

   (b)   by a county court under ss. 30, 127 or 157 of the County Courts Act 1959; or

   (c)   by any superior court for contempt in the face of that or any other court or tribunal,

the court may order that he shall be given legal aid for the purposes of the proceedings.

(12) In the following provisions of this Part of this Act "legal aid order" means an order made under any provision of this section and "legally assisted person" means a person to whom legal aid is ordered to be given by such an order.

(as amended by the Children Act 1975, s. 65 and the Bail Act 1976, s. 11, the Contempt of Court Act 1981, sch. 1, the Criminal Justice Act 1982, s. 25(2)).

COMMENTARY

Subsection (2): Charged with an offence. *See* the extended definition of this term in subs. (10) and (11) of s. 30, *infra*. Legal aid ordered under this subsection includes proceedings on an application for bail to the Crown Court following a full argument certificate: s. 30(1A). Counsel are not included for this purpose except where they were allowed in the magistrates' court: s. 30(1B).

To be dealt with. Defined in s. 30(12), *infra*.

The proceedings before the court. Examining justices can make a "through" order which covers both the committal proceedings and the proceedings in the Crown Court: Legal Aid Act 1982, s. 2. This term includes, by virtue of the European Communities Act 1972, s. 2(1), proceedings before the European Court upon a reference by a magistrates' court to that court: *R. v. Marlborough Street Stipendiary Magistrate, ex parte Bouchereau* (1977) 142 J.P. 27.

Subsection (5). The wide terminology of this subsection ("desires to appeal") suggests that legal aid may be granted before notice of appeal has been served. It could thus cover an application for leave to appeal out of time.

   Legal aid may only be granted on appeals to the Crown Court under this Part of the Act. Appeals by way of case stated are dealt with under Part I, even where they arise from criminal proceedings.

A person convicted. This includes a juvenile found guilty: Children & Young Persons Act 1933, s. 59.

Sentenced. Defined in s. 30(12), *infra*.

Appeal. For the documents to be transmitted to the Crown Court *see* reg. 17 of the (General) Regulations, *infra*. Notes of any evidence taken must be supplied to the defence: reg. 16, *ibid*.

The other party to the appeal. Presumably this would extend to the original prosecutor in third party proceedings: *R. v. Recorder of Derby, ex parte Spalton* (1944) 108 J.P. 193; *R. v. Epsom JJ., ex parte Dawnier Motors, Ltd.* (1961) 125 J.P. 40.

Subsection (7): Committed . . . for trial. Defined in the Interpretation Act 1978, sch. 1 as meaning, committed in custody or on bail by a magistrates' court pursuant to s. 6 of the Magistrates' Courts Act 1980, or by any Judge, or other authority having power to do so with a view to trial before a Judge and jury.

   For the documents to be transmitted to the Crown Court *see* reg. 17 of the (General) Regulations, *infra*.

Committed . . . for . . . sentence. Defined in s. 40(1), *infra*. For the documents to be transmitted to the Crown Court *see* reg. 17 of the (General) Regulations, *infra*.

Subsection (11A). Counsel may be allowed: s. 30(4A).

Circumstances in which legal aid may be ordered to be given

29. (1) Subject to the following provisions of this sction, the power to make a legal aid order shall be exercisable by a court having that power under s. 28 above where it appears to the court desirable to do so in the interests of justice, and a court having that power shall make such an order—

(a) where a person is committed for trial on a charge of murder; or

(b) . . .

or (c) where a person charged with an offence before a magistrates' court is brought before the court in pursuance of a remand in custody on an occasion when he may be again remanded or committed in custody and is not (but wishes to be) legally represented before the court, not having been legally represented before the court when he was so remanded;

or (d) where a person who is to be sentenced or dealt with for an offence before a magistrates' court or the Crown Court is to be kept in custody to enable inquiries or a report to be made to assist the court in sentencing or dealing with him for the offence;

(e) where a child is brought before a juvenile court under s. 21A of the Child Care Act 1980 and is not (but wishes to be) legally represented before that court.

(1A) Nothing in subs. (1) above shall require a magistrates' court, in the circumstances mentioned in para. (c) of that subsection, to order that the person charged before it be given legal aid for the purposes of the proceedings before that court and any juvenile court (as distinct from legal aid for the purpose of so much of those proceedings as relates to the grant of bail) or, in those circumstances, to make a legal aid order after the conviction of that person.

(2) A court shall not make a legal aid order for the giving of aid to any person for any purpose unless it appears to the court that his disposable income and disposable capital are such that he requires assistance in meeting the costs which he may incur for that purpose.

(3) (*Repealed*).

(4) Without prejudice to subs. (2) above, before a court makes a legal aid order for the giving of aid to any person, the court shall require him to furnish a written statement of his means in a prescribed form unless it appears to the court that he is by reason of his physical or mental conditions incapable of doing so.

(5) Subsections (3) and (4) above shall have effect in their application to a person who has not attained the age of 16, as if the words "he", "him" and "his" referred to that person and a person who is an appropriate contributor in relation to him or such of them as the court selects, and as if in subs. (4) for the word "shall" there were substituted the word "may" and the words from "unless" onwards were omitted; and the court may require that a statement furnished by an appropriate contributor in pursuance of subs. (4) shall specify both his means and those of the person who has not attained the age of 16.

(5A) Paragraphs (c) and (d) of subs. (1) above shall have effect in their application to a person who has not attained the age of 18 as if the references to a remand in custody and to being remanded, committed or kept in custody included references to being committed under s. 23 of the Children and Young Persons Act 1969 to the care of a local authority or to a remand centre.

(6) Where a doubt arises whether a legal aid order should be made for the giving of aid to any person, the doubt shall be resolved in that person's favour.

(as amended by the Bail Act 1976, s. 11, the Criminal Law Act 1977, sch. 12, the Legal Aid Act 1982, s. 10, sch., the Criminal Justice Act 1982, s. 25(2)).

12 LEGAL AID

COMMENTARY

Subsection (1): A legal aid order. Defined in s. 28(12), *supra*.

The interests of justice. *See* under this heading in the introduction.

Committed for trial. *See* the note to s. 28, *supra*.

Subsection (2): Any indictable offence. It was formerly held that this includes an offence which can be tried either summarily or on indictment: *R.* v. *Guildhall Justices, ex parte Marshall* (1976) 140 J.P. 274. The present definition of "indictable offence" in the Interpretation Act 1978, sch., confirms this decision.

Subsection (4): A written statement of his means. The penalty for false statements is in s. 90 of the Criminal Justice Act 1967 as applied by s. 42(3) of this Act.
   In the case of persons under 16 *see* the Legal Aid Act 1982, s. 7(4).

   For the treatment of persons who fail to furnish a statement of means *see* the Legal Aid Act 1982, s. 7(5).

Attained the age of 16. For juveniles who subsequently attain this age *see* s. 40(3), *infra*.

Appropriate contributor. Defined in s. 40(1), *infra*.

Scope of legal aid and supplementary provisions as to legal aid orders

30. (1) For the purposes of this Part of this Act legal aid, in relation to any proceedings to which a person is party, shall be taken, subject to the following provisions of this section, as consisting of representation by a solicitor and counsel assigned by the court, including advice on the preparation of that person's case for those proceedings.

(1A) Legal aid which may be ordered to be given to any person for the purpose of any proceedings by a legal aid order under s. 28(2) above, whether or not in the circumstances mentioned in s. 29(1)(c) above, shall include, in the event—

   (a) of his being remanded in custody in those proceedings; and

   (b) of the court issuing a certificate under s. 5(6A) of the Bail Act 1976 (refusal of fully argued bail application),

legal aid for the purpose of proceedings in connection with an application for bail to the Crown Court.

(1B) Notwithstanding anything in subs. (1) above, legal aid in connection with an application for bail to the Crown Court shall not include representation by counsel except in a case where by virtue of subs. (2)(a) below legal aid ordered to be given for the purposes of the proceedings before the magistrates' court included representation by counsel.

(2) Notwithstanding anything in subs. (1) above, legal aid ordered to be given for the purposes of any proceedings before a magistrates' court shall not include representation by counsel except—

   (a) in the case of any indictable offence, where the court is of the opinion that, because of circumstances which make the case unusually grave or difficult, representation by both solicitor and counsel would be desirable; and

   (b) ....

and legal aid ordered to be given for the purpose of so much of any proceedings before a magistrates' court as relates to the grant of bail shall not include representation by counsel.

(3) Where the Crown Court makes a legal aid order under s. 28(5), (6) or (7) above, the court may, in cases of urgency where it appears to the court that there is no time to instruct a solicitor, order that the legal aid to be given shall consist of

representation by counsel only, and where a magistrates' court or the Crown Court makes a legal aid order under any of those subsections for the purpose of proceedings in the Crown Court, being proceedings at which solicitors have a right of audience, the court may order that the legal aid to be given shall consist of representation by a solicitor only.

(4) . . .

(4A) Where a court makes a legal aid order under s. 28(11A) above, the court may order that the legal aid to be given shall consist of representation by counsel only or, in any court where solicitors have a right of audience, by a solicitor only; and the court may assign for the purpose any counsel or solicitor who is within the precincts of the court at the time when the order is made.

(5) A legal aid order under s. 28(2) or (3) above for the purpose of proceedings before a magistrates' court shall be authority for the solicitor assigned by the court to give advice on the question whether there appear to be reasonable grounds of appeal from any determination in those proceedings and assistance by him in the giving of a notice of appeal or making of an application for a case to be stated, being a notice given or application made within the ordinary time for doing so.

(6) Where legal aid is ordered to be given to any person for the purpose of an appeal to the Crown Court by a legal aid order under s. 28(5) or (6) above and the Crown Court—

(a)   in the case of an order under s. 28(5), confirms or varies his conviction or sentence, or

(b)   in the case of an order under s. 28(6), dismisses the appeal or otherwise alters the order to which the appeal relates,

the legal aid order shall be authority for counsel or the solicitor assigned to him to give advice on the question whether there appear to be reasonable grounds of appeal from the decision of the Crown Court and, if such grounds appear to exist, assistance in the making of an application for a case to be stated.

(7) Legal aid which may be ordered to be given to any person for the purpose of any proceedings by a legal aid order under s. 28(7) above shall, in the event of his being convicted or sentenced in those proceedings, include advice on the question whether there appear to be reasonable grounds of appeal and—

(a)   if such grounds appear to exist, assistance in the preparation of an application for leave to appeal or in the giving of a notice of appeal;

(b)   while the question is being considered, assistance in the making of a provisional application or the giving of a provisional notice.

(7A) Where a certificate that a case is fit for appeal has been issued under the Criminal Appeal Act 1968 or under s. 81(1B) of the Supreme Court Act 1981, legal aid which may be ordered to be given by a legal aid order under s. 28(7) above shall include legal aid for the purposes of an application for the grant of bail by the Crown Court.

(8) Legal aid which may be ordered to be given to any person for the purpose of any appeal by a legal aid order under s. 28(8) or (9) above may, without prejudice to subs. (1) above, consist in the first instance of advice, by counsel or a solicitor assigned by the court, on the question whether there appear to be reasonable grounds of appeal and assistance by that solicitor in the preparation of an application for leave to appeal or in the giving of a notice of appeal.

(9) . . .

(10) The reference in s. 28(2) above to a person charged with an offence before a magistrates' court includes a reference to a person summoned or arrested for an offence and under a duty to appear or a liability to be brought before a magistrates'

court in respect of that offence; and the power to make a legal aid order under that subsection shall, in the case of a person arrested for an offence who has not appeared or been brought before a magistrates' court, be exercisable by the magistrates' court to which an application for legal aid is made in pursuance of regulations under this Part of the Act.

(11) Any reference in s. 28(2) above to a person charged with an offence includes a reference to a person against whom proceedings are instituted under s. 115 of the Magistrates' Courts Act, 1980 (binding over), in respect of an actual or apprehended breach of the peace or other misbehaviour, and any such reference to a person brought before a magistrates' court to be dealt with includes a reference to a person brought before a metropolitan stipendiary magistrate to be dealt with under s. 9 of the Extradition Act 1970, or s. 7 of the Fugitive Offenders Act 1967 (hearing of extradition and similar proceedings).

(12) In ss. 28 and 29 above—
"dealt with" means dealt with under ss. 6, 8, 16, 17(1) or (2), 23 or 27 of the Powers of Criminal Courts Act 1973 or s. 47(3) of the Criminal Law Act 1977, or dealt with for a failure to comply with a condition of a recognizance to keep the peace or be of good behaviour;

"sentence" includes an order of a court in respect of which an appeal lies (with or without leave) to another court, and "sentenced" shall be construed accordingly.

(as amended by the Bail Act 1976, s. 11, the Administration of Justice Act 1977, sch. 1, the Magistrates' Courts Act 1980, sch. 7, the Contempt of Court Act 1981, sch. 1, the Criminal Justice Act 1982, ss. 29, 60, the Legal Aid Act 1982, s. 4.)

COMMENTARY

Subsection (1): Solicitor and counsel assigned by the court. *See* s. 38, *infra*. the court must assign any solicitor willing to act who is selected by the assisted person: reg. 8 of the General Regulations 1968, except that the court may assign a single counsel or solicitor to two or more persons whose cases are heard together unless the interests of justice require separate representation: reg. 14, *ibid*. Except a solicitor excluded by the complaints tribunal: reg. 7, *ibid*. As to the selection of counsel *see* regs, 9 and 10, *ibid*.

Not more than one counsel may be assigned in magistrates' courts (General Regulations, reg. 13) and only in the circumstances stipulated in subs. (2). Two counsel may be assigned for proceedings in the Crown Court, but where the legal aid order is made by the magistrates' court, only on a charge of murder: r. 13 of the General Regulations.

Subsection (2). Except in a murder case, before justices can exercise their discretion affirmatively to order representation by counsel under s. 30(2)(*a*) the applicant has to show both that the case is of unusual gravity or difficulty and that that circumstance leads to the conclusion that such representation is desirable in the particular proceedings under consideration—whether for summary trial before the justices or for committal proceedings. Where there is no conceivable reason for opposing a s. 6(2) committal, no matter how grave or difficult the case might be, it is difficult to see how there can be any conceivable reason for assigning counsel at that stage. Certainly, the mere multiplicity of simple, straightforward charges cannot make it desirable for counsel to be instructed. However, the facts in relation to a single charge may be so complex that it is desirable that counsel should at least advise whether there are good grounds for opposing a committal under s. 6(2): *R.* v. *Guildford Justices, ex parte Scott* (1975) *The Times*, February 24; [1975] Crim. L.R. 286. In the case of committal proceedings for alleged murder it should be recognized as a rule of practice that legal aid should include representation by counsel: *R.* v. *Derby JJ., ex parte Kooner* (1970) 134 J.P. 680.

An application under this subsection may be referred to the appropriate criminal legal aid committee: r.14A(2) of the Regulations.

Indictable offence. Defined in the Interpretation Act 1978, sch. 1 as meaning an offence which, if committed by an adult, is triable on indictment, whether it is exclusively so triable or triable either way.

Subsection (3): Proceedings at which solicitors have a right of audience. The *Practice Direction* [1972] 1 All E.R. 708 states that:

    1. A solicitor may appear in, conduct, defend and address the court in (*a*) criminal proceedings in the Crown Court on appeal from a magistrates' court or on committal of a person for sentence or to be dealt with, if he, or any partner of his, or any solicitor in his employment or by whom he is employed, appeared on behalf of the defendant in the magistrates' court; (*b*) civil proceedings in the Crown Court on appeal from a magistrates' court if he, or any partner of his, or any solicitor in his employment or by whom he is employed, appeared in the proceedings in the magistrates' court.

    2. The rights of audience conferred by this direction are in addition to and not in derogation from the rights of audience conferred by the *Practice Direction* dated December 7, 1971; (which concerned sittings of the Crown Court at Caernarvon, Barnstaple, Bodmin, Doncaster and (in certain respects) Lincoln.

Subsection (5): The ordinary time. That is, 21 days after the day on which the decision was given: Crown Court Rules 1971, r. 7 (appeal to the Crown Court) and Magistrates' Courts Act 1980, s. 111 (appeal by way of case stated).

Subsection (11). Alleged breaches of bind-over are dealt with under ss. 28(2) and 30(12) of this Act.

Subsection (12): Dealt with. These provisions of the Powers of Criminal Courts Act 1973 refer to breach of probation (s. 6) commission of further offence when on probation or conditional discharge (s. 8), breach of community service order (s. 16) and certain amendments thereto (s. 17(1) and (2)), dealing with suspended sentences (s. 23) and suspended sentence supervision orders (s. 27). The Criminal Law Act 1977, s. 47(3) deals with partly suspended sentences.

Amendment and revocation of legal aid orders

31. (1) A court having power to make a legal aid order may on the application of the legally assisted person or otherwise amend any such order by substituting for any legal representative or representatives previously assigned to him any legal representative or representatives whom the court could have assigned to him if it had been making the legal aid order.

(2) A court having power to make a legal aid order may revoke any such order—

(*a*)   on the application of the legally assisted person; or

(*b*)   if the only legal representative or all the legal representatives for the time being assigned to him withdraws or withdraw from the case and it appears to the court that, because of his conduct, it is not desirable to amend the order under subs. (1) above.

(3) The amendment or revocation of a legal aid order under this section shall not affect the right of any legal representative previously assigned to the legally assisted person to remuneration for work done before the date of the amendment or revocation, as the case may be.

(as amended by the Legal Aid Act 1982, sch.)

COMMENTARY

Subsections (1) and (2) of this section are two quite different methods of dealing with a legal aid order: the first one is simply of substitution, the second of revocation, *per* Slynn J. in *R. v. Swindon Justices, ex parte Preece* (1977) 141 J.P.N. 529. A copy of the amending or revoking order must be sent or delivered to the solicitor and the legally aided person must be notified: reg. 6 of the General Regulations, *infra*. An application under this subsection may be referred to the appropriate criminal legal aid committee: r.14A(2) of the Regulations.

Subsection (1): Court having power to make a legal aid order. *See* s. 28(2)-(11), *supra*.

Legal aid order/Legally assisted person. Defined in s. 28(12), *supra*.

Subsection (2): Before the court can execute its powers under this subsection either an application must be received from the legally aided person for revocation or alternatively the legal representative(s) must withdraw *and* it must appear to the court because of the conduct of the legally assisted person it is not desirable to amend the order under subs. (1): *R. v. Swindon Justices, ex parte Preece, supra*.

Power to order payment of contributions

32. (1)-(4) (*Repealed.*)

(5) In this Part of the Act "collecting court", in relation to a legal aid contribution order, means a magistrates' court specified in that order; and the court so specified shall be—

(a) in a case where the court making the order is itself a magistrates' court, that court;

(b) in a case where the order is made on an appeal from a magistrates' court, or in respect of a person who was committed (whether for trial or otherwise by a magistrates' court) to the Crown Court, the court from which the appeal is brought or, as the case may be, which committed him; and

(c) in any other case, a magistrates' court nominated by the court making the order.

(*as amended by the Criminal Law Act 1977, sch. 12, the Legal Aid Act 1982, sch.*)

Enforcement of legal aid contribution orders

35. (1) Subject to subs. (4) below, any sum required to be paid by a legal aid contribution order shall be recoverable as if it had been adjudged to be paid by an order of the collecting court, subject to and in accordance with the provisions of sch. 3 to this Act.

(2) Without prejudice to subs. (1) above, but subject to the following subsections, payment of any sum required to be paid by a legal aid contribution order shall be enforceable by the High Court or a county court (otherwise than by issue of a writ of *fieri facias* or other process against goods or by imprisonment or attachment of earnings) as if the sum were due to the clerk of the collecting court in pursuance of a judgment or order of the High Court or county court, as the case may be.

(3) Subsection (2) above shall not authorize the enforcement by a county court of payment of any sum exceeding the limit for the time being in force under s. 40 of the County Courts Act 1959 on the amount of any penalty recoverable by statute in a county court.

(4) Where a legal aid contribution order has been made in respect of a member of Her Majesty's armed forces and the Secretary of State notifies the collecting court that any sum payable under the order will be recovered by deductions from the person's pay, the collecting court shall not enforce payment of any sum unless and until the Secretary of State subsequently notifies it that the person is no longer a member of those forces and that sum has not been fully recovered.

(5) The clerk of the collecting court shall not take proceedings by virtue of subs. (2) above to recover any sum required to be paid by a legal aid contribution order unless authorized to do so.

(6) Any expenses incurred by the clerk of the magistrates' court in recovering any sum so required to be paid shall be treated for the purposes of Part VI of the Justices of the Peace Act 1979, as expenses of the magistrates' court committee.

(7) Any sum paid by way of contribution towards costs to a clerk of the

magistrates' court shall be paid by him to the Lord Chancellor and subs. (4) of s. 61 of the Justices of the Peace Act 1979 (regulations as to accounts of justices' clerks) shall apply in relation to sums payable to the Lord Chancellor under this subsection as it applies in relation to sums payable to the Secretary of State under that section.

(8) . . .

(as amended by the Justices of the Peace Act 1979, sch. 2, S.I. 1980 No 705).

COMMENTARY

Subsection (1): A legal aid contribution order. That is, an order under the Legal Aid Act 1982, ss. 7 or 8(2).

Recoverable as if it had been adjudged to be paid by an order. That is, in accordance with the Magistrates' Courts Act 1980, s. 76.

The collecting court. Defined in s. 32(5), *supra*.

Subsection (2): A write of *fieri facias* etc. These remedies are excluded because corresponding remedies are available under sch. 3.

The collecting court. Defined in s. 32(5), *supra*.

Subsection (7). *See* the Justices' Clerks (Accounts) Regulations 1973. (Not printed herein).

Solicitors and counsel

38. (1) Any practising barrister or solicitor may be assigned to act for a legally assisted person unless he is for the time being excluded by virtue of subs. (2) below as being unfit so to act by reason of his conduct when acting for legally assisted persons or his professional conduct generally.

(2) *(Rules)*

(3) . . .

(4) *(Rules)*

(5), (6) . . .

COMMENTARY

Excluded. That is, by the Complaints Tribunal set up under the Legal Aid in Criminal Proceedings (Complaints Tribunal) Rules 1968: reg. 7 of the General Regulations, *infra*.

Interpretation of Part II

40. (1) In this Part of this Act, except so far as the context otherwise requires—

"appropriate contributor", in relation to a person who has not attained the age of 16, means his father, any person who has been adjudged to be his putative father, and (whether or not he is legitimate) his mother;

"committed for sentence" means committed under the Vagrancy Act, 1824, ss. 37 or 38 of the Magistrates' Courts Act, 1980, s. 67 of the Mental Health Act, 1959, s. 62(6) of the Criminal Justice Act 1967 or ss. 6, 8 16, 17(2)(*b*) or 24 of the Powers of Criminal Courts Act 1973;

"legal aid contribution order" means an order under ss. 7 or 8(2) of the Legal Aid Act 1982;

"legal aid fund" means the legal aid fund established under Part I of this Act;

"prescribed" means prescribed by regulations made under this Part of this Act.

(2) Any power to make an application in pursuance of this Part of this Act which is exercisable by a person who has not attained the age of 17 shall also be exercisable by his parent or guardian on his behalf, without prejudice to any powers of the parent or guardian apart from this subsection; and in this subsection "guardian" has the same meaning as in s. 70(2) of the Children and Young Persons Act 1969.

(3) A person who attains the age of 16 after a legal aid order is made in respect of him or, in a case where such an order is made in pursuance of an application, after the application is made, shall be treated for the purposes of this Part of this Act, in relation to the order, as not having attained that age.

(4) . . .

(as amended by the Magistrates' Courts Act 1980, sch. 7, the Legal Aid Act 1982, s. 14).

COMMENTARY

Subsection (2): Guardian. Section 70(2) of the 1969 Act provides that this term "includes any person who was a guardian of the child or young person in question at the time when any supervision order, care order or warrant to which the application relates was originally made."

Subsection (2): Attains the age of 17. For the ascertainment of age *see* the Magistrates' Courts Act 1980, s. 150(3).

SCHEDULE 3

ENFORCEMENT OF LEGAL AID CONTRIBUTION ORDERS

General provisions as to enforcement

1. In this schedule "collecting court" and "legal aid contribution order" have the same meanings as in Part II of this Act.

2. The collecting court may, in relation to a legal aid contribution order, exercise the power of s. 75 of the Magistrates' Courts Act 1980, (power to dispense with immediate payment); and for the purposes of that section any provision made by the court which made the order as to time for payment, or payment by instalments, shall be treated as made by the collecting court.

3. Sections 93 (complaint for arrears), 94 (effect of committal on arrears) and 95 (power to remit arrears) of the Magistrates' Courts Act 1980, shall apply as if a legal aid contribution order were enforceable as an affiliation order.

4. Any costs awarded, under s. 64 of the Magistrates' Courts Act 1980, on the hearing of a complaint for the enforcement of a legal aid contribution order shall be enforceable as a sum required to be paid by that order.

5. Sections 17 and 18 of the Maintenance Orders Act 1958, (not more than one committal for same arrears, and power to review committals), shall apply as if a legal aid contribution order were a maintenance order.

6. Section 80 of the Magistrates' Courts Act 1980, (application of money found on defaulter to satisfy sum adjudged) shall apply as if a legal aid contribution order were enforceable as an affiliation order.

Transfer of enforcement proceedings to different court

7. (1) Where it appears to the collecting court that a person subject to a legal aid contribution order is residing in a petty sessions area other than that for which the court acts, the court may make a transfer order under this paragraph, that is to say

an order making payment under the legal aid contribution order enforceable in that other petty sessions area (which area shall be specified in the transfer order).

(2) As from the date of a transfer order under this paragraph the court which made the order shall cease to be the collecting court for the purposes of the legal aid contribution order and of s. 35 above and this schedule and be replaced as such by a magistrates' court acting for the petty sessions area specified in the transfer order.

(as amended by the Magistrates' Courts Act 1980, sch. 7, the Legal Aid Act 1982, s. 14).

THE LEGAL AID ACT 1982

Advice and representation by duty solicitors.

1. (1) A scheme under s. 15 of the Legal Aid Act 1974 (in this Act referred to as "the principal Act") may provide–

    (*a*)   for the making, by committees set up under the scheme, of arrangements whereby advice and representation to which this section applies is provided by solicitors in attendance at magistrates' courts; and

    (*b*)   for the remuneration out of the legal aid fund or by the Lord Chancellor of solicitors providing advice and representation under the arrangements.

(2) This section applies to such advice and representation in connection with criminal proceedings before magistrates' courts as may be specified by the scheme, being advice and representation for persons, or any class of persons, in respect of whom no legal aid order is for the time being in force in relation to the proceedings in question and to whom advice and assistance in respect of those proceedings is not being given under s. 1 of the principal Act.

(3), (4) . . .

(5) A magistrates' court shall comply with such directions given to it by the Lord Chancellor as he thinks requisite for securing that effect is given at that court to any such arrangements as are mentioned in subs. (1) above.

(6) . . .

(7) Sections 2(5), 15(1), 20(1) and (2)(*a*), (*c*) and (*d*), 22 and 23 of the principal Act (ancillary provisions relating to advice and assistance under s. 1 of that Act) shall apply also in relation to advice and representation provided pursuant to this section.

Legal aid for committal proceedings and trials.

2. (1) A magistrates' court inquiring into an offence as examining justices may make a legal aid order under s. 28(2) of the principal Act which applies, or amend an order already made by the court under that provision so that it applies, both to the proceedings before the court and, in the event of the defendant being committed for trial, to his trial before the Crown Court.

(2) Legal aid ordered to be given to a person by virtue of this section shall, in the event of his being convicted by the Crown Court, include such advice and assistance as is mentioned in s. 30(7) of the principal Act.

COMMENTARY

Subsection (1). This is a discretionary power. The court can still limit the legal aid order to the committal proceedings only, if that seems desirable.

Examining justices. Thus, in the case of an offence triable either way a "through" legal aid order cannot be made until the mode of trial decision has been taken.

Legal aid contribution orders.

7. (1) Where a court makes a legal aid order giving legal aid to a person whose disposable income or disposable capital exceeds the limits prescribed in relation to such income and capital respectively the court shall, subject to the provisions of this section, make an order ("a legal aid contribution order") requiring him to make a payment (in this Act referred to as "a contribution") in respect of the costs of the legal aid.

(2) The contribution which a legal aid contribution order requires a person to make shall be of such amount as is applicable in his case in accordance with regulations made for the purposes of this section; and any such contribution shall be paid in one sum or by instalments as may be prescribed.

(3) In a case where the legally assisted person has not attained the age of sixteen, the court may, instead of or in addition to making a legal aid contribution order against him, make such an order against any person who is an appropriate contributor in relation to him and whose disposable income or disposable capital exceeds the limits referred to in subs. (1) above.

(4) Where a court makes a legal aid order for the giving of legal aid to a person who has attained the age of sixteen and does so without first requiring him to furnish a statement of his means under s. 29(4) of the principal Act because it appears to the court that he is by reason of his physical or mental condition incapable of doing so—

(a)   no legal aid contribution order need be made at the time when the legal aid order is made; but

(b)   if it subsequently appears to the court having power to make a legal aid contribution order under s. 8(2) below that he has become capable of furnishing such a statement, that court may require him to do so.

(5) Where a person fails to furnish a statement which he is required to furnish under subs. (4) above or under s. 29(5) of the principal Act (statements by appropriate contributors) he shall be treated, for the purposes of any legal aid contribution order made in connection with the legal aid order in relation to which the requirement was imposed, as if his disposable income and disposable capital exceeded the limits referred to in subs. (1) above and as if the amount of the contribution applicable in his case were such as the court may determine.

(6) Subject to s. 13(5) below, where the costs of the legal aid in respect of which a legal aid contribution was made are less than the contribution made under the order, the difference between the contribution and those costs shall be repaid—

(a)   where the contribution was made by one person only, to him; and

(b)   where the contribution was made by two or more persons, to them in proportion to the amounts contributed by them.

(7), (8) (*Regulations*).

COMMENTARY

The amount of a legal aid contribution order must be determined in accordance with the Legal Aid in Criminal Proceedings (General) Regulations 1968, rr. 18-20 and the second Schedule.

Subsection (3): Appropriate contributor. The definition in the Legal Aid Act 1974, s. 40(1) is applied by s. 16(4) of this Act.

Variation and revocation of legal aid contribution orders.

8. (1) A legal aid contribution order made against a person in connection with a legal aid order may be varied–

(a)   in the light of any further information as to his disposable income or disposable capital at the time when the legal aid contribution order was made; or

(b)   in the light of any change in his disposable income or disposable capital at any time within such period beginning with the date of the legal aid order as may be prescribed for the purposes of this section ("the prescribed period").

(2) Where no legal aid contribution order has been made against a person in connection with a legal aid order at the time when that order was made–

(a)   because his disposable income or disposable capital did not exceed (or was then believed not to exceed) the limits referred to in subs. (1) of s. 7 above; or

(b)   because of subs. (4)(a) of that section,

a legal aid contribution order may be made against that person at any subsequent time if it appears that his disposable income or disposable capital at any time within the prescribed period exceeds or exceeded the limits referred to in subs. (1) of that section.

(3) Where a legal aid contribution order has been made against a person and it subsequently appears that his disposable income or disposable capital at the time when the order was made was such that no legal aid contribution order should have been made in his case, the order shall be revoked; but if the order is revoked subs. (2) above shall apply as if the order had never been made.

(4) The powers conferred by the foregoing provisions of this section shall be exercisable by the court that made the legal aid order in question except that–

(a)   where the relevant proceedings are being heard or have been concluded in a different court, those powers shall, subject to para. (b) below, be exercisable by that court; and

(b)   where any sum in respect of a contribution under a legal aid contribution order falls due at a time after the conclusion of the relevant proceedings, the power conferred by subs. (1) above to vary the order so far as relates to any sum falling due as aforesaid shall be exercisable by the collecting court.

(5) At the conclusion of the relevant proceedings the court in which those proceedings are concluded may, if it thinks fit–

(a)   remit any sum due under a legal aid contribution order from a legally assisted person which falls to be paid after the conclusion of those proceedings or, if that person has been acquitted, remit or order the repayment of any sum due from or paid by him under such an order;

(b)   remit or order the repayment of any sum due from or paid by an appropriate contributor under such an order;

and where a legally assisted person successfully appeals against his conviction the court which allows his appeal may remit or order the repayment of any sum due from or paid by him or an appropriate contributor under such an order.

(6) Where the legal aid order in connection with which a legal aid contribution order was made is revoked, the foregoing provisions of this sec-

tion shall have effect as if the relevant proceedings had then been concluded.

(7) Where a legal aid contribution order is revoked, or is varied to an amount less than what has already been paid, any sum paid or, as the case may be, overpaid under the order shall be repaid.

(8) For the purposes of this section the relevant proceedings, in relation to a legal aid contribution order, are the proceedings for the purposes of which legal aid was ordered to be given by the legal aid order in connection with which the legal aid contribution order was made except that where those proceedings are proceedings before a magistrates' court which result—

  (a) in the legally assisted person being committed to the Crown Court for trial or sentence; or

  (b) in his case being remitted to a juvenile court in pursuance of s. 56(1) of the Children and Young Persons Act 1933 or s. 2(11) of the Children and Young Persons Act 1969,

the relevant proceedings include the proceedings before the Crown Court or that juvenile court.

Enforcement of legal aid contribution orders.

9. (1) Any sum due under a legal aid contribution order shall not be recoverable, and payment of any such sum shall not be enforced, under s. 35 of the principal Act until—

  (a) the conclusion of the relevant proceedings; or

  (b) if earlier, the revocation of the legal aid order in connexion with which the legal aid contribution order was made.

(2) Where a sum in respect of a contribution under a legal aid contribution order made in connection with a legal aid order is required to be paid on the making of the legal aid contribution order, the court may direct that the legal aid order shall not take effect until that sum is paid.

(3) Where a sum in respect of a contribution under a legal aid contribution order made in connection with a legal aid order is required to be paid by the legally assisted person at any subsequent time before the conclusion of the relevant proceedings and is not paid at that time, the court in which those proceedings are being heard may revoke the legal aid order but shall not do so unless satisfied, after affording the legally assisted person an opportunity of making representations in such manner as may be prescribed—

  (a) that he was at that time able to pay the sum in question; and

  (b) that he is able to pay the whole or part of it but has failed or refused to do so.

(4) The revocation of a legal aid order under subs. (3) above shall not affect the right of any legal representative previously assigned to the legally assisted person to remuneration for work done before the date of the revocation.

(5) The collecting court may defer recovering any sum due under a legal aid contribution order if an appeal is pending in respect of the relevant proceedings or if the legally assisted person has been ordered to be retried.

(6) In this section "the relevant proceedings" has the same meaning as in s. 8 above.

THE LEGAL AID IN CRIMINAL PROCEEDINGS (GENERAL) REGULATIONS 1968

S.I. 1968, No. 1231

(as amended by S.I. 1970, No. 1980, S.I. 1976, No. 790, S.I. 1980 No. 705, 1651 S.I. 1983 No. 1863)

Many of the terms used in these regulations are defined in reg. 31, *infra*.

NOTE: These and the succeeding regulations made under former legislation are kept in effect by the Legal Aid Act 1974, s. 42(2). References have been altered so as to refer to this Act.

Proceedings in a magistrates' court

1. *(1) An application for a legal aid order in respect of proceedings in a magistrates' court under s.73(2) or (3A) of the Act (magistrates' court proceedings) may be made to the justices' clerk–*

   (a)   *If the application is made by a parent or guardian on behalf of a person who has not attained the age of seventeen years, in Form 1 in the Schedule of these Regulations,*

   (b)   *if the application is made by any other person, in Form 1 in the Schedule to these Regulations.*

(2) An application for a legal aid order may be made orally to the court.

(3) A legal aid order shall not be made until the court, a justice of the peace or the justices' clerk has considered the statement of means of the applicant except where the applicant is not required unde s.29(4) and (5) of the 1974 Act to furnish a statement of means.

(4) Subject to the provisions of this regulation, the powers of the court to determine an application for a legal aid order may be exercised by the justices' clerk or a justice of the peace to whom the clerk has referred the application.

(5) Where an application for a legal aid order is made orally to the court, the court may refer it to the justices' clerk for determination.

(6) The justices' clerk considering an application for a legal aid order:
   (a)   *shall make an order or refer the application to the court or a justice of the peace; or*
   (b)   *may, where review under reg 6H would be available, refuse to make an order.*

(7),(8) **(Repealed)**.

(9) In this regulation the expression "justice of the peace" means a justice of the peace who is entitled to sit as a member of the magistrates' court and "legal aid order" means a legal aid order within the meaning of para (1) of this regulation.

Proceedings in the Crown Court

2. *(1) An application for a legal aid order under 73(3), (3B) or (4) of the Act (proceedings in the Crown Court) may be made–*
   (a)   (i)   *to the appropriate officer of the Crown Court, or*
         (ii) *in the case of an appeal to the Crown Court, to the justices' clerk;*
   (b)   (i)   *if the application is made by a parent or guardian on behalf of a person who has not attained the age of seventeen years, in Form 2 in the Schedule to these Regulations.*
         (ii) *if the application is made by any other person, in Form 2 in the Schedule to these Regulations.*

(2) An application for a legal aid order may be made orally to the Crown

Court, or to the magistrates' court at the conclusion of the proceedings in that court.

(3) . . .

(4) A legal aid order shall not be made until the court, a judge of the court, the proper officer of the court or, where the application is made to the magistrates' court or justices' clerk, a justice of the peace has considered the statement of means of the applicant except where the applicant is not required under 29(4) and (5) of the 1974 Act to furnish a statement of means.

(5) Subject to the provisions of this regulation, the powers of the court to determine an application for a legal aid order may be exercised by a judge of the court, the proper officer of the court, or, where the application is made to the magistrates' court or justices' clerk, a justice of the peace.

(6) Where an application for a legal aid order is made orally to the court, the court may refer it to the proper officer of the court for determination.

(7) The proper officer of the court considering an application for a legal aid order shall—

  (a)   *make an order; or*
  (b)   **(repealed)**
  (c)   *except where the proper officer of the court is a justices' clerk, refer the application to a judge of the court, or, if he is, to the magistrates' court or a justice of the peace.*

(8) (9) **(Repealed)**

  (10) In this regulation the expression "magistrates' court" means the court which committed or convicted the applicant, "justice of the peace" means a justice of the peace who is entitled to sit as a member of the magistrates' court, "justices' clerk" means the clerk to the magistrates' court, and "legal aid order" means a legal aid order within the meaning of para (1) or (3) of this regulation, as the case may be.

  3 . . .

Statement of means

4. *(1) A statement of means submitted by an applicant or an appropriate contributor shall be in Form 5 in the Schedule to these Regulations.*

  (2) **(Repealed)**

  (3) If an applicant who has attained the age of sixteen years does not furnish a statement of means at the time that he makes an application for legal aid, he shall be required to do so by a proper officer of the court to whom or to whose court he is making the application, unless he has already submitted such a statement in pursuance of a previous application in respect of the same case where no legal aid order has previously been made and revoked.

  (4) If a statement of means of an applicant who has not attained the age of sixteen years or an appropriate contributor is not furnished at the time that the applicant makes an application for legal aid, either or both, may be required to furnish one by the proper officer of the court to whom or to whose court the application is made unless the person who has not furnished a statement at that time has already submitted a statement in pursuance of a previous application in respect of the same case where no legal aid order has previously been made or revoked.

Provison of information

4A *(1) The court or the proper officer of the court may require the applicant,* *the legally assisted person or the appropriate contributor to provide evdence of any information given in a statement of means or of any change in his financial circumstances at any time after the submission of a statement of means and such additional information as the court or the proper officer of the court may require.*

(2) Where the applicant, the legally assisted person or the appropriate contributor fails to provide evidence or information required under para (1), he may be treated as though his disposable income and disposable capital exceeded the limits prescribed in reg 19(3) and as if the contribution payable by him were such amount as the court or the proper officer of the court may determine or redetermine.

General powers to make legal aid order

5. *Subject to the provisions of reg 4 of these Regulations, nothing in reg 1, 2, 3 or 25D of these Regulations shall affect the power of a court or a judge of the court or the Registrar (subject to the provisions of 75 of the Act) to make a legal aid order, whether an application has been made for legal aid or not, or the right of an applicant whose application has been refused or whose legal aid order has been revoked under s. 9(3) of the 1982 Act.*

Legal aid orders

6. *A legal aid order shall be in Form 6A or 6B in the Schedule and a copy of it shall, subject to reg 6H(3) and 22(3), be sent to:*

(a) *the legally assisted person or, where the application was made by his parent or guardian, the parent or guardian;*
(b) *the solicitor assigned or counsel (where counsel only is assigned); and*
(c) *where the legal aid order is made by a criminal legal aid committee, to the proper officer of the court to which the application for legal aid was made.*

Amendment of legal aid orders

6A. *(1) An order amending a legal aid order shall be in Form 7 in the Schedule and a copy of it shall be sent to—*

(a) *the legally assisted person or, where the application was made by his parent or guardian;*
(b) *the solicitor assigned by the legal aid order or to counsel (where counsel only is assigned) and to any solicitor and counsel assigned by the amended legal aid order; and*
(c) *where the legal aid order is amended by the criminal legal aid committee, to the proper officer of the court to which the application for amendment was made.*

(2) Where a new solicitor or counsel (where counsel only was assigned) is assigned by an order amending a legal aid order—

(a) *counsel originally assigned shall send all papers and other things in his possession relating to the proceedings to the solicitor who instructed him or to counsel newly assigned (where counsel only was assigned); and*
(b) *the solicitor originally assigned shall send all papers and other things in his possession relating to the proceedings to the solicitor who instructed him or to counsel newly assigned (where counsel only was assigned); and*
(c) *the solicitor originally assigned shall send all papers and other things in his possession relating to the proceedings to the solicitor newly assigned or to counsel (where counsel only is assigned by the amended legal aid order).*

Revocation of legal aid orders

6B. *(1) An order revoking a legal aid order shall be in Form 8 in the Schedule and a copy of it shall be sent to—*

(a)   *the legally assisted person or, where the application was made by his parent or guardian, the parent or guardian;*

(b)   *the solicitor assigned or to counsel (where counsel only is assigned), and*

(c)   *where the legal aid order is revoked by the criminal legal aid committee, to the proper officer of the court to which the application for revocation or amendment was made.*

(2) Where a legal aid order is revoked—

(a)   *the counsel assigned shall send all the papers and other things in his possession relating to the proceedings to the solicitor assigned or (whether no solicitor was assigned) to the legally assisted person; and*

(b)   *the solicitor assigned shall send all papers and other things in his possession relating to the proceedings to the legally assisted person.*

Notification of refusal of legal aid

6C. *(1) Where an application for a legal aid order is refused, the court or the proper officer of the court shall notify the applicant or, where the application was made by his parent or guardian, the parent or guardian, stating that the application has been refused on one or both of the following grounds, that—*

(a)   *it does not appear to the court or the proper officer of the court desirable to make an order in the interests of justice; or*

(b)   *it does not appear to the court or the proper officer of the court that the applicant's disposable income and disposable capital are such that he requires assistance in meeting the costs he may incur.*

and shall inform him of the provisions, if any, of these Regulations which relate to the circumstances in which he may apply to a criminal legal aid committee for the decision to be reviewed.

(2) Notification of refusal, and determination of contribution under reg 6D, shall be in Form 14A in the Schedule.

(3) A copy of Form 14A and, where an application for review under regulation 6E may be made, of Form 1 shall be sent to the applicant or, where the application was made by his parent or guardian, the parent or guardian and to his solicitor, if any.

Determination of contribution where legal aid is refused

6D. *Where a magistrates' court, justice of the peace or a justices' clerk has refused to make a legal aid order on the grounds specified in reg 6C(1)(a) above, there shall nevertheless be determined, where an application for a review under reg 6E may be made, and in accordance with reg 18, 19 and 22, the applicant's disposable income, disposable capital and the amount of any contribution that would have been payable and the manner in which it would be so payable by the applicant or an appropriate contributor had a legal aid order been made.*

Application for review

6E. *(1) Where an application for a legal aid orde has been refused after being considered for the first time by a magistrates' court, justice of the peace or a justices' clerk, the applicant may, subject to para (2), apply for review to the appropriate criminal legal aid committee.*

(2) An application for review shall only lie to a criminal legal aid committee where—

(a)   *the applicant is charged with an indictable offence or an offence triable either way; and*

(b)   *the application for a legal aid order has been refused on the grounds specified in reg 6C(1)(a); and*

(c)   *the application for a legal aid order was made no later than 21 days before the date fixed for the trial of an information or the inquiry into an offence as examining justices, where such a date had been fixed at the time that the application was made.*

Procedure for application for review

6F. *(1) An application for review shall be made by giving notice in Form 14B in the Schedule to the appropriate criminal legal aid committee within 14 days of the date of notification of refusal to make a legal aid order.*

(2) The applicant or, where the application was made by his parent or guardian, the parent or guardian shall also send to the appropriate criminal legal aid committee the following documents—

(a)   *a copy of the application for legal aid; and*

(b)   *a copy of Form 14A (notification of refusal and determination of contribution).*

(3) The time limit within which the application for review must be made may, for good reason, be waived or altered by the criminal legal aid committee.

Provision of information

6G. *The justices' clerk and the applicant or, where the application was made by his parent or guardian, the parent or guardian shall supply such further particulars, information and documents as the criminal legal aid committee may require.*

Determination of review

6H. *(1) The criminal legal aid committee shall, on a review, reconsider the application for legal aid and*

(a)   *refuse the application; or*

(b)   *make a legal aid order.*

(2) Where the criminal legal aid committee makes a legal aid order, it shall make a legal aid contribution order in accordance with any determination made under regulation 6D.

(3) Where the magistrates' court, justice of the peace or justices' clerk has made a determination under reg. 6D that any legal aid order granted be withheld until a contribution from disposable capital is paid, the criminal legal aid committee shall send the legal aid order to the appropriate justices' clerk.

(4) The criminal legal aid committee shall give notice of its decision and the reason for it to—

(a)   *the applicant or, where the application was made by his parents or guardian, to the parent or guardian;*

(b)   *his solicitor, if any; and*

(c)   *the justices' clerk of the magistrates' court to which the application for legal aid was made.*

Exclusion of solicitors and counsel

7. *(1) The proper officer of each court shall keep a list of solicitors and counsel, notified to him by the Lord Chancellor,* who are for the time being excluded from acting for legally assisted persons under s.82 of the Act.

(2) Any reference in these Regulations to solicitors or counsel shall not apply to solicitors or counsel so excluded.

Assignment of solicitor

8. *Subject to the provisions of reg 11 and 14 of these Regulations, any person in respect of whom a legal aid order is made, entitling him to the services of a solicitor, may select any solicitor who is willing to act and such solicitor shall be assigned to him.*

Selection of counsel

9. *Where a legal aid order is made in respect of the services of solicitor and counsel, the solicitor may instruct any counsel who is willing to act:*
Provided that in the case of proceedings in the Court of Appeal or House of Lords, counsel may be assigned by the court or person making or amending the legal aid order.

Assignment of counsel only

10. *(1) Where a legal aid order in respect of proceedings in the Crown Court is made or amended so as to provide for representation by counsel only, counsel shall be assigned by the court or person making or amending the legal aid order.*

(2) Where a legal aid order in respect of proceedings in the Court of Appeal is made or amended so as to provide for representation by counsel only, counsel shall be assigned by the court, a judge of the court or the Registrar.

11, 12 . . .

Assignment of two counsel

13. *(1) Except as provided by para (2) of this regulation, a legal aid order shall not provide for the services of more than one counsel.*

(2) In trials in the Crown Court or appeals to the House of Lords or the Court of Appeal, an order may provide for the services of two counsel—

(a)   *on a charge of murder; or*
(b)   *where it appears to the court or person making the legal aid order that the case is one of exceptional difficulty, gravity or complexity and that the interests of justice require that the legally assisted person shall have the services of two counsel,*

but an order made by a magistrates' court (or amended by such a court under para (3) of this regulation) may not provide for the services of more than one counsel except on a charge of murder.

(3) Where, in such a case as is specified in para (2) of this regulation, a legal aid order provides for the services of one counsel, it may be amended to provide for the services of two counsel.

Assignment of one solicitor or counsel to more than one legally assisted person

14. *A solicitor may be assigned to two or more legally assisted persons whose cases are heard together, unless the interests of justice require that such persons be separately represented.*

Applications in respect of legal representation

14A. *(1) An application by a legally assisted person or his solicitor for—*

    (a) representation by counsel in accordance with s.30(2) of the 1974 Act; or

    (b) the amendment or revocation of a legal aid order under s.31 of the 1974 Act,

shall be made to the proper officer of the court.

(2) The proper officer of the court considering an application under para (1) shall—

    (a) grant it; or

    (b) where para (3) applies, refer it to the appropriate criminal legal aid committee; or

    (c) refer it to the court.

(3) Any application under para (1) which is not granted shall be referred to a criminal legal aid committee unless—

    (a) an application under the same sub-paragraph of para (1) has previously been refused by a criminal legal aid committee in the same proceedings; or

    (b) the application was made—

        (i) in the case of proceedings in the Crown Court, more than 14 days after the committal for trial or sentence or the date of giving of notice of appeal; or

        (ii) in the case of proceedings in the magistrates' court, less than 14 days before the date fixed for the trial of an information or the inquiry into an offence as examining justices, where such a date had been fixed at the time the application was made; or

    (c) the application is an application in respect of proceedings in the Court of Appeal or in the House of Lords.

Reference to criminal legal aid committee

14B. *(1) The proper officer of the court, in referring an application to a criminal legal aid committee, shall send to the secretary the following documents—*

    (a) a copy of the legal aid order;

    (b) any papers presented to the proper officer of the court by the legally assisted person or his solicitor in support of the application; and

    (c) any other relevant documents or information.

(2) The proper officer of the court and the legally assisted person or his solicitor shall supply such further particulars, information and documents as the criminal legal aid committee may require.

14C. *(1) The criminal legal aid committee shall consider any application referred to it under reg 14A and any further particulars, information or documents submitted to it under reg 14B and any other relevant information and shall grant or refuse the application and, where necessary, amend or revoke the legal aid order accordingly.*

(2) The criminal legal aid committee shall notify the proper officer of the court and the legally assisted person and his solicitor of its decision.

Power of criminal legal aid committee to authorise expenditure

14D. *(1) Where it appears to a legally assisted person's solicitor necessary for*

the proper conduct of proceedings in a magistrates' court or in the Crown
Court to incur costs by taking any of the following steps—

(a) obtaining a report or opinion of one or more experts or tendering expert
evidence;

(b) employing a person to provide a report or opinion (otherwise than as an
expert);

(c) bespeaking transcripts of shorthand notes or tape recordings of any
proceedings, including police questioning of suspects; or

(d) performing an act which is either unusual in its nature or involves
unusually large expenditure;

he may apply to the appropriate criminal legal aid committee for authority to
do so.

(2) If a criminal legal aid committee authorises the taking of any step
specified in paragraph (1), it shall also authorise the maximum fee payable for
any such report, opinion, expert evidence, transcript or act.

Restriction on payment

14E. Where a legal aid order has been made, the legally assisted person's
solicitor or counsel shall not receive or be a party to any payment for work done
in connection with the proceedings in respect of which the legal aid order was
made except such payments as are made—

(a) out of the legal aid fund or by the Lord Chancellor in accordance with
s.37 of the 1974 Act; or

(b) in respect of any expenses or fees incurred in

(i) preparing, obtaining or considering any report, opinion or further
evidence, whether provided by an expert witness or otherwise; or

(ii) bespeaking transcript of shorthand notes or tape recordings of any
proceedings, including police questioning of suspects;

provided that the assisted person's solicitor or counsel (where counsel only is
assigned) has previously made an application under reg 14D for authority to incur such expenses or fees which has been refused by the criminal legal aid committee.

Powers exercisable by secretaries

14F. (1) Where a criminal legal aid committee is required or entitled to perform any function under these Regulations, that function may, subject to para
(2), be performed on behalf of the committee by the secretary.

(2) Paragraph (1) shall not empower a secretary to—

(a) refuse an application to the committee under reg 14A; or

(b) refuse an application for review under reg 6H(1).

15 . . .

Notes of evidence and depositions

16. Where a legal aid order is made in respect of an appeal to the Crown
Court, the justices' clerk shall supply, on the application of the solicitor
assigned to the appellant or respondent on whose application such an order was
made, copies of any notes of evidence or depositions taken in the proceedings in
the magistrates' court.

Transfer of documents

17. *Where a person is committed by a lower court to a higher court or appeals or applies for leave to appeal from a lower court to a higher court, the proper officer of the lower court shall send to the proper officer of the higher court the following documents (if any):—*

(a)   *a copy of any legal aid order previously made in the same case;*
(b)   *a copy of any contribution order previously made;*
(c)   *a copy of any legal aid application which has been refused;*
(d)   *any statement of means already submitted.*

Determination of contributions

18. *(1) The court or the proper officer of the court shall, in making a legal aid order or where reg 25 applies, determine the amount of any contribution payable in respect of the costs of the legal aid by the applicant, the legally assisted person or the appropriate contributor in accordance with reg 19.*

(2) Where the applicant or the legally assisted person has paid or is liable to pay a contribution under 4(2) of the 1974 Act in respect of legal advice and assistance in the same proceedings, any contribution he is liable to make, or an appropriate contributor is liable to make on his behalf, under 7(1) of the 1982 Act shall be reduced by the total amount of any contribution already paid or liable to be paid under s.4(2) of the 1974 Act.

19. *(1) The court or the proper officer of the court shall consider the statement of means of the applicant, the legally assisted person or the appropriate contributor, and any other relevant information, and, subject to para (2), determine his disposable income and disposable capital in accordance with the Second Schedule.*

(2) The court or the proper officer of the court shall not determine—

(a)   *disposable income and disposable capital where the applicant, the legally assisted person or the appropriate contributor is in receipt of supplementary benefit; or*
(b)   *disposable income where the applicant, the legally assisted person or the appropriate contributor is in receipt of family income supplement;*

unless he is required to make a re-determination under reg 24A below.

(3) The applicant, the legally assisted person or the appropriate contributor shall make a contribution—

(a)   *if his disposable income exceeds the average weekly sum of £42, of such an amount as shall be determined by the proper officer in accordance with the Third Schedule; and*
(b)   *if his disposable capital exceeds £3,000, of such an amount as is equal to the excess.*

Legal aid contribution orders

20. *(1) The court or the proper officer of the court shall make a legal aid contribution order in respect of any contribution determined under reg 18 above.*

(2) A legal aid contribution order shall be in Form 9 in the Schedule and a copy shall be sent to the person ordered to make the contribution, to the legally assisted person's solicitor and to the collecting court.

21. . . .

Payment of contributions

22. *(1) Any contribution payable out of disposable income shall be payable by weekly instalments (or, at the discretion of the court or the proper officer of the court, by two-weekly or monthly instalments) within a period not exceeding the contribution period, with the first such instalment falling due 7 days from the making of the legal aid order or of the legal aid contribution order, whichever is the later.*

(2) Any contribution payable out of disposable capital shall be paid immediately if the sum is readily available or, if it is not, at such time as the court or the proper officer of the court considers to be reasonable in all the circumstances.

(3) Where a contribution out of disposable capital is payable immediately, the court or the proper officer of the court may withhold the legal aid order until such payment is made.

(4) Where a legal aid order is withheld under para (3), the court or the proper officer of the court shall give notice of this fact in Form 10 in the Schedule to—

(a)   *the assisted person or, where the application was made by his parent or guardian, the parent or guardian; and*
(b)   *the solicitor assigned or counsel (where counsel only is assigned).*

Determination where no contribution previously payable

23. *(1) Except where para (2) applies, contributions shall be payable to the proper officer of the collecting court.*

(2) Where the legal aid order is withheld until a contribution out of disposable capital is made, such payment shall be made to the proper officer of the court making the legal aid order, unless that court otherwise directs.

Change in financial circumstances

24. *The legally assisted person or the appropriate contributor shall inform the court or the proper officer of the court of any change in his financial circumstances which has occurred since the submission of his statement of means which he has reason to believe—*

(a)   *might make him liable to pay a contribution in respect of the costs of the legal aid, where such a contribution is not already payable; or*
(b)   *might affect the terms of any legal aid contribution order made in connection with a legal aid order.*

Determination where no contribution previously payable

25. *The court or the proper officer of the court shall determine the amount of any contribution payable in respect of the costs of the legal aid by a legally assisted person or an appropriate contributor who is not already liable to make such a contribution where—*

(a)   *further information has become available as to the amount of disposable income and disposable capital available at the time when the legal aid order was made; or*
(b)   *the circumstances upon which the disposable income or disposable capital were determined at the time the legal aid order was made have altered within the contribution period;*

and it appears likely that, were such determination to be made, the legally assisted person or the appropriate contributor would be liable to make a contribution in respect of the costs of the legal aid.

Redetermination of contribution

25A. *The court or the proper officer of the court shall redetermine the amount of any contribution payable by a legally assisted person or an appropriate contributor under a legal aid order where—*

(a) *further information has become available as to the amounts of disposable income and disposable capital available at the time when the legal aid contribution order was made; or*

(b) *the circumstances upon which the disposable income or disposable capital were determined at the time when the legal aid contribution order was made have altered within the contribution period so that—*

    (i) *his disposable income may have increased by an amount greater than £400 or decreased by an amount greater than £200; or*

    (ii) *his disposable capital may have increased by an amount greater than £200;*

unless it appears to be unlikely that any significant change in the liability to make a contribution would result from such a redetermination, and shall vary or revoke the legal aid contribution order accordingly.

Effect of error or mistake

25B. *Where it appears to the court or the proper officer of the court that there has been some error or mistake in the determination of the legally assisted person's or the appropriate contributor's disposable income, disposable capital or contribution and that it would be just and equitable to correct the error or mistake, the court or the proper office of the court may vary or revoke the legal aid contribution order accordingly.*

Variation and revocation of legal aid contribution orders

25C. *(1) Where the legal aid contribution order is revoked or varied to an amount less than that already paid the court or the proper officer of the court shall order the repayment of any sum paid or overpaid as the case may be.*

(2) Where—

(a) *the legal aid contribution order is varied to an amount greater than that previously payable; or*

(b) *a legal aid contribution order is made after a determination under reg 25,*

and any payment is to be made out of disposable income, the court or the proper officer of the court may, for the purposes of such payment, extend the period provided in reg 22 within which such payment must be made.

(3) An order varying or revoking a legal aid contribution order shall be in Form 11 in the Schedule and a copy of it shall be sent to the person ordered to make the contribution, to the legally assisted person's solicitor and to the proper officer of the collecting court.

Refusal to pay contributions

25D. *(1) When any sums due under a legal aid contribution order before the conclusion of the proceedings have not been paid by the legally assisted person, the court or the proper officer of the court may—*

(a) *serve notice on the legally assisted person requiring him to comply with the legal aid contribution order and pay any sums due under it within 7 days of receiving such notice; and,*

(b) *if he does not do so, serve notice on him inviting him to make represen-*

tations giving reasons for not complying with the legal aid contribution order.

(2) A notice under para (1)(a) shall be in Form 12 and a notice under paragraph (1)(b) in Form 13 of the Schedule and copies shall be sent to the legally assisted person and to his solicitor or counsel (where counsel only is assigned).

(3) The court shall consider any representations made under para 1(b) above and, if satisfied that it would be just so to do, may revoke the legal aid order in accordance with s.9(3) of the 1982 Act.

Termination of contribution period

25E. *(1) Where the contribution period has not ended and—*

(a) *the court remits any sum due under a legal aid contribution order which falls to be paid after the conclusion of the relevant proceedings; or*

(b) *the legally assisted person is sentenced to an immediate term of imprisonment or a sentence of youth custody or detention in a detention centre,*

the contribution period shall be deemed to have ended on the date of that remission or sentence.

(2) The court making any such remission or passing any such sentence shall inform the collecting court that the contribution period is to be deemed to have ended on the date of that remission or sentence.

Disposal of sums received from legally assisted persons after conviction

26. *(1) Where a legally assisted person or an appropriate contributor to whom this regulation applies has been ordered to make a contribution, any amounts falling due under the legal aid contribution order after the conclusion of the relevant proceedings shall, unless remitted or specifically appropriated by the person paying the money to payment of the contribution, when paid be applied in the first place in accordance with the provisions of s.139 of the Magistrates' Court Act 1980 and any sum paid in addition to the sums referred to in para (2) below shall be paid to the Lord Chancellor in accordance with s.35(7) of the 1974 Act.*

(2) This regulation applies to a legally assisted person who is ordered to pay any sum adjudged to be paid by a conviction and to an appropriate contributor who is ordered to pay a fine, damages, compensation or costs under the provisions of s.55 of the Children and Young Persons Act 1933 or s.3(6) of the Children and Young Persons Act 1969.

Repayment of contributions

26A. *The collecting court or the proper officer of the collecting court, on receiving notification of the amount of the costs of the legal aid determined by the appropriate authority under the 1982 Regulations, shall, in accordance with s.7(6) of the 1982 Act, repay to the legally assisted person or the appropriate contributor, as the case may be, the amount, if any, by which any contribution paid exceeds those costs.*

Recovery of costs

27. *Where a court makes an order that the costs of a legally aided person shall be paid by any other person, the proper officer of that court shall notify the*

*authority from whose funds the costs of legal aid are to be paid or, in the case
of an order made by a magistrates' court, the Law Society, of the order and of
the name and address of the person by whom the costs are to be paid.*

Enforcement of orders for payment of costs

28. *Where a person ordered to pay the costs of a legally aided person does not
pay them in accordance with s.79(1) of the Act, they may be recovered summarily by the aforesaid authority referred to in reg 27 of these Regulations or
the Law Society, as the case may be, as a sum adjudged to be paid as a civil
debt by order of a magistrates' court.*

Notification of fund into which costs are to be paid

29. *Where any court makes such an order as is referred to in reg 27 of these
Regulations, the court shall cause the person against whom the order is made
to be informed of the fund into which the payment must be made in accordance
with s.79(1) of the Act.*

Legal aid records

30. *(1) The proper officer of each court shall keep a record, in the manner and
form directed from time to time by the Lord Chancellor, of all cases in which
an application for legal aid was made to the court or a legal aid order was
made, under reg 5 of these Regulations, by the court without application; and
shall send to the Lord Chancellor such information from such record as the
Lord Chancellor shall from time to time direct.*

Interpretation

31. *(1) In these Regulations, unless the context otherwise requires—*

"*the Act*" *means the Criminal Justice Act 1967;*
"*the 1974 Act*" *means the Legal Aid Act 1974;*
"*the 1982 Act*" *means the Legal Aid Act 1982;*
"*applicant*" *means, in relation to an application for legal aid made on
behalf of a person who has not attained the age of seventeen years by his
parent or guardian, that person and in the case of any other application
for legal aid the person making the application;*

"*appropriate authority*" *means an officer or body authorised to determine
costs under the 1982 Regulations;*

"*appropriate contributor*" *has the meaning assigned to it by s.84(1) of the
Act;*

"*appropriate criminal legal aid committee*" *means the criminal legal aid
committee in whose area is situated the court to which an application for
or concerning a legal aid order has been made;*

"*collecting court*" *has the meaning assigned to it by s.32(5) of the 1974
Act;*

"*contribution*" *means a payment in respect of the costs of the legal aid;*

"*contribution period*" *means the period of 6 months commencing with the
date of the making of the legal aid order;*

"*Court of Appeal*" *means the criminal division of the Court of Appeal;*

"*criminal legal aid committee*" *means a criminal legal aid committee appointed by the Council of the Law Society under the provisions of a
scheme made under s.15 of the 1974 Act;*

"disposable capital" means capital calculated in accordance with the Second Schedule which is available for the making a contribution;

"disposable income" means income calculated in accordance with the Second Schedule which is available for the making of a contribution;

"family income supplement" means any supplement under the Family Income Supplements Act 1970;

"guardian" has the same meaning as in s.87 of the Child Care Act 1980;

"judge of the court" means–

(i)   in the case of the Court of Appeal, a Lord Justice of Appeal or a judge of the Queen's Bench Division of the High Court;
(ii)   in the case of the Crown Court, a judge of the High Court, a circuit judge, a recorder or an assistant recorder;

"justices' clerk" includes a person duly authorised by the justices' clerk to act on the justices' clerk's behalf to the extent that he is so authorised;

"legal aid contribution order" means an order made under s. 7(1) of the 1982 Act;

"legal aid fund" has the meaning assigned to it by s.84 of the Act;

"legal aid order" means an order made under s.73 of the Act and includes an order made solely for the purpose described in s. 74(8) of the Act;

"legally assisted person has the meaning assigned to it by s.73(9) of the Act;

"person concerned" means the person whose disposable income and disposable capital are to be determined or the person whose resources are to be treated as the resources of any other person under these Regulations;

"proper officer" means the Clerk of the Parliaments, the Registrar of Criminal Appeals, the appropriate officer of the Crown Court or the justices' clerk (as the case may be);

"Registrar" means the Registrar of Criminal Appeals;

"the 1982 Regulations" means the Legal Aid in Criminal Proceedings (Costs) Regulations 1982;

"secretary" means the secretary of the appropriate criminal legal aid committee and includes any person duly authorised to act on the secretary's behalf to the extent that he is so authorised;

"statement of means" means a statement of means submitted in accordance with reg 4 of these Regulations;

"supplementary benefit" means supplementary benefit under the Supplementary Benefits Act 1976.

(1A) An applicant who attains the age of sixteen years after the date on which the application is made shall be treated for the purposes of these Regulations as not having attained that age.

(2) The Interpretation Act 1978 shall apply to the interpretation of these Regulations as it applies to the interpretation of an Act of Parliament.

(3) Any reference in these Regulations to an enactment is a reference thereto as amended.

Determination in private and in absence of legally assisted person

32. Where it is provided by these Regulations that any matter may be determined otherwise than by a court, it may be determined in private and in the absence of the applicant or legally assisted person or appropriate contributor.

32 . . .

33. *(Repealed.)*

34 . . .

THE SECOND SCHEDULE
(Regulation 19(1))

Part I: General

1. *(1) In computing the disposable income and disposable capital of the person concerned the resources of any spouse of his shall be treated as his resources unless—*

(a) *the person concerned and the spouse are living separate and apart; or*

(b) *the spouse has a contrary interest in the proceedings in respect of which an application for legal aid has been made; or*

(c) in all the circumstances of the case it would be inequitable to do so.

(2) If the spouse fails to provide information as to his resources at the request of the proper officer, the proper officer may make an estimate, on the basis of any information then available, of the likely resources of the spouse.

2. *If it appears to the proper officer that the person concerned has with intent to reduce the amount of his disposable income or disposable capital—*

(a) *directly or indirectly deprived himself of any resources; or*

(b) *converted any part of his resources into resources which under these Regulations are to be wholly or partly disregarded, or in respect of which nothing is to be included in determining the resources of that person;*

the resources of which he has so deprived himself or which he has so converted shall be treated as part of his resources or as not so converted as the case may be.

Part II: Disposable Income

1. *(1) The income of the person concerned shall be that which he receives during the contribution period.*

(2) The income received during the contribution period may be estimated on the basis of the income received by the person concerned during the three months prior to the commencement of the contribution period.

2. *(1) Income from any trade, business or gainful occupation other than employment at a wage or salary shall be the profit therefrom which accrues during the contribution period.*

(2) The income received during the contribution period may be estimated on the basis of the profits made in the last accounting period for which accounts have been made up.

3. *In computing disposable income there shall be disregarded—*

    (a)   *attendance allowance paid under the Social Security Acts 1975–1980;*

    (b)   *mobility allowance paid under the Social Security Acts 1975–1980;*

    (c)   *any rebate or allowance paid under Part II of the Social Security and Housing Benefits Act 1982 and any rebate; and*

    (d)   *constant attendance allowance paid as an increase to a disablement pension under section 61 of the Social Security Act 1975.*

4. *In computing disposable income there shall be deducted—*

    (a)   *the total amount of any tax payable on that income;*

    (b)   *the total amount of any contributions payable under the Social Security Acts 1975–1980;*

    (c)   *reasonable expenses of travelling to and from the place of employment;*

    (d)   *the amount of any contribution paid, whether under a legal obligation or not, to an occupational pension scheme within the meaning of the Social Security Pensions Act 1975; and*

    (e)   *reasonable expenses in respect of the making of reasonable provision for the care of any dependant child living with the person concerned because of that person's absence from home by reason of employment.*

5. *In computing disposable income there shall be a deduction in respect of the main or only dwelling in the case of a householder of the amount of the net rent payable, or such part thereof as is reasonable in the circumstances.*

    (2) In this rule "rent" means—

    (a)   *the annual rent payable; and*

    (b)   *a sum in respect of yearly outgoings borne by the householder including, in particular, rates, a reasonable allowance towards any necessary expenditure on repairs and insurance and any annual instalment (whether of interest or of capital) payable in respect of a mortgage debt or heritable security charged on the house in which the householder resides or has an interest therein.*

    (3) Where any amount of the rent or rates is met by a rebate or allowance under Part II of the Social Security and Housing Benefits Act 1982, or by any rate rebate, the amount so met shall be deducted from the rent to be considered under paragraph (1) of this rule.

6. *If the person concerned is not a householder, there shall be a deduction in respect of the costs of his living accommodation of such an amount as is reasonable in the circumstances.*

7. *(1) In computing disposable income, there shall be a deduction in respect of the maintenance of the spouse of the person concerned, if the spouses are living together, in respect of the maintenance of any dependant child and in respect of the maintenance of any dependant relative of the person concerned being (in either of such cases) a member of his household at the following rates—*

    (a)   *in the case of a spouse at the rate equivalent to 50% above the amount specified for the time being in column (3) of paragraph 6 of Part IV of Schedule 4 to the Social Security Act 1975 (increase for adult dependant of Category A retirement pension); and*

(b) *in the case of a dependant child or a dependant relative, at the rate equivalent to 50% above the amount specified for the time being in paragraph 3 of Schedule 1 to the Supplementary Benefit (Requirements) Regulations 1980 appropriate to the age of the child or relative;*

provided that the proper officer may reduce such rate by taking into account the income and other resources of the dependant child or other dependant to such extent as appears to the officer to be just and equitable.

(2) In ascertaining whether a child is a dependant child and whether a person is a dependant relative regard shall be had to their income and other resources.

8. *If the person concerned is making and, throughout such period as the proper officer may consider adequate, has regularly made bona fide payments for the maintenance of a spouse who is living apart, of a former spouse, of a child or of a relative who is not (in any such cases) a member of the household of the person concerned there shall be a deduction at the rate of such payments or at such rate, not exceeding the rate of such payments, as in all the circumstances is reasonable.*

9. *In computing disposable income, there shall be a deduction in respect of any sum or sums payable by the person concerned under an order made by or arising from any conviction before the High Court, county court, Crown Court or a magistrates' court in proceedings otherwise than those in respect of which the legal aid order was granted.*

10. *Where the person must or may reasonably provide for any other matter the proper officer may make an allowance of such amount he considers to be reasonable in the circumstances of the case.*

11. *In computing the income from any source there shall be disregarded such amount, if any, as the proper officer considers to be reasonable having regard to the nature of the income or to any other circumstances of the case.*

Part III: Disposable Capital

1. *(1) In computing the capital of the person concerned there shall be included the amount or value of every resource of a capital nature belonging to him on the date of the assessment.*

(2) So far as any such resource does not consist of money, the amount or value thereof shall be taken to be the amount which that resource would realise if sold in the open market, or if there is only a restricted market for the resource, the amount which it would realise in that market, after deduction of any expenses incurred in the sale, or if such amount cannot be ascertained, an amount which appears to the proper officer to be reasonable.

2. *In computing such capital there shall be disregarded–*

(a) *a death grant payable to a person under section 32 of the Social Security Act 1975;*

(b) *any maternity grant payable under section 21 of the Social Security Act 1975;*

(c) *any savings of mobility allowance paid under the Social Security Act 1975 which the person concerned intends to use in connection with mobility; and*

(d) *for a period not exceeding 12 months from the date of receipt, any arrears of–*

    (i)i   *attendance or mobility allowance paid under the Social Security Act 1975; and*

    (ii) *supplementary benefit.*

3. *Save where it is reasonable in the circumstances, nothing shall be included in the amount of capital of the person concerned in respect of the value of the assets of any business owned in whole or in part by him.*

4. *Save in exceptional circumstances, nothing shall be included in the amount of capital of the person in respect of—*

    (a) *the household furniture and effects of the main or only residence occupied by him;*

    (b) *articles of personal clothing; and*

    (c) *the personal tools and equipment of his trade.*

5. *In computing the amount of capital of the person concerned, the value of any interest in the main or only residence in which he resides shall be wholly disregarded.*

6. *In computing such capital there shall be disregarded such an amount of capital, if any, as the proper officer considers to be reasonable having regard to the nature of the capital or to any other circumstances of the case.*

THE THIRD SCHEDULE
(Regulation 19(3))

CONTRIBUTIONS FROM DISPOSABLE INCOME

The weekly instalment payable by the applicant or the appropriate contributor under section 7(1) of the 1982 Act, where his disposable income falls within a range specified in the first column of the following table, is the amount specified in relation to that range in the second column.

Average Weekly Disposable Income	Weekly Contribution
Exceeding £42 but not exceeding £48	£1
Exceeding £48 but not exceeding £52	£2
Exceeding £52 but not exceeding £56	£3
Exceeding £56 but not exceeding £60	£4
Exceeding £60 but not exceeding £64	£5

The weekly instalment of contribution shall be increased by £1 for each £4 or part of £4 by which average weekly disposable income exceeds £64."

CHAPTER 13

APPEAL

CONTENTS

INTRODUCTION

There are three methods by which the decisions of magistrates may be questioned: appeal to the Crown Court, appeal to the High Court by way of case stated and proceedings for judicial review in the High Court.

Appeal to the Crown Court

A person convicted by a magistrates' court may appeal to the Crown Court, if he pleaded guilty, against sentence, and if he pleaded not guilty, against conviction and sentence: Magistrates' Courts Act 1980, s. 108. "Sentence" is defined in subs. (3), *ibid*, as including, with certain exceptions, any order made on conviction. Other orders of magistrates may be the subject of separate rights of appeal: *see*, for example, the Magistrates' Courts (Appeal from Binding Over Orders) Act 1956. Appeal is made by giving written notice to the magistrates' clerk and to the prosecutor not later than 21 days after the day on which the decision appealed against was given: Crown Court Rules, 1982, r. 7(3). Where the hearing was adjourned after conviction time runs from the date of sentence. This period may be extended by the Crown Court: *ibid*, r. 7(5).

Justices have a right to appear at the appeal and support their decision without rendering themselves liable to costs: *R*. v. *Kent Justices, ex parte Commissioner of Metropolitan Police* (1936) 100 J.P. 17; *R*. v. *Goodall and Others, Sussex JJ* (1874) 38 J.P. 616.

On appeal, which is by way of rehearing, the powers of the Crown Court are as set out in the Supreme Court Act 1981, s. 48. Its decisions are enforced by the magistrates' court, except in so far as they are dealt with by process already issued: Magistrates' Courts Act 1980, s. 110.

An appeal to the Crown Court may be abandoned by notice in writing to the clerk and prosecutor not later than the third day before the day fixed for hearing: Crown Court Rules 1982, r. 11. For the effect of abandonment *see* the Magistrates' Courts Act 1980, s. 109.

There is no corresponding right of appeal to the Crown Court on the part of the prosecutor. However, such an appeal may, rarely, be conferred by statute as, for example, by the Customs and Excise Act 1952, s. 283 (4) and the Animal Health Act 1981, s. 78.

Appeal by Way of Case Stated

Any party or any person aggrieved by the conviction, order, determination or other proceeding of a magistrates' court may question any proceeding before a magistrates' court on the ground that it is wrong in law or is in excess of jurisdiction by applying to the justices to state a case for the opinion of the High Court: Magistrates' Courts Act 1980, s. 111. The justices may refuse to state a case where they consider the application frivolous: subs. (5), *ibid*. If they agree to state a case, they may require the appellant to enter into recognizances conditioned for the prosecution of his appeal: s. 114, *ibid*. There is no statutory procedure for abandonment analogous to that in s. 109, nor have magistrates power to order costs against an appellant who fails to prosecute his appeal. They may however forfeit his recognizance under s. 120, *ibid*.

When there is a denial of natural justice the correct remedy is by way of a prerogative order: *R*. v. *Wandsworth Justices, ex parte Read* (1942) 106 J.P. 50. (And *see R*. v. *Dorking Justices, ex parte Harrington* [1983] 3 W.L.R. 370).

When an interlocutory matter arises it is more convenient if the justices continue the hearing and so enable the Divisional Court to dispose of the case in its final form: *Piggott* v. *Simms* [1972] Crim. L.R. 595; *Davies* v. *May* (1937) 101 J.P. 250. It cannot be intended that the proceedings should be held up while a case on such an intermediate matter as the admissibility of evidence is stated and determined, *per* Lord Reid in *Atkinson* v. *U.S. Government* [1969] 3 All E.R. 1317 at p. 1324: An application to state a case must be made within 21 days after the day on which the decision of the magistrates' court was given, Magistrates' Courts Act 1980, s. 111(2). Thereafter the drawing up of the case proceeds by strictly regulated time limits contained. in the Magistrates' Courts Rules 1981, rr. 77, 79. Once received by the appellant the case must be lodged with the Crown Office within 10 days and within four days of lodging notice of entry and a copy of the case must be served on the respondent: R.S.C. Ord. 56, r. 6. The appeal is heard by a Divisional Court of the Queen's Bench Division: r. 5, *ibid.* It has power to send the case back for amendment: Summary Jurisdiction Act 1857, s. 10. The magistrates have no right to be heard at the appeal: *Smith* v. *Smith* (1886) 50 J.P. 260.

Once a defendant has applied for a case to be stated he forfeits his right to appeal to the Crown Court against the decision in question: Magistrates' Courts Act 1980, s. 111(4).

The powers of the High Court in respect of a case stated are set out in the Summary Jurisdiction Act 1857, s. 6, which provides that the magistrates shall not be liable to costs. (But *see* the note to that section.) The order of the High Court is enforceable as if it were a decision of the magistrates' court: Magistrates' Courts Act 1980, s. 112.

Judicial Review

The High Court also exercises a controlling jurisdiction over the actions of magistrates by way of the prerogative orders of *mandamus, prohibition* and *certiorari* (formerly prerogative writs of the same names: Administration of Justice (Miscellaneous Provisions) Act 1933, s. 11). A prerogative order is obtained by way of an application for judicial review under R.S.C. Ord. 53. The leave of the court must first be obtained under r. 3, *ibid.* Application must be made promptly and normally within three months from the date when grounds for the application first arose: r. 4, *ibid.*

When the facts are complicated it is far more convenient if proceedings are commenced by way of case stated rather than for judicial review: *R.* v. *Felixstowe Justices, ex parte Baldwin* (1980) October 22, unreported.

Mandamus

The order of *mandamus* is appropriate when the High Court is asked to compel an inferior tribunal such as a magistrates' court to perform its duty, as, for example, where it has wrongly declined jurisdiction. *Mandamus* will not be granted in committal proceedings to review the decisions of the magistrate (in this case allowing a particular line of cross examination) until the proceedings have run their course: *R.* v. *Wells Street Stipendiary Magistrate, ex parte Seillon* [1978] 3 All E.R. 257.

Prohibition

Prohibition may be used to restrain magistrates from exceeding their jurisdiction so long as the matter is still capable of being corrected and has not been finally determined: *R.* v. *North, ex parte Oakey* (1927) 43 T.L.R. 60. *Prohibition* has been granted to prevent oppressive and unfair prosecutions: *R.* v. *Cwmbran Justices, ex parte Pope* (1979) 143 J.P. 638.

Certiorari

An order of *certiorari* removes to the High Court any decision or action of justices for review, for example, where there has been an abuse of natural justice: *R. v. Wandsworth Justices, ex parte Read* (1942) 106 J.P. 50. Instead of quashing a conviction upon which an unlawful sentence was imposed the High Court may amend the conviction by substituting any sentence which the magistrates' courts had power to impose: Administration of Justice Act 1960, s. 16; *R. v. Birmingham Justices, ex parte Wyatt* [1975] 3 All E.R. 897. *Certiorari* will not be granted if an objection was not taken before the court below, unless the party was unaware of the absence of jurisdiction: *R. v. Inner London Quarter Sessions, ex parte D'Souza* [1969] 54 Cr. App. R. 193; nor on the ground of fresh evidence: *R. v. West Sussex Quarter Sessions, ex parte Albert and Maud Johnson Trust Ltd and Others* (1973) 137 J.P. 784. *Certiorari* will not issue as a matter of course where there is a more convenient statutory remedy: *R. v. Brighton Justices, ex parte Robinson* (1972) *The Times*, November 3. (Case heard without defendant's knowledge may be rectified by the Magistrates' Courts Act 1980, s. 14(1)). In *R. v. Wells St. Justices, ex parte Collett* [1981] R.T.R. 272 *certiorari* was refused where the accused had not availed herself of the remedy in the Magistrates' Courts Act 1980, s. 142 (power of magistrates to re-open cases). The High Court refused *certiorari* to review sentence where the applicant had not exercised his right of appeal to the Crown Court: *R. v. Battle Justices, ex parte Shepherd and Another* [1983] Crim. L.R. 550. A mistakenly announced "conviction" by justices following a submission of no case to answer does not make them *functi officio* and *certiorari* is therefore unnecessary: *R. v. Midhurst Justices, ex parte Thompson and Another* (1974) 138 J.P. 359. *Certiorari* will not issue where a conflict of evidence has to be resolved: *R. v. Abingdon (County) Magistrates' Court, ex parte Lenard Arthur Clifford* [1978] Crim. L.R. 165. *Certiorari* was issued to quash a conviction where there was no fault on the part of the magistrates, merely the prosecutor, on the basis that this had caused a clear denial of natural justice: *R. v. Leyland Justices, ex parte Hawthorn* [1979] 68 Cr. App. R. 269.

The High Court will not interfere by way of *certiorari* while proceedings before a magistrate are in progress and not yet finally determined, whether those proceedings are committal proceedings (*R. v. Carden* (1879) Q.B.D. 1) or summary trial (*R. v. Rochford Justices, ex parte Buck* [1979] 68 Cr. App. R. 114.) *Certiorari* may be used to correct a breach of the rules of natural justice even when this constitutes a refusal to grant an adjournment: *R. v. Thames Magistrates' Court, ex parte Polemis* (1974) 138 J.P. 672.

However, unless the proceedings are a nullity, the High Court will not interfere by way of judicial review to upset an acquittal: *R. v. Dorking Justices, ex parte Harrington* [1983] 3 W.L.R. 370. The appropriate remedy is an appeal by way of case stated.

The justices may make and file an affidavit setting forth the grounds of the decision and any material facts: Review of Justices Decisions Act, 1872, s. 2, but if they appear by counsel they may be liable in costs. In a circular letter dated June 17, 1981 the Lord Chancellor's Secretary of Commissions reminded justices' clerks that it is generally unnecessary and even undesirable for the justices to be represented, but that if the Divisional Court indicates that they should be, the Treasury Solicitor will normally make the necessary arrangements. When justices have appeared at the suggestion of the court and costs have been awarded against them or their clerk the Lord Chancellor has power at his discretion to defray such costs out of moneys provided by Parliament. (Justices of the Peace Act 1979, s. 54(2)).

Bail on Appeal

After an appellant has given notice of appeal to the Crown Court or has applied to a magistrates' court to state a case, the magistrates may release him on bail: Magistrates' Courts Act 1980, s. 113. There is no power in magistrates to grant bail pending the hearing of an application for a prerogative order: *Blyth* v. *Lancaster Appeal Committee* [1944] 1 All E.R. 587.

The general right to bail (Bail Act 1976, s. 4) does not apply to bail pending appeal. The practice of the Court of Appeal is not to grant bail on appeal save in exceptional circumstances but to ensure the expedited hearing of the appeal: *R.* v. *Imdad Shah* (1980) 144 J.P. 460; *R.* v. *Priddle* [1981] Crim. L.R. 114.

The High Court has power to admit to bail anyone refused bail by magistrates or offered it on unacceptable terms: Criminal Justice Act 1967, s. 22. Also anyone convicted and sentenced by a magistrates' court who has applied for an order of *certiorari* or who has applied for leave to make such application: Criminal Justice Act, 1948, s. 37. The Crown Court may grant bail to anyone who has appealed to it: Supreme Court Act 1981, s. 81.

THE SUMMARY JURISDICTION ACT, 1857

Superior Court to determine the questions on the case
6. The Court to which a case is transmitted under the Magistrates' Courts Act 1980, shall hear and determine the question or questions of law arising thereon, and shall thereupon reverse, affirm, or amend the determination in respect of which the case has been stated, or remit the matter to the justice or justices, with the opinion of the Court thereon, or may make such other order in relation to the matter, and may make such orders as to costs, as to the Court may seem fit; and except as provided by the Administration of Justice Act, 1960, all such orders shall be final and conclusive on all parties: Provided always, that no justice or justices of the peace, who shall state and deliver a case in pursuance of the Magistrates' Courts Act, 1980, shall be liable to any costs in respect or by reason of such appeal against his or their determination. (*as amended by the Magistrates' Courts Act, 1952, s. 131, the Administration of Justice Act, 1960, s. 19(1), the Magistrates' Courts Act 1980, sch. 7*).

COMMENTARY

The appellant is not to be deprived of his right to appeal merely by reason of the prosecutor's death: *Garnsworthy* v. *Pyne* (1870) 35 J.P. 21. A case was struck out where the respondent had died before argument: *Finchley U.D.C.* v. *Blyton* (1913) 77 J.P.N. 556 (but without reference to *Garnsworthy* v. *Pyne, supra*). In *Hodgson* v. *Lakeman* (1943) 107 J.P. 27, the Divisional Court held that they had jurisdiction to allow the appellant's executors to proceed with his appeal after his death. But there must be some legal interest, such as a pecuniary penalty, to justify the action of the executor: a sentence of imprisonment is not enough: *R.* v. *Rowe* 1955) 119 J.P. 349. "We take it to be a general principle that whenever a party to proceedings dies, the proceedings must abate, unless his personal representatives both have an interest in the subject matter and can by virtue of the express terms of a statute (or by rules of court made by virtue of jurisdiction given by a statute) take the appropriate steps to have themselves substituted for the deceased as a party to the proceedings", *per* Widgery LJ in *R.* v. *Jeffries* [1968] 3 All E.R. 238 (appeal to the House of Lords).

The authority and jurisdiction vested in a superior court by this section may be exercised by a Judge in chambers: s. 8 of the Act.

Certiorari is not necessary for a case to be stated: s. 10, *ibid.*

For the court's power to award costs *see* the Costs in Criminal Cases Act 1973, s. 5.

Appeal from the decision of the High Court lies, with leave, to the House of Lords, where a point of law of general public importance is involved: Administration of Justice Act 1960, s. 1.

Shall hear and determine. The High Court have power, on application, to send a case back to the justices to repair an omission: *Yorkshire Tyre and Axle Co.* v. *Rotherham Board of Health* (1858) 22 J.P. 625; *Christie* v. *St. Luke's Chelsea* (1858) 22 J.P. 496; *Townsend* v. *Read* (1861) 25 J.P. 455; *Spicer* v. *Warbey* (1953) 117 J.P. 92.

Remit the matter to the magistrates. Who can be compelled to act thereupon by *mandamus: R.* v. *Corser* (1892) 8 T.L.R. 563. Where the remission contains a suggestion that the case shall be heard by a fresh bench the new bench need not begin the hearing *de novo* but may start at the moment when evidence is first called, omitting the preliminaries regarding choice of venue and the taking of the plea: *R.* v. *Bradfield and Sonning Justices, ex parte Jones* [1976] R.T.R. 144.

There is no power in the High Court to order a retrial, although they may order that a hearing shall be resumed if, for example, the magistrates wrongfully failed to hear the defence: *Rigby* v. *Woodward* (1957) 121 J.P. 129.

In an Irish case (*R.* v. *Waterford Justices* (1900) 2 Ir. R. 307) it was held that when a case is remitted to justices with a direction to convict on the basis that they came to a wrong conclusion from the facts, there remained a right to appeal to quarter sessions against the findings of facts.

Make such other order. When substituting a conviction for an acquittal this provision was held to be wide enough to allow the making of an order of absolute discharge: *Coote* v. *Winfield* [1980] R.T.R. 42.

Costs. But *see Edge* v. *Edwards* (1932) 96 J.P.N. 350. (Costs awarded when the justices failed to amend the case by removing admittedly erroneous matters). Although not stated, this decision presumably rested on the fact that the justices had not "stated and delivered a case in pursuance of" the Act.

Amendment of case

7. The court for the opinion of which a case is stated shall have power, if they think fit, to cause the case to be sent back for amendment and thereupon the same shall be amended accordingly, and judgment shall be delivered after it shall have been amended.

THE REVIEW OF JUSTICES' DECISIONS ACT 1872

Affidavit of ground of justice's decision.

2. Whenever the decision of any justice or justices is called in question in any Superior Court of Common Law by a rule to show cause or other process issued upon an ex parte application, it shall be lawful for any such justice to make and file in such court an affidavit setting forth the grounds of the decision so brought under review, and any facts which he may consider to have a material bearing upon the question at issue, without being required to pay any fee in respect of filing such affidavit and such affidavit may be forwarded by post to one of the Masters of the Court for the purpose of being so filed.

(as amended by the Statute Law Revision (No. 2) Act 1893, the Finance Act 1949, s. 52, sch. 11).

COMMENTARY

A dissenting justice has no right to file an affidavit: *R.* v. *Waddingham etc., Gloucestershire Justices and Tustin* (1896) 60 J.P.N. 372.

Consideration of affidavit.

3. Whenever any such affidavit has been filed as aforesaid, the Court shall, before making the rule absolute against the justice or justices, or otherwise determining the matter so as to overrule or set aside the acts or decisions of the justice or justices to which the application relates, take into consideration the matter set forth in such affidavit, notwithstanding that no counsel appear on behalf of the said justices.

THE MAGISTRATES' COURTS ACT 1980

Right of appeal to the Crown Court

108. (1) A person convicted by a magistrates' court may appeal to the Crown Court —

(*a*) if he pleaded guilty, against his sentence;
(*b*) if he did not, against the conviction or sentence.

(1A) Section 13 of the Powers of Criminal Courts Act 1973 (under which a conviction of an offence for which a probation order or an order for conditional or absolute discharge is made is deemed not to be a conviction except for certain purposes) shall not prevent an appeal under this section, whether against conviction or otherwise.

(2) A person sentenced by a magistrates' court for an offence in respect of which a probation order or an order for conditional discharge has been previously made may appeal to the Crown Court against the sentence.

(3) In this section "sentence" includes any order made on conviction by a magistrates' court, not being —

(*a*)   (*Repealed*)
(*b*) an order for the payment of costs;
(*c*) an order under s. 2 of the Protection of Animals Act 1911 (which enables a court to order the destruction of an animal); or
(*d*) an order made in pursuance of any enactment under which the court has no discretion as to the making of the order or its terms.

(*as amended by the Criminal Justice Act 1982, s. 66, sch. 16.*)

COMMENTARY

The right of appeal to the Crown Court is of statutory origin: *R.* v. *Warwickshire Justices,* (1856) 20 J.P. 693. Save where given by statute, the Crown Court has no jurisdiction to hear an appeal, *per* Lord Widgery CJ in *R.* v. *Crown Court at Lewes, ex parte Rogers* (1974) 138 J.P. 249. The rights given by this Act are not in derogation of any other statutory right of appeal: *Harris* v. *Cooke* (1918) 83 J.P. 72; *Mittelmann and Anr.* v. *Dennman (1920) 84 J.P. 30; Cockhill* v. *Davies* (1943) 107 J.P. 130, but *see* s. 111(4), *infra.*

Magistrates have power to grant legal aid in an appeal to the Crown Court both to the defendant and to "the other party": Legal Aid Act 1974, s. 28(5).

An appellant who is in custody may be released on bail after giving notice of appeal: s. 113, *infra.*

For notice of appeal *see* the Crown Court Rules 1982, r. 7. For the documents to be sent to the Crown Court *see* the Magistrates' Courts Rules 1981, r. 74. For the abandonment of appeal *see* the Crown Court Rules 1982, r. 11, *infra.*

It was held in *Hawkins* v. *Bepey and Others* (1980) 144 J.P. 203, that the death of the police officer who had preferred the information did not cause the appeal to lapse when the officer was acting on behalf of the chief constable whose order he had to obey.

Subsection (1): Pleaded guilty.

Ambiguous plea.

The Crown Court may determine whether a defendant's plea was correctly recorded by the magistrates: *R.* v. *Durham Quarter Sessions, ex parte Virgo* (1952) 116 J.P. 157 and may then remit the case to the magistrates for rehearing as a plea of not guilty. The terms of the order of remission are immaterial: *R.* v. *Tottenham Justices, ex parte Rubens* (1970) 134 J.P. 285. The same principles apply to appeals against conviction following committals for sentence: *R.* v. *Fareham Justices, ex parte Long* (1976) 140 J.P.N. 256; [1976] Crim. L.R. 269.

When, on appeal against sentence, a defendant wishes to change his plea to one of not guilty, asserting that the previous guilty plea was equivocal, the Crown Court should first be satisfied that there was credible prima facie evidence that the original plea was one of "guilty, but . . .". If there was no such evidence that was the end of the matter and the court could proceed to deal with the appeal against sentence. There might, however, be rare cases when prima facie evidence of equivocality was produced. If the Crown Court then remitted the matter to the justices with a view to a retrial, the justices, having before them their own opinion of what happened, would be likely to say that there was no equivocality and decline to act. Thus an unseemly conflict would arise between the two courts. It was essential that in such cases the Crown Court should seek help from the justices by way of affidavits from the justices' clerk or the chairman of the bench or both as to what occurred in the magistrates' court. Only when it had considered such evidence, should the Crown Court come to a conclusion as to the equivocality of the plea. It should not remit before such evidence had been considered. Cases in which it would be proper to remit were likely to be out of the ordinary; and it might well be that in most cases the proper forum for determining the question of equivocality was the Divisional Court rather than the Crown Court, *per* Lord Lane, CJ, in *R.* v. *Rochdale Justices, ex parte Allwork* (1982) 146 J.P. 33. And *see R.* v. *Plymouth Justices, ex parte Whitton* [1980] 71 Cr. App. R. 322. But when the ground of appeal is the ambiguity of the plea the Crown Court exceed their jurisdiction by remitting a case to magistrates with a direction that a plea of not guilty should be entered if they fail to make any inquiry to ascertain whether anything took place before the magistrates' court which would cast doubt on the plea of guilty. The inquiry in each case is as to what took place before the magistrates' court to see whether the court acted properly in accepting an apparent plea of guilty as an equivocal plea and where no such inquiry is held the magistrates act properly in refusing to accept the remission:*R.* v. *Marylebone Justices, ex parte Westminster City Council* (1971) 135 J.P. 239; *R.* v. *Coventry Crown Court and Another, ex parte Manson* [1978] L.S. Gaz., April 5.

Plea under duress

When the accused is making a plea of guilty under pressure and threats he does not make a free plea and the trial starts without there being a proper plea at all: *R.* v. *Inns* [1975] 60 Cr. App. R. 231 (pressure from the judge).

Sentence. Does not include a committal in default of payment of any sum of money, or for want of sufficient distress to satisfy any sum of money, or for failure to do or abstain from doing anything required to be done or left undone: s. 150(1) of the Act. It includes a recommendation for deportation: Immigration Act 1971, s. 66(5)(*a*). And *see* subs. (3) of this section.

The mere fact that the sentence is invalid does not deprive the Crown Court of the power to hear an appeal: *R.* v. *Birmingham Justices, ex parte Wyatt* [1975] 3 All E.R. 897.

Conviction. Includes a finding of guilt in respect of a juvenile: Children and Young Persons Act, 1933, s. 59.

Subsection (3): Order made on conviction. This means an order made as a consequence of conviction and not simply at the time of conviction: *R.* v. *London Sessions Appeal Committee, ex parte Beaumont* (1951) 115 J.P. 104; *R.* v. *Harmann* (1959) 123 J.P. 399. Thus, it excludes a binding over to be of good behaviour, even though made at the time of conviction: *R.* v. *London Sessions, supra;* although appeal against such an order is now provided for separately by the Magistrates' Courts (Appeal From Binding Over Orders) Act, 1956.

A committal for sentence under s. 38 of this Act is not an order made on conviction: *R.* v. *London Sessions, ex parte Rogers* (1951) 115 J.P. 108.

There is a right of appeal under this section from a discretionary order of disqualification for holding or obtaining a driving licence: *R.* v. *Surrey Quarter Sessions, ex parte Commissioner of Police of the Metropolis* (1962) 126 J.P. 269. The Road Traffic Act 1972, s. 94(1), gives a separate right of appeal against "mandatory" orders of disqualification.

A direction under s. 40(3) of the Education Act, 1944, that a child should be brought before a juvenile court in respect of his failure to attend school regularly is not, it is submitted, an order made on conviction.

The payment of costs. The prosecutor has a right of appeal when costs ordered against him in committal proceedings exceed £25: Costs in Criminal Cases Act 1973, s. 2(5). This applies only to a discharge, not to a case when the prosecution is not proceeded with: *R.* v. *Crown Court at Lewes, ex* *parte Rogers* (1974) 138 J.P. 249.

Abandonment of appeal

109. (1) Where notice to abandon an appeal has been duly given by the appellant —

> (*a*) the court against whose decision the appeal was brought may issue process for enforcing that decision, subject to anything already suffered or done under it by the appellant; and
>
> (*b*) the said court may, on the application of the other party to the appeal, order the appellant to pay to that party such costs as appear to the court to be just and reasonable in respect of expenses properly incurred by that party in connexion with the appeal before notice of the abandonment was given to that party.

(2) In this section "appeal" means an appeal from a magistrates' court to the Crown Court, and the reference to a notice to abandon an appeal is a reference to a notice shown to the satisfaction of the magistrates' court to have been in accordance with Crown Court rules.

COMMENTARY

Unless an abandonment of appeal is a nullity by virtue of mistake or fraudulent inducement, the Crown Court cannot entertain an appeal once it has been validly abandoned: *R.* v. *Essex Quarter Sessions, ex parte Larkin* (1961) 126 J.P. 29.

Subsection (1): Notice to abandon. Under the Crown Court Rules 1982, r. 11, *infra.* And *see* subs. (2) of this section.

Costs. Costs on appeal are enforceable by whatever magistrates' court is specified in the order as sums adjudged to be paid on a conviction of that court: Administration of Justice Act 1970, s. 41 and sch. 9.

Enforcement of decision of the Crown Court

110. After the determination by the Crown Court of an appeal from a magistrates' court the decision appealed against as confirmed or varied by the Crown Court, or any decision of the Crown Court substituted for the decision appealed against, may, without prejudice to the powers of the Crown Court to enforce the decision, be enforced —

> (*a*) by the issue by the court by which the decision appealed against was given of any process that it could have issued if it had decided the case as the Crown Court decided it;
>
> (*b*) so far as the nature of any process already issued to enforce the decision appeal against permits, by that process;

and the decision of the Crown Court shall have effect as if it had been made by the magistrates' court against whose decision the appeal is brought.

COMMENTARY

Any process. Such enforcement action to be commenced within six months of the completion of taxation: *McVittie* v. *Rennison* (1941) 104 J.P. 455.

When a defendant has been released on bail after notice of appeal, the warrant is exhausted and the sentence, if confirmed on appeal, requires a fresh warrant: *R.* v. *Pentonville Prison Governor* (1902) 67 J.P. 206; *Demer* v. *Cook* (1903) 88 L.T. 629.

Statement of case by magistrates' court

111. (1) Any person who was a party to any proceeding before a magistrates' court or is aggrieved by the conviction, order, determination or other proceeding of the court may question the proceeding on the ground that it is wrong in law or is in excess of jurisdiction by applying to the justices composing the court to state a case for the opinion of the High Court on the question of law or jurisdiction involved; but a person shall not make an application under this section in respect of a decision against which he has a right of appeal to the High Court or which by virtue of any enactment passed after December 31, 1879 is final.

(2) An application under subs. (1) above shall be made within 21 days after the day on which the decision of the magistrates' court was given.

(3) For the purpose of subs. (2) above, the day on which the decision of the magistrates' court is given shall, where the court has adjourned the trial of an information after conviction, be the day on which the court sentences or otherwise deals with the offender.

(4) On the making of an application under this section in respect of a decision any right of the applicant to appeal against the decision to the Crown Court shall cease.

(5) If the justices are of opinion that an application under this section is frivolous, they may refuse to state a case, and, if the applicant so requires, shall give him a certificate stating that the application has been refused; but the justices shall not refuse to state a case if the application is made by or under the direction of the Attorney General.

(6) Where justices refuse to state a case, the High Court may, on the application of the person who applied for the case to be stated, make an order of mandamus requiring the justices to state a case.

COMMENTARY

"The stating of the case, like any other form of appeal, is a matter arising entirely from statute", *per* Lord Goddard CJ, in *Card* v. *Salmon* [1953] 1 All E.R. 324. For the powers of the High Court upon hearing a case stated *see* s. 6 of the Summary Jurisdiction Act, 1857, *supra*.

A legal aid order for proceedings before magistrates is authority for the solicitor to give assistance in the making of an application for a case to be stated within the ordinary time for doing so: Legal Aid Act 1974, s. 30(5). Legal aid for the conduct of the proceedings themselves is available under the civil scheme contained in Part I of the Act.

Subsection (1): A magistrates' court. This means any justice or justices of the peace acting under any enactment or by virtue of his or their commission or under the common law: Magistrates' Courts Act 1980, s. 148. The consolidating Act of 1952 did not change the previously established rule in *Card* v. *Salmon* (1953) 117 J.P. 110 that examining magistrates have no power to state a case: *Atkinson* v. *United States Government* [1969] 3 All E.R. 1317 (an extradition case) followed in *Dewing* v. *Cummings* [1971] R.T.R. 295.

Person . . . aggrieved. Not necessarily a party, but "persons whose legal rights are directly affected by the decision", *per* Bruce J, in *Drapers' Co.* v. *Hadder* (1892) 57 J.P. 200. Thus a person adversely affected by an order of restitution of stolen property may be a person aggrieved: *Moss* v. *Hancock* (1899) 63 J.P. 517.

Although the prosecutor is not a person aggrieved, he is a party to the proceedings: *R.* v. *Newport (Salop) Justices, ex parte Wright* (1929) 93 J.P. 179. An informant under s. 3 of the Obscene Publications Act 1959, is not a "person aggrieved" though he is a "party to the proceedings": *Burke* v. *Copper* (1962) 126 J.P. 319.

"Where the prosecution ask for a case against a defendant who has taken advantage of [third party proceedings], it is essential that the prosecution should join the third party as a party to the case if the result of the case may be a remission to the justices for re-hearing or with a direction to convict, because otherwise the defendant will lose his right to proceed against the third party at the rehearing", *per* Lord Goddard CJ, in *Elkington* v. *Kesley* (1948) 112 J.P. 228 (a case turning upon what is now s. 113 of the Food and Drugs Act 1955).

For a discussion of the term "person aggrieved" in the context of a civil appeal *see R.* v. *London Sessions Appeal Committee, ex parte Westminster City Council* (1951) 115 J.P. 350 and *R.* v. *Dorset Quarter Sessions Appeal Committee, ex parte Weymouth Corporation* (1960) 124 J.P. 337.

Wrong in law. The applicant must identify the question(s) of law or jurisdiction on which the opinion of the High Court is sought: Magistrates' Courts Rules 1981, r. 76.

It is a question of law when justices fail to draw the only conclusion which could be drawn from the facts by reasonable persons honestly applying their minds to the question; where. in other words, the decision is perverse: *Bracegirdle* v. *Oxley* (1974) 111 J.P. 31.

A point of law constituting a valid defence to a criminal charge may be entertained providing it depends on the facts stated in the case: *Knight* v. *Halliwell* (1874) 38 J.P. 470; which no evidence could alter; *Kates* v. *Jeffrey* (1914) 78 J.P. 310; but not otherwise: *Mottram* v. *Eastern Counties Rail. Co.* (1859) 24 J.P. 40. Despite dicta to the contrary in *Ross* v. *Moss* (1965) 129 J.P. 37, it was held in *Whitehead* v. *Haines* (1964) 128 J.P. 372, that it would not be right for the Divisional Court to decline to entertain and determine a.point of law open on the facts found in the case to an appellant convicted on a criminal charge which, if sound, might afford him a defence, merely because that legal objection to the charge had first been appreciated after his conviction.

Excess of jurisdiction. The applicant must identify the question(s) of law or jurisdiction on which the opinion of the High Court is sought: Magistrates' Courts Rules 1981, r. 76. A refusal of jurisdiction should be challenged by way of case stated: *R.* v. *Wisbech Justices* (1890) 54 J.P. 743; *R.* v. *Clerkenwell Metropolitan Stipendiary Magistrate, ex parte Director of Public Prosecutions* (1983) *The Times,* August 4.

Applying to the justices composing the court. The application must be in writing and signed and must be sent to the magistrates' clerk: Magistrates' Courts Rules 1981, r. 76. Even under the former law the names of the justices need not be stated and error in naming them is not fatal provided the application is clearly made: *R.* v. *Oxford (Bullingdon) Justices, ex parte Bird* [1949] 1 K.B. 100.

State a case. The procedure for stating the case is laid down in the Magistrates' Courts Rules 1981, rs. 76 - 80. The contents of the case are prescribed by r. 81. There is no reason why half a dozen different cases heard by the same magistrate on the same day against different people should not be included in one case stated, assuming always. of course, that they raise precisely the same point: *Director of Public Prosecutions* v. *Lamb* (1941) 105 J.P. 251.

It is not for the inferior court to direct what shall be done upon hearing of the case: *R.* v. *Headington Union* (1883) 47 J.P.N. 756.

The High Court will not offer a decision on a hypothetical question at the request of the parties which is "essentially in the nature of an *obiter dictum* and would not be binding upon any other court": *Tindall* v. *Wright* (1922) 86 J.P. 108. Nor will a special case be entered by the Crown Office where it is stated in alternative form: *Sheffield Waterworks Co.* v. *Sheffield Union* (1887) 31 Sol. Jo. 271.

Subsection (2): Within 21 days after. That is, not counting the day of decision but including the 21st day: *Goldsmiths' Co.* v. *West Metropolitan Rail. Co.* (1904) 68 J.P. 41; *Stewart* v. *Chapman* (1951) 115 J.P. 473, Sunday must be counted even though it is the last of the days: *Peacock* v. *R.* (1858) 22 J.P. 403; *Ex parte Simpkin* (1859) 24 J.P. 262; *Wynne* v. *Ronaldson* (1865) 29 J.P. 566. The High Court has no power to extend the period: *Michael* v. *Gowland* (1977) 141 J.P. 343. Nor, it is submitted, have the magistrates any discretion to state a case where application is made outside this period. As to the need for the question(s) of law or jurisdiction to be identified within the 21 days *see* the notes to the Magistrates' Courts Rules 1981, r. 76, *infra.*

Subsection (4). This provision is not avoided by simultaneously asking for a case to be stated and appealing to the Crown Court: *R.* v. *Winchester Crown Court, ex parte Lewington* [1982] 1 All E.R. 1277. However, an appeal by case stated does not bar an appeal to the Crown Court against sentence: *ibid* and *Sivalingham* v. *D.P.P.* [1975] C.L. 2037 (Judge Box QC).

Subsection (5): Frivolous. Justices cannot refuse to state a case on an arguable point of law: *R.* v. *Petersfield Justices, ex parte Levy* [1981] R.T.R. 204.

A magistrate may decline to state a case where he has followed a decision binding upon him on the same point from which there is no right of appeal: *R.* v. *Shiel* (1900) 19 Cox 507; 82 L.T. 587; but this does not apply where the authority followed was not the final court of appeal: *R.* v. *Watson, ex parte Bretherton* (1944) 109 J.P. 38. For an example of a frivolous point *see R.* v. *Newport (Salop) Justices, ex parte Wright* (1929) 93 J.P. 179. And compare the meaning of this term in the Court of Appeal in *R.* v. *Taylor* [1979] Crim. L.R. 649. (Not confined to foolish or silly but extends to a point of law which cannot possibly succeed on argument). If the justices refuse improperly to state a case they may be ordered to do so by *mandamus*.

Effect of decision of High Court on case stated by magistrates' court

112. Any conviction, order, determination or other proceeding of a magistrates' court varied by the High Court on an appeal by case stated, and any judgment or order of the High Court on such an appeal, may be enforced as if it were a decision of the magistrates' court from which the appeal was brought.

Bail on appeal or case stated

113. (1) Where a person has given notice of appeal to the Crown Court against the decision of a magistrates' court or has applied to a magistrates' court to state a case for the opinion of the High Court, then, if he is in custody, the magistrates' court may grant him bail.

(2) If a person is granted bail under subs. (1) above, the time and place at which he is to appear (except in the event of the determination in respect of which the case is stated being reversed by the High Court) shall be —

(*a*) if he has given notice of appeal, the Crown Court at the time appointed for the hearing of the appeal;

(*b*) if he has applied for the statement of a case, the magistrates' court at such time within 10 days after the judgment of the High Court has been given as may be specified by the magistrates' court;

and any recognizance that may be taken from him or from any surety for him shall be conditioned accordingly.

(3) Subsection (1) above shall not apply where the accused has been committed to the Crown Court for sentence under s. 37 or 38 above.

(4) Section 37(6) of the Criminal Justice Act 1948 (which relates to the currency of a sentence while a person is released on bail by the High Court) shall apply to a person released on bail by a magistrates' court under this section pending the hearing of a case stated as it applies to a person released on bail by the High Court under s. 22 of the Criminal Justice Act 1967.

COMMENTARY

See generally the note Bail on Appeal in the introduction.

Subsection (1): Notice of appeal. That is, under the Crown Court Rules 1982, r. 7, *infra*.

Applied . . . to state a case. That is, under s. 111, *supra*.

May grant him bail. Although it is not obligatory, the Home Office recommend that a defendant refused bail should be informed of his right to apply to a High Court Judge: circ. 88/49 dated April 26, 1949.

Subsection (2): Within 10 days after. That is, excluding the day of judgment but including the 10th day.

Subsection (4). The effect of this is to exclude time spent on bail from any sentence of imprisonment. As to the effect of bail on appeal to the Crown Court *see R. v. Pentonville Prison Governor* (1903) 67 J.P. 206.

Recognizances and fees on case stated

114. Justices to whom application has been made to state a case for the opinion of the High Court on any proceeding of a magistrates' court shall not be required to state the case until the applicant has entered into a recognizance, with or without sureties, before the magistrates' court, conditioned to prosecute the appeal without delay and to submit to the judgment of the High Court and pay such costs as that Court may award; and (except in any criminal matter) the clerk of a magistrates' court shall not be required to deliver the case to the applicant until the applicant has paid him the fees payable for the case and for the recognizances.

COMMENTARY

Shall not be required. Thus magistrates may state a case before or even without a recognizance.

A recognizance. *See* form 118.

The recognizance will be in time if entered into before the case is stated and delivered: *Stanhope* v. *Thorsby* (1866) 30 J.P. 342; but not later: *Walker* v. *Delacombe* (1894) 58 J.P. 88. When a recognizance was entered into with a surety and the appellant went bankrupt and his surety died, the magistrates could not insist on a further recognizance: *R. v. Kettle, ex parte Ellis* (1905) 69 J.P. 55.

In the case of a corporation, a director or other agent may be appointed by the board of directors under the Law of Property Act, 1925, s. 74(2), to enter into the recognizance: *Southern Counties Deposit Bank, Ltd* v. *Boaler* (1895) 59 J.P. 536.

Failure to prosecute the appeal without delay renders the recognizance liable to forfeiture in accordance with the Magistrates' Courts Act, 1980, s. 120. An order of forfeiture of such a recognizance may seemingly be made without complaint.

The fees. No fees are chargeable in any criminal matter: sch. 6, Part II, para. 2 of the Act. That provision applies to fees on a case stated in a criminal matter: *R. v. Preston Justices, ex parte Pamplin* [1981] Crim. L.R. 338.

THE SUPREME COURT ACT 1981

Appeals to Crown Court

48. (1) The Crown Court may, in the course of hearing any appeal, correct any error or mistake in the order or judgment incorporating the decision which is the subject of the appeal.

(2) On the termination of the hearing of an appeal the Crown Court —

(*a*) may confirm, reverse or vary the decision appealed against; or

(*b*) may remit the matter with its opinion thereon to the authority whose decision is appealed against; or

(*c*) may make such other order in the matter as the court thinks just, and by such order exercise any power which the said authority might have exercised.

(3) Subsection (2) has effect subject to any enactment relating to any such appeal which expressly limits or restricts the powers of the court on the appeal.

(4) If the appeal is against a conviction or a sentence, the preceding provisions of this section shall be construed as including power to award any punishment, whether more or less severe than that awarded by the magistrates' court whose decision is appealed against, if that is a punishment which that magistrates' court might have awarded.

(5) This section applies whether or not the appeal is against the whole of the decision.

(6) In this section "sentence" includes any order made by a court when dealing with an offender, including —

(a)   a hospital order under Part III of the Mental Health Act 1983 with or without a restriction order and an interim hospital order under that Act; and

(b)   a recommendation for deportation made when dealing with an offender.

(7) The fact that an appeal is pending against an interim hospital order under the said Act of 1983 shall not affect the power of the magistrates' court that made it to renew or terminate the order to deal with the appellant on its termination; and where the Crown Court quashes such an order but does not pass any sentence or make any other order in its place the Court may direct the appellant to be kept in custody or released on bail pending his being dealt with by that magistrates' court.

(8) Where the Crown Court makes an interim hospital order by virtue of subs. (2)—

(a)   the power of renewing or terminating the order and of dealing with the appellant on its termination shall be exercisable by the magistrates' court whose decision is appealed against and not by the Crown Court; and

(b)   that magistrates' court shall be treated for the purposes of s. 38(7) of the said Act of 1983 (absconding offenders) as the court that made the order.

(as amended by the Mental Health (Amendment) Act 1982, sch. 3, the Mental Health Act 1983, sch. 4.)

COMMENTARY

The death of the informant does not abate the appeal: *R.* v. *Truelove* (1880) 44 J.P. 346. And *see* also the case of *R.* v. *Jefferies* noted under the Summary Jurisdiction Act 1857, s. 6, *supra*.

For the court's power to award costs *see* the Costs in Criminal Cases Act 1973, s. 3.

An appeal to quarter sessions was always treated as a rehearing, although there was no statutory authority for this, but in an appeal against sentence it is usual to hear only the matters affecting sentence: *Paprika, Ltd* v. *Board of Trade* (1944) 108 J.P. 104. And *see Rugmann* v. *Drover* (1950) 114 J.P. 452, concerning juveniles, and *Sirros* v. *Moore* (1975) 139 J.P. 29.

Subsection (2): With opinion. The fact that the phraseology is used by the superior court does not make its decision any less binding on the magistrates: *R.* v. *Tottenham Justices, ex parte Rubens* [1971] 1 All E.R. 879.

Make such other order . . . as the court thinks just. Compare the similar wording of an appeal provision in a civil matter in *Fulham Metropolitan Borough Council* v. *Santilli* (1933) 97 J.P. 174.

The Crown Court have no power on appeal to commit an offender to themselves for sentence under s. 38 of the Magistrates' Courts Act, 1980: *R.* v. *Bullock* (1964) 128 J.P. 3; [1963] 3 All E.R. 506.

The Crown Court have no power to amend after conviction an information which is bad on its face: *Meek* v. *Powell* (1952) 116 J.P. 116, *Garfield* v. *Maddocks* (1973) 137 J.P. 461 (explaining *Wright* v. *Nicholson* (1970) 134 J.P. 85 as being *per incuriam* on this point).

Exercise any power. The substitution of a suspended for a forthwith sentence of imprisonment has the effect of a new order under para. (c) which runs from the date of the Crown Court order: *R.* v. *Burn* [1976] Crim. L.R. 754.

Subsection (4). Thus, if the defendant was not legally represented or otherwise within the terms of s. 21 of the Powers of Criminal Courts Act 1973 when he appeared before the magistrates' court the Crown Court may not on appeal pass a first sentence of imprisonment: *R.* v. *Birmingham Justices, ex parte Wyatt* [1975] 3 All E.R. 897.

RULES OF THE SUPREME COURT 1965
S.I. 1965 No. 1776, as amended

ORDER 53
APPLICATIONS FOR JUDICIAL REVIEW

Cases appropriate for application for judicial review
1. (1) *An application for* —

(a) *an order of mandamus, prohibition or certiorari, or*
(b) *an injunction under s. 30 of the Act restraining a person from acting in any office in which he is not entitled to act.*

shall be made by way of an application for judicial review in accordance with the provisions of this Order.

(2) *An application for a declaration or an injunction (not being an injunction mentioned in para. (1)(b) may be made by way of an application for judicial review, and on such an application the Court may grant the declaration or injunction claimed if it considers that, having regard to* —

(a) *the nature of the matters in respect of which relief may be granted by way of an order of mandamus, prohibition or certiorari,*
(b) *the nature of the persons and bodies against whom relief may be granted by way of such an order, and*
(c) *all the circumstances of the case,*

it would be just and convenient for the declaration or injunction to be granted on an application for judicial review.

Joinder of claims for relief
2. *On an application for judicial review any relief mentioned in r. 1(1) or (2) may be claimed as an alternative or in addition to any other relief so mentioned if it arises out of or relates to or is connected with the same matter.*

Grant of leave to apply for judicial review
3. (1) *No application for judicial review shall be made unless the leave of the court has been obtained in accordance with this rule.*

(2) *An application for leave must be made ex parte to a Judge by filing in the Crown Office* —

(a) *a notice in form No. 86A containing a statement of*
  (i) *the name and description of the applicant,*
  (ii) *the relief sought and the grounds upon which it is sought,*
  (iii) *the name and address of the applicant's solicitors (if any), and*
  (iv) *the applicant's address for service; and*
(b) *an affidavit verifying the facts relied on.*

(3) *The Judge may determine the application without a hearing, unless a hearing is requested in the notice of application, and need not sit in open court; in any case, the Crown Office shall serve a copy of the Judge's order on the applicant.*

(4) *Where the application for leave is refused by the Judge, or is granted on terms, the applicant may renew by applying* —

(a) *in any criminal cause or matter, to a Divisional Court of the Queen's Bench Division;*
(b) *in any other case, to a single Judge sitting in open court or, if the Court so directs, to a Divisional Court of the Queen's Bench Division:*

Provided that no application for leave may be renewed in any non-criminal cause or matter in which the Judge has refused leave under para. (3) after a hearing.

(5) *In order to renew his application for leave the applicant must, within 10 days of being served with notice of the Judge's refusal, lodge in the Crown Office notice of his intention in Form No. 86B.*

(6) *Without prejudice to its powers under Order 20, r. 8, the Court hearing an application for leave may allow the applicant's statement to be amended whether by specifying different or additional grounds or relief or otherwise, on such terms, if any, as it thinks fit.*

(7) *The Court shall not grant leave unless it considers that the applicant has a sufficient interest in the matter to which the application relates.*

(8) *Where leave is sought to apply for an order of certiorari to remove for the purpose of its being quashed any judgment, order, conviction or other proceeding which is subject to appeal and a time is limited for the bringing of the appeal, the Court may adjourn the application for leave until the appeal is determined or the time for appealing has expired.*

(9) *If the Court grants leave, it may impose such terms as to costs and as to giving security as it thinks fit.*

(10) *Where leave to apply for judicial review is granted, then —*

  (a) *if the relief sought is an order of prohibition or certiorari and the Court so directs, the grant shall operate as a stay of the proceedings to which the application relates until the determination of the application or until the Court otherwise orders;*
  (b) *if any other relief is sought, the Court may at any time grant in the proceedings such interim relief as could be granted in an action begun by writ.*

Delay in applying for relief
4. (1) *An application for judicial review shall be made promptly and in any event within three months from the date when grounds for the application first arose unless the Court considers that there is good reason for extending the period within which the application shall be made.*

(2) *Where the relief sought is an order of certiorari in respect of any judgment, order, conviction or other proceeding, the date when grounds for the application first arose shall be taken to the date of that judgment, order, conviction or proceeding.*

(3) *Paragraph (1) is without prejudice to any statutory provision which has the effect of limiting the time within which an application for judicial review may be made.*

Mode of applying for judicial review
5. (1) *In any criminal cause or matter where leave has been granted to make an application for judicial review, the application shall be made by originating motion to a Divisional Court of the Queen's Bench Division.*

(2) *In any other such cause or matter, the application shall be made by originating motion to a judge sitting in open court, unless the Court directs that it shall be made —*

  (a) *by originating summons to a judge in chambers; or*

(b) *by originating motion to a Divisional Court of the Queen's Bench Division.*

Any direction under subpara. (a) shall be without prejudice to the Judge's powers under Order 32, r. 13.

(3) *The notice of motion or summons must be served on all persons directly affected and where it relates to any proceedings in or before a court and the object of the application is either to compel the court or an officer of the court to do any act in relation to the proceedings or to quash them or any order made therein, the notice or summons must also be served on the clerk or registrar of the court and, where any objection to the conduct of the judge is to be made, on the judge.*

(4) *Unless the Court granting leave has otherwise directed, there must be at least 10 days between the service of the notice of motion or summons and the hearing.*

(5) *A motion must be entered for hearing within 14 days after the grant of leave.*

(6) *An affidavit giving the names and addresses of, and the places and dates of service on, all persons who have been served with the notice of motion or summons must be filed before the motion or summons is entered for hearing and, if any person who ought to be served under this rule has not been served, the affidavit must state that fact and the reason for it; and the affidavit shall be before the Court on the hearing of the motion or summons.*

(7) *If on the hearing of the motion or summons the Court is of opinion that any person who ought, whether under this rule or otherwise, to have been served has not been served, the Court may adjourn the hearing on such terms (if any) as it may direct in order that the notice or summons may be served on that person.*

Statements and affidavits
6. (1) *Copies of the statement in support of an application for leave under rule 3 must be served with the notice of motion or summons and, subject to para. (2), no grounds shall be relied upon or any relief sought at the hearing except the grounds and relief set out in the statement.*

(2) *The Court may on the hearing of the motion or summons allow the applicant to amend his statement, whether by specifying different or additional grounds or relief or otherwise, on such terms, if any, as it thinks fit and may allow further affidavits to be used if they deal with new matters arising out of an affidavit of any other party to the application.*

Claim for damages
7 (1) *On an application for judicial review the Court may, subject to para. (2), award damages to the applicant if —*

(a) *he has included in the statement in support of his application for leave under r. 3 a claim for damages arising from any matter to which the application relates, and*

(b) *the Court is satisfied that, if the claim had been made in an action begun by the applicant at the time of making his application, he could have been awarded damages.*

(2) *Order 18, r. 12, shall apply to a statement relating to a claim for damages as it applies to a pleading.*

Application for discovery, interrogatories, cross-examination, etc.
8. (1) *Unless the Court otherwise directs, any interlocutory application in proceedings on an application for judicial review may be made to any Judge or a master of the Queen's Bench Division, notwithstanding that the application for judicial review has been made by motion and is to be heard by a Divisional Court.*

In this paragraph "interlocutory application" includes an application for an order under Order 24 or 26 or Order 38, r. 2(3) or for an order dismissing the proceedings by consent of the parties.

(2) *In relation to an order made by a master pursuant to para. (1), Order 58, r. 1, shall, where the application for judicial review is to be heard by a Divisional Court, have effect as if a reference to that court were substituted for the reference to a Judge in chambers.*

(3) *This rule is without prejudice to any statutory provision or rule of law restricting the making of an order against the Crown.*

Hearing of application for judicial review
9. (1) *On the hearing of any motion or summons under r. 5, any person who desires to be heard in opposition to the motion or summons, and appears to the Court to be a proper person to be heard, shall be heard, notwithstanding that he has not been served with notice of the motion or the summons.*

(2) *Where the relief sought is or includes an order of certiorari to remove any proceedings for the purpose of quashing them, the applicant may not question the validity of any order, warrant, commitment, conviction, inquisition or record unless before the hearing of the motion or summons he has lodged in the Crown Office a copy thereof verified by affidavit or accounts for his failure to do so to the satisfaction of the Court hearing the motion or summons.*

(3) *Where an order of certiorari is made in any such case as is referred to in para. (2), the order shall, subject to para. (4), direct that the proceedings shall be quashed forthwith on their removal into the Queen's Bench Division.*

(4) *Where the relief sought is an order of certiorari and the Court is satisfied that there are grounds for quashing the decision to which the application relates, the Court may, in addition to quashing it, remit the matter to the court, tribunal or authority concerned with a direction to reconsider it and reach a decision in accordance with the findings of the Court.*

(5) *Where the relief sought is a declaration, an injunction or damages and the Court considers that it should not be granted in an application for judicial review but might have been granted if it had been sought in an action begun by writ by the applicant at the time of making his application, the Court may, instead of refusing the application, order the proceedings to continue as if they had been begun by writ; and Order 28, r. 8, shall apply as if, in the case of an application made by motion, it had been made by summons.*

Saving for person acting in obedience to mandamus
10. *No action or proceeding shall be begun or prosecuted against any person in respect of anything done in obedience to an order of mandamus.*

Consolidation of applications

12. *Where there is more than one application pending under s. 30 of the Act, or s. 92 of the Local Government Act 1972, against several persons in respect of* the same office, and on the same grounds, the Court may order the applications to be consolidated.

Appeal from Judge's order

13. *No appeal shall lie from an order made under para. (3) of r. 3 on an application for leave which may be renewed under para. (4) of that rule.*

Meaning of "Court"

14. *In relation to the hearing by Judge of an application for leave under r. 3 or of an application for judicial review, any reference in this Order to "the Court" shall, unless the context otherwise required, be construed as a reference to the Judge.*

ORDER 56
APPEALS, ETC. TO HIGH COURT BY CASE STATED: GENERAL

Appeal from magistrates' court by case stated

5. (1) *Except as provided by para. (2), all appeals from a magistrates' court by case stated shall be heard and determined—*

(2) *An appeal by way of case stated against an order or determination of a magistrates' court shall be heard and determined by a single judge or . . . .*

Case stated by magistrates' court: lodging case, etc.

6. (1) *Where a case has been stated by a magistrates' court the appellant must—*

(a) *within 10 days after receiving the case, lodge it in the Crown Office or, if the appeal falls to be heard by a Divisional Court of the Family Division the principal registry of the Family Division, and*

(b) *within 4 days after lodging the case as aforesaid serve on the respondent a notice of the entry of appeal together with a copy of the case.*

(2) *Unless the Court having jurisdiction to determine the appeal otherwise directs, the appeal shall not be heard sooner than 8 clear days after service of notice of the entry of the appeal.*

COMMENTARY

A single Judge has jurisdiction to extend the time for lodging a case: *Devlin* v. *F.* (1982) 145 J.P. 252.

Application for order to state a case

8. (1) *An application to the Court for an order directing a Minister, tribunal or other person to state a case for determination by the Court or to refer a question of law to the Court by way of case stated must be made by originating motion; and the persons to be served with a notice thereof are the Minister, secretary of the tribunal or other person, as the case may be, and every party (other than the applicant) to the proceedings to which the application relates.*

(2) *The notice of such motion must state the grounds of the application, the question of law on which it is sought to have the case stated and any reasons given by the Minister, tribunal or other person for his or its refusal to state a case.*

(3) *The motion must be entered for hearing, and the notice thereof served, within 4 days after receipt by the applicant of notice of the refusal of his request to state a case.*

Signing and service of case

9. (1) *A case stated by a tribunal must be signed by the chairman or president of the tribunal, and a case stated by any other person must be signed by him or by a person authorised in that behalf to do so.*

(2) *The case must be served on the party at whose request, or as a result of whose application to the Court, the case was stated; and if a Minister, tribunal, arbitrator or other person is entitled by virtue of any enactment to state a case, or to refer a question of law by way of case stated, for determination by the High Court without request being made by any party to the proceedings before that person, the case must be served on such party to those proceedings as the Minister, tribunal, arbitrator or other person, as the case may be, thinks appropriate.*

(3)*When a case is served on any party under para. (2), notice must be given to every other party to the proceedings in question that the case has been served on the party named, and on the date specified, in the notice.*

Proceedings for determination of case

10. (1) *Proceedings for the determination by the High Court of a case stated, or a question of law referred by way of case stated, by a Minister, tribunal, arbitrator or other person must be begun by originating motion by the person on whom the case was served in accordance with r. 9(2).*

(2) *The persons to be served with the notice of such motion are —*

    (a) *the Minister, secretary of the tribunal, arbitrator or other person by whom the case was stated, and*

    (b) *any party (other than the applicant) to the proceedings in which the question of law to which the case relates arose;*

and a copy of the case stated must be served with the notice on any such party.

(3) *The notice of such motion must set out the applicant's contentions on the question of law to which the case stated relates.*

(4) *The motion must be entered for hearing, and the notice thereof served, within 14 days after the case stated was served on the applicant.*

(5) *If the applicant fails to enter the motion within the period specified in para. (4), then, after obtaining a copy of the case from the Minister, tribunal, arbitrator or other person by whom the case was stated, any other party to the proceedings in which the question of law to which the case relates arose may, within 14 days after the expiration of the period so specified, begin proceedings for the determination of the case, and paras. (1) to (4) shall have effect accordingly with the necessary modifications.*

The references in this paragraph to the period specified in para. (4) shall be construed as including references to that period as extended by any order of the Court.

(6)*The documents required to be lodged in accordance with Order 57, r. 2, before entry of the motion include a copy of the case stated.*

(7) *Unless the Court having jurisdiction to determine the case otherwise directs, the motion shall not be heard sooner than 7 days after service of notice of the motion.*

Amendment of case

11. *The Court hearing a case stated by a Minister, tribunal, arbitrator or other person may amend the case or order it to be returned to that person for amendment, may draw inferences of fact from the facts stated in the case.*

ORDER 57
DIVISIONAL COURT PROCEEDINGS, ETC.:
SUPPLEMENTARY PROVISIONS

Application

1. (1) *Subject to para. (2), this Order shall apply to—*
- (a) *any proceedings before a Divisional Court,*
- (b) *any proceedings before a single judge under Order 52, r. 2, Order 53, Order 54 or Order 79,*
- (c) *any proceedings before a single judge, being proceedings which consist of or relate to an appeal to the High Court from any court, tribunal or person including an appeal by case stated and the references of a question of law by way of case stated.*

(2) *The following rules of this Order shall not apply to an appeal from a county court to a Divisional Court of the High Court under s. 108(2) of the Bankruptcy Act 1914.*

Entry of motions

2. (1) *Every motion in proceedings to which this Order applies must be entered for hearing in the appropriate office; and entry shall be made when a copy of the notice of motion, and any other documents required to be lodged before entry, have been lodged in that office.*

(2) *The party entering the motion for hearing must lodge in the appropriate office copies of the proceedings for the use of the judges.*

(3) *Except where it relates to proceedings in the Admiralty Court every motion entered for hearing by a Divisional Court of the Queen's Bench Division shall be entered in the Divisional Court list.*

(4) *In this rule "the appropriate office" means —*

- (a) *in relation to proceedings in the Queen's Bench Division (including the Admiralty Court), the Crown Office of the Admiralty Registry, as the circumstances of the case require . . .*

Issue, etc., of originating summons

3. *An originating summons by which any proceedings to which this Order applies are begun must be issued —*

- (a) *in the case of proceedings in the Family Division, out of the principal registry of the Family Division, and*
- (b) *in the case of any other proceedings, out of the Crown Office or the Admiralty Registry, as the circumstances of the case require;*

and such summons shall be in Form No. 10 in Appendix A.

Filing of affidavits and drawing up of orders

4. (1) *Except as provided by Order 41, r. 9(2) and (3), every affidavit used in proceedings to which this Order applies must be filed in the Crown Office or the Admiralty Registry, as the circumstances of the case require.*

(2) *Every order made in proceedings to which this Order applies in the Queen's Bench Division shall be drawn up in the Crown Office or the Admiralty Registry, as the circumstances of the case require, and a copy of any order made by a judge in chambers in any such proceedings must be filed in that office.*

Issue of writs

5. (1) *Every writ issued in proceedings to which this Order applies shall be issued out of the Crown Office or the principal registry of the Family Division, as the circumstances of the case require and must be prepared by the party seeking to issue it.*

(2) *Every such writ must be filed in the Crown Office or the principal registry of the Family Division, as the circumstances of the case require together with the return thereto and a copy of any order made thereon.*

Custody of records

6. *The Master of the Crown Office or the Admiralty Registry, as the circumstances of the case require shall have the custody of the records of or relating to proceedings in the Queen's Bench Division to which this Order applies.*

THE MAGISTRATES' COURTS RULES 1981
S.I. 1981 No 552

Form of conviction or order

16. (1) *A form of summary conviction or order made on complaint shall be drawn up if required for an appeal or other legal purpose, and if drawn up shall be in such one of the prescribed forms as is appropriate to the case.*

(2) *Where the conviction is of an offence that could not have been tried summarily without the consent of the accused, the conviction shall contain a statement that the accused consented to the summary trial.*

COMMENTARY

Note also the effect of r. 100, which applies to convictions: *Cole* v. *Wolkind* [1981] Crim. L.R. 252.

"The courts have always been more particular about the necessity for accuracy and more rigid in their decisions with regard to convictions than they have been with regard to processes of the court . . . which are designed to bring persons before the court", *per* Humphrey, J, in *Atterton* v. *Browne* (1945) 109 J.P. 25. But the record is never conclusive in matters of a criminal nature, *per* Lord Denning MR in *Sirros* v. *Moore* (1975) 139 J.P. 29.

The decision should set out with sufficient particularity the nature of the offence. It is not sufficient merely to recite the wording of the statute: the conviction must include sufficient details to identify the ingredients necessary to constitute the offence: *Newman* v. *Lord Hardwicke* (1838) 8 Ad. & El. 124; *Charter* v. *Greame* (1849) 13 J.P. 232; *R.* v. *Mackenzie* (1892) 56 J.P. 712; *Smith* v. *Moody* (1903) 67 J.P. 69. The conviction should also (i) show the jurisdiction: *R.* v. *Fuller* (1845) 9 J.P. 140; (ii) state the venue: *R.* v. *Casterton (Inhabitants)* (1844) 6 Q.B. 507; and (iii) state the costs ordered: *R.* v. *Hampshire Justices* (1862) 32 L.J.M.C. 46; 7 L.T. 391. It is not necessary to recite the date of laying of the informations: *Wray* v. *Toke* (1848) 12 J.P. 804.

A number of defendants may be included in the same conviction so long as the separate penalties are stated clearly: *R.* v. *Cridland* (1857) 21 J.P. 404; but it is not enough to recite "Messrs. Harrison and Company": *R.* v. *Harrison & Co.* (1800) 8 Term. Rep. 508.

A conviction may be drawn up in correct form even after one has been delivered to the defendant so long as the earlier conviction has not been quashed for informality: *R.* v. *Allen* (1812) 15 East 333; *Charter* v. *Greame* (1849) 13 J.P. 232.

Paragraph (1): Other legal purpose. A defendant has a right to a copy of his conviction: *R.* v. *Midlam* (1765) 3 Burr. 1720.

Documents to be sent to Crown Court

74. (1) *A clerk of a magistrates' court shall as soon as practicable send to the appropriate officer of the Crown Court any notice of appeal to the Crown Court given to the clerk of the court.*

(2) *The clerk of a magistrates' court shall send to the appropriate officer of the*

Crown Court, with the notice of appeal, a statement of the decision from which the appeal is brought and of the last known or usual place of abode of the parties to the appeal.

(3) *Where any person, having given notice of appeal to the Crown Court, has been granted bail for the purposes of the appeal the clerk of the court from whose decision the appeal is brought shall before the day fixed for the hearing of the appeal send to the appropriate officer of the Crown Court —*

(a) *in the case of bail in criminal proceedings, a copy of the record made in pursuance of s. 5 of the Bail Act 1976 relating to such bail;*

(b) *in the case of bail otherwise than in criminal proceedings, the recognizance entered into by the appellant relating to such bail.*

(4) *Where, in any such case as is referred to in para. 3(b), the recognizance in question has been entered into otherwise than before the magistrates' court from whose decision the appeal is brought, or the clerk of that court, the person who took the recognizance shall send it forthwith to that clerk.*

(5) *Where a notice of appeal is given in respect of a hospital order or guardianship order made under s. 60 of the Mental Health Act 1959, the clerk of the magistrates' court from which the appeal is brought shall send with the notice to the appropriate officer of the Crown Court any written evidence considered by the court under subs.(1)(a) of the said s. 60.*

(6) *Where a notice of appeal is given in respect of an appeal against conviction by a magistrates' court the clerk of the court shall send with the notice to the appropriate officer of the Crown Court any admission of facts made for the purposes of the summary trial under s. 10 of the Criminal Justice Act 1967.*

COMMENTARY

Save for specific statutory exceptions there is no general obligation upon clerks to keep notes of evidence of summary trial. However, where notes have been taken, "We hope . . . that clerks to justices will send their notes to the clerk of the peace when there is an appeal, so that he can show them to the chairman or recorder if he requires them before the hearing . . . and also will give them to the court during the hearing if it becomes necessary or desirable for the court to see what happened below": *Practice Note* [1956] 1 All E.R. 448. The purpose of this is to help decide applications for legal aid and estimate the length of the case. It is undesirable when trying an appeal for the court to have before it any notes of the hearing in the magistrates' court unless this is necessary to see what a witness had said or what had transpired in the court below: *ibid.* There is no power in the Queen's Bench Division to order a justices' clerk to produce his notes to the Crown Court: *R.* v. *Lancaster Justices, ex parte Hill* (1983) *The Times*, 9 August.

Notice of appeal. That is, under the Crown Court Rules, 1982, r. 7. So long as the document is a "notice of appeal" there is seemingly a duty on the clerk to transmit it to the Crown Court even if he believes it to be invalid, eg. because it is out of time.

Statement of the decision. *See* r. 16 as to the form of conviction or order.

Abandonment of appeal

75. *Where notice to abandon an appeal has been given by the appellant, any recognizance conditioned for the apperance of the appellant at the hearing of the appeal shall have effect as if conditioned for the appearance of the appellant before the court from whose decision the appeal was brought at a time and place to be notified to the appellant by the clerk of that court.*

COMMENTARY

Notice to abandon. That is, under the Crown Court Rules 1982, r. 11.

Application to state case

76. (1) *An application under s. 111(1) of the Act of 1980 shall be made in writing and signed by or on behalf of the applicant and shall identify the question or questions of law or jurisdiction on which the opinion of the High Court is sought.*

(2) *Where one of the questions on which the opinion of the High Court is sought is whether there was evidence on which the magistrates' court could come to its decision, the particular finding of fact made by the magistrates' court which it is claimed cannot be supported by the evidence before the magistrates' court shall be specified in such application.*

(3) *Any such application shall be sent to the clerk of the magistrates' court whose decision is questioned.*

COMMENTARY

Paragraph (1): Identify the question. Despite a line of cases which suggests that the appeal may not proceed unless the question or questions of law or jurisdiction have been identified within the period laid down by the Act (*Shippington* v. *Gouvenot-Gardiner* (1977) February 15; *Taylor* v. *Phillips* (1977) February 15; 141 J.P.N. 711; *R.* v. *Flint Justices, ex parte Baker* (1980) March 25; 144 J.P.N. 303; *The Bristol & West Building Society and Brian Simmons* v. *Hickmott* (1981) 144 J.P. 443) the better view would seem to be that this rule is directory rather than mandatory (*R.* v. *Bromley Magistrates' Court, ex parte Waitrose Ltd.* (1981) 144 J.P. 444; *Robinson* v. *Whittle* (1980) 144 J.P. 444) in the sense that there must be a "substantial compliance" with the rule: *R.* v. *Croydon Justices, ex parte Lefore Holdings Ltd* (1980) 144 J.P. 435. (In that case the clerk must have realized that there could not have been any other question because that was the only question at the hearing). Each case has to be looked at on its merits but the object of the rule was the speeding up of justice, not to curtail the opportunities for doing justice, *per* Lawton LJ, *ibid.*

Consideration of draft case

77. (1) *Within 21 days after receipt of an application made in accordance with r. 76, the clerk of the magistrates' court whose decision is questioned shall, unless the justices refuse to state a case under s. 111(5) of the Act of 1980, send a draft case in which are stated the matters required under r. 81 to the applicant or his solicitor and shall send a copy thereof to the respondent or his solicitor.*

(2) *Within 21 days after receipt of the draft case under para. (1), each party may make representations thereon. Any such representations shall be in writing and signed by or on behalf of the party making them and shall be sent to the clerk.*

(3) *Where the justices refuse to state a case under s. 111(5) of the Act and they are required by the High Court by order of mandamus under s. 111(6) to do so, this rule shall apply as if in paragraph (1) —*

(a) *for the words "receipt of an application made in accordance with r. 76" there were substituted the words "the date on which an order of mandamus under s. 111(6) of the Act of 1980 is made"; and*

(b) *the words "unless the justices refuse to state a case under s. 111(5) of the Act of 1980" were omitted.*

COMMENTARY

Although these rules are directory rather than mandatory the High Court will refuse to hear a case when the party seeking to have the case heard has himself been the author of the delay: *Parsons* v. *F. W. Woolworth & Co. Ltd* [1980] 1 W.L.R. 1472.

Paragraph (1): Within 21 days after. That is, not counting the day of the decision but including the 21st day: *Goldsmith's Co.* v. *West Metropolitan Railway* (1904) 68 J.P. 41; *Stewart* v. *Chapman* (1951) 115 J.P. 473. Sunday must be counted even though it is the last day: *Peacock* v. *R.* (1858) 22 J.P. 403; *Ex parte Simpkin* (1859) 24 J.P. 262; *Wynne* v. *Ronaldson* (1865) 29 J.P. 566.

The clerk of the magistrates' court. That is, the justices' clerk. "The intention is that as a general rule, but not invariably, the justices' clerk should prepare the first draft of the case, unless the justices wish to do so themselves. The Lord Chief Justice has expressed the view that this will usually be the most expeditious way of proceeding". Home Office circ. 55/1975 dated April 8, 1975.

Send. *See* r. 80.

Preparation and submission of final case.

78. (1) *Within 21 days after the latest day on which representations may be made under r. 77, the justices whose decision is questioned shall make such adjustments, if any, to the draft case prepared for the purposes of that rule as they think fit, after considering any such representations, and shall state and sign the case.*

(2) *A case may be stated on behalf of the justices whose decision is questioned by any two or more of them and may, if the justices so direct, be signed on their behalf by their clerk.*

(3) *Forthwith after the case has been stated and signed the clerk of the court shall send it to the applicant or his solicitor, together with any statement required by r. 79.*

COMMENTARY

Paragraph (2): Any two or more. Not necessarily the majority in the case of a majority decision. The fact that the decision was that of the majority should not appear in the case: *More O'Ferrall, Ltd.* v. *Harrow U.D.C.* (1946) 110 J.P. 357.

Send. *See* r. 80.

Extension of time limits

79. (1) *If the clerk of a magistrates' court is unable to send to the applicant a draft case under para. (1) of r. 77 within the time required by that paragraph, he shall do so as soon as practicable thereafter and the provisions of that rule shall apply accordingly; but in that event the clerk shall attach to the draft case, and to the final case when it is sent to the applicant or his solicitor under r. 78(3), a statement of the delay and the reasons therefor.*

(2) *If the clerk of a magistrates' court receives an application in writing from or on behalf of the applicant or the respondent for an extension of the time within which representations on the draft case may be made under paragraph (2) of r. 77, together with reasons in writing therefor, he may by notice in writing sent to the applicant or respondent as the case may be extend the time and the provisions of that paragraph and of r. 78 shall apply accordingly; but in that event the clerk shall attach to the final case, when it is sent to the applicant or his solicitor under r. 78(3), a statement of the extension and the reasons therefor.*

(3) *If the justices are unable to state a case within the time required by para. (1) of r. 78, they shall do so as soon as practicable thereafter and the provisions of that rule shall apply accordingly; but in that event the clerk shall attach to the final case, when it is sent to the applicant or his solicitor under r. 78(3), a statement of the delay and the reasons therefor.*

Service of documents

80. *Any document required by rr. 76 to 79 to be sent to any person shall either be delivered to him or be sent by post in a registered letter or by recorded delivery service and, if sent by post to an applicant or respondent, shall be addressed to him at his last known or usual place of abode.*

Content of case

81. (1) *A case stated by the magistrates' court shall state the facts found by the court and the question or questions of law or jurisdiction on which the opinion of the High Court is sought.*

(2) *Where one of the questions on which the opinion of the High Court is sought is whether there was evidence on which the magistrates' court could come to its decision, the particular finding of fact which it is claimed cannot be supported by the evidence before the magistrates' court shall be specified in the case.*

(3) *Unless one of the questions on which the opinion of the High Court is sought is whether there was evidence on which the magistrates' court could come to its decision, the case shall not contain a statement of evidence.*

COMMENTARY

"It is necessary to draw attention to [r. 81 of the Magistrates' Courts Rules 1981], the terms of which are frequently disregarded. Every magistrates' case should contain a full statement of the facts proved or admitted, and should not contain any statement of the evidence unless it is to be contended that there was no evidence to support a particular finding of fact. The case should follow [Form 155 of the Schedule to the Magistrates' Courts (Forms) Rules 1981] as closely as possible."
Practice Note (1972) 136 J.P. 39.

If a respondent thinks that certain facts found by the justices — and not merely evidence which was submitted to them — have been omitted from the case, he can apply to (the High Court) for a re-assessment of the case on stating in an affidavit the findings of fact which, in his opinion, have been omitted; *per* Lord Goddard CJ in *Spicer* v. *Warbey* (1953) 117 J.P. 92. And *see* the Summary Jurisdiction Act 1857, s. 7.
State the facts found. This is inappropriate where the appeal is founded on a submission of no case to answer, as to which *see* the unreported case of *Smith and Smith v. Luck* (1976) 140 J.P.N. 384. (And *see* the article at 143 J.P.N. 299).

THE CROWN COURT RULES 1982

S.I. 1982 No. 1109

Application of Part III

6. (1) Subject to the following provisions of this Rule, this Part of these Rules shall apply to every appeal which by or under any enactment lies to the Crown Court from any court, tribunal or person.

(2) Without prejudice to r. 7(5), this Part of these Rules shall have effect subject to the provisions of the enactments specified in Part I of Sch. 3 (being enactments which make special procedural provisions in respect of certain appeals) and those enactments shall have effect subject to the amendments set out in Part II of that Schedule (being amendments reproducing amendments made by r. 6(2) of, and Part II of Sch. 1 to, the Crown Court Rules 1971).

Notice of appeal

7. (1) An appeal shall be commenced by the appellant's giving notice of appeal in accordance with the following provisions of this rule.

(2) The notice required by the preceding paragraph shall be in writing and shall be given—
  (a) in a case where the appeal is against a decision of a magistrates' court, to the clerk of the magistrates' court;
  (b) in the case of an appeal under s. 81B of the Licensing Act 1964 against a decision of licensing justices, to the clerk to the justices;
  (c) in any other case, to the appropriate officer of the Crown Court; and
  (d) in any case, to any other party to the appeal.

(3) Notice of appeal shall be given not later than 21 days after the day on which the decision appealed against is given and, for this purpose, where the court has adjourned the trial of an information after conviction, that day shall be the day on which the court sentences or otherwise deals with the offender:

Provided that, where a court exercises its power to defer sentence under s. 1(1) of the Powers of Criminal Courts Act 1973, that day shall, for the purposes of an appeal against conviction, be the day on which the court exercises that power.

(4) A notice of appeal shall state–

    (a)   in the case of an appeal arising out of a conviction by a magistrates' court, whether the appeal is against conviction or sentence or both; and

    (b)   in the case of an appeal under an enactment listed in Part III of Sch. 3, the grounds of appeal.

(5) The time for giving notice of appeal (whether prescribed under paragraph (3), or under an enactment listed in Part I of Sch. 3) may be extended, either before or after it expires, by the Crown Court, on an application made in accordance with para. (6).

(6) An application for an extension of time shall be made in writing, specifying the grounds of the application and sent to the appropriate officer of the Crown Court.

(7) Where the Crown Court extends the time for giving notice of appeal, the appropriate officer of the Crown Court shall give notice of the extension to–

    (a)   the appellant;

    (b)   in the case of an appeal from a decision of a magistrates' court, to the clerk of that court;

    (c)   in the case of an appeal under s. 81B of the Licensing Act 1964 from a decision of licensing justices, to the clerk to the justices,

and the appellant shall give notice of the extension to any other party to the appeal.

COMMENTARY

For the documents to be sent to the Crown Court *see* the Magistrates' Courts Rules 1981, r. 74, *supra.*

    It would be "exceedingly improper" for a justice to issue process to enforce a sentence after notification of appeal: *Kendal* v. *Wilkinson* (1855) 19 J.P. 467.

Notice of appeal. It was held in relation to the previous legislation that the superior court is exclusive judge of the sufficiency of the description of the notice and that, therefore, *certiorari* will not lie: *R.* v. *Durham Justices,* (1981) 55 J.P.N. 277.

Any other party. Service on his solicitor is insufficient if he is no longer instructed: *R.* v. *Oxfordshire Justices,* (1983) 57 J.P. 712.

    In third party proceedings it is necessary that substantive notice of appeal be given to the original prosecutor as well as to the third party: *R.* v. *The Recorder of Derby, ex parte Spalton* (1944) 108 J.P. 193, and this applies even where the third party procedure goes only to penalty: *R.* v. *Epsom Justices, ex parte Dawnier Motors, Ltd* (1960) 125 J.P. 40. (And *see* the notes to s. 111 of the Magistrates' Courts Act, 1980).

Paragraph (5). For the exercise of the higher court's discretion, *see R.* v. *Middlesex Quarter Sessions Chairman, ex parte M.* [1967] Crim. L.R. 474.

Entry of appeal and notice of hearing

8. On receiving notice of appeal, the appropriate officer of the Crown Court shall enter the appeal and give notice of the time and place of the hearing to–

    (a)   the appellant;

    (b)   any other party to the appeal;

    (c)   in the case of an appeal from a decision of a magistrates' court, to the clerk of that court;

    (d)   in the case of an appeal under s. 81B of the Licensing Act 1964 from a decision of licensing justices, to the clerk to the justices.

9. 10. . . . .

Abandonment of appeal

11. (1) Without prejudice to the power of the Crown Court to give leave for an appeal to be abandoned, an appellant may abandon an appeal by giving notice in writing, in accordance with the following provisions of this Rule, not later than the third day before the day fixed for hearing the appeal.

(2) The notice required by the preceding paragraph shall be given—

(a) in a case where the appeal is against a decision of a magistrates' court, to the clerk of the magistrates' court;

(b) in the case of an appeal under s. 21 of the Licensing Act 1964, or in the case of an appeal under s. 81B of that Act against a decision of licensing justices, to the clerk to the licensing justices;

(c) in any other case, to the appropriate officer of the Crown Court; and

(d) in any case, to any other party to the appeal;

and, in the case of an appeal mentioned in sub-para. (a) or (b), the appellant shall send a copy of the notice to the appropriate officer of the Crown Court.

(3) For the purposes of determining whether notice of abandonment was given in time there shall be disregarded any Saturday, Sunday and any day which is specified to be a bank holiday in England and Wales under s. 1(1) of the Banking and Financial Dealings Act 1971.

COMMENTARY

Any other party. *See* the note to r. 7, *supra*.

The only right that an appellant has to abandon an appeal is the right which he exercises by giving notice in writing not later than the third day before the hearing. Any other application may or may not be granted in the court's discretion. It will only be in the most exceptional circumstances that the judge would be entitled to decline to give leave to abandon where the application is made before the hearing begins. Once the hearing has started it will only be in exceptional circumstances that leave will be granted: *R.* v. *Manchester Crown Court, ex parte Welby and Smith* [1981] 3 Cr. App. R. (S) 194.

CHAPTER 14

MAGISTRATES AND THEIR COURTS

CONTENTS

INTRODUCTION

A Magistrates' Court

A magistrates' court is any justice or justices of the peace acting under any enactment or by virtue of his or their commission or under the common law: Magistrates' Courts Act 1980, s. 148(1); Interpretation Act 1978, sch. 2.

It follows that a magistrates' court may comprise a single justice except where statute otherwise provides. In particular, a magistrates' court may not try an information or hear a complaint or hold a means inquiry except when composed of at least two justices: Magistrates' Courts Act 1980, s. 121(1), (2). The number of justices sitting to deal with a case as a magistrates' court may not exceed seven: The Justices of the Peace (Size and Chairmanship of Bench) Rules 1964.

Certain statutes give power to a single justice, but limitations are imposed by subs. (5), *ibid*. The justices composing the court must be present throughout the proceedings: *ibid*., s. 121(6); except that a differently constituted bench may sentence following an adjournment after conviction provided that full inquiry is made of the facts and circumstances: *ibid*., s. 121(7).

Except where the contrary is expressed or implied, anything required or authorized by the Magistrates' Courts Act 1980 to be done by justices may be done by one on behalf of the others present: *ibid*., s. 150(2).

Court Houses

A magistrates' court may only try a summary offence, hold a means inquiry or impose imprisonment when sitting in a petty sessional court house or occasional court house, but the summary trial of an indictable offence may take place only in the former: Magistrates' Courts Act 1980, s.121(3).

A petty sessional court house is a court house or place at which justices are accustomed to assemble for holding special or petty sessions or for the time being appointed as a substitute for such a court house or place (including, where justices are accustomed to assemble for either special or petty sessions at more than one court house or place in a petty sessional division, any such court house or place) and a court house or place at which a stipendiary magistrate is authorized by law to discharge any act authorized to be done by more than one justice of the peace: Magistrates' Courts Act 1980, s.150(1).

The justices acting for a petty sessions area may appoint as an occasional court house any place that is not a petty sessional court house for each petty sessions area and an occasional court house may be outside the area for which it is appointed: s.147, *ibid*.

Times of Sitting

There are no statutory limits upon the times when magistrates' courts may sit. In practice, they arrange their sittings at fixed hours which are published locally, but these do not prevent them sitting at any other time to discharge their duties. They are authorized to sit if they think fit on any day of the year including Christmas Day, Good Friday and Sundays: Magistrates' Courts Act 1980, s.153.

Open Court

Whenever magistrates are required to sit in a petty sessional or occasional court house they must sit in open court: Magistrates' Courts Act 1980, s. 121.

This and similar provisions are merely declaratory of the common law. "Every court of justice is open to every subject of the King", *per* Lord Halsbury in *Scott* v.

Scott [1913]A.C. 1417; [1911–13] All E.R. Rep. 1 at p.11. But "while the broad principle is that the courts in this country must, as between parties administer justice in public, this principle is subject to apparent exceptions (*which however*) are themselves the outcome of a yet more fundamental principle that the chief object of courts of justice must be to secure that justice is done", *per* Viscount Haldane, L.C., *ibid.*, at p.9. "The actual presence of the public is never, of course, necessary", *per* Lord Blanesburgh in *McPherson* v. *McPherson* [1935] All E.R. Rep. 105 at p. 109 (a divorce case). The injunction to the judge or magistrate is for him to do his best to enable the public to come in and see what was happening, having proper commonsense regard to the facilities available and the necessity for keeping order, security and the like. Although it is difficult to imagine a case which could be said to be held publicly if the press had been actively excluded, the fact that the press is present is not conclusive the other way because one must not overlook the other factor of an open and public proceeding; one to which members of the public could come if they had sufficient interest in the proceedings to make it worth their while to do so. If, having regard to all the prevailing circumstances, the judge or magistrate on the spot had shown himself conscious of his duty and reached a reasonable conclusion the Divisional Court would not substitute their own views as to whether the facilities were sufficient or not: *R.* v. *Denbigh Justices, ex parte Williams and Evans* (1974) 138 J.P. 645.

"It is one of the essential qualities of a court of justice that its proceedings should be public, and that all persons who may be desirous of hearing what is going on, if there be room in the place for that purpose—provided they do not interrupt the proceedings and provided there is no specific reason why they should be removed—have a right to be present for the purpose of hearing what is going on": *Daubney* v. *Cooper (1829)* 10 B. & C. 237. "The court may be closed or cleared if such a precaution is necessary for the administration of justice. Tumult or disorder or the just apprehension of it, would certainly justify the exclusion of all from whom such interruption is expected, and if such discrimination is impossible, the exclusion of the public in general", *per* Lord Loreborn in *Scott* v. *Scott* [1911–13] All E.R. Rep. 1 at p. 13.

Where magistrates have power to sit in private it is an acceptable alternative in a proper case to allow a witness to conceal his identity by a pseudonym ("Colonel X"). Where this is done a warning should be given as to the intended effects of this ruling: *Attorney-General* v. *Leveller Magazine Ltd. and Others (1979)* 143 J.P. 260.

Justices have power in a proper case to hear mitigation *in camera*. It follows that the application to so hear should be heard *in camera*, although the decision (to hear *in camera*) should be announced in open court: *R.* v. *Ealing Justices, ex parte Weafer* [1982] 74 Cr. App. R. 206. Mitigation can also be submitted in a sealed form although the prosecution are entitled to see it, *per* Donaldson L.J., *ibid.* The hearing of mitigation *in camera* should be a very exceptional step and should be avoided if there is any alternative, for example by the advocate drawing the court's attention to relevant passages in written documents: *R.* v. *Reigate Justices, ex parte Argus Newspapers Ltd. and Another* (1983) *The Times,* May 20; [1983] Crim L.R. 564.

Restrictions on Publication

The court may order that publication of any legal proceedings held in public or any part of those proceedings be postponed, but only where it appears necessary for avoiding a substantial risk of prejudice to the administration of justice in those or other proceedings: Contempt of Court Act 1981, s. 4(2).

Statutory Exceptions

Examining justices must sit in open court except when any enactment contains an express provision to the contrary and except where it appears to them as respects the whole or any part of committal proceedings that the ends of justice would not be served by their sitting in open court: Magistrates' Courts Act 1980, s.4(2). The court may on the application of the prosecutor order that all or any portion of the public may be excluded during any part of the hearing of proceedings under the Official Secrets Acts on the grounds that the publication of evidence would be prejudicial to public safety: Official Secrets Act 1920, s.8(4).

The public, but not the press, may be excluded during the evidence of a juvenile witness in proceedings in relation to an offence against or any conduct contrary to decency or morality: Children & Young Persons Act 1933, s. 37. Children other than babes in arms may not in general be allowed in court except as witnesses: Children & Young Persons Act 1933, s. 36.

The Privacy of the Retiring Room

Justices should not receive a record of previous convictions in their retiring room even though they have already come to a decision to convict: *Hastings* v. *Ostle* (1930) 94 J.P. 209; *Hill* v. *Tothill* [1936] W.N. 126. A witness even as to character only may not be interviewed by justices in their retiring room: *R.* v. *Bodmin JJ., ex parte McEwen* (1947) 111 J.P. 47. Nor may a social worker even after conviction: *R.* v. *Aberdare JJ., ex parte Jones* [1973] Crim. L.R. 45. *Certiorari* will not issue simply because anyone, even the informant, enters the justices' retiring room, but the conviction will be quashed where it appears he did so specifically to make a point: *R.* v. *Stratford Upon Avon JJ., ex parte Edmunds* [1973] Crim L.R. 241.

Views

There is nothing improper in magistrates viewing an immovable exhibit outside the court or inspecting the scene of a crime. A view is a part of the evidence and evidence must be given in the presence of both parties. The only exception is when a judge goes by himself to see some public place, such as the site of a road accident, *per* Denning, L.J. in *Goold* v. *Evans & Co.* (1951) 2 T.L.R. 1189 (a civil case). This applies to a magistrates' court: *see* for example *Houghton* v. *Schofield* [1973] R.T.R. 239.

There would be no objection to a witness who had already given evidence attending and taking part in a view so long as he is recalled to be cross-examined, if desired: *Karamat* v. *R.* (1957) 120 J.P. 136.

It is improper to conduct a view after a jury (and thus, seemingly, the magistrates) have retired: *R.* v. *Lawrence* (1968) 132 J.P. 173, but this was waived where the view took place at the express wish of the defence: *R.* v. *Nixon* (1968) 132 J.P. 309.

Exhibits

Exhibits are looked at by the court but are not shown to the public who have no claim to see them. This includes the showing of films the subject of prosecution, *per* Lawton L.J., in *R.* v. *Waterfield* (1975) 139 J.P. 400. This judgment also contained advice on the circumstances when the public or press should be allowed to see such films.

Disorder in Court

It is a contempt of court for anyone wilfully to insult the justices, witnesses, officers of the court or advocates or wilfully to interrupt the proceedings of the court: Contempt of Court Act 1981, s. 12(1). The court may order any officer of the court or any constable to take the offender into custody and detain him until the rising of the court and may commit him for a specified period not exceeding one month or impose a fine not exceeding £1,000 or both: *ibid.,* s. 12(2).

The court may also have power to bind over: *see* under this title in the introduction to Ch. 10.

Photography, etc.

Photography and sketching in court are prohibited by the Criminal Justice Act 1925, s. 41. The use without leave of sound recorders in court is prohibited by the Contempt of Court Act 1981, s. 9, which also forbids the playing of recordings in public and gives the court power to forfeit the instrument. Practice governing the use of tape recorders is contained in the *Practice Direction* [1982] 1 W.L.R. 1475 noted under the Contempt of Court Act 1981, s. 9.

Justices of the Peace

The term "magistrate" in relation to a county or London commission area or the City of London means a justice of the peace for the county, London commission area or the City as the case may be other than a justice whose name is for the time being entered in the supplement list, and in relation to a part of a county or of a London commission area, means a person who is a magistrate for that county or area and ordinarily acts in and for that part of it: Justices of the Peace Act 1979, s. 70.

A justice of the peace holds his office by virtue of the commission of the peace. There is a commission of the peace for each commission area addressed generally and not by name to all such persons as may from time to time hold office as justice of the peace for the area: Justices of the Peace Act 1979, s.5. Each county, London commission area and the City of London is a commission area: s.1, *ibid*. Although a justice is appointed to a commission area he is assigned by the Lord Chancellor administratively to a petty sessions area. Outside Greater London every non-metropolitan county not divided into petty sessional divisions, every petty sessional division of a non-metropolitan county and every metropolitan district not divided into petty sessional divisions, is a petty sessions area: s. 4(1), *ibid*. For Greater London *see* subs. (2), *ibid*. A justice of the peace for any commission area may act as a justice for that area in any adjoining commission area: s. 66(1), *ibid*.

A justice of the peace must reside in or within 15 miles of his commission area, but no act of his is invalidated by reason only of his being disqualified thereby: Justices of the Peace Act 1979, s.7. Once a justice becomes 70 his name is normally entered in the supplemental list: s.8, *ibid*. His powers thereafter are limited to those specified in s.10(2), *ibid*, but other acts are not disqualified: s.10(4), *ibid*.

Stipendiary Magistrate

A stipendiary magistrate sitting at a place appointed for that purpose has power to do any act and to exercise alone any jurisdiction which can be done or exercised by two justices under any law other than any law made after August 2, 1858 which expressly provides to the contrary: Justices of the Peace Act 1979, s.16(3). The term "stipendiary magistrate" includes a metropolitan stipendiary magistrate: s. 70 of the Act. Metropolitan stipendiary magistrates are appointed under s. 13 of the Act. Each is by virtue of his office a justice of the peace for each of the London Commission areas and for the counties of Essex, Hertfordshire, Kent and Surrey: s. 13(4) of the Act. The Lord Chancellor may appoint acting stipendiary magistrates for any area under s. 15 of the Act. While so acting they have the same jurisdiction, powers and duties as if appointed stipendiary magistrate in that area: s. 15(2) of the Act.

Disqualification of Justices

Justices may be disqualified from acting as such in court by failing to conform to residence qualifications (Justices of the Peace Act 1979, s.7), sitting in proceedings in which they are interested as members of local authorities (s. 64, *ibid*.) or when on the supplemental list (s. 10(1), *ibid*). But such disqualifications do not *in themselves* invalidate their acts (s. 10(4), *ibid.*). Solicitor justices are restricted from practising before their own bench by the Solicitors Act 1974, s. 38 and there are many other statutory restrictions upon justices sitting to hear cases with which they have a connexion.

The Lord Chancellor's Department have offered advice to magistrates in cases (a) where the solicitor prosecuting or defending is the magistrate's personal and/or business adviser; and (b) where the firm in which a justice's son is a partner or salaried assistant in another office. See the August 1982 issue of *The Magistrate*, at p.121.

Pecuniary Interest

The common law distinguishes, somewhat cynically perhaps, between pecuniary and non-pecuniary interest. Any direct pecuniary interest, however small, in the subject of inquiry disqualifies a person from acting as a judge in the matter, *per* Blackburn, J, in *R. v. R and. R. v. Justices of Blandford* (1866) 30 J.P. 293 (a civil case). If a justice "has a pecuniary interest or an interest capable of being measured pecuniarily the law raises a conclusive presumption of bias", *per* Vaughan Williams, LJ, in *R. v. Sunderland JJ.* (1901) 65 J.P. 594, 598. (But *see R. v. Burton, ex parte Young* (1897) 61 J.P. 727.)

The fact that a magistrate is a ratepayer does not disqualify him from ordering costs against a party: *Sierzant* v. *Anderton* (1982) July 14. Exemptions or disqualifications of this type only apply where there is an interest in the subject matter of the proceedings and have no application to ancillary matters such as costs or sentence, *per* Ormrod L.J., *ibid.*

Non-Pecuniary Interest

On the other hand, other interests not of a pecuniary nature disqualify only where there is "a real likelihood" of bias: *R. v. Sunderland JJ, supra*. The question is one of degree as to whether the position of the person attacked is such as to give rise to a reasonable suspicion of bias in reasonable minds: *R. v. London JJ, ex parte South Metropolitan Gas Co.* (1908) 72 J.P. 137 (a rating appeal). "There are some people whose minds are so perverse that they will suspect without any ground whatever. The question of incapacity is to be one of 'substance and fact'," *per* Lord Esher, M.R., in *Allinson* v. *General Council of Medical Education* (1894) 58 J.P. 542. In all cases of alleged non-pecuniary bias "the question is, what would occur to the mind of an ordinary person . . ." *per* Lord Goddard, CJ in *R. v. Caernarvon Licensing JJ, ex parte Bensen* (1948) 113 J.P. 23; or, as Lord Widgery, CJ, said in *R. v. McLean, ex parte Aiken and Others* (1975) 139 J.P. 261 at p. 266, would a reasonable and fair minded person sitting in court have come to the conclusion that the magistrate had shown such bias against the applicants that a fair trial was not to be had?

Justices who are interested in a criminal proceeding should not act therein: *R. v. Glamorganshire JJ.* (1857) 21 J.P. 773; *R. v. Hammond* (1863) 27 J.P. 793 (shareholders in the victim company). The reason for this is that "It is highly desirable that justice should be administered by persons who cannot be suspected of improper motives", *per* Mellor, J, in *R. v. Allan* (1864) 4 B. & S. 915 at p. 926. The most flagrant example of this rule is where a magistrate adjudicates in a matter to which he is substantially a party, since no man may be a judge in his own cause: *R. v. Hoseason* (1811) 14 East 605. It is bias for a magistrate to declare his preference for police evidence: *R. v. Bingham Justices, ex parte Jowitt* (1974) *The Times*, July 3.

A conviction was quashed when a presiding magistrate was a member of the education committee whose schools were said to have been short weighted by a firm of contractors: *R. v. Altrincham Justices, ex parte Pennington and Another* (1975) 139 J.P. 434 in which Bridge J, said that, if one visualized almost any kind of association between a magistrate and a private victim of an offence, it would be obvious that it ought to disqualify. If the plain outcome of an association between a magistrate and a private commercial undertaking which was the victim of the offence to be tried was that he should not sit without disclosing his position, the same outcome should result from a comparable association between a magistrate and a non-commercial undertaking, such as an education authority, which was the victim. In the same case Lord Widgery, CJ observed *obiter* that the situation of a magistrate member of a police authority is wholly different: the police authority are concerned with the administration of the force; they are not concerned with the rights and wrongs of the individual prosecution. They are not given such an interest merely because the prosecutor is a police officer. An acquittal was quashed where the husband of one of the justices had formerly been a member of the defendant local authority: *R. v. Smethwick Justices, ex parte Hands* (1980) *The Times*, December 4.

Bias and the Justices' Clerk

The same principles would appear to apply to the clerk of the court: *R. v. Camborne Justices, ex parte Pearce* (1954) 118 J.P. 488.

In *R. v. Uxbridge Justices, ex parte Bowbridge* (1972) *The Times*, June 20 it was held that an alleged remark of a clerk out of court which might have disclosed bias could not affect all the magistrates on a particular bench when the clerk did not sit in the proceedings.

Waiver of Objection

Objection on ground of interest can be waived: *R. v. Cheltenham Commissioners* (1841) 10 L.J.M.C. 99; and cannot be made afterwards unless the objector shows that both he and his advocate were unaware of the interest: *R. v. Justices of Richmond* (1860) 24 J.P. 422; *R. v. Justices of Kent* (1880) 44 J.P. 298 (a licensing case). There can be no waiver in ignorance of the interest: *R. v. Cumberland JJ., ex parte Midland Rail Co.* (1880) 52 J.P. 502.

An advocate in under no duty to put "fishing" questions to justices when he suspects interest: *R. v. Barnsley Licensing JJ, ex parte Barnsley & District L.V.A.* (1959) 123 J.P. 365.

The Avoidance of Bias

The proper course for any magistrate with a multiplicity of outside interests before embarking on a judicial task on the day when he or she was sitting, is to look at the list of cases to see whether there is something which involves an organization with which he or she has an interest. If in the list there is a case involving an organization in which the magistrate is actively employed, then the magistrate ought either to disqualify himself or herself, or at all events bring the matter to the parties' attention before the case is opened to see if there is any objection—which is really doing the same thing, *per* Lord Widgery CJ, in *R. v. Altrincham Justices, ex parte Pennington and Another*, (1975) 139 J.P. 434

Magistrates who are interested should not even appear to form part of a court or place themselves in a position where they could exert any influence: *R. v. Byles & Others, ex parte Hollidge* (1912) 77 J.P. 40. (*See* also *R. v. Suffolk JJ.* (1852) 16 J.P. 296—a rating appeal). If an interested justice remains upon the bench that is sufficient to invalidate the proceedings, *per* Kay, LJ, in *R. v. Budden & Others, Kent JJ* (1896) 60 J.P. 166 (notes passed from interested magistrate to bench). The Lord Chancellor in a letter dated January 12, 1967 has condemned the practice of "sitting back" and expressed the view that magistrates who do not sit as a member of a court should remove themselves completely from its vicinity.

Knowledge of the Parties

As to a justice's personal knowledge of the parties before him, it was said in a civil case that it would be a preposterous thing if a suggestion were made that there was bias or a possibility of bias because of the mere fact that some sort of acquaintance exists between a justice and parties, or even the fact that they have discussed business matters entirely unconnected with the case. "The whole essence of the local administration of justice and the great value of the functions of justices are that they do administer justice amongst people with whom they are acquainted and of whose lives and family history they know something", *per* Sir Boyd Merriman P in *Cottle* v. *Cottle* [1939] 2 All E.R. 535 at p. 539. (Decision quashed where there was sufficient evidence upon which the litigant husband might reasonably have formed the impression that the justice, who was a friend of the wife's mother, could not give the case an unbiased hearing.) It is desirable in criminal proceedings that an accused should come before a magistrate who does not have an intimate knowledge of his record or background, but that desirability cannot be elevated into a proposition of law: *R.* v. *Metropolitan Stipendiary Magistrate, ex parte Gallagher and Another* (1972) 136 J.P.N. 80. Thus, there is no rule of law that a magistrate is disqualified from hearing a case by reason of his having been concerned with the same defendant in other proceedings: *R.* v. *McLean, ex parte Aikens and Others* (1975) 139 J.P. 261.

Knowledge of the Circumstances

While magistrates may without hearing evidence take cognizance of any matter covered by the doctrine of judicial notice (*see* the article at 127 J.P.N. 418), they may not otherwise act on their own local knowledge. Thus, it is proper on the one hand for magistrates to make use of their general local knowledge in deciding whether a car park known to all three members of the bench was a public place or not (*Clift* v. *Lang* [1961] Crim. L.R. 121). Similarly, justices in dealing with local geography in the sense that they are dealing with matters which are notorious locally and which are within their own local knowledge, are entitled to supplement the evidence (as to road user) by their knowledge that the journey in question inevitably involved passage over public roads, *per* Lord Widgery, C.J. in *Borthwick* v. *Vickers* [1973] R.T.R. 390. On the other hand, the private knowledge of one member of the bench as to the use to which a car park was put on a particular occasion cannot be a substitute for evidence: *Williams* v. *Boyle* (1962) 126 J.P.N. 732; [1963] Crim. L.R. 204.

Magistrates may not act on their own expert evidence by taking a tyre gauge with them into the retiring room for the purpose of measurement: *R.* v. *Tiverton Justices, ex parte Smith* (1981) 145 J.P. 177.

Specialized Knowledge

It is not improper for a justice with specialized knowledge, such as a doctor, to draw on that knowledge in interpreting the evidence. However, he should not go on as it were, to give evidence to himself in contradiction of that heard in court. In the retiring room, a justice with such knowledge ought to wait until asked to make a contribution on his specialty: *Wetherall* v. *Harrison* (1976) 140 J.P. 143. *See*, for example, *Kent* v. *Stamps* [1982] R.T.R. 273 (Knowledge of road).

Magistrates' Conduct on the Bench

If a responsible observer seriously believes a justice to have been asleep on the bench the justice should withdraw from the case even if the belief is unfounded: *R.* v. *Weston-Super-Mare Justices, ex parte Taylor* (1980) *The Times*, November 4; [1981] Crim. L.R. 179.

Magistrates' Names

The justices' clerk is under no duty to supply even a party with the justices' names: *Newton* v. *Saunders* (1972) October 31; 137 J.P.N. 432. And *see* the opinion of the Justices' Clerks' Society in *The Justices' Clerk* of May, 1973.

The Liability of Justices

No action is maintainable against a justice for anything said or done within his jurisdiction. Nor is he liable for acts done outside his jurisdiction provided that he acted judicially and in the honest belief that he was within his jurisdiction: *per* Denning LJ, in *Sirros* v. *Moore & Others* (1975) 139 J.P. 29. No action against a justice for anything done within his jurisdiction can succeed unless the plaintiff alleges and proves that the act was done maliciously and without reasonable and probable cause: Justices of the Peace Act 1979, s. 44. There are limitations on his liability for acts done outside or in excess of his jurisdiction: ss. 45, 52, *ibid.*

The Clerk to the Justices

The functions of the clerk to the justices, i.e. the person or persons appointed to this post under the Justices of the Peace Act 1979, s. 25 (not printed herein), are only partially defined by statute. They include the giving to the justices to whom he is clerk or any of them, at the request of the justices or justice, of advice about law, practice or procedure on questions arising in connexion with the discharge of their or his functions, including questions arising when the clerk is not personally attending on the justices or justice. In particular the clerk may, at any time when he thinks he should do so, bring to the attention of the justices or justice any point of law, practice or procedure that is or may be involved in any question so arising: Justices of the Peace Act 1979, s. 28(3). This provision does not define or in any respect limit the powers and duties of the justices' clerk or the matters on which justices may obtain assistance from him: *ibid,* s. 28(4).

Certain things authorized to be done by, to or before a single justice may be done by, to or before a justices' clerk: Justices' Clerks Rules 1970. In acting under those Rules any enactment or rule of law regulating the exercise of any jurisdiction or powers of justices or relating to the exercise of such jurisdiction or powers applies to the clerk as if he were one of the justices: Justices of the Peace Act 1979, s. 28(2).

Where outside Inner London someone acts as a substitute for the clerk to the justices he is treated as acting as deputy to the clerk and must make a return to the latter: Justices of the Peace Act 1979, s. 30. Except in Inner London there is no statutory post of deputy to the clerk to the justices, although such appointments are commonly made.

The Court Clerk

From the earliest days justices of the peace have sat in court with a clerk. For a long time this was usually the person holding the office of clerk to the justices, but with the growth in work of the modern magistrates' courts increasingly this role has come to be assumed by his assistants. Although there is no requirement that justices must have the assistance of a clerk when sitting in court, no person may be employed as a clerk in court unless he is (a) qualified (any age limits apart) to be appointed a justices' clerk by virtue of s. 27 of the Justices of the Peace Act 1979; or (b) he is qualified by virtue of r. 4 of the Justices' Clerks (Qualifications of Assistants) Rules 1979 (not reproduced herein): Justices of the Peace Act 1979, s. 30. A person who is not so qualified may be employed as a clerk in court if he holds a valid training certificate granted by a magistrates' courts' committee: Justices' Clerks (Qualifications of Assistants) Rules 1979, r. 5. The Secretary of State may grant authority for any such person as may be specified by him to be employed as a clerk in court for such period not exceeding six months as may be specified if he is satisfied that the person is in the circumstances a suitable person to be so employed and that no other arrangements can reasonable be made for the hearing of proceedings before the court: r. 6, *ibid*.

Any staff provided for a justices' clerk work under his direction: Justices of the Peace Act 1979, s. 27(6).

The role of the clerk in court is governed by the following *Practice Direction* [1981] 2 All E.R. 831:

1. A justices' clerk is responsible to the justices for the performance of any of the functions set out below by any member of his staff acting as court clerk and may be called in to advise the justices even when he is not personally sitting with the justices as clerk to the court.

2. It shall be the responsibility of the justices' clerk to advise the justices as follows:
    (a)   on questions of law or of mixed law and fact;
    (b)   as to matters of practice and procedure.

3. If it appears to him necessary to do so, or he is so requested by the justices, the justices' clerk has the responsibility to:
    (a)   refresh the justices' memory as to any matter of evidence and to draw attention to any issues involved in the matters before the court;
    (b)   advise the justices generally on the range of penalties which the law allows them to impose and on any guidance relevant to the choice of penalty provided by the law, the decisions of the superior courts or other authorities.
    If no request for advice has been made by the justices, the justices' clerk shall discharge his responsibility in court in the presence of the parties.

4. The way in which the justices' clerk should perform his functions should be stated as follows:
    (a)   The justices are entitled to the advice of their clerk when they retire in order that the clerk may fulfill his responsibility outlined above.
    (b)   Some justices may prefer to take their own notes of evidence. There is, however, no obligation upon them to do so. Whether they do so or not, there is nothing to prevent thm from enlisting the aid of their clerk and his notes if they are in any doubt as to the evidence which has been given.
    (c)   If the justices wish to consult their clerk solely about the evidence or his notes of it, this should ordinarily, and certainly in simply cases, be done in open court. The object is to avoid any suspicion that the clerk has been involved in deciding issues of fact.

5, 6.   (*Domestic Proceedings*)

A failure to comply strictly with the *Practice Direction* which caused no material injustice, just a question of appearances, nevertheless resulted in a conviction being quashed in *R. v. Warley Justices, ex parte S.J. Nash* July 13, 1982; [1982] 8 C.L. 170a (clerk failed to return to court before magistrates on an issue of fact.) But cf. *R. v. Southampton Justices, ex parte Atherton* (1973) 137 J.P. 571, where a different view was taken.

It is normal for the clerk to conduct the ordinary arrangements inside the court and in doing so he does not usurp the judicial function of the bench, *per* Lord Parker C.J. in *R. v. Consett Justices, ex parte Postal Bingo* (1967) 131 J.P. 196 (not improper for a clerk to retire with his justices for substantially the whole two and a half hours of their retirement and to call his shorthand writer in with him) where questions of fact and law were closely interwoven. Lord Parker CJ, added that "there is hardly a decision which fails to be made which is not mixed law and fact."

Since the magistrates and not their clerk are in theory responsible for all decisions, including decisions of law, there is no division corresponding to that between judge and jury in the Crown Court. The magistrates may for example have to read a document themselves before deciding whether it is admissible before them. However, in *R.* v. *Weston-super-Mare Justices, ex parte Townsend* (1968) 132 J.P. 526, Lord Parker, CJ dealing with the problems that arise under the Criminal Evidence Act 1898 said that where an unrepresented defendant attacks prosecution witnesses the prosecutor should ask for an adjournment and in the justices' absence enlist the help of their clerk in warning the defendant of the risk he runs.

The extent to which the clerk in court should assist the parties was considered in *Simms* v. *Moore* (1970) 134 J.P. 573 where Lord Parker CJ laid down the following points:

(1) In general, neither the court nor the justices' clerk should take an active part in the proceedings except to clear up ambiguities in the evidence. (2) So far as examining witnesses is concerned, this should never be done if the party concerned is legally represented: see *Hobby* v. *Hobby* (1954) 118 J.P. 331 where Sachs J said:

'Both parties were represented at the trial by solicitors. Accordingly neither of them was in need of assistance as to how to present the case to the court. Both parties were entitled within the limits of relevancy and reasonableness, so to conduct their cases as seemed best to their legal representatives in court. In those circumstances a justices' clerk is no more entitled to step into the arena and conduct a litigant's case for him than is a justice himself. Indeed, it is important in the interests of justice that the clerk should not give even the appearance of seeking himself to conduct the case of either party or to limit the way in which the case is conducted.'

Nor in my opinion should this be done where a party, although unrepresented, is competent to and desires to examine the witnesses himself. (3) Where however, the unrepresented party, whoever he may be, is not competent through a lack of knowledge of court procedure or rules of evidence or otherwise, to examine the witnesses properly, the court can at its discretion permit the clerk to do so. (4) When this is permitted, there is no reason why the clerk should not do so by reference to a proof of evidence or statement handed in to him, provided always that an opportunity is given to the other side to see it or to have a copy. (5) Where notes of evidence have to be or are taken, care should be taken not to use the proof or statement as the basis of the notes: see *Hobby* v. *Hobby*, already referred to. The best course is for it to be arranged that someone else, possibly a member of the court itself, should take the note. (6) Generally, the discretion in the court should be so exercised that examination of witnesses by the clerk should only be permitted when there are reasonable grounds for thinking that thereby the interests of justice would be best promoted, care being taken to see that nothing is done which conflicts with the rules of natural justice or the principle that justice must manifestly be seen to be done.

Notes of Evidence.

Although the clerk of the court will often keep such a note of evidence as will enable him to discharge his duties and will sometimes keep a full note it is submitted that he is under no obligation to take notes in criminal cases: see the articles at 142 J.P.N. 512, 552.

THE CRIMINAL JUSTICE ACT, 1925

Prohibition on taking photographs, etc., in court

41. (1) No person shall—
  (a) take or attempt to take in any court any photograph, or with a view to publication make or attempt to make in any court any portrait or sketch, of any person, being a judge of the court or a juror or a witness in or a party to any proceedings before the court, whether civil or criminal; or
  (b) publish any photograph, portrait or sketch taken or made in contravention of the foregoing provisions of this section or any reproduction thereof;
and if any person acts in contravention of this section he shall, on summary conviction, be liable in respect of each offence to a fine not exceeding level 3 on the standard scale.
  (2) For the purposes of this section—
  (a) the expression "court" means any court of justice, including the court of a coroner:
  (b) the expression "judge" includes registrar, magistrate, justice and coroner;
  (c) a photograph, portrait or sketch shall be deemed to be a photograph, portrait or sketch taken or made in court if it is taken or made in the court-room or in the building or in the precincts of the building in which the court is held, or if it is a photograph, portrait or sketch taken or made of the person while he is entering or leaving the court-room or any such building or precincts as aforesaid.
(as amended by the Courts Act 1971, sch. 11. the Criminal Justice Act 1982, ss. 38, 46)

COMMENTARY

Subsection (2): Precincts. The first meaning given in the *Shorter Oxford Dictionary* is "the space enclosed by the walls or other boundaries of a particular place or building, or by an imaginary line drawn about it, *esp*. the ground immediately surrounding a religious house or place of worship."

THE SOLICITORS ACT 1974

Solicitor who is justice of the peace not to act in certain proceedings

38. (1) Subject to the provisions of this section, it shall not be lawful for any solicitor who is one of the justices of the peace for any area, or for any partner of his, to act in connexion with proceedings before any of those justices as solicitor or agent for the solicitor for any person concerned in those proceedings.

  (2) Where the area for which a solicitor is a justice of the peace is divided into petty sessional divisions, his being a justice for the area shall not subject him or any partner of his to any disqualification under this section in relation to proceedings before justices acting for a petty sessional division for which he does not ordinarily act.

  (3) Where a solicitor is a justice of the peace for any area, that shall not subject him or any partner of his to any disqualification under this section if his name is entered in the supplemental list kept under s. 80 of the Justices of the Peace Act 1979.

  (4) Where a solicitor is, as being Lord Mayor or alderman, a justice of the peace for the City of London, that shall not subject him or any partner of his to any disqualification under this section, if he is in accordance with the proviso to s. 39(1) of the Justices of the Peace Act 1979 excluded from the exercise of his functions as a justice for the City.
(as amended by the Justices of the Peace Act 1979, sch. 2).

COMMENTARY

As a matter of conduct the Law Society consider that the prohibition from acting imposed by this section upon a solicitor who becomes a J.P. and his partner should apply to any assistant solicitor employed by the firm in question. See the August 1982 issue of *The Magistrate* at p. 122.

THE JUSTICES OF THE PEACE ACT 1979

General form of commissions of the peace

5. (1) The commission of the peace for any commission area shall be a commission under the Great Seal addressed generally, and not by name, to all such persons as may from time to time hold office as justices of the peace for the commission area.

(2) . . .

COMMENTARY

The present commission of the peace reads as follows:

ELIZABETH THE SECOND by the Grace of God of the United Kingdom of Great Britain and Northern Ireland and of Our other Realms and Territories Queen Head of the Commonwealth Defender of the Faith To all such persons as may from time to time hold office as justices of the peace for Our County of . . . .

GREETING Know ye that you are and each of you is by these Presents assigned to keep Our peace in Our said county and to keep and cause to be kept in all points in Our said County the rules of law and enactments from time to time obtaining for the good of Our peace and for the preservation of the same and for the quiet rule and government of Our people And to deal according to law with all persons that offend against any of those rules of law or enactments And also to cause to come before you and to deal according to law with all persons against whom anything is alleged giving just cause under any rule of law or enactment for the time being in force why they should find security to keep the peace or be of good behaviour towards Us and Our people And to exercise all such other jurisdiction and powers as by any rule of Law or enactment may from time to time belong to justices of the peace And therefore We command you and each of you that you diligently apply yourselves in Our said county to the keeping of Our peace and of the rules of law and enactments aforesaid and to the other matters hereinbefore mentioned doing therein what to justice appertains according to law

In Witness whereof We have caused these Our Letters to be made Patent
WITNESS Ourself at Westminster the   day of   in the year of Our Reign.

The Crown Office (Commissions of the Peace) Order 1973, S.I. 1973 No. 2099.

Residence qualification

7. (1) Subject to the provisions of this section, a person shall not be appointed as a justice of the peace for a commission area in accordance with s. 6 of this Act, nor act as a justice of the peace by virtue of any such appointment, unless he resides in or within 15 miles of that area.

(2) If the Lord Chancellor is of the opinion that it is in the public interest for a person to act as a justice of the peace for a particular area though not qualified to do so under subs. (1) above, he may direct that, so long as any conditions specified in the direction are satisfied, that subsection shall not apply in relation to that person's appointment as a justice of the peace for the area so specified.

(3) Where a person appointed as a justice of the peace for a commission area in accordance with s. 6 of this Act is not qualified under the preceding provisions of this section to act by virtue of the appointment, he shall be removed from office as a justice of the peace in accordance with s. 6 of this Act if the Lord Chancellor is of opinion that the appointment ought not to continue having regard to the probable duration and other circumstances of the want of qualification.

(4) No act or appointment shall be invalidated by reason only of the disqualification or want of qualification under this section of the person acting or appointed.

COMMENTARY

Subsection (1): Commission area. Defined in s. 1 of the Act (not printed).

15 miles. Measured in a straight line on a horizontal plane: Interpretation Act 1978, s. 8.

Subsection (2): Lord Chancellor. In the counties of Greater Manchester, Merseyside and Lancashire this refers to the Chancellor of the Duchy of Lancaster: s. 68(1) of the Act.

Place of sitting and powers of stipendiary magistrates

16. (1) Subject to subs. (5) below, nothing in the Magistrates' Courts Act 1980 requiring a magistrates' court to be composed of two or more justices, or to sit in a petty sessional court-house, or limiting the powers of a magistrates' court composed of a single justice, or when sitting elsewhere than in a petty sessional court-house, shall apply to any stipendiary magistrate sitting in a place appointed for that purpose.

(2) A stipendiary magistrate appointed under s. 13 of this Act in any commission area shall sit at such court houses in the area, on such days and at such times as may be determined by, or in accordance with, directions given by the Lord Chancellor from time to time.

(3) Subject to subs. (5) below, a stipendiary magistrate so appointed, sitting at a place appointed for the purpose, shall have power to do any act, and to exercise alone any jurisdiction, which can be done or exercised by two justices under any law, other than any law made after August 2, 1858 which contains an express provision to the contrary; and all the provisions of any Act which are auxilliary to the jurisdiction exercisable by two justices of the peace shall apply also to the jurisdiction of such a stipendiary magistrate.

(4) Subsection (3) above shall apply to cases where the act or jurisdiction in question is expressly required to be done or exercised by justices sitting or acting in petty sessions as it applies to other cases; and any enactment authorizing or requiring persons to be summoned or to appear at petty sessions shall in the like cases authorize or require persons to be summoned or to appear before such a stipendiary magistrate at the place appointed for his sitting.

(5) (*Domestic proceedings*)

(*as amended by the Magistrates' Courts Act 1980, sch. 7*)

COMMENTARY

See under Stipendiary Magistrate in the introduction.

Chairman and deputy chairman of justices

17. (1) In any petty sessions area there shall be a chairman and one or more deputy chairmen of the justices chosen from amongst themselves by the magistrates for the area by secret ballot.

(2) Subject to subs. (3) below, if the chairman or a deputy chairman of the justices for a petty sessions area is present at a meeting of those justices, he shall preside unless he requests another justice to preside in accordance with rules made under the next following section.

(3) Subsection (2) above shall not confer on the chairman and deputy chairman of the justices as such any right to preside in a juvenile or domestic court or at meetings of a committee or other body of justices havings its own chairman, or at

meetings when any stipendiary magistrate is engaged as such in administering justice.

COMMENTARY

Subsection (2): Meeting. That is. any sitting of the court.

Before exercising the power to ask another to preside the chairman must satisfy himself of the justice's suitability: Justices of the Peace (Size and Chairmanship of Bench) Rules 1964.

General powers and duties of justices' clerks

28. (1) (*Rules*).

(2) Any enactment (including any enactment contained in this Act) or any rule of law regulating the exercise of any jurisdiction or powers of justices of the peace, or relating to things done in the exercise or purported exercise of any such jurisdiction or powers, shall apply in relation to the exercise or purported exercise thereof by virtue of subs. (1) above by the clerk to any justices as if he were one of those justices.

(3) It is hereby declared that the functions of a justices' clerk include the giving to the justices to whom he is clerk or any of them, at the request of the justices or justice, of advice about law, practice or procedure on questions arising in connexion with the discharge of their or his functions, including questions arising when the clerk is not personally attending on the justices or justice, and that, the clerk may, at any time when he thinks he should do so, bring to the attention of the justices or justice any point of law, practice or procedure that is or may be involved in any question so arising.

In this subsection the reference to the functions of justices or a justice is a reference to any of their or his functions as justices or a justice of the peace, other than functions as a judge of the Crown Court.

(4) The enactment of subs. (3) above shall not be taken as defining or in any respect limiting the powers and duties belonging to a justices' clerk or the matters on which justices may obtain assistance from their clerk.

(*as amended by the Magistrates' Courts Act 1980, sch. 7.*)

COMMENTARY

Subsection (3); Justices' clerk. Means a clerk to the justices for a petty sessions area: s. 70 of the Act.

Questions of law, including questions of mixed law and fact. Compare the *Practice Direction* [1982] 2 All E.R. 831 and *R.* v. *Consett Justices, ex parte Postal Bingo* (1967) 131 J.P. 196.

Person acting as substitute clerk to justices.

30. (1) The provisions of this section shall have effect where, in any petty sessions area outside the inner London area, a person who is not the justices' clerk or one of the justices' clerks appointed in that petty sessions area by the magistrates' courts committee acts as clerk to the justices for that petty sessions area.

(2) Subject to any rules made under s. 144 of the Magistrates' Courts Act 1980 and to subs. (3) below, the person so acting shall be treated as having acted as deputy to the justices' clerk appointed by the magistrates' courts committee in that petty sessions area, and shall make a return to the justices' clerk so appointed of all matters done before the justices and of all matters that the clerk to the justices is required to register or record.

(3) In relation to a petty sessions area in which there are two or more justices' clerks appointed by the magistrates' courts committee, any reference in subs. (2) above to the justices' clerk so appointed shall be construed as a reference to such one of them as may be designated for the purpose by the committee.
(*as amended by the Magistrates' Courts Act 1980, sch. 7*).

COMMENTARY

Subsection (1): Petty sessions area. Defined in s. 4 of the Act.

Justices' clerk. Means a clerk to the justices for a petty sessions area: s. 70 of the Act.

Disqualification in certain cases of justices who are members of local authorities.

64. (1) A justice of the peace who is a member of a local authority within the meaning of the Local Government Act 1972 or the Local Government (Scotland) Act 1973 shall not act as a member of the Crown Court or of a magistrates' court in any proceedings brought by or against, or by way of appeal from a decision of, the authority or any committee or officer of the authority.

(2) For the purposes of subs. (1) above—

(a) any reference to a committee of a local authority includes a joint committee, joint board, joint authority or other combined body of which that authority is a member or on which it is represented; and

(b) any reference to an officer of a local authority refers to a person employed or appointed by the authority, or by a committee of the authority, in the capacity in which he is employed or appointed to act.

(3) A justice of the peace who is a member of the Common Council of the City of London shall not act as a member of the Crown Court or of a magistrates' court in any proceedings brought by or against, or by way of appeal from a decision of, the Corporation of the City or the Common Council or any committee or officer of the Corporation or Common Council; and subs. (2) above shall apply for the purposes of this subsection, with the substitution, for references to a local authority, of references to the Corporation or the Common Council.

(4) Nothing in this section shall prevent a justice from acting in any proceedings by reason only of their being brought by a police officer.

(5) No act shall be invalidated by reason only of the disqualification under this section of the person acting.

COMMENTARY

Subsection (1): Local authority. To be construed as a reference to a local authority as defined in the Local Government Act 1972, s. 270(1): sch. 29, *ibid*. Although a person co-opted to a committee of a local authority may not be a member of that authority the same principle would seemingly apply.

Magistrates' court. Defined in the Interpretation Act 1978, s. 5, sch. 1.

Acts done by justices outside their commission area.

66. (1) A justice of the peace for any commission area may act as a justice for that area in any commission area which adjoins the commission area for which he is a justice.

(2) Justices for the county of Surrey or the county of Kent may hold special or petty sessions for any division of their county at any place in Greater London; and for all purposes relating to sessions so held the place at which they are held shall be deemed to be within the county and the division for which the justices holding them are justices.

COMMENTARY

Subsection (1): Commission area. Defined in s. 1 of the Act (not printed).

THE MAGISTRATES' COURTS ACT 1980

Orders other than for payment of money

63. (1) Where under any Act passed after 31st December 1879 a magistrates' court has power to require the doing of anything other than the payment of money, or to prohibit the doing of anything, any order of the court for the purpose of exercising that power may contain such provisions for the manner in which anything is to be done, for the time within which anything is to be done, or during which anything is not to be done, and generally for giving effect to the order, as the court thinks fit.

(2) The court may by order made on complaint suspend or rescind any such order as aforesaid.

(3) Where any person disobeys an order of a magistrates' court made under an Act passed after 31st December 1879 to do anything other than the payment of money or to abstain from doing anything the court may—

(a) order him to pay a sum not exceeding £50 for every day during which he is in default or a sum not exceeding £2,000, or

(b) commit him to custody until he has remedied his default or for a period not exceeding two months;

but a person who is ordered to pay a sum for every day during which he is in default or who is committed to custody until he has remedied his default shall not by virtue of this section be ordered to pay more than £1,000 or be committed for more than two months in all for doing or abstaining from doing the same thing contrary to the order (without prejudice to the operation of this section in relation to any subsequent default).

(4) Any sum ordered to be paid under subs. (3) above shall for the purposes of this Act be treated as adjudged to be paid by a conviction of a magistrates' court.

(5) The preceding provisions of this section shall not apply to any order for the enforcement of which provision is made by any other enactment.

(as amended by S.I. 1984 No. 447)

COMMENTARY

The power under this section may be exercised either of the court's own motion or lay order on complaint: Contempt of Court Act 1981, s. 17(1).

There is no power to make consecutive commitments to prison under this section: *Head* v. *Head* [1982] 3 All E.R. 14.

Instead of being committed to prison a person under 21 but not less than 17 may be detained under s. 9 of the Criminal Justice Act 1982.

Constitution and place of sitting of court.

121. (1) A magistrates' court shall not try an information summarily or hear a complaint except when composed of at least two justices unless the trial or hearing is one that by virtue of any enactment may take place before a single justice.

(2) A magistrates' court shall not hold an inquiry into the means of an offender for the purposes of s. 82 above except when composed of at least two justices.

(3) A magistrates' court shall not—

(a) try summarily an information for an indictable offence or hear a complaint except when sitting in a petty-sessional court-house;

(b) try an information for a summary offence or hold an inquiry into the means of an offender for the purposes of s. 82 above, or impose imprisonment, except when sitting in a petty-sessional court-house or an occasional court-house.

(4) Subject to the provisions of any enactment to the contrary, where a magistrates' court is required by this section to sit in a petty-sessional or occasional court-house, it shall sit in open court.

(5) A magistrates' court composed of a single justice, or sitting in an occasional court-house, shall not impose imprisonment for a period exceeding 14 days or order a person to pay more than £1.

(6) Subject to the provisions of subs. (7) below, the justices composing the court before which any proceedings take place shall be present during the whole of the proceedings; but, if during the course of the proceedings any justice absents himself, he shall cease to act further therein and, if the remaining justices are enough to satisfy the requirements of the preceding provisions of this section, the proceedings may continue before a court composed of those justices.

(7) Where a trial of an information is adjourned after the accused has been convicted and before he is sentenced or otherwise dealt with, the court which sentences or deals with him need not be composed of the same justices as that which convicted him; but, where among the justices composing the court which sentences or deals with an offender there are any who were not sitting when he was convicted, the court which sentences or deals with the offender shall before doing so make such inquiry into the facts and circumstances of the case as will enable the justices who were not sitting when the offender was convicted to be fully acquainted with those facts and circumstances.

(8) ...

COMMENTARY

Subsection (1): At least two justices. "The number of justices sitting to deal with a case as a magistrates' court shall not be greater than seven: Justices of the Peace (Size and Chairmanship of Bench) Rules 1964, r. 2(2), *infra*. It is the Lord Chancellor's opinion that only in special circumstances should more than five justices constitute a court: circular letter of November 30, 1950. There should preferably be an odd number of justices, *per* Lord Goddard, C.J., in *Barnsley* v. *Marsh* (1947) 111 J.P. 363. Today, the normally accepted number is three.

By virtue of any enactment. For example, the Vagrancy Act, 1982, ss. 3 and 4 and the Licensing Act, 1872, s. 12. For a full list *see* 29 *Halsbury's Law* 4th edn. at para. 244. But note the restrictions of subs. (5).

Subsection (3): Indictable/summary offence. Defined in the Interpretation Act 1978, sch. 1.

Petty sessional court-house. Defined in the Justices of the Peace Act 1979, s. 70. Licensed premises may not be used as a petty sessional court-house: Licensing Act 1964, s. 190.

Occasional court-house. Appointed under s. 147, *infra*.

Subsection (4): Any provision to the contrary. *See*, for example, the Official Secrets Act, 1920, s. 8(4); the Magistrates' Courts Act 1980, s. 4(2) (examining justices); the Children & Young Persons Act, 1933, s. 37 (evidence of juveniles in certain cases) and s. 47(2), *ibid.*, not reproduced herein (juvenile courts).

Open court. See under this title in the introduction.

Subsection (6): Present during the whole of the proceedings. Thus if even one justice joins the others the hearing must be begun afresh. A conviction has been quashed where a justice who had not heard the case joined the bench and appeared to (though did not actually) participate in the adjudication: *R.* v. *Walton, ex parte Dutton* (1911) 75 J.P. 558. And *see* subs. (7).

Fees

137.   (1) Subject to the provisions of this section, the court fees set out in Part I of sch. 6 to this Act, and no others, shall be chargeable by clerks of magistrates' courts; and any enactment providing for the payment of any fees for the payment of which provision is made in the said Part I shall have effect accordingly.

(2) No fee shall be chargeable by a clerk of a magistrates' court in respect of any matter specified in Part II of the said Schedule.

(3) - (6) . . .

Clerks to justices.

141. (1) Any reference in this Act to a clerk of any magistrates' court shall be construed as a reference to the clerk to the justices for the petty sessions area for which the court is acting, or was acting at the relevant time.

(2) Where there is more than one clerk to the justices for any petty sessions area, anything that this Act requires or authorizes to be done by or to the clerk to the justices shall or may be done by or to any of the clerks or by or to such of the clerks as the magistrates' courts committee having power over the apointment of clerks to justices for that area generally or in any particular case may direct.

(3) Subsections (1) and (2) above shall apply to the justices' clerks for the inner London area as if the reference in subs. (2) to the magistrates' courts committee were a reference to the committee of magistrates.

COMMENTARY

Subsection (1): Petty sessions area. Defined in s. 150(1) of the Act, (not printed herein).

Occasional court-house

147. (1) The justices acting for a petty sessions area may appoint as an occasional court-house any place that is not a petty-sessional court-house.

(2) A place appointed as an occasional court-house after May 31, 1953 shall not be used as such unless public notice has been given that it has been appointed.

(3) There may be more than one occasional court-house for each petty sessions area; and an occasional court-house may be outside the petty sessions area for which it is appointed, and if so shall be deemed to be in that area for the purpose of the jurisdiction of the justices acting for that area.

COMMENTARY

Subsection (1): Occasional court-house. For the powers of justices sitting in occasional court-houses *see* s. 121, *supra*.

Petty sessional court house. *See* the note to s. 121 *supra*.

Subsection (2): Public notice. No method of giving notice is prescribed. *Chislett* suggests a notice by the clerk in newspapers circulating in the district.

"Magistrates' court".

148. (1) In this Act the expression "magistrates' court" means any justice or justices of the peace acting under any enactment or by virtue of his or their commission or under the common law.

(2) Except where the contrary is expressed, anything authorized or required by this Act to be done by, to or before the magistrates' court by, to or before which any other thing was done, or is to be done, may be done by, to or before any magistrates' court acting for the same petty sessions area as that court.

COMMENTARY

Subsection (1): Magistrates' court. As to where and in what numbers justices sit to form a magistrates' court *see* s. 121, *supra*. This term includes examining justices: *Atkinson* v. *United States Government* (1971) 135 J.P. 617.

Interpretation of other terms.

150. (1)...

(2) Except where the contrary is expressed or implied, anything required or authorized by this Act to be done by justices may, where two or more justices are present, be done by one of them on behalf of the others.

(3) – (7)...

Magistrates' court may sit on Sundays and public holidays.

153. It is hereby declared that a magistrates' court may sit on any day of the year, and in particular (if the court thinks fit) on Christmas Day, Good Friday or any Sunday.

COMMENTARY

This declaratory provision is in permissive and not mandatory terms.

SCHEDULE 6

(Section 137)

FEES

PART II

MATTERS IN RESPECT OF WHICH NO FEES ARE CHARGEABLE

1. . . .

2. Any criminal matter, but this paragraph shall not prevent the charging of a fee for supplying, for use in connexion with a matter which is not a criminal matter, a copy of a document prepared for use in connexion with a criminal matter.

THE CONTEMPT OF COURT ACT 1981

Contemporary reports of proceedings.

4. (1)...

(2) In any such proceedings the court may, where it appears to be necessary for avoiding a substantial risk of prejudice to the administration of justice in those proceedings, or in any other proceedings pending or imminent, order that the publication of any report of the proceedings, or any part of the proceedings, be postponed for such a period as the court thinks necessary for that purpose.

(3), (4)...

COMMENTARY

Despite the existence of a separate (but different) power to restrict the reporting of committal proceedings this section may also be used for that purpose: *R.* v. *Horsham Justices, ex parte Farquharson and Another* [1982] 2 All E.R. 269.

Any such proceedings. That is, legal proceedings held in public.

The court. Includes any tribunal or body exercising the judicial power of the State and "legal proceedings" must be construed accordingly: s. 19 of the Act.

Substantial risk of prejudice. The only relevant risk to be considered is the risk to the proceedings being heard at the relevant time which, in the case of committal proceedings, is the committal proceedings. The proceedings at the Crown Court may be considered as "proceedings pending or imminent": *R. v. Horsham Justices, ex parte Farquharson and Another, supra.*

Order. Disobedience to such an order is punishable either on complaint or on the court's own motion under the Magistrates' Courts Act 1980, s. 63(3).

Under s. 4(2) of the Contempt of Court Act 1981, a court may, where it appears necessary for avoiding a substantial risk of prejudice to the administration of justice in the proceedings before it or in any other pending or imminent, order that publication of any report of the proceedings or part thereof be postponed for such period as the court thinks necessary for that purpose. Section 11 of the Act provides that a court may prohibit the publication of any name or other matter in connexion with the proceedings before it which (having power to do so) it has allowed to be withheld from the public.

It is necessary to keep a permanent record of such orders for later reference. For this purpose all orders made under s. 4(2) must be formulated in precise terms, having regard to the decision of *Reg. v. Horsham Justices, ex parte Farquharson* [1982] 2 All E.R. 269, and orders under both sections must be committed to writing either by the judge personally or by the clerk of the court under the judge's directions. An order must state (a) its precise scope, (b) the time at which it shall cease to have effect, if appropriate, and (c) the specific purpose of making the order. Courts will normally give notice to the press in some form that an order has been made under either section of the Act and court staff should be prepared to answer any inquiry about a specific case, but it is, and will remain, the responsibility of those reporting cases, and their editors, to ensure that no breach of any order occurs and the onus rests with them to make inquiry in any case of doubt. *Practice Direction* [1982] 1 W.L.R. 1475.

Publication. This term is defined in s. 2(1) of the Act as including any speech, writing, broadcast or other communication in whatever form, which is addressed to the public at large or any section of the public: *ibid*, s. 19.

Use of tape recorders.

9. (1) Subject to the subs. (4) below, it is a contempt of court—

(a) to use in court, or bring into court for use, any tape recorder or other instrument for recording sound, except with the leave of the court;
(b) to publish a recording of legal proceedings made by means of any such instrument, or any recording derived directly or indirectly from it, by playing it in the hearing of the public or any section of the public, or to dispose of it or any recording so derived, with a view to such publication;
(c) to use any such recording in contravention of any conditions of leave granted under para. (a).

(2) Leave under para. (a) of subs. (1) may be granted or refused at the discretion of the court, and if granted may be granted subject to such conditions as the court thinks proper with respect to the use of any recording made pursuant to the leave; and where leave has been granted the court may at the like discretion withdraw or amend it either generally or in relation to any particular part of the proceedings.

(3) Without prejudice to any other power to deal with an act of contempt under para. (1) of subs. (1), the court may order the instrument, or any recording made with it, or both, to be forfeited; and any object so forfeited shall (unless the court otherwise determines on application by a person appearing to be the owner) be sold or otherwise disposed of in such manner as the court may direct.

(4) This section does not apply to the making or use of sound recordings for purposes of official transcripts of proceedings.

COMMENTARY

The following *Practice Direction* [1981] 3 All E.R. 848 has been issued in the Supreme Court but its principles would seem to be of equal application in the magistrates' courts:

1. Section 9 of the Contempt of Court Act 1981 contains provisions governing the unofficial use of tape recorders in court. Among other things it provides that it is a contempt of court to use in court, or bring into court for use, any tape recorder or other instrument for recording sound, except with the leave of the court; and it is also a contempt of court to publish a recording of legal proceedings or to use any such recording in contravention of any conditions which the court may have attached to the grant of permission to use the machine in court. These provisions do not apply to the making or use of sound recordings for purposes of official transcripts of proceedings, on which the Act imposes no restriction whatever.

2. The discretion to the court to grant, withhold or withdraw leave to use tape recorders or to impose conditions as to the use of the recording is unlimited, but the following factors may be relevant to its exercise: (a) the existence of any reasonable need on the part of the applicant for leave, whether a litigant or a person connected with the press or broadcasting, for the recording to be made; (b) in a criminal case, or a civil case in which a direction has been given excluding one or more witnesses from the court, the risk that the recording could be used for the purpose of briefing witnesses out of court; (c) any possibility that the use of a recorder would disturb the proceedings or distract or worry any witnesses or other participants.

3. Consideration should always be given whether conditions as to the use of a recording made pursuant to leave should be imposed. The identity and role of the applicant for leave and the nature of the subject matter of the proceedings may be relevant to this.

4. The particular restriction imposed by s. 9(1)(*b*) of the 1981 Act applies in every case, but may not be present to the mind of every applicant to whom leave is given. It may, therefore, be desirable on occasion for this provision to be drawn to the attention of those to whom leave is given.

5. The transcript of a permitted recording is intended for the use of the person given leave to make it and is not intended to be used as, or to compete with, the official transcript mentioned in s. 9(4) of the 1981 Act.

Sources of information

10. No court may require a person to disclose, nor is any person guilty of contempt of court for refusing to disclose, the source of information contained in a publication for which he is responsible, unless it be established to the satisfaction of the court that disclosure is necessary in the interests of justice or national security or for the prevention of disorder or crime.

Publication of matters exempted from disclosure in court

11. In any case where a court (having power to do so) allows a name or other matter to be withheld from the public in proceedings before the court, the court may give such directions prohibiting the publication of that name or matter in connexion with the proceedings as appear to the court to be necessary for the purpose for which it was so withheld.

COMMENTARY

See the *Practice Direction* [1982] 1 W.L.R. 1475 noted under s. 4, *supra*. Breach of directions is a contempt of court which may be punished by the High Court or by the magistrates' court under the Magistrates' Court Act 1980, s. 63(3) and in accordance with the Contempt of Court Act 1981, s. 17.

Offences of contempt of magistrates' courts.

12. (1) A magistrates' court has jurisdiction under this section to deal with any person who—

(a) wilfully insults the justice or justices, any witness before or officer of the court or any solicitor or counsel having business in the court, during his or their sitting or attendance in court or in going to or returning from the court; or

(b) wilfully interrupts the proceedings of the court or otherwise misbehaves in court.

(2) In any such case the court may order any officer of the court, or any constable, to take the offender into custody and detain him until the rising of the court; and the court may, if it thinks fit, commit the offender to custody for a specified period not exceeding one month or impose on him a fine not exceeding £1,000, or both.

(3) (Repealed)

(4) A magistrates' court may at any time revoke an order of committal made under subs. (2) and, if the offender is in custody, order his discharge.

(5) The following provisions of the Magistrates' Courts Act 1980 apply in relation to an order under this section as they apply in relation to a sentence on conviction or finding of guilty of an offence, namely: s. 36 (restriction on fines in respect of young persons); ss. 75 to 91 (enforcement); s. 108 (appeal to Crown Court); s. 136 (overnight detention in default of payment); and s. 142(1) (power to rectify mistakes).

(as amended by the Criminal Justice Act 1982, sch. 16, S.I. 1984 No. 447)

COMMENTARY

Legal aid is available where anyone is liable to be fined under this section: Legal Aid Act 1974, s. 28(11A).

Subsection (1). It has been held under the corresponding County Court legislation that abuse of a judge in a newspaper did not take place "in court": R. v. Lefray (1873) 37 J.P. 566.

Wilfully. Despite conflicting decisions in other fields it is submitted that this term imports mens rea of all the elements of the offence.

Officer of the court. It is submitted that this includes the clerk to the justices and his staff and any probation officer attached to the court.

Court. It is submitted that this is confined to the court room and its adjacent offices rather than the whole building in which the court room is situated.

Misbehaves. It is submitted that this is not confined to interruptions. Note that misbehaviour (unlike an interruption) must take place in court.

Subsection (2). In Balogh v. Crown Court at St. Albans [1972] 3 All E.R. 283 Lord Denning M.R. said that the power to commit summarily for contempt should be exercised by the judge of his own motion "only when it is urgent and imperative to act immediately - so as to maintain the authority of the court - to prevent disorder - to enable witnesses to be free from fear . . . and the like".

No procedure is laid down for the punishment of contempt in a magistrates' court. It is suggested that where the contempt was in the face of the court and is not denied the magistrates may proceed to punishment immediately although they will often be wise first to exercise their power to confine the offender to afford time for reflection on their part and apology on his. Where the identity or acts of the contemner are denied the issue must be tried under the usual criminal procedure. Upon a finding of guilt it is desirable for the court to announce the facts it finds and the process of reasoning by which they were arrived at: cf. R. v. Goult [1983] 76 Cr. App. R. 140.

Commit the offender to custody. The restrictions on the use of prison sentences (Powers of Criminal Courts Act 1973, ss. 20, 20A and 21) do not apply, nor may the sentence be suspended in whole or in part. Young offenders may be committed to be detained under s. 9 of the Criminal Justices Act 1982 (s. 9, *ibid*). For the place of detention *see* s. 12(10), *ibid* Note ss. 1(5), 2(1), (5), (7).

It would seem that the order and warrant of commitment should specify the particular matter of contempt: cf. *McIlraith* v. *Grady* [1967] 3 All E.R. 625.

A specified period. Presumably a magistrates' court shares the power of the superior courts to release a contemnor before the end of the period: cf. *Enfield London Borough Council* v. *Mahoney* [1983] 1 W.L.R. 749

Proceedings in England and Wales

14. (1), (2) . . .

(2A) In the exercise of jurisdiction to commit for contempt of court or any kindred offence the court shall not deal with the offender by making an order under s. 17 of the Criminal Justice Act 1982 (an attendance centre order) if it appears to the court after considering any available evidence, that he is under 17 years of age.

(3) (*Repealed*).

(4), (5) . . .

(as amended by the Criminal Justice Act 1982, sch. 14, 16).

Disobedience to certain orders of magistrates' courts.

17. (1) The powers of a magistrates' court under subs. (3) of s. 63 of the Magistrates' Courts Act 1980 (punishment by fine or committal for disobeying an order to do anything other than the payment of money or to abstain from doing anything) may be exercised either of the court's own motion or by order on complaint.

(2) In relation to the exercise of those powers the provisions of the Magistrates' Court Act 1980 shall apply subject to the modifications set out in sch. 3 to this Act.

COMMENTARY

The courts' own motion. If the court acts of its own motion natural justice demands that the person to be punished is first given notice of the court's intention and the opportunity to make representations to the court.

SCHEDULE 3

(Section 17)

APPLICATION OF MAGISTRATES' COURTS ACT 1980 TO CIVIL CONTEMPT PROCEEDINGS UNDER SECTION 63(3)

1. (1) Where the proceedings are taken of the court's own motion the provisions of the Act listed in this sub-paragraph shall apply as if a complaint had been made against the person against whom the proceedings are taken, and subject to the modifications specified in sub-paras. (2) and (3) below. The enactments so applied are:—

      s. 51 (issue of summons)
      s. 53(1) and (2) (procedure on hearing)
      s. 54 (adjournment)
      s. 55 (non-appearance of defendant)
      s. 97(1) (summons to witness)
      s. 101 (onus of proving exceptions etc.)
      s. 121(1) and (3)(a) (constitution and place of sitting of court)
      s. 123 (defect in process).

(3) In s. 123, in subs. (1) and (2) the words "adduced on behalf of the prosecutor or complainant" shall be omitted.

2. Where the proceedings are taken by way of complaint for an order, s. 127 of the Act (limitation of time) shall not apply to the complaint.

(2) In. s. 55, in subsection (1) for the words "the complainant appears but the defendant does not" there shall be substituted the words "the defendant does not appear", and in subs. (2) the words "if the complaint has been substantiated on oath, and" shall be omitted.

(3) . . .

THE JUSTICES OF THE PEACE (SIZE AND CHAIRMANSHIP OF BENCH) RULES 1964

S.I. 1964 No. 1107, as amended by S.I. 1969 No. 1272

2. (1)...

(2) *The number of justices sitting to deal with a case as a magistrates' court shall not be greater than seven.*

4. (1) *In this rule:—*

the expression "justice" means any justice who ordinarily acts in and for the petty sessions area, other than any person whose name has been entered in the Supplemental List; and the expression "clerk to the justices" includes any person acting as such.

(2) - (13) . . .

(14) *In the absence of a chairman or deputy chairman elected under these rules nothing in this rule shall prevent the appointment by justices present (in any manner which has been customary) of one of their number to preside at a court sitting to deal with any case.*

(15) *Before a chairman or deputy chairman of the justices for a petty sessions area who is present at a meeting of those justices requests another justice to preside under the provisions of s. 17(2) of the Justices of the Peace Act 1979, he shall satisfy himself as to the suitability of that justice for this purpose.*

COMMENTARY

Rule 2(2). See the note "At least two justices" to the Magistrates' Courts Act 1980, s. 121, *supra.*

THE JUSTICES' CLERKS RULES 1970

S.I. 1970 No. 231, as amended by S.I. 1971 No. 809, S.I. 1975 No. 30, S.I. 1976. No. 1767, S.I. 1978 No. 754, S.I. 1983 No. 527

3. *The things specified in the schedule to these rules, being things authorized to be done by, to or before a single justice of the peace for a petty sessions area, may be done by, to or before the justices' clerk for that area.*

SCHEDULE

1. *The laying of an information or the making of a complaint, other than an information or complaint substantiated on oath.*

2. *The issue of any summons, including a witness summons.*

3. ...

4. (1) *The further adjournment of criminal proceedings with the consent of the prosecutor and the accused if, but only if,*

(a) *the accused, not having been remanded on the previous adjournment, is not remanded on the further adjournment; or*
(b) *the accused, having been remanded on bail on the previous adjournment is remanded on bail on the like terms and conditions.*

(2) *The remand of the accused on bail at the time of further adjourning the proceedings in pursuance of subpara. (1) (b) above.*

5. ...

6. *The allowing of further time for payment of a sum enforceable by a magistrates' court.*

6A. *The varying of the number of instalments payable, the amount of any instalment payable and the date on which any instalment becomes payable where a magistrates' court has ordered that a sum adjudged to be paid by a conviction shall be paid by instalments.*

7. *The making of a transfer of fine order, that is to say, an order making payment by a person of a sum adjudged to be paid by a conviction enforceable in the petty sessions area in which he is residing.*

8. *The making of an order before an inquiry into the means of a person under s. [84 of the Magistrates' Courts Act 1980] that that person shall furnish to the court a statement of his means in accordance with s. [84(1)].*

9. (Repealed)

10. *The giving of consent for another magistrates' court to deal with an offender for an earlier offence in respect of which, after the offender had attained the age of 17 years, the court had made a probation order or an order for conditional discharge, where the justices' clerk is the clerk of the court which made the order or, in the case of a probation order, of that court or of the supervising court.*

11. *The amending, in accordance with para. 2(1) of sch. 1 to the Powers of Criminal Courts Act 1973, of a probation order made after the probationer had attained the age of 17 years by substituting for the petty sessions area named in the order the area in which the probationer proposes to reside or is residing.*

12. *The signing of a certificate given to the Crown Court under s. 16(4) of the Powers of Criminal Courts Act 1973 as to non-compliance with a community service order.*

13., 14., 15. ...

16. *The acceptance under subs. [(3) of s. 14 of the Magistrates' Courts Act 1980] (which relates to process for minor offences) of service of such statutory declaration as is mentioned in [subs. (1)] of that section.*

17. *The fixing under s. [86(3) of the Magistrates' Courts Act 1980] of a later day in substitution for a day previously fixed for the appearance of an offender to enable an inquiry into his means to be made under [s. 82] of that Act or to enable a hearing required by [subs. (5) of s. 82] to be held.*

COMMENTARY

See the Justices of the Peace Act 1979, s. 28(2).

THE MAGISTRATES' COURTS RULES 1981
S.I. 1981 No. 552, as amended by S.I. 1983 No. 523.

Register of convictions, etc.

66. (1) *The clerk of every magistrates' court shall keep a register in which there shall be entered—*

(a) *a minute or memorandum of every adjudication of the court;*
(b) *a minute or memorandum of every other proceeding or thing required by these rules or any other enactment to be so entered.*

(2) *The register shall be in the prescribed form, and entries in the register shall include, where relevant, such particulars as are provided for in the said form.*

(3) *Particulars of any entry relating to a decision about bail or the reasons for any such decision or the particulars of any certificate granted under s. 5(6A) of the Bail Act 1976 may be made in a book separate from that in which the entry recording the decision itself is made, but any such separate book shall be regarded as forming part of the register.*

(3A) *Where, by virtue of subs. (3A) of s. 128 of the Act of 1980, an accused gives his consent to the hearing and determination in his absence of any application for his remand on an adjournment of the case under ss. 5, 10(1) or 18(4) of that Act, the court shall cause the consent of the accused, and the date on which it was notified to the court, to be entered in the register.*

(3B) *Where any consent mentioned in para. (3A) is withdrawn, the court shall cause the withdrawal of the consent and the date on which it was notified to the court to be entered in the register.*

(4) *On the summary trial of an information the accused's plea shall be entered in the register.*

(5) *Where a court tries any person summarily in any case in which he may be tried summarily only with his consent, the court shall cause his consent to be entered in the register and, if the consent is signified by a person representing him in his absence, the court shall cause that fact also to be entered in the register.*

(6) *Where a person is charged before a magistrates' court with an offence triable either way the court shall cause the entry in the register to show whether he was present when the proceedings for determining the mode of trial were conducted and, if they were conducted in his absence, whether they were so conducted by virtue of s. 18(3) of the Act of 1980 (disorderly conduct on his part) or by virtue of s. 23(1) of that Act (consent signified by person representing him).*

(7) *In any case to which s. 22 of the Act of 1980 (certain offences triable either way to be tried summarily if value involved is small) applied, the court shall cause its decision as to the value involved or, as the case may be, the fact that it is unable to reach such a decision to be entered in the register.*

(8) *Where a court has power under s. 53(3) of the Act of 1980 to make an order with the consent of the defendant without hearing evidence, the court shall cause any consent of the defendant to the making of the order to be entered in the register.*

(9) *The entry in the column of the register headed "Nature of Offence" shall show clearly, in case of conviction or dismissal, what is the offence of which the accused is convicted or, as the case may be, what is the offence charged in the information that is dismissed.*

(10) *An entry of conviction in the register shall state the date of the offence.*

(11) *The entries shall be signed by one of the justices, or the justice, before whom the proceedings to which they relate took place, or by the clerk who was present when those proceedings took place or, in the case of an entry required by paras. (3A) and (3B), where the consent or withdrawal of consent was not given or made (as the case may be) when the accused was present before the court, by the clerk or justice who received the notification:*

Provided that, where the proceedings took place before a justice or justices sitting elsewhere than in a petty sessional court-house, the justice or, as the case may be, one of the justices may instead of signing an entry in the register, send to the clerk whose duty it is to keep the register a signed return of the proceedings containing the particulars required to be entered in the register; and the clerk shall enter the return in the register.

(12) *Every register shall be open to inspection during reasonable hours by any justice of the peace, or any person authorized in that behalf by a justice of the peace or the Secretary of State.*

COMMENTARY

Para. 1: Clerk of . . . magistrates' court. *See* s. 141 of the principal Act.

Para. 12. A request to justices' clerks to afford the police access to the register for statistical purposes was made by the Secretary of State. *See* Home Office circular dated February 9, 1893 reproduced in *The Justices' Clerk,* September 1980.

Proof of proceedings.

68.   *The register of a magistrates' court, or any document purporting to be an extract from the register and to be certified by the clerk as a true extract, shall be admissible in any legal proceedings as evidence of the proceedings of the court entered in the register.*

COMMENTARY

Extract. *See* form 154.

Signature of forms prescribed by rules made under the Act of 1980.

109.   (1) *Subject to para. (2), where any form prescribed by Rules made or having effect as if made under s. 144 of the Act of 1980 contains provision for signature by a justice of the peace only, the form shall have effect as if it contained provision in the alternative for signature by the clerk of a magistrates' court.*

(2) *This rule shall not apply to any form of warrant, other than a warrant of commitment or of distress, or to any form prescribed in the Magistrates' Court (Forms) Rules 1981.*

COMMENTARY

In addition to the provisions of this rule the clerk of a magistrates' court may sign any document in the Schedule to the Magistrates' Courts (Forms) Rules 1981 which admits of his signature.

The clerk of a magistrates' court. That is, the clerk to the justices: Magistrates' Courts Act 1980, s. 141(1).

CHAPTER 15

LIST OF COMMON OFFENCES
INCLUDING MAXIMUM PENALTIES AND MODE
OF TRIAL
arranged in alphabetical order of statute

Section	Offence	Mode of trial	Maximum punishment

THE BAIL ACT 1976

6.(7)	Absconding by person released on bail.	If committed for sentence or dealt with as for a contempt. Summarily.	12 months or a fine or both. 3 months or a fine not exceeding level 5 on the standard scale; or both

THE BRITISH TELECOMMUNICATIONS ACT 1981

48	Fraudulent use of a public telecommunications system	(a) on indictment	a fine or imprisonment not exceeding two years or both
		(b) summarily	6 months imprisonment or a fine not exceeding the statutory maximum (£2,000); or both

The standard scale of fines is as follows:—

Level on the scale	Amount of fine
1	£50
2	£100
3	£400
4	£1,000
5	£2,000

Criminal Justice Act, 1982, s. 37

Section	Offence	Mode of trial	Maximum punishment
	THE BRITISH TRANSPORT COMMISSION ACT 1949		
55.	Trespass on the railway.	Summarily.	a fine not exceeding level 3 on the standard scale
	THE CRIMINAL ATTEMPTS ACT 1981		
9.	Interference with vehicles.	Summarily	a fine not exceeding level 4 on the standard scale or both.
	THE CRIMINAL DAMAGE ACT 1971		
1.(1)	Destroying or damaging property.	On indictment. Summarily*.	10 years. 6 months or £2000 or both.
1.(2)	Destroying or damaging property with intent to endanger life etc.	On indictment.	Life (s.4(3)).
1.(3)	Destroying or damaging property by fire (arson).	On indictment. Summarily*.	Life (s.4(1)). 6 months or £2000 or both.
2.	Threats to destroy or damage property.	On indictment. Summarily.	10 years. 6 months or £2000 or both.

*Triable only on indictment if defendant is also charged before the court with an offence under s. 17(1) or 17(2) of the Firearms Act 1968: para. 2 of Part II of sch. 6. *ibid.*

3. Possessing anything with intent to destroy or damage.

On indictment. 10 years.

Summarily. 6 months or £2000 or both.

THE CRIMINAL JUSTICE ACT 1925

39.(1) Common assault.

Summarily. 2 months or a fine not exceeding level 3 on the standard scale (Power to bind over in addition: s. 39(3)).

THE FAMILY INCOME SUPPLEMENTS ACT 1970

11. False statements.

Summarily. 3 months or a fine not exceeding level 5 on the standard scale; or both.

The standard scale of fines is as follows:—

Level on the scale	Amount of fine
1	£50
2	£100
3	£400
4	£1,000
5	£2,000

Criminal Justice Act, 1982, s. 37

THE FIREARMS ACT 1968

SCHEDULE 6
PROSECUTION AND PUNISHMENT OF OFFENCES

(as amended by the Criminal Justice Act 1972, s. 28, sch. 6, Criminal Law Act 1977, s. 28(2))

PART I
TABLE OF PUNISHMENTS

Section	General nature of offence	Mode of prosecution	Punishment	Additional provisions
1.(1)	Possessing etc. firearm or ammunition without firearm certificate.	(a) Summary	6 months or a fine or £2000 or both.	
		(b) On indictment	(i) where the offence is committed in an aggravated form within the meaning of s.4(4) of this Act, 5 years, or a fine; or both. (ii) in any other case, 3 years or a fine; or both.	(Scotland.)
1.(2)	Non-compliance with condition of firearm certificate.	Summary	6 months or a fine not exceeding level 5 on the standard scale; or both.	(Scotland.)
2.(1)	Possessing etc. shot gun without shot gun certificate.	Summary	6 months or a fine not exceeding level 5 on the standard scale; or both.	(Scotland.)
2.(2)	Non-compliance with condition of shot gun certificate.	Summary	6 months or a fine not exceeding level 5 on the standard scale; or both.	(Scotland.)

Section	General nature of offence	Mode of prosecution	Punishment	Additional provisions
3.(1)	Trading in firearms without being registered as firearms dealer.	(a) Summary	6 months or a fine of £2,000; or both.	
		(b) On indictment	3 years or a fine; or both.	
3.(2)	Repairing, testing etc., firearm for person without a certificate.	(a) Summary	6 months or a fine of £2000; or both.	
		(b) On indictment	3 years or a fine; or both.	
3.(6)	Pawnbroker taking firearm in pawn.	Summary	3 months or a fine not exceeding level 3 on the standard scale; or both.	
4.(1) (3)	Shortening a shot gun; conversion of firearms.	(a) Summary	6 months or a fine of £2000; or both.	
		(b) On indictment	5 years or a fine; or both.	

The standard scale of fines is as follows:—

Level on the scale	Amount of fine
1	£50
2	£100
3	£400
4	£1,000
5	£2,000

Criminal Justice Act, 1982, s. 37

Section	General nature of offence	Mode of prosecution	Punishment	Additional provisions
5.(1)	Possessing or distributing prohibited weapons or ammunition.	(a) Summary	6 months or a fine of £2000, or both.	
		(b) On indictment	5 years or a fine; or both	
5.(5)	Non-compliance with condition of Defence Council authority.	Summary	6 months or a fine not exceeding level 5 on the standard scale; or both.	
5.(6)	Non-compliance with requirement to surrender authority to possess, etc., prohibited weapon or ammunition.	Summary	A fine not exceeding level 3 on the standard scale.	
6.(3)	Contravention of order under s.6 (or corresponding Northern Irish order) restricting removal of arms.	Summary	¾ months or, for each firearm or parcel of ammunition in respect of which the offence is committed, a fine not exceeding level 3 on the standard scale; or both.	Para. 2 of Part II of this schedule applies.
7.(2)	Making false statement in order to obtain police permit.	Summary	6 months or a fine not exceeding level 5 on the standard scale; or both.	
9.(3)	Making false statement in order to obtain permit for auction of firearms etc.	(a) Summary	6 months or fine of £2000; or both	
		(b) On indictment	3 years or a fine; or both.	

13.(2)	Making false statement in order to obtain permit for removal of signalling apparatus.	Summary	6 months or a fine not exceeding level 5 on the standard scale; or both.
16.	Possession of firearm with intent to endanger life or injure property.	On indictment	Life imprisonment or a fine; or both.
17.(1)	Use of firearms to resist arrest.	On indictment	Life imprisonment or a fine; or both.	Paras. 3 to 5 of Part II of this schedule apply.
17.(2)	Possessing firearm while committing an offence specified in sch. 1 or, in Scotland, an offence specified in sch. 2.	On indictment	14 years or a fine; or both.	Paras. 3 and 6 of Part II of this schedule apply.
18.(1)	Carrying firearm or imitation firearm with intent to commit indictable offence (or, in Scotland, an offence specified in sch. 2) or to resist arrest.	On indictment	14 years or a fine; or both
19.	Carrying loaded firearm in public place	(a) Summary	6 months or a fine of £2000; or both.
		(b) On indictment (but not if the firearm is an air weapon).	5 years or a fine; or both.

The standard scale of fines is as follows:—

Level on the scale	Amount of fine
1	£50
2	£100
3	£400
4	£1,000
5	£2,000

Criminal Justice Act, 1982, s. 37

Section	General nature of offence	Mode of prosecution	Punishment	Additional provisions
20.(1)	Trespassing with firearm in a building	(a) Summary	6 months or a fine of £2000; or both.	
		(b) On indictment (but not if the firearm is an air weapon).	5 years or a fine; or both.	
20.(2)	Trespassing with firearm on land.	Summary	3 months or a fine not exceeding level 4 on the standard scale; or both.	
21.(4)	Contravention of provisions denying firearms to exprisoners and the like.	(a) Summary	6 months or a fine of £2000; or both.	
		(b) On indictment	3 years or a fine, or both.	
21.(5)	Supplying firearms to person denied them under s. 21.	(a) Summary	6 months or a fine of £2000; or both	
		(b) On indictment	3 years or a fine; or both.	
22.(1)	Person under 18 acquiring firearm.	Summary	6 months or a fine not exceeding level 5 on the standard scale; or both.	
22.(2)	Person under 14 having firearm in his possession without lawful authority.	Summary	6 months or a fine not exceeding level 5 on the standard scale; or both.	
22.(3)	Person under 15 having with him a shot gun without adult supervision.	Summary	A fine not exceeding level 3 on the standard scale.	Para. 8 of Part II of this schedule applies.

22.(4)	Person under 14 having with him an air weapon or ammunition therefor.	Summary	A fine not exceeding level 3 on the standard scale.	Paras. 7 and 8 of Part II of this schedule apply.
22.(5)	Person under 17 having with him an air weapon in a public place.	Summary	A fine not exceeding level 3 on the standard scale.	Paras. 7 and 8 of Part II of this schedule apply.
23.(1)	Person under 14 making improper use of air weapon when under supervision; person supervising him permitting such use.	Summary	A fine not exceeding level 3 on the standard scale.	Paras. 7 and 8 of Part II of this schedule apply.
24.(1)	Selling or letting on hire a firearm to person under 17.	Summary	6 months or a fine not exceeding level 5 on the standard scale; or both.	Paras. 7 and 8 of Part II of this schedule apply.
24.(2)	Supplying firearm or ammunition (being of a kind to which s. 1 of this Act applies) to person under 14.	Summary	6 months or a fine not exceeding level 5 on the standard scale; or both.	

The standard scale of fines is as follows:—

Level on the scale	Amount of fine
1	£50
2	£100
3	£400
4	£1,000
5	£2,000

Criminal Justice Act, 1982, s. 37

Section	Offence	Mode of trial	Maximum punishment
24.(3)	Making gift of shot gun to person under 15.	Summary	A fine not exceeding level 3 on the standard scale. Para. 9 of Part II of this schedule applies.
24.(4)	Supplying air weapon to person under 14.	Summary	A fine not exceeding level 3 on the standard scale. Paras. 7 and 8 of Part II of this schedule apply.
25.	Supplying firearm to person drunk or insane.	Summary	3 months or a fine not exceeding level 3 on the standard scale; or both.
26.(5)	Making false statement in order to procure grant or renewal of a firearm or shot gun certificate.	Summary	6 months or a fine not exceeding level 5 on the standard scale; or both.
29.(3)	Making false statement in order to procure variation of a firearm certificate.	Summary	6 months or a fine not exceeding level 5 on the standard scale; or both.
30.(4)	Failing to surrender certificate on revocation.	Summary	A fine not exceeding level 3 on the standard scale.
38.(8)	Failure to surrender a certificate of registration on removal of firearms dealer's name from register.	Summary	A fine not exceeding level 3 on the standard scale.

39.(1) Making false statement in order to secure registration or entry in register of a place of business.

Summary — 6 months or a fine not exceeding level 5 on the standard scale; or both.

39.(2) Registered firearms dealer having place of business not entered in the register.

Summary — 6 months or a fine not exceeding level 5 on the standard scale; or both.

39.(3) Non-compliance with condition of registration.

Summary — 6 months or a fine not exceeding level 5 on the standard scale; or both.

40.(5) Non-compliance by firearms dealer with provisions as to register of transactions; making false entry in register.

Summary — 6 months or a fine not exceeding level 5 on the standard scale; or both.

42. Failure to comply with instructions in firearm certificate when transferring firearm to person other than registered dealer; failure to report transaction to police.

(a) Summary — 6 months or a fine of £2000; or both.

(b) On indictment — 3 years or a fine; or both.

The standard scale of fines is as follows:—

Level on the scale	Amount of fine
1	£50
2	£100
3	£400
4	£1,000
5	£2,000

Criminal Justice Act, 1982, s. 37

Section	Offence	Mode of trial	Maximum punishment
47.(2)	Failure to hand over firearm or amm- unition on demand by constable.	Summary	3 months or a fine not exceeding level 4 on the standard scale; or both.
48.(3)	Failure to comply with requirement of a constable that a person shall declare his name and address.	Summary	A fine not exceeding level 3 on the standard scale.
49.(3)	Failure to give constable facilities for examination of firearms in transit, or to produce papers.	Summary	3 months or, for each fire- arm or parcel of ammunition in respect of which the offence is committed, a fine not exceeding level 3 on the standard scale; or both. Para. 2 of Part II of this schedule applies.
52.(2)	Failure to surrender firearm or shot gun certificate cancelled by court on conviction.	Summary	A fine not exceeding level 3 on the standard scale.

PART II

SUPPLEMENTARY PROVISIONS AS TO TRIAL
AND PUNISHMENT OF OFFENCES
(as amended by the Criminal Law Act 1977, sch. 12,
the Magistrates' Courts Act 1980, sch. 7.)

1. (*Scotland.*)

2. In the case of an offence against ss. 6(3) or 49(3) of this Act, the court before which the offender is convicted may, if the offender is the owner of the firearms or ammunition, make such order as to the forfeiture of the firearms or ammunition as the court thinks fit.

3. (1) Where in England or Wales a person who has attained the age of 17 is charged before a magistrates' court with an offence triable either way listed in sch. 1 to the Magistrates' Courts Act 1980 ('the listed offence') and is also charged before that court with an offence under s.17(1) or (2) of this Act, the following provisions of this paragraph shall apply.

(2) Subject to the following sub-paragraph the court shall proceed as if the listed offence were triable only on indictment and s.18 to 23 of the said Act of 1980 (procedure for determining mode of trial of offences triable either way) shall not apply in relation to that offence.

(3) If the court determines not to commit the accused for trial in respect of the offence under s.17(1) or (2), or if proceedings before the court for that offence are otherwise discontinued, the preceding sub-paragraph shall cease to apply as from the time when this occurs and—

(*a*) If at that time the court has not yet begun to inquire into the listed offence as examining justices, the court shall, in the case of the listed offence, proceed in the ordinary way in accordance with the said s.18 to 23; but

(*b*) if at that time the court has begun so to inquire into the listed offence, those sections shall continue not to apply and the court shall proceed with its inquiry into that offence as examining justices, but shall have power in accordance with s.25(3) and (4) of the said Act of 1980 to change to summary trial with the accused's consent.

4. Where a person commits an offence under s.17(1) of this Act in respect of the lawful arrest or detention of himself for any other offence committed by him, he shall be liable to the penalty provided by Part I of this schedule in addition to any penalty to which he may be sentenced for the other offence.

5. If on the trial of a person for an offence under s.17(1) of this Act the jury are not satisfied that he is guilty of that offence but are satisfied that he is guilty of an offence under s.17(2), the jury may find him guilty of the offence under s.17(2) and he shall then be punishable accordingly.

6. The punishment to which a person is liable for an offence under s.17(2) of this Act shall be in addition to any punishment to which he may be liable for the offence first referred to in s.17(2).

7. The court by which a person is convicted of an offence under s.22(4) or (5), 23(1) or 24(4) of this Act may make such order as it thinks fit as to the forfeiture or disposal of the air weapon or ammunition in respect of which the offence was committed.

8. The court by which a person is convicted of an offence under s.22(3), (4) or (5), 23(1) or 24(4) may make such order as it thinks fit as to the forfeiture or disposal of any firearm or ammunition found in his possession.

9. The court by which a person is convicted of an offence under s.24(3) of this Act may make such order as it thinks fit as to the forfeiture or disposal of the shot gun or ammmunition in respect of which the offence was committed.

COMMENTARY

Paragraph 3. Sch. 1, as amended by the Criminal Damage Act 1971, lists the following offences to which this paragraph and s.17(2) of the Act (use of firearm to resist arrest) apply:

1. Offences under s.1 of the Criminal Damage Act 1971.
2. Offences under any of the following provisions of the Offences against the Person Act 1861:—

ss.20 to 22 (inflicting bodily injury; garrotting; criminal use of stupefying drugs);

s.30 (laying explosive to building etc.);s.32 (endangering railway passengers by tampering with track);

s.38 (assault with intent to commit felony or resist arrest);

s.47 (criminal assaults);

s.56 (child-stealing and abduction).

3. Offences under such of the provisions of s.4 of the Vagrancy Act 1824, as are referred to in and amended by s.15 of the Prevention of Crimes Act 1871, and s.7 of the Penal Servitude Act 1891 (suspected persons and reputed thieves being abroad with criminal intent).
4. Theft, burglary, blackmail and any offence under s.12(1) (taking of motor vehicle or other conveyance without owner's consent) of the Theft Act 1968.
5. Offences under s. 51(1) of the Police Act 1964, or s. 41 of the Police (Scotland) Act 1967 (assaulting constable in execution of his duty).
6. Offences under any of the following provisions of the Sexual Offences Act, 1956:—

s.1 (rape);

ss.17, 18 and 20 (abduction of women).

7. (*Repealed*)
8. Aiding or abetting the commission of any offence specified in paras. 1 to 6 of this schedule.
9. Attempting to commit any offence so specified.

THE FORGERY AND COUNTERFEITING ACT 1981

Section	Offence	Mode of trial	Maximum punishment
1.	Forgery		10 years (s. 6)
2.	Copying a false instrument		
3.	Using a false instrument		
4.	Using a copy of a false instrument.		
5.(1)	Having custody or control of a false instrument with intent	On indictment Summarily	A fine not exceeding the statutory maximum (£2000) or 3 months imprisonment or both. (s. 6)
5.(2)	Having custody or control of a false instrument without lawful authority or excuse	On indictment	Two years. (s. 6)
5.(3)	Offences related to machines etc. adapted etc. for making a false instrument	On indictment Summarily	Six months or a fine not exceeding the statutory maximum (£2000) or both. (s. 6).
5.(4)	Making or controlling such machine etc.	On indictment	Two years
14.(1)	Making counterfeit notes or coins with intent to pass as genuine	On indictment Summarily	10 years or a fine or both.(s. 22). Six months or a fine not exceeding the statutory maximum (£2000) or both. (s. 22).

Section	Offence	Mode of trial	Maximum punishment
14.(2)	Making counterfeit notes or coin without lawful authority or excuse	On indictment	2 years or a fine or both.
		Summarily	Six months or a fine not exceeding the statutory maximum (£2000) or both.
15.(1)	Passing or delivering as genuine counterfeits	On indictment	10 years or a fine
		Summarily	Six months or a fine not exceeding the statutory maximum (£2000) or both.
15.(2)	Delivering counterfeits without lawful authority or excuse	On indictment	Two years or a fine or both.
16.(1)	Having custody or control of counterfeit with intent	On indictment	10 years or a fine
		Summarily	Six months or a fine not exceeding the statutory maximum. (£2000) or both.
16.(2)	Having custody or control of counterfeit without lawful authority or excuse	On indictment	Two years or a fine or both.
		Summarily	Six months or a fine not exceeding the statutory maximum (£2000) or both.

17.(1)	Making etc. things for purpose of counterfeiting	On indictment	10 years or a fine or both
		Summarily	Six months or a fine not exceeding the statutory maximum (£2000)) or both.
17.(2)	Making etc. any thing specially designed or adapted for counterfeiting	On indictment	Two years or a fine or both.
		Summarily	Six months or a fine not exceeding the statutory maximum (£2000)) or both.
17.(3)	Making etc. any implement capable of making a resemblance	On indictment	Two years or a fine or both.
		Summarily	Six months or a fine not exceeding the statutory maximum (£2000)) or both.
18.	Reproducing British currency notes	On indictment	A fine.
		Summarily	A fine not exceeding the statutory maximum (£2000).
19.	Making etc. imitation British coins	On indictment	A fine.
		Summarily	A fine not exceeding the statutory maximum (£2000).

The standard scale of fines is as follows:—

Level on the scale	Amount of fine
1	£50
2	£100
3	£400
4	£1,000
5	£2,000

Criminal Justice Act, 1982, s. 37

Section	Offence	Mode of trial	Maximum punishment
		THE HIGHWAYS ACT 1835	
72.	Riding or driving on footpath.	Summarily.	A fine not exceeding level 2 on the standard scale.
		THE HIGHWAYS ACT 1980	
137.	Wilful obstruction.	Summarily.	A fine not exceeding level 1 on the standard scale.
155.	Straying animals.	Summarily.	A fine not exceeding level 3 on the standard scale.
148.(1)	Depositing things on highway.	Summarily.	A fine not exceeding level 3 on the standard scale.
161.(2)	Discharging firearms or firework	Summarily	A fine not exceeding level 3 on the standard scale
		THE INDECENCY WITH CHILDREN ACT 1960	
1.	Indecent conduct towards children.	On indictment. Summarily.	2 years 6 months or £2000 or both.

15 LIST OF COMMON OFFENCES

THE LICENSING ACT 1872

| 12. | Found drunk. | Summarily. | A fine not exceeding level 1 on the standard scale |

THE LICENSING ACT 1964

168.	Children in bars.	Summarily.	A fine not exceeding level 2 on the standard scale
169.(1)	Serving liquor to minors.	Summarily.	A fine not exceeding level 2 on the standard scale* ‡
169.(2)	Minors, etc., buying liquor.	Summarily.	A fine not exceeding level 3 on the standard scale (s. 169(9)).
169.(3)	Buying liquor for minors.	Summarily.	A fine not exceeding level 3 on the standard scale* ‡
169.(5)	Delivering liquor to minors for consumption off the premises.	Summarily.	A fine not exceeding level 2 on the standard scale* ‡

The standard scale of fines is as follows:—

Level on the scale	Amount of fine
1	£50
2	£100
3	£400
4	£1,000
5	£2,000

Criminal Justice Act, 1982, s. 37

Section	Offence	Mode of trial	Maximum punishment
170.	Employing minor in bar.	Summarily.	A fine not exceeding level 1 on the standard scale (s. 169(9)) ‡
172.	Permitting drunkenness in licensed premises.	Summarily.	A fine not exceeding level 2 on the standard scale (s. 172(4)). ‡

*s. 169(8), applies which gives power to forfeit a licence on a person's second or subsequent conviction if the offence was committed by him as the holder of a justices' licence.

† Any conviction which took place more than five years previously must be disregarded: s.194(2), *ibid*. ‡

THE LITTER ACT 1983

1.	Leaving litter.	Summarily.	A fine not exceeding level 3 on the standard scale.

THE NATIONAL ASSISTANCE ACT 1948

52.	False statements.	Summarily.	3 months or a fine not exceeding level 3 on the standard scale; or both.

THE OFFENCES AGAINST THE PERSON ACT 1861

16.	Threats to kill.	On indictment. Summarily.	10 years 6 months or £2000 or both.

18.	Wounding with intent to do grievous bodily harm.	On indictment.	Life.
20.	Inflicting bodily injury with or without a weapon.	On indictment. Summarily.*	5 years. 6 months or £2000 or both.
27.	Exposing child.	On indictment. Summarily.	5 years. 6 months or £2000 or both.
38.	Assault with intent to resist apprehension.	On indictment. Summarily.*	2 years. 6 months or £2000 or both.
47.	Assault occasioning actual bodily harm.	On indictment. Summarily.	5 years. 6 months or £2000 or both.
47.	Common assault.	On indictment. Summarily ‡	1 year. 6 months or £2000 or both.
57.	Bigamy.	On indictment. Summarily.	2 years. 6 months or £2000 or both.
60.	Concealing the birth of a child.	On indictment. Summarily.	2 years. 6 months or £2000 or both.

‡ For the summary offence see the Criminal Justice Act 1925, s.39

* Triable only on indictment if the defendant is also charged before the court with an offence under ss.17(1) or 17(2) of the Firearms Act 1968: para. 3 of Part II of sch. 6, *ibid*.

The standard scale of fines is as follows:—

Level on the scale	Amount of fine
1	£50
2	£100
3	£400
4	£1,000
5	£2,000

Criminal Justice Act, 1982. s. 37

Offence	Mode of Trial	Maximum Punishment

THE POLICE ACT 1964

Offence	Mode of Trial	Maximum Punishment
51.(1) Assault on constable.	Summarily.*	6 months or a fine not exceeding level 5 on the standard scale; or both.
51.(3) Resisting or obstructing a constable.	Summarily.	1 month or a fine not exceeding level 3 on the standard scale; or both.

*Triable only on indictment if the defendant is charged before the court with an offence under the Firearms Act 1968, s. 17(1) or 17(2): para.3 of Part II of sch. 6, *ibid*.

THE PREVENTION OF CRIME ACT 1953

Offence	Mode of Trial	Maximum Punishment
1. Carrying offensive weapons.	On indictment. Summarily.	2 years or a fine or both. 3 months or £2000 or both. Power to order forfeiture or disposal of any weapon in respect of which the offence was committed (s.1(2)).

THE PUBLIC ORDER ACT 1936

Offence	Mode of Trial	Maximum Punishment
5. Offensive conduct.	Summarily.	6 months or £2000 or both.

THE PUBLIC PASSENGER VEHICLES ACT 1981

24. Breach of regulations concerning drivers, inspectors and conductors — Summarily — A fine not exceeding level 3 on the standard scale.

25. Breach of regulations concerning passengers — Summarily — A fine not exceeding level 3 on the standard scale.

THE REGULATION OF RAILWAYS ACT 1889

5.(3) Avoiding payment of fare with intent. — Summarily. — A fine not exceeding level 2 on the standard scale.

THE ROAD TRAFFIC ACT 1972

See Ch. 9.

The standard scale of fines is as follows:—

Level on the scale	Amount of fine
1	£50
2	£100
3	£400
4	£1,000
5	£2,000

Criminal Justice Act, 1982. s. 37

THE ROAD TRAFFIC REGULATION ACT 1967

Offence		Mode of Trial	Maximum Punishment
1.(8)	Contravention of traffic regulation order.	Summarily.	A fine not exceeding level 3 on the standard scale.
14(2)	Breach of order—one way traffic on trunk roads.	Summarily.	A fine not exceeding level 3 on the standard scale.
16.(5)	Breach of order—restriction of vehicle on certain classes of roads.	Summarily.	A fine not exceeding level 3 on the standard scale.
23.(5)	Breach of pedestrian crossing regulations.	Summarily.	A fine not exceeding level 3 on the standard scale.
25.(2)	Failing to stop for school crossing patrol.	Summarily.	A fine not exceeding level 3 on the standard scale.
26.(6)	School playgrounds.	Summarily.	A fine not exceeding level 3 on the standard scale.
31.(3)	Contravention of order	Summarily.	A fine not exceeding level 2 on the standard scale.

Interfering with ap-
paratus etc.

Summarily.

A fine not exceeding
level 3 on the standard
scale.

71.(1) Speeding.

Summarily.

A fine not exceeding
level 3 on the standard
scale (s. 78A).

* For the duty to endorse and the power to disqualify *see* the Road Traffic Act 1972, sch.4, Pt.3, *infra*.

THE SEXUAL OFFENCES ACT 1956
SCHEDULE 2

(The fifth column of this schedule (alternative verdicts) has been omitted.)

TABLE OF OFFENCES, MODE OF PROSECUTION, PUNISHMENTS, ETC.

PART I

(a) Rape s.1
(b) An attempt to commit this offence.

On indictment.
On indictment.

Life.
7 years.

(a) Intercourse with girl under 13 (s.5).
(b) An attempt to commit this offence.

On indictment.
On indictment.

Life.
7 years.

The standard scale of fines is as follows:—

Level on the scale	Amount of fine
1	£50
2	£100
3	£400
4	£1,000
5	£2,000

Criminal Justice Act, 1982, s. 37

Offence	Mode of Trial	Maximum Punishment
(a) Buggery (s.12).	On indictment.	If with a boy under the age of 16 or with a woman or an animal, life; otherwise the relevant punishment prescribed by s.3 of the Sexual Offences Act 1967. If with a boy under the age of 16 or with a woman or an animal, 10 years.
(b) An attempt to commit this offence.	On indictment.	
Abduction of woman by force or for the sake of her property (s.17).	On indictment.	14 years.
Permitting girl under 13 to use premises for intercourse (s.25).	On indictment.	Life.
(a) Procurement of woman by threats (s.2).	On indictment.	2 years.
(b) An attempt to commit this offence.	On indictment.	2 years.
Procurement of woman by false pretences (s.3).	On indictment.	2 years.
Administering drugs to facilitate intercourse (s.4).	On indictment.	2 years.
(a) Intercourse with girl under 16 (s.6).	(i) On indictment: a prosecution may not be commenced more	2 years.

(b) An attempt to commit this offence.

than 12 months after the offence charged.

(ii) Summarily.
[As above.]

6 months and/or £2000.
[As above.]

(a) Intercourse with defective (s. 7).

On indictment.

2 years.

(b) An attempt to commit this offence.

On indictment.

2 years.

(a) Procurement of defective (s. 9).

On indictment.

2 years.

(b) An attempt to commit this offence.

On indictment.

2 years.

If with a girl under 13 who is stated to have been so in the indictment, 7 years; otherwise 2 years.

On indictment; a prosecution may not be commenced except by or with the consent of the Director of Public Prosecutions.

If with a girl under 13, and so charged in the indictment, life; otherwise 7 years.

(a) Incest by a man (s. 10).

On indictment; a prosecution may not be commenced except by or with the consent of the Director of Public Prosecutions.

The standard scale of fines is as follows:—

Level on the scale	Amount of fine
1	£50
2	£100
3	£400
4	£1,000
5	£2,000

Criminal Justice Act, 1982, s. 37

Offence	Mode of Trial	Maximum Punishment
(a) Incest by a woman (s.11).	On indictment; a prosecution may not be commenced except by or with the consent of the Director of Public Prosecutions.	7 years.
(b) An attempt to commit this offence.	On indictment; a prosecution may not be commenced except by or with the consent of the Director of Public Prosecutions.	2 years.
(a) Indecency between men (s.13).	(i) On indictment.	If by a man of or over the age of 21 with a man under that age, 5 years; otherwise 2 years.
	(ii) Summarily.	6 months and/or £2000.
(b) An attempt to procure the commission by a man of an act of gross indecency with another man.	(i) On indictment.	If the attempt is by a man of or over the age of 21 to procure a man under that age to commit an act of gross indecency with another man, 5 years; otherwise 2 years.
	(ii) Summarily	6 months and/or £2000.

Indecent assault on a woman (s.14).

   (i) On indictment.

     If on a girl under 13 who is stated to have been so in the indictment, 5 years; otherwise 2 years.

   (ii) Summarily (by virtue of s17(1) of the Magistrates' Courts Act 1980).

     As provided by s.32(1) of that Act, that is to say, 6 months or the prescribed sum within the meaning of that section. (£2000) or both.

Indecent assault on a man (s.15).

   (i) On indictment.

     10 years.

   (ii) Summarily (by virtue of s17(1) of the Magistrates' Courts Act 1980).

     As provided by s.32(1) of that Act, that is to say, 6 months or the prescribed sum within the meaning of that section (£2000) or both.

Assault with intent to commit buggery (s.16).

   On indictment.

     10 years.

The standard scale of fines is as follows:—

Level on the scale	Amount of fine
1	£50
2	£100
3	£400
4	£1,000
5	£2,000

Criminal Justice Act, 1982, s. 37

Offence	Mode of Trial	Maximum Punishment
Abduction of girl under 18 from parent or guardian (s.19).	On indictment.	2 years.
Abduction of girl under 16 from parent or guardian (s.21).	On indictment.	2 years.
Abduction of defective from parent or guardian (s.20).	On indictment.	2 years.
(a) Causing prostitution of a woman (s.22).	On indictment.	2 years.
(b) An attempt to commit this offence.	On indictment.	2 years.
Detention of woman in brothel. (s.27).	On indictment.	2 years.
Permitting girl under 16 to use premises for intercourse (s.26).	(i) On indictment. (ii) Summarily.	2 years. 6 months and/or £2000.
Permitting defective to use premises for intercourse (s.27).	On indictment.	2 years.
Causing or encouraging prostitution, etc., of girl under 16 (s.28).	On indictment.	2 years.
Causing or encouraging prostitution of defective (s.29).	On indictment.	2 years.
Living on earnings of prostitution (s.30).	(i) On indictment. (ii) Summarily.	7 years. 6 months and/or £2000.

Controlling a prostitute (s.31).

(i) On indictment.
(ii) Summarily.

7 years.
6 months and/or £2000.

Solicitation by a man (s.22).

(i) On indictment.
(ii) Summarily.

2 years.
6 months and/or £2000.

Keeping a brothel (s.33).

Summarily.

6 months or a fine not exceeding level 4 on the standard scale; otherwise 3 months or a fine not exceeding level 3 on the standard scale; or both.

Letting premises for use as brothel (s.34).

Summarily.

For an offence committed after a previous conviction 6 months or a fine not exceeding level 4 on the standard scale or both; otherwise, 3 months or a fine not exceeding level 3 on the standard scale or both.

The standard scale of fines is as follows:—

Level on the scale	Amount of fine
1	£50
2	£100
3	£400
4	£1,000
5	£2,000

Criminal Justice Act, 1982, s. 37

Section	Offence	Mode of Trial	Maximum Punishment
	Tenant permitting premises to be used as brothel (s.35).	Summarily.	For an offence committed after a previous conviction 6 months or a fine not exceeding level 4 on the standard scale or both; otherwise 3 months or a fine not exceeding level 3 on the standard scale or both.
	Tenant permitting premises to be used for prostitution (s.36).	Summarily.	For an offence committed after a previous conviction 6 months, or a fine not exceeding level 4 on the standard scale or both; otherwise 3 months or a fine not exceeding level 3 on the standard scale or both.

THE SOCIAL SECURITY ACT 1975

Section	Offence	Mode of Trial	Maximum Punishment
146.	Failing to pay contribution.	Summarily.	A fine not exceeding level 3 on the standard scale. Unpaid contributions must be ordered under s. 150: *R. v. Melksham Justices ex parte Williams* (1983) 147 J.P. 283.

THE STREET OFFENCES ACT 1959

| 1.(2) | Loitering or soliciting. | Summarily. | A fine not exceeding level 2 on the standard scale or, for an offence committed after a previous conviction, a fine not exceeding level 3 on the standard scale. |

THE SUPPLEMENTARY BENEFITS ACT 1976

| 21. | False statements. | Summarily. | 3 months or a fine not exceeding level 5 on the standard scale. |
| 25. | Failure to maintain. | Summarily. | 3 months or a fine not exceeding level 4 on the standard scale. |

THE THEFT ACT 1968

| 7. | Theft. | On indictment. | 10 years. |
| | | Summarily.* | 6 months or £2000 or both. |

The standard scale of fines is as follows:—

Level on the scale	Amount of fine
1	£50
2	£100
3	£400
4	£1,000
5	£2,000

Criminal Justice Act, 1982, s. 37

Section	Offence	Mode of trial	Maximum punishment
8.	Robbery or assault with intent to rob.	On indictment.	Life.
9.	Burglary. Burglary except burglary comprising the commission of or an intention to commit an offence which is triable only on indictment and burglary in a dwelling if any person in the dwelling was subjected to violence or the threat of violence: Magistrates' Courts Act 1980, sch.1.	On indictment. Summarily.*	14 years. 6 months or £2000 or both.
10.	Aggravated burglary.	On indictment.	Life.
11.	Removal of articles from place open to the public.	On indictment. Summarily.	10 years. 6 months or £2000 or both.
12.(1)	Taking motor vehicle or other conveyance without authority.	On indictment. Summarily.*	3 years. 6 months or £2000 or both.
12.(5)	Taking, etc., pedal cycle.	Summarily.	A fine not exceeding level 3 on the standard scale.
13.	Abstracting electricity.	On indictment. Summarily.	5 years. 6 months or £2000 or both.
15.	Obtaining property by deception.	On indictment. Summarily.	10 years. 6 months or £2000 or both.

16. Obtaining pecuniary advantage by deception.

On indictment.
Summarily.

5 years.
6 months or £2000 or both.

17. False accounting.

On indictment.
Summarily.

7 years.
6 months or £2000 or both.

19. False statements by company directors etc.

On indictment.
Summarily.

7 years.
6 months or £2000 or both.

20.(1) Suppression of documents.

On indictment.
Summarily.

7 years.
6 months or £2000 or both.

20.(2) Procuring the execution of a valuable security.

On indictment.
Summarily.

7 years.
6 months or £2000 or both.

21. Blackmail.

On indictment.

14 years.

22. Handling stolen goods.

On indictment.
Summarily.

14 years.
6 months or £2000 or both.

23. Advertising reward for goods stolen or lost.

Summarily.

A fine not exceeding level 3 on the standard scale.

25. Going equipped for stealing.

On indictment.
Summarily.

3 years.
6 months or £2000 or both.

The standard scale of fines is as follows:—

Level on the scale	Amount of fine
1	£50
2	£100
3	£400
4	£1,000
5	£2,000

Criminal Justice Act, 1982, s. 37

Section	Offence	Mode of trial	Maximum punishment
sch. 1, para. 2.(1)	Taking or destroying fish.	Summarily.	3 months or a fine not exceeding level 3 on the standard scale or both.
sch. 1, para. 2.(2)	Taking or destroying fish by angling in the daytime.	Summarily.	A fine not exceeding level 1 on the standard scale.

THE THEFT ACT 1978

Section	Offence	Mode of trial	Maximum punishment
1.	Obtaining services by deception.	On indictment. Summarily.	5 years. 6 months or £2000 or both.
2.	Evasion of liability by deception.	On indictment. Summarily.	5 years. 6 months or £2000 or both.
3.	Making off without payment.	On indictment. Summarily.	2 years. 6 months or £2000 or both.

THE TRADE DESCRIPTIONS ACT 1968

Section	Offence	Mode of trial	Maximum punishment
	All offences except s.29(1)	On indictment. Summarily.	2 years or a fine or both. £2000
29.(1)	Obstruction of authorized officers.	Summarily.	A fine not exceeding level 3 on the standard scale.

THE TRANSPORT ACT 1968

96.(11) Breaches of domestic drivers' code.

Summarily.

A fine not exceeding level 4 on the standard scale.

96.(11A) Breach of Community rules

Summarily

A fine not exceeding level 4 on the standard scale.

98.(4) Written records of driving hours— breach of regulations.

Summarily.

A fine not exceeding level 4 on the standard scale.

99.(5) False entries on written records.

On indictment. Summarily.

2 years. £2000.

THE VAGRANCY ACT 1824

3. Idle and disorderly person (various offences).

Summarily.

1 month or a fine not exceeding level 3 on the standard scale (Magistrates' Courts Act 1980, s. 34(3).)

The standard scale of fines is as follows:—

Level on the scale	Amount of fine
1	£50
2	£100
3	£400
4	£1,000
5	£2,000

Criminal Justice Act, 1982, s. 37

Section	Offence	Mode of trial	Maximum punishment
4.	Rogues and vagabonds (various offences).	Summarily.	3 months or a fine not exceeding level 3 on the standard scale (Magistrates' Courts Act 1980, s. 34(3).)
5.	Incorrigible rogues.	On indictment.	1 year.

THE VEHICLES (EXCISE) ACT 1971

Section	Offence	Mode of trial	Maximum punishment
8.	Using and keeping vehicles without a licence.	Summarily.	An excise penalty not exceeding level 3 on the standard scale or of an amount equal to five times the amount of the duty chargeable in respect of the vehicle. The court must order payment of an amount calculated in accordance with s. 8(2)-(4): s. 9(1). There is a corresponding provision governing written pleas of guilty under s. 34.
12.(4)	Failure to exhibit licence.	Summarily.	A fine not exceeding level 1 on the standard scale.

16.(7)	Misuse of trade plates.	Summarily.	An excise penalty of level 3 on the standard scale or of an amount equal to five times the amount of the duty chargeable in respect of the vehicle or vehicles.
18.	Higher rate of duty chargeable.	Summarily.	An excise penalty not exceeding level 3 on the standard scale or of an amount equal to five times the amount of the duty chargeable in respect of the vehicle or vehicles.
22.	Failure to fix and obscuration of marks and signs.	Summarily.	A fine not exceeding level 3 on the standard scale.
26.(1)	Fraudulent alteration or use.	On indictment. Summarily.	2 years. £2000.
26.(2)	False or misleading details.	On indictment. Summarily.	2 years. £2000.

THE WIRELESS TELEGRAPHY ACT 1949

| 1. | Unlicensed use or installation. | Summarily. | A fine not exceeding level 3 on the standard scale (s. 14). |

The standard scale of fines is as follows:—

Level on the scale	Amount of fine
1	£50
2	£100
3	£400
4	£1,000
5	£2,000

Criminal Justice Act, 1982, s. 37

Appendix A

THE JUDGES' RULES*

NOTE

The origin of the Judges' Rules is probably to be found in a letter dated October 26, 1906, which the then Lord Chief Justice, Lord Alverstone, wrote to the Chief Constable of Birmingham in answer to a request for advice in consequence of the fact that on the same circuit one judge had censured a member of his force for having cautioned a prisoner, whilst another judge had censured a constable for having omitted to do so. The first four of the pre-1964 Rules were formulated and approved by the judges of the King's Bench Division in 1912; the remaining five in 1918. They were much criticized *inter alia* for alleged lack of clarity and of efficacy for the protection of persons who were questioned by police officers; on the other hand it was maintained that their application unduly hampered the detection and punishment of crime. A committee of judges devoted considerable time and attention to producing, after consideration of representative views, a new set of rules which was approved by a meeting of all the Queen's Bench Judges and issued in 1964.

The judges control the conduct of trials and the admission of evidence against persons on trial before them; they do not control or in any way initiate or supervize police activities or conduct. As stated in paragraph (*e*) of the introduction to the present rules, it is the law that answers and statements made are only admissible in evidence if they have been voluntary in the sense that they have not been obtained by fear of prejudice or hope of advantage, exercised or held out by a person in authority, or by oppression. The rules do not purport to envisage or deal with the many varieties of conduct which might render answers and statements involuntary and therefore inadmissible. The rules merely deal with particular aspects of the matter. Other matters such as affording reasonably comfortable conditions, adequate breaks for rest and refreshment, special procedures in the case of persons unfamiliar with the English language or of immature age or feeble understanding, are proper subjects for administrative directions to the police.

Judges' Rules

These rules do not effect the principles:

(*a*) That citizens have a duty to help a police officer to discover and apprehend offenders;

(*b*) That police officers, otherwise than by arrest, cannot compel any person against his will to come to or remain in any police station;

(*c*) That every person at any stage of an investigation should be able to communicate and to consult privately with a solicitor. This is so even if he is in custody provided that in such a case no unreasonable delay or hindrance is caused to the processes of investigation or the administration of justice by his doing so;

(*d*) That when a police officer who is making inquiries of any person about an offence has enough evidence to prefer a charge against that person for the offence, he should without delay cause that person to be charged or informed that he may be prosecuted for the offence;

(*e*) That it is a fundamental condition of the admissibility in evidence against any person, equally of any oral answer given by that person to a question put by a police officer and of any statement made by that person, that it shall have been voluntary, in the sense that it has not been obtained from him by fear of prejudice or hope of advantage, exercised or held out by a person in authority, or by oppression.

* Promulgated as appendices to Home Office circ. 89/1978 dated June 1978.

The principle set out in paragraph (*e*) above is overriding and applicable in all cases. Within that principle the following rules are put forward as a guide to police officers conducting investigations. Non-conformity with these rules may render answers and statements liable to be excluded from evidence in subsequent criminal proceedings.

Rules

I. When a police officer is trying to discover whether, or by whom, an offence has been committed he is entitled to question any person, whether suspected or not, from whom he thinks that useful information may be obtained. This is so whether or not the person in question has been taken into custody so long as he has not been charged with the offence or informed that he may be prosecuted for it.

II. As soon as a police officer has evidence which would afford reasonable grounds for suspecting that a person has committed an offence, he shall caution that person or cause him to be cautioned before putting to him any questions, or further questions, relating to that offence.
The caution shall be in the following terms:-

> "You are not obliged to say anything unless you wish to do so but what you say may be put into writing and given in evidence."

When after being cautioned a person is being questioned, or elects to make a statement, a record shall be kept of the time and place at which any such questioning or statement began and ended and of the persons present.

III (*a*) When a person is charged with or informed that he may be prosecuted for an offence he shall be cautioned in the following terms:-

> "Do you wish to say anything? You are not obliged to say anything unless you wish to do so but whatever you say will be taken down in writing and may be given in evidence."

(*b*) It is only in exceptional cases that questions relating to the offence should be put to the accused person after he has been charged or informed that he may be prosecuted. Such questions may be put where they are necessary for the purpose of preventing or minimizing harm or loss to some other person or to the public or for clearing up an ambiguity in a previous answer or statement.   Before any such questions are put the accused should be cautioned in these terms:-

> "I wish to put some questions to you about the offence with which you have been charged (*or* about the offence for which you may be prosecuted). You are not obliged to answer any of these questions, but if you do the questions and answers will be taken down in writing and may be given in evidence."

Any questions put and answers given relating to the offence must be contemporaneously recorded in full and the record signed by that person or if he refuses by the interrogating officer.

(*c*) When such a person is being questioned, or elects to make a statement, a record shall be kept of the time and place at which any questioning or statement began and ended and of the persons present.

IV. All written statements made after caution shall be taken in the following manner-

(*a*) If a person says that he wants to make a statement he shall be told that it is intended to make a written record of what he said. He shall always be asked whether he wishes to write down himself what he wants to say; if he says that he cannot write or that he would like someone to write it for him, a police officer may offer to write the statement for him. If he accepts the offer the police officer shall, before starting, ask the person making the statement to sign, or make his mark to, the following-

> "I, ... , wish to make a statement. I want someone to write down what I say. I have been told that I need not say anything unless I wish to do so and that whatever I say may be given in evidence."

(b) Any person writing his own statement shall be allowed to do so without any prompting as distinct from indicating to him what matters are material.

(c) The person making the statement, if he is going to write it himself, shall be asked to write out and sign before writing what he wants to say, the following-

> "I make this statement of my own free will. I have been told that I need not say anything unless I wish to do so and that whatever I say may be given in evidence."

(d) Whenever a police officer writes the statement, he shall take down the exact words spoken by the person making the statement, without putting any questions other than such as may be needed to make the statement coherent, intelligible and relevant to the material matters; he shall not prompt him.

(e) When the writing of a statement by a police officer is finished the person making it shall be asked to read it and to make any corrections, alterations or additions he wishes. When he has finished reading it he shall be asked to write and sign or make his mark on the following certificate at the end of the statement-

> "I have read the above statement and I have been told that I can correct, alter or add anything I wish. This statement is true. I have made it of my own free will."

(f) If the person who has made the statement refuses to read it or to write the above mentioned certificate at the end of it or to sign it, the senior police officer present shall record on the statement itself and in the presence of the person making it, what has happened. If the person making the statement cannot read, or refuses to read it, the officer who has taken it down shall read it over to him and ask him whether he would like to correct, alter or add anything and to put his signature or make his mark at the end. The police officer shall then certify on the statement itself what he has done.

V. If at any time after a person has been charged with, or has been informed that he may be prosecuted for an offence a police officer wishes to bring to the notice of that person any written statement made by another person who in respect of the same offence has also been charged or informed that he may be prosecuted, he shall hand to that person a true copy of such written statement, but nothing shall be said or done to invite any reply or comment. If that person says that he would like to make a statement in reply, or starts to say something, he shall at once be cautioned or further cautioned as prescribed by Rule III(a).

VI. Persons other than police officers charged with the duty of investigating offences or charging offenders shall, so far as may be practicable, comply with these rules.

EVIDENCE OF IDENTIFICATION

Rules of Evidence

Evidence of Identification

In a considered judgment in the case of *R*. v. *Turnbull* (1976) 140 J.P. 648 Lord Widgery CJ laid down the following guidelines.

"(evidence of visual identification in criminal cases) can bring about miscarriages of justice and has done so in a few cases in recent years. The number of such cases, although small compared with the number in which evidence of visual identification is known to be satisfactory, necessitates steps being taken by the courts, including this court, to reduce that number as far as is possible. In our judgment the danger of miscarriages of justice occurring can be much reduced if trial judges sum up to juries in the way indicated in this judgment.

"First, whenever the case against an accused depends wholly or substantially on the correctness of one or more identifications of the accused which the defence alleges to be mistaken, the judge should warn the jury of the special need for caution before convicting the accused in reliance on the correctness of the identification or identifications. In addition he should instruct them as to the reason for the need for such a warning and should make some reference to the possibility that a mistaken witness can be a convincing one and that a number of such witnesses can all be mistaken. Provided this is done in clear terms the judge need not use any particular form of words. "Secondly, the judge should direct the jury to examine closely the circumstances in which the identification by each witness came to be made. How long did the witness have the accused under observation? At what distance? In what light? Was the observation impeded in any way, as for example by passing traffic or a press of people? Had the witness ever seen the accused before? How often? If only occasionaly, had he any special reason for remembering the accused? How long elapsed between the original observation and the subsequent identification to the police? Was there any material discrepancy between the description of the accused given to the police by the witness when first seen by them and his actual appearance? If in any case, whether it is being dealt with summarily or on indictment, the prosecution have reason to believe that there is such a material discrepancy they should supply the accused or his legal advisors with particulars of the description the police were first given. In all cases if the accused asks to be given particulars of such descriptions, the prosecution should supply them. Finally, he should remind the jury of any specific weaknesses which had appeared in the identification evidence. Recognition may be more reliable than identification of a stranger; but, even when the witness is purporting to recognise someone whom he knows, the jury should be reminded that mistakes in recognition of close relatives and friends are sometimes made.

"All these matters go to the quality of the identification evidence. If the quality is good and remains good at the close of the accused's case, the danger of a mistaken identification is lessened; but the poorer the quality, the greater the danger. In our judgment, when the quality is good, as for example when the identification is made after a long period of observation, or in satisfactory conditions by a relative, a neighbour, a close friend, a workmate and the like, the jury can safely be left to assess the value of the identifying evidence even though there is no other evidence to support it; provided always, however, that an adequate warning has been given about the special need for caution. Were the courts to adjudge otherwise, affronts to justice would frequently occur. A few examples, taken over the whole spectrum of criminal activity, will illustrate what the effects on the maintenance of law and order would be if any law were enacted that no person could be convicted on evidence of visual identification alone.

"Here are the examples. A had been kidnapped and held to ransom over many days. His captor stayed with him all the time. At last he was released but he did not know the identity of his kidnapper nor where he had been kept. Months later the police arrested X for robbery and as a result of what they had been told by an informer they suspected him of the kidnapping. They had no other evidence. They arranged for A to attend an identity parade. He picked out X without hesitation. At X's trial, is the trial judge to rule at the end of the prosecution's case that X must be acquitted?

"This is another example. Over a period of a week two police officers, B and C, kept observations in turn on a house which was suspected of being a distribution centre for drugs. A suspected supplier, Y, visited it from time to time. On the last day of the observation B saw Y enter the house. He at once signalled to other waiting police officers, who had a search warrant to enter. They did so; but by the time they got in, Y had escaped by a back window. Six months later C saw Y in the street and arrested him. Y at once alleged that C had mistaken him for someone else. At an identity parade he was picked out by B. Would it really be right and in the interests of justice for a judge to direct Y's acquittal at the end of the prosecution's case?

"A rule such as the one under consideration would gravely impede the police in their work and would make the conviction of street offenders such as pickpockets, car thieves and the disorderly very difficult. But it would not only be the police who might be aggrieved by such a rule. Take the case of a factory worker, D, who during the course of his work went to the locker room to get something from his jacket which he had forgotten. As he went in he saw a workmate, Z, whom he had known for years and who worked near him in the same shop, standing by D's open locker with his hand inside. He hailed the thief by name. Z turned round and faced D; he dropped D's wallet on the floor and ran out of the locker room by another door. D reported what he had seen to the chargehand. When the chargehand went to find Z, he saw him walking towards his machine. Z alleged that D had been mistaken. A directed acquittal might well be greatly resented not only by D but by many others in the same shop.

"When, in the judgment of the trial judge, the quality of the identifying evidence is poor, as for example when it depends solely on a fleeting glance or on a longer observation made in difficult conditions, the situation is very different. The judge should then withdraw the case from the jury and direct an acquittal unless there is other evidence which goes to support the correctness of the identification. This may be corroboration in the sense lawyers use the word; but it need not be so if its effect is to make the jury sure that there has been no mistaken identification. For example, X sees the accused snatch a woman's handbag; he gets only a fleeting glance of the thief's face as he runs off but he does see him entering a nearby house. Later he picks out the accused in an identity parade. If there was no more evidence than this, the poor quality of the identification would require the judge to withdraw the case from the jury; but this would not be so if there was evidence that the house into which the accused was alleged by X to have run was his father's. Another example of supporting evidence not amounting to corroboration in a technical sense is to be found in R. v. Long [1973] 57 Cr. App. R. 871. The accused, who was charged with robbery, had been identified by three witnesses in different places on different occasions, but each had only a momentary opportunity for observation. Immediately after the robbery the accused had left his home and could not be found by the police. When later he was seen by them he claimed to know who had done the robbery and offered to help to find the robbers. At his trial he put forward an alibi which the jury rejected. It was an odd coincidence that the witnesses should have identified a man who had behaved in this way. In our judgment odd coincidences can, if unexplained, be supporting evidence.

"The trial judge should identify to the jury the evidence which he adjudges is capable of supporting the evidence of identification. If there is any evidence or circumstance which the jury might think was supporting when it did not have this quality, the judge should say so. A jury, for example, might think that support for identification evidence could be found in the fact that the accused had not given evidence before them. An accused's absence from the witness box cannot provide evidence of anything and the judge should tell the jury so. But he would be entitled to tell them that when assessing the quality of the identification evidence they could take into consideration the fact that it was uncontradicted by any evidence coming from the accused himself.

"Care should be taken by the judge when directing the jury about the support for an identification which may be derived from the fact that they have rejected an alibi. False alibis may be put forward for many reasons: an accused, for example, who has only his own truthful evidence to reply on may stupidly fabricate an alibi and get lying witnesses to support it out of fear that his own evidence will not be enough. Further, alibi witnesses can make genuine mistakes about dates and occasions like any other witnesses can. It is only when the jury are satisfied that the sole reason for the fabrication was to deceive them and there is no other explanation for its being put forward, that fabrication can provide any support for identification evidence. The jury should be reminded that proving the accused has told lies about where he was at the material time does not by itself prove that he was where the identifying witness says he was.

"In setting out these guide lines for trial judges, which involve only changes of practice, not law, we have tried to follow the recommendations set out in the report which Lord Devlin's committee made to the Secretary of State for the Home Department in April 1976. We have not followed that report in using the phrase 'exceptional circumstances' to describe situations in which the risk of mistaken identification is reduced. In our judgment, the use of such a phrase is likely to result in the build-up of case law as to what circumstances can properly be described as exceptional and what cannot. Case law of this kind is likely to be a fetter on the administration of justice when so much depends on the quality of the evidence in each case. Quality is what matters in the end. In many cases the exceptional circumstances to which the report refers will provide evidence of good quality, but they may not; the converse is also true.

"A failure to follow these guidelines is likely to result in a conviction being quashed and will do so if in the judgment of this court on all the evidence the verdict is either unsatisfactory or unsafe."

This advice should be followed with great care by justices: *McShane* v. *Northumbria Chief Constable* [1981] 72 Cr. App. R. 28; but it does not make any new principles of law. (Court could convict when constable saw back of man's head in good light for a quarter of an hour). The judgment in *Turnbull* should not be applied inflexibly: *R.* v. *Keane* [1977] 65 Cr. App. R. 247. *Turnbull* is intended to deal with "the ghastly risk run in fleeting encounters", not the suggestion that a constable may be confused as to whether the man who knocked him down was the man standing beside him when he got up: *R.* v. *Oakwell* (1978) 142 J.P. 259. When the quality of the identification evidence is such that a jury can safely be left to assess its value they may be directed that an identification by one witness can constitute support for the identification by another, provided that they are warned that even a number of honest witnesses can be mistaken: *R.* v. *Weeder* [1980] 71 Cr. App. R. 228.

DIRECTIONS GIVEN BY THE LORD CHIEF JUSTICE WITH THE CONCURRENCE OF THE LORD CHANCELLOR UNDER [S. 75 OF THE SUPREME COURT ACT 1981]

(Practice Note [1971] 3 All E.R. 829, as amended by *Practice Direction* [1971] 3 All E.R. 1312, *Practice Direction* [1972] 2 All E.R. 1057, *Practice Direction* [1974] 2 All E.R. 121, *Practice Direction* [1978] 2 All E.R. 912)

Classification of offences

1. *For the purposes of trial in the Crown Court, offences are to be classified as follows—*

Class 1: *The following offences, which are to be tried by a High Court judge:*

(1)   Any offences for which a person may be sentenced to death.
(2)   Misprision of treason and treason felony.
(3)   Murder
(4)   Genocide.
(5)   An offence under the Official Secrets Act 1911, s. 1.
(6)   Incitement, attempt or conspiracy to commit any of the above offences.

Class 2: *The following offences, which are to be tried by a High Court judge unless a particular case is released by or on the authority of a presiding judge, that is to say, a High Court judge assigned to have special responsibility for a particular circuit:*

(1)   Manslaughter.
(2)   Infanticide.
(3)   Child destruction.
(4)   Abortion (Offences against the Person Act 1861, s. 58).
(5)   Rape.
(6)   Sexual intercourse with girl under 13.
(7)   Incest with girl under 13.
(8)   Sedition.
(9)   An offence under the Geneva Conventions Act 1957, s. 1.
(10)   Mutiny.
(11)   Piracy.
(12)   Incitement, attempt or conspiracy to commit any of the above offences.

Class 3: *All offences triable only on indictment other than those in classes 1, 2 and 4. They may be listed for trial by a High Court judge or by a circuit judge or by a recorder.*

Class 4:
(a)   Wounding or causing grievous bodily harm with intent (Offences Against the Person Act 1861, s. 18).
(b)   Robbery or assault with intent to rob. (Theft Act 1968, s. 8).
(c)   Offences under para. (a) of s. 2(2) of the Forgery Act 1913 where the amount of money or the value of goods exceeds £1,000.
(d)   Offences under para. (a) of s. 7 of the Forgery Act 1913, where the amount of money or the value of the property exceeds £1,000.
(e)   Incitement or attempt to commit any of the above offences.
(f)   Conspiracy at common law or conspiracy to commit any offence other than one included in classes 1 and 2.
(g)   All offences triable either way and any offence in class 3, if included in class 4 in accordance with directions, which may be either general or particular, given by a presiding judge or on his authority.

When tried on indictment offences in class 4 may be tried by a High Court judge, circuit judge or recorder but will normally be listed for trial by a circuit judge or recorder.

Committals for Trial

2.

    (i)   *A magistrates' court on committing a person for trial under the [Magistrates' Courts Act 1980, s. 6(1) or (2)] shall, if the offence, or any of the offences is included in classes 1 to 3, specify the most convenient location of the Crown Court where a High Court judge regularly sits, and if the offence is in class 4 shall, subject to para. 2(ii), specify the most convenient location of the Crown Court;*

    (ii)   *If in the view of the justices, when committing a person for trial for an offence in class 4, the case should be tried by a High Court judge, they shall indicate that view, giving reasons, in a notice to be included with the papers sent to the Crown Court, and shall commit to the most convenient location of the Crown Court where a High Court judge regularly sits.*

The following considerations should influence the justices in favour of trial by a High Court judge, namely where

    (i)   *the case involves death or serious risk to life (excluding cases of dangerous driving, or causing death by dangerous driving, having no aggravating features);*

    (ii)   *widespread public concern is involved;*

    (iii)   *the case involves violence or threat of violence of a serious nature;*

    (iv)   *the offence involves dishonesty in respect of a substantial sum of money;*

    (v)   *the accused holds a public position or is a professional or other person owing a duty to the public;*

    (vi)   *the circumstances are of unusual gravity in some respect other than those indicated above;*

    (vii)   *a novel or difficult issue of law is likely to be involved, or a prosecution for the offence is rare or novel.*

3. *In selecting the most convenient location of the Crown Court, the justices shall have regard to the considerations referred to in paras. (a) and (b) of s. 7(1) of the Courts Act 1971 and to the location or locations of the Crown Court designated by a presiding judge as the location or locations to which cases should normally be committed from their petty sessions area.*

4. *Where on one occasion a person is committed in respect of a number of offences, all the committals shall be to the same location of the Crown Court and that location shall be one where a High·Court judge regularly sits if such a location is appropriate for any of the offences.*

Committals for sentence or to be dealt with

5. *Where*

    (1)   *a probation order or order for conditional discharge has been made, and the offender is committed to be dealt with for the original offence; or*

    (2)   *a suspended sentence has been passed and the offender is committed to be dealt with in respect of the suspended sentence; or*

    (3)   *a community service order has been made and the offender is committed (a) to be dealt with for failure to comply with any of the requirements of s. 15 of the Powers of Criminal Courts Act 1973, or*

(b) because it appears to the magistrates' court specified in the order that the order should be revoked or that the offender should be dealt with in some other manner for the offence in respect of which the order was made;

the offender shall be committed in accordance with paras. 6 to 9 of these directions.

6. *If the order was made or the sentence was passed by the Crown Court, he shall be committed to the location of the Crown Court where the order was made or suspended sentence passed, unless it is inconvenient or impracticable to do so.*

7. *If he is not so committed and the order was made by a High Court judge or, before the appointed day, by a court of Assize, he shall be committed to the most convenient location of the Crown Court where a High Court judge regularly sits.*

8. *In all other cases where a person is committed for sentence or to be dealt with he shall be committed to the most convenient location of the Crown Court.*

9. *In selecting the most convenient location of the Crown Court the justices shall have regard to the location or locations of the Crown Court designated by a presiding judge as the location or location to which cases should normally be committed from their petty sessions area.*

Appeals and proceedings under the Crown Court's original civil jurisdiction

10. *The hearing of an appeal or of proceedings under the civil jurisdiction of the Crown Court, shall take place at the location of the Crown Court designated by a presiding judge as the appropriate location for such proceedings originating in the areas concerned.*

Application for removal of a driving disqualification

11. *Application should be made to the location of the Crown Court where the order of disqualification was made, or, if it was made by a court of Assize or quarter sessions, to the location of the Crown Court which is most convenient to the place where the order was made.*

Allocation of proceedings at locations of the Crown Court

12.

(i)   *Class 1 and class 2 offences shall be tried by a High Court judge, unless in the case of a class 2 offence the case is released by or under the authority of a presiding judge having regard to all the circumstances. Where the prosecution of such an offence has been undertaken by the Director of Public Prosecutions the Director's views shall, where practicable, be obtained before the case is considered for release;*

(ii)   *Class 3 offences shall be listed for trial by a High Court judge unless, after having regard to the considerations set out in para. 2 above, the officer responsible for listing decides that the case should be listed for trial by a circuit judge or recorder. Such a decision shall only be taken after consultation with a presiding judge (or a judge acting for him) or in accordance with directions, which may be either general or particular, given by a presiding judge;*

(iii)   *Class 4 offences shall be listed for trial by a circuit judge or recorder unless, bearing in mind the considerations set out in para. 2 above and the views, if any, put forward by justices, the officer responsible for listing decides that the case should be tried by a High Court judge.*

Such a decision shall be taken only after consultation with a presiding judge (or a judge acting for him) or in accordance with directions, either general or particular, given by a presiding judge including, in the case of any specified offence, directions relating to further considerations to be borne in mind by the officer responsible for listing;

(iv) *Where a probation order, care order, community service order or order for conditional discharge has been made, or a suspended sentence passed, by a High Court judge, and the offender is committed to or brought before the Crown Court, his case should be listed for hearing by a High Court judge unless, in accordance with the decision of the officer responsible for listing, his case is listed for hearing by a circuit judge or recorder.*

Such a decision shall only be taken after consultation with a presiding judge (or a judge acting for him) or in accordance with directions, either general or particular, given by a presiding judge;

(v) *All other proceedings before the Crown Court (excluding an application under s. 7(3) of the Courts Act 1971 for a direction, or further direction, varying the place of trial) including appeals, committals for sentence or to be dealt with, and proceedings under the original civil jurisdiction of the Crown Court shall normally be listed for hearing by a court presided over by a circuit judge or recorder.*

Allocation of proceedings to a court comprising lay justices

13. *In addition to the classes of case specified in the Courts Act 1971, s. 5(1) (appeals and proceedings on committals for sentence) any other proceedings which, in accordance with these directions, are listed for hearing by a Circuit judge or recorder are suitable for allocation to a court comprising justices of the peace.*

Transfer of proceedings between locations of the Crown Court

14. *Without prejudice to the provisions of the Courts Act 1971, s. 7(2) and (3) (transfer of trials on indictment), the Crown Court may give directions for the transfer from one location of the Crown Court to another of—*

(i) *appeals;*
(ii) *proceedings on committal for sentence, or to be dealt with;*
(iii) *proceedings under the original civil jurisdiction of the Crown Court*

where this appears desirable for the expediting of the hearing or the convenience of the parties.

Such directions may be given in a particular case by an officer of the Crown Court, or generally, in relation to a class or classes of case, by the presiding judge or a judge acting on his behalf.

If dissatisfied with such directions given by an officer of the Crown Court, any party to the proceedings may apply to a judge of the Crown Court who may hear the application in chambers.

Where the Crown Court has deferred passing sentence under [s. 1(1) of the Powers of Criminal Courts Act 1973], and before the expiration of the period of deferment the offender is convicted in a different location of the Crown Court of another offence, the power to pass sentence for the original offence under [s. 1(4)] may be exercised in the location of the Crown Court where he was convicted of the subsequent offence.

Application to the Crown Court for bail

15.   *(1)(a) Notice of intention to apply for bail shall be given to the appropriate officer at the location of the Crown Court where the proceedings in which the application for bail arises took place or are pending.*

(b) Where a person gives notice in writing that he wishes to apply for bail and requests that the Official Solcitor shall act for him in the application, the application shall be heard by a judge of the Crown Court in London.

(c) In any other case, the application shall be heard at the location of the Crown Court where the proceedings in respect of which it arises took place or are pending, or at any other location which the court may direct.

(2) Subject to such directions as may be given in any case by or on behalf of the Lord Chief Justice with the concurrence of the Lord Chancellor, any application for bail—

(a) by a person charged with a Class 1 offence, or in any case where a presiding judge so directs, shall be heard by a High Court judge or by a circuit judge nominated by a presiding judge for this purpose;

(b) by a person charged with a Class 2 offence may be heard by a High Court judge or by a circuit judge or (on the authority of a presiding judge) by a recorder;

(c) in any other case may be heard by any judge of the Crown Court.

WITNESS,
   admission, formal, 49
   adverse, contradictory statements by, 55
   arrest of, 75, 84
   children as, 45, 65
   committal proceedings, in, 146
     before examining justices, recall of, 185
     order for attendance in, 84
   competency, 58-61
   compulsion, 44, 75-7
   convictions, previous, of, 55
   discrediting of, 55
   evidence of, on oath, 45
   exclusion of, from court, 44
   husbands and wives, 53-4
   name and address of, 45
   refreshment of memory, 46
   written statements by, 48, 72
     cross-examination on, 55

Y

YOUNG PERSONS *see* JUVENILES
YOUTH CUSTODY, 215, 261, 297-8